POSTCARDS FROM

⊙Frommer's
Australia

P9-DND-691

You'll have no problem finding a patch of sand all to yourself, like here on Fitzroy Island in Queensland. See chapter 1 for a list of our favorite beaches and chapter 6 for Fitzroy Island. © Queensland Tourist & Travel Corporation.

Your gateway to Australia most likely will be Sydney, home of the world-famous Opera House, shown here with its white sails aglow. For details on touring the House and seeing a performance, see chapter 3. © *Paul Chesley/Tony Stone Images.*

Sydney Harbour buzzes with activity at the start of the annual ferry race. See chapter 3 for details on getting around by ferry and taking sightseeing cruises. © *George Hall/Tony Stone Images.*

The Walls of China, a shimmering cliff formation skirting dry Lake Mungo, is typical of the eerie, red-streaked desertscapes you'll find in the Outback. For tours that visit this area, see chapter 4; for information on Outback tours, see chapter 2. © Dave G. Houser/Houserstock, Inc.

Stretching for more than 1,250 miles, the Great Barrier Reef is not just great, it's awesome; see chapter 6. Australia, in fact, has two barrier reefs—the other is off the coast of Western Australia; see chapter 9. © Carl Roessler Photography.

There's no better place than Australia to get face to face with the fishes. For a list of our favorite diving and snorkeling sites, see chapter 1. © Kelvin Aitken/Peter Arnold, Inc.

Like a 'roo unexpectedly bounding across the road, the mighty monolith of Uluru (Ayers Rock) seems to pop up out of nowhere from the red desert floor. See chapter 7.
© Doug Armand/Tony Stone Images.

The haunting sounds of the didgeridoo capture the spirit of Aboriginal culture. You can learn to play one at the Aboriginal Art and Culture Centre in Alice Springs. See chapter 7.
© Paul Souders/Tony Stone Images.

For a true-blue Aussie experience, spend a few days on a cattle station like Runnymeade, in New South Wales. For more information, see chapters 2 and 4. © Dave G. Houser/Houserstock, Inc.

You can swim with dolphins at Monkey Mia in Western Australia; see chapter 9. Dolphins and migrating whales can also be spotted off the coasts of New South Wales and Queensland; see chapters 4 and 6. © Thomas Schmitt/The Image Bank.

Picturesque today, Port Arthur, on the island-state of Tasmania, was once Australia's most notorious penal colony. You can tour the remains of the church, guard tower, and model prison. See chapter 14. © Greg Probst Photography.

Kakadu National Park in the Northern Territory has some 5,000 Aboriginal art sites. Aborigines used paintings such as these to tell stories and show their ownership of the land. See chapter 8. © Tom Till Photography.

When should I travel to get the best airfare?
Where do I go for answers to my travel questions?
What's the best and easiest way to plan and book my trip?

frommers.travelocity.com

Frommer's, the travel guide leader, has teamed up with **Travelocity.com**, the leader in online travel, to bring you an in-depth, easy-to-use resource designed to help you plan and book your trip online.

At **frommers.travelocity.com**, you'll find free online updates about your destination from the experts at Frommer's plus the outstanding travel planning and purchasing features of Travelocity.com. Travelocity.com provides reservations capabilities for 95 percent of all airline seats sold, more than 47,000 hotels, and over 50 car rental companies. In addition, Travelocity.com offers more than 2,000 exciting vacation and cruise packages. Travelocity.com puts you in complete control of your travel planning with these and other great features:

> **Expert travel guidance from Frommer's** - over 150 writers reporting from around the world!
>
> **Best Fare Finder** - an interactive calendar tells you when to travel to get the best airfare
>
> **Fare Watcher** - we'll track airfare changes to your favorite destinations
>
> **Dream Maps** - a mapping feature that suggests travel opportunities based on your budget
>
> **Shop Safe Guarantee** - 24 hours a day / 7 days a week live customer service, and more!

Whether traveling on a tight budget, looking for a quick weekend getaway, or planning the trip of a lifetime, Frommer's guides and Travelocity.com will make your travel dreams a reality. You've bought the book, now book the trip!

A New Star-Rating System & Other Exciting News from Frommer's!

In our continuing effort to publish the savviest, most up-to-date, and most appealing travel guides available, we've added some great new features.

Frommer's guides now include a new **star-rating system.** Every hotel, restaurant, and attraction is rated from 0 to 3 stars to help you set priorities and organize your time.

We've also added **seven brand-new features** that point you to the great deals, in-the-know advice, and unique experiences that separate travelers from tourists. Throughout the guide look for:

Finds	Special finds—those places only insiders know about
Fun Fact	Fun facts—details that make travelers more informed and their trips more fun
Kids	Best bets for kids—advice for the whole family
Moments	Special moments—those experiences that memories are made of
Overrated	Places or experiences not worth your time or money
Tips	Insider tips—some great ways to save time and money
Value	Great values—where to get the best deals

We've also added a **"What's New"** section in every guide—a timely crash course in what's hot and what's not in every destination we cover.

Other Great Guides for Your Trip:

Frommer's Australia from $50 a Day

Frommer's Portable Sydney

Frommer's Portable Australia's Great Barrier Reef

Frommer's Adventure Guides: Australia & New Zealand

Frommer's®

Australia

8th Edition

by Natalie Kruger, Marc Llewellyn &
Lee Mylne

Here's what the critics say about Frommer's:

"Amazingly easy to use. Very portable, very complete."

—Booklist

"The only mainstream guide to list specific prices. The Walter Cronkite of guidebooks—with all that implies."

—Travel & Leisure

"Complete, concise, and filled with useful information."

—New York Daily News

"Detailed, accurate, and easy-to-read information for all price ranges."
—Glamour Magazine

Hungry Minds™

Best-Selling Books • Digital Downloads • e-Books • Answer Networks
e-Newsletters • Branded Web Sites • e-Learning
New York, NY • Cleveland, OH • Indianapolis, IN

About the Authors

Natalie Kruger (chapters 1, 2, 7, 8, and 9), another Sydneysider, spent 7 years as a public relations consultant for international and Australian airlines, global hotel chains, tourist promotion boards, and tourism industry organizations, until she realized it is more fun to be a travel writer—that way, you get to say what you *really* think. She contributes travel pieces to Australia's top newspapers and magazines, including the prestigious *Weekend Australian,* and is a member of the Australian Society of Travel Writers. She is the author of *Frommer's Portable Australia's Great Barrier Reef.*

Sydney resident **Marc Llewellyn** (chapters 1, 3, 4, 10, 11, 12, 13, 14, and "Australia in Depth") is one of Australia's premier travel writers and a regular contributor to all of Australia's leading newspaper travel sections and travel magazines. As a member of the Australian Society of Travel Writers, he keeps his suitcase ready packed beneath his bed. He is also the author of *Frommer's Portable Sydney* and co-author of *Frommer's Australia from $50 a Day.*

Lee Mylne (chapters 1, 5, and 6) is a Brisbane-based freelance travel writer who writes for a broad range of Australian and international publications, including the national travel trade magazine *Travel Week Australia.* She has lived in Queensland for the past 15 years and is currently president of the Australian Society of Travel Writers.

Published by:

Hungry Minds, Inc.

909 Third Ave.
New York, NY 10022

ISBN 0-7645-6533-8
ISSN 1040-9408

Editor: Kelly Regan
Special thanks to Kimberly Perdue
Production Editor: Donna Wright
Cartographer: Nicholas Trotter
Photo Editor: Richard Fox
Production by Hungry Minds Indianapolis Production Services

Special Sales

For general information on Hungry Minds' products and services please contact our Customer Care department; within the U.S. at 800-762-2974, outside the U.S. at 317-572-3993 or fax 317-572-4002. For sales inquiries and reseller information, including discounts, bulk sales, customized editions, and premium sales, please contact our Customer Care department at 800-434-3422.

Manufactured in the United States of America
5 4 3 2 1

Contents

List of Maps ix

What's New in Australia 1

1   The Best of Australia 5

1 The Top Travel Experiences 5
2 The Best Outdoor Adventures . . .9
3 The Best Places to View
  Wildlife 10
4 The Best Places to Experience
  the Outback 12
5 The Best Beaches 13
6 The Best Diving & Snorkeling
  Sites .14
7 The Best Places to Bushwalk
  (Hike) 15
8 The Best Places to Learn About
  Aboriginal Culture 16

9 The Best of Small-Town
  Australia 17
10 The Best Museums 18
11 The Best Luxury
  Accommodations 19
12 The Best Moderately Priced
  Accommodations 20
13 The Best Alternative
  Accommodations 21
14 The Best B&Bs &
  Guest Houses 22
15 The Best Restaurants 24

2   Planning Your Trip to Australia 26

by Natalie Kruger

1 The Regions in Brief 26
2 Visitor Information 30
3 Entry Requirements &
  Customs 31
4 Money 33
  *The Australian Dollar, the U.S.
  Dollar & the British Pound* 34
5 When to Go 35
  Australia Calendar of Events . . .37
  Calling All City Slickers 39
6 The Active Vacation Planner . . .40
7 Health & Insurance 49

*Warning: Sunshine May Be
Hazardous to Your Health* 50
8 Tips for Travelers with
  Special Needs 51
9 Booking a Package or
  Escorted Tour 53
10 Flying to Australia 54
11 Getting Around Australia 57
12 Planning Your Trip Online 70
  *Frommers.com: The Complete
  Travel Resource* 71
13 Tips on Accommodations 72
  Fast Facts: Australia 74

3   Sydney 80

by Marc Llewellyn

1 Orientation 81
  Neighborhoods in Brief 85

2 Getting Around 89
  Fast Facts: Sydney 96

3 Where to Stay 99

4 Where to Dine 117

What to Know About BYO . . .117

Something Fishy 129

5 What to See & Do in
Sydney 135

Great Deals on Sightseeing . . .138

6 Harbor Cruises & Organized
Tours 154

7 Staying Active 156

8 Spectator Sports 158

9 Shopping 159

10 Sydney After Dark 166

4   New South Wales   173

by Marc Llewellyn

1 The Blue Mountains 174

2 The Hunter Valley: Wine
Tasting & More 186

*Bunking down in a Caravan,
Man* 190

*Something Special: A Cattle Station
in the Upper Hunter* 192

3 Port Stephens: Dolphin & Whale
Watching 195

4 North of Sydney Along the
Pacific Highway: Australia's
Holiday Coast 198

5 South of Sydney Along the
Princes Highway 208

6 The Snowy Mountains:
Australia's Ski Country 215

7 Outback New South Wales . . .217

5   Brisbane   225

by Lee Mylne

1 Orientation 225

Neighborhoods in Brief 229

2 Getting Around 229

Fast Facts: Brisbane 233

3 Where to Stay 235

4 Where to Dine 237

5 Exploring Brisbane 240

6 Organized Tours 243

7 Enjoying the Great
Outdoors 245

8 The Shopping Scene 246

9 Brisbane After Dark 246

10 Brisbane's Moreton Bay
& Islands 249

6   Queensland & the Great Barrier Reef   253

by Lee Mylne

1 Exploring the Great Barrier
Reef 255

2 Cairns 261

You Too Can Be a Survivor . . .274

3 Port Douglas, Daintree &
the Cape Tribulation Area 282

4 The North Coast: Mission Beach,
Townsville & the Islands 294

5 The Whitsunday Coast &
Islands 307

Come Sail with Me 312

6 The Capricorn Coast &
the Southern Reef Islands 320

*Up Close & Personal with
a Turtle* 326

7 Fraser Island: Eco-Adventures
& Four-Wheel-Drive Fun 329

8 The Sunshine Coast 333

9 The Gold Coast 341

10 The Gold Coast Hinterland:
Back to Nature 350

7 The Red Centre   356

by Natalie Kruger

1 Exploring the Red Centre 356

2 Alice Springs 359

*Earning a Degree from
Didgeridoo University* 364

3 Road Trips from Alice
Springs 372

*Road-Trip Tips for the East
& West Macs* 373

4 Kings Canyon 375

5 Uluru-Kata Tjuta National Park
(Ayers Rock/The Olgas) 377

Dinner in the Desert 381

8 The Top End   386

by Natalie Kruger

1 Exploring the Top End 386

2 Darwin 390

Cheap Eats & More! 398

3 Kakadu National Park 401

*Never Smile at a
You-Know-What* 403

4 Katherine 408

5 The Kimberley: A Far-Flung
Wilderness 412

9 Perth & Western Australia   427

by Natalie Kruger

*Tiptoeing Through the
Wildflowers* 430

1 Perth 431

Neighborhoods in Brief 434

A Free Ride 436

Fast Facts: Perth 437

2 Side Trips from Perth 455

3 Margaret River & the Southwest:
Wine Tasting in the Forests 461

Taking a Dip with Flipper 462

4 The Goldfields 468

5 The Midwest & the Northwest:
Where the Outback Meets
the Sea 471

10 Adelaide & South Australia   479

by Marc Llewellyn

1 Adelaide 480

*The Adelaide & Womadelaide
Festivals* 484

Fast Facts: Adelaide 486

2 Side Trips from Adelaide 499

*So Much Wine, So Little
Time* 499

3 Kangaroo Island 507

*Culling Koalas—A National
Dilemma* 511

4 Outback South Australia 515
*A Fabulous Four-Wheel-Drive
Adventure* 520

5 The Coorong 520

11 Melbourne   523

by Marc Llewellyn

1 Orientation 523
Neighborhoods in Brief 526
2 Getting Around 528
Fast Facts: Melbourne 529
3 Where to Stay 530
4 Where to Dine 538
5 Seeing the Sights 545

6 Enjoying the Great Outdoors or
Catching an Aussie Rules
Football Match 550
7 Shopping 552
Death by Chocolate 554
8 Melbourne After Dark 555
9 Side Trips from Melbourne 559

12 Victoria   568

by Marc Llewellyn

1 Ballarat: Gold-Rush City 570
2 The Great Ocean Road: One of
the World's Most
Scenic Drives 573
3 The Murray River 577

4 The Southeast Coast 580
5 The High Country 582
6 The Northwest: Grampians
National Park 587

13 Canberra   589

by Marc Llewellyn

1 Orientation 589
2 Getting Around 592
Fast Facts: Canberra 593
3 Where to Stay 594
4 Where to Dine 597

5 Seeing the Sights 599
Up, Up & Away 600
6 Outdoor Pursuits 602
7 Canberra After Dark 603

14 Tasmania   604

by Marc Llewellyn

1 Exploring Tasmania 604
2 Hobart 608
Tasmania by Raft 620
3 Port Arthur: Discovering
Tasmania's Convict Heritage . .621
4 Freycinet National Park 623

5 Launceston 625
6 Cradle Mountain &
Lake St. Clair National Park . . .630
Hiking the Overland Track 632
7 The West Coast 634

Appendix: Australia in Depth   637

by Marc Llewellyn

1 Australia's Natural World 637
2 The People of Oz 639
3 Australian History 101 641
   Dateline 641

4 Aussie Eats & Drinks 644
5 Recommended Books & Films . . .645
   *Witchetty Grubs, Lilly-Pillies
   & Other Good Eats* 646

Index   648

List of Maps

Australia 6

Greater Sydney 82

Sydney Harbour 86

Sydney Transportation Systems 90

Sydney Ferries 95

Where to Stay in Central
   Sydney 100

Where to Dine in Central
   Sydney 118

Where to Dine in The Rocks 123

Central Sydney Attractions 136

New South Wales 175

The Blue Mountains 176

The Hunter Valley 187

Greater Brisbane 227

Brisbane Hotels, Restaurants &
   Attractions 230

The Great Barrier Reef 257

Cairns 263

Port Douglas, Daintree & Cape
   Tribulation 283

The Whitsunday Region 309

The Sunshine Coast 334

The Gold Coast 343

The Red Centre 357

Alice Springs 360

The Northern Territory 387

Darwin 391

The Kimberley Region 413

Western Australia 429

Perth 433

South Australia 481

Adelaide 483

The Barossa 501

Greater Melbourne 525

Where to Stay in Melbourne 531

Where to Dine in Melbourne 539

Melbourne Attractions 547

Victoria 569

Canberra 591

Tasmania 605

Hobart 609

An Invitation to the Reader

In researching this book, we discovered many wonderful places—hotels, restaurants, shops, and more. We're sure you'll find others. Please tell us about them, so we can share the information with your fellow travelers in upcoming editions. If you were disappointed with a recommendation, we'd love to know that, too. Please write to:

Frommer's Australia, 8th Edition
Hungry Minds, Inc. • 909 Third Avenue • New York, NY 10022

An Additional Note

Please be advised that travel information is subject to change at any time—and this is especially true of prices. We therefore suggest that you write or call ahead for confirmation when making your travel plans. The authors, editors, and publisher cannot be held responsible for the experiences of readers while traveling. Your safety is important to us, however, so we encourage you to stay alert and be aware of your surroundings. Keep a close eye on cameras, purses, and wallets, all favorite targets of thieves and pickpockets.

New! Frommer's Star Ratings & Icons

Every hotel, restaurant, and attraction listing in this guide has been ranked for quality, value, service, amenities, and special features using a star-rating scale. In country, state, and regional guides, we also rate towns and regions to help you narrow down your choices and budget your time accordingly. Hotels and restaurants in the Very Expensive and Expensive categories are rated on a scale of one (highly recommended) to three stars (exceptional). Those in the Moderate and Inexpensive categories rate from zero (recommended) to two stars (very highly recommended). Attractions, towns, and regions are rated according to the following scale: zero stars (recommended), one star (highly recommended), two stars (very highly recommended), and three stars (must-see).

In addition to the rating system, we also use seven icons to highlight insider information, useful tips, special bargains, hidden gems, memorable experiences, kid-friendly venues, places to avoid, and other useful information:

(Finds (Fun Fact (Kids (Moments (Overrated (Tips (Value

The following abbreviations are used for credit cards:

AE	American Express	DISC	Discover	V	Visa
DC	Diners Club	MC	MasterCard		

FROMMERS.COM

Now that you have the guidebook to a great trip, visit our website at **www.frommers.com** for travel information on nearly 2,000 destinations. With features updated regularly, we give you instant access to the most current trip-planning information available. At Frommers.com, you'll also find the best prices on airfares, accommodations, and car rentals—and you can even book travel online through our travel booking partners. At Frommers.com, you'll also find the following:

- Daily Newsletter highlighting the best travel deals
- Hot Spot of the Month/Vacation Sweepstakes & Travel Photo Contest
- More than 200 Travel Message Boards
- Outspoken Newsletters and Feature Articles on travel bargains, vacation ideas, tips and resources, and more!

What's New in Australia

Perhaps it's the success of reality TV's *Survivor: The Australian Outback,* but interest in the Outback has taken a dramatic upturn. Australia has even declared 2002 the **Year of the Outback,** and activities and events are being staged in celebration. One of the key events is a Great Australian Outback Cattle Drive through the South Australian desert, in which visitors can take part. (See "Calling All City Slickers" in chapter 2 for more information.) You'll find plenty of other new Outback adventures in South Australia, a state that's generally overlooked by most tourists. **Banksia Adventures** (© **08/8236 9141;** www.banksia-adventure.com.au) runs camping trips to the craggy Flinders Rangers in South Australia. **South Australian Scenic Tours** (© **08/8289 3970;** jpayne@camtech.net.au) takes adventurers up the Birdsville Track in the arid interior; while **Wayward Bus** (© **1800/882 823** in Australia, or 08/8232 6646; www.waywardbus.com.au) offers a trip all the way from Adelaide to Alice Springs, complete with camping under the stars.

Checking on things further south: Nothing much is new in Tasmania—it's that kind of place, really—and Melbourne ticks along nicely as always. Read on for a quick rundown on other noteworthy developments in the rest of the country:

PLANNING YOUR TRIP See chapter 2 for more information. As mentioned, the popularity of the *Survivor* franchise has sent tour operators rushing to cash in. Cairns-based **The Adventure Company** (© **800/388-7333** in the U.S., or 07/4051 4777) is offering an action-oriented 8-day holiday package to the same scenic location where the TV show was filmed. The package is loosely based on the TV show—but unlike the program contestants, you get to actually eat and have fun.

Australia's major domestic airline, Qantas, now has a competitor in no-frills airline **Virgin Blue** (© **07/3295 2296**) on some major east coast routes. Virgin Blue's fares can be considerably lower than those offered by the two "big guys," Though at press time there was talk that Virgin Blue would merge with Qantas.

And speaking of regional air service in Australia, in late 2001, **Ansett Australia** and its subsidiaries (Hazelton Airlines, Kendell Airlines, Skywest Airlines, and Aeropelican) suspended operations, as the airline looked for a buyer to bail them out of bankruptcy. Ansett was, after Qantas, the country's major airline, offering international and extensive regional service. Qantas announced plans to take over some of Ansett's regional routes, but as this book went to press, new schedules and destinations were not available. Now that two other carriers—Impulse and Flight West—have also folded, local plane service may be hard to come by in some of Australia's more remote areas. Contact **Qantas** (© **13 13 13** in Australia, 800/227-4500 in the United States and Canada,

457/747 767 in the UK; www. qantas.com.au) and the tourist bureaus of areas where you are planning to travel for the latest updates on regional air service.

A new aerial tour company, **Connoisseur Tours** (© 02/9964-9220), offers upscale tours right around the country in a chartered Boeing 737.

Great Southern Railway (© 08/ 8213 4592), operator of the upmarket trains *Indian Pacific* (between Sydney and Perth) and *The Ghan* (between Sydney and Alice Springs), has launched rail packages under a new "Trainways" package holiday banner. The packages incorporate a good range of activities, sightseeing and accommodation, both in major cities as well as in quirky Outback spots like Coober Pedy, Kalgoorlie, and Broken Hill.

Orient Express Trains & Cruises (© 800/524 2420 in the U.S., or 1800/000 395 in Australia) is now keeping its ultra-luxurious *Great South Pacific Express* train in cooler Sydney during January, February, and March, when tropical Cairns gets too humid for comfortable travel. In these months, the company will offer packages that include rail travel, sightseeing, upscale experiences like helicopter flights over Sydney Harbour and stays in luxury resorts in the lovely Blue Mountains, as well as visits to the Hunter Valley wine region and Canberra, the nation's capital.

National coach operator **McCafferty's** has bought out its only rival, **Greyhound Pioneer.** It doesn't look like fares will rise now that competition has been eliminated; if anything, they seem to be the same, or even a little lower, as the companies streamline their operations.

SYDNEY See chapter 3 for more information. Dozens of hotels opened up in the lead-up to the 2000 Sydney Olympics, but those still causing a stir are the excellent apartment complexes

run by Medina, particularly the **Medina Grand Harbourside,** corner of Shelley and King streets, King Street Wharf, at Darling Harbour (© 1300 300 232 in Australia, or 02/9249 7000). Medina routinely offers excellent rates, so make sure to ring ahead to inquire about specials. Another apartment complex worth considering is the **Quay Grand Suites Sydney,** 61 Macquarie St., East Circular Quay, on the pedestrian walkway leading up to the Sydney Opera House (© 1800 091 954 in Australia, or 02/9256 4000). The rooms overlooking the harbor are terrific.

The pedestrian walkway was completely upgraded in the lead up to the Olympics but it's only really come into its own post-Games. This is a restaurant scene worth exploring— and while in the area, why not stop off for a movie at the new art house **Dendy Cinema,** virtually next door at 2 East Circular Quay (© 02/9247 3800).

On the action front, Sydney Harbour has cranked up the gears with the recent addition of two jet-boat companies. **Harbour Jet** (© 02/9929 7373; www.harbourjet.com) offers fast and furious rides along with pumping rock music. A more relaxed experience comes with **Aussie Duck** (© 02/9251 7774; www.aussieduck. com), a purpose-built amphibious people-carrier that operates on water and land. The Duck takes in the heart of Sydney before rolling into the water for a harbor tour.

NEW SOUTH WALES See chapter 4 for more information. For this edition of *Frommer's Australia* I have added coverage of Ulladulla, a fishing town on the south coast. It's well worth popping down here—and taking in Jervis Bay on the way—even if you don't intend to drive the whole south coast route. Pebbly Beach, not far to the south of Ulladulla, is famous for the kangaroos on the beach.

BRISBANE & QUEENSLAND
See chapters 5 and 6 for more information. Getting from Brisbane Airport to the city and Gold Coast has been made easier and, perhaps more importantly, cheaper with the introduction of **Airtrain,** a new rail link. Fares to the Brisbane Central Business District are A$9 (U.S.$5.85) and to the Gold Coast A$17.90 (U.S.$11.65). Stations can be found inside the airport terminal, and helpful "red-coat" staff members are on hand to assist.

Major changes on the accommodation scene have largely centered on Queensland's island resorts, several of which have undergone major overhauls to add even more luxury touches. The super-luxe **Hayman** (© 800/223-6800 in the U.S. and Canada, or 1800/075 175) has spent a whopping A$12 million (U.S.$7.8 million) to refurbish all rooms, create new ones and add a beachfront restaurant. At **Bedarra Island** (© 800/225-9849 in the U.S. and Canada, or 1800/737 678), the resort has been given a more contemporary style, with larger verandas for the private villas and revamped public areas.

While in the Whitsunday Islands, don't forget to check out the new A$8 million (U.S.$5.2 million) **lagoon at Airlie Beach,** which is the best place to swim during stinger season!

At press time, **Daydream Island Resort** was ready to reopen under the Accor hotel group's Novotel banner after a A$30-million (U.S.$19.5-million) renovation. Stay tuned to the "Updates" page on frommers.travelocity.com for more information and a review. **Great Keppel Island,** off the central Queensland coast, is also now an Accor-managed property; reservations are now being accepted before its reopening as a Mercure resort in October 2001 (© 1800/221-4542 in the U.S. and Canada, or 1300/65 65 65).

On fabulous **Heron Island** (© 800/225-9849 in the U.S. and Canada, or 1800/737 678), the old wooden bunkbed "Turtle Cabins" have been replaced with duplex-style "Turtle Rooms," and a new restaurant with sea views has opened as part of major work completed in September 2001.

Silky Oaks Lodge, in Daintree (© 800/225-9849 in the U.S. and Canada, or 1800/737 678), and **Sheraton Noosa Resort,** on the Sunshine Coast (© 1800/073 535, or 07/5449 4888), have both launched extensive day spas for those who want a pampering after a hard day in the rain forest or at the beach.

Never one to be outdone, the Gold Coast has welcomed the opening of the grandiose **Palazzo Versace** resort (© 1800/098 000, or 07/5509 8000), a monument to the late Gianni and his particular style. It may be the world's first, but they say it won't be the last!

THE RED CENTRE See chapter 7 for more information. If you've always harbored a secret hankering to feed bugs to snakes or walk around with a frill-necked lizard on your shoulder, you can satisfy it at the new **Alice Springs Reptile Centre** (© 08/8952 8900).

Rockayer, the company that provided aerial day trip service to King's Canyon, has ceased operation. The routes have been picked up by **Ayers Rock Scenic Flights** (© 08/8956 2345). The company also offers 110-minute Uluru/Olgas/Lake Amadeus/Kings Canyon "joyflights." Another firm, **Wright's Air** (© 08/8995 5670), also offers aerial day trips on a charter basis from Alice Springs.

Ayers Rock Resort (© 02/9339 1040) is planning a lavish new luxury safari camp to open in the dunes some time this year. We're not talking nylon zip-up two-person tents with sleeping bags, either; instead, think luxuriously appointed floored "tents" with beds, air-conditioning, and bathrooms. The camp is part of an A$55-million

(U.S.$30-million plus) refurbishment to the whole resort complex that will see the conversion of a budget-minded Spinifex Lodge into a groovy new hotel, most likely in the mid- to high-price bracket.

THE TOP END See chapter 8 for more information. The well-heeled folks who can afford to stay in the luxurious homestead digs at **El Questro Wilderness Park,** via Kununurra (✆ **1800/221-4542** in the U.S. and Canada, or 1300/65 65 65), can now choose to have their private dinner table set up wherever they like: on the veranda overlooking beautiful Chamberlain Gorge; in their room, out under the stars by the pool; or even down the side of the gorge cliff above the croc-infested river.

PERTH & WESTERN AUSTRALIA See chapter 9 for more information. Fans of one of Perth's best chefs (make that one of Australia's best chefs), Kate Lamont, no longer have to make the 20-minute drive out to Lamont's Winery, Restaurant & Gallery in the Swan Valley to sample her hearty fare. She has opened a second restaurant downtown in East Perth, **Lamont's,** at 11 Brown St. (✆ **08/9202 1566**). Samples of the **gold, silver, and bronze medals** won by athletes at the Sydney 2000 Olympic Games are on show at the **Perth Mint,** 310 Hay St. (✆ **08/9421 7277**).

Fremantle's excellent **Maritime Museum** (✆ **08/9431 8444**) is being split into two this year. The existing museum (on Cliff Street) becomes the **Shipwrecks Museum,** housing displays of treasure recovered from wrecks along the state's coast, while a bold new **Maritime Museum,** at Forrest Landing on the western end of Victoria Quay, will focus on a wider picture of seamanship and sailing.

Naturaliste Charters (✆ **08/9755 2276**) is conducting its whale-watching cruises in the Southwest in a new vessel that sports an underwater camera. Passengers can now view the whales from their deckside perch, and can check out underwater images beamed to a closed-circuit TV monitor in the cabin.

The modernistic newly opened **Mining Hall of Fame** (✆ **08/9091-4074**) in the Outback gold mini town of Kalgoorlie looks like it will be one of Australia's best museums.

Northwest Regional Airlines (✆ **08/9192 1369**) has started up flights from the pearling port of Broome to Exmouth near Ningaloo Reef on the Northwest Cape; it is the first direct air link between these two wonderful Outback locations.

CANBERRA See chapter 13 for more information. The nation's capital is now the proud home of the brand new **National Museum of Australia** (✆ **1800/026 132**, or 02/6208 5000), featuring state-of-the-art technology and hands-on exhibits centered around Australian history, environment, and Aboriginal and Torres Strait Islander cultures and histories.

The Best of Australia

Maybe we shouldn't say so, being Aussies ourselves, but Australia has a lot of bests. World bests, that is. It's got some of the best natural scenery, the weirdest wildlife, the most brilliant scuba diving and snorkeling, the best beaches (shut up, California), the oldest rain forest (110 million years and counting), the oldest human civilization (some archaeologists say 40,000 years, some say 120,000; who cares?—it's old), the best wines (okay, stop focusing on Napa or Bordeaux and come see what we mean), the best weather (give or take the odd Wet Season in the north), the most innovative east-meets-west-meets-someplace-else cuisine—all bathed in sunlight that brings everything up in Technicolor.

"Best" means different things to different people, but scarcely a visitor lands on these shores without having the Great Barrier Reef at the top of their "Best Things to See in Australia" list. So they should, because it really is a glorious natural masterpiece that no one should die without seeing. Also high on most folks' must-see list is Ayers Rock. This monolith must have some kind of magnet inside it designed to attract planeloads of tourists. We're not saying the Rock isn't special, but we think the vast Australian desert all around it is even more so. The third attraction on most visitors' lists is Sydney, the Emerald City that glitters in the Antipodean sunshine on—here we go with the "bests" again—the best harbor, spanned by the best bridge in the world (shut up, San Francisco).

But as planes zoom overhead delivering visitors to these "big three" attractions, Aussies in charming country towns, on far-flung beaches, on rustic sheep stations, in rain-forest villages, and in mountain lodges shake their heads and say sadly, "They don't know what they're missin'." Well, that's the aim of this chapter—to show you what you're missin'. Read on, and consider the road less traveled.

1 The Top Travel Experiences

- **Hitting the Rails on the *Indian Pacific* Train:** This 3-day train journey across the Outback regularly makes it onto the "Top Rail Journeys in the World" lists compiled by glossy travel magazines. The desert scenery ain't all that magnificent—it's the unspoiled, empty vastness that passengers appreciate. It includes the longest straight stretch of track in the world, 478 kilometers (299 miles) across the treeless Nullarbor Plain. Start in Sydney and end in Perth, or vice versa, or just do a section. See "Getting Around Australia," in chapter 2.

- **Experiencing Sydney** (NSW): Sydney is more than just the magnificent Harbour Bridge and Opera House. For one thing, no other city has beaches in abundance like Sydney, and few have such a magnificently scenic harbor. Our advice is to get aboard a ferry, walk from one side of the bridge to the other, and try to spend a week here, because you're going to need it. See chapter 3.

Australia

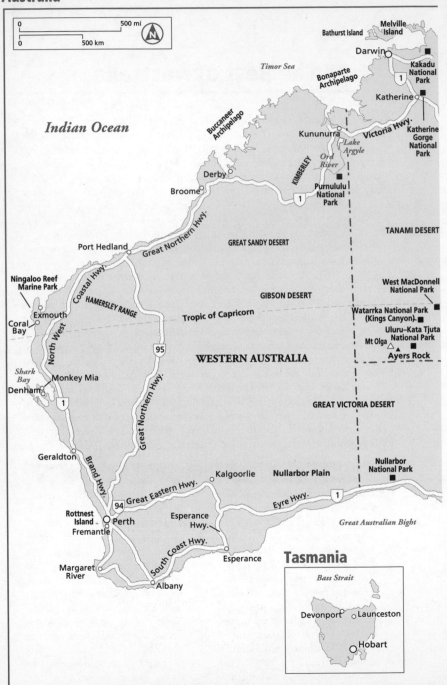

0 500 mi
0 500 km

Indian Ocean

Timor Sea

Melville Island

Bathurst Island

Darwin

Kakadu National Park

Katherine

Bonaparte Archipelago

Buccaneer Archipelago

Kununurra

Victoria Hwy.

Katherine Gorge National Park

Lake Argyle

Ord River

KIMBERLEY

Derby

Broome

Purnululu National Park

1

TANAMI DESERT

GREAT SANDY DESERT

Port Hedland

Great Northern Hwy.

Coastal Hwy.

Ningaloo Reef Marine Park

HAMERSLEY RANGE

GIBSON DESERT

West MacDonnell National Park

Tropic of Capricorn

Watarrka National Park (Kings Canyon)

Exmouth

Coral Bay

North West

Uluru–Kata Tjuta National Park

Mt Olga

Ayers Rock

95

WESTERN AUSTRALIA

Shark Bay

Monkey Mia

Denham

1

Great Northern Hwy.

GREAT VICTORIA DESERT

Geraldton

Kalgoorlie

Nullarbor Plain

Nullarbor National Park

Brand Hwy.

Great Eastern Hwy.

Eyre Hwy.

1

94

Rottnest Island

Perth

Fremantle

Esperance Hwy.

Great Australian Bight

South Coast Hwy.

Esperance

Margaret River

Albany

Tasmania

Bass Strait

Devonport

Launceston

Hobart

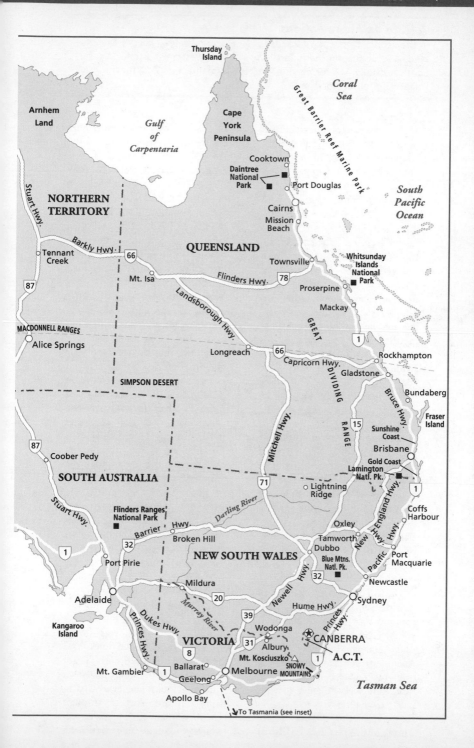

A Note on Abbreviations

In the listings below, NSW stands for New South Wales, QLD for Queensland, NT for the Northern Territory, WA for Western Australia, SA for South Australia, VIC for Victoria, TAS for Tasmania, and ACT for the Australian Capital Territory.

- **Seeing the Great Barrier Reef** (QLD): It's a glorious 2,000-kilometer-long (1,250-mile-long) underwater coral fairyland with electric colors and bizarre fish life—*and* it comes complete with warm water and year-round sunshine. This is what you came to Australia to see. When you're not snorkeling over stunning coral and giant clams almost as big as you, scuba diving, calling in at tropical towns, or lazing on deserted island beaches, you're trying out the sun lounges or enjoying the first-rate food aboard this intimate white liner. See chapter 6.
- **Exploring the Wet Tropics Rain Forest** (QLD): Folks who come from skyscraper lands like Manhattan or Los Angeles can't get over the moisture-dripping ferns, the neon-blue butterflies, and the primeval peace of this World Heritage patch of rain forest stretching north, south, and west from Cairns. Hike it, four-wheel-drive it, or glide over the treetops in the Skyrail gondola from Cairns. See chapter 6.
- **Bareboat Sailing in the Whitsundays** (QLD): Bareboat means unskippered—that's right, even if you think port is an after-dinner drink, you can charter a yacht, pay for a day's instruction from a skipper, and then take over the helm yourself and explore these 74 island gems. It's easy, really. Anchor in deserted bays, snorkel over dazzling reefs, fish for coral trout, and feel the wind in your sails. See chapter 6.
- **Exploring the Olgas (Kata Tjuta) and Ayers Rock (Uluru)** (NT): Just why everyone comes thousands of miles to see the big red stone of Ayers Rock is a mystery—that's probably why they come, because the Rock is a mystery. Just 50 kilometers (31 miles) from Ayers Rock are the round red heads of the Olgas, a second rock formation more significant to Aborigines and more intriguing to many visitors than Uluru. See chapter 7.
- **Taking an Aboriginal Culture Tour** (Alice Springs, NT): Eating female wasps, contemplating a hill as a giant resting caterpillar, and imagining that the stars are your grandmother smiling down at you will give you a new perspective on Aboriginal culture. See what we mean on a half-day tour from the Aboriginal Art & Culture Centre in Alice Springs. See chapter 7.
- **Discovering the Kimberley** (WA): Australia's last frontier, the Kimberley is a romantic cocktail of giant South Sea pearls, red mountain ranges, aqua seas, deadly crocodiles, striking Aboriginal rock art, and million-acre farms in a never-ending wilderness. Cross it by four-wheel-drive, stay in safari tents on a cattle ranch, swim under ferny waterfalls, ride a camel along the beach in Broome, and more. See chapter 8.
- **Rolling in Wildflowers** (WA): Imagine Texas three times over and covered in wildflowers. That's what much of the state of Western Australia looks like every spring from around August through October when pink, mauve, red, white, yellow, and blue wildflowers

bloom. Aussies flock here big-time for this spectacle, so book ahead. See chapter 9.

- **Drinking in the Barossa Valley** (SA): One of Australia's four largest wine-producing areas, this German-speaking region less than an hour's drive from Adelaide is also the prettiest. Adelaide's restaurants happen to be some of the country's best, too, so test out your wine purchases with the city's terrific food. See chapter 10.

- **Getting Dusty in the Desert** (SA): Head inland from Adelaide to the Outback to visit remote pubs and settlements, the craggy ridges of the Flinders ranges, as well as dry salt lakes and stony deserts. See chapter 10.

- **Seeing the Sights Along the Great Ocean Road** (VIC): This 106-kilometer (64 ½-mile) coastal road carries you past wild and stunning beaches, forests, and dramatic cliff-top scenery—including the Twelve Apostles, 12 pillars of red rock standing in splendid isolation in the foaming Southern Ocean. See chapter 12.

- **Driving Around Tasmania:** The "Apple Isle" is Australia's prettiest state, a picturesque Eden of lavender fields, wineries, snow-topped granite tors, white-water wildernesses, and haunting historic prisons. A bonus is that it's small enough to drive around in a few days. See chapter 14.

2 The Best Outdoor Adventures

- **Horse Trekking in the Snowy Mountains** (NSW): Ride the ranges like the Man from Snowy River, staying in bush lodges or camping beneath the stars. See chapter 4.

- **Abseiling (rappelling) in the Blue Mountains** (NSW): Careering backward down a cliff face with the smell of eucalyptus in your nostrils is not everyone's idea of fun, but you sure know you're alive. Several operators welcome both novices and the more experienced. See chapter 4.

- **Game Fishing:** Battle a black marlin off Cairns and you might snare the world record; that's how big they get down there. Marlin and other game catches run around much of the Australian coastline—Exmouth on the Northwest Cape in Western Australia (see chapter 9), and Broome and Darwin in the Top End (see chapter 8) are two other hotspots.

- **White-Water Rafting on the Tully River** (Mission Beach, QLD): The Grade 3 to 4 rapids of the Tully River swoosh between lush, rain-forested banks. The guides are professional, and the rapids are just hairy enough to be fun. A good choice for first-time rafters. See chapter 6.

- **Four-Wheel-Driving on Fraser Island** (QLD): Burning down 75-Mile Beach in a 4×4 on the biggest sand island in the world is liberating, if not great for the environment. Paradoxically, the island is ecologically important and popular with nature lovers. Hike its eucalyptus and rain forests, swim its clear lakes, and fish off the beach. See chapter 6.

- **Canoeing the Top End** (NT): Paddling between the sun-drenched ochre walls of Katherine Gorge sharpens the senses, especially when a (harmless) freshwater crocodile pops up! **Gecko Canoeing** will take you down-river to the rarely explored Flora and Daly River systems to meet

Aboriginal communities, shower under waterfalls, hike virgin bushland, and camp in swags on the banks. See chapter 8.

- **Surfing in Margaret River** (WA): A 90-minute surf lesson with four-time Western Australia surf champ Josh Parmateer is a great introduction to the sport—if only to hear Josh's Aussie accent! In July and August, Josh shifts his classes to Cable Beach in Broome. See chapters 8 and 9.
- **Sea Kayaking:** Kayaking is a great way to explore Queensland's Whitsunday Islands as well as Dunk Island off Mission Beach in Queensland. **Rivergods** in Perth even takes you on a sea-kayaking day trip to snorkel with wild sea lions and watch penguins feeding. This Western Australian company also runs multiday expeditions past whales, dolphins, and sharks in Shark Bay, and over coral at Ningaloo Reef on the Northwest Cape. See chapters 2 and 6.
- **Skiing in the Victorian Alps** (VIC): Skiing in Australia? Sure. When you've had enough coral and sand, you can hit the slopes in Victoria. Where else can you swish down the mountain between gum trees? See chapter 12.

3 The Best Places to View Wildlife

- **Pebbly Beach** (NSW): The eastern gray kangaroos which inhabit Murramarang National Park, 20 minutes south of Ulladulla on the south coast of New South Wales, tend to congregate along this pristine ocean beach and the adjoining grassy dunes. See chapter 4.
- **Montague Island** (Narooma, NSW): This little island just offshore from the seaside town of Narooma, on the south coast, is a haven for nesting seabirds, but it's the water around it that's home to the main attractions. Dolphins are common, fairy penguins, too; in whale-watching season, you're sure to spot southern right and humpback whales. See chapter 4.
- **Jervis Bay** (NSW): This is probably the closest place to Sydney where you're certain to see kangaroos in the wild and where you can pet them, too. The national park here is home to hundreds of bird species, including black cockatoos, as well as plenty of possums. See chapter 4.
- **Lone Pine Koala Sanctuary** (Brisbane, QLD): Cuddle a koala (and have your photo taken doing it) at this park, the world's first and largest koala sanctuary. Apart from some 130 koalas, lots of other Aussie wildlife—including wombats, Tasmanian devils, 'roos (which you can hand-feed), and colorful parakeets—are on show. See chapter 5.
- **Hervey Bay** (QLD): The warm waters off Hervey Bay, and in particular the lovely Platypus Bay, on the Queensland coast, are where the humpback whales come each year between June and October in increasing numbers to give birth. The long journey from Antarctica brings them up the coast to frolic with their young for several months before making the return trip. Hervey Bay's many cruises can bring you closer to these gentle giants than you'll ever come elsewhere. See chapter 6.
- **Australian Butterfly Sanctuary** (Kuranda, near Cairns, QLD): Walk through the biggest butterfly "aviary" in Australia and see some of Australia's most gorgeous butterflies, including the electric-blue Ulysses. See many species of butterfly feed, lay eggs, and mate,

and inspect caterpillars and pupae. Wearing pink, red, or white encourages the butterflies to land on you. See chapter 6.

• **Wait-a-While Environmental Tours** (QLD): Head into the World Heritage–listed Wet Tropics rain forest behind Cairns or Port Douglas with this ecotour operator to spotlight possums, lizards, pythons, even a platypus, so shy that most Aussies have never seen one in the wild. About once a month one group will spot the rare, bizarre Lumholtz's tree kangaroo. See chapter 6.

• **Mon Repos Turtle Rookery** (Bundaberg, QLD): Most nights November through January, giant green, loggerhead, and hawksbill turtles crawl up Mon Repos Beach in Bundaberg to lay their eggs. From late January to March, the babies hatch at night and scamper down to the water. Rangers lead inexpensive tours to watch these magical spectacles. See chapter 6. Heron Island in Queensland (also in chapter 6) and the Northwest Cape in Western Australia (see chapter 9) are two other good turtle-watching sites.

• **Currumbin Wildlife Sanctuary** (The Gold Coast, QLD): Tens of thousands of unbelievably pretty red, blue, green, and yellow rainbow lorikeets have been screeching into this park for generations to be hand-fed by delighted visitors every morning and afternoon. There are 'roos and other Australian animals at the sanctuary, too, but the birds steal the show. See chapter 6.

• **Kakadu National Park** (NT): One-third of Australia's bird species live in Kakadu; so do lots of dangerous saltwater crocs. A cruise on the Yellow Waters Billabong, or aboard the Original Jumping Crocodiles cruise en route to the park, are some of the best places to see them in the wild. See chapter 8.

• **The Northwest Cape** (WA): For the thrill of a lifetime, go snorkeling with a whale shark. No one knows where they come from, but these mysterious monsters up to 18 meters (60 ft.) long surface in the remote Outback waters off Western Australia every year from March to early June. A mini-industry takes snorkelers out to swim alongside the sharks as they feed (on plankton, not snorkelers). See chapter 9.

• **Bunbury and Monkey Mia** (WA) and **Tangalooma** (QLD): There are several places you can see, hand-feed or swim with wild dolphins Down Under. At Bunbury, south of Perth, you can swim with them or join cruises to see them (they come right up to the boat). If you want an almost guaranteed dolphin sighting, head to Tangalooma Wild Dolphin Resort, a day trip from Brisbane, where you can hand-feed them, or to Monkey Mia on the lonely Outback coast, where they cruise past your legs. Even better is a cruise on the *Shotover* catamaran to see some of the area's 10,000 dugongs (manatees), plus turtles, sea snakes, sharks—and more. See chapters 5 and 9.

• **Kangaroo Island** (SA): You're sure to see more native animals here—including koalas, wallabies, birds, echidnas, reptiles, seals, and sea lions—than anywhere else in the country, apart from a wildlife park. Another plus: The distances between major points of interest are not great, so you won't spend half the day just getting from place to place. See chapter 10.

4 The Best Places to Experience the Outback

- **Broken Hill** (NSW): There's no better place to experience real Outback life than in Broken Hill. There's the city itself, with its thriving art scene and the Royal Flying Doctor service; a historic ghost town on its outskirts; a national park with Aboriginal wall paintings; an opal mining town nearby; and plenty of kangaroos, emus, and giant wedge-tailed eagles. See chapter 4.

- **Lightning Ridge** (NSW): This opal-mining town is as rough and ready as the stones they pull out of the ground. Meet amazing characters, share in the eccentricity of the place, and visit opal-rush areas with mole-hill scenery made by the old sun-bleached mine tailings. See chapter 4.

- **Uluru-Kata Tjuta National Park** (Ayers Rock, NT): Sure, Ayers Rock will enthrall you with its eerie beauty; but the nearby Olgas are more soothing, more interesting, and actually taller than the Rock, so make the time to wander through them, too. Hike the Rock's base, burn around it on a Harley-Davidson, saunter up to it on a camel, climb it if you must. Don't go home until you've felt the powerful heartbeat of the desert. See chapter 7.

- **The MacDonnell Ranges** (NT): The Aborigines say these red rocky hills were formed by the Aboriginal "Caterpillar Dreaming" that wriggled from the earth here. To the west of Alice Springs are dramatic gorges, idyllic (and bloody cold) waterholes, and cute wallabies. To the east are Aboriginal rock carvings, and the Ross River Homestead, where you can crack a stockwhip, throw a boomerang, feast on damper and billy tea, and ride a horse or camel in the bush. See chapter 7.

- **Kings Canyon** (NT): Anyone who saw the cult flick *The Adventures of Priscilla, Queen of the Desert* will remember the scene where the transvestites climb a soaring orange cliff and survey the desert floor. That was Kings Canyon, about 320 kilometers (200 miles) from Alice Springs in one direction and Ayers Rock in the other. Trek the dramatic rim or take the easier shady route along the bottom. Don't forget your lipstick, guys. See chapter 7.

- **Elsey Station** (NT): This vast farm got more than its 15 minutes of fame as the setting of the Australian book *We of the Never Never,* an account of isolated Outback life written in 1902 by the station's owner, Mrs. Jeannie Gunn. The title originated in visitors' desire to "never never" leave such remote beauty. Visit for a day and meet the resident Aboriginal kids, or stay longer and canoe the isolated Roper River to Red Lily Lagoon. See chapter 8.

- **The Northwest Cape** (WA): This treeless moonscape of red anthills, spiky spinifex, and blazing heat seems to go on forever, so it's all the more amazing to find a beautiful coral reef offshore. Drive the rugged hills in a four-wheel-drive, dodging kangaroos on the way; swim with giant manta rays; snorkel right off the beach; scuba dive coral outcroppings; and laze on blindingly white beaches. This is where the Outback meets the sea. See chapter 9.

- **Coober Pedy** (SA): It may be hot and dusty, but you'll get a true taste of the Outback as you tag along with the local mail carrier as he makes his rounds to the area's remote cattle stations (ranches). It's a 12-hour, 600-kilometer (372-mile) journey along sun-baked dirt roads. See chapter 10.

5 The Best Beaches

- **Palm Beach** (Sydney): At the end of a string of beaches stretching north from Sydney, Palm Beach is long and very white, with some good surfing and a golf course. See chapter 3.
- **Hyams Beach** (Jervis Bay, NSW): This beach in pretty, off-the-beaten-path Jervis Bay is said to be the whitest in the world. You need to wear sunblock if you decide to stroll along it, because the reflection from the sun, even on a cloudy day, can give you a nasty sunburn. The beach also squeaks as you walk. See chapter 4.
- **Four Mile Beach** (Port Douglas, QLD): The sea is turquoise, the sun is warm, the palms sway, and the low-rise hotels starting to line this country beach can't spoil the feeling that it is a million miles from anywhere. But isn't there always a serpent in paradise? In this case the "serpents" are north Queensland's seasonal, potentially deadly marine stingers. Come June through September to avoid them, or confine your swimming to the area in the stinger net the rest of the year. See chapter 6.
- **Mission Beach** (QLD): Azure blue water, islands dotting the horizon, and white sand edged by tangled vine forests make this beach a real winner. The bonus is that hardly anyone ever comes here. Cassowaries (giant emu-like birds) hide out in the rain forest, and the tiny town of Mission Beach makes itself invisible behind the leaves. Visit June through September to avoid deadly marine stingers. See chapter 6.
- **Whitehaven Beach** (Whitsunday Island, QLD): It's not a surf beach, but this 6-kilometer (3¾-mile) stretch of white silica sand on uninhabited Whitsunday Island is pristine and peaceful. Bring a book, curl up under the rain forest lining its edge, and fantasize that the cruise boat is going to leave without you. See chapter 6.
- **Surfers Paradise Beach** (Gold Coast, QLD): Actually, all 35 of the beaches on the 30-kilometer (19-mile) Gold Coast strip in south Queensland are worthy of inclusion here. Every one has sand so clean it squeaks, great surf, and fresh breezes—ignore the tacky high-rises. Surfers will like Kirra and Burleigh Heads. See chapter 6.
- **Cable Beach** (Broome, WA): Is it the South Sea pearls they pull out of the Indian Ocean, the camels loping along the sand, the sunsets, the surf, or the red earth meeting the green sea that gives this beach an exotic appeal? Maybe it's the 26 kilometers (16 miles) of glorious white sand. The only time to swim here is June through September, when deadly marine stingers aren't around. See chapter 8.
- **Cottesloe Beach** (Perth, WA): Perth has 19 great beaches, but this petite crescent is the prettiest. After you've checked out the scene, join the fashionable set for brunch in the Indiana Tea House, a mock-Edwardian bathhouse fronting the sea. Surfers head to Scarborough and Trigg. See chapter 9.

6 The Best Diving & Snorkeling Sites

- **Port Douglas** (QLD): Among the fabulous dive sites found off the shores of Port Douglas, north of Cairns, are Split-Bommie, with its delicate fan corals and schools of colorful fusiliers; Barracuda Pass, with its coral gardens and giant clams; and the swim-through coral spires of the Cathedrals. Snorkelers can glide over abundant coral and reef fish life of Agincourt Reef. See chapter 6.

- **Lizard Island** (QLD): Snorkel over 150-year-old giant clams—as well as gorgeous underwater coral—in the Clam Garden, just off this exclusive resort island northeast of Cairns. Nearby is the famous Cod Hole, where divers can hand-feed a school of giant potato cod. See chapter 6.

- **Cairns** (QLD): Moore, Norman, Hardy, Saxon, and Arlington reefs and Michaelmas and Upolu cays—all about 90 minutes off Cairns—offer great snorkeling and endless dive sites. Explore on a day trip from Cairns or join a live-aboard adventure. See chapter 6.

- **Coral Sea** (QLD): In this sea east of the Great Barrier Reef off north Queensland, you'll see sharks feeding at Predator's Playground; 1,000-meter (3,280-ft.) drop-offs in the Abyss; large reefs covering hundreds of square miles; and tropical species not found on the Great Barrier Reef. This is not a day-trip destination; numerous dive operators run multiday trips on live-aboard vessels. Visibility is excellent—up to 100 meters (328 ft.). See chapter 6.

- *Yongala* **wreck** (QLD): Sunk by a cyclone in 1911, the 120-meter (394-ft.) SS *Yongala* lies in the Coral Sea off Townsville. Big schools of trevally, kingfish, barracuda, and batfish surround the wreckage; giant Queensland grouper live under the bow, lionfish hide under the stern, turtles graze on the hull, and hard and soft corals make their home on it. It's too far for a day trip; live-aboard trips run from Townsville and Cairns. See chapter 6.

- **The Whitsunday Islands** (QLD): As well as Blue Pearl Bay, these 74 breathtaking islands offer countless dive sites both among the islands themselves and on the Outer Great Barrier Reef 90 minutes away. Bait Reef on the Outer Reef is popular for its cascading drop-offs. Snorkelers can explore not just the Outer Reef, but also patch reefs among the islands and rarely visited fringing reefs around many island shores. See chapter 6.

- **Heron Island** (QLD): Easily the number-one snorkel and dive site in Australia. If you stayed in the water for a week, you couldn't snorkel all the acres of coral stretching from shore. Take your pick of 22 dive sites: the Coral Cascades, with football trout and anemones; the Blue Pools, favored by octopus, turtles, and sharks; and Heron Bommie, with its rays, eels, and Spanish dancers; and more. Absolute magic. See chapter 6.

- **Lady Elliot Island** (QLD): Gorgeous coral lagoons, perfect for snorkeling, line this tiny coral cay island off the town of Bundaberg. Boats take you farther out to snorkel above manta rays, plate coral, and big fish. Divers can swim through the blow hole, 16 meters (52 ft.) down, and see Gorgonian fans, soft and hard corals, shark, barracudas, and loads of reef fish. See chapter 6.

- **Rottnest Island** (WA): Just 19 kilometers (12 miles) off Perth, this former prison island has excellent snorkeling and more than 100 dive sites. Wrecks, limestone overhangs, and myriad fish will keep divers entertained. There are no cars, so snorkelers should rent a bike and snorkel gear, buy a visitor center map of suggested snorkel trails, and head off to find their own private coral garden. The sunken grotto of Fishhook Bay is great for fish life. See chapter 9.

- **Ningaloo Reef** (WA): A well-kept secret is how we'd describe Australia's second great barrier reef, stretching some 260 kilometers (163 miles) along the Northwest Cape halfway up Western Australia. Coral starts right on shore, not 90 minutes out to sea as at the Great Barrier Reef. Snorkel or dive with manta rays, and dive to see sharks, angelfish, turtles, eels, grouper, potato cod, and much more. Snorkel with whale sharks up to 18 meters (60 ft.) long, every year from March to early June. See chapter 9.

7 The Best Places to Bushwalk (Hike)

- **Blue Mountains** (NSW): Many bushwalks in the Blue Mountains National Park offer awesome views of valleys, waterfalls, cliffs, and forest. All are easily reached from Sydney. See chapter 4.
- **Whitsunday Islands** (QLD): Most people think of snorkeling and water sports when they come to these subtropical national-park islands clad in dense rain forest and bush, but every resort island we recommend in chapter 6 has hiking trails. Some are flat; some are hilly. Wallabies and butterflies are common sights en route. South Molle has the best network of trails and 360° island views from its peak. See chapter 6.
- **Lamington National Park** (QLD): Few other national parks in Australia have such a well-marked network of trails (160 kilometers/100 miles in all) as this one, just 90 minutes from the Gold Coast. Revel in dense subtropical rain forest, marvel at mossy 2,000-year-old Antarctic beech trees, delight in the prolific wallabies and birds, and soak up the cool mountain air. See chapter 6.
- **Larapinta Trail** (The Red Centre, NT): Soon you will be able to start at Alice Springs and walk this entire 250-kilometer (156-mile) semi-desert trail that winds through the stark crimson Mac-Donnell Ranges. The trail is still under construction, but plenty of day-length and multiday sections are waiting for you now. This one's for the cooler months only (Apr–Oct). See chapter 7.
- **Kakadu National Park** (NT): Whether a pleasant wetlands stroll or a tough overnight hike in virgin bushland, you can find it in this World Heritage–listed park. You'll see red cliffs, cycads, waterfalls, lily-filled lagoons hiding man-eating crocodiles, what sometimes looks like Australia's entire bird population, and Aboriginal rock art. See chapter 8.
- **Cape-to-Cape** (WA): Rugged sea cliffs, a china-blue sea, eucalyptus forest, white beaches, and coastal heath are what you will find hiking between Cape Naturaliste and Cape Leeuwin, in the southwest corner of Western Australia. In season, you'll see whales and wildflowers. See chapter 9.
- **Freycinet National Park** (TAS): The trek to Wine Glass Bay passes warty pink granite outcrops, with views over an ocean sliced by a

crescent of icy sand. It's prehistorically beautiful. See chapter 14.

• **Cradle Mountain & Lake St. Clair National Park** (TAS): The 80-kilometer (50-mile) Overland Track is the best hike in Australia.

The trek, from Lake St. Clair to Cradle Mountain, takes anywhere from 5 to 10 days, depending on your fitness level. Shorter walks, some lasting just half an hour, are also accessible. See chapter 14.

8 The Best Places to Learn About Aboriginal Culture

• **The Umbarra Aboriginal Cultural Centre** (Wallaga Lake, near Narooma, NSW): This center offers boomerang- and spear-throwing instruction, painting with natural ochres, discussions on Aboriginal culture, and guided walking tours of Aboriginal sacred sites. See chapter 4.

• **Tjapukai Aboriginal Cultural Park** (Cairns, QLD): This multi-million-dollar center showcases the history of the local Tjapukai people—their Dreamtime creation history and their often-harrowing experiences since the white man arrived—using a film, a superb theatrical work, and a dance performance. Its Aboriginal art and crafts gift shop is one of the country's biggest and best. See chapter 6.

• **Native Guide Safari Tours** (Port Douglas, QLD): Hazel Douglas, an Aborigine who was raised in the 110-million-year-old Daintree rain forest, takes you on a full-day four-wheel-drive rain-forest safari. She shows you how to rustle up a roast dinner using a termites nest, tells you how to know you're in for rain (it's in the way lizards sit on trees), and teaches you how to know when a crocodile is in the water. It's a fabulous insight into the world's oldest culture—one that's almost lost. See chapter 6.

• **Aboriginal Art & Culture Centre** (Alice Springs, NT): You'll taste bush food, see a dance, throw boomerangs and spears and learn about Aboriginal family values in one half-day tour of this Aborigine-owned center in Alice Springs. Be sure to hang around for the 1-hour didgeridoo lesson at the end. See chapter 7.

• **Anangu Tours** (Ayers Rock, NT): The Anangu are the owners of Ayers Rock, or Uluru, as it is called in their native tongue. Join them for walks around the Rock as you learn about the poisonous "snake men" who fought battles here, pick bush food off the trees, throw spears, visit rock paintings, and watch the sun set over the monolith. Their Cultural Centre near the base of the Rock has good displays about the Aboriginal Dreamtime. See chapter 7.

• **Manyallaluk: The Dreaming Place** (Katherine, NT): This Aboriginal community welcomes visitors to their bush home and teaches them to paint, weave, throw boomerangs, and other tasks of daily life. A low-key day and the chance to chat one-on-one with Aboriginal people. See chapter 8.

• **Mangarrayi People** (Katherine, NT): Mike Keighley of **Far Out Adventures** takes tours to beautiful Elsey Station (a ranch) near Katherine, where you visit with the children of the local Mangarrayi people. Sample bush tucker, learn a little bush medicine, and swim in a natural "spa-pool" in the Roper River. See chapter 8.

• **Yamatji Bitja Aboriginal Bush Tours** (Kalgoorlie, WA): Geoffrey Stokes, brought up the traditional

Aboriginal way in the bush, takes you out to track emus, forage for bush food, and maybe even hunt a 'roo for dinner (with a gun, not a boomerang!). Explore the bush, learn about Aboriginal Dreamtime creation myths, and find out more about his childhood. See chapter 9.

- **Tandanya Aboriginal Cultural Institute** (Adelaide, SA): This is a great place to experience life through Aboriginal eyes. You might catch one of the dance or other performances, although there are plenty of other opportunities to find out more about Aboriginal culture. See chapter 10.

9 The Best of Small-Town Australia

- **Central Tilba** (NSW): Just inland from Narooma on the south coast, this tiny historic hamlet is one of the cutest you'll ever see, complete with its own blacksmiths and leather-work outlets. The ABC cheese factory offers free tastings, and you can spend hours browsing antique stalls or simply admiring the period buildings. See chapter 4.
- **Broken Hill** (NSW): Known for its giant silver mines, the quirky town of Broken Hill has more pubs per capita than just about anywhere else. It's also the home of the School of the Air—a "classroom" that transmits lessons by radio to isolated communities spread over thousands of miles of Outback. Here you'll also find the eccentric Palace Hotel, made famous in *The Adventures of Priscilla, Queen of the Desert,* as well as plenty of colonial mansions and heritage homes. See chapter 4.
- **Port Douglas** (QLD): What happens when Sydneysiders and Melburnites discover a quaint one-street fishing village in tropical north Queensland? Come to Port Douglas and find out. A strip of groovy restaurants and a championship golf course have not diminished "Port's" old-fashioned air. Four Mile Beach is at the end of the street, and boats depart daily for the Great Barrier Reef from the marina. See chapter 6.

- **Mission Beach** (QLD): You'd never know this tidy village, hidden in lush rain forest off the highway, existed if you weren't well-informed. Aussies know it's here, but few bother to patronize its dazzling beach, offshore islands, and secluded rain-forest trails, so you'll have the place all to yourself. There's great white-water rafting on the nearby Tully River, too. See chapter 6.
- **Broome** (WA): This romantic pearling port on the far-flung Kimberley coast on the Indian Ocean blends Aussie corrugated-iron architecture with red pagoda roofs left by the Chinese pearl divers who settled here. The town fuses a sophisticated international ambience with a rough Outback attitude. Play on beautiful Cable Beach (see "The Best Beaches," above) and stay at glamorous Cable Beach Club Resort. This is the place to add to your South Sea pearl collection. See chapter 8.
- **Kalgoorlie** (WA): This is it, the iconic Australian country town. Vibrant Kalgoorlie sits on what used to be the richest square mile of gold-bearing earth ever. It still pumps around 2,000 ounces *a day* out of the ground. Have a beer in one of the gracious 19th-century pubs, peer into the world's biggest open-cut gold mine, and wander the ghost-town streets of its sister town, Coolgardie. See chapter 9.

• **Hahndorf** (SA): A group of Lutheran settlers founded this German-style town, located in the Adelaide Hills just outside the Adelaide, in the 1830s. You'll love the churches, the wool factory and craft shops, and the delicious German food served up in the local cafes, restaurants, and bakeries. See chapter 10.

• **Coober Pedy** (SA): For an Outback experience that's *fair dinkum* (genuine), few places are as weird and wonderful as this opal-mining town in the middle of nowhere. Visit mines, see wacky museums, and stay in a hotel underground— not all that unusual, considering that the locals live like moles anyway. See chapter 10.

• **Launceston** (TAS): Tasmania's second city is not much larger than your average European or American small town, but it's packed with Victorian and Georgian architecture and plenty of remnants of Australia's convict past. Spend a few days here and discover the local scenery, splurging a little on a stay in a historic hotel. See chapter 14.

10 The Best Museums

• **Australian National Maritime Museum** (Sydney, NSW): The best things about this museum are the ships and submarines often docked in the harbor out front. You can climb aboard and explore what it's like to be a sailor. Inside are some fascinating displays relating to Australia's dependence on the oceans. See chapter 3.

• **Alice Springs Telegraph Station Historical Reserve** (NT): It's not called a museum, but that's what this restored telegraph-repeater station out in the picturesque hills by a spring—Alice Springs— really is. From the hot biscuits turned out of the wood-fired oven to the old telegraph equipment tapping away, this 1870s settlement is as real as history can get. See chapter 7.

• **Australian Aviation Heritage Centre** (Darwin, NT): The pride of this hangar is a B-52 bomber on permanent loan from the United States. But there's loads more, and not just heaps of planes, engines, and other aviation paraphernalia—there are detailed stories, jokes, and anecdotes associated with the exhibits that will appeal even if you don't have avgas (aviation fuel) running in your veins. See chapter 8.

• **Warradjan Aboriginal Cultural Centre** (NT): Reader Mari Fagin of Oklahoma City, Oklahoma, wrote that this small, stylish museum in Kakadu National Park makes for a "very memorable and moving experience!! This museum is one of the best of its type we've ever seen." Learn about Dreamtime myths and day-to-day life of Aboriginal people living in Kakadu. See chapter 8.

• **Western Australian Maritime Museum** (to be renamed Shipwrecks Museum after mid-2002) (Perth, WA): Housed in a two-level warehouse in the historic port precinct of Fremantle, Perth, this museum tells tales of the harsh Western Australian coastline since the Dutch first bumped into it and abandoned it as useless in the 1600s. Anyone who ever dreamed of finding a shipwreck laden with pieces of eight will relish the displays of treasure recovered from the deep. See chapter 9.

• **New Norcia Museum and Art Gallery** (New Norcia, WA): The collection of European Renaissance art in this tiny country museum in the Spanish Benedictine monastery town of New Norcia is mind-boggling. The museum also has all kinds of memorabilia from the monks' past— manuscripts, clothing, musical instruments, and gifts from Queen Isabella of Spain. See chapter 9.

- **The Migration Museum** (Adelaide, SA): This fascinating museum gives visitors insight into the people who came to Australia, how and where they settled, and how many suffered getting here.

Don't expect a lot of musty displays, because this museum is full of hands-on activities. See chapter 10.

- **Australian War Memorial** (Canberra, ACT): Given its name, you might think this museum is a bleak sort of place, but you'd be wrong. The museum gives important insight into the Anzac (Australian and New Zealand Army Corps) spirit, including an evocative exhibit on the tragic battle of Gallipoli. There's also a pretty good art collection. See chapter 13.

11 The Best Luxury Accommodations

- **Sir Stamford at Circular Quay, Sydney** (© 1300/301 391 in Australia, or 02/9252 4600): This grand five-star city hotel combines old-world luxury with a wonderful bar and nice views. I like the top-hatted doorman who valet-parked my rusting 1976 Toyota without a comment. See chapter 3.
- **Park Hyatt Sydney** (© 13 12 34 in Australia, or 02/9241 1234): You'll have to book well in advance to snag a room at Sydney's best-positioned property, located at the edge of the city's historic Rocks district. Many rooms have fabulous views across the harbor to the Sydney Opera House. See chapter 3.
- **Lizard Island** (off Cairns, QLD; © 1800/737 678 in Australia, 800/225-9849 in the U.S. and Canada, or 020/7805 3875 in the U.K.): Exclusive Lizard Island has long been popular with Americans for its game fishing, wonderful coral and diving, smart food, and simple upscale lodge accommodations. See chapter 6.
- **Sebel Reef House** (Cairns, QLD; © 1800/079 052 in Australia): Everyone who stays here says the same thing: "It feels like home."

Airy rooms look into tropical gardens, waterfalls cascade into the pools, mosquito nets drape over the beds, and you could swear pith-helmeted colonial officers will be back any minute to finish their gin-and-tonics in the clubby Brigadier Bar. Idyllic Palm Cove Beach is just across the road. See chapter 6.

- **Bedarra Island** (off Mission Beach, QLD; © 1800/737 678 in Australia, 800/225-9849 in the U.S. and Canada, or 020/7805 3875 in the U.K.): Presidents and princesses in need of a little time out come to this small rain-forest island ringed by beaches. The timber villas are cozy, and the ultra-discreet staff assures privacy. Best of all, though, is the extravagant 24-hour open bar. See chapter 6.
- **Orpheus Island Resort** (off Townsville or Cairns, QLD; © 1800/077 167 in Australia): Beloved of film stars and others who relish privacy, this resort has simple, attractive rooms; good food; a marvelous sense of seclusion; and a particularly beautiful location in the curve of a palm-lined bay. The only way in is by seaplane. See chapter 6.

• **Hayman** (Whitsunday Islands, QLD; ℂ **1800/075 175** in Australia, or call Leading Hotels of the World at ℂ 800/223-6800 in the U.S. and Canada, 0800/181 123 in the U.K., 1800/409 063 in Ireland, or 0800/44 1016 in New Zealand): Located on Hayman Island in the sybaritic Whitsundays, this is Australia's most glamorous resort. It's got classy rooms, excellent restaurants, staff keen to please, a superb hexagonal swimming pool, and a fleet of gleaming charter boats waiting to spirit you off to the Reef or your own deserted isle. See chapter 6.

• **El Questro Homestead** (The Kimberley, WA; ℂ Accor, **1300/ 65 65 65** in Australia, 1800/ 221-4542 in the U.S. and Canada, 020/8283 4500 in the U.K., 0800/44 4422 in New Zealand, or 08/9169 1777): Charming country decor spiced up with Indonesian antiques, good cooking, and a dramatic gorge location make this glamorous homestead on a remote million-acre cattle station popular with international jet-setters. Cruise wild gorges, heli-fish for barramundi, and hike to Aboriginal rock art while you're here. See chapter 8.

• **Cable Beach Club Resort Broome** (Broome, WA; ℂ **1800/ 099 199** in Australia, or 08/9192 0400): Chinatown meets the Outback at this elegant corrugated-iron-and-pagoda-studded resort lying low along glorious Cable Beach in the romantic pearling port of Broome. Three to-die-for suites, decorated with superb Asian antiques and paintings by luminaries of the Australian art world. See chapter 8.

• **The Hotel Como** (Melbourne, VIC; ℂ **1800/033 400** in Australia, or 03/9825 2222): Great service, nice rooms, and free plastic ducks make this one of our favorite top-flight Australian hotels. See chapter 11.

• **Hyatt Hotel Canberra** (Canberra, ACT; ℂ **800/233-1234** in the U.S. and Canada, or 02/6270 1234): Visiting heads of state and pop stars make this their residence of choice when staying in Canberra. It's only a 2-minute drive from the central shopping district, and a stone's throw from both Lake Burley Griffin and the Parliamentary Triangle. See chapter 13.

12 The Best Moderately Priced Accommodations

• **Explorers Inn Hotel** (ℂ **1800/ 62 3288** in Australia) and **Hotel George Williams** (ℂ **1800/064 858** in Australia), both in Brisbane, QLD: These two hotels just around the corner from each other in Brizzie are shining examples of what affordable hotels should be—trendy, clean, and bright with useful facilities like 24-hour front desk, hair dryers, helpful staff, and a pleasant, inexpensive restaurant attached. See chapter 5.

• **The Reef Retreat** (Cairns, QLD; ℂ **07/4059 1744**): It's not often you find so much decorating taste—wooden blinds, teak furniture, and colorful upholstery—at a price you want to pay, but that's what you get at the apartments in trendy Palm Cove, one of Cairns's most desirable beachfront suburbs. There's a swimming pool in the lovely landscaped grounds, but the beach is just a block away. See chapter 6.

• **Archipelago Studio Apartments** (Port Douglas, QLD; ℂ **07/4099 5387**): They may be tiny, but these pretty apartments have a homey atmosphere and are just seconds from spectacular Four Mile Beach. Some units have sea views. The solicitous proprietor is a font of advice on things to see and do. See chapter 6.

• **South Molle Island** (Whitsunday Islands, QLD; ℃ **1800/075 080** in Australia): At first glance this pretty island resort ain't all that moderately priced, but for an island, it is. Hearty buffet meals, non-motorized water sports, and other activities are included in the price. See chapter 6.

• **Bahia Beachfront** (the Gold Coast, QLD; ℃ **07/5538 3322**): They're no shakes in the glamour-puss stakes, but these comfortable apartments are big, clean, and airy, and most have great views of the beach right opposite—all for just A$127 (U.S.$82.55) for a double in high season. See chapter 6.

• **Miss Maud Swedish Hotel** (Perth, WA; ℃ **1800/998 022** in Australia): Staying at this slightly musty hotel in the heart of Perth is like staying at grandma's—even if your grandma's house doesn't have Swedish murals on the walls. Friendly staff members who actually look pleased to see you and a

huge buffet breakfast (included in the rate) complete the picture. See chapter 9.

• **North Adelaide Heritage Group** (Adelaide, SA; ℃ **08/8272 1355**): These accommodations actually consist of 18 separate fabulous properties in North Adelaide and Eastwood. The former Friendly Meeting Chaple Hall resembles a small church stocked with Victorian antiques. Another memorable place is the George Lowe Esq. Apartment, done up in the style of a 19th-century gentleman's bachelor pad. See chapter 10.

• **Macquarie Manor** (Hobart, TAS; ℃ **1800/243 044** in Australia, or 03/6224 4999): This lovely place in the heart of Hobart has a variety of heritage rooms with individual appeal. It's just a short walk to the waterfront. See chapter 14.

• **York Mansions** (Launceston, TAS; ℃ **03/6334 2933**): If you feel that where you stay is as important to your visit as what you see, then don't miss out on a night or two here. This National Trust–classified building has five spacious apartments, each with a distinct character. It's like living the high life in the Victorian age. See chapter 14.

13 The Best Alternative Accommodations

• **Underground Motel** (White Cliffs, NSW; ℃ **1800/02 1154** in Australia, or 08/8091 6677): All but two of this motel's rooms are underground in this fascinating opal-mining town. Rooms are reached by a maze of spacious tunnels dug out of the rock. See chapter 4.

• **Daintree Eco Lodge & Spa** (near Port Douglas, QLD; ℃ **1800/808 010** in Australia): These 15 luxury cabins perched high in the tree canopy by a gushing waterfall are Australia's premier rain-forest

getaway. Walk the trails, have the tour desk book a jungle river cruise, or enjoy an aromatherapy facial in the spa. See chapter 6.

• **Whitsunday Wilderness Lodge** (The Whitsunday Islands, QLD; ℃ **07/3357 3843**): The 10 comfy beachfront cabins are basic, but your vacation at this island eco-retreat will be anything but. Sea kayak, sail, snorkel, hike rain-forest trails, dine with other guests outside under the Milky Way, and maybe even swim with Myrtle, the pet kangaroo.

Considering you'll only shell out for wine and maybe a sea-plane trip to the Reef, this is a great value. See chapter 6.

- **Kingfisher Bay Resort** (Fraser Island, QLD; ✆ **1800/072 555** in Australia): If it weren't for the ranger station and natural-history videos in the lobby, the wildlife walks, the guided four-wheel-drive safaris, and other eco-activities taking place, you'd hardly know that this hotel is an eco-resort, so comfortable and modern is it. See chapter 6.

- **Binnaburra Mountain Lodge** (✆ **1800/074 260** in Australia) and **O'Reilly's Rainforest Guesthouse** (✆ **1800/688 722** in Australia): both in the Gold Coast Hinterland, QLD: Tucked snugly almost 1,000 meters (3,000 ft.) up on rain-forested ridges, these cozy retreats offer fresh mountain air, daily activities, and instant access to the hiking trails of Lamington National Park. At O'Reilly's you can hand-feed brilliantly colored rain-forest birds every morning. See chapter 6.

- **Emma Gorge Resort** (The Kimberley, WA; ✆ **1800/221-4542** in the U.S. and Canada, or 08/9169 1777): At this spic-and-span little safari camp on the 1-million-acre El Questro cattle station, guests stay in cute tents with wooden floors and electric lights, eat at a rustic gourmet restaurant, and join in the many hikes, bird-watching tours, river cruises, and more. See chapter 8.

- **Prairie Hotel** (Flinders Ranges, SA; ✆ **08/8648 4844**): This remarkable tin-roofed, stone-walled Outback pub in the Flinders Ranges has quaint rooms, a great bar out front where you can meet the locals, and some of the best food in Australia. See chapter 10.

- **Cradle Mountain Lodge** (Cradle Mountain, TAS; ✆ **03/6492 1303**): Just minutes from your comfortable cabin are 1,500-year-old trees, moss forests, craggy mountain ridges, limpid pools and lakes, and hordes of scampering marsupials. See chapter 14.

- **Freycinet Lodge** (Freycinet National Park, Coles Bay, TAS; ✆ **03/6257 0101**): These eco-friendly bush cabins are right next to one of the nation's best walking tracks. The ocean views from the magnificent restaurant and the surrounding balconies are spectacular. See chapter 14.

14 The Best B&Bs & Guest Houses

- **The Russell** (The Rocks, Sydney; ✆ **02/9241 3543**): This B&B, wonderfully positioned in the city's old quarter, is the coziest place to stay in all of Sydney. It's got creaky floorboards, a ramshackle feel, brightly painted corridors, and rooms with immense character. See chapter 3.

- **Echoes Guesthouse** (Katoomba, Blue Mountains, NSW; ✆ **02/ 4782 1966**): Echoes is right on the edge of a dramatic drop into the Jamison Valley. The views from the balconies are breathtaking. See chapter 4.

- **Barrington Guest House** (Barrington Tops National Park, The Hunter, NSW; ✆ **02/4995 3212**): Nestled in a valley just outside the Barrington Tops National Park, this charming guest house and luxury cabin property offers magnificent rain-forest walks, plenty of native animals, and excellent activities, such as horseback riding through the bush. See chapter 4.

- **Ulladulla Guest House** (Ulladulla, NSW; ℂ **02/4455 1796**): Works of art on the walls, fabulous food and a lagoon-like pool among the palm trees—all this and lovely rooms with hosts that can't do enough for you. See chapter 4.
- **Waverley** (Brisbane, QLD; ℂ **07/ 3369 8973**): This gorgeous old timber Queenslander house has pretty rooms, and a cool deck within earshot of rainbow lorikeets chirping in the mango trees. And the cute shops and galleries of fashionable Paddington are right outside your door. See chapter 5.
- **Lilybank Bed & Breakfast** (Cairns, QLD; ℂ **07/4055 1123**): This rambling 1890s homestead used to be the Cairns mayor's residence. Today, owners Pat and Mike Woolford welcome guests to its comfy rooms, wide verandas, and blooming gardens. You can also stay in the renovated gardener's cottage. See chapter 6.
- **The Rocks** (Townsville, QLD; ℂ **07/4771 5700**): Victorian charm has been poured into this old Queenslander with stylish, not frilly, results. Eat off valuable china in the old dining room, bathe in a claw-foot tub in the main bathroom, and meet other guests for sherry on the wide old veranda at dusk. See chapter 6.
- **Marae** (near Port Douglas, QLD; ℂ **07/4098 4900**): Lush bushland full of butterflies and birds is the setting for this gorgeous contemporary Queenslander house with hip rooms and an outdoor plunge pool. Host Andy Morris serves a wonderful breakfast, and Cactus, the crazy pet cockatoo, gives you a warm welcome, too. See chapter 6.

- **The Summer House** (Darwin, NT; ℂ **08/8981 9992**): Groovy guest rooms with hip furniture, funky bathrooms, louvered windows, and tropical gardens make this small converted apartment block an oasis of cool—in both senses of the word. See chapter 8.
- **Hansons Swan Valley** (near Perth, WA; ℂ **08/9296 3366**): Good-bye faded lace, hello Art Deco—here is a B&B with cutting-edge style for young sophisticates. Jon and Selina Hanson have created a stylish retreat nestled among the Swan Valley vineyards, an easy drive from Perth. See chapter 9.
- **Heritage Trail Lodge** (Margaret River, WA; ℂ **08/9757 9595**): How many B&Bs do you know that provide a double Jacuzzi in every room? These salmon-pink cabins abut tall karri forest where parrots flit. 'Roos hop into the parking lot on occasion, and the fabulous Margaret River wineries surround you. See chapter 9.
- **Collingrove Homestead** (Angaston, the Barossa Valley, SA; ℂ **08/ 8564 2061**): This country house, built in 1856, has a real air of colonial manor farm living, with hallways festooned with hunting trophies, rifles, and oil paintings, and plenty of oak paneling and antiques scattered about. See chapter 10.
- **Robinson's by the Sea** (St. Kilda, Melbourne; ℂ **03/9534 2683**): This 1870s heritage B&B just across the road from St. Kilda beach has a comfortable living room and dining room stocked with antiques and five individually decorated bedrooms. It's a very friendly place and a good value. See chapter 11.

15 The Best Restaurants

• **Mezzaluna** (Sydney, NSW; ℂ 02/ 9357 1988): Come here for exquisite food, flawless service, and a great view across the city's western skyline. The main dining room opens onto a all-weather terrace kept warm in winter by giant, overhead fan heaters. Don't miss it. See chapter 3.

• **MG Garage** (Sydney, NSW; ℂ 02/9383 9383): Causing a stir in Sydney with the fashionable crowd, MG Garage is set in a car showroom and serves up great Modern Australian cuisine. See chapter 3.

• **Quay** (Sydney, NSW; ℂ 02/9251 5600): Sydney's best seafood restaurant offers perhaps the loveliest view in Sydney. Gaze through the large glass windows towards the Opera House, the city skyline, the North Shore suburbs, and the Harbour Bridge. See chapter 3.

• **Tetsuya's** (Sydney, NSW; ℂ 02/ 9267 2900): Chef Tetsuya Wakuda is arguably Sydney's most famous chef, and his nouveau Japanese creations are imaginative enough to guarantee that this hip eatery is a constant number one in Australia. See chapter 3.

• **Salt** (Sydney, NSW; ℂ 02/9332 2566): You'll need to dress up in your coolest outfit to fit into the scene happening at this modernist restaurant in the Kirketon Hotel in Darlinghurst. Inside it's all sleek and chrome, and the menu is innovative Mod Oz all the way. See chapter 3.

• **e'cco bistro** (Brisbane, QLD; ℂ 07/3831 8344): Simple food, elegantly done, has won this small but elegant bistro a stack of awards, and you'll soon see why. Not least among its titles is Australia's top restaurant award, the

Remy Martin Cognac/Gourmet Traveller Restaurant of the Year. Booking ahead is almost essential. See chapter 5.

• **Fishlips Bar & Bistro** (Cairns, QLD; ℂ 07/4041 1700): Clever ways with fresh seafood and other Aussie ingredients— think crocodile—make this cheerful blue beach house on a busy Cairns highway a real winner. This place is the pick of the bunch in Cairns. See chapter 6.

• **Fraser's** (Perth, WA; ℂ 08/9481 7100): The city center and Swan River sparkling in the sunshine seem so close that you can almost reach out and touch them from the terrace of this parkland restaurant. Sensationally good Mod Oz food turned out with flare and flavor is what you come here for; seafood is a specialty. See chapter 9.

• **Newtown House** (Vasse, near Margaret River, WA; ℂ 08/9755 4485): Chef Stephen Reagan makes intelligent, flavorsome food that beautifully partners with premium Margaret River wines. Stay in his homestead B&B overnight and explore the wineries the next day. See chapter 9.

• **Lamont's** (in the Swan Valley near Perth, WA; ℂ 08/9296 4485): Hearty, tasty, yet sophisticated fare is what this rustic restaurant in the vineyards is all about. It's worth the 20-minute drive from Perth, but if you can't make the trip, the chef has a second Lamont's in East Perth. She also does a mean takeout from her Perth deli, Lamont's City Store. See chapter 9.

• **Prairie Hotel** (Flinders Ranges, SA; ℂ 08/8648 4844): Chef Darren ("Bart") Brooks serves up some very high-class cuisine in the middle of nowhere. His "feral" foods, such as kangaroo tail soup and a mixed grill of emu sausages, camel steak, and kangaroo, is remarkable. See chapter 10.

- **Flower Drum** (Melbourne, VIC; ℂ **03/9662 3655**): Praise pours in for this upscale eatery serving Cantonese food. The food is exquisite and the service impeccable. See chapter 11.

- **The Tryst** (Canberra, ACT; ℂ **02/ 6239 4422**): Canberra has far grander and more expensive restaurants, but this place has found a spot in our hearts for its constantly delicious food. It's also relaxed, feeling almost communal on busy nights. See chapter 13.

2

Planning Your Trip to Australia

by Natalie Kruger

This chapter aims to answer all of those practical questions that may pop up as you're planning your trip: how will you get there, how much will it cost, the ins and outs of traveling Down Under, and myriad other pesky details. We've done all the legwork—ferreting out ways to nail down smart deals on airfares, listing package companies, locating outdoor adventure operators, and more—so you won't have to.

1 The Regions in Brief

People who have never visited Australia always wonder why such a huge country has a population of just 19 million people. The truth is, Australia can barely support that many. The vast majority of Australia is harsh Outback country, characterized by spiky spinifex grass plains, arid brown crags, shifting sand deserts, and dry salt lakes. The soil for the most part is poor; it hardly ever rains, and some rivers don't even make it to the ocean. The only decent rainfall occurs along a thin strip of land around the country's eastern coastal fringe. Some 84% of Australia's population huddles in cities around the coast in an area covering a mere 1% of the continent. Few roads traverse the inland; most travel is done around the continent's edge, or by air.

If Australia knows the harsh hand of Mother Nature, though, it also knows its bounty. It is blessed with one of the greatest natural attractions in the world—the Great Barrier Reef—plus ancient rain forests in Queensland, alpine scenery in Tasmania, wildflowers in Western Australia, Outback deserts in South Australia, a great coastal drive in Victoria, bird-filled wetlands in the Northern Territory, and countless sand beaches more or less everywhere, even right in the heart of Sydney.

Australia is made up of six states—New South Wales, Queensland, Victoria, South Australia, Western Australia, and Tasmania—and two internal "territories"—the Australian Capital Territory (ACT) and the Northern Territory. The political capital is Canberra, which lies within the boundaries of the ACT.

This book isn't organized strictly along state and territory lines. It's organized more in accordance with the way Australians think of the country and the way travelers experience it.

See the map in chapter 1 or the map on the inside back cover to visualize the regions described here.

NEW SOUTH WALES Australia's most populated state is also the one most visited by tourists. Principally they come to see Sydney, undoubtedly one of the most glamorous cities in the world, with dozens of harbor and ocean beaches scattered within and around the city, and a dramatic mixture of bushland and city development around Sydney Harbour itself. Sydney is also a good base for day trips or overnight excursions inland, especially

---

Tips   Size Does Matter

People are often surprised when they hear that Melbourne and Brisbane are a long day's drive from Sydney, and that it takes the best part of a week to drive from Sydney to Perth. When planning your trip, keep in mind that Australia is as big as the whole of western Europe and about the same size as the 48 contiguous U.S. states.

---

to the scenic Blue Mountains and the wineries of the Hunter Valley.

Farther afield is a string of quaint beachside towns stretching all the way down the southern coast into Victoria. Along the north coast are remnant areas of rain forest and a more tropical air in the laid-back hangout of Byron Bay, where "Croc Dundee" himself, movie star Paul Hogan, has a home.

Inland New South Wales is dry and sparsely forested. Highlights include the far west mining town of Broken Hill (known for abundant wildlife, art galleries, and Aboriginal influences), and the Outback opal-mining towns of White Cliffs and Lightning Ridge, which exist in a wacky underground world of their own.

QUEENSLAND   Without a doubt, the biggest draw in Queensland is the Great Barrier Reef. Coming to Australia and not visiting the Reef is a bit like going to Paris and skipping the Eiffel Tower. Ogling the tropical fish, weird sea creatures, and gardens of rainbow-hued corals will be a highlight of your holiday. The Reef stretches for more than 2,000 kilometers (1,250 miles) right along Queensland's coast down to Bundaberg, 384 kilometers (241 miles) north of Brisbane. Alluring island resorts are dotted along the coast; while most are expensive, we've found a few that won't break the bank.

Queensland is also known for its white-sand beaches. The best are on the Gold Coast in the state's south (just over an hour's drive from Brisbane), though the Sunshine Coast, a 2-hour drive north of Brisbane, has some lovely ones. Cairns and Port Douglas in the north have their fair share of beaches, too, but there is a BIG drawback to them. Deadly box jellyfish, or "stingers," call a halt to all ocean swimming at beaches in roughly the whole northern third of the country October through May. In Queensland, stingers infest the waters north of Gladstone. It is unspeakably frustrating, but there is a way to beat these spoilsport critters—head to an island. Stingers are mangrove creatures that like mainland currents, and their jelly-ish bodies break up a few miles from shore. Island swimming is therefore stinger-free all the time. That steps up the appeal of another Queensland aquatic playground—the 74 tropical Whitsunday Islands in the Great Barrier Reef Marine Park. These mostly uninhabited islands are a paradise for sea kayaking, snorkeling, diving, fishing, hiking through rain forest, water sports, bird-watching, and, best of all, bareboat sailing.

Another big attraction in the state is the lush 110-million-year-old Daintree Rain Forest, just north of Port Douglas. The capital, Brisbane, has Australia's largest koala sanctuary, where you can cuddle a cutie, and you can hand-feed wild dolphins on a day trip across Brisbane's bay. In the Gold Coast hinterland lies Lamington National Park, a rain-forested mountain region great for hiking and spotting wildlife.

THE RED CENTRE   The eerie silence of Uluru, more commonly known as Ayers Rock, is what pulls everyone to the sprawling crimson sands of the Red Centre, the heart of the Northern Territory. Most folks discover that they like a nearby giant pebble even more, the towering domes of Kata Tjuta, or "the Olgas." A half day's drive from the Rock brings you to Kings Canyon, an orange desert gorge popular with hikers. If you visit the Red Centre, try to schedule some time in Alice Springs. This laid-back Outback town has the best Aboriginal arts-and-crafts shopping in Australia, Aboriginal tours, a good desert wildlife park, pretty scenery, hikes through the stark MacDonnell Ranges, an Outback ranch to stay at, and even camel rides down a dry riverbed.

THE TOP END The northwest reaches of Oz, from the dramatic rocky red ranges of the Kimberley in Western Australia to the northern third of the Northern Territory, encompass what Aussies eloquently dub "the Top End." This is Crocodile Dundee territory, a remote, vast, and hot semi-desert region where men are heroes and cows probably outnumber people. Near the tropical city of Darwin, the territory's capital, is Kakadu National Park, where you can cruise past crocodiles on inland billabongs, bird-watch, and visit ancient Aboriginal rock-art sites. Even closer to Darwin is Litchfield National Park, where you can take a dip in fern-fringed swimming holes surrounded by majestic red cliffs—stuff straight from Eden. You can cruise the orange walls of Katherine Gorge, a few hours' drive south of Darwin, or explore them by canoe. Near Katherine you can even learn to make your own didgeridoo, and canoe rarely explored, croc-infested inland rivers.

In the Western Australia section of the Top End, you can visit age-old Geikie and Windjana gorges, pearl farms where the world's best South Sea pearls grow, and the charming (in a corrugated-iron sort of way) beachside Outback town of Broome. This tract of the country is so little populated and so underexplored that most Aussies think of it almost as a foreign land. Getting around it is expensive, just because it's so big. Near Kununurra, on the eastern edge of the Kimberley, is a fun million-acre cattle station, El Questro, where you can camp in comfy safari tents (or stay in an upmarket but very expensive homestead), fish for barramundi, hike through the bush to Aboriginal rock art, take all kinds of active tours from horseback riding to four-wheel-drive jaunts, and dine every night on terrific modern Oz cuisine. From Kununurra you can fly over or hike into the beehive-shaped rock formation of the Bungle Bungles (a great photo op), cruise on the bird-rich, croc-haunted Ord River, and tour the Argyle Diamond Mine, the world's biggest.

WESTERN AUSTRALIA Perhaps the least-visited state (largely because distance and high airfares work against it), Western Australia is also the state with the most untamed natural beauty. The seas teem with whales in season, and thrill seekers can swim alongside gentle giant whale sharks on the Northwest Cape every fall (Mar–June). This cape is home to one of Australia's best-kept secrets, a second barrier reef called Ningaloo Marine Park, which runs for 260 kilometers (163 miles) along its western shore, one of the few reefs in the world to grow on a western coast. You can snorkel with giant manta rays here, and the diving is great. Just 19 kilometers (12 miles) off Perth, snorkelers can gawk at corals and fish on pretty Rottnest Island, and in World Heritage–listed Shark Bay, tourists greet wild dolphins at Monkey Mia.

In the southwest "hook" of the continent lies the Margaret River wine region. Its wild forests, thundering surf, dramatic cliffs, rich bird life, and wild 'roos make it one of the country's most attractive wine regions. The state's capital, Perth, has surf beaches and a wonderfully restored 19th-century port with a fun atmosphere and some great museums, Fremantle. One or two hours' drive from the city brings you to some cute towns, like the Spanish Benedictine monastery town of New Norcia. Inland, the state is mostly wheat fields and desert, but if you have the time and inclination, head west 600 kilometers (375 miles) from Perth to the gold-mining boom-town of Kalgoorlie, where you'll find the world's largest open-cast gold mine. With its gracious old pubs lining the wide bustling streets, it's just what you think the perfect Aussie country town should look like.

SOUTH AUSTRALIA Stretched out between Western Australia and Victoria is the nation's breadbasket, South Australia. The capital, Adelaide, is a stately affair known for its conservatism, parks, and churches. It's a delightful stopover, and it's a base for exploring Australia's most illustrious wine region, the Barossa Valley. Big labels like Penfolds, Seppelts, and Wolf Blass are here, but take time to sniff out the many smaller but no less outstanding vineyards. And it's less than an hour from the city!

Bring your binoculars for the giant waterbird sanctuary called the Coorong. Stay in an underground hotel in the offbeat opal-mining town of Coober Pedy (it's too hot above ground), or order a 'roo-burger at the historic Prairie Hotel tour in the craggy, ancient arid lands of the Flinders Ranges in the South Australian Outback.

But the greatest of South Australia's attractions (apart from wine, of course!) is Kangaroo Island, likely the best place in Australia to see native animals. In a single day you can spot wallabies and 'roos, wild koalas, oodles of birds from black swans to kookaburras, echidnas, penguins, and walk along a beach loaded with sea lions. It's a must-see.

VICTORIA Australia's second-largest city, Melbourne, is the capital of Victoria. Melbourne is more stately than Sydney, more "old-world" than "Californian," and offers an exciting mix of ethnicity and the country's best fashion shopping. Nearby Phillip Island is world-famous for its Penguin Parade, where hundreds of tiny penguins dash up the beach to their burrows at dusk; and the historic gold-mining city of Ballarat is not far away. Victoria is also the site of one of Australia's greatest road trips, the Great Ocean Road, which stretches for 106 kilometers (64½ miles) along the southern coast, where the eroded rock towers named the Twelve Apostles stand tall in the foamy sea. Then there's the inland "high country," which is *The Man from Snowy River*'s stomping ground.

AUSTRALIAN CAPITAL TERRITORY (ACT) Surrounded entirely by New South Wales is the tiny Australian Capital Territory. The ACT is made up of bush land and the nation's capital, Canberra, a planned city that's very similar in architectural concept to Washington, D.C. Many Australians consider the capital boring, but Canberra can surprise you. It has some of the country's best museums, so don't automatically exclude it from your itinerary.

TASMANIA The last port before Antarctica is the island state of Tasmania. Visit the Apple Isle for its beautiful national parks, enormous stretches of alpine wilderness and gloomy forests, fruit and lavender farms, the world's best trout fishing, and an exquisitely slow pace of life rarely experienced anywhere else. If you're up to it, you could tackle the Overland Track, an 85-kilometer (53-mile) hiking trail between Cradle Mountain and Lake St. Clair that passes through highland moors, dense rain forests, and several mountains. A more leisurely option is a visit to the picturesque stone ruins of Port Arthur, Australia's version of Devil's Island, where thousands of convicts brought in to settle the new British colony were imprisoned and died. All of Tasmania is spectacular, but you haven't seen anything until you've experienced Freycinet National Park, with its pink granite outcrops set against an emerald-green sea.

2 Visitor Information

The Australian Tourist Commission (ATC) is the best source of information on traveling Down Under. Its excellent website, **www.australia. com**, has more than 10,000 pages of listings for tour operators, hotels, car-rental companies, specialist travel outfitters, public holidays, maps, distance charts, suggested itineraries, and much more. It provides you with information tailored to travelers from your country of origin, including good-value packages and deals. By signing up for the free online Travel Club, you will be e-mailed news of hot deals, major events, and the like on a regular basis. The ATC operates only a website to dispense information on Australia, not telephone lines.

The ATC publishes a general brochure called the *Australian Vacation Planning Kit,* but you may find it too general to be of much use. You can order it online, along with a range (limited so far, but growing) of brochures from some state tourism marketing bureaus, various Australian cities or regions, accommodation chains, car and motorhome-rental companies, airlines, and vacation package companies.

Another excellent information source is the websites of Australia's official state tourism marketing offices. You can contact them at:

- **Canberra Tourism:** www. canberratourism.com.au
- **Northern Territory Tourist Commission:** www.Ntholidays. com, or www.insidetheoutback. com, which is written for North Americans.
- **South Australian Tourism Commission:** www.southaustralia.com
- **Tourism New South Wales:** www.visitnsw.com.au, or www. seesydney.com if you live in the U.S., or www.sydneyaustralia.co. uk if you live in Great Britain.
- **Tourism Queensland:** www. queensland-holidays.com.au; or www.destinationqueensland.com, which is written for North Americans.
- **Tourism Tasmania:** www. discovertasmania.com.au
- **Tourism Victoria:** www.visit victoria.com
- **Western Australian Tourism Commission:** www.western australia.net

---

Tips Get Help from the ATC

The ATC maintains a network of "Aussie Specialist" travel agents in several hundred cities across the United States, Canada, the United Kingdom, New Zealand, and several other countries. These agents are trained on the best destinations, hotels, deals, and tours in Oz. Get a referral to the nearest two Aussie Specialists by clicking the "Aussie Specialist" button on the home page on the ATC's website, www.australia.com.

3 Entry Requirements & Customs

ENTRY REQUIREMENTS

Along with a current passport valid for the duration of your stay, the Australian government requires a visa from visitors of every nation (New Zealand citizens are issued a visa on arrival in Australia). To speed up the visa-application process, the Australian government has introduced the Electronic Travel Authority (ETA)—an electronic or "paperless" visa that takes the place of a rubber stamp in your passport.

Here's how the ETA works: You give your passport details in person or over the phone to your travel agent or to your airline reservationist when you book your plane ticket. This information will be entered into the airline's reservations system, which is linked to the Australian Department of Immigration and Multicultural Affairs computer system. Assuming you are not wanted by Interpol, your ETA should be approved in about 6 to 8 seconds while you wait. You can also apply for an ETA at Australian embassies, high commissions, and consulates (see below).

Note the fees mentioned in this section are in Australian dollars; the exact amount charged by the Australian embassy, consulate, or high commission in your country will depend on the foreign currency exchange rate.

Tourists should apply for a Visitor ETA. It's free and is valid for as many visits to Australia as you like of up to 3 months each within a 1-year period. Tourists may not work in Australia, so if you are visiting for business, you have two choices: apply for a free Short Validity Business ETA, which is valid for a single visit of 3 months within a 1-year period, or pay A$60 (U.S.$33) to apply for a Long Validity Business ETA, which entitles you to as many 3-month stays in Australia as you like for the life of your passport.

By the time you read this, you should be able to apply for an ETA yourself online at www.eta.immi.gov.au, instead of having your travel agent or airline reservations office do it for you. There will likely be a A$20 (U.S.$11) charge to apply online.

There are still some situations in which you will need to apply for a visa the old-fashioned way—by taking or mailing your passport, a completed visa application form, and the appropriate payment to your nearest Australian embassy or consulate. This will be the case if your travel agent, airline, or cruise ship (if you plan to arrive in Australia by boat) is not connected to the ETA system. In the United States, Canada, the United Kingdom, Ireland, and many other countries, most agents and airlines are ETA-compatible, but your cruise lines may not be yet. You will also need to apply for a visa the old-fashioned way if you plan to enter Australia as something other than a tourist or a business traveler—for example, as a student studying in Australia; a business person staying longer than 3 months; a long-term resident; a sportsperson; a member of the media; a performer; or a member of a social group or cultural exchange. If you fall into one of these categories, you will need to apply for a Temporary Residence visa. There is a A$60 (U.S.$33) processing fee for non-ETA tourist and business visas for stays of up to 3 months, and A$155 (U.S.$85.25) for business visas for stays between 3 months and 4 years. Non-ETA visa application fees for other kinds of travelers vary, from nil to thousands of dollars. Before shooting off a check, contact the nearest Australian embassy, consulate, or high commission to check what forms of payment they accept.

Apply for non-ETA visas at Australian embassies, consulates, and high commissions. In the United States, your state of residence determines where you apply. From Alaska, Arizona, California, Colorado, New Mexico, Hawaii, Idaho, Montana, Nevada, New Mexico, Oregon, the U.S. South Pacific Territories, Utah, Washington, and Wyoming, apply to the **Australian Consulate-General,** 2049 Century Park E., Level 19, Los Angeles, CA 90067-3238 (© **310/ 229-4800;** dima-los.angeles@dfat. gov.au). From anywhere else in the United States, apply to the Australian Embassy, 1601 Massachusetts Ave. NW, Washington, DC 20036-2273 (© 202/797-3000; dima-washington@ dfat.gov.au). The website of the Australian Embassy in North America is www.austemb.org. In Canada, contact the Australian High Commission, 50 O'Connor St., no. 710, Ottawa, ON K1P 6L2 (© 613/783 7665; www. ahc-ottawa.org). For business-visa inquiries in the United States and Canada, call © 800/579 7664. In the United Kingdom, contact the Australian High Commission, Australia House, The Strand, London WC2B 4LA (© 09001/600 333 for 24-hr. recorded information, or 020/7379 4334; www.australia.org.uk). In Ireland, contact the Australian Embassy, Fitzwilton House, Wilton Terrace, Dublin 2, Ireland (© 1/676 1517; www.australianembassy.ie, dima-dublin@dfat.gov.au). Travelers from Northern Ireland can lodge their applications in Dublin.

You can obtain an application form for a non-ETA visa via the Internet at the Australian Department of Immigration and Multicultural Affairs website (www.immi.gov.au). This site also has a good explanation of the ETA system.

Allow at least a month for processing of non-ETA visas.

CUSTOMS & QUARANTINE
WHAT YOU CAN BRING IN   Anyone over 18 can bring into Australia no more than 250 cigarettes or 250 grams of cigars or other tobacco products, 1.125 liters (41 fl. oz.) of alcohol, and "dutiable goods" to the value of A$400 (U.S.$220), or A$200 (U.S.$110) if you are under 18. Broadly speaking, "dutiable goods" are luxury items like perfume concentrate, watches, jewelry, furs, plus gifts of any kind. Keep this in mind if you intend to come bearing presents for family and friends in Australia; gifts given to you also count toward the dutiable limit. Your own personal goods that you're taking with you when you leave are usually exempt from duty. Customs officers do not collect duty of less than A$50 (U.S.$27.50) as long as you declared the goods in the first place. If you have something you think may be dutiable but are not sure, contact the nearest Australian embassy or consulate (see above). You can also call the Australian Customs Service in Canberra, Australia (© **02/6275 6666;** www.customs. gov.au).

Cash in any currency, and other currency instruments such as traveler's checks, under a value of A$10,000 need not be declared. Firearms in Australia are strictly controlled; contact the nearest Australian diplomatic post for advice on importing a handgun.

Australia is a signatory to the Convention on International Trade in Endangered Species (CITES), which restricts or bans the import of products made from protected wildlife. Examples of the numerous restricted items are coral, giant clam, wild cats, monkey, zebra, crocodile or alligator, bear, some types of caviar, American ginseng, and orchid products. Banned items include ivory, tortoise (marine turtle) shell, products from rhinoceros or tiger, and sturgeon caviar. Bear this in mind if you stop in other countries en route to Australia where souvenirs from items such as these may be widely sold. Australian authorities may seize and not return the items to you.

Because Australia is an island, it is free of many agricultural and livestock diseases. To keep it that way, strict quarantine applies to importing plants, animals, and their products, including food. Some items may be held for treatment and returned to you; others may be confiscated; others may be held over for you to take with you when you leave the country. Amnesty trash bins are available before you reach the immigration counters in airport arrivals halls for items such as fruit. Don't be alarmed if, just before landing, the flight attendants spray the aircraft cabin (with products approved by the World Health Organization) to kill potentially disease-bearing insects that entered the plane in a foreign country. For more information on what is and is not allowed entry, contact the nearest Australian embassy or consulate, or contact Australia's Department of Agriculture, Fisheries and Forestry, which runs the Australian Quarantine and Inspection Service (✆ 02/6272 3933; www.affa. gov.au). Its website contains a list of many restricted or banned foodstuffs, animal and plant products, and other items.

WHAT YOU CAN BRING HOME
Check with your country's Customs or Foreign Affairs department for the latest guidelines—including information on items that are not allowed to be brought into your home country—just before you leave home.

Returning U.S. citizens who've been away for 48 hours or more are allowed to bring back, once every 30 days, $400 worth of merchandise duty-free. Be sure to have your receipts handy. You can mail gifts worth up to $100 to people in the United States on any single day (as long as the gifts are not alcohol, perfume, or tobacco). You may want to register certain personal items that would normally attract duty—such as laptops and watches—to avoid having to prove to customs officers that you did not buy them on your trip Down Under. United States customs officers will look with suspicion on fresh foodstuffs; tinned foods, however, are usually allowed (although not tinned meat). It's worth contacting the U.S. Customs Service (✆ 202/927-8727; www.customs.ustreas.gov) to request the helpful free pamphlet *Know Before You Go* (or read the whole thing online).

U.K. citizens should contact the National Advice Service (✆ 0845/010 9000), which handles calls regarding HM Customs & Excise, or visit www.hmce.gov.uk.

For a clear summary of Canadian rules, visit the comprehensive website of the Canada Customs and Revenue Agency at www.ccra-adrc.gc.ca, or call the agency's information line (✆ 800/461-9999).

For New Zealand customs information, contact the New Zealand Customs Service at ✆ 0800/428 786 or 09/300-5399, or go online to www.customs.govt.nz.

4 Money

See the "Taxes" section under "Fast Facts: Australia," at the end of this chapter, for details on Australia's Goods & Services Tax (GST).

CASH & CURRENCY
The Australian dollar is divided into 100 cents. Coins come in 5¢, 10¢, 20¢, and 50¢ pieces (all silver in color) and $1 and $2 pieces (gold in color).

The Australian Dollar, the U.S. Dollar & the British Pound

For U.S. Readers   The rate of exchange used to calculate the dollar values given in this book was U.S.$1 = approximately A$1.80 (or A$1 = U.S.55¢).

For British Readers   The rate of exchange used to calculate the pound values in the accompanying table was 1 British pound = A$2.85 (or A$1 = 35p).

Note: International exchange rates for the Australian dollar can fluctuate markedly. Check the latest rate when you plan your trip. The table below, and all the prices in this book, should be used only as a guide.

A$	U.S.$	U.K.£	A$	U.S.$	U.K.£
0.25	0.14	0.09	30.00	16.50	10.50
0.50	0.28	0.18	35.00	19.25	12.30
1.00	0.55	0.35	40.00	22.00	14.00
2.00	1.10	0.70	45.00	24.75	15.80
3.00	1.65	1.05	50.00	27.50	17.55
4.00	2.20	1.40	55.00	30.25	19.30
5.00	2.75	1.75	60.00	33.00	21.05
6.00	3.30	2.10	65.00	35.75	26.00
7.00	3.85	2.45	70.00	38.50	24.55
8.00	4.40	2.80	75.00	41.25	26.30
9.00	4.95	3.15	80.00	44.00	28.10
10.00	5.50	3.50	85.00	46.75	29.80
15.00	8.25	5.25	90.00	49.50	31.60
20.00	11.00	7.00	95.00	52.25	33.35
25.00	13.75	8.75	100.00	55.00	35.10

Prices in Australia often end in a variant of 1¢ and 2¢ (for example, 78¢ or $2.71), a relic from the days before 1-cent and 2-cent pieces were phased out. Prices are now rounded up or down to the nearest 5¢—so 77¢ rounds down to 75¢, and 78¢ rounds up to 80¢). Bank notes come in denominations of $5, $10, $20, $50, and $100.

ATMS

The safest and easiest method of managing money Down Under is to withdraw money directly from your home bank account at an Australian ATM. That way you can get cash when banks and currency exchanges are closed, and your money is safely residing in your bank account back home until you withdraw it. It also means you get the bank exchange rate, not the higher commercial rate charged at currency exchanges. You will be charged a fee for each withdrawal, usually A$4 (U.S.$2.20) or so. (It's your bank back home that's tacking on this charge, not the Aussie bank, so ask your bank what it is.)

All of the biggest banks in Australia—ANZ, Commonwealth, National, and Westpac—are connected to the Cirrus and Plus ATM networks, which have hundreds of thousands of ATMs around the world. Both Cirrus (© **800/424-7787;** www.mastercard. com) and Plus (for overseas ATM locations, go to www. visa.com) networks have automated ATM locators that list the banks in each country that will accept your card. The locators are unwieldy to use, though; instead, ask your bank at home for a directory of international ATM locations where your card is accepted. Most ATMs in Australia accept both four- and six-digit PINs (personal identification numbers), but it's a good idea to request a four-digit PIN from your bank, because these are the most common, not just in Australia but throughout the rest of the world.

Not all ATMs may have letters on the keypads, so memorize your PIN by number.

In Outback areas, carry cash and a credit card because while ATMs are widely available in cities and towns, they can be conspicuous by their absence in small country towns, and small merchants in remote parts may not cash traveler's checks.

CREDIT CARDS

Visa and MasterCard are universally accepted in Australia, but American Express and Diners Club are considerably less so. Always carry at least a little cash, because many merchants in Australia will not take cards for purchases under A$15 (U.S.$8.25) or so. If your credit card is linked to your bank account, it is good for withdrawing emergency cash from an ATM (just keep in mind that interest starts accruing immediately on credit-card cash advances).

Almost every credit-card company has an emergency toll-free number that you can call if your wallet or purse is stolen. Here are the Australia-wide numbers for the three major cards: **American Express** (℃ 1800/230 100), **MasterCard** (℃ 1800/120 113), and **Visa** (℃ 1800/125 440). Report your stolen wallet to the police, because your credit-card company may require a police report number.

TRAVELER'S CHECKS

Traveler's checks are something of an anachronism from the dark days before a global ATM network. Major towns and all cities in Australia have 24-hour ATMs, and virtually every establishment, even remote Outback gas stations, accepts credit cards and EFTPOS (electronic funds transfer at point of sale), which you can use internationally if your ATM card is linked to the Maestro network. Arrange this with your bank before leaving home. Traveler's checks are not as widely accepted in Australia.

If you opt to buy traveler's checks, get them in Australian dollars. Checks in U.S. dollars are widely accepted at banks, big hotels, currency exchanges, and shops in major tourist regions, but chances are shops, restaurants, and other businesses will have no idea what the current exchange rate is when you present a U.S. check. Another advantage of Australian-dollar checks is that the two largest Aussie banks, ANZ and Westpac, cash them for free.

It will cost you around A$5 (U.S.$2.75) to A$7 (U.S.$3.85) to cash checks in foreign currency at most Australian banks.

If you opt to carry traveler's checks, keep a record of their serial numbers, separately from the checks of course. To report lost or stolen American Express traveler's checks call ℃ 1800/ 251 902 anywhere in Australia.

5 When to Go

When the Northern Hemisphere has winter, Australia, in the Southern Hemisphere, has summer, and vice versa. That means midwinter in Australia is July and August, and the hottest months are November through March. Remember, unlike in the Northern Hemisphere, the farther

---

Tips Steer Clear of the Vacation Rush

Try to avoid Australia from Boxing Day (Dec 26) to the end of January, when Aussies take their summer vacations. In popular seaside holiday spots, hotel rooms and airline seats get scarce as hen's teeth, and it's a rare airline or hotel that will discount even 1 dollar off their full tariffs.

---

south you go in Australia, the colder it gets.

THE TRAVEL SEASONS

Airfares to Australia offered by U.S. airlines are lowest from mid-April to late August—that's just the time when it's best to travel in the Red Centre, the Top End, and the Great Barrier Reef!

HIGH SEASON It might surprise you to learn that the peak travel season in the most popular parts of Australia is the Aussie winter. In much of the country—Queensland from around Townsville and northward, all of the Top End and the Red Centre, and most of Western Australia—the most pleasant time to travel is April to September, when daytime temperatures are 19°C to 31°C (66°F–89°F) and it rarely rains. June, July, and August are the busiest months in these parts; you'll need to book accommodations and tours way in advance, and you will pay higher rates then, too.

On the other hand, summer is a nice time to visit the southern states— New South Wales, Victoria, South Australia, Western Australia from Perth on south, and Tasmania. Even in winter, temperatures rarely dip below freezing here, and snow falls only in parts of Tasmania, in the ski-fields of Victoria, and in the Snowy Mountains in southern New South Wales.

If I had to pick the one best month to visit Australia, I'd say September or October, when it's warm enough to hit the beach in the southern states (on a warm day), it's cool enough to tour Ayers Rock (on a cool day), and the humidity and rains have not yet come

to Cairns and the Top End (although it will be very hot by October). It's also smack in the middle of Western Australia's wildflower season.

LOW SEASON October through March (summer) it is just too darn hot, too darn humid, too darn wet, or all three to tour in the Red Centre, the Top End, and anywhere in Western Australia except Perth and the South-west. The Top End, the Kimberley, and North Queensland, including Cairns, suffer an intensely hot, humid Wet Season November or December through March or April. In the Top End and Kimberley, this is preceded by an even stickier "build-up" in October and November. Some attractions and tour companies close up shop, floodwaters render others off-limits, and hotels drop their rates, often dramatically. I'm not saying touring is no fun in summer—people can and do travel at this time—but be prepared to take the heat, the inconvenience of floods, and in tropical coastal areas, the slight chance of encountering cyclones.

HOLIDAYS

In addition to the period from December 26 to the end of January, when Aussies take their summer vacations, the 4 days at Easter (from Good Friday to Easter Monday) and all school holiday periods are very busy, so book ahead. The school year in Australia is broken into four semesters, with 2-week holidays falling around the last half of April, the last week of June and the first week of July, and the last week of September and the first week of October. Some states break at slightly different dates. There's a 6-week summer/Christmas vacation from mid-December to the end of January.

Almost everything shuts down on Boxing Day (Dec 26) and Good Friday, and much is closed New Year's Day, Easter Sunday, and Easter Monday. Most things are closed until 1pm, if not all day, on Anzac Day, a World War I commemorative day on April 25.

Among the major national holidays are: New Year's Day (Jan 1); Australia Day (Jan 26); Labor Day (Second Mon in Mar, WA); Eight Hours Day (First Mon in Mar, TAS); Labor Day (Second Mon in Mar, VIC); Canberra Day, (Third Mon in Mar, ACT); Good Friday; Easter Sunday; Easter Monday; Anzac Day (Apr 25); May Day (First Mon in May, NT); Labour Day (First Mon in May, QLD); Adelaide Cup (Third Mon in May, SA); Foundation Day (First Mon in June, WA); Queen's Birthday (Second Mon in June, except WA); Royal National Show Day (second or third Wed in Aug, QLD); Queen's Birthday (Mon in late Sept/early Oct, WA); Labour Day (First Mon in Oct, NSW/SA); Melbourne Cup Day (First Tues in Nov, Melbourne only); Christmas (Dec 25); Boxing Day (Dec 26, or celebrated on the next Mon if 26th falls on a weekend; if Christmas Day is a Sat and Boxing Day a Sun, then both the following Mon and Tues are holidays)

AUSTRALIA CALENDAR OF EVENTS

January

New Year's Eve. Watching the Sydney Harbour Bridge light up with New Year's Eve fireworks is a treat. The main show is at 9pm, not midnight, so young kids don't miss out. Pack a picnic and snag a Harbourside spot by 4pm, or even earlier at the best vantage point—Mrs. Macquarie's Chair in the Royal Botanic Gardens.

Sydney Festival. Highlights of Sydney's visual and performing-arts festival are the free jazz or classical music concerts held outdoors on 2 Saturday nights in the Domain near the Royal Botanic Gardens (take a picnic and arrive by 4pm to snare a place). Contact the organizers (✆ 02/8248 6500) or go to www.sydneyfestival.org.au. 3 weeks in January (Jan 5–26, 2002).

Hyundai Hopman Cup, Perth. Tennis greats from the world's nine top tennis nations are invited to battle it out in a 7-day mixed-doubles competition. Contact the booking agent, BOCS Ticketing (✆ 08/9484 1133), or check www.hopmancup.com.au. Late December or early January.

Tamworth Country Music Festival, Tamworth (459km/287 miles northwest of Sydney), New South Wales. It may look like an Akubra Hat Convention, but this 10-day gathering of rural folk and city folk who would like to be rural folk is Australia's biggest country music festival. The Tamworth Information Centre (✆ 02/6755 4300; www.tamworth.nsw.gov.au) takes bookings. Second half of January.

Australia Day. Australia's answer to the Fourth of July marks the landing of the First Fleet of convicts at Sydney Cove in 1788. Most Aussies celebrate by heading to the nearest beach. Every town puts on some kind of celebration in its own small way; in Sydney, there are ferry races and tall ships on the harbor, food and wine stalls in Hyde Park, open days at museums and other attractions, and fireworks in the evening. January 26.

Johnnie Walker Classic, Perth. The country's richest golf tournament with £800,000 (around A$2 million, or U.S.$1.1 million) up for grabs will draw top players to Perth in 2002. Tiger Woods held the 2001 title. Ticketing details were not set at press time; contact event managers IMG (© **03/9639 2333**) or check the Western Australian Tourism Commission's events site at www.eventscorp.com.au. January 24 through 27, 2002.

March

Sydney Gay & Lesbian Mardi Gras. A spectacular street parade of costumed dancers and gaudily decorated floats, watched by several hundred thousand onlookers, followed by a giant warehouse party (the party is for gays and their invited friends only). Contact Sydney Gay & Lesbian Mardi Gras (© **02/9557 4332;** www.mardigras.com.au). Usually the last Saturday night in February or the first Saturday in March (it'll be Mar 2 in 2002).

Adelaide Festival of Arts. This huge event on the international arts scene features enthusiastic performance art, music, dance, and outdoor concerts, as well as a writers' week. A summer-party atmosphere takes over Adelaide's city streets every night until late. Contact the organizers (© **08/8216 4444;** www.adelaidefestival.org.au). Over 2½ weeks in March every 2nd year (the next is Mar 1–17, 2002).

Australian Formula One Grand Prix, Melbourne. The first Grand Prix of the year on the international FIA Formula One World Championship circuit is battled out on one of its fastest circuits, in Melbourne. Contact Australian Grand Prix Corporation (© **03/9258 7100**); or order online at www.grandprix.com.au. Four days in the 1st or 2nd week of March.

April

Australian Surf Life Saving Championships, Kurrawa Beach, Gold Coast, Queensland. As many as 6,000 bronzed Aussie and international men and women swim, ski paddle, sprint relay, pilot inflatable rescue boats, parade past admiring crowds, and resuscitate "drowning" swimmers in front of 10,000 spectators. Contact Surf Life Saving Australia (© **02/9597 5588;** www.slsa.asn.au). Over 4 days in late March or early April.

June

Sydney Film Festival. World and Australian premieres of leading Aussie and international flicks are shown in the ornate State Theatre and other venues. Contact the Sydney Film Festival (© **02/9660 3844;** www.sydneyfilmfestival.org). Over 2 weeks from 1st or 2nd Friday in June.

August

Sun-Herald City to Surf, Sydney. Fifty thousand Sydneysiders pound the pavement (or walk, or wheelchair it) in this 14-kilometer (9-mile) "fun run" from the city to Bondi Beach. For an entry form, write to the Sun-Herald City to Surf, 201 Sussex St., Sydney, NSW 2000 (© **1800/555 514** in Australia, or 02/9282 2833). If numbers have not reached their limit, you can enter on the day of the race. The entry fee is around A$25 (U.S.$13.75). The 2nd Sunday in August.

September

Floriade, Canberra. A million tulips, daffodils, hyacinths, and other blooms carpet the banks of Canberra's Lake Burley Griffin in stunning themed flowerbed designs at this spring celebration, which also features performing arts and other entertainment. Among the

Calling All City Slickers

Australia celebrates the Year of the Outback in 2002 with a host of festivals and activities across the country. One of the most exciting events will be a 6-week, 514-kilometer (321-mile) Great Australian Outback Cattle Drive from tiny Birdsville, in far western Queensland, to Marree, in South Australia, which ain't much bigger. As one of 100-plus cowboys, you can join the drive for sectors lasting from 3 to 11 days. Drove the herd through the Lake Eyre wetlands, over the pebbly plains of the Sturt Stony Desert, over dry white salt lakes, and across the vast, arid, flat inland of Australia. En route you can join in festivals; the drive kicks off with a weekend droving celebration in Birdsville, there is a country music festival at Mungerannie Station 300 kilometers (188 miles) to the south, and the drive winds up with a bush horserace meeting, an Outback ball and a carnival in Marree. Every night will feature bush poetry and music, Aboriginal cultural talks, or some other kind of social activity, and you can take four-wheel-drive side trips and scenic flights. Experience in the saddle is not a must; accomplished drovers will be on hand to show novice riders the ropes. The drove takes place from May 4 to June 9, 2002. Contact the South Australian Tourism Commission (© 08/8303-2033; www.southaustralia.com).

themes in 2001 were Aboriginal culture and 1970's "flower power." Contact Canberra Tourism (© 02/6205 0044; www.canberratourism.com.au) and see www.floriade australia.com. Over a month from the 2nd or 3rd week of September.

Henley-on-Todd Regatta, Alice Springs. Sounds sophisticated, doesn't it? It's actually a harum-scarum race down the dry bed of the Todd River in hilarious home-made "boats" made from anything you care to name—an old four-wheel-drive chassis, say, or beer cans lashed together. The only rule is the vessel has to look *vaguely* like a boat. Contact the organizers at © 08/8955 1253; www.henleyontodd.com.au. One Saturday in late September.

October

Honda Indy 300 Carnival, Surfers Paradise, Queensland. The world's best Indy-car drivers race a street circuit around Surfers Paradise on the glitzy Gold Coast, as part of the international FedEx Championship champ car motor-sport series. Contact Ticketek in Brisbane (© 13 19 31 in Queensland, or 07/3404 6700; www.ticketek.com), or check the event's website at www.indy.com.au. Four days in mid- or late October.

November

Melbourne Cup. If you're not glued to the TV to watch this A$3.385 million (U.S.$1.86 million) horse race in Melbourne, well, you're probably not an Australian. Women wear hats to the office, files on desks all over the country make way for a late chicken and champagne lunch, and don't even think about flagging a cab at the 3:20pm race time. First Tuesday in November.

December

Sydney-to-Hobart Yacht Race. Find a cliff-top spot near the Heads to watch the glorious show of spinnakers as a hundred or so yachts leave Sydney Harbour for this grueling world-class event. The organizer is the Sydney-based Cruising Yacht Club of Australia (© 02/ 9363 9731; www.cyca.com.au). The event's website is www.sydney hobart.telstra.com. Starts December 26.

6 The Active Vacation Planner

Australia's generally warm, dry climate and wide-open spaces cry out to even the most dedicated couch potatoes. Most of the operators and outfitters listed below specialize in adventure vacations for small groups. Meals, accommodation, equipment rental, and guides are included in their packages as a rule, though international airfares are usually not. Where you end up spending the night varies depending on the package you select—on a sea-kayaking trip you almost always camp on the beach; on a hiking expedition you may stay at a wilderness lodge, and on a biking trip you often stop over at B&B-style lodgings.

You will find additional information on the outdoor activities discussed below in the relevant regional chapters. Before you hit the outdoors, review the tips on safety later in this section.

SCUBA DIVING

Diving Down Under is one of the best travel experiences in the world. Don't think all of Australia's dive spots are on the Great Barrier Reef, though. Good sites are found all around the coastline—even right in Sydney. A second barrier reef in Ningaloo Reef Marine Park stretches 260 kilometers (163 miles) off the coast of Western Australia. (See chapter 9 or check out Exmouth Diving Centre's website at www.exmouthdiving.com.au for a good description of dive sites there.) Not all the good sites are on coral. In Tasmania, for instance, you can dive giant kelp beds popular with seals, and in South Australia you can cage-dive with great white sharks. For a rundown on the country's truly outstanding dive areas, see "The Best Diving & Snorkeling Sites," in chapter 1.

Wherever you find coral in Australia (which is a lot of places), you'll find dive companies offering learn-to-dive courses, day trips, and, in some cases, extended journeys on live-aboard vessels. Most international dive certificates, including PADI, NAUI, SSI, and BSAC, are recognized. It's easy to rent gear and wet suits wherever you go, or you can bring your own.

Beginners' courses are known as "open-water certification" and usually require 2 days of theory in a pool at the dive company's premises on land, followed by 2 or 3 days on a live-aboard boat where you make between four and nine dives, including a night dive if you opt for the 5-day course. Open-water certification courses range from an intensive 3 to 5 days, for which you can expect to pay between about A$350 and $600 (U.S.$192.50 and $330). A 5-day course is seen as the best. When comparing the value offered by various dive schools, keep in mind that if the practical section of your course does not take place on a live-aboard boat but is land-based, you will also have to budget for accommodation and meals. Most operators offer courses right up to instructor level. If you're pressed for time, a PADI Referral course might suit you. It allows you to do your theory work at home, do a few hours of pool work at a PADI dive center near you in your home country, and then spend 2 or 3 days in the Australian ocean doing your qualifying dives. Remember to allow time in your itinerary for a medical exam in

Australia, and expect the dive instructor to grill you on your theory again before you hit the water.

If you're already a certified diver, remember to bring your "C" card and log book. If you're going to do a dive course, you'll need a medical certificate from an Australian doctor that meets Australian standard AS4005.1, specifically stating that you are fit for scuba diving (an all-purpose physical is not enough). Virtually all dive schools will arrange the medical for you; expect to pay around A$50 (U.S.$27.50) for the consultation. Remember, you can fly before you dive, but you must complete your last dive 24 hours before you fly in an aircraft. This catches a lot of people off guard when they are preparing to fly on to their next destination the day after a visit to the Reef. You won't be able to helicopter off the Reef back to the mainland, either. Check to see if your travel insurance covers diving. The Divers Alert Network (© 800/446-2671; www.diversalertnetwork.org) sells diving insurance and has diving and non-diving medical emergency hot lines, and an information line for dive-related medical questions.

If you've never been diving before and don't plan to become qualified, you can see what all the fuss is about on an "introductory" dive. That lets you dive in the company of an instructor on a one-off basis, with a briefing beforehand. Most dive operators on the Great Barrier Reef and other popular dive locations offer introductory dives.

Section 1 of chapter 6 contains more information on diving the Great Barrier Reef.

For information on dive regions and operators, you could try the Australian Tourist Commission website (www.australia.com, or see "Visitor Information," earlier in this chapter) for diving anywhere in Australia. The site is not as comprehensive or helpful as it could be where diving is concerned, though. Better are some of the state tourism marketing boards' websites (see "Visitor Information," earlier in this chapter). Tourism Queensland's website (www.queensland-holidays.com.au; hit the "Special Interests" tab) links to most dive operators working the Great Barrier Reef. If you know exactly where you want to dive, you may obtain an even more detailed list of operators by bypassing the big tourism boards and contacting the nearest local tourist office for a list of local dive operators. **Dive Queensland** (the Queensland Dive Tourism Association; © 07/4051 1510; fax 07/4033 7906; www.great-barrier-reef.net.au) will put you in touch with member dive operators in that state who stick to a code of ethics. Its website is practically a fossil, so it may be better to telephone or fax for an up-to-date list. A good source is **DIVErsion Dive Travel & Training** (© 07/4039 0200; www.diversionoz.com) a Cairns-based travel agent that specializes in dive holidays on the Great Barrier Reef, as well as in lots of other good dive spots in Australia. It books diving day trips and extended diving excursions on a big choice of live-aboard vessels, as well as dive courses, island resorts with diving, accommodation, and non-diving tours. It also sells diving insurance. Its proprietors are both dive instructors, and one of

---

(*Tips* **Peak Time on the Reef**

August through January is peak visibility time on the Great Barrier Reef, but the marine life will wow you any time of year.

them is trained as a Handicapped Diving Instructor for divers with disabilities.

Peter Stone's *Dive Australia* is a 608-page guidebook to more than 2,000 dive sites all over Australia. It by no means lists every fabulous site, but it does contain many sites off the dive-tourist trail (many of them not on the Great Barrier Reef), so keen divers in search of new territory may find it handy. It also contains a lot of background such as dive operators and associations, a chapter on Australian diving law, the nearest hyperbaric chambers, and travel tips. Order from the publisher, Oceans Enterprises (© **03/5182 5108;** www.oceans.com. au). It costs A\$36 (U.S.\$19.80) plus postage.

BUSHWALKING (HIKING)

With so much unique scenery and so many rare animals and plants, it's not surprising Australia is full of national parks crisscrossed with hiking trails. You're never far from a park with a bushwalk, whether it's an easy stroll to a lookout, or a 6-day odyssey on the Cape-to-Cape coastal trail in Western Australia's Southwest.

The best place to get information about bushwalking is the National Parks & Wildlife Service, or its equivalent in each state, which are listed below. A good Australian bushwalking Web page is at www.bushwalking. org.au.

- **NSW National Parks & Wildlife Service** (© **02/9585 6444** administration; www.npws.nsw. gov.au). It has a visitor information center at 110 George St., The Rocks, Sydney (© **02/9253 4600**).
- **Environmental Protection Agency** (QLD Parks & Wildlife Service; © **07/3227 8185;** www. env.qld.gov.au).
- **Parks & Wildlife Commission of the Northern Territory** (© **08/8999 5511;** www.nt.gov. au/paw). The Northern Territory

Tourist Commission (see "Exploring the Red Centre," at the beginning of chapter 7) is the official dispenser of information on parks and wildlife matters.

- **Western Australian Department of Conservation and Land Management** (CALM; © **08/9442 0300;** www.calm.wa.gov.au).
- **South Australian Department for Environment and Heritage** (© **08/8204 1910;** www.denr.sa. gov.au).
- **Parks Victoria** (© **03/9637 8325;** www.parkweb.vic.gov.au).
- **Tasmania Parks and Wildlife Service** (www.parks.tas.gov.au). An information officer is on duty, during summer only, at the Tasmanian government's information line, Service Tasmania (© **1300/ 135 513** in Australia); outside summer, there is no information shopfront or telephone enquiry service. If you know which park you want more information on, call that park direct. There are too many parks to list all their numbers here; the best way to find out the park's telephone number is to call one of Tasmania Parks and Wildlife's field centers and ask for it—the field center at one of the biggest parks, Cradle Mountain National Park (© **03/6492 1133**), will be able to provide you with the number you seek.

Some parks charge a daily or one-time entry fee; it's usually around A\$5 to \$8 (U.S.\$2.75 to \$4.40) but is occasionally as much as A\$16 (U.S.\$8.80) or so.

MORE ACTIVE VACATIONS FROM A TO Z

ABSEILING Rappelling is another name for this sport that involves backing down vertical cliff faces on a rope and harness. The ruggedly beautiful Blue Mountains near Sydney are

> (Fun Fact **Something Different: Camel Trekking**
>
> Camels Down Under? You bet. Australia has one of the world's largest camel populations. The country even exports racing camels to the Middle East. Camels were imported to negotiate waterless deserts in the 1900s but were later set free. They are now a popular way to trek the country. Short rambles of an hour or two in Alice Springs and at Ayers Rock are a novel way to see the Outback, or you can join extended camel treks through Outback deserts offered by a number of operators. Several companies in Broome lead guided rides along beautiful Cable Beach.

Australia's abseiling capital. In the Margaret River region in Western Australia, you can do it as mighty breakers crash on the cliffs below. You can even do it in the heart of Brisbane on riverside cliffs.

BIKING Australia's flat countryside is ideal for cycling, as Aussies call biking, but consider the heat and the vast distances before trying to cycle from point to point. There are plenty of biking trails. The rain-forest hills behind Cairns hosted the world mountain-biking championships in 1996, and Sydney's Blue Mountains have good mountain-biking trails. On pretty Rottnest Island off Perth, it's the only mode of transport from one coral-filled bay to the next. All major towns and most resort centers rent regular bikes and mountain bikes.

If you're interested in taking an extended biking trip, you may find it useful to have a copy of *Cycling Australia: Bicycle Touring Throughout the Sunny Continent*, by Australian Ian Duckworth (Motorbooks). This 224-page touring guide outlines short trips and eight long trips with maps and detailed route descriptions. Any large bookstore can order it, or it is available for U.S.$5.98 from the Adventurous Traveler Bookstore (© **800/282-3963** in the U.S. and Canada; www. adventuroustraveler.com), or for £9.95 from the Quayside Bookshop in the U.K. (© 01626/77-5436; or order at www.cycling.uk.com).

Remote Outback Cycle Tours (© **08/9279 6969;** www.cycletours. com.au) takes novice and expert bike riders, young and old, on extended biking tours across the country. The distances are vast, but the trip is combined with four-wheel-drive travel in parts. Itineraries include the Red Centre, the historic Oodnadatta Track cattle-droving route from Alice Springs to Adelaide via the underground opal-mining town of Coober Pedy in South Australia, and from Adelaide to Perth across the treeless Nullarbor Plain desert and through the pretty Margaret River wine region in southern Western Australia.

BIRD-WATCHING Australia's unique geography as an island continent ensures it has species you won't see anywhere else. It is probably best known for its many brilliant parrots, but you will see species from the wetlands, savannah, mulga scrub, desert, oceans, dense bushland, rain forest, mangroves, rivers, and other habitats. More than half of the country's species have been spotted in the Daintree Rain Forest area in north Queensland, and one-third of Australia's species live in wetlands-rich Kakadu National Park in the Top End. The Coorong in South Australia and Broome in the Top End are home to marvelous waterfowl populations.

To get in touch with bird-watching clubs all over Australia, contact **Birds Australia** (© **03/9882 2622;** www. birdsaustralia.com.au).

Kirrama Wildlife Tours (℗ 07/4065 5181; www.gspeak.com.au/kirrama/) operates extended birding expeditions to remote regions in northern Australia from a base near Cairns. Broome-based ornithologist George Swann of Kimberley Birdwatching, Wildlife & Natural History Tours (℗ 08/9192 1246; www.4.tpgi.com.au/users/kimbird/) tailor-makes extended birding trips throughout the Kimberley and parts of the Northern Territory. Fine Feather Tours (℗ 07/4094 1199; www.ozemail.com.au/~fifetour/) based near Port Douglas near the Daintree rain forest, operates bird-watching day trips and morning river cruises.

CANOEING & SEA KAYAKING Katherine Gorge in the Northern Territory offers some of the most spectacular flat canoeing in the country. You'll find delightful flat canoeing on the magnificent bird-rich Ord River in the Top End, too. Katherine Gorge and the Ord are full of generally harmless freshwater crocodiles, but never canoe in saltwater-crocodile territory. White-water canoeing can be found in Barrington Tops National Park north of Sydney.

A growing number of operators all around the coastline rent kayaks and lead guided expeditions. Popular spots are the Whitsunday Islands in north Queensland, the cold southern seas around Tasmania, and Byron Bay, where you can take a 3-hour "dolphin kayaking" trip to see wild dolphins (and whales June–Oct) and "kayak-surf" the waves.

Rivergods (℗ 08/9259 0749; www.rivergods.com.au) conducts multiday sea kayaking, canoeing, and white-water-rafting adventures throughout Western Australia's pristine ocean and rivers, in which whales, sharks, dugongs (manatees), sea snakes, turtles, and dolphins abound. They also run a "sea kayak with wild seals" day outing from Perth. Gecko

Canoeing (℗ 08/8972 2224; www.geckocanoeing.com.au) leads canoeing trips of 1 to 12 days from Katherine along remote crocodile-infested Top End rivers.

CAVING Australia doesn't have a lot of caves, but the ones it has are spectacular. The best spots are the Blue Mountains west of Sydney, and the Margaret River region in southwest Western Australia. For tourists who want to see caves and stay clean and safe at the same time (as opposed to spelunkers), the best caves are the spectacular Jenolan Caves in the Blue Mountains, a honeycomb of caverns bursting with intricate stalactites and stalagmites; and the 350 limestone caves in Margaret River, of which five are open to the public. Two of them are "adventure caves," which any novice caver (as opposed to an experienced spelunker) can explore on a tour of 2 or 3 hours.

FISHING Reef, game, deep sea, beach, estuary, and river fishing—Australia's massive coastline lets you do it all. Drop a line for coral trout on the Great Barrier Reef; go for the world record black marlin off Cairns; hook a fighting "barra" (barramundi) in the Northern Territory or the Kimberley; or cast for trout in Tasmania's highland lakes. Charter boats will take you out for the day from most towns all around the coast.

GOLF Australians are almost as passionate about golf as they are about football and cricket—after all, before Greg Norman was a Yank, he was an Aussie! Queensland has the lion's share of the most stunning resort courses, like the Sheraton Mirage in Port Douglas, Laguna Quays Resort near the Whitsundays, and the Hyatt Regency Sanctuary Cove Resort on the Gold Coast. The Gold Coast alone is studded with more than 40 courses. The Vines near Perth was voted Number One Resort Course in Australia by Golf Australia magazine in 2001. One of the world's best desert courses is at Alice Springs.

Most courses rent clubs for around A$30 (U.S.$16.50). Greens fees start at around A$20 (U.S.$11) for 18 holes but average A$65 (U.S.$37.75) or more on a championship course. Koala Golf (© **415/727 853** is the company's cell phone in Australia; www.koalagolf.com) offers a tee-time booking service, escorted day trips and accommodated package tours to excellent golf courses in major cities and holiday areas around Australia.

HORSEBACK RIDING Horseback-riding operators are everywhere in Australia. A particularly pleasant vacation is a multiday riding and camping trek in "The Man From Snowy River" country in the Snowy Mountains in New South Wales.

SAILING The 74 island gems of the Whitsundays in Queensland are an out-of-this-world backdrop for sailing. And you don't have to know how to sail—the Whitsundays are Australia's "bareboating" capital. Bareboating means you can charter an unskippered yacht by the day or the week and sail yourself among the islands. Even folks without a stitch of sailing experience can do it, although it's best to have at least one person on board who knows aft from fore. Perth and Sydney are mad about sailing; head down to the nearest yacht club and see what on-board places are going, especially during summer twilight races. The clubs are often short of sailors and most will welcome out-of-towners.

SURFING You'll have no trouble finding a good surf beach almost all along the Australian coast. Perth and Sydney are blessed with loads of good ones right in the city. Other popular spots include the Gold Coast in Queensland, the legendary Southern Ocean swells along Victoria's southern coast, and the magnificent sets off Margaret River in Western Australia. Just don't take your board much north of the Sunshine Coast in Queensland—the Great Barrier Reef puts a stop to the swell from there all the way to the northern tip of Queensland. Loads of companies rent surf gear. Beginner's lessons are offered at many popular surf beaches. Remember, surf only at patrolled beaches and never surf alone.

WHITE-WATER RAFTING The best rapids are the Grade 5 torrents on the Nymboida and Gwydir rivers behind Coffs Harbour in New South Wales. More Grade 5 rapids await you on the Johnstone River in north Queensland, although they must be accessed by helicopter. Loads of tourists who have never held a paddle hurtle down the Grade 3 to 4 Tully River or the gentler Grade 2 to 3 Barron River on a day trip from Cairns. The Snowy River National Park in Victoria and the Franklin River in the wilds of Tasmania are other popular spots. See also "Canoeing & Sea Kayaking," above.

MORE AUSTRALIA-BASED OUTFITTERS & OPERATORS

The Adventure Company (© **800/ 388-7333** in the U.S., or 07/4051 4777; www.adventures.com.au) does day trips and extended trips that incorporate all kinds of activities—hiking, biking, canoeing, rafting, snorkeling, sea kayaking, scuba diving, sailing, and four-wheel-driving—mostly on the Great Barrier Reef and in the Daintree rain forest and other wilderness areas in North Queensland. The company is based in Cairns.

Auswalk (© **02/6457-2220;** www. auswalk.com.au) offers self-drive or escorted accommodated walking tours throughout many picturesque parts of Australia such as the Great Ocean Road in Victoria, tropical Magnetic Island in Queensland, and the Fraser Island wilderness.

Fun Fact **The Tribe Has Spoken**

Think you could do better than the contestants on the hit TV program, "Survivor: The Australian Outback?" In 2001, The Adventure Company (see p. 45) launched the official 8-day "Survivor" tour featuring biking, canoeing, and hiking in the location where the show was filmed. It's a much less strenuous experience than the show contestants endured!

Tasmanian Expeditions (© 03/6334 3477; www.tas-ex.com.au) conducts day trips and extended expeditions featuring hiking, cycling, rafting, abseiling, canoeing, sea kayaking, and rock-climbing throughout Tasmania's national parks and unspoiled rural areas.

World Expeditions (© 415/989-2212 in the U.S., 020/8870-2600 in the U.K., 09/522-9161 in New Zealand, or 02/9264-3366; www.worldexpeditions.com.au) runs trekking expeditions in many parts of Australia, including to places less traveled such as Hinchinbrook Island in the Great Barrier Reef Marine Park, and the long-distance Bibbulmun Track in Western Australia's forested Southwest. Some trips incorporate other pursuits like rafting, sailing, or biking.

MORE U.S.-BASED OUTFITTERS & OPERATORS

The **Great Outdoor Recreation Pages** (G.O.R.P.) site at www.gorp.com not only has links to many adventure-tour operators to Australia, but also contains articles, sells books and maps, and has links to heaps of sites on Australia with an action slant.

Adventure Express (© 800/443-0799, or 206/441 3482; www.adventureexpress.com) sells scuba-diving packages and custom-built itineraries on the Great Barrier Reef.

Outer Edge Expeditions (© 800/322-5235, or 517/552 5300; www.outer-edge.com) and **The World Outdoors** (© 800/488-8483, or 303/413-0938; www.theworldoutside.com)

both offer ecologically minded multi-sport diving, hiking, mountain-biking, canoeing, and sea-kayaking packages to the Great Barrier Reef and surrounding North Queensland rain forest.

TIPS ON HEALTH, SAFETY & OUTDOOR ETIQUETTE

Australia has a lot of remote territory typified by incredibly high temperatures, scarce water or none at all, little shade, and the occasional flash flood or bushfire. Extreme heat and ultraviolet rays can lead to exhaustion, dehydration, sunstroke, and severe sunburn quickly, even if you expend only a small amount of energy. Add to that the deadly snakes and spiders you might meet, and the thought that the nearest gas station, telephone, or person could be hundreds of miles away, and you may wonder that anyone ventures 10 miles from the airport! Actually, Australia is one of the safest places in the world to travel, as long as you act sensibly and keep yourself prepared.

Follow the tips below, and you should make it back home unscathed.

GENERAL RULES OF THUMB

- **Don't disturb wildlife,** take plant cuttings, or remove rocks, shells, coral, or other pieces of the wilderness. These are offenses in national and marine parks.
- In the Outback and national parks, **tell someone where you are going,** whether you're taking a 2-hour hike or a 3-week cross-country four-wheel-drive safari. If

you are hiking in a national park, register in the National Parks & Wildlife Service logbook if there is one at the start of the walk (don't forget to deregister, or a search party will be out looking for you while you're back at your hotel having dinner). On a trip in remote Outback parts, leave your travel plans with friends, relatives, the local tourist bureau, or the police.

- **Carry extra water.** It's easy to dehydrate without even knowing it in Australia's extremely hot and arid Outback. Two liters per person per day should be your minimum ration anywhere in the country; 1 liter per person per hour is the rule in the Outback and the Top End in summer.
- **Don't feed animals, birds, and fish.** It makes them unhealthy and causes them to lose hunting skills.
- **Obey fire restrictions.** Bushfires are a major threat across Australia in summer. In hot, dry weather, a total fire ban may apply, which means you cannot light a naked flame. Many national parks permit only camp ovens, not campfires. If you use a campfire, burn only fallen wood, not standing dead trees that could house animals. Extinguish all campfires thoroughly.
- **Look at, but don't touch, historic Aboriginal sites** like rock-art walls and middens (shell mounds). It can be an offense to disturb them.

BUSHWALKING BASICS

- **Stay on the track.** Cutting corners can damage vegetation and cause soil erosion. Australia's ecology is more fragile than it looks.
- **Whatever you take in, take out.** Leave no rubbish, even organic stuff like an apple core (it takes a long time to degrade, it's not the right food for native animals, and

it might self-seed and become a pest among native vegetation). For the same reason, don't bury your rubbish.

- **Check track conditions** and the weather forecast before you go.
- **Wear a broad-brimmed hat,** sunglasses, sunscreen, sturdy shoes, and a comfortable backpack. Insect repellent should be a key item on your list, because flies can reach plague proportions in dry areas and mosquitoes are common in rain forests.

BEACH SAVVY FOR SWIMMERS & SURFERS

- **The signal for "help"** in the water is to raise one arm high above your head.
- **Never swim alone** at beaches not patrolled by lifesavers (lifeguards).
- **Always swim between the red and yellow flags** denoting a safe swimming zone. Crossed flagpoles or a red flag mean the beach is closed due to dangerous swimming conditions. A yellow flag means conditions are dangerous and swimming is not advised.
- **"Rips" are powerful currents at all beaches** that can carry even the strongest swimmer out to sea. Beach lifesavers rescue thousands of swimmers from them every year, sometimes dozens of swimmers at one beach in a single day. If caught in one, don't fatigue yourself struggling. Remain calm, raise one arm high above your head, and wait for help. Try to swim diagonally against the current to shore.
- **If you get a cramp,** raise one arm and keep the cramped part still.

DANGEROUS WILDLIFE & OTHER HAZARDS

Aussies love terrorizing wide-eyed visitors with tales of the country's two **deadly spiders,** the funnel web and the red-back, but truth is most Australians

---

(Tips Taking the Sting out of Getting Stung

Follow this golden rule to avoid a fatal sting or bite from a marine creature: Look but don't touch!

---

never come across these spiders and wouldn't know what one looked like if it, well, bit them. Spider bites are not common. If you go bushwalking, check your whole body carefully. **Ticks** are common, especially in eastern Australia, and can cause severe itching and fever. If you find one attached to you, dab it with methylated spirits or some other noxious chemical. Wait for a while, then pull the tick gently out with tweezers, carefully ensuring you don't leave its head buried inside the wound.

Many Aussie marine creatures are deadly. Fish to avoid are **stingrays, stonefish** (which look exactly like stones, so avoid walking on underwater rocks), **lionfish,** and **puffer fish.** Never touch a **blue-ringed octopus** (it has blue circles all over its body), or a **cone shell** (a large shellfish shaped like a blunt cone). Unfortunately, the mainland seas in the northern third of the country are home to **marine stingers** (also called box jellyfish) in summer. They inhabit the waters within a few miles of the coastline. Their sting is very painful and can cause heart failure and death. If you happen to brush past one of these creatures, pour vinegar over the affected site immediately—local councils leave bottles of vinegar on the beach specifically for this purpose. In beaches in Sydney and many other areas, you might come across **"blue bottles."** These long-tentacled blue jellyfish inflict a generally harmless but painful sting that can last for hours. Sometimes you'll see warning signs on patrolled beaches. The best remedy if you are stung is to apply vinegar or have a very hot shower.

All cuts obtained in the marine environment must be taken seriously, because the high level of bacteria present can quickly cause the cut to become infected. The most common cuts are from **coral.** The best way to prevent cuts is to wear a wet suit, gloves, and reef shoes when diving. Never, under any circumstances, should you touch a coral head; not only can you get cut, but you will damage a living organism that took decades to grow. The symptoms of a coral cut can range from a slight scratch to severe welts and blisters. Gently pull the edges of the skin open and remove any embedded coral or grains of sand with tweezers, and scrub the cut well with fresh water. Never use ocean water to clean a cut. If the wound is bleeding, press a clean cloth against it until it stops. If bleeding continues, or the edges of the injury are jagged or gaping, seek medical treatment.

Snakes are common throughout Australia, but you will very rarely see one. If by the remotest chance you are bitten, do these three things in this order: 1. Keep calm; moving as little as possible may save your life. 2. Demobilize the limb, wrap that whole section of the limb quite tightly (but not tight enough to restrict the blood flow) with a wide cloth or bandage (not a narrow tourniquet). 3. Send someone to the nearest hospital, where antivenom should be available.

There are two types of **crocodiles** in Australia, the freshwater crocodile, which grows to almost 3 meters (10 ft.), and the highly dangerous Estuarine (or saltwater) crocodile, which reaches 5 to 7 meters (16–23 ft.). Freshwater crocs eat fish and are considered harmless; unfortunately, Estuarine crocs aren't so picky. Estuarine crocs are called "saltwater" crocs but they live mostly in freshwater rivers, wetlands, gorges, and billabongs (ponds). They are extremely ferocious, move at lightning speed, and are invisible even an inch beneath the water; it is unlikely you would survive an attack. Never swim in, or stand near the bank of, any river, swamp, or pool in the northern third of Australia, unless you know for certain it's croc-free. Don't swim at beaches near stream or river mouths, as crocs hang out in estuaries.

7 Health & Insurance

You don't have a lot to worry about healthwise on a trip to Australia. Hygiene standards are high, hospitals are modern, and doctors and dentists are all well educated. Australia's immense distances mean you can sometimes be a long way from a hospital or a doctor, but help is never far away thanks to the Royal Flying Doctor Service. No vaccinations are needed to enter the country unless you have been in a yellow-fever danger zone—that is, South America or Africa—in the past 6 days.

WHAT TO DO IF YOU GET SICK AWAY FROM HOME

If you worry about getting sick away from home, you may want to consider medical travel insurance (see the section on travel insurance later in this chapter). In most cases, however, your existing health plan will provide all the coverage you need, except perhaps for medical evacuation. Be sure to carry your identification card in your wallet.

If you suffer from a chronic illness, consult your doctor before your departure. For conditions like epilepsy, diabetes, or heart problems, wear a **Medic Alert Identification Tag** (© **888/633-4289;** www.medic alert.org), which will immediately alert doctors to your condition and give them access to your records through Medic Alert's 24-hour hot line. Membership is U.S.$35, then U.S.$20 for annual renewal.

Pack prescription medications in your carry-on luggage. Carry written prescriptions in generic, not brand-name, form, and dispense all prescription medications from their original labeled vials. Also bring along copies of your prescriptions in case you lose your pills or run out. Usually a 3-month supply is the maximum quantity of prescription drugs you are permitted to carry in Australia, so if you are carrying large amounts of medication, contact the Australian embassy or consulate in your home country to check that your supply does not exceed the maximum. If you need more medication while you're in Australia, you will need to get an Australian doctor to write the prescription for you.

If you wear contact lenses, pack an extra pair in case you lose one.

If you do get sick, you may want to ask the concierge at your hotel to recommend a local doctor—even his or her own. If you can't find a doctor who can help you right away, try the emergency room at the local hospital. Doctors are listed under "M" for Medical Practitioners in the Australian Yellow Pages. Most large towns and cities have 24-hour medical clinics.

A WORD ABOUT SMOKING

Smoking in many public areas, such as museums, cinemas, and theaters, is restricted if not banned. Increasingly Oz restaurants are totally banning smoking (those in Western Australia and New South Wales do); though in many states, restaurants just have smoking and no-smoking sections. Pubs are a territorial victory for smokers; after a night in one, non-smokers go home smelling as if they smoked the whole pack (which they probably

Tips **Warning: Sunshine May Be Hazardous to Your Health**

There's a reason Australians have the world's highest death rate from skin cancer—the country's intense sunlight. Limit your exposure to the sun, especially during the first few days of your trip, and always from 11am to 3pm in summer and 10am to 2pm in winter, when the stronger UVB kind of rays hit the earth. Scattered UV rays can bounce off surfaces such as city walls, water, and even the ground, and can burn you, even when you're not in direct sunlight. Use a broad-spectrum sunscreen with a high protection factor (SPF 30+). Wear a broad-brimmed hat that covers the back of your neck, ears, and face (*not* a baseball cap), and a long-sleeved shirt to cover your forearms. Kids need more protection than adults do.

And don't even think about coming to Oz without sunglasses, or you'll spend your entire vacation with your eyes shut against Australia's "diamond light" that cuts your eyes like, well, a diamond!

did, secondhand). Most hotels have smoking and no-smoking rooms. Australian aircraft on all domestic and international routes are completely nonsmoking.

INSURANCE

There are three kinds of travel insurance: trip-cancellation, medical, and lost-luggage coverage. Rule number one: Check your existing policies before you buy any additional coverage.

Trip-cancellation insurance is a good idea if you've paid a large portion of your vacation expenses up front (say, by purchasing a package deal), and it should cost approximately 6% to 8% of the total value of your vacation.

Your existing health insurance should cover you if you get sick while on vacation—though if you belong to an HMO, you should check to see whether you are fully covered when away from home. If you need hospital treatment, most health-insurance plans and HMOs will cover out-of-country hospital visits and procedures, at least to some extent. However, most make you pay the bills up front at the

time of care, and you'll get a refund after you've returned and filed all the paperwork.

Medical care in Australia is expensive. One of the most potentially financially ruinous situations arising from getting sick in Australia is needing to be evacuated back to your home country. Your policy should cover the cost to fly you back home in a stretcher, along with a nurse, should that be necessary. A stretcher takes up three coach-class seats, plus you may need extra seats for a nurse and medical equipment. Also make sure your policy covers medical evacuation by helicopter or Australia's Royal Flying Doctor Service airlift (you might well need this if you become sick or injured in the wilds of the Outback). The United States Medicare system only covers U.S. citizens traveling in Mexico and Canada.

Australia has a reciprocal medical-care agreement with Great Britain and a limited agreement with Ireland and New Zealand. Under this, travelers are covered for medical expenses for immediately necessary treatment in a public hospital (but not evacuation to your home country, ambulances, funerals, and dental care) by Australia's national health system, called Medicare like it is in the U.S. It's still crucial to buy insurance, though, because Australia's national health-care system typically covers only 85%, sometimes much less, of treatment; you will not be covered for treatment in a private hospital; and evacuation insurance is a must. Foreign students of all nationalities except Sweden and Norway must take out the Australian government's Overseas Student Health Cover as a condition of entry.

Your homeowner's or renter's insurance should cover lost or stolen luggage. The airlines are responsible for only a minimal amount if they lose your luggage on an international flight (and for a maximum A$1,600/ U.S.$880 for checked-in baggage on domestic flights in Australia).

Some credit- and charge-card companies may insure you against travel accidents if you buy plane, train, or bus tickets with their cards, for baggage protection, or they may provide theft and collision (but not liability) insurance for car rentals. American Express offers its cardholders a free 24-hour Global Assist hot line (✆ **800/ 554-AMEX** in the U.S., or call collect 312/935 3600 from overseas or in Illinois) for any travel query—medical, emergency, or even pre-trip planning.

If you do require additional insurance, try one of the following companies: **Access America** (✆ 800/ 284-8300; www.accessamerica.com); **Travel Guard International** (✆ 800/ 826-1300; www.travel-guard.com); **Columbus Direct** (✆ 020/7375-0011 in the U.K.; www.columbus direct.com), which insures U.K. residents only; and **The Divers Alert Network** (✆ 800/446-2671; www. diversalertnetwork.org), which insures scuba divers and provides diving and non-diving medical emergency hot lines, and a non-emergency medical question information line.

8 Tips for Travelers with Special Needs

FOR TRAVELERS WITH DIS-ABILITIES Most hotels, major stores, attractions, and public rest rooms have wheelchair access. Many smaller lodges and even B&Bs are starting to cater to guests with disabilities, and some diving companies cater to scuba divers with disabilities. National parks make an effort to include wheelchair-friendly pathways, too. Taxi companies in bigger cities can usually supply a cab equipped for wheelchairs. TTY facilities are still limited largely to government services.

For information on all kinds of facilities and services in Australia for people with disabilities (not just travel-related organizations), contact **National Information Communication Awareness Network** (NICAN), P.O. Box 407, Curtin, ACT 2605 (✆ **1800/806 769** voice and TTY in Australia, or 02/6285 3713; www. nican.com.au). This free service can put you in touch with accessible accommodations and attractions throughout Australia, as well as with travel agents and tour operators who understand your needs.

A World of Options, a 600-plus-page book of resources for travelers with disabilities, costs U.S.$35 from Mobility International USA (✆ **541/ 343-1284,** voice and TTY; www. miusa.org).

FOR GAY & LESBIAN TRAVELERS Sydney is the most gay-friendly city in the world after San Francisco, and across most of Australia, the gay community has a high profile and lots of support services. There are plenty of gay and lesbian bars, and most Saturday nights see a privately operated gay dance party taking place in an inner-city warehouse somewhere. The cafes and pubs of Oxford Street in Darlinghurst, a short cab ride or long stroll from Sydney's downtown area, are the most lively gay spots. The annual Sydney Gay & Lesbian Mardi Gras, culminating in a huge street parade and gay-only party on the last Saturday in February, is a high point on the city's calendar. In rural areas of Australia, you may still encounter a little conservative resistance to gays and lesbians, but Australians everywhere are generally tolerant.

Some services you may find useful are the **Gay & Lesbian Counselling Service** of NSW (© **02/9207 2888** for the administration office), which runs a hot line from 4pm to midnight daily (© **1800/805 379** in Australia, or 02/9207 2800). The **Albion Street Centre** (© **02/9332 1090** for administration, or 1800/451 600 in Australia outside Sydney and 02/9332 4000 in Sydney for the information line) in Sydney is an AIDS clinic and information service.

FOR SENIORS Seniors—often referred to as "pensioners" by Aussies—visiting Australia from other countries don't always qualify for the discounted entry prices to tours, attractions, and events that Australian seniors enjoy, but mostly they do. Always inquire about discounts when booking hotels, airline flights, train or bus tickets, and so on. The best ID to bring is something that shows your date of birth, or something that marks you as an "official" senior, like a membership card from the **American Association of Retired Persons** (AARP; © **800/424-3410** in the

U.S.; www.aarp.org). Membership in AARP is open to working or retired people over 50 and costs U.S.$10 a year. AARP's Privileges program entitles members to discounts of around 10% to 25%, sometimes more, on a range of travel products.

Elderhostel (© **877/426-8056** toll-free in the U.S. and Canada; www.elderhostel.org) is a non-profit organization that sells educational package tours, including ones to Australia, for travelers 55 years and over. Recent itineraries in Australia included Great Barrier Reef study cruises, Outback camping trips, bushwalking tours in Tasmania, and visits to Lord Howe Island and Kangaroo Island.

FOR FAMILIES Australians travel widely with their own kids, so facilities for families, including family passes to attractions, are common.

A great accommodation option for families is Australia's huge stock of serviced or unserviced apartments. Often less expensive than a hotel room, they offer a living room, a kitchen, sometimes two bathrooms, and the blissful privacy of a separate bedroom for adults. "Tips on Accommodations," later in this chapter, has details on the major apartment chains. Just about all hotels in Australia will arrange babysitting given a day's notice.

International airlines and domestic airlines within Australia charge 67% of the adult fare for kids under 12. Most charge 10% for infants under 2 not occupying a seat. Australian transport companies, attractions, and tour operators typically charge half price or 60% for kids under 12 or 14 years.

⌐Value The Benefits of Hostel Membership

Members of Hostelling International not only receive discounted rates at Australia's YHA (Youth Hostels Association) hostels, but also myriad other discounts—on car rentals, bus travel, and tours, for example—that can repay the membership fee many times over.

(*Value* Consider Booking a Package Tour

A package tour to Australia might include airfare and, say, 5 nights in a decent hotel for less than the cost of the airfare alone. Because each element of a package—airfare, hotel, tour, car rental—costs the package company much less than if you had booked the same components yourself, packages are a terrific value.

Rascals in Paradise (℃ **800/U RASCAL** in the U.S. and Canada; www.rascalsinparadise.com) sells family vacation packages to Australia.

These places have great kids clubs: Mercure Resort Surfers Paradise on the Gold Coast, and Hamilton Island and South Molle Island, which are both in the Whitsunday Islands (see chapter 6).

FOR STUDENTS STA Travel (℃ **800/781-4040** in the U.S. and Canada, 08701/600 599 or 0161/830 4713 [northern region] in the U.K., and 1300/360 960 in Australia; www.statravel.com) and **Council Travel** (℃ **800/2-COUNCIL** in the U.S.; www.counciltravel.com) both specialize in affordable airfares, bus and rail passes, accommodation, insurance, and tours and packages for students and young travelers. Both issue **International Student Identity Cards** (ISIC). This is the most widely recognized proof in Australia that you really are a student. As well as assuring you of discounts on a huge range of travel, accommodations, tours, and attractions, it comes with a 24-hour emergency help line, accident and sickness insurance, and a global voice/fax/e-mail messaging system with discounted international telephone calls. It is available to any full-time student 12 and over (and there is also a version for anyone aged 12–25). In the United States, both versions cost U.S.$22.

Ask STA Travel for a list of its many offices across Australia so you can keep the discounts flowing (and aid lines open) as you travel.

The **Australian Youth Hostels Association** (YHA; ℃ **02/9261 1111;** www.yha.org.au), the Australian arm of Hostelling International, has more than 150 hostels in Australia. Rates range from A$10 to $24 (U.S.$5.50 to $13.20), more for a private double/twin room.

You can join Hostelling International at state offices and major youth hostels in Australia, but it's best to join before you leave your home country. In the United States, contact **Hostelling International** (℃ **202/783-6161;** www.hiayh.org). The 12-month membership is free if you are 17 or under, U.S.$25 if you are 18 to 54, and U.S.$15 if you are 55 years or older.

9 Booking a Package or Escorted Tour

There are two kinds of "package tours"—independent and escorted. Independent packages usually include some combination of airfare, accommodations, and car rental, with an occasional tour or shopping discount voucher book thrown in. Aside from the cost savings, the main advantage is that you travel on your own pace and according to your own interests—no tour buses and no group sightseeing. Your car and hotel arrangements are already booked, leaving you free to get on with your day instead of fussing about finding a hotel for the night.

Escorted tours have different advantages—you don't have to carry your own luggage or constantly plan ahead, and the tour leader is on hand to advise on fun things to do, sort out hassles like lost passports, and even to make tour or dinner bookings for you. An argument for escorted tours is that your guide is usually well-informed and can offer interesting tidbits about the country as you go along, so you'll probably learn more than you would on your own. You also get to meet and travel with other people, though your time won't be your own to schedule flexibly and a lot of your enjoyment may depend on whether you like your guide and your fellow travelers. Escorted tours tend to be more expensive because you're paying for the guide, but most meals are included.

The airlines themselves are often a good source of package tours. Check newspaper ads, the Internet, or your travel agent.

Austravel (✆ **800/633-3404** in the U.S. and Canada, or 0870/055 0239 in the U.K.; www.austravel.net) is one American company offering independent packages Down Under. The following companies offer both independent and escorted tours: **ATS Tours** (✆ 800/423-2880 in the U.S. and Canada; www.atstours.com); **Collette Vacations** (✆ 800/340-5158 in the U.S., 416/626 1661 in Canada, or 0189/581 2333 in the U.K. through Adventures Unlimited, Inc.; www.collettevacations.com); **Goway** (✆ 800/387-8850 in the U.S. and Canada; www.goway.com); **Inta-Aussie South Pacific Tours** (✆ 800/531-9222 in the U.S. or 310/568-2060; www.inta-oz.com); **Maupintour** (✆ 800/ 255-4266 in the U.S. and Canada; www.maupintour.com); **Qantas Vacations** (✆ 800/348-8139 in the U.S. and 800/268-7525 in Canada; www. qantasvacations.com); **Sunbeam Tours** (✆ 800/955-1818 in the U.S. and Canada; www.sunbeam tours. com); **Swain Australia Tours** (✆ 800/22-SWAIN in the U.S. and Canada; www.swainaustralia.com); Swain Australia's budget-travel division, **Downunder Direct** (✆ 800/ 642-6224 in the U.S. and Canada; www.downunderdirect.com); and **United Vacations** (✆ 800/917-9246 in the U.S. and Canada; www.united vacations.com). Swain Australia is operated and largely staffed by Aussies. Collette Vacations, Inta-Aussie South Pacific, Sunbeam Tours, Swain Australia, and Goway have offices in Australia.

Connections for 18 to 35's (call Adventure Centre, ✆ 510/654 1879 in the U.S.; Goway, ✆ 800/387-8850 in Canada; The Imaginative Traveller, ✆ 020/8742 8612 in the U.K.; or 1800/077 251 in Australia or 07/3839 7877; www.connections1835.com.au) and **Contiki** (✆ 800/CONTIKI in the U.S. and Canada, 020/8290 6777 in the U.K., or 02/9511 2200 in Australia; www.contiki.com) specialize in escorted tours for 18- to 35-year-olds. These trips attract a lot of Australians, too, so they are a good way to meet locals. Connections for 18 to 35's also does a Connections Plus range of active holidays for people of any age. It is an Australian company.

ANZA Travel (✆ **800/269-2166** in the U.S., or 800/667-4329 in Canada; www.anza-travel.com) specializes in special-interest vacations with an active bent, such as golfing, sailing, and fishing. **Premier Vacations** (✆ **800/321-6720** in the U.S. and Canada; www.premierdownunder.com) is another reliable escorted tour operator.

10 Flying to Australia

Australia is a loooong flight from anywhere except New Zealand. Sydney is a 14-hour non-stop flight from Los Angeles, longer if your flight stops in

Honolulu. From the east coast, add 5½ hours. If you're coming from the states via Auckland, add transit time in New Zealand plus another 3 hours for the Auckland–Sydney leg. If you are coming from the United Kingdom, brace yourself for a flight of more or less 12 hours from London to Asia; then possibly a long day in transit, because flights to Australia have a nasty habit of arriving in Asia early in the morning and departing around midnight; and finally the 8- to 9-hour flight to Australia.

Sydney, Cairns, Melbourne, Brisbane, Adelaide, Darwin, and Perth are all international gateways, but most airlines fly only into Sydney, and some also fly to Melbourne.

THE MAJOR CARRIERS

Here are toll-free reservations numbers and websites for the major international airlines serving Australia. The "13" prefix in Australia means the number is charged at the cost of a local call from anywhere in the country.

CARRIERS FLYING FROM NORTH AMERICA

- **Air Canada** (© 888/247-2262 in the U.S. and Canada, 02/9286 8900 in Sydney, or 1300/655 767 from elsewhere in Australia; www.aircanada.ca)
- **Air New Zealand** (© 800/262-1234 in the U.S., or 310/615-1111 in the Los Angeles area, www.airnewzealand.com; in Canada: 800/663-5494 for English, 800/799-5494 for French, or 604/606-0150 in Vancouver, www.ca.airnz.com; or 13 24 76 in Australia)
- **Canada 3000** (© 888/828 9797 in the U.S. and Canada, or 1300/55 3301 in Australia; www.canada3000.com)
- **Qantas** (© 800/227-4500 in the U.S. and Canada; 13 13 13 in Australia; www.qantas.com.au)

- **United Airlines** (© 800/241 6522 in the U.S. and Canada, www.ual.com in the U.S. or www.united.ca, or 13 17 77 in Australia)

CARRIERS FLYING FROM THE U.K.

- **British Airways** (© 0845/773-3377 in the U.K.; 1800/626-747 in Ireland; or 02/8904 8800 in Sydney, 07/3223 3123 in Brisbane, 1300/134 001 in Canberra, 03/9603 1133 in Melbourne, 08/8238 2138 in Adelaide, and 08/9425 7711 in Perth; www.britishairways.com)
- **Cathay Pacific** (© 0845/758 1581 in the U.K.; 13 17 47 in Australia; www.cathaypacific.com/uk)
- **Malaysia Airlines** (© 0870/607-9090 in the U.K.; 1/676-1561 in Ireland; 13 26 27 in Australia; www.malaysiaairlines.com.my or www.malaysiaairlineseurope.com)
- **Qantas** (© 0845/7-747-767 in the U.K.; 13 13 13 in Australia; www.qantas.com.au)
- **Singapore Airlines** (© 0870/608 8886 in the U.K.; 1/671-0722 in Ireland; 13 10 11 in Australia; www.singaporeair.com/uk)
- **Thai Airways International** (© 0870/6060-911 in the U.K.; 1300/651 960 in Australia; www.thaiair.com)

FINDING THE BEST AIRFARE

If you're flying from the United States, keep in mind that the airlines' low season is from mid-April to the end of August—this is when you'll find the cheapest fares, and this happens to be the best time to travel most parts of Australia. High season is December through February, and shoulder season is September through November, and again from March to mid-April.

Keep an eye out for special deals offered throughout the year. Unexpected lows in airline passenger loads

---

Tips Plan Wisely to Avoid Jet Lag

Jet lag is a foregone conclusion on the long trip to Australia, so don't plan to climb Ayers Rock the first morning you arrive, or book opera tickets for your first evening. Help beat it by getting plenty of sleep on the flight, eating light, staying up as long as you can the first day in Australia, then trying to wake up at a normal hour the next morning.

---

often lead airlines to put cheap offers on the market. The catch is these usually have a short lead time, requiring you to travel in the next 6 weeks or so. Some deals involve taking a circuitous route, via Fiji or Japan, for instance. Canada 3000 has good rates from Vancouver in low season and often has promotional specials, although its route can involve a number of stops en route.

Some travel agents specializing in cheap fares to Australia include **Austravel** (℡ **800/633-3404** in the U.S. and Canada, or 0870/055 0239 in the United Kingdom; www.austravel.net); **Downunder Direct,** a division of Swain Australia (℡ **800/642 6224** in the U.S. and Canada; www.downunderdirect.com); and **Goway** (℡ **800/387-8850** in the U.S. and Canada; www.goway.com).

Consolidators, also known as "bucket shops," are another good source for low fares. Consolidators buy seats in bulk from the airlines and then sell them back to the public at low prices, sometimes even below even the airlines' discounted rates. There's nothing shady about the reliable ones—basically, they're just big travel agents that get discounts for buying in bulk and pass some of the savings on to you. Before you pay, however, ask for a confirmation number from the consolidator and then call the airline itself to confirm your seat. Be prepared to book your ticket with a different consolidator—there are many to choose from—if the airline can't confirm your reservation. Also be aware that consolidator tickets are usually non-refundable or come with stiff cancellation penalties. Some of the more reliable consolidators include: **Cheap Tickets** (℡ **888/922 8849;** www.cheaptickets.com); **Fly-Cheap** (℡ 800-FLY-CHEAP; www.flycheap.com); **Council Travel** (℡ **800/2COUNCIL;** www.counciltravel.com); and **STA Travel** (℡ **800/781-4040;** www.statravel.com). Although Council Travel and STA Travel aim primarily at student travelers, you don't have to be a student to buy their fares or use their services.

You can also search the Internet for cheap fares. See "Planning Your Trip Online," below, for valuable advice on how to make the web work for you.

IN-FLIGHT COMFORT

Wear loose clothing and a roomy pair of shoes, because your feet will swell en route. Drink plenty of water and go easy on the alcohol. To while away the hours, consider traveling with an airline that offers in-seat videos. Requesting a bulkhead or exit-door seat will give you more leg room. Some airlines allow you to request seats when you book, but others allocate seats only at check-in—in that case, be early to beat savvy Aussies queuing for the same thing!

On such a long journey, it makes sense to break up the trip with a 1-night stopover if you have time. If you're coming from the United States, this will be Honolulu or maybe Fiji; if you're coming from Europe, you have any number of Asian cities—Bangkok, Singapore, Hong Kong—in which to spend a night or two. If you're coming from Europe and you have a long layover in Asia, I recommend you book a day room at a hotel with a 6pm checkout. Wandering around a humid, crowded city at 2pm when your body thinks it's 3am is *not* fun.

CRUISING TO AUSTRALIA

Australia mostly only crops up on cruise itineraries when the liner is making a world voyage. These cruise lines have ships that call at Australia, usually at least once a year: **Cunard** (© 800/7-CUNARD; www.cunard. com), **Crystal Cruises** (© 31/785-9300; www. crystalcruises.com), **Holland America** (© 800/426-0327; www.hollandamerica.com), **Princess Cruises** (© 800-PRINCESS; www. princess cruises.com), and **Royal Caribbean** (© 800/398-9819; www. royalcaribbean.com).

11 Getting Around Australia

The one big mistake tourists make Down Under (apart from getting sunburned) is failing to comprehend the vast distances between the most popular locations. Every Sydney hotelier has a tale to tell about the tourist who comes down to the front desk complaining their room doesn't have a view of Ayers Rock, 2,841 kilometers (1,765 miles) away, or asking what time the afternoon boat to the Great Barrier Reef leaves from Cairns, about 2,800 kilometers (1,750 miles) to the north. Don't try to cram too much in one trip.

While traveling overland may make sense in Europe or North America, flying in Australia is the best way to go. People who go by train, bus, or car are often disappointed at Australia's flat, unchanging vistas of desert, wheat fields, and gum trees—and this dull scenery literally goes on for days. A good compromise is to take to the air for long trips and save the land travel for short hops of no more than a few hours. Try not to backtrack, because it eats up valuable time and money.

BY PLANE

Australia is a big country with a small population to support its air routes—hence, high airfares. This section contains some tips to help you save.

Domestic travel is mainly operated by **Qantas** (© **800/227-4500** in the U.S. and Canada; 0845/7747-767 in the U.K.; 09-357-8900 in Auckland, or 0800/808-767 in New Zealand;

Tips Changes to Regional Plane Service

In late 2001, **Ansett Australia** and its subsidiaries (Hazelton Airlines, Kendell Airlines, Skywest Airlines, and Aeropelican) suspended operations, as the airline looked for a buyer to bail them out of bankruptcy. Ansett was, after Qantas, the country's major airline, offering international and extensive regional service. Qantas announced plans to take over some of Ansett's regional routes, but as this book went to press, new schedules and destinations were not available. Now that two other national carriers—Impulse and Flight West—have also folded, local plane service may be hard to come by in some of Australia's more remote areas. Contact **Qantas** (© **13 13 13** in Australia, 800/227-4500 in the United States and Canada, 457/747 767 in the UK; www.qantas.com.au) and the tourist bureaus of areas where you are planning to travel for the latest updates on regional air service.

13 13 13 in Australia; www.qantas. com.au). You may get a much cheaper fare with the no-frills airline, **Virgin Blue,** based in Brisbane (© **13 67 89** in Australia, or 07/3295 2296; www. virginblue.com.au). It operates an East Coast network covering Townsville, Brisbane, the Gold Coast, Sydney, Melbourne, and Adelaide. It started taking on the big guys in 2000—in fact, there has been talk of Virgin Blue margining with one of the more established national airlines. As its network is growing all the time, it may have added more cities by the time you read this.

Most of the time Qantas airfares on the same route match each other to within a dollar, and both airlines maintain virtually identical standards of in-flight service and safety. Both own or are affiliated with a number of regional airlines covering almost every part of Australia, whose schedules and fares are linked into the parents' reservations systems. Australia's air network is not as well developed as that of North America or Europe, so don't assume there is a direct flight to your chosen destination, or that there is a flight every hour or even every day. *Note:* All flights in Australia are nonsmoking.

FARES FOR INTERNATIONAL TRAVELERS Qantas typically offers international travelers a discount of around 30% off the full fares that Australians pay for domestic flights. So if the full fare for Australians is A$1,000, international visitors pay only around A$700—which works out to U.S.$385! Not bad. To qualify for these fares if you find yourself buying a ticket once you arrive in Australia, quote your passport number and international ticket number when making your reservation. Don't assume the fare for international travelers is the best deal you'll get, though—the latest hot special in the market that day (or even better, perhaps, a package deal with

accommodation thrown in) may be cheaper still.

AIR PASSES If you are planning on whipping around to more than one city, purchasing a Qantas **Boomerang Pass** is much cheaper than buying regular fares. You must buy these passes before you arrive in Australia; residents of Australia cannot purchase them. (New Zealand residents can't buy passes from Qantas).

With Qantas's Boomerang Pass, for example, you must purchase a minimum of two coupons (and a maximum 10) priced at U.S.$160/ Can$240 or U.S.$190/Can$280 per coupon for travel within a zone, or U.S.$200/Can$300 or U.S.$240/ Can$360 per coupon for travel between zones. The difference between the higher and lower fares depends on the airline's yield management system, so your coupons may cost the lower or higher amount depending on the day you buy them. Air passes are a great value when you consider that the regular Sydney–Cairns fare is A$606.10 or $666.60 (it differs from day to day, depending on the airline's yield management system)—which works out to U.S.$333.35 or $366.65, compared to the coupon fare of just U.S.$160 or $190!

Coupons are also good for travel to and from New Zealand and to the most popular South Pacific nations. The pass is also good for travel around the South Pacific with Air Pacific. Zone 1 covers Western Australia; Zone 2 covers the Red Centre and Darwin; Zone 3 covers major towns in South Australia, Tasmania, Victoria, New South Wales, and Queensland; and Zone 4 covers many small towns in the east coast states, including island gateways like Hayman Island, Hamilton Island, and Gladstone. You must book your first two coupon destinations before you arrive, but you can book the rest as you go. Another beauty of these fares is that they are refundable and changeable; you will incur a U.S.$45/Can$50 fee to change destinations after the coupons have been ticketed. Many small towns, some island resorts, and many airports served by subsidiaries of Qantas are not covered by the air passes, but passes will still get you loads of places.

AERIAL TOURS The great thing about aerial touring around Australia is that it allows you to whiz around the vast Australian continent to see many highlights, and you get to skip all the dreary, featureless countryside that typically separates Australia's most fascinating bits. Much of the Australian landscape is best seen from the air, anyhow (such as the weird Bungle Bungles formations in the Kimberley). **Aircruising Australia** ✒ (© 02/ 9693-2233; www.aircruising.com.au) operates upscale aerial tours of 8 to 19 days in a private aircraft, usually a 40-passenger Fokker Friendship which is nimble enough to "flight-see" at a low 500 feet. One factor you may see as a plus is that the company mainly markets within Australia, so your fellow passengers are likely to be Aussies. Perhaps because the tours are expensive for Australians, most of the passengers are over 55. I have traveled a 5-day Outback leg on one of the company's tours, and highly recommend them. It was extremely well organized, with lots of time for the organized land-based sightseeing, some free time, and a maximum 2 hours in the air most days. Accommodation was usually the best available, and the itinerary included fun extras like a dry riverbed barbecue in Alice Springs. Fares in 2001 for a 12-day Great Australian Aircruise around the Outback, departing from Sydney, were A$8,998 to $9,390 (U.S.$4,948.90 to $5,164.45) per person, twin-share, **depending on the season.**

Connoisseur Tours (© 1800/ 50-7777 in Australia, or 02/9964-9220; www.connoisseurtours.com) started up in 2001 offering luxury aerial tours around Australia aboard chartered Qantas Boeing 737's, carrying up to 88 passengers. It only made two departures in 2001, but that frequency may grow. Connoisseur's tours are more lavish and expensive than Aircruising Australia's including, for example, a firelight dinner in a North Queensland rain forest and a private first-class train journey from Adelaide to the Barossa Valley wine region.

BY TRAIN

The rail network in Australia is mostly good only for travel in a single line traveling from Perth through Adelaide, Melbourne, Canberra, Sydney, Brisbane, and up to Cairns, and from Adelaide to Alice Springs. A few rural towns, such as Broken Hill, are also served by trains. Australia's trains are clean, comfortable, and safe, and service standards and facilities are perfectly adequate. Trains generally cost more than buses, but are still reasonably priced. The exception are three trains which promote themselves as "experiences" rather than a mere mode of transport—the *Indian Pacific,* The *Ghan,* and the *Great South Pacific Express* (described below)—which can be frightfully expensive.

Most long-distance trains have smart sleepers with big windows, electric outlets, wardrobes, hand basins, and fresh sheets and blankets. First-class sleepers have en-suite bathrooms, and meals are often included in the fare. Second-class sleepers use shared shower facilities, and meals are not included. Some second-class sleepers are private cabins; on other trains you share with strangers. Single cabins are usually of broom-closet dimensions but surprisingly comfy. The food ranges from okay to pretty darn good. Smoking is usually banned, or allowed only in the club cars.

Tips Plan Carefully for the Train

Australian rail schedules are no match for the snappy frequency of European rail travel—some trains operate only once a week—so check the timetable before you get your other travel arrangements in place. And because Australia doesn't have that many trains, they're often fully booked—so make reservations well in advance.

Australia's rail routes are managed either by the private enterprise **Great Southern Railway** (© 13 21 47 in Australia, or 08/8213 4592; www.gsr.com.au), which runs the Indian Pacific, the Overland, and the Ghan, or by one of the following government bodies. **Traveltrain,** the long-distance train division of Queensland Rail (© 13 22 32 in Australia, or 07/3235 1122; www.traveltrain.qr.com.au), handles rail within that state. **Countrylink** (© 13 22 32 in Australia, or 02/9379 1298; www.countrylink.nsw.gov.au), manages travel within New South Wales and from Sydney to Canberra, Melbourne, and Brisbane. **WAGR (Western Australian Government Railways** (© 13 10 53 in Western Australia, 1800/099 150 from elsewhere in Australia, or 08/9326 2000; www.wagr.wa.gov.au), operates trains in Western Australia.

Outside Australia, the umbrella organization **Rail Australia** (www.railaustralia.com.au) handles inquiries and makes reservations for all long-distance trains, with the exception of WAGR and the Great South Pacific Express (see below) through its overseas agents: **ATS Tours** (© 800/423-2880) in the United States; **Goway** (© 800/387-8850) in Canada; **Leisurail** (© 0870/750 0222) in the United Kingdom; and **Tranz Rail** (© 03/339 3809) in New Zealand.

The *Great South Pacific Express* is an ultra-opulent locomotive with lavish turn-of-the-20th-century decor, plush cabins, and a romantic open-sided car at the tail (unlike Australia's other long-distance trains). It's a joint venture between the Queensland government and Venice Simplon-Orient-Express. It plies the Sydney-Brisbane-Cairns route, incorporating the scenic rail trip to Kuranda (see chapter 6) and a side trip by seaplane or helicopter to a private snorkeling pontoon on the Great Barrier Reef. The scenery is dull, dull, dull; you make this trip for the romance and excitement of the train journey itself. Passengers I have met always speak highly of it. In the summertime wet season January through March, the train avoids steamy Cairns and stays in the cooler south, operating rail-package tours that incorporate sightseeing in Sydney, the Blue Mountains, the Hunter Valley Wine region, and Canberra, plus stays in luxury hotels. Fares for the Brisbane–Cairns leg range from A$2,970 to $4,950 (U.S.$1,633.50 to $2,722.50) per person, twin-share. Contact **Orient Express Trains & Cruises** (© 1800/000 395 in Australia, or 07/3247 6555; 800/524 2420 in the U.S.; 020/7805 5100 in the U.K.; or 09/379 3708 in New Zealand; www.orient-expresstrains.com).

Great Southern Railway's *Indian Pacific* ✿ does not match the Great South Pacific Express' luxury, but it is nonetheless a rather glamorous train linking Sydney, Broken Hill, Adelaide, and Perth in an epic 3-day Outback run twice a week. The slightly less posh *Ghan* (named after "Afghani," actually Pakistani, camel trainers who traveled the Outback in the 19th century) traverses a loop between Sydney,

Melbourne, Adelaide, and Alice Springs once or twice a week. Both trains have a choice of economy seats and second- or first-class sleepers.

Great Southern Railway's third train, the *Overland,* is a more prosaic journey linking Adelaide and Melbourne four times a week. Countrylink runs daily trains from Sydney to Melbourne, Canberra, and Brisbane, and to a number of New South Wales country towns.

Queensland Rail operates two trains on the Brisbane–Cairns route: the weekly *Queenslander* in all-first-class-sleepers configuration or economy seat, the comfortable Sunlander does the same route three times a week with a choice of seats or second- and first-class sleepers. Queensland Rail's *Spirit of the Tropics* runs Brisbane–Townsville twice a week and is popular with the backpacker set headed to one of their favorite haunts, the Whitsunday Islands; it has economy seats and second- and first-class sleepers. Queensland Rail also operates a service at least daily from Brisbane to Rockhampton (most days aboard the 160kmph/100 mph Tilt train service), and other trains to small Outback towns. All Queensland Rail and most Countrylink long-distance trains stop at most towns en route, so they're a good tool for exploring the eastern mainland states.

PACKAGES Great Southern Railway, Countrylink, and Queensland Rail (see above) offer rail packages that include accommodations and sightseeing. Look into Great Southern Railways' "Trainways" packages, as I think they will give you a fun first-hand experience of the Outback. For example, a 10-day "Outback Odyssey" features rail travel aboard the Ghan from Alice Springs to Adelaide, Melbourne, or Sydney, sightseeing at Uluru and the Olgas, the Kings Canyon walk, a choice of tours in Alice from a camel-back dinner to a

visit to ancient Palm Valley, a tour of the underground opal-mining town of Coober Pedy, and a full-day Outback aerial mail run with the pilot/postman to deliver mail to remote cattle ranches.

RAIL PASSES National, East Coast and Queensland rail passes are available from Rail Australia (see above) at its overseas agents. National passes must be bought before you arrive and are available only to holders of non-Australian passports. East Coast (Melbourne-Sydney-Brisbane-Cairns) and Queensland passes can be purchased before or after you arrive in Australia. Passes are not valid for first-class travel.

The national **Austrail Pass** is good for economy seats and second-class sleepers on all long-distance trains (except WAGR services in Western Australia) and is even good for suburban city train networks. It comes in 14-, 21-, and 30-day versions and costs between A$660 and $1,035.10 (U.S.$363 and $569.30). You can buy 7-day extensions for A$345.40 (U.S.$190). An alternative version, the **Austrail Flexipass,** allows you to travel for any 8, 15, 22, or 29 days, consecutive or not, within a 6-month period. An 8-day Flexipass is A$550 (U.S.$302.50), with the price going up to A$1,439.90 (U.S.$791.95) for a 29-day Flexipass. *Note:* You cannot use the 8-day pass on the Indian Pacific or the Ghan, meaning, not on the Adelaide–Perth or on the Sydney–, Melbourne–, or Adelaide–Alice Springs routes.

BY BUS

Bus travel in Australia is a big step up from the low-rent affair it can be in the United States. Terminals are centrally located and well lit, the coaches are clean and air-conditioned, you sit in comfy adjustable seats, videos are shown on board, and the drivers are polite and even comment on points of interest along the way sometimes. Some buses even have rest rooms. Unlike Australia's train service, there are few places the extensive bus network won't take you. Buses are totally no-smoking.

Australia has two national coach operators: **Greyhound Pioneer Australia** (© **13 20 30** in Australia or 07/3329-7777; www.greyhound.com. au; no relation to Greyhound in the U.S.) and **McCafferty's** (© **13 14 99** in Australia, or 07/3329-7777; www.mccaffertys.com.au). In 2000, McCafferty's bought Greyhound Pioneer (hence both share the same telephone number, above). While the coach lines will operate as separate brands with their own networks and pass products, by the time you read this book, it is likely that passengers will be able to use tickets and passes interchangeably on either network. The coaches and service standards of both companies are virtually identical. The only real difference between them is that McCafferty's does not travel in Western Australia, while Greyhound Pioneer does (although McCafferty's reservations offices can book your travel in Western Australia aboard Greyhound Pioneer buses, anyhow).

Neither bus company operates within Tasmania; however, McCafferty's provides a bookings and transfer service from Melbourne across the Bass Strait aboard the *Spirit of Tasmania* ferry to connect with one of Tasmania's major coach companies, Redline Coaches. As well as point-to-point services, both coach companies offer a limited range of tours at popular locations on their networks. McCafferty's/Greyhound Pioneer have many international agents, including **Inta-Aussie South Pacific** (© **310/568-2060**) in the United States, **Goway** (© **800/387-8850**) in Canada, and **Bridge the World** (© **020/7911 0900**) in the United Kingdom.

BUS PASSES   Bus passes are a great value. There are several kinds—Day passes, Pre-set Itinerary passes, and Kilometre passes. Look into the one that suits you best. Note that even with a pass, you may still need to book the next leg of your trip 12 or 24 hours ahead as a condition of the pass, and in school vacation periods, which are always busy, it may be smart to book as much as 7 days ahead.

McCafferty's **"Discover Australia"** day pass is good for 7, 10, 15, 21, or 30 days of travel, consecutive or not, within a 1- to 2-month period depending on how many days you buy. The passes are valid for unlimited travel, and backtracking is allowed. Fares range from A$683 (U.S.$375.65) for a 7-day pass

---

Sample Travel Times & Bus Fares

Here are some sample bus fares and travel times, to give you an idea of what you're getting yourself into as you step aboard. McCafferty's and Greyhound's fares are usually identical. All fares and travel times are one-way.

Route	Travel Time (Approx.)	Fare
Broome–Darwin	27 hr.	A$230 (U.S.$126.50)
Sydney–Brisbane	17 hr.	A$85 (U.S.$46.75)
Cairns–Brisbane	29 hr.	A$173 (U.S.$95.15)

Note: Fares and some passes will be considerably cheaper if you're a student, a senior, a backpacker cardholder, or a Hostelling International/YHA member. Take note, though, that you sometimes have to buy passes before you leave home to qualify for discounts.

to A$1,643 (U.S.$903.65) for a 30-day pass. Note the pass must be bought before you arrive in Australia. Greyhound Pioneer does not sell a day pass.

If you know where you are going and are willing to obey a "no backtracking" rule, consider a **Travel Australia** (McCafferty's) or **Aussie Explorer** (Greyhound Pioneer) predetermined itinerary pass. These passes allow unlimited stops in a generous time frame on a preset one-way route (you are permitted to travel the route in either direction). Both McCafferty's and Greyhound have a huge range of pre-set itinerary passes to choose from. As an example, McCafferty's **"Sun and Centre"** pass takes in Ayers Rock, Alice Springs, Katherine, Darwin, Mt. Isa, Cairns, and the whole east coast down to Sydney. The pass is valid for 6 months and costs A$888 (U.S.$488.40) from Sydney for travel only, or A$988 (U.S.$543.40) with optional tours to Kakadu National Park and Kings Canyon. You don't have to start in Sydney; you can start at any point along any of the pass routes, in which case the pass may be cheaper. In the case of the Sun and Centre pass, that means you could start further up the track at Brisbane (in which case the pass costs A$727/U.S.$399.85, or A$910/U.S.$500.50 with tours) or Cairns (from where the pass costs A$494/U.S.$271.70, or A$611/U.S.$336.05 with tours). McCafferty's does not serve Western Australia, so if you want a pass that covers the whole country, go for Greyhound Pioneer's All Australian Pass for A$2,102 (U.S.$1,156.10); it's valid for a year.

Greyhound Pioneer has an **Aussie Kilometre Pass** that allows unlimited stops in any direction within the mileage you buy. Passes are available in increments of 1,000 kilometers (625 miles). Prices range from A$281 (U.S.$154.55) for 2,000 kilometers

(1,250 miles)—enough to get you from Cairns to Brisbane—to A$1,975 (U.S.$1,086.25) for a whopping 20,000 kilometers (12,500 miles). McCafferty's has a similar product called an **Australian Roamer Pass,** but note it is available only to students, holders of selected backpacker cards, and members of Hostelling International/YHA.

BY CAR

Not only are Australia's roads not great, but there are not many of them. The taxes of the population of 19 million people get spread pretty thin when it comes to maintaining roads in a country roughly the size of the continental United States. Most highways are two-lane affairs with the occasional rut and pothole, often no outside line markings, and sometimes no shoulders to speak of.

When you are poring over the map of Australia, remember that what looks like a road may be an unsealed (unpaved) track suitable for four-wheel-drive vehicles only. Many roads in the Top End are passable only in the Dry Season (about Apr–Nov). If you plan long-distance driving, get a road map (see below for sources) that marks paved and unpaved roads.

You cannot drive across the middle of the country (except along the north-south Stuart Highway linking Adelaide and Darwin) because most of it is desert. In most places you must travel around the edge on Highway 1. The map on the inside back cover of this book marks the major highways.

Your current driver's license or an international driver's permit is fine in every state of Australia. By law you must carry your license with you when driving. The minimum driving age is 16 or 17, depending on which state you visit, but some rental-car companies require you to be 21, or even 26 sometimes, if you want to rent a four-wheel-drive vehicle.

CAR RENTALS

Think twice about renting a car in tourist hot spots such as Cairns. In these areas most tour operators pick you up and drop you back at your hotel door, so having a car may not be worth the expense.

The "big four" car-rental companies all have extensive networks across Australia:

- **Avis** (© **13 6333** in Australia, www.avis.com.au; 800/230-4898 in the U.S., www.avis.com; 800/ 272-5871 in Canada; 0870/90 77300 in the U.K., www.avis.co. uk; 21/428 1111 in Ireland; 09/ 526 2847 in New Zealand, www. avis.co.nz)
- **Budget** (© **1300/36 2848** in Australia, www.budget.com.au; 800/527-0700 in the U.S., www. budget.com; 800/268-8900 in Canada, www.budget.ca; 0800/ 328 2831 in the U.K., www. budget-rent-a-car.co.uk; 903 27711 in Ireland, www.budget-ireland.com; 0800/652 227 in New Zealand, www.budget.co.nz)
- **Hertz** (© **13 30 39** in Australia, www.hertz.com.au; 800/654-3001 in the U.S., www.hertz. com; 800/263-0600 in English, 800/263-0678 in French in Canada, or 416/620-9620 in Toronto, www.hertz.ca; 0870/844 8844 in the U.K., www.hertz.co. uk; 1/676 7476 in Ireland; 0800/ 654 321 in New Zealand)

- **Thrifty** (© **1300/367 227** in Australia, www.thrifty.com.au; 800/THRIFTY in the U.S. and Canada, www.thrifty.com; 01494/ 751 600 in the U.K., www.thrifty. co.uk; 1800/51 5800 in Ireland, www.thrifty.ie; 0800/73 7070 in New Zealand, www.thrifty.co.nz)

Two large Australian companies are:

- **Delta EuropCar** (© **1300/13 13 90** in Australia, or 03/9330 6122; www.deltacarrentals.com.au). It is a national chain with the third largest fleet in Australia.
- **Red Spot Car Rentals** (© **1800/ 633 936** in Australia, or 02/9211 1144; www.redspotrentals.com. au). It has depots in Sydney, Melbourne, Brisbane, and Cairns.

A small sedan good for zipping around a city or touring a wine region will cost around A$70 to $80 (U.S.$38.50 to $44) a day. A feistier vehicle with enough grunt to get you hundreds of miles from state to state will cost around A$80 to $100 (U.S.$38.50 to $55) a day. Rentals of a week or longer usually reduce by A$5 (U.S.$2.75) a day or so.

A regular car will get you to most places in this book, but because the country has a high number of unpaved roads, it can make sense to rent a four-wheel-drive (4WD) vehicle. All of the major car-rental companies rent them. They are more expensive than a regular car at around A$150 (U.S.$82.50) per day, or

Sample Driving Distances & Times

Here are a few sample road distances between popular points and the minimum time it takes to drive between them.

Route	Distance	Approx. Driving Time
Cairns–Sydney	2,495km (1,559 miles)	29 hr. (allow 4–5 days)
Sydney–Melbourne	873km (546 miles)	15 hr. (allow 1–2 days)
Sydney–Perth	4,131km (2,581 miles)	51 hr. (allow 6–7 days)
Adelaide–Darwin	3,024km (1,890 miles)	31 hr. (allow 4–6 days)
Perth–Darwin	4,163km (2,602 miles)	49 hr. (allow 6–8 days)

⌒Tips Insurance Alert

Damage to a rental car caused by an animal (hitting a kangaroo, for instance) is not covered by car-rental companies' insurance policies, nor is driving on an unpaved road—and Australia has a lot of those.

---

around A$130 (U.S.$71.50) a day for rentals of a week or longer.

The rates quoted here are only a guide. Many smaller local companies, and the big guys, too, do competitive specials, especially in tourist areas with distinct off-seasons. Advance purchase rates, usually 7 to 21 days, can offer significant savings.

INSURANCE   Insurance for loss of, or damage to, the car, and third-party property insurance are usually included in the rate, but read the rental agreement before you set off, because the fine print contains key information the smiling front-desk staff never tell you. For example, damage to the car body may be covered, but not damage to the windshield or tires, or damage caused by water or driving too close to a bushfire.

The deductible, known as "excess" in Australia, on insurance may be as high as A$2,000 (U.S.$1,100) for regular cars and up to A$5,500 (U.S.$3,025) on four-wheel-drives and campervans. You can reduce it, or avoid it altogether, by paying a premium of around A$7 to $16 (U.S.$3.85 to $8.80) per day on a car or four-wheel-drive, and around A$22 to $44 (U.S.$12.10 to $24.20) per day on a campervan. The amount of the excess reduction premium depends on the vehicle type and the extent of reduction you choose. Your rental company may bundle personal accident insurance and baggage insurance into this premium. And again, check the conditions; some excess reduction payments do not reduce excesses on single-vehicle accidents, for example.

ONE-WAY RENTALS   Australia's great distances often make one-way rentals a necessity, for which car-rental companies can charge a hefty penalty amounting to hundreds of dollars. A one-way fee usually applies to campervan renters, too—for example, Hertz charges a A$175 (U.S.$96.25) fee, and Britz charges A$200 (U.S.$110).

CAMPERVANS   Campervans (as Aussies call motorhomes) are popular in Australia. Generally a good deal smaller than the enormous RVs in the United States, they come in two-, three-, four-, or six-berth versions, and they usually have everything you need, such as a minifridge/freezer (icebox in the smaller versions), microwave oven, gas cooker, cooking and cleaning utensils, linen, and touring information including maps and campground guides. All have showers and toilets, except for some two-berthers. Most have air-conditioned driver's cabins, but not all have air-conditioned living quarters, a necessity in most parts of the country November through March. Four-wheel-drive campers are available, but they tend to be small and some lack hot water, toilet, shower, and air-conditioning. Minimum driver age for campervans is usually 21.

Australia's biggest national campervan-rental companies are **Apollo Motorhome Holidays** (✆ 1800/777 779 in Australia, or 07/3260 5466; www.apollocamper.com), **Britz Campervan Rentals** (✆ 1800/331 454 in Australia, or 03/8379 8890; www.britz.com), **Hertz Campervans** (✆ 1800/33 5888 in Australia, or 08/ 8271 8281; www.hertzcampervans. com.au), and **Maui** (✆ 1300/363 800

in Australia, or 02/9667 0402; www.
maui-rentals.com).

Frustratingly, most local councils
take a dim view of "free camping," the
practice of pulling over by the roadside
to camp for the night. Instead, you will
likely have to stay in a campground.

For a two-berth campervan with
shower and toilet, Britz's 2001/2002
rates were between A$105 and $213
(U.S.$57.75 and $117.15) per day,
over a 4- to 20-day rental period. For a
four-berth with shower and toilet over
the same period, you are looking at
between A$158 and $278 (U.S.$86.90
and $152.90) per day. Rates vary with
the seasons. May and June are the
slowest months; December and January are the busiest. It's sometimes possible to get better rates by booking in
your home country before departure.
Renting for longer than 3 weeks
knocks around A$10 (U.S.$5.50) off
the daily rate. Most companies will
demand a minimum 4- or 5-day
rental. Give the company your itinerary before booking, because some
routes, such as the ferry across to
Tasmania, or in a four-wheel-drive
campervan's case, the Gibb River Road
in the Kimberley, may need the company's special permission. Campervan-
rental companies may not permit you
to drive your two-wheel-drive campervan on unpaved roads; for example,
Britz and Hertz do not, while Maui
does allow two-wheel-drive campers to
travel up to 100 kilometers (63 miles)
from an unpaved road.

ON THE ROAD

GAS   The price of petrol (gasoline)
will elicit a cry of dismay from Americans and a whoop of delight from
Brits. Prices go up and down a lot, but
very roughly, you're looking at around
A90¢ a liter (or U.S.$1.87 per U.S.
gallon) for unleaded petrol in Sydney,
and A$1 a liter (or U.S.$2.08 per U.S.
gallon), or more, in the Outback. One
U.S. gallon equals 3.78 liters. Most
rental cars take unleaded gas, and

campervans run on diesel, which costs
around A90¢ to $1.20 a liter
(U.S.$1.87 to $2.49 per U.S. gallon),
depending on your location.

DRIVING   RULES   Australians
drive on the left, which means you
give way to the right. Left turns on a
red light are not permitted unless a
sign says so.

Roundabouts (traffic circles) are
common at intersections; approach
these slowly enough to stop if you
have to, and give way to all traffic on
the roundabout. You are supposed to
flash your indicator light as you leave
the roundabout (even if you're going
straight ahead, as technically that's a
left turn), but most Aussies never
bother and it's not an enforced rule.

The only strange driving rule is
Melbourne's requirement that drivers
turn right from the left lane. This
allows the city's trams to carry on
uninterrupted in the right lane. Pull
into the left lane opposite the street
you are turning into, and make the
turn when the traffic light in the street
you are turning into becomes green.

The maximum permitted blood
alcohol level when driving is 0.05,
which equals approximately two 200
milliliter (6.6 fl. oz.) drinks in the first
hour for men, one for women, and
one drink per hour for both sexes after
that. The police set up random breath-
testing units (RBTs) in cunningly dis-
guised and unlikely places all the time,
so it is easy to get caught. You will face
a court appearance if you do.

The speed limit is 60 kilometers per
hour (37.5 mph) in urban areas and
100 kilometers per hour (63 mph) or
110 kilometers per hour (69 mph) in
most country areas. Speed-limit signs
are black numbers circled in red on a
white background.

Drivers and passengers, including
taxi passengers, must wear a seatbelt at
all times when the vehicle is moving
forward, if a belt is fitted in the car.
Young children are required to sit in

the rear seat in a child-safety seat or harness; car-rental companies will rent these to you, but be sure to book them. Tell the taxi company you have a child when you book a cab so that they can send a car with the right restraints.

MAPS The maps published by the state automobile clubs listed later in "Auto Clubs" will likely be free if you are a member of an affiliated auto club in your home country. None will mail them to you overseas; you will have to pick them up on your arrival. Remember to bring your auto-club-membership card to qualify for discounts or free maps.

Two of the biggest map publishers in Australia are **HEMA Maps** (© 07/ 3340 0000; www.hemamaps.com.au) and **Universal Press** (© 02/9857 3700; www.universalpress-online. com). Both publish an extensive range of national, state, regional and city maps. HEMA has an especially strong list of regional maps ("Gold Coast and Region" and "The Red Centre" are just a few), while Universal produces a complete range of street directories by city, region, or state under the "UBD" and "Gregory's" labels. HEMA produces national four-wheel-drive and motorbike road atlases and many regional four-wheel-drive maps— good if you plan to go off the trails— an atlas of Australia's national parks, and maps to Kakadu and Lamington National Parks.

Both companies produce a range of national road atlases. Universal's "UBD Motoring Atlas of Australia" helpfully publishes street maps of small regional towns in each state. Hema publishes a national road atlas on CD. As Australia is such as big country, a national atlas is good for overall trip planning and long-distance or interstate journeys, but sometimes of limited use on day trips or short journeys because it is not detailed enough. Then, you may find it worthwhile to purchase a map to the local area—say, a "Cairns to Cooktown" map if you wanted to explore Cairns, Kuranda, Port Douglas, and other towns within an hour or two's drive of Cairns.

Both HEMA and Universal Press maps are distributed in the United States by **Map Link** (© 805/ 692-6777; www.maplink.com). Hema Maps are also distributed in Canada, by **ITMB (International Travel Maps and Books)** (© 604/879-3621; www. itmb.com) and in the United Kingdom by **World Leisure Marketing** (© 01332/57-3737; www.mapguides.com). Both Universal Press and HEMA maps are sold in the United Kingdom by **Edward Stanford's** (© 020/7836-1321).

In Australia, auto clubs (see below), bigger newsagents, and bookstores are your best source of maps. Petrol stations stock a limited range relating to the route they are on, and visitor information centers sometimes stock a range to the area and the whole state.

ROAD SIGNS Australians navigate by road name, not road number. The easiest way to get where you're going is to familiarize yourself with the major towns along your route and follow the signs toward them.

AUTO CLUBS Every state and territory in Australia has its own auto club. Your auto association back home almost certainly has a reciprocal agreement with Australian clubs, possibly entitling you to free maps, accommodation guides, and emergency roadside assistance. Don't forget to bring your membership card.

Even if you're not a member, the clubs are a good source of advice on local traffic regulations, touring advice, road conditions, traveling in remote areas, and any other motoring questions you may have. They sell maps, accommodation guides, and camping guides to non-members at reasonable prices. You can drop into numerous regional offices as well as the head office locations listed here.

- **New South Wales & ACT: National Roads and Motorists' Association (NRMA)**, 74–76 King St. (at George Street), Sydney, NSW 2000 (© **13 21 32** in New South Wales, or 02/9848 5201)
- **Victoria: Royal Automobile Club of Victoria (RACV)**, 550 Princes Hwy., Noble Park, VIC 3174 (© **13 19 55** in Australia, or 03/9790 2211). A more convenient city office is located at 360 Bourke St., Melbourne.
- **Queensland: Royal Automobile Club of Queensland (RACQ)**, 300 St. Pauls Terrace, Fortitude Valley, QLD 4006 (© **13 19 05** in Australia, or 07/3361 2444). A more convenient city office is in the General Post Office building at 261 Queen St., Brisbane.
- **Western Australia: Royal Automobile Club of WA (RAC)**, 228 Adelaide Terrace, Perth, WA 6000 (© **08/9421 4444**)
- **South Australia: Royal Automobile Association of South Australia (RAA)**, 41 Hindmarsh Sq., Adelaide, SA 5000 (© **08/8202 4600**)
- **Northern Territory: Automobile Association of the Northern Territory (AANT)**, 79–81 Smith St., Darwin, NT 0800 (© **08/8981 3837**)
- **Tasmania: Royal Automobile Club of Tasmania (RACT)**, corner of Murray and Patrick streets, Hobart, TAS 7000 (© **13 27 22** in Tasmania, or 03/6232 6300)

All these clubs except the AANT can be accessed on the Web via www.aaa.asn.au.

ROAD CONDITIONS & SAFETY

Here are some common motoring dangers and ways to avoid them:

FATIGUE Fatigue is a killer on Australia's long roads. The rule is to take a 20-minute break every 2 hours, even if you don't feel tired.

KANGAROOS & OTHER WILDLIFE It's a sad fact, but Skippy is a road hazard. Avoid driving between dusk and dawn in country areas, because this is when 'roos feed and are most active. If you hit one, always stop and check its pouch for live joeys (baby kangaroos), because females usually have one in the pouch. Wrap the joey tightly in a towel or old sweater, don't feed or overhandle it, and take it to a vet in the nearest town or call one of the following wildlife care groups: **Wildlife Information & Rescue Service (WIRES)** in New South Wales (© 1800/641 188 or 02/8977 3333); **Wildlife Care Network** in Victoria (© 0500/540 000); **Wildcare** in Queensland (© 07/5527 2444); **RSPCA Wildlife** in the ACT (© 02/6287 8100); **FAWNA Inc.** in Western Australia (© 08/9334 0333); **Wildcare Inc.** in the Northern Territory (© 08/8999 4536); the **Kangaroo (& Wildlife) Information & Rescue Service** (KRIS; © 08/8556 5464) or **Fauna Rescue of S.A.** (© 08/8289 0896) in South Australia; or **Wildcare** in Tasmania (© 03/6233 6556). Most vets will treat native wildlife free of charge.

Some highways run through unfenced stations (ranches), where sheep and cattle pose a threat. Cattle like to rest on the warm bitumen road at night, so put your lights on high beam to spot them. If an animal does loom up before you, slow down but never swerve or you may roll, and, if you have to, hit it. Tell station owners within 24 hours if you have hit their livestock.

Car-rental companies will not insure for animal damage to the car, which should give you an inkling of how common an occurrence this is.

ROAD TRAINS Road trains consist of as many as three big truck carriages linked together to make a "train" up to 53.5 meters (175 ft.) long. If you're in front of one, give them plenty of warning when you brake, because they need a lot of distance in which to slow down. Allow at least 1 clear kilometer (over half a mile) before you pass one, but don't expect the driver to make it easy for you—"truckies" are notorious for their lack of concern for motorists.

UNPAVED ROADS Many of Australia's country roads are unsealed (unpaved). They are usually bone-dry, which makes them a lot more slippery than they look, so travel at a moderate speed on these—35 kilometers per hour (20 mph) is not too cautious and anything over 60 kilometers per hour is dangerous. Don't over-correct if you veer to one side. Keep well behind any vehicles in front because the dust they throw up can block your vision.

FLOODS Floods are common in the Top End and north of Cairns November or December through March or April (the Wet Season). Never cross a flooded road unless you are sure of its depth. Crocodiles may be in the water, so do not wade in to test it! Fast-flowing water is dangerous, even if very shallow. When in doubt, stay where you are and wait for the water to drop, because most flash floods subside in 24 hours. Check the road conditions ahead at least once a day in the Wet Season.

RUNNING OUT OF GAS Petrol stations (also called "roadhouses" in rural areas) can be few and far between in the Outback, so fill up at every opportunity.

WHAT IF YOUR VEHICLE BREAKS DOWN?

If you break down or get lost, *NEVER* leave your vehicle. Many a motorist, often an Aussie who should know better, has died wandering off on some crazy quest for help or water, knowing full well that neither is to be found for maybe hundreds of miles. Most people who get lost do so in hot Outback spots; if that happens to you, conserve your body moisture level by doing as little as possible and staying in the shade of your car. Put out distress signals in patterns of three—three yells, three columns of smoke, and so on. The traditional Outback call for help is "coo-ee," with the accent on the "ee" and yodeled in a high pitch; the sound travels a surprisingly long way.

The state auto clubs listed above provide free breakdown emergency assistance to members of many affiliated automobile associations around the world.

EMERGENCY ASSISTANCE

The emergency breakdown assistance telephone number for every Australian auto club is ✆ **13 11 11** from anywhere in Australia. It is billed as a local call. If you are not a member of an auto club back home that has a reciprocal agreement with the Australian clubs, you'll have to join the Australian club on the spot before they will come tow/repair your car. This usually costs only around A$60 (U.S.$33), not a big price to pay when you're stranded (although in the Outback, the charge may be considerably higher). Most car-rental companies also have emergency assistance numbers.

TIPS FOR FOUR-WHEEL DRIVERS

Always keep to the four-wheel-drive track as going off-road causes soil erosion, which is a significant environmental problem in Australia. Leave gates as you found them. Obtain permission from the owners before venturing onto private station (ranch) roads. On an extended trip or in very remote areas, be prepared. Carry 5 liters (1.3 gal.) of drinking water per person per day (dehydration occurs fast in the Australian heat); enough food to last

3 or 4 days more than you think you will need; a first-aid kit; spare fuel; a jack and two spare tires; spare fan belts, radiator hoses, and air-conditioner hoses; a tow rope; and a good map that marks all gas stations. In seriously remote areas outside the scope of this book, carry a high-frequency and CB radio (even if you have a cell phone, it may not work in the Outback). Advise a friend, your hotel manager, the local tourist bureau, or a police station of your route and your expected time of return or arrival at your destination.

12 Planning Your Trip Online

With a mouse, a modem, and a certain determination, Internet users can tap into the same travel-planning databases that were once accessible only to travel agents. Sites such as **Travelocity, Expedia,** and **Orbitz** allow consumers to comparison shop for airfares, book flights, find last-minute bargains, and reserve hotel rooms and rental cars.

But don't fire your travel agent just yet. Although online booking sites offer tips and hard data to help you bargain shop, they cannot endow you with the hard-earned experience that makes a seasoned, reliable travel agent an invaluable resource, even in the Internet age. And for consumers with a complex itinerary, a travel agent is still the best way to arrange the most direct flights to and from the best airports.

The benefits of researching your trip online can be well worth the effort:

• **Last-minute specials,** known as "E-savers," such as weekend deals or Internet-only fares, are offered by airlines to fill empty seats. Most of these are announced on Tuesday or Wednesday and must be purchased online. They are only valid for travel that weekend (not much help when it comes to flying to another continent like Australia), but some can be booked weeks or months in advance. Sign up for weekly e-mail alerts at airline websites (see below) or check megasites that compile comprehensive lists of E-savers, such as Smarter Living (smarterliving.com) or WebFlyer (www.webflyer.com).

• Some sites will send you **e-mail notification** when a cheap fare becomes available to your favorite destination. Some will also tell you when fares to a particular destination are lowest.

• The best of the travel planning sites are now **highly personalized;** they track your frequent-flier miles, and store your seating and meal preferences, tentative itineraries, and credit-card information, letting you plan trips or check agendas quickly.

• All major airlines offer **incentives**—bonus frequent-flier miles, Internet-only discounts, sometimes even free cell phone rentals—when you purchase online or buy an E-ticket.

• Advances in mobile technology provide business travelers and other frequent travelers with **the ability to check flight status, change plans, or get specific directions** from handheld computing devices, mobile phones, and pagers. Some sites will e-mail or page a passenger if a flight is delayed.

TRAVEL-PLANNING & BOOKING SITES

The best travel-planning and booking sites cast a wide net, offering domestic and international flights, hotel and rental-car bookings, plus news, destination information, and deals on cruises and vacation packages. Keep in

Tips Frommers.com: The Complete Travel Resource

For an excellent travel-planning resource, we highly recommend **Arthur Frommer's Budget Travel Online** (www.frommers.com). Among the special features are: **"Ask the Expert"** bulletin boards, where Frommer's authors answer your questions via online postings; **Arthur Frommer's Daily Newsletter,** for the latest travel bargains and inside travel secrets; and Frommer's **Destinations Archive,** where you'll get expert travel tips, hotel and dining recommendations, and advice on the sights to see for more than 200 destinations around the globe. Once your research is done, the **Online Reservation System** (www.frommers.com/booktravelnow) takes you to Frommer's favorite sites for booking your vacation at affordable prices.

mind that free (one-time) registration is often required for booking. Because several airlines are no longer willing to pay commissions on tickets sold by online travel agencies, be aware that these online agencies will either charge a $10 surcharge if you book a ticket on that carrier—or neglect to offer those air carriers' offerings.

The sites in this section are not intended to be a comprehensive list, but rather a discriminating selection to get you started. Recognition is given to sites based on their content value and ease of use and is not paid for—unlike some website rankings, which are based on payment. Remember: This is a press-time snapshot of leading websites—some will have evolved or moved by the time you read this.

- **Travelocity** (www.travelocity.com or frommers.travelocity.com) and **Expedia** (www.expedia.com) are the most longstanding and reputable sites, each offering excellent selections and searches for complete vacation packages. Travelers search by destination and dates coupled with how much they are willing to spend.
- The latest buzz in the online travel world is about **Orbitz** (www.orbitz.com), a site launched by United, Delta, Northwest, American, and Continental airlines. It shows all possible fares for your desired trip, offering fares lower than those available through travel agents.
- **Qixo** (www.qixo.com) is another powerful search engine that allows you to search for flights and hotel rooms on 20 other travel-planning sites (such as Travelocity) at once. Qixo sorts results by price, after which you can book your travel directly through the site.

SMART E-SHOPPING

The savvy traveler is one armed with good information. Here are a few tips to help you navigate the Internet successfully and safely.

- **Know when sales start.** Last-minute deals may vanish in minutes. If you have a favorite booking site or airline, find out when last-minute deals are released to the public. (For example, Southwest's specials are posted every Tues at 12:01am Central Time.)
- **Shop around.** Compare results from different sites and airlines—and against a travel agent's best fare, if you can. If possible, try a range of times and alternate airports before you make a purchase.

- **Follow the rules of the trade.** Book in advance, and choose an off-peak time and date if possible. Some sites will tell you when fares to a particular destination tend to be cheapest.
- **Stay secure.** Book only through secure sites (some airline sites are not secure). Look for a key icon (Netscape) or a padlock (Internet Explorer) at the bottom of your web browser before you enter credit-card information or other personal data.
- **Avoid online auctions.** Sites that auction airline tickets and frequent-flier miles are the number-one perpetrators of Internet fraud, according to the National Consumers League.
- **Maintain a paper trail.** If you book an E-ticket, print out a confirmation, or write down your confirmation number, and keep it safe and accessible—or your trip could be a virtual one!

AIRLINE WEBSITES

Below are the websites for the major airlines that service Australia. These sites offer schedules and booking, and most have E-saver alerts for weekend deals and late-breaking bargains.

- **Air Canada.** www.aircanada.ca
- **Air New Zealand.** www.airnewzealand.com
- **British Airways.** www.britishairways.com
- **Canada 3000.** www.canada3000.com
- **Cathay Pacific.** www.cathaypacific.com
- **Malaysia Airlines.** www.malaysiaairlines.com.my or www.malaysiaairlineseurope.com
- **Qantas.** www.qantas.com.au
- **Singapore Airlines.** www.singaporeair.com/uk
- **Thai Airways International.** www.thaiair.com
- **United Airlines.** www.ual.com

13 Tips on Accommodations

Note: All accommodations listed in this book have private bathrooms unless otherwise noted.

HOTELS   It's a rare hotel room that does not have reverse-cycle air-conditioning for heating and cooling, a telephone, a color TV, a clock-radio, a minirefrigerator if not a minibar, an iron and ironing board, and self-serve tea and coffee. Private bathrooms are standard, although they often have only a shower, not a tub. Many of the world's international lodging chains have properties in Australia.

SERVICED APARTMENTS   Serviced apartments are the accommodation of choice for many Aussie families and business travelers. That is because you get a fully furnished apartment with one, two, or three separate bedrooms, a spacious living room, a kitchen or kitchenette, a laundry, and often two bathrooms—in other words, all the facilities of a hotel suite and more, often for less than the cost of a four-star hotel room. It's a terrific value. You can easily find a nice two-bedroom apartment for between A$120 and $220 (U.S.$66 to $121). (Note that not every apartment kitchen stretches to a dishwasher, so check yours does if that's important to you). Australia's apartment inventory is enormous and ranges from clean and comfortable, if a little dated, to luxurious. Most apartments can be rented for just 1 night, especially in cities, but in popular vacation spots, some proprietors will insist on a minimum 3-night stay, or even a week in high season.

   Medina Serviced Apartments (© **1300/300 232** in Australia, or 02/9356 1000; www.medinaapartments.com.au) has a chain of mid-range to upscale properties in Sydney, Melbourne, Brisbane, Canberra, and, from 2002, Adelaide. Australia's biggest apartment chain is the **Quest Serviced Apartments** (© **0800/944 400** in New Zealand, 1800/334 033 in Australia, or 03/9347 8622; www.questapartments.com.au). It has two brands, the upscale Quest Establishment and the mid-range Quest Inns, in every state and territory except the Northern Territory.

MOTELS & MOTOR INNS Australia's plentiful motels are neat and clean, if often a little dated. You can count on them to provide air-conditioning, a telephone, a color TV, a clock-radio, a minirefrigerator or minibar, and self-serve tea and coffee. Most have only showers, not bathtubs. Some have restaurants attached, and many have swimming pools. Motor inns offer a greater range of facilities and a generally higher standard of rooms than motels. Rates average A$70 to $110 (U.S.$38.50–$60.50) double.

BED-&-BREAKFAST INNS B&Bs are cheap and plentiful in Australia. It is easy to find charming rooms for A$80 (U.S.$44) or less for a double. Bathroom facilities are often shared, although more and more properties now offer private, if not always ensuite, bathrooms.

Travel agents rarely list B&Bs because the establishments are not big enough to pay commission, so they can be hard to find. I find the best source is *The Australian Bed & Breakfast Book,* by James Thomas (published by Moonshine Press: © **02/ 9985 8500,** or the Pelican Publishing Company in the U.S.), which lists over 600 B&Bs across Australia. Although the B&B's pay to be in the book, they have to meet standards required by the editors. The entire book is posted on the Web at www.bedandbreakfastbook.com.au. In Australia, it's widely available in

bookshops and newsagents; you can also order it easily on www.amazon. com or with Barnes & Noble at www. bn.com, or contact Moonshine Press, which retails it for A$16.95 (U.S.$9.35) plus A$10 (U.S.$5.50) for overseas postage.

Orangewood, a Northern Territory B&B, provides an index of Australian B&B directories at this rather ungainly Web address: http://members. ozemail.com.au/~orangewo/owdirdir. htm.

What Next? Productions Pty. Ltd. (© **03/9537 0833;** whatnext@ bigpond.net.au) publishes a color guide titled *Beautiful B&Bs & Small Hotels,* 190 exquisite properties in Victoria and Tasmania, many in charming rural areas. The properties listed are more upscale than most, roughly in the A$100 to $200 (U.S.$55 to $110) The guide sells for A$29.65 (U.S.$16.30) in Australian bookstores.

PUBS Aussie pubs are really made for drinking in, not spending the night, but many offer rooms upstairs, usually with shared bathroom facilities. Because most pubs are decades old, the rooms may be either cutely old-fashioned or just plain old. Pub accommodations are dying out in the cities but are still common in the country. Australians are rowdy drinkers, so sleeping over the front bar can be hellishly noisy; but the pub's saving grace is incredibly low rates. Most charge per person, not per room, and you will rarely pay more than A$50 (U.S.$27.50) per person a night. I have found rooms for as little as A$20 (U.S.$11) a night.

MEET THE PEOPLE DOWN UNDER

If you want to see an Australian Rules football game in the company of a knowledgeable local in the game's birthplace of Melbourne or swim at Bondi Beach with a Sydneysider, get in touch with **Friends Overseas— Australia,** 68–01 Dartmouth St.,

Forest Hills, NY 11375 (© **718/261 0534;** FOverseas@aol.com). This meet-the-people program is designed to match visitors to Oz with friendly Aussies of like age and interests, so you can spend time with them, without staying in their homes. Send a stamped, self-addressed envelope to the above address. The membership fee is U.S.$25.

If you want to stay with an Aussie family and really get involved in their life, even sitting at their table, **Homestay Network** (© **02/9498 4400;** the network@bigpond.com) can place you in one of some 2,000 homes in the greater Sydney area. They can try to match your interests with your host's. Prices vary, but expect to pay as little as A$32 (U.S.$17.60) up to about A$150 (U.S.$82.50) per single, per night. That will usually include one or two meals a day. Double rates are a little higher.

FARMSTAYS The Aussie answer to the dude ranch is a farmstay. Australian farmstays are rarely as well set up for tourists as the dude ranch visited by Billy Crystal's character in the movie, "City Slickers." Most are farms first, tourist operations second, so you may have to find your own fun and know how to take care of yourself on a farm, at least to a degree. Accommodations on farms can be anything from a basic bunkhouse (ask if it's air-conditioned, because most farms are in very hot areas) to rustically luxurious digs that would do Ralph Lauren proud. Do some research on your chosen farm—a lot of activities are seasonal, some farmers will not allow you to get involved in dangerous work, not all will offer horseback riding, and "farm" means different things in different parts of Australia. If you like green fields and black-and-white dairy cows, Victoria may be the place for you. If checking fences on a dusty 500,000-acre (202,000-hectare) Outback station (ranch) sounds wildly romantic, head to Western Australia or the Northern Territory.

Australian Farm & Country Tourism (© 03/9614 0892; www.farmstaysaustralia.com) is a co-operative marketing organization for farmstay properties. It dispenses free brochures, one each for Victoria, New South Wales, Queensland, South Australia, and Western Australia, that detail the style of accommodation, activities, and rates at a huge range of farmstay properties. Rates vary enormously, but you will find many properties charging between A$100 and $140 (U.S.$55 and $77) for a double, which sometimes includes breakfast. Meals are often available as an optional extra.

 FAST FACTS: Australia

American Express For all travel-related customer inquiries regarding any American Express service, including reporting a lost card, call © **1800/230 100.** To report lost or stolen traveler's checks there is a separate line (© **1800/251 902**).

Business Hours Banks open Monday through Thursday from 9:30am to 4pm, 5pm on Friday. General business hours are Monday through Friday from 8:30am to 5:30pm. Shopping hours are usually from 8:30am to 5:30pm weekdays and 9am to 4 or 5pm on Saturday. Many shops close Sundays, although major department stores and shops in tourist precincts are open 7 days.

Car Rentals See "Getting Around Australia," earlier in this chapter.

Climate See "When to Go," earlier in this chapter.

Currency See "Money," earlier in this chapter.

Customs See "Entry Requirements & Customs," earlier in this chapter.

Dates Australians write their dates day, month, year: January 5, 1968 is 05/01/68.

Driving Rules See "Getting Around Australia," earlier in this chapter.

Drugstores These are called "chemists" or "pharmacies." Australian pharmacists are permitted to fill only prescriptions written by Australian doctors.

Electricity The current is 240 volts AC, 50 hertz. Sockets take two or three flat, not rounded, prongs. North Americans and Europeans will need to buy a converter before they leave home (don't wait until you get to Australia, because Australian stores are only likely to stock converters for Aussie appliances to fit American and European outlets). Some large hotels have 110V outlets for electric shavers or dual voltage, and some will lend converters; but don't count on it in smaller, less expensive hotels, motels, or B&Bs. Power does not start automatically when you plug in an appliance; you need to flick the switch located beside the socket to the "on" position.

Embassies/Consulates Most diplomatic posts are in Canberra: British High Commission, Commonwealth Avenue, Canberra, ACT 2600 (✆ **02/6270 6666**); Embassy of Ireland, 20 Arkana St., Yarralumla, ACT 2600 (✆ **02/6273 3022**); High Commission of Canada, Commonwealth Avenue, Yarralumla, ACT 2600 (✆ **02/6270 4000**); New Zealand High Commission, Commonwealth Avenue, Canberra, ACT 2600 (✆ **02/6270 4211**); and the United States Embassy, 21 Moonah Place, Yarralumla, ACT 2600 (✆ **02/6214 5600**). Embassies or consulates with posts in state capitals are listed in "Fast Facts" in the relevant state chapters.

Emergencies Dial ✆ **000** anywhere in Australia for police, ambulance, or the fire department. This is a free call from public and private telephones and needs no coins. The TTY emergency number is ✆ **106**.

Holidays See "When to Go," earlier in this chapter.

Information See "Visitor Information," earlier in this chapter.

Liquor Laws Hours vary from pub to pub, but most are open daily from around 10am or noon, to 10pm or midnight. The minimum drinking age is 18. Random breath tests to catch drunk drivers are common, and drunk-driving laws are strictly enforced. Getting caught drunk behind the wheel will mean a court appearance, not just a fine. The maximum permitted blood alcohol level is 0.05. Alcohol is sold only in liquor stores, or in the "bottle shops" attached to every pub, and rarely in supermarkets.

Mail A postcard costs A$1 (U.S.55¢) to the United States, Canada, the United Kingdom, or New Zealand.

Maps See "Getting Around," earlier in this chapter.

Pets Leave 'em at home. You will be back home planning your next vacation before Fluffy clears quarantine in Oz.

Police Dial ✆ **000** anywhere in Australia. This is a free call from public and private telephones and requires no coins.

Safety Violent crime is uncommon, and the political situation is highly stable. Guns are strictly controlled. Purse snatchers are the same threat that they are all over the world.

Taxes Australia applies a 10% consumption tax called Goods and Services Tax (GST) on most products and services. Your international airline ticket to Australia is not taxed, nor are your domestic airline tickets for travel within Australia *if you bought them outside Australia*. If you buy more domestic Australian airline tickets once you arrive in Australia, you will pay GST on them.

Through the Tourist Refund Scheme (TRS), Australians and international visitors can claim a refund of the GST (and of a 14.5% wine tax called Wine Equalisation Tax, or WET) paid on a purchase worth more than A$300 (U.S.$165) from a single outlet, within the last 30 days before you leave Australia. More than one item may be included in that A$300. For example, you can claim back the GST you paid on 10 T-shirts each worth A$30 (U.S.$16.50), as long as they were bought from a single store. You do this as you leave Australia by presenting your receipt, known in tax office parlance as a "tax invoice," to the Australian Customs Service's TRS booths, located beyond passport control in the international terminal departure areas at most international airports (listed below). If you buy several things on different days from one store, which individually are worth less than A$300 but together add up to A$300 or more, you must ask the store to total all purchases on one tax invoice (or receipt)—now there's a nice piece of bureaucracy to remember Australia by! Carry the items in your carry-on baggage, as you must show them to Customs. You can use the goods before you leave Australia and still claim the refund, but you cannot claim a refund on things you have consumed (film you shoot off in the camera, say, or food). You cannot claim a refund on alcohol other than wine. Allow an extra 15 minutes to stand in line and get your refund.

You can also claim a refund if you leave Australia as a cruise passenger from these ports: Circular Quay or Darling Harbour in Sydney, Cairns, Darwin, or Fremantle (Perth). If your cruise departs from elsewhere in Australia, or if you are flying out from an airport other than Sydney, Melbourne, Brisbane, Adelaide, Cairns, Perth, Darwin, Coolangatta (Gold Coast), or Broome, telephone the Australian Customs Service (✆ **1300/363 263** in Australia, or 02/6275-6666) to see if you can still claim the refund.

Items bought in duty-free stores will not be charged GST. Nor will items you export—such as an Aboriginal painting, say, that you buy in a gallery in Alice Springs and have shipped straight to your home outside Australia.

Basic groceries are not GST-taxed, but restaurant meals are.

Other taxes include departure tax of A$38 (U.S.$20.90) for every passenger 12 years and over, included in the price of your airline ticket when you bought it in your home country; landing and departure taxes at some airports, also included in the price of your ticket; and "reef tax," officially dubbed the Environmental Management Charge, of A$4 (U.S.$2.20) for every person over the age of 4 every time he or she enters the Great Barrier Reef Marine Park (this charge goes toward park upkeep).

Telephone & Fax The primary telecommunications network in Australia is Telstra (www.telstra.com). To call the operator, dial ✆ **12 552.**

To call Australia from North America: Dial the international access code (011), then Australia's country code (61), then the two-digit area code (we've given the area code for every number listed in this book), then the local number. The local area codes found throughout this book all begin with "0"; you drop the "0" if you're calling from outside Australia, but you need to dial it as part of the area code if you're calling from another city or town within Australia. For example, to ring the Sydney Opera House (✆ 02/9250 7111) from the United States, dial 011-61-2-9250-7111.

To call Australia from the United Kingdom: Dial the international access code (00), and then follow the instructions above.

To make an international call from Australia: Dial the international access code (0011—note it has two zeros, unlike the international access code from North America), then the country code (1 for the U.S. and Canada, 44 for the U.K., 353 for Ireland, 64 for New Zealand, 27 for South Africa), then the area code, and finally the local number. To find out the per-minute international call charges to any country, dial ✆ **12552.** To find a country code, call ✆ **1222** or look in the back of the Australian White Pages.

To make an international credit-card or collect call from Australia: Dial one of the following access codes to your country. United States: AT&T Direct (✆ **1800/881 011**), Sprint (✆ **1800/881 877**), MCI (✆ **1800/881 100**), Worldcom (✆ **1800/881 212**), or Verizon (✆ **1800/881 152**). Canada: ✆ **1800/881 150.** United Kingdom: BT (✆ **1800/881 440,** or 1800/881 441 for automated service only) or Mercury (✆ **1800/881 417**). Ireland: ✆ **1800/881 353.** New Zealand: ✆ **1800/881 640.** If your country is not listed here, dial Telstra's Country Direct service (✆ 1800/801 800) to find out how to get connected to an operator in your country.

To make a long-distance call within Australia: Dial the area code, including the initial zero, followed by the number you are calling. Australia's area codes are New South Wales and the A.C.T., 02; Victoria and Tasmania, 03; Queensland, 07; and South Australia, Western Australia, and the Northern Territory, 08. Long-distance calls within Australia are usually cheaper at night and on weekends; for example, long-distance calls on Telstra's network are cheaper before 7am and after 7pm Monday through Friday and anytime on weekends.

Australia's toll-free numbers: Australian phone numbers starting with 1800 are toll-free; numbers starting with 13 or 1300 are charged at the local fee of 25¢ from anywhere in Australia. Numbers beginning with 1900 (or 1901, 1902, and so on) are pay-for-service lines (like 900 numbers in the United States); expect to be charged as much as A$5 (U.S.$2.75) a minute.

Local Calls: Local calls in Australia are untimed and cost a flat A40¢ from a public telephone, or A25¢, sometimes a little less, from a private phone in a home or office.

To avoid juggling for change to use at pay phones, consider buying one of the many phone cards, which you use by dialing access codes printed on the card. The cards typically contain a prepaid allotment of call time for local, long-distance, international, and cell-phone calls. They are widely sold at newsagents. Telstra's PhoneAway phone card can also be used to call Australia from more than 40 overseas countries, including the United States and the United Kingdom. PhoneAway cards have a personalized Voicemail voice and fax box. They are sold at newsagents, Telstra shops, tourist information booths, and Traveland travel agencies. Australia's second major telecommunications network, Optus, sells a similar card at Optus stores, Australia Post post offices, newsagents, Kmart, and other outlets.

Mobile Calls: Australia is reputed to have the world's biggest per-capita uptake of cellular or "mobile" telephones. They are available for daily rental at major airports and in big cities, and increasingly from car- and campervan-rental companies. The cell network is digital, not analog. Calls to, or from, a mobile telephone are generally more expensive than a call to, or from, a fixed telephone—A60¢ a minute is a ballpark guide, although the price varies widely depending on the telephone company, the time of day, the distance between caller and callee, and the pricing plan on the telephone used to make the call.

Operator Assistance: To reach the operator for help making a call, dial 𝄡 **1234**. To make a collect call, called a "reverse charges" call in Australia, dial the operator at 𝄡 **12550**.

To find out a telephone number, call Directory Assistance at 𝄡 **12 455** for numbers within Australia, or 𝄡 **1225** for overseas numbers.

To book a wake-up call, dial 𝄡 **12 454**.

Time   Eastern Standard Time (EST, also written as AEST sometimes) covers Queensland, New South Wales, the Australian Capital Territory, Victoria, and Tasmania. Central Standard Time is used in the Northern Territory and South Australia, and Western Standard Time (WST) is the standard in Western Australia. When it's noon in New South Wales, the A.C.T., Victoria, Queensland, and Tasmania, it's 11:30am in South Australia and the Northern Territory and 10am in Western Australia. All states except Queensland, the Northern Territory, and Western Australia observe daylight saving time, usually from the last Sunday in October (the first Sun in Oct in Tasmania's case) to the last Sunday in March. However, not all states switch over to daylight saving on the same day or in the same week.

The east coast of Australia (including Cairns, Brisbane, Sydney, and Melbourne) is GMT (Greenwich Mean Time) plus 10 hours. When it is noon on the east coast, it is 2am in London that morning, and 6pm in Los Angeles and 9pm in New York the previous night. These times are based on standard time, so allow for daylight saving in the Australian summer, or in the country you are calling. New Zealand is 2 hours ahead of the east coast of Australia.

Tipping   Waiters get paid decently enough in Australia that you are not expected to supplement their income. It is customary to tip around 5% or round up to the nearest A$10 for a substantial meal in a restaurant (but not for a casual sandwich and cup of coffee). Some passengers round up to the nearest dollar in a cab, but it's okay to insist on every last 5-cent piece of change back from the driver. Tipping bellboys and porters is sometimes done but not really expected. No one tips bar staff, barbers, or hairdressers.

Water Water is fine to drink everywhere except Port Douglas, where you should stick to the bottled variety. In the Outback, the taps may carry warm brackish water from underground called "bore water" for showers and laundry, while drinking water is collected in rainwater tanks.

3

Sydney

by Marc Llewellyn

Sunny, sexy, and sophisticated, Sydney (pop. 4 million) basks in its worldwide recognition as the shining star of the southern hemisphere. The "emerald city" is without question one of the most attractive on earth. Some people compare it to San Francisco—it certainly has that relaxed Californian feel—but the gateway to Australia is far from a clone of an American city.

First, of course, there's the Sydney Opera House, one of the most recognized buildings in the world. This white-sailed construction on Sydney Cove, designed by Danish architect Jørn Utzon, is the pride of the city—but there's far, far more on offer.

For example, you can walk across that other great icon, the Sydney Harbour Bridge, on the pathway beside the trains and traffic and catch the CityRail train back into town from the other end. Those with a daredevil spirit can venture across catwalks and ladders to the top of the main arch for 360° views across the Opera House and the ferries and boats below.

Sydney is one of the biggest cities in the world—it can take 2 hours' of driving to break free of its outskirts—but fortunately most of the interesting things are concentrated in a relatively compact area around one of the finest urban harbors in the world.

As it is, there's so much to do in Sydney that you could easily spend a week here and still find yourself crashing into bed at night exhausted by trying to fit all the main attractions in.

Sydney's greatest summer experience, of course, is on the beaches—and with over 20 strung along the city's oceanfront and dozens more dotted around the harbor, you'll be spoiled for choice. The most famous of them all is Bondi, a long strip of golden sand legendary for its Speedo-clad lifesavers and surfboard riders. From here a "must do" is the 2-mile coastal path which leads off across the cliff tops, via cozy Tamarama Beach (dubbed "Glamourama" for its chic sun worshippers), to glorious Bronte Beach, where you can cool down again in the crashing waves of the Pacific.

Another beach favorite is Manly, just a 30-minute ferry trip from Circular Quay. Pick up some fish-and-chips and head for the main beach, flanked by a row of giant pines that chatter with hundreds of colorful lorikeets at dusk.

The best time to return to the city is in the early evening, when the fluorescent lights of the skyscrapers around Circular Quay are streaked like rainbows across the inky water of the harbor, and the sails of the Opera House and the girders of the Harbour Bridge are lit up—it's magical.

History is also enshrined in its many museums and art galleries, while modern Sydney comes alive in the more recent developments around Darling Harbour and the restaurant and entertainment area nearby at Cockle Bay. It's at Darling Harbour that you'll find the world-class Sydney Aquarium. It's also here you can start your gourmet tour of Sydney's renowned "Modern Australian" cooking style, which encompasses the best of freshness with spices from the Orient and flavors from the Mediterranean.

Add to all this the side trips to the dramatic gorges and cliffs of the Blue Mountains, the wineries of the Hunter Valley, and the dolphin- and whale-watching around Port Stephens (see chapter 4), and you'll see why Sydney gets so much praise.

The frugal traveler will find that, compared to other major cities around the world, Sydney offers good value for money spent. Food and public transport are quite cheap, and attractions are generally not prohibitively expensive (senior and student prices are almost always available if you have identification). The price of a hotel room is far cheaper than in other major population centers such as New York and London.

1 Orientation

ARRIVING

BY PLANE **Sydney International Airport** is 8 kilometers (about 5 miles) from the city center. The international and domestic terminals are separate but linked by regular free shuttle buses. In both terminals, you'll find luggage carts (they cost A$2 when departing Australia, but are free otherwise), wheelchairs, a post office (open Mon–Fri 9am–5pm), mailboxes, duty-free shops (including one before you go through customs on arrival), restaurants, bars, stores, showers, luggage lockers and a Baggage Held Service for larger items, ATMs, and tourist information desks. There is also a State Transit Kiosk where you can exchange travel vouchers into tickets if you have them, and where you can buy the SydneyPass (see below) and Airport Express tickets (see below); a Sydney Visitors Centre desk offering cheap deals on hotels (see "Where to Stay," below); and a currency exchange. The airport is very efficient, has some of the world's strictest quarantine procedures, and is completely nonsmoking.

GETTING INTO TOWN The **Sydney Airport Train Link** connects both the international and domestic airports to the City stations of Central, Museum, St James, Circular Quay, Wynyard, and Town Hall. You'll need to change trains for all other Sydney stations. Unfortunately, the line uses existing rolling stock, has no dedicated luggage areas and, as it's on a scheduled route into the city from the outer suburbs, it gets very crowded during rush hours (approximately 7–9am and 4–6:30pm). If you have lots of luggage and you're traveling into the city at these times, it's probably best to take an airport bus (below) or a taxi. Otherwise take a chance and walk to the end of the platform where there should be more room onboard. There are elevators at the Airport Train Link stations and supposedly some at the city train stations (but the crowds and lack of staff and

---

Tips Tourist Refund Scheme

Visitors to Australia are entitled to claim back any Goods and Services Tax (GST) paid on items worth more than A$300 (U.S.$165). The GST component is 10% of the sale price. You do this at the refund booth located past Customs. After filling in the paperwork—you need to have the goods and receipt with you, not in your checked-in luggage—you will be refunded by check on the spot. You can convert this to cash at any foreign exchange booth at Sydney Airport.

Greater Sydney

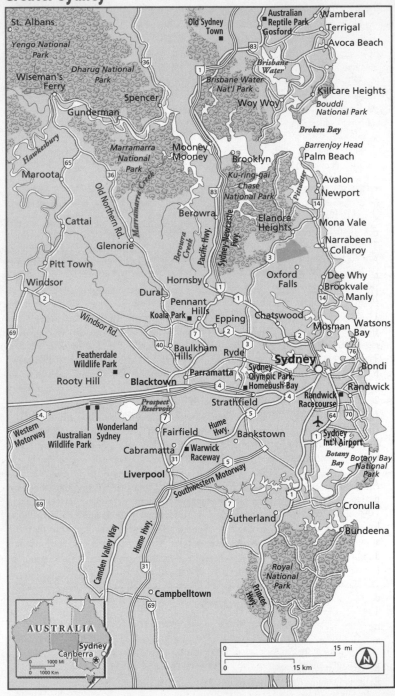

St. Albans

Yengo National Park

Wiseman's Ferry

Dharug National Park

Gunderman

Spencer

Maroota

Marramarra National Park

Cattai

Glenorie

Pitt Town

Windsor

Dural

Pennant Hills

Koala Park

Baulkham Hills

Featherdale Wildlife Park

Rooty Hill

Blacktown

Parramatta

Australian Wildlife Park

Wonderland Sydney

Fairfield

Cabramatta

Warwick Raceway

Liverpool

Campbelltown

Old Sydney Town

Australian Reptile Park
Gosford

Wamberal
Terrigal
Avoca Beach

Brisbane Water

Brisbane Water Nat'l Park

Woy Woy

Killcare Heights

Bouddi National Park

Broken Bay

Mooney Mooney

Brooklyn

Ku-ring-gai Chase National Park

Barrenjoy Head
Palm Beach

Avalon
Newport

Berowra

Elanora Heights

Mona Vale

Narrabeen
Collaroy

Hornsby

Oxford Falls

Dee Why
Brookvale
Manly

Epping

Chatswood

Watsons Bay

Ryde

Mosman

Bondi

Sydney

Sydney Olympic Park, Homebush Bay

Strathfield

Randwick Racecourse

Randwick

Bankstown

Sydney Int'l Airport

Botany Bay

Botany Bay National Park

Cronulla

Sutherland

Bundeena

Royal National Park

Hawkesbury

Old Northern Rd.

Marramarra Creek

Berowra Creek

Pacific Hwy.

Sydney-Newcastle Fwy.

Pittwater

Windsor Rd.

Western Motorway

Hume Hwy.

Southwestern Motorway

Camden Valley Way

Prospect Reservoir

AUSTRALIA

Sydney
Canberra

1000 Mi
1000 Km

0   15 mi
0   15 km

N

82

A Taxi Tip

Especially in busy periods, taxi queues can be long, and cab drivers may try to cash in by insisting you share a cab with other passengers waiting in line at the airport. Here's the scam: After dropping off the other passengers, the cab driver will then attempt to charge you the full price of the journey, despite the fact that the other passengers paid for their sections. You certainly won't save any money sharing a cab if this happens, and your journey will be a long one. I find it's often better to wait until you can get your own cab, or catch an airport bus to the city center (and then take a taxi from there to your hotel, if necessary). If you are first in line in the taxi rank, the law states that you can refuse to share the cab with anyone else.

signs mean you'll probably end up lugging it all up loads of steps anyway). The train takes 10 minutes to reach Central and then continues on to Circular Quay. Trains leave every 15 minutes or so and cost A$10 (U.S.$6.50) one-way and A$15 (U.S.$9.75) return. Special "Group Fares" mean 3 or 4 people can travel together to the city for just A$20 (U.S.$13).

Fast and comfortable green-and-yellow **Airport Express buses** travel between the city center and both the international and domestic terminals from 5am to 11pm. The number 300 bus runs to and from Circular Quay, The Rocks, Wynyard, and Town Hall every 15 minutes Monday through Friday and approximately every 30 minutes early mornings, nights, weekends, and public holidays. The trip to Circular Quay takes about 45 minutes. Bus 350 runs to and from Kings Cross, Potts Point, and Elizabeth Bay every 20 minutes and takes around 30 minutes to reach Kings Cross. Both buses travel via Central Station (around 20 min. from the International Terminal). One-way tickets for these buses cost A$7 (U.S.$4.55) for adults, A$4.50 (U.S.$2.90) for kids under 16, and A$15 (U.S.$9.75) for families (any number of children). A round-trip ticket costs A$10 (U.S.$6.50) for adults, A$5 (U.S.$3.25) for kids, and A$25 (U.S.$16.25) for families. You must use the return portion within 2 months. Buy your tickets from the Airport Express booth outside the airport terminal, or on the bus. The Airport Express buses also travel between the international and domestic terminals every 15 minutes and cost A$3 (U.S.$1.95).

The **Kingsford Smith Airport Coach** also operates to the city center from bus stops outside the terminals. This service will drop you off (and pick you up) at your hotel (pickups require at least 1 hr. advance notice; call ✆ **02/9667 3221**). Tickets cost A$7 (U.S.$4.55) one-way and A$11 (U.S.$7.15) round-trip (the return portion can be used at any time in the future).

The **Bondi Jetbus** (✆ **0500/886 008** mobile phone; fax 02/9487 3554) will deliver you anywhere on the eastern beaches, including Bondi and Bronte. Tickets are A$10 (U.S.$6.50) for single adult, A$8 (U.S.$5.20) each for two or more, and A$4 (U.S.$2.60) for children. Call when you arrive at the airport, and they'll come pick you up within 15 minutes or less.

A **taxi** from the airport to the city center costs about A$20 (U.S. $13). To Kings Cross, expect to pay around A$25 (U.S.$16.25). A new expressway, the Eastern Distributor, opened in 2000 and is a faster way to reach the city from the airport. Most taxis use this route, but it's best to ask them to take it just in case. There's a $3.30 (U.S.$2.15) toll from the airport to the city (the taxi driver pays it, and you pay at the end of the trip), but there is no toll to the airport. *Note:* A dispute with Visa means this credit card isn't accepted by Australian taxis.

BY TRAIN   Central Station (© **13 15 00** for CityRail, and © **13 22 32** for Countrylink interstate trains) is the main city and interstate train station. It's at the top of George Street in downtown Sydney. All interstate trains depart from here, and it's a major CityRail hub. Many city buses leave from neighboring Railway Square for places like Town Hall and Circular Quay.

BY BUS   The **Greyhound-Pioneer Australia terminal** is on the corner of Oxford and Riley streets in Darlinghurst (© **13 20 30** in Australia, or 02/9283 5977). **McCafferty's** (© **13 14 99** in Australia) operates from the **Sydney Coach Terminal** (© **02/9281 9366**) on the corner of Eddy Avenue and Pitt Street, bordering Central Station.

BY CRUISE SHIP   Cruise ships dock at the **Overseas Passenger Terminal** in The Rocks, just opposite the Sydney Opera House, or in Darling Harbour if The Rocks facility is already occupied by another vessel.

BY CAR   Drivers coming into Sydney from the north enter the city on the Pacific Highway, drivers approaching from the south enter the city via the Hume and Princes highways, and those coming from the west enter the city via the Great Western Highway.

VISITOR INFORMATION

The **Sydney Visitor Centre,** 106 George St., The Rocks (© **02/9255 1788**), is a good place for maps, brochures, and general tourist information, including for region towns in New South Wales; it also has two floors of excellent displays on The Rocks. The office is open daily from 9am to 6pm. Also in The Rocks is the **National Parks & Wildlife Centre** (© **02/9247 8861**), in Cadmans Cottage, 110 George St. If you are in Circular Quay, the **CityRail Host Center** (no phone), opposite No. 5 jetty, has a wide range of brochures and a staff member on hand to help with general inquiries. It's open daily from 9am to 5pm. Elsewhere, the **Sydney Convention and Visitors Bureau** (© **02/9235 2424**) operates an information kiosk in Martin Place, near Castlereagh Street, Monday through Friday from 9am to 5pm. The **Manly Visitors Information Centre** (© **02/9977 1088**), right opposite Manly beach near the Corso, offers general information, but specializes in Manly and the northern beaches. If you want to inquire about destinations and holidays within Sydney or the rest of New South Wales, call **Tourism New South Wales'** help line at © **13 20 77** in Australia.

Electronic information on cinema, theater, exhibitions, and other events can be accessed through **Talking Guides** (© **13 16 20** in Australia). You'll need a code number for each topic, which you can find on page 3 of the A-K section of the *Sydney Yellow Pages.* The service costs the same as a local call.

Good **websites** include **CitySearch Sydney** (www.sydney.citysearch.com.au), for events, entertainment, dining, and shopping; and **City of Sydney** (www.cityofsydney.nsw.gov.au), the official information site. Also try www.viewsydney.com.au; www.visitnsw.com.au; and www.sydney.sidewalk.com.au for latest events info.

CITY LAYOUT

Sydney is one of the largest cities in the world by area, covering more than 1,730 square kilometers (668 sq. miles) from the sea to the foothills of the Blue

Mountains. Thankfully the city center is compact. The jewel in Sydney's crown is its harbor, which empties into the South Pacific Ocean though head lands known simply as North Head and South Head. On the southern side of the harbor are the high rises of the city center; the Sydney Opera House; a string of beaches, including Bondi; and the inner-city suburbs. The Sydney Harbour Bridge and a tunnel connect the city center to the high rises of the North Sydney business district and the affluent northern suburbs and beautiful ocean beaches beyond.

MAIN ARTERIES & STREETS The city's main thoroughfare, **George Street,** runs up from **Circular Quay** (pronounced "key"), past Wynyard CityRail station, Town Hall, and to Central Station. A whole host of streets bisect the city parallel to George, including Pitt, Elizabeth, and Macquarie streets. **Macquarie Street** runs up from the Sydney Opera House, past the Royal Botanic Gardens, colonial architecture, and Hyde Park. **Martin Place** is a pedestrian thoroughfare that stretches from Macquarie to George streets. It's about halfway between Circular Quay and Town Hall—in the heart of the city center. The easy-to-spot **AMP Centerpoint Tower,** facing onto the pedestrian-only **Pitt Street Mall,** is the main city-center landmark. Next to Circular Quay and across from the Opera House is **The Rocks,** a cluster of small streets that was once city slums but is now a tourist attraction. Roads meet at Town Hall from Kings Cross in one direction and Darling Harbour in the other.

NEIGHBORHOODS IN BRIEF

South of the Harbour

Circular Quay This transport hub for ferries, buses, and CityRail trains is tucked between the Harbour Bridge and the Sydney Opera House. The Quay, as it's known to the locals, is a good spot for a stroll, and its outdoor restaurants and buskers are popular. The Rocks, the Royal Botanic Gardens, the Contemporary Art Museum, and the start of the main shopping area (centered on Pitt and George streets) are all just a short walk away. To reach the area via public transport, take a CityRail train, ferry, or city-bound bus to Circular Quay.

The Rocks This small historic area, just a short stroll west of Circular Quay, is closely packed with colonial stone buildings, intriguing back streets, boutiques, popular pubs, tourist stores, and top-notch restaurants and hotels. It's the most exclusive place to stay in the city because of its beauty and its proximity to the Opera House and the harbor. Shops here are geared toward Sydney's yuppies and wealthy Asian tourists—don't expect bargains. On weekends a portion of George Street is blocked off for The Rocks Market, with street stalls selling tourist-orientated souvenirs and crafts. To reach the area via public transportation, take any bus bound for Circular Quay or The Rocks (via George Street) or a CityRail train or ferry to Circular Quay

Town Hall Right in the heart of the city, this area is home to the main department stores and to two Sydney landmarks, the Town Hall and the Queen Victoria Building (QVB). In this area are also the AMP Centerpoint Tower and the boutique-style chain stores of Pitt Street Mall. Farther up George Street are major movie houses, the entrance to Sydney's Spanish district (around Liverpool Street), and the city's small Chinatown. To

Sydney Harbour

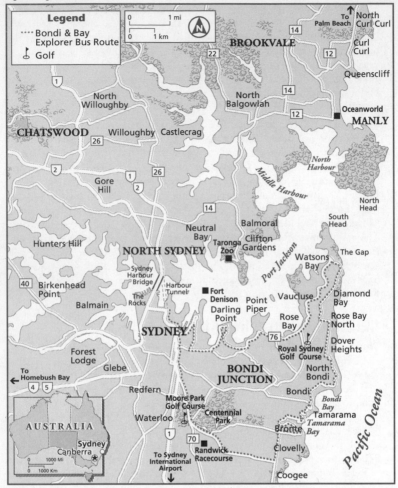

Legend
···· Bondi & Bay Explorer Bus Route
⛳ Golf

0   1 mi
0   1 km

N

To Palm Beach North Curl Curl
BROOKVALE
Curl Curl
Queenscliff
North Willoughby
North Balgowlah
Oceanworld
MANLY
CHATSWOOD Willoughby Castlecrag
Gore Hill
North Harbour
North Head
Hunters Hill
Neutral Bay Balmoral
Taronga Zoo Clifton Gardens
South Head
NORTH SYDNEY
The Gap
Sydney Harbour Bridge
Harbour Tunnel
Port Jackson
Watsons Bay
Birkenhead Point
The Rocks
Fort Denison
Darling Point
Point Piper
Vaucluse
Diamond Bay
Balmain
SYDNEY
Rose Bay
Rose Bay North
Forest Lodge
Royal Sydney Golf Course
Dover Heights
To Homebush Bay
Glebe
BONDI JUNCTION
North Bondi
Redfern
Bondi
Moore Park Golf Course
AUSTRALIA
Waterloo
Centennial Park
Brontë
Tamarama
Tamarama Bay
Bondi Bay
Sydney
Canberra
To Sydney International Airport
Randwick Racecourse
Clovelly
Pacific Ocean
Coogee

reach the area via public transportation, take any bus from Circular Quay via George Street, or take a CityRail train to the Town Hall stop.

Darling Harbour Designed from scratch as a tourist precinct, Darling Harbour now features Sydney's main convention, exhibition, and entertainment centers; a huge waterfront promenade; the Sydney Aquarium; the giant screen Panasonic IMAX Theatre; the Australian Maritime Museum; the Powerhouse Museum; a major food court; and

plenty of shops. Star City, Sydney's casino and theater complex, opened in Darling Harbour in late 1997. To reach the area via public transportation, take a ferry from Circular Quay (Wharf 5), the monorail from Town Hall, or the light rail (tram) from Central Station.

Kings Cross & the Suburbs Beyond "The Cross," as it's known, is famous as the city's red-light district—though it's also home to some of the city's best-known nightclubs and restaurants. It houses plenty of backpacker hostels, a few bars, and some upscale hotels. The main drag, Darlinghurst Road, is short but crammed with seedy strip joints, prostitutes, drug addicts, drunks, and such. Also here are cheap e-mail centers that offer discount overseas phone rates. Fortunately, there's a heavy police presence, but still take care. Beyond the strip clubs and glitter, the attractive suburbs of Elizabeth Bay, Double Bay, and Rose Bay hug the waterfront. To reach the area via public transportation, take Bus 324, 325, or 327 from Circular Quay; Bus 311 from Railway Square, Central Station; or a CityRail train to Kings Cross station.

Paddington/Oxford Street This inner-city suburb, centered on trendy Oxford Street, is known for its expensive terrace houses, off-the-wall boutiques and bookshops, and popular restaurants, pubs, and nightclubs. It's also the heart of Sydney's large gay community (the largest after San Francisco) and has a liberal scattering of gay bars and dance spots. To reach the area via public transportation, take Bus 380 or 382 from Circular Quay (via Elizabeth Street); 378 from Railway Square, Central Station; or 380 and 382 from Bondi Junction.

Darlinghurst Wedged between grungy Kings Cross and upscale Oxford Street, this extroverted and grimy terraced suburb is home to some of Sydney's finest cafes. It's probably wise not to walk around here at night. Take the CityRail train to Kings Cross and head right from the exit.

Central The congested and badly polluted crossroads around Central Station, the city's main train station, has little to recommend it. Buses run from here to Circular

Quay, and it's a 20-minute walk to Town Hall. The Sydney Central YHA is located here.

Newtown This popular student area is centered around car-clogged King Street, lined with alternative shops, bookstores, and cheap ethnic restaurants. People-watching is the thing to do—see how many belly-button rings, violently colored hairdos, and Celtic arm tattoos you can spot. To reach the area via public transportation, take Bus 422, 423, 426, or 428 from Circular Quay (via Castlereagh Street and City Road), or take the CityRail train to Newtown Station.

Glebe Young professionals and students come to this inner-city suburb for the cafes, restaurants, pubs, and shops spread out along the main thoroughfare, Glebe Point Road. All this, plus a location just 15 minutes from the city and 30 minutes from Circular Quay, makes it a good place for budget-conscious travelers. To reach Glebe via public transportation, take Bus 431, 433, or 434 from Millers Point, The Rocks (via George Street), or Bus 459 from behind Town Hall.

Bondi & the Southern Beaches Some of Sydney's most glamorous surf beaches—Bondi, Bronte, and Coogee—can be found along the South Pacific Ocean coastline southeast of the city center. Bondi is a disappointment to many who expect more than this former working-class suburb has to offer. It does have a wide sweep of beach (crowded in summer), some interesting restaurants and bars, and plenty of attitude and beautiful bodies. To reach the beaches via public transportation, take Bus 380 or 382 to Bondi Beach from Circular Quay—it takes up to an hour—or, a quicker alternative is a

CityRail train to Bondi Junction to connect with same buses. Bus 378 from Railway Square, Central Station goes to Bronte, and Bus 373 or 374 travels to Coogee from Circular Quay.

Watsons Bay Watsons Bay is known for The Gap—a section of dramatic sea cliffs—as well as several good restaurants, such as Doyles on the Beach, and the popular Watsons Bay Hotel beer garden. It's a terrific spot to spend a sunny afternoon. To reach the area via public transportation, take Bus 324 or 325 from Circular Quay. There's a limited ferry service daily from Circular Quay (Wharf 2), starting at 10:15am on weekdays and 9:15am on weekends and public holidays.

North of the Harbour

North Sydney Just across the Harbour Bridge, the high rises of North Sydney attest to its prominence as a major business area. There's little to offer for tourists here, except the possibility of being knocked over on some busy thoroughfare. Take a CityRail train to the North Sydney stop. Chatswood (take a CityRail train from Central or Wynyard stations) has some pretty good suburban-type shopping, and Milsons Point, just across the bridge, has a fairly decent pub called the Kirribilli Hotel and a couple of restaurants and cafes.

The North Shore Ferries and buses provide reliable access to these wealthy neighborhoods across the Harbour Bridge. The gorgeous Balmoral Beach, Taronga Zoo, and upscale boutiques are the attractions in Mosman. Take a ferry from Circular Quay (Wharf 2) to Taronga Zoo—10 minutes—and a bus from there to Balmoral Beach (another 10 min.).

Manly & The Northern Beaches Half an hour away by ferry, or just 15 minutes by the faster JetCat, Manly is famous for its beautiful ocean beach and scores of cheap food outlets. Farther north are more beaches popular with surfers. Unfortunately, CityRail train line does not go to the northern beaches. The farthest beach from the city, Palm Beach, has magnificent surf and lagoon beaches, nice walking paths, and a scenic golf course. To reach the area via public transportation, take the ferry or JetCat from Circular Quay (wharves 2 and 3) to Manly. Change at Manly interchange for various buses to the northern beaches, numbers 148 and 154 through 159. You can also take Bus L90 from Wynyard Station.

West of the City Center

Balmain Located west of the city center, a short ferry ride from Circular Quay, Balmain was once Sydney's main ship-building area. In the last few decades the area has become trendy and expensive. The suburb has a village feel about it, is filled with restaurants and pubs, and hosts a popular Saturday market at the local church. Take Bus 441, 442, or 432 from Town Hall or George Street, or a ferry from Circular Quay (Wharf 5), and then a short bus ride up the hill to the main shopping area.

Homebush Bay This was the main site of the 2000 Olympic Games. Here you'll find the Olympic Stadium, the Aquatic Center, and the Homebush Bay Information Center, as well as parklands and a water-bird reserve. To reach the area via public transportation, take a CityRail train from Circular Quay to the Olympic Park station.

2 Getting Around

BY PUBLIC TRANSPORTATION

State Transit operates the city's buses and the ferry network, CityRail runs the urban and suburban trains, and Sydney Ferries runs the public passenger ferries. Some private bus lines operate buses in the outer suburbs. In addition, a monorail connects the city center to Darling Harbour and a light rail line (tram) runs between Central Station and Wentworth Park in Pyrmont.

MONEY-SAVING TRANSIT PASSES   Several passes are available for visitors who will be using public transportation frequently—all work out to be much cheaper than buying individual tickets.

The **SydneyPass** includes return Airport Express transfers, unlimited travel on Sydney Explorer coaches and Bondi & Bay Explorer coaches, unlimited travel on any or each of four Sydney Harbour cruises (see "What to See & Do in Sydney"), unlimited travel on the JetCat to Manly and the high-speed River-Cat to Parramatta (linking the city center to this important heritage and business center along an historic waterway), and unlimited travel on all Sydney Buses, Sydney Ferries, and CityRail trains (within the "Red TravelPass" travel zone, which includes the entire city center, as well as to Bondi Junction). The SyndeyPass costs A$90 (U.S.$58.50) for adults and A$45 (U.S.$29.25) for children for 3 days travel over a 7-day period; A$120 (U.S.$78) for adults and A$60 (U.S.$39) for children for 5 days over a 7-day period; and A$140 (U.S.$91) for adults and A$70 (U.S.$45.50) for children for 7-days' consecutive travel. Buy the tickets on the Airport Express bus, or on Sydney Explorer and Bondi & Bay Explorer buses.

A **Weekly Travel Pass** allows unlimited travel on buses, trains, and ferries. There are six different passes (denoted by color) depending on the distance you need to travel. The passes most commonly used by visitors are the Red Pass and the Green Pass. The Red Pass costs A$28 (U.S.$18.20) for adults and A$14 (U.S.$9.10) for kids and covers all transportation within the city center and near surroundings. This pass will get you aboard inner harbor ferries, for example, but not the ferry to Manly. The Green Pass, which costs A$36 (U.S.$23.40) for adults and A$18 (U.S.$11.70) for kids, will take you to more far-flung destinations, including Manly (aboard the ferry but not the JetCat before 7pm). You can buy either pass at newsagents or bus, train, and ferry ticket outlets.

The **Day Tripper** ticket gives you unlimited bus, train, and ferry travel for 1 day. Tickets cost A$13 (U.S.$8.45) for adults and A$6.50 (U.S.$4.20) for children. The pass is available at all bus, train, and ferry ticket outlets.

A **Travelten ticket** offers 10 bus or ferry rides for a discounted price. A blue Travelten covers two sections on the bus route and costs A$10.40 (U.S.$6.75) for adults and A$5.20 (U.S.$3.40) for children; a BrownTravelten covers up to

---

Tips Transit Information

For timetable information on buses, ferries, and trains, call the **Infoline** at ① **13 15 00** daily from 6am to 10pm. Otherwise check the relevant website for Sydney buses and ferries (www.sydneybuses.nsw.gov.au), or CityRail (www.staterail.nsw.gov.au). Pick up a **Sydney Transport Map** (a guide to train, bus, and ferry services) at any rail, bus, or ferry information office.

Sydney Transportation Systems

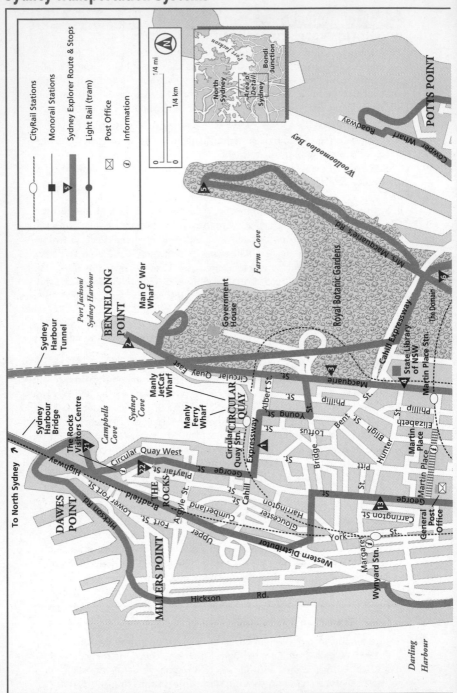

Legend:
- CityRail Stations
- Monorail Stations
- Sydney Explorer Route & Stops
- Light Rail (tram)
- Post Office
- (i) Information

1/4 mi
1/4 km

Area of Detail Sydney
North Sydney
Port Jackson
Bondi Junction

POTTS POINT

Cowper Wharf
Cowper Wharf Roadway
Woolloomooloo Bay

Mrs. Macquarie's Rd.

Royal Botanic Gardens

Farm Cove

Government House

The Domain

Cahill Expressway

State Library of NSW

Martin Place Stn.

BENNELONG POINT

Man O' War Wharf

Port Jackson/Sydney Harbour

Sydney Harbour Tunnel

Manly JetCat Wharf
Manly Ferry Wharf

CIRCULAR QUAY

Circular Quay Stn.

Circular Quay East

Circular Quay West

Sydney Cove

Campbells Cove

The Rocks Visitors Centre

Sydney Harbour Bridge

To North Sydney

DAWES POINT

Bradfield Highway

Hickson Rd.
Lower Fort St.
Upper Fort St.
Argyle St.
Cumberland St.
Gloucester St.
Harrington St.
George St.
Playfair St.

THE ROCKS

MILLERS POINT

Western Distributor

Cahill Expressway

Albert St.
Young St.
Phillip St.
Macquarie St.
Bligh St.
Bent St.
Hunter St.
Bridge St.
Loftus St.
Pitt St.
Phillip St.
Elizabeth St.

Martin Place

General Post Office

Wynyard Stn.

Margaret St.
York St.
Carrington St.

Darling Harbour

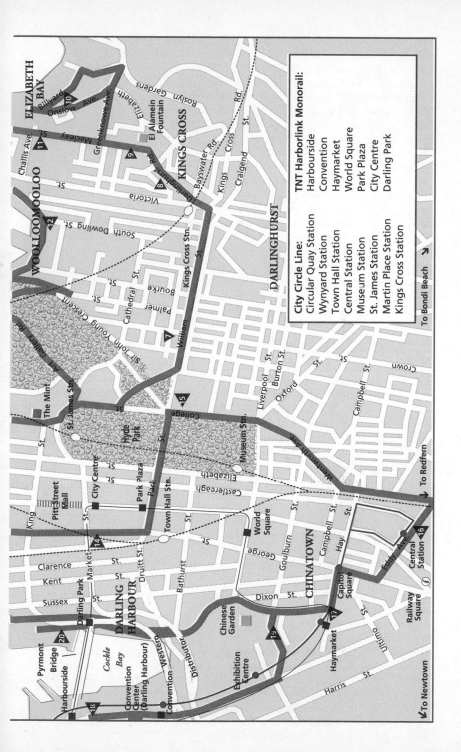

City Circle Line:
Circular Quay Station
Wynyard Station
Town Hall Station
Central Station
Museum Station
St. James Station
Martin Place Station
Kings Cross Station

TNT Harborlink Monorail:
Harbourside
Convention
Haymarket
World Square
Park Plaza
City Centre
Darling Park

nine sections and costs A$17.60 (U.S.$12.30) for adults and A$8.80 (U.S.$6.15) for children. The Travelten ferry ticket costs A$25.30 (U.S.$16.45) for adults and A$12.60 (U.S.$8.20) for kids for 10 trips within the inner harbor (this excludes Manly). The Manly ferry Travelten costs A$37.40 (U.S.$24.30) for adults and A$18.70 (U.S.$12.15) for children, while the JetCat Travelten to Manly (before 7pm) costs A$52 (U.S.$33.80) for adults (no kids' price). Buy Travelten tickets at newsagents, bus depots, or at the Circular Quay ferry terminal. Tickets are transferable, so if two or more people travel together, you can use the same ticket.

A 7-day **Rail Pass** costs A$16.40 (U.S.$10.65) for adults and A$8.20 (U.S.$5.30) for children, traveling within the city center. For a full day's unlimited travel by bus, you can't go wrong with the One-Day Bus Tripper. It costs A$9 (U.S.$5.85) for adults and A$4.50 (U.S.$2.90) for children 4 to 15, and can be bought from newsagents and at bus depots. An unlimited One-Day Bus/ferry Tripper costs A$13 (U.S.$8.45) for adults and A$6.50 (U.S.$4.20) for children.

BY PUBLIC BUS   Buses are frequent and fairly reliable and cover a wide area of metropolitan Sydney—though you might find the system a little difficult to navigate if you're visiting some of the outer suburbs. The minimum fare (which covers most short hops within the city) is A$1.40 (U.S.90¢) for adults and A70¢ (U.S.45¢) for children for a 4-kilometer (2½-mile) "section." The farther you go, the cheaper each section is. For example, the 44-kilometer (27-mile) trip to beautiful Palm Beach, way past Manly, costs just A$4.40 (U.S.$3) for adults and $2.20 (U.S.$1.40) for kids. Sections are marked on bus-stand signs (though most Sydneysiders are as confused about the system as you are sure to be).

Most buses bound for the northern suburbs, including night buses to Manly and the bus to Taronga Zoo, leave from Wynyard Park on Carrington Street, behind the main Wynyard CityRail station on George Street. Buses headed to the southern beaches, such as Bondi and Bronte, and the western and eastern suburbs leave from Circular Quay. Buses to Balmain leave from behind the Queen Victoria Building.

Call the **Transport Info Line** on ✆ **13 15 00** for timetable and fare information, or ask the staff at the bus information kiosk on the corner of Alfred and Loftus streets, just behind Circular Quay CityRail station (✆ **02/9219 1680**). The kiosk is open Monday through Saturday from 8am to 8pm and Sunday from 8am to 6pm. Buses run from 4am to around midnight during the week, less frequently on weekends and public holidays. Some night buses to outer suburbs run after midnight and throughout the night. You can purchase single tickets onboard from the driver; exact change is not required.

BY RED SYDNEY EXPLORER BUS   These bright red buses operate every day, traveling a 28-kilometer (17¼-mile) circuit and stopping at 21 places of interest. These include Sydney Opera House, the Royal Botanic Gardens, the State Library, Mrs. Macquarie's Chair, the Art Gallery of New South Wales, Kings Cross, Elizabeth Bay House, Wynyard CityRail Station, Martin Place, the Queen Victoria Building, AMP Sydney Tower, the Australian Museum, Central Station, Chinatown, and Darling Harbour. Buses depart from Circular Quay at 15-minute intervals from 8.40am with the last "round-trip" service departing Circular Quay at 5.25pm. This service returns to Circular Quay at 6.50pm. Board anywhere along the route where you see the distinctive red Sydney Explorer stop sign, and leave at any attraction along the way. If you want to stay on the bus from start to finish, the full circuit takes 1½ hours to complete. Your Sydney Explorer ticket entitles you to free travel on regular "blue and white" Sydney Buses services within the same zone covered by your Sydney Explorer Ticket until midnight. When planning your itinerary for the day, remember that some attractions, such as museums, close at 5pm. Tickets cost A$30 (U.S.$19.50) for adults, A$15 (U.S.$9.75) for children, and A$75 (U.S.$48.75) for a family. Buy tickets onboard the bus.

BY BONDI & BAY EXPLORER BUS   The Bondi & Bay Explorer operates every day, traveling a 30-kilometer (18½-mile) circuit around the eastern harborside bays and coastal beaches and back to the city. Stops along the way include Kings Cross, Double Bay, Watsons Bay, Bondi Beach, Bronte Beach, Coogee Beach, Paddington, Oxford Street, and Martin Place. The bus departs from Circular Quay at 25-minute intervals from 9:15am, with the last "round-trip" service departing Circular Quay at 4:20pm. This service returns to Circular Quay at 5:55pm. Board anywhere along the route where you see the Bondi & Bay Explorer stop sign, and leave at any attraction along the way. If you wish to stay on board from start to finish without making any stops, the entire circuit takes 1½ hours to complete. Your ticket entitles you to free travel on regular "blue and white" Sydney Buses services within the same zone covered by your Bondi & Bay Explorer ticket until midnight. The 1-day fare is A$30 (U.S.$19.50) for adults, A$15 (U.S.$9.75) for children under 16, and A$75 (U.S.$48.75) for families. Buy the ticket onboard.

BY FERRY & JETCAT   The best way to get a taste of a city that revolves around its harbor is to jump aboard a ferry. The main ferry terminal is at Circular Quay. Tickets can be bought at machines at each wharf (there are also change machines) or at the main Circular Quay ticket offices just opposite Wharf 4. For ferry information call ✆ **13 15 00,** or visit the ferry information office opposite Wharf 4. Timetables are available for all routes.

One-way journeys within the inner harbor (virtually everywhere except Manly and Parramatta) cost A$4 (U.S.$2.60) for adults and A$2 (U.S.$1.30) for children. The ferry to Manly takes 30 minutes and costs A$5 (U.S.$3.25) for adults and A$2.50 (U.S.$1.60) for children. It leaves from Wharf 3. The rapid JetCat service to Manly takes 15 minutes and costs A$6.30 (U.S.$4) for adults and children alike. After 7pm all trips to and from Manly are by JetCat at ferry prices. Ferries run from 6am to midnight.

BY CITYRAIL   Sydney's publicly owned train system is a cheap and relatively efficient way to see the city. The system is limited, though, with many tourist areas—including Manly, Bondi Beach, and Darling Harbour—not connected to the railway network. CityRail trains have a reputation of running late and out of timetable order. All train stations have automatic ticket machines, and most have ticket offices.

The single fare within the city center at any time of day is A$2.20 (U.S.$1.40) for adults and A$1.10 (U.S.70¢) for kids. An off-peak (after 9am) return ticket costs A$2.60 (U.S.$1.70) for adults and A$2.20 (U.S.$1.40) for kids, while a peak return will cost A$4.40 (U.S.$2.85) for adults and A$2.20 (U.S.$1.45) for kids. Information is available from **InfoLine** (✆ **13 15 00**) and at the CityRail Host Centers located opposite Wharf 4 at Circular Quay (✆ **02/9224 2649**) and at Central Station (✆ **02/9219 1977**); both centers are open daily from 9am to 5pm.

Comfortable and efficient **Countrylink** trains operating out of Central Station link the city with the far suburbs and beyond. For reservations call ℂ **13 22 32** between 6:30am and 10pm, or visit the **Countrylink Travel Center** (ℂ **02/9224 2742**), Station Concourse, Wynyard CityRail Station for brochures and bookings.

BY METRO MONORAIL   The metro monorail, with its single overhead line, is seen by many as a blight on the city and by others as a futuristic addition. The monorail connects the central business district to Darling Harbour. The system operates Monday through Wednesday from 7am to 10pm, Thursday and Friday from 7am to midnight, Saturday from 7am to midnight, and Sunday from 8am to 10pm. Tickets are A$3.50 (U.S.$2.30); children under 5 ride free. An all-day monorail pass costs A$7 (U.S.$4.50) for adults and A$20 (U.S.$13) for a family. The trip from the city center to Darling Harbour takes around 12 minutes. Look out for the gray overhead line and the plastic tube-like structures that are the stations. Call **Metro Monorail** at ℂ **02/8584 5288** (www. metrolightrail.com.au) for more information.

BY METRO LIGHT RAIL   A system of "trams" opened in late 1997 with a route that traverses a 3.6-kilometer (2¼-mile) track between Central Station and Wentworth Park in Pyrmont. It provides good access to Chinatown, Paddy's Markets, Darling Harbour, the Star City casino, and the Sydney Fish Markets. The trams run every 10 minutes. The one-way fare is A$2.20 (U.S.$1.45) or $4.50 (U.S.$2.90), depending on distance. There are no child fares. A family-of-five day pass costs A$20 (U.S.$13). Call **Metro Light Rail** at ℂ **02/8584 5288** (www.metrolightrail.com.au) for details.

BY TAXI

Taxis are a relatively economical way to get around Sydney. Several taxi companies service the city center and suburbs. All journeys are metered. If you cross either way on the Harbour Bridge or through the Harbour Tunnel, it will cost you an extra (A$2.20/U.S.$1.40), and if you take the Eastern Distributor from the airport, it's A$3.30 (U.S.$2.15). An extra 10% will be added to your fare if you pay by credit card (*important note:* Visa cards are not accepted in Australian taxis due to an ongoing dispute over charges).

Taxis line up at ranks in the city, such as those found opposite Circular Quay and Central Station. They are also frequently found in front hotels. A small yellow light on top of the cab means it's vacant. Cabs can be particularly hard to get on Friday and Saturday nights and between 2 and 3pm everyday, when tired cabbies are changing shifts after 12 hours on the road. Tipping is not necessary, but appreciated. Some people prefer to sit up front with the driver, but it's certainly not considered rude if you don't. It is compulsory for all passengers to wear seat belts in Australia. The **Taxi Complaints Hotline** (ℂ **1800/648 478** in Australia) deals with problem taxi drivers. Taxis are licensed to carry four people.

The main cab companies are **A** (ℂ **132 522**); **Taxis Combined Services** (ℂ **02/9332 8888**); **RSL Taxis** (ℂ **02/9581 1111**); **Legion Cabs** (ℂ **13 14 51**); and **Premier** (ℂ **13 10 17**).

BY WATER TAXI

Harbour Taxis, as they are called, operate 24 hours a day and are a quick and convenient way to get to waterfront restaurants, harbor attractions, and some suburbs. They can also be hired for private cruises of the harbor. A journey from Circular Quay to Watsons Bay, for example, costs about A$55 (U.S.$35.75) for

Sydney Ferries

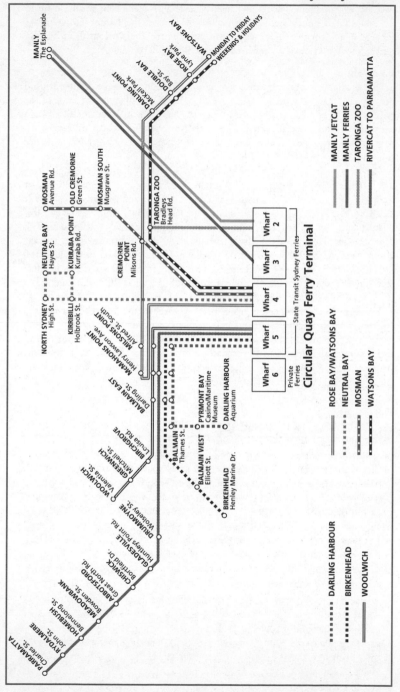

Circular Quay Ferry Terminal

State Transit Sydney Ferries

Private Ferries

Wharf 2
Wharf 3
Wharf 4
Wharf 5
Wharf 6

Legend (right):
- MANLY JETCAT
- MANLY FERRIES
- TARONGA ZOO
- RIVERCAT TO PARRAMATTA

- ROSE BAY/WATSONS BAY
- NEUTRAL BAY
- MOSMAN
- WATSONS BAY

Legend (bottom):
- DARLING HARBOUR
- BIRKENHEAD
- WOOLWICH

Stops:

MANLY — The Esplanade

WATSONS BAY
ROSE BAY — Lyne Park
DOUBLE BAY — Bay St.
DARLING POINT — McKell Park
MONDAY TO FRIDAY
WEEKENDS & HOLIDAYS

TARONGA ZOO — Bradleys Head Rd.

MOSMAN — Avenue Rd.
OLD CREMORNE — Green St.
MOSMAN SOUTH — Musgrave St.

NEUTRAL BAY — Hayes St.
KURRABA POINT — Kurraba Rd.

CREMORNE POINT — Milsons Rd.

NORTH SYDNEY — High St.
KIRRIBILLI — Holbrook St.

MCMAHONS POINT — Alfred St. South
MILSONS POINT — Henry Lawson Ave.

BALMAIN EAST — Darling St.

BIRCHGROVE — Louisa Rd.
GREENWICH — Mitchell St.
WOOLWICH — Valentia St.
DRUMMOYNE — Wolseley St.

PYRMONT BAY — Casino/Maritime Museum
DARLING HARBOUR — Aquarium

BALMAIN — Thames St.
BALMAIN WEST — Elliott St.
BIRKENHEAD — Henley Marine Dr.

GLADESVILLE — Huntleys Point Rd.
CHISWICK — Bortfield Dr.
ABBOTSFORD — Great North Rd.
MEADOWBANK — Bowden St.
HOMEBUSH — Bennelong St.
RYDALMERE — John St.
PARRAMATTA — Charles St.

95

two. An extra passenger costs just A$6 (U.S.$3.90); some taxis can hold up to 28 people. An hour's sightseeing excursion around the harbor costs A$181 (U.S.$117.65) for two. The two main operators are **Taxis Afloat** (☎ **02/9955 3222**) and **Water Taxis Combined** (☎ **02/9810 5010**).

BY CAR

Traffic restrictions, parking problems, and congestion can make getting around the city center by car a frustrating experience, but if you plan to visit some of the outer suburbs or take excursions elsewhere in New South Wales, then renting a car will give you more flexibility. The **NRMA's** (National Roads and Motorists' Association—the New South Wales auto club) emergency breakdown service can be contacted at ☎ **13 11 11.**

Car-rental agencies in Sydney include **Avis,** 214 William St., Kings Cross (☎ **02/9357 2000**); **Budget,** 93 William St., Kings Cross (☎ **13 28 48,** or 02/9339 8888); **Dollar,** Domain Car Park, Sir John Young Car Park (☎ **02/ 9223 1444**); **Hertz,** corner of William and Riley streets, Kings Cross (☎ **02/ 9360 6621**); and **Thrifty,** 75 William St., Kings Cross (☎ **02/9380 5399**). Avis, Budget, Hertz, and Thrifty also have desks at the airport. Rates average about A$60 (U.S.$39) per day for a small car. One of the best value car rental operations is **Bayswater Car Rentals,** 180 William St., Kings Cross (☎ **02/ 9360 3622**), which has small cars costing A$48 (U.S.$31.20) a day, and A$25 (U.S.$16.25) a day for 6 days or more.

You can rent a campervan from **Britz Campervans,** 182 O'Riordan St., Mascot, NSW 2020 (☎ **1800/331 454** in Australia, or 02/9667 0402; www.britz.com.au). Plan on about A$105 (U.S.$68.25) a day for a two-person van in winter and around $145 (U.S.$94.25) in summer. Both companies allow you to drop off your van at most state capitals and Cairns. It costs an extra A$200 (U.S.$130) for this convenience.

 FAST FACTS: Sydney

American Express The main Amex office is at Level 3, 130 Pitt St., near Martin Place (☎ **02/9236 4200**). You can cash traveler's checks here, and it also acts as a travel booking service. It's open Monday through Friday from 8:30am to 5pm and Saturday from 9am to noon. Another foreign exchange office is located on the walkway leading up to the Sydney Opera House (☎ **02/9251 1970**). If you've lost your traveler's checks, then you need to go to the head office at 175 Liverpool St. (☎ **02/9271 1111**). It's a locked security building so you'll need to call ahead first.

Babysitters Dial an Angel (☎ **02/9416 7511,** or 02/9362 4225) offers a well-regarded babysitting service.

Business Hours General office and banking hours are Monday through Friday from 9am to 5pm. Many banks, especially in the city center, are also open from around 9.30am to 12:30pm on Saturdays. Shopping hours are usually 8:30am to 5:30pm daily (9am–5pm Sat), and most stores stay open until 9pm on Thursdays. Most city-center stores are open from around 10am to 4pm on Sundays.

Camera Repair The **Camera Service Centre,** 1st Floor, 203 Castlereagh St. (☎ **02/9264 7091**), is a tiny place up a flight of stairs not far from the Town

Hall CityRail station. It repairs all kinds of cameras on the spot, or within a couple of days if parts are needed.

Car Rentals See "Getting Around," earlier in this chapter.

Currency Exchange Most major bank branches offer currency exchange services. Small foreign-currency-exchange offices are clustered at the airport and around Circular Quay and Kings Cross. **Thomas Cook** can be found at the airport; at 175 Pitt St. (℗ **02/9231 2877**), open Monday through Friday from 6:45am to 5:15pm and Saturday from 10am to 2pm; and on the lower ground floor of the Queen Victoria Building (℗ **02/9264 1133**), open Monday through Friday from 9am to 6pm (until 9pm Fri), Saturday from 9am to 6pm, and Sunday from 11am to 5pm.

Dentist A well-respected dentist office in the city is **City Dental Practice,** Level 2, 229 Macquaire St. (near Martin Place) (℗ **02/9221 3300**). For dental problems after hours, call **Dental Emergency Information** (℗ **02/9369 7050**).

Doctor The **Park Medical Centre,** Shop 4, 27 Park St. (℗ **02/ 9264 4488**), in the city center near Town Hall, is open Monday through Friday from 8am to 6pm; consultations cost A$40 (U.S.$26) for 15 minutes. (*Note:* If you plan to take a dive course while in Australia, get your medical exam done here. It costs A$70/U.S.$45.50, which is about the cheapest in Australia.) The **Kings Cross Travelers' Clinic,** Suite 1, 13 Springfield Ave., Kings Cross, just off Darlinghurst Road (℗ **1300/369 359** in Australia, or 02/9358 3066), is a great place for travel medicines and emergency contraception pills among other things. Hotel visits in the Kings Cross area cost A$80 (U.S.$52); consultations cost A$40 (U.S.$26). The **Travelers' Medical & Vaccination Centre,** Level 7, 428 George St., in the city center (℗ **02/ 9221 7133**), stocks and administers all travel-related vaccinations and medications.

Drugstores See "Pharmacies," below.

Embassies/Consulates All foreign embassies are based in Canberra. You'll find the following consulates in Sydney: **United Kingdom,** Level 16, Gateway Building, 1 Macquarie Place, Circular Quay (℗ 02/9247 7521); **New Zealand,** 55 Hunter St. (℗ 02/9223 0144); **United States,** Level 59, MLC Centre, 19–29 Martin Place (℗ 02/9373 9200); **Canada,** Level 5, 111 Harrington St., The Rocks (℗ 02/9364 3000).

Emergencies Dial ℗ **000** to call police, the fire service, or an ambulance. Call the **Emergency Prescription Service** (℗ **02/9235 0333**) for emergency drug prescriptions, and the NRMA for car breakdowns (℗ **13 11 11**).

Eyeglass Repair **Perfect Vision,** Shop C22A, in the Centerpoint Tower, 100 Market St. (℗ **02/9221 1010**), is open Monday through Friday from 9am to 6pm (until 9pm Thurs) and Saturday from 9am to 5pm. It's the best place to replace lost contact lenses, but bring your prescription.

Holidays See "When to Go" in chapter 2. New South Wales also observes Labour Day on the first Monday in October.

Hospitals Make your way to **Sydney Hospital,** on Macquarie Street, at the top end of Martin Place (℗ **02/9382 7111** for emergencies). **St. Vincents Hospital** is on Victoria and Burton streets in Darlinghurst (near Kings Cross) (℗ **02/9339 1111**).

Hot Lines Contact the **Poisons Information Center** at ✆ 13 11 26; the **Gay and Lesbian Counseling Line** (4pm–midnight) at ✆ 02/9207 2800; the Rape Crisis Center at ✆ 02/9819 6565; and the **Crisis Center** at ✆ 02/9358 6577.

Information See "Visitor Information" earlier in this chapter.

Internet Access Several Internet/e-mail centers are scattered around the Kings Cross area.

Lost Property There is no general lost property bureau in Sydney. Contact the nearest police station if you think you've lost something. For items lost on trains, contact the **Lost Property Office, 494** Pitt St., near Central Railway Station (✆ **02/9379 3000**). The office is open Monday through Friday from 8:30am to 4:30pm. For items left behind on planes or lost at the airport, go to the Federal Airport Corporation's administration office on the top floor of the international terminal at Sydney International Airport (✆ **02/9667 9583**). For stuff left behind on buses or ferries, call ✆ **02/9245 5777**. Each taxi company has its own lost property office.

Luggage Storage You can leave your bags at the International Terminal at the airport. A locker here costs A$5 (U.S.$3.25) per day, or you can put them in the storage room for A$7 (U.S.$4.55) per day per piece. The storage room is open from 4:30am to the last flight of the day. Call ✆ **02/9667 9848** for information. Otherwise, leave luggage at the cloakroom at Central Station, near the front of the main building off George Street (✆ 02/9219 4395). Storage at the rail station costs A$4.50 (U.S.$2.90) per article per day. The **Travelers Contact Point,** 7th floor, 428 George St. (above the Dymocks bookstore) (✆ **02/9221 8744**), stores luggage for A$15 (U.S.$9.75) per piece per month. It also operates a poste restante service, has Internet access, a travel agency, and a jobs board, and freights items back to the UK and Ireland.

Newspapers The *Sydney Morning Herald* is considered one of the world's best newspapers—by its management at least—and is available throughout metropolitan Sydney. The equally prestigious *Australian* is available nationwide. The metropolitan *Daily Telegraph* is a more casual read and has a couple of editions a day. The *International Herald Tribune, USA Today,* the British *Guardian Weekly,* and other U.K. newspapers can be found at Circular Quay newspaper stands and most newsagents.

Pharmacies Most suburbs have pharmacies that are open late. For after-hours referral, contact the **Emergency Prescription Service** (✆ **02/9235 0333**).

Police In an emergency dial ✆ **000.** Make non-emergency police inquiries through the Sydney Police Centre (✆ **02/9281 0000**).

Post Office The General Post Office (G.P.O.) is at 130 Pitt St., not far from Martin Place (✆ **13 13 17** in Australia). It's open Monday through Friday from 8:30am to 5:30pm and Saturday from 8am to noon. Letters can be sent c/o Poste Restante, G.P.O., Sydney, NSW 2000, Australia (✆ **02/9244 3733**), and collected at 310 George St., on the 3rd floor of the Hunter Connection shopping center. It's open Monday through Friday from 8:15am to 5:30pm. For directions to the post office nearest you, call ✆ **1800/043 300.**

Restrooms These can be found in the Queen Victoria Building (second floor), most department stores, at Central Station and Circular Quay, near the escalators by the Sydney Aquarium, and in the Harbourside Festival Marketplace in Darling Harbour.

Safety Sydney is an extremely safe city overall, but as anywhere else, it's good to keep your wits about you and your wallet hidden. If you wear a moneybelt, keep it underneath your shirt. Be wary in Kings Cross and Redfern at all hours and around Central Station and the cinema strip on George Street near Town Hall station in the evening—the latter is a hangout for local gangs, though they're usually busy holding each other up for their sneakers. Other places of concern are the back lanes of Darlinghurst and along the Bondi restaurant strip when the drunks spill out after midnight. Several people have reported thieves operating at the airport on occasions. If traveling by train at night, travel in the carriages next to the guard's van, marked with a blue light on the outside.

Taxes Beginning July 1, 2000, Australia adopted a 10% Goods and Services Tax (GST) on most goods sold in Australia and most services. The GST applies to most travel-related goods and services, including transport, hotels, tours, and restaurants. By law, the tax has to be included in the advertised price of the product, though it doesn't have to be displayed independently of the pre-tax price.

Taxis See "Getting Around," earlier in this chapter.

Telephones Sydney's public phone boxes take coins (A40¢ or U.S. .25¢ for local calls), while many also take credit cards and A$10 (U.S.$6.50) phonecards available from newsagents.

Transit Information Call the **InfoLine** at ✆ **13 15 00** (daily 6am–10pm).

Useful Telephone Numbers For news, dial ✆ **1199**; for the time, ✆ **1194**; for Sydney entertainment, ✆ **11 688**; for phone directory/assistance, ✆ **12 455**; for Travelers Aid Society, ✆ **02/9211 2469**.

Weather For the local forecast call ✆ **1196**.

3 Where to Stay

Sydney's success in winning the 2000 Olympic Games, and the increased media exposure the city has received as a result, have led to more visitors to the city and more hotels to cater to them. Although it's unlikely you'll find the city's hotels completely booked if you simply turn up looking for a bed for the night, it's probably wise to reserve rooms in advance.

DECIDING WHERE TO STAY The choice location for lodging in Sydney is in The Rocks and around Circular Quay—just a short stroll from the Sydney Opera House, the Harbour Bridge, the Royal Botanic Gardens, and the ferry terminals.

Hotels around Darling Harbour offer good access to the local facilities, including museums, the Sydney Aquarium, and the Star City casino. Most Darling Harbour hotels are a 10- to 15-minute walk, or a short monorail or light rail trip, from Town Hall and the central shopping district in and around Centerpoint Tower and Pitt Street Mall.

Where to Stay in Central Sydney

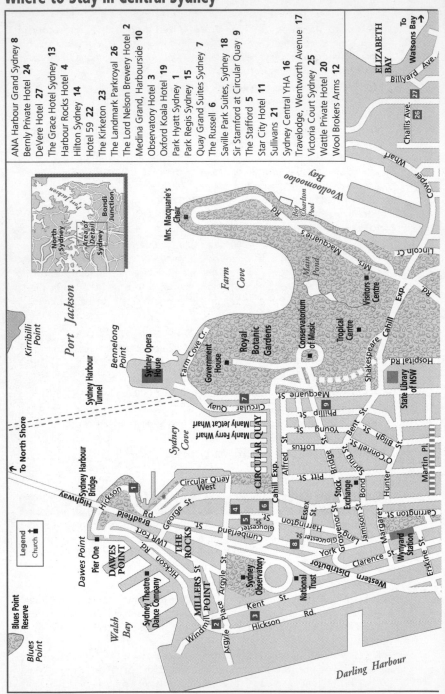

ANA Harbour Grand Sydney **8**
Bernly Private Hotel **24**
DeVere Hotel **27**
The Grace Hotel Sydney **13**
Harbour Rocks Hotel **4**
Hilton Sydney **14**
Hotel 59 **22**
The Kirketon **23**
The Landmark Parkroyal **26**
The Lord Nelson Brewery Hotel **2**
Medina Grand, Harbourside **10**
Observatory Hotel **3**
Oxford Koala Hotel **19**
Park Hyatt Sydney **1**
Park Regis Sydney **15**
Quay Grand Suites Sydney **7**
The Russell **6**
Saville Park Suites, Sydney **18**
Sir Stamford at Circular Quay **9**
The Stafford **5**
Star City Hotel **11**
Sullivans **21**
Sydney Central YHA **16**
Travelodge, Wentworth Avenue **17**
Victoria Court Sydney **25**
Wattle Private Hotel **20**
Wool Brokers Arms **12**

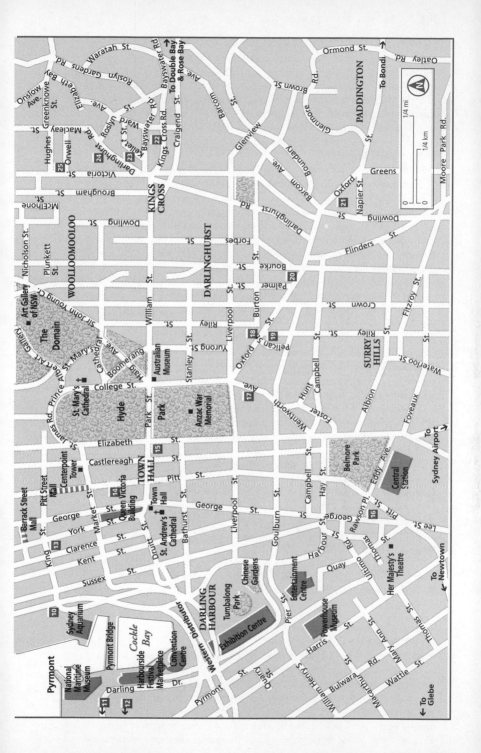

Waratah St.
Onslow Ave.
Greenknowe St.
Elizabeth Bay
Roslyn Gardens Rd.
Bayswater Rd
To Double Bay & Rose Bay
Ormond St.
To Bondi
Oatley Rd.
Brown St.
Glenmore
PADDINGTON
Moore Park Rd.

Hughes St.
Macleay St.
Orwell St.
Ward Ave.
Roslyn St.
Kellett St.
Bayswater Rd.
Kings Cross Rd.
Craigend St.
Barcom
Glenview
Barcom Ave.
Greens
Napier St.
Dowling
Oxford St.

25
24 Darlinghurst St.
23
22

Victoria St.
Brougham St.
KINGS CROSS
Darlinghurst Rd.

Nicholson St.
McElhone St.
Plunkett St.
Dowling St.
WOOLLOOMOOLOO
DARLINGHURST
Forbes St.
Bourke St.
Palmer St.
Flinders St.

21

20

William St.
Riley St.
Stanley St.
Yurong St.
Liverpool St.
Burton St.
Crown St.
Fitzroy St.

Art Gallery of NSW
The Domain
Sir John Young C.
Boomerang
Australian Museum
Oxford St.
Pelican St.
Campbell St.
Riley St.
SURRY HILLS
Waterloo St.

18
19

Gilbert Art Gallery
Prince Albert Rd.
St. Mary's Ave.
Cathedral Ave.
Haig Ave.
College St.
Park St.
St. Mary's Cathedral
Hyde Park
Anzac War Memorial
Hunt St.
Albion St.
Foster St.
Foveaux St.

17

Wentworth Ave.
Belmore Park
Eddy Ave.
Central Station
To Sydney Airport

St. James Rd.
Elizabeth St.
Centerpoint Tower
Castlereagh St.
TOWN HALL
Pitt St.
George St.
Hay St.
Campbell St.

15

Barrack Street Mall
Pitt Street Mall
Market St.
Queen Victoria Building
14
Town Hall
St. Andrew's Cathedral
Bathurst St.
George St.
Liverpool St.
Goulburn St.
Harbour St.
Rawson Pl.
Pitt St.
Lee St.
To Newtown

George St.
York St.
Clarence St.
Kent St.
Sussex St.
13
King St.
Druitt St.
Quay St.
Ultimo Rd.
Thomas St.
Her Majesty's Theatre

Sydney Aquarium
10
Pyrmont Bridge
Cockle Bay
DARLING HARBOUR
Western Distributor
Tumbalong Park
Chinese Gardens
Exhibition Centre
Entertainment Centre
Powerhouse Museum
Harris St.
Mary Ann St.
Thomas St.

Pyrmont
National Maritime Museum
Harbourside Festival Marketplace
Convention Centre
Darling Dr.
Pyrmont St.
Quarry St.
William Henry St.
Bulwara Rd.
Wattle St.
Macarthur St.
To Glebe

11
12

N
1/4 mi
1/4 km
0
0

101

LAST-MINUTE ROOM DEALS

If you turn up in town without a reservation, you should definitely make use of the Sydney Visitors Centre—Sydney Airport desk (© **02/9667 6050**) in the arrivals hall of the airport's International Terminal. It negotiates deals with many of Sydney's hotels (but not hostels) and offers exceptional value discounts on rooms that haven't been filled that day—you can save up to 50% on a room this way. The desk is open from 6am to the last flight of the day and also offers discounts on tours (to the Blue Mountains, for example), and cheap tickets for flights within Australia.

More hotels are grouped around Kings Cross, Sydney's red-light district. While some of the hotels found here are among the city's best, in this area you'll also find a range of cheaper lodgings, including several backpacker hostels. Kings Cross can be unnerving at any time, but especially so on Friday and Saturday nights when the area's strip joints and nightclubs are doing their best business. Staying here does have it's advantages, though: you get a real inner-city feel and it's close to some excellent restaurants and cafes centered around the Kings Cross/Darlinghurst and Oxford Street areas.

Glebe, with its ethnic restaurants, is another inner-city suburb popular with tourists. It's well served by local buses, as well as Airport Express Bus route 352.

If you want to stay near the beach, check out the options in Manly and Bondi, though you should consider their distance from the city center and the lack of CityRail trains to these areas. A taxi to Manly from the city will cost around A$33 (U.S.$21.45), and to Bondi around A$22 (U.S.$14.30).

The prices given below for very expensive and expensive hotels are the "**rack rates,**" the official published rates, which almost nobody pays. Always ask about discounts rates, package deals, and any other special offerings when booking a hotel, especially if you are traveling in winter when hotels are less likely to be full. Ask about weekend discounts, corporate rates, and family plans. **Serviced apartments** are also well worth considering, because you can save a bundle by cooking your own meals; many also have free laundry facilities.

Almost all hotels offer nonsmoking rooms; inquire when you make a reservation if it's important to you. Most moderately priced to very expensive rooms will have tea- and coffee-making facilities. Like elsewhere, there's an increasing trend to rip off guests with pay-per-view movie channels (around A$14/U.S.$9.10 per movie), rather than to provide full access to a range of free cable TV channels. In Australia, by the way, a "double" room means you get one double, queen-size, or king-size bed in a room.

The price categories used below are defined as follows (for a double room): Very Expensive, A$250 (U.S.$162) and up; Expensive, A$150 to $250 (U.S.$97–$162); Moderate, A$80 to $150 (U.S.$52–$97); Inexpensive, below A$80 (U.S.$52).

THE ROCKS/CIRCULAR QUAY
VERY EXPENSIVE

ANA Harbour Grand Sydney 🏨🏨   For a room with a view, you're not going to do better than this ultra-modern landmark hotel situated a 5-minute walk to Circular Quay. All rooms look out onto either Darling Harbour, or across the Opera House and Harbour Bridge. Try to book a room on the 20th floor or above, because from here Sydney is laid out at your feet, with the ferries buzzing around below you like wind-up bathtub toys. If you really want to splurge, book a corner room for an extraordinary vista. Rooms are comfortably furnished and decorated to blend with sky, city, and sea. The hotel is popular with tour groups, particularly from Japan.

176 Cumberland St., The Rocks, Sydney, NSW 2000. ℂ 1800/801 088 in Australia, or 02/9250 6000. Fax 02/9250 6250. www.anahotel.com.au. 563 units. A$430–$475 (U.S.$279–$308) double depending on view; deluxe corner rooms with views A$705 (U.S.$458); suites from A$705–A$4,800 (U.S.$458–$3120). Extra person A$55 (U.S.$35.75). Children stay free in parents' room. Ask about packages. AE, DC, MC, V. Parking A$21 (U.S.$13.65). CityRail or ferry: Circular Quay. **Amenities:** 2 restaurants (Modern Australian, Japanese), lounge, 2 bars; heated indoor pool; spa; sauna; exercise room; concierge; business center; salon; 24-hr. room service; babysitting; laundry service; currency exchange; early-arrivals/late-departures lounge. In room: A/C, TV with pay movies, dataport, minibar, hair dryer, iron, safe.

Harbour Rocks Hotel   This four-story, heritage-listed boutique hotel is right in the heart of Sydney's historical Rocks district. Rooms are clean and well appointed, but there is no elevator, so guests have to climb the stairs. Rooms vary in size, with some being quite large and others much smaller; bathrooms also vary in size, and none (except the penthouse suite) has a tub. The more expensive rooms look over the Sydney Opera House. There's one room equipped for travelers with disabilities on the ground floor. While its position is almost perfect, the staff are a little brusque.

34–52 Harrington St., The Rocks, Sydney, NSW 2000. ℂ 1800/251 210 in Australia, or 02/9251 8944. Fax 02/9251 8900. www.harbourrocks.com.au. 55 units. A$235–$279 (U.S.$153–$181) double; A$550 (U.S.$357.50) penthouse suite. Extra person A$33 (U.S.$21.45). Children under 12 stay free in parents' room. AE, DC, MC, V. Parking A$18 (U.S.$11.70) across the road. CityRail or ferry: Circular Quay. **Amenities:** Cafe, bar; secretarial services; limited room service (breakfast daily, and dinner Mon–Sat); babysitting; laundry service; coin-operated laundry. In room: TV with complimentary in-house movies, minibar, coffeemaker, iron.

Observatory Hotel 𝘈𝘈𝘈   This exclusive hotel, a 10-minute walk uphill from The Rocks and George Street, is a turn-of-the-20th-century beauty competing for top-hotel-in-Sydney honors (in 2001, U.S.-based customer-response surveyor, Zagats, named it hotel of the year in Australia, and the 11th-best hotel in the world). Up there with the Ritz-Carlton Sydney for unadulterated style, it's fitted out with antiques, objets d'art, and the finest carpets, wallpapers, and draperies, and is renowned for its personalized service. Rooms are plush and quiet, and the huge bathroom is a great place for a glass of champagne and some take-out sushi. Some rooms have city views while others look out over the harbor. If you don't fancy the walk into town, then take advantage of the hotel's free BMW limo service, which delivers guests to the central business district on weekdays. The pool here is one of the best in Sydney: Note the Southern Hemisphere constellations on the roof. The health club offers a free float in the flotation tank for early arrivals coming in from overseas.

89–113 Kent St., Sydney, NSW 2000. ℂ 1800/806 245 in Australia, or 02/9256 2222. Fax 02/9256 2233. www.observatoryhotel.com.au. 100 units. A$415–$450 (U.S.$270–$292) double; from A$510 (U.S.$331) suite. Extra person A$66 (U.S.$42.90). Children under 14 stay free in parents' room. AE, DC, MC, V. Parking A$30. Bus: 339, 431, or 433 to Millers Point. **Amenities:** Restaurant (Modern Australian), bar; very special chemical-free heated indoor pool; floodlit tennis court; sauna; health club with floatation tank; concierge; courtesy limo; business center; 24-hr. room service; dry-cleaning/laundry service. In-room: TV with pay movies, VCR, CD player, dataport, minibar, hair dryer, safe.

Park Hyatt Sydney 𝘈𝘈   This artistically curving property on The Rocks foreshore is without a doubt the best-positioned hotel in Sydney. It's literally right on the water, with some rooms having fantastic views directly across the harbor to the Sydney Opera House. Its location and general appeal mean it's usually full and frequently has to turn guests away. The room rates have rocketed here in recent years, and unless you have money to burn, there are plenty of places around that are far cheaper and just as nice.

The building itself is a pleasure to look at, and from a ferry on the harbor it looks like a wonderful addition to the toy town feel of The Rocks. Every possible luxury has been incorporated into the good-size rooms. Room rates here really depend on views; the least expensive units have only glimpses of the harbor (the most expensive rooms look over the Opera House). Each of the 33 executive suites has two balconies with a telescope.

The Verandah on the Park restaurant offers good buffet food either indoors or in a fabulous location on the edge of the harbor, and is worth a visit even if you don't stay here.

7 Hickson Rd., The Rocks, Sydney, NSW 2000. ⓒ **02/9241 1234.** Fax 02/9256 1555. www.sydney.hyatt.com. 158 units. A$650–$700 (U.S.$422–$455) double depending on view; A$820–$920 (U.S.$533–$598) executive studio; from A$1,000 (U.S.$650) suite. Extra person A$55 (U.S.$35.75). Children under 18 stay free in parents' room. Ask about lower weekend rates and packages. AE, DC, MC, V. Parking A$22 (U.S.$14.30). CityRail, bus, or ferry: Circular Quay. **Amenities:** 2 restaurants (casual & formal, International), bar/lounge; heated outdoor pool; health club/spa; concierge; business center; 24-hr. room service; babysitting; laundry service. *In room:* A/C, TV, dataport, minibar, coffeemaker, hair dryer, iron, safe.

Quay Grand Suites Sydney 🐾🐾

The very best serviced-apartment complexes, like this one, can even outdo superior five-star hotels. This building, located on the pedestrian concourse leading up to the Sydney Opera House, also houses private apartments costing upwards of A$750,000 (U.S.$487,500)— so you know you are in exclusive territory. The apartments here are very spacious and ultra-modern, and face either onto the Botanic Gardens or have fantastic views looking across the ferry terminals and the Sydney Harbour Bridge. Rooms are fully self-contained and come with a balcony to admire the views. The noises from the CityRail train station, including the train announcements as well as the ferry hooters, are captivating but can easily be shut out. Bathrooms are large and feature a good-size Jacuzzi. You might want to eat at the hotel's Quadrant restaurant, which serves up palatable Modern Australian food; otherwise there are two separate and excellent eateries—Aqua Luna and Aria—on the promenade down below. The Dendy cinema, in the same strip, has good art house movies.

61 Macquarie St., E. Circular Quay, Sydney, NSW 2000. ⓒ **1800/091 954** in Australia, or 02/9256 4000. Fax 02/9256 4040. www.mirvachotels.com.au. A$385–$443 (U.S.$250–$288) 1-bedroom apt depending on view. Extra person A$35 (U.S.$22.75). Ask about weekend packages and rates for long-term stays. AE, DC, MC, V. Parking A$20 (U.S.$13). CityRail, bus, or ferry: Circular Quay. **Amenities:** Restaurant (Modern Australian), bar (the trendy ECQ); small health club; concierge; business center; 24-hr. room service; massage; babysitting; laundry service; nonsmoking rooms. *In room:* A/C, TV with pay movies, kitchen, minibar, coffeemaker, hair dryer, iron, laundry.

Sir Stamford at Circular Quay 🐾🐾🐾

Talk about plush! This is Sydney's most deluxe hotel—from the moment the doorman doffs his top hat to you, you enter the world of aristocracy, complete with the slight scent of cigar smoke and aged brandy in the air. This hotel, formally the Ritz Carlton, has a prime location, just a short walk from Circular Quay and the Opera House, and just across the road from the Royal Botanic Gardens. Rooms are exceptionally large and luxurious with good-size marble bathrooms. Most rooms have a small balcony. The rooms on the east side of the hotel have the best views across the Botanic Gardens. Most rooms are accessible to wheelchairs.

93 Macquaire St., Sydney, NSW 2000. ⓒ **1300 301 391** in Australia, or 02/9252 4600. Fax 02/9252 4286. www.stamford.com.au. 106 units. A$540 (U.S.$351) double, A$570 (U.S.$370) deluxe harbor-view double; A$2,500 (U.S.$1625) suite. AE, DC, MC, V. Parking A$25 (U.S.$16.25). CityRail, bus, or ferry: Circular Quay. **Amenities:** Restaurant (international), gentleman's club-type bar; heated indoor pool; excercise room; sauna;

concierge; business center with secretarial services; salon; 24-hr. room service; massage; babysitting; laundry service; currency exchange. *In room:* A/C, TV with pay movies, fax, dataport, minibar, hair dryer, iron, safe.

EXPENSIVE

The Lord Nelson Brewery Hotel

Sydney's oldest pub was established in 1841 after serving as a private residence since its construction in 1836. It's an attractive, three-story sandstone building with a busy pub on the ground floor, a good brasserie on the second, and hotel accommodations on the third. The rooms were totally renovated in 1999 and while compact are spacious enough to swing your bags around without hitting the walls. From its creaky floorboards and bedroom walls made from convict-hewn sandstone blocks, to the narrow corridors, the wood fire, and homemade beer down in the bar, the Lord Nelson positively wallows in colonial atmosphere.

At the corner of Kent and Argyle sts., The Rocks, Sydney, NSW 2000. © 02/9251 4044. Fax 02/9251 1532. 9 units, 8 with bathroom. A$160 (U.S.$104) double without bathroom, A$180 (U.S.$117) double with bathroom. Extra person A$30. Rates include continental breakfast. AE, DC, MC, V. Parking not available. CityRail or ferry: Circular Quay. **Amenities:** 2 restaurants (Modern Australian, bar food), bar. *In room:* TV, fax, coffeemaker, hair dryer, iron.

The Stafford

The Stafford offers some of the best-positioned serviced apartments in Sydney, right in the heart of The Rocks, very close to the harbor and Circular Quay, and a short stroll from the central business district. The property consists of modern apartments in a six-story building (the best units, for their harbor and Opera House views, are on the top three floors) and 7 two-story terrace houses dating from 1870 to 1895. The Stafford is highly recommended for its location, spacious rooms, and fully equipped kitchen.

75 Harrington St., The Rocks, Sydney, NSW 2000. © 02/9251 6711. Fax 02/9251 3458. www.citysearch.com.au/syd/thestafford. 61 units. A$235–$275 (U.S.$153–$179) studio double; A$280 (U.S.$182) 1-bedroom apt; A$320 (U.S.$208) executive 1-bedroom apt; A$295 (U.S.$192) terrace house; A$370 (U.S.$240) 1-bedroom penthouse. Extra person A$15 (U.S.$9.75). Children under 12 stay free in parents' room. Ask about lower weekly rates. AE, DC, MC, V. Parking A$15 (U.S.$9.75). CityRail or ferry: Circular Quay. **Amenities:** Small outdoor pool; exercise room; spa; sauna; complimentary self-service laundry. *In room:* A/C, TV, kitchen, minibar, coffeemaker, hair dryer, iron.

MODERATE

The Russell ★★ *Finds*

This is the coziest place to stay in The Rocks, and perhaps in all of Sydney. It's more than 100 years old, and it shows its age wonderfully in the creak of the floorboards and the ramshackle feel of its brightly painted corridors. Every room is totally different in style, size, and shape; all come with a queen-size bed and most have cable TV (others can have a TV moved in if requested). All rooms have immense character, including a series of rooms added on in 1990 above the Fortune of War Hotel next door. There are no harbor views, but from some rooms you can see the tops of the ferry terminals at Circular Quay. Guests have the use of a comfortable sitting room, a living room scattered with magazines and books, and a rooftop garden. The apartment is large and open plan with a king-size bed and a small kitchen suitable for three people (there's a double sofa bed). It overlooks Circular Quay. The whole place was refurbished in 2000 and 2001.

143A George St., The Rocks, Sydney, NSW 2000. © 02/9241 3543. Fax 02/9252 1652. www.therussell.com.au. 29 units, 19 with bathroom. A$130–$180 (U.S.$84–$117) double without bathroom; A$215–$260 (U.S.$140–$169) double with bathroom; A$285 (U.S.$185) suite and apartment. Extra person A$15 (U.S.$9.75). Rates include continental breakfast. AE, DC, MC, V. Parking not available. CityRail or ferry: Circular Quay. **Amenities:** Restaurant (Modern Australian); lounge. *In room:* TV, coffeemaker, iron.

CITY CENTRE
VERY EXPENSIVE

The Grace Hotel Sydney 🎇🎇   Situated within the historic Grace Building, a replica of the Chicago Tribune Building in the United States and one of Australia's finest examples of commercial Gothic architecture, The Grace is one of the city's newest centrally located hotels. The 11-story building's L-shaped lobby has marble flagstones, stained-glass windows, a lace ironwork balcony, Art-Deco furniture and light fittings, and high ceilings supported by marble columns. Guest rooms vary in size (the more expensive doubles being labeled "deluxe," the cheaper "executive"), with either king-size beds or a pair of doubles, and are fronted by almost surreally wide corridors. Three rooms are suitable for travelers with disabilities.

77 York St., Sydney, NSW 2000. © 1800/682 692 in Australia, or 02/9299 8777. Fax 02/9299 8189. www.gracehotel.com.au. 382 units. A$374–$396 (U.S.$243–$257) double; A$572 (U.S.$371) suite. Extra person A$49.50 (U.S.$32.20). Children under 17 stay free in parents' room. AE, DC, MC, V. Parking A$27.50 (U.S.$17.90). CityRail: Wynyard. **Amenities:** 2 restaurants (brasserie, deli), bar; good heated outdoor pool; sauna; gym; concierge; business services; 24-hr. room service; massage; babysitting; laundry service; currency exchange. *In room:* A/C, TV, dataport, minibar, coffeemaker, hair dryer, iron, safe.

Hilton Sydney 🎇   Right in the middle of town and close to all major shops, the Hilton is a 1970s conglomerate with a decidedly ugly facade rearing onto both Pitt and George streets. The lackluster gold lobby—if you can find it (the main entrance is hidden away in a warren of concrete)—is dimly lit and houses a popular cafe and boutique shops. The rooms were refurbished in 1999, and are the first in Australia to have a fully electronic minibar system (aimed at preventing disputes with guests). The hotel is due for major external renovations in 2000. Many rooms, especially from the 32nd floor up, have panoramic views of the A.M.P. Centrepoint Tower, the Harbour Bridge, and neighboring skyscrapers. The higher priced doubles are "executive" rooms and have access to a meeting room and evening buffet food.

259 Pitt St., Sydney, NSW 2000. © 02/9266 2000, or 1800/222 255 in Australia. Fax 02/9265 6065. 585 units. A$420–$465 (U.S.$273–$302.25) double; A$550–$1,500 (U.S.$357.50–$975) suite. Extra person A$45 (U.S.$29.25). Children under 18 stay free in parents' room. AE, DC, MC, V. Parking $27 (U.S.$17.55). CityRail: Town Hall. **Amenities:** 2 restaurants (Modern Australian, bistro), 3 bars; outdoor pool; exercise room; sauna; spa; concierge; tour desk; business center; 24-hr. room service; massage; babysitting; laundry service; currency exchange. *In room:* A/C, TV, minibar, dataport, iron, coffeemaker, hair dryer.

EXPENSIVE

Park Regis Sydney   This hotel occupies the top 15 floors of a 45-story building and is well placed in the central business district, just 2 blocks from Hyde Park and Town Hall. There's nothing spectacular about the place, but the

---

Where to Stay During Gay & Lesbian Mardi Gras

The **Saville Park Suites** (see below) is a fabulous place from which to watch Sydney's annual Gay and Lesbian Mardi Gras, held every February (the parade is usually on the last Saturday in February or the first Saturday in March). Make your plans early, though, as most rooms are booked a year in advance. Four-night Mardi Gras packages range from around A$1,538 to $1,992 (U.S.$999.70–$1,295). Sullivans hotel (see below) on Oxford Street is also another popular place to stay during Mardi Gras.

rooms are light, modern, and equally practical. The bathrooms have a shower and no tub. Many of the guests are business travelers, which gives the hotel a corporate feel. Nevertheless, it's a relatively good value considering the location. Rooms at the front have views over the city and park.

27 Park St. (at Castlereagh St.), Sydney, NSW 2000. © **02/9267 6511**, or 1800/221 138 in Australia. Fax 02/9264 2252. www.parkregis.com.au. 120 units. A$165 (U.S.$72.80) double; A$198 (U.S.$128.70) suite. Extra person A$22 (U.S.$14.30). Children under 14 stay free in parents' room. Ask about lower rates available through Aussie auto clubs. AE, DC, MC, V. Free parking. CityRail: Town Hall. Monorail: Park Plaza. **Amenities:** Small pool; concierge; tour desk; massage; babysitting; laundry service. *In room:* A/C, TV, coffeemaker, hair dryer, iron.

Saville Park Suites, Sydney 𝓰

Although the serviced apartments here are pleasant and nicely furnished and the complex is very well situated right at the start of Oxford Street and just a short walk across Hyde Park from the Pitt Street Mall shopping area, I feel it's overpriced. You may be able to negotiate a cheaper rate with the management, though; it never hurts to ask. All rooms have a sofa and a couple of armchairs, a separate kitchen, a balcony, and a bathroom with a smallish tub and separate shower. Guests get free membership at a gym just down the road.

16–32 Oxford St., Sydney, NSW 2010. © **02/8268 2599**, or 1800/221 2599 in Australia. Fax 02/8268 2599. www.savillesuites.com.au. 135 units. A$230 (U.S.$149.50) 1-bedroom apt; A$255 (U.S.$165.75) 2-bedroom apt. Extra person A$25 (U.S.$16.25). Children under 15 stay free in parents' room. Ask about special rates. AE, DC, MC, V. Parking A$5 (U.S.$3.25). CityRail: Museum. **Amenities:** Restaurant (International); small outdoor pool; sauna; spa. *In room:* A/C, TV, minibar, iron, laundry.

MODERATE

Travelodge, Wentworth Avenue 𝓰

This typical business-orientated hotel is pretty cheap for Sydney, but it's comfortable and well located nevertheless—making it a very good option for the average traveler. The clean, brown-colored rooms are motel-like in appearance, with a queen-size bed. Many also come with a sofa. From here it's a short walk to Oxford Street, Town Hall, Hyde Park, and the monorail to Darling Harbour.

27–33 Wentworth Ave., Sydney, NSW 2000. © **02/8267 1700**. Fax 02/8267 1800. www.travelodge.com.au. 406 units. A$119 (U.S.$77) double and twin rooms. Extra person A$16 (U.S.$10.40). AE, DC, MC, V. Parking around corner A$16.50 (U.S.$10.75). CityRail: Museum. **Amenities:** Restaurant (Modern Australian); massage; babysitting; nonsmoking rooms. *In room:* A/C, TV, dataport, kitchenette, refrigerator, coffeemaker, hair dryer, iron.

INEXPENSIVE

Sydney Central YHA 𝓰𝓰 (Value)

This multi-award-winning youth hostel is one of the biggest and busiest in the world. With a 98% year-round occupancy rate, you'll have to book early to secure a place. Opened in 1987 in a historic nine-story building, it offers far more than standard basic accommodation. In the basement is the Scu Bar, a very popular drinking hole with pool tables and occasional entertainment. There's also an entertainment room with more pool tables and e-mail facilities, TV rooms on every floor, and an audio-visual room showing movies. Try the heated swimming pool and the sauna! Rooms are clean and basic. The YHA is completely accessible to travelers with disabilities. Check the YHA website for other great hotels in Sydney—including the Glebe Point YHA in Glebe, the Sydney Beachhouse YHA in the beachside suburb of Collaroy, and Pittwater YHA in Ku-ring-gai Chase National Park (only accessible by boat and a fabulous way to experience the "bush" around Sydney).

11 Rawson Place, Sydney, NSW 2000. © **02/9281 9111**. Fax 02/9281 9199. www.yha.com.au. 151 rooms, or 532 beds (54 twin rooms). A$24–$29 (U.S.$15.60–$18.85) dorm bed; A$72 (U.S.$46.80) twin without

bathroom, A$80 (U.S.$52) twin with bathroom. Non-YHA members pay A$3 (U.S.$1.95) extra. MC, V. Parking A$10 (U.S.$6.50). It's located on the corner of Pitt St., right outside Central Station. CityRail: Central. **Amenities:** Restaurant (bistro), bar; swimming pool; sauna; 2 kitchens; TV room.

AT DARLING HARBOUR
VERY EXPENSIVE

Star City Hotel 𝕰𝕰𝕰   Opened at the end of 1997, this A$900-million (U.S.$585-million) gambling and entertainment complex includes a five-star hotel, with rooms overlooking both Darling Harbour and the architecturally interesting Pyrmont Bridge. Although the four split-level Royal Suites are quite spectacular, each with three TVs, a giant spa, a full kitchen, two bathrooms, its own sauna, and the services of the former butler to the governor of Queensland, the standard rooms are somewhat small and sterile. Executive suites are very nice though. If you do stay here, pay the extra money for a room with truly spectacular views over Darling Harbour.

80 Pyrmont St., Pyrmont, Sydney, NSW 2009. ℭ **1800/700 700** in Australia, or 02/9777 9000. Fax 02/9657 8344. www.starcity.com.au. 491 units. A$350–$370 (U.S.$154.70–$163.80) double, depending on view; from A$510 (U.S.$331.50) and way up for apts. Extra person A$40 (U.S.$26). Ask about special packages. AE, DC, MC, V. Parking A$15 (U.S.$9.75). Ferry: Pyrmont Bay. Monorail: Harbourside. Light Rail: Star City. Free shuttle buses run from the central business district. **Amenities:** 4 restaurants (Modern Australian, Italian, Chinese, bistro); large outdoor pool; sauna; spa; gaming rooms; 2 theaters; concierge; business center; shopping arcade; salon; 24-hr. room service; massage; laundry service; currency exchange. *In room:* A/C, TV, dataport, minibar, coffeemaker, hair dryer.

MODERATE

Wool Brokers Arms   You'll find this friendly 1886 heritage building on the far side of Darling Harbour, next to the prominent four-star Novotel hotel and hidden behind a monstrous above-ground parking garage. It's set on a noisy road, so unless you're used to traffic avoid the rooms at the front. Rooms are simply furnished with a double bed and a sink. Room 3 is one of the nicer ones. Family rooms have a king-size bed, a set of bunks, and two singles through an open door way. There are 19 shared bathrooms. It's adequate for a few nights.

22 Allen St., Pyrmont, NSW 2009. ℭ **02/9552 4773.** Fax 02/9552 4771. woolbrokers@ozemail.com.au. 26 units, none with bathroom. A$79 (U.S.$51) double; A$98(U.S.$63.70) triple; A$120 (U.S.$78) family room for 4. These discounted prices are for Frommer's readers only. Rates include continental breakfast. Extra person A$20 (U.S.$13). AE, MC, V. Parking A$9 (U.S.$5.85) nearby. Bus: 501 from central business district or Central Station. Light Rail: Convention Centre. **Amenities:** Coin-op laundry. *In room:* TV, refrigerator, coffeemaker, hair dryer.

SERVICED APARTMENTS

Medina Grand, Harbourside 𝕰𝕰   This very impressive serviced hotel offers modern and very comfortable rooms at very competitive prices. It's a little oddly placed—reached by an offshoot road and a short, unattractive walk from the Sydney Aquarium in Darling Harbour—but it makes up for it by being very close to all the Darling Harbour, Cockle Bay and Town Hall attractions and shops. You can choose from between studio and one-bedroom apartments, which all come with Italian designer furniture, large windows, and balconies (some with good harbor views). Studio units come with a kitchenette, and one-bedroom units with a fully equipped kitchen and a second TV. All have dataports. Medina offers very good package and weekend rates, which mean this place can work out to be a real bargain.

Medina has a series of other serviced-apartment complexes in Sydney, including the Medina Executive, Sydney Central (ℭ **02/8396 9800**), in a lovely historic building near Central station; the pleasant Medina Classic in Martin

Place (© **02/9224 6400**); the coastal Medina Executive, near Coogee Beach (© **02/9578 6000**); the gorgeous Medina Executive in Paddington (© **02/ 9361 9000**); and the five-star Medina Grand, Sydney (© **02/9274 0000**), between Town Hall and Darling Harbour. Check the website below for more details on all these highly recommended properties.

Corner of Shelley and King sts., King Street Wharf, Sydney, NSW 2000. © **1300 300 232** in Australia, or 02/9249 7000. Fax 02/9249 6900. www.medinaapartments.com.au. 114 units. AE, DC, MC, V. CityRail: Town Hall. **Amenities:** Small pool; exercise room; concierge; tour desk; business center; laundry service; nonsmoking rooms. *In room:* A/C, TV, dataport, kitchenette, minibar, coffeemaker, hair dryer, iron.

IN KINGS CROSS & THE SUBURBS BEYOND
VERY EXPENSIVE
The Landmark Parkroyal ⊗⊗   This top-flight, four-star hotel is where airline pilots stay when they're stopping off in Sydney. Though not slap bang in the city center, it's just a 5-minute walk from Kings Cross station and very close to some of the city's best restaurants. The guest rooms are good-size and have large windows that open. Some rooms have spectacular views over the inner harbor, the Heads, and parts of the city; others have good skyline views; while still others look over the Sydney Opera House and the Harbour Bridge. Depending on the room, it will have either one or two queen-size beds, or a single king-size bed. Bathrooms are small but come with a tub/shower combination. Guests on the two club floors (the 16th and 17th) receive complimentary breakfast and drinks every evening.

81 Macleay St., Potts Point, NSW 2011. © **02/9368 3000.** Fax 02/9357 7600. www.sphc.com.au. 463 units. A$327–$439 (U.S.$212–$285) double; A$950 (U.S.$617) suite. Extra bed A$30 (U.S.$19.50). Children under 14 stay free in parents' room. Ask about weekend and excellent money-saving packages. AE, DC, MC, V. Parking A$15 (U.S.$9.75). CityRail: Kings Cross, then about a 1-km (½-mile) walk. Bus: 311 from Circular Quay. **Amenities:** Restaurant (seafood/Asian); small outdoor pool; free access to nearby gym; concierge; courtesy limo; 24-hr. room service; babysitting; laundry service; nonsmoking rooms; executive rooms. *In room:* A/C, TV, minibar, coffeemaker, hair dryer.

Stamford Plaza Double Bay ⊗⊗   Madonna, the late Princess Diana, Tom Jones, George Bush, Neil Diamond—they've all stayed in this five-star darling of the establishment, situated about 4 kilometers (2½ miles) from the city center in Sydney's poshest harborside suburb—that's when the hotel was called the Ritz-Carlton Double Bay. Taken over in 2001, the grand lobby still retains its maritime theme, the corridors are still somberly lit, and antiques and Persian rugs are scattered tastefully here and there. The large guest rooms are done in Regency style and are almost unnervingly quiet. Everything you would expect at the best in town is here, from the enormous TV and the fluffy bathrobes down to designer bathtub salts and a perfect, single rose. Most rooms have balconies with water views. Ferries to the city leave from just around the corner.

33 Cross St., Double Bay, NSW 2028. © **02/9362 4455,** or 1300/301 391 in Australia. www.stamford.com.au. 140 units. A$349–$409 (U.S.$226.85–$265.85) double; from A$499 (U.S.$324.35) and up for suites. A$399–$449 (U.S.$259–$291) Club floor. AE, DC, MC, V. Parking A$15 (U.S.$9.75). CityRail: Edgecliff, then about a 1-km (½-mile) walk. Bus: 325 or 324 from Circular Quay. Ferry: Double Bay. **Amenities:** Restaurant (International), bar, lounge; heated rooftop pool; fitness center; concierge; business center; 24-hr. room service; babysitting; separate kosher kitchen; currency exchange. *In room:* A/C, TV, minibar, coffeemaker, iron.

EXPENSIVE
The Kirketon ⊗   If you want to stay somewhere a bit off-beat, and class yourself as a "hip, fashionable type," then this boutique hotel in busy Darlinghurst is a fascinating option. Rooms come with either a king, queen, double, or twin

beds, and are lightly stocked with modernist furniture and custom-made fittings, including mirrored headboards, sleek bathrooms hidden away behind mirrored doors, and interestingly textured bedspreads and areas of wallpaper. All in all it's quite fun if you like this sort of thing, though personally I found it jarred with my more conventional taste. Junior rooms are quite compact, some of the Premium rooms come with a tub as well as shower, and the quite large Executive rooms have a VCR, with some having a small balcony overlooking the main road (it can be quite noisy at night). The inside scoop is that the best Junior room is number 330, the best Premium room number 340, and the best Executive room number 323. I would definitely ask for a room away from the main road.

229 Darlinghurst Rd., Darlinghurst. ℂ 02/9332 2011. Fax: 02/9332 2499. www.kirketon.com.au. 40 rooms. Junior rooms A$220 (U.S.$143); Premium rooms A$275 (U.S.$178.75); Executive rooms A$365 (U.S.$237.25). Rooms cater only for 1 or 2 people. AE, DC, MC, V. Free parking in garage around the corner (ask in advance for directions). **Amenities:** Restaurant—the hip Salt (see "Where to Dine," later in this chapter), bar. *In room:* A/C, TV, dataport, minibar, hair dryer.

MODERATE

DeVere Hotel   The DeVere has been recommended by several readers who comment on the friendly staff and the bargain-basement room prices when booked at the Tourism New South Wales Travel Centre at the Sydney airport. Although the rooms are very modern, they are a little too standard gray corporate for my liking (though the owner says some are now yellow). Superior rooms are a bit larger, and the executive room is larger still and comes with nicer furniture. However, they are certainly a bargain compared to similar, but far more expensive, rooms elsewhere in Sydney. The suites have views of Elizabeth Bay, a spa bath, and a king-size bed rather than a queen. Some suites have a pretty useless kitchenette with no cooking facilities. Some standard rooms have an extra single bed. Breakfast is available from A$8 (U.S.$5.20).

44–46 Macleay St., Potts Point, NSW 2011. ℂ 1800/818 790 in Australia, 0800/441 779 in New Zealand, or 02/9358 1211. Fax 02/9358 4685. www.devere.com.au. 98 units. A$107.90 (U.S.$70) double; superior room $140.60 (U.S.$91.40); executive room $162.40 (U.S.$105.50); A$206 (U.S.$133.90) suite. Extra person A$32.70 (U.S.$21.25). Children under 12 stay free in parents' room. AE, DC, MC, V. Parking at nearby Landmark Hotel A$12 (U.S.$7.80) per exit. CityRail: Kings Cross. Bus: 311 from Circular Quay. *In room:* A/C, TV.

Hotel 59 *Kids*   This popular and friendly B&B is well worth considering if you want to be near the Kings Cross action, but just far enough away to get a decent night's sleep. Deluxe rooms have either a queen- or king-size bed and a combined shower and tub, while the smaller standard rooms come with a double bed and a shower (no tub). The two large superior rooms come with a separate living room, two single beds, and two more that can be locked together to form a king. The two large superior rooms come with two single beds and two more that can be locked together to form a king, and a separate living room. One comes with a small kitchen with a microwave and hot plates. All rooms are very clean and comfortable, and have private bathrooms. A fully cooked breakfast is served up in the cafe below. A flight of stairs and no elevator (lift) might make this a bad choice for older travelers or those with disabilities.

59 Bayswater Rd., Kings Cross, NSW 2011. ℂ 02/9360 5900. Fax 02/9360 1828. www.interspace.net. au/inns/hotel59. 8 units. A$115 (U.S.$74.75) standard double, A$125 (U.S.$81.25) deluxe double; A$135 (U.S.$87.75) superior room. Extra person A$15 (U.S.$9.75), extra children 2–12 A$10 (U.S.$6.50). Rates include cooked breakfast. MC, V. Limited parking A$5 (U.S.$3.25). CityRail: Kings Cross. **Amenities:** TV lounge. *In room:* A/C, TV.

Victoria Court Sydney ⚔ This cute, good value little place is made up of two 1881 terrace houses joined together; it's situated near a string of backpacker hostels and popular cafes in a leafy street running parallel to sleazy Darlinghurst Road. The glass-roofed breakfast room on the ground floor is a work of art decked out with hanging ferns, giant bamboo, wrought-iron tables and chairs, and a trickling fountain. Just off this is a peaceful guest lounge stacked with books and newspapers. The very plush rooms come with either king- or queen-size beds, but lack a tub in the bathroom. There's a coin-op laundry just down the road.

122 Victoria St., Potts Point, NSW 2011. ℂ **1800/630 505** in Australia, or 02/9357 3200. Fax 02/9357 7606. www.VictoriaCourt.com.au. 22 units. A$99–$115 (U.S.$64.35–$74.75) double, depending on the season; A$165 (U.S.$107.25) deluxe double with sun deck; A$250 (U.S.$162.50) honeymoon suite with balcony. Rates include buffet breakfast. Extra person A$20 (U.S.$13). AE, DC, MC, V. Free parking in secured lot. CityRail: Kings Cross. **Amenities:** Guest lounge. *In room:* A/C, TV.

INEXPENSIVE
Bernly Private Hotel *(Finds* This place, tucked away just off Darlinghurst Road, is a real find. It's an ants' nest of rooms run by very friendly staff, catering to everyone from short-term travelers to newly arrived immigrants. All rooms are new and clean. The more expensive rooms here are superior to most others of their price in the area. Budget rooms are a bit scruffier and smaller than the standards, but are perfectly livable. Some come with a microwave oven, and all have a small TV. Backpacker rooms have two sets of bunk beds, though just two people seem to occupy most. Some of the backpacker rooms also have a shower. There's a good rooftop sun deck and a lounge with cable TV. Five family rooms come with double beds and two singles.

15 Springfield Ave., Potts Point, NSW 2011. ℂ **02/9358 3122.** Fax 02/9356 4405. www.bernleyprivatehotel. com.au. 95 units, 12 with bathroom (shower only). A$49 (U.S.$31.85) single without bathroom; $55 (U.S.$35.75) budget double without bathroom; A$82.50 (U.S.$53.60) budget double with bathroom; A$93.50 (U.S.$60.80) standard double with bathroom; A$132 (U.S.$85.80) triple with bathroom. A$20 (U.S.$13) dorm bed. Additional person A$22 (U.S.$14.30) extra. AE, DC, MC, V. On-street meter parking. CityRail: Kings Cross. **Amenities:** Rooftop sun deck; TV lounge. *In room:* TV.

OXFORD STREET/DARLINGHURST
MODERATE
Oxford Koala Hotel ⚔ You won't find many three-star hotels that offer as much value for your dollar as the Oxford Koala. A very popular tourist hotel, it is well placed just off trendy Oxford Street, a 5- to 10-minute bus trip from the city center and Circular Quay. There are 13 floors of rooms in this tower block; rooms on the top floor have reasonable views over the city. Superior rooms are very comfortable and more spacious than standard rooms and have better furniture. All come with a shower/tub combination or just a shower. Apartments are good-size, come with a full kitchen, and are serviced daily. On the premises are a swimming pool, a restaurant, and a cocktail bar.

Corner of Oxford and Pelican sts., Darlinghurst (P.O. Box 535, Darlinghurst, NSW 2010). ℂ **02/9269 0645,** or 1800/222 144 in Australia (outside Sydney). Fax 02/9283 2741. www.oxfordkoala.com.au. 330 units (including 78 apts). A$135–$155 (U.S.$87.75–$100.75) double; A$185–$205 (U.S.$120.25–$133.25) 1-bedroom apt. Extra person A$25 (U.S.$16.25). Children under 12 stay free in parents' room. AE, DC, MC, V. Parking A$15 (U.S.$9.75) a day. Bus: 380 or any bus traveling via Taylor Square. **Amenities:** Restaurant (Modern Australian), bar; small swimming pool; tour desk. *In room:* A/C, TV. In apartments only: kitchen.

Sullivans About half of this boutique hotel's guests come from overseas, mainly from the United Kingdom, Europe, and the United States. There's also a small corporate following. Sullivans is right in the heart of the action in one of

Sydney's most popular shopping, entertainment, restaurant, and gay pub and club areas. The hotel is particularly popular with Americans during the Gay and Lesbian Mardi Gras, held over the month of February. Rooms are cozy, with queen-size beds and a refrigerator; all have an en-suite bathroom with a shower (no tub). There's a pleasant garden courtyard.

21 Oxford St., Paddington, NSW 2021. ℂ **02/9361 0211.** Fax 02/9360 3735. www.sullivans.com.au. sydney@sullivans.com.au. 64 units. A$125 (U.S.$81.25) double. AE, DC, MC, V. Limited free parking. Bus: 378 or 380 from Circular Quay. **Amenities:** Small swimming pool; bike rental. *In room:* A/C, TV, refrigerator.

Wattle Private Hotel   This attractive Edwardian-style house built between 1900 and 1910 offers homey accommodations in the increasingly fashionable inner-city suburb of Darlinghurst, known for its great cafes, nightlife, and restaurants. Rooms are found on four stories, but there's no elevator (lift), so if you don't fancy too many stairs try to get a room on the lower floor. Rooms are smallish but are opened up by large windows. Twin rooms have a better bathroom, with a tub. The decor is a jumble of Chinese vases, ceiling fans, and contemporary bedspreads. The owners are very friendly.

108 Oxford St. (at corner of Palmer St.), Darlinghurst, NSW 2010. ℂ **02/9332 4118.** Fax 02/9331 2074. wattlehotel@yahoo.com.au. 12 units. A$99 (U.S.$64.35) double. Extra person A$11 (U.S.$7.15). Rates include continental breakfast. MC, V. No parking. Bus: Any to Taylor Square from Circular Quay. **Amenities:** Coin-op laundry. *In room:* A/C, TV, stocked minibar.

IN NEWTOWN

Billabong Gardens   For that real inner city feel you can't beat Newtown with busy street happenings, cheap restaurants and "grunge" look. It's also easily accessed by buses and Newtown CityRail Station. Billabong gardens is located just of the main drag, King Street, and is classed with a five-star backpackers rating. While there is dormitory accommodation here, you might also consider the double or twin rooms, which offer pretty good value. The more expensive rooms have their own bathroom. It's a friendly place with lots of native plants scattered around and a pool set in a pleasant courtyard. Rooms are simply furnished in pine and have exposed brickwork. They are cleaned daily. On the property is a comfortable TV lounge and a large kitchen. It's very secure and offers 24-hour access.

5-11 Egan St., Newtown, NSW 2042. ℂ **02/9550 3236.** Fax 02/9550 4352. www.billabonggardens.com.au. 37 units. A$20–$23 (U.S.$13–$15) dorm; A$66–$88 (U.S.$43–$57) double/twin. MC, V. Free parking. CityRail: Newtown. Bus: 422, 423, 426, or 428. **Amenities:** Swimming pool; laundry; TV room; barbecue; fax; free Internet; kitchen; pay phones; safe.

IN GLEBE
EXPENSIVE

Tricketts Luxury Bed & Breakfast 𝄞𝄞   As soon as I walked into this atmospheric old place, I wanted to ditch my modern Sydney apartment and move in. Your first impression as you enter the tessellated, tiled corridor of this 1880s Victorian mansion is the amazing jumble of plants and ornaments, the high ceilings, the Oriental rugs, and the leaded windows. Guests play billiards over a decanter of port or relax among magazines and wicker furniture on the balcony overlooking the fairly busy Glebe Point Road. The bedrooms are quiet and homey (no TVs). My favorites are number 2, with its wooden floorboards and king-size bed, and number 7, with its queen-size bed, extra single bed, and very large bathroom. Rooms all have showers. There's a nice courtyard out the back with a barbecue.

270 Glebe Point Rd., Glebe, NSW 2037. ℂ **02/9552 1141.** Fax 02/9692 9462. www.citysearch. com.au/syd/trickettsbandb. 7 units. A$154–A$176 (U.S.$100–$114) double; A$198 (U.S.$128.70) honeymoon

suite. Rates include continental breakfast. No credit cards. Free parking. Bus: 431 from George Street, or Airport Express Bus 352 from airport. **Amenities:** Tour desk. *In room:* Coffeemaker, iron.

MODERATE

Alishan International Guest House

The Alishan is another quiet place with a real Aussie feel. It's at the city end of Glebe Point Road, just 10 minutes by bus from the shops around Town Hall. Standard dorm rooms are spotless, light and bright, and come with two sets of bunks. Doubles have a double bed, a sofa and armchair, and an en-suite shower. Grab room 9 if you fancy sleeping on one of two single mattresses on the tatami mat floor, Japanese-style.

100 Glebe Point Rd., Glebe, NSW 2037. ℂ **02/9566 4048.** Fax 02/9525 4686. www.alishan.com.au. 19 units. A$30 (U.S.$19.50) dorm bed; A$100 (U.S.$65) double; A$145 (U.S.$94.25) family room. Extra person A$15 (U.S.$9.75). AE, MC, V. Secured parking available for 6 cars; otherwise, free on-street parking. Bus: 431 or 433 from George St., or Airport Express route 352 from airport. **Amenities:** Coin-op laundry; BBQ area; TV room; Internet access. *In room:* TV.

IN BONDI

Bondi Beach is a good place to stay if you want to be close to the surf and sand, though if you're getting around by public transport you'll need to catch a bus to Bondi Junction, then a train to the city center (you can stay on the bus all the way, but it takes forever).

As well as the properties recommended below, there's a good backpacker hostel called **Indy's** (ℂ **02/9365 4900**), at 35a Hall St., which offers four- to eight-person dorm rooms for A$16 (U.S.$11.20) in winter and A$20 (U.S.$14) in summer, and double rooms in a separate building opposite North Bondi Surf Club for the same price per person.

VERY EXPENSIVE

Bondi Beachside Inn ⚡

With such a great location, right on the beachfront, you can't get much better value than this. A modern seven-story hotel which prides itself on being family-friendly, the Beachside Inn has quite large rooms with compact bathrooms. The more expensive rooms have a balcony with ocean views. It's well loved by return travelers, so it's very advisable to book well ahead, especially during the Australian summer.

152 Campbell Parade, Bondi Beach, NSW 2026. ℂ **02/9130 5311.** Fax 02/9365 2646. www.bondiinn. com.au. 70 units. A$100–A$120 (U.S.$63–U.S.$76) double. AE, DC, MC, V. Free parking. Bus: 380 or 382 from Circular Quay. **Amenities:** 24-hr. reception; free security parking. *In room:* A/C, TV, fridge, tea/coffeemaking facilities, toaster.

Ravesi's on Bondi Beach ⚡

Right on Australia's most famous golden sands, this Art-Deco boutique property offers Mediterranean-influenced rooms with a beachy decor. Standard doubles are spacious, quite basic, and don't have air-conditioning—though you hardly need it with the ocean breeze. The one-bedroom suite is good for families, with two sofa beds in the living room. The split-level one-bedroom room has a bedroom upstairs and a single sofa bed in the living area. Rooms 5 and 6 and the split-level suite have the best views of the ocean. All rooms have Juliet balconies, and the split-level suite has its own terrace. If you're a light sleeper, request a room on the top floor because the popular Ravesi's Restaurant can cook up quite a bit of noise on busy nights.

Corner of Hall St. and Campbell Parade, Bondi Beach, NSW 2026. ℂ **02/9365 4422.** Fax 02/9365 1481. Ravesis@wheretostay.com.au. 16 units. A$115.50 (U.S.$75) standard double; A$176–$181.50 (U.S.$114–$118) double with side view; A$209–$236.50 (U.S.$135.85–$153.75) split-level 1-bedroom with side view; A209–$236.50 (U.S.$135.85–$153.75) 1-bedroom suite with ocean view. Penthouse $324.50 (U.S.$210). Extra person A$20 (U.S. $13). Two children under 12 stay free in parents' room. AE, DC, MC, V.

Parking at the Swiss-Grand Hotel nearby for A$5 (U.S.$3.25) for 24 hr. CityRail: Bondi Junction; then Bus 380. Bus: 380 from Circular Quay. **Amenities:** Restaurant; tour desk. *In room:* TV, iron.

Swiss-Grand Hotel 🏖🏖 Situated right on Bondi Beach, overlooking the Pacific, the Swiss-Grand is the best hotel in Bondi. The lobby is grand indeed, with high ceilings and stylish furniture. Rooms are spacious, and all come with a separate tub and shower in a rather luxurious bathroom. All rooms have two TVs; some have spas. All ocean-fronting rooms have balconies.

Corner of Campbell Parade and Beach Rd. (P.O. Box 219, Bondi Beach, NSW 2026). © 02/9365 5666, or 1800/655 252 in Australia, 800/344-1212 in the U.S., 0800/951 000 in the U.K., or 0800/056 666 in New Zealand. Fax 02/9365 9710. www.swissgrand.com.au. 230 units. A$297 (U.S.$193) double, A$341 (U.S.$221) double with ocean view; suites from A$385(U.S.$250). Extra person A$44 (U.S.$28.60). AE, DC, MC, V. Free parking. Bus: 380 from Circular Quay. **Amenities:** 2 restaurants (Modern Australian, brasserie); rooftop and indoor swimming pools; fitness center; spa, tour desk. *In room:* A/C, TV, coffeemaker, hair dryer, iron.

SERVICED APARTMENTS
Bondi Serviced Apartments If you plan on staying a week or more in Sydney then these pleasant privately-owned but managed apartments could be ideal. They're located on busy Bondi Road, a 25-minute walk to the beach, and right opposite you'll find a post office (with phones—the apartment complex doesn't have any), an Internet parlor, and a 24-hour supermarket. The rooms at the front of the hotel suffer from traffic noise, but are larger than the quieter ones out back. That said, all are good-size and have a nice feel about them. Each has a double bed (the front rooms also have an extra single), and a full kitchen. There's no air-conditioning (though the sea breeze does tend to cool Bondi down a bit in summer). You must book for a week or more, but if there are free rooms you can negotiate a 4-night stay. The owner describes it as a "no frills" complex—hence the lack of phones, Internet address, fax number, credit-card payments, and once-weekly servicing.

164–166 Bondi Rd., Bondi Beach, NSW 2026. © 02/9363 5529. No fax. 12 apts. 12 units. $385–$550 (U.S.$250–$357) apt, per week. Ask about cheaper rates for longer stays. No credit cards. Free parking. Bus 380 or 382 from city centre and Bondi Junction. **Amenities:** Laundry; weekly servicing. *In room:* TV, kitchen, iron and ironing board.

IN MANLY
If you decide to stay at my favorite beachside suburb, then you'll need to be aware that ferries from the city stop running at midnight. If you get stranded, you'll be facing either an expensive taxi fare (around A$35/U.S.$22.75), or you'll need to make your way to the bus stand behind Wynyard CityRail station to catch a night bus. Consider buying a Ferry Ten or JetCat Ten ticket, which will save you quite a bit of money in commuting expenses if you're staying in Manly for a few days.

As well as the recommendations below, Manly has several backpacker places worth checking out. The best of the bunch are **Manly Backpackers Beachside,** 28 Ragland St. (© **02/9977 3411;** fax: 02/9977 4379), which offers dorm beds for A$24 (U.S.$15.60), doubles without bathroom for A$70 (U.S.$45.50) and doubles with bathroom for A$80 (U.S.$52). There's a A$30 (U.S.$19.50) returnable key deposit.

VERY EXPENSIVE
Manly Pacific Parkroyal 🏖🏖 If you could bottle the views from this top-class hotel—across the sand and through the Norfolk Island Pines to the Pacific Ocean—you'd make a fortune. Standing on your private balcony in the evening with the sea breeze in your nostrils and the chirping of hundreds of lorikeets is

nothing short of heaven. The Manly Pacific is the only hotel of its class in this wonderful beachside suburb. There's nothing claustrophobic here, from the broad expanse of glittering foyer to the wide corridors and spacious rooms. Each standard room is light and modern with two double beds, a balcony, limited cable TV, and all the necessities from bathrobes to an iron and ironing board. Views over the ocean are really worth the extra money. The hotel is a 10-minute stroll, or a A$4 (U.S.$2.60) taxi ride, from the Manly ferry.

55 North Steyne, Manly, NSW 2095. ℂ **02/9977 7666**, or 800/835-7742 in the U.S. and Canada. Fax 02/9977 7822. www.parkroyal.com.au. 169 units. A$283–$327 (U.S.$184–$212) double, depending on view; A$512 (U.S.$332.80) suite. Extra person A$32 (U.S.$20.80). AE, DC, MC, V. Parking: $10 (U.S.$6.50). Ferry or JetCat: Manly. **Amenities:** 2 restaurants (International, buffet), 2 bars; rooftop pool; spa; exercise room; sauna; concierge; tour desk; 24-hr. room service; laundry service. *In room:* A/C, TV, dataport, minibar, coffeemaker, hair dryer, iron.

MODERATE

Manly Lodge ⚘ *(Kids)*   At first sight this ramshackle building halfway between the main beach and the harbor doesn't look like much—especially the cramped hostel-like foyer bristling with tourist brochures. But don't let the taint of tattiness put you off. Some of the rooms here are lovely, and the whole place has a nice atmosphere about it and plenty of character. Double rooms are not exceptional and come with a double bed, stone or carpet floors, a TV and VCR, and either a spa or a tub/shower combination. Some of the standard doubles, and all of the deluxe doubles have a kitchen. Family rooms have a set of bunk beds and a double in one room, and a shower. Family suites are very classy; each has a small kitchen area, one double and three singles in the bedroom, and two sofa beds in the living area. The lodge also has a table tennis table, and even an Olympic-size trampoline.

22 Victoria Parade, Manly, NSW 2095. ℂ **02/9977 8655.** Fax 02/9976 2090. www.manlylodge.com.au. 24 units. Standard double A$132–$154 (U.S.$85.80–$100) peak season, A$107.80–$132 (U.S.$69.70–$85.80) off-season; deluxe double A$154–$198 (U.S.$100–$128) peak season, A$132–$154 (U.S.$85.50–$100) off-season; family suite with spa A$264–$330 (U.S.$171.60–$214.50) peak season, A$187–$262 (U.S.$121.55–$170) off-season. Peak season is Christmas, Easter, and school holidays. Rates include continental breakfast. Extra person A$30 (U.S.$19.50); children under 10 A$16.50 (U.S.$10.70) extra. Ask about weekly rates; management will also negotiate off-season prices. AE, MC, V. Free parking. Ferry or JetCat: Manly. **Amenities:** Exercise room; spa; sauna; coin-op laundry. *In room:* A/C, TV.

Manly Paradise Motel and Beach Plaza Apartments ⚘   I walked into this place after taking a good look around the modern Manly Waterfront Apartment Hotel next door and immediately felt more at home here. The motel and the apartment complex are separate, but share the same reception area. Though there is one motel room that goes for A$90 (U.S.$58.50), it's a bit small for my liking; the rest of the irregularly shaped rooms are big yet cozy, and come with a shower (no tub) and a springy double bed. Though there is no restaurant, you can get breakfast in bed. My only concern is that the traffic outside can make it a little noisy during the day (but, hey, you'll probably be on the beach anyway) Some rooms have glimpses of the sea. A swimming pool (with views) on the roof is shared with the apartment complex.

The apartments are magnificent—very roomy, with thick carpets. They're stocked with everything you need, including a private laundry, a full kitchen with dishwasher, and two bathrooms (one with a tub). The sea views from the main front balcony are heart-stopping.

54 North Steyne, Manly, NSW 2095. ℂ **1800/815 789** in Australia, or 02/9977 5799. Fax 02/9977 6848. www.manlyparadise.com.au. 40 units. A$95–$145 (U.S.$61.75–$94.25) double motel unit; A$265

(U.S.$172.25) 2-bedroom apt. Extra person A$20 (U.S.$13). Ask about lower rates for long-term stays. AE, DC, MC, V. Free secured parking. Ferry or JetCat: Manly. **Amenities:** Swimming pool. *In room:* A/C, TV.

Periwinkle-Manly Cove Guesthouse   Nicely positioned just across the road from one of Manly's two harbor beaches, the Periwinkle is just a short walk from the ferry, the shops along the Corso, and the main ocean beach. Rooms are small and come with a double bed. Some have a shower and toilet attached (these go for the higher prices noted above), but otherwise you'll have to make do with one of four separate bathrooms (one has a tub). A full kitchen next to a pleasant-enough communal lounge means you could save money by not eating out. Rooms 5 and 10 are the nicest and have screened balconies overlooking the harbor (but no bathrooms). For atmosphere I prefer the Manly Lodge (see above). No smoking inside.

18–19 E. Esplanade, Manly, NSW 2095. ℰ **02/9977 4668.** Fax 02/9977 6308. 18 units, 11 with bathroom. A$126 (U.S.$81.90) double without bathroom; A$165 (U.S.$107.25) double with bathroom; A$148 (U.S.$96.20) triple without bathroom; A$176 (U.S.$114.40) triple with bathroom; A$160.50 (U.S.$104.30) quad without bathroom; A$192.50 (U.S.$125) quad with bathroom. Units with harbor views A$11 (U.S.$7.15) extra. Extra person A$33 (U.S.$21.45). Rates include continental breakfast. MC, V. Free parking. Ferry or JetCat: Manly. **Amenities:** Kitchen; common lounge. *In room:* TV, refrigerator.

IN MOSMAN
MODERATE
Buena Vista Hotel   If you want to see how wealthy Sydneysiders live, then come and stay in this upmarket northern suburb just a 10-minute walk from Taronga Zoo. The rooms above this popular local pub, just down the road from some of Sydney's most exclusive boutiques, are clean and comfortable, and a bargain by Sydney standards. Each comes with a springy queen-size bed or two singles, a small TV, and a sink; a few have balconies. All except room 13 have good city views. The best is room 1, which is larger and brighter than the rest, and comes with a large balcony with good views. Family rooms come with a double bed, a foldout sofa bed, and a trundle bed—all in one room. All rooms share nice bathrooms. The fabulous Balmoral Beach is a 10-minute walk away, or just 5 minutes by bus. Ask hotel staff for ferry times and bus/ferry connection details from Taronga Zoo and Mosman wharves. The taxi from city is around A$22 (U.S.$14.30). If you stay here I highly recommend the Japanese restaurant, Kyushu, at Shop 5, 9–11 Grosvenor St., Neutral Bay (ℰ **02/9953 8272**), about 5 minutes away by taxi.

76 Middle Head Rd., Mosman, NSW 2095. ℰ **02/9969 7022.** Fax 02/9968 2879. 14 units (5 doubles, 6 single, 1 twin, 1 family room) none with bathroom. A$82.50 (U.S.$53.60) double; A$150 (U.S.$97.50) double over Christmas and New Year's period; A$99 (U.S.$65) family room; A$200 (U.S.$130) family room over Christmas and New Year's. Rates include continental breakfast. AE, DC, MC, V. Ferry: Taronga Zoo, then a 5-min. bus ride. Bus: Taronga Zoo from Wynyard Station. **Amenities:** Restaurant, 2 bars. *In room:* TV.

AT THE AIRPORT
Stamford Sydney Airport 𝒻𝒻   This is the best airport hotel and the only five-star airport hotel in Australia. Opened in 1992, it has the largest rooms, each with a king-size bed or two doubles, access to airport information, and a good-size bathroom with tub. It's just 7 minutes from the airport via a free pickup service. Day-use rates for 2 to 4 hours cost A$85 (U.S.$55.25) and from 4 to 8 hours A$115 (U.S.$74.75).

Corner of O'Riordan and Robey sts. (P.O. Box 353, Mascot, Sydney, NSW 2020). ℰ **1300/301 391** in Australia, or 02/9317 2200. Fax 02/9317 3855. www.stamford.com.au. 314 units. A$270 (U.S.$175.50) double; from A$370 (U.S.$240) and up for suites. Extra person A$25 (U.S.$16.25). Children under 17 stay free in parents' room. Ask about discount packages and weekend rates. AE, DC, MC, V. A$5 (U.S.$3.25) self-parking fee for up to 10 days. **Amenities:** 2 restaurants (snacks, Modern Australian buffet), bar; good-size pool; fitness center; spa; sauna; concierge; business center 24-hr. room service; babysitting; laundry service; currency exchange; nonsmoking rooms; executive rooms. *In room:* A/C, TV, minibar, dataport, coffeemaker, hair dryer, iron.

4 Where to Dine

Sydney is a gourmet paradise, with an abundance of fresh seafood, a vast range of vegetables and fruit always in season, prime meats at inexpensive prices, and top-quality chefs making an international name for themselves. You'll find that Asian and Mediterranean cooking have had a major influence on Australian cuisine, with spices and herbs finding their way into most dishes. Immigration has brought with it almost every type of cuisine you could imagine, from African to Tibetan, from Russian to Vietnamese, with whole areas of the city dedicated to one type of food, while other areas are a true melting pot of styles.

Sydney is a great place to try "Modern Australian," or "Mod Oz," cuisine, which has been applauded by chefs and food critics around the world as one of the most important food trends going. Modern Australian cuisine emphasizes very fresh ingredients and a creative blend of European styles with Asian influence. (Some foodies complain, however, that some restaurants use the label "Modern Australian" as an excuse to serve skimpy portions—like one lamb chop atop a miniscule mound of mashed potatoes sprinkled with curry sauce). At its best, Modern Australian food is world-class, but you'll probably have to go to the best of Sydney's restaurants to really see what the scene is all about.

Value What to Know About BYO

Most moderate and inexpensive restaurants in Sydney are **BYO,** as in "bring your own" bottle, though some places may also have extensive wine and beer lists of their own. More and more moderately priced restaurants are introducing "corkage" fees, which mean you pay anywhere from A$1 to $4 (U.S.65¢ to $2.60) per person for the privilege of the waiter opening your bottle of wine. Very expensive restaurants discourage BYO.

Sydney's **cheap eats** are congregated in inner-city areas such as along King Street in Newtown, Crown Street in Darlinghurst, and Glebe Point Road in Glebe. There are also inexpensive joints scattered among the more upscale restaurants in Kings Cross and along trendy Oxford Street. There are some good food courts around Chinatown, including the **Sussex Street Food Court,** on Sussex Street, which offers Chinese, Malay, Thai, Japanese, and Vietnamese meals for between A$4 and $7 (U.S.$2.60 and $4.55).

I would avoid, however, the take-out booths found along the ferry wharves at Circular Quay, after revelations showed that some of them harbored nasty bugs. The fish-and-chip shop opposite the "bottle shop" (the Australian name for liquor store) is an exception—it also has some of the best french fries (chips) in Sydney.

Smoking is banned in all Sydney restaurants, except if you're eating from sidewalk tables.

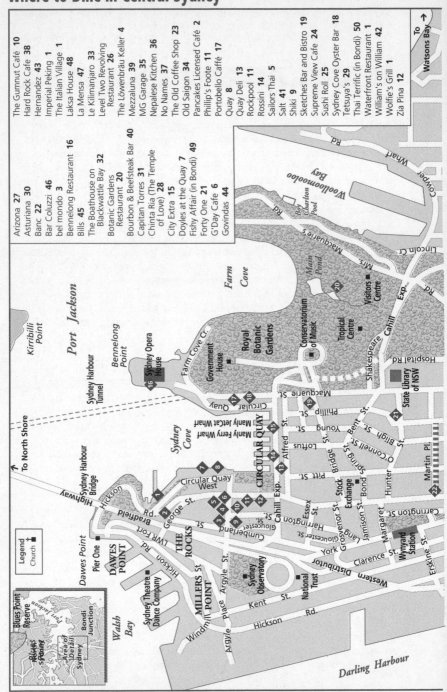

Arizona 27
Asturiana 30
Banc 22
Bar Coluzzi 46
bel mondo 3
Benelong Restaurant 16
Bills 45
The Boathouse on Blackwattle Bay 32
Botanic Gardens Restaurant 20
Bourbon & Beefsteak Bar 40
Capitan Torres 31
Chinta Ria (The Temple of Love) 28
City Extra 15
Doyles at the Quay 7
Fishy Affair (in Bondi) 49
Forty One 21
G'Day Cafe 6
Govindas 44

The Gumnut Café 10
Hard Rock Café 38
Hernandez 43
Imperial Peking 1
The Italian Village 1
Laksa House 48
La Mensa 47
Le Kilimanjaro 33
Level Two Revolving Restaurant 26
The Löwenbräu Keller 4
Mezzaluna 39
MG Garage 35
Nepalese Kitchen 36
No Names 37
The Old Coffee Shop 23
Old Saigon 34
Pancakes Licensed Café 2
Phillip's Foote 11
Portobello Caffè 17
Quay 8
Quay Deli 13
Rockpool 11
Rossini 14
Sailors Thai 5
Salt 41
Shiki 9
Sketches Bar and Bistro 19
Supreme View Cafe 24
Sushi Roll 25
Sydney Cove Oyster Bar 18
Tetsuya's 29
Thai Terrific (in Bondi) 50
Waterfront Restaurant 1
William's on William 42
Wolfie's Grill 1
Zia Pina 12

Jugglers, dancers and an assortment of acrobats fill the street.

She shoots you a wide-eyed look as a seven-foot cartoon character approaches.

What brought you here was wanting the kids

to see something magical while they still believed in magic.

America Online Keyword: Travel

With 700 airlines, 50,000 hotels and over 5,000 cruise and vacation getaways, you can now go places you've always dreamed of.

Travelocity.com
A Sabre Company
Go Virtually Anywhere.

"WORLD'S LEADING TRAVEL WEB SITE, 5 YEARS IN A ROW." WORLD TRAVEL AWARDS

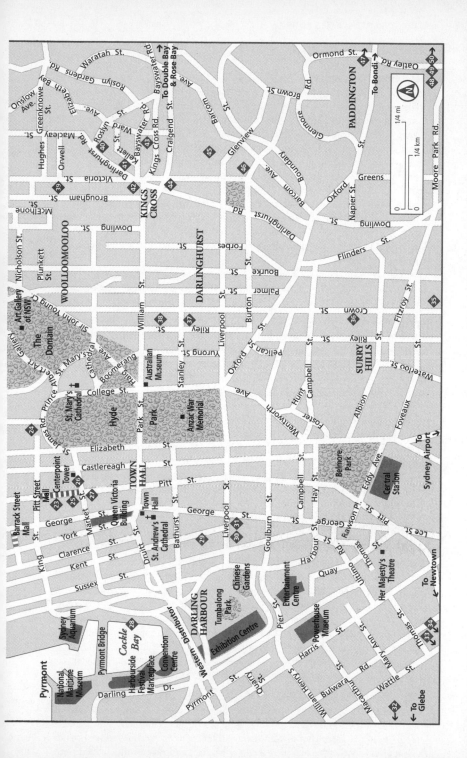

NEAR CIRCULAR QUAY
VERY EXPENSIVE

Bennelong Restaurant ⬌ MODERN AUSTRALIAN   If you go to Bondi, you have to swim in the Pacific; if you see the Harbour Bridge, you have to walk across it; if you visit the Opera House, you have to eat at Bennelong. The restaurant is as uniquely designed as the building itself, with tall glass windows that furrow around in an arch and grab the harbor and Circular Quay by the throat. Diners munch on main courses, such as roasted tuna steak with tomato-and-chili jam, or red emperor with sweet-and-sour eggplant baked in clay. Many would rather miss the first half of the opera they've paid a fortune to see rather than leave the Bennelong before eating dessert. One drawback is the continuing reports of slapdash service—places spoiled by tourism are sometimes like that. And keep in mind that all that Sydney sunlight plus all those windows can make lunch an uncomfortably hot experience in summer. *Note:* At press time, Bennelong was closed for renovations but scheduled to reopen shortly; to be safe, call ahead.

In the Sydney Opera House, Bennelong Point. ⓒ **02/9250 7548**, or 02/9250 7578. Reservations recommended. Main courses A$30–$37 (U.S.$19.50–$24). AE, DC, MC, V. Fri noon–2:30pm; Mon–Sat 7–10:30pm. CityRail, bus, or ferry: Circular Quay.

Forty One ⬌⬌ MODERN AUSTRALIAN   Powerful people, international celebrities, and average Sydneysiders out for a special celebration all come here to feel exclusive. It's won plenty of awards including the Amex Best Restaurant in Sydney City 2000 and the Best Restaurant in New South Wales 2000. The views over the city are terrific, the service is fun, the cutlery is the world's best, and Swiss chef Dietmar Sawyere has given the food a wickedly good Asian slant. In all, it's a very glamorous place to experience the best of Australian cuisine. Try the specialty crown roast wild hare, with braised Belgian endive and chartreuse jus. The seared yellow-fin tuna on sesame and miso English spinach is another favorite. If there are 6 to 10 people in your group, rent one of the three special private dining rooms.

Level 41, Chifley Tower, 2 Chifley Sq. ⓒ **02/9221 2500**. forty.one@chifleytower.com.au. Reservations required. Lunch main courses Mon–Fri A$28 (U.S.$18.20). Sun lunch: 3 courses A$85 (U.S.$55.25), 4 courses A$95 (U.S.$61.75), 5 courses A$110 (U.S.$71.50). Mon–Sat dinner: 3 courses A$75 (U.S.$48.75), 4 courses A$85 (U.S.$55.25), 5 courses A$95 (U.S.$61.75). AE, DC, MC, V. Mon–Fri noon–4pm; Mon–Sat 7–10pm. CityRail: Wynyard.

EXPENSIVE

Botanic Gardens Restaurant MEDITERRANEAN   You couldn't ask for a better walk to get to a restaurant than through the Royal Botanic Gardens, next to the Sydney Opera House. Enjoying lunch on the wisteria-covered balcony in the middle of Sydney's most beautiful park is a treat every visitor should enjoy. Main courses include the very popular roast loin of lamb with warm salad and couscous. The desserts such as the rhubarb compote with zabaglione and shortbread make my mouth water just reminiscing.

In the Royal Botanic Gardens. ⓒ **02/9241 2419**. Reservations recommended. Main courses A$18–$25 (U.S.$11.70–$16.25). AE, DC, MC, V. Daily noon–2:30pm. Bus or ferry: Circular Quay.

City Extra ITALIAN/AUSTRALIAN   Because this place stays open 24 hours, it's convenient if you get the munchies at a ridiculous hour. It's also nicely placed right next to the Manly ferry terminal. The plastic chairs and tables placed outside make it a pleasant spot to while away an inexpensive meal. A range of pastas are on offer as well as salads, pies, steaks, ribs, fish, and Asian-influenced dishes.

Finds A Great Place for Picnic Grub

If you're looking for a sandwich or something to take with you on a harbor cruise or on a stroll through the Royal Botanic Gardens, you can't go wrong with **Quay Deli**, E5 Alfred St. (next to the pharmacy under the Circular Quay CityRail station, facing the road; © **02/9241 3571**). Everything is fresh and tasty, and there are all sorts of goodies to choose from, including gourmet sandwiches and simple take-out foods such as olives, Greek dishes, pasta, fruit salads, green salads, meat pies, and the best English-style custard tarts around. Lunch items go for A$1.80 to $4.50 (U.S.$1.25 to $3.15). It's open Monday through Friday from 5am to 6:45pm, Saturday from 9am to 4pm. No credit cards.

There's also a fat selection of desserts. The food is much nicer and a better value next door at Rossini (see below).

Shop E4, Circular Quay. © 02/9241 1422. Main courses A$10.30–$17.65 (U.S.$6.70–$11.50). 10% surcharge midnight–6am, Sundays, and public holidays. AE, DC, MC, V. Daily 24 hr. CityRail, bus, or ferry: Circular Quay.

Portobello Caffé PIZZA/SANDWICH   Sharing the same address as the Sydney Cove Oyster Bar (and the same priceless views), the Portobello Caffé offers first-class gourmet sandwiches on Italian wood-fired bread, small but delicious gourmet pizzas, breakfast croissants, snacks, cakes, and hot and cold drinks. Walk off with sensational ice cream in a cone for around A$3 (U.S.$1.95).

No.1 Eastern Esplanade, Circular Quay East. © 02/9247 8548. Main courses A$8 (U.S. $5.20). 10% surcharge Sun and public holidays. AE, DC, MC, V. Minimum credit-card purchase A$30 (U.S.$19.50). Daily 8am–11:50pm. CityRail, bus, or ferry: Circular Quay.

Rossini *⋒ Kids* ITALIAN   This cafeteria-style Italian restaurant opposite Ferry Wharf 5 at Circular Quay is wonderfully positioned for people-watching. The outside tables are perfect spots for breakfast or a quick bite before a show at the Opera House. Breakfast croissants, Italian donuts, muffins, and gorgeous Danish pastries cost just A$2 (U.S.$1.30), and bacon and eggs just A$8 (U.S.$5.20). Wait to be seated for lunch or dinner, make your choice, pay your money at the counter, take a ticket, and then pick up your food. Meals, including veal parmigiana, cannelloni, ravioli, chicken crêpes, and octopus salad, are often huge. You could easily get away with one meal between two—ask for an extra plate—and while not the best Italian you'll ever eat, they are tasty enough. Coffee fanatics I know rate the Rossini brew as only average.

Shop W5, Circular Quay. © 02/9247 8026. Main courses A$10–$15 (U.S.$6.50–$9.75). Cash only. Daily 7am–10pm. CityRail, bus, or ferry: Circular Quay.

Sketches Bar and Bistro *⋒* PASTA   Sketches is a favorite with people on their way to the Opera House and those who really know a cheap meal when they taste one. Here's how it works: After getting the barman's attention, point to one of three different sized plates stuck to the bar above your head—the small size is adequate if you're an average eater, the medium plate is good for filling up after a hard day of sightseeing (and no lunch), but I've yet to meet a man who can handle the large serving with its accompanying bread, pine nuts, and Parmesan cheese. Then, with ticket in hand, head toward the chefs in white hats and place your order. There are 12 pastas to choose from and several sauces, including carbonara, marinara, pesto, vegetarian, and some unusual ones to dishearten pasta purists, such as south Indian curry. Meals are cooked in front of you in a few minutes while you wait.

In the Hotel Inter-Continental, 117 Macquarie St. (enter from Bridge St.). ⓒ **02/9240 1210.** Reservations recommended. Pasta A$10.90–$17 (U.S.$7–$11). AE, DC, MC, V. Mon–Fri 5:30–9:30pm, Sat 5:30–10:30pm. CityRail, bus, or ferry: Circular Quay.

Sydney Cove Oyster Bar SEAFOOD   Just before you reach the Sydney Opera House you'll notice a couple of small shed-like buildings with tables and chairs set up to take in the stunning views of the harbor and the Harbour Bridge. The first of these is a Sydney institution, serving some of the best oysters in town. Light meals such as Asian-style octopus and seared tuna steak are also on the menu.

No. 1 Eastern Esplanade, Circular Quay East. ⓒ **02/9247 2937.** Main courses A$20–$23.50 (U.S.$13–$15.30). 10% surcharge weekends and public holidays. AE, DC, MC, V. Mon–Sat 11am–11pm, Sun 11am–8pm. CityRail, bus, or ferry: Circular Quay.

IN THE ROCKS
VERY EXPENSIVE
bel mondo 𝞙𝞙 NORTHERN ITALIAN   With its uncomplicated northern Italian cuisine, bel mondo has deservedly positioned itself alongside the very best of Sydney's upscale restaurants. At this family-run affair, chef Stefano Manfredi is helped out in the kitchen by his mum, Franca, a pasta diva in her own right. The restaurant is large and long with high ceilings, and the energetic pace and the banging and clashing coming from the open kitchen give the place a New York feel. Standout appetizers include grilled sea scallops with soft polenta and pesto. Favorite main courses include roast lamb with rosemary and roast potatoes, potato gnocchi with burnt butter and Parmesan, and barbecued duck with balsamic vinegar. The wine list is very extensive. bel mondo's **Antibar** is cheaper and more relaxed; it offers some of the best antipasto I've ever tasted, as well as light meals (from A$13.50–$21.50/U.S.$8.80–$14) and features jazz on Friday evenings from 5:30 to 7:30pm.

3rd floor in the Argyle Department Store, 18–24 Argyle St., The Rocks. ⓒ **02/9241 3700.** reservations@ belmondo.com.au. Reservations recommended well in advance. Main courses A$26.50–$45.50 (U.S.$17.20–$29.60). 10% surcharge Sun and public holidays. AE, DC, MC, V. Mon–Fri 12:30–2:30pm; Mon–Thurs 6:30–10:30pm, Fri–Sat 6:30–11pm, Sun 6:30–10pm. CityRail, bus, or ferry: Circular Quay.

Quay 𝞙𝞙 SEAFOOD   Without question, Quay (formerly known as Bilson's) is Sydney's best fish and seafood restaurant—and with its enviable location on top of the cruise-ship terminal, it offers perhaps the loveliest view in Sydney, too. In good weather the sun sparkles off the water and through the large glass windows the Opera House, the city skyline, the North Shore suburbs, and the Harbour Bridge all look magnificent. At night, when the lights from the city wash over the harbor and the bridge and the Opera House's sails are all lit up, the view is even better. The signature dishes are the basil-infused tuna, the Kangaroo Island roast chicken with ravioli and truffles, and the popular chargrilled beef tenderloin on mashed potatoes. The service is exemplary. Expensive, yet select, this restaurant has tempted all the big-name visitors to Sydney. Believe me, they tell all their friends.

On the upper level of the Overseas Passenger Terminal, Circular Quay West, The Rocks. ⓒ **02/9251 5600.** Reservations recommended well in advance. Main courses A$38–$50 (U.S.$24–$31). A$6 (U.S.$3.90) per-person surcharge Sun and public holidays. AE, DC, MC, V. Mon–Fri noon–2:30pm; Mon–Sun 6–10pm. CityRail, bus, or ferry: Circular Quay.

Where to Dine in The Rocks

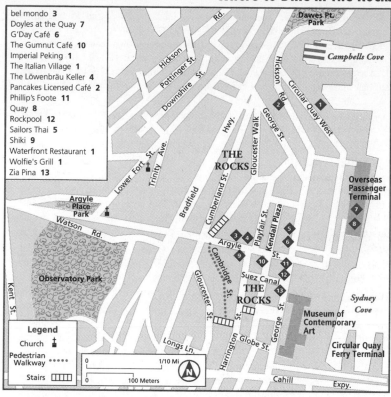

bel mondo **3**
Doyles at the Quay **7**
G'Day Café **6**
The Gumnut Café **10**
Imperial Peking **1**
The Italian Village **1**
The Löwenbräu Keller **4**
Pancakes Licensed Café **2**
Phillip's Foote **11**
Quay **8**
Rockpool **12**
Sailors Thai **5**
Shiki **9**
Waterfront Restaurant **1**
Wolfie's Grill **1**
Zia Pina **13**

Legend

Church ✝

Pedestrian Walkway •••••

Stairs ⊞⊞⊞

0 _____ 1/10 Mi
0 _____ 100 Meters
Ⓝ

Rockpool 👁👁 MODERN AUSTRALIAN   The Rockpool is an institution in Sydney, known for its inventive food. It's approached by a steep ramp and opens up into two stories of ocean-green carpet, designer chairs, and stainless steel. Along with the bar, the kitchen—with its busy chefs and range of copper pots and pans—is very much at the center of things. Menus change regularly, but you can expect to find anything from a dozen fresh oysters and spanner crab with lemon ravioli to fish cooked with coconut milk and Indian garam masala and served with snow peas and semolina noodles. On my last visit, the desserts were a letdown after the fabulous main courses.

109 George St., The Rocks. ☏ 02/9252 1888. Reservations required. Main courses A$38 (U.S.$24.70). AE, DC, MC, V. Mon–Sat 6–11pm. CityRail, bus, or ferry: Circular Quay.

EXPENSIVE

Doyles at the Quay SEAFOOD   Just below Quay (see above) is Doyles, a name synonymous with seafood in Sydney. Most customers sit outside to enjoy the fabulous views across the harbor, though a set of thick green railings does somewhat interrupt the view of the Opera House. Businesspeople and tourists come here if they don't want to lay out the cash for Quay or if they fancy a more relaxed style. The most popular dish here is basically pricey fish-and-chips (choose between ocean trout, garfish, John Dory, swordfish, whiting, and salmon). You can also pick up a dozen oysters for A$20 (U.S.$13) or a lobster for A$65 (U.S.$42.25). A second Doyles, **Doyles on the Beach** 👁👁

(© **02/9337 2007**), at Watsons Bay, serves fabulous food. Nearby is a third Doyles, **Doyles Fisherman's Wharf** (© **02/9337 1572**), located on the ferry wharf; it used to be a take-out joint, but now has sit-down service. Ferries run to Watsons Bay from Circular Quay in time for lunch at 10:30, 11:30am, and 12:30pm Monday through Friday, and at 11:15am and 1:15pm on Saturday, Sunday, and public holidays. On weekdays the last ferry returns at 3:50pm, and on weekends at 4:15 and 6:10pm.

Overseas Passenger Terminal, Circular Quay. © **02/9252 3400**. Main courses A$20–$33 (U.S.$13–$21.45). DC, MC, V. Daily 11:30am–2:45pm; Mon–Sat 5:30–9:30pm, Sun 5:30–9pm. CityRail, bus, or ferry: Circular Quay.

G'Day Café *Value* CAFE   According to the manager, about half the tourists who visit Sydney visit this little place in the heart of The Rocks. That's not surprising considering it offers simple but satisfying food at around half the price you'd expect to pay in such a tourist precinct. The interior is uninspiring, but out the back there's a pleasant leafy courtyard. Among the offerings are foccacia sandwiches, hearty soups, salads, burgers, lasagna, chili con carne, and beef curry.

83 George St., The Rocks. © **02/9241 3644**. Main courses A$3–$7 (U.S.$1.95–$4.55). AE. Sun–Thurs 5am–midnight, Fri–Sat 5am–3am. CityRail, bus or ferry: Circular Quay.

The Gumnut Café *Kids* MODERN AUSTRALIAN   A hearty lunch in a courtyard shaded from the sun by giant cream umbrellas—ah, heaven. With a great location in the heart of The Rocks, this restaurant also has an extensive indoor seating area, so it's a perfect place to take a break from all that sightseeing. The breakfast specials (A$8.50/U.S.$5.50) are very popular with guests from surrounding hotels, while at lunchtime it's always bustling with tourists and local office workers. Lunchtime blackboard specials cost A$11 (U.S.$7.15). More regular fare includes the disappointing Ploughman's Lunch (why spoil a traditional English meal of bread, cheese, and pickles by limiting the bread and adding unappealing vegetables and salad?), the better chicken and leek pies, and quite good pasta and noodle dishes. Filling Turkish bread sandwiches cost between A$7.70 and $9 (U.S.$5 to $5.85). The courtyard is heated in winter, making it quite cozy.

28 Harrington St., The Rocks. © **02/9247 9591**. Main courses A$6.90–$13 (U.S.$4.50–$8.45). AE, DC, MC, V. Daily 8am–5pm. CityRail, bus, or ferry: Circular Quay.

The Löwenbräu Keller ☆ BAVARIAN   Renowned for celebrating Oktoberfest every day for the past 20 years, this is the place to come to watch Aussies let their hair down. You can come for lunch and munch a club sandwich or focaccia in the glassed-off atrium while watching the daytime action of The Rocks. For a livelier scene, head here on a Friday or Saturday night, when mass beer-sculling (chugging) and yodeling are accompanied by a brass band, and costumed waitresses ferry foaming beer steins about the atmospheric, cellar-like inside. Hearty southern German and Austrian fare and no less than 17 varieties of German beers in bottle or on draught (tap), are served. There's a good wine list, and, surprisingly, vegetarians are well catered for, too.

18 Argyle St. (at Playfair St.), The Rocks. © **02/9247 7785**. Reservations recommended. Main courses A$15–$21.50 (U.S. $9.75–$14). AE, DC, MC, V. Daily 9:30am–2am (kitchen closes at 11pm.) CityRail, bus, or ferry: Circular Quay.

Pancakes Licensed Café AMERICAN COFFEE-SHOP FARE/PANCAKES   Buttermilk and chocolate pancakes, and French crêpes filled with seafood,

chicken, and mushrooms, vegetables in a basil-cream sauce, or smoked ham and
cheese are the most popular dishes served up in this old warehouse done up in
Art-Deco style. The beef ribs, pastas, and pizzas are also good sellers.

10 Hickson Rd. (enter from Hickson Rd. or George St.), The Rocks. © 02/9247 6371. Reservations not
accepted. Main courses A$12.95–$21.95 (U.S.$8.40–$14.30); breakfast (served 24 hr.) A$8.95–$11.95
(U.S.$5.80–$7.80). AE, DC, MC, V. Daily 24 hr. CityRail, bus, or ferry: Circular Quay.

Phillip's Foote BARBECUE   Venture behind this historic pub and you'll find
a popular courtyard strung with tables and benches and large barbecues. Choose
your own steak, lemon sole, trout, chicken, or pork and throw it on the "barbie." It's fun, it's filling, and you might even meet some new friends while your
meal's sizzling.

101 George St., The Rocks. © 02/9241 1485. Main courses A$21 (U.S.$13) weekdays, A$22 (U.S.$14) weekends. AE, MC, V. Mon–Sat noon–midnight; Sun noon–10pm. CityRail, bus, or ferry: Circular Quay.

Sailors Thai ✿ THAI   With a reputation as hot as the chilies in its jungle
curry, Sailors Thai canteen attracts lunchtime crowds who come to eat great-
tasting noodles and the likes of pork and prawn won ton soup, red curry with
lychees, and Thai salads at its single, stainless steel table lined with some
40 chairs. Four other tables overlook the cruise-ship terminal and the quay.
Downstairs, the a la carte restaurant serves inventive food which is a far cry from
your average Thai restaurant, like stir-fried pineapple curry with chilies and
cashew nuts and a wonderfully glutenous coconut ash pudding, made from the
ash of burnt coconuts cooked with licorice root, coconut water, rice flower, and
sugar.

106 George St., The Rocks. © 02/9251 2466. Reservations required well in advance in restaurant; not
accepted in canteen. Main courses A$14–$34 (U.S.$9.10–$22.10) in restaurant, A$11–$16 (U.S.$7.15–
$10.40) in canteen. AE, DC, MC, V. Restaurant Mon–Fri noon–2pm, Mon–Sat 6–10pm; canteen daily
noon–8pm. CityRail, bus, or ferry: Circular Quay.

Shiki ✿ TRADITIONAL JAPANESE   Shiki is making a name for itself as a
top-flight traditional Japanese eatery. Though you can eat at Western-style
tables, or the sushi bar, there are also five tatami rooms available, where you sit
around a raised table on Japanese mats. Either way you can enjoy some good
views over The Rocks (it's especially magical at night when the ferry lights strung
across the area's trees are lit up). There are plenty of sushi, sashimi, and sukiyaki
dishes on the menu, but "pot-cooking" at the table is very popular. Of these the
Tobanyaki, where customers simmer a combination of beef and seafood on their
own burner, steals the show. If you want your main meal during the day consider the lunch menu, costing between A$13.50 (U.S.$8.80) and A$20
(U.S.$13). The sushi plate—with seven pieces of sushi, six pieces of tuna roll, a
salad, and miso soup—costs A$20 (U.S.$13).

Clock Tower Square, corner of Argyle and Harrington sts., The Rocks. © 02/9252 2431. Reservations recommended well in advance. Meals around A$25–$40 (U.S.$16–$25) per person. AE, DC, MC, V. Mon–Fri
noon–2:30pm; Mon–Sun 6–10pm.

Waterfront Restaurant ✿   You can't help but notice the mast, rigging, and
sailing ship sails that mark this restaurant, one of four in a row right next to the
water below the main spread of The Rocks. It's very popular at lunchtime when
businesspeople snap up the best seats outside in the sunshine, but at night with
the colors of the city washing over the harbor it can be magical. Most main
courses cost a hefty A$25 (U.S.$16.25) or so, but for that you get a choice of
such things as steaks, mud crab, fish fillets, prawns, or a seafood platter. The

food is nice and simple, with the markup added for the glorious position and views.

In the same building you'll find the Waterfront's sister restaurants **Wolfie's Grill** (© **02/9241 5577**), which serves good chargrilled beef and seafood dishes for A$22 to $26 (U.S.$14.30–$16.90), and **The Italian Village** (© **02/9247 6111**), which serves regional Italian cuisine for A$22 to $30 (U.S.$14.30–$19.50). The third in the line is an excellent Chinese restaurant, the **Imperial Peking** (© **02/9247 7073**), which serves excellent food for similar prices. All four restaurants offer fantastic water views and indoor and outdoor dining.

In Campbell's Storehouse, 27 Circular Quay West, The Rocks. © **02/9247 3666**. Reservations recommended. Main courses A$23.90–$42.50 (U.S.$15.50–$27.60). A$3 (U.S.$1.95) per person surcharge weekends and public holidays. AE, DC, MC, V. Daily 11am–10pm. CityRail, bus, or ferry: Circular Quay.

Zia Pina PIZZA/PASTA   With ten tables crammed downstairs and another 24 upstairs, there's not much room to breathe in this cramped traditional pizzeria and spaghetti house. But squeeze in between the close-fit bare-brick walls and wallow in the clashes and clangs coming from the hard-working chefs in the kitchen. Pizzas come in two sizes; the larger feeds two people. Servings of delicious gelato go for a cool A$4 (U.S.$2.60).

93 George St., The Rocks. © **02/9247 2255**. Reservations recommended well in advance. Main courses A$7.80–$19 (U.S.$5–$12.35). AE, DC, MC, V. Daily noon–3pm; Sun–Mon 5–9pm, Tues–Thurs 5–10:30pm, Fri–Sat 5–11:30pm. CityRail, bus, or ferry: Circular Quay.

NEAR TOWN HALL
VERY EXPENSIVE

BANC MODERN FRENCH   Winner of "Best Restaurant" in the 2001 *Sydney Morning Herald* Good Food Awards, Banc is an upmarket establishment which serves up top-class French-inspired food in a formal atmosphere of columns and white linen-clothed tables. It's popular with business executives and high flyers. Service is excellent, and the cellar holds more than 900 wine labels from Australia and abroad. The advertised dishes are a mouthful in themselves, among them an "Assiette of Lamb with Haricot Blanc and a Ragout of Vegetables," an "Open Ravioli of Crustacea with a Vanilla and Oyster Nage," and "Pan-Fried John Dory and Roasted Scallops with a Curry Emulsion." Dress to impress.

53 Martin Place. © **02/9233 5300**. Reservations essential. Main courses A$38–$45 (U.S.$24.70–$29.25); 8-course meal with wines A$125 (U.S.$81); vegetarian option A$110 (U.S.$71.50). AE, DC, MC, V. Tues–Fri noon–2:30pm; Tues–Sat 6.30–10.30pm. CityRail: Martin Place.

Tetsuya's MODERN JAPANESE   Chinese chef Tetsuya Wakuda is arguably Sydney's most famous chef, and his food is certainly cutting edge. This is not Japanese food as you might know it, but instead a fusion of eastern and western styles that has made him the darling of Australian cuisine. Everybody who is anybody wants to eat here—so much so that it's very difficult to get a table. To have a chance you need to book 4 weeks in advance (they don't take bookings before this time). The restaurant is stylish and light, and the food mind-blowing. The menu is constantly changing, but to give you an idea think tofu with duck foie gras and sherry vinegar; marinated roast breast of duck with coffee; tartare of tuna with olive oil and wasabi jelly; and seared fillet of veal with porcini mushrooms, sautéed green beans, and asparagus.

529 Kent St., Sydney. © **02/9267 2900**. Lunch A$100 (U.S.$65) per person (8 courses); dinner $155 (U.S.$100.75) per person (12 courses). AE, DC, MC, V. Fri noon–3pm; Tues–Sat 6–10pm. CityRail: Town Hall.

EXPENSIVE

Level Two Revolving Restaurant *(Kids* GRILLS/ROASTS/SEAFOOD/ ASIAN   For those not scared of heights, Level Two offers a self-service all-you-can-eat buffet—ideal for those who don't want to pay for the a la carte goodies a floor down at its sister restaurant, Level One. This place is very popular with tourists, who come here for the stupendous views right across Sydney and, on a clear day, as far as the Blue Mountains. The dining area takes about an hour to fully rotate, but even going this slowly I find it a bit off-putting—especially when you're some 250 meters (820 ft.) up. You can heap your plate with a selection of five appetizers, then choose between 15 main courses, including steaks, roasts, pork knuckles, beef Stroganoff, seafood, and Asian dishes. There are also five desserts to choose from.

In Centerpoint Tower, Market St. (between Pitt and Castlereiagh sts.). *(C)* **02/9233 3722.** Reservations recommended. Lunch Mon–Sat A$34 (U.S.$23.80); lunch Sun A$37 (U.S.$25.90); early dinner A$37 (U.S.$25.90); regular dinner A$40 (U.S.$28). A$15 (U.S.$10.50) for children 3–12 at lunch and early dinner. 10% surcharge (on drinks only) weekends and public holidays. AE, DC, MC, V. Daily 11:30am–2:15pm and 5–11:45pm. CityRail: St. James. Monorail: City Centre.

MODERATE

Arizona TEX-MEX   Cactus-strewn frescoes, a split-log-cabin exterior, and Native American figurines leave no doubt about where Arizona is coming from. Split into two separate venues, opposite each other on the second floor of a low-rise on Pitt Street (just across from the Pitt Street Mall), Arizona is a fun place with pretty good food and a youthful atmosphere. Main meals include T-bone steak, chargrilled salmon steak, Cajun chicken burger, and Texas barbecued pork ribs and wings.

Corner of Pitt and Market sts. *(C)* **02/9261 1077.** Main courses A$12–$18 (U.S.$8.40–$12.60). The Cowboy Bar: Mon noon–10pm, Tues noon–10:30pm, Wed noon–11pm, Thurs–Fri noon–2am, Sat noon–3:30am, Sun noon–8pm. Arizona 101 Bar & Grill: Mon–Sat noon–3pm, Mon–Wed 5–9pm, Thurs–Fri noon–10pm, Sat 5–10pm. AE, DC, MC, V. CityRail, bus, or monorail: Town Hall.

Capitan Torres SPANISH   Sydney's Spanish quarter, based on Liverpool Street (a 10-min. walk from Town Hall station on your right just past Sydney's main cinema strip) offers some great restaurants, of which Capitan Torres is my favorite. Downstairs is a tapas bar with traditional stools, Spanish serving staff, and lots of authentic dark oak. Upstairs on two floors is a fabulous restaurant with heavy wooden tables, chairs, and an atmosphere thick with sangria and regional food. The garlic prawns are incredible, and the whole snapper a memorable experience. The tapas are better, though, at **Asturiana** (*(C)* **02/9264 1010**), another Spanish restaurant a couple of doors down on the same street. Make sure you insist on eating at the bar for that authentic experience.

   Though Capitan Torres is a favorite, one Frommer's reader recently complained of bad service and mediocre food. I hope it was simply an off day.

73 Liverpool St. (just past the cinema strip on George St., near Town Hall). *(C)* **02/9264 5574.** Main courses A$16.50–$19 (U.S.$10.70–$12.35); tapas A$5.50–$9.90 (U.S.$3.60–$6.40). AE, DC, MC, V. Daily noon–3pm; Mon–Sat 6–11pm; Sun 6–10pm. CityRail: Town Hall.

Supreme View Café *(K* *(Finds* CAFE   If you happen to be in the city center, then this fabulous, largely undiscovered restaurant/cafe is a must for the great value food and absolutely fantastic views reaching over Hyde Park and even to the harbor. It's very large inside, has panoramic windows, and serves meals from the counter. Breakfasts are hearty and include bacon and eggs, omelets, and cereals. It's particularly handy if you are staying in the lower Oxford street area. All day dishes include the likes of sandwiches, Caesar salad, homemade pies, pastas, and lasagna. Even if you're not hungry it's well worth popping in for a coffee.

Level 14. Law Courts Building, 184 Pillip St. (Queens Square). ⓒ **02/9230 8224**. Main courses A$8–$13. Coffee and cake $5. Cash only. Open 7am–5pm Mon–Fri.

Sushi Roll ⓕ SUSHI   The fresh, simple food served up at this bargain-basement take-out booth is certainly a healthy alternative to the greasy edibles which many travelers end up satisfying their hunger on. A large range of sushi and nori rolls peek out from behind the counter here, and you can eat at the tables opposite. The gourmet sandwiches and meals served up by other establishments in the food court here make it a worthwhile stopover after a hard morning's shopping and sightseeing.

Sydney Central Plaza (downstairs in the food hall next to Grace Brothers dept. store on Pitt Street Mall). ⓒ **02/9233 5561**. Sushi rolls A$1.70 (U.S.$1.10) each. No credit cards. Mon–Wed and Sat 8am–7pm, Thurs 8am–10pm, Sun 10am–6pm.

DARLING HARBOUR

Chinta Ria (The Temple of Love) ⓕ MALAYSIAN   Cockle Bay's star attraction for those who appreciate good food and a fun ambience without paying a fortune, Chinta Ria is on the roof terrace of the three-story Cockle Bay development. In a round building dominated by a giant golden Buddha in the center, Chinta Ria serves up fairly good "hawker-style" (read: cheap and delicious) Malaysian food. While the food is indeed good, the atmosphere is even more memorable. The service is slow, but who cares in such an interesting space, with plenty of nooks, crannies, and society folk to look at. There are seats outside (some get the noise of the highway), but the best views unfold inside. The hot-and-sour soup—a broth made with tofu, mushrooms, bamboo shoots, and preserved cabbage—makes an interesting starter, and I recommend the chili prawns and the *Hokkeien Char* (soft-cooked egg noodles with extras) as main dishes.

Cockle Bay Wharf Complex. ⓒ **02/9264 3211**. Main courses A$12–$25 (U.S.$7.80–$16.25). AE, DC, MC, V. Daily noon–2:30pm and 6–11pm. Ferry or monorail: Darling Harbour.

SURRY HILLS
VERY EXPENSIVE

MG Garage ⓕⓕⓕ MODERN AUSTRALIAN   This fine-dining restaurant has caused quite a stir in Sydney, and not just because it's in a car showroom. It's a glamorous, modern eatery with good service and a fashionable crowd. Tables are difficult to get, so you'll need to book at least a week in advance. Among the offerings you might find are the steam fillet of beef with dumplings, and roast pigeon with pine mushrooms. Best to get here by taxi, or a shortish walk from Central station.

490 Crown St., Surry Hills. ⓒ **02/9383 9383**. dpearce@trivettclassic.com.au. Reservations essential. Main courses A$28–$36 (U.S.$18.20–$23.40). AE, DC, MC, V. Mon–Fri noon–2:30pm; Mon–Sat 6:30–10pm.

MODERATE

Nepalese Kitchen NEPALESE   Adventurous gourmands around here dig into this somewhat mildly spiced cuisine, which is something like a mixture of Indian and Chinese. Steamed dumplings, called "momo," and stuffed crispy pancakes made with black-lentil flour are interesting to start with, and the goat curry is the pick of the main courses. Also popular is the chargrilled lamb or chicken marinated in roasted spices. The curries are very tasty, and there's a large

Something Fishy

If you like fresh seafood at cheap prices, then saunter down to the **Sydney Fishmarket** (*, on the corner of Bank Street and Pyrmont Bridge Road, Pyrmont (© **02/9660 1611,** or call the **Fishline** at © **02/ 9552 2180** for information on special events such as seafood cooking classes). The major fish retailers here sell sashimi at the cheapest prices in Sydney, but if you prefer your seafood cooked, then don't miss these two fabulous outlets.

Musumeci Seafoods, found outside the large blue retail arcade, is a little more than a stall with a hotplate, but you won't find baby octopus cooked better in any of Sydney's glitzy restaurants. Seafood combinations are also offered, with a small plate (easily enough for one person) costing just A$5.50 (U.S.$3.60), and a large plate A$11 (U.S.$7.15). Musumeci's is open Friday and Sunday from 7am to 4pm and Saturday from 6am to 4pm.

Also mouthwatering are the stir-fries at nearby **Christies,** a seafood retailer inside the main retail building. Here you pick your own seafood, such as fresh calamari or mussels, and your own sauce, and they just throw it straight in a wok and cook it for you on the spot. Stir-fries or great Asian-style seafood noodle dishes cost just A$5.50 (U.S.$3.60). Christies cooks are on the job daily from 7am to 7pm.

To get to the Fishmarket, take the light rail (tram) from Central Station, Chinatown, or Darling Harbour to the Fishmarket stop, or you can walk from Darling Harbour (follow the signs).

selection of vegetarian dishes, including flavorsome eggplant curry. Accompany your food with "achars," or relishes, to highlight the flavors of your dishes.

481 Crown St., Surry Hills. © 02/9319 4264. Main courses A$8–$12 (U.S.$5.60–$8.40); 2-course meal A$18 (U.S.$12.60). AE, DC, MC, V. Daily 6–11pm. CityRail: Central, then a 10-min. walk up Devonshire St.

IN KINGS CROSS/DARLINGHURST
EXPENSIVE
Mezzaluna (*(* MODERN ITALIAN   Exquisite food, flawless service, and an almost unbeatable view across the city's western skyline have all helped Mezzaluna position itself firmly among Sydney's top restaurants. A cozy, candlelit place with plain white walls and polished wooden floorboards, the main dining room opens up onto a huge, all-weather terrace kept warm in winter by giant, overhead fan heaters. The restaurant's owner, well-known Sydney culinary icon Beppi Polesi, provides an exceptional wine list to complement a menu that changes daily. There's always a fabulous risotto on the menu though, while other delights may include rack of lamb roasted with olives and oregano and served with baked baby eggplant, or grilled fillet of Atlantic salmon on rocket with a borlotti-bean purée. Whatever you choose, you can't go wrong. I highly recommend this place—of all Sydney's restaurants I chose this to take my long-term girlfriend for her birthday.

123 Victoria St., Potts Point. © 02/9357 1988. www.mezzaluna.com.au. Reservations recommended. Main courses A$19.50–$31 (U.S.$12.70–$20). A$3 (U.S. $2) surcharge Sun. AE, DC, MC, V. Tues–Sun noon–3pm and 6–11pm. Closed public holidays. CityRail: Kings Cross.

Salt ⟨R⟩⟨R⟩ MODERN AUSTRALIAN   This is the really "in" place for the fashion crowd; you'll need to dress up in your coolest outfit to fit into the scene happening here. Inside it's all sleek and chrome, with tables just big enough for two. The food is innovative and cutting-edge, and could include anything from quails eggs encrusted with salt and sugar to a delicate raw belly of salmon lacquered with shallot and ginger. A Martini is the drink of choice. Some people though might find it all a bit pretentious.

229 Darlinghurst Rd., Darlinghurst (in the Kirketon Hotel). ℂ 02/9332 2566. Reservations essential. Main courses A$28–$35 (U.S.$18.20–$22.75). AE, DC, MC, V. Open Sun–Fri noon–3pm; Daily 6–11pm.

MODERATE

Bourbon & Beefsteak Bar INTERNATIONAL   The Bourbon & Beefsteak has been a popular Kings Cross institution for more than 30 years, and it still attracts everyone from visiting U.S. sailors and tourists to businesspeople and ravers. The fact that it's open 24 hours means many people never seem to leave—occasionally you'll find someone taking a nap in the bathroom. The American-themed restaurant is busy at all hours, churning out steaks, seafood, salads, Tex-Mex, ribs, seafood specials, and pasta. Breakfast is served daily from 6 to 11am.

Every night there's live music in the Piano Bar from 5 to 9pm, followed by a mixture of jazz, Top 40, and rock 'n' roll until 5am. A disco downstairs starts at 11pm every night (finishing at 6am), and a larger one takes off in The Penthouse at the Bourbon bar on Friday and Saturday nights. The music is geared toward the 18-to-25 crowd of locals and tourists.

24 Darlinghurst Rd., Kings Cross. ℂ 02/9358 1144. Reservations recommended Fri–Sun. Main courses A$8.50–$23.95 (U.S.$5.50–$15.60). A$2 (U.S.$1.30) surcharge weekends and public holidays. AE, DC, MC, V. Daily 24 hr. (happy hour 4–7pm). CityRail: Kings Cross.

Govindas VEGETARIAN   When I think of Govindas, I can't help smiling. Perhaps it's because I'm reliving the happy vibe from the Hare Krishna center it's based in, or maybe it's because the food is so cheap! Or maybe it's because they even throw in a decent movie with the meal (the movie theatre is on a different floor). The food is simple vegetarian, served buffet style and eaten in a basic room off black-lacquer tables. Typical dishes include pastas and salads, lentil dishes, soups, and casseroles. It's BYO and doctrine-free.

112 Darlinghurst Rd., Darlinghurst. ℂ 02/9380 5155. Dinner A$13.90 (U.S.$9), including free movie. AE, MC, V. Daily 6–11pm. CityRail: Kings Cross.

Hard Rock Cafe AMERICAN   The obligatory half a Cadillac through the wall beckons you into this shrine to rock 'n' roll. Among the items on display are costumes worn by Elvis, John Lennon, and Elton John, as well as guitars from Sting and the Bee Gees, drums from Phil Collins and The Beatles, and one of Madonna's bras. The mainstays here are the burgers, with ribs, chicken, fish, and salads, and T-bone steaks on the menu, too. Most meals come with french fries or baked potatoes and a salad. It's really busy on Friday and Saturday evenings from around 7:30 to 10:30pm, when you might have to queue to get a seat.

121–129 Crown St., Darlinghurst. ℂ 02/9331 1116. Reservations not accepted. Main courses A$9.95–$21.95 (U.S.$6.50–$14.30). 10% surcharge weekends and public holidays. AE, DC, MC, V. Daily noon–midnight. Shop daily 10am–midnight. Closed Christmas. CityRail: Museum; then walk across Hyde Park, head down the hill past the Australian Museum on William St., and turn right onto Crown St. Sydney Explorer Bus: Stop 7.

INEXPENSIVE

No Names ITALIAN   This fabulous cafeteria-style Italian joint is the place to go in Sydney for a cheap and cheerful meal. Downstairs you can nibble on cakes or drink good coffee, but upstairs you have a choice between spaghetti and several meat or fish dishes. The servings are enormous and often far more than you can eat. You get free bread, and simple salads are cheap. Help yourself to water and cordials.

2 Chapel St. (or 81 Stanley St.), Darlinghurst. ℂ **02/9360 4711**. Main courses A$6–$14 (U.S.$3.90–$9.10). Cash only. Daily noon–2:30pm and 6–10pm. CityRail: Kings Cross or Town Hall, then a 10-min. walk.

William's on William CAFE/PASTA   Just around the corner from the Kings-X Hotel, which itself is right opposite the huge Coca-Cola sign, you'll come across this remarkably scruffy little eatery. The walls need a bit of a paint, the floors need to be swept, and the tacky plastic tablecloths look like they survived the last war. If you can get past all this, though, you'll be very satisfied. The pastas at A$5 to $6 (U.S.$3.50 to $4.20) are huge and delicious, and the all-day breakfast of bacon, egg, toast, and homemade french fries is a fantastic value at A$3.90 (U.S.$2.75). Tea and coffee come in at a very cheap A$1.50 (U.S.$1.05).

242 William St., Kings Cross. ℂ **02/9358 6680**. Main courses A$3.90–$11.90 (U.S.$2.75–$8.35). AE, MC, V. Daily 7:30am–11pm. CityRail: Kings Cross.

IN GLEBE

The Boathouse on Blackwattle Bay ⭐ *Finds* SEAFOOD   Located above Sydney University's rowing club and looking over a working area of Sydney Harbour, this converted boatshed offers fascinating water views across to the city and the remarkable Anzac Bridge. Terrific French-inspired seafood is served up in an elegant, yet informal, atmosphere of white tablecloths and good natural lighting. The service is good, and you can see the chefs at work in the adjoining open-plan kitchen. You can't go wrong with the fabulous snapper fish pie with roasted tomatoes and mashed potato, the signature dish here, while there are usually around 10 varieties of oysters on offer. A good wine list and delicious deserts cap off a truly memorable experience. I highly recommend The Boathouse, particularly as a lunchtime treat.

End of Ferry Rd., Glebe. ℂ **02/9518 9011**. Main courses A$25–$27 (U.S.$16.25–$17.55). AE, DC, MC, V. Tues–Sun noon–2:30pm and 6:30–10:30pm. Bus 431, 433, or 434 from Millers Point, The Rocks (via George St.), or 459 from behind Town Hall.

IN PADDINGTON

The top end of Oxford Street, which runs from Hyde Park in central Sydney toward Bondi, has a profusion of trendy bars and cafes and a scattering of cheaper eateries among the more glamorous ones.

MODERATE

La Mensa ITALIAN/MEDITERRANEAN   Though I find clean-cut, minimal interiors like the one here to be increasingly boring, at La Mensa it has the added zest of a gourmet food and vegetable store tacked on. There's a communal table seating about 20 people, as well as other smaller tables both inside and out. Mains might include a salad of salmon, asparagus and poached egg; a pumpkin, pea and leg ham risotto; grilled swordfish with chickpeas and braised tomatoes; and Tuscan-style baby chicken and potatoes.

257 Oxford St., Paddington. ℂ **02/9332 2963**. Reservations recommended. Main courses A$10.50–$19.50 (U.S.$6.90–$12.70). AE, DC, MC, V. Mon–Thurs 11am–10pm, Fri 11am–11pm, Sat 9am–11pm, Sun 9am–10pm. Bus: Oxford St.

INEXPENSIVE

Laksa House MALAYSIAN   The dining room here is simple but friendly, and the food is wonderfully authentic. The specialty is *laksa,* a spicy Asian soup cooked with coconut milk with chicken, prawn, vegetables, or tofu. You can also try the peanut-sauce satays, the Singapore noodles, the Indonesian rice and noodle staples of *nasi goreng* and *gado gado,* as well as a range of spicy curries.

In the Windsor Castle Hotel, 72 Windsor St. 🕐 02/9328 0741. Reservations not accepted. Main courses A$6–$9 (U.S.$4.20–$6.30). No credit cards. Open daily noon–3pm and 6–9:30pm. Bus: Oxford St.

CAFE CULTURE

Debate rages over which cafe serves the best coffee in Sydney, which has the best atmosphere, and which has the tastiest snacks. The main cafe scenes are centered around Victoria Street in Darlinghurst, Stanley Street in East Sydney, and King Street in Newtown. Other places, including Balmoral Beach on the north shore, Bondi Beach, and Paddington, all have their favored hangouts as well.

Note: Americans will be sorry to learn that, unlike in the States, free refills of coffee are rare in Australian restaurants and cafes. Sip slowly.

Here are a few of my favorites around town:

Balmoral Boatshed Kiosk 🕏 *(Finds*   A real find, this beautiful rustic cafe is right on the water beside the dinghies and sailing craft of the wooden Balmoral Boatshed. It's a heavenly place for enjoying a breakfast muffin or a ham-and-cheese croissant while basking in the sun. This place is popular with families on weekend mornings, so if you hate kids, find another place.

2 The Esplanade, Balmoral Beach. 🕐 02/9968 4412. Daily 8am–7pm in summer, 8am–6pm in winter. Ferry to Taronga Zoo, then bus to Balmoral Beach.

Bar Coluzzi   Although it may no longer serve the best coffee in Sydney, this cafe's claim to fame is that long ago it served up real espresso when the rest of the city was drinking Nescafe. People-watching is a favorite hobby at this fashionably worn-around-the edges spot in the heart of Sydney's cafe district.

322 Victoria St., Darlinghurst. 🕐 02/9380 5420. Daily 4:45am–7:30pm. CityRail: Kings Cross.

Bill's   Bill's is on everyone's lips. The bright and airy place, strewn with flowers and magazines, serves fantastic nouveau cafe–style food. It's so popular, you might have trouble finding a seat. The signature breakfast dishes—including ricotta hotcakes with honeycomb butter and banana, and sweet corn fritters with roast tomatoes and bacon—are the stuff of legends. Last time I was here I asked for fried eggs instead of the scrambled eggs and was bruskly told I had to stick to the menu, so be warned.

433 Liverpool St., Darlinghurst. 🕐 02/9360 9631. Mon–Sat 7:30am–3pm. CityRail: Kings Cross.

Hernandez 🕏 *(Finds*   The walls of this tiny, cluttered cafe are crammed with eccentric fake masterpieces, and the air is permeated with the aroma of 20 types of coffee roasted and ground on the premises. It's almost a religious experience for discerning inner-city coffee addicts. The Spanish espresso is a treat.

60 Kings Cross Rd., Potts Point. 🕐 02/9331 2343. Daily 24 hr. CityRail: Kings Cross.

The Old Coffee Shop 🕏   Sydney's oldest coffee shop opened in the charming Victorian Strand Arcade in 1891. The shop may or may not serve Sydney's best java, but the old-world feel of the place and the sugary snacks, cakes, and pastries make up for it. It's a good place to take a break from shopping and sightseeing.

Ground floor, The Strand Arcade. 🕐 02/9231 3002. Mon–Fri 7:30am–5:30pm, Sat 8:30am–5pm, Sun 10:30am–4pm. CityRail: Town Hall.

IN NEWTOWN: GREAT ETHNIC EATS

Inner-city Newtown is three stops from Central Station on CityRail, and 10 minutes by bus from central Sydney. On Newtown's main drag, King Street, many inexpensive restaurants offer food from all over the world.

Le Kilimanjaro AFRICAN   With so many excellent restaurants to choose from in Newtown—they close down or improve quickly enough if they're bad—I picked Kilimanjaro because it's the most unusual. It's a tiny place, with very limited seating on two floors. Basically, you enter, choose a dish off the blackboard menu (while standing), and then you are escorted to your seats by one of the waiters. On a recent visit I had couscous, some African bread (similar to an Indian chapatti), and the *Saussou-gor di guan* (tuna in a rich sauce). Another favorite dish is *Yassa* (chicken in a rich African sauce). All meals are served on traditional wooden plates.

280 King St., Newtown. ℂ 02/9557 4565. Reservations not accepted. Main courses A$8.50–$9.50 (U.S.$5.50–$6.20). No credit cards. CityRail: Newtown.

Old Saigon VIETNAMESE   Another Newtown establishment bursting with atmosphere, the Old Saigon was owned until 1998 by a former American Vietnam War correspondent who loved Vietnam so much he ended up living there and marrying a local, before coming to Australia. Just to make sure you know about it, he's put up his own photos on the walls, and strewn the place with homemade tin helicopters. His Vietnamese brother-in-law has taken over the show, but the food is still glorious, with the spicy squid dishes among my favorites. A popular pastime is grilling your own thin strips of venison, beef, wild boar, kangaroo, or crocodile over a burner at your table, then wrapping the meat up in rice paper with lettuce and mint, then dipping it in a chili sauce. I highly recommend this place for a cheap night out.

107 King St., Newtown. ℂ 02/9519 5931. Reservations recommended. Main courses A$10–$40 (U.S.$6.50–$26). AE, DC, MC, V. Wed–Fri noon–3pm; Tues–Sun 6–11pm. BYO only. CityRail: Newtown.

AT BONDI BEACH

The seafront drag of Campbell Parade is packed with restaurants. For a super-cheap meal at the beach, you could try the bistro at the **North Bondi R.S.L. Club,** located at 120 Ramsgate Ave., North Bondi, at the far end of Bondi Beach to your left as you look at the ocean (ℂ **02/9130 3152**). Daily lunches—including fish-and-chips, roast meats, and schnitzel—served between noon and 2:30pm, go for just A$3 (U.S.$2.10). The dinner menu, offered from 5 to 8:30pm daily, is good value, too. Because of its "club" status, alcohol is very cheap in the bar here.

Fishy Affair SEAFOOD   Just one of many good restaurants, cafes, and take-out joints along the beach's main drag, the Fishy Affair is nevertheless a stand-out. Sitting outside and munching on tasty fish-and-chips while watching the beach bums saunter past is a great way to spend an hour or so. The herb-crusted Atlantic salmon steak and the smoked salmon salad are both truly delicious.

152–162 Campbell Parade, Bondi Beach. ℂ 02/9300 0494. Main courses A$14.40–$21 (U.S.$10.10–$14.70). AE, MC, V. Mon–Thurs noon–3pm and 6–10pm; Fri–Sat noon–3pm and 6–10:30pm; Sun noon–10pm. Bus: Bondi Beach.

North Indian Flavour NORTH INDIAN   I've lost count of the times the North Indian Flavour restaurants around Sydney have satisfied a curry craving. Don't expect first-class Indian food, but it'll do if you really want to fill up on something a little spicy. The curries and breads are displayed just inside the doorway, and you can either eat on the premises or take your food down to the grassy strip in front of the beach. Most people tend to choose a selection of three curries on rice and mop it up with naan bread. A medium-size serving is big enough to plug a very large appetite. Wash it down with a mango *lassi* yogurt drink for A$1.70 (U.S.$1.20). You'll find almost identical outlets on King Street in Newtown (© **02/9550 3928**), under the Grace Brothers department store on Pitt Street Mall (© **02/9221 4715**), and on Broadway opposite Central Station (© **02/9212 3535**).

138 Campbell Parade, Bondi Beach. © **02/9365 6239**. Main courses A$4.90–$7.90 (U.S.$3.45–$5.55). No credit cards. Mon–Fri noon–11pm, Sat–Sun 11:30am–11:30pm.

Thai Terrific ☆ THAI Thai Terrific by name, terrific Thai by nature. This truly superb place just around the corner from the Bondi Hotel is run with flair and coolly efficient service. The large back room can be very noisy, so if you prefer less din with your dinner, sit at one of the small sidewalk tables. The servings here are enormous—three people could easily fill up on just two mains. The *tom yum* soups and the prawn or seafood *laksa* noodle soups (spicy soup made with coconut milk) are the best I've tasted in Australia and are very filling. I also highly recommend the red curries.

Equally as nice (and quieter) is the Bangkok-style **Nina's Ploy Thai Restaurant** ☆, at 132 Wairoa Ave. (© **02/9365 1118**), at the corner of Warners Ave. at the end of the main Campbell Parade strip. Main courses here cost between A$8 and $12.50 (U.S.$5.60 and $8.75); cash only.

147 Curlewis St., Bondi Beach. © **02/9365 7794**. Reservations recommended Fri–Sat nights. Main courses A$10–$18 (U.S.$7–$12.60). AE, DC, MC, V. Daily noon–11pm. Bus: 380 to Bondi Beach.

IN MANLY

Manly is 30 minutes from Circular Quay by ferry, or 15 minutes by JetCat. The take-out shops that line the Corso, the pedestrian mall that runs between the ferry terminal and the main Manly Beach, offer everything from Turkish kebabs to Japanese noodles.

Ashiana ☆ INDIAN You'll be hard-pressed to find a better cheap Indian restaurant in Sydney. Tucked away up a staircase next to the Steyne Hotel (just off the Corso and near the main beach), Ashiana has won a few prizes for its traditional spicy cooking. Portions are large and filling, and the service is very friendly. The butter chicken is magnificent, while the *Malai Kofta* (cheese and potato dumplings in a mild, creamy sauce) is the best this side of Bombay. Beer is the best drink with everything. My only gripe is that it's hard to avoid cigarette smoke in such a cozy place, especially on Friday and Saturday nights when the place is packed. Clear your lungs and work off the heavy load in your stomach with a beachside stroll afterwards. Check out the soda machine in Woolworth's just across the road for A80¢ (U.S.56¢) cold drinks—the cheapest in Sydney.

2 Sydney Rd., Manly. © **02/9977 3466**. Reservations recommended. Main courses A$9.90–$15.90 (U.S.$6.95–$11.15). AE, MC, V. Daily 5:30–11pm. Ferry or JetCat: Manly.

Finds **Sydney's Best Fries**

If you're looking for the best french fries in Sydney, head to **Manly Ocean Foods**, three shops down from the main beach on the Corso. Avoid the fish-and-chips here, though (the shark is not the best in my opinion), and spend a couple of dollars extra on barramundi, salmon, perch, or snapper.

INEXPENSIVE

Howe's Restaurant ☆ THAI/INDONESIAN/MALAYSIAN Mr. Howe has been phenomenally successful on the Manly food circuit with his cram 'em in and keep it cheap philosophy. The restaurant is right across from Manly's main beach (to the right as you leave the Corso), but it makes no use of its position at all. What it does do is serve simple Southeast Asian dishes, including various curries, noodles, and rice-based dishes. Mr. Howe himself is generally around offering huge smiles. Tables are lined up in long rows, so don't be surprised if you are elbow to elbow with strangers. On weekend evenings, the place is swamped with a generally young crowd. Don't leave without tasting the sticky rice with mango desert.

33 South Steyne, Manly. ℭ **02/9977 1877.** Reservations required Fri–Sat nights. Main courses A$6.20–$9.90 (U.S.$4.35–$6.95). AE, MC, V. Tues–Sun 5–11:30pm. Closed Mon except national holiday weekends. Ferry or JetCat: Manly.

VEGETARIAN

Green's Eatery VEGETARIAN Of the many eateries in Manly, this nice little vegetarian place, just off The Corso on the turnoff just before the Steyne Hotel, does the best lunchtime business. The food is healthy and good quality. The menu includes 11 different vegetarian burgers, vegetable curries and noodle dishes, patties and salads, soups, smoothies, and wraps. They serve some exceptionally nice cakes here, too, which despite being incredibly wholesome are still surprisingly tasty. On a nice day you can sit outside.

1–3 Sydney Rd., Manly. ℭ **02/9977 1904.** Menu items A$2–$6.20 (U.S.$1.30–$4). Cash only. Daily 8am–6pm. Ferry or JetCat: Manly.

NORTH SYDNEY

L'Incontro Italian Restaurant ☆☆ NORTHERN ITALIAN Less than 10 minutes by train from the city center—plus a 5-minute stroll up Miller Street (turn right up the hill as you exit the train station and take the first right)—this little beauty in an easy-to-miss turn-of-the-20th-century house is a good place for moderately priced Italian. Dishes are beautifully prepared and served in this stylish trattoria as far removed from the modern yuppie bistro as you can get. The food is exquisite. The courtyard, with its vines and ferns, is delightful in summer. Menus change regularly, so pray for the baked rainbow trout cooked with almonds and red wine butter—it's simply the best fish I've ever tasted.

196 Miller St. (at McLaren St.), North Sydney. ℭ **02/9957 2274.** Reservations recommended. Main courses A$19.50–$36.50 (U.S.$12.70–$23.70). AE, DC, MC, V. Mon–Fri noon–3pm; Mon–Sat 6–10pm. CityRail: North Sydney.

5 What to See & Do in Sydney

The only problem with visiting Sydney is fitting in everything you want to do and see. Of course, you won't want to miss the "icon" attractions—the **Opera House** and the **Harbour Bridge.** Everyone seems to be climbing over the arch of the bridge these days on the BridgeClimb Tour, so look up for the tiny dots of people waving to the ferry passengers below.

You should also check out the native wildlife in **Taronga Zoo** and the **Sydney Aquarium,** stroll around the "tourist" precinct of **Darling Harbour** and get a dose of Down Under culture at the not-too-large **Australian Museum.** Also try to take time out to visit one of the nearby national parks for a taste of the Australian bush, and if it's hot take your "cozzie" and towel to **Bondi Beach** or **Manly.**

Central Sydney Attractions

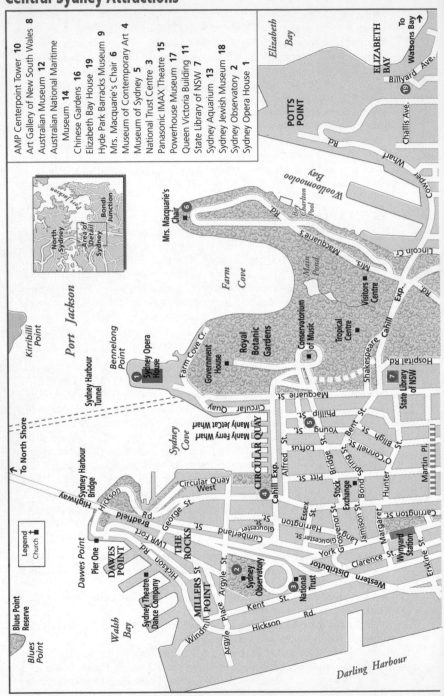

AMP Centerpoint Tower **10**
Art Gallery of New South Wales **8**
Australian Museum **12**
Australian National Maritime Museum **14**
Chinese Gardens **16**
Elizabeth Bay House **19**
Hyde Park Barracks Museum **9**
Mrs. Macquarie's Chair **6**
Museum of Contemporary Art **4**
Museum of Sydney **5**
National Trust Centre **3**
Panasonic IMAX Theatre **15**
Powerhouse Museum **17**
Queen Victoria Building **11**
State Library of NSW **7**
Sydney Aquarium **13**
Sydney Jewish Museum **18**
Sydney Observatory **2**
Sydney Opera House **1**

Legend
Church ✝

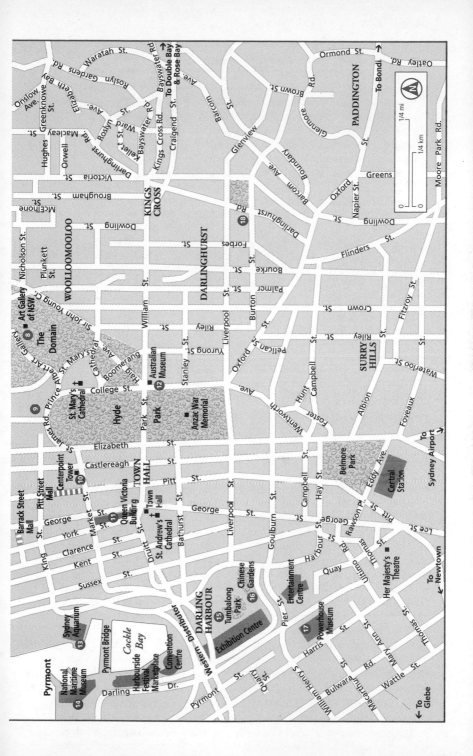

> ⌒*Value* **Great Deals on Sightseeing**
>
> The **Privileges Card** is a great way to save money if you plan to visit
> Sydney's biggest attractions. The card costs A$25 (U.S.$16.25), is good
> for up to 1 month, and can be used in Sydney, Canberra, and
> Melbourne. In Sydney, all the major attractions offer some sort of dis-
> count if you show a Privileges Card, such as two-for-one admission or
> reduced-price admission if you're traveling alone, and buy-one-get-
> one-free reductions. With the card you'll also get discounts on harbor
> cruises (typically 20%), as well as discounts at certain restaurants (some-
> times a free main course if two of you are dining, or a 20% rebate off
> the total bill for the cardholder and three others). To get a card, you'll
> need to fill out an application form, available on the Internet
> (www.privilegescard.com) or at tourist information centers in Sydney;
> you'll receive a booklet with details on where you can save. Call Privi-
> leges at ℭ **1800 675 500,** or fax at 02/6254 8788. If you book in
> advance, the company can arrange to have the card sent to your hotel.

I also recommend a quick trip out of town. Go bushwalking in the **Blue
Mountains,** wine tasting in the **Hunter Valley,** or dolphin-spotting at **Port
Stephens** (see chapter 4 for details on all three).

Whatever you decide to do, you won't have enough time. Don't be surprised
if you start planning ahead for your next visit before your first is even finished.

THE OPERA HOUSE & SYDNEY HARBOUR

Officially called Port Jackson, **Sydney Harbour** is the focal point of Sydney and
one of the features—along with the beaches and the easy access to surrounding
national parks—that makes this city so special. It's entered through **the Heads,**
two bush-topped outcrops (you'll see them if you take a ferry or JetCat to
Manly), beyond which the harbor laps at some 240 kilometers (149 miles) of
shoreline before stretching out into the Parramatta River. Visitors are often
awestruck by the harbor's beauty, especially at night when the sails of the Opera
House and the girders of the Harbour Bridge are lit up, and the waters are
swirling with the reflection of lights from the abutting high-rises—reds, greens,
blues, yellows, and oranges. During the day, it buzzes with green-and-yellow
ferries pulling in and out of busy Circular Quay, sleek tourist craft, fully-rigged
tall ships, giant container vessels making their way to and from the wharves of
Darling Harbour, and hundreds of white-sailed yachts. The greenery along the
harbor's edges is perhaps a surprising feature, and all thanks to the **Sydney
Harbour National Park,** a haven for native trees and plants, and a feeding and
breeding ground for lorikeets and other nectar-eating bird life. In the center of
the harbor is a series of islands, the most impressive being the tiny isle supporting
Fort Denison, which once housed convicts and acted as part of the city's
defense.

THE HARBOUR ON THE CHEAP   The best way to see Sydney Harbour,
of course, is from the water. Several companies operate tourist craft for fare-
paying customers (see "Harbor Cruises & Organized Tours," later in this chapter), but it's easy enough just to hop on a regular passenger ferry (see "Getting

Around," earlier in this chapter). The best ferry excursions are over to the beach-side suburb of **Manly** (come back after dusk to see the lights ablaze around The Rocks and Circular Quay); to **Watsons Bay,** where you can have lunch and wander along the cliffs; to **Darling Harbour,** for all the area's entertainment and the fact that you travel right under the Harbour Bridge; and to **Mosman Bay,** just for the ride and to see the grand houses that overlook exclusive harbor inlets.

NEW ACTION ON THE HARBOR   A recent addition to the Sydney Harbour scene is a 420-horsepower jet boat which zooms about on three high-speed waterway tours. **Harbour Jet** (© **02/9929 7373;** www.harbourjet.com) offers a 35-minute Jet Blast Adventure departing at 1, 2, and 3pm Monday through Friday and 1 and 2pm on weekends. It costs A$35 (U.S.$22.75) for adults, and A$20 (U.S.$13) for kids under 15. A 50-minute Sydney Harbour Adventure spin leaves at 11am and 5pm daily and costs A$50 (U.S.$32.50) for adults and A$30 (U.S.$19.50) for kids; a 1-hour-and-20-minute Middle Harbour Adventure cruise costs A$70 (U.S.$45.50) for adults and A$40 (U.S.$26) for kids. Rides are fast and furious and pump with rock music. The boat leaves from the Convention Jetty, between the Convention Centre and the Harbourside Shopping complex on the far side of Darling Harbour.

Another newcomer is the **Aussie Duck,** a custom-built amphibious people-carrier that can power through water and cruise on land. The Duck, as big and tough as a tank, weaves through the heart of Sydney on huge wheels, then like a duck-to-water transforms itself to a sea-going vehicle as two roof-mounted pontoons are lowered by hydraulic arms. The 2-hour tour departs from outside the Clock Tower building, 35 Argyle St., The Rocks, at 10:30am, 12:30, and 2:30pm every Saturday and Sunday; show up 20 minutes early. The tour costs A$55 (U.S.$35.75) for adults; A$42.50 (U.S.$27.50) for seniors and students; and A$30 (U.S.$19.50) for children under 13. For details contact Aussie Duck at © **13 10-07** in Australia or 02/9251 7774, or surf to www.aussieduck.com.

Sydney Harbour Bridge ⭐⭐⭐ *(Moments)*   One thing so few tourists do, but which only takes an hour or so, is to walk right across the Harbour Bridge. The bridge, completed in 1932, is 1,150 meters (3,795 ft.) long and spans the 503-meter (1,600-ft.) distance from the south shore to the north. It accommodates pedestrian walkways, two railway lines, and an eight-lane road. The 30-minute stroll across offers some excellent harbor views. Once on the other side, you can take a CityRail train from Milsons Point train station back to the city (to Wynyard—change here for Circular Quay, Town Hall, or Central stations).

As you walk across the bridge, you should stop off at the **Pylon Lookout** (© **02/9247 3408**), located at the southeastern pylon. Admission is A$5 (U.S.$3.25) for adults, A$3 (U.S.$1.95) for children and A$12 (U.S.$7.80) for a family. From the top of this bridge support, you are 89 meters (591 ft.) above the water and get panoramic views of Sydney Harbour, the ferry terminals of Circular Quay, and beyond. An interesting museum here charts the building of the bridge. Reach the pylon by walking to the far end of George Street in The Rocks toward the Harbour Bridge. Just past the Mercantile Pub on your left you'll see some stone steps that take you onto Cumberland Street. From there, it's a 2-minute walk to the steps underneath the bridge on your right. Climb four flights of stairs to reach the bridge's Western Footway, then walk along to the first pylon. *Note:* Climbing up inside the pylon involves 200 steps. The Pylon Lookout is open daily from 10am to 5pm (closed Christmas).

(*Moments* **A Walk on the Wild Side: Climbing the Harbour Bridge**

At one time, only bridge workers who painted the Harbour Bridge had the opportunity to view Sydney from the top of the main bridge arch. But since October 1998, Sydneysiders and tourists have been able to experience the spectacular view and the exhilarating achievement of climbing to the top of one of Australia's icons. The experience takes 3 hours from check-in at the **BridgeClimb** base at 5 Cumberland St., The Rocks (© **02/ 9240 1100,** or 02/8274 7777; fax 02/9240 1122; www.bridgeclimb.com; admin@bridgeclimb.com) to the completion of the climb. The office is open daily from 8am to 6pm, and climbers leave in small groups every 10 minutes or so. Climbers wear specially designed "Bridge Suits" and are harnessed to a static line. Participants are also breath-tested for alcohol and are banned from carrying anything on the climb, including cameras or video recorders. Climbs cost A$117 (U.S.$76) for adults and A$96 (U.S.$62.40) for children ages 12 to 16 on weekdays during the day; A$142 (U.S.$92.30) for adults and $118 (U.S.$76.70) for children for night climbs Monday through Friday and weekend day climbs; and A$164 (U.S.$106.60) for adults and $140 (U.S.$91) for children on Saturday and Sunday nights. Children under 12 are not allowed to climb.

Sydney Opera House ☆☆☆   Only a handful of buildings around the world are as architecturally and culturally significant as the Sydney Opera House. But what sets it apart from, say, the Taj Mahal and the Great Pyramids of Egypt is that this white-sailed construction caught mid-billow over the waters of Sydney Cove is a working building. Most are surprised to learn it's not just an Opera House, but a full-scale performing-arts complex with five major performance spaces. The biggest and grandest of the lot is the 2,690-seat **Concert Hall,** which has the best acoustics of any man-made building of its type in the world. Come here to experience opera, but also chamber music, symphonies, dance, choral performances, and even rock 'n' roll. The **Opera Theatre** is smaller, seating 1,547, and is home to operas, ballets, and dance. The **Drama Theatre,** seating 544, and the **Playhouse,** seating 398, specialize in plays and smaller-scale performances. In March 1999 the Boardwalk, a new theater that seats 300, opened on the site of the old library, to be used for dance and experimental music.

The history of the building is as intriguing as the design. The New South Wales Government raised the money needed to build it from a public lottery. Danish Architect Jørn Utzon won an international competition to design it. From the start, the project was controversial, with many Sydneysiders believing it was a monstrosity. Following a disagreement, Utzon returned home, without ever seeing his finished project, and the interior fell victim to a compromise design, which, among other things, left too little space to perform full-scale operas. And the cost? Initially the project was budgeted at a cool A$7 million (U.S.$5.44 million), but by the time it was finished in 1973 it had cost a staggering A$102 million (U.S.$66.3 million), most raised through a series of lotteries. Since then, continual refurbishment and the major task of replacing the asbestos-infected grouting between the hundreds of thousands of white tiles that make up its shell has cost many millions more.

Tours & Tickets: Guided tours of the Opera House last about an hour and are conducted daily from 9am to 4pm, except Good Friday and Christmas. Though guides try to take groups into the main theaters and around the foyers, if you don't get to see everything you want it's because the Opera House is not a museum but a workplace, and there's almost always some performance, practice, or setting up to be done. Reservations are essential. Tours include approximately 200 stairs (tours for people with disabilities can be arranged). Specialized tours, focusing on the building's architecture and engineering, for example, can also be arranged.

The Tourism Services Department at the Sydney Opera House can book **combination packages,** including dinner and a show; a tour, dinner, and a show; or a champagne interval performance. Prices vary depending on shows and dining venues. Visitors from overseas can buy tickets by credit card and then pick them up at the box office on arrival, or contact a local tour company specializing in Australia—a good idea, as performances are very popular. The views from the back rows are hardly worth the effort and expense if you turn up on the day of performance. Tickets for performances vary from as little as A$12 (U.S.$7.80) for children's shows to A$180 (U.S.$117) for good seats at the opera. Plays cost between A$40 and $60 (U.S.$26 to $39) on average.

Free performances are given outside on the Opera House boardwalks on Sunday afternoons and during festival times. The shows range from musicians and performance artists, to school groups.

Bennelong Point. ℂ 02/9250 7250 for guided tours & inquiries. www.soh.nsw.gov.au. For box office bookings, call ℂ 02/9250 7777; fax 02/9251 3943; bookings@soh.nsw.gov.au. Box office open Mon–Sat 9am–8:30pm; Sun 2 hrs. before performance. Tours A$15.40 (U.S.$10) adults, A$10.60 (U.S.$6.90) children (family prices available on application); Backstage tours A$25.20 (U.S.$16.40) (no children's price). Tours run Mon–Sun 8.30am–5pm (around every 45 min.) subject to theater availability (tour sizes are limited, so be prepared to wait). CityRail, bus, or ferry: Circular Quay. Sydney Explorer bus. Parking: Daytime A$7 (U.S.$4.50) per hr.; evening A$23 (U.S.$15) flat rate.

ATTRACTIONS AT DARLING HARBOUR

Many tourists head to Darling Harbour for the Harbourside Festival Marketplace, a huge structure beside the Pyrmont pedestrian and monorail bridge that's crammed full of cheap eateries and a few interesting shops. However, Sydney's tourist precinct has a lot more to offer.

Australian National Maritime Museum ⚐ *Kids*   Modern Australia owes almost everything to the sea, so it's not surprising there's a museum dedicated to the ships, from Aboriginal vessels to submarines. Here you'll also find ships' logs, things to pull and tug at, and the fastest boat in the world, the "Spirit of Australia." Docked in the harbor are a fully-rigged tall ship and an Australian Naval Destroyer, *The Vampire,* which you can clamber over, and an Oberon Class submarine. By the time you read this, the museum should have the yacht belonging to Kay Cottee, the first woman to sail solo around the world. Allow 2 hours.

Darling Harbour. ℂ 02/9298 3777. www.anmm.gov.au. A$10 (U.S.$6.50) adults, A$6 (U.S.$3.90) children, A$25 (U.S.$16.25) families (for entry without access to navy ships). A$14 (U.S.$9.10) adults, A$7 (U.S.$4.55) children and A$30 (U.S.$19.50) families (for museum entry and navy ships). Daily 9:30am–5pm (until 6:30pm in Jan). Ferry: Darling Harbour. Monorail: Harbourside. Sydney Explorer bus.

Chinese Garden   The largest Chinese garden of its type outside China offers a pleasant escape from the city concrete. It was designed by expert gardeners from

China's Guangdong Province to embody principles of garden design dating back to the 5th century. Allow 30 minutes.

Darling Harbour (adjacent to the Entertainment Centre). ☎ **02/9281 6863**. Admission A$4.50 (U.S.$2.90) adults, A$2 (U.S.1.30) children, A$10 (U.S.$6.50) families. Daily 9:30am–dusk. Ferry: Darling Harbour. Monorail: Convention. Sydney Explorer bus.

Panasonic IMAX Theatre   Four different IMAX films are usually showing on the gigantic eight-story-high screen. Each flick lasts about 50 minutes or so. If you've ever been to an IMAX theater before, you know what to expect. As you watch, your mind is tricked into feeling that it's right in the heart of the action. Also shown are 3-D movies, which cost A$1 (U.S.65¢) extra.

Southern Promenade, Darling Harbour. ☎ **02/9281 3300**. Admission A$15 adults (U.S.$9.75), A$12 (U.S.$7.80) students, A$10 children (U.S.$6.50) 3–15, A$35 (U.S.$22.75) families. Daily 10am–10pm (until 11:30pm Fri–Sat). Ferry: Darling Harbour. Monorail: Convention. Sydney Explorer bus.

Powerhouse Museum *(Kids)*   Sydney's most interactive museum is also one of the largest in the Southern Hemisphere. Inside the post-modern industrial interior you'll find all sorts of displays and gadgets relating to the sciences, transportation, human achievement, decorative art, and social history. The many hands-on exhibits make this fascinating museum worthy of a couple of hours of your time.

500 Harris St., Ultimo (near Darling Harbour). ☎ **02/9217 0111**. Admission A$8 (U.S.$5.20) adults, A$3 (U.S.$1.95) students, A$2 (U.S.$1.30) children 5–15, A$18 (U.S.$11.70) families. Free admission 1st Sat of every month. Daily 10am–5pm. Ferry: Darling Harbour. Monorail: Harbourside. Sydney Explorer bus.

Sydney Aquarium *(R̂R̂)* *(Kids)*   This is one of the world's best aquariums and should be near the top of any Sydney itinerary. The main attractions are the underwater walkways through two enormous tanks—one with an impressive collection of creatures found in Sydney Harbour, the other full of giant rays and gray nurse sharks. Other excellent exhibits include a giant Plexiglas room suspended inside a pool patrolled by rescued seals, and a magnificent section on the Great Barrier Reef, where thousands of colorful fish school around coral outcrops. Also on display are two saltwater crocodiles and some fairy penguins. Try to visit during the week when it's less crowded. Allow around 2 hours.

Aquarium Pier, Darling Harbour. ☎ **02/9262 2300**. Admission A$22 (U.S.$14.30) adults, A$13 (U.S.$8.45) students, A$10 (U.S.$6.50) children 3–15, A$48 (U.S.$31.20) families. The Aquarium Link ticket, available from CityRail train stations, is a combined discount rail and Aquarium ticket that includes a ferry ride. Daily 9am–10pm. Seal Sanctuary closes at 7pm in summer. CityRail: Town Hall. Ferry: Darling Harbour. Sydney Explorer bus.

OTHER TOP ATTRACTIONS: A SPECTACULAR VIEW, SYDNEY'S CONVICT HISTORY & MORE

A.M.P. Centrepoint Tower *(R̂)*   The tallest building in the Southern Hemisphere is not hard to miss—it resembles a giant steel pole skewering a golden marshmallow. Standing more than 300 meters (1,860 ft.) tall, it offers stupendous 360° views across Sydney and as far as the Blue Mountains. Fortunately, an elevator takes you to the indoor viewing platform. Unfortunately, prices have rocketed in recent years, too. Don't be too concerned if you feel the building tremble slightly, especially in a stiff breeze—I'm told it's perfectly natural. Below the tower are three floors of stores and restaurants. Allow 1 hour.

Pitt and Market sts. ☎ **02/9229 7444**. Admission A$19.80 (U.S.$12.90) adults, A$13.20 (U.S.$7.95) children 5–16, A$55 (U.S.$35.75) families (up to 3 kids). Daily 9am–10:30pm. CityRail: St. James or Town Hall. Sydney Explorer bus.

Fox Studios Australia   This major working movie studio has been used for the production of such flicks as *The Matrix, Mission Impossible,* and *Babe II.* A 4-hour or so self-guided Backlot Tour shows off the Babe set and has a re-creation of a scene from the *Titanic.* You also get an insight into working studios, audio and animation effects, and costumes and makeup. Here, too, is a 16-screen movie complex and a range of shops, bars and restaurants. Between 10am and 5pm there's a market selling movie and retro bric-a-brac, furniture, and books. Altogether it makes for an interesting outing if you're into movies.

Lang Rd. and Driver Ave. Moore Park. © 02/9383 4000, or 1300 369 849. www.foxstudios.com.au. Open daily 10am–5pm, except Christmas Day. Admission A$24.95 (U.S.$16.25) adults, A$14.95 (U.S.$9.75) children 5–15. Bus: 336, 337, 339, or 340 from Circular Quay, and 372 from Pitt St., or via the Bondi & Bay Explorer.

Hyde Park Barracks Museum ✾   These Georgian-style barracks were designed in 1819 by the convict/architect Francis Greenway. They were built by convicts and inhabited by fellow prisoners. These days they house relics from those early days in interesting, modern displays, including log books, early settlement artifacts, and a room full of ships' hammocks in which visitors can lie and listen to fragments of prisoner conversation. If you are interested in Sydney's early beginnings, then I highly recommend a visit—the displays are also far more straightforward that those at the Museum of Sydney (see below). The courtyard cafe is excellent. Allow for 1 hour or more.

Queens Sq., Macquarie St. © 02/9223 8922. Admission A$7 (U.S.$4.55) adults, A$3 (U.S.$1.95) children, A$17 (U.S.$11.05) families. Daily 9:30am–5pm. CityRail: St. James or Martin Place. Sydney Explorer bus.

Museum of Contemporary Art (MCA)   This imposing sandstone museum set back from the water on The Rocks side of Circular Quay offers wacky, entertaining, inspiring, and befuddling displays of what's new (and dated) in modern art. It houses the J. W. Power Collection of more than 4,000 pieces, including works by Andy Warhol, Christo, Marcel Duchamp, and Robert Rauschenberg, as well as temporary exhibits. As it's relatively new and still building up its collection, don't expect it to be as impressive as major modern art museums in say London or New York. In mid-2001 there was talk of the museum closing because of financial concerns. Guided tours are offered Monday through Saturday at noon and 2pm, and Sunday at 2pm. Worth at least an hour.

140 George St., Circular Quay West. © 02/9252 4033. www.mca.com.au. Free general admission. Daily 10am–6pm (5pm in winter). CityRail, bus, ferry: Circular Quay. Sydney Explorer bus.

Old Sydney Town ✾   You can spend quite a few hours on a nice day wandering around this outdoor theme park. Actors mill about dressed up like convicts, sailors, and the like. You'll see stores, buildings, and ships from the old days of the colony. Performances are put on throughout the day. It's the Australian version of an American Wild West–theme town. Allow half a day.

Pacific Hwy., Somersby. © 02/4340 1104. Admission A$22 (U.S.$14.30) adults, A$13 (U.S.$8.45) children, A$50 (U.S.$32.50) families. Wed–Sun 10am–4pm; daily during school holidays. Somersby is near the town of Gosford, 84km (52 miles) north of Sydney. To reach Gosford by car, take the Pacific Hwy. and the Sydney-Newcastle Fwy. (F3); the trip takes about an hr. CityRail trains leave from Central Station for Gosford every 30 min. From Gosford, take the bus marked Old Sydney Town (15-min. ride).

Sydney Olympic Park ✾   The site of the 2000 Sydney Olympic Games is still very much a tourist attraction, as well as a major sporting venue. Most of the Olympic venues are at this dedicated Olympic precinct at Homebush Bay, which also has plenty of bars and restaurants. First port of call should be the

Homebush Bay Information Centre (℃ **02/9714 7888**), which offers displays, walking maps, and tour tips. It's open daily from 9am to 5pm.

Nearby is **Stadium Australia** (℃ **02/8765 2300;** www.stadiumaustralia. com.au), the site of the Olympic Opening and Closing ceremonies, the track and field events, and some Olympic soccer games. Today it stages Australian Rules games, rugby league, rugby union, and soccer matches. A 20-minute tour of the stadium costs A$15 (U.S. $9.50) for adults, A$7.50 (U.S.$4.90) for children and A$42 (U.S.$27.30) for a family. A 1-hour "behind the scenes" tour is A$26 (U.S.$17) for adults, A$13 (U.S.$8.45) for children and A$60 (U.S.$39) for a family.

Also around here is the **Sydney International Aquatic Centre** (℃ **02/9752 3666;** www.siac.nsw.gov.au), which comprises the Olympic pool, diving pool and training facilities. To swim here costs A$5.50 (U.S.$3.60) for adults and A$4.40 (U.S.$2.90) for children.

There are wonderful views of the Sydney Olympic Park and the city from Level 17 of the **Novotel hotel** (℃ **02/8762 1111**), located in the park. Entry to the observation area costs A$3 (U.S.$1.95) for adults and A$2.50 (U.S.$1.60) for children.

One of the best ways to get to the Olympic Site is via the Sydney Explorer bus; otherwise FJ Tours runs a daily afternoon Olympic Site tour from outside McDonald's at Circular Quay leaving at 1pm. It includes a tour of Stadium Australia and the Sydney International Aquatic Centre, as well as a river cruise, and costs A$72 (U.S.$46.80) for adults; A$66 (U.S.$43) for students, and A$36 (U.S.$23.40) for children.

Sydney 2000 Olympic Site, Olympic Park, Homebush Bay. CityRail: Olympic Park. Explorer bus.

Wonderland Sydney   If you're used to big Disneyesque extravaganzas, then this theme park (until recently called Australia's Wonderland) might be a bit of a disappointment—though I guarantee The Demon roller coaster will more than satisfy in the terror department. Other big rides are Space Probe 7, which is basically a heart-stopping drop, and a cute and rattly wooden roller coaster called the Bush Beast. Live shows and bands round out the entertainment options. The entry ticket also includes admission to a wildlife park, with all the old favorites—koalas, wombats, kangaroos, wallabies, and more. Allow half a day.

Wallgrove Rd., Eastern Creek. ℃ **02/9830 9100.** Admission (includes all rides and entrance to the Australian Wildlife Park) A$44 (U.S.$28.60) adults, A$29.30 (U.S.$19) children, family tickets only available for wildlife park. Daily 10am–6pm. CityRail: Rooty Hill (trip takes less than an hr.); Wonderland buses leave from Rooty Hill station every ½-hr. on weekends, and at 8:55, 9:32, 10:10, 11:35am, and 12:14pm weekdays.

'ROOS, KOALAS & OTHER AUSSIE WILDLIFE

The Sydney Aquarium is discussed above in "Attractions at Darling Harbour."

Australian Reptile Park   What started off as a one-man operation supplying deadly snake antivenin in the early 1950s has ended up a nature park teeming with the slippery-looking creatures. But it's not all snakes and lizards here; you'll also find saltwater crocodiles, American alligators, as well as plenty of somewhat cuddlier creatures, such as koalas, platypuses, wallabies, dingoes, and flying foxes. The park is set in beautiful bushland dissected by nature trails. A truly devastating fire burned down the entire park in mid-2000, killing all the animals. The staff have worked valiantly to start up a new collection.

Pacific Hwy., Somersby. ℃ **02/4340 1022.** Admission A$15.50 (U.S.$10) adults, A$8 (U.S.$5.20) children, A$40 (U.S.$26) families. Daily 9am–5pm. Closed Christmas. Somersby is near the town of Gosford, 84 km (52 miles) north of Sydney. To reach Gosford by car, take the Pacific Hwy. and the Sydney-Newcastle Fwy. (F3);

the trip takes about an hr. CityRail trains leave from Central Station for Gosford every 30 min. From Gosford, take the bus marked Australian Wildlife Park (10-min. ride).

Featherdale Wildlife Park 🐨🐨 *(Kids)*   If you only have time to visit one wildlife park in Sydney, make it this one. The selection of native Australian animals is excellent, and, most importantly, the animals are very well cared for. You could easily spend a couple of hours here despite the park's compact size. You'll have the chance to hand feed plenty of friendly kangaroos and wallabies, and get a photo taken next to a koala (there are many here, both the New South Wales variety and the much larger Victorian type). It's a bit of a hassle to get here by public transport, so ring the park in advance to get times for its twice-daily bus tours, which include hotel pickup and drop-off.

217 Kildare Rd., West Pennant Hills. ℂ 02/9622 1644. Admission A$15 (U.S.$9.75) adults, A$7.50 (U.S.$4.90) children 4–14, A$38 (U.S.$24.70) families. Daily 9am–5pm. CityRail: Blacktown station, then take Bus 725 to park (ask driver to tell you when to get off). By car: take the M4 motorway to Reservoir Rd., turn off, travel 4km (2½ miles), then turn left at Kildare Rd.

Koala Park   This is probably the only place in the country (unless you travel all the way to Kangaroo Island in South Australia), where you'll be able to spot this many koalas in one place. In all, there are around 55 koalas roaming within the park's leafy boundaries. Koala cuddling sessions are free, and take place at 10:20, 11:45am, 2, and 3pm daily. There are also wombats, dingoes, kangaroos, wallabies, emus, and native birds here, too. You can hire a private guide to take you around for A$70 (U.S.$45.50) for a 2-hour session, or hitch onto one of the free "hostess" guides who wander around the park like Pied Pipers.

84 Castle Hill Rd., West Pennant Hills. ℂ 02/9484 3141, or 02/9875 2777. Admission A$14 (U.S.$9.10) adults, A$7 (U.S.$4.55) children, A$36 (U.S.$23.40) families. Daily 9am–5pm. Closed Christmas. CityRail: Pennant Hills station via North Strathfield (45 min.), then take any bus nos. 651–655 to park.

Oceanworld Manly *(Kids)*   Though not as impressive as the Sydney Aquarium, Oceanworld can be combined with a visit to the wonderful Manly Beach (see below) for a nice day's outing. There's a decent display of Barrier Reef fish, and more giant sharks. Shark feeding is at 11am on Monday, Wednesday, and Friday.

West Esplanade, Manly. ℂ 02/9949 2644. Admission A$15.90 (U.S.$10.30) adults, A$8 (U.S.$5.20) children, A$39.90 (U.S.$26) families. Daily 10am–5:30pm. Ferry or JetCat: Manly.

Taronga Zoo 🐨 *(Kids)*   Taronga has the best view of any zoo in the world. Set on a hill, it looks out over Sydney Harbour, the Opera House, and the Harbour Bridge. The main attractions here are the fabulous chimpanzee exhibit, the gorilla enclosure, and the Nocturnal Houses, where you can see some of Australia's many nighttime marsupials out and about, including the platypus and the cuter-than-cute bilby (the official Australian Easter bunny). There's an interesting reptile display, a couple of rather impressive Komodo dragons, a scattering of indigenous Australian beasties—including a few koalas, echidnas, kangaroos, dingoes, and wombats—and lots more. The kangaroo and wallaby exhibit is unimaginative; you'd be better off going to Featherdale Wildlife Park (see above) for happier-looking animals. Animals are fed at various times during the day. The zoo can get crowded on weekends, so I strongly advise visiting during the week or going very early in the morning on weekends. Interestingly, the three sun bears near the lower ferry entrance/exit were rescued by an Australian businessman, John Stephens, from a restaurant in Cambodia, where they were to have their paws cut off and served up as an expensive soup. Allow around 2 hours.

Bradley's Head Rd., Mosman. ℂ 02/9969 2777. Admission A$21 (U.S.$13.65) adults, A$11.50 (U.S.$7.50) children 4–15. Ask about family prices. A money-saving Zoopass (includes entry, round-trip ferry from

Circular Quay, and Aerial Safari cable-car ride from ferry terminal to upper entrance of zoo) is available from CityRail stations. Daily 9am–5pm (Jan 9am–9pm). Ferry: Taronga Zoo. At the Taronga Zoo wharf, a bus to the upper zoo entrance is A$1.30 (U.S.85¢), or you can take a cable car to the top for A$2.50 (U.S.$1.60). The lower zoo entrance is a 2-min. walk up the hill from the wharf; it's better on the legs to explore the zoo from the top down.

HITTING THE BEACH

One of the big bonuses of visiting Sydney in the summer months (Dec–Feb) is that you get to experience the beaches in their full glory.

Most major city beaches, such as Manly and Bondi, have lifeguards on patrol, especially during the summer months. They check the water conditions and are on the lookout for **"rips"**—strong ocean currents that can easily pull a swimmer far out to sea. Safe places to swim are marked by red and yellow flags. You must always swim between these flags, never outside them. If you are using a foam or plastic body board or "boogie board," it's also advisable to use them between the flags. Fiberglass surfboards must always be used outside the flags (expect a warning from the beach loudspeakers and an A$100 (U.S.$65) fine if you fail to take notice). For more tips on safe swimming, see the section on "Beach Savvy for Swimmers & Surfers," in chapter 2.

WHAT ABOUT SHARKS & OTHER NASTIES?   One of the first things visitors wonder when they hit the water in Australia is: *Are there sharks?* The answer is yes, but fortunately they are rarely spotted inshore. In reality, sharks have more reason to be scared of us than we of them; most of them end up as the fish in your average packet of fish-and-chips (shark fillets are often sold as "flake"). Though some beaches—such as the small beach next to the Manly ferry wharf in Manly and a section of Balmoral Beach in Mosman—have permanent shark nets, but most rely on portable nets that are moved from beach to beach.

Another common problem off Sydney's beaches are **"blue bottles"**—small blue jellyfish, often called "stingers" in Australia, and "Portuguese-Man-o'-Wars" elsewhere. You'll often find these creatures washed up along the tide line on the beach; they become a hazard for swimmers when there's a strong breeze coming off the ocean and they're blown in to shore (watch out for warning signs erected on the shoreline). Minute individual stinging cells often break off the main body of the creature, and they can cause minor itching or stinging. Or you might be hit by the full force of a blue bottle, which will often stick to your skin and wrap its tentacles around you. Blue bottles deliver a hefty punch from their many stinging cells, causing a severe burning sensation almost immediately. If you are stung, ask a lifeguard for some vinegar to neutralize any stinging cells that haven't yet sprung into action. Otherwise, a very hot bath or shower can help relieve the pain, which can be intense and last for up to a day. Wearing a T-shirt in the water reduces the risk somewhat (though a pair of waterlogged jeans isn't a good idea).

SOUTH OF SYDNEY HARBOUR

Sydney's most famous beach is **Bondi** 𝒦𝒦. In many ways it's a raffish version of a Californian beach, with plenty of tanned skin and in-line skaters. Though the beach is nice, it's cut off from the cafe and restaurant strip that caters to beach-goers by a road that pedestrians have to funnel across in order to reach the sand. On summer weekend evenings it's popular with souped-up cars and groups of disaffected youths from the far western suburbs of Sydney. To reach Bondi Beach, take the CityRail train to Bondi Junction, then transfer to Bus 380 (a 15-min. bus journey). You can also catch Bus 380 directly from Circular Quay (but it can take an hr. or so in peak time).

If you follow the water along to your right at Bondi, you'll come across a very scenic cliff-top trail that takes you to **Bronte Beach** (a 20-min. walk), via gorgeous little **Tamarama,** nicknamed "Glamourama" for its trendy sun-worshippers. This boutique beach is known for its dangerous rips. Bronte has better swimming than Bondi. To get to Bronte, catch Bus 378 from Circular Quay, or pick up the bus at the Bondi Junction CityRail station.

Clovelly Beach, farther along the coast, is blessed with a large rock pool carved into a rock platform and sheltered from the force of the Tasman Sea. This beach is accessible for visitors in wheelchairs via a series of ramps. To reach Clovelly, take Bus 339 from Circular Quay.

The cliff walk from Bondi will eventually bring you to **Coogee,** which has a pleasant strip of sand with a couple of hostels and hotels nearby. To reach Coogee, take Bus 373 or 374 from Circular Quay (via Pitt, George, and Castlereagh streets, and Taylor Square on Oxford Street) or Bus 314 or 315 from Bondi Junction.

NORTH OF SYDNEY HARBOUR

On the north shore you'll find **Manly** 𝒜𝒜, a long curve of golden sand edged with Norfolk Island pines (don't be fooled by the two small beaches either side of the ferry terminal as some people have been—including the famous novelist Arthur Conan Doyle, who traveled to Manly by ferry and presuming the small beach near the ferry station was the best the suburb had to offer did not bother to disembark). Follow the crowds shuffling through the pedestrianized "Corso" to the main ocean beach. You'll find one of Sydney's nicest walks here, too. Looking at the ocean, head to your right along the beachfront and follow the coastal path to the small and sheltered **Shelly Beach** 𝒜, a nice area for snorkeling and swimming (there's also a small take-out outlet here selling drinks and snacks, next to the good, but pricey, Le Kiosk beachfront restaurant). Follow the bitumen path up the hill to the carpark. Here, a track cuts up into the bush and leads toward a fire wall, which marks the entrance to Sydney Harbour National Park. Around here you'll get some spectacular ocean views across to Manly and the northern beaches (the headland further in the distance is Palm Beach). The best way to reach Manly is on a ferry or JetCat from Circular Quay.

Farther along the north coast are a string of ocean beaches, including the surf spots of **Curl Curl, Dee Why, Narrabeen, Mona Vale, Newport, Avalon,** and finally **Palm Beach** 𝒜, a long and beautiful strip of sand cut from the calmer waters of **Pittwater** by sand dunes and a golf course. Here you'll also find the Barrenjoey Lighthouse, which also offers fine views along the coast (see the "Greater Sydney" map earlier in this chapter for a map of this area). Bus numbers 136 and 139 run from Manly to Curl Curl, while Bus 190 runs from Wynyard to Newport and then via the other northern beaches as far as Palm Beach.

The best harbor beach can be found at **Balmoral** 𝒜, a wealthy North Shore hangout complete with some good cafes (The Sandbar is the best for food) and two very good, upmarket beach-view restaurants—the **Bathers Pavillion** (© **02/9969 5050**) and **The Watermark** (© **02/9968 3433**). The beach itself is split into three parts. As you look towards the sea, the middle section is the most popular with sunbathers, while the wide expanse of sand to your left and the sweep of surreally beautiful sand to your right have a mere scattering. There's a caged pool area for swimming. Reach Balmoral via a ferry to Taronga Zoo and then a 5-minute ride on a connecting bus from the ferry wharf, or catch the bus from the stop outside the zoo's top entrance.

> **Fun Fact Grin & Bare It**
>
> If getting an all-over tan is your scene, you have a couple of options in Sydney. Head either to the nudist beach at **Lady Jane Bay,** a short walk from Camp Cove Beach (accessed from Cliff Street in Watsons Bay, reached by walking along the strip of sand—to the right as you look at the sea—at the back of the Watsons Bay Hotel). Or, you can try **Cobblers Beach,** accessed via a short, but steep, unmarked bush track that leads from the far side of the playing field oval next to the main HMAS *Penguin* naval base at the end of Bradley's Head Road in Mosman (follow the procession of men in shorts). Be prepared for a largely male-orientated scene—as well as the odd boatload of beer-swigging peeping toms.

MUSEUMS, GALLERIES, HISTORIC HOUSES & MORE

Art Gallery of New South Wales 🍳   The numerous galleries here present some of the best of Australian art and many fine examples by international artists, including good displays of Aboriginal and Asian art. You enter from The Domain parklands on the third floor of the museum. On the fourth floor you will find an expensive restaurant and a gallery often showing free photography displays. On the second floor is a wonderful cafe overlooking the wharves and warships of Wooloomooloo. Every January and February there is a fabulous display of the best work created by school students throughout the state. Allow at least 1 hour.

Art Gallery Rd., The Domain. ℭ **02/9225 1744.** www.artgallery.nsw.gov.au. Free admission to most galleries. Special exhibitions vary, though expect to pay around A$12 (U.S.$7.80) adults, A$7 (U.S.$4.55) children. Daily 10am–5pm. Tours of general exhibits Tues–Fri 11am, noon, 1, and 2pm and Monday 1 and 2pm, call for weekend times. Tours of Aboriginal galleries Tues–Fri 11am, Sat–Sun at 1pm. Free Aboriginal performance Tues–Sat at noon. CityRail: St. James. Sydney Explorer bus.

Australian Museum   Though nowhere near as impressive as, say, the Natural History Museum in London, Sydney's premier natural history museum is still worth a look. Displays are presented thematically, the best being the Aboriginal section with its traditional clothing, weapons, and everyday implements. There are some sorry examples of stuffed Australian wildlife, too. Temporary exhibits run from time to time. Allow 1 to 2 hours.

6 College St. ℭ **02/9320 6000.** www.austmus.gov.au. Admission A$8 (U.S.$5.20) adults, A$3 (U.S.$1.95) children, A$19 (U.S.$12.35) families. Special exhibits cost extra. Daily 9:30am–5pm. Closed Christmas. CityRail: Museum, St. James, or Town Hall. Sydney Explorer bus.

Customs House   This museum, in the sandstone building with the clock and flags across the large square opposite the Circular Quay CityRail station and the ferry wharves, opened in December 1998. It's worth a look inside if you're interested in architecture. You might be hooked by the series of modern-art objects displayed on the ground floor, and the traveling exhibits on the third floor—though often you won't be. Outside in the square is a popular cafe selling reasonably priced coffee, cakes, sandwiches, and the like. Allow 15 minutes.

Alfred St., Circular Quay. ℭ **02/9320 6429.** Free general admission. Open daily 9:30am–5pm. CityRail, bus, or ferry: Circular Quay.

Elizabeth Bay House   This good example of colonial architecture was built in 1835 and was described at the time as the "finest house in the colony." Visitors can tour the whole house and get a real feeling of the history of the fledgling settlement. The house is situated on a headland and has some of the best harbor views in Sydney. Allow 1 hour.

7 Onslow Ave., Elizabeth Bay. © 02/9356 3022. Admission A$7 (U.S.$4.55) adults, A$3 (U.S.$1.95) children, A$17 (U.S.$11.05) families. Tues–Sun 10am–4:30pm. Closed Good Friday and Christmas. Bus: 311 from Circular Quay. Sydney Explorer bus.

Museum of Sydney   You'll need your brain in full working order to make the most of the contents of this three-story post-modern building near Circular Quay, which encompasses the remnants of Sydney's first Government House. This place is far from being a conventional showcase of history; instead, it houses a rather minimalist collection of first-settler and Aboriginal objects and multimedia displays that "invite" the museum-goer to discover Sydney's past for him- or herself. Some Frommer's readers have criticized the place, saying it's not just minimalist—it's simply unfathomable. By the way, that forest of poles filled with hair, oyster shells, and crab claws in the courtyard adjacent to the industrial-design cafe tables is called *Edge of Trees*. It's a metaphor for the first contact between Aborigines and the British. There's a reasonable cafe out the front. Allow anywhere from an hour to a lifetime to understand.

37 Phillip St. © 02/9251 5988. Admission A$7 (U.S.$4.55) adults, A$3 (U.S.$1.95) children under 15, A$17 (U.S.$11) family. Daily 9:30am–5pm. CityRail, bus, or ferry: Circular Quay. Sydney Explorer bus.

St James Church   Sydney's oldest surviving colonial church, begun in 1822, was designed by the Government architect, and former convict, Francis Green-way. At one time the church's spire served as a landmark for ships coming up the harbor, but today it looks totally lost amidst the skyscrapers. It's well worth seeking out though, especially for the plaques on the wall, which pay testament to the hard early days of the colony when people were lost at sea, "speared by blacks," and died while serving the British Empire overseas.

Queens Sq., Macquarie St. © 02/9232 3022. Daily 9am–5pm.

St Mary's Cathedral   Sydney's most impressive worship place is a giant sandstone construction wedged between The Domain and Hyde Park. The original St Mary's was built in 1821, but the chapel was destroyed by fire. Work on the present cathedral began in 1868, but due to lack of funds remained unfinished until work began in 1999 to build the two spires. The stained-glass windows inside are particularly impressive. St. Mary's is Roman Catholic and was built for Sydney's large population of Irish convicts. In perhaps Sydney's worst pre-Olympic planning, the beautiful brown sandstone building was marred by a wide stretch of dark gray paving outside—now the battleground of skateboarders and city council rangers. The two spires were completed in extra-quick time for the Olympics, too.

College and Cathedral sts. © 02/9230 1414. Mon–Tues 6:30am–6:30pm; Sat 8am–7:30pm; Sun 6:30am–7:30pm.

State Library of NSW   The state's main library is divided into two sections, the Mitchell and Dixon Libraries, which are located next door to one another. A newer reference-library complex nearby has two floors of reference materials, local newspapers, and microfiche viewers. Leave your bags in the free lockers downstairs (you'll need an A$2/U.S.$1.30 coin, which is refundable). I highly recommend the library's leafy **Glasshouse Café,** in my opinion one of the best walk-in lunch spots in Sydney. The older building contains many older and more valuable books on the ground floor, and often hosts free art and photography displays in the upstairs galleries. A small library section in the Sydney Town Hall building has international newspapers.

Macquarie St. ℰ **02/9273 1414.** Free admission. Mon–Fri 9am–9pm; Sat–Sun and selected holidays 11am–5pm. Closed New Year's Day, Good Friday, Christmas, and Boxing Day (Dec 26). CityRail: Martin Place. Sydney Explorer bus.

Sydney Jewish Museum   Harrowing exhibits here include documents and objects relating to the Holocaust and the Jewish culture, mixed with sound-scapes, audio-visual displays, and interactive media. There's also a museum shop, a resource center, a theaterette, and a traditional kosher cafe. It's considered one of the best museums of its type in the world. Allow 1 to 2 hours.

148 Darlinghurst Rd. (at Burton St.), Darlinghurst. ℰ **02/9360 7999.** Admission A$7 (U.S.$4.55) adults, A$4 (U.S.$2.60) children, A$16 (U.S.$10.40) families. Cash only. Mon–Thurs 10am–4pm; Fri 10am–2pm; Sun 11am–5pm. Closed Jewish holidays, Christmas, and Good Friday. CityRail: Kings Cross.

Sydney Observatory   The city's only major museum of astronomy offers vis-itors a chance to see the southern skies through modern and historic telescopes. The best time to visit is during the night on a guided tour, when you can take a close-up look at some of the planets. Night tours are offered at 8:15pm from the end of May to the end of August and at 6:15 and 8:15pm the rest of the year; be sure to double-check the times when you book your tour. The planetarium and hands-on exhibits are also interesting.

Observatory Hill, Watson Rd., Millers Point. ℰ **02/9217 0485.** Admission free in daytime; guided night tours (reservations essential) A$10 (U.S.$6.50) adults, A$5 (U.S.$3.25) children, A$25 (U.S.$16.25) families. Daily 10am–5pm. CityRail, bus, or ferry: Circular Quay.

Vaucluse House   Also looking over Sydney Harbour, this house includes lavish entertainment rooms and impressive stables and out-buildings. It was built in 1803 and was the home of Charles Wentworth, the architect of the Aus-tralian Constitution. It's set in 27 acres (11 hectares) of gardens, bushland, and beach frontage—perfect for picnics. Allow 1 hour.

Wentworth Rd., Vaucluse. ℰ **02/9337 1957.** www.hht.nsw.gov.au. Admission A$7 (U.S.$4.55) adults, A$3 (U.S.$1.95) children. House Tues–Sun 10am–4:30pm. Grounds daily 7am–5pm. Free guided tours. Closed Good Friday and Christmas. Bus: 325 from Circular Quay, or Bondi & Bay Explorer.

PARKS & GARDENS
IN SYDNEY

ROYAL BOTANIC GARDENS ℛ   If you are going to spend time in one of Sydney's green spaces, then make it the **Royal Botanic Gardens** (ℰ **02/9231 8111**), next to Sydney Opera House. The gardens were laid out in 1816 on the site of a farm dedicated to supplying food for the fledgling colony. They're in-formal in appearance with a scattering of duck ponds and open spaces, though there are several areas dedicated to particular plant species, such as the rose garden, the cacti and succulent display, and the central palm and the rain-forest groves (watch out for the thousands of large fruit bats which chatter and argue amongst the rain-forest trees). **Mrs. Macquarie's Chair,** along the coast path, offers superb views of the Opera House and the Harbour Bridge (it's a favorite stop for tour buses). The giant sandstone building dominating the gardens nearest to the Opera House is **Government House,** once the official residence of the Governor of New South Wales (he moved out in 1996 in the spirit of republicanism). The pleasant gardens are open to the public daily from 10am to 4pm, and the house is open Friday through Sunday from 10am to 3pm. Entrance to both is free. If you plan to park around here it's well to note that

PACIFIC RIM   PACIFIC HEIGHTS

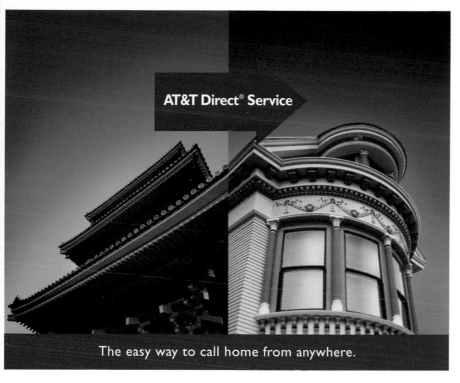

AT&T Direct® Service

The easy way to call home from anywhere.

Global
connection
with the AT&T
Network

AT&T
direct
service

For the easy way to call home, take the attached wallet guide.

www.att.com/traveler

AT&T Calling Card, AT&T Corporate Card, AT&T Universal Card, MasterCard,® American Express,® VISA,® Diners Club,® and Discover® cards accepted. Credit card calling subject to availability. Payment terms subject to your credit card agreement. ©2001 AT&T

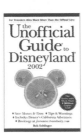
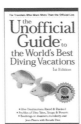
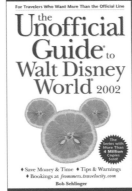
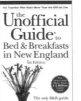

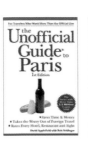

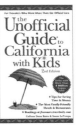

parking meters cost upwards of A$3 (U.S.$1.95) per hour, and you need A$1 coins.

A popular walk takes you through the Royal Botanic Gardens to the **Art Gallery of New South Wales.** The gardens are open daily from 7am to dusk. Admission is free.

HYDE PARK   In the center of the city is Hyde Park, a favorite with lunching businesspeople. Of note here are the **Anzac Memorial** to Australian and New Zealand troops killed in the wars, and the **Archibald Fountain,** complete with spitting turtles and sculptures of Diana and Apollo. At night, avenues of trees are lit up with twinkling lights giving the place a magical appearance.

MORE CITY PARKS   Another Sydney favorite is giant **Centennial Park** (✆ 02/9339 6699), usually accessed from the top of Oxford Street. It opened in 1888 to celebrate the centenary of European settlement, and today encompasses huge areas of lawn, several lakes, picnic areas with outdoor grills, cycling and running paths, and a cafe. It's open from sunrise to sunset. To get there, take Bus 373, 374, 378, 380, or 382 from the city, or via the Bondi & Bay Explorer.

A hundred years later, **Bicentennial Park,** at Australia Avenue, in Homebush Bay, came along. Forty percent of the park's total 100 hectares (247 acres) is general parkland reclaimed from a city rubbish tip; the rest is the largest remaining remnant of wetlands on the Parramatta River and is home to many species of both local and migratory wading birds, cormorants, and pelicans. Follow park signs to the **visitor information office** (✆ 02/9763 1844), open Monday through Friday from 10am to 4pm, and Saturday and Sunday from 9:30am to 4:30pm. To reach the park, take a CityRail train to Homebush Bay station.

BEYOND SYDNEY

SYDNEY HARBOUR NATIONAL PARK   You don't need to go far to experience Sydney's nearest national park. The Sydney Harbour National Park stretches around parts of the inner harbor and includes several small harbor islands (many first-time visitors are surprised at the amount of bushland still remaining in prime real-estate territory). The best walk through the Sydney Harbour National Park is the **Manly to Spit Bridge Scenic Walkway** (✆ 02/9977 6522). This 10-kilometer (6-mile) track winds its way from Manly (it starts near the Oceanarium), via Dobroyd Head to Spit Bridge (where you can catch a bus back to the city). The walk takes around 3 hours at a casual pace, and the views across busy Sydney Harbour are fabulous. There are a few Aboriginal stone carvings, which are signposted along the route. Maps are available from the **Manly Visitors Information Bureau,** right opposite the main beach (✆ 02/9977 1088).

Other access points to the park include tracks around Taronga Zoo (ask the zoo staff to point you toward the rather concealed entrances), and above tiny Shelly Beach, opposite the main beach at Manly.

Also part of the national park is the recently restored **Fort Denison,** the easily recognizable fortified outcrop in the middle of the harbor between Circular Quay and Manly. The fort was built during the Crimean War due to fears of a Russian invasion, and later acted as a penal colony. One- to two-hour **Heritage Tours** of the island leave from Cadmans Cottage, in The Rocks (✆ 02/9247 5033). They cost A$22 (U.S.$14.30) for adults and A$18 (U.S.$11.70) for students and children. Call ahead for times and bookings. Pick up maps of Sydney Harbour National Park at Cadmans Cottage.

Another great walk in Sydney can be combined with lunch or a drink at Watsons Bay. A 15-minute bush stroll to **South Head** is accessed from the small beach outside the Watsons Bay Hotel. Walk to the end of the beach (to your right as you look at the water) then up the flight of steps into Short Street, then left along Cliff Street to the end of Camp Cove beach. Continue along the coast past the nudist Lady Bay beach to the lighthouse at South Head, where there are some great views (of the coastline, not the nudists). Across the road in front of the Watsons Bay Hotel is another section of the national park, known for its fabulous cliff-top views. Here you'll find The Gap, a spectacularly sheer cliff popular for suicides. Watsons Bay is reached by ferries from Circular Quay, and via the Bondi and Bay Explorer.

MORE NATIONAL PARKS   Forming a semicircle around the city are Sydney's biggest parks of all. To the west is the **Blue Mountains National Park** (see chapter 4), to the northeast is **Ku-ring-gai Chase National Park,** and to the south is the magnificent **Royal National Park.** All three parks are home to marsupials such as echidnas and wallabies, numerous bird and reptile species, and a broad range of native plant life. Walking tracks, whether they stretch for half an hour or a few days, make each park accessible to the visitor.

   Ku-ring-gai Chase National Park (☎ **02/9457 9322** or 02/ 9457 9310) is a great place to take a bushwalk through gum trees and rain forest on the lookout for wildflowers, sandstone rock formations, and Aboriginal art. There are plenty of tracks through the park, but one of my favorites is a relatively easy 2.5-kilometer (1½-mile) tramp to **The Basin** (Track 12). The well-graded dirt path takes you down to a popular estuary with a beach and passes some significant Aboriginal engravings. There are also some wonderful water views over Pittwater from the picnic areas at **West Head.** Pick up a free walking guide at the park entrance, or gather maps and information in Sydney at the National Parks & Wildlife Service's center at **Cadmans Cottage,** 110 George St., The Rocks (☎ **02/9247 8861**). The park is open from sunrise to sunset, and admission is A$10 (U.S.$6.50) per car. You can either drive to the park or catch a ferry from Palm Beach to The Basin (from where you can walk up Track 12 and back). Ferries run on the hour (except at 1pm) from 9am to 5pm daily and cost A$4 (U.S.$2.60) one-way; call ☎ **02/9918 2747** for details. Shorelink Bus 577 runs from the Turramurra CityRail station to the nearby park entrance every hour on weekdays and every 2 hours on weekends; call ☎ **02/9457 8888** for details. There is no train service to the park. Camping is allowed only at The Basin (☎ **02/9457 9853**), and costs A$12 (U.S.$7.80) for two people booked in advance.

   If you have a car you could visit the **Ku-ring-gai Wildflower Garden,** 420 Mona Vale Rd., St Ives (☎ **02/9440 8609**), which is essentially a huge area of natural bushland and a center for urban bushland education. There are plenty of bushwalking tracks, self-guided walks, and a number of nature-based activities. It's open daily from 8am to 4pm. Admission is A$2.50 (U.S.$1.60) for adults, A$1 (U.S.65¢) for children, and A$6 (U.S.$3.90) for families.

   To the south of Sydney is the remarkable **Royal National Park,** Farrell Avenue, Sutherland (☎ **02/9542 0648**). It's the world's oldest national park, having been gazetted as such in 1879 (the main competitor to the title is Yellowstone in the United States, which was set aside for conservation in 1872 but not designated as a national park until 1883). Severe bushfires almost destroyed the whole lot in early 1994, but the trees and bush plants have recovered remarkably. There's no visitor center, but you can get park information at park entrances, where you'll have to pay a A$10 (U.S.$6.50) per-car entry fee.

There are several ways to access the park, but my favorites are the little-known access points from Bundeena and Otford. To get to Bundeena, take a CityRail train from Central Station to Cronulla. Just below the train station you'll find Cronulla Wharf. From there, hop on the delightful ferry run by **National Park Ferries** (© **02/9523 2990**) to Bundeena; ferries run hourly on the half hour (except 12:30pm). After you get off the ferry, the first turn on your left just up the hill will take you to **Bundeena Beach.** It's another 5 kilometers (3 miles) or so to the wonderfully remote **Little Marley Beach,** via Marley Beach (which has dangerous surf). The ferry returns to Cronulla from Bundeena hourly on the hour (except 1pm). The fare is A$3 (U.S.$1.95) each way.

An alternative way to reach the park is to take the train from Central Station to **Otford,** then climb the hill up to the sea cliffs. If you're driving, you might want to follow the scenic cliff-edge road down into Wollongong. The entrance to the national park is a little tricky to find, so you may have to ask directions— but roughly it's just to the left of a cliff top popular for hang gliding, radio-controlled airplanes, and kites. A 2-hour walk from the sea cliffs through beautiful and varying bushland and a palm forest will take you to **Burning Palms Beach.** There is no water along the route. The walk back up is steep, so only attempt this trek if you're reasonably fit. Trains to the area are irregular, and the last one departs around 4pm, so give yourself at least 2½ hours for the return trip back to the train station to make sure you don't get stranded. It's possible to walk the 26 memorable kilometers (16 miles) from Otford to Bundeena, or vice versa, in 2 days (take all your food, water, and camping gear). The track sticks to the coast, crosses several beaches, and is relatively easy to follow.

ESPECIALLY FOR KIDS

There are plenty of places kids can have fun in Sydney, but my choices below are particularly suitable for youngsters (all of the places are reviewed in full above).

Taronga Zoo (see p. 145) is an all-time favorite with kids, where the barn-yard animals, surprisingly, get as much attention as the koalas. If your kids want hands-on contact with the animals, though, then you'd better head to **Feather-dale Wildlife Park** (see p. 145), where they can get their photo taken next to a koala, and hand feed and stroke kangaroos and wallabies. You can't stroke koalas in New South Wales. Even more interactive are the exhibits just crying out to be touched and bashed at the **Powerhouse Museum** (see p. 142).

The sharks at **Oceanworld** (see p. 145) in Manly and at the **Sydney Aquarium** (see p. 142) in Darling Harbour are big lures for kids, too, and the thrill of

---

Tips **A Stroll on The Rocks**

Sydney is relatively compact, so it's a wonderful city for exploring on foot. I particularly recommend a wander through The Rocks, site of the oldest settlement in Australia, a rough-and-tumble place where prostitutes, gang members, and other shady characters loitered more than a century ago. **The Rocks Walking Tour** (© **02/9247 6678**) has an organized stroll (see "Walking Tours," below). For my own take on the neighborhood, consult the self-guided walk that appears in *Frommer's Portable Sydney*.

walking through a long plexiglass tunnel as giant manta rays perch over their heads will lead to more squeals of excitement.

Another fascinating outing for both adults and children is to crawl around inside boats and submarines at the **Australian National Maritime Museum** (see p. 141).

And, of course, what kid wouldn't enjoy a day at the beach, and Sydney's got plenty to choose from, like **Bondi** or **Manly.**

6 Harbor Cruises & Organized Tours

For details on the Red Sydney Explorer bus, see "Getting Around," earlier in this chapter.

HARBOR CRUISES

The best thing about Sydney is the harbor, so you shouldn't leave without taking a harbor cruise. **Sydney Ferries** (© **13 15 00** or 02/9245 5600; www.sta.nsw. gov.au) offers a 1-hour morning harbor cruise with commentary departing Circular Quay, Wharf 4, daily at 10 and 11:15am. It costs A$15 (U.S.$9.75) for adults, A$7.50 (U.S.$4.90) for children under 16, and A$37.50 (U.S.$24.40) for families (any number of children under 16). A 2½-hour afternoon cruise explores more of the harbor and leaves from Wharf 4 at 1pm on weekdays and 1:30pm on weekends and public holidays. This tour costs A$22 (U.S.$14.30) for adults, A$11 (U.S.$7.15) for children, and A$55 (U.S.$35.75) for families. The highly recommended 1½-hour **Evening Harbour Lights tour,** which takes in the city lights as far east as Double Bay and west to Goat Island, leaves Monday through Saturday at 8pm from Wharf 5. The 1½-hour evening tour costs A$19 (U.S.$12.35) for adults, A$9.50 (U.S.$6.20) for children, and A$47.50 (U.S.$30.90) for families.

If you are missing the Mississippi, another option is a trip on the paddle-steamer The *Sydney Showboat* (© **02/9552 2722;** www.bluelinecruises. com.au). A daily lunch cruise on this oddly placed vessel starts at either 11.15am or 1:15pm and costs A$51 (U.S.$33.15) for adults and A$30.60 (U.S.$20) for children 4 to 12; it includes a good buffet lunch, a jazz band, and commentary. A daily 2½-hour dinner cruise and variety show runs from 7:30pm and costs A$133 (U.S.$87) for adults and A$79.80 (U.S.$52) for children. Check with the company about other cruises, including afternoon excursions.

HARBOR CRUISE TICKETS & INFO

The one-stop shop for tickets and information on all harbor cruises is the **Australian Travel Specialists** (© **02/9247 5151;** www.atstravel.com.au). Find outlets at Jetty no. 6 at Circular Quay; at the Harbourside Festival Marketplace at Darling Harbour; and on the Podium Level of the A.M.P. Centerpoint Tower.

If you're going to splurge on a cruise, though, the best are aboard the fully rigged replica of **Captain Bligh's** *Bounty* ✿ (© **02/9247 1789;** www. thebounty.com). Based at Campbell's Cove in The Rocks, the Bounty was built for the movie *The Bounty,* which starred Mel Gibson and Anthony Hopkins. Standard 2-hour and lunch cruises run from 12:30pm Monday through Friday and cost A$65 (U.S.$42.25). Two-and-a-half-hour dinner cruises depart daily at 7pm in high season (Sept 1–Apr 30) and Friday and Saturday only from May 1 to August 31, and cost A$99 (U.S.$64.40) for adults. On Saturday and Sunday (and public holidays) a 2½-hour Buffet Lunch Sail starts at 12:30pm and costs A$95 (U.S.$61.75), and a 1½-hour pre-dinner sail on Saturdays from 4pm costs

A$53 (U.S.$34.45). An extra 1½-hour brunch sail on Sundays and public holidays also costs A$53 (U.S.$34.45). There's a 40% discount for children under 12 on all cruises.

Alternatively, you can cruise like a millionaire aboard the **MV *Oceanos*** (② 02/9555 4599), a 21.5-meter (72-ft.) luxury motor cruiser. A 3-hour cruise, which leaves Campbells Cove at 12.30pm Tuesday, Thursday, and Sunday, costs A$75 (U.S.$48.75) per person and includes a quality seafood lunch. It's essential to book 2 days in advance. **Sail Venture Cruises** (② 02/9262 3595) also has a range of cruises aboard their catamarans.

Captain Cook Cruises, departing Jetty no. 6, Circular Quay (② 02/9206 1111; www.captaincook.com.au), offers several harbor excursions on its sleek vessels, with commentary along the way. The Harbour Highlights cruise operates several times daily and takes in most of the main points of interest in 1¼ hours, for A$20 (U.S.$13) for adults and A$10 (U.S.$6.50) for children. Another offering is the *Sydney Harbour Explorer* cruise which departs at 9:30, 11:30am, 1:30, and 3:30pm and combines visits to five major Sydney attractions with a 2-hour cruise. You can get off where you want and join the boat again later. Tickets cost A$25 (U.S.$16.25) for adults and A$15 (U.S.$9.75) for children. An Aquarium & Zoo Cruise, costing A$36.50 (U.S.$23.70) for adults and A$19 (U.S.$12.35) for children, includes the *Sydney Harbour Explorer* cruise and admission to either the Sydney Aquarium or Taronga Zoo.

The company also offers a 1½-hour Lunch Cruise, which leaves daily at 12:30pm. It costs A$49 (U.S.$31.85) for adults and A$29 (U.S.$18.85) for children. A Starlight Dinner Cruise leaves nightly at 7:30pm and costs A$59 (U.S.$38.35) for adults and A$35 (U.S.$22.75) for children.

Alternatively, its nightly 1½-hour "Sunset Cruise" aboard the **John Cadman Cruising Restaurant boat,** departing just before sunset costs A$69 (U.S.$44.85) for adults and A$35 (U.S.$22.75) for children, and includes a two-course meal and drinks. Yet another option is the Opera Afloat Dinner (including opera singers of course). This costs A$97 (U.S.$63) for adults and A$55 (U.S.$35.75) for children.

Matilda Cruises (② 02/9264 7377; www.matilda.com.au) offers a 1-hour Matilda Rocket sightseeing tour leaving the pontoon at the far end of Sydney Aquarium at Darling Harbour eight times daily beginning at 9:30am (six times daily in winter—Apr 1–Sept 30—beginning at 10:30am). You can stay on for the full hour, or get off and on again at Circular Quay, the Opera House, Watsons Bay, and Taronga Zoo. The last boat leaves Taronga Zoo at 5:10pm in summer (4:10pm in winter). There's commentary and tea and coffee on board. The cruise costs A$20.50 (U.S.$13.30) for adults, A$10.50 (U.S.$6.80) for children 5 to 12, and A$49.50 (U.S.$32) for a family. The company also runs morning and afternoon cruises, and lunch and dinner cruises with good food.

WALKING TOURS

The center of Sydney is surprisingly compact, and you'll find you can see a lot in a day on foot. If you want to learn more about Sydney's early history, then you should book a guided tour with **The Rocks Walking Tour** (② 02/9247 6678), based at the Shop K4, Kendall Lane (off Argyle St., The Rocks). Excellent walking tours leave Monday through Friday at 10:30am, 12:30, and 2:30pm, and Saturday and Sunday at 11:30am and 2pm (in Jan only 10:30am and 2:30pm on weekdays). The 1½-hour tour costs A$16 (U.S.$10.40) for adults, A$10.70 (U.S.$6.95) for children 10 to 16, and A$41.25 (U.S.$26.80) for families. Accompanied children under 10 are free.

For other historical walks contact **Sydney Guided Tours** (☎ 02/9660 7157). The company's owner, Maureen Fry, has been in the business for over 12 years and employs trained guides qualified in specific disciplines, such as history, architecture, and botany. She offers a range of tours including an introductory tour of Sydney, a tour of historic Macquarie Street, and many others. Walking tours cost A$17 (U.S.$11) for 2 hours as part of a group (call in advance to find out what's available).

A journey with a difference is **Weird Sydney Ghost and History Tours** (☎ 02/9555 2700; www.destinytours.com.au). The tour—in a hearse—is fascinating and fun, an explores a large section of historic Sydney (and more modern additions) including a former VD Clinic, the Sydney Opera House, and some of the buildings along Macquarie Street. It costs A$149 (U.S.$96.85) for the 1½- to 2-hour trip.

MOTORCYCLE TOURS

Blue Thunder Motorcycle Tours (☎ 02/9977 7721 or 0414/278 983) runs chauffeured Harley-Davidson tours of Sydney, the Blue Mountains, and other places around New South Wales. A 1-hour ride (you sit on the back of the bike) around the city costs A$90 (U.S.$58.50). A half-day trip to the northern beaches or down the south coast through the Royal National Park costs A$265 (U.S.$172.25), including lunch. Full-day trips cost A$370 (U.S.$240) including lunch and snacks, and go to either the Hunter Valley, the south coast, Bathurst, or the Blue Mountains.

Another Harley-Davidson tour specialist is **Dream Legends Motor Cycle Tours** (☎ 02/9584 2451). One-hour city trips cost A$75 (U.S.$48.75), half-day jaunts go for A$225 (U.S.$146.25), and a full-day excursion "wherever you want to go" costs A$400 (U.S.$260) with lunch and drinks. A side car is available.

A third mean-machine operator is **Eastcoast Motorcycle Tours** (☎ 02/9247 5151). One-hour city tours cost A$99 (U.S.$65), and four-hour trips to the south coast, Royal National Park, and Pittwater cost A$270 (U.S.$175.50).

7 Staying Active

BIKING   The best place to cycle in Sydney is in Centennial Park. Rent bikes from Centennial Park Cycles, 50 Clovelly Rd., Randwick (☎ 02/9398 5027), which is 200 meters (656 ft.) from the Musgrave Avenue entrance. (The park has five main entrances). Mountain bikes cost A$9 (U.S.$5.85) for the first hour, A$13 (U.S.$8.45) for 2 hours, and A$20 (U.S.$13) for 4 hours.

Bicycles in The City, 722 George St. (near Central Station) (☎ 02/9280 2229), rents mountain bikes from A$5 (U.S.$3.25) per hour, or $25 ($16.25) per day. You can rent in-line skates here, too, for the same daily rate with all protective clothing. Helmets are compulsory in Australia.

GOLF   Sydney has more than 90 golf courses and plenty of fine weather. The 18-hole championship course at **Moore Park Golf Club,** at Cleveland Street and Anzac Parade, Waterloo (☎ 02/9663 1064), is the nearest to the city. Visitors are welcome every day except all day Friday and Sunday mornings. Greens fees are A$24 (U.S.$15.60) Monday through Friday, and A$27 (U.S.$17.55) Saturday and Sunday.

One of my favorite courses is **Long Reef Golf Club,** Anzac Avenue, Colloroy (☎ 02/9982 2943). This northern beaches course is surrounded by the Tasman

Sea on three sides and has gorgeous views. Greens fees are A$25 (U.S.$16.25) midweek, and A$35 (U.S.$22.75) on weekends.

For general information on courses call the **New South Wales Golf Association** (© **02/9264 8433**).

FITNESS CLUBS   The **City Gym,** 107 Crown St., East Sydney (© **02/9360 6247**), is a busy gym near Kings Cross. Drop-in visits are A$10 (U.S.$6.50), and it's open daily 24 hours.

IN-LINE SKATING   The best places to go in-line skating are along the beachside promenades at Bondi and Manly beaches and in Centennial Park. **Manly Blades,** 49 North Steyne (© **02/9976 3833**), rents skates for A$12 (U.S.$7.80) for the first hour and A$6 (U.S.$3.90) for each subsequent hour, or A$25 (U.S.$16.25) per day. Lessons are A$25 (U.S.$16.25) including 1-hour skate rental and a half-hour lesson. **Bondi Boards & Blades,** 148 Curlewis St., Bondi Beach (© **02/9365 6555**), rents skates for A$11 (U.S.$7.15) for the first hour, A$5.50 (U.S.$3.60) for each subsequent hour, and A$20 (U.S.$13) for 24 hours. Ask about a free lesson. **Total Skate,** 36 Oxford St., Paddington, near Centennial Park (© **02/9380 6356**), rents skates for A$10 (U.S.$6.50) for the first hour and A$5 (U.S.$3.25) for subsequent hours, and A$30 (U.S.$19.50) for 14 hours. Ask about a free lesson.

JOGGING   The **Royal Botanic Gardens, Centennial Park,** or any **beach** are the best places to kick-start your body. You can also run across the Harbour Bridge, though you'll have to put up with the car fumes. Another popular spot is along the sea cliffs from Bondi Beach to Bronte Beach.

PARASAILING   If being strapped to a parachute 100 meters (328 ft.) above Sydney Harbour while being towed along by a speed boat is your idea of fun, contact **Sydney Harbour Parasailing and Scenic Tours** (© **02/99776781**). A regular flight will see you in the air for 8 to 10 minutes at the end of a 100-meter (328-ft.) line. Flights cost A$55 (U.S.$35.75) per adult. Tandem rides, for children and adults, are also available. The boat departs next to the Manly ferry wharf in Manly.

SCUBA DIVING   Plenty of people learn to dive in Sydney before taking off for the Barrier Reef. Don't expect beautiful coral reefs, though. **Pro Dive** (27 Alfreda St., Coogee © **02/9665 6333**), offers a 4-day learn-to-dive program costing $A345 (U.S.$224.25). A day of diving for registered divers costs A$105 (U.S.$68.25).

SURFING   **Bondi Beach** and **Tamarama** are the best surf beaches on the south side of Sydney Harbour, while **Manly, Narrabeen, Bilgola, Colloroy, Long Reef,** and **Palm** beaches are the most popular on the north side. Most beach suburbs have surf shops where you can rent a board. At Bondi Beach, the **Bondi Surf Co.,** 72 Campbell Parade (© **02/9365 0870**), rents surfboards for A$45 (U.S.$29.25) for 4 hours or A$60 (U.S.$39) all day. Body boards cost A$20 (U.S.$13) for 2 hours and A$60 (U.S.$39) all day. In Manly, **Aloha Surf,** 44 Pittwater Rd., Manly (© **02/9977 3777**), also rents surfboards. **Manly Surf School** (© **02/9977 6977**) offers 2-hour surf classes for A$40 (U.S.$26), 2-day sessions for A$70 (U.S.$45.50) and 3-day classes for A$90 (U.S.$58.50). **Wave Action Surf School** (© **02/9970 6813,** or mobile 0413/177 242) offers a similar service with the same rates as Manly Surf School, but this time on the breakers at Palm Beach. Also, it offers a 1-day surf tour from central Sydney to Palm

Beach and other northern Sydney beaches with sightseeing and a restaurant lunch for A$100 (U.S.$65).

SWIMMING   The best place to swim indoors in Sydney is the **Sydney International Aquatic Centre,** at Olympic Park, Homebush Bay (℃ **02/9752 3666**). It's open Monday through Friday from 5am to 9:45pm, and Saturday, Sunday, and public holidays from 6am to 7:45pm (6:45pm May–Oct).

Another good bet is the **North Sydney Olympic Pool,** Alfred South Street, Milsons Point (℃ **02/9955 2309**). It's just over the Harbour Bridge to your left, near the amusement park, so why not have a swim after a walk over from the city. Swimming here costs A$3.50 (U.S.$2.30) for adults and A$1.65 (U.S.$1.10) for children. More world records have been broken in this pool than in any other pool in the world. In 1999, the pool went through major renovations, and now has a separate indoor pool, too.

TENNIS   There are hundreds of places around the city to play one of Australia's most popular sports. A nice spot is the **Miller's Point Tennis Court,** Kent Street, The Rocks (℃ **02/9256 2222**). It's run by the Observatory Hotel and is open daily from 7:30am to 10pm. The court costs A$25 (U.S.$16.25) per hour. The **North Sydney Tennis Centre,** 1A Little Alfred St., North Sydney (℃ **02/9371 9952**), has three courts available daily from 6am to 10pm. They cost A$16 (U.S.$10.40) until 5pm on weekdays and A$20 (U.S.$13) other times.

WINDSURFING   My favorite spot to learn to windsurf or to set out onto the harbor is at **Balmoral Beach,** in Mosman on the North Shore. Rent boards at **Balmoral Windsurfing, Sailing and Kayaking School & Hire,** 3 The Esplanade, Balmoral Beach (℃ **02/9960 5344**). Windsurfers cost A$27 (U.S.$17.55) per hour for beginners and A$38 (U.S.$27.70) for advanced windsurfing equipment. Lessons cost A$175 (U.S.$113.75) for 5 hours teaching over a weekend, for beginners, and A$195 (U.S.$126.75) for advanced lessons. This place also rents fishing boats.

YACHTING   **Balmoral Boat Shed,** Balmoral Beach (℃ **02/9969 6006**), rents catamarans, 3.5-meter (12-ft.) aluminum runabouts, canoes, and surf skis. The catamarans and runabouts cost A$35 (U.S.$22.75) for the first hour (with an A$80/U.S.$52 deposit); a full day costs A$120 (U.S.$78). Other vessels, such as canoes, cost A$12 (U.S.$7.80) per hour with an A$10 (U.S.$6.50) deposit.

Sydney by Sail (℃ **02/9280 1110,** or 0419/367 180 mobile phone) offers daily introductory sailing cruises on the harbor aboard luxurious 10.25- and 11.5-meter (34- and 38-ft.) yachts. A maximum of six people sail aboard each boat, which leave from the National Maritime Museum at Darling Harbour. Ninety-minute introductory sails cost A$54 (U.S.$35.10) per person with the more popular 3-hour sail costing A$98 (U.S.$63.70). Reservations are essential.

8 Spectator Sports

CRICKET   The **Sydney Cricket Ground,** at the corner of Moore Park and Driver Avenue, is famous for its 1-day and test matches, played generally October through March. Phone the **New South Wales Cricket Association** at ℃ **02/9339 0999** for match details, and **Sportspace Tours** (℃ **02/9380 0383**) for stadium tours.

Finds **A Surf Adventure**

If you've always fancied learning to surf then a great option is with Waves Surf School (© **1800/851 101** in Australia, or 0414 682 228 mobile; www.surfschool.com.au). Waves takes budding surfers on 1-day trips from Sydney to the Royal National Park with all equipment and lunch provided. They cost A$59 (U.S.$38.35) weekdays and A$64 (U.S.$41.60) on weekends. For A$199 (U.S.$129.35) you get a 2-day excursion to Seal Rocks, north of Sydney, for surf lessons, powerboat riding, and other activities. You camp out on the beach, and all meals and gear are provided.

FOOTBALL   In this city, "football" means rugby league. If you want to see burley chaps pound into each other while chasing an oval ball, then be here between May and September. The biggest venue is the **Sydney Football Stadium,** Moore Park Road, Paddington (© **02/9360 6601**). Match information is available at © **1900 963 133.** Buy tickets at **Ticketek** (© **02/9266 4800**).

HORSE RACING   Sydney has four horse-racing tracks: Randwick, Canterbury, Rosehill, and Warwick Farm. The most central and most well known is **Randwick Racecourse,** Alison Street, Randwick (© **02/9663 8400**). The biggest race day of the week is Saturday. Entry costs A$9 (U.S.$5.85) per person. Call the **Sydney Turf Club** at © **02/9930 4000** with questions about Rosehill and Canterbury, and the Randwick number above for Warwick Farm.

SURFING CARNIVALS   Every summer these uniquely Australian competitions bring large crowds to Sydney's beaches, as surf clubs compete against each other in various water sports. Contact the **Surf Lifesaving Association** (© **02/ 9597 5588**) for times and locations. Other beach events include Iron Man and Iron Woman competitions, during which Australia's fittest struggle it out in combined swimming, running, and surfing events.

YACHT RACING   While sailing competitions take place on the harbor most summer weekends, the start of the **Sydney to Hobart Yacht Race** on Boxing Day (Dec 26) is something not to be missed. The race starts from the harbor near the Royal Botanic Gardens. Contact **Tourism New South Wales** (© **02/ 9931 1111;** fax 02/9931 1490) or **Tourism Tasmania** (© **03/6230 8169;** fax 03/6230 8353) for more information.

9 Shopping

You'll find plenty of places to keep your credit cards in action in Sydney. Most shops of interest to the visitor are located in The Rocks and along George and Pitt streets (including the shops below the A.M.P. Centerpoint Tower and along the Pitt Street Mall). Other shopping precincts worth checking out are Mosman on the North Shore and Double Bay in the eastern suburbs for exclusive boutique shopping, Chatswood for its general shopping centers, the Sydney Fishmarket for the sake of it, and the various weekend markets (listed below).

You won't want to miss the **Queen Victoria Building (QVB),** on the corner of Market and George streets. This Victorian shopping arcade is one of the prettiest in the world and has some 200 boutiques—mostly men's and women's fashion—on four levels. The arcade is open 24 hours, but the shops do business Monday through Saturday from 9am to 6pm (Thurs to 9pm) and Sunday from 11am to 5pm.

SHOPPING HOURS　Regular shopping hours are generally Monday through Wednesday and Friday from 8:30 or 9am to 6pm, Thursday from 8:30 or 9am to 9pm, Saturday from 9am to 5 or 5:30pm, and Sunday from 10 or 10:30am to 5pm. Exceptions are noted in the store listings below.

Several other arcades in the city center also offer good shopping potential, including the **Royal Arcade** under the Hilton Hotel; the **Imperial Arcade** near the A.M.P. Centerpoint Tower; **Sydney Central Plaza,** beside the Grace Brothers department store on Pitt Street Mall; and the **Skygarden Arcade,** which runs from Pitt Street Mall to Castlereagh Street. The **Strand Arcade** (running between Pitt Street Mall and George Street) was built in 1892 and is interesting for its architecture and small boutiques, food stores and cafes, and the Down Town Duty Free store on the basement level.

On **Pitt Street Mall** you'll find record shops, including HMV, a branch of The Body Shop, and boutiques such as Just Jeans, Jeans West, Katies, and Esprit.

SYDNEY SHOPPING FROM A TO Z
ABORIGINAL ARTIFACTS & CRAFTS
Aboriginal & Tribal Art Centre　This center carries a wide range of desert paintings and bark paintings, mostly of very high quality. Collectibles such as didgeridoos, fabrics, books, and boomerangs are on sale, too. Open daily from 10am to 5pm. 1st floor, 117 George St., The Rocks. ☎ **02/9247 9625.** Fax 02/9247 4391.

Coo-ee Aboriginal Art Gallery and Shop　The proprietors of Coo-ee collect artifacts and fine art from more than 30 Aboriginal communities and dozens of individual artists throughout Australia. The gallery also stocks the largest collection of limited-edition prints in Australia. There are also plenty of hand-painted fabrics, T-shirts, didgeridoos, boomerangs, sculpture, bark paintings, jewelry, music, and books. Don't expect bargain prices, though; you pay for the quality here. Open Monday through Saturday from 10am to 6pm and Sunday from 11am to 5pm. 98 Oxford St., Paddington. ☎ **02/9332 1544.**

Didj Beat Didjeridoo's　Here you'll find the most authentic and well-priced didgeridoos in Sydney. Open daily from 10am to 6:30pm. Shop 2, The Clock Tower Sq., corner of Argyle and Harrington sts. ☎ **02/9251 4289.**

Gavala Aboriginal Art & Cultural Education Centre　I'd head here first if I were in the market for a decent boomerang or didgeridoo. Gavala is entirely owned and operated by Aborigines, and there are plenty of authentic Aboriginal crafts for sale, including carved emu eggs, grass baskets, cards, and

---

⏺ *Value* Discount Shopping

If you're looking for bargains, head to **Foveraux Street** between Elizabeth and Waterloo streets in Surry Hills for factory clearance shops selling last season's fashions and seconds at deep discounts. If you're keen on bargain shopping, consider joining up with **Shopping Spree Tours** (☎ **1800/625 969** in Australia, or 02/9360 6220; fax 02/9332 2641), which offers tours to outlets and warehouses selling everything from clothes to cookware to electrical appliances. Full-day tours cost A$70 (U.S.$45.50) for adults and A$20 (U.S.$13) for children 3 to 12 and include pickup at your hotel, visits to 8 to 10 outlets and warehouses, and a two-course lunch at a good restaurant. Tours depart at 8:15am daily except Sunday and public holidays.

books. A first-rate painted didgeridoo will cost anywhere from A$100 to $450 (U.S.$65 to $292.50). Gavala also sponsors cultural talks, didgeridoo-making lessons, and story-telling sessions. Open daily from 10am to 9pm. Shop 377, Harbourside Festival Marketplace, Darling Harbour. 📞 02/9212 7232.

Original & Authentic Aboriginal Art   Quality Aboriginal art is on sale here from some of Australia's best-known painters, including Paddy Fordham Wainburranga, whose paintings even hang in the White House in Washington, and Janet Forrester Nangala, whose work has been exhibited in the Australian National Gallery in Canberra. Expect to pay in the range of A$1,000 to $4,000 (U.S.$650 to $2,600) for the larger paintings. There are some nice painted pots here, too, costing from A$30 to $80 (U.S.$19.50 to $52). Open daily from 10am to 6.30pm. 79 George St., The Rocks. 📞 02/9251 4222.

ART PRINTS & ORIGINALS

Done Art and Design   The art is by Ken Done, who's well known for having designed his own Australian flag, which he hopes to raise over Australia should it abandon its present one following the formation of a republic. The clothing designs—which feature printed sea- and beachscapes, the odd colorful bird, and lots of pastels—are by his wife Judy. Ken Done's gallery is in Hickson Road, just off George Street, in the Rocks. Open daily from 10am to 5:30pm. 1 Hickson Rd., The Rocks. 📞 02/9247 2740.

Ken Duncan Gallery   This photographer-turned-salesman is making a killing from his exquisitely produced large-scale photographs of Australian scenery. Open daily from 9am to 8pm. 73 George St., The Rocks (across from The Rocks Visitor Centre). 📞 02/9241 3460. Fax 02/9241 3462.

BOOKS

You'll find a good selection of specialized books on Sydney and Australia for sale at the **Art Gallery of New South Wales**, the Garden Shop in the **Royal Botanic Gardens**, the **Museum of Sydney**, the **Australian Museum**, and the **State Library of New South Wales.**

Abbey's Bookshop   This interesting, centrally located bookshop specializes in literature, history, and mystery, and has a whole floor on language and education. 131 York St. (behind the Queen Victoria Building). 📞 02/9264 3111.

Angus & Robertson Bookworld   One of Australia's largest bookshops, with two stories of books—including a good guidebook and Australiana section— and games. 168 Pitt St., Pitt Street Mall. 📞 02/9235 1188.

Dymocks   One of the largest book department stores in the city, Dymocks has three levels of general books and stationery. There's a reasonable travel section with plenty of guides. Open Monday through Wednesday and Friday from 9am to 6pm, Thursday from 9am to 9pm, Saturday from 9am to 5pm, and Sunday from 10am to 5pm. 424–428 George St. (just north of Market St.). 📞 02/9235 0155.

Gleebooks Bookshop   Specializing in art, general literature, psychology, sociology, and women's studies, Gleebooks also has a secondhand store (with a large children's department) down the road at 191 Glebe Point Rd. Open daily 8am to 9pm. 49 Glebe Point Rd., Glebe. 📞 02/9660 2333.

Goulds Book Arcade   Come here to search for unusual dusty volumes. Located about a 10-minute walk from the Newtown CityRail station, the place is bursting at the seams with many thousands of secondhand and new books all in a very rough order. You can browse for hours here. Open daily from 8am to midnight. 32–38 King St., Newtown. ℂ 02/9519 8947.

Travel Bookshop   Hundreds of travel guides, maps, Australiana titles, coffee-table books, and travel accessories line the shelves of this excellent bookshop. There's also an Amex counter here. Open Monday through Friday from 9am to 6pm and Saturday from 10am to 5pm. Shop 3, 175 Liverpool St. (across from the southern end of Hyde Park, near the Museum CityRail station). ℂ 02/9261 8200.

CRAFTS

Australian Craftworks   This place showcases some of Australia's best arts and crafts, collected from some 300 Australian artists from around the country. It's all displayed in a former police station built in 1882, a time of economic depression when mob riots and clashes with police were common in this area. The cells and administration areas are today used as gallery spaces. Open daily from 8:30am to 7pm. 127 George St., The Rocks. ℂ 02/9247 7156.

The Puppet Shop at the Rocks *(Finds*   I can't believe I kept walking past the sign outside this place for so many years without looking in. Deep down in the bowels of a historic building I eventually came across several cramped rooms absolutely packed with puppets, costing from a couple of dollars to a couple of hundred. The owners make their own puppets—mostly Australian in style (emus, koalas, and that sort of thing)—as well as import things from all over the world. Wooden toys abound, too. It's the best shop in Sydney! Open daily from 10am to 5:30pm. 77 George St., The Rocks. ℂ 02/9247 9137.

Telopea Gallery   This shop is run by the New South Wales Society of Arts and Crafts, which exhibits works made by its members, all of whom are New South Wales residents. There are some wonderful glass, textile, ceramic, jewelry, fine-metal, and wood-turned items for sale. Open daily from 9:30am to 5:30pm. Shop 2 in the Metcalfe Arcade, 80–84 George St., The Rocks. ℂ 02/9241 1673.

DEPARTMENT STORES

The two big names in Sydney shopping are David Jones and Grace Brothers. **David Jones** (ℂ 02/9266 5544) is the city's largest department store, selling everything from fashion to designer furniture. You'll find the women's section on the corner of Elizabeth and Market streets, and the men's section on the corner of Castlereagh and Market streets.

Grace Brothers (ℂ 02/9238 9111) is similar to David Jones, but the building is newer and flashier. It's located on the corner of George and Market streets. Both stores are open Monday through Wednesday and Friday through Saturday from 9am to 6pm, Thursday from 9am to 9pm and Sunday from 11am to 5pm.

DUTY-FREE SHOPS

Sydney has several duty-free shops selling goods at a discount. To take advantage of the bargains, you need a passport and a flight ticket, and you must export what you buy. The duty-free shop with the best buys is **Downtown Duty Free,** which has two city outlets, one on the basement level of the Strand Arcade, off Pitt Street Mall (ℂ 02/9233 3166) and one at 105 Pitt St. (ℂ 02/9221 4444). Five more stores are found at Sydney International Airport and are open from the first to the last flight of the day.

FASHION

The best places to shop for fashion are the Queen Victoria Building and the Sydney Central Plaza (on the ground floor of the mall next to the Grace Brothers department store on Pitt Street Mall). Otherwise, the major Pitt Street Mall outlets will keep you up-to-date. For really trendy clothing head to Paddington, and for alternative clothes, go to Newtown.

Australian Outback Clothing

R.M. Williams Moleskin trousers may not be the height of fashion at the moment, but you never know. R.M. Williams boots are famous for being both tough and fashionable. You'll find Akubra hats, Driza-bone coats, and kangaroo-skin belts here, too. 389 George St. (between Town Hall and Central CityRail stations). © 02/9262 2228.

Thomas Cook Boot & Clothing Company Located on George Street between Town Hall and central CityRail stations, this place specializes in Australian boots, Driza-bone coats, and Akubra hats. There's another shop at 129 Pitt St., near Martin Place (© **02/9232 3334**). 790 George St., Haymarket. © 02/9212 6616. www.thomascookclothing.com.au.

Unisex Fashion

Country Road This chain store has outlets all across Australia as well as in the United States. The clothes, for both men and women, are good quality but tend to be quite expensive (though you might find something smart if you forgot to pack something). You'll find other branches in the Queen Victoria Building and the Skygarden Arcade, and in Bondi Junction, Darling Harbour, Double Bay, Mosman, and Chatswood. 142–146 Pitt St. © 02/9394 1818.

Mostrada If you're looking for good-quality leather items at very reasonable prices, then this is your place. Leather jackets for men and women go for between A$199 and $899 (U.S.$129.35–$584.35), with an average price of around A$400 (U.S.$260). There are also bags, belts, and other leather accessories on offer. Store 15G, Sydney Central Plaza, 450 George St. © 02/9221 0133.

Men's Fashion

Esprit Mens Not so cheap, but certainly colorful clothes come out of this designer store where bold hues and fruity patterns are the in thing. Quality designer shirts cost around A$60 (U.S.$39). Shop 10G, Sydney Central Plaza, 450 George St. © 02/9233 7349.

Gowings Probably the best all-round men's clothing store in Sydney, Gowings sells quality clothing on several levels. There's also an eclectic mix of gardening equipment, gourmet camping gear, odds and ends for the extrovert, a good range of Australian bush hats, and R.M. Williams boots (at around A$250/U.S.$162.50 a pair). If you want to risk it, you can even get a cheap haircut here. There's a similar store at 319 George St. (© **02/9262 1281**), near Wynyard CityRail station. 45 Market St. © 02/9264 6321.

Outdoor Heritage Quality clothing with a yachting influence is what you'll find at this good-looking store specializing in casual, colorful gear. Shop 13G, Sydney Central Plaza, 450 George St. © 02/9235 1560.

Women's Fashion

In addition to the places listed below, head to Oxford Street (particularly Paddington), for more avant-garde designers.

Carla Zampatti There are some 30 Carla Zampatti stores around Australia offering stylish fashions at hard-to-swallow prices. Open Monday through Saturday from 10am to 5pm. 143 Elizabeth St. © 02/9264 3257.

Dorian Scott   Probably the best place to go for hand-knitted sweaters—called "jumpers" in Australia—Dorian Scott has a wide range of colorful garments from more than 200 leading Australian designers. While some items go for A$80 (U.S.$52), others will set you back several hundred. You'll also find clothing accessories for men, women, and children in this two-story emporium, including Hot Tuna surfware and Thomas Cook adventure clothing. Open Monday through Saturday from 9:30am to 7pm and Sunday from 10am to 6pm. There are also two Dorian Scott stores at Sydney International Airport (© **02/9667 3255**) and another at the Inter-Continental Hotel at 117 Macquarie St. (© **02/ 9247 1818**). 105 George St., The Rocks. © **02/9221 8145**. Fax 02/9251 8553.

FOOD
The goodies you'll find in the downstairs food section of **David Jones** department store on Castlereagh Street (the men's section) are enough to tempt anyone. The store sells the best local and imported products to the rich and famous.

Coles   One of the few supermarkets in the city center, this place is a good bet if you want to cater for yourself or are after ready-made food (including tasty sandwiches) and cheap soft drinks. There's another Coles beneath the giant Coca-Cola sign on Darlinghurst Road, Kings Cross. Open daily from 6am to midnight. Wynyard Station, Castlereagh St., Wynyard (directly opposite the Menzies Hotel and the public bus stands). © **02/9299 4769**.

Darrell Lea Chocolates   This is the oldest location of Australia's most famous chocolate shop. Pick up some wonderful handmade chocolates as well as other unusual candies, including the best liquorice this side of the Kasbah. At the corner of King and George sts. © **02/9232 2899**.

Sydney Fishmarket   Finding out about what people eat can be a good introduction to a new country, and, in my opinion, nowhere is this more fascinating than a visit to the local fish market. Here you'll find seven major fish retailers selling everything from shark to Balmain bugs (a kind of squat crayfish), with hundreds of species in between. Watch out for the local pelicans being fed the fishy leftovers. There's also a Doyles restaurant and a sushi bar, a couple of cheap seafood eateries, a fruit market, and a good deli. The retail sections are open daily from 7am to 4pm. Get here by Light Rail (get off at the Fishmarket stop), or walk from Darling Harbour. Parking costs A$2 (U.S.$1.30) for the first 3 hours. At the corner of Bank St. and Pyrmont Bridge Rd., Pyrmont. © **02/9660 1611**.

GIFTS & SOUVENIRS
The shops at **Taronga Zoo**, the **Oceanarium** in Manly, the **Sydney Aquarium,** and the **Australian Museum** are all good sources for gifts and souvenirs. There are many shops around **The Rocks** worth browsing, too.

Australian Geographic   A spin-off from the Australian version of *National Geographic* magazine, this store sells good-quality crafts and Australiana. On hand are camping gadgets, telescopes and binoculars, garden utensils, scientific oddities, books and calendars, videos, music, toys, and lots more. Harbourside Festival Marketplace, Darling Harbour. © **02/9212 6539**. A.M.P. Centerpoint Tower, Pitt St. © **02/9231 5055**.

Ikonstore   This interesting little store located on the pedestrian pathway to the Sydney Opera House from Circular Quay has a fascinating collection of watches and gadgets for the gourmet collector. Shop 16, Opera Quays, East Circular Quay. © **02/9252 6352**.

National Trust Gift and Bookshop   You can pick up some nice souvenirs, including books, Australiana crafts, and indigenous foodstuffs here. An art gallery on the premises presents changing exhibits of paintings and sculpture by Australians. There's also a cafe. Closed Monday. Observatory Hill, The Rocks. ℂ 02/ 9258 0154.

The Wilderness Society Shop   Australiana is crawling out of the woodwork at this cute little craft emporium dedicated to spending all its profits on saving the few remaining untouched forests and wilderness areas of Australia. You'll find some quality craft items, cute children's clothes, books, cards, and knick-knacks. A.M.P. Centerpoint Tower, Castlereagh St. ℂ 02/9233 4674.

MARKETS

Balmain Market   Active from 8:30am to 4pm every Saturday, this popular market has some 140 vendors selling crafts, jewelry, and knickknacks. Take the ferry to Balmain (Darling Street); the market is a 10-minute walk up Darling Street. On the grounds of St. Andrew's Church, Darling St., Balmain ℂ 02/9555 1791.

Paddington Bazaar   At this Saturday-only market you'll find everything from essential oils and designer clothes to new age jewelry and Mexican hammocks. Expect things to be busy from 10am to 4pm. Take Bus 380 or 389 from Circular Quay. On the grounds of St. John's Church on Oxford St., on the corner of Newcome St. (just follow the crowds). ℂ 02/9331 2646.

Paddy's Markets   A Sydney institution, Paddy's Markets has hundreds of stalls selling everything from cheap clothes and plants to chickens. It's open Friday through Sunday from 9am to 4:30pm. Above Paddy's Markets is **Market City** (ℂ 02/9212 1388), which has three floors of fashion stalls, food courts, and specialty shops. Of particular interest is the largest Asian-European super-market in Australia, on level 1, and the **Kam Fook yum cha** Chinese restaurant on level 3, also the largest in Australia. At the corner of Thomas and Hay sts., in Haymarket, near Chinatown. ℂ 1300/361 589 in Australia or 02/9325 6924.

The Rocks Market   Held every Saturday and Sunday, this very touristy market has more than 100 vendors selling everything from crafts, housewares, posters, jewelry, and curios. The main street is closed to traffic from 10am to 4pm to make it easier to stroll around. On George St., The Rocks. ℂ 02/9255 1717.

MUSIC

Birdland   This is the best store in Sydney for jazz and blues, and it stocks a sizable collection of rare items. The staff is very knowledgeable. 3 Barrack St. ℂ 02/ 9299 8527. www.birdland.com.au.

HMV   This is one of the best music stores in Sydney. The jazz section is impressive. CDs in Australia are not cheap, with most new releases costing around A$30 to $35 (U.S.$19.50 to $22.75). Pitt Street Mall. ℂ 02/9221 2311.

Red Eye Records   These two shops, tucked away downstairs in a small arcade not far from Pitt Street Mall and the Strand Arcade, are directly across from one another. The larger store sells a wide range of modern CDs, but the smaller store sells a great collection of quality secondhand and end-of-the-line CDs for around A$20 (U.S.$13) each. Tank Stream Arcade (downstairs), at the corner of King and Pitt sts. (near Town Hall). ℂ 02/9233 8177 (new recordings), or 02/9233 8125 (secondhand CDs). www.redeye.com.au.

Sounds Australian   Anything you've ever heard that sounds Australian you can find here. From rock and pop to didgeridoo and country, it's all here.

Fortunately, if you haven't a clue what's good and what's bad you can spend some time listening before you buy. The management is extremely knowledgeable. In the Argyle Stores department store, The Rocks. ℂ 02/9247 7290. Fax 02/9241 2873.

OPALS

There are plenty of opal shops around in Sydney, but don't expect to walk away with any bargains. Best just to choose one you like and haggle.

Altman & Cherny   A good selection of opals—black, white and boulder varieties—as well as opal jewelry are on sale here. Ask the staff to see the world's biggest black opal. 19–31 Pitt St. (near Circular Quay). ℂ 02/9251 9477.

Australian Opal Cutters   Learn more about opals before you buy at this shop. The staff here will give you lessons about opals to help you compare pieces. Suite 10, Level 4, National Building, 250 Pitt St. ℂ 02/9261 2442.

WINE

Australian Wine Centre   This is one of the best places in the country to pick up Australian wines by the bottle or the case. The shop stocks a wide range of wines from all over Australia, including bottles from small boutique wineries you're unlikely to find anywhere else. Individual tastings are possible at any time, though there are formal tastings every Thursday and Friday from 4 to 6pm. Wine is exported all over the world from here, so if you want to send home a crate of your favorite, you can be assured it will arrive in one piece. The center owns the wine bar and bistro next door, which is open Monday through Saturday from 6am until 10pm. You can drink here without dining. 1 Alfred St., Shop 3 in Goldfields House, Circular Quay. ℂ 02/9247 2755.

10 Sydney After Dark

Australians are party animals when they're in the mood; whether it's a few beers around the barbecue with friends or an all-night rave at a trendy dance club, they're always on the lookout for the next event. You'll find that alcohol plays a big part in the Aussie culture.

WHERE TO FIND OUT WHAT'S ON

The best way to find out what's on is to get hold of the "Metro" section of the Friday *Sydney Morning Herald* or the "Seven Days" pullout from the Thursday *Daily Telegraph*.

THE PERFORMING ARTS

If you have an opportunity to see a performance in the **Sydney Opera House,** jump at it. The "House" is actually not that impressive inside, but the walk back after the show toward the ferry terminals at Circular Quay, with the Sydney Harbour Bridge lit up to your right and the crowd all around you debating the best part of this play or who dropped a beat in that performance—well, it's like hearing Gershwin while on the streets of New York—you'll want the moment to stay with you forever. For details on Sydney's most famous performing-arts venue, see section 5 earlier in this chapter.

THE OPERA, SYMPHONY & BALLET

Australian Ballet   Based in Melbourne, the Australian Ballet tours the country with its performances. The Sydney season, at the Opera House, is from mid-March until the end of April. A second Sydney season runs November through December. Level 15, 115 Pitt St. (C) 02/9223 9522. www.austballet.telstra.com.au.

Australian Chamber Orchestra   Based in Sydney, this well-known company performs at various venues around the city, from nightclubs to specialized music venues, including the Concert Hall in the Sydney Opera House. Opera Quays, 2 East Circular Quay. (C) 02/9357 4111; box office (C) 02/8274 3888. www.aco.com.au.

Opera Australia   Opera Australia performs at the Sydney Opera House's Opera Theatre. The opera season runs January through March and June through November. 480 Elizabeth St., Surry Hills. (C) 02/9699 1099; bookings (C) 02/9319 1088. www.opera-australia.org.au.

Sydney Symphony Orchestra   Sydney's finest symphony orchestra is conducted by the renowned Edo de Waart. It performs throughout the year in the Opera House's Concert Hall. The main symphony season runs March through November, and there's a summer season in February. Level 5, 52 William St., East Sydney. (C) 02/9334 4644; box office 02/9334 4600. www.symphony.org.au.

THEATER

Sydney's blessed with plenty of theaters, many more than I have space for here—check the *Sydney Morning Herald,* especially the Friday edition, for information on what's currently in production.

Belvoir Street Theatre   The hallowed boards of the Belvoir are home to Company B, which pumps out powerful local and international plays upstairs in a wonderfully moody main theater, formerly part of a tomato-sauce factory. Downstairs, a smaller venue generally shows more experimental productions, such as Aboriginal performances and dance. 25 Belvoir St., Surry Hills. (C) 02/9699 3444. Tickets around A$34 (U.S.$22.10).

Capital Theatre   Sydney's grandest theater plays host to major international and local productions like, cough, Australian singing superstar Kylie Minogue. It's also been the Sydney home of musicals such as *Miss Saigon* and *My Fair Lady.* 13–17 Campbell St., Haymarket (near Town Hall). (C) 02/9320 5000. Ticket prices vary.

Her Majesty's Theatre   A quarter of a century old, this large theater is still trawling in the big musicals. Huge productions that have run here include *Evita*

It's a Festival!

If you happen to be in Australia in January, then plan to attend one of the many events that take place as part of the annual Sydney Festival. The festival kicks off just after New Year's and continues until the last week of the month, with recitals, plays, films, and performances held at venues throughout the city, including Town Hall, the Royal Botanic Gardens, the Sydney Opera House, and Darling Harbour. Some events are free. "Jazz in The Domain" and "Symphony in The Domain" are two free outdoor performances held in the Royal Botanic Gardens outside the Art Gallery of New South Wales; each event (which generally takes place on the third and fourth weekend in Jan) attracts thousands of Sydneysiders. For more information on the Sydney Festival, contact **Festival Ticketek** ((C) **02/9266 4111;** fax 02/9267 4460). Buy tickets and find out about performances on the Web at **www.sydneyfestival.org.au.**

and *Phantom of the Opera*. 107 Quay St., Haymarket (near Central Station). ℂ **02/9212 3411**. Ticket prices average A$55–$75 (U.S.$35.75–$48.75).

Wharf Theatre   This wonderful theater is situated on a refurbished wharf on the edge of Sydney Harbour, just beyond the Harbour Bridge. The long walk from the entrance of the pier to the theater along old creaky wooden floorboards builds up excitement for the show. The Sydney Theatre Company is based here, a group well worth seeing whatever production is running. Dinner before the show at the Wharf's restaurant offers special views of the harbor. Pier 4, Hickson Rd., The Rocks. ℂ **02/9250 1777**. www.sydneytheatre.com.au. Ticket prices vary.

THE CLUB & MUSIC SCENE
JAZZ, FOLK & BLUES

The Basement   Australia's hottest jazz club also manages to squeeze in plenty of blues, folk, and funk. Pick up a leaflet showing who's playing when at the door. Acts appear every night, and it's best to book ahead. 29 Reiby Place, Circular Quay. ℂ **02/9251 2797**. Cover A$15–$20 (U.S.$9.75–$13) for local acts, A$20–$40 (U.S.$13–$26) for international performers.

The Bridge Hotel & Brasserie   Come on a Sunday afternoon and you're assured of getting the blues. Friday and Saturday nights offer blues, rock, or house music depending on the whim of the management. The three-level beer garden out back is nice on a sunny day. 135 Victoria St., Rozelle. ℂ **02/9810 1260**. Cover A$5–$25 (U.S.$3.25–$16.25).

The Harbourside Brasserie   Eat to the beat of soul and rhythm-and-blues at this not-bad eatery. Comedy nights attract big acts. Drinks are expensive. Pier One, Hickson Rd., Walsh Bay (behind The Rocks). ℂ **02/9252 3000**. Cover A$8–$20 (U.S.$5.20–$13) depending on performer.

Soup Plus   It seemed such a pity on my last visit to this cavernous jazz bar that the cover charge forced me to eat the bistro-style food on hand, which really was poor. However, some mellow blues cheered our non-plussed group in the end. 383 George St. (near the Queen Victoria Building). ℂ **02/9299 7728**. Cover A$6 (U.S.$3.80). Mon–Thurs; A$28 (U.S.$18) Fri–Sat, including 2-course meal & show.

ROCK

Metro   A medium-size rock venue with space for 1,000, the Metro is the best place in Sydney to see local and international acts. Tickets sell out quickly. 624 George St., ℂ **02/9264 2666**. Cover varies.

DANCE CLUBS

Clubs come and go, and change names and music, so check the latest by planning ahead with a phone call. You can also check the Metro section in *Sydney Morning Herald* on Friday, otherwise you might find free giveaway newspapers in some bars along Oxford Street that have info about latest clubs.

Blackmarket   This wacky place is known for its Friday night Hellfire Club (11pm–4am every first and third Fri), where Sydneysiders of all persuasions hang out to watch "non-stop fetish performances" and live sadomasochism shows. It's all in (relatively) good taste, with nothing too brutal, and it attracts a fun-loving crowd from students to office workers (about 50/50 male and female). Some people dress up. There's some good music, too, in the dark and moody interior. Ravers continue on, or drop in after working the nightshift, at the Day Club, offering dance music from 4am to 2pm on Saturday and 4am to

6pm on Sunday. 111–113 Regent St., Chippendale, at the corner of Meagher St. (5-min. walk from Central Station). © **02/9698 8863.** Cover A$20 (U.S.$13).

Bourbon & Beefsteak Bar Right in the middle of Sydney's red-light district, this 24-hour restaurant and nightspot freaks out to dance music downstairs nightly from 11pm to 5am. It's popular with both young backpackers and the 25-to-35 crowd. 24 Darlinghurst Rd., Kings Cross. © **02/9358 1144.** Weekend cover charge varies, but roughly A$8–$10 (U.S.$5.20–$6.50) Fri–Sat.

Chinese Laundry A couple of dance floors, one with rock walls to enhance the beat of the hip-hop, trance, and dance. Club wear—for example, dress like you want to un-impress. Sussex Street (turn right as you face the bridge from Cockle Bay across to Darling Harbour, and it's a 2-min. walk, below the Slip Inn bar). © **02/9299 4777.** Fri–Sat 11pm–4am. Cover A$12 (U.S.$7.80) Fri, A$18 (U.S.$11.70) Sat.

Home Cave-like in shape and feel with a balcony to look down upon the throng, Home has a reputation for bad bouncers—like the time the *Sydney Morning Herald* newspaper had a Christmas party there and even the influential journalists were abused. Still it's managed to survive—hope you can. Funk, and heavy drum-and-bass-style music, good for the serious clubber. Cockle Bay Wharf, Darling Harbour. © **02/9266 0600.** Cover A$25 (U.S.$16.25).

Mister Goodbar A young, trendy, local crowd inhabits Mister Goodbar's two good-size dance floors, which offers a range of rap, funk, and hip-hop music Wednesdays through Saturdays. 11a Oxford St., Paddington. © **02/9360 6759.** Cover A$10 (U.S.$6.50) Wed; A$5 (U.S.$3.25) Thurs; A$10 (U.S.$6.50) Fri; and A$15 (U.S.$9.75) Sat.

Riche Nightclub This hot spot for dancing is popular with the local over-25 club set, as well as with hotel guests wanting to shake their booties to typical "dance" music. Open only Friday and Saturday. In the Sydney Hilton, 259 Pitt St. © **02/9266 2000.** Cover A$11 (U.S.$7.15) Fri and Sun, A$16.50 (U.S.$10.70) Sat. Free for hotel guests.

Tantra "Upmarket nightclubbing for the likes of models and beautiful people from the [affluent] north shore of Sydney," is how the manager describes this place. The interior is pseudo-Roman with lots of pillars. The club offers hardcore club/dance music. Dress code is fashionable, with a shirt collar required for men and no sneakers. "70s Boogie Wonderland" night Friday; commercial house music Saturday, and "funky" house music Sunday. 169 Oxford St., Darlinghurst. © **02/9331 7729.** Cover A$15 (U.S.$9.75) Fri–Sat; A$5 (U.S.$3.25) Sun.

GAY & LESBIAN CLUBS

Sydney has the largest gay community outside San Francisco, so it's no wonder there's a happening scene here. The center of it all is Oxford Street, though Newtown has established itself as a major gay hangout, too. For information on events concerning gays and lesbians pick up a copy of the *Sydney Star Observer,* available at art-house cinemas and cafes and stores around Oxford Street.

Albury Hotel An institution, the Albury is a grande dame offering drag shows nightly in the public bar, and knockout Bloody Marys in the cocktail lounge. Dancing, too. 2–6 Oxford St. (near Barcom Ave.). © **02/9361 6555.** A$5 (U.S.$3.25) cover Fri–Sat nights.

Imperial Hotel A few minutes from King Street in Newtown, the Imperial is a no-attitude gay venue with a pool and cocktail bar out front and a raging cabaret venue out back. Sydney's best full-production drag shows happen late on Thursday, Friday, Saturday and Sunday, with dancing in between. 35–37 Erskineville Rd., Erskineville (near Union St.). © **02/9519 9899.** No cover.

Newtown Hotel   The octagonal bar here is the center of a casual drinking and cruising scene. The place kicks up its heels during late-night drag shows and powerfully camp discos. 174 King St., Newtown. © 02/9557 1329. No cover.

Taxi Club   "Tacky Club," as it's affectionately known, is another Sydney institution good for "handbag music"—or old pop and new pop. 40 Flinders St., Darlinghurst (near Taylor Sq., Oxford St.). © 02/9331 4256. No cover.

THE BAR SCENE

Most of Australia's drinking holes are known as "hotels," after the tradition of providing room and board alongside a good drink in the old days. Occasionally you might hear them referred to as pubs. You tend to find the term "bar" used in upscale hotels and trendy establishments. Bars close at various times, generally from midnight to around 3am.

Bondi Hotel   This huge, whitewashed conglomerate across the road from Bondi Beach offers pool upstairs, a casual beer garden outside, and a resident DJ Thursday through Sunday from 8pm to 4am. There's also a free nightclub on Friday nights. Watch yourself; too much drink and sun turns some people nasty here. 178 Campbell Parade, Bondi Beach. © 02/9130 3271. No Cover.

The Friend in Hand   In the same location as the fantastically cheap Caesar's No Names spaghetti house, The Friend in Hand offers cheap drinks, poetry readings on Tuesday evenings from 8:30pm, a trivia night on Thursday evenings from 8:30pm, and the distinctly unusual Crab Racing Party every Wednesday from around 8pm. Crab fanciers buy a crustacean for around A$4 (U.S.$2.60), give it a name, and send it off to do battle in a race against around 30 others. There are heats and finals, and victorious crustaceans win their owners prizes. 58 Cowper St., Glebe. © 02/9660 2326.

Henry the Ninth Bar   This mock-Tudor drinking hole gets very busy on Friday and Saturday nights. They serve up some good ales in an oaky atmosphere. An Irish band whips up the patrons on Thursday and Friday nights, and a cover band does the same on Wednesday and Saturday nights. A good-value happy hour brings beer prices tumbling Monday through Thursday from 5:30 to 7:30pm, Friday 5:30 to 8:30pm, and Saturday 8 to 10pm. In the Sydney Hilton, 259 Pitt St. © 02/9266 2000.

Hero of Waterloo Hotel   This sandstone landmark, built in 1845, was once allegedly the stalking ground of press gangs, who'd whack unsuspecting land-lubbers on the head, push them down a trapdoor out the back, and cart them out to sea. Today, this strangely shaped sandstone drinking hole is popular with the locals, and hosts old-time jazz bands (the musicians are often in their 70s and 80s) on Saturday and Sunday afternoons from 1:30 to 6:30pm, and Irish and cover bands Friday to Sunday evenings from 8:30pm. 81 Lower Fort St., The Rocks. © 02/9252 4553.

Jacksons on George   A popular drinking spot, this place has four floors of drinking, eating, dancing, and pool playing, and is a popular haunt with tourists and after-work office staff. Pool is expensive here at A$3 (U.S.$1.95) a game (you'll need to ask the rules, as Australians have their own), and drinks have a nasty habit of going up in price without warning as the evening wears on. The nightclub plays commercial dance, and there's a smart/casual dress code. Happy hour is Monday through Friday from 5 to 7pm, when drinks cost around one-third less than normal. 178 George St., The Rocks. © 02/9247 2727. Cover A$10 (U.S.$6.50) for nightclub Fri–Sat after 10pm.

Lord Dudley Hotel   The best way to get to this great English-style pub is via the Edgecliff CityRail station (between Kings Cross and Bondi Junction). From there, bear right along the edge of the bus station, walk up the hill for 5 minutes and then take a right onto Jersey Road—ask the railway staff for the correct exit if you can find anyone working. The Lord Dudley has the best atmosphere of just about any drinking hole in Sydney, with log fires in winter, couches to relax in, three bars, and a restaurant. 236 Jersey Rd., Woollahra. ℂ 02/9327 5399.

Lord Nelson Hotel (*Value*   Another Sydney sandstone landmark, the Lord Nelson rivals the Hero of Waterloo for the title of Sydney's oldest pub. The drinks are sold English-style, in pints and half-pints, and the landlord even makes his own prize-winning beers. Of these beers, Three Sheets is the most popular, but if you can handle falling over on your way home you might want to try a drop of Quail (a pale beer), Victory (based on an English bitter), and a dark beer called Admiral. You can get some good pub grub here, too. Upstairs there's a more formal brasserie. At Kent and Argyle sts., The Rocks. ℂ 02/9251 4044.

Marble Bar   Once part of a hotel demolished in the 1970s, the Marble Bar is unique as the only grand-cafe-style drinking hole in Australia. With oil paintings, marble columns, and brass everywhere, it's the picture of 15th-century Italian Renaissance architecture, a tourist attraction in itself. Live music, generally jazz or soul, is played here Tuesday through Saturday beginning at 8:30pm. Dress smart on Friday and Saturday evenings. Drinks are normally very expensive, but the happy hour (daily 7–9pm) cuts prices down to what you'd pay during normal drinking hours elsewhere. In the Sydney Hilton, 259 Pitt St. ℂ 02/9266 2000.

The Mercantile   Sydney's original Irish bar is scruffy and loud when the Irish music's playing in the evening, but an essential stop on any self-respecting pub crawl in The Rocks. The Guinness is some of the best you'll taste in Sydney. Irish bands kick off every night at around 8pm. 25 George St., The Rocks. ℂ 02/9247 3570.

Slip Inn   This multifunctioning bar and bistro set-up is a popular city place to drink and meet. There's a garden bar downstairs set in a courtyard, along with a trattoria selling pizzas. Upstairs there's a Thai bistro open for lunch and a large square bar. It's crowded on Friday evenings, but you'll never feel like a sardine. Sussex Street, a 2-min. walk towards the city from the Town Hall/Cockle Bay side of the pedestrian bridge across to Darling Harbour. ℂ 02/9299 4777.

Watsons Bay Hotel   If it's a sunny afternoon, get over to Watsons Bay for the best food you'll find in the sun anywhere. The beer garden serves good seafood and barbecue meat dishes, while you sip your expensive wine or beer overlooking the harbor. Nearby are the fabulous Doyles Wharf Restaurant and Doyles at the Beach take-out. 1 Military Rd., Watsons Bay. ℂ 02/9337 4299.

MOVIES

The city's major movie houses, **Hoyts** (ℂ **13 27 00** in Australia), **Greater Union** (ℂ **02/9267 8666**), and **Village** (ℂ **02/9264 6701**), are right next to each other on George Street just past Town Hall. They tend to show big-budget movie releases. Other options are the **Dendy Cinemas,** located at 19 Martin Place, City (ℂ **02/9233 8166**); 261–263 King St., Newtown (ℂ **02/9550 5699**); and the latest Dendy movie theatre located just before you reach the Opera House, at 2 East Circular Quay (ℂ **02/9247 3800**). All show art-house movies; the latter allows wine and beer bought on the premises to be consumed in the cinema.

Another exceptional art-house/recent blockbuster cinema is the **Hayden Orpheum Picture Palace,** 380 Military Rd., Cremorne (© **02/9908 4344**). This eight-screen Art-Deco gem is an experience in itself, especially on Saturday and Sunday evenings when a Wurlitzer pops up from the center of the Cinema 2 stage, and a musician in a tux gives a stirring rendition of times gone by. Eat "Jaffas," round candy-coated chocolates, if you want to fit in.

Movie prices hover around A$14.50 (U.S.$9.40), with a half-price night generally on Tuesdays.

THE CASINO

Star City This huge entertainment complex, which opened in 1997, has 15 main bars, 12 restaurants, 2 theaters—the Showroom, which presents Las Vegas–style revues, and the Lyric, Sydney's largest theater—and a huge complex of retail shops. All the usual gambling tables are here, in four main gambling areas. In all there are 2,500 slot machines to gobble your change. 80 Pyrmont St., Pyrmont (adjacent to Darling Harbour). © **02/9777 9000.** No cover. Open 24 hrs. Ferry: Pyrmont (Darling Harbour). Monorail: Casino.

4

New South Wales

by Marc Llewellyn

With so much to experience in a state as big as New South Wales, you're not going to see all the major attractions in one hit, so as with any trip to Australia you must prioritize. If you have just a few days to spare, you should certainly head out to the Blue Mountains, part of the Great Dividing Range that separates the lush eastern coastal strip from the more arid interior. Although they are more hills than mountains, they are spectacular, with tall eucalyptus trees, deep river valleys, waterfalls, and craggy cliffs. Or spend a day in the vineyards of the lower Hunter (also known as the Hunter Valley). If you have a few more days, I recommend heading to Barrington Tops National Park, north of the Hunter, for a taste of rain forest and native animals, or down to the pristine beaches of Jervis Bay on the south coast for gorgeous scenery and some great bushwalks.

For longer trips, you can head north toward the Queensland border on the 964-kilometer (600-mile) route to Brisbane. On the way you'll pass pretty seaside towns, deserted beaches, and tropical hinterland. Another option is to travel along the south coast 1,032 kilometers (640 miles) to Melbourne. Along the way are some of the country's most spectacular beaches, quaint hamlets, some good opportunities to spot dolphins and whales, and extensive national parks. If you want to experience another side of Australia— the Outback—then head west across the Blue Mountains. You are sure to see plenty of kangaroos, emus, reptiles, and giant wedge-tailed eagles. The main Outback destinations are the extraordinary opal-mining town of Lightning Ridge, where you can meet some of the most eccentric *fair-dinkum* (that means "authentic" or "genuine") Aussies you'll come across anywhere.

EXPLORING THE STATE

VISITOR INFORMATION   The **Sydney Visitors Centre,** 106 George St., The Rocks (**℄ 13 20 77** in Australia; www.tourism.nsw.gov.au) will give you general information on the what to do and where to stay throughout the state. Otherwise, **Tourism New South Wales** (**℄ 02/9931 1111**), will direct you to the regional tourist office in the town or area you are interested in.

GETTING AROUND   By Car   From Sydney, the **Pacific Highway** heads along the north coast into Queensland, and the **Princes Highway** hugs the south coast and runs into Victoria. The **Sydney–Newcastle Freeway** connects Sydney with its industrial neighbor and the vineyards of the Hunter. The **Great Western Highway** and the **M4 Motorway** head west to the Blue Mountains, while the **M5 Motorway** and the **Hume Highway** are the quickest (and least interesting) ways to get to Melbourne.

The state's automobile association, the **National Roads and Motorists' Association (NRMA),** 151 Clarence St., Sydney (✆ **13 11 22** in Australia), offers free maps and touring guides to members of overseas motoring associations, including the AAA in the United States, the CAA in Canada, the AA and RAC in the United Kingdom, and the NZAA in New Zealand.

By Train   Countrylink (✆ **13 22 32** in Australia) trains travel to most places of interest in the state and as far south as Melbourne in Victoria and across the border into southern Queensland. Countrylink also has special rates for car rental through Thrifty.

By Plane   Qantas (✆ **13 13 13** in Australia) and **Eastern Australia Airlines** (book through Qantas) fly to most major cities and towns within the state.

1 The Blue Mountains ⭑⭑

Although the **Blue Mountains** are today where Sydneysiders go to escape the humidity and crowds of the city and suburbs, in the early days of the colony, the mountains kept at bay those who would explore the interior. In 1813, three explorers—Gregory Blaxland, William Charles Wentworth, and William Lawson—managed to conquer the sheer cliffs, valleys, and dense forest, and cross the mountains (which are hardly mountains at all, but rather a series of hills covered in bush and ancient fern trees) to the plains beyond. There they found land urgently needed for grazing and farming. The Great Western Highway and Bells Line of Road are the access roads through the region today— winding and steep in places, they are surrounded by Blue Mountains and Wollemi national parks.

The area is known for its spectacular scenery, particularly the cliff-top views into the valleys of gum trees and across to craggy outcrops that tower up from the valley floor. It's colder up here than down on the plains, and the clouds can sweep in and fill the canyons with mist in minutes, while waterfalls cascade down sheer drops, spraying the dripping fern trees that cling to the gullies. You'll need at least a couple of days up here to get the best out of it—a single-day tour, with all the traveling involved, can only just scratch the surface.

The Blue Mountains is also one of Australia's best-known adventure playgrounds. Rock climbing, caving, abseiling (rappelling), bushwalking, mountain biking, horseback riding, and canoeing are practiced here year round.

BLUE MOUNTAIN ESSENTIALS
VISITOR INFORMATION   You can pick up maps, walking guides, and other information and book accommodations at **Blue Mountains Tourism,** with locations at Echo Point Road, Katoomba, NSW 2780 (✆ **1300/653 408** in Australia, or 02/4739 6266), and on the Great Western Highway at Glenbrook, a small settlement 61 kilometers (42 miles) from Sydney (same telephone number). The Katoomba information center is an attraction in itself, with giant glass windows overlooking a gum forest and cockatoos and colorful lorikeets feeding on seed dispensers. Be sure to pick up a copy of the *Blue Mountains*

⌐*Fun Fact* **Color Me Blue**

The Blue Mountains derive their name from the ever-present blue haze that is caused by light striking the droplets of eucalyptus oil that evaporate from the leaves of the dense surrounding forest.

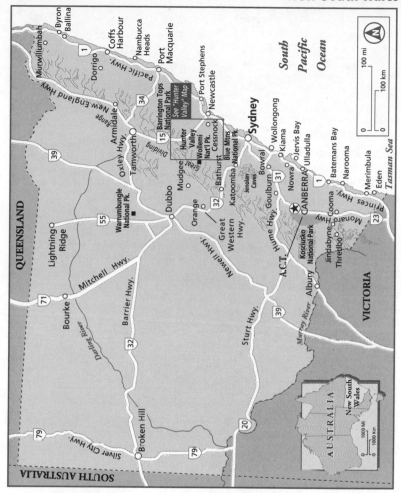

Pocket Guide, a free guide to dining, accommodations, bushwalking, and entertainment in the area. Both offices are open from 9am to 5pm daily (the office at Glenbrook closes at 4:30pm Sat and Sun).

The **National Park Shop,** Heritage Centre, the end of Govetts Leap Rd., Blackheath (© 02/4787 8877; www.npws.nsw.gov.au), is run by the National Parks and Wildlife Service and offers detailed information about the Blue Mountains National Park. The staff can also arrange personalized guided tours of the mountains. It's open daily from 9am to 4:30pm (closed Christmas).

Check the website, www.bluemts.com.au, for more information on the area.

GUIDED TOURS FROM SYDNEY Many private bus operators offer day trips from Sydney, but it's important to shop around because some offer a guided coach tour where you just stretch your legs occasionally, while others let you get the cobwebs out of your lungs with a couple of longish bushwalks. One highly recommended operator is **Oz Trek Adventure Tours,** P.O. Box 319, Potts Point, NSW 2011 (© 02/9360 3444; fax 02/9664 9134;

The Blue Mountains

www.oztrek.com.au; info@oztrek.com.au). Their trips include a tour of the Olympic Site, a visit to Glenbrook National Park (where you'll see kangaroos and wallabies in the wild), tours of all the major Blue Mountain sites, and a 1½-hour bushwalk. It costs just A$54 (U.S$35) for adults and A$43 (U.S.$28) for kids.

Wonderbus (© **02/9555 9800;** fax 02/9555 1345; www.wonderbus.com. au) tours are good fun for all ages and include most of the major sites and a short bush walk. The basic Blue Mountains Trip costs A$50 (U.S.$32.50), while a new Blue Mountains Discovery Tour, which also takes in Featherdale wildlife park and includes lunch, costs A$80 (U.S.$52). Overnight packages are also available. Ask about backpacker rates.

Cox's River Escapes, P.O. Box 81, Leura, NSW 2780 (© **02/4784 1621,** or mobile 0407 400 121; www.bluemts.com.au/CoxsRiver/), offers highly recommended tours for those wanting to get off the beaten track. Half-day trips with morning or afternoon tea cost A$110 (U.S$71.50); full-day trips with morning tea, lunch, and afternoon refreshments and entry into Jenolan Caves cost A$220 (U.S.$143).

AAT Kings, Shop 1, corner of Alfred St. and Ferry Wharf no. 1, Circular Quay (© **02/9518 6095;** www.aatking.com.au), operates three typical big bus tours of the mountains, taking in all the usual sights, with a couple of short walks included. One tour includes a visit to Jenolan Caves. Tours range in cost from A$85 to $113 (U.S.$55.25–$73.45) for adults, and A$43 to $86

> **Tips** **Timing Is Everything: When to Visit**
>
> If you can, try to visit the Blue Mountains on **weekdays,** when most Sydneysiders are at work and the prices are much lower. Note, too, that the colder winter months (June, July, and Aug) are the busiest time in the Blue Mountains. This period is known as **Yuletide**—the locals' version of the Christmas period, when most places offer traditional Christmas dinners and roaring log fires.

(U.S.$28–$60) for children. Another large operator, **Australian Pacific Tours** (© **1300 655 965;** fax 02/9660 5016), offers a similar trip with a visit to the Australian Wildlife Park and a quick visit to the Sydney Olympic site at Homebush Bay. This tour costs A$94 (U.S$61.10) for adults and A$47 (U.S.$30.55) for children. If you hate big-group travel then choose another option.

BUSHWALKING & OTHER ACTIVE ENDEAVORS

Whereas almost every other activity costs money, bushwalking (hiking) is the exception to the rule that nothing in life is free. There are some 50 walking trails in the Blue Mountains, ranging from routes you can cover in 15 minutes to the 3-day **Six Foot Track** 🎇 that starts just outside Katoomba and finishes at Jenolan Caves. If you are planning to do some bushwalking, I highly recommend picking up a copy of *Sydney and Beyond—Eighty-Six Walks in NSW* by Andrew Mevissen (Macstyle Publishing). It features eight walks in the Blue Mountains, from easy 1-hour treks to 6-hour tramps. Buy it at bookshops and tourist information centers. Otherwise the staff at the tourist offices and National Park office will be happy to point you in the right direction, whether it be for an hour's stroll or a full-day's hike.

Great Australian Walks, 81 Elliot St., Balmain, NSW 2041 (© **1300 360 499** in Australia, or 02/9555 7580; www.walkaustralia.com), is a superb operator offering walks in the Blue Mountains. I had great fun on their 3-day Six Foot Track Walk from Katoomba to Jenolan Caves. Though not a wilderness trek, it goes through nice pockets of rain forest and open gum forests and traverses pretty farming country.

One of the best adventure operators in the area, **High 'n' Wild,** Unit 3, No. 5 Katoomba St., Katoomba, NSW 2780 (© **02/4782 6224;** www.high-n-wild.com.au), offers a series of canyoneering expeditions, taking in scenic rainforest gullies and caverns made up of dramatic rock formations and fern-lined walls. Generally there's a bit of swimming and plenty of walking, wading, and squeezing through tight spaces involved—and sometimes abseiling—but fortunately being double-jointed is not a prerequisite.

If you really want to test your head for heights though, then try High 'n' Wild's 150-meter (492-ft.) "Mega Jump"—the highest continuous abseil in the Southern Hemisphere. This heart-pumping descent down a sheer cliff is suitable for the fearless beginner, but they assure me you soon settle in by learning the ropes on the 10-story-high junior slopes beforehand.

If that's too much to handle though then you could always try a day's rafting on an inflatable airbed between huge towering rock walls on the Wollangambe River. There are a few minor rapids to navigate, and the bushwalk down to the river and back up again can be a little testing, but it's certainly suitable for a family outing. Abseiling costs from A$69 (U.S.$44.85) and canyoning from $85 (U.S.$55.25). Airbed adventures cost $169 (U.S.$110).

Other excellent adventure operators are **The Blue Mountains Adventure Company,** P.O. Box 242, Katoomba, NSW 2780 (℗ **02/4782 1271;** bmac@bmac.com.au), located in Katoomba at 84a Bathurst Rd. (above The Summit Gear Shop); and the **Australian School of Mountaineering,** 166b Katoomba St., Katoomba, NSW 2780 (℗ **02/4782 2014).** Both offer rock climbing, abseiling, and canyoning trips. In addition, the Blue Mountains Adventure Company offers caving and mountain biking, and the Australian School of Mountaineering offers bushcraft and survival training. Expect to pay around A$100 (U.S.$65) for a full-day's introductory rock-climbing course including abseiling, and between A$99 to $125 (U.S.$64.35–$81.25) for a day's canyoning.

If you feel like some adventure on your own, you could always hire a mountain bike from **Cycletech,** 182 Katoomba St., Katoomba (℗ **02/4782 2800**). Standard mountain bikes cost A$19 (U.S.$12.35) for half a day and A$27.50 (U.S.$18) for a full day (superior front-suspension mountain bikes cost A$27.50/U.S.$18 for a half day and A$49.50/U.S.$32 for a full day).

KATOOMBA: GATEWAY TO THE BLUE MOUNTAINS
114km (71 miles) W of Sydney

Katoomba (pop. 11,200) is the largest town in the Blue Mountains and the focal point of the Blue Mountains National Park. It's an easy 1½- to 2-hour trip by train, bus, or car. The town is a low-socio-economic pocket in a very affluent region, with one of the highest unemployment rates in the State.

GETTING THERE   By car from central Sydney travel along Parramatta Road and turn off onto the M4 motorway (around 2 hr. to Katoomba). Another route is via the Harbour Bridge to the suburb of North Sydney, along the Warringah Freeway (following the signs to the M2). Then, travel along the M2 to its end and follow the signs to the M4, and the Blue Mountains. This route takes around 1½ hours.

Frequent rail services connect Sydney to Katoomba from Central Station; contact **CityRail** (℗ **13 15 00**) or **Countrylink** (℗ **13 22 32**) for details. The train trip takes 2 hours, leaving from platforms 12 and 13 of Central Station. Trains leave almost hourly, stopping at Katoomba, and then at Mt. Victoria and Lithgow. An adult day-return round-trip ticket costs A$11.80 (U.S.$7.70) off-peak and A$20 (U.S.$13) during commuter hours. A child's day-return round-trip tickets costs A$3 (U.S.$1.95).

GETTING AROUND   If you take the train to Katoomba from Sydney, walk up the stairs from the station onto Katoomba Street; at the top of the street you'll see the Savoy, a former theatre but now a restaurant. Coaches operated by **Mountain Link** (℗ **1800/801 577** in Australia, or 02/4782 3333) meet most trains from Sydney outside this theater or opposite at the Carrington Hotel (check the signs for your particular destination) and take passengers to the main Blue Mountains attractions, including Echo Point, the Three Sisters, the Skyway,

---

Bushwalking Safety Tip

Before setting off on a bushwalk, always tell someone where you are going—plenty of people get lost every year. For other outdoor safety advice, see "Tips on Health, Safety & Outdoor Etiquette," in section 6 of chapter 2.

Leura Village, the Gordon Falls, and Blackheath, as well as other drop-off points for good views. Single-ride tickets to one destination cost between A$1.40 and $6.30 (U.S.90¢ and U.S.$4) depending on the distance. The **Blue Mountains Bus Company** (📞 02/4782 4213) also runs buses between Katoomba, Leura, Wentworth Falls, and as far as Woodford every hour. Buses leave from either the Carrington Hotel or the Savoy. Fares are similar to Mountain Link's.

You can also connect with the **Blue Mountains Explorer Bus** (📞 02/4782 4807; www.explorerbus.com.au). This red double-decker bus leaves from outside Katoomba train station every hour from 9:30am until 4:30pm. It stops at 27 attractions, resorts, craft galleries, and tearooms in and around Katoomba and Leura. You can get on and off as often as you want. Tickets cost A$22 (U.S.$14.30) for adults, A$11 (U.S.$7.15) for children, and $55 (U.S.$35.75) for a family.

Another option is **Trolley Tours** (📞 1800/801 577 in Australia; www.trolleytours.com.au), which is a kind of tram car on wheels. An all-day pass costs A$9 (U.S.$5.85) and for this you get to see various attractions around Katoomba and Leura, too.

Combined rail/bus tours from Sydney can be purchased at any **CityRail** (📞 13 15 00 in Australia) station.

EXPLORING THE AREA

The most visited and photographed attractions in the Blue Mountains are the unusual rock formations known as the **Three Sisters** 𝒜𝒜. For the best vantage point, head to **Echo Point Road,** across from the Blue Mountains Tourism office. Or try Evans Lookout, Govetts Leap, and Hargreaves Lookout, all at Blackheath (see below)—none of which are serviced by the Blue Mountains Explorer Bus or Trolley Tours.

One thing you have to do in the Blue Mountains is ride the **Scenic Railway,** the world's steepest. It consists of a carriage on rails that is lowered 415 meters (1,360 ft.) down into the Jamison Valley at a maximum incline of 52°. Originally it was used to transport coal and shale in the 1880s from the mines below. The trip only takes a few minutes; at the bottom there are some excellent walks through forests of ancient tree ferns. Another popular attraction is the **Skyway,** a cable car that travels 300 meters (990 ft.) above the Jamison Valley. The trip takes 6 minutes round-trip. The Scenic Railway and the Skyway (📞 02/4782 2699) each cost A$8 (U.S.$5.20) round-trip for adults and A$3 (U.S.$1.95) for children, and operate from 9am to 5pm daily (last trip at 4:50pm). They leave from the ticket office at 1 Violet St., Katoomba (follow the signs).

Canyons, waterfalls, underground rivers—the Blue Mountains has them all, and before you experience them in person you can catch them on the (giant) silver screen in *The Edge* at the **MAXVISION Cinema,** 225–237 Great Western Hwy., Katoomba (📞 02/4782 8900). The special effects shown on the screen 18 meters (59 ft.) high and 24 meters (79 ft.) wide make you feel like you're part of the action. The 38-minute *The Edge* film is shown every 40 to 50 minutes from 10am to 5:45pm. Tickets are A$12.50 (U.S.$8.15) for adults, A$10.50 (U.S.$6.90) for students, and A$7.50 (U.S.$5) for children. The cinema is a 5- to 10-minute walk from the train station. Recent release movies are shown on part of the giant screen in the evenings. There is a restaurant and a snack bar on the premises.

To get back to Sydney I highly recommend taking the Bell's Line of Road through Bilpin. It's up to 3-hour's driving via this route, but you can stop off at the wonderful **Mt. Tomah Botanic Gardens** 𝒜 (you can't miss the large sign on

Seeing the Blue Mountains from the Back of a Harley

A thrilling way to see the Blue Mountains is on the back of a chauffeur-driven Harley-Davidson. **Blue Thunder Bike Tours** (© 02/4571 1154) leave from Manly Wharf in Sydney (but they'll pick you up anywhere in the city). Rides cost A$80 (U.S.$52) for the first hour, A$130 (U.S.$84.50) for 2 hours, A$255 (U.S.$165.75) for half a day, and A$360 (U.S.$234) for a full day with lunch. The same company runs **Hot Heritage Tours,** operating out of the Blue Mountains (pickup anywhere in the Mountains), for the same prices.

---

your right about 10 min. before you get to Bilpin). An adjunct of the Royal Botanic Gardens in Sydney, Mt. Tomah is dedicated to cold climate plants. It's compact and has a very good cafe serving lunch daily. Allow around 2 hours.

WHERE TO STAY

There are plenty of places to stay throughout the Blue Mountains, including historic guest houses, B&Bs, resorts, motels, and homestays.

Very Expensive

Echoes Guesthouse ☆ *Finds*   Lilianfels (see below) might be more expensive, but Echoes, just across the road and perched on a cliff overlooking the Jamison Valley, has far superior views. Large windows, balconies, and a sizeable deck allow guests to soak up the fantastic scenery. Rooms are simply furnished and smaller than those at Lilianfels; all have under-floor heating.

3 Lilianfels Ave., Katoomba, NSW 2780. © 02/4782 1966. Fax 02/4782 3707. www.ozemail.com.au/echoes. 12 units. Weekend $710 (U.S.$497) double for 2 nights, including 1 dinner and 2 breakfasts; midweek A$285 (U.S.$199.50) double with breakfast. AE, DC, MC, V. Free parking. **Amenities:** Restaurant (French), bar; sauna. *In-room:* TV, coffeemaker, iron.

Lilianfels Blue Mountains ☆☆   Set just over a road from Echo Point, this Victorian country-house hotel—a member of the Small Luxury Hotels of the World—is a full-service yet still cozy establishment. Rooms are spacious and furnished with antiques. Most come with king-size beds and both a tub and a shower. Those with views are more expensive. The living areas are just as grand, with roaring log fires and more antiques. Views are impressive, especially from the lounge, which overlooks the Jamison Valley. On the grounds is a free-standing 1889 cottage. Meant for two, it has a sitting room, a bedroom with a four-poster bed, a spa, an intimate fireplace, and its own private gardens. Among the other offerings at Lilianfels are a billiards room, a library and reading room, and a French boules lawn.

Lilianfels Ave., Katoomba, NSW 2780. © 1800/ 024 452 in Australia, or 02/4780 1200. Fax 02/4780 1300. www.slh.com. 85 units, 1 cottage. A$380–$470 (U.S.$247–$305) double; A$530–$685 (U.S.$344.60–$445) suite; A$1050 (U.S.$682) cottage. Extra person A$55 (U.S.$35.75). Ask about off-season packages. AE, DC, MC, V. Free parking. **Amenities:** 2 restaurants (Modern Australian, casual Modern Australian); small indoor swimming pool; health club with floatation tank; exercise room; spa; sauna; bike rental; tour desk; secretarial services; 24-hr. room service; massage; laundry service; same-day dry cleaning; nonsmoking rooms. *In room:* A/C, TV, minibar, coffeemaker, hair dryer, iron.

Moderate

The Carrington Hotel ☆☆   Construction started on this grand Victorian hotel in 1880, and it reopened in 2000 after a major 8-year renovation. A ramshackle building, The Carrington is a must-stay if you're into colonial buildings of the

British-Raj style. Downstairs is a restaurant/breakfast room that once acted as a ballroom, a couple of lounges scattered with antiques, and a gorgeous wood-paneled billiard room. Chandeliers and 1930s-style lamps reflecting off silver trophies won by the local Rifle Club give everything a warm glow. Unfortunately, heavy plexiglass doors greet you as you enter each of the many corridors—a necessary fire precaution. All the rooms are truly delightful, with royal gold and blue carpets and drapes which would probably be considered gaudy if they didn't seem to fit in nicely to the overall style. Traditional rooms share bathrooms; Colonial rooms come with a deep tub in the bathroom (with a noisy fan) and no view to speak of; Deluxe Colonial rooms have a balcony and mountain views; Premier rooms have spa baths and great views; and the suites are fit for a duke and duchess. Dinner here costs A$100 (U.S.$65) per person, and the full breakfast is one of the best I've encountered.

15–47 Katoomba St., Katoomba (P.O. Box 28, NSW 2780). © 02/4782 1111. Fax 02/4782 1421. www. the carrington.com.au. Traditional rooms Mon–Thurs A$100 (U.S.$65), Fri–Sat A$155 (U.S.$100.75); Colonial rooms Mon–Thurs A$150 (U.S.$97.50), Fri–Sat A$225 (U.S.$165.75); Deluxe Colonial rooms Mon–Thurs A$185 (U.S.$120), Fri–Sat A$300 (U.S.$195); Premier rooms Mon–Thurs A$225 (U.S.$146.25), Fri–Sat A$350 (U.S.$227.50); suites Mon–Thurs A$265–$450 (U.S.$172–$292.50), Fri–Sat A$410–$630 (U.S.$266.50–$409). Ask about weekend packages. Breakfast included. AE, DC, MC, V. **Amenities:** Restaurant (country cooking), bar; snooker room. *In room:* TV, coffeemaker, iron.

Echo Point Holiday Villas 🦆 These are the closest self-contained accommodations to the Three Sisters Lookout. The two front-facing villas are the best because of their beautiful mountain views. Some villas have one double and two single beds, plus a foldout double bed in the lounge room. Bathrooms contain a shower, with no tub. There are barbecue facilities in the backyard. The two cottage here are also fully self-contained, sleeping up to eight, and have a tub, central heating, and access to nice gardens.

36 Echo Point Rd., Katoomba, NSW 2780. © 02/4782 3275. Fax 02/4782 7030. 5 villas, 2 cottages (all with shower only). Fri–Sat and public holidays A$132 (U.S.$85.80) villa; Sun–Thurs A$105 (U.S.$68.25) villa. A$150 cottage for 2. Linen A$6 (U.S.$3.90) extra per person in villas. Min. 2-night stay required. Extra person A$12 (U.S.$7.80). AE, DC, MC, V. *In room:* TV, kitchen, unstocked refrigerator, coffeemaker, hair dryer, iron.

Inexpensive

Katoomba Mountain Lodge This two-star property is quite cozy, with rooms looking out across the mountains. Dorm rooms are clean and come with three to six beds. Doubles are basic and lack a TV, but are certainly adequate for a couple of nights. All share bathrooms. On the premises you'll find a TV lounge with a log fire, a BYO dining room, and a game room. The staff can arrange tour packages. Breakfast costs an additional A$9 to $10 (U.S.$5.85–$6.50) per person, and dinner and breakfast costs an extra A$30 to $32 (U.S.$19.59–$20.80) per person.

31 Lurline St., Katoomba, NSW 2780. © and fax 02/4782 3933. 23 units, none with bathroom. Sun–Thurs A$58 (U.S.$38) double; Fri–Sat A$78 (U.S.$50) double. A$11–$15 (U.S.$7.15–$9.75) dorm bed. Ask about packages. AE, DC, MC, V. **Amenities:** Tour desk; coin-op laundry.

Katoomba YHA Hostel This former guesthouse is fine for a couple of nights, if you don't mind things a little less than luxurious. It's friendly, clean, comfortable, well-located, and has log fires in the living areas, a communal kitchen, and dining room. The double rooms are simple, with a double, twin, or bunk beds and not much else but a small bathroom. The dorm rooms accommodate 4 to 12 people; the cheaper dorm rooms on the top floor share bathrooms.

66 Waratah St. (at Lurline St.), Katoomba, NSW 2780. ℂ 02/4782 1416. Fax 02/4782 6203. 80 beds in 16 rooms, most with bathroom. A$14–$19 (U.S.$9–$12.35) dorm bed; A$50 (U.S.$35) double/twin. Family rates available and guests under 18 half price. MC, V. **Amenities:** Tour desk; coin-op laundry.

WHERE TO DINE

Katoomba Street has many ethnic dining choices, whether you're hungry for Greek, Chinese, or Thai. Restaurants in the Blue Mountains are generally more expensive than equivalent places in Sydney.

Expensive

Lindsay's 🕸🕸 INTERNATIONAL   Swiss chef Beat Ettlin has been making waves in Katoomba ever since he left some of the best European restaurants behind to try his hand at dishes such as pan-fried crocodile nibbles on pumpkin scones with a ginger dipping sauce. The food in this upscale, New York speakeasy is as glorious as its decor—Tiffany lamps, sketches by Australian artist Norman Lindsay, and booths lining the walls. The three-level restaurant is warmed by a cozy fire surrounded by an antique lounge stage and resounds every night to piano, classical music, or a jazz band. The menu changes every few weeks, but a recent popular dish was grilled veal medallions topped with Balmain bugs (small, saltwater crayfish), with potato and béarnaise sauce.

122 Katoomba St., Katoomba. ℂ 02/4782 2753. Reservations recommended. Main courses A$14–$23.50 (U.S.$9.10–$15.30). AE, MC, V. Open for lunch on weekends from noon–3pm and dinner 7 days 6pm–midnight.

TrisElies TRADITIONAL GREEK   Perhaps it's the belly dancers and the plate smashing, or the smell of moussaka, but as soon as you walk through the door of this lively eatery you feel like you've been transported to an authentic Athenian taberna. The restaurant folds out onto three tiers of tables, all with a good view of the stage where every night Greek or international performances take place. The food is solid Greek fare—souvlaki, traditional dips, fried haloumi cheese, Greek salads, casseroles like mother could have made, whitebait (tiny fried fish), and sausages in red wine—with a few Italian and Spanish extras. If it's winter, come in to warm up beside one of two log fires.

287 Bathurst Rd, Katoomba. ℂ 02/4782 4026. Fax 02/4782 1128. Reservations recommended. Main courses A$17–$25.50. AE, MC, V. Open daily 5pm–midnight.

Inexpensive

Chork Dee Thai Restaurant TRADITIONAL THAI   Loved by the locals, Chork Dee offers good Thai food in a pleasant but modest eatery. Served up here is the usual Thai fare, including satay, spring rolls, and fish cakes to start, and lots of curries, noodles, and sweet-and-sour dishes for mains. While vegetarians won't find anything without meat or fish to start with, there are plenty of veggie and tofu dishes available as a main course. BYO.

216 Katoomba St., Katoomba. ℂ 02/4782 1913. Reservations not essential. Main courses A$7.70–$12.65. AE, MC, V. Sun–Thurs 5:30–9pm; Fri–Sat 5:30–10pm.

Paragon Café *Value* CAFE   The Paragon has been a Blue Mountains' institution since it opened for business in 1916. Inside, it's decked out with dark wood paneling, bas-relief figures guarding the booths, and chandeliers. The homemade soups are delicious. The cafe also serves pies, pastas, grills, seafood, waffles, cakes, and a Devonshire tea of scones and cream.

65 Katoomba St., Katoomba. ℂ 02/4782 2928. Menu items A$3–$10 (U.S.$1.95–$6.50). AE, MC, V. Tues–Fri 10am–3:30pm, Sat–Sun 10am–4pm.

LEURA
107km (66 miles) W of Sydney; 3km (2 miles) W of Katoomba

The fashionable capital of the Blue Mountains, Leura is known for its gardens, its pretty old buildings (many of them holiday homes for Sydneysiders), and its cafes and restaurants. The National Trust has classified Leura's main street as an urban conservation area. Just outside Leura is the **Sublime Point Lookout,** which has spectacular and unusual views of the Three Sisters formation in Katoomba. From the southern end of **Leura Mall,** a cliff drive takes you all the way back to Echo Point in Katoomba; along the way you'll get some spectacular views across the Jamison Valley.

WENTWORTH FALLS ☏☏
103km (62 miles) from Sydney; 7km (4 miles) from Katoomba

This pretty little town has numerous craft and antique shops, but the area is principally known for its magnificent 280.5-meter-high (935-ft.-high) waterfall, situated in **Falls Reserve.** On the far side of the falls is the **National Pass Walk**—one of the best in the Blue Mountains. It's cut into a cliff face with overhanging rock faces on one side and sheer drops on the other. The views over the Jamison Valley are spectacular. The track takes you down to the base of the falls to the **Valley of the Waters.** Climbing up out of the valley is quite a bit more difficult, but just as rewarding.

A NICE SPOT FOR LUNCH
Conservation Hut Café CAFE   This pleasant cafe is in the national park itself on top of a cliff overlooking the Jamison Valley. It's a good place for a bit of lunch on the balcony if you're famished after the Valley of the Waters walk, which leaves from just outside. It serves all the usual cafe fare—burgers, salads, sandwiches, and pastas. There are plenty of vegetarian options, too. There's a nice log fire inside in winter.

At the end of Fletcher St., Wentworth Falls. ☏ 02/4757 3827. Menu items A$6–$15 (U.S.$3.90–$9.75). MC, V. Daily 9am–5pm.

MEDLOW BATH
150km (90 miles) W of Sydney; 6km (3½ miles) E of Katoomba

In between Katoomba and Blackheath, Medlow Bath is a cozy place, with its own railway station, a secondhand bookstore, and a few properties hidden between the trees. Its one claim to fame is the **Hydro Majestic Hotel** (☏ 02/ 4788 1002), a must-do stop for any visitor to the Blue Mountains. The historic Hydro Majestic has fabulous views over the Megalong Valley; the best time to appreciate the views is at sunset with a drink on the terrace. Otherwise it sells Devonshire Tea all day, and plenty of cakes, snacks, coffee, and tea. Also drop into Medlow Bath's **Old Post Office,** now a wonderfully eccentric secondhand bookshop, with antique odds and ends, and tea, coffee, and Hungarian goulash among other things.

BLACKHEATH
114km (71 miles) W of Sydney; 14km (9 miles) W of Katoomba

Blackheath is the highest town in the Blue Mountains at 1,048.5 meters (3,495 ft.). The **Three Brothers** at Blackheath are not as big or as famous as the Three Sisters in Katoomba, but you can climb two of them for fabulous views. Or you could try the **Cliff Walk** from **Evans Lookout** to **Govetts Leap** (named after a surveyor who mapped the region in the 1830s), where there are magnificent views over the **Grose Valley** and **Bridal Veil Falls.** The 1½-hour tramp passes through banksia, gum, and wattle forest, with spectacular views of peaks and valleys. If you want a guide while you're in the area contact **Blue Mountains Magic** (✆ **02/4787 6354;** www.bluemts.com/bluemtmagic), based in Blackheath. The guide, Phil Foster, is a trained botanist.

Blackheath itself has some interesting tearooms and antique shops.

GETTING THERE The Great Western Highway takes motorists west from Katoomba to Blackheath. CityRail trains also stop at Blackheath.

VISITOR INFORMATION **The Heritage Centre** (✆ **02/4787 8877;** www.npws.nsw.gov.au), operated by the National Parks and Wildlife Service, is located close to Govetts Leap Lookout on Govetts Leap Road. It has information on guided walks, camping and hiking, as well as information on local European and Aboriginal historic sites. It's open daily from 9am to 4:30pm.

EXPLORING THE AREA ON HORSEBACK

One of the nicest ways to get around is on horseback. **Werriberri Trail Rides** (✆ **02/4787 9171;** fax 02/4787 6680), found at the base of the Blue Mountains, 10 kilometers (6 miles) from Blackheath on Megalong Road in the Megalong Valley, offers guided ½-hour to 3-hour rides through the Megalong Valley. Suitable for beginners to advanced riders. Half-hour rides cost A$17 (U.S.$11).

WHERE TO STAY

Jemby-Rinjah Lodge ✿ The Blue Mountains National Park is just a short walk away from this interesting alternative accommodation option. There are nine standard cabins (seven two-bedroom cabins, and two one-bedroom loft cabins), one deluxe cabin called Treetops Retreat, and three pole-frame lodges. The cabins are right in the bush, can sleep up to six people, and are well spaced. Each has a slow combustion heater, carpets, a bathroom, a fully equipped kitchen, and a lounge and dining area. There are also automatic laundry and barbecue areas nearby. The lodges each have five bedrooms, two bathrooms, and a common lounge area with a circular fireplace. You can rent linen, but bring your own food. Free pickup can be arranged from Blackheath train station. Treetops Retreat has a Japanese hot tub, TV, VCR, stereo, and three private balconies with bush views. It sleeps two, making it a perfect romantic getaway. The nearby walking tracks take you to the spectacular Grand Canyon; the Grose Valley Blue Gum forests; and Walls Cave, a resting place for local Aborigines 10,000 years ago.

336 Evans Lookout Rd., Blackheath, NSW 2785. ✆ **02/4787 7622.** Fax 02/4787 6230. jembyrin@pnc.com.au. 10 cabins, 3 lodges. Cabins (occupied by up to 2 adults and 2 children): Fri–Sun and public holidays A$160–$225 (U.S.$104–$146.25); Mon–Thurs A$115–$167 (U.S.$74.75–$108.55). Extra adult A$22 (U.S.$14.30), extra child A$14 (U.S.$9.10). Linen Hire A$13.50 (U.S.$8.80) per bed. AE, MC, V.

WHERE TO DINE

Cleopatra ✿✿ TRADITIONAL FRENCH The best place to eat in the mountains. *Sydney Morning Herald*'s "Good Food Guide" consistently rates this restaurant as the best outside Sydney. It also won the American Express restaurant award for the best restaurant in western New South Wales for 6 years. The dining room, in a hidden treasure of a National Trust house, is comfortable and warm and furnished with tasteful antiques. For good reason, the most popular appetizer is the salmon marinated in white wine and herbs. A standout among the main courses is the Daube of Beef (a hearty braised beef dish), while also getting full marks is the coral trout fillet with baby broad beans and capers.

A classic dessert is the hot chocolate pudding with a liquid chocolate center. Fully licensed, not BYO.

118 Cleopatra St., Blackheath, NSW 2785. ℂ 02/4787 8456. Fax 02/4787 6238. 3-course meal A$88 (U.S.$57); 2-course meal Tues–Thurs A$66 (U.S.$43). AE, DC, MC, V. Tues–Sun 7–11pm; Sun 12:30–3:30pm.

JENOLAN CAVES 🛉
182km (113 miles) W of Sydney; 70 (42 miles) W of Katoomba

The winding road from Katoomba eventually takes you to a spur of the Great Dividing Range and a series of underground limestone caves considered to be some of the world's best. Known to the local Aborigines as "Binoomea," meaning "dark place," the caves are an impressive amalgamation of stalactites, stalagmites, and underground rivers and pools. They have been open to the public since 1866.

GETTING THERE It's a 1½-hour drive from Katoomba to the caves. CityRail trains run to Katoomba and link up with daily Jenolan Caves excursions run by **Fantastic Aussie Tours** (ℂ 02/4782 1866). The CityRail Link Ticket, which is a combination train ticket/bus tour, costs A$60 (U.S.$39) for adults and A$30 (U.S.$19.50) for children. The tour alone from Katoomba costs A$64 (U.S.$41.60) for adults and A$32 (U.S.$20.80) for children, so the Link Ticket is well worthwhile to buy. These prices include cave entry. You can purchase Link Tickets at any rail station.

Day trips from Sydney are operated by **AAT King's** (ℂ 02/9252 2788) and **Australian Pacific Tours** (ℂ 02/9252 2988; fax 02/9247 2052). Coach tours depart from the coach terminal at Circular Quay. Since you end up spending 6 hours on a coach on these day trips, I recommend staying overnight in either Jenolan Village or somewhere else in the Blue Mountains.

EXPLORING THE CAVES
Nine caves are open for exploration, with guided tours operated by **Jenolan Caves Reserves Trust** (ℂ 02/6359 3311; www.jenolancaves.org.au). The first cave tour starts at 10am weekdays and 9:30am weekends and holidays. The final tour departs at 4:30pm (5pm in warmer months). Tours last 1 to 2 hours, and each costs between A$12 and $50 (U.S.$7.80–$32.50) for adults, and between A$8 (U.S.$5.20) and A$10 (U.S.$6.50) for children under 15. Family concessions and multiple cave packages are available. The best all-round cave is **Lucas Cave; Imperial Cave** is best for seniors. **Adventure Cave Tours,** which include canyoning, last from 3 hours to all day and cost from A$40 to $100 (U.S.$26–$65) per person.

WHERE TO STAY
The Gatehouse Jenolan The Gatehouse is a clean and cozy budget-style lodge, with a separate cottage nearby. It's located opposite the caves. The Gatehouse sleeps 66 people in all, in seven six-bed rooms and six four-bed rooms in the main building. The cottage can accommodate up to four couples. There are also two common rooms, lockers, washing machines and dryers, and basic kitchen facilities. There are outdoor barbecues on the premises, and apparently at least one ghost.

Jenolan Caves Village, NSW 2790. ℂ 02/6359 3322. Fax 02/6359 3227. 13 units. Weekend rates: 4-person dorm room A$88 (U.S.$57.20), 6-person dorm room A$110 (U.S.$71.50). Weekday rates: 4-person dorm room A$60.50 (U.S.$39), 6-person dorm room A$77 (U.S.$50) with linen rental of A$3.30 (U.S.$2.15) per person. AE, MC, V. **Amenities:** Coin-op laundry.

Jenolan Caves House   This heritage-listed hotel was built between 1888 and 1906 and is one of the most outstanding structures in New South Wales. The main part of the enormous three-story building is constructed of sandstone and fashioned in Tudor-style black and white. Around it are several scattered cottages and former servants quarters. Rooms vary within the main house from simple budget bunk rooms, to "traditional" rooms with shared bathrooms and "classic" rooms with private bathrooms. The traditional and classic rooms are both old-world and cozy, with heavy furniture and views over red-tile rooftops or steep vegetated slopes. Mountain Lodge rooms are found in a separate building behind the main house and are more motel-like.

Jenolan Caves Village, NSW 2790. ℂ 02/6359 3322. Fax 02/6359 3227. www.jenolancaves.com.au. 101 units, some with bathroom. Weekend rates: Grand Classic A$335.50 (U.S.$218), Classic A$265 (U.S.$172), Traditional A$165 (U.S.$107), Mountain Lodge A$209 (U.S.$136). Weekday rates: Grand Classic A$231.50 (U.S.$150), Classic A$187 (U.S.$121.50), Traditional A$110 (U.S.$71.50), Mountain Lodge A$132 (U.S.$85.80). Family rooms also available. AE, DC, MC, V. **Amenities:** 2 restaurants (Modern Australian, bistro [no vegetarian food]), bar; tour desk; nonsmoking rooms. *In room:* TV, coffeemaker, hair dryer.

2 The Hunter Valley: Wine Tasting & More

Cessnock: 190km (114 miles) N of Sydney

The Hunter Valley (or the Hunter as it's also called) is the oldest commercial wine-producing area in Australia, as well as a major site for coal mining. Internationally acclaimed wines have poured out of here since the early 1800s. Though the region falls behind the major wine-producing areas of Victoria in terms of volume, it has convenient advantage of being just 2 hours from Sydney.

People come here to visit the vineyards' "cellar doors" for free wine tasting, to enjoy the rural scenery, to sample the area's highly regarded cuisine, or to escape from the city for a romantic weekend. The whole area is dedicated to the grape and the plate, and you'll find many superb restaurants hidden away between the vineyards and farmland.

In the **Lower Hunter,** centered around the towns of Cessnock and Pokolbin, you'll find more than 50 wineries, including well-known producers such as Tyrell, Rothbury, Lindemans, Draytons, McGuigans, and McWilliams. Many varieties of wine are produced here, including semillon, shiraz, chardonnay, cabernet sauvignon, and pinot noir.

Farther north, the **Upper Hunter** offers the very essence of Australian rural life, with its sheep and cattle farms, historic homesteads, more wineries, and rugged bushland. The vineyards here tend to be larger than those in the south, and produce more aromatic varieties, such as traminers and rieslings. February through March is when the harvest takes place.

The Upper Hunter eventually gives way to the forested heights of the nearest World Heritage–listed site to Sydney, Barrington Tops National Park. The park is ruggedly beautiful and is home to some of the highest Antarctic beech trees in

A Wine-Buying Tip
The best year ever for red wines in this part of Australia was 1988, when a long, hot summer produced fewer, but more intensely flavored grapes. Stock up on anything you can find from this vintage. At the other end of the scale, 1997 was a very bad year in the Hunter, and 1996 produced an average vintage.

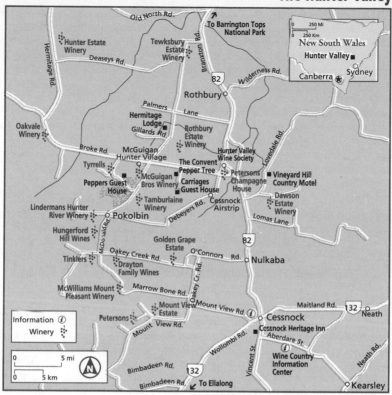

the country. It also abounds with animals, including several marsupial species and an abundance of bird life.

HUNTER VALLEY ESSENTIALS

GETTING THERE   To get to the wine-producing regions of the Hunter, leave Sydney via the Harbour Bridge or Harbour Tunnel and follow the signs for Newcastle. Just before Hornsby, turn off the highway and follow the signs for Cessnock. The trip will take about 2½ hours. Barrington Tops National Park is reached via the Upper Hunter town of Dungog.

Keynes Buses (✆ **1800/043 339** in Australia, or 02/6543 1322) run coaches to Scone in the Hunter Valley from Sydney's Central Station. Buses depart Monday through Saturday at 3pm and arrive in Scone at 6:50pm; a second service on Friday leaves at 6pm, and on Sunday the bus leaves at 6:40pm. Round-trip tickets are A$74 (U.S.$48.10) for adults and A$38 (U.S.$24.70) for children.

A rental car should cost you from A$45 (U.S.$29.25) a day from Sydney, and you might put in around A$40 (U.S.$26) worth of petrol or so for a couple of day's of touring (petrol in Australia hovers around A90¢ a liter, or U.S.$2.20 a gal.). In the Hunter, contact **Hertz,** 1A Aberdare Rd., Cessnock (✆ **13 30 39** in Australia, or 02/4991 2500).

CHECKED ORGANIZED TRIPS FROM SYDNEY   Several companies offer day trips to the Hunter Valley from Sydney. **Wonderbus Tours** (*©* 02/9555 9800; www.wonderbus.com.au) operates a fun trip that combines wine tasting in the Hunter Valley, a visit to Oakdale Farm (a native animal reserve) near Port Stephens, and dolphin spotting at Port Stephens. The trip costs A$99 (U.S.$64.35).

Wonderbus also offers a tour visiting five vineyards (instead of the three in the above trip), with lunch, costing A$130 (U.S.$84.50).

Boutique Wine Tours (*©* 02/9909 0822) also runs trips to the wineries daily from Sydney on a 10-seater BMW bus, costing A$89 (U.S.$57.85) per person. You get to choose which wineries you want to go to, up to a maximum of six. Pickup is from Sydney hotels or from outside Customs House near Circular Quay.

VISITOR INFORMATION   **Wine Country Visitors Information Centre,** Turner Park, Aberdare Road, Cessnock, NSW 2325 (*©* **02/4990 4477;** fax 02/4991 4518; www.winecountry.com.au), is open Monday through Friday from 9am to 5pm, Saturday from 9:30am to 5pm, and Sunday from 9:30am to 3:30pm. The staff can make accommodation bookings and answer any questions. The **Dungog Visitors Information Centre,** on Dowling Street, Dungog (*©* **02/4992 2212**), has plenty of information on the Barrington Tops area.

VISITING THE WINERIES

Many people start their journey through the Hunter by popping into the **Hunter Valley Wine Society,** at the corner of Broke and Branxton roads in Pokolbin (*©* **02/4998 7397**). The club basically acts as a Hunter Valley wine clearinghouse, sending bottles and cases to members all over Australia, and some overseas. It's also a good place to talk to the experts about the area's wines, and to taste a few of them. It's open daily from 9am to 5pm.

You might also like to visit the **Small Winemakers Centre,** McDonalds Road, Pokolbin (*©* **02/4998 7668**). At any one time it represents around six of the region's smaller producers.

Most of the wineries in the region are open for cellar-door tastings, and it's perfectly acceptable just to turn up, taste a couple of wines or more, then say your good-byes without buying anything. Though you will come across some unusual vintages, especially at the boutique wineries, don't expect to find any bargains—city bottle shops buy in bulk and at trade price, which means you can probably get the same bottle of wine for less in Sydney than at the cellar door in the Hunter.

Drayton Family Wines   Drayton's produces some spectacular shiraz. Oakey Creek Rd., Pokolbin. *©* **02/4998 7513.** Mon–Fri 9am–5pm; Sat–Sun 10am–5pm.

Hunter Estate Winery   The Hunter's largest winery crushes some 6,500 tons of grapes a year. Come here for excellent semillon and shiraz. Hermitage Rd., Pokolbin. *©* **02/4998 7777.** Daily 10am–5pm. Tours daily 11am and 2pm.

Tips **Don't Drink & Drive**

Australia's drunk-driving laws are strict and rigidly enforced. If you are interested in tasting some grapes in the Hunter Valley, choose a designated driver or take a guided tour (see above). Both easily identifiable and unmarked police cars patrol the vineyard regions.

A Wine-Tasting Tip

Some wineries routinely offer some of their inferior wines for tastings. I've made a habit of specifically asking for a list of their premium wines available for tasting. Most wineries usually have a bottle or two of their better wines uncorked for those with a serious interest.

Lindemans This famous winery offers an interesting sparkling red shiraz. McDonald Rd., Pokolbin. ℂ 02/4998 7684. Mon–Fri 9am–4:30pm; Sat–Sun 10am–4:30pm.

McGuigan Brothers Winery Another winery worth visiting in the area, McGuigan Brothers also has a cheese factory and bakery on the site. McDonald Rd., Pokolbin. ℂ 02/4998 7402. Daily 9:30am–5pm. Tours daily at noon.

McWilliams Mount Pleasant Famous for both its Elizabeth Semillon, which has won 15 trophies and 134 gold medals over 12 years, and its Lovedale Semillon, which has won 24 trophies and 38 gold medals. Marrowbone Rd., Pokolbin. ℂ 02/4998 7505. Daily 10am–4:30pm. Tours daily 11am.

Mount View Estate The pioneer of Verdelho wines in Australia—a grape attributed to Portugal, but it's also grown in small quantities in Italy and France. It's a very crisp and dry white wine, which I like with seafood. Mount View Rd., Mount View. ℂ 02/4990 3307. Daily 10am–5pm.

Peterson's Champagne House This is the only specialist champagne winery in the Hunter. At the corner of Broke and Branxton rds., Pokolbin. ℂ 02/4998 7881. Daily 9am–5pm.

Peterson's Vineyard Peterson's produces fine chardonnay, semillon, and shiraz. Mount View Rd., Mount View. ℂ 02/4990 1704. Mon–Sat 9am–5pm, Sunday 10am–5pm.

Rothbury Estate ✿ This very friendly winery produces the magnificent Brokenback Shiraz and the nice Mudgee Shiraz. The Rothbury Café (see "Where to Dine," below) serves meals. Broke Rd., Pokolbin. ℂ 02/4998 7555. Daily 9:30am–4:30pm.

Tamburlaine Don't miss this boutique winery, the winner of many wine and tourism awards. McDonald Rd., Pokolbin. ℂ 02/4998 7570. Daily 9:30am–5pm.

Tinklers If you want to taste the grapes in season, head to Tinklers. It sells some 30 different varieties of eating grapes between December and March, and nectarines, plums, peaches, and vegetables at other times of the year. It also offers wine tasting and free vineyard walks at 11am on Saturday and Sunday. Pokolbin Mountains Rd., Pokolbin. ℂ 02/4998 7435. Daily 10am–4pm.

Tyrell's Tyrell's has produced some famous wines and exports all over the world. Broke Rd., Pokolbin. ℂ 02/4993 7000. Tours daily 1:30pm.

DAY TOURS, HOT-AIR BALLOON RIDES & OTHER FUN STUFF

If you don't have a car, you'll have to get around as part of a tour, as there is no public transport running between the wineries.

Trekabout Tours (ℂ 02/4990 8277) offers half-day and full-day winery tours for a maximum of six people. Half-day tours cost A$28 (U.S.$18), with visits to five or six wineries, and full-day tours cost A$44 (U.S.$28.60), and take in up to nine wineries. The company can pick you up from your hotel in either Cessnock or Pokolbin.

Also offering local pickup is Hunter Vineyard Tours (© **02/4991 1659**) which has a full-day tour on either 12- or 21-seat buses, taking in five wineries. They charge A$38 (U.S.$24.70), or A$55 (U.S.$35.75) with a two-course meal.

A tranquil way to see the wineries is from above. **Balloon Aloft,** in Cessnock (© **1800/028 568** in Australia, or 02/4938 1955; fax 02/6344 1852), offers year-round dawn balloon flights that include a post-flight champagne and optional breakfast costing A$15 (U.S.$9.75). Flights last about an hour and cost A$205 (U.S.$133.25) for adults on weekdays and A$230 (U.S.$149.50) on weekends. Children ages 7 to 12 fly for A$130 (U.S.$84.50) daily.

If you like adventure, try **Grapemobile Bicycle and Walking Tours** (© **0500/ 804 039** in Australia, and 02/4991 2339 phone and fax). This company supplies you with a mountain bike, helmet, guide, and support bus, and takes you on a peaceful meander through the wineries. Tours cost A$98 (U.S.$63.70), including a restaurant lunch. The company also runs a walking tour for A$89 (U.S.$57.85), including wine tasting and lunch.

WHERE TO STAY

The Hunter Valley is far more expensive on weekends and during public holidays, when room prices jump significantly and some properties insist on a 2-night stay. It's worthwhile checking out the information board located inside the Wine Country Visitors Information Centre (see "Visitor Information," above) for special deals, but most of the rooms on offer tend to be in nondescript motels.

IN CESSNOCK

Staying in Cessnock is a good idea if you don't have a car and are relying on local tour companies to pick you up and show you around the area.

Cessnock Heritage Inn   This 1920s building, built as a pub, is right in the center of Cessnock, so there's easy access to all the local pubs and restaurants. All the rooms are done in country style, with dried grasses, floral bedspreads, and the like. All are quite large with high ceilings but differ greatly—the smallest room has a double bed, others have queen beds and singles, and there are two

 Bunking down in a Caravan, Man

Two caravan parks in the area offer reasonably comfortable accommodation in caravans and cabins. **Cessnock Cabins and Caravan Park** (© **02/4990 5819**; fax 02/4991 2944) Allandale/Branxton Road, Nulkaba (2km/1¼ miles north of Cessnock), has four on-site vans for A$30 to $40 (U.S.$19.50–$26); a double and 12 cabins with shower from A$48 to $69 (U.S.$3–$44.85); the more expensive prices are for weekends. There are also camping sites here for A$14 (U.S.$9) and powered sites for A$16 (U.S.$10.40).

The **Valley Vineyard Tourist Park** (© and fax **02/4990 2573**) on Mount View Road (on the way out to the vineyards) has five caravans for A$35 (U.S.$22.75) and 12 cabins with shower for A$55 (U.S.$35.75). Two two-bedroom units cost A$75 (U.S.$48.75). Powered sites cost A$16 to $20 (U.S.$10.40–$13) and a camping site A$12 (U.S.$7.80). There's a BYO restaurant, a camper's kitchen, and a swimming pool on the site.

Hermitage Lodge If you want to be right in heart of vineyard country, stay here. The property is surrounded by vineyards. Standard rooms are large, sunny, and nicely decorated, and come with a queen-size bed and a double sofa bed. The spa suites are larger with queen-size beds and double sofas, cathedral ceilings, spa baths, and separate showers. The more expensive suites have a separate bedroom and bathrobes. Breakfast is served in all rooms. Il Cacciatore restaurant is one of the best in the region.

At Gillards and McDonalds roads, Pokolbin, NSW 2320. © **02/4998 7639**. Fax 02/4998 7818. www. ozemail.com.au/~hlodge/. 10 units. Weekend A$180 (U.S.$117) standard double; A$240–$280 (U.S.$156–$182) spa suites. Midweek A$115 (U.S.$74.75) standard double, A$165–$170 (U.S.$107–$110.50) spa suites. Rates include continental breakfast. Extra person A$15 (U.S.$9.75). Min. 2-night stay on weekends. Ask about packages for midweek stays. AE, MC, V. **Amenities:** Restaurant (Italian), bar; medium-size outdoor pool; golf course nearby; bike hire (free for Frommer's readers); babysitting; free self-service laundry; non-smoking rooms. *In room:* A/C, TV, unstocked refrigerator, coffeemaker, hair dryer, iron.

Peppers Guest House This tranquil escape is set in beautiful bush gardens. So peaceful is it that kangaroos hop up to the veranda in the evenings looking for treats. The "classic" rooms downstairs have French doors that you can fling open in abandonment, while upstairs rooms express just a tad more old-fashioned charm and come with air-conditioning. All rooms have king-size beds and are furnished with colonial antiques. Guests don't come here for action; they come to relax. The Pampering Place offers massages and facials, while a gentle 30-minute track winds through the bush. There's a pleasant guest lounge with an open fireplace and a bar. The inn's restaurant, Chez Pok, is an upscale establishment with mismatched china and pretty good country food.

Ekerts Rd., Pokolbin, NSW 2321. © 02/4998 7596. Fax 02/4998 7739. www.peppers.com.au. 47 units, 1 cottage. Weekend rates (min. 2-night stay): A$277 (U.S.$180) colonial double; A$289 (U.S.$188) classic double; A$300 (U.S.$195) vintage double; A$347 (U.S.$225) heritage suite. Weekday rates: A$238 (U.S.$155) colonial

Something Special: A Cattle Station in the Upper Hunter

Located just off the Golden Highway, 1 hour north of Mudgee, 2½ hours west of Cessnock, and 4 hours northwest of Sydney, **Runnymeade**, Golden Highway, Runnymeade, Cassilis, NSW 2329 (© 02/ 6376 1183; fax 02/6376 1187), is a 2,000-acre sheep-and-cattle station where you can get a taste of Aussie ranch life. The ranch offers farm-style lodgings in a 1930s Californian bungalow. Two rooms have an en-suite shower, while the third shares the hosts' bathroom down the hall. The homestead has an open fire in the living room (and a rarely used TV). There are plenty of native birds in the gardens, and kangaroos are common. May is the best time to see sheep-shearing, and August is the best time to witness lambing and calving. Guest rave about the hosts, Libby and David Morrow. David offers 1-hour tours of property for around A$30 (U.S.$19.50) per "Toyota-load," and tours throughout the district.

ubles go for A$80 to $90 (U.S.$52–$58.50). Rates include break-
ut dinner is A$20 (U.S.$13) per person extra (BYO wine or beer).
dit cards.

family rooms (sleeping five). All have ceiling fans and free video movies. There's also a guest lounge where you can chat with the owners.

Vincent St., Cessnock (P.O. Box 714, NSW 2325). ✆ **02/4991 2744.** Fax 02/4991 2720. www.hunterweb.com.au/heritageinn.html. 13 units. Weekend A$110–$130 (U.S.$71.50–$84.50) per person with breakfast. Midweek A$88–$95 (U.S.$57–$61.75) double with full breakfast. AE, MC, V. **Amenities:** Tour desk; babysitting; laundry service; nonsmoking rooms. *In room:* A/C, TV, minibar, coffeemaker.

IN ELLALONG

Ellalong Hotel   This 1924 pub, located 11 kilometers (7 miles) from Cessnock, has a good Aussie country atmosphere. All rooms have a real out-in-the-country style with solid wood dressers and bouquets of dried flowers. Some have just a double bed, while others squeeze in an extra single. Rooms 1 and 2 are the best, as they've got fantastic views across to the Brokenback Ranges from their verandas.

80 Helena St., Ellalong, NSW 2325. ✆ and fax **02/4998 1217.** 10 units, none with bathroom. Sat A$79 (U.S.$51); Fri A$69 (U.S.$44.85); Sun–Thurs A$55 (U.S.$35.75) double. Rates include country breakfast. No credit cards. Inquire about dinner packages. **Amenities:** 2 restaurants (country cooking, bistro), bar. *In room:* coffeemaker.

IN POKOLBIN

Carriages Guest House 🌠🌠   Tucked away on 36 acres (14.5 hectares), a kilometer off the main road, Carriages is a secluded retreat in the heart of Pokolbin. A two-suite cottage called the Gatehouse is on a separate part of the grounds. In the main two-story house, a veranda circles downstairs rooms, which are furnished with antique country pine. Upstairs, the two lofty gable suites are centered around huge fireplaces. The Gatehouse suites offer five-star luxury; although relatively new, the stained-glass windows and rescued timber give them a rustic feel (these two spa rooms share a lounge with a full kitchen and an open fire). There are open fires in six of the rooms (the two standard doubles don have them). Breakfast is served in your room, and Robert's restaurant is just n door. The friendly owner, Ben Dawson, assures me he'll take Frommer's re up to the top of a nearby hill where they can see plenty of wild kangaroo

Halls Rd., Pokolbin, NSW 2321. ✆ **02/4998 7591.** Fax 02/4998 7839. 10 units. A$170 (U.S.$110.5 A$220–$245 (U.S.$126.75–$236.50) suite; A$270 (U.S.$175.50) spa suite. Rates include bre 2-night stay on weekends. Ask about 10%–20% discounts midweek. AE, MC, V. **Amenities:** pool; tennis court; babysitting; laundry service; nonsmoking rooms. *In room:* A/C, TV, unstoc coffeemaker, hair dryer.

The Convent Pepper Tree 🌠🌠   Originally a convent for Br the early part of the 20th century, this building was transporte meters (372 miles) from Coonamble in central New South W location in 1990. A year later, it opened as a hotel. Rooms cious, with baroque decor, including plaster frieze ceili drapes. French doors open onto private verandas overloc land. King rooms are larger and have wicker lounge ar sitting area where drinks are served, and a light and ai the best breakfasts in the Hunter. The Pepper Tree Tree Wines and the excellent Robert's restaurant.

In the Pepper Tree Complex, Halls Rd., Pokolbin, NSW 2320. ✆ 0' peppers.com.au. 17 units. Weekend A$323–$387 (U.S.$210–$252) Fri–Sat, or Sat–Sun). Midweek A$291–$332 (U.S.$189–215.80) room; children 5–15 A$22 (U.S.$14.30) extra. AE, DC, MC, V medium-size outdoor pool; tennis court; spa; bike rental (free A/C, TV, minibar, coffeemaker, hair dryer, iron.

double; A$248 (U.S.$161) classic double; A$257 (U.S.$167) vintage double; A$297 (U.S.$193) heritage suite. AE, DC, MC, V. **Amenities:** Restaurant (Modern Australian); small indoor pool; tennis court; bike rental; laundry service; nonsmoking rooms. *In room:* A/C, TV, minibar, coffeemaker, hair dryer, iron.

Vineyard Hill Country Motel ⟨ Motel is a bit of a misnomer for this place; it's more aptly described as a "fully self-contained chalet." Units are modern, with a separate bedroom, lounge and dining area, a full kitchen, and a balcony with views across a valley of vineyards to the Brokenback Ranges in the distance. It's all terrifically rural, with cows wandering about and kangaroos and possums creeping around at dusk. There's no restaurant, but there is a gourmet deli on the premises. In the garden are a large swimming pool and a spa.

Lovedale Rd., Pokolbin, NSW 2321. ⟨© 02/4990 4166. Fax 02/4990 4431. www.vineyardhill.com.au. 8 units. Weekend A$141 (U.S.$91.60) 1-bedroom unit; A$218 (U.S.$142) 2-bedroom unit (for 4 people). Midweek A$97 (U.S.$63) 1-bedroom unit, A$165 (U.S.$107) 2-bedroom unit. Extra person A$16.50 (U.S.$10.75). Ask about midweek and long-weekend packages. AE, MC, V. **Amenities:** Large outdoor pool; spa; free laundry service; nonsmoking rooms. *In room:* A/C, TV, kitchen, minibar, coffeemaker, hair dryer.

IN THE UPPER HUNTER

Barrington Guest House ⟨⟨ *Value* Barrington Guest House is nestled in a valley just outside the Barrington Tops National Park—the nearest World Heritage site to Sydney. It retains an old-world charm and serves bacon and eggs for breakfast, scones and cream, and vegetables boiled soft enough for your dentures. The place has lace tablecloths in the dining room, a log fire beneath a higgledy-piggledy brick chimney, dark mahogany walls, high ceilings, and personalized service—despite the communal mealtimes and the lack of a menu. Rooms range from the original guesthouse chambers adjoining the dining room, to new and almost luxurious two-story self-contained cottages (sleeping up to five) that cling to a hillside. I highly recommend the latter—the former are basic, with no TV and can be noisy if a party's in full swing in the dining room. This place is very popular with older travelers during the week but attracts a range of ages on the weekends. The guest-house grounds attract plenty of animals from the surrounding national park and act as a wildlife reserve for several rescued kangaroos. Activities include horseback riding, guided walks through the magnificent rain forest, "billy tea" tours, and night spotting for quolls (native cats) and possums, not to mention bush dancing, tennis, film evenings, and skeet shooting. It can be a very social scene, too.

Salisbury (via Dungog), NSW 2420. ⟨© 02/4995 3212. Fax 02/4995 3248. 20 rain-forest cottages, 21 guest-house units (13 with bathroom). A$152 (U.S.$99) per person in cottage midweek, including meals and activities; A$220 (U.S.$143) self-catering cottage midweek, including activities (min. 2-night stay; 2nd night A$199 (U.S.$129). A$79 (U.S.$51) per adult in a guesthouse room without bathroom, including meals and activities; A$120 (U.S.$78) per adult in a guesthouse room with bathroom, including meals and activities. Ask about packages. AE, MC, V. The guesthouse is about 3½ hours from Sydney and 1½ hours from the main Hunter wine region. Free pickup from Dungog railway station. **Amenities:** Restaurant (home cooking), bar; tennis court; laundry service; nonsmoking rooms. *In room:* Cottages only: TV, kitchen, unstocked refrigerator, coffeemaker, hair dryer, iron.

WHERE TO DINE
IN CESSNOCK

Amicos MEXICAN/ITALIAN PIZZERIA You can't mistake the Mexican influence in the decor, with bunches of chili peppers, cow skulls, ponchos, masks, and frescoes, but the Mediterranean/Italian connection is more evident in the menu. Mexican dishes include the usual nachos, enchiladas, burritos, barbecued chicken, and the like, while there are a few pastas and Mediterranean dishes, such as crumbed lamb brains, too. The pizzas are pretty good, and one could just about serve four people.

138 Wollombi Rd., Cessnock. ✆ 02/4991 1995. Reservations recommended. Main courses A$11.90–$19.90 (U.S.$7.70–$13); pizzas A$14–$18 (U.S.$9.10–$11.70). 10% discount for take-out orders. MC, V. Daily 6–10pm.

IN POKOLBIN

The three restaurants in the Hunter with the biggest reputations are Robert's, which is part of the Pepper Tree Complex (see "Where to Stay," above) along with the Convent guest house; Chez Pok in Peppers Guest House (see "Where to Stay," above); and Casuarina (see below).

Blaxland's Restaurant 𝕽 MODERN INTERNATIONAL This very atmospheric restaurant revolves around a winery theme, with pictures of vineyards on the walls, one of the most comprehensive Hunter wine lists in the area, and even the owner's homemade vintages on the menu. Parts of the building date from 1829, with wooden trusses holding up the ceiling and exposed sandstone block walls. Popular here is the roast spatchcock and the steamed balcak mussels. A large open fire brings a glow to the white tablecloths in winter.

Broke Rd., Pokolbin. ✆ 02/4998 7550. Reservations recommended. Main courses A$19.50–$25. A$2 (U.S.$1.40) per person surcharge weekends and public holidays. AE, DC, MC, V. Daily 11am–10pm.

Café Enzo MODERN AUSTRALIAN This charming little cafe offers a nice ambience and good cuisine. Pastas, pizzettas, antipasti, and steaks dominate the menu. The pizzetta with chargrilled baby octopus, squid, and king prawns, Kalamata olives, fresh chili and onion, and freshly shaved parmigiano is particularly nice. Cakes and cheese plates are a specialty.

At the corner of Broke and Ekerts roads. (adjacent to Peppers Creek Antiques, near Peppers Guest House), Pokolbin. ✆ 02/4998 7233. Main courses A$10–$18 (U.S.$6.50–$11.70). Devonshire tea A$7.50 (U.S.$4.90). AE, DC, MC, V. Wed–Sun 10am–5pm (until 10pm Sat).

Casuarina Restaurant 𝕽𝕽 MODERN AUSTRALIAN This superb restaurant has taken a slew of awards for its cooking in recent years. The surroundings are elegant, with lots of antiques below the very high wooden ceilings. Flambés are the signature meal here, the most popular being a flambé of chili lobster and prawn (for two people). Other meals to write home about are the Thai-style chicken curry and the Caesar salad.

Hermitage Rd., Pokolbin. ✆ 02/4998 7888. Reservations recommended. Main courses A$27–$34 (U.S.$17.55–$22.10). A$3 (U.S.$1.95) per-person surcharge weekends and public holiday. AE, DC, MC, V. Daily 7–11pm.

Robert's Restaurant 𝕽𝕽 MODERN AUSTRALIAN Chef and owner Robert Molines has become a legend in Hunter Valley gourmet circles for consistently coming up with great dishes that perfectly complement the region's wines. His restaurant is known for its eclectic mix of antiques and his country-style dishes, such as rabbit with olives and vegetables, rack of lamb from the wood-fired oven, and twice-roasted duckling. The meat-free specialty is the wild mushroom risotto.

In the Pepper Tree complex, Halls Rd., Pokolbin. ✆ 02/4998 7330. Main courses A$29–$34 (U.S.$18.85–$22). A$4 (U.S.$2.60) per-person surcharge weekends and public holidays. AE, DC, MC, V. Daily noon–5pm and 7–midnight.

The Rothbury Café 𝕽 MODERN AUSTRALIAN This second-floor cafe has some of the best views across the valley; occasionally you can even spot kangaroos grazing in the farmers' fields across the way. The cafe has a Mediterranean feel about it, with timber tables loaded with bread and olives. Signature dishes are the chickpea-battered squid with yogurt and eggplant relish for a first course, and the venison and beetroot pie or the braised oxtail with orange, walnuts, olives, and polenta for main courses. Desserts include the fabulously rich chocolate-chestnut torte with berries.

Upstairs at the Rothbury Estate, Broke Rd., Pokolbin. (C) 02/4998 7363. Main courses A$16–$18 (U.S.$10.40–$11.70). AE, DC, MC, V. Daily noon–3pm.

3 Port Stephens: Dolphin & Whale Watching ⭐⭐

209km (130 miles) N of Sydney

Port Stephen's Bay, just 2½ hours north of Sydney, should be at the top of any New South Wales itinerary. It's a perfect add-on to a trip to the Hunter Valley (see above). Though you can come up from Sydney for the day, I highly recommend staying in the general area for at least one night. The sheltered Port Stephen's Bay itself is more than twice the size of Sydney Harbour, and is as clean as a newly poured bath. The sea literally jumps with fish, and the creamy islands and surrounding Tomaree National Park boast more species of birds than even Kakadu National Park in the Northern Territory. Two pods of bottle-nosed dolphins, around 70 individuals in all, call the bay home, and you are almost certain to see some on a dolphin-watching cruise. Port Stephens is also a fabulous place to watch whales during their migration to the breeding grounds farther north (roughly from June 1 to mid-Nov—though they are less frequently seen in Aug). There is also a large breeding colony of koalas in Lemon Tree Passage on the south side of the Tomaree Peninsula, which makes up the southern shoreline of the bay.

The main town, **Nelson Bay** (pop. 7,000) is on the northern side of the peninsula. The township of Shoal Bay, farther along the peninsula, has a nice beach edged with wild flowers. Another small resort town, **Anna Bay,** is the largest development on the southern side of the peninsula, and has good surf beaches nearby. The Stockton Bight stretches some 35 kilometers (22 miles) from Anna Bay south to the large industrial town of Newcastle. The beach here is popular with ocean fishermen, who have the awful habit of driving their four-wheel-drives along it. The Stockton Sand Dunes, which run behind the beach, are the longest in the Southern Hemisphere.

Opposite the Tomaree Peninsula, across the bay, are the small tourist townships of Tea Gardens and Hawks Nest, both at the mouth of the Myall River. See the Wonderbus tour of The Hunter (above) for details on a tour to Port Stephens.

ESSENTIALS

GETTING THERE   To get to Port Stephens, take the Sydney–Newcastle Freeway (F3) to its end, then follow the Pacific Highway signs to Hexham and Port Stephens. **Port Stephens Coaches** (ⓒ **1800/045 949** in Sydney, or 02/4982 2940) travel between Port Stephens and Newcastle, and to Nelson Bay from Sydney daily at 2pm. Buses from Sydney leave from Eddy Avenue, near Central Station; the journey takes 3½ hours. Return tickets costs A$43 (U.S.$27.40) for adults and A$30 (U.S.$19.10) for children.

VISITOR INFORMATION   The **Port Stephens Visitor Information Centre,** Victoria Parade, Nelson Bay (ⓒ **1800/808 900** in Australia, or 02/4981 1579; fax 02/4984 1855; www.portstephens.org.au) is open Monday through Friday from 9am to 5pm and Saturday and Sunday from 9am to 4pm.

A Horse Ride Through the Dunes

You can ride a horse through the dunes with **Sahara Horse Trails** (ⓒ 02/ 4981 9077). A 2-hour trip costs A$40 (U.S.$26), and a half-day excursion is A$60 (U.S.$39). Bookings required 1 day in advance.

SEEING THE AREA

Several operators have vessels offering **dolphin- and whale-watching cruises.** Some of the best are aboard *Imagine* (ⓒ 02/4984 9000; www. imagine.com.au), a 15-meter (50-ft.) catamaran operated by Frank Future and Yves Papin, two real characters. They offer a daily "Island Discovery" trip that includes dolphin watching and a trip around the offshore islands. The 4-hour cruise departs from **D'Albora Marina** in Nelson Bay daily at 11am and costs A$39 (U.S.$25.35) for adults, and A$19 (U.S.$12.35) for children 4 to 14, including lunch.

Four-hour whale-watching tours cost the same and leave at 11am from June 1 to November 15. You are most likely to spot humpback whales, but there's also a chance to see minke and southern right whales.

A morning dolphin-watching cruise runs from 9 to 10:30am daily during summer and costs A$15 (U.S.$9.75) for adults, A$7 (U.S.$4.55) for children, and A$38 (U.S.$24.70) for families. If you happen to be around on the weekend nearest a full moon, ask about the company's overnight "**Full Moon Tours.**"

Another operator, *Advance II* (ⓒ 02/4981 0399), offers 2-hour dolphin cruises for A$18 (U.S.$11.70), and a 3-hour whale-watching cruise for A$43 (U.S.$27.95). The **Port Stephens Ferry Service** (ⓒ 02/4981 3798, or 0419/417 689 mobile phone) operates a 2½-hour "Early Bird Dolphin Watch" daily at 8:30am with a stop off at Tea Gardens. A similar 3½-hour cruise departs at noon (you can eat lunch at Tea Gardens), and a 2-hour dolphin-watching cruise departs at 3:30pm. All cruises cost A$15 (U.S.$9.75) for adults, A$8 (U.S.$5.20) for children, and A$35 (U.S.$22.75) for families.

WHERE TO STAY

Port Stephens is very popular with Sydneysiders, especially during the Christmas holidays, the month of January, and Easter, so you'll need to book well in advance at those times.

Peppers Anchorage Port Stephens 𝒜𝒜   This low-rise resort, split into a main guest house and four separate lodges, is built onto a headland and runs almost directly into the bay—it's only stopped from sliding in by a boardwalk and a picturesque marina. Rooms are light and luxurious; the suites each have a good-size spa, perfect for two. Rooms on the top floor have a large balcony, from which you have uninterrupted views across the bay and the islands; those below have their own private verandas. Two rooms are designed for wheelchairs. A nearby beach is the perfect spot for a sunset stroll.

Corlette Point Rd., Corlette, NSW 2315. ⓒ 1800/809 142 in Australia, or 02/4984 2555. Fax 02/4984 0300. www.peppers.com.au. 80 units. Weekend A$323 (U.S.$210) double; A$418 (U.S.$271) suite. Midweek A$248 (U.S.$161) double; A$351 (U.S.$228) suite. Ask about midweek packages. AE, DC, MC, V. **Amenities:** Restaurant (seafood/vegetarian), bar; good-size outdoor pool; exercise room; spa; children's program (public holidays only); tour desk; babysitting; laundry service; nonsmoking rooms. *In room:* A/C, TV, minibar, coffeemaker, hair dryer, iron.

Port Stephens Motor Lodge   Surrounded by tall trees and gardens, this motor lodge is a peaceful place to stay and a short stroll from the main township. The standard rooms are quite plain with raw-brick walls, a comfy double (and an extra single bed in most rooms), a private balcony, and an attached shower with half-tub. Adjacent to the lodge is a self-contained family unit with two bedrooms, a laundry, and water views. There's a barbecue area on the grounds.

44 Mangus St., Nelson Bay, NSW 2315. ℂ **02/4981 3366.** Fax 02/4984 1655. www.portstephens. org.au/index1. 17 units. A$60–$120 (U.S.$39–$78) standard double (Christmas holiday period most expensive); A$88 (U.S.$57) family unit on weekdays and A$120 (U.S.$78) on weekends. Extra person A$10 (U.S.$6.50), extra person under 15 A$5 (U.S.$3.25). AE, DC, MC, V. **Amenities:** Outdoor swimming pool; coin-op laundry; nonsmoking rooms. In room: A/C, TV, coffeemaker, hair dryer, iron.

Salamander Shores ℂ Salamander Shores looks like a beached, ramshackle paddle steamer—it's all white-painted bricks and rails and stairs, fixed to the bay by a jetty. Set in a well-tendered, sloping garden, this five-story hotel retains a certain 1960s charm, despite undergoing selective modernization. Standard rooms are similar to most motel rooms, but you really should throw caution to the wind and get a sea-view room—you won't regret it. These rooms have spas and large balconies with extensive views of the bay. When the sun rises over the water and the garden is full of lorikeets and corellas, it couldn't be more picture-book perfect. There's a pub and bottle shop down below.

147 Soldiers Point Rd., Soldiers Point, NSW 2317. ℂ **1800/655 029** in Australia, or 02/4982 7210. Fax 02/4982 7890. 90 units. A$109 (U.S.$80) standard double; A$142 (U.S.$92) garden-view double; A$160.60 (U.S.$104) sea-view double; A$229 (U.S.$149) family suite; $264 (U.S.$172) penthouse. A$17.60 (U.S.$11.50) extra person. Ask about packages. AE, DC, MC, V. **Amenities:** 2 good restaurants (seafood, Modern Australian), bar; small outdoor pool; sauna; tour desk; babysitting; laundry service; nonsmoking rooms. In room: A/C, TV, minibar, coffeemaker, hair dryer, iron.

WHERE TO DINE

Most people head down to Nelson Bay for their meals because of the great views across the bay. You'll also find a host of cheap take-out joints here, including **The Pure Pizza Café,** D'Albora Marina (ℂ **02/4984 2800**), offering pizzas for around A$10 to $24 (U.S.$6.50–$15.60), depending on toppings, pastas for between A$10 and $15 (U.S.$6.50–$9.75), and salads, too.

Rob's on the Boardwalk CAFE You can pick up a hearty American breakfast at this busy cafe overlooking the bay, or a snack throughout the day. The Caesar salad is popular, as are the half-dozen oysters for A$12.50 (U.S.$8.20). One of the best mains is the mixed seafood bouillabaisse, while the prime scotch fillet with sautéed forest mushrooms, Jerusalem artichokes, gratin potatoes, and a red wine sauce, would tempt the most red-blooded carnivore.

D'Albora Marina. ℂ **02/4984 4444.** Main courses A$11.50–$22.50 (U.S.$7.50–$14.60). AE, DC, MC, V. Daily 8am until the last customer leaves.

Rock Lobster SEAFOOD Eat inside or out at this peaceful yet stylish restaurant. The plump Port Stephens Oysters should be enough to tempt you to start, while main courses such as smoked salmon in layers of wonton pastry with salad and wasabi sauce, or calamari flavored with chili and coriander in breadcrumbs with spicy passion-fruit dip should fill you up. There are usually a couple of meat dishes and a vegetarian option on the menu, too.

D'Albora Marina. ℂ **02/4981 1813.** Main courses A$15–$29 (U.S.$9.75–$18.85). Seafood platter for 2 A$95 (U.S.$61.75). AE, DC, MC, V. Daily 11:30am–2:30pm; 5:30–9pm.

4 North of Sydney Along the Pacific Highway: Australia's Holiday Coast

The Pacific Highway leads over the Sydney Harbour Bridge and merges into the Sydney-Newcastle Freeway. It continues to the industrial coast town of Newcastle, bypassing Tuggerah Lake and Lake Macquarie (neither of real interest compared to what follows). From here, the Pacific Highway stays close to the coast until it reaches Brisbane, some 1,000 kilometers (620 miles) from Sydney.

Though the road is gradually being upgraded, the conditions vary, and the distances are long. Travelers should be aware that the route is renowned for its accidents. Though you could make it to Brisbane in a couple of days, you could also easily spend more than a week stopping off at the attractions along the way. The farther north you travel the more obviously tropical the landscape gets. By the time visitors reach the coastal resort town of Coffs Harbour, temperatures have noticeably increased, and banana palms and sugarcane plantations start to appear.

Along the coast, you'll find excellent fishing and some superb beaches, most of them virtually deserted. Inland, the Great Dividing Range, which separates the wetter eastern plains from the dry interior, throws up rain forests, extinct volcanoes, and hobby farms growing tropical fruit as you head even farther north toward the Queensland border. Along the way, too, are a series of national parks, most of them requiring detours of several kilometers. Those you shouldn't miss out on include the Dorrigo and Mount Warning national parks, both of which offer some of the country's best and most accessible rain forests.

PORT MACQUARIE

423km (262 miles) N of Sydney

Port Macquarie (pop. 28,000), about halfway between Sydney and the Queensland border, boasts some fabulous beaches; Flynn's Beach in particular is a haven for surfers. Boating and fishing are other popular pastimes.

ESSENTIALS

GETTING THERE   From Sydney, motorists follow the Pacific Highway and then the Sydney–Newcastle freeway (F3). **Eastern Australia Airways** (© 02/ 9691 2333) flies between Sydney and Port Macquarie. The coach trip from Sydney takes about 7 hours.

VISITOR INFORMATION   The **Port Macquarie Visitor Information Centre,** at the corner of Clarence and Hay streets, under the Civic Centre (© 1800/025 935 in Australia, or 02/6581 8000; www.portmacquarieinfo. com.au), is open Monday through Friday from 8:30am to 5pm and Saturday and Sunday from 9am to 4pm.

EXPLORING THE AREA

The Billabong Koala and Wildlife Park, 61 Billabong Dr., Port Macquarie (© 02/6585 1060), is a family-owned nature park where you can get up close to hand-raised koalas, kangaroos, emus, wombats, many types of birds, and fish. You can pat the koalas at 10:30am, 1:30, and 3:30pm. There are also barbecue facilities, picnic grounds, and a restaurant. Allow 2 hours to fully experience this recommended wildlife park. It's open daily from 9am to 5pm; admission is A$8 (U.S.$5.20) for adults and A$5 (U.S.$3.25) for children.

The 257-passenger vessel **Port Venture** (© 02/6583 3058) leaves from the wharf at the end of Clarence Street Tuesday and Thursday through Sunday at

10am and 2pm, for a 2-hour scenic cruise on the Hastings River. Cruises cost A$20 (U.S.$13) for adults, A$8 (U.S.$5.20) or children 6 to 14, and A$49 (U.S.$32) for families. Reservations are essential. The boat also travels up the river on a 5-hour Barbecue Cruise every Wednesday morning leaving at 10am. It docks at a private bush park along the way and passengers can tuck into a traditional Aussie barbecue of steaks, fish, and salad. You can then fish, take a bushwalk, go swimming, or take a 20-minute four-wheel-drive trip. The cruise costs A$37 (U.S.$24) for adults, A$18 (U.S.$11.70) for children, and A$94 (U.S.$61) for families. A 4-hour cruise also leaves on Monday at 10am. It costs A$35 (U.S.$22.75) for adults, A$15 (U.S.$9.75) for children, and A$88 (U.S.$57.20) for families.

WHERE TO STAY

El Paso Motor Inn   Located right on the waterfront, this motel offers standard-motel type rooms; the more expensive deluxe doubles are a little larger and have newer furniture and a fresher coat of paint after being refurbished in 1998. Two rooms come with spas, and some come with kitchenettes. The third-floor three-room suite has good ocean views and a kitchenette.

29 Clarence St., Port Macquarie, NSW 2444. (℃ **1800/027 965** in Australia, or 02/6583 1944. Fax 02/6584 1021. 55 units. A$87 (U.S.$56.55) standard double; A$97 (U.S.$63) deluxe double; A$130 (U.S.$84.50) spa rooms; A$150 (U.S.$97.50) suite. Extra person A$10 (U.S.$6.50). A$30 (U.S.$19.50) per-room surcharge Easter, Christmas, and some long weekends. DC, MC, V. **Amenities:** Restaurant (seafood/Modern Australian), bar; good heated pool; sauna; spa; game room; tour desk; babysitting; nonsmoking rooms. *In room:* A/C, TV, minibar, coffeemaker, hair dryer, iron.

COFFS HARBOUR: BANANA CAPITAL OF OZ ⊛

150km (93 miles) N of Port Macquarie; 572km (355 miles) N of Sydney; 427km (265 miles) S of Brisbane

The relaxed capital of Australia's Holiday Coast is bounded by rain forests, beaches, and sand. The state's "banana republic" headquarters—the area produces more bananas than anywhere else in Australia—is bordered by hillsides furrowed with neat rows of banana palms. Farther inland, the rolling hills plateau into the mystical Dorrigo National Park, one of the best examples of accessible rain forests anywhere in the world. Also inland is the Nymboida River, known for its excellent white-water rafting.

Coffs Harbour is a rather disjointed place, with an old town-center retail area; the Jetty Strip (with restaurants and fishing boats) near the best swimming spot, Park Beach; and a new retail area called The Plaza. Wide sweeps of suburbia separates these three areas; it's a difficult town to negotiate if you don't have a car.

ESSENTIALS

GETTING THERE   It takes around 7 hours to drive from Sydney to Coffs Harbour without stops; from Brisbane it takes around 5 hours. The Pacific Highway in this region is notoriously dangerous; there have been many serious accidents in recent years involving drivers enduring long hours behind the wheel. Ongoing road-widening projects should hopefully improve things. **Qantas** (℃ **13 13 13** in Australia) flies non-stop to Coffs Harbour from Sydney. Several coach companies, including **Greyhound-Pioneer** (℃ **13 20 30** in Australia) and **McCafferty's** (℃ **13 14 99** in Australia), make the trip from Sydney in about 9 hours. A **Countrylink** (℃ **13 22 32** in Australia) train from Sydney costs A$75 (U.S.$48.75).

VISITOR INFORMATION   The **Coffs Harbour Visitors Information Centre** (℃ **1800/025 650** in Australia, or 02/6652 1522) is just off the Pacific

Highway, at the corner of Rose Avenue and Marcia Street, 2 blocks north of the city center. It's open daily from 9am to 5pm.

GETTING AROUND   If you don't have a car, you can get around on the **Coffs Harbour Coaches** (✆ 02/6652 2877), which runs day trips around the local area on weekdays (including a town tour on Mon, and a trip to the magnificent Dorrigo National Park on Wed). **Blue Tongue Transport** ✆ (✆ 02/6651 8566, or 1800 258 386 in Australia) offers smaller group tours of Dorrigo National Park daily costing A$50 (U.S.$32.50) for adults and A$40 (U.S.$26) for children; a morning city tour for A$11 (U.S.$7.15); and an upmarket afternoon champagne tour of town for A$22 (U.S.$14.30).

CHECKING OUT THE BIG BANANA & OTHER THINGS TO DO

You can't miss the 10-meter (33-ft.) reinforced concrete banana alongside the highway at the **Big Banana Theme Park** (✆ 02/6652 4355), 3 kilometers (2 miles) north of town. The park includes an air-conditioned, diesel-powered train that takes visitors on a 1-hour tour of the 45-acre (18-hectare) banana plantation that contains some 18,000 banana trees. Along the route it passes various off-the-wall exhibits relating to farming, Aborigines, and local history. It stops at the property's hydroponic glasshouses and at a viewing platform and cafeteria, which serves up all things banana—cakes, breads, splits, shakes, and so on. The park is open daily from 9am to 4:30pm (3pm in winter). Admission is free, but the train tour costs A$10 (U.S.$6.50) for adults, A$6 (U.S.$3.90) for children, and A$25 (U.S.$16.25) for families. I had my doubts about this place before I visited, but I ended up charmed—even if it was simply by the wackiness of the place.

The **Coffs Harbour Zoo** (✆ 02/6656 1330), 10 minutes north of town on the Pacific Highway, has plenty of breeding koalas (you can pet them), as well as wombats, kangaroos, dingoes, Tasmanian devils, water birds, and aviaries. The award-winning native gardens are full of wild birds expecting a feed. The zoo is open daily from 8:30am to 4pm. Admission is A$12 (U.S.$7.80) for adults, A$6 (U.S.$3.90) for children, and A$30 (U.S.$19.50) for families.

A free natural attraction is **Mutton Bird Island,** which you can get to via the Coffs Harbour jetty. A steep path leads up the side of the island, but views from the top are worth it. Between September and April the island is home to thousands of shearwaters (or mutton birds), which make their nests in burrows in the ground.

If you prefer fish, try diving with gray nurse sharks, manta rays, and moray eels with **Island Snorkle and Dive** (✆ 02/6654 2860) or **Dive Quest** (✆ 02/6654 1930). The *Pamela Star* (✆ 02/6658 4379) offers good-value deep-sea-fishing trips including all tackle and bait, and lunch, for A$60 (U.S.$39). The boat leaves Coffs Harbour jetty at 7:30am and returns at 1:30pm daily.

For a taste of gold-rush fever, head to **George's Gold Mine,** 40 kilometers (25 miles) west of Coffs Harbour on Bushman's Range Road (✆ 02/6654 5355 or 02/6654 5273). You get to go into a typical old-timer gold mine, see the "stamper battery" crushing the ore, and pan for gold yourself. The mine is open Wednesday through Sunday (daily during school and public holidays) from 10:30am to 4pm. Admission is A$9 (U.S.$5.85) for adults, A$4.50 (U.S.$2.90) for children, and A$26 (U.S.$16.90) for families.

You might also like to visit **Kiwi Down Under Farm** (✆ 02/6653 4449), a fascinating organic farm growing kiwi fruit and macadamia nuts, among other things. No nasty sprays are used here. Free 30- to 45-minute guided tours of the property leave at 2, 3, and 4pm on weekends and school holidays. The tea shop on the premises serves amazing scones and jam for A$4.50 (U.S.$2.90) and excellent vegetarian lunches for A$8.50 (U.S.$5.50). The farm is 14 kilometers (8½ miles) south of Coffs Harbour; turn off at Gleniffer Road, just south of Bonville, and follow the signs for 4 kilometers (2½ miles).

SHOPPING FOR ARTS & CRAFTS

There are several recognized "craft drives" in the area, where tourists can go in search of quality souvenirs. Pick up a free copy of *Discover the Coffs Harbour Region* from the tourist information center for more details on the dozens of craft shops in the area. One of the best is the **Australian Wild Flower Gallery** (℗ **02/6651 5763**), just of West High Street and Bennetts Road. Wolfgang Shultze carves intricate designs out of pewter, silver, and gold to make detailed animal- and plant-inspired jewelry, charms, and spoons. Pieces cost between A$5 and $36 (U.S.$3.25–$23.40). The gallery is open daily from 9am to 5pm.

On the way to or from the Dorrigo rain forest, stop off at the township of **Bellingen,** 20 minutes south of Coffs Harbour on Waterfall Way. It's a pleasant place with several interesting craft shops. Among the best is **The Old Church** (℗ **02/6655 0438**), 8 Church St. (just off the main road), crammed full of wooden craft items, cards, furniture, wacky mobiles, incense, hats and knick-knacks, and surrounded by gardens and fruit trees. It's open daily from 8:30am to 5:30pm.

EXPLORING THE RAIN FORESTS & OTHER OUTDOOR ADVENTURES

Coffs Harbour's main tourist attraction is its position as a good base for exploring the surrounding countryside. You must see the World Heritage–listed **Dorrigo National Park** 𝕽𝕽, 68 kilometers (42 miles) west of Coffs Harbour, via Bellingen. Perched on the Great Dividing Range that separates the lush eastern seaboard from the arid interior, the rain forest here is one of the best I've seen in Australia (it's a desperate pity that so much of it fell to the axes of early settlers). Entry to the rain forest is free.

The **Dorrigo Rainforest Centre** (℗ **02/6657 2309**) is the gateway to the park and has extensive information on the local rain forest. Just outside is the 21-meter-high (69-ft.-high) **Skywalk,** which offers a bird's-eye view of the forest canopy. There are several rain-forest walks leaving either the Rainforest Centre, the Glade Picnic Area (about 1km/½ mile away), and the Never-Never Picnic Area (a 10-km/6¼-mile drive along Dome Road). Most tracks are suitable for wheelchairs. Bring a raincoat or an umbrella; it's not called a rain forest for nothing. The **Dorrigo Tourist Information** office (℗ **02/6657 2486**) is in the center of Dorrigo township.

One of the best tour operators in the area is the award-winning **Mountain Trails 4WD Tours** (℗ **02/6658 3333;** fax 02/6658 3299). Full-day tours that include visits to two rain-forest areas and a good lunch cost A$80 (U.S.$52) for adults and A$60 (U.S.$39) for children under 16. Half-day tours of one rain forest cost A$56 (U.S.$36.40) for adults and A$40 (U.S.$26) for children.

For a bit more personal action, try horseback riding through the rain forest 23 kilometers (14 miles) southwest of Coffs Harbour with **Valery Trails** (℗ **02/ 6653 4301**). Two-hour rides leave at 10am and 2pm daily and cost A$35 (U.S.$22.75) per person, bookings essential.

More hectic still are **white-water rafting trips** ₡ through the wilderness on the furious Nymboida River with **Wow Rafting,** 1448 Coramba Rd., Coramba via Coffs Harbour, NSW 2450 (₢ **1800/640 330** in Australia, or 02/6654 4066). Full-day trips, including morning tea, high-energy snack, and a barbecue meal, cost A$153 (U.S.$99.45). These adventurous trips operate year-around, depending on water levels. A 2-day trip costs A$325 (U.S.$211.25), including all meals and overnight camping. If the water level in the Nymboida is low then you raft on the Goolang Creek, a shorter but still exciting run. Most of the rapids are grade 3; some of them can be pretty hairy. The rafting guides are real characters; although they're safety-conscious, you're sure to be dunked a few times.

Rapid Rafting 2,000 (₢ **1800/629 797** in Australia, or 02/6652 1741) also runs rafting trips on the Goolang River, costing $77 (U.S.$50) for a half-day trip, and A$120 (U.S.$78) for a full day.

Looking for yet another adrenaline rush? Then head to the **Raleigh International Raceway** (₢ **02/6655 4017**), where you can zip around the track behind the wheel of your very own . . . go-kart. It's located 23 kilometers (14 miles) south of Coffs Harbour and 3 kilometers (2 miles) along Valery Road off the Pacific Highway north of Nambucca Heads. Six high-speed laps cost A$16 (U.S.$10.40), 11 cost A$23 (U.S.$14.95), and 16 cost A$32 (U.S.$20.80). It's open daily from 9am to 5pm (6pm in summer).

The *Pacific Explorer* catamaran (₢ **0418/663 815** mobile phone, or 02/6652 7225 after working hours) operates **whale-watching trips** between June and October; the 2½-hour cruises cost A$44 (U.S.$28.60). Between November and May, they run half-day dolphin-watching cruises for the same price

WHERE TO STAY

Coffs Harbour is a popular beachside holiday spot with plenty of motels along the Pacific Highway offering standard roadside rooms from A$35 to $49 (U.S.$22.75–$31.85) per night. Vacancy signs are common outside Australian school holiday periods and the Christmas and Easter periods (when Coffs really fills up). A few to try are the **Caribbean Motel,** 353 High St., Coffs Harbour, NSW 2450 (₢ **02/6652 1500;** fax 02/6651 4158), with doubles ranging from A$55 to $120 (U.S.$35.75 to $78) depending on the season and the view; and the **Coffs Harbour Motor Inn,** 22 Elizabeth St., Coffs Harbour, NSW 2450 (₢ **02/6652 6388;** fax 02/6652 6493), with doubles ranging from A$72 to $108 (U.S.$46.80–$70.20) depending on the season.

Pelican Beach Centre Resort ₡ *Value*   This Bali-style resort complex is situated 7 kilometers (4¼ miles) north of Coffs Harbour beside a long stretch of creamy sand (the beach is dangerous for swimming). Terraced over six levels, the resort's rooms all have balconies and many have ocean views. Standard rooms are light and modern, with either twin or queen beds. Family rooms have a kitchenette, dining area, and one queen and two single beds divided by a half wall. Suites have a separate bedroom, kitchenette, lounge area, and spa bath. Two rooms are equipped for travelers with disabilities. Outside in the landscaped gardens is a minigolf course and a volleyball court.

Pacific Hwy., Coffs Harbour, NSW 2450. ₢ 1800/02 8882 in Australia, 800/835-7742 in the U.S. and Canada, or 02/6653 7000. Fax 02/6653 7066. 112 units. A$112–$180 (U.S.$73–$117) standard room for 1 or 2 depending on season; A$156–$295 (U.S.$101–$192) family room for up to 4; A$200–$375 (U.S.$130–$244) suite. Extra person A$27 (U.S.$17.55). Ask about packages and discounts. The highest rates apply Dec 26–Jan 18. AE, DC, MC, V. **Amenities:** Restaurant (Modern Australian), bar; large lagoon-style swimming pool; exercise room; 2 spas; sauna; game room; children's center (weekends); tour desk; babysitting; free guest laundry; nonsmoking rooms. *In room:* A/C, TV, minibar, coffeemaker, hair dryer, iron.

Sanctuary Resort If you like animals you'll love this animal-sanctuary/ guest-house complex 2 kilometers (1¼ miles) south of town. Wandering around the grounds are wallabies, kangaroos, peacocks, and several species of native birds. The rooms are comfortable, with the more expensive rooms being larger and more recently renovated. The executive room comes with a spa.

Pacific Hwy., Coffs Harbour, NSW 2450. © 02/6652 2111. Fax 02/6652 4725. 37 units. A$88 (U.S.$57.20) standard double; A$93.50 (U.S.$60.80) superior double; A$150 (U.S.$97.50) executive double. Extra person A$13.50 (U.S.$8.80). Holiday surcharges. Ask about lower rates through Aussie auto clubs. AE, DC, MC, V. **Amenities:** Restaurant (Modern Australian/International), bar; large outdoor swimming pool; spa and sauna; room service 6–8pm; coin-op laundry. *In room:* TV with pay channels, coffeemaker.

WHERE TO DINE
Seafood Mama's ⚘ ITALIAN/SEAFOOD This charming, informal award-winning Italian restaurant packs a mean barbecue seafood dish of octopus, prawns, fish, calamari, and mussels. Also on the menu in this rustic, bottles-hanging-from-the-ceiling Italian joint are some well-regarded veal and steak dishes, and plenty of pastas. Seafood Mama's is right on the ocean, near the Pelican Beach and the older Nautilus resorts, 7 kilometers (4¼ miles) north of Coffs Harbour. The restaurant will do takeout and deliver to your hotel.

Pacific Hwy. © 02/6653 6733. Reservations recommended. Main courses A$12.50–$25 (U.S.$8.10–$16.25). AE, DC, MC, V. Tues–Sat 6–10pm.

BYRON BAY: A BEACH BOHEMIA ⚘
78km (48 miles) SE of Murwillumbah

Being the most easterly point on the Australian mainland, the sun's rays hit Byron before anywhere else. This geographical position is good for two things: you can spot whales close to shore as they migrate north in June and July, and it's holistically attractive to the town's "alternative" community. Painters, crafts-people, glass blowers, and poets are so plentiful they almost fall from the macadamia nut trees. The place is loaded with float tanks, "pure body products," beauty therapists, and massage centers. Though it attracts squadrons of roving backpackers each summer to its party scene and discos, many of the locals simply stay at home, sipping their herbal tea and preparing for the healing light of the coming dawn. Families love Byron Bay for the beautiful beaches, and surfers flock here for some of the best surfing in the world.

ESSENTIALS
GETTING THERE If you're driving up the north coast, leave the Pacific Highway at Ballina and take the scenic coast road via Lennox Head. It's around 10 hours by car from Sydney (790km/490 miles), and 2 hours (200km/124 miles) south of Brisbane. Byron Bus Transfers (© **02/6681 3354**) meets all flights and transfers to Byron bay for A$20 (U.S.$13) single and A$435 (U.S.$22.75) return. **Coolangatta airport** is 1 hour north of Byron Bay (112km/69½ miles). **Countrylink** (© **13 22 32** in Australia) runs daily trains from Sydney to Byron Bay; the one-way fare is A$92 (U.S.$59.80) one-way for adults and A$46 (U.S.$29.90) for children. **Greyhound-Pioneer** (© **13 20 30** in Australia) buses from Sydney take around 13½ hours; the one-way coach fare is A$69 (U.S.$44.85).

ORGANIZED TOURS FROM SYDNEY An unusual way to get to Byron is on a 5-day surf safari from Sydney with Surfaris (© **1800 634 941** in Australia;

www.surfaris.com). You can learn to surf along the way as you stop of at several beaches, with camping overnight. Trips leave Sydney on Monday mornings and Byron Bay on Sunday mornings. It costs A$449 (U.S.$291.90) all-inclusive—though you need to bring a sleeping bag.

Another great trip is with Ando's Outback Tours (© **1800 228 828** in Australia; www.outbacktours.com.au), which operates from Sydney every Sunday and heads inland deep into the Outback on a 5-day trip. Among the highlights are visits to Lightning Ridge and the wild Glengarry opal fields (see "Outback New South Wales" later in this chapter). The trip costs A$435 (U.S.$283). A return trip back to Sydney costs A$35 (U.S.$22.75).

VISITOR INFORMATION   The **Byron Visitors Centre,** 80 Jonson St., Byron Bay, NSW 2481 (© **02/6680 9271**), is open daily from 9am to 5pm. A half-hour farther south is the **Ballina Tourist Information Centre,** on the corner of Las Balsas Plaza and River Street, Ballina (© **02/6686 3484**), open daily from 9am to 5pm. Two good websites on the area are **www.byronbay. net.au** and **www.byrontobush.com.au**.

SPECIAL EVENTS   Byron really goes to town during 4 days over the Easter weekend with the **East Coast Blues & Roots Festival** (www.bluesfest.com.au). Up to 30,000 people camp out to listen to up to 80 acts, including the likes of Ben Harper, Midnight Oil, and Joan Armatrading. Book tickets on the web. The first Sunday of every month when the extraordinary local **craft market** brings hippies and funky performers out from the hinterland.

HITTING THE SURF & SAND

Many accommodations in Byron Bay offer free surfboards for guests, or else head to the **Byron Bay Surf Shop,** on Lawson Street at the corner of Fletcher Street (© **02/6685 7536**), which rents boards for A$12 (U.S.$7.80) for 4 hours and A$20 (U.S.$13) for 24 hours. The shop can also arrange surf lessons for around A$25 (U.S.$16.25) per hour.

Wategos Beach and an area off the tip of Cape Byron called **"The Pass"** are two particularly good surf spots, though since each of Byron's main beaches faces a different direction, you are bound to find the surf is up on at least one. **Main Beach,** which stretches along the front of the town (it's actually some 50km/ 31 miles long), is good for swimming. West of Main Beach is **Belongil Beach,** the unofficial nudist beach (when authorities aren't cracking down on covering up). **Clarke's Beach** curves away to the east of Main Beach toward Cape Byron.

The **Cape Byron Lighthouse** on Cape Byron is one of Australia's most powerful. It's eerie to come up here at night to watch the stars and see the light reach some 40 kilometers (25 miles) out to sea. A nice walk just south of town goes through the rain forest of the **Broken Heads Nature Reserve.**

The best place to dive around Byron Bay is at **Julian Rocks,** about 3 kilometers (2 miles) offshore. Cold currents from the south meet warmer ones from the north here, which makes it a good spot to find a large variety of marine sea life. **Byron Bay Dive Centre,** 111 Jonson St. (© **02/6685 7149**) charges A$70 (U.S.$45.50) for the first dive and A$35 (U.S.$22.75) for each subsequent dive. **Sundive,** in the Byron Hostel complex on Middleton Street (© **02/6685 7755**), has cheaper initial dives at A$60 (U.S.$39) each.

EXPLORING THE HILLS & RAIN FORESTS

Behind Byron you'll find hills that could make the Irish weep, as well as rain forests, waterfalls, and small farms burgeoning with tropical fruits. A good operator taking trips inland is **Forgotten Country Ecotours** (℡ **02/6687 7843**). **Byron Bay to Bush Tours** (℡ **02/6685 6889,** or 0418/662 684 mobile; bush@mullum.com.au) operates day trips to the hippy hangout of **Nimbin** ℟— where I was approached on four separate occasions in 10 minutes last time I was there by people wanting me to buy marijuana—and up into the rain forest, visiting a macadamia-nut farm on the way and having a barbecue on their own organic farm. The trip leaves at 11am Monday through Saturday and costs A$30 (U.S.$19.50). This company also operates trips to the Sunday market at Channon on the second Sunday of each month and the one at Bangalow on the fourth Sunday. These trips cost A$15 (U.S.$9.75).

WHERE TO STAY

Real-estate agents **Elders R Gordon & Sons** (℡ **02/6685 6222;** eldersbb@omcs.com.au) can book rooms and cottages in Byron Bay and in the hinterland. Rates vary.

The Byron Bay Waves Motel (The Waves) ℟   This exceptional motel is just 60 meters (195 ft.) from Main Beach and just around the corner from the town center. The rooms are very nice, and all come with a queen-size bed, a marble bathroom with shower, and a king-size tub. Four rooms on the ground floor have a courtyard, and one room is suitable for travelers with disabilities. Toasters, in-house massage, and beauty treatments are also available. The suites have a king-size bed and a large balcony. The penthouse is very plush and fully self-contained one-bedroom apartment. There are six family rooms sleeping three adults, or two adults and two children.

Corner of Lawson and Middleton sts. (P.O. Box 647, Byron Bay 2481). ℡ **02/6685 5966.** Fax 02/6685 5977. www.byronwaves.com. 19 units. A$150–$320 (U.S.$97.50–$208) double depending on season; A$250–$380 (U.S.$162–$247) suite; A$250–$480 (U.S.$162.50–$312) penthouse. Extra person A$20 (U.S.$13), extra child under 16 A$20 (U.S.$13). AE, DC, MC, V. **Amenities:** Massage; babysitting; laundry service; nonsmoking rooms. *In room:* A/C, TV, unstocked refrigerator, coffeemaker, hair dryer, iron, safe.

Byron Central Apartments   If you don't want to eat out all the time then this is the best place for you. The fully self-contained apartments here come with a queen-size sofa bed and free in-house movies. Those on the first floor come with balconies. There are also a few loft-style apartments with separate dining, lounge, and sleeping areas. Units for people with disabilities are available. The landscaped garden has a barbecue. The apartments are a 2-minute walk from the main beach and town.

Byron St., Byron Bay, NSW 2481. ℡ **02/6685 8800.** Fax 02/6685 8802. www.byronbay.com/bca. 26 units. A$120–$260 (U.S.$78–$169) standard apt 1 night (depending on season). Higher rates apply Christmas/New Year period; low season is Apr–Sept. Ask about discounts for multiple-night stays. AE, DC, MC, V. **Amenities:** Medium-size saltwater pool; coin-op laundry, nonsmoking rooms. *In room:* TV, kitchen, unstocked refrigerator, coffeemaker, hair dryer.

Holiday Village Backpackers ℟   Byron Bay's original hostel is still one of the best. It's located in the center of town next door to Woolworth's supermarket and only a few minutes' walk from the bus and train stops, the main beach, and the town center. It's classified as a five-star backpackers, which is as good as it gets. Dorm rooms are clean, and doubles in the hostel are above average and come with a double bed, a fan, and a wardrobe. For a couple of dollars more you can stay in a fully self-contained unit with a separate bedroom, lounge, and kitchen area. On the premises are a volleyball court, spa and pool, TV and video lounge (there's a video library), barbecues, basketball hoop, Internet and e-mail, and free surfboards, body boards, and bicycles.

116 Jonson St., Byron Bay, NSW 2481. (C) **02/6685 8888.** Fax 02/6685 8777. 42 units, 13 with bathroom. A$55–$65 (U.S.$35.75–$42.25) double in hostel; A$70–$85 (U.S.$45.50–$55.25) self-contained double. A$21–$29 (U.S.$13.65–$18.85) dorm bed. DC, MC, V. **Amenities:** Medium-size pool; bike hire; tour desk; coin-op laundry.

Taylor's Guest House 𝕮𝕮 This truly beautiful guesthouse is set in 5 secluded acres of gardens and rain forest. Rooms here vary in price depending on whether you stay for 1 night or more. The guest rooms are lavishly decorated in a country style and come with either a queen- or king-size bed. The cottage is huge, has wraparound verandas and long French windows, and is done up in bright Santa Fe–style colors. The cottage also comes with a laundry and has the largest bed in Australia—a (8-ft.-by 7-ft., or 2.4m-by-2.1m) antique English "Emperor" bed. The guesthouse is renowned for its cooking.

160 McGettigan's Lane, Ewingsdale, Byron Bay, NSW 2481. (C) **02/6684 7436.** Fax 02/6684 7526. www. taylors.net.au. 5 units, 1 cottage. A$220 (U.S.$143) double; A$330 (U.S.$214.50) cottage. Rates include breakfast, cakes, and biscuits, and pre-dinner champagne cocktails. Dinner is A$60 (U.S.$39) a head. Surcharge of 20% for doubles and 50% for cottage at Christmas and Easter. AE, DC, MC, V. Not suitable for children. **Amenities:** Restaurant (Modern Australian), lounge; very large swimming pool; nonsmoking rooms. *In room:* TV, hair dryer, iron.

WHERE TO DINE

Beach Hotel BarbecuePUB/BARBECUE The outdoor meals served at this pub near the beach make it very popular with visitors and locals alike. About the cheapest thing on the menu is the burger, and the most expensive a steak. The Beach Hotel Bistro here is open from 10am to 9pm daily and serves coffee, cakes, and snacks throughout the day; a full lunch menu is served from noon to 3pm and dinner from 6 to 9pm.

In the Beach Hotel, at Bay and Johnson sts. (C) **02/6685 6402.** Main courses A$3.90–$13.50 (U.S.$2.50–$8.80). No credit cards. Daily noon–3pm.

Earth 'n' Sea PIZZA/PASTA This popular spot has been around for years and offers a fairly extensive menu of pastas and pizzas, including some unusual combinations such as prawns, banana, and pineapple. Pizzas come in three sizes, and the small is just enough to satisfy the average appetite.

11 Lawson St. (C) **02/6685 6029.** Reservations recommended. Main courses A$9.50–$23.50 (U.S.$6.20–$15.30). AE, MC, V. Daily 5:30–11pm.

The Pass Café 𝕮 MEDITERRANEAN Though not as well positioned as Rae's Restaurant and Bar (see below), the Pass Café rivals Rae's for breakfasts and lunches, and if you happen to be heading to or from the local rain forest on the Cape Byron Walking Track, you'll find this a great place to stop off. Breakfast items range from simple fresh fruit and muffins to gourmet chicken sausages. Lunch specials include Cajun chicken, octopus, and calamari salad, as well as fresh fish, meat dishes, and plenty of good vegetarian options.

At the end of Brooke Dr., on Cape Byron Walking Track, Palm Valley. (C) **02/6685 6074.** Main courses A$10–$25 (U.S.$6.50–$16.25). MC, V. Daily 8am–3pm (Thurs–Sat until 6pm).

Rae's Restaurant and Bar 𝕮MODERN AUSTRALIAN/SEAFOOD You can't beat Rae's for either its location or its food. It's right on the beach, about a 2-minute drive from the town center, and has a secluded, privileged air about it in the nicest of ways. Inside it's all Mediterranean blue and white, which complements perfectly the incoming rollers hitting the sand. The menu changes daily, but you may find the likes of grilled Atlantic salmon, red curry of roast beef fillet, braised lamb shanks, and yellow-fin tuna. If you have any special dietary requirements, tell the chef, and he will go out of his way to please you. Next door to the restaurant, but part of the same establishment, is Rae's on Watago's, an exclusive guesthouse offering luxury accommodations.

Watago's Beach, Byron Bay. (C) **02/6685 5366.** Reservations recommended. Dinner main courses A$37–$60 (U.S.$24–$39); lunch A$30–$35 (U.S.$19.50–$22.75). AE, DC, MC, V. Daily 7–10pm; Sat–Sun noon–3pm.

Raving Prawn ⊛ SEAFOOD   Fish cover the walls at this excellent place, but there's more than that on the menu. You can tuck into veal, chicken, or vegetarian dishes if you want to, but I wouldn't miss out on the fabulous signature dish, the jewfish (a kind of grouper) with an herb-mustard crust. The forestberry tart is the best dessert on the menu.

Feros Arcade (between Jonson and Lawson sts.). (C) **02/6685 6737.** Reservations recommended. Main courses A$19–$27 (U.S.$12.35–$17.55). AE, DC, MC, V. Tues–Sat 6–10pm (until around 9pm in winter). Open daily during school holidays.

MURWILLUMBAH

321km (200 miles) N of Coffs Harbour; 893km (554 miles) N of Sydney; 30km (19 miles) S of Queensland border

The main town of the Tweed Valley, Murwillumbah is a good base for touring the surrounding area, which includes **Mount Warning,** picturesque country towns, and countryside dominated by sugarcane and banana.

ESSENTIALS
GETTING THERE   Murwillumbah is inland from the Pacific Highway. The nearest airport is at **Coolangatta,** 34 kilometers (21 miles) away, just over the Queensland border. **Countrylink** trains ((C) **13 22 42** in Australia) link Murwillumbah with Sydney, taking 12 hours and 40 minutes. **Greyhound-Pioneer** ((C) **13 20 30** in Australia) buses run from Sydney to Murwillumbah; the trip takes 14½ hours.

VISITOR INFORMATION   The **Murwillumbah Visitors Centre,** at the corner of the Pacific Highway and Alma Street, Murwillumbah, NSW 2484 ((C) **02/6672 1340**), is worth visiting before heading out to see more of the Tweed Valley or the beaches to the east. Another option is the **Tweed Heads Visitors Centre,** at the corner of Bay and Wharf streets, Tweed Heads, NSW 2485 ((C) **07/5536 4244**). Both are open Monday through Friday from 9am to 5pm, and Saturday from 9am to 1pm.

SEEING THE AREA
If you're looking for a Big Avocado to go with your Coffs Harbour Big Banana, then head for **Tropical Fruit World,** on the Pacific Highway ((C) 02/6677 7222), 15 kilometers (9 miles) north of Murwillumbah and 15 kilometers (9 miles) south of Coolangatta. The Tweed Valley's top attraction grows some 400 varieties of tropical fruit, which can be discovered on an interesting 1½-hour tractor-train tour of the 200-acre (81-hectare) tropical fruit plantation, as well as on four-wheel-drive rain-forest drives and riverboat rides. It's open daily from 10am to 5pm. Also on the property are a kiosk, fruit market, and gift shop. Admission to food and shopping areas is free. Guided tours cost A$22 (U.S.$14.50) for adults, A$12 (U.S.$7.80) for children 4 to 12.

The 1,154-meter (3,815-ft.) **Mount Warning** is part of the rim of an extinct volcano that formed from volcanic action some 20 to 23 million years ago. You can hike around the mountain and to the top of it on trails in the Mount Warning World Heritage Park.

WHERE TO STAY & DINE

Crystal Creek Rainforest Retreat 🐨🐨   Crystal Creek is tucked away in a little valley of rain forest just 25 minutes by car from the Pacific Highway. Self-contained cabins skirt the edge of the rain forest that borders the Border Ranges National Park, a World Heritage Site. There are plenty of native birds, possums, echidnas, wallabies, and bandicoots around and about. Though the water is always cold, guests can swim in the natural pools and laze around on hammocks strung up in the bush. Cabins have two comfortable rooms, a balcony, kitchen, barbecue, and plenty of privacy. Two glass-terrace cabins overlook the rain forest and mountain. All rooms have a king-size bed and a double spa—no curtains in the bathroom because the rain forest gives enough privacy. Several tours are offered, including four-wheel-drive rain-forest tours and visits to local country markets and arts-and-crafts galleries, as well as walking tours around the property. Guests cook their own food or eat at the casual restaurant.

Brookers Rd., Upper Crystal Creek, Murwillumbah, NSW 2484. ℂ 02/6679 1591. Fax 02/6679 1596. www.crystalcreekrainforestretreat.com.au. 7 cabins. A$230–$245 (U.S.$149.50–$159.25). Ask about mid-week specials. MC, V. Not suitable for children. Pick-up service from the airport and bus and train stations is available. **Amenities:** Restaurant (Modern Australian/regional food); nonsmoking rooms. *In room:* TV, CD player, kitchen, refrigerator, coffeemaker, hair dryer, iron.

AFTER DARK

The clubs up here on the border of Queensland are huge and offer cheap bistro meals as well as pricier ones in the more upscale restaurants, inexpensive drinks at the bar, entertainment, and hundreds of poker machines. The biggest in New South Wales is the **Twin Towns Services Club,** Wharf Street, Tweed Heads (ℂ **07/5536 2277**). Another worth checking out is **Seagulls Rugby League Club,** Gollan Drive, Tweed Heads (ℂ **07/5536 3433**). Major entertainers such as Tom Jones, Joe Cocker, and Bob Hope have played here over the last few years. It's open 24 hours. To gain admittance to these "private" clubs, you must sign the registration book just inside the door.

5 South of Sydney Along the Princes Highway

There are two main roads leading south out of Sydney: the Hume Highway and the Princes Highway. Both routes connect Sydney to Melbourne, but the Hume Highway is quicker. A favorite with truckers and anyone in a hurry, the Hume Highway will get you to Melbourne in about 12 hours. The Princes Highway is a scenic coastal route that can get you to Melbourne in 2 days, though the many attractions along the route make it well worth taking longer.

KIAMA

119km (74 miles) S of Sydney

Kiama (pop. 10,300) is famous throughout the nation for its **blowhole.** In fact, there are two, a large one and a smaller one, but both spurt sea water several meters into the air. The larger of the two can jet water up to 60 meters (195 ft.), but you need a large swell and strong southeasterly winds to force the sea through the rock fissure with enough force to achieve that height. The smaller of the two is more consistent, but fares better with a good northeasterly wind.

Pick up a map from the Kiama Visitors Centre (see below) to guide you on a Heritage Walk through the historic district of this quaint village, where you can tour a row of National Trust workers' cottages built in 1896. There's little reason to stay in Kiama the night, as plenty more scenic places await further south.

ESSENTIALS

GETTING THERE   From Sydney, travel south on the Princes Highway via the steel-works city of Wollongong. There's also a regular train service from Sydney and a Greyhound-Pioneer (℃ **13 20 30** in Australia) coach service. The trip by coach takes about 2 hours, the train trip a little less.

VISITOR INFORMATION   The **Kiama Visitors Centre** at Blowhole Point, Kiama (℃ **02/4232 3322;** fax 02/4226 3260; www.kiama.net/tourism.htm), is open daily from 9am to 5pm.

JERVIS BAY: AN OFF-THE-BEATEN-TRACK GEM ⋔⋔
182km (113 miles) S of Sydney

Booderee National Park (formally known as Jervis Bay National Park), at Jervis Bay, is nothing short of spectacular. You should come here even if it means missing out on some of Sydney's treasures. How does this grab you—miles of deserted beaches, the whitest sand imaginable, kangaroos you can stroke, lorikeets who mob you for food during the day time and possums who do the same at night, pods of dolphins, some great walks through gorgeous bushland, and a real Aboriginal spirituality-of-place? I could go on, but see for yourself.

ESSENTIALS

GETTING THERE   It's best to reach Jervis Bay via Huskisson, 24 kilometers (15 miles) southeast of Nowra on the Princes Highway. Approximately 16 kilometers (10 miles) south of Nowra, turn left onto the Jervis Bay Road to Huskisson. The entrance to Booderee National Park is just after Huskisson. It's about a 3-hour drive from Sydney. You'll probably need at least 2 days to get to know the area. Watch out for the black cockatoos.

Australian Pacific Tours (℃ **02/9247 7222;** fax 02/9247 2052; www. aptours.com.au) runs a dolphin-watching cruise to Jervis Bay from Sydney every day between early October and mid-April, and Monday and Thursday in winter. The 12-hour trip—7 of which are on the coach—includes a visit to the Kiama blowhole, a 3-hour luncheon cruise looking for bottlenose dolphins, and a stop off on the way back at Fitzroy Falls in the Southern Highlands. The trip costs A$116.50 (U.S.$75.70) for adults, and A$108.50 (U.S.$70.50) for children.

VISITOR INFORMATION   For information on the area, contact the **Shoalhaven Visitors Centre,** at the corner of Princes Hwy. and Pleasant Way, Nowra (℃ **1800/024 261** in Australia, or 02/4421 0778; www.shoalhaven.nsw.gov.au). Pick up maps and book camping sites at the **Booderee National Park** office (℃ **02/4443 0977;** www.booderee.np.gov.au), located just beyond Huskisson; it's open daily from 9am to 4pm. **Hyams Beach Store** (℃ **02/4443 0242**) has an accommodation guide listing 34 rental properties from A$100 (U.S.$65) a weekend.

SEEING THE AREA

If you want to see the best spots, you'll need to pay the rather extortionate park-entrance fee of A$10 (U.S.$6.50) a day. Some of the places you could visit include **Hyams Beach** ⋔, reputed to have the whitest sand in the world. Notice how it squeaks when you walk on it. Wear sunscreen! The reflection off the beach can burn your skin in minutes on a sunny day. **Hole in the Wall Beach** has interesting rock formations and a lingering smell of natural sulfur. **Summer Cloud Bay** is secluded and offers excellent fishing.

Dolphin Watch Cruises, 74 Owen St., Huskisson (© **1800/246 010** in Australia, or 02/4441 6311), runs a hardy vessel out of Huskisson on the lookout for the resident pod of bottle-nosed dolphins—you have "more than a 95% chance of seeing them," the company claims. Lunch cruises run daily at 1pm, and a coffee cruise runs at 10am on Saturdays and Sundays, public holidays, and school holidays. The 2½-hour lunch cruise costs A$35 (U.S.$22.75) for adults and A$19.50 (U.S.$12.70) for children, including lunch. The 2-hour coffee cruise costs A$20 (U.S.$13) for adults and A$10 (U.S.$6.50) for children. It's possible to see humpback and southern right whales June through October.

WHERE TO STAY & DINE

If you have a tent and camping gear, all the better. **Caves Beach** is a quiet spot (except when the birds chorus at dawn) located just a stroll away from a good beach; it's home to resident eastern gray kangaroos. A campsite here costs A$8 (U.S.$5.20) per tent in winter and A$10 (U.S.$6.50) in summer and on public holidays, though at the time of writing moves were afoot to increase prices. It's about a 250-meter (¼-mile) walk from the carpark to the campground. **Greenpatch** is more dirt than grass, but you get your own area and it's suitable for campervans. It's infested with over-friendly possums around dusk. A camp spot here costs A$13 (U.S.$8.45) in winter and A$16 (U.S.$10.40) in summer.

For supplies head to the area's main towns, **Huskisson** (pop. 930) and **Vincentia** (pop. 2,350). The **Huskisson RSL Club,** overlooking the wharf area on Owen Street (© **02/4441 5282**), has a good cheap bistro and a bar. You'll have to sign in just inside the main entrance door. The Huskissson Hotel (also called the "Husskie Pub") is just down the road and has a nice beer garden and cheapish meals at lunchtime.

Huskisson Beach Tourist Resort   This resort is the very pinnacle of cabin accommodation on this part of the east coast. Cabins vary in price depending on size, but even the smallest has room enough for a double bed, triple bunks, and a small kitchen with microwave. Larger cabins have two separate bedrooms. There's a game room and barbecue facilit:es on the grounds.

Beach St., Huskisson, Jervis Bay, NSW 2540. © and fax **02/4441 5142.** 38 units. Fri–Sat A$75–$105 (U.S.$49–$68.25) cabin; Sun–Thurs A$60–$95 (U.S.$39–$61.75) cabin. DC, MC, V. **Amenities:** Small outdoor pool; tennis court; coin-op laundry; nonsmoking rooms. *In room:* TV, kitchen, unstocked refrigerator, coffeemaker, hair dryer, iron.

Jervis Bay Guest House ♟   After the Jervis Bay Hotel, take the second road to the left—Nowra Street—and follow it to the end. This relatively new guest house has four distinctly different rooms (different color schemes, beds, and so on), all with private bathroom. One room has a Jacuzzi, and two rooms face the water. Breakfast is a hearty affair and could include emu sausages and thick slabs of bacon followed by a tropical fruit platter. Children under 16 not allowed.

1 Beach St., Huskisson, NSW 2540 © **02/4441 7658.** Fax 02/4441 7659. www.jervisbayguesthouse.com.au. 4 units. A$130–$220 (U.S.$84.50–$143) double depending on season. Rates include breakfast. DC, MC, V. **Amenities:** Lounge; nonsmoking rooms. *In room:* A/C, coffeemaker, hair dryer.

ULLADULLA

220km (134miles) south of Sydney.

Very much a supply town on the south coast as well as a major fishing center, especially for tuna, Ulladulla is a pleasant stopover on your journey south. This

A Safety Warning

Jervis Bay is notorious for its car break-ins, a situation the local police force has been unable to control. If you park your car anywhere in the national park, remove all valuables, including things in the trunk.

is also a good place to stock up on supplies from the local supermarkets. On the outskirts of town (just to the south) are a series of beautiful saltwater lakes that make for good fishing, though you'll have competition from the pelicans. Inland from here is the giant Morton National Park, marked by the prominent peak of Pigeonhouse Mountain. The 3- to 4-hour walk to the top and back starts at a carpark a 30-minute drive from Ulladulla. The going is steep at first but levels out as it crosses a sandstone plateau. Another upward climb and you're rewarded with a magnificent view of peaks and ocean.

Several side roads worth exploring spur off between Ulladulla and Batemans Bay (see below). These lead to the tiny villages of Bawley Point and Kioloa, where holiday cottages nestle between isolated beaches, gum forests, and green patches studded with gray kangaroos.

There are more kangaroos at the pristine **Pebbly Beach** 🐾 in Murramarang National Park, a short hop—20 minutes south—of Ulladulla. These furry creatures actually wander around the beach and adjacent campsite, or gather on the grassy dunes to graze. It's a good area for bird watching, too.

ESSENTIALS
GETTING THERE   Ulladulla is about a 3-hour drive from Sydney Central Business District down the Pacific Highway.

VISITOR INFORMATION   **Ulladulla Visitors Centre,** Civic Center, Princes Highway (© **02/4455 1269;** www.shoalhaven.nsw.gov.au), is open Monday through Friday from 10am to 5pm and Saturday and Sunday from 9am to 5pm.

WHERE TO STAY & DINE
Ulladulla is well known for its food (particularly seafood and beef) and wine (there are a few boutique wineries in the area). For some of the best fish in Australia, head to one of the fish-and-chip shops on Wason Street, close to the harbor. The best of these is **Tiger Fish and Chips** (no phone). On the same street is **Torys Takeaway** (© **02/4454 0888**), where you can buy good fish-and-chips on the ground floor at about a third of the price of the very nice restaurant above—**Torys Seafood Restaurant** (open in the evenings, same number) and take them down to the harbor to eat amongst the seagulls.

Ulladulla Guest House 🐾🐾🐾   This fabulous property is one of the best places to stay in Australia. Run by the friendly Andrew and Elizabeth Nowosad—try and guess his accent—the Ulladulla Guest House is an impressive five-star establishment. It's surrounded by small but lovely tropical gardens—Andrew insists his coconut palms are the only ones this far south—and overlooks the harbor. Unusually, the house is also a registered art gallery, and the walls are festooned with paintings for sale. Past the cozy lounge are three types of rooms. Two self-contained units with private entrances to the garden are the lowest in price. The one-bedroom unit has a queen-size bed and a foldout sofa bed, and the two-bedroom unit has a double bed in one room, two singles in another, and a double foldout sofa bed in the lounge. Luxury rooms have a queen-size bed, custom-made furniture, and original artwork. Executive rooms come with a marble bathroom and a private spa. There are three masseurs on standby.

39 Burrill Street, Ulladulla, NSW 2539. ℂ **02/4455 1796.** Fax 02/4454 4660. www.guesthouse.com.au. 10 units. Self-contained 1-bedroom unit: A$98 (U.S.$63.70) midweek standby, A$188 (U.S.$122) weekend and peak period (see below). 2-bedroom unit: A$120 (U.S.$78) midweek, A$228 (U.S.$148) weekend/peak. Luxury units A$118 (U.S.$76.70) midweek, A$188 (U.S.$122) weekend/peak. Executive units A$138 (U.S.$90) midweek, A$228 (U.S.$148) weekend/peak. Peak periods: weekends, public holidays, Easter, and Christmas school holidays. AE, DC, MC, V. **Amenities:** Restaurant (French Provincial); very nice lagoon-style outdoor pool; golf course nearby; exercise room; spa; water-sport rental; bike rental; room service (7am–10pm); in-room massage; babysitting; free laundry room; laundry service; same-day dry cleaning; nonsmoking rooms. *In room:* A/C, TV, fax, dataport, kitchenette (2 rooms), minibar, unstocked refrigerator, coffeemaker, hair dryer, iron.

BATEMANS BAY
275km (171 miles) S of Sydney

This laid-back holiday town offers good surfing beaches, arts-and-crafts galleries, boat trips up the Clyde River, good game fishing, and bushwalks in Morton and Deua national parks.

ESSENTIALS
GETTING THERE   Batemans Bay is about a 3- to 4-hour drive from Sydney, depending on the traffic (avoid leaving Sydney at rush hour, and prepare for long delays on public holidays). **Premier Motor Service** (ℂ **1300/368 100** in Australia, or 02/4423 5233) runs coaches to Batemans Bay from Sydney's Central Station.

VISITOR INFORMATION   **Batemans Bay Visitor Information Centre,** at the corner of Princes Highway and Beach Road (ℂ **1800/802 528** in Australia, or 02/4472 6800), is open daily from 9am to 5pm.

GAME FISHING & A RIVER CRUISE
If you fancy some serious fishing contact **OB1 Charters,** Marina, Beach Road, Batemans Bay (ℂ **1800/641 065** in Australia, 02/4471 2738, or 0416/241 586 mobile; www.southcoast.com.au/ob1). The company runs full-day game-fishing trips and morning snapper-fishing trips (afternoon snapper trips in summer, too). Expect to encounter black marlin, blue marlin, giant kingfish, mako sharks, albacore tuna, yellow-fin tuna, and blue tuna from November through June. The trip includes all tackle, bait, and afternoon and morning teas, but you must provide your own lunch. It costs A$900 (U.S.$585) to hire the six-person boat (so it's worth booking way in advance with general dates in order to get other people to go with you and share the cost). Snapper (a nice-tasting fish) trips include all gear, bait, and morning or afternoon tea for A$80 (U.S.$52) per person.

A river cruise on the **MV *Merinda,*** Innes Boatshed, Orient St., Batemans Bay (ℂ **02/4472 4052;** fax 02/4472 4754), is a pleasant experience. The 3-hour cruise leaves at 11:30am daily and travels inland past townships, forests, and farmland. It costs A$22 (U.S.$14) for adults, A$11 (U.S.$7.15) for children, and A$50 (U.S.$32.50) for families; a fish-and-chip lunch is A$6 (U.S.$3.90) extra and a seafood basket for two is A$12 (U.S.$7.80).

A NICE PLACE TO STAY
The Esplanade 𝒦   This four-star hotel is right on the Batemans Bay river estuary and close to the town center. Rooms are light and well furnished, and all have balconies (some with good water views). Some doubles and suites have

spas; they cost the same as non-spa rooms, so specify if you want one when booking. Eat at the hotel's restaurant or at the Batemans Bay Soldiers' Club just opposite, which has a restaurant, a bistro, cheap drinks, and a free evening kids club.

23 Beach Rd. (P.O. Box 202), Batemans Bay, NSW 2536. © 1800/659 884 in Australia, or 02/4472 0200. Fax 02/4472 0277. Esplanade.com.au. 23 units. A$104.50–$176 (U.S.$68–$114) double, depending on season; A$176–$203.50 (U.S.$114–$132) suite. Extra person A$11.50 (U.S.$7.50). Children under 18 stay free in parents' room. AE, DC, MC, V. **Amenities:** Restaurant (seafood); laundry facilities; nonsmoking rooms. *In room:* A/C, TV, kitchenette, unstocked refrigerator, coffeemaker, hair dryer, iron.

NAROOMA ℛ
345km (214 miles) from Sydney

Narooma is a seaside town with beautiful deserted beaches, an golf course right on a headland, a natural rock formation in the shape of Australia (popular with camera-wielding tourists), and excellent fishing. However, its major attraction is **Montague Island** ℛℛ, the breeding colony for thousands of shearwaters (or mutton birds, as they're also called) and a hangout for juvenile seals.

Just 18 kilometers (11 miles) farther south is **Central Tilba** ℛ, one of the prettiest towns in Australia and the headquarters of the boutique **ABC Cheese Factory.** You'll kick yourself if you miss this charming historical township (pop. 35; 1 million visitors annually).

ESSENTIALS
GETTING THERE   Narooma is a 7-hour drive from Sydney down the Princes Highway. **Premier Motor Service** (© **1300/368 100** in Australia, or 02/4423 5233) runs coaches to Narooma from Sydney's Central Station.

VISITOR INFORMATION   The **Narooma Visitors Centre,** Princes Highway, Narooma (© **02/4476 2881;** fax 02/4476 1690; www.naturecoast-tourism.com.au), is open daily from 9am to 5pm.

WHAT TO SEE & DO: WHALES, GOLF & MORE
A must if you're visiting the area is a boat tour with **Narooma Charters** (© **02/ 4476 2240;** www.acr.net/~charters). It offers spectacular tours of the coast on the lookout for dolphins, seal colonies, and little penguins, and also includes a tour of Montague Island. Morning and afternoon tours take 3½ hours and cost A$66 (U.S.$42.90) for adults, A$49.50 (U.S.$32.20) for children, and A$198 (U.S.$128.70) for families. A 4½-hour tour includes some of the world's best whale-watching (between mid-September and early December) and costs A$88 (U.S.$57.20) for adults, A$71.50 (U.S.$46.50) for children, and A$297 (U.S.$193) for families. The last time I went on this trip we saw no fewer than eight humpback whales, some of them mothers with calves. The company also offers game fishing from February to the end of June and scuba diving in the seal colonies from August to the end of December. Dives cost A$66 (U.S.$42.90) for a double dive, plus approximately A$33 (U.S.$21.45) for gear rental.

Narooma Golf Club, Narooma (© **02/4476 2522**), has one of the most interesting and challenging coastal courses in Australia. A round of golf will cost you A$25 (U.S.$16.25).

While in the area I recommend stopping off at the **Umbarra Aboriginal Cultural Centre** ℛ, Wallaga Lake, just off the Princes Highway on Bermagui Road (© **02/4473 7232;** www.umbarra.com.au). The center offers activities such as boomerang and spear throwing, and painting with natural ochres for A$6.25 (U.S.$4) per person, or A$20 (U.S.$13) for a family. There are also discussions, Aboriginal archival displays, and a retail store. It's open Monday through Friday from 9am to 5pm and Saturday and Sunday from 9am to 4pm (closed Sun in winter). The center's guides also offer 2- to 4-hour four-wheel-drive/walking trips of nearby **Mount Dromedary** 🏃 and **Mumbulla Mountain,** taking in sacred sites. The tours cost A$45 (U.S.$29.25) per person. Reservations are essential.

If you want to attempt Mt. Dromedary without a guide, ask for directions in Narooma. The hike to the top takes around 3 hours.

WHERE TO STAY

Whale Motor Inn 🏃   This nice and quiet motor inn has the best panoramic ocean views on the south coast and the largest rooms in town. Standard rooms have a queen-size and a single-person sofa bed. The standard suites have a separate bedroom, two additional sofa beds, and a kitchenette. Executive and spa suites are very spacious, better furnished, and have a kitchenette and a large balcony or patio.

Princes Hwy., Narooma, NSW 2546. ℂ **02/4476 2411.** Fax 02/4476 1995. 17 units. A$90–$145 (U.S.$58.50–$94.25). Extra person A$10 (U.S.$6.50). AE, DC, MC, V. **Amenities:** Restaurant (seafood); small outdoor pool; nonsmoking rooms. *In room:* A/C, TV, kichenette (in all rooms except A$90/U.S.$58.50 rooms), unstocked refrigerator, coffeemaker, hair dryer, iron.

MERIMBULA
480km (385 miles) S of Sydney; 580km (464 miles) NE of Melbourne

This seaside resort (pop. approx. 7,000) is the last place of interest before the Princes Highway crosses the border into Victoria. Merimbula is a good center from which to discover the surrounding **Ben Boyd National Park** and **Mimosa Rocks National Park;** both offer bushwalking. Another park, **Bournda National Park,** is situated around a lake and has good walking trails and a surf beach.

Golf is the game of choice in Merimbula itself, and the area's most popular venue is the **Pambula-Merimbula Golf Club** (ℂ **02/6495 6154**), where you can spot kangaroos grazing on the fairways of the 27-hole course. It costs A$14 (U.S.$9.10) for nine holes, or A$25 (U.S.$16.25) for the day. Another favorite is **Tura Beach Country Club** (ℂ **02/6495 9002**), which is known for its excellent coastal views. A round of 18 holes costs A$20 (U.S.$13).

Eden, 20 kilometers (12½ miles) south of Merimbula, was once a major whaling port. The rather gruesome **Eden Killer Whale Museum,** on Imlay Street in Eden (ℂ **02/6496 2094**), is the only reason to stop off here. It has a dubious array of relics, including boats, axes, and remnants of the last of the area's killer whales, called Old Tom. The museum is open Monday through Saturday from 9:15am to 3:45pm, Sunday from 11:15am to 3:45pm. In January it's open daily from 9:15am to 4:45pm daily. Admission is A$5.50 (U.S.$3.60) for adults and A$1.50 (U.S.$1) for children. Thankfully, you can still see a scattering of whales off the coast in October and November.

ESSENTIALS
GETTING THERE   The drive from either Sydney or Melbourne takes about 7 hours. The **Greyhound-Pioneer** (ℂ **13 20 30** in Australia) bus trip from Sydney takes more than 8 hours.

VISITOR INFORMATION   The **Merimbula Tourist Information Centre,** at Beach Street, Merimbula (ℂ **1800/150 457** in Australia, or 02/6495 1129; fax 02/6495 1250), is open daily from 9am to 5pm (10am–4pm in winter).

SYDNEY'S TOP ATTRACTIONS...

FOR THE CLIMB OF YOUR LIFE!™

T hree hour guided Climbs to the top of the Sydney Harbour Bridge. Experience the breathtaking 360° view of the world's most beautiful harbour by day, or the magic of Sydney lights by night.

WINNER
1999 AUSTRALIAN
TOURISM AWARDS

TICKET HOTLINE
61 2 8274-7777
7AM-7PM SEVEN DAYS

TICKETS ONLINE
www.bridgeclimb.com

BRIDGECLIMB
S Y D N E Y ®

IT&P BRIDG 1116-1

5 CUMBERLAND STREET, THE ROCKS, SYDNEY, 2000
Fax: 61 2 9240 1122 Email: admin@bridgeclimb.com

SHARKS!

AT ONE OF THE WORLD'S GREAT AQUARIUMS

OPEN EVERY DAY FROM 9.00am to 10.00pm

Over 11,000 All Australian Aquatic Animals World famous shark display **Fairy penguins** Crocodiles **Platypus** Seals **Underwater tunnels** Massive Great Barrier Reef complex **Touch pools**

www.sydneyaquarium.com.au

Darling Harbour Enquiries: 02 9262 2300

PRESENT THIS ADVERTISEMENT AND RECEIVE:

BRIDGECLIMB:
A FREE GIFT WITH EVERY CLIMB PURCHASED

SYDNEY AQUARIUM:
10% DISCOUNT ON ADMISSION PRICES

Offers expire 31 December 2002. Cannot be used with any other offer.

SPECIAL EVENTS   Jazz fans should head for the **Merimbula Jazz Festival** held over the long Queens Birthday weekend, the second weekend in June. A country-music festival takes place the last weekend in October.

WHERE TO STAY
Ocean View Motor Inn   This pleasant motel has good water views from 12 of its rooms (the best are numbers 9, 10, and 11). The rooms are spacious and modern, with plain brick walls, patterned carpets, and one long balcony serving the top six rooms. Fourteen rooms have kitchenettes. All have showers. It's a friendly place. Breakfast is served to your room for A$7.70 (U.S.$5) extra.

Merimbula Dr. and View St., Merimbula, NSW 2548. © **02/6495 2300.** Fax 02/6495 3443. oceanview@asitis.net.au. 20 units. A$66–$120 (U.S.$43–$78) double (depending on season). Extra person A$11 (U.S.$6.50). MC, V. **Amenities:** Medium-size solar-heated outdoor pool; coin-op laundry; nonsmoking rooms. *In room:* A/C, TV, kitchenette, refrigerator, coffeemaker.

6 The Snowy Mountains: Australia's Ski Country ⓐ

Thredbo: 519km (322 miles) SW of Sydney; 208km (129 miles) SW of Canberra; 543km (331 miles) NE of Melbourne

Made famous by Banjo Patterson's 1890 poem the "Man from Snowy River," the Snowy Mountains are most commonly used for what you'd least expect to happen in Australia—skiing. It starts to snow around June and carries on until September. During this time hundreds of thousands of people from all over the country flock here to ski at the major ski resorts—Thredbo and Perisher Blue, and to a lesser extent Charlotte Pass and Mount Selwyn. It's certainly different skiing here, with ghostly white gums as the obstacles instead of pine trees.

The whole region is part of the **Kosciuszko** (pronounced ko-zi-*os*-co) **National Park,** the largest alpine area in Australia. During the summer months the park is a beautiful place for walking, and in spring the profusion of wild-flowers is exquisite. A series of lakes in the area, including the one in the resort town of Jindabyne, are favorites with trout fishermen.

Visitors either stay at **Jindabyne,** 62 kilometers (39 miles) south of Cooma, or **Thredbo Village,** 36 kilometers (20 miles) southwest of Jindabyne. Jindabyne is a pretty bleak-looking resort town on the banks of the man-made Lake Jindabyne, which came into existence when the Snowy River was dammed to provide hydroelectric power.

Thredbo Village is set in a valley of Mt. Crackenback and resembles European-style resorts. From here, the Crackenback Chairlift provides easy access to the top of Mt. Kosciuszko, which at 2,228 meters (7,352 ft.) is Australia's highest peak. The mountain has stunning views of the alpine region and some good walks.

SNOWY MOUNTAIN ESSENTIALS
GETTING THERE   From Sydney, the Parramatta Road runs into the Hume Highway in the suburb of Ashfield. Follow the Hume Highway south to Goulburn, where you turn onto the Federal Highway toward Canberra. From there take the Monaro Highway to Cooma, then follow the Alpine Way through Jindabyne and on to Thredbo. Chains may have to be used on the slopes in winter and can be rented from local service stations. The trip takes around 7 hours from Sydney with short breaks.

Qantas (© **13 13 13** in Australia) has daily flights from Sydney to Cooma. A connecting bus to the ski fields takes about 1 hour and is available June through October. It's run by **Snowy Mountain Hire Cars** (© **02/6456 2957**) and costs A$48 (U.S.$31.20) one-way.

In winter only (from around June 19 to October 5), **Greyhound-Pioneer** (© **13 20 30** in Australia) operates daily buses between Sydney and Cooma, via Canberra. The journey takes around 7 hours from Sydney and 3 from Canberra. A one-way ticket costs A$50 (U.S.$32.50).

VISITOR INFORMATION   Pick up information about the ski fields and accommodation options either at the **Cooma Visitors Centre,** 119 Sharp St., Cooma, NSW 2630 (© **02/6450 1740;** fax 02/6450 1798), or at the **Snowy Region Visitor Centre,** Kosciuszko Rd., Jindabyne, NSW 2627 (© **02/6450 5600;** fax 02/6456 1249).

HITTING THE SLOPES & OTHER ADVENTURES

Obviously, skiing is the most popular activity around here. More than 50 ski lifts serve the combined fields of Perisher Valley, Mt. Blue Cow, Smiggins Holes, and Guthega. Perisher Valley offers the best overall ski slopes; Mt. Blue Cow is generally very crowded; Smiggins Holes offer good slopes for beginners; and Guthega has nice light, powdery snow and less-crowded conditions. Thredbo has some very challenging runs and the longest downhill runs, but I still prefer Perisher for atmosphere. A day's ski pass costs around A$62 (U.S.$40.30) for adults, and A$36 (U.S.$23.40) for children.

A ski-tube train midway between Jindabyne and Thredbo on the Alpine Way travels through the mountains to Perisher Valley and then to Blue Cow. It costs A$10 (U.S.$6.50) a day for adult skiers and A$6 (U.S.$3.90) for child skiers; A$22 (U.S.$14.30) for non-skiing adults and A$11 (U.S.$7.15) for non-skiing children. Prices are cheaper in summer. Ski gear can be rented at numerous places in Jindabyne and Thredbo.

In the summer, the region is popular for hiking, canoeing, fishing, and golf. Thredbo Village has tennis courts, a nine-hole golf course, and mountain-bike trails.

WHERE TO STAY

You'll have to book months ahead to find a place to stay during the ski season (especially on weekends). And don't expect to find a lot of bargains. The **Kosciuszko Accommodation Centre,** Nuggets Crossing, Jindabyne, NSW 2627 (© **1800/026 354** in Australia, or 02/6456 2022; fax 02/6456 2945), can help find and book accommodations in the area. Other private agents who can help find you a spot for the night include **The Snowy Mountains Reservation Centre** (© **02/6456 2633**) and the **Thredbo Resort Centre** (© **1800/020 622** in Australia).

IN THREDBO

Riverside Cabins   These fully self-contained studio and one-bedroom cabins are above the Thredbo River and overlook the Crackenback Range. They're also a short walk from the Thredbo Alpine Hotel and local shops. Most rooms have

---

Ski Condition Updates

For up-to-date ski field information call **Perisher Blue** (© 02/6459 4485); **Thredbo** (© 02/6459 4100); **Charlotte Pass** (© 02/6457 5247); or **Mt. Selwyn** (© 02/6454 9488).

Moments **Following in the Footsteps of the Man from Snowy River**

Horseback riding is a popular activity for all those wanting to ride like the "Man from Snowy River." **Reynella Kosciusko Rides,** located in Adamanaby, 44 kilometers (27 miles) northwest of Cooma (© **1800/029 909** in Australia, or **02/6454 2386;** fax 02/6454 2530; reynellarides.com.au), offers multinight rides through the Kosciuszko National Park from October to the end of April. Three-day/4-night rides costs A$799 (U.S.$519), and the 5-day/6-night ride A$1,207 (U.S.$784). Transfers from Cooma cost A$33 (U.S.$21.45) each way. The trips are all-inclusive and include camping and homestead accommodations. Shorter rides are offered by **Jindabyne Trail Rides** (© **02/6456 2421;** fax 02/6456 1254). Gentle, 1½-hour rides on the slopes above Jindabyne cost A$25 (U.S.$16.25) per person.

balconies. Rates vary wildly from weekday to weekend and season, so check before you come here.

Thredbo, NSW 2625. © **1800/026 333** in Australia, or 02/6459 4299. Fax 02/6459 4195. 36 units. Winter A$160–$516 (U.S.$104–$335) double. Summer A$117–$164 (U.S.$76–$106.60) double. Ask about weekly rates. AE, DC, MC, V. *In room:* TV, kitchen, laundry, unstocked refrigerator, coffeemaker, hair dryer, iron.

Thredbo Alpine Apartments These apartments are very similar to the Riverside Cabins (see above) and are managed by the same people. All have balconies with mountain views. Some have queen-size beds. There's a limited daily maid service and in-house movies.

Thredbo, NSW 2628. © **1800/026 333** in Australia, or 02/6459 4299. Fax 02/6459 4195. 35 units. Winter weekends A$210–$441 (U.S.$136.50–$286.65) 1-bedroom apt; A$289–$628 (U.S.$188–$408) 2-bedroom apt; A$394–$770 (U.S.$256–$500) 3-bedroom apt; midweek rates approx. 20% cheaper. Higher rates apply July 30–Sept 2. Summer A$127–$164 (U.S.$82.55–$106.60) 1-bedroom apt; A$159–$190 (U.S.$103–$123.50) 2-bedroom apt; A$180–$210 (U.S.$117–$136.50) 3-bedroom apt. Ask about weekly rates. AE, DC, MC, V. Undercover parking. *In room:* TV, kitchen, laundry, unstocked refrigerator, cofeemaker, hair dryer, iron.

Thredbo Alpine Hotel The center of activity in Thredbo after the skiing is finished for the day is this large resort-style lodge. Rooms vary; those on the top floor of the three-story hotel have a king-size bed instead of a standard queen. The rooms are all wood-paneled. Thredbo's only nightclub is here. There's also a swimming pool, sauna, and spa.

Thredbo, (P.O. Box 80, Thredbo NSW 2625). © **02/6459 4200.** Fax 02/6459 4201. www.thredbo.com.au. 65 units. Winter A$220–$498 (U.S.$143–$324) double. Summer A$149–$189 (U.S.$99–$123) double. Ask about weekly rates and packages. Rates include breakfast. AE, DC, MC, V. **Amenities:** Small indoor swimming pool; spa; sauna; tour desk; massage; coin-op laundry; nonsmoking rooms. *In room:* TV, minibar, coffeemaker, hair dryer.

7 Outback New South Wales

The Outback is a powerful Australian image. Hot, dusty and prone to flies, it can also be a romantic place where wedge-tailed eagles float in the shimmering heat as you spin in a circle, tracing the unbroken horizon. If you drive out here, you have to be constantly on the lookout for emus, large flightless birds that dart across roads open-beaked and wide-eyed. When you turn off the car engine, it's so quiet you can hear the scales of a sleepy lizard, as long as your forearm, scraping the rumpled track as it turns to taste the air with its long, blue tongue.

Outback Driving Tips

Most of the places covered below are accessible by two-wheel-drive cars, though you should never attempt to travel on dirt tracks after a rain. Always make sure you have plenty of water and fuel, and never wander off the main tracks unless you have a detailed local map of the area and have told someone when to expect to hear from you.

The scenery is a huge canvas with a restricted palette; blood red for the dirt, straw yellow for the blotches of Mitchell grass, a searing blue for the surreally large sky. There is room to be yourself in the Outback, and you'll soon find that personalities often tilt toward the eccentric. It's a hard-working place, too, where miners, sheep and cattle farmers, try to eke out a living in Australia's hard center.

BROKEN HILL ☆☆

1,157km (717 miles) W of Sydney; 508km (315 miles) NE of Adelaide

At heart, Broken Hill—or "Silver City" as it's been nicknamed—is still very much a hard-working, hard-drinking mining town. Its beginnings date back to 1883 when the trained eye of a boundary rider named Charles Rasp noticed something odd about the craggy rock outcrops at a place called the Broken Hill. Today, the city's main drag, Argent Street, bristles with finely crafted colonial mansions, heritage homes, hotels, and public buildings. Look deeper and you see the town's quirkiness. Around one corner you'll find the radio station built to resemble a giant wireless set with round knobs for windows, and around another the headquarters of the Housewives Association, which ruled the town with an iron apron for generations. Then there's the Palace Hotel—made famous in the movie *The Adventures of Priscilla, Queen of the Desert*—with its high painted walls and a mural of Botticelli's *Birth of Venus* on the ceiling two flights up.

Traditionally a hard-drinking but religious town, Broken Hill has 23 pubs (down from 73 in its heyday around the turn of the 20th century) and plenty of churches, as well as a Catholic cathedral, a synagogue, and a mosque to serve its 24,500 inhabitants.

ESSENTIALS

GETTING THERE   By car, take the Great Western Highway from Sydney to Dubbo, then the Mitchell Highway to the Barrier Highway, which will take you to Broken Hill. **Southern Australian Airlines** (book through Qantas, ☎ 13 13 13 in Australia) also connects Broken Hill to Adelaide, Melbourne, and Mildura.

The *Indian Pacific* train stops here on its way to Perth twice a week. The fare from Sydney is A$415 (U.S.$270) for adults and A$283 (U.S.$184) for children in a first-class sleeper, A$329 (U.S.$214) for adults and A$198 (U.S.$128.70) for children in an economy sleeper, and A$117 (U.S.$76) for adults and A$53 (U.S.$34.45) for children in an economy seat. Call **Great Southern Railways** (☎ 08/8213 4530) for more information and bookings, or check out the timetables and fares on their website (www.gsr.com.au).

Greyhound-Pioneer (☎ 13 20 30 in Australia) runs buses from Adelaide for A$69.30 (U.S.$45); the trip takes 7 hours. The 16-hour trip from Sydney costs A$111.10 (U.S.$71.50).

VISITOR INFORMATION   The **Broken Hill Visitors Information Centre,** at Blende and Bromide streets, Broken Hill, NSW 2880 (☎ 08/8087 6077; fax

08/8088 5209; www.murrayoutback.org.au; tourist@pcpro.net.au), is open daily from 8:30am to 5pm. The **National Parks & Wildlife Service** (NPWS) office is at 183 Argent St. (© **08/8088 5933**), and the **Royal Automobile Association of South Australia,** which offers reciprocal services to other national and international auto-club members, is at 261 Argent St. (© **08/8088 4999**).

Note: The area code in Broken Hill is **08,** the same as the South Australia code, not 02, the New South Wales code.

GETTING AROUND   Silver City Tours, 380 Argent St. (© **08/8087 3144**), conducts tours of the city and surrounding Outback. City tours take around 4 hours and cost A$45 (U.S.$26) for adults and A$20 (U.S.$13) for children. They also offer a range of other tours of the area.

Broken Hill Corner Country Adventure Tours (© **08/8087 5142;** www.cornercountryadventure.com.au), operates several small group tours into the desert from Broken Hill, staying in rural properties and bush pubs. The regular 4-day/3-night Corner Country Tour takes in a sheep station, White Cliffs, Mootwingee, and the red-sand Sturt National Park. It costs A$850 (U.S.$552) all-inclusive. Other offerings include a 5-day trip to the Flinders Ranges and the Lake Eyre—usually a vast dry bowl of clay, which sometimes floods—for A$1,235 (U.S.$803); and an 8-day Birdsville and Outback tour, May through October, stopping off at the very impressive red sand dunes on the edge of the Simpson Desert, as well as the one-camel bush towns of Birdsville, Marree, and Innamincka in South Australia. This costs A$1,790 (U.S.$1,163).

Another recommended small group tour operator, **Goanna Safari** (© **08/ 8087 6057;** www.goanna-safari.com.au) offers personalized tours of the Outback from Broken Hill, and a range of regular camping (with good camp beds and cooking fires) or accommodated tours. Among them is a 3-day/2-night trip to Mootwingee, White Cliffs, and Menidee Lakes, where giant dams on the Darling River bristle with the half-drowned skeletons of gum trees and flutter with numerous species of wading birds, pelicans, and ducks. This trip costs A$582 (U.S.$378.30) camping and A$693 (U.S.$450) accommodated. Also on the agenda is a 5-day trip to Sturt National Park—where wildflowers poke out of the red sand in abundance—as well as White Cliffs and Mootwingee. This costs A$971 (U.S.$631) camping and A$1,215 (U.S.$790).

Broken Hill Outback Tours (© **08/8087 7800;** www.outbacktours.net), also runs a range of accommodated trips in the area, among them a 4-day journey to Mootwingee, White Cliffs, and Menindee, with Mungo National Park added on. Lake Mungo, a dry lake famous for the 45,000-year-old skeletons and artifacts discovered there, is also known for a semicircle of huge sand dunes and shimmering white cliffs known as the Walls of China. This costs A$1,125 (U.S.$731) all-inclusive.

Hertz (© **08/8087 2719;** fax 08/8087 4838) rents four-wheel-drive vehicles suitable for exploring the area.

EXPLORING THE TOWN: GALLERIES, A MINE TOUR & THE WORLD'S LARGEST SCHOOLROOM

With the largest regional public gallery in New South Wales and 27 private **galleries,** Broken Hill has more places per capita to see art than anywhere else in Australia. The **Broken Hill City Art Gallery,** Chloride Street, between Blende and Beryl streets (© **08/8088 5491**), houses an extensive collection of Australian colonial and Impressionist works. Look for the *Silver Tree,* a sculpture created out of the pure silver mined from beneath Broken Hill. This is also a good place to see works by the "Brushmen of the Bush," a well-known group of artists, including Pro Hart, Jack Absalom, Eric Minchin, and Hugh Schultz, who spend many days sitting around campfires in the bush trying to capture its essence in paint. The gallery is open Monday through Friday from 10am to 5pm, and Saturday and Sunday from 1 to 5pm. Admission is A$3 (U.S.$1.95) adults, A$2 (U.S.$1.30) for children, and A$6 (U.S.$3.90) for families.

Other galleries worth visiting around town include **Absalom's Gallery,** 638 Chapple St. (© **08/8087 5881**), and the **Pro Hart Gallery,** 108 Wyman St. (© **08/8087 2441**). All are open daily. Pro Hart's gallery is really worth a look. Apart from his own works—including works based on incidents and scenes relating to Broken Hill—his gallery is crammed with everything from a bas-relief of Salvador Dalí to a landscape by Claude Monet.

To get a real taste of mining in Broken Hill, take an underground tour at **Delprat's Mine** (© **08/8088 1604**). Visitors go 120 meters (396 ft.) below the surface. Children under 6 are not allowed. Tours run Monday through Friday at 10:30am and Saturday at 2pm. The 2-hour tour costs A$23 (U.S.$14.95) for adults and A$18 (U.S.$11.70) for children.

Be sure not to miss the School of the Air and the Royal Flying Doctor Service base, both of which help show the enormity of the Australian interior. The **School of the Air**—the largest school room in the world, with students scattered over 800,000 square kilometers (312,000 sq. miles)—conducts lessons via two-way radios. Visitors can listen in on part of the day's first teaching session Monday through Friday at 8:30am (except public holidays). Bookings are essential and must be made through the **Broken Hill Tourist and Travelers Centre** (see "Visitor Information," above). Tours costs A$2 (U.S.$1.30) per person. The **Royal Flying Doctor Service base** is at the Broken Hill Airport (© **08/8080 1777**). The service maintains communication with more than 400 outback stations, ready to fly at once in case of an emergency. The base at Broken Hill covers 25% of New South Wales, as well as parts of Queensland and South Australia. Continuous explanatory lessons are held at the base Monday through Friday from 9am to noon and 1 to 5pm; Saturday and Sunday from 10am to 4pm. Admission is A$3 (U.S.$1.95) for adults, free for children.

OTHER THINGS TO SEE & DO NEARBY

VISITING A GHOST TOWN   At least 44 movies have been filmed in the Wild West town of **Silverton** ✵ (pop. 50), 23 kilometers (14 miles) northwest of Broken Hill. It's the Wild West Australian-style, though, with camels instead of horses sometimes placed in front of the **Silverton Pub,** which is well worth a visit for its kitchy Australian appeal. Silverton once had a population of 3,000 following the discovery of silver here in 1882, but within 7 years almost everyone had left. There are some good art galleries here, as well as a restored jail and hotel.

DISCOVERING ABORIGINAL HANDPRINTS   **Mootwingee National Park** ✵, 130 kilometers (80 miles) northeast of Broken Hill, was one of the

---

What Time Is It, Anyway?

Broken Hill runs its clocks to Central Standard Time, to correspond with South Australia. The surrounding country, however, runs half an hour faster at Eastern Standard Time.

> ### *Finds* A Fabulous Place to Enjoy the Sunset
>
> Just outside Broken Hill in the **Living Desert Nature Park** is the best col-
> lection of sculptures this side of Stonehenge. Twelve sandstone obelisks,
> up to 3 meters (10 ft.) high and carved totem-like by artists from as far
> away as Georgia, Syria, Mexico, and the Tiwi Islands, make up the Sculp-
> ture Symposium. Surrounding them on all sides is brooding mulga scrub.
> It's fantastic at sunset.

most important spiritual meeting places for Aborigines on the continent. Groups came from all over the country to peck out abstract engravings on the rocks with sharpened quartz tools and to sign their hand prints to show they belonged to the place. The ancient, weathered fireplaces are still here, laid out like a giant map to show where each visiting group came from. Hundreds of ochre outlines of hands and animal paws, some up to 30,000 years old, are sten- ciled on rock overhangs. The fabulous 2-hour Outback trip from Broken Hill to Mootwingee is along red-dirt tracks not really suitable for two-wheel-drives and should not be attempted after a heavy rain.

Mootwingee Heritage Tours (© **08/8088 7000**) organizes inspections of the historical sites every Wednesday and Saturday morning at 10:30am Broken Hill time (11am Mootwingee, or Eastern Standard, time). The tours may be canceled in very hot weather. The **NPWS office** in Broken Hill (© **08/8088 5933**) also has details. You can camp at the **Homestead Creek** campground for A$11 (U.S.$7.15) a night. It has its own water supply.

EXPLORING WHITE CLIFFS 𝔎𝔎   White Cliffs, 290 kilometers (180 miles) east of Broken Hill, is an opal-mining town bigger than it looks. Unlike Light- ning Ridge (below), which produces mainly black opals, White Cliffs is known for its less valuable white opals (as is Coober Pedy in South Australia). To escape the summer heat, most houses are built underground in mine shafts, where the temperature is a constant 23°C (73°F). Prospecting started here in 1889, when kangaroo shooters found the colorful stones scattered on the ground. A year later the rush was on and by the turn of the century about 4,000 people were digging and sifting in a lawless, waterless hell of a place. White Cliffs is smaller than Coober Pedy and less touristy—which is its great charm. You also have a lot more freedom to wander around the old opal tailings here, whereas in Coober Pedy they discourage it. However, given the hard choice between White Cliffs and Lightning Ridge (below), I'd opt for the latter (though if you have time you certainly should see both).

If you fancy an after-hours round of golf in the dirt (and who doesn't?), con- tact the secretary of the **White Cliffs Golf Club,** John Painter (© **08/8091 6715** after hours). He'll be happy to supply you with a golf club or two and a couple of balls for A$2 (U.S.$1.30). Otherwise, put A$2 (U.S.$1.30) in the black box at the first tee if you have your own clubs—but be warned, bush playing can damage your clubs, and crows often make off with the balls. Visitors can play daily day or night, but if you want some company, then turn up on Sunday when club members shoot it out.

Today, the countryside looks like an inverted moonscape, pimpled with bone- white heaps of gritty clay dug from the 50,000 mine shafts that surround the town. These days, White Cliffs is more renowned for its eccentricity. Take **Jock's Place,** for instance, an underground museum full to the beams with junk pulled from old mine shafts. Then there's a house made of beer flagons and a nine-hole **dirt golf course** where locals play at night with fluorescent green golf balls.

WHERE TO STAY: ABOVE GROUND & BELOW

One option is to rent a local cottage from **Broken Hill Historic Cottages** (© **08/8087 9966**) for A$80 (U.S.$52) a night, or **Sue Spicer's Holiday Cottages** (© **08/8087 8488**), which rents fully equipped cottages for A$65 (U.S.$42.25) per night and up.

Broken Hill Overlander Motor Inn   This is my favorite place to stay in Broken Hill, although admittedly that's not really saying much in this Outback town. It's set way back from the road, has nice green areas and barbecue facilities, and is very quiet. The more expensive four-star-rated rooms are much nicer than the cheaper variants, and considerably larger. Two family rooms sleep up to six in a combination of single and queen-size beds. You can order off several menus supplied by local restaurants, and with the hotel supplying plates and cutlery.

142 Iodide St., Broken Hill, NSW 2880. © **08/8088 2566.** Fax 08/8088 4377. www.murrayoutback.org.au. Reservations can be made through Best Western (© **800/780-7234** in the U.S. and Canada, 0800/39 3130 in the U.K., 0800/237 893 in New Zealand, or 13 17 79 in Australia). 15 units. A$82–$105 (U.S.$53–$68) double; A$130 (U.S.$84.50) 2-bed unit. Extra person A$10 (U.S.$6.50). AE, DC, MC, V. **Amenities:** Small pool; spa; sauna; nonsmoking rooms. *In room:* A/C, TV, coffeemaker, unstocked refrigerator, hair dryer, iron.

Mario the Palace Hotel *(Value)*   With its high painted walls, a mural of Botticelli's *Birth of Venus* on the ceiling two flights up, and an office crammed with stuffed animal heads and crabs, the Palace Hotel is an intriguing sanctuary for the night. The owners have put a lot of work into restoring the place. The more expensive doubles are larger and come with a small lounge area, but all are comfortable and cool. Ten double rooms come with an attached shower. The Priscilla Suite is famous because that's where the transvestites stayed in *The Adventures of Priscilla Queen of the Desert*. Mario owned the place for "donkey's years," as he says, but he's now retired. It's still run by his family.

227 Argent St., Broken Hill, NSW 2880. © **08/8088 1699.** Fax 08/8087 6240. www.mariospalace.com. 51 units, 10 with bathroom. A$44 (U.S.$28.60) double without bathroom; A$53–$70 (U.S.$34.50–$45.50) double with bathroom. Priscilla suite $90 (U.S.$58.50) for 2. AE, DC, MC, V. *In room:* A/C, TV, unstocked refrigerator, coffeemaker.

Underground Motel *(★★)*   I love this place; it's worth making the scenic trip out to White Cliffs just to stay here for the night. All but two of the rooms are underground; they're reached by a maze of spacious tunnels dug out of the rock and sealed with epoxy-resin to keep out the damp and the dust. The temperature below ground is a constant 22°C (71°F), which is decidedly cooler than a summer day outside. Rooms are comfortable though fairly basic, and toilets and showers are shared. Turn the light off, and it's as dark as a cave. Every night guests sit around large round tables and dig into the roast of the day (vegetarians are catered to, also).

Smiths Hill, White Cliffs (P.O. Box 427), NSW 2836. © **1800/02 1154** in Australia, or 08/8091 6677. Fax 08/8091 6654. 30 units, none with bathroom. A$83 (U.S.$54) double. A$25 (U.S.$16.25) 3-course meal. Extra person A$24 (U.S.$15.60). MC, V. **Amenities:** Restaurant (country cooking), bar; small outdoor pool; coin-op laundry; nonsmoking rooms.

WHERE TO DINE

The best place for a meal Aussie-style is at one of the local clubs. You'll find one of the best bistros at the **Barrier Social & Democratic Club,** at 218 Argent St. (© **08/8088 4477**). It serves breakfast, lunch, and dinner. There's also a whole host of Chinese restaurants around town, including the **Oceania Chinese Restaurant** on Argent Street (© **08/8087 3695**), which has a A$7 (U.S.$4.55) lunch special.

LIGHTNING RIDGE: OPALS GALORE ⟨★★⟩
765km (474 miles) NW of Sydney; 572km (355 miles) SW of Brisbane

Lightning Ridge, or "The Ridge" as the locals call it, is perhaps the most fascinating place to visit in all of New South Wales. Essentially, it's a hard-working opal-mining town stuck out in the arid far northern reaches of New South Wales—where summer temperatures regularly hover around the 45°C (113°F) mark. Lightning Ridge thrives off the largest deposit of black opal in the world. Good quality opals from here can fetch a miner around A$8,000 (U.S.$5,200) per carat, and stones worth upwards of A$500,000 (U.S.$325,000) each are not unheard of. Tourists come here to get a taste of life in Australia's "Wild West." A popular tourist activity in the opal fields is to pick over the old white heaps of mine tailings. Stories (perhaps tall tales) abound of tourists finding overlooked opals worth thousands of dollars.

I strongly recommend you visit the **Grawin** and **Glengarry opal fields** ⟨★★⟩, each about an hour or so from Lightning Ridge on a dirt track barely suitable for two-wheel-drive cars (check with locals before you go). These full-on frontier townships are bristling with drills and hoists pulling out bucket-loads of dirt and buzzing with news of the latest opal rush. If you can convince a local to take you there all the better, as the tracks can be misleading. Unfortunately, no local firm runs trips to these opal fields, though **Ando's Outback Tours** (see the section on Byron Bay earlier in this chapter) takes in Glengarry and Lightning Ridge on its 5-day trip.

ESSENTIALS
GETTING THERE   From Sydney it takes about 9 hours to drive to Lightning Ridge, via Bathurst, Dubbo, and the fascinating town of Walgett. **Countrylink Holidays** (© **13 28 29** in Australia) offer a 3-night/4-day Lightning Ridge tour from Sydney for A$492 (U.S.$320) for adults, and A$261 (U.S.$169.65) for children, including accommodation, some meals, and entrance fees; train fare is additional; ask about specials. **Hazelton Airlines** (© **13 17 13** in Australia) also flies to Lightning Ridge.

VISITOR INFORMATION   The **Lightning Ridge Tourist Information Centre** on Morilla Street, P.O. Box 1779, Lightning Ridge, NSW 2834 (© **02/ 6829 0565;** fax 02/6829 0565), is open Monday through Friday from 8:30am to 4pm.

SPECIAL EVENTS   If you're in Australia around Easter, make sure you come to Lightning Ridge for the **Great Goat Race** and the rodeo.

SEEING THE TOWN
Any visit to Lightning Ridge should start with an orientation trip with **Black Opal Tours** (© **02/6829 0368;** fax 02/6829 1206). The company offers a 5-hour tour of the opal fields for A$65 (U.S.$42.25) per person. Also ask about their shorter tours as well as their 2- and 3-day tours of the area.

Among the many points of interest is the 15-meter-tall (50-ft.-tall) home-made **Amigo's Castle,** which dominates the worked-out opal fields immediately surrounding the modern township of Lightning Ridge. Complete with turrets, battlements, dungeons, and a wishing well, the castle has been rising out of these arid lands for the past 17 years, with every rock scavenged from the surrounding area and lugged in a wheelbarrow or in a rucksack on Amigo's back. The wonderful Amigo hasn't taken out insurance on the property, so there are no official tours, though if he feels like a bit of company he'll show you around.

The **Artesian Bore Baths,** 2 kilometers (1 mile) from the post office on Pandora Street, are free, open 24 hours a day, and said to have therapeutic value. The water temperature hovers between 40°C and 50°C (104°F–122°F). A visit at night when the stars are out is amazing.

The **Bevan's Black Opal & Cactus Nursery** (ⓒ **02/6829 0429**) contains more than 2,000 species of cactus and succulent plants, including many rare specimens. Betty Bevan cuts here own opals, and many are on display. Admission is A$4 (U.S.$2.60).

There are plenty of opal shops, galleries, walk-in opal mines, and other distinctly unique things to see in Lightning Ridge. You might want to take a look at **Gemopal Pottery** (ⓒ **02/6829 0375**), on the road to the Bore Baths. The resident potter makes some nice pots out of clay mine tailings and lives in one of his five old Sydney railway carriages.

WHERE TO STAY & DINE

If you want to stay at the Glengarry opal fields then your only option is at the Glengarry Hilton, a rustic outback pub (not associated with the major hotel chain). Here you stay in mobile units sleeping 24. A night costs A$10 (U.S.$6.50).

The Wallangulla Motel The best motel in town offers two standards of rooms, the cheaper rooms being in an older section of the property. Newer rooms are better furnished and generally nicer; they're worth the extra money. Two large family rooms each have two bedrooms and a living room; one has a spa bath. Guests can use the barbecue facilities, and there is a special arrangement with the bowling club over the road for meals there to be charged back to your room. The Bowling Club has a restaurant with pretty good food and a very cheap bistro.

Morilla St. (at Agate St.), Lightning Ridge, NSW 2834. ⓒ **02/6829 0542.** Fax 02/6829 0070. 43 units. A$60–$80 (U.S.$39–$52) double; A$70–A$90 (U.S.$45.50–$58.50) triple; A$90–A$110 (U.S.$58.50–$71.50) family room with spa. AE, DC, MC, V. **Amenities:** Coin-op laundry; nonsmoking rooms. *In room:* A/C, TV, coffeemaker.

5

Brisbane

by Lee Mylne

Queensland's capital is relaxed and laid-back, as a subtropical city should be. Set along the banks of the wide, brown Brisbane River, Brisbane has grown up in recent years, confident in its appeal. It's one of those places that people don't always appreciate until they spend time there; once you do, you'll be greeted with a welcome as warm as the weather. The city is green and leafy; huge Moreton Bay fig trees give shade, and in summer the purple haze of jacarandas competes with the blaze of blooming poinciana trees. For residents, having a mango tree in the backyard is practically *de rigueur.*

To find major commercial tourist attractions, you have to head south of the city to the theme parks which line the Brisbane–Gold Coast corridor. And Brisbane folk don't consider that a drawback. They'll urge you to discover this city, rich in history and character, and to get to know the locals. It's easy, because Queenslanders will strike up a conversation with just about anyone.

Brisbane (pronounced *Briz*-bun) is known for its timber "Queenslander" cottages and houses—structures set high on stumps to catch the breeze, with wide shady verandas to keep out the midday sun. In some inner city suburbs, Queenslanders have been converted to trendy cafes and restaurants, or into shops selling antiques, clothes, and housewares.

In the city center, gracious colonial sandstone buildings stand next to modern glass towers. Wander in the city botanic gardens, in-line skate or bike along the riverfront pathways, have a cool drink in a pub beer garden, or get out on the river on a City-Cat. There are several bridges across the river, the most famous and attractive being the Story Bridge, on the Town Reach of the river. Getting around is cheap and easy, good food—including fantastic seafood—is abundant, and accommodations are affordable, especially in some of the city's comfortable, elegant B&Bs.

Brisbane is on the southern coast of the state, flanked by both the Sunshine Coast, less than 2 hours' drive to the north, and the Gold Coast, 1 hour to the south. The Brisbane River flows into Moreton Bay, dotted with islands that offer yet another dimension to the city's attractions.

1 Orientation

ARRIVING

BY PLANE More than 30 international airlines flying into **Brisbane International Airport** from Europe, Asia, and New Zealand, including Qantas, Air New Zealand, Canada 3000, Singapore Airlines, and Cathay Pacific. From North America you will most likely fly to Sydney and connect on one of several daily direct flights made by Qantas, or fly direct from Auckland, in New Zealand. Canada 3000 offers direct flights to Brisbane from Vancouver.

Qantas (© **13 13 13** in Australia; www.qantas.com.au) operates flights throughout the day from state capitals, Cairns, and several other regional towns. One newcomer on the domestic airline front, **Virgin Blue** (© **13 67 89;** www. virginblue.com.au), offers cheaper fares than the established airlines. Virgin Blue flies between Sydney, Brisbane, Townsville, Melbourne and Adelaide.

Brisbane International Airport is 16 kilometers (10 miles) from the city, and the domestic terminal is 2 kilometers (1¼ miles) farther away. The Arrivals Floor, on Level 2, has an information desk open to meet all flights, help you with flight inquiries, dispense tourist information, and make your hotel bookings. It also has lockers that cost A$5 to $10 (U.S.$3.25 to $6.50) for 24 hours, and a check-in counter for passengers transferring to domestic flights. Travelex currency-exchange bureaus are located on both the departures and arrivals floors. **Avis** (© **07/3860 4200**), **Budget** (© **07/ 3860 4466**), **Hertz** (© **07/ 3860 4522**), and **Thrifty** (© **07/3860 4588**) have desks on Level 2; in the airport there is also a free-call board connecting you to smaller local car-rental companies that sometimes offer better rates. Showers and baby change rooms are located on levels 2, 3, and 4; Level 4 has an ATM.

The domestic terminal has lockers (A$6/U.S.$3.90 for 24 hours), a Travelex currency-exchange bureau, showers, and the big four car-rental desks (call the telephone numbers above). An inter-terminal shuttle runs every 15 minutes and costs A$2.50 (U.S.$1.60).

Coachtrans (© **07/3236 1000;** fax 07/3236 3870; www.coachtrans.com.au) runs a shuttle between the airport and Roma Street Transit Centre every 30 minutes from 5am to 2pm and every 45 minutes from 2 to 8:45pm. The cost is A$9 (U.S.$5.85) per person, or A$15 (U.S.$9.75) for two people and A$20 (U.S.$13) for three to Roma St. Transit Centre, or A$11 (U.S.$7.15) for hotel drop-off. Kids ages 4 to 14 pay A$5 (U.S. $3.25). Return fare is A$15 (U.S.$9.75), or same-day return fare is A$12 (U.S.$7.80). The trip takes about 40 minutes, and bookings are not needed. No public buses serve the airport. A taxi to the city costs around A$20 (U.S.$13) from the international terminal and around A$24 (U.S.$15.60) from the domestic terminal.

Airtrain (© **07/3211 2855;** www.airtrain.com.au), a rail link between the city and Brisbane's domestic and international airport terminals, runs every 15 minutes from 5:30am to 11:30pm daily, with a fare from Central Station to the airport costing A$9 (U.S.$5.85) and taking about 20 minutes. Airtrain also links the airport with the Gold Coast.

BY TRAIN   Queensland Rail (© **13 22 32** in Queensland, or 07/3235 1122; www.qr.com.au) operates several long-distance trains most days of the week to Brisbane from Cairns. The 32-hour trip from Cairns costs A$162.80 (U.S.$105.30) for a sitting berth, and A$201.30 (U.S.$130.85) for an economy-class sleeper. **Countrylink** (© **13 22 32** in New South Wales, or 02/ 9379 1298; www.countrylink.nsw.gov.au) runs daily train service to Brisbane from Sydney. The 14-hour trip from Sydney costs A$110 to $154 (U.S.$71.50 to $100.10) in a sitting berth, and A$231 (U.S.$150.15) for a sleeper. Be sure to book the through-service; some services transfer to coach in Murwillumbah, south of the border, tacking an extra 2 hours to the trip. This train/coach service has no sleepers.

All intercity and interstate trains pull into **Brisbane Transit Centre at Roma Street** (in the city center), often called the Roma Street Transit Centre. From here,

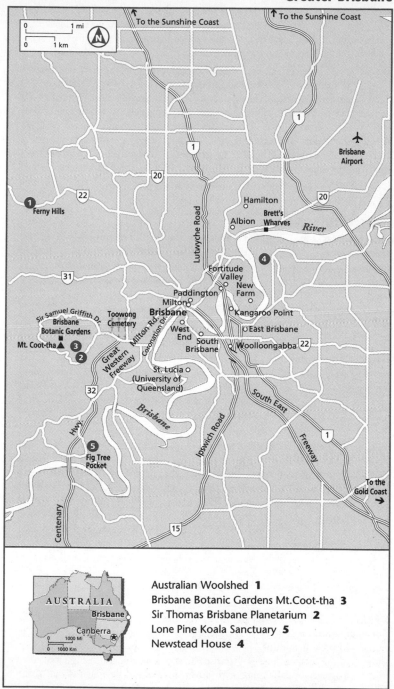

Greater Brisbane

To the Sunshine Coast
To the Sunshine Coast

1 Ferny Hills

Hamilton
Albion
Brett's Wharves
River

Brisbane Airport

Lutwyche Road

Fortitude Valley
New Farm
Paddington
Milton
Brisbane
Toowong Cemetery
Kangaroo Point
Sir Samuel Griffith Dr.
Brisbane Botanic Gardens
Mt. Coot-tha **3**
2
West End
South Brisbane
East Brisbane
Woolloongabba
Coronation Dr.
Milton Rd.
Great Western Freeway
St. Lucia (University of Queensland)
Brisbane
South East Freeway
Ipswich Road

5 Fig Tree Pocket

Centenary Hwy.

To the Gold Coast

AUSTRALIA
Brisbane
Canberra

Australian Woolshed **1**
Brisbane Botanic Gardens Mt.Coot-tha **3**
Sir Thomas Brisbane Planetarium **2**
Lone Pine Koala Sanctuary **5**
Newstead House **4**

most city and Spring Hill hotels are a few blocks' walk or a quick cab ride away. The Transit Centre has food outlets, showers, tourist information, and lockers.

Queensland Rail CityTrain (℡ 07/3235 5555) provides a daily train service from the Sunshine Coast, and plentiful services from the Gold Coast.

BY BUS All intercity and interstate coaches pull into the Brisbane Transit Centre (see "By Train," above). **McCafferty's** (℡ 13 14 99 in Australia, or 07/ 3236 3035; www.mccaffertys.com.au) and **Greyhound Pioneer** (℡ 13 20 30 in Australia, or 07/3258 1800; www.greyhound.com.au) serve the city several times daily. A one-way Cairns–Brisbane ticket costs around A$173 (U.S.$112.45), and the trip takes 28½ hours. The Sydney–Brisbane trip takes 18 hours and costs A$85 (U.S.$55.25) one-way. Coachtrans provides daily services from the Gold Coast. Call **Transinfo** (℡ 13 12 30) for details.

BY CAR The Bruce Highway from Cairns enters the city from the north. The Pacific Highway enters Brisbane from Sydney in the south.

VISITOR INFORMATION

Brisbane Marketing (℡ 07/3006 6200) has an information booth in the Queen Street Mall at Albert Street. It's open from 9am to 5:30pm Monday through Thursday, to 7pm or later Friday, and to 4pm Saturday; Sunday it's open from 10am to 4pm. The **Roma Street Transit Centre** is another source of tourist information (℡ 07/3236 2020).

CITY LAYOUT

The city center's glass office towers shimmer in the sun on the north bank of a curve of the Brisbane River. In the tip of the curve are the lush Brisbane City Gardens. The 30-meter (98-ft.) sandstone cliffs of Kangaroo Point rise on the eastern side of the south bank; to the west are the delightful South Bank Parklands and the Queensland Cultural Centre, known collectively as South Bank. Five kilometers (3 miles) to the west, Mt. Coot-tha (pronounced Coo-tha) looms out of the flat plain, providing a great vantage point for gazing over the city.

MAIN ARTERIES & STREETS It's easy to find your way around central Brisbane once you know that all the east-west streets are named after female British royalty, and all the north-south streets are named after their male counterparts. The "female" streets start with Ann in the north, followed by Adelaide, Queen, Elizabeth, Charlotte, Mary, Margaret, and Alice. From east to west, the streets are Edward, Albert, George, and William. William becomes North Quay, flanking the river's northeast bank. Brunswick Street is the main thoroughfare running through Fortitude Valley and New Farm.

Queen Street is the main thoroughfare; it becomes a pedestrian mall between Edward and George streets. Roma Street exits the city diagonally to the northwest. Ann Street leads all the way east into Fortitude Valley. The main street in Fortitude Valley is Brunswick St., which runs right into New Farm.

STREET MAPS The **Brisbane Map,** free from Brisbane Marketing (see "Visitor Information, above") or your concierge, is a lightweight map that shows the river and outlying suburbs, as well as the city. It's great for drivers because it shows parking lots and one-way traffic directions on the confusing city-center grid. Rental cars usually come with street directories. Newsagents and some bookstores sell this map, and the state auto club, the **R.A.C.Q.,** in the General Post Office, 261 Queen St. (℡ 13 19 05) is also a good source.

NEIGHBORHOODS IN BRIEF

City Center The vibrant city center is where residents eat, shop, and socialize. Queen Street Mall, right in the heart of town, is popular with shopaholics and cinemagoers, especially on weekends and Friday nights (when stores stay open until 9pm). The Eagle Street financial/legal office precinct houses some great restaurants with river views to match, and on Sundays there are fashionable markets by the Riverside office tower here. Much of Brisbane's elegant colonial architecture is in the city center, too. Strollers, bike riders, and in-line skaters shake the sticky summer heat in the green haven of the Brisbane City Gardens at the central business district's southern end.

Fortitude Valley Ten years ago, this suburb of derelict warehouses just east of the city center was one of the sleazier parts of town. Today, "the Valley" is a stomping ground for street-smart young folk who meet in restored pubs and eat in cool cafes. The lanterns, food stores, and shopping mall of Chinatown are here, too. Take Turbot Street to the Valley's main drag, Brunswick Street.

New Farm Always an appealing residential suburb, New Farm is fast becoming the city's "in" destination for cafe-hopping, shopping, and cinema-going. Merthyr Street is where the action is, especially on Friday and Saturday nights. From the intersection of Wickham and Brunswick streets, follow Brunswick southeast for 13 blocks to Merthyr.

Paddington This hilltop suburb, a couple of miles northwest of the city, is the prettiest in Brisbane. Cute, brightly painted Queenslander cottages line the main street, Latrobe Terrace, as it winds west along a ridge top. Many of the houses have been turned into shops and cafes, and the streets are full of people browsing for antiques, enjoying coffee and cake, or just admiring the charming architecture.

Park Road A street rather than a neighborhood, this is Brisbane's answer to Rome! Italian restaurants line the street, buzzing with white-collar office workers who down cappuccinos at alfresco restaurants, scout interior design stores for a new objet to grace the living room, and stock up on European designer rags.

West End This small inner-city enclave is alive with ethnic restaurants, cafes, and the odd, interesting houseware or fashion store. Most action is centered at the intersection of Vulture and Boundary streets, where Asian grocers and delis abound.

Bulimba One of the emerging fashionable suburbs, Bulimba has a long connection with the river through the boat-building industry, and one of the nicest ways to get there is by CityCat. Oxford Street is emulating Park Road, with a profusion of cafes and trendy shops springing up.

2 Getting Around

BY PUBLIC TRANSPORTATION

Bus, train, and ferry service is coordinated by **Brisbane Transport**. For timetable and route inquiries, call **Transinfo** (② **13 12 30;** www.transinfo. qld.gov.au; 6am–9pm Mon–Fri; 7am–9pm weekends). The most convenient places to buy passes and to pick up timetables and route maps are the Brisbane

Brisbane Hotels, Restaurants & Attractions

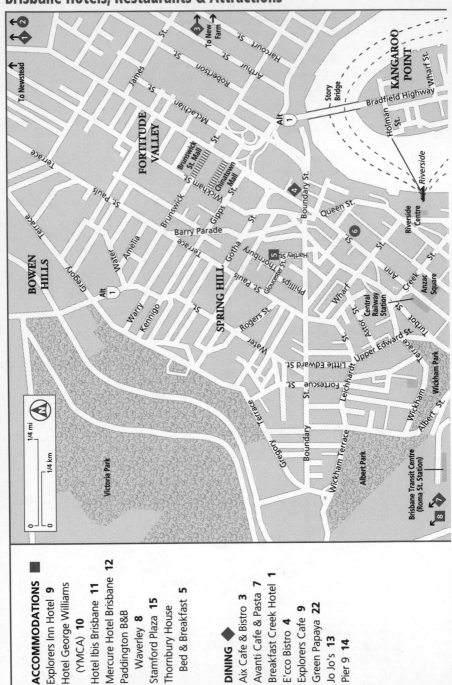

ACCOMMODATIONS ■

Explorers Inn Hotel **9**
Hotel George Williams
(YMCA) **10**
Hotel Ibis Brisbane **11**
Mercure Hotel Brisbane **12**
Paddington B&B
Waverley **8**
Stamford Plaza **15**
Thornbury House
Bed & Breakfast **5**

DINING ◆

Aix Cafe & Bistro **3**
Avanti Cafe & Pasta **7**
Breakfast Creek Hotel **1**
E'cco Bistro **4**
Explorers Cafe **9**
Green Papaya **22**
Jo Jo's **13**
Pier 9 **14**

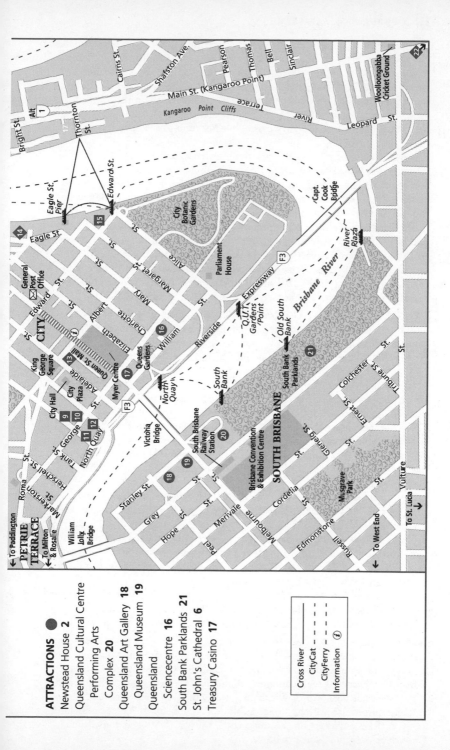

ATTRACTIONS ●

Newstead House **2**
Queensland Cultural Centre
Performing Arts
Complex **20**
Queensland Art Gallery **18**
Queensland Museum **19**
Queensland
Sciencecentre **16**
South Bank Parklands **21**
St. John's Cathedral **6**
Treasury Casino **17**

Cross River ————
CityCat – – – –
CityFerry – – – –
Information ⓘ

Transport outlets on the Elizabeth Street level of the Myer Centre, which fronts Queen Street Mall; at Brisbane Transport's Brisbane Administration Centre, 69 Ann St.; at the Roma Street Transit Centre; or at Brisbane Marketing's information kiosk in the Queen Street Mall. You can also buy passes on the bus, at the train station (if the pass has a train component), or on the CityCat or ferry. Any news agency displaying a yellow-and-white BUS & FERRY TICKETS SOLD HERE banner sells bus/ferry passes, but not train passes, special tour tickets, or family passes.

A single sector or zone on the bus, train, or ferry costs A$1.60 (U.S.$1.05). Whether they buy a single ticket or a pass, kids under age 5 travel free, kids ages 5 to 15 pay half fare; all seniors except Queensland residents and all students pay full fare. If you plan on doing lots of bussing and ferrying around, weekly passes and Ten Trip Saver tickets are available from the outlets described above.

The **Brisbane Mobility Map,** produced by the Brisbane City Council, outlines wheelchair access to buildings in the city center, and includes a detailed guide to the Queen Street Mall and a map of the Brisbane Botanic Gardens at Mt. Coot-tha. The council's disability services unit also has a range of other publications including a Braille Trail and an access guide to parks. These can all be obtained from council customer service centers (© **07/3403 4268**).

TRANSPORT PASSES   The **Rover Link pass** is good for 1 day of travel on most trains, ferries, and buses. The pass cannot be used on weekday trains before 9am, and there are limits to how far you can go on the trains, but the pass will get you as far as the Australian Woolshed, which is probably as far as you will be traveling anyhow. The Rover Link costs A$9 (U.S.$5.85).

It's possible you won't use trains to get around Brisbane, as most attractions are on the bus and ferry networks. In that case, get a Day Rover pass, which allows unlimited travel on buses, CityCats, and ferries for A$8 (U.S.$5.20).

On weekends and public holidays, it's cheaper to buy an Off-Peak Saver pass, which lets you travel on buses and ferries all day for A$4.40 (U.S.$2.85) for adults. The Off-Peak Saver is also available on weekdays, but it is probably too inconvenient for sightseeing because it cannot be used before 9am and between 3:30pm and 7pm.

Note that passes can't be used on the City Circle bus line (see "By Bus," below) or on tour buses like City Sights (see "Organized Tours," later in this chapter).

If you see peak-hour buses displaying a full-fare-only sign, that does not mean you cannot travel on them with a discounted ticket or pass. It just means you cannot purchase a ticket or pass on the bus; you will have to purchase your ticket or pass from a ticket agent before boarding the bus.

The excellent **City Sights** bus tour entitles you to unlimited travel on buses, ferries, and CityCats for the day, and at the same time gets you around to 19 points of interest—see "Organized Tours," later in this chapter, for details.

BY BUS   Buses operate from around 5am to 11pm weekdays, with fewer services on weekends. On Sunday many routes stop around 5pm. Midweek, the smart way to get around the city center is aboard City Circle Bus no. 333, which does a loop every 10 to 15 minutes around Eagle, Alice, George, Roma and Albert streets as far north as Wickham Terrace, then up Ann Street and down Adelaide Street. It's wheelchair-accessible, too. Look for the blue-and-white stops. A ticket anywhere on the route costs A80¢ (U.S.50¢). It runs Monday through Friday from 7am to 5:40pm.

Most buses depart from City Hall at King George Square, from Adelaide or Ann streets.

BY FERRY   The fast **CityCat** ferries run to many places of interest, including South Bank and the Queensland Cultural Centre; the restaurants and Sunday markets at the Riverside Centre; and New Farm Park, not far from the cafes of Merthyr Street. They run every half hour between Queensland University, approximately 9 kilometers (5½ miles) along the river to the south, and Brett's Wharf, about 9 kilometers (5½ miles) to the north. Slower but more frequent Inner City and Cross-River ferries stop at a few more points, including the south end of South Bank Parklands, Kangaroo Point, and Edward Street right outside the City Botanic Gardens. Ferries run from around 6am to 10:30pm daily.

To stop people from riding the CityCats all day—a real temptation—you cannot travel on them for more than 2 hours at a time, even with a transit pass; you are free to do another 2 hours later in the day if you wish. Two hours on the CityCat takes you the entire length of the run.

BY TRAIN   Brisbane's suburban rail network is fast, quiet, safe, and clean. Trains run from around 5am to midnight, stopping at about 11pm on Sundays. All trains leave Central Station, between Turbot and Ann streets at Edward Street.

BY CAR OR TAXI

Brisbane's grid of one-way streets can be confusing, so plan your route before you set off. Brisbane's biggest car park is at the Myer Centre (enter from Elizabeth Street) and is open 24 hours (© **07/3229 1699,** or 07/3221 4199). Most hotels and motels have free parking for guests.

Avis (© **13 63 33** or 07/3221 2900) and **Budget** (© **1300 362848** or 07/3220 0699) have outlets in the city center. **Thrifty** (© **1300 367 227**) is on the edge of the city center at 49 Barry Parade, Fortitude Valley.

For taxi service, call **Yellow Cabs** (© **13 19 24** in Australia) and **Black and White Taxis** (© **13 10 08** in Australia). There are major taxi ranks at each end of the Queen Street Mall, on Edward Street and George Street (outside the Treasury Casino).

 FAST FACTS: Brisbane

American Express   The office at 131 Elizabeth St. (© **07/3229 2729**) cashes traveler's checks, exchanges foreign currency, and refunds lost traveler's checks.

Business Hours   Banks are open Monday through Thursday from 9:30am to 4pm, and until 5pm on Fridays. See "The Shopping Scene," later in this chapter, for store hours. Some restaurants close Monday and/or Tuesday nights, and bars are generally open from 10 or 11am until midnight.

Currency Exchange   Travelex, Lennons Plaza, Queen Street Mall between Albert and George streets (© **07/3229 8610**), is open Monday through Friday from 9am to 6pm, Saturday from 9:30am to 5pm, and Sunday from 10:30am to 4:30pm.

Dentist   The Adelaide and Albert Street Dental Centre, located next to the Travellers Medical Service (see "Doctor," below), is open Monday through Friday from 8.30am to 5.30pm (© **07/3229 4121**).

Doctor City Mall 24 Hour Medical Service is located upstairs at 245 Albert St. (at Adelaide St.), diagonally opposite City Hall (© **07/3211 3611**). It's open Monday through Friday from 7:30am to 7pm, Saturday from 9am to 5pm, and Sunday from 10am to 4pm; for after-hours emergencies call © **0412/452 400.**

Drugstores (Chemist Shops) The T&G Corner Day & Night Pharmacy, 141 Queen Street Mall (© **07/3221 4585**) is open Monday through Friday from 7:30am to 9pm, Saturday from 8am to 9pm, and Sunday from 9:30am to 5:30pm. There is also a pharmacy under the City Mall 24 Hour Medical Service (see "Doctor," above).

Embassies/Consulates The United States, Canada, and New Zealand have no representation in Brisbane; see chapter 3, "Sydney," for those countries' nearest offices. The British Consul General is at Level 26, Waterfront Place, 1 Eagle St. (© **07/3223 3200**).

Emergencies Dial © **000** for fire, ambulance, or police help in an emergency. This is a free call from a private or public telephone.

Hospitals The nearest public hospital is at Royal Brisbane Hospital, about a 15-minute drive from the city at Herston Road, Herston (© **07/3636 8111**).

Hot Lines Lifeline (© **13 11 14**) is a 24-hour emotional crisis counseling service.

Internet Access **The Hub Internet Café**, 125 Margaret St. (© **07/3229 1119**), is open from 8am to 8.30pm weekdays and from 9am to 6pm weekends. You can also try **Dial Up Cyber Lounge,** in the Mayfair Arcade, 126 Adelaide St (© **07/3211 9095**), open from 10am to 7pm Monday through Thursday and Saturday, and to 8pm Friday. In Paddington, **The Computer Cafe,** 95 Latrobe Terrace (© **07/3368 3190**), is open Monday, Tuesday, and Thursday from 10am to 9pm, and Wednesday, Friday, and Saturday from 10am to 6pm.

Luggage Storage/Lockers Lockers are on Level A (use the Albert Street entrance) in the Myer Centre, Queen Street Mall (© **07/3221 4199**). The Brisbane Transit Centre on Roma Street also has baggage lockers.

Newspapers/Magazines The *Courier-Mail* (Monday through Saturday) and the *Sunday Mail* are Brisbane's daily newspapers. The free weekly *Brisbane News* is a good guide to dining, entertainment, and shopping.

Police Dial © **000** in an emergency, or © **07/3364 6464** for police headquarters. Police are stationed 24 hours a day beside the Brisbane Marketing information booth on Queen Street Mall at Albert Street (© **07/3224 4444**).

Safety Brisbane is relatively crime free, but as in any large city, personal safety should be considered especially when out at night. Stick to well-lit streets and busy precincts.

Time Zone Brisbane is GMT plus 10 hours. It does not observe daylight saving time, which means it's on the same time as Sydney and Melbourne in winter, and 1 hour behind those cities October through March, when they go to daylight saving. For the exact local time, call © **1194.**

Weather Call © **1196** for the southeast Queensland weather forecast.

3 Where to Stay
IN THE CITY CENTER
VERY EXPENSIVE

Stamford Plaza Brisbane 𝒦𝒦𝒦   The recently rebranded Stamford is one of Brisbane's most beautiful hotels; its marble lobby is dotted with brocade chairs and sofas, enormous still-life oils, gilt mirrors, and palms. It's also one of the few city hotels to have river views from every room—especially stunning at night from the southern rooms when the Story Bridge lights up. The plush rooms are not enormous, but all fit a king-size bed or two twins. What must be the biggest bathrooms in Brisbane sport small TVs to watch from the tub. A riverside boardwalk leads from the hotel to the Eagle Street Pier restaurants on one side, and the Brisbane City Gardens abut the hotel on the other. Queen Street Mall is an easy 6-block walk. In an historic sandstone building adjacent to the hotel is one of Brisbane's grandest fine-dining restaurants, Siggi's, which also boasts a wine bar where you can puff on cigars with your cognac.

Edward & Margaret sts. (adjacent to the Brisbane City Gardens), QLD 4000. © **1800/773 700** in Australia, or 07/3221 1999. Fax 07/3221 6895. www.stamford.com.au. 252 units. A$415 (U.S.$269.75) double; A$630–$3,080 (U.S.$409.50–$2,002) suite. Extra person A$38 (U.S.$24.70). Children under 12 stay free with existing bedding. Ask about packages. AE, DC, MC, V. Free valet parking. Train: Central, then taxi or walk 6 blocks. Bus: City Circle 333. Ferry: Edward St. **Amenities:** 3 restaurants (Japanese, fine dining, brasserie), 3 bars; smallish outdoor heated lap pool and sun deck; health club; spa; sauna; concierge; tour desk; car-rental desk; business center; 24-hour room service; in-room massage; babysitting; dry cleaning; 24-hr. butler service; nonsmoking rooms. *In room:* A/C, TV with pay movies, dataport, minibar, coffeemaker, hair dryer, iron.

EXPENSIVE

Mercure Hotel Brisbane 𝒦   Sweeping views of the Brisbane River come with many of the rooms at this bright little 14-story hotel across the water from South Bank. Renovated in 1998, the compact rooms are not grand, but they have comfortable, unassuming furniture and new bathrooms. Rooms without water views have nice city outlooks. Roma St. Transit Centre, Queen Street Mall, South Bank Parklands, and Queensland Cultural Centre are a walk away.

85–87 North Quay (between Ann and Turbot sts.), Brisbane, QLD 4000. © **1300/65 6565** in Australia, or 800/221-4542 in the U.S. and Canada, 020/8283 4500 in the U.K., 0800/44 4422 in New Zealand, 07/3236 3300. Fax 07/3236 1035. www.mercurebrisbane.com.au. 194 units. A$120–$180 (U.S.$78–$117) double; A$168–$195 (U.S.$109.20–$126.75) studio suite; A$178–$210 (U.S.$115.70–$136.50) executive suite. Extra person A$22 (U.S.$14.30). Children under 16 stay free in parents' room with existing bedding. Ask about packages. AE, DC, MC, V. Parking A$9.50 (U.S.$6.17) per day. Airport shuttle. Train: Roma St. Bus: City Circle 333. Ferry: North Quay (CityCat and CityFerry). **Amenities:** Restaurant, bar; small outdoor pool, recently renovated; access to nearby YMCA health club; concierge; 24-hr. room service; babysitting; nonsmoking rooms. *In room:* A/C, TV with pay movies, stocked minibar, coffeemaker, hair dryer, iron.

MODERATE

Hotel Ibis Brisbane   What you get is what you pay for at this sister property to the Mercure, just around the corner (see above). In this case, it is basically a room, with few amenities you'd possibly expect in a large hotel. But if you don't mind doing without river views, porters, minibar, pool, or other small luxuries, this could be the place for you. Rebuilt inside a gutted office building in 1998, the hotel has rooms furnished in a contemporary decor with sizable work desks and small but smart bathrooms.

27–35 Turbot St. (between North Quay and George St.), Brisbane, QLD 4000. © **1300/65 6565** in Australia, or 800/221-4542 in the U.S. and Canada, 020/8283 4500 in the U.K., 0800/44 4422 in New Zealand, 07/3237 2333. Fax 07/3237 2444. www.accorhotels.com.au. 218 units. A$109 (U.S.$113.10) double. Extra person A$22 (U.S.$14.30). Children under 16 stay free in parents' room with existing bedding. Ask about packages. AE, DC, MC, V. Parking A$10 (U.S.$6.50) daily maximum in Queensland Place open-air public car park 1 block away (enter off Roma St.) or use Mercure Hotel Brisbane's parking arrangements (see above) at A$9.50 (U.S.$6.20) per day. Airport shuttle. Train: Roma St. Bus: City Circle 333. Ferry: North Quay (CityCat and CityFerry). **Amenities:** Restaurant; some nonsmoking rooms. *In room:* A/C, TV, fridge, coffeemaker, hair dryer, iron.

INEXPENSIVE

Explorers Inn Hotel 🏵 You'll be astonished to find such spruce decor and terrific value in one place—and in the heart of the city! Each tiny room at this former YWCA was designed by its architect owners to contain just the neccessities—including a narrow desk. The front desk lends hair dryers and the friendly staff is on hand to help with booking tours and sending e-mails. Downstairs is the good-value Explorers Cafe restaurant and bar. South Bank, the casino, the Roma Street Transit Centre, and Queen Street Mall are all close by.

63 Turbot St. (near George St.), Brisbane, QLD 4000. ℰ 1800/62 3288 in Australia, or 07/3211 3488. Fax 07/3211 3499. www.powerup.com.au/~explorer. 58 units (all with shower only). A$75 (U.S.$44.85) double; A$97 (U.S.$57.85) family (sleeps 4). AE, DC, MC, V. No parking; council car park opposite charges a maximum of A$10 (U.S.$3.90) per day. Train: Roma St. Bus: City Circle 333. **Amenities:** Restaurant; tour desk; car-rental desk; secretarial services; coin-operated laundry; laundry and dry-cleaning service; all rooms are nonsmoking, but there is a smokers' lounge. *In room:* A/C, TV, fridge, coffeemaker.

Hotel George Williams 🏵 It's hard to believe this smart hotel is a YMCA. Your room has vivid bedcovers, chrome chairs, and artsy bedside lamps on chrome stands. Rooms are small, but each can accommodate up to four adults. By the time you get there, another whole floor of rooms will have been added, and the current upstairs reception area will have moved to an easier-to-find ground floor location. Among the useful facilities are a 24-hour front desk, safe-deposit boxes, a hip cafe, and even conference facilities. Three rooms are designed for guests with disabilities. The City Y health club, downstairs in the same building, offers aerobics and circuit classes, personal trainers, and massage.

317–325 George St. (between Turbot and Ann sts.), Brisbane, QLD 4000. ℰ 1800/064 858, or 07/3308 0700. Fax 07/3308 0733. www.ymca.org.au. 42 units (most with shower only). A$90 (U.S.$58.50) double; additional person A$22 (U.S.$14.30). Children 4 and under stay free. Rates include continental breakfast. Ask about packages. AE, DC, MC, V. Limited free parking. Airport shuttle. Train: Roma St. Bus: City Circle 333. Ferry: North Quay (CityCat and CityFerry). **Amenities:** Restaurant; bar; free access to YMCA health club downstairs; tour desk; car-rental desk; babysitting; coin-operated laundry and valet laundry service; same-day dry cleaning; nonsmoking rooms. *In room:* A/C, TV, fridge, coffeemaker.

Thornbury House Bed & Breakfast 🏵 *Finds* A 15-minute walk to nearby Spring Hill from the city center brings you to this charming 1886 Queenslander cottage on a quiet street in this semi-commercial area. Hostess Michelle Bugler has decked out every room individually with Oriental rugs, comfortable beds, bathrobes, and lovely old furniture and knickknacks. Those without en-suite bathrooms have their own pretty, impeccably clean private bathrooms down the hall. Downstairs is a self-contained apartment with contemporary decor. Michelle serves a scrumptious breakfast in the ferny courtyard, a cool and restful place to be on a humid Brisbane day, where you can help yourself to tea, coffee, cookies, and the newspaper all day long. She's also on hand to help with booking tours and activities and can organize car rental.

1 Thornbury St., Spring Hill, Brisbane, QLD 4000. ℰ 07/3832 5985. Fax 07/3832 7255. www.babs.com.au/thornbury.htm. 6 units (all with bathroom, 5 with shower only). A$99–$110 (U.S.$64.35–$71.50) double; A$420 (U.S.$273) apt weekly. Rates include full breakfast. AE, MC, V. Free on-street parking (with permit provided by host). Airport bus stop at front door. Train: Central. **Amenities:** Dinner on request; access to nearby public swimming pools, golf club, and health club; spa; children's play area and toys; dry cleaning; free access to laundry, iron, fridge and microwave; fax, computer and dataport available; pay phone. *In room:* A/C (2 rooms only), TV, hair dryer.

IN PADDINGTON

Waverley ☆☆ *finds*   Right on the main shopping strip in trendy Paddington, this lovely three-story 1888 residence retains most of its original features such as bay windows, tongue-and-groove walls, soaring ceilings, and polished timber floors. The two delightful, air-conditioned front rooms, renovated in 1995, are spacious and individually furnished with supportive mattresses, comfy sofas, and attractive bathrooms. You can also stay in two self-contained apartments (with fans) downstairs. Your hostess, Annette Henry, cooks a hearty breakfast in the homey yellow kitchen (her fresh muffins are popular). There's also a lounge with soaring ceilings and a rear deck on both levels overlooks two old mango trees, busy with possums at night and visited regularly by day by a pair of native butcher-birds. No smoking indoors.

5 Latrobe Terrace at Cochrane St., Paddington, Brisbane, QLD 4064. ℂ **07/3369 8973**, or 0419/741 282 mobile phone. Fax 07/3876 6655. www.babs.com.au/paddington. 4 units (all with en-suite shower only). A$105–$110 (U.S.$68.25–$71.50) double; self-contained apts A$425 (U.S.$276.25) per week. Additional person A$25 (U.S.$16.25) extra. Rates include full breakfast. AE, DC, MC, V. Limited free parking. Pickup available on request from Roma St. transit center. **Amenities:** Laundry facilities. *In room:* TV, hair dryer, kitchenette and fridge (apts only), coffeemaker, iron.

4 Where to Dine

Visitors are often surprised to find Brisbane has a sophisticated dining scene. Stylish bistros and cafes are beginning to line Merthyr Street in New Farm; cute cafes are plentiful in Paddington; Asian eateries are a good choice around the intersection of Vulture Street and Boundary Street in West End; and in Fortitude Valley ("the Valley" for short), you'll find Chinatown. There's a street full of upscale but laid-back restaurants under the kitsch replica Eiffel Tower on Park Road in Milton, many with a Mediterranean flavor, and in the city center you can find slick riverfront restaurants at Eagle Street Pier and Riverside. The intersection of Albert and Charlotte streets buzzes with inexpensive, good-quality cafes.

IN THE CITY CENTER
EXPENSIVE

e'cco bistro ☆☆☆ MODERN AUSTRALIAN   This multi-award-winning bistro counts the title of Australia's top restaurant award (the Remy Martin Cognac/Gourmet Traveller Restaurant of the Year) among its claims to fame. Well-known for doing simple food exceptionally well, the restaurant is in a renovated former tea warehouse on the city fringe. Large windows, bold colors, and modern furniture make it a pleasant setting in what is becoming a small but popular restaurant enclave in this part of town. There's a nice, simple price structure (each course's offerings are all the same price), and there's an extensive wine list, but you can BYO wine for a corkage fee of A$5.50 (U.S.$3.57) per bottle. Bookings are recommended, as it can be difficult to get a table.

100 Boundary St. (at Adelaide St.). ℂ **07/3831 8344**. Fax 07/3831 8460. www.eccobistro.com. Reservations required. Main courses A$26.50 (U.S.$17.22). AE, DC, MC, V. Tues–Fri noon–2:30pm; Tues–Sat 6–10:30pm. Also open Mon, mid-Nov to Christmas. On-street meter parking. Closed for 10 days from Christmas.

Pier Nine ☆☆☆ MODERN AUSTRALIAN SEAFOOD   Ask the locals for the best seafood restaurant in town, and this light-filled contemporary restaurant overlooking the river and Story Bridge is where they'll send you. The menu changes daily, but among the specialties are fresh local Moreton Bay bugs (a kind of crustacean) and oysters shucked to order and served several ways (say, with sesame, wakame salad, and soy jelly, or au naturel for the purist). Another is Atlantic salmon (from Tasmania), which might be done with asparagus roe and hollandaise. I'm a fan of the sand crab omelet. It's always busy, so prepare to cool your heels at the oyster bar if you turn up without a reservation.

Eagle Street Pier, 1 Eagle St. © 07/3229 2194. www.piernine.com.au. Reservations recommended. Main courses A$20.75–$37.85 (U.S.$13.50–$24.60). AE, DC, MC, V. Daily 11:30am–midnight. Bus: City Circle 333. Ferry: Riverside (CityCat); Edward St. or Riverside (CityFerry); Eagle Street Pier (Cross River Ferry). Underground parking, but charges are steep.

MODERATE

Jo Jo's INTERNATIONAL/CAFE FARE   A spectacular new timber, limestone, and glass bar dominates the center of this casual cafe-style eating spot overlooking the mall, housing more than 1,000 bottles of wine. Three different menus—chargrill, Thai, and Mediterranean—are on offer, and the locals have been dropping in here for years to take a shopping pit stop, or to eat after the cinema. The food is well priced and good. You order at the bar, but meals are delivered to the table. Among your options are steaks and seafood from the char grill, curries, soups and stir-fries from the Thai menu, and pastas and designer sandwiches from the Mediterranean. An update of the kitchens this year means by the time you visit, the menu will also include wood-fired pizzas and roasts.

2nd floor, Queen Street Mall at Albert St. © 07/3221 2113. www.jojos.com.au. Reservations not needed. Main courses A$8–$22 (U.S.$5.20–$14.30). AE, DC, DISC, MC, V. Daily 9:30am–midnight. Happy Hour daily 4:30–6:30pm. Train: Central.

INEXPENSIVE

Explorers Cafe *(Value* CAFE FARE   After 5 years with one of the best-value a la carte menus in town, this basement restaurant under the Explorers Inn (see "Where to Stay," above) is moving towards what it calls "a city barbecue." That means gourmet sausages, steaks, and chicken dishes, with a choose-and-pay-at-the-counter format but still retaining table service. There'll still be soup, pasta, and vegetarian dishes for non-meat eaters, and the prices will still be great value, but by the time you visit the place will have been done over by interior designers.

63 Turbot St. (near corner of George St.) © 07/3211 3488. Fax 07/3211 3499. www.powerup.com. au/~explorer. Reservations recommended at lunch. Main courses A$7–$11 (U.S.$5.85–$10.35); A$5–$9.90 (U.S.$3.25–$6.45) breakfast. AE, DC, MC, V. Daily 7–9:30am, noon–2pm, and 6–8:30pm; open for coffee all day. Happy hour Mon–Fri 5–6pm. Train: Roma St. Bus: City Circle 333.

IN NEW FARM

Aix Café + Bistro MODERN AUSTRALIAN/CAFE/BISTRO   Chic decor, affordable dishes, and a "drop in anytime" atmosphere attract a wide range of locals to this open-fronted eatery and bar on New Farm's hip strip. Chef Mitch Thompson turns out dishes with flair and fresh ingredients, whether it's a rib fillet with saffron braised leeks, crisp mushrooms ravioli and roasted garlic jus or his signature chargrilled Atlantic salmon with salade niçoise. Loads of inexpensive and stylish pastas, pizzas, and sandwiches on Turkish flat bread, panini, and bruschetta are an alternative to a main course. Many good Aussie wines are sold by the glass. Take note—the breakfast menu includes pancakes with bacon and maple syrup!

83 Merthyr Rd. © 07/3358 6444. Fax: 07/3358 6155. info@aixbistro.com. Reservations recommended on weekends. Main courses A$11.90–$17.90 (U.S.$7.75–$11.65); sandwiches and light meals from A$5 (U.S.$3.25). AE, DC, MC, V (minimum charge A$20 (U.S.$13). Daily 7am–midnight. Sheltered parking. Bus: 190.

IN MT. COOT-THA

The Summit *रिरि* MODERN AUSTRALIAN   It would be hard to find a better view or a nicer setting in Brisbane. A teahouse of some kind has been on this mountaintop for more than a century. Part 19th-century Queenslander house and part sympathetic new extension, the restaurant sports wraparound covered decks with a superb view to the city and Moreton Bay. A changing menu features local produce, each dish teamed with an award-winning Queensland wine. Try pan-fried Moreton Bay prawns tossed in Italian parsley, or grilled kangaroo loin on rosemary skewers with sweet potato cakes. When you've finished dining, spend some time on the observation deck or in the gift shop. At night the city lights provide a glittering panorama.

At the Mt. Coot-tha Lookout, Sir Samuel Griffith Dr., Mt. Coot-tha. ⓒ 07/3369 9922. Fax 07/3369 8937. www.mtcoot-tha.com. Reservations recommended Fri and Sat nights. Main courses A$21.90–$25.90 (U.S.$14.25–$16.85); Chef's Selection 3-course menu A$43.80 (U.S.$28.50); 3-course early-bird menu A$21.90 (U.S.$14.25) available from 3pm if you finish by 7pm. AE, DC, MC, V. Daily 11:30am–midnight; Sun brunch from 8am. Free parking. Bus: 471. From Roma Street Transit Centre, take Upper Roma St. and Milton Rd. 3.5km (2 miles) west to the Western Freeway roundabout at Toowong Cemetery, veer slightly right into Sir Samuel Griffith Dr., and go approx. 3km (2 miles).

IN EAST BRISBANE

Green Papaya *रि* *Value* NORTH VIETNAMESE   Clean, fresh, and simple are the key words to describe owner/chef Lien Yeoman's approach to her native cuisine. Two cheerful rooms—painted yellow and blue—are usually crowded with a faithful clientele. If you don't know your Bo xao cay ngot (spicy beef) from your Nom du du (green papaya salad), the staff willingly gives advice. The restaurant is licensed, but you can bring your own bottled wine only (no beer or spirits) for a corkage charge of A$3 (U.S.$1.95) per person. Cooking classes are also run from time to time, so call for a schedule. They also do take-out.

898 Stanley St. East (at Potts St.), East Brisbane. ⓒ 07/3217 3599. www.greenpapaya.com.au. Reservations recommended. Main courses A$15–$28 (U.S.$9.750–$18.20). Banquet menus (for min. of 4 people) A$30–$35 (U.S.$19.50–$22.75). AE, DC, MC, V. Tues–Sun 6–10pm. Lunch for booked groups of 12 or more. Parking at rear of restaurant and on-street. Closed Good Friday, and from Christmas to early Jan. Located a 10-min. drive from town and 1 block from the Woolloongabba Cricket Ground. Train: Woolloongabba station.

IN ALBION

Breakfast Creek Hotel *रि* STEAK   Listed by the National Trust, the Breakfast Creek Hotel has been treasured by Brisbane people since 1889. Known fondly as the Brekky Creek—or simply The Creek—it is quintessentially Queensland. Overlooking the Brisbane River, it is famed for its gigantic steaks—all served with mushroom, chili, or pepper sauce. Order a XXXX (Fourex) beer "off the wood" (from the keg), sit in the beer garden on plastic seats under umbrellas, and check out the blackboard menu. Steak is what most people come for, but they have fish and chicken dishes, too. Every meal is served with an Idaho potato with bacon sauce, coleslaw, and tomato. On footy nights (Aussie Rules Football, Rugby League, or Rugby Union) be prepared for big crowds. There's a band on Sunday afternoons.

2 Kingsford Smith Dr. (at Breakfast Creek Rd.), Albion. ⓒ 07/3262 5988. Main courses A$17–$25 (U.S.$11.05–$16.25). AE, DC, MC, V. Meals daily noon–2:30pm; Mon–Fri 5:30–9:30pm; Sat 5–9:30pm; Sun 5–8:30pm. Pub: Sun–Thurs 10am–10pm; Fri–Sat 10am–11pm. Bus: 300 or 322. Wickham St. becomes Breakfast Creek Rd; the hotel is just off the route to the airport.

IN SHORNCLIFFE

The Full Moon *Finds* INTERNATIONAL   With views across Moreton Bay from its perch above Sandgate Beach, this is one of the north side's most stylish and popular eating places. Renovated a year or so ago, the once run-down old pub is now a casual lunch spot. It has a bistro-style menu that includes gourmet pizzas (try the satay chicken with roast peppers, red onion, bok choy, and peanuts) from the wood-fired oven, and an oyster bar with 24 beers on offer. Choose a seat inside (there's a gaming lounge as well) or out on the terrace with the changing moods of the bay in front of you. Fresh seafood, bought direct from the trawlers, is always on the menu, as well as a selection of steaks, noodles, curries, and pasta.

118 Eagle Terrace, Sandgate. ℭ 07/3869 0544. Main courses A$14.50–$19.90 (U.S.$9.40–$12.90). AE, DC, MC, V. Daily from 10:30am–10:30pm, or until the last patrons leave, breakfast weekends from 8:30am. Ample free on-site and street parking. Train: Sandgate station, then a 5-min. walk to the top of Eagle Terrace.

5 Exploring Brisbane
CUDDLING A KOALA & OTHER TOP ATTRACTIONS

Australian Woolshed   If you've never seen a sheep or visited a farm, this might be a novelty for you, but don't be surprised if your Aussie friends cringe when you mention your intention to visit it. That said, this is a hugely popular attraction with overseas visitors and school groups, and you may have to contend with busloads of them. The ram show features eight trained rams from the major Australian breeds who answer to their name and walk through the audience to take their place beside their named spots on the stage. There's also sheep-shearing, spinning, and sheepdog demonstrations, and you can get your hands dirty classing wool, milking cows, bottle-feeding baby farm animals, feeding kangaroos, and cuddling koalas. The gift shop has won awards for its all-Australian-made quality souvenirs. A rustic restaurant serves Aussie specialties, including billy tea and damper. Some Friday and Saturday nights the Woolshed hosts a traditional bush dance and dinner, featuring country dancing, spoon-playing, sing-a-longs, a live bush band, and three-course dinner. Tickets cost A$38.50 (U.S.$25) per person. The fun starts at 7pm and goes until midnight. You must book to attend the dance, and you must be aged 18 or over to attend.

148 Samford Rd., Ferny Hills. ℭ 07/3872 1100. www.auswoolshed.com.au. Admission to ram show A$15.70 (U.S.$10.20) adults, A$11.60 (U.S.$7.55) seniors and students, A$10.40 (U.S.$6.75) children 3–14, A$44.50 (U.S.$28.90) family. AE, MC, V. Admission to billy tea and damper A$6.50 (U.S.$4.20) adults, A$4.10 (U.S.$2.65) children 3–14. Water slide A$5.50 (U.S.$3.60) for 1 hr.; A$7.50 (U.S.$4.90) for 4 hr. Minigolf A$5.50 (U.S.$3.25) for 9 holes. Daily 7am–5pm (Ram show 8, 9:30, 11am, 1, and 2:30pm) except Christmas Day and Anzac Day (Apr 25) morning. Train: Ferny Grove (station is 800m/¹⁄₂ mile) from the Woolshed). Car: Kelvin Grove Rd. from the city becomes Enoggera Rd., then Samford Rd.; the trip is 14km (8¹⁄₂ miles). Large off-street free car park.

Brisbane Botanic Gardens Mt. Coot-tha   These 52-hectare (130-acre) gardens at the base of Mt. Coot-tha feature diverse Aussie natives and exotics you probably won't see at home, including an arid zone, a glass Tropical Dome conservatory housing lush rain-forest plants, a cactus house, bonsai house, fragrant plants, a Japanese garden, African and American plants, wetlands, pine forests, and a bamboo grove. There are lakes and walking trails, usually a horticultural show or arts-and-crafts display in the auditorium on weekends, and a cafe. Free 1-hour guided tours leave the kiosk at 11am and 1pm Monday through Saturday (except public holidays).

Mt. Coot-tha Rd., Toowong, 7km (4 miles) from the city. ℭ 07/3403 2533. Fax 07/3403 2552. www.brisbane.qld.gov.au. Free admission to Botanic Gardens. Gardens open daily 8am–5pm (5:30pm in summer). Bus: 471. See "Organized Tours," below, for details on Brisbane Transport's daily bus tour. Free parking.

City Hall Once the tallest building in Brisbane, City Hall is now dwarfed by the office blocks that surround it. Nevertheless, a ride in the old elevator to the top of the sandstone clock tower gives you a whole different perspective on the city center. Take a peek into the small but spacious art gallery on the ground floor, then take the elevator from outside the gallery entrance to the third floor. A cheery lift operator will give you a history of the building on your short ride up before letting you out into the glassed-in observation floor in the bell tower. If you're there on the quarter hour you'll get a close-up experience of the chimes. Try not to be there at midday, when the clock chimes 12—it's deafening.

King George Square (Ann and Adelaide sts.). © 07/3403 8888. Mon–Sat 10am–4pm.

Lone Pine Koala Sanctuary 𝕽𝕽 *(Kids)* This is the best place in Australia to cuddle a koala—and one of the few places where koala cuddling is still allowed. Banned in New South Wales and Victoria, koala cuddling is allowed in Queensland under strict conditions which ensure each animal is handled for less than 30 minutes a day and they get every third day off! When it opened in 1927, Lone Pine had only two koalas, Jack and Jill, but is now home to more than 130 of the furry marsupials. You can cuddle them any time of the day for free, and have your photo taken holding one for A$12.60 (U.S.$8.20); once you've purchased one photograph, your companions can take as many photos of you as they like with their own cameras. Koalas sleep about 18 hours a day, which has led to the myth that they get "stoned" on the eucalyptus oil in the leaves they eat. Lone Pine isn't just koalas—you can also hand-feed kangaroos and wallabies (A50¢/U.S.32¢ for a bag of food), and get up close with emus, parrots, wombats, Tasmanian devils, skinks, lace monitors, frogs, bats, turtles, possums, and other native wildlife. There is currency exchange, a gift shop, restaurant and cafe, or take advantage of the picnic and barbecue facilities overlooking the river.

Jesmond Rd., Fig Tree Pocket. © 07/3378 1366. Fax 07/3878 1770. www.koala.net. Admission A$14.50 (U.S.$9.40) adults, A$9.50 (U.S.$6.15) children 3–13, family pass A$35 (U.S.$22.75), A$12 (U.S.$7.80) seniors, backpackers, and students with ID, A$9 (U.S.$5.85) pensioners. AE, DC, MC, V. Daily including Christmas 7:30am–5pm; 1:30–5pm on Anzac Day (Apr 25). **Getting There:** The nicest way to get to Lone Pine is a cruise down the Brisbane River aboard the *M.V. Miramar* (© 07/3221 0300), which leaves North Quay at the top end of Queen Street Mall, next to Victoria Bridge, at 10am. The 19-km (12-mile) trip to Lone Pine takes 90 min. and includes a commentary. You have 2 hours to explore Lone Pine before returning downriver, arriving in the city at 2:45pm. The fare is A$33 (U.S.$21.45) for adults and A$19 (U.S.$12.35) for children ages 3–13, including a map, transfers from city hotels when available, and discounted entry to Lone Pine. Cruises are every day except Christmas and Anzac Day. By car, take Milton Road to the roundabout at Toowong cemetery, and then the Western Freeway toward Ipswich. Signs will direct you to Fig Tree Pocket and Lone Pine. The sanctuary is 20 min. from the city center by car. There's a huge free car park. Bus 430 goes directly to the Sanctuary from the Koala platform "N" at the Myer Centre, Queen St. Mall, and leaves hourly from 8:45am–3:45pm weekdays; 8:30am–4.30pm weekends and public holidays. Bus fare is A$2.80 (U.S.$1.80) adults and A$1.40 (U.S.$0.91) children.

Newstead House 𝕽 Brisbane's oldest surviving home has been restored to its late Victorian splendor in a peaceful park overlooking the Brisbane River. Wander the rooms, admire the gracious exterior dating from 1846, and on Sundays and public holidays between March and November, take Devonshire tea. The U.S. Army occupied the house during World War II, and the first American war memorial built in Australia stands on Newstead Point on the grounds.

Newstead Park, Breakfast Creek Rd., Newstead. © 07/3216 1846, or 1800 061 846. A$4.40 (U.S.$2.85) adults, A$3.30(U.S.$2.15) seniors and students, A$2.20 (U.S.$1.45) children 6–16, $11 (U.S.$7.15) family pass. Mon–Fri 10am–4pm; Sun and most public holidays 2–5pm. Closed Christmas, Boxing Day (Dec 26), Good Friday, and Anzac Day (Apr 25). Bus: 300, 306, or 322. Limited parking.

Queensland Cultural Centre *(Kids)*   This low-rise, modern complex stretching along the south bank of the Brisbane River houses many of the city's performing arts venues as well as the state art gallery, museum, and library in a series of interlinked buildings. Thanks to plenty of open plazas and fountains inserted by thoughtful architects, it is a pleasing place to wander or to just sit and watch the river and the city skyline.

The **Queensland Performing Arts Complex** (© **07/3840 7444** administration, or 07/3840 7431 backstage tours) houses the 2,000-seat Lyric Theatre for musicals, ballet, and opera; the 1,800-seat Concert Hall for orchestral performances; the 850-seat Optus Playhouse Theatre for plays; and the 315-seat Cremorne Theatre for theater-in-the-round, cabaret, and experimental works. The complex has a restaurant and a cafe. Free 40-minute front-of-house tours leave from the ticket sales foyer at noon Monday through Friday; no bookings are needed. Backstage tours must be booked and cost A$5.50 (U.S.$3.55) adults, A$2.75 (U.S.$1.80) children, concessions, and students.

The **Queensland Art Gallery** *(® (© **07/3840 7303**) is one of Australia's most attractive galleries, with vast light-filled spaces and interesting water features both inside and out. It is a major player in the Australian art world, attracting international blockbuster exhibitions of works by the likes of Renoir, Picasso, and van Gogh, and showcasing diverse modern Australian painters, sculptors, and other artists. It also has a strong collection of Aboriginal art. Admission is free. Free guided tours run Monday through Friday at 11am, 1, and 2pm; Saturdays at 11am, 2, and 3pm; Sundays at 11am, 1, and 3pm. There is a gift shop and bistro. The gallery is open daily from 10am to 5pm; closed Good Friday, Christmas, and until noon on Anzac Day (Apr 25).

The **Queensland Museum** on the corner of Grey and Melbourne streets (© **07/3840 7555**) displays an eclectic assortment ranging from natural history specimens and fossils to a World War I German tank, and is a great place to learn more about Queensland. Children will like the blue whale model suspended from the entrance and the dinosaurs, which include Queensland's own Muttaburrasaurus. The museum has a cafe and gift shop. Admission is free, except to traveling exhibitions, and it is open daily from 9:30am to 5pm; closed Christmas and Good Friday.

Adjacent to South Bank Parklands, across Victoria Bridge at western end of Queen St. © **07/3840 7595.** Ferry: South Bank (CityCat) and Old South Bank (Inner City Ferry). Bus: Countless bus routes depart Adelaide St. near Albert St., cross the Victoria Bridge, and stop outside. Plentiful underground parking. The Centre is a 7-min. walk from town.

Sciencentre *(Kids)*   My kids love this hands-on science museum, and it doesn't matter how often they go back, there's always something to capture and hold their interest. Designed for children 12 and younger, the Sciencentre is nevertheless also a place where the adults have as much fun—or frustration—as the kids. Everything is interactive, and it's as much fun watching someone as they work out what's happening as it is doing it yourself. Become part of a battery, see walls expand before your eyes, watch shadows float in space, carry a briefcase with a mind of its own—these and other amazing feats demonstrating the principles of science cover three floors. Twenty-minute interactive shows run during the day.

110 George St. between Mary and Charlotte sts. © **07/3220 0166.** Admission A$8 (U.S.$5.20) adults, A$6 (U.S.$3.90) seniors, students, and children 5–15, A$2.50 (U.S.$1.60) children 3–4, A$28 (U.S.$18.20) family pass. Daily 10am–5pm. Closed Good Friday and Christmas, and until 1pm Anzac Day (Apr 25). Bus: City Circle 333. Ferry: Queensland University of Technology (QUT) Gardens Point (CityCat and Inner City Ferry).

Sir Thomas Brisbane Planetarium & Cosmic Skydome *Kids* The plane-
tarium is part of the Botanic Gardens at Mt. Coot-tha. A fascinating 45-minute
astronomical show re-creates the Brisbane night sky using the Ziess projector.
Kids over 6 will like this.

At the Botanic Gardens of Mt. Coot-tha. © **07/3403 2578**. A$10 (U.S.$6.50) adults, A$8.50 (U.S.$5.50) sen-
iors and students, A$6 (U.S.$3.90) children under 15 (not recommended for children under 6), A$28
(U.S.$18.20) family. Show times Wed–Fri 3:30 and 7:30pm; Sat 1:30, 3:30, and 7:30pm; Sun 1:30 and 3:30pm.
Reservations not necessary but advisable. Wed–Sun noon–7pm.

South Bank Parklands Follow the locals' lead and spend some time at this
delightful 16-hectare (40-acre) complex of parks, restaurants, souvenir shops,
playgrounds, street theater, and weekend markets. The former World Expo 88
site has been happily transformed into a people's place that really works. There's
even a man-made beach, lined with palm trees, with real waves and sand, where
you can swim, stroll, and cycle the meandering pathways; sit over a caffe latte in
one of the cafes; enjoy the city views; and maybe take in a 3-D movie at the
IMAX cinema. From the parklands it's an easy stroll to the museum, art gallery,
and other buildings of the adjacent Queensland Cultural Centre (see above).

From the Queen St. Mall, walk across the Victoria Bridge to South Bank. © **07/3867 2051** for Visitor Information Centre, or 07/3867 2020 for recorded entertainment information. Free admission. Park: daily 24 hr.;
Visitor Information Centre: Sun–Thurs 8am–6pm, Fri 8am–10pm, Sat 8am–8pm. Train: South Brisbane. Ferry:
South Bank (CityCat) and Old South Bank (Inner City Ferry). Bus: Countless bus routes depart Adelaide St.
near Albert St., cross the Victoria Bridge, and stop at the Queensland Cultural Centre; walk through the Centre to South Bank Parklands. Plentiful underground parking in Queensland Cultural Centre. The Parklands are
a 7-min. walk from town.

St. John's Anglican Cathedral *★★* Brisbane's stunning neo-Gothic Angli-
can cathedral is in the final stages of its completion—a mere 100 years after it
was begun. Don't be put off by the scaffolding which will most likely still be
swaddling it when you visit—from a glassed off area inside, you can watch the
stonemasons as they continue working on the western transept of the building
(fronting Ann St.), due to be completed in 2006. Friendly and knowledgeable
volunteer guides run tours and will point out some of the detail which makes
this cathedral uniquely Queensland—like the carved possums on the organ
screen and the hand-stitched cushions.

373 Ann St. (between Wharf and Queen sts). © **07/3835 2231**. www.anglicanbrisbane.gil.com.au. Daily
9am–5pm; free tours 10am and 2pm Mon–Sat; Sun 2pm only.

TAKING A CITY STROLL
Because Brisbane is leafy, warm, and full of colonial-era Queenslander architecture, it is a great city for strolling. Pick up one of the free Heritage Trail Maps
from the Brisbane Marketing information booths (see "Visitor Information,"
earlier in this chapter) and set off to explore on your own. The map books have
a history of the area you are about to walk, and excellent detailed information
and illustrations of historic buildings and other sights along the way. Free guided
walks of the **Brisbane City Gardens** (© **07/3403 7913**) at Alice Street leave
from the rotunda at the Albert Street entrance Tuesday through Sunday at 11am
and 1pm (except public holidays).

For organized walking tours, see below.

6 Organized Tours

RIVER CRUISES The best way of cruising the river, in my view, is aboard
the fast **CityCat** ferries *★★*. Board at Riverside and head downstream under the

Story Bridge to New Farm Park, past Newstead House to the restaurant row at Brett's Wharves; or cruise upriver past the city and South Bank to the University of Queensland's lovely campus (take a peek at its impressive Great Court while you're there). This trip in either direction will set you back a whole A$3.60 (U.S.$2.35). Or you can stay on for the full trip, which takes about 2 hours. For those who'd like a commentary and maybe a meal as they cruise, the **Club Crocodile River Queen** paddle wheeler (© 07/3221 1300) is a good option. You can choose from a lunch or dinner cruise, and from a three-course menu or a seafood platter. Lunch prices are A$35 (U.S.$22.75), or A$55 (U.S.$35.75) for the seafood, or A$49 (U.S.$31.85) and A$65 (U.S.$42.25) for dinner. Children eat for half-price, and prices are slightly higher on Friday and Saturday nights and on public holidays. The boat departs from the Eagle Street Pier. Parking is available under the City Rowers tavern in Eagle St. A A$22 (U.S.$14.30) "coffee, tea and cookies" fare is part of the lunch cruise, but without the full meal.

BUS TOURS   For a good introduction to Brisbane, look no further than a **City Sights** or **City Nights** bus tour, both run by Brisbane Transport (© **13 12 30** in Australia). City Sights stops at 19 points of interest in a continuous loop around the city center, South Bank, and Fortitude Valley, including Chinatown, South Bank Parklands, the Queensland Cultural Centre, Sciencentre, the Riverside Centre (where markets are held Sun), the City Botanic Gardens, the casino, and various historical buildings. The driver of the distinctive blue and yellow bus gives a commentary, and you can hop on and off at any stop you like, getting onto the next bus that comes along. The tour is also good value as your ticket also gives unlimited access to buses, ferries, and CityCats for the day. The bus departs every 45 minutes from 9am to 4:15pm daily except Christmas, Good Friday, and Anzac Day. The whole trip, without stopping, takes 90 minutes. Tickets cost A$18 (U.S.$11.70) for adults, A$12 (U.S.$7.80) for children ages 5 to 15. Buy your ticket on board. You can join anywhere along the route, but the most central stop is City Hall, Stop 2 on Adelaide Street at Albert Street. Daily except Christmas, Good Friday, and Anzac Day (Apr 25).

The City Nights tour shows you the city lights from Mt. Coot-tha, the Brisbane River at South Bank, the illuminated cliffs at Kangaroo Point, New Farm Park, and Fortitude Valley. It departs City Hall, Stop 2 on Adelaide Street, at 6pm daily (Mar–Oct) and 6:30pm (Nov–Feb) and takes about 2½ hours. Daily except Christmas, New Year's Eve, Good Friday, and Anzac Day. Tickets are A$18 (U.S.$11.70) for adults, A$12 (U.S.$7.80) for kids ages 5 to 15. The trip also includes a sector by CityCat from South Bank to New Farm Park, where the bus is waiting to pick you up again.

WALKING TOURS   The Brisbane City Council has a wonderful program called **Walking for Pleasure** (© 07/3403 8888): Most days a free guided walk departs from somewhere in the city or suburbs, exploring all kinds of territory from bushland to heritage buildings to riverscapes to cemeteries. The beauty of the walks is that they are aimed at locals, not tourists, so you get to explore Brisbane side-by-side with the townsfolk. Every walk has a flexible distance option and usually lasts about 2 hours. Most are easy, but some are more demanding. Most start and finish near public transport and end near a food outlet of some kind. **Historical Walking Tours** are run by local history expert Brian Ogden (© 07/3217 3673), who leads visitors on a journey into Brisbane's past, regaling them with entertaining tales dating from convict settlement right to the present day. Four different routes are taken and each tour takes about 2 hours.

Prepare for shivers up your spine if you take a **Brisbane Ghost Tours** ✨ (✆ 07/ 3272 6234), and relive the city's gruesome past with guide Jack Sim. City walking tours are run every Friday night and other haunted activities include ghost tours, sleepovers, and haunted film nights in the now-disused Boggo Road Gaol.

7 Enjoying the Great Outdoors
OUTDOOR ACTIVITIES

ABSEILING & ROCK CLIMBING   The Kangaroo Point cliffs just south of the Story Bridge are a breeze for first-time abseilers (rappellers) to scale—so they say. Outdoor Pursuits (✆ 07/3391 8776) stages rock climbs up the cliffs every second Sunday from 8:30am. The experience lasts 3½ hours and costs A$39 (U.S.$25.35) per person. At 1pm you can abseil back during a 4-hour session for A$39 (U.S.$25.35) per person. You will fit in four or five abseils in the course of the afternoon. If you want to climb in the morning and abseil in the afternoon, you can buy both experiences as a package for A$59 (U.S.$38.35).

BIKING   Bike tracks stretch for 400 kilometers (219 miles) around Brisbane, often shared with pedestrians and in line skaters. One great scenic route—about 9 kilometers (5½ miles) long—starts just west of the Story Bridge, sweeps through the City Botanic Gardens, and follows the river all the way to the University of Queensland campus at St Lucia. **Brisbane Bicycle Sales and Hire,** 87 Albert St. (✆ 07/3229 2433), will rent you a bike and furnish you with the Brisbane City Council's free detailed bike maps. Rentals start at A$9 (U.S.$5.85) for 1 hour and go up to A$20 (U.S.$13) for the day; overnight and weekly rentals are available. The price includes helmets, which are compulsory in Australia, and a lock for your bike. **Hotel Cycle Hire** (✆ 0408 003 198 mobile phone) rents bikes, helmets, and maps for A$30 (U.S.$19.50) for a half day, A$40 (U.S.$26) full day, and A$70 (U.S.$45.50) for 2 days. The company also operates an easy escorted tour each afternoon for about 3 hours, departing from the Brisbane City Gardens, which costs A$38 (U.S.$24.70). The **Brisbane City Council** at City Hall (✆ 07/3403 8888) and Brisbane Marketing's information booths (see "Visitor Information," earlier in this chapter) also give out bike maps.

BUSHWALKING   **Brisbane Forest Park** ✨✨, a 28,500-hectare (71,250-acre) expanse of bushland, waterfalls, and rain forest a 20-minute drive north of the city, has hiking trails ranging from just a few hundred meters up to 8 kilometers (5 miles). Some tracks have themes—one highlights the native mammals that live in the park, for example, and another, the 1.8-kilometer (just over 1-mile) **Mt. Coot-tha Aboriginal Art Trail**, showcases contemporary Aboriginal art with tree carvings, rock paintings, etchings, and a dance pit. Because the park is so big, most walks depart from seven regional centers that are up to a 20-minute drive from headquarters, so you will need a car. Make a day of it and pack a picnic. Park Headquarters (✆ 07/3300 4855) is at 60 Mt. Nebo Rd., The Gap. Here you will find a wildlife display, a restaurant, a crafts shop, and an information center.

IN-LINE SKATING   In-line skaters can use the network of bike/pedestrian paths. See "Biking," above, for locations of where to find a map, or just head down to the City Botanic Gardens at Alice Street and find your own way out along the river. **SkateBiz,** 101 Albert St. (✆ 07/3220 0157), rents blades, scooters, and protective gear for A$11 (U.S.$7.15) (the price goes up to A$13/U.S.$8.45 Sun) for 2 hours. All-day rental is A$25 (U.S.$16.25). Take photo ID. The store is open daily from 10am to 4pm, and later on weekdays.

8 The Shopping Scene

Brisbane's best shopping is centered on **Queen Street Mall,** which has around 500 stores to choose from. Fronting the mall at 171–209 Queen St., under the Hilton, is the three-level **Wintergarden** shopping complex (© **07/3229 9755**), housing upscale jewelers and Aussie fashion designers. Farther up the mall at 91 Queen St. (at Albert Street) is the **Myer Centre** (© **07/3221 4199**), which has Brisbane's biggest department store and five levels of moderately priced stores, mostly fashion. The historic **Brisbane Arcade,** 160 Queen Street Mall, (© **07/ 3221 5977**) is lined with the boutiques of highly regarded local Queensland designers. Just down the mall from it you will find the **Broadway on the Mall** arcade (© **07/3229 5233**), which stocks affordable fashion, gifts, and accessories on two levels.

The trendy suburb of **Paddington,** just a couple of miles from the city by cab (or take the no. 144 bus to Bardon), is the place for antiques, books, art, crafts, one-of-a-kind clothing designs, and unusual gifts. The shops—colorfully painted Queenslander cottages—line the main street, Given Terrace, which becomes Latrobe Terrace. Don't miss the second wave of shops around the bend.

SHOPPING HOURS   Brisbane shops are open from 8:30am to 5:30pm Monday through Friday, 8:30am to 5pm on Saturday, and 10:30am to 4pm on Sunday. They stay open until 9pm Friday in the city, when the Queen Street Mall is abuzz with cinema-goers and revelers, and Thursday in Paddington. In the suburbs stores often close Sundays.

MARKETS   Authentic retro '50s and '60s fashion, off-beat stuff like old LPs (vinyl lives), secondhand crafts, and all kinds of junk and treasure are all up for sale at Brisbane's only alternative markets, **Brunswick Street Markets,** Brunswick Street next to Chinatown Mall, in Fortitude Valley (© **0418/ 886 400** mobile phone). Hang around in one of the many coffee shops and listen to live folk bands. It's held Saturday from 7am to 4pm.

Friday night is a fun time to visit the **South Bank Craft and Lantern Markets,** Stanley Street Plaza, South Bank Parklands (© **07/3870 2807**), when the buzzing outdoor handcrafts market is lit by lanterns. The market is held Friday from 5 to 10pm, Saturday from 11am to 5pm, and Sunday from 9am to 5pm.

Brisbane's glamour set likes trawling the **Riverside Markets** ⊕ at the Riverside Centre, 123 Eagle St. (© **07/3289 7077,** or 0414/888 041 mobile phone), to buy attractive housewares, colorful pottery, wooden blanket chests, handmade toys, painted flowerpots, and other stylish wares. It's held Sunday from 8am to 4pm.

For an authentic taste of Queensland's best produce, the **Farmers Markets** ⊕⊕ operate on the second Saturday of each month, 6am to 1pm, in the grounds of the Brisbane Powerhouse, Lamington St., New Farm. Here you'll find much to tempt your palate, brought into the city fresh that morning by farmers from around the south east of the state. There's everything from fresh fruit and vegetables to homemade chutneys, quail, fresh seafood, free-range eggs, and patés. Foodies will find themselves in heaven.

9 Brisbane After Dark

You can find out about other festivals, concerts, and performing-arts events, and book tickets, through **Ticketek** (© **13 19 31** in Queensland, 07/3404 6700 outside Queensland; www.ticketek.com.au). You can book in person at Ticketek agencies, the most convenient of which are on Level E at the Myer Centre at

91 Queen Street Mall, in the Roma Street Transit Centre, and in the Visitor Information Centre at South Bank Parklands. Or try **TicketMaster** (℃ **13 16 00;** www.ticketmaster.com.au).

QTIX (℃ **13 62 46** in Australia) is a major booking agent for performing arts and classical music, including all events at the Queensland Performing Arts Complex (QPAC). There is a A$6.60 (U.S.$4.30) fee per booking, not per ticket. You can also inquire and book in person at the box office at QPAC between 9am and 9pm Monday through Saturday, and at its outlet at the South Bank Parklands Visitor Information Centre.

The free, color weekly newspaper *Brisbane News* lists performing arts; jazz and classical music performances; art exhibitions; rock concerts; and public events. The free weekly *TimeOff,* which comes out Wednesdays and can be found in bars and cafes, is a good guide to live music, as is Thursday's *Courier-Mail* newspaper.

THE PERFORMING ARTS

Many of Brisbane's performing-arts events are held at the **Queensland Performing Arts Complex** (QPAC) in the Queensland Cultural Centre (see "Exploring Brisbane," earlier in this chapter), but the city also has a lively independent theatre scene, with smaller companies making an increasing impact on cultural life. To find out what's playing and to book tickets, call QTIX (see above) or visit www.qtix.com.au.

Queensland Theatre Company, the state theater company, offers about seven productions a year, from Shakespeare to premiere Australian works, attracting some of the country's best actors and directors. Most performances are at either the Optus Playhouse or Cremorne Theatre at the Queensland Performing Arts Complex (QPAC), South Bank. Call ℃ **07/3840 7000** for administration and information. Tickets cost A$27 to $45 (U.S.$17.55–$29.25); student rush tickets are available 1 hour before the performance for A$18 (U.S.$11.70).

La Boite Theatre ⋬, 57 Hale St, Petrie Terrace (℃ **07/3369 1622**), is a well-established innovative company which performs contemporary all-Australian plays in an intimate theater-in-the-round on the edge of the city center. Tickets are A$27 (U.S.$17.55), previews A$15 (U.S.$9.75). A newcomer to the arts scene is the past year is the **Brisbane Powerhouse-Centre for the Live Arts,** 119 Lamington St., New Farm (℃ **07/3358 8600**). A former electricity powerhouse, this massive brick factory has been transformed into a dynamic new art space for exhibitions, contemporary performance, and live art. The building retains its unique character, an industrial mix of metal, glass, and stark surfaces etched with 20 years of graffiti. It's a short walk from the New Farm ferry terminal along the riverfront through New Farm Park.

The state opera company, **Opera Queensland,** performs a lively repertoire of works, such as Bizet's *The Pearl Fishers,* Mozart's *The Magic Flute,* and Verdi's *Rigoletto,* as well as modern works, musicals, and choral concerts. Free talks on the opera you are about to see start in the foyer 45 minutes before every performance, and free close-up tours of the set are held after every performance (except the final night). Performances take place at the Lyric Theatre at the Queensland Performing Arts Complex (QPAC). Call ℃ **07/3875 3030** for administration. Tickets average A$30 to $105 (U.S.$19.50–$68.25).

The **Queensland Ballet** (℃ **07/3846 5266** administration) performs a mix of classical and modern works at the Cremorne Theatre, Optus Playhouse Theatre at the Performing Arts Complex (QPAC) and studio performances at the company's offices, Drake Street at Montague Road, West End, and other venues. Tickets A$45 to $55 (U.S.$29.25–$22.75), studio performances A$22 (U.S.$14.30).

The state's symphony and philharmonic orchestras merged last year, forming the **Queensland Orchestra** (ℂ 07/3377 5000 for administration), which continues to provide classical music lovers with a diverse mix of orchestral and chamber music. They also make the odd foray into fun material, such as Cole Porter hits and gospel music. Free talks are given in the foyer 1 hour before all major performances. The occasional "Tea and Symphony" concerts at City Hall include tea and coffee. The orchestra plays at the Concert Hall in the Queensland Performing Arts Complex (QPAC), City Hall, though more intimate works are staged at its studios at 53 Ferry Rd., West End. Tickets cost A$32 to $42 (U.S.$20.80–$27.30); student rush tickets are available 30 minutes before the start of the performance A$10 (U.S.$6.50).

NIGHTCLUBS

Fridays   This indoor/outdoor bar, restaurant, and nightclub complex overlooking the Brisbane River is a haunt for professionals in their 20s and for university students. Every night sees some kind of unbeatable happy-hour deal, cocktail club, or drinks special, and the dance action starts pumping around 11pm. Every second Wednesday from 6pm the Wine Club welcomes over-30s with all the wine, champagne, spirits, beer, food, and live bands they can take for A$25 (U.S.$16.25). Live music plays on the impressive riverfront terrace from 3:30pm or so on Sunday. Upstairs in Riverside Centre, 123 Eagle St. ℂ 07/3832 2122. Cover A$5–$7 (U.S.$3.25–$4.55). CityCat to Riverside.

Margaux's   A smart mid-30s to mid-40s crowd gathers to dance and chat over cocktails and supper at this clubby joint. It's open Friday and Saturday from 9:30pm to 3am. 5th fl., Brisbane Hilton, 190 Elizabeth St. ℂ 07/3234 2000. Happy hour 9:30–10:30pm. Cover A$5 (U.S.$3.25) Sat night.

COOL SPOTS FOR JAZZ & BLUES

Brisbane Jazz Club 🔆 *Finds*   Right on the riverfront under the Story Bridge, this is the only Australian jazz club still featuring big band dance music (three bands every Sun night). Watch out for the slightly sloping dance floor—it was once a boat ramp! About once a month on Thursday nights, Queensland Conservatorium students play modern jazz, and Friday nights jump to Latin jazz. Traditional and mainstream jazz is featured on Saturday nights. Once a month on Sunday afternoons guest artists play at a jazz brunch (noon–4pm) on the deck. 1 Annie St., Kangaroo Point (ℂ 07/3391 2006). 7:30–11:30pm Fri and Sat, 7–10:30pm Sun. A$8 (U.S.$5.20) most nights, with higher cover charges for some guest acts. CityCat to Holman St. Free car park.

Centra Brisbane Jazz-n-Blues Bar   One of Brisbane's leading live jazz venues is in the unlikely setting of this busy hotel. A mixed crowd in their 20s to 40s listens to jazz on Tuesday, a lucky dip of styles on Wednesday, blues on Thursday, and funk on Friday and Saturday. Ground floor of the Centra hotel, next to Roma Street Transit Centre, Roma St. ℂ 07/3238 2222. Cover A$5 (U.S.$3.25), and varying cover charges for major visiting acts. No cover Tues.

PUBS & BARS

City Rowers Tavern   Downstairs is a modern tavern with great river views from the terrace, pool tables, a big sports screen, and sometimes live bands; upstairs is a nightclub playing the latest disco hits. Waterfront workers (the kind that wear Italian suits, not the sort that shift cargo) drink up big at the 5-to-9pm happy hour. Eagle St. Pier, 1 Eagle St. ⓒ 07/3221 2888. Cover varies.

Empire Hotel   Friday and Saturday nights find this heritage-listed pub packed with the hip, the young, and the beautiful. Don't come here in a suit, and forget about it if you're over 35—you're not welcome. Most nights a DJ plays in the downstairs Art-Nouveau bar. By day, the place is more like a friendly country pub. 339 Brunswick St. at Ann St., Fortitude Valley. ⓒ 07/3852 1216.

Jameson's Restaurant & Bar   This downstairs wine bar leads a chameleon-like existence—it might host a literary night with a famous Aussie novelist one night, comedy cabaret the next, a Great Debate, live jazz bands, and '80s dance tunes. No matter what's going on, the mood is always friendly and stylish. 475 Adelaide St. ⓒ 07/3831 7633.

Treasury Casino   This lovely heritage building—built in 1886 as, ironically enough, the state's Treasury offices—houses a modern casino. Three levels of 100 gaming tables offer roulette, blackjack, baccarat, craps, sic-bo, and traditional Aussie two-up. There are more than 1,000 slot machines, five restaurants and seven bars, and it's open 24 hours. Live bands appear nightly in the Livewire Bar. Ask about Ride and Dine deals, in which your bus, train, ferry, or taxi fare entitles you to buy a package of cheap gaming chips and a meal. Queen St. between George and William sts. ⓒ 07/3306 8888. Must be 18 years old to enter; neat casual attire required (no beachwear or thongs). Closed Christmas, Good Friday, and until 1pm Anzac Day (Apr 25).

10 Brisbane's Moreton Bay & Islands

The Brisbane River runs into beautiful Moreton Bay, which is studded with hundreds of small islands—and a few large ones. Some of them can only be reached by private vessel. Others are national parks, and some are easily accessible either by tour boat or public ferry.

NORTH STRADBROKE ISLAND 𝔸𝔸

Affectionately called "Straddie" by the locals, the island was once home to a large Aboriginal population and still retains much of their history. Dunwich was later used as a convict outstation, a Catholic mission, quarantine station, and benevolent institution. The historical museum at Dunwich has a display of historic photographs, items salvaged from shipwrecks, and information about the early settlement of the island; it's open 10am to 2pm Wednesdays and Saturdays. A self-guided historical walk begins at the information center, where you can pick up a free map. Point Lookout, at the northern tip of the island, is Queensland's most easterly point. A "must" for all visitors is the North Gorge Headlands Walk, for breathtaking views and for spotting turtles, dolphins, and whales.

GETTING THERE & GETTING AROUND   Stradbroke Ferries (ⓒ 07/ 3286 2666), operates a water-taxi service from Toondah Harbour, Middle Street, Cleveland, to Dunwich (about 30 min.) for A$10.50 (U.S.$6.80) return (round-trip) adult fare. The vehicle barge takes walk-on passengers for A$8.50 (U.S.$5.50) return (this takes about an hour). A bus service meets almost every water taxi or ferry, and operates between the three main settlements, Dunwich, Amity, and Point Lookout. The trip takes about 30 minutes to either place and costs A$8.60 (U.S.$5.60) for adults.

VISITOR INFORMATION   The Visitor Information Centre (ⓒ 07/4309 9555) is on Junner Street, Dunwich (about 200m/656 ft. from the ferry terminal), and is open weekdays from 8:30am to 5pm and weekends 9am to 3pm.

SOUTH STRADBROKE ISLAND 🐾🐾

A turn-of-the-20th-century shipwreck (with a cargo of whiskey and explosives) weakened the link between this lovely island and North Stradbroke, and nature did the rest. South Stradbroke is less well-known than its sister island, but that's changing. There are four camping grounds and three resorts on the island. South Stradbroke Island is accessible from Runaway Bay near Southport, at the Gold Coast—about 45 minutes drive south of Brisbane city.

GETTING THERE & GETTING AROUND   From Brisbane, take the Pacific Highway exit after Dreamworld, follow signs to Sanctuary Cove/Hope Island and then to the marina. The resorts run boats for guests only, so the only other way to get there is by water taxi. **Gold Coast Water Taxi** (© **0418 759 789**) takes groups to the campgrounds and resorts for about A$10 (U.S.$6.50) per person (minimum of six people plus camping gear, if necessary). **Couran Cove Resort** runs day tours starting from A$50.45 (U.S.$32.80) per person which includes return transfers from Runaway Bay, morning tea, guided rainforest tour, lunch, and use of resort facilities for the rest of the afternoon. Fastcat leaves Runaway Bay at 10am, and you can return on either the 3 or 5pm boat.

MORETON ISLAND 🐾🐾

At more than 200 square kilometers (122 sq. miles) in area, Moreton is the second-largest sand mass in the world (after Queensland's Fraser Island) and has the world's largest sandhill, Mt. Tempest. There are three settlements and the Tangalooma Wild Dolphin Resort, where guests and visitors on a special extended day cruise can take part in hand-feeding a pod of wild dolphins which come in to the jetty each evening. It's an experience for which they line up in great anticipation, but be warned—it is highly regulated, you can't touch the dolphins, and it's over in a few seconds! Moreton has other claims to fame that are just as exciting. For instance, you can visit the 42-hectare (103-acre) "desert" and spend hours tobogganing down the towering sand dunes. Or you can snorkel around the 12 wrecks just north of the resort, and visit historic points of interest including the sandstone lighthouse at Cape Moreton, built in 1857. A four-wheel-drive is essential for getting around, but tours are run from the resort. Permits for access and camping are available from National Park rangers and ferry operators.

GETTING THERE & GETTING AROUND   The high-speed catamarans **Tangalooma Flyer** and **Tangalooma Express** leave Brisbane's Pinkenba wharf twice daily, at 10am and 5pm (10am and 2pm on Sat).The trip takes 75 minutes. Coaches pick up from Roma Street Transit Centre at 9am daily to connect with the Flyer and will pick up from city and Spring Hill hotels on request. Return transfers leave Tangalooma at 3:30pm daily except Saturday, when they leave at noon and 4:30pm. The return fare is A$52 (U.S.$33.80) adults and A$26 (U.S.$16.90) children aged 3 to 14. The **Combie Trader** vehicular and passenger ferry (© **07/3203 6399;** www.moreton-island.com) departs from Scarborough on the Redcliffe Peninsula in Brisbane's northern suburbs for Bulwer daily except Tuesday. The trip takes about 2 hours and costs A$26 (U.S.$16.90) adults, A$23 (U.S.$14.95) high school students 16 and over, and A$15 (U.S.$9.75) children (5–15 years) round-trip for walk-on passengers. The cost to take a four-wheel-drive and up to five passengers is A$122 (U.S.$79.30). Day trips operate on Saturdays (11am–4pm) and cost A$18 (U.S.$11.70) adults, A$10 (U.S.$6.50) children, and A$66 (U.S.$42.90) for a family of four. Combie Trader also runs four-wheel-drive trips to the island on Mondays,

Fridays, and Saturdays. The cost of A$79 (U.S.$51.35) adults and A$60 (U.S.$39) children under 14, includes the ferry crossing, tour, and lunch. Timetables are subject to change so check first.

ST. HELENA ISLAND 𝔯𝔯

For 65 years, from 1867 to 1932, St. Helena was a prison island, known as "the hell-hole of the Pacific" to the nearly 4,000 souls incarcerated there. Today, the prison ruins are a tourist attraction, with a small museum in the restored and reconstructed Deputy Superintendent's Cottage.

GETTING THERE & GETTING AROUND   Entry to the island—now a National Park—is by guided tour only. Excellent tours, most involving a re-enactment of life on the island jail, are run by **AB Sea Cruises** (℃ 07/ 3396 3994; 7am–7pm daily), leaving from Manly Boat Harbour. The cost is A$55 (U.S.$35.75) adults, A$48 (U.S.$31.20) concessions, A$27 (U.S.$17.55) children, and $119 (U.S.$77.35) for a family of four. The tour leaves at 9:30am weekdays, returning at 2:30pm, and 11am to 4pm on weekends and public holidays and includes a picnic box lunch. St. Helena By Night tours on the aptly named launch Cat-o-Nine Tails include live on-board entertainment, three-course dinner with licensed bar, and a dramatized version of life in the prison. Night tours—usually on Friday and Saturday nights—cost A$67 (U.S.$43.55) adults, A$35 (U.S.$22.75) children, or A$139 (U.S.$90.35) for a family of four.

GETTING THERE & GETTING AROUND   The Bay Islands taxi service (℃ 07/3409 1145) leaves from the Victoria Point jetty (Colburn Ave.) and Cleveland. The trip takes about 5 minutes from Victoria Point and costs A$2 (U.S.$1.30) each way. From Cleveland, it takes about 20 minutes and costs A$9 (U.S.$5.85) return.

WHERE TO STAY ON THE ISLANDS

Moreton and South Stradbroke islands have resorts, while North Stradbroke has plenty of existing low-key accommodation and is likely to have a major resort development in the next year or so. The smaller islands offer a variety of motels, cabins, caravan parks, and camping grounds.

Couran Cove Resort 𝔯𝔯𝔯 *Finds*   If you're lucky you might run into some of the world's elite athletes at this quietly luxurious South Stradbroke resort, unique for its range of more than 30 recreational and sporting activities. Developed in 1998 under the guidance of former Australian Olympic runner Ron Clarke (who lit the flame at the 1956 Melbourne Olympics), the resort is also strongly committed to environmentally-friendly practices. Hire a bicycle to get around on during your stay, walk, or catch a shuttle. Bike paths extend to the fantastic surf beach on the eastern side of the island, and the facilities include a 9-meter (29½-ft.) rock-climbing wall, three-lane sprint track, baseball and softball pitching cage, and a High Ropes Challenge course. There's also a beach volleyball court, bocce and lawn bowls, shuffleboard, surfing, fishing, and a star-gazing observatory. If all that sounds like hard work, there are also extensive spa facilities and a resident artist who'll give you lessons. There are lots of accommodation choices. My favorite is an eco-cabin in the bush, but for water views and closer access to the restaurants and spa, choose one of colorful waterfront units. All have kitchen facilities, and there's a general store and "pantry service" which will deliver supplies to your room. In line with the health and environmental tenets of the resort, smoking is only allowed in designated outdoor areas and on balconies, and tobacco is not sold at the resort.

South Stradbroke Island, Moreton Bay, QLD or P.O. Box 224, Runaway Bay, QLD 4216. ℂ **1800 632 211,** or 07/5597 9000. Fax 07/5597 9090. www.couran-cove.com.au. 357 units. Nature cabins (sleep from 3–8) from A$157 (U.S.$102.05) per night with a min 3-night stay; waterfront rooms from A$205 (U.S.$133.25) per night (no min. stay); 10% discount for 7 nights or more. AE, DC, MC, V. **Amenities:** 3 restaurants and poolside cafe; Olympic standard 10-lane heated pool, children's swimming pool; golf driving range and putting green, free transfers to mainland golf courses; 2 tennis courts; small but fully equipped exercise room; spa; extensive water-sports-equipment rentals; bike rental; children's programs and ½-acre adventure playground; game room; tour desk; massage; babysitting; laundry and dry-cleaning service. *In room:* A/C (waterfront units only, others have ceiling fans), TV with pay movies, VCR, fax, dataport, kitchen, minibar (marine resort only), hair dryer, safe.

Tangalooma Wild Dolphin Resort 𝄞 *Kids*   Once the southern hemisphere's largest whaling station, Tangalooma is the only resort on Moreton Island. The resort's big attraction is the pod of wild bottle-nosed dolphins that comes into the jetty each evening. Guests are guaranteed one chance during their visit to hand-feed the dolphins; but be warned—you can't swim with, or touch, the dolphins. The feeding is highly regulated for the health of the pod, your turn is over in a few seconds. Tangalooma is a good base for exploring the rest of the island, and a variety of good tours are available, among them, ironically, seasonal (June–Oct) whale-watching cruises (A$55/U.S.$35.75 adults, A$32/U.S.$20.80 children). A dolphin research center is also based here. The 48 modern two-story family villas added to the resort in the last few years are more pricey than regular rooms, and are a little further from the resort facilities. Units in the main resort area each sleep four to five people, and each has a private balcony. Rooms are not air-conditioned, but do have ceiling fans. A general store is on site for those who want to self-cater, and hair dryers are available from reception.

Moreton Island, off Brisbane, QLD or P.O. Box 1102, Eagle Farm, QLD 4009. ℂ **1300/652 250,** or 07/3268 6333. Fax 07/3268 6299. www.tangalooma.com. 192 units (all with shower only). A$334 double (U.S.$217.10), including return catamaran transfers, breakfast, and dolphin feeding. Ask about special packages and meal packages. AE, DC, MC, V. **Amenities:** 2 restaurants, cafe; 2 outdoor swimming pools; golf driving range and putting green; archery; tennis and squash courts; Jacuzzi; water-sports-equipment rental; children's programs and playground; tour desk; four-wheel-drive rental; in-room and poolside massage; babysitting; coin-op washers and dryers. *In room:* TV, kitchenette in all rooms and full kitchen in villas, fridge, coffeemaker.

Queensland & the Great Barrier Reef

by Lee Mylne

With a landscape three times the size of Texas and a population that hugs the coast but embraces the Outback, Queensland is a sprawling amalgam of stunning scenery, fantastic yarns, and eccentric personalities. Its most famous attraction is the Great Barrier Reef—but that's by no means the only thing worth seeing. Great beaches and tropical weather make it hard to decide where to go first, and for how long.

White sandy beaches grace almost the entire Queensland coastline, and a string of lovely islands and coral atolls dangle just offshore. At the southern end of the state, Gold Coast beaches and theme parks keep tourists happy. In the north, from Townsville to Cape York, the rain forest teems with exotic flora and fauna.

Brisbane is the state capital, a former penal colony that today brims with style. While Brisbane boasts world-class theater, shopping, markets, art galleries, and restaurants, it still conveys the relaxed warmth of a country town. For more, see chapter 5.

Less than an hour's drive south of Brisbane is the **Gold Coast** "glitter strip," with its 35 kilometers (22 miles) of rolling surf and sandy beaches. North of Brisbane lies the aptly named **Sunshine Coast**—more white sandy beaches, crystal-clear waters, and rolling mountains dotted with villages. Don't miss the wild beauty of the largest sand island in the world, World

Heritage–listed **Fraser Island.** Each year from August to October, magnificent humpback whales come to frolic in the sheltered waters between Fraser Island and Hervey Bay.

As you travel north along the coast, you'll be tempted by one tropical island after another until you hit the cluster of 74 which make up the **Whitsunday** and **Cumberland** groups.

Then you enter a land where islands, rain forest, mountains, and rivers unite. Green sugarcane fields are everywhere—**Mackay** is the largest sugar-producing region in Australia. This attractive city has its own beach, but the harbor is a departure point for cruises to the Great Barrier Reef and the Whitsunday Islands. The Whitsundays are on the same latitude as Tahiti, and for my money are equally lovely. The idyllic island group is laced with coral reefs rising out of calm, blue waters teeming with colorful fish—warm enough for swimming year round.

North of the Whitsundays is popular **Dunk Island** and the lovely rainforest settlement of **Mission Beach**—a perfect illustration of the regional contrasts found in Tropical North Queensland. The port city **Townsville** boasts 320 days of sunshine per year, and marks the start of the Great Green Way—an area of lush natural beauty on the way to Cairns.

Then you come to **Cairns,** with rain-forest hills and villages to explore and a harbor full of cruise and dive boats waiting to take you to the Reef.

Cairns is fine as a base, but the savvy these days head an hour north to the trendy village of **Port Douglas.**

EXPLORING THE QUEENSLAND COAST

VISITOR INFORMATION The **Queensland Travel Centre** is a great resource on traveling and touring the entire state, including the Great Barrier Reef. For information visit the Destination Queensland website at www.queensland-holidays.com.au (click on the "North American site" for advice for travelers from the U.S.) or call © **13 18 01.** Tourism Queensland has offices in the United States and the United Kingdom—see "Visitor Information" in chapter 2.

You will also find excellent information on the **Great Barrier Reef Visitors Bureau's** website at www.great-barrier-reef.com. This is not an official tourist office but part of a private company, **Travel Online** (© **07/3876 4644;** fax 07/3876 4645), which offers itinerary planning and booking services for a wide range of accommodations and tours throughout north Queensland.

For information on B&Bs and farmstays in Cairns, Port Douglas, Mission Beach, and Townsville, contact the **Bed & Breakfast and Farmstay Association of Tropical North Queensland Inc.,** c/o Lilybank Bed & Breakfast, 75 Kamerunga Rd., Stratford, Cairns, QLD 4870 (© **07/4058 1227;** fax 07/4058 1990; www.bnbnq.com.au).

WHEN TO GO Australia's winter (June–Aug) is high season in Queensland; the water can be chilly, but its temperature rarely drops below 22°C (72°F). August through January is peak visibility time for divers. Summer is hot and sticky across the state. North Queensland (Mission Beach, Cairns, and Port Douglas) gets a monsoonal Wet Season November or December through March or April, which brings heavy rains, high temperatures, extreme humidity, and cyclones. It's no problem to visit then, but if the Wet turns you off, consider the beautiful Whitsundays, which are generally beyond the reach of the rains and the worst humidity (but not of cyclones).

GETTING AROUND   By Car The Bruce Highway travels along the coast from Brisbane all the way to Cairns. It is mostly a narrow two-lane highway, and the scenery most of the way is eucalyptus bushland, but from Mackay north you will pass through sugarcane fields adding some variety to the trip.

Tourism Queensland publishes regional motoring guides. All you are likely to need, however, is a state map from the **Royal Automobile Club of Queensland** (RACQ), 300 St. Pauls Terrace, Fortitude Valley, Brisbane, QLD 4006 (© **13 19 05** in Australia, or 07/3361 2444). If you are already in Brisbane, you can get maps and motoring advice from the more centrally located RACQ office in the General Post Office (GPO) building at 261 Queen St. For road condition reports, call © **07/3219 0900.** The state's Department of Natural Resources (© **07/3896 3216**) publishes an excellent range of "Sunmap" maps that highlight tourist attractions, national parks, and the like, although they are of limited use as road maps. You can get them at newsagents and gas stations throughout the state.

By Train   Queensland Rail (© **13 22 32** in Queensland, or 07/3235 1122) operates several long-distance trains of varying degrees of luxury along the Brisbane–Cairns route, a 32-hour trip. See the "Getting Around" section in chapter 2 for more details.

By Plane   This is the fastest way to see a lot in such a big state. Beware the "milk run" flights that stop at every tiny town en route; these can chew up time. Qantas and regional airline Sunstate serve most coastal towns from Brisbane, and a few from Cairns. Virgin Blue flies between Brisbane and Townsville.

1 Exploring the Great Barrier Reef

It's the only living structure on Earth visible from the moon; at 348,700 square kilometers (238,899 sq. miles), it's bigger than the United Kingdom; it's over 2,000 kilometers (1,250 miles) long, stretching from Lady Elliot Island off Bundaberg to just south of Papua New Guinea; it's home to 1,500 kinds of fish, 400 species of corals, 4,000 kinds of clams and snails, and who knows how many sponges, worms, starfish, and sea urchins. Today, the Great Barrier Reef is listed as a World Heritage Site and is the biggest Marine Park in the world.

The Reef is not a plant, but a massive conglomeration of tiny animals called coral polyps. They coat themselves in limestone to keep safe, and as they die, their limestone bodies cement into a reef on which more living coral grows. And so it goes on, slowly constructing a megametropolis of coral polyp skyscrapers just under the surface of the water.

There are three kinds of reef on the Great Barrier Reef—fringing, ribbon, and platform. **Fringe reef** is the stuff you will see just off the shore of islands and along the mainland. **Ribbon reefs** create "streamers" of long, thin reef along the outer edge of the Reef, and are only found north of Cairns. **Platform** or **patch reefs** are splotches of coral emerging up off the continental shelf all the way along the Queensland coast. Platform reefs, the most common kind, are what most people are thinking of when they refer to the Great Barrier Reef. Island resorts in the Great Barrier Reef Marine Park are either "continental," meaning part of the Australian landmass, or "cays," crushed dead coral and sand amassed over time by water action. Cays are surrounded by dazzling coral and fish life. Continental islands may have terrific coral, some coral, or none at all.

Apart from the dazzling fish life around the corals, the Reef is home to large numbers of green and loggerhead turtles, one of the biggest dugong (manatee) populations in the world, sharks, giant manta rays, and sea snakes. In winter (July–Sept), humpback whales gather in the warm waters around the Hervey Bay and the Whitsunday Islands to give birth to calves.

To see the Reef you can snorkel, dive, fish, or fly over it. When most people say Great Barrier Reef they mean the "Outer Reef," the network of platform and ribbon reefs that lies an average of 65 kilometers (41 miles) off the coast (about 1 hr.–90 min. by boat from the mainland). You should get out and see that, but there is plenty of fringing reef to explore around islands closer to the mainland.

Learning about the Reef before you get there will enhance your visit. **Reef Teach** (☎ 07/4031 7794) is an evening multimedia presentation by Paddy Colwell, an enthusiastic marine biologist and scuba diver. He tells you everything

---

Tips When to Visit the Reef

April through November is the best time to visit. December through March can be uncomfortably hot and humid, particularly as far north as the Whitsundays, Cairns, and Port Douglas. In the winter months (June–Aug), the water can be a touch chilly (Aussies think so, anyway), but it rarely drops below 22° C (72° F).

The Reef Tax

Every passenger over 4 years old must pay a A$4 (U.S.$2.60) Environmental Management Charge (EMC), commonly called "reef tax," every time they visit the Great Barrier Reef. This money goes towards the management and conservation of the Reef. Your tour operator will collect it from you when you pay for your trip.

you need to know about the Reef, from how it was formed to how coral grows, from what dangerous creatures to avoid, to how to take successful underwater photos. It takes place throughout the year at 14 Spence St., Cairns, Monday through Saturday at 6:15pm, and costs A$13 (U.S.$8.45) per person.

Townsville is the headquarters of the Great Barrier Reef Marine Park Authority, and a visit to its showcase, Reef HQ (see "The North Coast: Mission Beach, Townsville & the Islands," later in this chapter) is a superb introduction. The star attraction at the aquarium is a re-created living-reef ecosystem in a massive viewing tank. If you want to learn more about the Reef, write to the **Great Barrier Reef Marine Park Authority,** P.O. Box 1379, Townsville, QLD 4810 (© **07/4750 0700;** fax 07/4772 6093; www.gbrmpa.gov.au, or www.reefHQ.org.au).

DISCOVERING THE REEF

Snorkeling the Reef can be a wondrous experience. Green and purple clams, pink sponges, red starfish, purple sea urchins, and fish from electric blue to neon yellow to lime are a truly magical sight. The rich colors of the coral only survive with lots of light, so the nearer the surface, the brighter and richer the marine life. That means snorkelers are in a prime position to see it at its best.

If your Reef cruise offers a guided snorkel tour, often called a "snorkel safari," take it. They are worth the extra cost of A$25 (U.S.$16.25) or so. Most safaris, which are suitable for both beginners and advanced snorkelers, are led by marine biologists who tell you heaps about the fascinating sea creatures before you. Snorkeling is an easy skill to master, and the crew on cruise boats are always happy to tutor you if you are unsure.

A day trip to the Reef also offers you a great opportunity to go scuba diving—even if you have never dived before. Every major cruise boat listed in "Day Trips to the Reef" (below) and many dedicated dive boats listed in "Diving the Reef" (below) offer introductory dives that allow you to dive without certification to a depth of 6 meters (20 ft.) in the company of an instructor. You will need to complete a medical questionnaire on board and then undergo a 30-minute briefing session on the boat. Intro dives are also referred to as "resort dives" because many resorts offer something similar, giving you 1 or 2 hours' instruction in their pools before taking you to a nearby reef to dive.

CHOOSING A GATEWAY TO THE REEF

A popular belief among overseas travelers is that **Cairns** and **Port Douglas** are the best places from which to access the Reef. They are both great places from which to see it, but the quality of the coral is just as good off any town along the coast between **Gladstone** and Cairns. The Reef is pretty much equidistant from any point on the coast—about 90 minutes away by high-speed catamaran. An exception is **Townsville,** where the Reef is about 2½ hours away. Think carefully about where you would like to base yourself.

The Great Barrier Reef

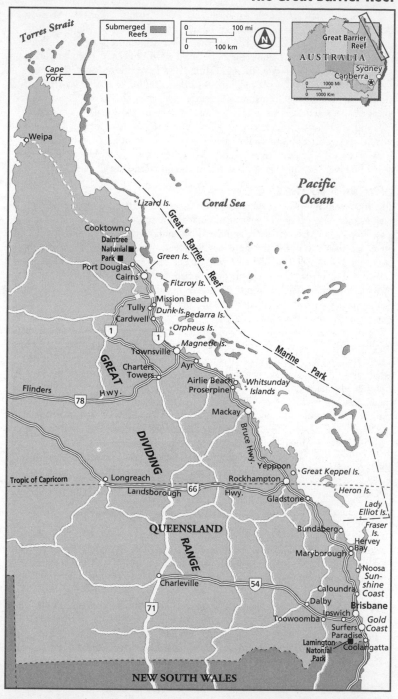

Torres Strait

Submerged Reefs

0   100 mi
0   100 km

Great Barrier Reef

AUSTRALIA

Sydney
Canberra

0   1000 Mi
0   1000 Km

Cape York

Weipa

Lizard Is.

Coral Sea

Pacific Ocean

Cooktown
Daintree National Park
Port Douglas
Cairns

Green Is.

Great Barrier Reef

Fitzroy Is.

Mission Beach
Tully
Cardwell
Dunk Is.
Bedarra Is.
Orpheus Is.

Magnetic Is.

Townsville

Marine   Park

GREAT

Charters Towers
Ayr
Airlie Beach
Proserpine
Whitsunday Islands

Flinders

Hwy.

78

DIVIDING

Mackay

Bruce Hwy.

Yeppoon

Tropic of Capricorn   Longreach   Great Keppel Is.

Landsborough   66   Rockhampton
Hwy.   Gladstone   Heron Is.

Lady Elliot Is.

QUEENSLAND

RANGE

Bundaberg   Fraser Is.
Hervey Bay
Maryborough

Noosa
Sun-
shine
Coast

Charleville   54   Caloundra

Dalby   Brisbane

71   Toowoomba   Ipswich   Gold Coast
Surfers Paradise
Lamington National Park   Coolangatta

NEW SOUTH WALES

The main gateways, north to south, are **Port Douglas, Cairns, Mission Beach, Townsville, the Whitsunday Islands, Gladstone** (for Heron Island), and **Bundaberg.** The Whitsundays has the added attractions of dazzling islands to sail among; beautiful island resorts offering a wealth of water sports and other activities; and a large array of diving, fishing, and day cruises. Most important, you can snorkel every day off your island or join a sailing or cruise day trip to a number of magnificent inner reefs much nearer than the main Outer Reef. Many people stay in Cairns simply because of easy international airport access.

If you are a non-swimmer, choose a Reef cruise that visits a coral cay, because a cay slopes gradually into shallow water and the surrounding coral. The **Low Isles** at Port Douglas; **Green Island, Michaelmas Cay,** or **Upolu Cay** off Cairns; **Beaver Cay** off Mission Beach and **Heron Island** are all good locations.

DAY TRIPS TO THE REEF

The most common way to get to the Reef is on one of the big motorized catamarans that carry up to 300 passengers each and depart from Cairns, Port Douglas, Townsville, Mission Beach, and the Whitsunday mainland and islands. The boats are air-conditioned and have a bar, videos, and educational material on board, as well as a marine biologist who gives a brief talk on the Reef's ecology en route. The boats tie up at their own private permanent pontoons anchored to a platform reef. The pontoons have glass-bottom boats for folks who don't want to get wet, dry underwater viewing platforms, usually a bar, sun decks, shaded seats, and often showers.

An alternative to traveling on a big tour boat is to go on one of the many smaller boats. These typically visit two or three Reef sites rather than just one. There are usually no more than 20 passengers, so the crew offers you personal attention, and you get to know the other passengers and have a fun, friendly time. Another advantage of going in a small boat is that you will have the coral pretty much all to yourself. The drawbacks of a small boat are that you have only the cramped deck to sit on when you get out of the water, and your traveling time to the Reef may be longer. If you're a nervous snorkeler, you may feel safer going in a big boat where you are surrounded by 300 other passengers in the water.

Most day-trip fares include snorkel gear—fins, mask, and snorkel, and wet suits in winter, although you rarely need them—free use of the underwater viewing chambers and glass-bottom-boat rides, a plentiful buffet or barbecue lunch,

---

Tips Reef Health & Safety Warnings

Coral is very sharp and coral cuts get infected quickly and badly. If you do cut yourself, ask your cruise boat for antiseptic cream and apply it to grazes as soon as you come out of the water.

The sun and reflected sunlight off the water can burn you fast. Remember to put sunscreen on your back and the back of your legs, especially around your knees and the back of your neck, even behind your ears, all places that rarely get exposed to the sun but which will be exposed as you swim face down. Apply more when you leave the water.

And remember the Great Barrier Reef is a Marine Park. Removing coral (living or dead), shells, or any other natural item is an offense. If everyone who has ever visited the Reef took a piece, it would not be worth your coming to see what's left.

Tips **Feeling Green?**

If you are inclined to be seasick, come prepared with medication. Some boats sell a ginger-based natural anti-seasickness pill, but it doesn't always work!

---

and morning and afternoon refreshments. Diving is an optional activity for which you pay extra. The big boats post snorkeling scouts to keep a lookout for anyone in trouble and to count heads periodically. If you wear glasses, check whether your boat offers prescription masks as this could make a big difference to the quality of your experience! Don't forget, you can travel as a snorkel-only passenger on most dive boats, too.

The major launching points for day trips to the Reef are Port Douglas, Cairns, Mission Beach, Townsville, and the Whitsundays (see individual sections on these regions later in this chapter).

MULTIDAY CRUISES ALONG THE REEF

Down Under Dive (© **1800/079 099** in Australia, or 07/4052 8300; fax 07/4031 1373; www.downunderdive.com.au) in Cairns offers a chance to "sleep on the Reef" aboard a glamorous 42.6-meter (140-ft.) 1890s-style brigantine, the S.V. *Atlantic Clipper*. It's a sleek, romantic sailing ship with towering masts, a roomy Jacuzzi on the foredeck, a cocktail bar, a comfortable dining room, and single, double, triple or quad-share air-conditioned cabins. A motorized launch takes you from Cairns to the ship's reef mooring; from there you sail up to the four popular reef complexes of Norman, Hastings, and Saxon reefs, and Michaelmas Cay. The emphasis is on fun and relaxation, with lots of snorkeling and diving. Trips range from a 2-day/1-night stay in a two-, three- or four-berth cabin for A$210 (U.S.$136.50) for snorkelers or A$290 (U.S.$188.50) for divers, to a 4-day/3-night journey for A$420 (U.S.$273) for snorkelers or A$550 (U.S.$357.50) for divers. Add a surcharge of A$20 (U.S.$13) per person per night for a double cabin and A$30 (U.S.$19.50) for a double cabin with shower. The all-inclusive prices include all dive and snorkel gear (including prescription masks), meals, and pickups from your Cairns city accommodation. Transfers from Port Douglas available for an extra A$12 (U.S.$7.80).

DIVING THE REEF *₰*

Divers have a big choice of dive boats that make 1-day runs to the Outer Reef and live-aboard dive boats making excursions that last up to a week. As a general rule, on a typical 5-hour day trip to the Reef, you will fit in about two dives.

The companies listed next give you an idea of what kinds of diving trips are available and how much they cost. This is by no means an exhaustive list of the dive operators up and down the Reef, for there are far too many to include here. The section on "The Active Vacation Planner" in chapter 2 has more pointers for locating a dive operator. The prices quoted here include full gear rental; knock off about A$20 (U.S.$13) if you have your own gear.

FROM CAIRNS **Tusa Dive** (© **07/4031 1248;** www.tusadive.com) runs two 20-meter (65-ft.) dive boats daily to two dive sites from a choice of 21 locations on the Outer Reef. A day's diving costs A$175 (U.S.$113.75) with wet suits, guided snorkel tours, lunch, and transfers from your Cairns or northern beaches hotel. For an extra A$65 (U.S.$42.25) you can get a video done of the day's dive. If you want to be shown the best spots under the water, you can take a guided dive with the dive team for an extra A$15 (U.S.$9.75). Day trips for introductory divers cost A$175 (U.S.$113.75) for one dive or A$205 (U.S.$133.25) for two. The groups are kept to a maximum of 25 people, so you get personal attention. The company is the Nitrox and Rebreather facility for north Queensland, and certified divers can take two introductory dives on Nitrox/Safe Air in 1 day for A$200 (U.S.$113.75).

FROM PORT DOUGLAS   The waters off Port Douglas are home to dramatic coral spires and swim-throughs at the Cathedrals; giant clams at Barracuda Pass; a village of parrot fish, anemone fish, unicorn fish, and two moray eels at the soaring pinnacle of Nursery Bommie; fan corals at Split-Bommie; and many other wonderful sites.

Poseidon (© 07/4099 4772; www.poseidon-cruises.com.au) is a fast 18-meter (58-ft.) vessel that visits three Outer Reef sites. The day-trip price of A$125 (U.S.$81.25) for adults, A$90 (U.S.$58.50) for kids ages 3 to 12, includes snorkel gear, a marine biology talk, snorkel safaris, lunch, and pickups from Port Douglas hotels. Certified divers pay A$22 (U.S.$14.30) extra per dive, plus A$30 (U.S.$19.50) gear rental. Guides will accompany you, free of charge, to show you great locations. Introductory divers pay A$70 (U.S.$45.50) for one dive, and A$40 (U.S.$26) each for the second and third. The vessel carries no more than 48 passengers, one-third its capacity, and gets you to the Reef in just over an hour, giving you 5 hours on the coral. The boat departs Marina Mirage daily at 8:30am.

FROM MISSION BEACH   Quick Cat Dive Adventures (see "Day Trips to the Reef," above) takes divers on its day cruises to the Reef.

FROM TOWNSVILLE   Off Townsville, you can dive not only the Reef but also a wreck, the **Yongala** ⚓, which lies off the coast in 30 meters (98 ft.) of water with good visibility. A cyclone sent the *Yongala* with 49 passengers and 72 crew members to the bottom of the sea in a cyclone in 1911. Today it's surrounded by a mass of coral and rich marine life, including barracuda, grouper, rays, and turtles. **Diving Dreams** (© 07/4721 2500; fax 07/4721 2549; www.divingdreams.com) runs 2- or 3-day trips which include dives at the *Yongala*, with prices at around A$350 to $450 (U.S.$227.50–$292.50).

FROM THE WHITSUNDAYS   In and around the Whitsunday Islands, you can visit the Outer Reef and explore the many excellent Reef dive sites close to shore. Two of the more established companies are **Reef Dive** (© 1800/075 120 in Australia, or 07/4946 6508) and **Kelly Dive** (© 1800/063 454 in Australia, or 07/4946 6122). A day trip with scuba and snorkel gear, two dives, lunch, and a pickup from your Airlie Beach accommodations costs around A$135 (U.S.$87.75) per person.

DIVE COURSES   Many dive companies in Queensland offer dive courses, from initial open-water certification right up to dive master, rescue diver, and

---

Tips Pressed for Time?

If you don't have time for a full day on the Outer Reef, don't forget that you can dive the coral cay of Green Island, just 27 kilometers (16 miles) off Cairns, in half a day (see "Exploring the Islands" in the Cairns section in this chapter).

Diving Tips
Don't forget to bring your "C" certification card, and it's a good idea to bring along your dive log also. Remember not to fly for 24 hours after diving.

instructor level. To take a course, you will need to have a medical exam done by a Queensland doctor (your dive school will arrange it). You will also need two passport photos for your certificate, and you must be able to swim! Some courses take as little as 3 days, but 5 days is generally regarded as the best. Open-water certification usually requires 2 days of theory in a pool, followed by 2 or 3 days out on the Reef, where you make between four and nine dives.

Deep Sea Divers Den (© 07/4031 2223; fax 07/4031 1210) has been in operation since 1974 and claims to have certified about 55,000 divers. The 5-day open-water course involves 2 days of theory in the pool in Cairns, and 3 days and 2 nights on a live-aboard boat. The course costs A$545 (U.S.$354.25) per person, including all meals on the boat, nine dives (including a guided night dive), all your gear and a wet suit, and transfers from your city hotel. The same course over 4 nights, with 1 night on the boat and four dives, costs A$435 (U.S.$282.75). New courses begin every day of the week.

Virtually every Great Barrier Reef dive operator offers dive courses. Most island resorts offer them, too. You will find dive schools in Cairns, Port Douglas, Mission Beach, Townsville, and the Whitsunday Islands.

Most dive companies teach from beginner level ("open-water certification") through to Advanced, Rescue, Dive Master, and Dive Instructor level. Courses usually commence every day or every week. Prices vary quite a bit, but a rough guide is around A$550 (U.S.$357.50) for a 5-day open-water certification course, or A$440 (U.S.$286) for the same course over 4 nights.

Companies offering dive courses appear under the relevant regional sections throughout this chapter.

2 Cairns

346km (207½ miles) N of Townsville; 1,807km (1,084 miles) N of Brisbane

This is the only place in the world where two World Heritage–listed attractions—the Great Barrier Reef and the Wet Tropics Rainforest—lie side by side. In parts of the far north, the rain forest touches the reef, reaching right down to sandy beaches from which you can snorkel the reef. Cairns is the gateway to these natural attractions, plus to man-made tourist attractions such as the Skyrail Rainforest Cableway. It's also a stepping stone to islands of the Great Barrier Reef and the grasslands of the Gulf Savannah.

When international tourism to the Great Barrier Reef boomed a decade or two ago, Cairns boomed with it. The result is that this small sugar-farming town now boasts five-star hotels, island resorts off shore, big Reef-cruise catamarans in the harbor, and too many souvenir shops.

The 110-million-year-old rain forest, the Daintree, where plants that are fossils elsewhere in the world exist in living color, is just a couple of hours north of Cairns. The Daintree is part of the Wet Tropics, a World Heritage–listed area that stretches from north of Townsville to south of Cooktown, beyond Cairns, and houses half of Australia's animal and plant species.

If you are spending more than a day or two in the area, consider basing your-self on the city's pretty northern beaches, in Kuranda, or in Port Douglas (see "Port Douglas, Daintree & the Cape Tribulation Area," later in this chapter). Although prices will be higher in the peak season (Australian winter and early spring, July–Oct), the town has affordable accommodations year-round.

ESSENTIALS

GETTING THERE   By Plane   Qantas (© 13 13 13 in Australia) has direct flights throughout the day to Cairns from Sydney and Brisbane, and between them at least one flight a day from Alice Springs and Darwin. Qantas also flies direct from Ayers Rock once or twice a day. From Melbourne you can fly direct some days, but most flights connect through Sydney or Brisbane. **Sunstate Airlines** (book through Qantas) also flies several times a day from Townsville, and **Airlink** (book through Qantas) has flights from Alice Springs and Ayers Rock. Several international carriers fly to Cairns from various Asian cities, and from New Zealand.

Cairns Airport is 8 kilometers (5 miles) north of downtown, and a 5-minute walk or a A$2 (U.S.$1.30) shuttle ride separates the domestic and international terminals. The **Australia Coach** (© 07/4031 3555) shuttle, which costs A$4.50 (U.S.$2.90), A$3 (U.S.$1.95) children 2 to 12 years, meets major flights at both terminals for transfers to city hotels. Bookings are not needed. **Coral Coaches** (© 07/4031 7577) meets most flights between 6am and 8:15pm and does frequent drop-offs and pickups at city, northern beaches, and Port Douglas accommodations. Some trips require reservations; others are on a first-come, first-served basis, but booking is a good idea. The adult one-way fare is A$7.40 (U.S.$4.80) to the city, A$11.40 (U.S.$7.40) to Trinity Beach, A$14.80 (U.S.$9.60) to Palm Cove. Children ages 4 to 14 pay half price, seniors get a 40% discount.

A taxi from the airport costs around A$10.50 (U.S.$6.80) to the city, A$26 (U.S.$16.90) to Trinity Beach, and A$34 (U.S.$22.10) to Palm Cove. Call **Black & White Taxis** (© 13 10 08, or 07/4051 5333 in Cairns).

Avis, Budget, Hertz, and Thrifty all have car-rental offices at the domestic and international terminals (see "Getting Around," below).

By Train   Long-distance trains operate from Brisbane several times a week, calling at most towns and cities along the way on a route that is loosely parallel to the Bruce Highway. All services are operated by **Queensland Rail Traveltrain** (© 1800 806 468 in Australia, or 07/3235 1000; www.qr.com.au). Trains pull into the Cairns Central terminal (© 13 22 32 in Australia for reservations or inquiries 24 hours a day, or 07/4052 6297 for the terminal from 8am to 6pm, 07/4052 6203 after hours) on Bunda Street in the center of town. It has no showers, lockers, or currency exchange booths, but you will find 24-hour ATMs outside the Cairns Central shopping mall, right above the terminal.

The trip from Brisbane takes around 30 hours. A seat on the *Sunlander* or *Spirit of the Tropics* costs A$162.80 (U.S.$105.80). Sleeping berths only on the *Sunlander* cost A$305.80 (U.S.$198.25) for a private cabin. The most comfortable choice is The *Queenslander* (Mar to mid-Dec only), which provides silver-service meals and sleepers for A$558.80 (U.S.$362.70).

For details on the opulent Great South Pacific Express that runs from Sydney or Brisbane to Cairns, see "Getting Around Australia," in chapter 2.

By Bus   McCafferty's (© 13 14 99, or 07/4051 5899 for Cairns terminal) and **Greyhound-Pioneer** (© 13 20 30, or 07/4051 3388 for Cairns terminal) buses pull into Trinity Wharf Centre on Wharf Street in the center of town.

Cairns

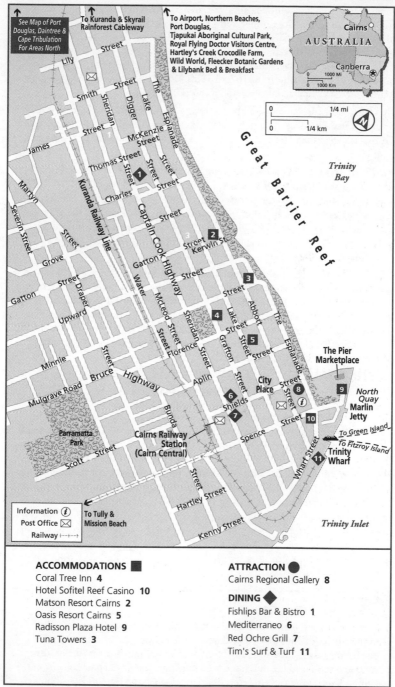

See Map of Port Douglas, Daintree & Cape Tribulation For Areas North

To Kuranda & Skyrail Rainforest Cableway

To Airport, Northern Beaches, Port Douglas, Tjapukai Aboriginal Cultural Park, Royal Flying Doctor Visitors Centre, Hartley's Creek Crocodile Farm, Wild World, Fleecker Botanic Gardens & Lilybank Bed & Breakfast

AUSTRALIA

Cairns

Canberra

0   1000 Mi
0   1000 Km

0   1/4 mi
0   1/4 km

Trinity Bay

Great Barrier Reef

Lily Street

Smith Street

Sheridan Street

Digger Street

The Esplanade

Lake Street

James Street

McKenzie Street

Thomas Street

Charles Street

Martyn Street

Severin Street

Kuranda Railway Line

Captain Cook Highway

Grove Street

Gatton Street

Draper Street

Upward Street

Water Street

Gatton Street

Kerwin St

Street

Street

McLeod Street

Sheridan Street

Florence Street

Grafton Street

Lake Street

Abbott Street

The Esplanade

Minnie Street

Bruce Highway

Mulgrave Road

Aplin Street

Shields Street

Spence Street

City Place

The Pier Marketplace

North Quay

Marlin Jetty

Parramatta Park

Bunda Street

Cairns Railway Station (Cairn Central)

Scott Street

Wharf Street

Trinity Wharf

To Green Island

To Fitzroy Island

Information ⓘ To Tully &
Post Office ✉ Mission Beach
Railway ⊢–⊢–⊣

Hartley Street

Kenny Street

Trinity Inlet

ACCOMMODATIONS ■
Coral Tree Inn **4**
Hotel Sofitel Reef Casino **10**
Matson Resort Cairns **2**
Oasis Resort Cairns **5**
Radisson Plaza Hotel **9**
Tuna Towers **3**

ATTRACTION ●
Cairns Regional Gallery **8**

DINING ◆
Fishlips Bar & Bistro **1**
Mediterraneo **6**
Red Ochre Grill **7**
Tim's Surf & Turf **11**

Buses travel from the south via all towns and cities on the Bruce Highway, and from the west from Alice Springs and Darwin via Tennant Creek on the Stuart Highway and the Outback mining town of Mt. Isa to Townsville, where they join the Bruce Highway and head north.

The 46-hour Sydney–Cairns trip costs A$249.70 (U.S.$162.30), the 28½-hour trip from Brisbane is A$167.20 (U.S.$108.70), and from Darwin, the journey takes 41 hours and costs A$335.50 (U.S.$218).

By Car   From Brisbane and all major towns in the south, you'll enter Cairns on the Bruce Highway. To reach the northern beaches or Port Douglas from Cairns, take Sheridan Street in the city center, which becomes the Captain Cook Highway.

VISITOR INFORMATION   Tourism Tropical North Queensland is at 51 The Esplanade, Cairns, QLD 4870 (✆ **07/4051 3588;** fax 07/4051 0127; www.tnq.org.au). Its Visitor Information Center has information not just on Cairns and its environs, but also on Mission Beach, Port Douglas, the Daintree Rain Forest, Cape York, and Outback Queensland. It's open daily from 8:30am to 5:30pm. Closed Christmas and Boxing Day (Dec 26) and after 1pm on public holidays.

CITY LAYOUT   Cairns' downtown precinct is laid out on a grid 5 blocks deep bounded in the east by the Esplanade on the water, and in the west by McLeod Street, where the train station and the Cairns Central shopping mall are located. In between are shops, offices, and restaurants. Cruises to the Great Barrier Reef and other tour boats leave from the edge of this 5-block area, either from Trinity Wharf on Wharf Street, beside the Hilton, or from the adjacent Marlin Marina beside the Pier Mall.

GETTING AROUND   By Bus   Local Sunbus (✆ **07/4057 7411**) buses depart City Place Mall at the intersection of Lake and Shields streets. Buy all tickets and passes on board, and try to have correct change. You can hail buses anywhere it's convenient for the driver to stop. Buses 1, 1A, and 2X (a seasonal June–Nov express service) travel to Trinity Beach; and 1, 1B, 1X (weekend express), and 2X travel to Palm Cove. The "N" route runs along the highway from the city to Palm Cove all night until dawn on Friday and Saturday nights, stopping at all beaches in between. Most other buses run from early morning until almost midnight. A "Beaches" pass allowing 24-hours' unlimited travel as far as the northern beaches is A$8.95 (U.S.$5.80).

By Car   Avis (✆ 07/4051 5911), **Budget** (✆ 07/4051 9222), **Hertz** (✆ 07/4051 6399), and **Thrifty** (✆ 07/4051 8099) all have offices in Cairns city and at the airport. One long-established local outfit, **Sugarland Car Rentals,** has reasonable rates and offices in Cairns (✆ 07/4052 1300) and Palm Cove

---

⟨Tips⟩ Staying Connected

You can surf the Web and check your e-mail at **Travellers' Contact Point,** in the offices of The Adventure Company, 2nd floor, 13 Shields St. (✆ **07/ 4041 4677;** fax 07/4041 1338), for A$1 (U.S.65¢) per hour. You can also send and receive faxes, and have snail mail sent here. It's open daily from 8am to 8pm. Other central Internet access is at **Global Gossip,** 125 Abbott St (✆ 07/4031 6411) and **internetcafe@thepier** (✆ 07/4051 7941), which as its name implies is at the Pier.

Croc Alert!
Dangerous crocodiles inhabit Cairns waterways. Do not swim in, or stand on the bank of, any river or stream.

(℅ 07/4059 1087). **Britz Australia** (℅ 1800/33 1454 in Australia), **Budget Campervan Rentals** (℅ 07/4032 2065), **Koala Campervan Rentals** (℅ 07/4053 6740), and **Maui Rentals** (℅ 07/4051 3010) rent motor-homes. Britz and most major rental-car companies rent four-wheel-drives.

By Taxi or Limousine   Call **Black & White Taxis** at ℅ **13 10 08**. For a transfer or guided tour by town car or stretch limo, try **Black & White Limousines** (℅ **13 19 08** in Cairns, or 07/4051 5074). Cairns has several limousine operators.

DAY TRIPS TO THE REEF

Cairns passengers can board the most luxurious vessel visiting the Reef, the **Quicksilver Cruises** wavepiercer in Cairns (℅ **07/4031 4299;** www.quicksilver-cruises.com) at the Marlin Marina at 8am and at Palm Cove Jetty on Cairns' northern beaches at 8:30am. It arrives at Port Douglas at 9:30am and leaves for the Reef at 10am. All of these trips run daily except Christmas. The fare for the whole day for Cairns and Palm Cove passengers is A$160 (U.S.$104) for adults, A$82.50 (U.S.$53.60) for kids ages 4 to 14. A free pickup from your hotel is included in the price.

If you prefer to visit the Reef straight from Cairns, large-scale operator **Great Adventures** (℅ **07/4044 9944;** www.greatadventures.com.au) does daily cruises in fast, air-conditioned catamarans to a three-level pontoon on the Outer Reef. The pontoon has a children's swimming area, a semi-submersible, and an underwater observatory. You get at least 3 hours on the Reef. The cost for the day is A$144 (U.S.$93.60) for adults, A$72 (U.S.$46.80) for children ages 4 to 14, and A$360 (U.S.$234) for a family of two adults and two kids. Hotel transfers are available from Cairns and the northern beaches for an extra cost. The boat departs the Great Adventures terminal at Trinity Wharf near the Hilton.

You have an option to depart Cairns with Great Adventures at 8:30am and spend 2 hours on Green Island en route. This gives you time to walk nature trails, rent snorkel gear and water-sports equipment, or laze on the beach before continuing to the Outer Reef. This cruise costs an extra A$16 (U.S.$10.40) per adult and A$8 (U.S.$5.20) per child.

Sunlover Cruises (℅ **1800/810 512** in Australia, or 07/4050 1333; www.sunlover.com.au) has a choice of Outer Reef trips aboard its large, fast catamarans. One trip stops at Fitzroy Island for a guided rain-forest walk before heading on to Moore Reef on the Outer Reef. Transfers from city and northern beaches hotels are included. The day costs A$142 (U.S.$92.30) adults, A$71 (U.S.$46.15) for children ages 4 to 14, and A$335 (U.S.$217.75) for a family of four. This trip consists of 1 hour on Fitzroy and about 3 on the Reef and includes a guided snorkel safari.

Another Sunlover trip departs Cairns and picks up passengers at Palm Cove before heading to Arlington Reef. In total, you spend about 4 hours on the Reef. The price is A$126 (U.S.$81.90) for adults, A$63 (U.S.$40.95) for kids, and A$315 (U.S.$204.75) for a family.

Introductory dives on either trip cost A$93 (U.S.$60.45), while certified divers pay A$83 (U.S.$53.95), including all gear. Both cruises include lunch and transfers from Cairns and northern beaches hotels. Both boats depart Trinity Wharf in Cairns at 9:30am daily.

Great Adventures, Quicksilver, and Sunlover all offer helicopter flights over the Reef from their pontoons—a truly spectacular experience. There are also fly/cruise and fly/fly day trips (in which you travel both ways by plane).

An alternative to motoring to the Reef is to sail to it. **Ocean Spirit Cruises** (© 07/4031 2920; www.oceanspirit.com.au) operates two sailing cats that take no more than or 100 or 150 passengers to Michaelmas Cay or Upolu Cay, lovely white-sand cays on the Outer Reef surrounded by rich reefs. This trip is a good value, since it includes a pleasant 2 hours sailing to either cay, a guided snorkeling safari, guided beach walk, and a free glass of bubbly and live music on the way home—in addition to the usual reef ecology talks, semi-submersible rides, lunch, and transfers from your Cairns or northern beaches hotel. Another plus is that you spend your out-of-water time on a beautiful beach, not on a pontoon or boat deck. You get about 4 hours on the Reef.

The day trip to Michaelmas Cay is A$150 (U.S.$97.50) for adults, A$75 (U.S.$48.75) for children ages 4 to 14, and A$415 (U.S.$269.75) for a family of two adults and two kids. The day trip to Upolu Cay costs A$122 (U.S.$79.30) for adults, A$61 (U.S.$39.65) for kids, and A$330 (U.S.$214.50) for a family. Transfers from Cairns and the northern beaches are free, but from Port Douglas they cost an extra A$37.50 (U.S.$24.40) adults and A$18.50 (U.S.$12) children. Introductory dives cost A$85 (U.S.$55.25) and certified divers pay A$53 (U.S.$34.45) for one or A$85 (U.S.$55.25) for two, all gear included. An introductory dive/sail package to Upolu costs A$180 (U.S.$117) per person. The boats depart Marlin Marina at 8:30am daily.

WHAT TO SEE & DO IN & AROUND CAIRNS

If you're staying in Cairns, also check out what there is to see and do in and around Port Douglas (see section 3 of this chapter) and Mission Beach (see section 4 of this chapter). Many tour operators in Port Douglas, and a few in Mission Beach, offer transfers from Cairns.

LEARNING ABOUT ABORIGINAL CULTURE

Tjapukai Aboriginal Cultural Park ⋒⋒⋒   Don't miss this. The Tjapukai (pronounced Jab-oo-gai) cultural park is one of the best chances you'll have to discover the history and culture of the Aboriginal people without going to Central Australia. The center was founded in 1987 by American theater director and accountant Don Freeman and his French Canadian show-dancer wife, Judy. The Freemans worked closely with local Aborigines, including acclaimed dancer and songwriter David Hudson, to establish a small dance theater in Kuranda, which has evolved into the multi-award-winning cultural park you see today. Don and Judy are still heavily involved, but the park is 51% owned by the Aboriginal people who work in it.

Housed in a striking modern building that incorporates Aboriginal themes and colors, the Tjapukai experience needs at least 2 to 3 hours, but you will leave with insight into the history and culture of the traditional people of the Kuranda region.

The Creation Theatre is a mix of culture and technology, where the latest in illusion, theatrics, and technology are used to tell the story of the creation of the world according to the spiritual beliefs of Tjapukai people. Actors interact with spectacular special effects and holographic images, sometimes up to 3 meters

Travel Tip
Unless you are sure which tours you want to take, it often pays to wait until you get to Cairns to book them. Local travel agents, your hotel or B&B host, and other travelers in Cairns are the best sources of advice. Cairns has about 600 tour operators, so even in peak season, it is rare for a tour to be booked up more than 24 hours in advance.

(9¾ ft.) high, to illustrate the legends. The production is performed in the Tjapukai language, translated through headsets.

Move on through the Magic Space museum and gallery section of the complex to the History Theatre, where a 20-minute film relates the history of the Tjapukai people since the coming of white settlers 120 years ago.

Outside, a suspension bridge links the main building with a cultural village where you can try boomerang and spear throwing, fire-making and didgeridoo playing, and learn about bush foods and medicines. In the open-sided Dance Theatre, Aboriginal men and women perform dances incorporating ancient and modern steps. Shows and demonstrations are planned so visitors can move from one to another easily, without missing anything. The complex also includes a restaurant and coffee shop, and an arts-and-crafts gallery and shop is stocked with the work of local Aboriginal artists and crafts workers.

Captain Cook Hwy. (beside the Skyrail terminal), Smithfield. ☎ 07/4042 9999. Fax 07/4042 9988. www.tjapukai.com.au. Admission A$28 (U.S.$18.20) adults, A$14 (U.S.$9.10) children 4–14, A$67.50 (U.S.$43.90) family of 4. AE, DC, MC, V. Ask about packages that include transfers, lunch and a guided Magic Space tour, or Skyrail and/or Scenic Rail travel to and from Kuranda on the same day. Daily 9am–5pm. Closed Christmas and New Year's Day. Bus: 1C, 1E, 1G, or 1H. Book shuttle transfers from Cairns and northern beaches hotels (A$15/U.S.$9.75 adults and A$7.50/U.S.$4.90 children) through the park. Park is 15 min. north of Cairns and 15 min. south of Palm Cove along the Captain Cook Hwy. Free parking.

MORE ATTRACTIONS IN CAIRNS
Hartley's Creek Crocodile Farm   The star of the show at this modest working crocodile farm is Charlie, a giant croc who's been in residence (and captivity) since 1934, when he was estimated to be about 10 years old. Hartley's claims to be the original Australian croc show, and the best time to visit is for the 3pm "croc attack" show, when you can witness the infamous saltwater crocodile "death roll" during the 45-minute performance. At 11am you can see these monsters get hand-fed or hear an eye-opening talk on the less aggressive freshwater crocodiles. Kids will enjoy patting koalas and learning about dingoes and other Aussie animals at the 30-minute mammal talk at 1pm; at 2pm there is a snake show about Australia's venomous reptiles; and at 4pm it's koala-feeding time. This attraction makes a good stop en route to Port Douglas, and is also the place to ensure you get to see a cassowary. Crocodiles never move much except when they eat, so go at show time to see them in action.

Capt. Cook Hwy. (40km/24 miles north of Cairns, 25km/15 miles south of Port Douglas). ☎ 07/4055 3576. Fax 07/4059 1017. www.hartleyscreek.com. Admission A$16 (U.S.$10.40) adults, A$14 (U.S.$9.10) students, A$8 (U.S.$5.20) children 4–14, A$40 (U.S.$26) family pass for 2 adults and unlimited kids. Daily 8:30am–5pm. Closed Christmas. Transfers available through Coral Coaches (☎ 07/ 4031 7577).

Royal Flying Doctor Visitors Centre   The Royal Flying Doctor Service (RFDS), the free aeromedical service that provides a "mantle of safety" for all Outback Australians, has a base in Cairns. You can watch a film and attend a talk on how the service began, browse through memorabilia, and board a former RFDS plane. Allow about 45 minutes.

1 Junction St., Edge Hill. (© 07/4053 5687. Admission A$5 (U.S.$3.25) adults, A$2.50 (U.S.$1.60) children, A$15 (U.S.$9.75) family pass for 2 adults and unlimited kids. Mon–Sat 9am–5pm. Closed Good Friday and Christmas. Bus: 6 or 6A

Wild World-The Tropical Zoo   Get a dose of your favorite Aussie wildlife here—some kind of talk or show takes place just about every 15 or 30 minutes throughout the day, including koala cuddling and talks (have your photo taken cuddling one for an extra A$12/U.S.$7.80), saltwater crocodile feeding and talks, lorikeet feeding, cane toad racing, and snake talks. Lots of other animals are on show, too, like kangaroos (which you can hand-feed for A$1/U.S.65¢ a bag), emus, cassowaries, dingoes, and native birds in a walk-through aviary. The park also runs a nocturnal tour, in which you can see many of the more elusive creatures on show. To take the park's Cairns Night Zoo tour, book by 4pm that day, earlier if you want transfers. The evening includes: a wildlife spotlighting walk, where you can pat a koala and a possum and feed kangaroos; a stargazing interlude; a barbecue dinner with beer and wine, billy tea and damper and supper; and dancing to an Aussie bush band.

Captain Cook Hwy. (22km/13 miles north of the city center), Palm Cove. (© 07/4055 3669. Fax 07/4059 1160. www.wildworld-aus.com.au. Admission A$22 (U.S.$14.30) adults, A$11 (U.S.$7.15) children 4–15. Cairns Night Zoo experience A$69 (U.S.$44.85) adults, A$34.50 (U.S.$22.40) children 4–15. AE, DC, DISC, MC, V. Daily 8:30am–5pm. Closed Christmas. Bus: 1B. Cairns Night Zoo transfers through All In A Day ((© 07/4032 5050), or Beaches Meet & Greet ((© 07/4055 7575). Free parking.

EXPLORING THE ISLANDS

You don't have to go all the way to the outer Reef to see coral. Less than an hour from the city wharf, Green Island has snorkeling equal to that on the Great Barrier Reef. Fitzroy Island has rain-forest walks, coral accessible by dive and snorkel boat trips from the island, and water sports. See "Where to Stay," later in this section, for details of the resorts on both islands.

GREEN ISLAND   This 15-hectare (37-acre) coral cay, surrounded by dazzling coral and marine life, is just 27 kilometers (17 miles) east of Cairns. You can rent snorkel gear, windsurfers, and paddle-skis; take glass-bottom-boat trips; go parasailing; take an introductory or certified dive; walk vine-forest trails; or laze on the beach. The beach is coral sand, so it's a little rough underfoot. Day visitors can use one of Green Island Resort's pools, its main bar, casual or upscale restaurants, and lockers and showers; they can buy basics, ice cream, and beachwear. Ask beach staff for their recommendations for the best snorkeling spots. If you don't snorkel, it's worth the meager admission charge to see the magical display of clown fish, potato cod, and anemones at the little underwater observatory, despite its cloudy old viewing windows. The island has a small attraction called Marineland Melanesia, where you can see old nautical artifacts, primitive art, a turtle and reef aquarium, and live crocodiles, including Cassius, said to be the biggest saltwater croc in captivity. Admission is A$8.50 (U.S.$5.55) adults, A$4 (U.S.$2.60) kids; croc shows are at 10:30am and 1:45pm.

Great Adventures (© 07/4044 9944; www.greatadventures.com.au) and **Big Cat Green Island Reef Cruises** (© 07/4051 0444; www.bigcat-cruises. com.au) both make trips to Green Island from Cairns. Expect to pay around A$60 (U.S.$39) for a half-day trip with snorkel gear or a glass-bottom-boat cruise. A full-day trip can be as much as A$90 (U.S.$58.50), but Big Cat makes a day trip for as little as A$52 (U.S.$33.80). Big Cat's boat is slower, but you still get 5½ hours on the island. Both companies pick up from hotels in Cairns, the northern beaches, and Port Douglas for an extra cost; Big Cat also runs to the island direct from Palm Cove.

FITZROY ISLAND Scenic Fitzroy Island is a rain-forested national park 45 minutes from Cairns, offering good diving. You can rent windsurfers, catamarans, and canoes; hike to the mountain-top lighthouse; view coral from a glass-bottom boat or take a short boat trip from the island to snorkel it; take a beginner's or certified dive; and swim in the pool. A day trip is simply the price of the ferry fare at A$36 (U.S.$23.40) round-trip, A$18 (U.S.$11.70) for kids 4 to 14, or A$90 (U.S.$58.50) for a family of four. There are three departures a day. Book on ℭ **07/4030 7907,** or through **Raging Thunder Adventures** (ℭ **07/4030 7990;** www.ragingthunder.com.au). Raging Thunder also runs guided sea-kayak expeditions around Fitzroy Island. The trips include transfers from your Cairns hotel and a boat transfer to the island, 3 hours of kayaking, snorkeling gear, lunch on a deserted beach, and a rain-forest walk to the lighthouse. The full-day trip costs A$135 (U.S.$107.25). You can also stay on the island for as little as A$31 (U.S.$20.15) per person per night in multishare bunkhouse accommodation (See "Where to Stay," later in this chapter).

EXPLORING THE WET TROPICS RAIN FOREST

The 110-million-year-old World Heritage–listed Daintree Rain Forest, 2 hours north of Cairns, gets most of the attention (see the "Port Douglas, Daintree & the Cape Tribulation Area" section, later in this chapter), but tracts of rain forest closer to Cairns are just as pristine. These rain forests and the Daintree are part of the Wet Tropics, a World Heritage area that stretches from Cape Tribulation to Townsville. This dense, lush environment has remained unchanged by Ice Ages and other geological events, and today the plants and animals here retain primitive characteristics. Within the tract's mangroves, eucalyptus woodlands, and tropical rain forest are 65% of Australia's bird species, 60% of its butterfly species, and many of its frogs, reptiles, bats, marsupials, and orchids.

Because so much rain-forest wildlife is nocturnal and often difficult to spot, consider joining **Wait-A-While Environmental Tours** (ℭ **07/4033 1153**). Wait-A-While's naturalist guides take you into restricted parts of the forest to spot a range of wildlife: musky-rat kangaroos, platypus, ring-tailed possums, cassowaries, amethystine pythons, birds, and tree frogs. They use only low-wattage bulbs and quiet four-wheel-drive or off-road vehicles to minimize their impact on the animals. Tours, which go to either the Atherton Tableland or the Daintree wilderness, depart Cairns daily at 2pm and return around midnight or 1am. The cost, A$132 (U.S.$85.80) for adults and A$97 (U.S.$63.05) for children under 15, includes binoculars, torches (flashlights), reference books, National Park permits, dinner (either in a country restaurant or a picnic dinner), and candlelit supper in the rain forest. Tour groups include no more than eight people. The Atherton Tableland trip is best for viewing wildlife; the Daintree trip is more about getting back to a true wilderness.

Just over 50 kilometers (30 miles) southwest of Cairns in the Wooroonooran National Park are the rain-forested slopes of Mt. Bartle Frere, at 1,622 meters (5,320 ft.) the highest peak in Queensland. **The Adventure Company** (ℭ **07/ 4051 4777;** www.adventures.com.au) runs 2- and 4-day hikes on the mountain, camping out in hammocks.

A SIDE TRIP TO KURANDA, A RAIN-FOREST VILLAGE ✿

Few travelers visit Cairns without making at least a day trip to the mountain village of Kuranda, 34 kilometers (20½ miles) west of Cairns near the Barron

Wildlife-Viewing Tip

If you want to spot wildlife, be careful which rain-forest tour you pick. To avoid contact with humans on the coast, rain-forest animals are increasingly retreating to higher altitudes; however, most tour operators to the Daintree and Cape Tribulation National Parks customarily stick to the lowlands. Many people on those day tours end up saying "But where are all the animals?" The afternoon-into-night trips offered by Wait-a-While Environmental Tours offer the most wildlife-viewing-for-your-buck.

Gorge National Park. Although it's undeniably touristy, the cool mountain air and mist-wrapped rain forest refuse to be spoiled, no matter how many tourists clutter the streets. The shopping in Kuranda—for leather goods, Australian-wool sweaters, opals, crafts, and more—is more individual and unusual than in Cairns, and the handful of cafes and restaurants are much more atmospheric. The town is easily negotiated on foot, so pick up a visitors' guide and map at the Skyrail gondola station or train station (see below for how to get there) when you arrive.

GETTING THERE

Getting to Kuranda is part of the fun. Some people drive up the winding 25-kilometer (15-mile) mountain road, but undoubtedly the most popular routes are to chuff up the mountainside in a scenic train, or to glide silently over the rain-forest canopy in the world's longest gondola cableway, the Skyrail Rainforest Cableway.

The most popular way to get there is to go one way on the Skyrail (mornings are best for photography from the Skyrail) and the other way on the train.

BY SKYRAIL   The **Skyrail Rainforest Cableway** ☆☆☆ (© **07/4038 1555;** www.skyrail.com.au) is a magnificent feat of engineering and one of Australia's top tourism attractions. About 114 six-person gondolas leave every few seconds from the terminal in the northern Cairns suburb of Smithfield for the 7.5-kilometer (4½-mile) journey. The view of the coast as you ascend is so breathtaking that even those afraid of heights will find it worthwhile overcoming their nervousness. As you rise over the foothills of the coastal range, watching the lush green of the rain forest take over beneath you. Looking back, there are spectacular views over Cairns and north towards Trinity Bay. On a clear day, you can see Green Island. There are two stops along the way—at Red Peak and Barron Falls—and about 90 minutes is needed to make the trip properly. After about 10 minutes, you reach Red Peak. You are now 545 meters (1,787½ ft.) above sea level, and massive kauri pines dominate the view. You must change gondolas at each station, so take the time to stroll around the boardwalks for the ground view of the rain forest. Guided walks are run every 20 minutes.

On to Barron Falls station, built on the cleared site of an old construction camp for workers on the first hydroelectric power station on the Barron River in the 1930s. A rain-forest information center has been established here, and there are boardwalks to the lookouts for wonderful views of the Barron Gorge and Falls. From Barron Falls station, the gondola travels over the thickly rain-forested range, and it's easy to spot ferns and orchids and the brilliant blue butterflies of the region. As you reach the end of the trip, the gondola passes over the Barron River and across the Kuranda railway line into the station. A one-way ticket is A$30 (U.S.$19.50) for adults and A$15 (U.S.$9.75) for children ages 4 to 14; a round-trip ticket, including transfers from your Cairns or northern beaches hotel, is A$60 (U.S.$39) for adults, A$30 (U.S.$19.50) for children, or A$150 (U.S.$97.50) family, and A$73 (U.S.$47.45) for adults, A$36.50 (U.S.$23.70) for children or A$182.50 (U.S.$118.60) family from Port Douglas. You must make a reservation to travel within a 15-minute segment. Don't worry if it rains on the day you've chosen to go—one of the best trips I've made on Skyrail was in a misty rain, which added a new dimension to the rain forest. The cableway operates from 8am to 5pm, with last boarding at the Cairns end at 3:45pm. The Skyrail terminal is on the Captain Cook Highway at Kamerunga Road, Caravonica Lakes, 15 kilometers (9 miles) north of Cairns' city center.

BY SCENIC RAILWAY The 34-kilometer (20½-mile) Kuranda Scenic Railway (© 1800/620 324 in Australia, or 07/4031 3636; www.traveltrain.qr.com.au) is rated as one of the top five scenic rail journeys in the world. The train snakes through the magnificent vistas of the Barron Gorge National Park, past gorges and waterfalls on the 90-minute trip from Cairns to Kuranda. It rises 328 meters (1,076 feet) and goes through 15 tunnels before emerging at the pretty Kuranda station, which is smothered in ferns. Built by hand over 5 years in the late 1880s, the railway track is today a living monument to the 1,500 men who toiled to link the two towns, and the ride on the historic steam train adds to the atmosphere. It departs Cairns Central at 8:30 and 9:30am Sunday through Friday every day except Christmas and leaves Kuranda at 2 and 3:30pm Sunday through Friday. (Saturday departure from Cairns Central is at 8:30am only, with return trip at 3:30pm only.) The fare is A$29.60 (U.S.$19.25) one-way for adults, A$19.50 (U.S.$12.70) for Australian seniors and students (no discounts for international visitors), and A$15 (U.S.$9.75) for children ages 4 to 14. A pass for a family of four (only available Mon and Thurs–Sat) is A$74.20 (U.S.$48.10) one-way.

SKYRAIL/TRAIN COMBINATION TICKETS In most cases, these packages represent convenience rather than savings. A package combining one-way travel on the Skyrail and a trip back on the Scenic Railway is A$59.60 (U.S.$38.75) for adults and A$30 (U.S.$19.50) for children; A$66.60 (U.S.$43.30) for adults and A$33.50 (U.S.$21.80) for kids with round-trip transfers from Cairns or the northern beaches. A shuttle bus operates between the Skyrail terminal and the nearest train station at Freshwater, 7 kilometers (4 miles) away, for A$4 (U.S.$2.60) adults, A$2 (U.S.$1.30) kids one-way. A three-way package including the Skyrail, the Scenic Railway, and entry to the Tjapukai Aboriginal Cultural Park (see above) is A$86.60 (U.S.$56.30) for adults and A$43.50 (U.S.$28.30) for kids, or A$100.60 (U.S.$65.40) for adults and A$50.50 (U.S.$32.80) for kids including transfers from Cairns/northern beaches. A Skyrail/Scenic Railway/Rainforestation option is A$98.10 (U.S.$63.75) for adults. Book packages through Skyrail, Queensland Rail, or the Tjapukai Aboriginal Cultural Park.

BY BUS White Car Coaches (© 07/4091 1855) operates several daily bus services to Kuranda departing from 48 Spence St., Cairns. The fare is A$7 (U.S.$4.55) for adults, A$3.50 (U.S.$2.25) for kids ages 4 to 12.

EXPLORING KURANDA

Kuranda is known for its markets that sell locally made arts and crafts, fresh produce, boomerangs, T-shirts, and jewelry. There are two markets—the small "original" markets behind Kuranda Market Arcade (open Wed–Fri and Sunday; © 07/4093 8060), which mainly sell cheap imports; and the 90-stall Heritage markets (open daily 9am–3pm), which offer better quality and a wider variety of goods. Try to visit Kuranda Wednesday through Friday or Sunday when both markets are open.

Even the Heritage markets are being invaded by commercial imported products, and in response, a group of about 50 local artisans sell their work in the **Kuranda Arts Co-Operative** ⚓, 20 Coondoo St. (✆ **07/4093 9026**), open from 10am to 4pm daily. You will find quality furniture crafted from recycled Australian hardwoods, jewelry, handcrafts, and all kinds of stuff here.

You can explore the rain forest, the river esplanade, or Barron Falls along a number of easy walking tracks. If you want to learn about the rain forest, explore it with Brian Clarke of **Kuranda Riverboat & Rainforest Tours** (✆ **07/4093 7476**), who runs informative 45-minute river cruises. The cruises depart regularly from 10:15am to 2:30pm from the riverside landing across the railway footbridge near the train station. He also runs a daily 400-meter (1,312-ft.) walk through the rain forest, leaving at 11:45am and returning at 12:45pm. Brian is a former professional crocodile hunter and has lived in the rain forest for more than 30 years. The cruise or the walk costs A$12.50 (U.S.$8.10) for adults, A$6 (U.S.$3.90) for children 5 to 15, and A$30 (U.S.$19.50) for families. Buy your tickets on board.

KURANDA'S NATURE PARKS

Of Kuranda's two walk-through aviaries, **Birdworld** (✆ **07/4093 9188**), behind the Heritage Markets off Rob Veivers Drive, is probably the most interesting, as it has eye-catching macaws and a cassowary. **The Aviary,** 8 Thongon St. (✆ **07/4093 7411**), is good if you want to see a bigger range of Australian species. Birdworld is open daily from 9am to 4pm; admission is A$11 (U.S.$7.15) for adults, A$4 (U.S.$2.60) for children. The Aviary is open from 10am to 4pm; admission is A$10 (U.S.$6.50) for adults, A$9 (U.S.$5.85) for seniors and students, A$4.50 (U.S.$2.90) for kids ages 4 to 16, and A$25 (U.S.$16.25) for a family of four. Both aviaries are closed Christmas.

Australian Butterfly Sanctuary ⚓ A rainbow-hued array of 1,500 tropical butterflies—including the electric blue "Ulysses" and Australia's largest species, the Cairns birdwing—is housed in a lush walk-through enclosure here. Take the free guided tour and learn about the butterfly's fascinating life cycle. The butterflies will land on you if you wear pink, red, and other bright colors.

8 Rob Veivers Dr. ✆ 07/4093 7575. Fax 07/4093 8923. www.australianbutterflies.com. Admission A$12 (U.S.$7.80) adults, A$11 (U.S.$7.15) seniors, A$5 (U.S.$3.25) children 5–16; family pass A$28 (U.S.$18.20) for 2 adults and 2 kids; extra child A$4 (U.S.$2.60). AE, DC, MC, V. Daily 9:45am–4pm. Free guided tours every 15 min.; last tour departs 3:15pm. Closed Christmas. On-street parking. Bus stop 7-min. walk away.

Rainforestation Nature Park At this 40-hectare (100-acre) nature and cultural complex, you can take a 45-minute ride into the rain forest in a World War II amphibious Army Duck. You'll hear commentary on orchids and other rain-forest wildlife along the way. You can also see a performance by Aboriginal dancers; learn about Aboriginal legends and throw a boomerang on the Dreamtime Walk; or have your photo taken cuddling a koala in the wildlife park. You can do any of these activities separately, or do them all (except cuddle a koala) in a package that costs A$32.50 (U.S.$21.10) for adults, A$16.25 (U.S.$10.55) for kids ages 4 to 14, or A$81.25 (U.S.$52.80) for a family of five. Koala photos are A$11.50 (U.S.$7.50). The Army Duck runs on the hour beginning at 10am; the Aboriginal dancers perform at 11:30am and 2pm; and the 30-minute Dreamtime Walk leaves at 11am, noon, 1:30, and 2:30pm.

Travel Tip

If you visit Kuranda, don't forget to bring some warm clothing in winter. It can get nippy in the mountains, especially at night.

On the Kennedy Hwy., a 5-min. drive from the center of Kuranda. ℭ 07/4093 9033. Fax 07/4093 7578. www.rainforest.com.au. Shuttle from outside Skyrail/train terminal 9:45–11am and the Australian Butterfly Sanctuary 10am–2:45pm. A$6 (U.S.$3.90) adults, A$3 (U.S.$1.95) children, and A$15 (U.S.$8.95) family, round-trip. AE, DC, MC, V. Daily 9am–4pm. Closed Christmas. Ample parking.

WHITE-WATER RAFTING & OTHER THRILLS

The **Adventure Company** (see below) offers a wide range of outdoor adventures, from hiking or biking through the rain forest to sea kayaking in the Great Barrier Reef Marine Park. It also offers white-water rafting, bungee jumping, hot-air ballooning, four-wheel-driving, sky diving, and other high-octane thrills.

RnR Rafting ⚜ (ℭ 07/4051 7777) and **Raging Thunder Adventures** (ℭ 07/4030 7990; www.ragingthunder.com.au) serve as one-stop booking shops for action pursuits in and around Cairns, including hot-air ballooning, skydiving, jet-boating, horse riding, ATV (All-Terrain Vehicle) safaris, parasailing, and rafting. Ask them about multipursuit packages.

BIKING   **Dan's Mountain Biking** (ℭ 07/4033 0128) runs a wide range of full- and half-day guided tours in small groups from A$65 to $125 (U.S.$42.25–$81.25) per person.

BUNGEE JUMPING   Contact **A. J. Hackett Bungy** (ℭ 07/4057 7188). The cost is A$99 (U.S.$64.35) per person. Free transport is provided to the site, which is 20 minutes north of town on McGregor Road.

FISHING   Cairns is the world's giant black marlin capital. Catches of more than 1,000 pounds hardly raise an eyebrow in this neck of the woods. The game-fishing season is September through December, with November the busiest. Book early, as game boats are reserved months in advance. Game fishers can also battle Pacific sailfish, dogtooth and yellow-fin tuna, Spanish mackerel, wahoo, dolphinfish, barracuda, and tiger shark. Reef anglers can expect to land coral trout, red emperor (sea perch), and sweetlip. Mangrove jack, barramundi, and tarpon lurk in the estuaries. Call **Destination Cairns Marketing,** Shop 5 in the Hilton Hotel complex, Wharf Street (ℭ **1800/807 730** in Australia, or 07/4051 4107), to book a charter. Expect to pay around A$400 (U.S.$260) per person per day for heavy-tackle game fishing, A$190 to $250 (U.S.$123 to $162) for light tackle stuff, A$100 to $145 (U.S.$65 to $95) for reef fishing, and A$120 (U.S.$78) for a day or A$60 (U.S.$39) for a half day in the Cairns Inlet estuary.

WHITE-WATER RAFTING   Several companies offer exciting white-water-rafting trips from Cairns on the Grade 3 to 4 **Tully River** ⚜⚜, 90 minutes south of Cairns near Mission Beach; the Grade 3 Barron River in the hills behind the city; and the Grade 4 to 5 rapids of the inland Johnstone River. One of the best is **RnR Rafting** (ℭ 07/4051 7777), or book through The Adventure Company, above.

One-day trips on the Tully are suitable for all ages and abilities and are the most popular (see the description in "The North Coast: Mission Beach, Townsville & the Islands" section, later in this chapter). The trip costs A$128 (U.S.$83.20) from Cairns, or A$138 (U.S.$89.70) from Port Douglas, including transfers.

Fun Fact **You Too Can Be a Survivor**

Always fancied yourself as a contestant on the hit TV series *Survivor?* Here's a chance to prove yourself, by taking a tour of the Queensland outback where *Survivor 2—The Australian Outback* was filmed.

There is only one tour that will take you to the exact location, on Goshen Station, about 3 hours southwest of Cairns, where the survivor tribes tested their mettle. Officially sanctioned by the producers of *Survivor* and the owners of Goshen Station, the tour visits the sites used by the Kucha and Ogakor tribes and explores the harsh but beautiful countryside.

The tour is run by the Cairns-based **Adventure Company Australia** (*℃* **07/4051 4777;** fax 07/40514888; www.adventures.com.au). For 8 days, participants pit their mental and physical skills against the Outback in an adventure tour which includes biking, canoeing, and hiking the Savannah lands surrounding the mighty Herbert River of North Queensland. On the 8th day, tour members vote for the "most likely survivor" among the group—but sadly, without the massive cash prize.

Tours depart Cairns every Sunday May through November, and are likely to run under the *Survivor* banner until at least 2003. The cost is A$1,590 (U.S.$1,033.50) for adults and A$1390 (U.S.$903.50) for children ages 8-13. The last Sunday departure of the month is available for families with children as young as 8 years. The minimum age on all other tours is 14. Cost includes all meals from lunch on day 1 to lunch on day 8, basic accommodation and camping, all equipment for listed activities including camping gear, safety equipment, bandanna, water bottle, and transfers.

Closer to Cairns, the gentler **Barron River** is good choice for the timid. The half-day trip with RnR Rafting costs about A$79 (U.S.$51) from Cairns or A$90 (U.S.$58) from Port Douglas, including pickup from your accommodations and 2-hours' rafting.

WHERE TO STAY

High season in Cairns includes 2 weeks at Easter, the period from early July to early October, and the Christmas holiday through January. Book ahead in those periods, and in low season (Nov–June) many hotels offer discount rates or are willing to negotiate.

Cairns has a good supply of affordable accommodations, both in the heart of the city and along the northern beaches. Or you can choose to stay in the peaceful village of Kuranda, or get away from it all at an island resort.

Don't think you have to stay in Cairns city if you don't have a car. Most tour and cruise operators will pick you up and drop you off in Cairns, on the northern beaches, or even in Port Douglas (see section 3, later in this chapter).

IN CAIRNS

Unless noted otherwise, all accommodations below are within walking distance of shops, restaurants, cinemas, the casino, the tourist office, bus terminals, the train station, and the departure terminals for Great Barrier Reef cruises.

Very Expensive

Hotel Sofitel Reef Casino   Arguably the most stylish five-star property in Cairns, this six-story hotel is 1 block from the water, with partial water views from some rooms, and nice city/hinterland outlooks from others. All the rooms, which have lots of light and higher-quality fittings than the average five-star digs, come with Jacuzzis, bathrobes, and small balconies with smart timber furniture. The Cairns casino is attached to the hotel (see "Cairns After Dark," below).

35–41 Wharf St., Cairns, QLD 4870. (℃) **1800/808 883** in Australia, 800/221 4542 in the U.S. and Canada, 020/8283 4500 in the U.K., 0800/44 4422 in New Zealand, or 07/4030 8888. Fax 07/4030 8777. www.accorhotel.com. 128 units. A$320–$600 (U.S.$208–$390) double; A$710–$2,000 (U.S.$461.50–$1,300) suite. Extra person A$33 (U.S.$21.45). Children under 15 stay free in parents' room using existing bedding. AE, DC, MC, V. Free valet and self-parking. Airport shuttle. **Amenities:** 3 restaurants; bar; smallish rooftop pool with sun deck; health club; Jacuzzi; sauna; concierge; tour desk; business center; 24-hr. room service; babysitting; dry cleaning/laundry service. *In room:* A/C, TV/VCR, dataport, minibar, hair dryer, iron, safe.

Radisson Plaza Hotel 🄖   There's a definite "wow!" factor to this hotel on Trinity Bay. When you walk into the lobby, you're surrounded by rain forest. Tall trees (real ones) and cockatoos (papier-mâché) give the place a great atmosphere. Sporting the best views of any city-center hotel, the rooms were renovated in 1999 with smart maple entryways and a gold, burgundy, and navy decor. Each has a VCR, a balcony, and a view of the harbor, the city, tropical gardens, or the big free-form pool. The bathrooms all have marble and maple fittings, and big corner tubs. The hotel is connected to The Pier shopping mall and is next to the Great Barrier Reef cruise terminals.

Pierpoint Rd., Cairns, QLD 4870. (℃) **1800/333 333** in Australia and New Zealand, 800/333-3333 in the U.S. and Canada, 0800/37 4411 in the U.K., 1800/55 7474 in Ireland, or 07/4031 1411. Fax 07/4031 3226. www.radisson.com/cairnsau. 219 units. A$368–$407 (U.S.$239–$264) double; A$539–A$1,012 (U.S.$350–$658) suite. Extra person A$33 (U.S.$21.45). Children under 17 stay free in parents' room using existing bedding. AE, DC, MC, V. Free outdoor and covered self-parking. Airport shuttle. **Amenities:** 2 restaurants (seafood, tropical, local cuisine); bar; large outdoor swimming pool and children's pool; nearby golf course; health club; Jacuzzi; sauna; concierge; tour desk; business center; shopping arcade; 24-hr. room service; in-room massage; babysitting; dry cleaning. *In room:* A/C, TV with pay movies, stocked minibar, coffeemaker, hair dryer, iron, safe.

Expensive

Matson Resort Cairns   Despite its lack of obvious glitz, the 14-story Matson has been the choice of a number of movie stars—most famously Marlon Brando—while on location in Cairns. A 20-minute waterfront walk from downtown, the hotel offers a range of accommodations, from hotel rooms to four-bedroom penthouses, which have been refurbished over the past 4 years. The one- and two-bedroom apartments look out to the sea; hotel rooms have sea or mountain views. The rooms are spacious, but the bathrooms are not, perhaps reflecting the hotel's Japanese market. Out back are cheaper studios and apartments, with newly upgraded furnishings, and out front is a pretty free-form pool and sun deck.

The Esplanade (at Kerwin St.), Cairns, QLD 4870. (℃) **1800/079 105** in Australia, or 07/4031 2211. Fax 07/4031 2704. www.matsonresort.com.au. 342 units. A$220–$260 (U.S.$143–$169) double; A$150 (U.S.$97.50) studio; A$165–$310 (U.S.$107.25–$201.50) apt (sleeps 2–5). Extra person A$25 (U.S.$16.25). Ask about Reef and golf packages. AE, DC, MC, V. Free covered parking. Courtesy transfers to and from airport, and there's a hotel-shuttle service around the city several times a day. Bus stop about 100 meters (328 ft.) from the hotel. **Amenities:** 2 restaurants and bars (International fine dining, International buffet); 3 outdoor swimming pools; golf course about 20 min. away; 2 day/night tennis courts; health club with facilities including aerobics classes; Jacuzzi; sauna; bike rental; concierge; tour and car-rental desk; 24-hr. room service; massage (in-room or at the health club); babysitting; coin-operated laundry and laundry service; same-day dry cleaning; nonsmoking rooms. *In room:* A/C, TV with pay movies, dataports in some rooms, kitchenette in studios and apts only, stocked minibar in hotel rooms and apts, unstocked refrigerator in studios, hair dryer, iron, safe.

Oasis Resort Cairns So what if downtown Cairns doesn't have a beach? You've got a neat little sandy one right here—and a swim-up bar to boot—at the large free-form swimming pool at this attractive six-story resort built in 1997. All the colorful, contemporary rooms have balconies with views over the tropical gardens, mountains, or the pool. The suites, with a TV in the bedroom and a large Jacuzzi bathtub, could well be the best-value suites in town.

122 Lake St., Cairns, QLD 4870. © 1300/65 6565 in Australia, 800/221-4542 in the U.S. and Canada, 020/8283 4500 in the U.K., 0800/44 4422 in New Zealand, or 07/4080 1888. Fax 07/4080 1889. www.oasis-cairns.com.au. 314 units. A$205 (U.S.$133) double; A$372 (U.S.$242) suite. Extra person A$32.50 (U.S.$21.15). Children under 17 stay free in parents' room using existing bedding. Free crib. Ask about packages. AE, DC, MC, V. Free valet and self-parking. Airport shuttle. **Amenities:** Restaurant, 2 bars; outdoor pool; health club; concierge; tour desk; room service (6:30am–10:30pm); babysitting; coin-operated laundry or laundry service; dry cleaning. *In room:* A/C, TV with pay movies, dataport, stocked minibar, hair dryer, iron, safe.

Moderate

Tuna Towers The harbor views at this multistory motel and apartment complex are better than those at most of the five-star hotels in Cairns. Two blocks from town, the accommodations are a good size, with fresh, appealing furnishings, and modern bathrooms. If your balcony does not have a water vista, it has a nice aspect of the city or mountains instead.

145 The Esplanade (at Minnie St.), Cairns, QLD 4870. © 1800 117 787 in Australia, or 07/4051 4688. Fax 07/4051 8129. www.tunatowers.com.au. 60 units. A$124 (U.S.$80.60) double, A$140 (U.S.$91) studio apt double; A$167 (U.S.$108.55) suite. Extra person A$10 (U.S.$6.50). AE, DC, MC, V. Limited free parking. Airport shuttle. **Amenities:** Restaurant; small outdoor pool; golf course (1km/¹⁄₂ mile away); 4 day/night tennis courts 200m (656 ft.) away; access to nearby health club; Jacuzzi; tour desk; car-rental desk; limited room service; massage; babysitting; coin-operated laundry; dry cleaning. *In room:* A/C, TV, dataport, kitchenettes in suites and studios, coffeemaker, hair dryer, iron.

Inexpensive

Coral Tree Inn The focal point of this airy, modern resort-style motel just a 5-minute walk from the city center is the clean, friendly communal kitchen that overlooks the small palm-lined pool and newly paved sun deck. It's a great spot to cook up a steak or reef fish fillet on the free barbecue and join other guests at the big communal tables. Local restaurants deliver, free fresh-roasted coffee is on the boil all day, and a vending machine sells wine and beer, so you don't even have to go down to the pub for supplies! The smallish, basic but neat motel rooms have painted brick walls, terra-cotta tile or carpeted floors, and clean new bathrooms sporting marble-look laminate countertops. In contrast, the eight suites are huge and stylish enough to do any corporate traveler proud. They are some of the best-value accommodations in town. All rooms have a private balcony or patio; some look out onto the drab commercial buildings next door, but most look out over the pool. Ask about packages that include cruises and other tours.

166–172 Grafton St., Cairns, QLD 4870. © 07/4031 3744. Fax 07/4031 3064. www.coraltreeinn.com.au. 58 units. A$110 (U.S.$71.50) double; A$136 (U.S.$88.40) suite. Additional person A$10 (U.S.$6.50). AE, DC, MC, V. Limited free parking; ample on-street parking. Airport shuttle. **Amenities:** Bar; outdoor pool; access to nearby health club; bike rental; tour desk; car-rental desk; babysitting; coin-operated laundry and laundry service; same-day dry cleaning; nonsmoking rooms. *In room:* A/C, TV, dataport, kitchenette in suites, fridge, coffeemaker, hair dryers, iron, safe (at reception).

Lilybank Bed & Breakfast ๙ This lovely 1870s Queenslander homestead, originally the mayor's residence, is in a leafy suburb 6 kilometers (3³⁄₄ miles) from the airport and a 10-minute drive from the city. Guests sleep in large, attractive rooms, all individually decorated with such features as wrought-iron beds and patchwork quilts. Each bathroom is different, too, although all are comfortable and a good size. The largest room has French doors opening onto a "sleep-out," an enclosed veranda with two extra beds. You can also stay in the gardener's cottage, renovated with slate floors, stained-glass windows, a king-size bed, and a bar. The house is set in gardens with a picturesque rock-lined salt-water pool. Breakfast is served in the relaxed garden room by the fishpond. Your hosts are Mike and Pat Woolford, and you share the house with three poodles, an irrepressible galah, and a giant green tree frog. There's a guest TV lounge, a guest kitchen, and phone, fax and e-mail access. Many tours pick up at the door, and several good restaurants are a stroll away, so you don't need a car to stay here. No smoking indoors.

75 Kamerunga Rd., Stratford, Cairns, QLD 4870. © 07/4055 1123. Fax 07/4058 1990. www.lilybank.com.au. 6 units (4 with shower only). A$88–$110 (U.S.$57.20–$71.50) double. Additional person A$33 (U.S.$21.45). Rates include full breakfast. AE, MC, V. Free parking. Bus: 1E or 1F. Taxi from airport approx. A$15 (U.S.$9.75). Children not permitted. **Amenities:** Outdoor pool; tour desk; car-rental desk; massage can be arranged; coin-operated laundry. *In room:* A/C, hair dryer.

ON THE NORTHERN BEACHES

Cairns has a string of white sandy beaches starting 15 minutes north of the city center. Trinity Beach, 15 minutes from the airport, is secluded, elegant, and scenic. The most upscale is Palm Cove, 20 minutes from the airport. Here rainbow-hued shops and tasteful apartment blocks nestle among giant paperbarks and palms fronting a postcard-perfect beach. It has several advantages over other beach suburbs: a nine-hole resort golf course and a gym are within walking distance, the Quicksilver Wavepiercer Great Barrier Reef cruise boat picks up passengers here daily, and it has the greatest choice of places to eat. Add 5 to 10 minutes to the traveling times above to reach the city.

Very Expensive

Sebel Reef House ☆☆☆   Picture yourself inside a Somerset Maugham novel—but substitute the Queensland tropics for Singapore—and you've almost got it right. This must be one of the most romantic hotels in Queensland, or all of Australia. The white walls are swathed in bougainvillea, and the beds with mosquito netting. Airy interiors are furnished with rustic handmade artifacts and white wicker furniture. The seven Veranda rooms, which have a Jacuzzi on the balcony, overlook the pool, waterfalls, and lush gardens and there are all the extra touches such bathrobes and CD player, as well as generous balconies within earshot of the ocean. Built in 1958, the Reef House's guest list has read like an excerpt from Who's Who—the most recent addition being Bob Dylan and his band. But no matter who you are, I guarantee you will never want to leave.

99 Williams Esplanade, Palm Cove, Cairns, QLD 4879. © 1800/079 052 in Australia, or 07/4055 3633. Fax 07/4055 3305. www.reefhouse.com.au. 69 units (14 with shower only). A$270–$440 (U.S.$175.50–$286) double; A$440–$560 (U.S.$286–$364) suite. Extra person A$30 (U.S.$19.50). Children under 14 stay free in parents' room using existing bedding. AE, DC, MC, V. Free undercover parking (for limited number of cars); ample on-street parking. Courtesy airport shuttle. Bus: 1, 1B, 1X, 2X, or N. **Amenities:** Restaurant, bar, cafe, honor bar; 3 small outdoor pools; nearby golf course; access to nearby health club; 2 Jacuzzis available on the beach opposite the hotel (run by independent operators); concierge; tour desk; room service (6:30am–9:30pm); resident massage therapist; babysitting; coin-operated laundry or laundry service; same-day dry cleaning. *In room:* A/C, TV/VCR, kitchenette, stocked minibar, coffeemaker, hair dryer, iron, safe

Expensive

Courtyard by Marriott Great Barrier Reef Resort   A huge, sprawling free-form pool and sun deck winding under a canopy of palms is the focal point of this comfortable four-story resort right opposite the beach. All the same reasonable size, the rooms were renovated in 1999. Pool-view rooms have the most restful vistas; the "ocean view" is largely obscured by trees, and some "garden views" really just look onto the street.

Tips **Safe Swimming**

All of the northern beaches have small, netted enclosures for safe swimming October through May, when deadly box jellyfish (stingers) render all mainland beaches in north Queensland off-limits.

Williams Esplanade (at Veivers Rd.), Palm Cove, Cairns, QLD 4879. © 800/321-2211 in the U.S. and Canada, 0800/221 222 in the U.K. or 171/591 1500 in London, 0800/441 035 in New Zealand, 1800/251 259 in Australia or 02/9251 5522 in Sydney, or 07/4055 3999 for the resort. Fax 07/4055 3902. www.courtyard.com. 189 units. A$237–$296.50 (U.S.$154.05–$192.75) double; A$312–$388 (U.S.$202.80–$252.20) suite. Extra person A$32.50 (U.S.$21). Children under 17 stay free in parents' room using existing bedding. Ask about packages. AE, DC, MC, V. Bus: 1, 1B, 1X, 2X, or N. Shuttle to and from airport, city wharf, and train station. Valet and self-parking. **Amenities:** Restaurant; coffee shop, bistro, 2 bars; outdoor pool; golf course nearby; day/night tennis court; health club; spa; water-sport rental; bicycle rental; concierge; tour desk; car-rental desk; room service (6:30am–10pm); massage available (must be pre-booked); babysitting (must be pre-booked); coin-op laundry; same-day dry cleaning; nonsmoking rooms. *In room:* A/C, TV with pay movies, dataport, stocked minibar, coffeemaker, hair dryer, iron, safe.

Moderate

The Reef Retreat 🐨🐨 Tucked back one row of buildings from the beach is this little gem—a low-rise collection of contemporary studios and suites built around a swimming pool in an almost mystically peaceful grove of palms and silver paperbarks. All the rooms in the newer or extensively renovated wings have cool tile floors and smart teak and cane furniture, and about half of them have been freshly painted. The studios are a terrific value and much larger than the average hotel room. In some of the studios, you can even lie in bed and see the sea. The extra-private honeymoon suites have a Jacuzzi and a kitchenette outside on the balcony, where you can hide behind timber blinds. There's a barbecue on the grounds and a Jacuzzi. There's no elevator. Serviced twice weekly; one free service for stays of 5 days or longer. Extra services A$16 (U.S.$10.40)

10–14 Harpa St., Palm Cove, Cairns, QLD 4879. © 07/4059 1744. Fax 07/4059 1745. www.reefretreat.com.au. 36 units (16 with shower only, 20 with shower and Jacuzzi). A$130 (U.S.$84.50) studio double; A$140–$160 (U.S.$91–$104)) suite; A$250 (U.S.$162.50) 2-bedroom apt (sleeps 4). Additional person A$22 (U.S.$14). Children under 3 stay free in parents' room if they use existing bedding; crib A$22 (U.S.$14). AE, DC, MC, V. Free parking. Bus: 1, 1B 1X, 2X, or N. Airport shuttle. **Amenities:** Pool; nearby golf course; 100m (328 ft.) to tennis courts; spa; tour desk; car-rental desk; coin-operated laundry and laundry service; dry cleaning. *In room:* A/C, TV, fax, dataport, kitchenette, fridge, coffeemakers, hair dryer, iron.

Inexpensive

Ellis Beach Oceanfront Bungalows 🐨 *Finds* Set on what is arguably the loveliest of the northern beaches, about 30 minutes from Cairns, these bungalows are set under waving palm trees between the Coral Sea and a backdrop of mountainous rain forest. The beach is patrolled by lifeguards, and there are stinger nets in season as well as a shady swimming pool and toddlers' wading pool. There's plenty of privacy and the one- and two-bedroom bungalows are basic but pleasant. You can sit on the veranda and gaze at the ocean (keep an eye out for dolphins). Each bungalow has full kitchen facilities (with microwave, fridge, and freezer), and there are coin-operated barbecues and phone and fax facilities.

Captain Cook Highway, Ellis Beach, QLD 4879 . © 1800 637 036 in Australia, or 07/4055 3538. Fax 07/4055 3077. www.ellisbeachbungalows.com.au. ellisbeach@internetnorth.com.au. 15 units (all with shower only). A$150 (U.S.$97.50) double per night. Extra person A$15 (U.S.$9.75) per night. Children under 3 stay free. Cribs A$5 (U.S.$3.25) per night. AE, MC, V. **Amenities:** Restaurant; 2 pools; golf course nearby; tour desk; car-rental desk, coin-operated laundry . *In room:* A/C and ceiling fans, TV, kitchen, iron.

ON AN ISLAND

Several island resorts are located off Cairns. They afford you safe swimming year-round, because the October-to-May infestations of deadly marine stingers don't make it to the islands.

Very Expensive

Green Island Resort ⚅   Step off the beach at this Great Barrier Reef national-park island, and you are surrounded by acres of coral. Green Island is a coral cay, not a continental island like most others off Cairns. The resort itself is a high-class cluster of rooms tucked away in a dense vine forest. Each room is private, roomy, and elegantly outfitted, with polished wooden floors and a balcony looking into the forest. Windsurfing, paddle skiing, canoeing, diving and snorkeling (both on the island and on day trips to the outer Reef), learn-to-dive courses, glass-bottom-boat trips, walking rain-forest trails, parasailing, and beach volleyball are among the activities available, or you can simply laze on the coarse white-coral sand. Helicopter and seaplane flights and cruises are available to the Outer Reef. Many activities and equipment are free for guests, such as non-motorized sports, snorkel gear, and glass-bottom-boat trips, while there's a charge for scuba diving and other activities using fuel. Both the island and the resort are small, so you can feel a bit cramped when the day-trippers from Cairns descend; but after most of them leave at 4:30pm, the place is blissfully peaceful.

27km (17 miles) east of Cairns. P.O. Box 898, Cairns, QLD 4870. © **1800/67 3366** in Australia, or 07/4031 3300. Fax 07/4052 1511. www.greenislandresort.com.au. 46 units. A$455 (U.S.$296) double; A$555 (U.S.$360.75) suite. Extra person A$69 (U.S.$45). Ask about packages. AE, DC, MC, V. Great Adventures (© 07/4044 9944) runs transfers (50 min.) from Cairns 3 times a day for A$46 (U.S.$30) adults, A$23 (U.S.$15) children 4–14, round-trip. Helicopter and seaplane transfers are available through resort. **Amenities:** 2 restaurants (International, seafood), bar; 2 outdoor freshwater pools; wide array of water-sports equipment available; tour desk; free guest laundry. *In room:* A/C, TV, free cable TV, minibar, hair dryer, safe.

Lizard Island ⚅⚅⚅   Black marlin, huge potato cod so tame divers can pet them, snorkeling right off the beach, and isolation—that's what lures well-heeled Americans, Europeans, and Aussies to this exclusive resort. Lizard is a rugged 1,000-hectare (2,470-acre) national-park island on the Great Barrier Reef, grassy and sparse but beautiful, ringed by 24 white sandy beaches, with stunning fringing reefs and giant clams. No day-trippers bother you. Many activities are free: snorkeling and glass-bottom-boat trips, windsurfing, sailing catamarans, paddle-skis, fishing tackle, tennis, and hiking trails, such as the muscle-straining 545-meter (⅓-mile) climb to Cook's Look, where Captain Cook spied his way out of the treacherous reefs in 1770. You pay for fishing and diving trips to nearby Reef sites, including Cod Hole. The dive shop conducts introductory dives, night dives, and 5-day learn-to-dive courses. Lizard's waters are home to the world-record black marlin; half- and full-day game-fishing trips are available.

The resort underwent a renovation in July 2000. Accommodations, which are freestanding lodges tucked under palms along the beach or up the cliff, are of elegant timber and stone construction, in a casual tropical style, with earth-toned finishes, a CD player, modem outlets, bathrobes, and a balcony facing the sea. The larger open-plan villas and one-bedroom suites, some of them split-level, have big decks and the best views. A guest lounge has fax and Internet facilities, and there's also a book and games library.

240km (149 miles) north of Cairns; 27km (16¾ miles) offshore. P&O Australian Resorts, G.P.O. Box 478, Sydney, NSW 2001. © **1800/737 678** in Australia, 800/225-9849 in the U.S. and Canada, 020/7805 3875 in the U.K., 02/9277 5050 (Sydney reservations office), or 07/4060 3999 (the island). Fax 02/9299 2477 (Sydney reservations office) or 07/4060 3991 (the island). www.poresorts.com.au. 40 units (all with shower only). A$1,200–$1,900 (U.S.$780–$1,235) double. Extra person A$350 (U.S.$227). Rates include all meals and many activities. Ask about packages; some combine stays at Silky Oaks Lodge (Port Douglas), Sebel Reef House (Cairns), and Bedarra Island (off Mission Beach). AE, DC, MC, V. Transfers are by twice-daily 1-hr. flight from Cairns (book through Qantas); round-trip advance purchase fare is A$380 (U.S.$247) per person. Aircraft luggage limit 15kg (33 lb.) per person. Air-charter transfers also available. No children under 10. **Amenities:** Restaurant (candlelit dinners by the sea can be arranged); freshwater pool; night/day tennis court; small exercise room; spa offering massage, facials, and other pampering treatments; laundry service (but no dry cleaning). *In room:* A/C and fans, dataport, stocked minibar, coffeemaker, hair dryer, iron.

Moderate/Inexpensive

Fitzroy Island Resort   This is probably the most affordable island resort on the Great Barrier Reef. It's targeted at a young crowd looking for action and eco-fun in a pristine, beautiful location. It's no glamour-puss palace, but the place was revamped in 2000 to sport a new Hard Rock Café–style restaurant, spruced-up linens and upholstery, and a makeover around the pool area. Fitzroy is a continental island offering little in the way of fringing coral and only a few narrow strips of coral sand. What it does have are catamarans, outrigger canoes, and surf skis; glass-bottom-boat rides; and hiking trails through dense national-park forest to a lighthouse. Divers can make drift dives over the reefs dotted around the island to see manta rays, reef sharks, turtles, and plenty of coral. There is good snorkeling at two points around the island that you can reach twice a day on the dive boat, at an extra fee. You can also catch the Sunlover Cruises day trip to the outer Great Barrier Reef. The dive shop runs introductory and certified dives and certification courses. Each of the modestly comfortable beach cabins has a queen-size bed and two bunks in the back, and the rooms have ceiling fans and a large balcony with views through the trees to the sea. The bunkhouse accommodations are basic fan-cooled carpeted rooms with bunks and/or beds. Bunkhouse guests can use the communal kitchen if they BYO supplies from the mainland.

The restaurant is moderately priced, a kiosk sells cheap take-out food, and the poolside grill and bar does casual meals. The Raging Thunder Beach Bar, billed as "the only nightclub on the Reef," really gets going Friday and Saturday nights.

35km (22 miles) southeast of Cairns. P.O. Box 1109, Cairns, QLD 4870. ℂ **07/4051 9588.** Fax 07/4052 1335. www.fitzroyislandresort.com.au. 52 cabins (all with shower only); 32 bunkhouses, none with private bathroom. Cabins A$220 (U.S.$143) double. Extra person A$35 (U.S.$22.75). Bunkhouses A$31 (U.S.$20.15) per person per bed (sharing with up to 3 other people); A$116 (U.S.$75.40) double (sole use); A$124 (U.S.$80) family bunkhouse. AE, DC, MC, V. Round-trip transfers 3–4 times daily from Cairns (approx. 45 min.) cost A$36 (U.S.$23.40) adults, A$18 (U.S.$11.70) children 4–14. **Amenities:** 2 restaurants, bar; small outdoor pool; water-sports equipment; tour desk. *In room* (cabins only): TV, minifridge, hair dryer, iron.

WHERE TO DINE
IN CAIRNS
Expensive

Fishlips Bar & Bistro 𝒜𝒜 MODERN AUSTRALIAN/SEAFOOD   Ask locals where they go for seafood—as opposed to where they send tourists—and they direct you to this 1920s bluebird-blue shack about 2 kilometers (1¼ miles) from town on a non-descript section of Sheridan Street. Chef Ian Candy is renowned for thinking up new ways to present seafood and cooking it with flair, and for the second year in a row Fishlips has won Cairns' best seafood restaurant award. All dishes come in small or large servings, and the popular local barramundi, or "barra," shows up in two incarnations, maybe beer-battered with rough-cut chips (fries) and fresh tartar sauce, or simply grilled. There are plenty of non-seafood options as well, such as wok-tossed crocodile with cumin and fenugreek spice in Chinese potato nest with garlic mayo and beetroot chutney.

There's a vegetarian choice on every menu, too, such as roast tomato risotto. How nice to see that more than 20 choices on the wine list come by the glass. Dine inside (air-conditioned for those humid nights) or on the front deck, with its bright blue pots and palm trees. Licensed Sunday through Thursday, and BYO wine only (no BYO beer or spirits).

228 Sheridan St. (between Charles and McKenzie sts.) ℂ 07/4041 1700. Reservations recommended. Main courses A$18.50–$32 (U.S.$12–$21). AE, DC, MC, V. Fri noon–2:30pm; daily 6pm–late

Red Ochre Grill ₢ GOURMET BUSH TUCKER You could accuse this restaurant/bar of using weird and wonderful Aussie ingredients as a gimmick to pull in crowds, but the diners who flock here know good food when they taste it. Daily specials are big on fresh local seafood, such as tempura bugs (a delectable crustacean) on lemongrass skewers. On the regular menu is emu pate with bush tomato-chili jam and fresh damper, and wallaby topside done over a mallee-fired grill (mallee is a wood) with sweet potato mash. You can even eat the Aussie coat of arms by ordering a game platter of kangaroo and emu served with native warrigal spinach and yam gratin. Although the place is slick enough for a night out, it is also informal enough for a casual meal.

43 Shields St. ℂ 07/4051 0100. www.redochregrill.com.au. Reservations recommended. Main courses A$8.50–$18 (U.S.$5.50–$11.70) at lunch, A$24–$30 (U.S.$11.40–$16.25) at dinner. Australian game platter A$38 (U.S.$20.80) per person; seafood platter A$48 (U.S.$27.30) per person. AE, DC, MC, V. Mon–Sat noon–3pm; daily 6–10:30pm or whenever the last diners leave.

Moderate

Mediterraneo ITALIAN Friendly, professional service and talented chefs keep the locals coming back here for more. Many of the menu's classic dishes come with a modern twist, and of course there are the traditional favorites, with all the pasta made fresh on the premises every day. The decor is trendy but not showy, just a polished concrete floor, framed sketches on the wall, and timber tables. There's also a courtyard out the back. BYO.

74 Shields St. ℂ 07/4051 4335. Reservations recommended on weekends. Main courses A$18.50–$23.80 (U.S.$12–$15.50); pasta A$13.50–$17.50 (U.S.$8.75–$11.40). MC, V. Tues–Sun 6–10:30pm or whenever the last diners leave.

Tim's Surf & Turf (Value STEAK/SEAFOOD For huge hearty meals at unbeatable prices, you can't go wrong at this cheerful chain outlet overlooking Trinity Inlet. The seafood platters, oysters, thick grain-fed steaks, pastas, roasts, quiche, and other simple fare are all cooked with skill.

Upstairs, Trinity Wharf 28–34 Wharf St (end of Abbott St.). ℂ 07/4031 6866. Reservations accepted only for groups of 8 or more. Main courses A$7.50–$27.90 (U.S.$4.90–$18); many dishes under A$15 (U.S.$10); kids' menu A$4.50–$4.90 (U.S.$2.90–$3.20). No credit cards. Daily noon–2:30pm and 5:30–9:30pm. Closed Christmas Day, Dec 26, and New Year's Day.

ON THE NORTHERN BEACHES

Colonies MODERN AUSTRALIAN It may not have the ocean frontage of the grander restaurants along Williams Esplanade, but you are still within earshot of the waves from the veranda of this cheery little aerie upstairs behind a seafront building. The atmosphere is simple enough for a morning coffee, and special enough at night for a full-fledged dinner banquet of mussels sautéed in white wine, followed by peppered lamb fillet in red wine and herbs with a port mint glaze. The long menu includes loads of inexpensive choices at both lunch and dinner, such as pastas, vegetable soups, green chicken curry, and hot savory scones (biscuits) with bacon and melted cheese. The yummy desserts include banana splits and "spacacamino," vanilla ice cream dressed with Scotch whisky, and freshly ground coffee beans. Licensed and BYO.

Upstairs in Paradise Village shopping center, Williams Esplanade, Palm Cove. (℗ **07/4055 3058**. Fax 07/4059 1559. www.palmcoveonline.com/colonies/. Reservations recommended at dinner. Main courses A$15–$26.90 (U.S.$10–$17.50). AE, DC, MC, V. Daily 7:30am–10:30pm. Closed mid-Jan to mid-Mar. Bus: 1, 1B, 1X, 2X, or N.

Far Horizons MODERN AUSTRALIAN   You can't quite sink your toes into the sand, but you are just yards from the beach at this pleasant restaurant within the Angsana Resort. The laid-back fine-dining fare includes plenty of fresh seafood—the catch of the day comes with chunky homemade chips and tartare, and there's interesting choices like Vietnamese salad with chargrilled reef fish. The restaurant sometimes sets up dining on the lawn among the palm trees beside the beach. The service is relaxed and friendly and the crowd is a mix of hotel guests from this and other nearby resorts. On Friday and Saturday nights a guitarist plays in the cocktail bar.

Angsana resort, 1 Veivers Rd. (southern end of Williams Esplanade), Palm Cove. (℗ **07/4055 3000**. Reservations recommended. Main courses A$23.50–$28.50 (U.S.$15.20–$18.50). AE, DC, MC, V. Daily 6:30pm–midnight (last orders at 9:30pm). Bus: 1, 1B, 1X, 2X, or N.

CAIRNS AFTER DARK

Cairns is not big on after-hours action. The **Hotel Sofitel Reef Casino,** 35–41 Wharf St. (℗ **07/4030 8888**), has two levels of blackjack, baccarat, reef routine, roulette, sic-bo, money wheel, paradise pontoon, Keno, and slot machines. It's open from 10am to 4am Monday through Thursday, and 24 hours from 10am Friday until 4am Monday (and closed Good Friday, Anzac Day, and Christmas). The hotel also puts on a dinner show, where you sit among rain-forest plants in a giant glass-domed conservatory. It takes place every night except Sunday and costs A$80 (U.S.$52) per person. The hotel also has Cairns's hottest nightclub, **Casino Nightclub 1936,** located underground. It's open Thursday through Saturday from 8pm to late; cover is A$5 (U.S.$3.25).

If you're over 18, but under 35 or so, and it's Friday or Saturday night, you may want to take the 7pm boat to the DJs or live bands at the **Raging Thunder Beach Bar** on Fitzroy Island (see "Where to Stay," above). The boat costs A$18 (U.S.$11.70) round-trip and departs for Cairns at midnight. Book through Raging Thunder Adventures (℗ **07/4030 7990**).

3 Port Douglas ⋆⋆, Daintree & the Cape Tribulation Area

Port Douglas is 67km (40 miles) N of Cairns; Mossman is 19km (11½ miles) N of Port Douglas; Daintree is 49km (29½ miles) N of Port Douglas; Cape Tribulation is 34km (20½ miles) N of Daintree

The tiny fishing village of Port Douglas is the only place in the world where two World Heritage areas—the Daintree Rain Forest and the Great Barrier Reef—lie side by side. This is truly where "the rain forest meets the reef." Just over an hour's drive from Cairns, through rain forest and along the sea, Port Douglas may be a one-horse town, but it's main street is lined with stylish shops and seriously trendy restaurants, and its beautiful Four Mile Beach is not to be missed.

People often base themselves in "Port," as the locals call it, rather than in Cairns, because they like the peaceful rural surroundings, the uncrowded beach, and the charmed absence of tacky development (so far, anyway). Don't think you will be isolated if you stay here—many reef and rain-forest tours originate in Port Douglas and many of the tours discussed in the Cairns section earlier in this chapter pick up from Port Douglas.

Port Douglas, Daintree & Cape Tribulation

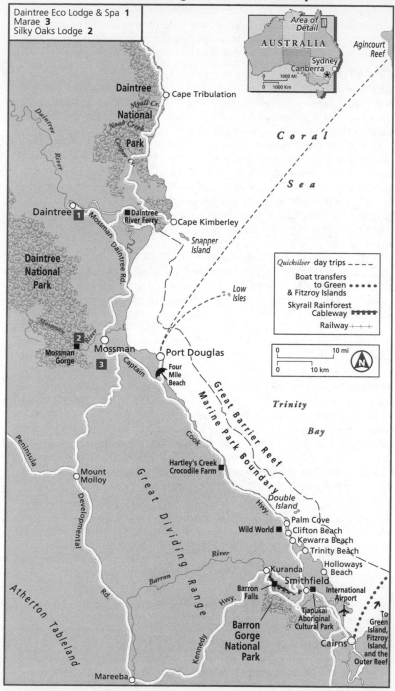

Daintree Eco Lodge & Spa **1**
Marae **3**
Silky Oaks Lodge **2**

Area of Detail

AUSTRALIA

Sydney
Canberra

0   1000 MI
0   1000 Km

Agincourt Reef

Daintree National Park

Cape Tribulation

Myall Cr.

Neab Creek

Coral

Sea

Daintree River

Daintree **1**

Daintree River Ferry

Cape Kimberley

Snapper Island

Mossman Daintree Rd.

Low Isles

Daintree National Park

Quicksilver day trips - - - -
Boat transfers
to Green
& Fitzroy Islands •••••
Skyrail Rainforest
Cableway ▪▪▪▪▪
Railway +–+–+

Mossman River

2

Mossman Gorge

Mossman

3

Captain

Port Douglas

Four Mile Beach

0   10 mi
0   10 km

N

Great Barrier Reef

Marine Park Boundary

Trinity

Bay

Peninsula

Cook

Mount Molloy

Hartley's Creek Crocodile Farm

Great Dividing Range

Developmental

Double Island

Palm Cove

Wild World

Clifton Beach

Kewarra Beach

Trinity Beach

River

Barron

Holloways Beach

Kuranda

Smithfield

Rd.

Barron Falls

International Airport

Barron Gorge National Park

Tjapukai Aboriginal Cultural Park

To Green Island, Fitzroy Island, and the Outer Reef

Atherton Tableland

Kennedy Hwy.

Cairns

Mareeba

283

Daintree National Park lies just north of Port Douglas; and just north of that is Cape Tribulation National Park, another wild tract of rain forest and hilly headlands sweeping down to the sea. Exploring these two national parks is easy on a four-wheel-drive day safari from Port Douglas.

ESSENTIALS

GETTING THERE   Port Douglas is a scenic 65-minute drive from Cairns, in part along a narrow winding road that skirts the coast. Take Sheridan Street north out of the city as it becomes the Captain Cook Highway; follow the signs to Mossman and Mareeba until you reach the Port Douglas turnoff on your right.

One of the most pleasant ways to get to Port Douglas is to take one of the giant **Quicksilver Wavepiercer** (© 07/4099 5500) catamarans along the coast. They depart Marlin Marina in Cairns at 8am, Palm Cove jetty at 8:30am, and arrive in Port Douglas at 9:30am. You can also stay onboard and go straight to the Great Barrier Reef for the day if you like, for an extra charge (see "Discovering the Great Barrier Reef," below). The cost of the trip from Cairns is A$22 (U.S. $14.30) one-way, A$32 (U.S.$21) round-trip, half price for kids ages 4 to 14.

A one-way ticket aboard **Coral Coaches** (© 07/4031 7577) to Port Douglas hotels is A$20.50 (U.S.$13.30) from Cairns city hotels, or A$25 (U.S.$16.25) from the Cairns airport. Fares for children 14 and under are half price. The coaches meet all major flights between 6am and 8:15pm. It's not strictly necessary, but it's a good idea to book; five buses per day are reservations only.

There is no train to Port Douglas, and no scheduled air service. A small airport handles light aircraft and helicopter charters. A **taxi** from Cairns would run around A$94 (U.S.$61.10); call **Black & White Taxis** (© 13 10 08 in Cairns). Limo or town-car transfers from Cairns are another option; try **Black & White Limousines** (© 13 19 08 in Cairns, or 07/4051 5074).

VISITOR INFORMATION   Write for information to the **Port Douglas Daintree Tourism Association,** P.O. Box 511, Port Douglas, QLD 4871 (© 07/4099 4588; www.pddt.com.au). The association has no visitor information office in Port Douglas. Instead, visitors should visit one of several private tour information and booking centers in town. One of the biggest and most centrally located is the **Port Douglas Tourist Information Centre,** 23 Macrossan St. (© 07/4099 5599), open from 7:30am to 6pm daily.

GETTING AROUND   Of the major rental companies, only **Budget** (© 07/4099 4690) and **Avis** (© 07/4099 4331) have offices in Port Douglas. Check out the local companies, including **Port Douglas Car Rental** (© 07/4098 5898) and **Crocodile Car Rentals** (© 07/4099 5555). All rent four-wheel-drives as well as regular vehicles, and these are needed if you plan to drive to Cape Tribulation. If you need a taxi, call **Port Douglas Taxis** (© 07/4099 5345).

Coral Coaches (© 07/4099 5351) makes a circuit of town that stops at most of the places you want to visit, such as the Rainforest Habitat, Four Mile Beach,

---

A Few Safety Tips

The tap water is not safe for drinking in Port Douglas. The water comes from local rivers and streams and can harbor harmful bacteria and tropical bugs. Most hotels provide free bottled water. Deadly marine stingers (jellyfish) infest the water from October through May; swim only in areas partitioned off by stinger nets during those months.

and Marina Mirage. Fares range from A$1.30 to $3.20 (U.S.85¢ to $2.10). The bus starts at 7:30am and runs hourly until 9am, then half hourly until midnight. A good way to get around the town's flat streets is by bike. **Port Douglas Bike Hire** (✆ 07/4099 5799), 40–42 Macrossan St. (opposite Westpac Bank) rents bikes for A$14 (U.S.$9.10) for 24 hours. The shop is open from 9am to 5pm.

EXPLORING THE REEF & THE RAIN FOREST

DISCOVERING THE GREAT BARRIER REEF   Without a doubt the most glamorous large vessels visiting the Outer Reef are the **Quicksilver Wavepiercers** (✆ 07/4099 5500) based in Port Douglas. These ultra-sleek high-speed, air-conditioned 37-meter (121-ft.) and 45.5-meter (149-ft.) catamarans carry 300 or 440 passengers to Agincourt Reef, a ribbon reef 39 nautical miles (72km/43 miles) from shore on the very outer edge of the Reef. After the 90-minute trip to the Reef you tie up at a two-story pontoon, where you spend 3½ hours on the Reef.

Quicksilver departs Marina Mirage at 10am daily except Christmas Day. The cost for the day is A$150 (U.S.$97.50) for adults and half price for kids ages 4 to 14. Coach transfers from your Port Douglas hotel are an extra A$5 (U.S.$3.25) adults, A$2.50 (U.S.$1.60) children. Guided snorkel safaris cost A$31 (U.S.$20.15) per person, and introductory dives cost A$107 (U.S.$69.55) per person. Qualified divers take a dive-tender boat to make two dives for A$104 (U.S.$67.60) per person, all gear included. Because Quicksilver carries so many passengers, it is a good idea to book snorkel safaris and dives in advance.

The dive boat *Poseidon* (see "Diving the Reef," earlier in this chapter) welcomes snorkelers. It presents a Reef ecology talk en route and takes you on a guided snorkel safari. Lunch and transfers from Port Douglas hotels are included in Poseidon's price of A$125 (U.S.$81.25) for adults and A$90 (U.S.$58.50) for children ages 3 to 12.

In addition to its proximity to the Outer Reef, Port Douglas offers easy day-trip access to the Low Isles, two pretty coral-wrapped cays close to shore on the Inner Reef.

Another way to spend a pleasant day on the Great Barrier Reef, closer to shore, is to visit the **Low Isles,** 15 kilometers (9 miles) northeast of Port Douglas. The isles are 3¾-acre (1.5-hectare) coral-cay specks of lush vegetation surrounded by white sand and 55 acres (22 hectares) of coral—which is what makes them so appealing. The coral is not quite as good as the outer Reef's, but the fish life is rich and the proximity makes for a relaxing day.

The trip aboard the 30-meter (98-ft.) luxury sailing catamaran *Wavedancer* (✆ 07/4099 5500), operated by Quicksilver, is A$100 (U.S.$65) per adult, kids 4 to 14 half price, and families A$250 (U.S.$162.50) You have the option of making an introductory scuba dive for an extra A$87 (U.S.$56.55) per person. The *Wavepiercer* departs Marlin Marina in Cairns at 8am and Palm Cove Jetty on the northern beaches at 8:30am to connect with *Wavedancer* departures from Port Douglas. The company picks you up free of charge from your hotel.

Snorkeling specialist boat *Wavelength* (✆ 07/4099 5031) does a half-day morning trip to the Low Isles for just A$83 (U.S.$53.95) for adults, A$60 (U.S.$39) for children ages 2 to 12, or A$223 (U.S.$145) for a family. The trip incorporates a guided beach walk and a snorkeling tour with a marine biologist and includes snorkel gear and transfers from your hotel. Both beginners and experienced snorkelers will like this trip. It departs Wednesday and Saturday from the Wavelength jetty in Wharf Street at 8:30am and returns at 1pm.

EXPLORING DAINTREE NATIONAL PARK & CAPE TRIBULATION

The World Heritage–listed Daintree Rain Forest has remained largely unchanged over the past 110 million years. It is now home to rare plants that provide key links in the evolution story. In the 56,000-hectare (140,000-acre) **Daintree National Park** you will find cycads, dinosaur trees, fan palms, giant strangler figs, and epiphytes like the basket fern, staghorn, and elkhorn. Nighttime croc-spotting tours on the Daintree River vie for popularity with early morning cruises to see the rich bird life. Pythons, lizards, frogs, and electric blue Ulysses butterflies attract photographers, and sport fishermen come here to do battle with the big barramundi.

Just about everyone who visits Port Douglas takes a guided four-wheel-drive day trip into the beautiful Daintree and Cape Tribulation rain forests. Although they are referred to as two separate national parks, the forests that cover them merge into one.

You can rent a four-wheel-drive and explore on your own, but you won't understand much about what you are seeing unless you have a guide to interpret it all for you. Most companies basically cover the same territory and sights, including a 1-hour Daintree River cruise to spot crocs, a visit to the lovely Mardja Botanical Walk, a stroll along an isolated beach, lunch at a pretty spot somewhere in the forest, and a visit to Mossman Gorge. Some tours also go to the picturesque Bloomfield Falls in Cape Tribulation National Park. Expect to pay about A$110 (U.S.$72) per adult and about A$75 (U.S.$49) per child. Trips that include Bloomfield Falls are about A$30 (U.S.$20) more. A plethora of tour operators offers such trips. Among the more established are **Trek North Safaris** (© 07/4051 4328), **BTS Tours** (© 07/4099 5665), and **De Luxe Safaris** (© 07/4098 2097). As is the case in most tourist hot spots, some tour operators battle each other fiercely to pay tour desks the highest commission to recommend their tours, even though those tours may not necessarily be the best ones for your needs. Take tour desks' recommendations with a grain of salt, and ask other travelers for their recommendations. You may not see too much wildlife, as rain-forest animals are either shy, camouflaged, nocturnal, or all three! Most four-wheel-drive tours will pick you up in Port Douglas at no charge, although there is usually a small fee from Cairns and the northern beaches. Floods and swollen creeks can quash your plans to explore the Daintree in the Wet Season (Dec–Mar or Apr), so keep your plans flexible.

If your chosen safari does not visit Mossman Gorge, 21 kilometers (12½ miles) northwest of Port Douglas near the sugar town of Mossman, try to get there under your own steam. The gushing river tumbling over boulders, and the network of short forest walks are magical. (Don't climb on the rocks or enter the river, as strong currents are extremely dangerous and have claimed at least one life in recent years). **Coral Coaches** (© 07/4099 5351) makes runs to the gorge from Port Douglas about 10 times a day for A$22 (U.S.$14.30) round-trip. Pack a picnic and make a pleasant couple of hours of it.

Most four-wheel-drive Daintree tours include a 1-hour cruise on the **Daintree River** 𝒜, but if yours does not, or you want to spend more time on the river, cruises are available on a variety of boats, ranging from open-sided "river trains" to small fishing boats. One of the best cruises is offered by **Dan Irby's Mangrove Adventures** (© 07/4090 7017), whose small open boat can get up side creeks the bigger boats can't. Dan is a wildlife artist and photographer; he takes no more than 10 people at a time on 2-, 3- and 4-hour cruises. Chances are you will spot lots of fascinating wildlife on his 2-hour night cruise. A 2-hour trip

---

Tips Drat Those Aussie Mozzies!

Mozzies, as Aussies call mosquitoes, love the rain forest as much as people do, so throw some insect repellent in your day pack when touring the Daintree and Cape Tribulation.

---

costs A$38.50 (U.S.$25). Night trips depart from the Daintree Eco Lodge, 20 Mossman Daintree Rd., 4 kilometers (2½ miles) south of Daintree village; day trips leave from the Daintree River ferry crossing. Take the Captain Cook Highway north to Mossman, where it becomes the Mossman Daintree Road, and follow it for 24 kilometers (15½ miles) to the signposted turnoff for the ferry on your right. The ferry is 5 kilometers (3 miles) from the turnoff. You'll need a car to get there.

Bird-watchers love the Wet Tropics rain forests of which the Daintree and Cape Tribulation national parks are part. More than half of Australia's bird species have been recorded within 200 kilometers (120 miles) of this area. **Fine Feather Tours** (© 07/4094 1199) offers a full-day bird-watching safari through the Wet Tropics to the edge of the Outback for A$145 (U.S.$94.25), and a morning cruise on the Daintree River for A$90 (U.S.$58.50).

Rainforest Habitat wildlife sanctuary (© 07/4099 3235) is a great place to get to see the animals that are too shy to be spotted in the wild. Here, 150 animal species from the Wet Tropics are gathered in one place for you to see up close. You can see saltwater and freshwater crocodiles, hand-feed kangaroos, and have your photo taken beside (but not holding) a koala (from 10–11am and 3–4pm for the cost of a donation). The highlight is the walk-through aviary, which houses 70 Wet Tropics bird species so tame you can almost touch them. You'll get the most out of your visit if you take one of the excellent free guided tours that leave every hour on the hour between 9am and 3pm. Rainforest Habitat is located on Port Douglas Road at the turnoff from the Captain Cook Highway. It's open daily from 8am to 5:30pm (last entry at 4:30pm); admission is A$18 (U.S.$11.70) for adults, A$16.20 (U.S.$10.50) seniors and students, A$9 (U.S.$5.85) for kids ages 4 to 14. Second child admitted free with a family. Between 8am and 11am, the park serves a champagne buffet breakfast for A$34 (U.S.$22) for adults and A$17 (U.S.$11) for kids, including admission. Allow 2 hours here.

One company that shows you plenty of rain-forest creatures in the wild is **Wait-A-While Environmental Tours** 🛈 (© 07/4033 1153) whose rain-forest wildlife-spotting walks are described in "Exploring the Wet Tropics," under "What to See & Do in & Around Cairns" earlier in this chapter. Port Douglas visitors can join the company's Daintree tour, which departs at 3pm Monday, Wednesday, and Thursday, and gets back around midnight or 1am; the tour costs A$121 (U.S.$79) for adults, A$88 (U.S.$57) for kids under 15.

DISCOVERING ABORIGINAL CULTURE   In addition to Native Guide Safari Tours (see "Exploring Daintree National Park & Cape Tribulation," above), the native KuKu-Yalanji tribe will teach you about bush medicines and foods, Dreamtime legends, and the sacred sites their families have called home for tens of thousands of years. **KuKu-Yalanji Dreamtime Tours** 🛈 (© 07/4098 1305) offers a 1-hour guided walk through the rain forest to see cave paintings and visit "special sites"; the tour is followed by a Dreamtime story over billy tea and damper in a bark warun (a kind of shelter). You can buy artifacts from the tribe's information center, gift shop, and art gallery. The tours depart Monday through Friday at 10, 11:30am, 1, and 2:30pm from the Kuku-Yalangi community on the road to Mossman Gorge (1km/½ mile before you reach the Gorge parking lot). Tours cost A$15 (U.S.$9.75) for adults, A$12 (U.S.$7.80) for seniors and A$7.50 (U.S.$4.90) for children.

Hazel Douglas of **Native Guide Safari Tours** ⚅ (© 07/4098 2206; www. nativeguidesafaritours.com.au) runs an excellent four-wheel-drive tour of the rain forest from an Aboriginal perspective. Hazel is a full-blooded Aboriginal who grew up in a tribal lifestyle in the Daintree. She imparts her traditional knowledge of the plants, animals, Dreamtime myths, and Aboriginal history on a full-day tour departing at 9:15am from your Port Douglas hotel. Passengers from Cairns transfer up on the Quicksilver catamaran and return either by coach (northern beaches) or catamaran (Cairns city). The trip costs A$120 (U.S.$78) for adults and A$80 (U.S.$52) for children ages 3 to 14 from Port Douglas, and A$10 (U.S.$6.50) extra from Cairns or the northern beaches.

MORE TO SEE & DO

Some companies in Cairns that offer outdoor activities will provide pick-ups from Port Douglas hotels. See "White-Water Rafting & Other Thrills" in the Cairns section above for details.

The best outdoor activity in Port Douglas, however, is to do absolutely nothing but laze on spectacular **Four Mile Beach** ⚅⚅. May through September the water is stinger-free. October through April, swim in the stinger safety net. **Get High Parafly** (© 07/4099 6366) offers parasailing, jet-skiing, inflatable tube rides, water-skiing, and other water sports on the beach. Expect to pay around A$30 to $60 (U.S.$19.50–$39) for each activity. A boat runs every hour on the hour between 9am and 5pm from the booking office at Berth C4 at Marina Mirage to the company's beach location at Four Mile Beach.

Visitor greens fees at the championship Sheraton Mirage golf course on Port Douglas Road are A$135 (U.S.$87.75) for 18 holes. Whacking a ball on the hotel's aquatic driving range costs A$6 (U.S.$3.90) for a small bucket of balls, A$12 (U.S.$7.80) for a big one, plus A$2 (U.S.$1.30) for club rental. Contact the **Pro Shop** (© 07/4099 5537).

Mowbray Valley Trail Rides (© 07/4099 3268), located 13 kilometers (8 miles) inland from Port Douglas, offers half-day rides through rain forest and sugarcane fields to Collards Falls, or to a swimming hole in the Hidden Valley, for A$60 (U.S.$39). It also runs full-day trips along the mountainous Bump Track, followed by a dip in a rain-forest pool and barbecue lunch at Mowbray Falls. Transfers from your Port Douglas accommodations are included. Transfers from Cairns are A$15 (U.S.$9.75) per person. **Wonga Beach Trail Rides** (© 07/4098 7583) does 3-hour rides through the rain forest and along Wonga Beach, 35 minutes north of Port Douglas, for A$65 (U.S.$42.25), including transfers from Port Douglas.

Bike 'n' Hike (© 07/4099 4650 for the booking agent) takes small groups biking, hiking, and swimming in natural lagoons in the Hidden Valley in the rain forest near Port Douglas. You don't need to be a strong cyclist to take part. Half-day tours cost A$60 (U.S.$39). Full-day tours cost A$82 (U.S.$53.30). Pickups from your Port Douglas hotel, a 21-speed mountain bike, a snack, drinks (and lunch on the full-day trip) are included. Transfers from Cairns and Palm Cove are extra. Experienced mountain bikers can descend the steep 14-kilometer (8½-mile) Bump Track through dense rain forest from the top of the Great Dividing Range on a half-day trip designed for a maximum of four riders.

> **Tips   The Secret of the Seasons**
>
> High season in Port Douglas is from roughly June 1 through October 31.

Every Sunday, a colorful handicrafts and fresh food market sets up on the lawns under the mango trees beside Dickson Inlet at the end of Macrossan Street. Stalls sell everything from foot massages to fresh coconut milk. It runs from 7:30am to 1pm. While you're here, take a peek, or attend a non-denominational service, inside the pretty timber St. Mary's By The Sea church.

WHERE TO STAY

Port Douglas Accommodation Holiday Rentals (© 1800/645 566 in Australia, or 07/4099 4488; www.portdouglasaccom.com.au) has a wide range of apartments and homes for rent.

VERY EXPENSIVE

Sheraton Mirage Port Douglas ✿✿✿   One of Australia's most luxurious properties, this low-rise Sheraton has 5 acres (2 hectares) of saltwater pools, and a championship Peter Thomson–designed 18-hole golf course. It helps to have a car to stay here: it is a bit too far from Port's main street to walk it, and though it's on the beach, the stinger nets and lifeguards are really too far up the sand to walk. If you're going to pay these rates, upgrade to an extra-large Mirage room with a corner Jacuzzi and king beds. They're better value than the unexciting standard rooms. The 101 privately owned two-, three-, and four-bedroom luxury villas with golf course, garden, or sea views are rented out by Sheraton; the decor varies, but all have a Jacuzzi and two bathrooms. A free shuttle runs from 9am to 6pm to the golf course's country club/health center, to Marina Mirage shopping center, and into town.

Davidson St. (off Port Douglas Rd.), Port Douglas, QLD 4871. © 1800/07 3535 in Australia; 800/325-3535 in the U.S. and Canada; 00800/325 353535 in the U.K., Ireland, and New Zealand; or 07/4099 5888. Fax 07/4099 4424 or Starwood Hotels reservation fax 07/4099 5398. www.sheraton-mirage.com.au. 394 units (including 101 villas). A$590–$790 (U.S.$383.50–$513.50) double; A$950–$1,150 (U.S.$617–$747) 2-, 3-, or 4-bedroom vIlla. Extra person A$70 (U.S.$45.50). Children under 17 stay free in parents' room using existing bedding. Rates include full breakfast. Discounted rates available. AE, DC, MC, V. Free valet and self-parking. Helicopter transfers available. **Amenities:** 3 restaurants, 2 bars; 25-m (82-ft.) outdoor lap pool; 18-hole championship golf course with country club and pro shop, aquatic driving range (with targets in a lake), putting green, and golf clinics; 9 day/night tennis courts; health club; spa; Jacuzzi; bike rental; daily day care for kids under 5, kids' club for children ages 5–15 during school vacations (for a fee); concierge; tour desk; car-rental desk; business center (with extra charge for Internet access); salon; 24-hr. room service; massage; babysitting; dry cleaning; nonsmoking rooms. *In room:* A/C, TV, kitchenette in villas only, stocked minibar in hotel rooms only, coffeemakers, hair dryer, iron, safe.

EXPENSIVE

Port Douglas Peninsula Boutique Hotel ✿✿   Built in 1999 over three levels, this intimate studio apartment hotel fronting Four Mile Beach is one of the nicest places to stay in town. Every apartment features an open-plan living room/bedroom, a contemporary kitchenette (with microwave and dishwasher), and a groovy bathroom boasting a giant double tub (or Jacuzzi, in some units). Corner apartments are a little bigger. The decor is a stylish melange of terracotta, mosaic tiles, granite, and wicker, with classy extra touches like a CD player and boxed Twining's teas. Most have great beach views from the roomy balcony or patio, while a few look onto the green and mauve complex of petite Art Deco–ish pools, waterfalls, hot and cold Jacuzzis, and sun deck rising and falling on several levels. A 2-minute walk brings you to the main street. There's also a picnic hamper service on offer.

9–13 The Esplanade, Port Douglas, QLD 4871. ℂ 1800/676 674 in Australia, or 07/4099 9100. Fax 07/4099 5440. www.peninsulahotel.com.au. 34 units. A$280–$320 (U.S.$182–$208) double. Rates include continental breakfast. Ask about packages. AE, DC, MC, V. Complimentary round-trip transfers from your Cairns hotel, Cairns airport, wharf, or train terminal. Undercover parking. **Amenities:** Restaurant, small bar; pool and Jacuzzi (no kids under 15 without an adult in either); bike rental; tour desk; laundry/dry cleaning. *In room:* A/C, TV/VCR, dataport, kitchenette, coffeemaker, hair dryer, iron, safe.

MODERATE
Archipelago Studio Apartments ⍟   You won't find a friendlier or more convenient place to stay in Port Douglas than these apartments, 10 seconds from the beach and less than 10 minutes' walk from town. Your hosts Wolfgang Klein and Christel Bader are eager to help with tour bookings and to give useful advice—and they also speak fluent German, conversational French and some Spanish. The apartments are on the small side (most suit only three people, at the most), but all are well cared for and were refurbished last year. You can opt for a tiny Garden apartment with a patio; or upgrade to a Balcony or Seaview apartment, both a bit larger and with private balconies. Seaview apartments are quite roomy, have just undergone a complete refurnishing and have side-on views along Four Mile Beach. Towels are changed daily and linen weekly, but general servicing will cost A$20 (U.S.$13) extra. No children under 3 catered for.

72 Macrossan St., Port Douglas, QLD 4871. ℂ 07/4099 5387. Fax 07/4099 4847. www.archipelago.com.au. 21 units (all with shower only). High season A$109–$159 (U.S.$70.85–$103) double; low season A$89–$131 (U.S.$58–$85) double. Additional person A$20 (U.S.$13). 3-night min. stay applies. AE, MC, V. Free undercover parking. **Amenities:** Outdoor saltwater pool; nearby golf course; 6 nearby tennis courts lit for night play; access to nearby health club; spa; tour desk; coin-operated laundry and laundry service; same-day dry cleaning can be arranged; nonsmoking rooms. *In room:* A/C, TV, kitchenette, fridge, coffeemaker, hair dryer.

Port Douglas Retreat   This well-kept two-story studio apartment complex on a quiet street, featuring the white-battened balconies of the Queenslander architectural style, is a good value, because even some of the ritzier accommodation houses in town can't boast its lagoon-like pool surrounded by dense jungle and wrapped by an ample shady sun deck that cries out to be lounged on with a good book and a cool drink. The apartments are not enormous, but are fashionably furnished with terra-cotta tile floors, wrought-iron beds, cane seating, and colorful bedcovers. All have large furnished balconies or patios looking into tropical gardens (some on the ground floor open onto the common-area boardwalk, so maybe ask for a first-floor unit). Town and the beach are a 5-minute walk away. No smoking indoors. The newly opened Cayman Villas (www.caymanvillas.com.au) next door are also run by the same management but are a bit more expensive.

31–33 Mowbray St. (at Mudlo St.), Port Douglas, QLD 4871. ℂ 07/4099 5053. Fax 07/4099 5033. www. portdouglasretreat.com.au. 36 units (all with shower only). High season A$143 (U.S.$93) double; low season A$102 (U.S.$66) double. Crib A$5.50 (U.S.$3.60) per night. AE, MC, V. Security undercover parking. **Amenities:** Outdoor pool; tour desk; car-rental desk; coin-operated laundry. *In room:* A/C, TV with free in-house movies, kitchenette, iron.

INEXPENSIVE
Port O'Call Lodge   There's a nice communal feeling to this modest motel, located on a suburban street a 10-minute walk from town. Backpackers, families, and anyone on a budget seems to treat it like a second home, swapping travel stories as they cook up a meal in the communal kitchen and dining room. The rooms are light, cool, and fresh with tile floors, loads of luggage and bench

space, air-conditioning, and small patios. The compact bathrooms are efficiently laid out with old but neat fixtures (BYO hair dryer). Only the deluxe rooms have a TV, clock radio, self-serve tea and coffee facilities, and a minirefrigerator. The dormitories have private bathrooms and no more than five beds and/or bunks to a room. A new 26-bed bunkhouse opened last year, which includes facilities for travelers with disabilities. At night the lively poolside bistro is the place to be (see "Where to Dine," below). Other facilities include free board games, a pay phone, Internet access, guest safe, and a kiosk.

Port St. at Craven Close, Port Douglas, QLD 4871. ℂ 1800/892 800 in Australia, or 07/4099 5422. Fax 07/ 4099 5495. 28 units (all with shower only). High season (June–Sept) A$89–$99 (U.S.$58–$65) double; low season (Nov–Apr) A$69–$79 (U.S.$45–$51) double. Additional person A$11 (U.S.$7). A$23 (U.S.$15) dorm bed (A$21.50/U.S.$14 for YHA/Hostelling International members). Children under 3 stay free. MC, V. Free minibus to and from Cairns Mon, Wed, and Sat. Free on-site parking. Bus stop at front door. **Amenities:** Restaurant; outdoor pool; 3 golf courses nearby; access to nearby health club; bike rental; tour desk; coin-operated laundry; nonsmoking rooms. *In room:* A/C, TV, refrigerator in double motel rooms.

A LUXURY B&B HIDEAWAY IN THE COUNTRY

Marae *☆☆*   Your hostess Andy Morris has turned her architecturally stunning timber home, on a rural hillside 15 kilometers (9 miles) from Port Douglas, into a glamorous and soothing retreat. The rustic-meets-sleek contemporary bedrooms have white mosquito nets and smart linens on timber beds, and elegant bathrooms. The downstairs room opens onto a plunge pool overlooking the valley. Wallabies and bandicoots (a kind of small marsupial) feed in the garden, kingfishers and honeyeaters use the pool, and butterflies are everywhere. You can laze on the two decks, or wander the rain-forest trails of Mossman Gorge just a few miles away.

Lot 1, Chook's Ridge, Shannonvale (P.O. Box 133, Port Douglas, QLD 4871). ℂ 07/4098 4900. Fax 07/4098 4099. www.marae.com.au. 3 bedrooms (2 with shower only). A$130 (U.S.$84.50) double. Min. 2-night stay. Rates include full breakfast. MC, V. From Port Douglas take Captain Cook Hwy. toward Mossman for 10km (6 miles), turn left onto Mt. Molloy turnoff for 1km (½ mile), then turn right onto Ponzo Rd. for 2km (1¼ miles); Chook's Ridge is on your left. You need your own transport. Undercover parking. Pets by arrangement. No children under 13 allowed. **Amenities:** Outdoor pool; nearby golf course; tour desk; use of laundry; nonsmoking rooms. *In room:* A/C, TV, hair dryer.

HIDEAWAYS IN THE RAIN FOREST

Daintree Eco Lodge & Spa *☆☆*   Acclaimed nature-documentary-maker David Attenborough described a stay at this luxury eco-resort as "one of the most magical experiences of my life." Who wouldn't think so, after waking up suspended over a burbling creek in a swish villa in the rain-forest canopy? A multi-award winner for "green tourism," this place hosts only a small number of guests and has a position right in the primeval forest (rather than on the forest's edge like Silky Oaks Lodge, below) that gives it a special sense of peace. Don't think "eco" means sacrificing creature comforts: the big rooms were refurbished in 2000 and boast marble floors, exotic timber and bamboo furniture, and smartly tiled bathrooms with robes. Five have Jacuzzis on the balcony. You may be disappointed to encounter the fine insect screens around your quarters, even the balcony, but they are essential for blocking mosquitoes. All drinking and shower water is pure rainwater from the waterfall.

The health spa offers all kinds of treatments, from the Jalaynba Rain Treatment (in which six shower heads pummel you as you recline on a timber "wet bed") to the Secret Sacred Treatment (a women-only "pilgrimage" to the lodge's waterfall for a body treatment involving natural ochres found at its base). You can join a yoga or Ki (based on Japanese Aikido) session, laze by the small solar-heated pool and sun deck, walk rain-forest trails leading from the lodge, join members of the local Aboriginal Kuku tribe on a bush tucker and native medicine stroll, or take a four-wheel-drive day trip to modern-day Aboriginal communities. The tour desk books four-wheel-drive jungle safaris, Daintree river-wildlife-spotting cruises, horseback riding, and snorkeling, diving, and fishing trips to the Great Barrier Reef. The Baaru House Restaurant and Bar, built over a lily-filled pond, serves gourmet bush tucker.

20 Daintree Rd., Daintree, QLD 4873 (4km/2½ miles south of Daintree village). © **1800/808 010** in Australia, or 07/4098 6100. Fax 07/4098 6200. www.daintree-ecolodge.com.au. 15 units (10 with shower only). A$476–$531(U.S.$309–$345) double. Extra person A$33–$50 (U.S.$21.50–$32.50). Cribs A$33 (U.S.$21.45) for duration of stay. Rates include full breakfast. Ask about 3- and 5-night packages. AE, DC, MC, V. Scheduled minibus picks up and drops off once a day at Port Douglas hotels, Cairns hotels, and Cairns airport for A$49.50 (U.S.$32.20) (Port Douglas) or A$55 (U.S.$35.75) (Cairns) per person, one-way. Transfers at any time are available at higher cost. Private car transfers A$143 (U.S.$92.95) from Port Douglas or A$165 (U.S.$107.25) from Cairns, per car, one-way. Stretch limousine transfers (A$242/U.S.$157 one way), and helicopter transfers can be arranged. The lodge is 98km (61 miles) north of Cairns and 40km (25 miles) north of Port Douglas. Take the Captain Cook Hwy. north to Mossman, where it becomes the Mossman-Daintree road; follow this all the way to the lodge. The road is paved all the way. **Amenities:** Restaurant; pool; spa; tour desk; laundry service. *In room:* A/C, TV, minibar, coffeemaker, hair dryer.

Silky Oaks Lodge 🌟🌟   From the main complex of this upscale lodge at Mossman Gorge, you look straight down onto the picturesque Mossman River, where you can swim (croc-free!). Despite its peaceful setting, the place has a rather bustling air because of the high number of guests, plus visitors to the restaurant. Accommodations are in chalets scattered through a mixture of rain forest and man-made gardens; a few have river frontage, and some have Jacuzzis. Each has elegant timber floors, attractive furnishings, bathrobes, a CD player, and a double hammock to string up on your veranda. The resort's most recent renovation was completed in September 2001, and included the addition of the Healing Waters Day Spa, named for the healing properties of the Mossman River. Guided nature walks, mountain bikes, and evening nature slide shows are free, and there are a daily activities program and a wallaby sanctuary where you can feed the animals. A car is necessary to access Mossman Gorge's lovely walking trails across the river.

7km (4 miles) west of Mossman; 27km (17 miles) from Port Douglas. c/o P&O Australian Resorts, G.P.O. Box 478, Sydney, NSW 2001. © **1800/737 678** in Australia, 800/225-9849 in the U.S. and Canada, 020/7805 3875 in the U.K., 02/9277 5050 (Sydney reservations office), or 07/4098 1666 (lodge). Fax 02/9299 2477 (Sydney reservations office) or 07/4098 1983 (lodge). www.poresorts.com.au. 60 units. A$440 (U.S.$286) double. Extra person A$65 (U.S.$42.25). Rates include continental breakfast. Ask about packages; some combine stays at Dunk, Bedarra, and Lizard islands and Sebel Reef House (all described in this chapter). AE, DC, MC, V. Free morning and afternoon shuttle from Port Douglas. Coral Coaches makes morning and afternoon transfers from Port Douglas for A$14.80 (U.S.$9.65) one-way, A$29.60 (U.S.$19.25) round-trip. Town-car transfers A$130 (U.S.$81.25) per car one-way from Cairns city or airport; stretch limousine transfers A$180 (U.S.$117). Take the Captain Cook Hwy. to Mossman, where it becomes the Mossman-Daintree Rd.; follow this approx. 3.5km (2 miles) past Mossman and turn left onto Finlayvale Rd. at the small white-on-blue silky oaks sign. No children under 6. **Amenities:** Restaurant, bar; lovely free form pool; day/night tennis court; spa; tour desk; in-room massage; coin-operated laundry; laundry service. *In room:* A/C, minibar, hair dryer.

Thala Beach Lodge 🌟🌟   "Where are the walls?" may be your first question on arriving at this Balinese-style luxury hideaway in the rain forest outside Port Douglas. The lodge's reception area and lobby are open, to stunning effect. And from the elevated restaurant the impact is even greater, with sweeping views from the Daintree to Cape Grafton, south of Cairns. Thala (pronounced Ta-la) Beach is set on a 145-acre (59-hectare) private peninsula, bordered on three sides by private beaches and coves. Owners Rob and Oonagh Prettejohn also own the well-established Kewarra Beach Resort on Cairns' northern beaches. Thala

Beach opened in 1998, taking its inspiration from the flora and fauna of the World Heritage area that surrounds it. The secluded bungalows are built on high poles in the trees, where dazzling lorikeets and small red-faced flying foxes feed on blossoms and hang contentedly from the branches. Some of the bungalows are a bit of a hike from the public areas, but I thought it was a small price to pay for the privacy and the rain-forest setting.

16km (10 miles) south of Port Douglas. P.O. Box 199, Smithfield, Cairns, QLD 4878. © 1800 251 958 in Australia (Small Luxury Hotels of the World), or 07/4098 5700 (lodge). Fax: 07/4098 5837. www.thalabeach. com.au. 85 units. A$317–$500 (U.S.$206–$325) double. AE, DC, MC, V. **Amenities:** Restaurant, bar; outdoor free-form pool; nearby golf course; tour desk. *In room:* A/C and ceiling fans, TV, minibar, coffeemaker, hair dryer, safe.

WHERE TO DINE IN PORT DOUGLAS

One of the more appealing newer restaurants in Port Douglas is **Lime,** 38 Macrossan St. (© **07/4099 6536**), which serves up Asian-inspired flavors with a casual tropical menu using local ingredients.

B.J.'s Salsa Bar & Grill *Kids* TEX MEX/SOUTH PACIFIC RIM/ASIAN This trendsetting restaurant may have moved house, but rest assured, nothing else has changed! There's still the same lively, fun service, great value prices and terrific food. What is new is the setting, in a timber Queenslander-style building with wraparound verandas. Try the Cajun tuna carpaccio, or the duck and macadamia nut nachos with nashi pear salsa and smoky fondue aïoli. Or maybe chargrilled Atlantic salmon on saffron risotto cake with asparagus, ponzu beurre blance and a tempura prawn fan. By day the tablecloths are brown paper; at night the white cloths come out. There's always lounge music playing, and the ultra-contemporary bar next door is a good place for a pre- or post-dinner cocktail.

26 Wharf St. © 07/4099 4922. Fax 07/4099 5338. Reservations recommended. Main courses A$20–$22.50 (U.S.$13–$14.60). AE, DC, MC, V. Mon–Sat 10am–midnight; Sundays 8am–midnight.

Nautilus *Ⓐ* TROPICAL/SEAFOOD   If it's good enough for Bill and Hillary, it might be good enough for you. The Clintons dined here during a visit Down Under, and by all accounts loved it. The restaurant, which has been keeping the locals happy since 1953, is extremely popular, with an appealing setting outdoors under the palm trees and stars and a reputation for cleverly cooked seafood. Melbourne-trained chef Gregory Bull makes the most of local produce and seafood, serving up such delights as the grilled yellow-fin tuna served on salt-cod mash and drizzled with green olive tapenade. Or you may prefer to go for the fresh mud crab, barramundi, or the barbecue tiger prawns. There are plenty of choices for non-seafood eaters, too.

17 Murphy St. (entry also from Macrossan St.), Port Douglas. © 07/4099 5330. Reservations recommended. Main courses A$25.90–$36 (U.S.$16.80–$23.40). AE, DC, MC, V. Daily 6:30–10:30pm or until the last diners leave.

Port O' Call Bistro *Kids* CAFE/BISTRO   Locals patronize this casual poolside bistro and bar at the Port O' Call Lodge (see "Where to Stay" above) almost as often as guests do, because it offers good, honest food in hearty portions at painless prices. The atmosphere is fun and friendly. There are pasta, curry, and roast nights as well as the chef's blackboard surprises every night, including local seafood and beef. Kids' meals are all A$6 (U.S.$3.90), and there are burgers, nachos and pastas to appeal to everyone.

Port St. at Craven Close. © 07/4099 5422. Main courses A$7.50–$14 (U.S.$4.90–$9). MC, V. Open 6–9pm. Happy hour 5–7pm. Bar opens 4pm.

4 The North Coast: Mission Beach ✶✶, Townsville & the Islands

For years the lovely town of **Mission Beach** was a well-kept secret. Farmers retired here; then those who liked to drop out and chill out discovered it; today, it's a small, prosperous and stunningly pretty rain-forest town. The beach here is one of the most beautiful in Australia, a long white strip fringed with dense tangled vine forests, the only surviving lowlands rain forest in the Australian tropics. It is also one of the least crowded and least spoiled, so clever has **Mission Beach** been at staying out of sight, out of mind, and off the tourist trail.

The nearby **Tully River** is white-water-rafting heaven for thrill-seekers. You can also bungee jump and tandem skydive when you're not rushing down the rapids, flanked by lush rain forest.

From Mission Beach it's a short ferry ride to **Dunk Island,** a large resort island that welcomes day-trippers. You can even sea kayak there from the mainland. Mission Beach is closer to the Great Barrier Reef than any other point along the coast—just an hour—and cruise boats depart daily from the jetty, stopping en route at Dunk Island.

A few hours' drive south brings you to the city of **Townsville,** also a gateway to the Great Barrier Reef, but more important to visitors as a gateway to Magnetic Island, a picturesque, laid-back haven for hikers and water-sports enthusiasts.

MISSION BEACH: THE CASSOWARY COAST
140km (84 miles) S of Cairns; 240km (144 miles) N of Townsville

Tucked away off the Bruce Highway, the township of Mission Beach has managed to duck the tourist hordes. It's actually a conglomeration of four beachfront towns: South Mission Beach, Wongaling Beach, Mission Beach proper, and Bingil Bay. Most commercial activity centers around the small nucleus of shops and businesses at Mission Beach proper. It's so isolated that signs on the way into town warn you to watch out for ultra-shy cassowaries emerging from the jungle to cross the road. Dense rain forest hides the town from view until you come around the corner to Mission Beach proper and discover tidy villages of appealing hotels, neat shops, and smart little restaurants. Just through the trees is the fabulous beach. A mile or so north of the main settlement of Mission Beach is Clump Point Jetty.

ESSENTIALS
GETTING THERE   From Cairns, follow the Bruce Highway south. The Mission Beach turnoff is at the tiny town of El Arish, about 15 kilometers (9 miles) north of Tully. Mission Beach is 25 kilometers (15 miles) off the highway. It's a 90-minute trip from Cairns. If you're coming from Townsville, there is an earlier turnoff just north of Tully that leads 18 kilometers (11 miles) to South Mission Beach.

Mission Beach Bus & Coach (© 07/4068 7400) operates four door-to-door shuttles a day from Cairns for A$28 (U.S.$18.20) per person, and from the Cairns airport for A$33 (U.S.$21.45) per person. One service a day runs from the northern beaches at A$38 (U.S.$24.70) per person. **McCafferty's** (© 13 14 99 in Australia) and **Greyhound-Pioneer** (© 13 20 30 in Australia) coaches both stop in Mission Beach proper (not South Mission Beach) several times daily on their Cairns–Brisbane–Cairns runs. Trip time from Brisbane is over 26 hours.

Four trains a week on the Cairns–Brisbane–Cairns route call at the nearest train station, Tully, about 20 kilometers (13 miles) away. The one-way fare is

---

Plan Ahead for Your Banking Needs
There is no bank in Mission Beach, and the only ATM is at Mission Beach Resort, Wongaling Beach, so come with enough cash, traveler's checks, and/or a credit card.

A$24.20 (U.S.$15.75) from Cairns for the 3¼-hour trip; from Brisbane it ranges from A$158.40 (U.S.$103) for a seat to A$547(U.S.$355) for a first-class sleeper on The *Queenslander*. Call Queensland Rail's long-distance division, **Traveltrain** (© 1800/806 468 in Australia, or 07/3235 1122). A taxi from Tully to Mission Beach with **Tully Taxis & Buses** (© 07/4068 3937) is about A$40 (U.S.$26).

A bus transfer to Mission Beach with **Mission Beach Bus & Coach** (© 07/ 4068 7400) is A$5 (U.S.$3.25).

VISITOR INFORMATION   The **Mission Beach Visitor Centre,** Porters Promenade, Mission Beach, QLD 4852 (© 07/4068 7099; fax 07/4068 7066; www.missionbch.com), is located at the northern end of town. It's open Monday through Saturday from 9am to 5pm, and Sunday from 9am to 4pm.

GETTING AROUND   The **local bus** (© 07/4068 7400, or call the bus driver while he's driving at 0419/745 875 mobile phone) travels day and night between the beach communities, stopping outside all the accommodation houses listed below, at Clump Point Jetty, and at Wongaling Beach near the water taxi to Dunk Island. **Sugarland Car Rentals** (© 07/4068 8272) is the only rental-car company in town. For Mission Beach taxi service, call © 07/4068 8155.

WHAT TO SEE & DO
EXPLORING THE REEF   Mission Beach is the closest point on the mainland to the Reef, just 1 hour by the high-speed **Quick Cat** catamaran (© 1800/ 654 242 in Australia, or 07/4068 7289). The trip starts with an hour at Dunk Island 20 minutes offshore, where you can walk rain-forest trails, play on the beach, or parasail or jet ski for an extra fee. Then it's a 1-hour trip to sandy Beaver Cay on the Outer Reef, where you have 3 hours to snorkel or to check out the coral from a semi-submersible or glass-bottom boat. There's no shade on the cay, so come prepared with a hat and sunscreen. The trip departs Clump Point Jetty at 10am; it departs daily in high season between July 1 and October 31, and every day except Sunday the rest of the year. It costs A$140 (U.S.$91) for adults and A$70 (U.S.$45.50) for children ages 4 to 14. An introductory scuba dive costs A$77 (U.S.$50.05) for the first dive and A$33 (U.S.$21.45) for the second. You should pre-book your introductory scuba dive to ensure a place. Qualified divers pay A$55 (U.S.$35.75) for the first dive, A$33 (U.S.$21.45) for the second, all gear included. Free pickups from Mission Beach are included. You can also join this trip from Cairns; coach connections from your Cairns hotel cost an extra A$15 (U.S.$9.75) for adults and A$7.50 (U.S.$4.85) for children. Ask about Sunday specials during high season.

WHITE-WATER RAFTING ON THE TULLY   A day's rafting through the rain forest on the Grade 3 to 4 Tully River is an adventure you won't soon forget. In raft-speak, Grade 4 means "exciting rafting on moderate rapids with a continuous need to maneuver rafts." On the Tully, that translates to regular hair-raising but manageable rapids punctuated by calming stretches that let you just float downstream. You don't need experience, just a decent level of agility and an enthusiastic attitude. **RnR Rafting** (© **07/4051 7777**), runs a trip which includes 5 hours on the river with fun, expert guides, a barbecue lunch in the rain forest, and a video screening of your adventure. With transfers, the day costs A$128 (U.S.$83.20) from Mission Beach, A$138 (U.S.$89.70) from Cairns or the northern beaches, and A$149 (U.S.$96.85) from Port Douglas, plus a A$10 (U.S.$6.50) national park fee. The trip runs daily; you must be 13 years or older.

EXPLORING THE RAIN FOREST & COAST   Walking, wildlife spotting, canoeing in the forest, and kayaking along the pristine coast are all well worth doing in these parts. Hiking trails abound through national-park rain forest, fan palm groves, and along the beach. The 8-kilometer (5-mile) **Licuala Fan Palm** track starts at the parking lot on the Mission Beach–Tully Road about 1.5 kilometers (1 mile) west of the turnoff to South Mission Beach. The track leads through dense forest, over creeks, and comes out on the El Arish–Mission Beach Road about 7 kilometers (4 miles) north of the post office. When you come out, you can cross the road and keep going on the 1.2-kilometer (less than 1-mile) Lacey Creek loop in the Tam O'Shanter State Forest. A shorter Rainforest Circuit option leads from the parking lot at the start of the Licuala Fan Palm track and makes a 1.2-kilometer (less than a mile) loop incorporating a fan palm boardwalk. There's also a 10-minute "follow the cassowary footprints to the nest" children's walk leading from the parking lot.

If you would rather see the sea than rain forest, take the 7-kilometer (4-mile) Edmund Kennedy track, which starts below the Horizon resort at the southern end of the Kennedy Esplanade in South Mission Beach. You get alternating views of the ocean and the rain forest on this trail. The Mission Beach Visitor Centre has free trail maps.

Ingrid Marker of **Sunbird Adventures** (© **07/4068 8229**) offers a range of sea-kayaking and trekking expeditions that interpret the rich environment around you. No more than eight people are allowed on each trip, so you get personal attention and time to ask questions. Her half-day sea-kayak expedition (A$48/ U.S.$31 per person) journeys around Bingil Bay. Her full-day rain-forest trek visits the Liverpool/Nyleta Creek area, and includes a dip in a natural swimming hole (A$59/U.S.$38 per person). Her night walks are held on Bicton Hill and are great for kids because they spot glow-in-the-dark fungi, and frogs and shrimps in the streams (A$25/U.S.$16 per person). The sea kayaks and full-day treks depart at 8am; the night walks depart at 7pm, returning around 9:30pm. Ingrid picks you up from your accommodation for free. All food on the trip is locally grown organic produce. Not all tours depart every day, so check her schedule.

Safety Tips When Encountering Wildlife

Endangered cassowaries (spectacular ostrich-like birds with a blue boney crown on their head) can kill with their enormous claws, so never approach one. If you disturb one, back off slowly and hide behind a tree.

Dangerous crocodiles inhabit the local waterways. Do not swim in, or stand on the bank of, any river or stream.

You will no doubt spend plenty of time lazing and strolling the area's 14 kilometers (8½ miles) of gorgeous beaches, but be careful about where you swim. Deadly marine stingers inhabit the sea October through April; in these times swim only in the stinger nets erected at the north and south ends of Mission Beach.

HITTING THE BEACH   Of course, lazing on the uncrowded beach is what everyone comes to Mission Beach for. June through September you can swim anywhere, and the water is warm; October through May stick to the safety nets at Mission Beach proper (behind Castaways resort) and South Mission Beach.

A DAY TRIP TO DUNK ISLAND   If you're a beachcomber at heart, Dunk will fulfill your dreams. Just 5 kilometers (3 miles) offshore from Mission Beach, Dunk was the inspiration for writer E.J. Banfield's book *Confessions of a Beachcomber*. Banfield moved to Dunk at the turn of the century to live out what he thought would be a short life. He lived on for another 23 years, which must say something about the restorative powers of a piece of paradise. Ed and Bertha Banfield's graves are alongside the track to Mt. Kootaloo.

Thick bushland and rain forest cover much of the island's 12 square kilometers (5 sq. miles), most of which is a national park. The island is renowned for its myriad birds and electric-blue Ulysses butterflies.

You can stay at the upscale Dunk Island resort (see "Where to Stay on the Island," in this section) or just pop over for the day to snorkel, hike in the forest, or do all sorts of water sports. **Dunk Island Ferry & Cruises (© 07/4068 7211,** or 07/4065 6333 after hours) runs round-trip cruises for A$26 (U.S.$16.90) for adults and A$13 (U.S.$8.45) for kids ages 10 to 14 (free for younger kids). This cruise costs the same as the regular water-taxi fare (see below) and includes free snorkeling gear (with a A$20/U.S.$13 refundable deposit). Daily departures from Clump Point Jetty at 8:45 and 10:30am. The trip takes about 40 minutes. You can also get to Dunk by the **water taxi** (© **07/4068 8310**), which runs six times a day from Wongaling Beach. The round-trip fare is A$22 (U.S.$14.30) for adults and A$11 (U.S.$7.15) for kids ages 4 to 14, but does not include snorkel gear, which costs A$10 (U.S.$6.50) extra per person. Ask at your accommodation about transfers between Clump Point and South Mission Beach.

Once on Dunk, you pay as you go for activities and equipment rental on the island. Everything from water-skiing to catamaran sailing is available, and Dunk has lovely beaches and half a dozen rain-forest walking trails, ranging in duration from 15 minutes to 4 hours. On Monday and Thursday mornings, you can visit an artist's gallery reached via a 40-minute trail through the rain forest; admission is A$4 (U.S.$2.60).

Ingrid Marker of Sunbird Adventures (see above) runs unusual full-day guided **sea-kayak expeditions** ⚘ to Dunk Island. Ingrid says if you can pedal a bike for an hour, you can sea kayak for the hour it takes to get to the island. You glide over reefs, looking for sea turtles; spend the morning snorkeling in Coconut Bay; have a picnic lunch of oysters, mussels, and fresh produce (all organic) in Hidden Palm Valley; then hike the rain forest. At morning and afternoon tea you get a choice of no less than nine organic teas and coffees. The trip costs A$80 (U.S.$52) per person.

WHERE TO STAY IN MISSION BEACH

The Horizon ⚘   With its beguiling views across the pool to Dunk Island, its rain-forest setting, and its impressive rooms, this resort perched on a steep hillside is one of the most comfortable and beautiful you will find. Even the least expensive rooms are spacious and have luxurious bathrooms. All but a handful of rooms have some kind of sea view; a half-dozen retain the older-style bathrooms from a previous resort development, but the sea views from these rooms are the best. It's just a minute or two down the rain-forest track to the beach.

Explorer Dr., South Mission Beach, QLD 4852. ℰ **1800/079 090** in Australia, or 07/4068 8154. Fax 07/4068 8596. www.thehorizon.com.au. 55 units. A$225–$420 (U.S.$146–$273) double. Children A$20 (U.S.$13). Ask about packages and specials. Rates are higher Dec 22–Jan 2. AE, DC, MC, V. **Amenities:** 3 restaurants, bar; large free-form saltwater pool; day/night tennis courts; tour desk. *In room:* A/C, TV with cable, minibar, coffeemaker, hair dryer, iron.

Mackays   This delightfully well-kept motel is one of the best-value places to stay in town. It's just 80 meters (260 ft.) from the beach and 400 meters (¼ mile) from the heart of Mission Beach. The friendly Mackay family repaints the rooms annually, so the place always looks brand new. All the rooms are pleasant and spacious with white-tiled floors, cane sofas, colorful bedcovers, and very clean bathrooms. Those in the newer section are air-conditioned, and some have views of the attractive granite-lined pool and gardens. Rooms in the older painted-brick wing have garden views from a communal patio and no air conditioning. Ask about special packages; they can be extremely good deals and may include extras like rafting on the Tully River and day trips to the Reef and Dunk Island.

7 Porter Promenade, Mission Beach, QLD 4852. ℰ **07/4068 7212.** Fax 07/4068 7095. www.mackaysmission beach.com. 22 units (12 with bathroom; 10 with shower only). A$88–$110 (U.S.$57–$71) double; A$110 (U.S.$71) 1- and 2-bedroom apt. Higher rates apply at Easter. Additional person A$16.50 (U.S.$10.70); children under 14 A$6.50 (U.S.$4.20). Crib A$6.60 (U.S.$4.30). Ask about special packages. AE, DC, MC, V. Free undercover off-street parking. **Amenities:** Outdoor pool; access to nearby tennis courts; access to bike rental; tour desk; car-rental desk; room service breakfast 7:30–8:30am; in-room massage; babysitting; coin-operated laundry; nonsmoking rooms. *In room:* A/C (in 12 units only), TV, fax, kitchenettes in 4 units only, fridge, safe.

WHERE TO STAY ON THE ISLAND

Dunk Island 𝒦 *Kids*   Families love Dunk Island because there's so much to do, but that doesn't mean it's not just as appealing for honeymooners or retired couples. Just 5 kilometers (3 miles) offshore from Mission Beach, Dunk is a thickly rain-forested 12-square-kilometer (7½-sq.-mile) island that attracts everyone. The island is renowned for bird life and neon-blue Ulysses butterflies, which you will see everywhere.

Among the free activities are snorkel gear and lessons, windsurfing, catamaran sailing, paddle skiing, a 6-hole golf course (pay for balls and tees), tennis and squash courts, fitness classes and aqua-aerobics, beach and pool volleyball, badminton, bocce and archery, to name just a few. You pay for a range of other activities, including guided jet-ski tours, parasailing, water-skiing, tube rides, tandem skydiving, game-fishing trips, motorboats, sunset wine-and-cheese cruises, and horse riding. A yacht calls to make trips around nearby islands, and a game-fishing boat picks up here regularly. The kids will love the playground and a visit to Coonanglebah (the island farm), as well as the kids club. A private artists' colony in the rain forest sells works Monday and Thursday, from 10am to 1pm.

All four kinds of low-rise accommodations are comfortable rather than glamorous, with tile floors, nice cane furniture, hair dryers, and colorful furnishings. Not all have sea views; those that do are the most recently renovated.

In 2000, A$2 million (U.S.$1.3 million) was spent to spruce up the restaurants and other public areas. Beach barbecues are also held from time to time. The Spa of Peace and Plenty was also added to the facilities, offering facials, massage, and body wraps among its treatments.

Off Mission Beach. c/o P&O Australian Resorts, G.P.O. Box 478, Sydney, NSW 2001. ℰ **1800/737 678** in Australia, 800/225-9849 in the U.S. and Canada, 020/7805 3875 in the U.K., 02/9277 5050 (Sydney sales and reservations office), or 07/4068 8199 (the island). Fax 02/9299 2477 (Sydney sales and reservations office) or 07/4068 8528 (the island). www.poresorts.com.au. 146 units (72 with shower only). A$440–$700 (U.S.$286–$455) double. Rates include full breakfast and dinner every day. Extra adult A$130 (U.S.$84.50), extra child 3–14 A$70 (U.S.$45.50). Ask about packages; some combine stays at Bedarra Island and Silky Oaks Lodge (both described elsewhere in this chapter). AE, DC, MC, V. Daily 45-min. flights operate from Cairns (book through Qantas or the resort). Aircraft luggage limit 16kg (35 lbs.) per person. Dunk Island Ferry & Cruises ((℮ 07/4068 7211) makes round-trip ferry transfers from Mission Beach for A$28 (U.S.$18) adults. Including the ferry fare, the company does daily door-to-door coach connections from Port Douglas for A$126 (U.S.$82), Cairns for A$84 (U.S.$55), and Cairns northern beaches for A$104 (U.S.$68) adult. Fares for children 4–14 are half price. Disembarkation from the ferry is sometimes into shallow water—be prepared to get your feet wet! Airport pickups must be booked. Transfers also available by air charter and "Quick Cat" Great Barrier Reef cruise boat (see earlier in this chapter). **Amenities:** 3 restaurants, bar; 2 pools (1 has a striking 3-tiered effect); 6-hole golf course; 3 day/night tennis courts (1 indoor); exercise room; spa; extensive water-sports equipment rental; bike rental; daily kids' club for ages 3–14 (at a fee); babysitting; coin-operated laundry. *In room:* A/C and ceiling fans, TV, minibar (beachfront units and suites only); fridge; coffeemaker; hair dryer; iron.

BEDARRA ISLAND: THE ULTIMATE LUXURY GETAWAY

Only a mile long, Bedarra is home to an exclusive 15-room resort favored by the rich, the famous, and anyone who treasures privacy. The Duchess of York has stayed here, and so has Princess Caroline of Monaco. The staff is discreet, and day-trippers are banned. Rain-forested and fringed by beaches, Bedarra is a few miles south of Dunk Island.

Bedarra Island 🐨🐨🐨 Bedarra is one of those rare and fabulous places that throws not just meals but vintage French champagnes, fine cognacs and wines, and other potable treats into the price, shocking though that price may be. If you feel like Louis Roederer Champagne at 3am, help yourself. Closed for a month in 2001, the new-look Bedarra has been injected with some contemporary style. The private villas now have larger verandas, and there's a new sense of light and space in the public areas. The lobby, restaurant, and 24-hour bar have ironbark and recycled timber beams, with feature panels of volcanic stone. Each villa is tucked into the rain forest with a balcony and sea views. All come with generous living areas, king beds, CD players, bathrobes, and the important things in life, like double hammocks on the veranda, big double bathtubs, and aromatherapy oil-burners.

The emphasis here is on relaxation. Walk along rain-forest trails, fish off the beach, snorkel, or take a catamaran, paddle-ski, or windsurf out on the water. These activities are free; chartering a yacht or game-fishing boat costs extra. To visit the Great Barrier Reef, you will need to transfer to Dunk Island to join the Quick Cat catamaran (see earlier in this chapter). Many guests do nothing more strenuous than have the chef pack a gourmet picnic with a bottle of bubbly and set off in a dinghy in search of a deserted beach. Dress at night is smart casual.

Off Mission Beach. c/o P&O Australian Resorts, G.P.O. Box 478, Sydney, NSW 2001. (℮ **1800/737 678** in Australia, 800/225-9849 in the U.S. and Canada, 020/7805 3875 in the U.K., 02/9277 5050 (Sydney sales and reservations office), or 07/4068 8233 (the island). Fax 02/9299 2477 (Sydney sales and reservations office) or 07/4068 8215 (the island). www.poresorts.com.au. 15 villas. A$1,680–$1,900 (U.S.$1,092–$1,235) double. Rates include all meals, 24-hr. open bar and transfers from Dunk Island. Ask about packages; some combine stays at Dunk Island (see above), Silky Oaks Lodge, and Lizard Island (both described in this chapter). AE, DC, MC, V. Air or coach/ferry transfer to Dunk Island from Cairns (see above), then 15-min. boat transfer. Water transfers can be arranged from Mission Beach. No children under 16. **Amenities:** Restaurant, bar; secluded swimming pool with timber decking and private Jacuzzi area; day/night tennis court; water sports (see above); massage (in room or on the beach); laundry service. *In room:* A/C and ceiling fan, TV/VCR, free minibar, hair dryer, iron.

WHERE TO DINE IN MISSION BEACH

Friends HOME COOKING The cozy interior and a hearty menu favoring local seafood make this place a long-standing favorite with locals. Appetizers include mussels Normandy, oysters done three ways, and garlic prawns; main courses feature lamb shanks; steak with Dianne, mushroom, or green peppercorn sauce; and chicken hotpot. Settle in with a homemade dessert and liqueur coffee after dinner. Licensed and BYO.

Porters Promenade (opposite Campbell St.), Mission Beach. Ⓒ 07/4068 7107, or 07/4068 7440 (9am–5pm). Reservations recommended. Main courses A$15–$25 (U.S.$9.75–$16.30). AE, MC, V. Mon–Sat 6:30–10:30pm or until the last diners leave. Open Sun on long weekends. Closed for 1 month during Feb–Mar.

TOWNSVILLE & MAGNETIC ISLAND
346km (207½ miles) S of Cairns; 1,371km (822½ miles) N of Brisbane

With a population of 140,000, Townsville claims to be Australia's largest tropical city. Because of its size, and an economy based on mining, manufacturing, education, and tourism, it is sometimes overlooked as a holiday destination. Unjustly so, I think. The people are friendly, the city pleasant, and there's plenty to do. The town is nestled by the sea below the pink face of Castle Rock, which looms 300 meters (about 1,000 ft.) directly above, and the beachfront has recently undergone a A$29-million (U.S.$18.8-million) revamp.

Townsville's major new attraction is the world-class **Museum of Tropical Queensland,** where a full size replica of the HMS *Pandora* is the stunning centrepiece. The museum is next door to one of the city's most enduring attractions, the Reef HQ aquarium.

Remnants of bygone times are still apparent in some of the surrounding towns, particularly **Charters Towers** and **Ravenswood,** where there are splendid examples of colonial architecture, historic hotels, museums, and displays of old gold mining machinery and cottages.

Cruises depart from the harbor for the Great Barrier Reef, about 2½ hours away, and just 8 kilometers (5 miles) offshore is Magnetic Island—"Maggie" to the locals— a popular place for water sports, hiking, and spotting koalas in the wild.

Although Townsville can be hot and humid in the summer—and sometimes in the path of cyclones—it is generally spared the worst of the Wet Season rains.

ESSENTIALS
GETTING THERE   Townsville is on the Bruce Highway, a 3-hour drive north of Airlie Beach and 4½ hours south of Cairns. The Bruce Highway breaks temporarily in the city. From the south, take Bruce Highway Alt. 1 route into the city. From the north, the highway leads into the city as Ingham Road.

Qantas (Ⓒ 13 13 13 in Australia) and their respective subsidiaries **Sunstate Airlines** (book through Qantas) have many flights a day from Cairns, and several from Brisbane. Sunstate flies from Proserpine and Hamilton Island airports in the Whitsundays. **Virgin Blue** (Ⓒ 136 789 in Australia) flies to Townsville from Brisbane daily.

Airport Transfers & Tours (Ⓒ 07/4775 5544) runs a door-to-door airport shuttle. It meets only flights from Brisbane, not from Cairns or elsewhere. A trip into town is A$6 (U.S.$3.90) one-way or A$10 (U.S.$6.50) return, less if there are two of you. Reservations are not needed.

Several **Queensland Rail** (Ⓒ 13 22 32 in Queensland, or 07/3235 1122) long-distance trains stop at Townsville each week. The twice-weekly Spirit of the Tropics operates between Brisbane and Townsville, and costs A$272.80 (U.S.$177). From Brisbane the journey takes just over 20 hours; fares range from A$141.90 (U.S.$92) for a sitting berth to A$509.80 (U.S.$330) for a first-class sleeper on The Queenslander.

Greyhound-Pioneer (Ⓒ 13 20 30 in Australia) and McCafferty's (Ⓒ 13 14 99 in Australia) coaches stop at Townsville many times a day on their

Cairns–Brisbane–Cairns routes. The fare from Cairns is about A$44 (U.S.$28.60); trip time is 6 hours. The fare from Brisbane is about A$130 (U.S.$84.50); trip time is 22½ hours.

VISITOR INFORMATION   For an information packet, contact **Townsville Enterprise Limited,** P.O. Box 1043, Townsville, QLD 4810 (© **07/4726 2728;** www.tel.com.au). It has two Information Centers. One is in the heart of town on Flinders Mall (© **1800/801 902** in Australia, or 07/4721 3660); it's open Monday through Friday from 9am to 5pm, and weekends from 9am to 1pm. The other is on the Bruce Highway 10 kilometers (6 miles) south of the city (© **07/4778 3555**); it is open daily from 9am to 5pm. Townsville Enterprise supplies information on Magnetic Island, but also check www.magnetic-island.com.au.

GETTING AROUND   Local **Sunbus** (© 07/4725 8482) buses depart Flinders Street Mall. Car-rental chains include **Avis** (© 07/4721 2688), **Budget** (© 07/4725 2344), **Hertz** (© 07/4775 5950), and **Thrifty** (© 07/4725 4600).

   Detours Coaches (© **07/4721 5977**) runs tours to most attractions in and around Townsville.

DAY TRIPS TO THE REEF

The only Reef cruise operator to offer fishing as well as snorkeling and diving trips from Townsville is **Pure Pleasure Cruises** (© **07/4721 3555**), which operates the large Wavepiercer 2001 catamaran to a pontoon on Kelso Reef, where you will find hundreds of types of hard and soft corals and 1,500 fish species. A marine biologist gives talks en route. The cruise costs A$124 (U.S.$81) for adults, A$112 (U.S.$73) for children ages 16 to 18 and A$62 (U.S.$40) for children ages 4 to 15, or A$309 (U.S.$200) for a family of 5. Price includes glass-bottom-boat trips, fishing, and unlimited snorkeling. Guided snorkeling tours are A$23 (U.S.$14.95). Introductory dives are an extra A$66 (U.S.$42.90), and qualified divers can make two dives for A$55 (U.S.$35.75). If you'd rather catch fish than look at them, you can head off to deeper water to cast a line for sweetlip, coral trout, and other reef beauties. The staff will clean and wrap your catch, and your hotel chef should be happy to cook it for you. Cruises depart from Reef HQ every day except Monday and Thursday at 9am and from Picnic Bay Jetty on Magnetic Island at 9:15am. Hotel pick-up can be arranged at a small extra cost. The boat takes 186 passengers, is air-conditioned, and has a video and bar. The trip takes 2½ hours each way, giving you 3½ to 4 hours on the Reef.

THE TOP ATTRACTIONS

Imax Dome Theatre   The films shown on the 21-meter (69-ft.) dome-shaped screen here are generally documentaries with a natural history or geographic theme about places like Everest, Africa, Alaska, and Egypt, or on topics like the oceans of the world.

Flinders St. (in the Reef HQ Centre) © 07/4721 1481. Admission A$12.60 (U.S.$8.20) adults, A$9.90 (U.S.$6.45) seniors and students, A$6.60 (U.S.$4.30) children 4–14, A$29.70 (U.S.$19.30) family. Open daily except Christmas. Movies shown hourly from 10am; last screening 4pm.

Museum of Tropical Queensland 🐾🐾   A stunning addition to Townsville's skyline is this new A$22-million (U.S.$14.3-million) museum, with its distinctive curved roof reminiscent of a ship in full sail. In pride of place is the amazing exhibition of relics salvaged from the wreck of HMS *Pandora,* which lies 33 meters (108¼ ft.) underwater on the edge of the Great Barrier Reef, 120 kilometers (75 miles) east of Cape York. The Pandora exhibit includes a built-to-scale replica of a section of the ship's bow and its 17 meters (55¾ ft.) high foremast. Standing three stories high, the replica and its copper-clad keel was crafted by local shipwrights for the museum. *Pandora* sank in 1791, and the wreck was discovered in 1977. The exhibition traces the ship's voyage and the retrieval of the sunken treasure. The museum has six galleries, including a hands-on science center, and a natural history display which looks at life in tropical Queensland—above and below the water. Another is dedicated to north Queensland's indigenous heritage, with items from Torres Strait and the South Sea Islands as well as stories from people of different cultures about the settlement and labor of north Queensland. Touring exhibitions change every 3 months.

70–102 Flinders St (next to Reef HQ). ℂ 07/4726 0600. www.mtq.qld.gov.au. Admission A$9 (U.S.$5.85) adults, A$5 (U.S.$3.25) children 4–16, A$6.50 (U.S.$4.20) seniors and students, A$24 (U.S.$15.60) family of 4. MC, V. Daily 9am–5pm. Closed Christmas, Good Friday, and Anzac Day morning (Apr 25).

Reef HQ *(⅄ (Kids* Reef HQ is the reef education center for the Great Barrier Reef Marine Park Authority's headquarters and is the largest living coral reef aquarium in the world. The highlight is walking through a 20 meters-long (66-ft.-long) see-through acrylic tunnel, gazing right into a giant predator tank where sharks cruise silently. The wreck of the SS *Yongala* provides an eerie backdrop for blacktip and whitetip reef sharks, leopard sharks, and nurse sharks, sharing their 750,000-liter (195,000-gal.) home with stingrays, giant trevally, and a green turtle. Watching them feed is quite a spectacle. The tunnel also reveals the 2.5-million-liter (650,000-gal.) coral reef exhibit, with its hard and soft corals providing a home for thousands of colorful fish, giant clams, sea cucumbers, sea stars, and other creatures. There's a regular scuba dive show where the divers speak to you via intercom while they feed the fish. Other highlights include a marine creature touch-tank, a wild sea-turtle rehabilitation center, plus great interactive activities for children. On weekends there are special kids' activities from 11am to noon and 3 to 4pm. Reef HQ is an easy walk from the city center.

2–68 Flinders St. ℂ 07/4750 0800. www.reefHQ.org.au Admission A$16 (U.S.$10.40) adults, A$13.80 (U.S.$9) seniors and students, A$7 (U.S.$4.55) children 4–14, A$38 (U.S.$24.70) family pass. AE, DC, MC, V. Daily 9am–5pm. Closed Christmas. Carpark 4-min. walk from Reef HQ costs A$4 (U.S.$2.60) per day. Bus stop 3-min. walk away.

MORE THINGS TO SEE & DO

The Strand is a 2.5-kilometer (1½-mile) strip with safe-swimming beaches, a fitness circuit, a great waterpark for the kids, and plenty of covered picnic areas and free gas barbecues. Stroll along the promenade or relax at one of the many cafes, restaurants, and bars while you gaze across the Coral Sea to Magnetic Island. For the more active, there are areas to in-line skate, cycle, walk, or fish, and a basketball half-court. Four rocky headlands and a picturesque jetty adjacent to Strand Park provide good fishing spots, and there are two surf lifesaving clubs to service the three swimming areas along The Strand. With 300 days of sunshine each year, Townsville is a place where you'll enjoy cooling off—in either the Olympic-size Tobruk Pool, the seawater Rockpool, or at the beach itself. During summer (Nov–Mar), three safe swimming enclosures operate to keep swimmers safe from marine stingers, and if water sports are on your agenda try a jet ski, hire a canoe, or take to the latest in pedal skis. A state-of-the-art water-park, complete with an assortment of wet and wild fun has waterfalls, hydrants, water slides, and water cannons, plus a huge bucket of water which continually fills until it overturns and dumps water on laughing children.

Don't miss the views of Cleveland Bay and Magnetic Island from **Castle Hill;** it's a 2.5-kilometer (1½ mile) drive or a shorter, but steep, walk up from town. To drive to the top, follow Stanley Street west from Flinders Mall to Castle Hill Drive; the walking trails up are posted en route.

At the **Billabong Sanctuary** (© 07/4778 8344; www.billabongsanctuary. com.au) on the Bruce Highway 17 kilometers (11 miles) south of town, you can see a range of Aussie wildlife in a natural setting; hold a koala, a (baby) crocodile, a python, a wombat, or a fruit bat; and hand-feed kangaroos (all for free). Bring your own camera. There are talks and shows continuously from 10am; one of the most popular is the saltwater-crocodile feeding at noon and 2:30pm. There are also Aboriginal cultural talks. Admission is A$19.80 (U.S.$12.87) for adults, A$15.40 (U.S.$10) for students and seniors, A$9.90 (U.S.$6.45) for kids ages 3 to 16, and A$47.30 (U.S.$30.75) for a family of five. The sanctuary is open every day except Christmas from 8am to 5pm. Take your swimsuit as there is a pool.

WHERE TO STAY

Holiday Inn Townsville   The "Sugar Shaker" (you'll know why when you see it) has been Townsville's favorite hotel for years, especially with the corporate set. Until last year, it was the Centra but despite the name change remains part of the Bass Hotels group. Right on Flinders Mall, it's a stroll from Reef HQ, Museum of Tropical Queensland, and Magnetic Island ferries. The rooms are fitted out in sleek blonde-wood decor, and because the 20-story building is circular, every one faces the city, the bay, or Castle Hill. The place is well run, with lots of extras like free tea and coffee in the lobby, and women's and men's gyms. The star attraction is the rooftop pool and sun deck with barbecues.

334 Flinders Mall, Townsville, QLD 4810. © **1800/079 903** in Australia, 800/835-7742 in the U.S. and Canada, 0345/581 666 in the U.K. or 020/8335 1304 in London, 0800/801 111 in New Zealand, or 07/4772 2477. Fax 07/4721 1263. www.centra.com.au. 197 units. A$240 (U.S.$156) double; A$240–$330 (U.S.$156–$214.50) suite. Extra person A$33 (U.S.$21.45). Children under 20 stay free in parents' room using existing bedding. Free crib. Ask about weekend rates, advance-purchase rates, and packages. AE, DC, MC, V. Free undercover valet parking. **Amenities:** Restaurant, 2 bars; roof-top pool; separate men's and women's exercise rooms; bike rental; secretarial services; 24-hr. room service; massage; babysitting; coin-operated laundry; laundry service; dry cleaning. *In room:* A/C, TV with pay movies, kitchenette (in suites only), minibar, coffeemaker, hair dryer, iron.

The Rocks (© *(Finds*   If you have a weakness for Victoriana, you will sigh with delight when you enter this exquisitely renovated old Queenslander home. The owners have fitted it with genuine 19th-century antiques, from the crimson velvet settee to the grandfather clock in the drawing room. Even your meals are served on collectible dinnerware. Every room is decorated with lovely linens, old trunks, and in a few, even original washbasins tastefully wrapped in muslin "gowns." One has an en-suite bathroom; the others share a historically decorated bathroom with a cast-iron claw-foot bath. Complimentary sherry is served at 6pm on the wide veranda, where you have lovely views of Magnetic Island and Cleveland Bay. Despite the old-world ambience, the house has telephone, fax, Internet, and e-mail access for guests (although not in your room). Free tea and coffee are available. There's also an outdoor Jacuzzi, a billiards table (antique, of course), and a guest laundry. The Strand is a minute's stroll away, and you are a 10- to 15-minute walk from town and the Magnetic Island ferries.

20 Cleveland Terrace, Townsville, QLD 4810. © 07/4771 **5700,** or 0416/044 409 mobile phone. Fax 07/4771 5711. www.therocksguesthouse.com.au. 8 units, 3 with private bathroom (shower only). A$99 (U.S.$64) double. Rates include continental breakfast. AE, DC, MC, V. Airport shuttle. Limited free on-street parking. **Amenities:** Outdoor Jacuzzi; tour desk; business center; laundry service. *In room:* A/C (five rooms only).

Seagulls Resort   This popular low-key resort, a 5-minute drive from the city, is built around an inviting free-form saltwater pool in 1.2 hectares (3 acres) of dense tropical gardens. Despite its Esplanade location, the motel-style rooms do not boast waterfront views, but they are comfortable and a good size. The larger Reef suites have painted brick walls, a sofa, dining furniture, and a kitchen sink. Apartments have a main bedroom and a bunk bedroom, a kitchenette, dining furniture, and a roomy balcony. The rooms were last refurbished in late 1997, and the modest fittings are in good condition. The foyer was reburbished in late 2000, and the whole resort is wheelchair-friendly, with bathroom facilities for people with disabilities. The accommodation wings surround the pool and its pretty open-sided restaurant, which is popular with locals. It's a 10-minute walk to The Strand; the resort makes free transfers to the city and Magnetic Island ferry terminals, and most tour companies pick up at the door.

74 The Esplanade, Belgian Gardens, QLD 4810. ℂ **1800/079 929** in Australia, or 07/4721 3111. Fax 07/4721 3133. www.seagulls.com.au. 70 units (all with shower only). A$99–$110 (U.S.$64.35–$71.50) double; A$139 (U.S.$90.35) 2-bedroom apt. Additional person A$15 (U.S.$9.75); extra children under 14 A$9 (U.S.$5.85). AE, DC, MC, V. Airport shuttle. Bus: 4, 5, 5A, or 7. Free parking. **Amenities:** Restaurant; bar; indoor pool; golf course 3km (1¾ miles) away; small tennis court; access to nearby health club; children's playground; tour desk; room service (6–9:30pm); coin-operated laundry; laundry service; dry cleaning. *In room:* A/C, TV, free in-house movies, dataport, fridge, hair dryer, iron.

WHERE TO DINE

Apart from the suggestions below, you will find more restaurants and cafes on Palmer Street, an easy stroll across the river from Flinders Mall.

Michel's Cafe and Bar MODERN AUSTRALIAN   This big contemporary space is popular with Townsville's "in" crowd. Owner/chef Michel Flores works in the open kitchen where he can keep an eye on the excellent service. You might choose a Louisiana blackened rib fillet, or kangaroo. There are also plenty of casual choices like the stylish pizzas or warm salads.

7 Palmer St. ℂ **07/4724 1460.** Reservations recommended. Main courses A$10.90–$23 (U.S.$7.10–$15). AE, DC, MC, V. Tues–Fri 11:30am–2pm; Tues–Sun 5:30–10pm.

Zouí Alto 🍴🍴 MODERN AUSTRALIAN   This is not just one of the best restaurants in Townsville, it's one of the best in the country. Chef Mark Edwards, who's cooked for the King of Norway, turns out terrific food, while his effusive wife Eleni runs the front of the house, which is idiosyncratically decked out in primary splashes and Greek urns. Main courses include ravioli with choice of filling—pumpkin and blue vein cheese, sweet potato and ginger, or sun-dried tomato and goat's cheese. Arrive before sunset, to make the most of the spectacular views of Castle Hill on one side and the bay on the other.

On 14th floor at Aquarius on the Beach, 75 The Strand. ℂ **07/4721 4700.** Reservations recommended. Main courses A$17.50–$22 (U.S.$11.40–$14.30). AE, MC, V. Tues–Sat 6:30–9:30pm. Bus: 1B.

A SIDE TRIP TO MAGNETIC ISLAND

8km (5 miles) E of Townsville

"Maggie" is a delightful 51-square-kilometer (20-sq.-mile) national-park island 20 minutes from Townsville by ferry. A population of 2,500 locals live here, but it's also popular with Aussies, who love its holiday atmosphere. It is a busy little place as visitors and locals zip about between the small settlements dotted around its coast; in fact, the island has a good range of restaurants, laid-back cafes, and take-out joints. But peace-seeking visitors will find plenty of unspoiled nature to restore their souls. Most people come for the 20 or so pristine (and amazingly uncrowded) bays and white beaches that rim the island, but hikers, botanists, and bird-watchers may want to explore the eucalyptus woods, patches of gully rain forest, and granite tors. (The island got its name when Captain Cook thought the "magnetic" rocks were interfering with his compass readings.) The place is famous for wild koalas that are easily spotted up in the gum trees by the side of the road; ask a local to point you to the nearest colony. Rock wallabies are often spotted in the early morning. Maggie, off the tourist trail by and large, is definitely a flip-flops kind of place; leave the Prada pumps in your suitcase.

GETTING THERE & GETTING AROUND   Sunferries (© 07/4771 **3855** for Flinders Street terminal, or 07/4721 4798 for Breakwater terminal) runs services from the 168–192 Flinders Street terminal and the Breakwater terminal on Sir Leslie Thiess Drive throughout the day. The company has a courtesy coach that will pick you up from your hotel for the 10:30am ferry. Round-trip tickets are A$14 (U.S.$9.10) for adults, A$12 (U.S.$7.80) for students, A$6.70 (U.S.$4.35) for seniors and children ages 5 to 15, and A$29 (U.S.$18.85) for a family of five. Combination tickets combining the ferry with an all-day Magnetic Island bus pass or minimoke (similar to a golf cart) rental can save you a couple of dollars.

You can take your own car across on the ferry, but most people get around by renting a fun open-sided minimoke from the many moke-rental outfits on the island. Minimokes are unlikely to send your speedometer much over 60 kilometers per hour (36 mph). **Holiday Moke Hire** (© 07/4778 5703) right near the jetty rents them for around A$35 (U.S.$22.75) a day, plus A30¢ (U.S.20¢) per kilometer. The frequent round-island bus service offers an all-day pass for A$11 (U.S.$7.15) for adults, A$5.50 (U.S.$3.60) for kids, or A$27.50 (U.S.$17.90) for a family of 4.

OUT & ABOUT ON THE ISLAND

There is no end to the things you can do on Maggie—snorkeling, swimming in one of a dozen or more bays, catamaran sailing, water-skiing, paraflying, horseback riding on the beach, biking, tennis or golf, scuba diving, sea kayaking, sailing or cruising around the island, taking a Harley-Davidson tour, fishing, and more. Equipment for all these activities is for rent on the island.

Most activities are spread out around Picnic Bay (where the ferry pulls in) and the island's three settlements: Arcadia, Nelly Bay, and Horseshoe Bay.

The island is not on the Great Barrier Reef, but surrounding waters are part of the Great Barrier Reef Marine Park. There is good reef snorkeling at Florence

---

Magnetic Island Travel Tips

If you're going over to Magnetic Island for the day, pick up a copy of the free "Magnetic Island Guide" from any tourist information center or hotel lobby or at the ferry terminal in Townsville before you go. Because there are so many choices of activities and tours, it will help if you plan your day before you arrive. Also, there is no bank on the island, so carry cash (not every business will cash traveler's checks) and a credit card.

Be warned: Deadly marine stingers make swimming and snorkeling a bad idea October through May, except at the safe swimming enclosure at Picnic Bay. You can still do water sports on top of the water, if your rental outlet provides a protective lycra stinger-suit, but you won't want to wear one of those in the sticky summer heat from November through March.

Bay on the southern edge, Arthur Bay on the northern edge, and Geoffrey Bay, where you can even reef-walk at low-tide (wear sturdy shoes and do not walk directly on coral to avoid damaging it). First-time snorkelers will have an easy time of it in Maggie's weak currents and softly sloping beaches. Outside stinger season there is good swimming at any number of secluded bays found all around the island. Alma Bay is a good choice for families as it is reef free and has shady lawns and a playground; Rocky Bay is a small, secluded cove.

One of the best, and therefore the most popular, of the island's 20 kilometers (12 miles) of hiking trails is the Nelly-Bay-to-Arcadia trail, a one-way journey of 5 kilometers (3 miles) that takes 2½ hours. The first 45 minutes, starting in rain forest and climbing gradually to a saddle between Nelly Bay and Horseshoe, are the most interesting. Another excellent walk is the 2-kilometer (1¼-mile) trail to the Forts, remnants of World War II defenses, which, not surprisingly, have great 360° sea views. The best koala spotting is on the track up to the Forts off Horseshoe Bay Road. Carry water when walking, as some bays and hiking trails are not near shops.

If you feel like splurging, consider the jet-ski circumnavigation of the island offered by **Adrenalin Jet Ski Tours & Hire** (℃ **07/4778 5533**). The 3-hour tour is conducted on two-seat jet skis and costs A$99 (U.S.$64.35), which includes your wet suit, life jacket, and stinger suits in season. Tours depart from Horseshoe Bay morning and afternoon. Keep your eyes peeled for dolphins, dugongs (manatees), and sea turtles.

ORPHEUS ISLAND
80km (50 miles) N of Townsville; 190km (119 miles) S of Cairns

In the 1930s, actress Vivien Leigh and novelist Zane Grey were among the stars who sought seclusion at this beautiful island. More recently, rock star Elton John vacationed here. One of the Great Barrier Reef's most exclusive retreats, Orpheus Island Resort is a popular getaway for executives, politicians, and any savvy traveler eager for peace and beauty. Although it takes 74 guests, guest numbers usually sit at around 40 or so. The surrounding waters are home to 340 of the 350 or so coral species found on the Great Barrier Reef, 1,100 species of fish, green and loggerhead turtles, dolphins, manta rays, and, from June through September, humpback whales. The only other people you will see are resort staff, a handful of guests, and the occasional scientist from the James Cook University marine research station in the next bay. Day-trippers are not allowed.

Transfers are by eight-seater Cessna seaplane. There are two flights a day from Townsville and one from Cairns. Fares are A$565 (U.S.$367.25) per person round-trip, from Cairns (trip time: 1 hr.), and A$350 (U.S.$227.50) per person round-trip, from Townsville (trip time: 30 min.). Book through the resort. Luggage limit is 25kg (55 lb.) per person.

Orpheus Island Resort ⓡ   The resort is simply a cluster of rooms lining one of the prettiest turquoise bays you'll find anywhere. Most guests spend their time snorkeling over coral reefs, chilling with a good book or magazine in the Polynesian-style Quiet Lounge, or lazing in a hammock. Free activities include water-skiing (and lessons), snorkeling, catamaran sailing, a "Discover Scuba" lesson, canoeing, windsurfing, paddle skiing, glass-bottom-boat rides, fishing, and taking a dinghy around the shore to explore some of the island's 1,300 national-park hectares (3,211 acres). You can pay to go game fishing, charter a boat or seaplane to the outer Reef, dive, or do a dive course.

Rooms do not contain TV or telephones, but a TV is hidden away in the gym. The smallest units are the beachfront Terraces; they are also the prettiest, with mosquito netting over the beds, tiled floors, and timber shutters. Beachfront Studio rooms are larger and smarter looking, with black-and-white tiled bathrooms with Jacuzzis, and walnut veneer fittings. Larger still are Beachfront Bungalows, more like traditional hotel rooms with Jacuzzis facing a little garden courtyard. Up on a hill are palatial two-bedroom villas (not air-conditioned), recently refurbished in terra cotta and Tuscan shades. Don't expect marbled splendor on Orpheus; the rooms and facilities are attractive and comfortable rather than luxurious—although the complimentary champagne, fruit and chocolates, and fresh flowers in your room when you arrive are extravagant touches. What you are paying for is seclusion and tranquility.

Orpheus Island, Great Barrier Reef via Townsville (PMB 15, Townsville Mail Centre, QLD 4810). © **1800/077 167** in Australia, or 07/4777 7377. Fax 07/4777 7533. www.orpheus.com.au. 31 units (8 with shower only). A$1,020–$1,430 (U.S.$663–$929.50) double. Extra person A$255–$360 (U.S.$165.75–$234). Rates include all meals and snacks; drinks cost extra. Ask about packages. AE, DC, MC, V. No children under 15. **Amenities:** Restaurant, bar; 2 small outdoor free-form pools, 1 with swim-up bar; day/night tennis court; Jacuzzi; watersports rentals (see above); tour desk; in-room massage. *In room:* A/C (beachfront units only), minibar, coffeemaker, hair dryer, iron.

5 The Whitsunday Coast & Islands

A day's drive or a 1-hour flight south of Cairns brings you to the dazzling collection of 74 islands known as the Whitsundays. No more than 3 nautical miles separates most of the islands, and altogether they represent countless bays, beaches, dazzling coral reefs, and fishing spots that comprise one fabulous Great Barrier Reef playground. Sharing the same latitude as Rio de Janeiro and Hawaii, the water is at least 22°C (72°F) year-round, the sun shines most of the year, and winter requires only a light jacket at night.

All the islands are composed of densely rain-forested national-park land, mostly uninhabited, and the surrounding waters belong to the Great Barrier Reef Marine Park. Don't expect palm trees and coconuts—these islands are covered with dry-looking pine and eucalyptus forests full of dense undergrowth, and rocky coral coves far outnumber the few sandy beaches. More than half a dozen islands have resorts that offer just about all the activities you could ever want—snorkeling, scuba diving, sailing trips, reef fishing, water-skiing, jet-skiing, parasailing, sea kayaking, hiking, rides over the coral in semi-submersibles, fish feeding, putt-putting around in dinghies to secluded beaches, tennis, squash, and aqua-aerobics classes. Accommodations range from small, low-key wilderness retreats to mid-range family havens to Australia's most luxurious resort, Hayman.

The village of Airlie Beach is the center of the action on the mainland. The Whitsundays are just as good a stepping stone to the outer Great Barrier Reef as Cairns—some people think it is better because you don't have to make the 90-minute trip to the Reef before you hit coral. Just about any Whitsunday island has fringing reef around its shores, and there are good snorkeling reefs between the islands, a quick boat ride away from your island or mainland accommodations.

ESSENTIALS

GETTING THERE   By Car   The Bruce Highway leads south from Cairns or north from Brisbane to Proserpine, 26 kilometers (16 miles) inland from Airlie Beach. Take the "Whitsunday" turnoff to reach Airlie Beach and Shute Harbour. Allow a good 8 hours to drive from Cairns. There are several car-storage facilities at Shute Harbour. Sandra and Roger Boynton of **Whitsunday Car Security** (© **07/4946 9955** or 0419/729 605) collect your car anywhere in the Whitsunday area and store it in locked undercover parking for A$13.50 (U.S.$8.80) per 24 hours.

By Plane   There are two air routes into the Whitsundays: Hamilton Island airport, and Proserpine airport on the mainland. **Qantas** (© **13 13 13** in Australia) flies direct to Hamilton Island from Sydney. Airlink (book through Qantas) flies daily from Brisbane. **Sunstate Airlines** (book through Qantas) flies daily from Cairns. Airlink and Sunstate Airlines (book through Qantas) fly to Proserpine direct from Brisbane, and from Cairns via Townsville.

If you stay on an island, the resort may book your launch transfers automatically. These may appear on your airline ticket, in which case your luggage will be checked through to the island.

By Train   Several **Queensland Rail** (© **13 22 32** in Queensland, or 07/3235 1122) long-distance trains stop at Proserpine every week. The one-way fare is A$73.70 (U.S.$47.90) from Cairns. From Brisbane fares range from A$125.40 (U.S.$81.50) for a sitting berth to A$467.50 (U.S.$304) for a first-class sleeper.

By Bus   Greyhound-Pioneer (© **13 20 30** in Australia) and **McCafferty's** (© **13 14 99** in Australia) operate plentiful daily services to Airlie Beach from Brisbane (trip time: around 18 hr.) and Cairns (trip time: 9–10½ hr.). The fare is A$124.30 (U.S.$80.80) from Brisbane and A$71.50 (U.S.$46.50) from Cairns.

Whitsunday Transit (© **1300/65 5449**, or 07/4945 4011) meets all flights and trains at Proserpine to provide door-to-door transfers to Airlie Beach hotels, or to Shute Harbour. The fare is A$12 (U.S.$7.80), half price for kids 4 to 14.

VISITOR INFORMATION   For information before you travel, contact **Tourism Whitsundays,** P.O. Box 83, Whitsunday, QLD 4802 (© **07/4946 6673;** fax 07/4946 7387; www.whitsundayinformation.com.au). Another useful website is www.whitsunday.net.au. **Tourism Whitsundays'** information center (© **1800/801 252** in Australia, or 07/4945 3711) is in Proserpine, on the Bruce Highway in the town's south. It's open Monday through Saturday from 8:30am to 5:30pm and Sunday from 10am to 5pm.

If you're staying in Airlie Beach, it's easier to pick up information from the countless private booking agents lining the main street, which all stock a vast range of cruise, tour, and hotel information, and which make bookings free of charge. They all have pretty much the same stuff; but because some manifest certain boats exclusively, and prices can vary a little from one to the next, shop around.

GETTING AROUND   Island ferries and Great Barrier Reef cruises leave from Shute Harbour, a 10-minute drive south of Airlie Beach on Shute Harbour Road. Most other tour-boat operators and bareboat charters anchor at Abel Point Marina, a 15-minute walk west from Airlie Beach.

Avis (© 07/4946 6318), **Hertz** (© 07/4946 4687), and **Thrifty** (© 07/4946 7727) have outlets in Airlie Beach and Proserpine Airport (telephone numbers serve both locations). Budget has no Whitsundays office.

Local bus company **Whitsunday Transit** (© **1300/655 449** or 07/4945 4011) runs a half-hourly service between Airlie Beach and Shute Harbour to meet all ferries. The fare is A$3.60 (U.S.$2.35).

Most tour-boat operators pick up guests free from Airlie Beach hotels and call at some or all island resorts.

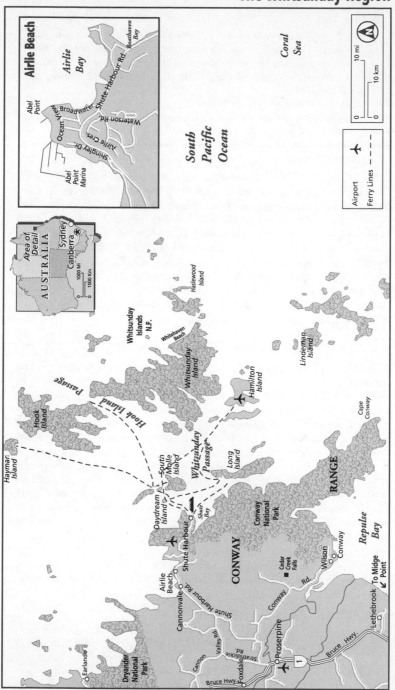

Airlie Beach

Airlie Bay

Boathaven Bay

Shute Harbour Rd.

Abel Point

Ocean View

Broadwater

Waterson Rd

Airlie Cres.

Shingley Dr.

Abel Point Marina

Coral Sea

South Pacific Ocean

N

10 mi

10 km

0

0

Airport

Ferry Lines

Area of Detail

Sydney

Canberra

AUSTRALIA

1000 Mi

1000 Km

0

Haslewood Island

Whitsunday Islands N.P.

Whitehaven Beach

Whitsunday Island

Hamilton Island

Lindeman Island

Hook Island Passage

Hook Island

Hayman Island

South Molle Island

Daydream Island

Shute Bay

Long Island

Whitsunday Passage

Cape Conway

RANGE

Shute Harbour

Airlie Beach

Cannonvale

Conway National Park

Cedar Creek Falls

Wilson

Conway

Repulse Bay

To Midge Point

CONWAY

Shute Harbour Rd.

Gannon Valley Rd.

Strathdickie Rd.

Conway Rd.

Letherbrook

Bruce Hwy.

Proserpine

Foxdale

Bruce Hwy.

1

Dryander National Park

Earlando

Safety Tips

Although they have not been sighted at Airlie Beach for 5 years, deadly marine stingers may inhabit the shoreline October through April. The best place to swim during these months is in the brand new Airlie Beach lagoon. Stingers do not make it to the islands, so swimming in the islands is safe year-round.

The rivers in these parts are home to dangerous saltwater crocodiles (which mostly live in fresh water, contrary to their name), so no swimming in streams, rivers, and water holes.

Whitsunday All Over (☎ **1300/366 494** in Australia, or 07/4946 9499), **Whitsunday Island Adventure Cruises** (☎ **07/4946 5255** for the booking agent), and **FantaSea Cruises** (☎ **1800/650 851** in Australia, or 07/4946 5111) make ferry transfers from Shute Harbour to the islands and between the islands. One-way transfers cost from A$8 (U.S.$5.20) for the short hop from Daydream Island to South Molle Island, to A$24 (U.S.$15.60) from Hamilton Island to the mainland. Children 4 to 14 pay around half price. It is not necessary to book, but do book your arrival and departure ferry so that you don't miss your connections. Most islands receive a boat only every 2 to 4 hours, some only once or twice a day, so it's a long wait if you miss your boat.

CHOOSING A WHITSUNDAY BASE

The advantages of staying on the mainland are cheaper accommodations, a choice of restaurants, and freedom to visit a different island each day. There is jet-skiing, kayaking, parasailing, catamaran rental, and windsurfing on the mainland.

The main advantage of staying on an island is that swimming, snorkeling, bushwalking, and a huge range of water sports, many of them free, are right outside your door. The deadly stingers that can infest Airlie's shores do not make it to the islands, so swimming in the islands is safe year-round. You won't be isolated if you stay on an island, as most Great Barrier Reef cruise boats, "sail & snorkel" yacht excursions, Whitehaven Beach cruises, dive boats, fishing tour vessels, and so on stop at the island resorts every day or on a frequent basis. Be warned, however, that once you're "captive" on an island, you may be slugged with high food and drink prices. Bear in mind, too, that although most island resorts offer non-motorized water sports, such as windsurfers and catamarans, free of charge, you will pay for activities that use fuel, such as parasailing, waterskiing, and dinghy rental.

In some places in the Whitsundays, extreme low tides may reveal rocky mud flats below the sand line. Water sports can be limited at low tide because of the low water level.

EXPLORING THE ISLANDS & THE REEF

REEF CRUISES FantaSea Cruises (☎ **07/4946 5111;** www.fantasea. com.au) makes a daily trip to Hardy Reef from Shute Harbour, near Airlie Beach, in a high-speed, air-conditioned catamaran. The boat has a bar, and a biologist gives a marine ecology talk en route. You anchor at the FantaSea Reefworld pontoon, and spend up to 3½ hours on the Reef. The day trip costs A$145 (U.S.$94.25) for adults, A$120 (U.S.$78) for seniors and students, A$75 (U.S.$48.75) for children ages 4 to 14, and A$336 (U.S.$218.40) for a family of four. Guided snorkel safaris cost A$22 (U.S.$14.30) extra. Cruise/dive packages are available for A$45 (U.S.$29.25) extra for both introductory and certified dives. Wet suit hire is A$7 (U.S.$4.55). Cruises departs at 8:15, 8:30, or 8:45am and pick up passengers at South Molle, Hamilton, Long, and Lindeman island resorts. If you're staying at Airlie Beach, the company provides free coach transfers to Shute Harbour.

A fun alternative to this day trip is FantaSea's 2-day, 1-night **ReefSleep,** in which you spend the night on the pontoon. This gives you a fabulous chance to snorkel at night when the coral is luminescent in the moonlight and nocturnal sea creatures get busy. The trip costs A$305 (U.S.$198.25) per person and includes a marine biologist's slide presentation, two scuba dives, plenty of night snorkeling, two buffet lunches, dinner under the stars with wine, and breakfast and more snorkeling on the second day. The accommodations are clean, comfortable bunkhouses. There's a limit of eight guests per night, so you have the Reef all to yourself.

SAILING & SNORKELING TRIPS 🐟 A cheaper alternative to skippering your own yacht—also called "bareboating"—around the Whitsundays (see "Come Sail with Me," below) is to join one of the numerous yachts offering 3-day, 2-night sailing adventures around the islands. You can get involved with sailing the boat as much or as little as you want, snorkel to your heart's content over one dazzling reef after another, beach-comb, explore national-park trails, learn to sail if you want, call into secluded bays, swim, sunbathe, and generally have a laid-back good time. A few companies offer introductory and qualified scuba diving for an extra cost per dive. Most boats carry a maximum of 12 passengers, so the atmosphere is always friendly and fun. The food is generally good, the showers are usually hot, and you sleep in comfortable but small berths off the galley. Some have petite private twin or double cabins.

In peak season, expect to pay around A$500 (U.S.$325) per person. Prices usually include all meals, any Marine Park entrance fees, snorkel gear, and courtesy transfers to the departure point (Abel Point Marina or Shute Harbour). In the off-season, the boats compete fiercely for passengers; you'll see signboards on the main street in Airlie Beach advertising standby deals. Among the better-known operators are *Ragamuffin II* (© 07/4946 7777), a 16.5-meter (55-ft.) ocean-going yacht; and *Prosail* (© 07/4946 5433; www.prosail.com.au), which runs trips on a fleet of 19 yachts. *Prosail* offers day trips (around A$90/ U.S.$58) as well as multiday sailing, specializing in 3-day, 2-night guided sailing trips through the Marine Park and Great Barrier Reef Marine Park for around A$470 (U.S.$300). All trips include sailing, snorkeling, scuba diving,

---

ⓘ Tips **The Secret of the Seasons**

High season in the Whitsundays is school vacations, which occur mid-April, from late June to early July, from late September to early October, late December, and all of January. The Aussie winter, June through August, is popular, too. You have to book months ahead to secure high-season accommodations, but at any other time you can get some very good deals indeed. Specials on accommodations, sailing trips, day cruises, and diving excursions fairly leap off the blackboards outside the tour-booking agents in Airlie Beach.

(Moments Come Sail with Me

If the bareboating is a mystery to you (and you're not alone), take heart. It simply means that you are sailing the boat yourself. And if that also seems pretty daunting, rest assured that thousands of people do it safely every year, with some instruction before they set out. Most of the many bareboat-yacht-charter companies in the islands will want one person on the boat to have a little experience at the helm of a vessel, but don't worry if you don't know one end of a boat from another. You do not need a license, and sailing is surprisingly easy in these uncrowded waters, where the channels are deep and hazard-free and the seas are protected from big swells by the Great Barrier Reef farther out to sea. The 74 islands are so close to each other that one is always in sight, and safe anchorages are everywhere.

If you have absolutely no boating experience, the company may require you to take a skipper along for the first day at a typical extra cost of A$140 (U.S.$91) a day. And if you think you know what you're doing but just want that extra reassurance, you can choose to have a skipper accompany you for an extra fee for the first couple of hours, or even overnight, to help you get the hang of things. In any case, most companies mail you a preparation kit before you leave home, and you receive a thorough 2- to 3-hour briefing before departure and are given easy-to-read maps marking channels, anchorage points, and the very few dangerous reefs. Your charter company will radio in once or twice a day to check that you're still afloat, and you can contact them any time for advice.

Most yachts are fitted for two to eight passengers. Try to get a boat with two berths more than you need if your budget will bear it, as space is always tight. The boats usually have a galley kitchen, a barbecue mounted to the stern, hot showers, toilet, linen, a radio and/or stereo, a motorized dinghy, and snorkeling equipment. Sleeping quarters are usually not all that luxurious and include a mix of single galley berths and one or two very compact private cabins. You can purchase your own provisions or have the charter company stock the boat for you at an extra cost of about A$30 (U.S.$20) per person per day. Most operators will load a windsurfer, fishing tackle, and scuba-diving equipment on request for an extra fee, if they are not already standard.

and bush walking and you can sail on world-famous maxi-yachts such as *Matador, Condor, Apollo* and *Hammer*. They also offer 2- and 5-day packages. Contact **Tourism Whitsundays** (see "Visitor Information," above) for details on other charters.

ISLAND HOPPING Day-trippers to Hamilton, Daydream, South Molle, Club Crocodile Long Island, and Hook Island resorts can rent the hotels' watersports equipment, laze by the beaches and pools, scuba dive, join the resorts' activities programs, hike their trails, and eat at some or all of their restaurants.

In peak season you may have to charter the boat for a week. At other times, most companies stipulate a minimum of 5 days, but many will in fact rent for 3 nights if you ask, rather than let a vessel sit idle in the marina. Five nights is a good length of time as it allows you to get familiar enough with the boat to relax and enjoy yourself.

For a 5-night rental in peak season, expect to pay around A$350 to $600 (U.S.$230–$390) for a four- to six-berth yacht, per boat, per night. Rates in the off-season, and even in the Whitsundays' busiest time June through August, will be anywhere from A$30 to $70 (U.S.$20–$45) less. If you are prepared to book within 14 days of when you want to sail, the deals can be even better; you should usually be able to find a boat at such late notice in the off-season. You will be asked to lodge a credit-card bond of around A$750 (U.S.$487). Mooring fees of A$20 to $65 (U.S.$13 to $43) per boat per night apply if you want to call into one of the half-dozen island resorts. A number of bareboat-charter companies offer "sail 'n' stay" packages that combine a few days sailing with a few days at an island resort.

Most bareboat charter companies will make complete holiday arrangements for you in the islands, including accommodations, transfers, tours, and sporting activities. Most companies operate out of Airlie Beach or Hamilton Island, or both. Some of the better-known bareboat-charter companies include: **Australian Bareboat Charters** (© 1800/075 000 in Australia, or 07/4946 9381; fax 07/4946 9220; www.ozemail.com.au/~bareboat); **Queensland Yacht Charters** (© 1800/075 013 in Australia, or 07/4946 7400; fax 07/4946 7698; www.yacht charters.com.au); **Sail Whitsunday** (© 1800/075 045 in Australia, or 07/4946 7070; fax 07/4946 7044; www.whitsunday.net.au/bareboat/sailwhit.htm); **The Moorings** (© 888/952 8420 in the U.S.; www.moorings.com; in Australia contact the company's booking agents, Club Seafarer © 1300/656 484 or 02/9389 5856; fax 02/9389 9341; www.seafarer.com.au); and **Whitsunday Rent-A-Yacht** (© 1800/075 111 in Australia, or 07/4946 9232; fax 07/4946 9512; www.rentayacht.com.au). Tourism Whitsundays (see "Visitor Information," above) can furnish you with a complete list of operators.

If you don't want to sail yourself, there are countless skippered sailing trips through the islands (see the "Sailing & Snorkeling Trips" section above for details).

See "The Whitsunday Island Resorts," below, for details on where to stay. Club Crocodile Long Island is a rather noisy, unpretentious resort that nonetheless has plentiful water sports, picturesque hiking trails, wild wallabies, and a large beach-cum-tidal flat where you can laze on sun lounges.

You can get to the islands on your own by ferry (see "Getting Around," above), or take an organized day trip that visits one, two, or even three islands in a day. **FantaSea Cruises** (© **1800/650 851** in Australia, or 07/4946 5111; www.fantasea.com.au), **Whitsunday All Over** (© **1300/366 494** in Australia, or 07/4946 6900), and **Whitsunday Island Adventure Cruises** (© **07/4946 5255** for the booking agent) all offer them, as do several yachts. Whitsunday All Over also does a day trip to Bali Hai, an uninhabited isle where you can snorkel, dive, view the coral from a large submersible, or laze on the sand. Rates for day trips range from A$36.50 to $75 (U.S.$23.75 to $48.75).

SCENIC FLIGHTS Expect to pay around A$180 (U.S.$117) for a 1-hour flight over the outer Reef (a spectacular sight from the air), about A$250 (U.S.$162.50) for a seaplane flight to a private Reef pontoon to snorkel for a couple of hours, way up to A$375 (U.S.$243.75), even more, for a helicopter to drop you on a deserted coral-edged island with a champagne seafood picnic and snorkel gear. **Hamilton Island Aviation** (© 07/4946 8249) and **Air Whitsunday Seaplanes** (© 07/4946 9111) both do a big range of such tours. Air Whitsunday also does day trips to posh Hayman (see "The Whitsunday Island Resorts," below), the only operator to do so.

FISHING Reef fishing is superb throughout the islands; red emperor, coral trout, sweetlip, and snapper are common catches. One of the most popular charter vessels is the 16.2-meter (54-ft.) timber cruiser *Moruya* (© 07/4946 6665, or 07/4946 7127 after hours). Day trips depart Shute Harbour daily at 9:45am and return at 5:45pm. They include lunch, bait, and hand reels. Fishing rods can be hired for A$15 (U.S.$9.75) for the day, or you can take your own. The crew will even clean your catch for you. Adults pay A$75 (U.S.$48.75), seniors A$70 (U.S.$45.50), children ages 4 to 14 A$37 (U.S.$24.05), and a family of four A$185 (U.S.$120.25).

The 12-meter (40-ft.) *Marlin Blue* (© 07/4948 0999 for the booking office) takes reef and game anglers out from Abel Point Marina and South Molle Island Resort for A$245 (U.S.$159.25) per person for a full day, based on a shared charter. That includes lunch, bait, and tackle; drinks are extra. The boat departs the mainland at 7am and returns around 5:30pm.

If you want to undertake your own fishing expedition, **Harbourside Boat Hire** (© 07/4946 9330), in Shute Harbour, rents motorized dinghies for A$50 (U.S.$32.50) for a half day or A$70 (U.S.$45.50) for a full day. Half-cabin cruisers cost A$70 (U.S.$45.50) for a half day or A$120 (U.S.$78) for a full day. They also sell tackle, bait, ice, and all your fishing needs.

ECO TOURS Visitors to the Whitsundays can get up-close-and-personal with crocodiles in their natural habitat on new tours run by Proserpine resident Steve Watson. **Proserpine River Eco Tours** (© 0408/071 544 mobile phone) combines an open-air wagon ride through pristine wetlands and a boat trip on the river to learn more about one of Queensland's major crocodile-breeding

---

Finds Hitting the Sand at Whitehaven Beach

The 6-kilometer (3¾-mile) stretch of pure-white silica sand on **Whitehaven Beach** 👀 will leave you in rapture. The beach, located on uninhabited Whitsunday Island, does not boast a lot of coral, but the swimming is good, and the densely forested shore is beautiful for strolling. Take a book and chill out. Some sailboat day trips visit it, as do several motorized vessel operators, including the *Lindeman Pacific* (© 07/4946 6922, or 07/4946 5580 after hours) and *Fantasea Cruises* (© 07/4946 5111). Expect to pay around A$65 (U.S.$42) per person for the day, with lunch.

Moments Whale-Watching in the Whitsundays

Humpback whales migrate to the Whitsundays every July through September to give birth to their calves. These curious and fearless giants of the deep come right up to the boat. **Fantasea Cruises (© 07/4946 5111; www.fantasea.com.au)** runs whale-watching cruises in season; trips feature an onboard whale talk and educational videos. The cost is about A$95 (U.S.$62) per adult, and if you don't see any whales on your day out, you can go again another day for free, or choose another of Fantasea's cruises as an alternative.

---

grounds. This is the only place to see crocs in safety in the wild south of the Daintree. Bus pickups operate from Airlie Beach, Cannonvale, and Proserpine for the morning and afternoon tours, which each run for about 4 hours, depending on tides, and cost A$48 (U.S.$31.20) per person.

HIKING & FOUR-WHEEL-DRIVE SAFARIS The hills behind Airlie Beach stretch into the nearby Conway State Forest and are rich in giant strangler figs, ferns, and palms. If you're lucky you'll spot a giant blue Ulysses butterfly. Several companies run half-day four-wheel-drive safaris. Hiking trails ranging in length from 1 kilometer (just over half a mile) to 5.4 kilometers (3¼ miles) lead through open forest or down to the beach in Conway National Park, which spans Shute Harbour Road between Airlie Beach and Shute Harbour. One trail has signboards explaining the Aboriginal uses of the plants you are passing; several trails offer impressive views of the islands. The trails depart from one of three parking lots along Shute Harbour Road. The **Queensland Parks and Wildlife Service information center (© 07/4946 7022)**, on Shute Harbour Road at Mandalay Road, 2.5 kilometers (1½ miles) northeast of Airlie Beach has maps and self-guiding brochures; it's open Monday through Friday from 8am to 5pm and most, but not all, Saturdays from 9am to 1pm.

GOLF Serious golfers should not miss a round on arguably Australia's best resort course, the championship **Turtle Point golf course** ✆ at Laguna Quays Resort, Kunapipi Springs Road, Midge Point (© **1800/812 626** in Australia, or 07/4947 7777), a 45-minute drive south of Airlie Beach. An 18-hole round dodging wallabies, goannas, and kookaburras on these difficult fairways will set you back A$55 (U.S.$35.75) midweek, A$66 (U.S.$42.90) weekends, plus A$30 (U.S.$19.50) for clubs, A$10 (U.S.$6.50) for shoes, and A$25 (U.S.$16.25) for a round-trip shuttle transfer.

SEA KAYAKING ✆ If you have strong arms, sea kayaking is a wonderful way to enjoy the islands. Daydream Island and the beaches and bays of the North, Mid, and South Molle group of islands are all within paddling distance of the mainland. It's common to see dolphins, turtles, and sharks along the way. One of the area's most established operators is **Salty Dog Sea Kayaking (© 07/4946 1388**, or 0419 544 841 mobile phone; www.saltydog.com.au; saltydog@mackay. net.au), which takes escorted day trips through the islands on Monday, Thursday, and Friday, departing at 8:30am and returning at 5pm. The trips usually depart from Shute Harbour but also run from the island resorts on request. Two-day expeditions depart Tuesday and Saturday. A day trip is A$80 (U.S.$52) per person, 2-day trips are A$235 (U.S.$152.75); rates include snorkel gear, meals, hotel pickup, and, on overnight trips, camping gear. They also deliver sea kayaks to you anywhere in the Whitsundays. A full day's rental is from A$40 (U.S.$26) for a single kayak, A$70 (U.S.$45.50) for a double, including delivery and pickup and all safety equipment.

AIRLIE BEACH
640km (384 miles) S of Cairns; 1,146km (687½ miles) N of Brisbane

The little town of Airlie Beach is the focal point of activity on the Whitsunday mainland. The town is only a few blocks long, but you will find an adequate choice of decent accommodations, a small selection of good restaurants and bars, a nice boutique or two, and facilities such as banks and a supermarket. Cruises and yachts depart from either Shute Harbour, a 10-minute drive south on Shute Harbour Road, or Abel Point Marina, a 10-minute walk west along the foreshore or a quick drive over the hill on Shute Harbour Road.

Airlie Beach has a new A$8-million (U.S.$5.2-million) artificial lagoon, off-set by sandy beaches and landscaped parkland, which resolves the problem of where to swim in stinger season. The lagoon is the size of about six full-size Olympic swimming pools, set in 4 hectares (10 acres) of botanic gardens, with a children's pool, plenty of shade, barbecues, picnic shelters, toilets and showers, and parking.

Perched on the edge of the Coral Sea, with views across Pioneer Bay and the Whitsunday Passage, Airlie Beach has a village atmosphere where life revolves around the beach and the marina by day, and the bars and restaurants by night.

The spit of land between Airlie Bay and Boathaven Bay is home to the Airlie Beach Sailing Club. Shute Harbour, 11 kilometers (7 miles) from Airlie Beach, is one of Queensland's busiest ports, filled with yachts, cruisers, water taxis, ferries and fishermen. For a bird's-eye view, head to the Lions Lookout.

WHERE TO STAY
Whitsunday Terraces Resort   These studio and one-bedroom apartments on a hillside a steep 2-minute walk above Airlie Beach give real "value with a view." The one-bedroom apartments have especially roomy, light-filled living rooms, and every apartment has a big balcony. All are furnished differently, but to a high standard, and serviced daily. The front desk lends hair dryers. Guests gather around the swimming pool/sun deck/restaurant/cocktail bar, which, like the rooms, has sweeping views over the town to the bay and Twin Cone Island.

Golden Orchid Dr. (off Shute Harbour Rd.), Airlie Beach, QLD 4802. © **1800/075 062** in Australia, or 07/4946 6788. Fax 07/4946 7128. www.whitsunday.net.au/terraces. 65 units. A$138 (U.S.$89.70) studio; A$149 (U.S.$96.85) 1-bedroom apt. Extra person A$15 (U.S.$9.75). Rates lower for stays of 3 nights or more. AE, DC, MC, V. **Amenities:** Restaurant, bar; 2 outdoor pools; 2 Jacuzzis; tour desk. *In room:* A/C and ceiling fans, TV, kitchenette.

Whitsunday Wanderers Resort *(Kids*   Set in 7 hectares (18 acres) of tropical gardens on the main street of Airlie Beach, this laid-back resort fits right in with the Airlie lifestyle. Accommodations are scattered around the grounds in blocks of four- to eight-rooms with open-air parking under the trees. The decor is old-fashioned, but you get plenty of space, a kitchenette, a decent-size bathroom, and a big balcony or patio for your money. Hair dryers are on loan at reception, and irons and ironing boards are in the communal laundry area. This is a good choice for families as there is plenty of room on the grounds for the kids to run around, as well as half- and full-size tennis courts, an 18-hole minigolf course, archery, Ping-Pong, volleyball, pools, and a kids' playground. All activities are free.

Shute Harbour Rd., Airlie Beach, QLD 4802. ℂ **1800/075 069** in Australia, or 07/4946 6446. Fax 07/4946 6761. 104 units (all with shower only). A$120 (U.S.$78) double. Ask about off-season discounts, overnight and honeymoon packages, and packages that include meals. AE, MC, V. Free parking. **Amenities:** Restaurant and bar; 3 outdoor pools; 5 tennis courts; Jacuzzi; exercise room; tour desk; free kids' club during school vacations; babysitting; coin-operated laundry. *In room:* A/C and ceiling fans, TV with satellite and free 24-hr. movies; kitchenette; unstocked fridge; coffeemaker.

WHERE TO DINE

Mangrove Jack's PIZZA/CAFE FARE   Bareboat sailors, local sugar farmers, Sydney yuppies, and European backpackers all flock to this big open-fronted sports bar/restaurant. The mood is upbeat but pleasantly casual, the surrounds are spic-and-span, and the food passes muster. Wood-fired pizza with trendy toppings is the specialty. There is no table service; just place your order at the bar and collect your food when your number is called. The more than 50 wines come by the glass.

In the Airlie Beach Hotel, 16 The Esplanade (enter via Shute Harbour Rd.). ℂ 07/4946 6233. Reservations recommended. Main courses A$7.90–$19.90 (U.S.$5.15–$12.95). AE, DC, MC, V. Daily 10am–midnight.

THE WHITSUNDAY ISLAND RESORTS

There are about 10 resorts of varying degrees of splendor; accommodations range from positively glitzy to comfortably mid-range to downright old-fashioned.

VERY EXPENSIVE

Hayman 𝆏𝆏𝆏   This is the most luxurious, glitzy, and glamorous resort in Australia. And by the time you get there, a A$12-million (U.S.$7.8 million) redevelopment will have ensured that it is even more so. Plans for Hayman's new look include refurbishment of its reception area, Lagoon suites and superior rooms, creation of 15 new Lagoon deluxe rooms, 16 Beach Garden rooms (each with private veranda, open patios, and outdoor rinse showers), a spa, and a contemporary beachfront restaurant.

Check-in is done over a glass of bubbly aboard the resort's sleek launch that meets you at Hamilton Island airport. On arrival, you won't take long to find your way through the open-air sandstone lanais, cascading ponds, and tropical foliage to the fabulous hexagonal complex of swimming pools by the sea. Despite the luxury, Hayman is relaxed. Dress is beachwear by day, smart casual at night (but pack something elegant for dinner, if you wish). An impressive lineup of activities is available, and it's probably fair to say the staff at Hayman can organize almost anything you desire.

While Hayman is renowned for the antiques, artworks, and fine objets gracing its public areas, the four-story accommodations are welcoming. Every room or suite has a balcony or terrace, bathrobes, and valet service (and butler service in the penthouses). Pool Wing rooms, which were renovated in 2000 with marble floors and bathrooms and tropically elegant furnishings, have views over the pool, and also to the sea from the third and fourth floors. Lagoon Wing rooms overlook a lagoon and have sea views from the third floor. As for the rest, you'll have to wait and see, but the betting is you won't be disappointed.

Hayman Island, Whitsunday Islands, QLD 4801. ℂ **1800/075 175** in Australia, or call Leading Hotels of the World (ℂ 800/223-6800 in the U.S. and Canada, 0800/181 123 in the U.K., 1800/409 063 in Ireland, 0800/44 1016 in New Zealand, 03/9866 8085 (Melbourne sales office), or 07/4940 1234 (the island). Fax 03/9866 8665 (Melbourne sales office) or 07/4940 1567 (the island). www.hayman.com.au. 245 units. A$544.50–$925 (U.S.$353–$601) double; A$1,485–$1,650 (U.S.$965–$1,072) suite; A$1,980–$3,630 (U.S.$1,287–$2,359) penthouse. Children under 15 stay free in parents' room. Children 4–14 charged 50% for all dining costs. Ask about packages. AE, DC, MC, V. Resort launch meets all flights at Hamilton Island Airport for the 55-min. transfer. Helicopter and seaplane transfers available. Hayman Island is 33km (21 miles) from Shute Harbour.

Amenities: 4 restaurants, 3 bars; 3 swimming pools (1 saltwater and 2 heated freshwater); beachside 9-hole golf putting green; 5 day/night tennis courts (with ball machine and coaching); extensive health club with massage and sauna; spa; outdoor Jacuzzi; water sports (including parasailing, water-skiing, windsurfing, and catamarans; dive center offering dive day trips, courses, and gear rental); free daily kids' club for children ages 5–14, and creche for younger kids; game room; concierge; tour desk; business center and secretarial services; upscale shopping arcade; salon; 24-hr. room service; babysitting; dry cleaning/laundry service. *In room:* A/C, TV with free and pay-per-view movies, fax, minibar, fridge, coffeemaker, hair dryer, iron, safe.

EXPENSIVE

Hamilton Island *Kids*   More a vacation village than a single resort, Hamilton has the widest range of activities, accommodation styles, and restaurants of any Great Barrier Reef island resort. Thanks to a A$40-million (U.S.$26-million) refurbishment over the past 4 years, the place is looking fresh. Accommodation choices are extra-large rooms and suites in the high-rise hotel, high-rise one- and two-bedroom apartments, Polynesian-style bungalows in tropical gardens (but too close to the road for real privacy), and glamorous rooms in the two-story, adults-only Beach Club, which sports minimalist decor and a personal "host" to cater to every whim. The best sea views come from the second-floor Beach Club rooms, from floors 5 to 18 of the hotel, and from most apartments. Amenities vary depending on your accommodation choice so check when booking.

On one side of the island is a marina village with cafes, restaurants, shops, and a yacht club. On the other are the accommodations, a large and inviting freeform pool and swim-up bar, and the wide curve of Cat's Eye Beach. Hamilton offers a huge range of water sports, fishing trips, and cruises, speedboat rides, Go-Karts, a "wire flyer" flying-fox hang glider, a pistol/clay target/rifle range, minigolf, an aquatic driving range, beach barbecue safaris in an army truck, hiking trails, an Aussie fauna park where you can cuddle a koala, and an extensive daily activities program. Because the resort is split by a steep hill, you need to get around by shuttle (which runs half-hourly or hourly between 10am and 8pm at A$5.50/U.S.$3.60 a day), by golf buggy (A$15/U.S.$9.75 per hr. or A$55/U.S.$35.75 for 24 hr.), by inexpensive taxi, or on foot. Despite the price, everyone seems to go for the buggies, so the place can feel like rush hour. To get away, hit the beach or the hiking trails, because most of the 750-hectare (1,853-acre) island is virgin bushland. The biggest drawback is that just about every activity—including non-motorized watercraft—costs big-time, whether it's A$25 (U.S.$16.25) an hour for a catamaran, A$40 (U.S.$26) for 50 pistol shots, or a frightening A$250 (U.S.$162.50) for a scuba-diving trip.

Hamilton Island (16km/10 miles SE of Shute Harbour), Whitsunday Islands, QLD 4803. ✆ **1800/075 110** in Australia, or 02/8353 8444 (reservations office in Sydney), or 07/4946 9999 (the island). Fax 02/8353 8499 (reservations office in Sydney) or 07/4946 8888 (the island). www.hamiltonisland.com.au. 737 units (some with shower only). A$250 (U.S.$162) bungalow or Palm Terrace; A$324–$649 (U.S.$210–$422) apt (to sleep 5 or 6); hotel A$347–$489 (U.S.$225–$318) double, A$672–$745 (U.S.$436–$484) suite; Beach Club A$486 (U.S.$315) double. Extra person A$27 (U.S.$17.55). Children under 12 stay free in parents' room using existing bedding and eat free from kids' menu at 5 restaurants. No children in Beach Club rooms. Ask about packages. AE, DC, MC, V. Airlines fly into Hamilton Island Airport. Free airport-resort transfers for all guests. FantaSea Cruises (✆ 1800/650 851 in Australia, or 07/4946 5111) provides launch transfers from Shute Harbour and most other islands. **Amenities:** 10 restaurants, 7 bars; 6 outdoor pools; minigolf and driving range; day/night tennis courts; health club and spa; extensive range of water sports and activities; bike rental; childcare center for kids from 6 weeks to 14 years (in 3 groups); concierge (hotel and Beach Club only); tour desk; business center and secretarial services; shopping arcade; salon; room service (18 hr. for Beach Club guests; 16 hr. for hotel guests); massage; babysitting; coin-operated laundry; laundry service (hotel only); *In room:* A/C, TV (some rooms have VCR, some have pay movies), fax, kitchen (apartments only), minibar, coffeemaker, hair dryer, iron, safe.

MODERATE

Hook Island Wilderness Resort   This humble collection of cabins and campsites on a white sandy beach is one of the few really affordable island resorts on the Great Barrier Reef. That makes it popular with backpackers and anybody who just wants to dive, rent canoes, play beach volleyball, visit the underwater observatory, hike, fish in the four-person flat-bottom boat, laze in the pool and Jacuzzi, and chill out. Good snorkeling is footsteps from shore, and the resort's dive center conducts first-time and regular dives off the beach. Hook is a national park and the second-largest Whitsunday island. You need to be able to get along without room service, in-room telephones, hair dryers and smart accommodations, because the cabins are just basic huts with beds or bunks sleeping six or eight. All come with fresh bed linen, but bring your own bath towels. A store sells essentials, but try to come with everything you need.

Hook Island (40km/25 miles NE of Shute Harbour), Whitsunday Islands. (Postal address: P.M.B. 23, Mackay, QLD 4741.) ℂ 07/4946 9380. Fax 07/4946 9470. www.hookislandresort.com.au. 20 tent sites; 2 10-bed dormitories; 10 cabins, 4 with bathroom (shower only). A$66 (U.S.$42.90) cabin without bathroom double; extra adult A$22 (U.S.$14.30), extra child 4–14 A$17.50 (U.S.$11.40). A$105 (U.S.$68) cabin with bathroom double; extra adult A$27.50 (U.S.$17.90), extra child A$22 (U.S.$14.30). Tent site A$14.30 (U.S.$9.30) adult, A$7.70 (U.S.$5) child 4–14. Dorm bed A$22 (U.S.$14.30) adult, A$17.50 (U.S.$11.40) child (linen supplied). Ask about packages. MC, V. Prosail Dive provides transfers from the mainland at A$36 (U.S.$23.40) per person, round-trip. Boat leaves Shute Harbour at 8:30am and leaves Hook Island for the return trip at 4:30pm (trip time: 45 min.). Book through the resort. **Amenities:** Cafe and bar; outdoor pool; Jacuzzi; water-sports equipment (snorkel gear, canoes, and sea kayaks); tour desk. *In room:* A/C, minifridge, coffeemaker.

South Molle Island ℱ   South Molle is a good-value island choice. It's not glamorous but it's pretty, with many free activities, and all meals included in the rates. The complex, built around a curving white-sand bay, is getting on in years, but beachfront units were refurbished in 1999 and the public areas in 2001, with the addition of a waterfall Jacuzzi pool and children's wading pool. The accommodations are modest, but well maintained and set in tropical gardens or along a hillside. Each unit has sea, garden, or golf-course views. The beachfront units, especially those with Jacuzzis, are positively trendy. Reception lends hair dryers.

The 405-hectare (1,000-acre) island is a hilly national park of grasslands, rain forest, and eucalypts with 16 kilometers (10 miles) of walking trails, including a steep climb to Mt. Jeffreys for fabulous 360° views. A packed daily activities program offers everything from parasailing to coconut-throwing competitions. The dive shop makes dive and snorkel day trips, takes first-timers diving in the bay, and runs courses. The island is rimmed with inlets accessible by hiking or rented dinghy. Snorkeling safaris are run some days to better reefs than those around the island. Rainbow lorikeets are everywhere, and you can feed them at 3pm every day at the golf bar.

Although the dining room lacks sea views, the buffet food is fine. If you don't choose a full-board rate, good meals are available at extra cost in Coral's restaurant some nights, and a cafe sells light meals. There's live entertainment every night in the large bar, from a staff song-and-dance show to cane-toad racing to the Friday-night "Flames of Polynesia" dinner show.

South Molle Island (7km/4 miles E of Shute Harbour), Whitsunday Islands. (Postal address: P.M.B. 21, Mackay, QLD 4741). ℂ 1800/075 080 in Australia, or 07/4946 9433. Fax 07/4946 9580. www.southmolleisland.com. au. 200 units (some with shower only, some also with Jacuzzi). A$342–$474 (U.S.$222.30–$308.10) double. Extra adult A$171–$237 (U.S.$111.15–$154.05); extra child 3–14 A$55 (U.S.$35.75). Family rates available in some rooms. Rates include all meals. Ask about packages. AE, DC, MC, V. FantaSea Cruises (ℂ 1800/650 851 in Australia, or 07/4946 5111) and Whitsunday All Over (ℂ 1300/366 494 in Australia, or 07/4946 9499) provide launch transfers from Shute Harbour and most other islands. **Amenities:** 2 restaurants, coffee shop, 3 bars; outdoor pool and children's wading pool; 9-hole golf course (small charge for balls); 2 day/night tennis courts; exercise room; Jacuzzi; water sports (catamarans, windsurfers, and paddle-skis are free; jet-skis, water skis and tube rides cost extra); free daily kids' club for 5 and unders, and for 6–12-year-olds during Australian school vacations; tour desk; salon; massage; babysitting; coin-operated laundry; dry cleaning/laundry service. *In room:* A/C, TV, stocked minibar, fridge, coffeemaker, hair dryer (on request), iron.

Whitsunday Wilderness Lodge ★★ This resort was designed to show off the Whitsundays' natural beauty. Tucked in a cove under towering hoop pines and palms, it is an environmentally sensitive lodge on a national-park island for people who want to explore the wilderness in basic comfort, but without the crowds, noisy water sports, or artificial atmosphere of a resort. It's also a great place to meet other travelers. A maximum 20 guests stay in simple but smart new (1999) cabins facing the sea, each with a double and single bed, modern bathrooms, and a private deck facing the sea. Solar power rules, so there is no air-conditioning, TV, hair dryer, iron, or other appliances. There is one public phone. Social life centers on an open-sided gazebo by the beach, equipped with a natural-history library and CDs, where everyone dines together at slab tables under the Milky Way on fabulous buffet-style campfire meals. Access is only by a short but stunning helicopter flight from Hamilton Island.

Every morning (except Sun), the resort managers decide what the day's excursion will be, usually aboard the lodge's gleaming 10.2-meter (34-ft.) catamaran. It could be sailing to tidal flats to look for red and purple rhinoceros starfish, sea kayaking the mangroves to spot giant green sea turtles (which are common around the lodge), snorkeling the fringing reef on uninhabited islands, or bush-walking to a magical milkwood grove no one else knows about. Or you may prefer to just laze in the hammocks, or head off with a free sea kayak and snorkel gear. The beach is more tidal flat than sand, but clean and firm enough to sunbathe on. Wildlife abounds, including Myrtle, the lodge's pet kangaroo. Those who stay here consider it a plus that no ferries or cruise boats call and that the lodge is inaccessible to day-trippers or hikers from other resorts on this 1,215-hectare (3,001-acre) island.

Long Island (16km/10 miles SE of Shute Harbour), Whitsunday Islands. ✆ **07/3221 7799.** Fax 07/3220 2250 (Brisbane reservations office) or 07/4946 9787 the island (all bookings and enquiries to Brisbane office, 9am–5pm weekdays only). www.southlongisland.com. 10 units (all with shower only). A$1,596 (U.S.$1,037) double for 4 nights (min. stay). Rates include all meals, helicopter transfers from Hamilton Island Airport (heli-transfers from Airlie Beach are A$30/U.S.$19.50 extra one-way), daily excursions, and equipment. Rates decrease with longer stays. On "Beachcomber Weeks," held several times a year, there's a 50% discount on 6-night rates—all that's asked is that you spend time helping clean up the island's shores. MC, V. No children under 15.

6 The Capricorn Coast & the Southern Reef Islands

South of the Whitsundays, the Bruce Highway travels through rural country until it hits the beaches of the Sunshine Coast just north of Brisbane. It may not be the tourism heartland of the state, but there's still plenty to discover. The most spectacular Great Barrier Reef island of them all, Heron Island, is off the coast from Gladstone. Heron's reefs are a source of enchantment for divers and snorkelers, its waters boasting 21 fabulous dive sites. In summer giant turtles nest on its beaches, and in winter humpback whales cruise by.

North of Gladstone is Rockhampton and the Capricorn Coast, named after the Tropic of Capricorn that runs through it. Rockhampton is also a stepping stone to Great Keppel Island, a friendly resort island popular with families, travelers, and young Aussies on holiday. To the south, off the small town of Bundaberg, lies another tiny coral cay, Lady Elliot Island, which is a nesting site for tens of thousands of sea birds, and has a first-rate fringing reef. Two little-known attractions in Bundaberg are its good shore scuba diving and a loggerhead turtle rookery that operates in summer on the beach. Farther south lies the world's largest sand island, the World Heritage–listed Fraser Island, which can be negotiated only on foot or by four-wheel-drive.

ROCKHAMPTON: THE BEEF CAPITAL
1,055km (633 miles) S of Cairns; 638km (383 miles) N of Brisbane

"Rocky" is the unofficial capital of the sprawling beef-cattle country inland, and the gateway to Great Keppel Island, which boasts some of the few inexpensive island retreats in Queensland. Heritage buildings line the Fitzroy River, where barramundi await keen fishermen. Every Friday night at the Great Western Hotel, bull-riding cowboys take to the rodeo ring to test their skills against local Brahman bulls.

ESSENTIALS
GETTING THERE   Rockhampton is on the Bruce Highway, a 3½-hour drive south of Mackay, and almost 2 hours north of Gladstone.

Qantas (© 13 13 13 in Australia) has flights from Brisbane, and from Cairns via Townsville and Mackay. Qantas also flies from Bundaberg and Gladstone.

Several **Queensland Rail** (© 13 22 32 in Queensland, or 07/3235 1122) trains call into Rockhampton weekly or daily on the Brisbane–Cairns route. The trip from Brisbane takes just 7 hours on the high-speed Tilt train; the fare is A$81.40 (U.S.$52.91) economy class and $173.80 (U.S.$113) business class.

McCafferty's (© 13 14 99 in Australia) and **Greyhound-Pioneer** (© 13 20 30 in Australia) call at Rockhampton on their many daily coach services between Brisbane and Cairns. The fare is A$66 (U.S.$42.90) from Brisbane (trip time: just over 11 hr.) and A$103 (U.S.$66.95) from Cairns (trip time: about 16½ hr.).

VISITOR INFORMATION   Drop by the **Capricorn Tourism bureau**, whose information center is at the city's southern entrance on Gladstone Road (at the Capricorn Spire; © 07/4927 2055). It's open daily from 9am to 5pm.

GETTING AROUND   **Avis** (© 07/4927 3344), **Budget** (© 07/4926 4888), **Hertz** (© 07/4922 2721), and **Thrifty** (© 07/4927 8755) have offices in Rockhampton

EXPLORING THE AREA: CAVERNS, ABORIGINAL CULTURE & MORE
Olsen's Capricorn Caverns ★ (© 07/4934 2883), 23 kilometers (13 miles) north of Rockhampton at Olsen's Caves Road, off the Bruce Highway, have been a popular attraction in this part of the world ever since Norwegian pioneer John Olsen stumbled upon them in 1882. The limestone caves have origins in an ancient coral reef (380 million years old) and today are a maze of small tunnels and larger chambers. The 1-hour tour, which winds through large caverns with stalactite and stalagmite formations before entering the 20-meter-high (65½-ft.-high) Cathedral Cave, is A$11 (U.S.$7.15) for adults, A$10 (U.S.$6.50) for seniors and students, and A$5.50 (U.S.$3.60) for children ages 5 to 15. It departs daily on the hour from 9am to 4pm (closing time is 5pm). Spelunkers (over 16 years) can squeeze through tunnels and chimneys and rock climb on a 4-hour adventure tour that costs A$45 (U.S.$29.25); book 24 hours ahead for this. Plan enough time here to walk the 30-minute dry rain-forest trail, watch the video on bats in the interpretive center, and feed the wild kangaroos. From December 1 to January 10, you can catch the Summer Solstice light cave

on a tour departing every morning at 11am. On the longest day of the year the sun moves slowly over the Tropic of Capricorn and a ray of pure light pours through a hole in the limestone caves. It's known as the Summer Solstice phenomenon and is the only time of year when the sun is directly over the Tropic of Capricorn. The caves are also home to thousands of small insectivorous bats, which leave the cave at sunset to feed. Three resident flying foxes housed near the kiosk also provide much interest for visitors of all ages. You can buy sandwiches from the kiosk to eat on the pleasant grounds, take a dip in the pool, and even camp if you like for A$10 (U.S.$6.50) double for a tent site or A$16 (U.S.$10.40) for a powered site. Rothery's Coaches (© **07/4922 4320**) provide transfers from town.

The **Dreamtime Cultural Centre** (© **07/4936 1655**), located on the Bruce Highway opposite the Yeppoon turnoff, 6 kilometers (3¾ miles) north of town, showcases Aboriginal culture. Ninety-minute tours of burial sites and rock art, with didgeridoo demonstrations and boomerang-throwing classes, run daily at 10:30am and 1pm. There's also a sandstone cave replica, a display on the dugong (manatee) culture of the Torres Strait Islanders, and an Aboriginal crafts shop. The center is open daily from 10am to 3:30pm. Closed Anzac Day, Christmas, and New Year's Day. Admission, including the tour, is A$12.10 (U.S.$7.85) for adults and A$5.50 (U.S.$3.60) for kids.

Rockhampton has two free public botanic gardens, both nice for a stroll and a barbecue picnic. The Kershaw Gardens, which display Aussie rain-forest, wetland, and fragrant plants from north of the 30th parallel, also have a monorail and a pioneer-style slab hut where Devonshire teas are served. Enter off Charles Street. Admission is free to the small zoo in the **Rockhampton Botanic Gardens** (© **07/4922 1654**), which features chimps, crocs, 'roos, koalas, monkeys, flying foxes, lorikeets, and a range of other creatures. It is open from 6am to 6pm daily. Enter off Ann Street or Spencer Street.

WHERE TO STAY
Rydges Capricorn Resort ⚲   The 20 kilometers (12½ miles) of unbroken beach which fronts this resort—and the fact that it is the only resort of any size or style in this region—are reason enough to visit. The resort is about 9 kilometers (5½ miles) from the pretty seaside town of Yeppoon, about 45 kilometers (28 miles) north of Rockhampton Airport. Open since 1986, the resort was built and is still owned by Japanese businessman Yohachiro Iwasaki, and you will still hear the locals refer to it as "the Iwasaki Resort" despite its several changes of name over the years. Now showing its age a little, the resort is nevertheless cheerful and pleasant, and the rooms are spacious. The best of the three accommodation blocks is The Palms for its views over the beach and out to Great Keppel Island. The main resort block is dominated by one of the largest freshwater swimming pools in the southern hemisphere, popular with visiting local families, especially at weekends. Set in 22,000 acres (8910 hectares) of bushland, the resort also has an extensive wetlands area which has great bird-watching. This is not the place for a quiet getaway—it is very popular with large and sometimes noisy conference groups—but there are lots of activities, and it may be just the place to break your coastal trek.

Farnborough Rd. (P.O. Box 350), Yeppoon, QLD 4703. © **1800 075 902** in Australia, or 07/4939 5111. Fax 07/4939 5666. www.capricornresort.com. 279 units. A$200 (U.S.$130) hotel room; A$250 (U.S.$162.50) junior suite; A$275 (U.S.$179) junior suite with kitchenette; A$325 (U.S.$211) Capricorn Suite; A$355 (U.S.$230) Capricorn Suite with kitchenette; A$270 (U.S.$175.50) 1-bedroom apt; A$345 (U.S.$224) 2-bedroom apt; A$350–$380 (U.S.$227.50–$247) interconnecting family rooms. Extra person A$30 (U.S.$19.50). Free cots. Packages available year-round, including golf packages. AE, DC, MC, V. Free undercover parking. **Amenities:**

5 restaurants, 2 bars; huge outdoor freshwater swimming pool, with adjoining heated beach-style pool; 2 18-hole world-class championship golf courses; 4 tennis courts; exercise room; outdoor Jacuzzi; sauna; extensive water sports and other activities available free of charge; bike rental; activities which cost include horseback riding, land yachting, fishing, canoeing, clay-pigeon shooting, wetlands tours, wave-runners, rifle shooting; free kids' club during the day (charges apply for evening sessions); game room for children over 14; children's playground; concierge; tour desk; car-rental desk; free transfers to airport, rail or coach terminal; business center; salon; room service (7am–10:30pm); massage (in-room and poolside); babysitting; laundry service; 2-bedroom apts and Capricorn Suites with kitchens have washing machine and dryer; laundry facilities are available in The Palms and Araucaria buildings; dry cleaning service Mon–Thurs only. *In room:* A/C, TV with pay movies, kitchenette in some suites and all apts., minibar in all hotel rooms and on request in apts, tea/coffeemaking facilities, hair dryer, iron, safe (Royal Palm building only).

GREAT KEPPEL ISLAND
15km (9 miles) E of Rockhampton

This 1,454-hectare (3,635-acre) island is home to Great Keppel Island Resort (see below), renowned among Australians for its array of water sports and activities. You can stay at the resort, or take a day trip from the mainland and pay to use many of the facilities including water-sports equipment, pools, and food outlets. Seventeen beaches on the island are accessible by walking trails or dinghy (which you can rent). The resort information center will book activities and provide walking trail maps. The shallow waters and fringing reef make the island a good choice for beginner divers; experienced divers will see corals, sea snakes, turtles, and rays. If you stay overnight, you will be most likely be rewarded with one of the spectacular sunsets for which the island is famous.

ESSENTIALS

GETTING THERE   A launch operated by **Keppel Tourist Services** (✆ 07/ **4933 6744**) makes the 30-minute crossing from Rosslyn Bay Harbour, approximately 55 kilometers (33 miles) east of Rockhampton, daily at 7:30, 9:15, 11:30am, and 3:30pm. It leaves the island at 8:15am, 2, and 4:30pm. An extra 6pm service runs Fridays, returning at 6:40pm. A$29 (U.S.$18.85) adults, A$15 (U.S.$9.75) children ages 5 to 14, and A$75 (U.S.$48.75) family of four.

From Rockhampton, take the Capricorn Coast scenic drive route "10" to Emu Park and follow the signs to Rosslyn Bay Harbour. If you're coming to Rockhampton from the north, the scenic drive turnoff is just north of the city, and from there it's 46 kilometers (27½ miles) to the harbor. You can leave your car in undercover storage at **Great Keppel Island Security Car Park** (✆ 07/ **4933 6670**) at 422 Scenic Hwy., near the harbor, for A$6.50 to $8 (U.S.$4.20– $5.20) per day.

Rothery's Coaches (✆ 07/4922 4320) runs a daily service from Kern Arcade on Bolsover Street in Rockhampton to Rosslyn Bay Harbour and back, three times a day. You can request a free pickup from the airport, train station, or your hotel. Round-trip fares from town are A$13.75 (U.S.$9) for adults, A$11 (U.S.$7.15) for seniors and students, A$7 (U.S.$4.55) for children ages 5 to 14. The round-trip fare to/from the airport is A$27.50 (U.S.$17.90) for adults, A$22 (U.S.$14.30) for seniors and students, A$13.75 (U.S.$8.95) for children, and A$68.75 (U.S.$44.70) families.

Guests at Great Keppel Island Resort can fly from Rockhampton on one of four daily 15-minute services with Queensland Air Services. The round-trip fare is A$130 (U.S.$84.50) adults and A$65 (U.S.$42.25) children 3 to 14. Book through the resort (see below).

VISITOR INFORMATION   The **Great Keppel Island Information Centre,** at the ferry terminal at Rosslyn Bay Harbour (✆ **1800/77 4488** in Australia) dispenses information about the island's activities and accommodations.

WHERE TO STAY & DINE

Great Keppel Island Resort *Kids* Despite its inability to shake a '70s advertising campaign which has left the resort firmly stuck with an image as a place for young party animals to "get wrecked," Great Keppel, for my money, is one of the best places to take a family. It's unpretentious, pretty, and there's plenty to do. Just about every water- and land-based sport you can name is offered at this friendly resort, as well as more unusual pursuits such as camel rides on the beach. Many activities, including catamarans, paddle-skis, and windsurfers, are free. Activities that cost extra include scuba diving, tandem sky-diving, parasailing, guided snorkeling safaris, jet-skiing, sunset champagne sails, and reef-fishing trips, to name only a few. The white-tiled Hillside Villas with sea or bush views have smart interiors and air-conditioning. Other units will have air-conditioning as part of a 2001 refurbishment. My pick is the beachfront units for their location. The palm-lined grass along the beachfront gives great shade between forays into the water.

The resort will be rebranded as one of the Accor hotel group's Mercure resorts from October 2001, following a A$3-million (U.S.$1.9-million) refurbishment of all rooms and public areas, so by the time you visit it should be even more appealing.

PMB 8001, North Rockhampton, QLD 4701. © **1800/245 658** in Australia, or 07/4939 5044. Fax 07/4939 1775. www.gkeppel.com.au. 193 units (133 with shower only). A$280–$360 (U.S.$182–$234) double; A$120–$180 (U.S.$78–$117) per person triple/quad-share. Extra child 3–14 A$39 (U.S.$25.35). Meal packages A$44–$59 (U.S.$28.60–$38.35) adult, A$18–$29 (U.S.$11.70–$18.85) child per day. Ask about packages. AE, DC, MC, V. **Amenities:** 3 restaurants, 4 bars; 4 outdoor pools; 9-hole golf course; 2 day/night tennis courts; 2 Jacuzzis; extensive water-sports equipment and rental; free kids' club for 3–12 year-olds; concierge; tour desk; salon; massage; babysitting; coin-operated laundry and laundry service; dry cleaning; nonsmoking rooms. *In room:* A/C (villas only), TV, minibar (villas and beachfront units only), coffeemaker, hair dryer, iron.

GLADSTONE: GATEWAY TO HERON ISLAND

550km (330 miles) N of Brisbane; 1,162 (697½ miles) S of Cairns

The industrial port town of Gladstone is the departure point for the breathtakingly beautiful Heron Island. It is also home to the delectable mud-crab, best savored over a glass of wine at the award-winning Flinders Seafood Restaurant. About 25 kilometer (16 miles) south of the town (but off the Bruce Highway) are the twin beach towns of Boyne Island and Tannum Sands, which are worth the detour.

ESSENTIALS

GETTING THERE & GETTING AROUND Gladstone is on the coast 21 kilometers (12½ miles) off the Bruce Highway. **Sunstate Airlines** (book through Qantas) has many flights a day from Brisbane (trip time: 85 min.) and one direct flight a day from Rockhampton. From Cairns it operates a "milk run" via Townsville, Mackay, and Rockhampton.

Queensland Rail (© **13 22 32** in Queensland, or 07/3235 1122) operates trains most days to Gladstone from Brisbane and Cairns. The fare from Brisbane (trip time: 6 hr. on the high-speed Tilt train) is A$69.30 (U.S.$45); fares from Cairns (trip time: 20 hr.) range from A$124.30 (U.S.$80.80) for a sitting berth to A$162.80 (U.S.$105.80) for an economy-class sleeper.

McCafferty's and **Greyhound-Pioneer** operate many daily coaches to Gladstone on their Brisbane–Cairns runs. The fare is A$57 (U.S.$37.05) from Brisbane (trip time: 10½ hr.) and A$105 (U.S.$68.25) from Cairns (trip time: 17½ hr.).

Avis (✆ 07/4978 2633), Budget (✆ 07/4972 8488), Hertz (✆ 07/4978 6899) and Thrifty (✆ 07/4972 5999) all have offices in Gladstone.

VISITOR INFORMATION   The **Gladstone Area Promotion & Development Bureau's** Information Centre is located in the ferry terminal at Gladstone Marina, Bryan Jordan Drive, Gladstone, QLD 4680 (✆ 07/4972 9922; fax 07/ 4972 5006). It's open from 8:30am to 5pm Monday through Friday, and from 9am to 5pm Saturday and Sunday.

WHERE TO STAY IN GLADSTONE

Country Plaza International   This four-level hotel in the center of town runs a free shuttle to the wharf for guests bound for Heron Island. Gladstone's best hotel, it caters primarily to business travelers, so it has ample facilities—spacious rooms with balconies, modern bathrooms, an upscale seafood restaurant, free tea and coffee in the lobby, and a pool and sun deck. Most rooms have views over the port or the city.

100 Goondoon St., Gladstone, QLD 4680. ✆ 07/4972 4499. Fax 07/ 4972 4921. 72 units. A$128 (U.S.$83.20) double. AE, DC, MC, V. Free parking. **Amenities:** Restaurant; bar; outdoor pool; 24-hr. room service; laundry service; free transfers from airport, coach terminal, marina, and train station. *In room:* A/C, TV with free movies, fax, dataport, minibar, coffeemaker, hair dryer, iron.

HERON ISLAND: JEWEL OF THE REEF ☆☆☆
72km (43¼ miles) NE of Gladstone

The difference between Heron and other islands is that once there, you have no need to travel further to the reef. Step off the beach, and you enter magnificent fields of coral that seem to stretch for miles. And the myriad lifeforms which abound here are accessible to everyone through diving, snorkeling, reef walks at low tide, or aboard a semi-submersible vessel which allows you to view the ocean floor without getting wet. When geologist Joseph Bette Jukes named this piece of paradise in 1843, he overlooked the turtles for which it is now famous and favored the reef herons which abounded on the island. There has been a resort on Heron since 1932, and in 1943 the island was made a National Park. It is a haven for wildlife and people alike, and an experience of a lifetime is almost guaranteed at any time of year. Heron is a rookery for giant green and loggerhead turtles. Resort guests gather on the beach from late November to February to watch the female turtles lay eggs, and from February to mid-April to see the hatched babies scuttle down the sand to the water. Humpback whales pass through June through September.

Three days on Heron gives plenty of time to see everything. The island is so small you can walk around it at a leisurely pace in about half an hour. One of the first things to do is to take advantage of the organized activities which operate several times a day and are designed so guests can plan their own days. Snorkeling and reef walking are major occupations for visitors—if they're not diving, that is, for the island is home to 21 of the world's most stunning dive sites.

Guided island walks provide another way to explore the island. Walks include a visit to the research station based on the island. As for the reef walk, just borrow a pair of sandshoes, a balance pole, and a viewing bucket, and head off with a guide at low tide. The walk can take up to 90 minutes, but there's no compulsion to stay and if it gets too hot you can head back for the sanctuary of your room or the shady bar area.

A fishing trip should also be put on the agenda, even for the most inexperienced. The reef fish seem to just jump onto the hook and the resort chef is happy to cook them for you for dinner!

⌐Moments Up Close & Personal with a Turtle

The egg in my hand is warm, soft, and about the size of a Ping-Pong ball. At our feet, a giant green turtle sighs deeply as she lays a clutch of about 120 eggs in a pear-shaped chamber dug from the sand. A large tear rolls from her eye. In the distance the wedge-tailed shearwaters call eerily to each other, backed by the sound of the ocean.

The egg-laying ritual of the turtles is central to a trip to Heron Island in the summer months. At night and in the early morning, small groups of people gather on the beaches to witness the turtles lumber up the beach, dig a hole in the sand, and lay their eggs. (The turtles are not easily disturbed, and you can get very close.) Every night during the season, volunteer guides from the University of Queensland research station based on the island are on hand; you can watch and ask questions as the researchers tag and measure the turtles before they return to the water. The laying season runs December through February, and only one in 5,000 hatchlings will live to return in about 50 years to lay their own eggs.

Another good place to watch the turtles nesting is at Mon Repos Beach, outside Bundaberg. Mon Repos Conservation Park is one of the two largest loggerhead-turtle rookeries in the South Pacific. The visitor center by the beach has a great display on the turtle life cycle and shows films at approximately 7:30pm each night in summer. Visitors can turn up anytime after 7pm; the action goes on all night, sometimes until as late as 6am. Nesting happens around high tide; hatching usually occurs between 8pm and midnight. Try to get there early to join the first group of 70 people, the maximum allowed at one laying or hatching. Take a flashlight if you can.

The **Mon Repos Turtle Rookery** ⌂ (© **07/4159 1652** for the visitor center) is 14 kilometers (8½ miles) east of Bundaberg's town center. Follow Bourbong Street out of town toward Burnett Heads as it becomes Bundaberg–Bargara Road. Take the Port Road to the left and look for the Mon Repos signs to the right. Admission to the visitor center is free April through November (8am–4pm), but when the turtles start nesting, you pay A$5 (U.S.$3.25) for adults, A$2 (U.S.$1.30) for children. November through March, the center is open from 7pm until 2am the next day.

GETTING THERE   A courtesy coach meets flights at 10:30am to take guests to Gladstone Marina for the 2-hour launch transfer to the island; it departs 11am daily (except Christmas). Round-trip boat transfer costs A$160 (U.S.$104) for adults, half price for kids ages 3 to 14. Make sure you take sea-sickness medication, especially for the outward bound trip. It is often rough, although for some reason the return journey is not as bad.

WHERE TO STAY ON HERON ISLAND

Heron Island Resort ⌂⌂⌂ *Kids*   Comfortable rather than glamorous is the best way to describe this resort. As one guest told me: "This is not a place where you have to dress up just to walk across the lobby." That is unlikely to change.

A stylish new look is promised, along with a restaurant designed to look like a Queenslander house with newly created ocean views. A focal point of the restaurant will be a vast communal table where solo travelers can dine with new friends (but don't worry, if you want a table for two, they'll still be there). Reef Suites, the standard motel-style rooms, will be upgraded as will the Heron and Point Suites. Heron Suites, near the beach, have screened-off sleeping quarters; and Point Suites, which have great views, are actually one big room with a king-size bed and a sitting area. The cheapest option, Turtle cabins, will be replaced by new duplex-style Turtle Rooms suitable for couples or families.

Heron Island, via Gladstone, QLD 4680 (P&O Resorts, G.P.O. Box 5287, Sydney, NSW 2001). ☎ 1800 737 678 in Australia, 800/225 9849 in the U.S. and Canada, 020 7805 3875 in the U.K., 02/9257 5050 or fax 02/9299 2477 (Sydney reservations office), or 07/4972 9055 (the island). www.poresorts.com. 109 units (some with shower only). Turtle Rooms A$364 (U.S.$236) double; Reef Suite A$532 (U.S.$345) double; Heron Suite A$620 (U.S.$403) double; Point Suite or private Beach House A$840 (U.S.$546) double. Extra adult A$140 (U.S.$91); extra children 3–14 A$80 (U.S.$52). No children allowed in Point suites or Beach House. Free crib. Rates include all meals and many activities. Ask about special packages. AE, DC, MC, V. **Amenities:** Restaurant, bar; outdoor pool; 2 day/night tennis courts; Jacuzzi; limited water-sports-equipment rental; kids' club in Australian school vacations only; game room; activities desk; babysitting; coin-operated laundry. In room: fridge, coffeemaker, hair dryer, no phone or TV (but there are public phones, a TV in the lounge, and Internet access is available at reception).

BUNDABERG: GATEWAY TO LADY ELLIOT ISLAND
384km (230½ miles) N of Brisbane; 1,439km (863½ miles) S of Cairns

The small sugar town of Bundaberg is the closest to the southern-most point of the Great Barrier Reef. If you visit the area between November and March, allow an evening to visit the Mon Repos turtle rookery. Divers may want to take in some of Australia's best shore diving right off Bundaberg's beaches.

GETTING THERE & GETTING AROUND   Bundaberg is on the Isis Highway, about 50 kilometers (31 miles) off the Bruce Highway from Gin Gin in the north and 53 kilometers (33 miles) off the Bruce Highway from just north of Childers in the south.

Sunstate Airlines (book through Qantas at ☎ 13 13 13 in Australia) flies from Brisbane. Sunstate also flies from Cairns via Townsville, Mackay, and Rockhampton, and direct from Gladstone.

Queensland Rail (☎ 13 22 32 in Queensland, or 07/3235 1122) trains stop in Bundaberg most days en route between Brisbane and Cairns. The fare is A$49.50 (U.S.$32.20) from Brisbane; fares range from A$135.30 (U.S.$87.95) for a sitting berth to A$257.40 (U.S.$167.30) for a first-class berth from Cairns.

McCafferty's (☎ 13 14 99 in Australia) and **Greyhound-Pioneer** (☎ 13 20 30 in Australia) call here many times a day on their coach runs between Brisbane and Cairns. The 7-hour trip from Brisbane costs around A$46 (U.S.$29.90). From Cairns it is a 22-hour trip, for which the fare is A$125 (U.S.$81.25).

Avis (☎ 07/4152 1877), **Budget** (☎ 07/4153 1600), **Hertz** (☎ 07/4155 2403), and **Thrifty** (☎ 07/4151 6222) all have offices in Bundaberg.

VISITOR INFORMATION   The **Bundaberg District Tourism and Development Board Information Centre** is at 271 Bourbong St. at Mulgrave Street, Bundaberg, QLD 4670 (☎ 1800/060 499 in Australia, or 07/4152 2333; www.tourgroups.net). It's open daily from 9am to 5pm.

WHAT TO SEE & DO
The best shore diving in Queensland is in **Bundaberg's Woongarra Marine Park.** It has soft and hard corals, urchins, rays, sea snakes, and 60 fish species,

plus a World War II Beaufort bomber wreck. There are several scuba operators. **Salty's Dive Centre** (© **1800/ 625 476** in Australia, or 07/4151 6422; fax 07/ 4151 4938; www.saltys.net) rents dive gear for A$45 (U.S.$29.25). They also run 4-day learn-to-dive courses priced from A$169 (U.S.$109.85) per person, and a 3-day/3-night southern Great Barrier Reef dive cruise for A$495 (U.S.$321.75). A 5-day diving course is A$580 (U.S.$377), which includes the 3-day/3-night cruise.

WHERE TO STAY

Acacia Motor Inn   This tidy motel is a short stroll from the town center. It offers slightly dated but clean, well-kept rooms and extra-large family rooms at a decent price. Local restaurants provide room service, and many are within walking distance. The five family units have kitchenettes.

248 Bourbong St., Bundaberg, QLD 4670. © **1800/35 1375** in Australia, or 07/4152 3411. Fax 07/4152 2387. acabund@fc-hotels.com.au. 26 units (all with shower only). A$79.20 (U.S.$51.50) double. Additional person A$11 (U.S.$7.15) adults, A$6 (U.S.$3.90) children under 12. A$5 (U.S.$3.25) crib. AE, DC, MC, V. **Amenities:** Outdoor saltwater pool; nearby golf course; access to nearby health club; room service; coin-operated laundry; laundry service and same-day dry cleaning; nonsmoking rooms. *In room:* A/C, TV with free movies, fax, stocked minibar, hair dryer, iron, safe.

LADY ELLIOT ISLAND *&*
80km (48 miles) NE of Bundaberg

The southernmost Great Barrier Reef island, Lady Elliot is a 42-hectare (105-acre) coral cay ringed by a wide shallow lagoon filled with dazzling coral life.

Reef walking, snorkeling, and diving are the main reasons people come to this coral cay that's so small you can walk across it in 15 minutes. You may snorkel and reef walk during only the 2 to 3 hours before and after high tide, so plan your schedule accordingly. You will see dazzling corals and brilliantly colored fish, clams, sponges, urchins, and anemones. Divers will see a good range of marine life, including green and loggerhead turtles (which nest on the beach November through March). Whales pass by June through September.

Lady Elliot is a sparse, grassy island rookery, not a lush tropical paradise, so don't expect white sand and palm trees. Some folks will find it too spartan; others will relish chilling out in a beautiful, peaceful location with reef all around. Just be prepared for the smell and constant noise of those birds.

GETTING THERE   You reach the island via a 25-minute flight from Bundaberg. Connections are available from Hervey Bay and Maroochydore. Book your air travel along with your accommodation. Round-trip fares are A$159 (U.S.$103.35) for adults and A$80 (U.S.$52) for children ages 3 to 14. There is a 10-kilogram (22-lb.) luggage limit. Day trips from Bundaberg or Hervey Bay cost A$219 (U.S.$142) per person, and include flights, snorkel gear, glass-bottom-boat ride, lunch, and guided activities.

WHERE TO STAY

Lady Elliot Island Resort *&*   Accommodation here is fairly basic, but visitors come for the reef, not the room. Reef units have a double bed (some also have two bunks), a chair or two, wardrobe space, and a deck with views through the trees to the sea. Island suites are more luxurious and have a tiny kitchenette, a diminutive living/dining area, one or two separate bedrooms, and great sea views from the deck. Both room types have modern bathrooms. Lodge rooms contain simply a bed or bunks and a small wardrobe. The permanent tents have electric lighting and a wooden floor, and are spacious and cool. Lodges and tents share the public toilets and showers. All accommodations have fans. There are

> ### *Tips* Look Out Below!
>
> When you land on the grass airstrip at Lady Elliot Island, you'll think you're on the set of Hitchcock's *The Birds*. The air is thick with tens of thousands of swirling noddy terns and bridled terns that nest in every available branch and leave their mark on every available surface—including you—so bring a big, cheap straw hat for "protection."

few facilities, other than a boutique, a swimming pool, a casual bar and snack area, and an education center. There is no air-conditioning, no keys (secure storage is at front desk), no TVs, no radio, and only one public telephone. The food is basic. The low-key activities program includes things like bush-tucker tours, fish feeding, guided snorkeling, badminton, and movie screenings, most of which are free. The island accommodates no more than 140 guests at any one time, so you pretty much get the reef to yourself.

Great Barrier Reef via Bundaberg. (P.O. Box 206, Torquay, QLD 4655). © 1800/072 200 in Australia, or 07/4125 5344. Fax 07/4125 5778. www.ladyelliot.com.au. 40 units, 20 with bathroom (shower only). A$280 (U.S.$182) double for tent cabins; A$370 (U.S.$240.50) double for Reef units; A$420 (U.S.$273) double for Island Suites. Ask about 2-, 4-, 5-, and 7-night packages, and dive packages. Rates include breakfast and dinner. AE, DC, MC, V.

7 Fraser Island: Eco-Adventures & Four-Wheel-Drive Fun

1,547km (928 miles) S of Cairns; 260km (156 miles) N of Brisbane; 15km (9 miles) E of Hervey Bay

The biggest sand island in the world, this 162,000-hectare (405,000-acre) World Heritage–listed island off the central Queensland coast attracts a mix of sensitive ecotourists and Aussie fishermen. Fraser is a pristine vista of eucalyptus woodlands, soaring dunes, clear creeks, ancient rain forest, blue lakes, ochre-colored sand cliffs, and a stunning 120.75-kilometer (75-mile-long) beach. For four-wheel-drive fans though, Fraser's true beauty lies in its complete absence of paved roads. On weekends when the fish are running, it's nothing to see 100 four-wheel-drives lining 75-Mile Beach, which is a authorized road. Pedestrians should beware!

You'll need more than a day here to see everything and to truly appreciate how stunning this place is. Allow at least 3 days to soak it all up, and to allow for the slow pace dictated by the sandy trails that call themselves roads.

ESSENTIALS

GETTING THERE   Hervey (pronounced Harvey) Bay is the main gateway to the island. Take the Bruce Highway to Maryborough, then the 34-kilometer (21-mile) road to Hervey Bay. If approaching from the north, turn off the highway at Torbanlea, north of Maryborough, and cut across to Hervey Bay. Allow 3 hours from the Sunshine Coast, a good 5 hours from Brisbane.

Guests at Kingfisher Bay Resort (see below) can get to the resort aboard the Kingfisher Bay Fastcat, which departs Urangan Boat Harbour at Hervey Bay six times a day between 8:30am and 6:30pm. Round-trip fare for the 40-minute crossing is A$35 (U.S.$22.75) adults and A$18 (U.S.$11.70) kids 4 to 14. The resort runs a courtesy shuttle from Hervey Bay's airport and coach terminal to the harbor. You can park free in the open at the Fastcat terminal; **Fraser Coast Secure Vehicle Storage,** at 629 The Esplanade (© 07/4125 2783), a 5-minute walk from the terminal, gives covered parking for A$7.70 to $9.90 (U.S.$5 to $6.45) per 24 hours.

Both **Greyhound-Pioneer** and **McCafferty's** coaches stop several times a day in Hervey Bay on their Brisbane–Cairns–Brisbane routes. The 6-hour trip from Brisbane costs around A$37.40 (U.S.$24.30). From Cairns, the fare is A$152.90 (U.S.$99.40) for a 23-hour trip.

The nearest train station is in **Maryborough West,** 34 kilometers (20¼ miles) from Hervey Bay. Passengers on the high-speed **Tilt train** (Sun–Fri) and the **Spirit of Capricorn** (Sat) can book a connecting bus service to Urangan Boat Harbour via **Queensland Rail** (© **13 22 32** in Queensland, or 07/3235 1122). The fare from Brisbane for the 2½-hour Tilt train trip or the 4½-hour Spirit of Capricorn trip is A$42.90 (U.S.$27.90), plus A$4.40 (U.S.$2.85) for the bus. Fares are A$144.10 (U.S.$93.65) in a sitting berth and A$182.60 (U.S.$118.70) in an economy-class sleeper from Cairns (trip time: just under 27 hr.). Train passengers from the north must take a courtesy shuttle to Maryborough Central, then take the next available local bus to Urangan Boat Harbour.

Sunstate Airlines (book through Qantas) has one or two direct daily flights from Brisbane to Hervey Bay.

GETTING THERE & AROUND BY FOUR-WHEEL-DRIVE 🚗 Four-wheel-drives are the only permissible mode of vehicle transportation on the island. Many four-wheel-drive-rental outfits are based in Hervey Bay. You'll pay between about A$100 and $160 (U.S.$65–$104) a day, plus around A$20 to $35 (U.S.$13–$22.75) per day to reduce the deductible, which is usually A$4,000 (U.S.$2,600), plus a bond (typically A$500/U.S.$325). You must also buy a Vehicle Access Permit, which costs A$30 (U.S.$19.50) from your rental-car company or Urangan Boat Harbour or the Mary River Heads boat ramp, or A$40 (U.S.$26) from a Queensland Parks and Wildlife Service office on the island. Both **Bay 4WD Centre** (© **07/4128 2981;** www.bay4wd.com.au) and **Ausbay 4WD Rentals** (© **1800/679 479** in Australia, or 07/4124 6177; www.ausbay4wd.com.au) rent four-wheel-drives, offer camping and accommodated four-wheel-drive packages; rent camping gear; organize Vehicle Access Permits, barge bookings, camping permits, and secure storage for your own car; and pick you up free from the airport, coach terminal, or your hotel. Ausbay 4WD

⟨Tips⟩ Four-Wheel-Drive Fundamentals

Driving a four-wheel-drive is great fun and not hard for a beginner to learn, but if you've never driven one before, get a good briefing from your rental company before you head out. Fraser's loose sand tracks can be tricky, and getting bogged is common. The beach can be dangerous for the novice—if you travel too high up on the beach, you can get trapped in soft sand; if you travel too low, a surprise wave can bog your vehicle in treacherously soft sand under the water (and rust your car). Car-rental companies don't like that, and they can smell salt on an axle a mile away! Stick to the firmest tracks, know the tides, and don't be afraid to ask for advice. You'll have to drive a lot slower on a four-wheel-drive trail than you would on a conventional road; take that into account when you plan your day. For example, it takes a full day to get to Indian Head and back, and then only when the tide is favorable. Look out for light planes landing on the beach (which is a runway as well as a road).

Rentals allows 1-day rental (at a slightly higher price); Bay 4WD Centre demands a minimum 2.

Four-wheel-drives transfer by **Fraser Venture** barge (© **07/4125 4444**), which runs at least three times a day from Mary River Heads, 17 kilometers (11 miles) south of Urangan Boat Harbour. The round-trip fare for vehicle and driver is A$77 (U.S.$50.05), plus A$5.50 (U.S.$3.60) per extra passenger. It is a good idea to book a place for the 10-minute crossing.

Kingfisher Bay 4WD Hire (© **07/4120 3366**) within Kingfisher Bay Resort (see below) rents four-wheel-drives for A$195 (U.S.$126.75) a day, plus a A$500 (U.S.$325) bond and a A$2,000 (U.S.$1,300) deductible. They allow 1-day rentals. Book well in advance.

Fraser Island Taxi Service (© **07/4127 9188**) will take you anywhere on the island—in a four-wheel-drive, of course. It's based at Eurong on the island's eastern side. A typical fare, from Kingfisher Bay Resort across the island to go fishing on 75 Mile Beach, say, is A$50 (U.S.$32.50). The taxi seats five.

VISITOR INFORMATION   Contact the **Hervey Bay Tourism & Development Bureau,** 10 Bideford St., Hervey Bay, QLD 4655 (© **1800/811 728** in Australia, or 07/4124 9609; www.herveybaytourism.com.au). A better source for Web-connected travelers is www.hervey.com.au. The **Marina Kiosk** (© **07/ 4128 9800**) at Urangan Boat Harbour is a one-stop booking and information agency for all Fraser-related travel. Several Queensland Parks and Wildlife Service information offices are on the island.

There are no towns and very few facilities, food stores, or services on the island, so if you're camping, take all supplies with you.

ECO-EXPLORING THE ISLAND

Fraser's gem-like turquoise lakes and tea-colored "perched" lakes in the dunes are among the island's biggest attractions. The brilliant blue **Lake McKenzie** is absolutely beautiful; a swim here may be the highlight of your visit. Lake Birrabeen is another popular swimming spot. Don't miss a refreshing swim in the fast-flowing clear shallows of **Eli Creek.** Wade up the creek for a mile or two and let the current carry you back down. You should also take the boardwalk through a verdant forest of palms and ferns along the banks of Wanggoolba Creek.

Don't swim at **75-Mile Beach,** which hugs the eastern edge of the island—there are dangerously strong currents and a healthy shark population to contend with. Instead, swim in the **Champagne Pools** (also called the Aquarium)— pockets of soft sand protected from the worst of the waves by rocks. The bubbling seawater turns the pools into miniature spas. The pools are just north of **Indian Head,** a 60-meter (197-ft.) rocky outcrop at the northern end of the beach.

View the island's famous colored sand in its natural setting—the 70-meter (230-ft.) cliffs called **the Cathedrals,** which stretch for miles north of the settlement of Happy Valley on the eastern side of the Island.

Some of Queensland's best fishing is on Fraser Island. Anglers can throw a line in the surf gutters off the beach (freshwater fishing is not allowed). Bream, whiting, flathead, and swallowtail are the beach catches. Indian Head is good for rock species and tailor; and the waters east off **Waddy Point** yield northern and southern reef fish. **Kingfisher Bay Resort** (see below) offers free fish clinics, rents tackle, and organizes half-day fishing jaunts.

August through October, tour boats crowd the straits to see humpback whales returning to Antarctica with calves in tow. Kingfisher Bay Resort runs a whale-watching cruise from Urangan Harbour.

Tips **Please Don't Feed the Dingoes**

The dingoes that roam the island are emboldened by visitors who have—sometimes deliberately and sometimes unwittingly—fed them over the years. These are dangerous wild animals and have been responsible for one death and several serious attacks in recent years. Do not feed them, and keep your distance.

WHERE TO STAY

Fraser Island Retreat *Finds*   This is the wild side of Fraser Island, just minutes from 75-Mile Beach. Don't come expecting a luxury resort, but one that has comfortable timber cottages and all the amenities you need. There's a small swimming pool, surrounded by a timber deck and deck chairs, and each cottage has a small veranda to sit out on. The rooms all have fans, limited cooking facilities, and VCR (you can rent videos). The bar and bistro is open for all meals, but be warned that it is used by day-tour buses as their lunch stop so can be crowded at those times. If you want to cook for yourself, there's a general store to buy food and you can also buy take-out liquor. The store also sells fuel, ice, and gas for campers. You can also hire a four-wheel-drive from the resort. There's a public phone to use. The only access is by plane (**Air Fraser Island,** *©* 07/4125 3600) or bus. **Fraser Island Top Tours** (*©* 07/4125 3933 or 1800/063 933) will transfer guests to the resort from Hervey Bay and also runs day tours of the island for A$82 (U.S.$53) adults and A$49 (U.S.$32) children.

Happy Valley, Fraser Island, QLD 4650. *©* **1800/446 655** in Australia, or 07/4127 9144. Fax 07/4127 9131. www.fraserislandretreat.com.au. 9 units (all with shower only). A$166 (U.S.$108) double. Ask about package deals. AE, MC, V. **Amenities:** Restaurant; bar; outdoor pool; tour desk; car-rental desk; babysitting; coin-operated laundry. *In room:* TV/VCR, kitchenette, small fridge, no phone.

Kingfisher Bay Resort *Kids*   This sleek, environment-friendly eco-resort lies low along Fraser's west coast. Hotel guest rooms are smart and contemporary, with a Japanese screen opening onto a balcony looking into the bush, but my pick is the two- and three-bedroom villas which are just a short walk from the main resort area and pools. The hillside villas, which have Jacuzzis on their balconies, are fairly luxurious, but there's that long haul up the hill to contend with. Budget-style lodge rooms are also an option, but guests there have limited use of the resort facilities. An impressive lineup of eco-educational activities includes daily four-wheel-drive tours with a ranger to points of interest around the island, free guided ranger walks daily, and an excellent free Junior Eco-Ranger program on weekends and school vacations. You can also join bird-watching tours, fly- and reef-fishing trips, guided canoe trips, sunset champagne sails, and dugong- (manatee) spotting cruises. Wildlife videos play continuously in the lobby, and the on-site ranger office lists the animals and plants you are most likely to spot.

Fraser Island (PMB 1, Urangan, QLD 4655). *©* **1800/072 555** in Australia, or 07/4120 3333. Fax 07/4120 3326. www.kingfisherbay.com. 262 units. A$250 (U.S.$162.50) double for hotel rooms; A$825 (U.S.$536.25) 3 nights in 2-bedroom villa (sleeps 5); A$1,260 (U.S.$819) 3 nights in 3-bedroom villa (sleeps 6); min. 3-night stay in villas. Additional person A$22 (U.S.$14.30). Free crib. Ask about package deals. AE, DC, MC, V. **Amenities:** 3 restaurants; 4 bars; 2 outdoor pools (with waterslide for the kids); day/night tennis courts; Jacuzzi; water-sports equipment and fishing tackle for hire; kids' club; game room; tour desk; babysitting; laundry (in villas only). *In room:* A/C (hotel rooms only), TV, kitchen (villas only), fridge, coffeemaker, hair dryer, iron.

8 The Sunshine Coast

Warm sunshine, miles of pleasant beaches, trendy restaurants, and a relaxed lifestyle attract Aussies to the Sunshine Coast in droves. Despite some rather unsightly commercial shop development that has sprung up in recent years, the Sunshine Coast is still a great spot if you like lazing on sandy beaches and enjoying a good meal.

The Sunshine Coast starts at **Caloundra,** 83 kilometers (50 miles) north of Brisbane and runs all the way to **Rainbow Beach,** 40 kilometers (24 miles) north of **Noosa Heads** ⚓, where the fashionable crowd goes. There's a wide range of accommodation choices, from inexpensive motels and holiday apartments to five-star hotels and resorts.

Most of the Noosa's sunbathing, dining, shopping, and socializing takes place on trendy Hastings Street, Noosa Heads, and on the adjacent Main Beach. The commercial strip of Noosa Junction is a 1-minute drive away; a 3-minute drive west along the river takes you to the low-key town of Noosaville, where Australian families rent holiday apartments. Giving Noosa a run for its money in recent years is the newly spruced up Mooloolaba, about 30 kilometers (18 miles) south which has a better beach and about 90 great restaurants.

A short drive away, in the hinterland, mountain towns like **Maleny, Montville,** and **Mapleton** lead to the stunning beauty of the **Glass House Mountains,** a dramatic series of 13 volcanic plugs.

SUNSHINE COAST ESSENTIALS

GETTING THERE   If you're driving from Brisbane, take the Bruce Highway north to Aussie World theme park at Palmview, then exit onto the Sunshine Motorway to Mooloolaba, Maroochydore or Noosa Heads. The trip takes about 2 hours.

Sunstate Airlines (book through Qantas) has many flights daily (trip time: 30 min.) from Brisbane to the Sunshine Coast Airport in Maroochydore, 42 kilometers (25 miles) south of Noosa Heads. **Qantas** flies from Sydney several times a day and has direct flights from Sydney and Melbourne on weekends. From Cairns, you will need to fly to Brisbane and back to Maroochydore. **Henry's Airport Bus Service** (✆ 07/5474 0199) meets all flights; door-to-door transfers to Noosa Heads are A$14 (U.S.$9.10) for adults and A$7 (U.S.$4.55) for kids ages 4 to 14, one-way. Bookings are not necessary.

The nearest train station to Noosa Heads is in **Cooroy,** 25 kilometers (15 miles) away, to which **Queensland Rail** (✆ 13 22 32 in Queensland, or 07/3235 1122) operates two daily services from Brisbane on its suburban **CityTrain** (✆ 07/3235 5555) network. The trip takes about 2 hours and 20 minutes and the fare is A$14.40 (U.S.$9.35). Queensland Rail's long-distance trains departing Brisbane pick up but do not drop off passengers in Cooroy, with the exception of the high-speed **Tilt** train (which runs Sun–Fri) and the **Spirit of Capricorn** (which runs Sat). The fare on both trains is A$24.20 (U.S.$15.75). Several Queensland Rail trains make the 29½-hour trip from Cairns each week; the fare is A$150.70 (U.S.$97.95) for a sitting berth, A$189.20 (U.S.$123) for an economy-class sleeper. Local bus company **Sunbus** (✆ 131 230 or 07/5492 8700) meets most trains at Cooroy station and travels to Noosa Heads; take bus no. 12.

Several coach companies have service to Noosa Heads from Brisbane, including **Sun-air** (✆ 1800/804 340 in Australia, or 07/5478 2811) and **Suncoast**

The Sunshine Coast

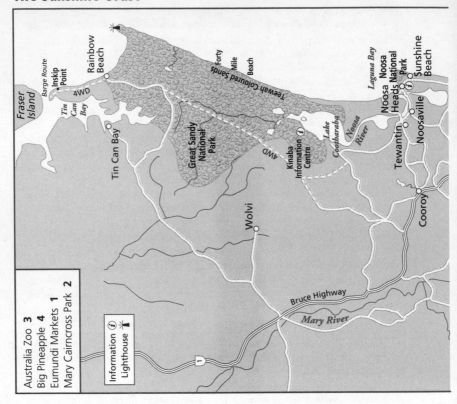

Australia Zoo **3**
Big Pineapple **4**
Eumundi Markets **1**
Mary Cairncross Park **2**

ⓘ Information
✲ Lighthouse

Pacific (ⓒ **07/5443 1011** on the Sunshine Coast, 07/3236 1901 in Brisbane) which also runs from Hervey Bay. McCafferty's and Greyhound-Pioneer have many daily services from all major towns along the Bruce Highway between Brisbane and Cairns. Trip time to Noosa Heads is 2 hours and 20 minutes from Brisbane, and just under 26 hours from Cairns. The single fare is A$16 (U.S.$10.40) from Brisbane and A$152 (U.S.$98.80) from Cairns.

VISITOR INFORMATION Write for information to **Tourism Sunshine Coast Ltd,** P.O. Box 264, Mooloolaba, QLD 4557 (ⓒ **07/5477 7311,** fax 07/ 5477 7322; www.sunshinecoast.org). In Noosa, drop into the **Tourism Noosa Information Centre** (ⓒ **07/5447 4988,** fax 07/5474 9494) at the eastern roundabout on Hastings Street where it intersects Noosa Drive. It's open daily from 9am to 5pm. Other tourist information centres are: **Nambour Information Centre,** Currie St., Nambour (ⓒ 07/5476 0199); **Maroochy Tourism,** Sixth Avenue and Aerodrome Rd., Maroochydore, (ⓒ 07/5479 1566); and **Caloundra City Information Centre,** 7 Caloundra Rd., Caloundra (ⓒ 07/5491 0202).

GETTING AROUND Major car-rental companies on the Sunshine Coast are **Avis** (ⓒ 07/5443 5055 Sunshine Coast Airport, 07/5447 4933 Noosa Heads), **Budget** (ⓒ 07/5448 7455 airport, 07/5474 2820 Noosa), **Hertz** (07/5448 9731 airport, 07/5447 2253 Noosa Heads), and **Thrifty** (ⓒ 07/5443 1733 airport, 07/5447 2299 Noosa Heads). Many local companies rent cars and four-wheel-drives, including **Trusty** (ⓒ 07/5447 4777).

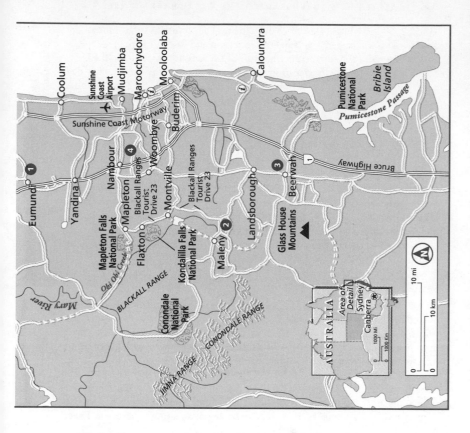

The local bus company is **Sunbus** (© **07/5492 8700,** or 13 1230 in Australia).

EXPLORING THE AREA

HITTING THE BEACH & OTHER OUTDOOR FUN Main Beach, Noosa Heads, is the place to swim, surf, and sunbathe. If the bikini-clad super-model look-alikes are too much for you, head to Sunshine Beach, just behind Noosa Junction off the David Low Way, about 2 kilometers (1¼ miles) from Noosa Heads. It's just as beautiful. Both beaches are patrolled 365 days a year.

Learn to surf with two-time Australian and World Pro-Am champion **Merrick Davis** (© **0418/787 577** mobile phone; www.learntosurf.com.au), who's lived in Noosa for the past 7 years. Merrick runs 2-hour lessons on Main Beach daily for A$35 (U.S.$22.75), 3-day certificate courses for A$95 (U.S.$61.75) and 5-day courses for A$125 (U.S.$81.25). He will pick you up and drop you off at your accommodation, and also rents surfboards and body boards.

If you want to rent a windsurfer, canoe, kayak, surf ski, catamaran, jet-ski, or canopied fishing boat—that you can play with on the Noosa River, or take upriver into Great Sandy National Park (see below)—check out the dozens of outfits along Gympie Terrace between James Street and Robert Street in Noosaville.

The **Aussie Sea Kayak Company** (© **07/5477 5335,** or 0407/049 747 mobile phone; rod&nat@ausseakayak.com.au), at The Wharf, Mooloolaba, runs a 2-hour sunset paddle on the Maroochy River every day for A$40

(U.S.$26)—including a glass of champagne on your return as reward for all the hard work! Owner/operators Natalie Stephenson and Rod Withyman are qualified kayak guides and instructors who worked for various companies in the U.S., Canada, and Mexico before returning to Australia to set up their tours. Half-day tours run every day for 3 to 4 hours at Mooloolaba (A$60/U.S.$39), day tours for 6 hours, Tuesday and Friday through Saturday at Noosa (A$105/U.S.$68). The company also runs overnight adventures to Moreton and North Stradbroke Islands, and to Fraser Island and the Whitsundays for up to 6 days.

EXPLORING NOOSA NATIONAL PARK A 10-minute stroll northeast from Hastings Street brings you to the 432-hectare (1,080-acre) **Noosa National Park.** Anywhere you see a crowd looking upwards, you're sure to spot a koala. They're often seen in the unlikely setting of the car park at the entrance to the park. A network of well-signposted walking trails leads through the bush. The most scenic is the 2.7-kilometer (1½-mile) coastal trail. The shortest trail is the 1-kilometer (just over ½-mile) Palm Grove circuit; the longest is the 4.7-kilometer (3-mile) Tanglewood trail inland to Hell's Gates—definitely worth the effort.

GREAT SANDY NATIONAL PARK Stretching north of Noosa along the coast is the 56,000-hectare (140,000-acre) Great Sandy National Park (often called Cooloola National Park), home to forests, beach, and freshwater lakes, including the state's largest, Lake Cootharaba. A popular thing to do is cruise the silent Everglades formed by the Noosa River and tributary creeks. The park's information office, the **Kinaba Information Center** (© 07/5449 7364), is on the western shore of Lake Cootharaba, about 30 kilometers (18 miles) from Noosaville. It has a display on the area's geography and a mangrove boardwalk to explore; it's accessible only by boat, which you can easily rent from the numerous boat-rental outfits in Noosaville. Several operators run half-day cruises into the Everglades, and guided kayak tours explore the park's lower reaches.

The other option is to take a four-wheel-drive along 40-Mile Beach, a designated highway with traffic laws, for a close-up view of the Teewah colored sand cliffs. This is a great place to get away from the crowds and enjoy nature's wonders. Lifeguards do not patrol the beach, so do not swim alone, and take care. Tours are available, or you can rent a four-wheel-drive and explore on your own. To reach the beach, cross Noosa River on the ferry at Tewantin, then take Maximilian Drive for 4 kilometers (2½ miles) to the beach. Stock up on water, food, and gas in Tewantin. The ferry (© 07/5449 8013) costs A$8 (U.S.$5.60) per vehicle round-trip; it operates from 6am to 10pm Sunday through Thursday, and 6am to midnight Friday and Saturday.

WILDLIFE PARKS & THEME PARKS Small theme parks seem to thrive on the Sunshine Coast. Don't expect thrill rides, but you might find some of them a pleasant way to spend a few hours.

A transparent tunnel with an 80-meter (256-ft.) moving walkway which takes you through a tank filled with sharks, stingrays, groupers, eels, and coral is the highlight at **Underwater World** (© 07/5444 8488), at The Wharf, Mooloolaba. Kids can pick up starfish and sea cucumbers in the touch pool, and there are static displays on whales and sharks, shark-breeding, and freshwater crocodile talks, an otter enclosure, and a 30-minute seal show. You can also swim with the seals (A$65/U.S.$42.25), dive with the sharks (A$94/U.S.$61 for certified divers, including gear, or A$110/U.S.$71.50 for non-divers), or get up close to a seal over Sunday breakfast for A$27 (U.S.$17.55) adults, A$21 (U.S.$13.65) children 3 to 15, A$25 (U.S.$16.25) seniors and students, or A$99 (U.S.$64.35) family of five. Breakfast with a seal prices include entry to Underwater World. It's open daily from 9am to 6pm (last entry at 5pm). Closed Christmas. Admission is A$21.50 (U.S.$14) for adults, A$14 (U.S.$9.10) for seniors and students, A$11 (U.S.$7.15) for children ages 3 to 15, and A$55 (U.S.$35.75) for a family of five. Allow 2 hours to see everything, more if you want to attend all the talks.

At the **Big Pineapple** (© 07/5442 1333; www.bigpineapple.com.au), 6 kilometers (3½ miles) south of Nambour on the Nambour Connection Road in Woombye—don't worry, you can't miss the 16-meter (52½-ft.) tall monument—you can take a train ride through a working pineapple plantation, ride through a rain forest and a macadamia farm in a macadamia-shaped carriage, and take a boat ride through a hydroponics greenhouse. The park also has a baby animal farm, kangaroos, koalas, a rain-forest walk, small but excellent nocturnal house called "Creatures of the Night," and a gift shop. It's open 365 days a year from 9am to 5pm (opens later on Christmas and Anzac Day; call for exact time). Entry is free; the plantation train, animal nursery, and macadamia tour each cost A$8.80 (U.S.$5.70) adults and A$7.70 (U.S.$5) children 4 to 14; the hydroponics-boat ride costs A$7.70 (U.S.$5) adults and A$6.60 (U.S.$4.30) children, and entry to Creatures of the Night costs A$5.50 (U.S.$3.55) adults and A$3.30 (U.S.$2.15) children. A family pass to all tours is A$62.70 (U.S.$40.75) for 2 adults and up to 4 children. Allow half a day if you do everything.

Farther south on the Glass House Mountains Tourist Drive 24 at Beerwah, off the Bruce Highway, is **Australia Zoo** (© 07/5494 1134; www.crocodile hunter.com), which showcases Australian animals in interactive demonstrations with their keepers. The zoo's owners, Steve and Terri Irwin, are renowned for manhandling dangerous saltwater crocs and achieved a measure of fame on their U.S. TV show **"Animal Planet's Crocodile Hunter."** Among items on the schedule are: otter feedings at 10:30am, 1pm and 3:30pm; a snake show at 11am; a Galapagos tortoise feeding at 11:30am; an American alligator show at noon; and a birds-of-prey demonstration at 3pm. The highlight is the saltwater croc show at 1:30pm. You can also hand-feed 'roos, pat a koala, check out foxes and camels, watch (even hold!) venomous snakes and pythons and see wild birds on the grounds. Admission is A$16.50 (U.S.$10.70) for adults, A$13.50 (U.S.$8.80) for seniors and students, A$8.50 (U.S.$5.50) for kids ages 3 to 14, and A$39.90 (U.S.$25.95) for a family of 5. The park is open daily from 8:30am to 4pm. Closed Christmas.

A "Funshine" pass giving discounted entry to three attractions—Australia Zoo, Underwater World, and Forest Glen Deer Sanctuary—is available from travel agents and automobile associations (in Queensland, that's the RACQ, © 07/3361 2406) for A$49.40 (U.S.$32.10) adults, A$25.50 (U.S.$16.60) children ages 3 to 15, and A$132.80 (U.S.$86.30) family of five.

A SCENIC MOUNTAINTOP DRIVE THROUGH THE SUNSHINE COAST HINTERLAND

A leisurely drive along the lush green ridge-top of the **Blackall Ranges** 𝄫 behind Noosa is a popular half- or full-day excursion. Cute mountain villages, full of crafts shops and cafes, and terrific views of the coast are the main attractions. Macadamia nuts, peaches, and other homegrown produce is often for sale by the road at dirt-cheap prices.

On Wednesdays and Saturdays, start at the colorful outdoor **Eumundi Markets** 𝒸𝒸 in the historical village of Eumundi, 13 kilometers (8 miles) west of Noosa along the Eumundi Road. Locals and visitors wander under the huge shady trees among dozens of stalls selling locally grown organic lemonade, fruit, groovy hats, teddy bears, antique linen, homemade soaps, handcrafted hardwood furniture—even live emu chicks! Get your face painted, your palm read, or your feet massaged. Listen to some didgeridoo music or bush poetry. When shopping's done, everyone pops into the trendy cafes on Eumundi's main street. The market runs from 6:30am to 2pm both days.

From Eumundi, take the Bruce Highway to Nambour and turn right onto the **Nambour–Mapleton road.** (The turnoff is just before you enter Nambour, so if you hit the town, you've gone too far.) A winding 12-kilometer (7¼-mile) climb up the range between rolling farmland and forest brings you to Mapleton. Stop at the pub for some spectacular views from the veranda. From here, detour almost 4 kilometers (2½ miles) to see the 120-meter (393½-ft.) Mapleton Falls. A 200-meter (656-ft.) bushwalk departs from the picnic grounds and ends with great views over the Obi Obi Valley. There is also a 1.3 kilometer (¾ mile) circuit.

Back on the main **Mapleton–Maleny Road,** head south 3.5 kilometers (2 miles) through lush forest and farms to Flaxton Gardens. Perched on the cliff with breathtaking coast views is a wine cellar offering tastings and sales, a pottery, cafe, and gift shop. A bit farther south you can detour right and walk the 4.6 kilometers (2¾ miles) round-trip trail to the base of the 80-meter (262-ft.) Kondalilla Falls. You can swim here, too. It's a slippery downhill walk, and the climb back up can be tough.

Take the main road south for 5.5 kilometers (3½ miles) to **Montville.** This English-style village has become such a tourist stop that it has lost some of its character and lots of people decry its touristy facade. But everyone still ends up strolling the tree-lined streets and browsing the gift shops and galleries.

About 13 kilometers (8 miles) down the road is **Maleny,** more modern and less commercialized than Montville. Be sure to follow the signs around to Mary Cairncross Park for spectacular views of the **Glass House Mountains** 𝒸𝒸, 11 volcanic plugs protruding out of the plains. The park has a kiosk, a playground, free wood barbecues, and a rain-forest information center; a 1.7-kilometer (1-mile) walking trail loops through the rain forest past some giant strangler figs. You can either return to Noosa the way you came or, if you're in a hurry, drive down to Landsborough and rejoin the Bruce Highway.

WHERE TO STAY
EXPENSIVE

Hyatt Regency Coolum 𝒸𝒸   A couple of hours under the expert care of the therapists at the Spa and you'll emerge feeling years younger! This is one of the reasons the well-heeled flock to this sprawling bushland resort. The other is its 18-hole Robert Trent Jones, Jr.–designed golf course. The Spa (there are entrance fees of around A$13/U.S.$8.45 a day as well as the cost of treatments) does everything from aromatherapy baths to triglyceride checks (130 treatments in all) and has massage rooms, aqua-aerobics, yoga, and much more. An almost-6 hour body detox costs A$400 (U.S.$260), but you can get a minifacial or a half-hour massage for A$60 (U.S.$39). The golf course was rated in Australia's top five resort courses by *Australian Golf Digest* in 2000. Golf widows and widowers can play tennis; do decoupage in the Creative Arts Center; take the twice-daily free shuttle into Noosa to shop; and surf at the resort's private patrolled beach. A nightly shuttle runs to Noosa Heads restaurants for A$15 (U.S.$9.75) per person, round-trip.

So spread out are the low-rise accommodations that guests rent a bike to get around, wait 15 minutes for the two free resort shuttles (frustrating sometimes!), or get into the healthy swing of things and walk. Accommodations all sport contemporary decor and come as "suites" (a single room divided into living and sleeping quarters); two-bedroom President's Villas with a kitchenette; villas within the Ambassador Club, which has its own concierge, pool, tennis court, and lounge; and two-story, three-bedroom Ambassador Club residences boasting rooftop terraces with a Jacuzzi.

The Village Square is just that: an attractive cluster of shops, restaurants, bars, and take-out joints that provides the heart of the resort.

Warran Rd., off David Low Way (approx. 2km/1¼ miles south of town), Coolum Beach, QLD 4573. (C) **13 12 34** in Australia, 800/633-7313 in the U.S. and Canada, 0845/758 1666 in the U.K. or 020/8335 1220 in London, 0800/44 1234 in New Zealand, or 07/5446 1234. Fax 07/5446 2957. www.coolum.hyatt.com. 323 units (some with Jacuzzis). A$265–$395 (U.S.$172–$256) double; A$355–$1,400 (U.S.$230–$910) villa; A$1,000–$2,200 (U.S.$650–$1,430) residence. Rates include continental breakfast. Extra person A$45 (U.S.$29.25). Children under 13 stay free in parents' room using existing bedding. Ask about golf, spa, and other packages. AE, MC, V. Valet parking A$18 (U.S.$11.70) or self-parking. Resort shuttle meets all flights at Sunshine Coast Airport for A$18 (U.S.$11.70) per person, one-way. Town car transfers from Brisbane Airport A$79 (U.S.$51) per person, one-way (shared service with other guests); limousine transfers available. **Amenities:** 4 restaurants, 3 bars; 9 outdoor pools, including 25-m (82-ft.) heated lap pool; 18-hole championship golf course; 9 night/day tennis courts; health club and spa; water-sports-equipment rental (body boards, canoes, and fishing tackle); bike rental; children's programs daily for kids 6 weeks–12 years old (for a fee); concierge; tour desk; car-rental desk; business center; shopping arcade; room service; massage; babysitting; same-day dry cleaning; nonsmoking rooms; executive rooms. In room: A/C, TV with pay movies, fax, dataport, kitchenette, stocked minibar, coffeemaker, hair dryer, iron, safe.

Sheraton Noosa Resort ✦✦✦
Noosa's first five-star resort has just taken itself one step further, with the opening of a day spa designed to bring in the locals as well as the visitors. Right in the heart of Hastings Street, the Sheraton has a prime spot among the chic boutiques and restaurants. There are several different styles of room, but the best in my book are those with views away from the beach but looking right down the Noosa River to the mountains. Sit on the balcony at sunset and drink it all in. All the rooms are extra-large, and all have Jacuzzis. You'll pay more for the two-level poolside villas, which have private access to the pool area, but there's no view. Some rooms have ocean (but not beach) views. The Aqua Day Spa has a Roman-bathhouse feel to it and offers a wide range of treatments in its seven treatment rooms. The hotel restaurant, Cato's—named for Australian novelist Nancy Cato, who lived in Noosa until her death a few years ago—fronts onto Hastings Street and is a great place to watch the world go by.

Hastings St, Noosa Heads, QLD 4567. (C) **1800/073 535** in Australia, or 07/5449 4888. Fax 07/5449 2230. www.sheraton.com. 169 units. A$274–$476 (U.S.$178–$309) double low season; A$576 (U.S.$374) double high season (Dec 25–Jan4). Secure undercover parking and valet parking. **Amenities:** Restaurant, 2 bars; outdoor heated pool; health club and sauna; spa; Jacuzzi; sauna; daily childcare center for ages 6 weeks–10 years; kids' club programs on weekends and during school vacations for ages 9–15 (at a fee); game room; concierge; tour desk; room service 6am–1am; massage (poolside and in-room); babysitting; guest laundry. In room: A/C, TV with free and pay-per-view movies, kitchenette with microwave, minibar, fridge, coffeemaker, hair dryer, iron, safe.

MODERATE
Noosa Village Motel
All the letters from satisfied guests pinned up on the wall here are a testament to owners John and Mary Skelton's hard work in continually sprucing up this clean, bright little motel in the heart of Hastings Street.

> ### *Tips* The Seasons of the Sunshine Coast
>
> Room rates on the Sunshine Coast are mostly moderate, but they jump sharply in the Christmas period from December 26 to January 26, during school holidays, and in the week following Easter. Book well ahead at these times. Weekends are often busy, too.

The pleasant rooms are spacious and freshly painted, with a cheerful atmosphere. There's no air-conditioning, but the rooms all have ceiling fans. Proprietors John and Mary Skelton are continually sprucing up the place. And at these rates, it must be one of Hastings Street's best values.

10 Hastings St., Noosa Heads, QLD 4567. © **07/5447 5800.** Fax 07/5474 9282. www.noosavillage.com.au. 11 units (9 with shower only). High season (Dec 24–Jan 14) A$175 (U.S.$113.75) double, A$230 (U.S.$149.50) family room. Low season A$100–$110 (U.S.$65–$71.50) double, A$155 (U.S.$100.75) family room. Additional person A$11–$15 (U.S.$7.15–$9.75). Discounts for longer stays. Ask about May/June specials. MC, V. Free parking. **Amenities:** Bike rental; tour desk; car-rental desk; room-service breakfast; free babysitting; coin-operated laundry; nonsmoking rooms. *In room:* TV, kitchenette, refrigerator, hair dryer.

IN THE HINTERLAND
Avocado Grove Bed & Breakfast   Noela and Ray Troyahn's modern red cedar Queenslander home is in a peaceful rural setting in the middle of an avocado grove just off the ridge-top road. The cozy, comfortable rooms have country-style furniture, full-length windows opening onto private verandas, and oil heaters for cool mountain nights. The big suite downstairs has a TV and kitchen facilities. Colorful parrots and other birds are a common sight. Guests are welcome to picnic on the peaceful sloping lawns that have wonderful views west to Obi Obi Gorge in the Connondale Ranges. Noela prepares a big country-style breakfast and provides tea and coffee any time.

10 Carramar Ct., Flaxton via Montville, QLD 4560. © and fax **07/5445 7585.** www.babs.com.au/avocado. 4 units, 3 with bathroom (shower only), 1 with private adjacent bathroom. A$120 (U.S.$78) double; A$140 (U.S.$91) suite. Rates include full breakfast. Ask about weekend and midweek packages. MC, V. Turn right off ridge-top road onto Ensbey Rd.; Carramar Ct. is the first left. **Amenities:** Tour desk; in-room massage; non-smoking rooms. *In room:* Ceiling fan, coffeemaker, hair dryer.

WHERE TO DINE
Noosa's Hastings Street comes alive at night with vacationers wining and dining at restaurants as sophisticated as those in Sydney and Melbourne. Just stroll along and see what appeals to you—but be prepared to need a booking at high seasons. For a great breakfast try Café Le Monde at the southern end of Hastings Street (opposite the back of the Surf Club), or Bistro C, one of the few restaurants which still has beachfront dining. Noosa Junction is a less attractive place to eat, but the prices are cheaper. There are about 90 restaurants at Mooloolaba to choose from.

Ricky Ricardo's ☾ MODERN AUSTRALIAN   Owners Leonie Palmer and Steven Fisher have been on the Noosa restaurant scene for years, and their latest restaurant is as popular as its predecessors. I'd choose it for lunch over dinner simply because of the fantastic setting; the food is sensational at any time. You can sit over a long lunch drinking in the view across the Noosa River while nibbling from an innovative tapas menu or something more substantial. The menu is Mediterranean style, with fresh seafood and regional produce used throughout.

2/2 Quamby Place (inside the shopping centre), Noosa Sound, QLD 4567. © **07/5447 2455.** Reservations recommended. Main courses A$19.50–$25.40 (U.S.$12.70–$16.50). AE, DC, MC, V. Daily noon–midnight.

Season ⟨⟩ MODERN AUSTRALIAN With a new beachfront location, chef Gary Skelton has secured his place as one of Noosa's most popular restaurants. The former Sydneysider's following has come with him, with happy vacationers from southern states rediscovering Season. A recent move to the beachfront (below the Tingerana apartments) from the other side of Hastings Street has given Season one of the best locations in town and the food remains superb. Breakfast dishes start from A$4 (U.S.$2.60) for muffins or you can indulge yourself with buttermilk and banana pancakes (with palm sugar butter and maple syrup) for A$12 (U.S.$7.80). For dinner? How about the roast deboned spatchcock, with feta and mint potato cake and tzatziki. BYO. Smoking is not permitted

25 Hastings St., Noosa Heads, QLD 4567. (© 07/5447 3747. Reservations only accepted on the day you dine. Light meals and main courses A$8–$28 (U.S.$5.20–$18.20). AE, DC, MC, V. Daily 8am–10pm.

9 The Gold Coast

Love it or hate it, the Gold Coast is one of Australia's icons. Bronzed lifeguards, bikini-clad meter maids, tanned tourists draped with gold jewelry, high-rise apartment towers that cast long shadows over some parts of the beach . . . but the glitz, the glitter and the overdevelopment pales into insignificance as soon as you hit the beach. The white sands stretch uninterrupted for 70 kilometers (18 miles), making up for the long strips of neon-lit motels and cheap souvenir shops. Since the '50s, Australians have been flocking to this strip of coastline, and that hasn't changed. Today, they're queuing up with tourists from all around the world to get in to the theme parks, but everyone can still find a quiet spot on the beach and the sun shines on.

The Gold Coast's theme parks are not as large or as sophisticated as Disneyland, but they're exciting enough. Apart from the three major parks—Dreamworld, Warner Bros. Movie World, and Sea World—there are of plenty of smaller-scale ones. If theme parks aren't your thing, there are also 40 golf courses, dinner cruises, and loads of adrenaline-based outdoor activities, from bungee jumping to jet-skiing. The best activity on the Gold Coast, though, is the natural kind, and it doesn't cost a cent—hitting the surf and lazing on the beach.

GOLD COAST ESSENTIALS

GETTING THERE By Car Access to the Gold Coast Highway, which runs the length of the Coast, is off the Pacific Highway from Sydney or Brisbane. The drive takes about 80 minutes from Brisbane. From Sydney it's an 11-hour trip, sometimes longer, on the crowded, rundown Pacific Highway.

By Plane Domestic flights land at Gold Coast Airport at Coolangatta, 25 kilometers (15 miles) south of Surfers Paradise. **Qantas** operates plenty of direct flights from Sydney, Melbourne, and Brisbane. **Coachtrans** airport shuttles (© **13 12 30** in Queensland, or 07/5588 8747) meet every flight; the fare to Surfers Paradise is A$11 (U.S.$7.15) one way and A$16.50 (U.S.$10.70) round-trip. A taxi from the airport to Surfers Paradise is about A$30 (U.S.$21), depending on the traffic, which can be heavy.

The nearest international gateway is Brisbane International Airport (see chapter 5). The Coachtrans Airporter bus meets most flights and makes about 20 trips a day from the domestic and international terminals at Brisbane Airport to Gold Coast accommodations for A$35 (U.S.$22.75) adults, A$18 (U.S.$11.70) children ages 4 to 14. The trip takes about 90 minutes to Surfers Paradise. You do not need to book in advance unless you are on an evening flight. The **Gold Coast Tourist Shuttle** (© 07/5574 5111) also runs transfers from Brisbane Airport, for A$27.50 (U.S.$17.90) adults, A$14.50 (U.S.$9.40) children 4 to 14, or A$69.50 (U.S.$45.15) family of four. You must book this service.

Airtrain services link Brisbane Airport and the Gold Coast and cost A$17.75 (U.S.$11.50) adults. Direct services between Brisbane's international and domestic terminals and Gold Coast stations run twice an hour in both directions. The trip from the airport to Robina on the southern end of the Gold Coast takes about 90 minutes.

By Bus Coachtrans (© 13 12 30 in Queensland, or 07/5588 8777) also runs regular public buses daily between Brisbane and the Gold Coast, leaving from the Brisbane Transit Centre on Roma Street. Every second service on average is express, which takes 1 hour 20 minutes to Surfers Paradise. The fare is A$13 (U.S.$9.10) one-way. Reservations are not necessary.

McCafferty's (© 13 14 99) and **Greyhound-Pioneer** (© 13 20 30) make daily stops at Surfers Paradise from Sydney and Brisbane. The trip from Sydney takes 15 to 16 hours, and the fare is A$82.50 (U.S.$53.60). Trip time from Brisbane is 90 minutes, and the fare is $15.40 (U.S.$10).

By Train Suburban trains (call **Queensland Rail Citytrain;** © 07/3235 5555) depart Brisbane Central and Roma Street stations every 30 minutes for the 80-minute trip to the Gold Coast suburb of Robina. The fare is A$9.10 (U.S.$5.90) adults, A$4.60 (U.S.$3) children ages 5 to 15. Numerous local buses meet the trains to take passengers to Surfers Paradise.

If you come by train to Surfers Paradise from Sydney or other southern cities (call **Countrylink** at © 13 22 32 in Australia, or 07/9379 1298), you will need to transfer to a connecting coach in Casino or Murwillumbah, which are just south of the Queensland border. The trip from Sydney takes 14 to 15 hours and the fare is A$98 (U.S.$63.70) for a sitting berth, and A$227 (U.S.$147.55) for a sleeper.

VISITOR INFORMATION The **Gold Coast Tourism Bureau** has an information kiosk on Cavill Avenue in Surfers Paradise (© 07/5538 4419). It is stacked with loads of brochures on things to see and do, and they will make book tours and arrange accommodations for you. The kiosk is open Monday through Friday from 8:30am to 5:30pm, Saturdays and public holidays from 9am to 5:30pm, and Sundays from 9am to 3:30pm. A second information booth is at the corner of Griffith and Warner streets, Coolangatta (© 07/5536 7765). It is open from 8am to 4pm weekdays, from 8am to 3pm Saturdays, from 8am to 1pm public holidays, and closed Sundays.

To obtain material in advance, write to the bureau at P.O. Box 7091, Gold Coast Mail Centre, QLD 9726 (© 07/5592 2699; fax 07/5570 3144; www.goldcoasttourism.com.au).

ORIENTATION The heart of the Gold Coast is **Surfers Paradise**—"Surfers" to the locals—a high-rise forest of apartment towers, shops, cheap eateries, taverns, and amusement parlors. The pedestrians-only Cavill Mall in the center of town connects the Gold Coast Highway to The Esplanade, which runs along the beach.

The Gold Coast Highway is the main artery that connects the endless beachside suburbs lining the coast. Just north of Surfers is **Main Beach** ⚓, where Tedder Avenue is lined with shops, restaurants, and cafes. Heading south from Surfers, the main beach centers are Broadbeach, where retail complexes and

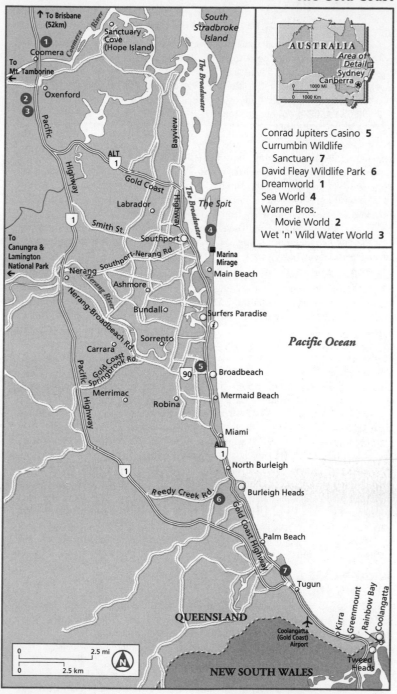

The Gold Coast

AUSTRALIA
Area of Detail
Sydney
Canberra

0   1000 Mi
0   1000 Km

Conrad Jupiters Casino **5**
Currumbin Wildlife
    Sanctuary **7**
David Fleay Wildlife Park **6**
Dreamworld **1**
Sea World **4**
Warner Bros.
    Movie World **2**
Wet 'n' Wild Water World **3**

↑ To Brisbane
(52km)

Coomera **1**

Sanctuary
Cove
(Hope Island)

South
Stradbroke
Island

To
Mt. Tamborine ←

Oxenford **2** **3**

Coomera River

Pacific

The Broadwater

Bayview

ALT **1**

Gold Coast

Highway

Labrador

The Broadwater

The Spit

To
Canungra &
Lamington
National Park ←

Smith St.

Southport-Nerang Rd.

Nerang

Ashmore

Nerang River

Bundall

Southport

4

Marina
Mirage

Main Beach

Surfers Paradise

Pacific Ocean

Nerang-Broadbeach Rd.

Sorrento

Carrara

*Gold Coast
Springbrook Rd.*

5

90

Broadbeach

Merrimac

Robina

Mermaid Beach

*Pacific
Highway*

Miami

ALT
1

North Burleigh

1

Reedy Creek Rd.

6

Burleigh Heads

Gold Coast Highway

Palm Beach

7

Tugun

Kirra
Greenmount
Rainbow Bay
Coolangatta

QUEENSLAND

Coolangatta
(Gold Coast)
Airport

Tweed
Heads

0   2.5 mi
0   2.5 km

N

NEW SOUTH WALES

> **⌐Tips The Secret of the Gold Coast Seasons**
>
> School holidays, especially the Christmas vacation from mid-December to
> the end of January, are peak season on the Gold Coast. Accommodations
> are booked months in advance at these times. The rest of the year, occu-
> pancy levels plummet and so do rates! Packages and deals abound in the
> off-season, and perfectly adequate motel rooms can go for as little as
> A$50 (U.S.$32.50) double on standby.

restaurants are mushrooming; family-oriented Burleigh Heads; and the twin
towns of Coolangatta in Queensland and Tweed Heads just over the border in
New South Wales. Coolangatta still has the sleepy small-town feel ideal for families, despite some major development in the past few years. Gold Coast Airport
is the other side of the highway from Coolangatta township.

West of Surfers Paradise and Broadbeach are the affluent suburbs of Ashmore
and Nerang, where luxury residential estates and many of the region's championship golf courses have sprung up.

GETTING AROUND   It's not necessary to have a car to get around. The
hotels listed below are within walking distance of the beach, shops, and restaurants, and many tour companies pick up at hotels. You can reach the theme
parks by bus. A car is handy for a day trip to the hinterland, and to get around
to restaurants and golf courses. Parking is cheap and plentiful in numerous parking lots and on the side streets between the Gold Coast Highway and The
Esplanade.

Avis (© **07/5539 9388**), **Budget** (© **97/5538 1344**), **Hertz** (© **07/5538
5366**), and **Thrifty** (© **07/5538 6511**) have outlets in Surfers Paradise and at
Gold Coast Airport. Endless local outfits rent cars at cheap rates.

Surfside Buslines (© **13 12 30** in Queensland) is the local bus company. Its
best deal is a Gold Pass that allows you to hop on and off the buses anytime you
like. It costs A$15 (U.S.$9.75) adults and A$8 (U.S.$5.20) children and seniors
for 24 hours and A$25/$13 (U.S.$16.25/$8.45) for 3 days; 5-, 7-, 10- and 14-
day passes are also available. This is a particularly good deal if you're planning to
visit the theme parks, as the company's Gold Coast Tourist Shuttle operates door
to door transfers 4 times every morning from anywhere on the coastal strip. You
must book for this, but if you are staying in Surfers Paradise or Broadbeach you
can just hop on the Surfside Theme Park Express, which leaves every 15 minutes from 8:30 to 11am from Pacific Fair shopping center at Broadbeach and
picks up at bus stops along the way.

WHAT TO SEE & DO ON THE COAST
HITTING THE BEACHES
Needless to say, the wide white sandy beaches are the number one attraction on
the Gold Coast. No fewer than 35 patrolled beaches stretch almost uninterrupted
from the Spit north of Surfers Paradise to Rainbow Bay, south of Coolangatta. In
fact, the Gold Coast is really just one long fabulous beach—all you need do is
step onto it at any point, and you will spot the nearest set of red and yellow flags
that signal safe swimming. The most popular beaches are **Main Beach** ✹✹,
**Surfers North, Elkhorn Avenue, Surfers Paradise, Mermaid Beach, Burleigh
Heads, Coolangatta,** and **Greenmount.** All are patrolled 365 days a year.

DOING THE THEME PARKS

The big three are **Dreamworld, Sea World,** and **Warner Bros. Movie World.**
Right next door to Movie World is **Wet 'n' Wild Water World.**

Sea World is the only major theme park in the center of town. The others are
in northern bushland on the Pacific Highway, about 15 to 20 minutes away
from Surfers Paradise. You can ride free to the theme parks and get a free Gold
Pass for unlimited bus travel for 24 hours if you buy your park entry ticket
aboard a **Surfside Buslines** (© **13 12 30** in Queensland) bus. Park tickets
bought on the bus cost the same as they do at the park gates, but you avoid the
entry queues. Take Bus 1A or 3 to Movie World and Wet 'n' Wild; Bus 1A or
10 to Dreamworld; and Bus 2 or 9 to Sea World.

Coachtrans (© **1800/426 224** in Australia, or 07/5592 3488) does daily
door-to-door transfers to the big three parks, as well as to Wet 'n' Wild, and Currumbin Bird Sanctuary. Round-trip fare is A$15 (U.S.$9.75) for adults, A$9
(U.S.$5.85) for kids, or A$39 (U.S.$25.35) for a family of four. The company
also does round-trip transfers to Sea World for A$9 (U.S.$5.85) for adults, A$5
(U.S.$3.25) for children, and A$23 (U.S.$14.95) for a family. Book a day ahead
if you can, especially in peak season.

You can also hail the regular Coachtrans buses that run daily every 30 to
45 minutes between the Gold Coast and Brisbane. They will be marked Brisbane, and you will find them on the Gold Coast Highway.

Dreamworld ᚷ *(Kids* Adrenaline-crazed thrill-seekers will love the action rides
here, such as the aptly named Giant Drop, in which you free-fall 39 stories in
5 seconds, or the Tower of Terror which propels you forwards and upwards at
4.5 G before falling backwards 38 stories in 7 seconds. They'll also get a kick out
of the Thunderbolt, Australia's fastest double-loop roller coaster; Wipeout,
which spins, twists, and tumbles you upside down in a random sequence (but
only exerts a sissy 2.5 G units of pressure); and Enterprise, which loops a loop
at 60 kilometers per hour (36 mph). These high-octane offerings make the park's
other offerings look tame. Dreamworld is a family fun park laid out Disney-
style—except that here giant koalas called Kenny and Belinda roam the streets
instead of Mickey Mouse. Other activities include an Imax theater, a native
wildlife park where you can cuddle a koala and hand-feed kangaroos, river
cruises livened up by a bushranger shoot-out, and a carousel and other rides for
young kids. A big highlight is to watch trainers swim, wrestle, and play with
Bengal tigers on Tiger Island. Souvenir stores, restaurants, cafes, and ice-cream
shops abound, and there's a water-slide park, so bring your swimsuit.

Pacific Hwy. (25km/15 miles north of Surfers Paradise), Coomera. © 1800/073 300 in Australia, 07/5588
1111, or 07/5588 1122 (24-hr info line). www.dreamworld.com.au. Admission (all-inclusive except skill
games, souvenir photos, and helicopter rides) A$52 (U.S.$33.80) adults, A$32 (U.S.$20.80) children 6–13.
Daily 10am–5pm; Main St., Plaza Restaurant, and Koala Country open at 9am. Closed Christmas and until
1:30pm Anzac Day. Extended hours during Dec–Jan.

Tips A Money-Saving Theme Park Pass

Sea World, Warner Bros. Movie World, and Wet 'n' Wild sell a 3 Park
Super Pass that gets you a full-day's entry to each park plus a free return
visit to the one you like best. It costs A$135 (U.S.$87.75) for adults and
A$86 (U.S.$55.90) and kids ages 4 to 13. You can only buy it from a travel
agency.

Sea World *Kids*   Two large polar bears called Ping Ping and Kanook are the new star attractions at this marine park, and the crowds are flocking to see them frolic, dive, and hunt for fish in a large deep pool. Make sure you get there for viewing times (10am and 2pm), and fit in the park's other attractions around the chance to see the big white bears. Sea World may not be as sophisticated as similar parks in the United States, but it's got its own charm and has all the things you'd expect to see—performing dolphins and sea lions, ski shows, an aquarium, shark feeding, and an array of rides. A monorail gets you around the grounds, and there's a free water-slide playground. Water-skiing, parasailing, WaveRunners, and banana rides are available for an extra fee. Adults (14 and over) can snorkel with dolphins, seals or sharks for A$80 to $105 (U.S.$52–$68.25), including a souvenir photo. Kids can attend a 30-minute dolphin talk, pat one, and have their photo taken with it for A$40 (U.S.$26).

Sea World Dr. (3km/2 miles north of Surfers Paradise), The Spit, Main Beach. © 07/5588 2222, or 07/5588 2205 for recorded show times. Fax: 07/5588 2180. www.seaworld.com.au. Admission (all-inclusive except dolphin experiences, helicopter rides, and powered water sports) A$52 (U.S.$33.80) adults, $A33 (U.S.$21.45) children 4–13. AE, DC, MC, V. Daily 9:30am–5pm; Anzac Day 1:30–6:30pm. Closed Christmas. Free parking.

Warner Bros. Movie World *Kids*   Australia's answer to Universal Studios just about matches its U.S. counterpart for thrills and spills. The park is based around working studios where *The Phantom,* starring Billy Zane; *20,000 Leagues Under the Sea,* with Michael Caine; and *Streetfighter,* with Jean-Claude Van Damme, were filmed. If you already know how Superman flies across skyscrapers and you've heard a Foley sound studio in action before, the train ride around the sets might not interest you, but it's a great introduction to cinema tricks for first-timers. Movie World has a couple of tummy-turning rides as well, including the Lethal Weapon roller coaster and Batman—The Ride, a simulated high-speed chase in the Batmobile. Don't miss the hilarious Police Academy Stunt Show. Other attractions include an illusion show, a bloopers cinema, and a Wild West flume ride. Young kids can take rides and see stage shows by Yosemite Sam and Porky Pig in the Looney Tunes Village, and there's a Looney Tunes Parade through the streets each day. If you can stomach Daffy Duck and Wonder Woman first thing in the morning, join them and other characters for "Breakfast with the Stars," at 9:50am. Most parades and shows take place between 11am and 4pm.

Pacific Hwy. (21km/12½ miles north of Surfers Paradise), Oxenford. © 07/5573 3999, or 07/5573 8485 for recorded information. www.movieworld.com.au. Admission (all-inclusive) A$52 (U.S.$33.80) adults, A$33 (U.S.$21.45) children 4–13. AE, DC, MC, V. Daily 9:30am–5:30pm; rides and attractions operate 10am–5pm. Closed Christmas. Extended hours during Dec–Jan.

Wet 'n' Wild Water World *Kids*   Hurtling down a seven-story piece of fiberglass at 70 kilometers per hour (44 mph) is just one of many water-slide options at this aquatic fun park. The rides have names like Double Screamer, Mammoth Falls, The Twister, Terror Canyon, and White Water Mountain. That just about says it all. Scaredy-cats can stick to the four regular white-water flumes, float gently past palm-studded "islands" at Calypso Beach, or swim in the artificial breakers in the Wave Pool or in the regular pool. There's also a water playground for young kids. Every night in January, and Saturday night September through April, is Dive-In Movie night, during which film fans can recline on a rubber tube in the pool while watching the flick on a giant screen. *Be warned:* It is very popular and very crowded, and to get a tube or a seat you have to get there early. A stunt show plays at 2:30pm (5pm on movie nights). The water is heated to 26°C (79°F) for year-round swimming.

Pacific Hwy (next to Warner Bros. Movie World), Oxenford. © 07/5573 6233, or 07/5573 2255 for recorded information. Fax 07/5529 7055. www.wetnwild.com.au. Admission A$31 (U.S.$20.15) adults, A$20 (U.S.$13) children 4–13. AE, DC, MC, V. Daily Jan 10am–9pm, Feb 10am–5pm, Mar–Apr 10am–4:30pm, May–Aug 10am–4pm, Sept–Oct 10am–4:30pm, Nov–Dec 10am–5pm. Open to 9pm on Dive-In Movie nights. Closed Christmas and open from 1:30pm Anzac Day (April 25). Take exit 60 on the M1 Pacific Motorway, 15 min. north of the Gold Coast or 40 min. south of Brisbane. Frequent bus services to the park from the Gold Coast and Brisbane with Coachtrans © 07/1800 426 224, or 07/3236 1000. Trains run to Coomera on the Brisbane–Gold Coast line, with bus connections from the station to the park.

EXPLORING THE WILDLIFE & AUSTRALIAN PARKS

Currumbin Wildlife Sanctuary ⓡ *Kids* Currumbin used to be called a bird sanctuary, and it is almost synonymous with the wild rainbow lorikeets which flock here in their hundreds twice a day for feeding. It's quite an experience, as flocks of chattering birds descend onto visitors holding trays of food for them. Photographers go crazy and the tourists love it. These amazingly beautiful birds have a vivid green back, blue head, and red and yellow chest. Lorikeet feeding is at 8am and 4pm. Don't miss it. You can also have your photo taken cuddling a koala, hand-feed kangaroos, stroll, or take a free miniature-steam-train ride through the park, and attend animal talks and feeding demonstrations. An Aboriginal song and dance show takes place daily. The park's 27 hectares (67 acres) are home to 1,400 native birds and animals, and lots of native birds are also drawn to the wetlands within the grounds. It also offers behind-the-scenes tours that take in the animal hospital and endangered-species-breeding area, a birds-of-prey display, and nighttime tours (Mon, Wed, and Sat, 7:30–9:45pm; cost A$35/U.S.$22.75 adult, A$18/U.S.$11.70 children 4–15, A$89/U.S.$57.85 family of four). Allow several hours to see everything.

28 Tomewin St., Currumbin (18km/11 miles south of Surfers Paradise). © 07/5534 1266. www.currumbin-sanctuary.org.au. Admission A$19 (U.S.$12.35) adults, A$11 (U.S.$7.15) seniors and children 4–15, A$49 (U.S.$32) family of 4. AE, DC, MC, V. Daily 8am–5pm. Closed Christmas and until 1pm ANZAC Day. Ample free off-street parking. Bus stop 15 m (49 ft.) from entrance.

David Fleay Wildlife Park ⓡ *Value* Established in 1952 by Australian naturalist David Fleay, this is one of Australia's premier wildlife parks. You'll see a platypus, saltwater and freshwater crocodiles, wallabies, kangaroos, glider possums, dingoes, wombats, the rare Lumholtz's tree kangaroo, and a big range of Australian birds, including emus, cassowaries, wedge-tailed eagles, black swans, and lorikeets. You walk on a series of raised boardwalks through picturesque mangrove, rain-forest, and eucalyptus habitats, where most of the animals roam free. The nocturnal house is open from 11am to 5pm daily, and this is where you'll see many of the most elusive native animals including Australia's answer to the Easter bunny, the bilby. A program of talks and feeding demonstrations throughout the day includes a reptile show and saltwater-croc feeding—usually only October through April, when the crocs are hungry. Aboriginal rangers from the local Gomberriberri and Bundjalung communities give talks about weaponry, bush medicine, and their links with this region. Volunteers also give free guided tours throughout the day. The park has been run by the Queensland National Parks and Wildlife Service since 1983, but David Fleay continued to live here until his death in 1993. Because the QNPWS frowns on handling animals, you can't cuddle a koala or hand-feed kangaroos here. There's a cafe, gift shop, and picnic tables.

West Burleigh Rd.(17km/10¼ miles south of Surfers Paradise), West Burleigh. © 07/5576 2411. Admission A$13 (U.S.$8.45) adults, A$8.50 (U.S.$5.50) seniors and students, A$6.50 (U.S.$4.20) children 4–17, A$33 (U.S.$21.45) for a family of 6. MC, V. Free re-entry if rained out. Daily 9am–5pm. Closed Christmas Day and until 1pm Anzac Day. Ample free parking.

WHERE TO STAY
VERY EXPENSIVE
Palazzo Versace   You almost have to see this to believe it. In the unlikely location of the Australian Gold Coast, fashion designer Donatella Versace has created a tribute to her late brother Gianni in the form of an extravagantly opulent resort, furnished exclusively with Versace gear. You'll either love it or hate it . . . there's no in-between. Everything has been imported from Italy, from the river stones that pave the porte-cochere to the massive antique chandelier that dominates the vast, marbled lobby. Vaulted ceilings are hand-detailed in gold and huge marble columns dominate. The rooms are decorated in four colors, red, blue, gold, and orange, but are less confronting than the public areas of the hotel. Everything in them—furniture, cutlery, crockery, toiletries, the lot—is Versace (either from the homewares collection or specially created for the hotel). Many of the rooms overlook the huge swimming pool, the Broadwater, and marina. As you'd expect, everything is beautifully appointed, and you'll enjoy strolling the corridors that are lined with Gianni's artwork and designs. The restaurants are run by one of Australia's top chefs, Russell Armstrong, and there's an extensive spa and health club in the basement. You can choose from eight room types (Donatella stays in the Imperial Suite when she comes) or from a letting pool of two or three bedroom condominiums. And of course, should you get the urge to shop, there's a Versace boutique.

94 Sea World Drive, Main Beach, QLD 4217. © **1800/098 000** in Australia, or 07/5509 8000. Fax 07/5509 8888. www.palazzoversace.com.au. 205 units and 72 condominiums. A$390 (U.S.$253.50) double Superior room; A$430 (U.S.$279.50) double Superior Lagoon View room; A$490 (U.S.$318.50) double Executive Suite; A$590 (U.S.$383.50) Deluxe Suite; A$840 (U.S.$546) Broadwater suite; condominiums A$1130–$1430 (U.S.$734.50–$929.50) per night. AE, DC, MC, V. **Amenities:** 3 restaurants, 2 bars; enormous 65 meter saltwater heated lagoon pool and 27 other pools (some of them exclusive to condos); health club and spa; Jacuzzis (some condominiums only); wet and dry sauna; concierge; tour desk; business center and secretarial services; salon; room service; massage; laundry service; dry cleaning; half the rooms are nonsmoking. *In room:* A/C, TV with pay movies, dataport and Sony playstation, kitchen, minibar, fridge, coffeemaker, hairdryer, iron, safe.

MODERATE
Calypso Plaza 𝄪 *Kids* *Finds*   Just 10 minutes from Gold Coast Airport, this is one of Coolangatta's newer developments but somehow manages not to spoil the old-fashioned seaside-town feel. It is just across the road from the beach but boasts its own huge free-form lagoon, complete with water slides, which the kids will love. There's also a separate swimming pool for smaller kids. The one- and two-bedroom apartments have sweeping views across the beach and ocean, and all have balconies with outdoor furniture, from which to enjoy them. All two-bedroom apartments have two bathrooms, and there's also a laundry in each apartment. Other services include a shuttle bus to local golf, tennis, and service clubs.

87–105 Griffith St., Coolangatta, QLD 4225. © **1800/062 189** in Australia, or 07/5599 0000. Fax 07/5599 0099. www.mirvachotels.com.au. reservationcalypsoplaza@mirvachotels.com.au. 155 units. A$140–$325 (U.S.$91–$211) double. AE, DC, MC, V. Free undercover parking. **Amenities:** Restaurant, bar; huge outdoor pool with water slide and Jacuzzi; tour desk; car-rental desk; business center and secretarial services; room service; babysitting. *In room:* A/C, TV with in-house movies, kitchen, hair dryer, iron, safe.

Mercure Resort Surfers Paradise 𝄪 *Kids* *Value*   If you're a parent and your idea of a holiday is to not even see your kids for most of the day, this place is for you. The resort has a licensed childcare center for little ones as young as 6 weeks up to 4 years old. For 5- to 12-year-olds, there's the Gecko Club, complete with pedal minicars, the Leonardo de Gecko painting room, and an underwater

> ⓘ *Tips* **Book Ahead for Indy & Easter Madness!**
>
> Most accommodations will require a 1-week minimum stay during school holiday periods, and a 4-day minimum stay at Easter. When the Gold Coast Indy car race takes over the town for 4 days in October, hotel rates skyrocket and most hostelries demand a minimum stay of 3 or 4 nights. Don't leave accommodation bookings to the last minute! Contact the Gold Coast Tourism Bureau (ⓒ **07/5538 4419**; fax 07/5570 3259) to find out the exact dates.

themed pirate adventure world. You can laze around the pleasant leafy pool area and watch the kids play on the water slide. The childcare center charges a moderate fee, but the Gecko Club is free; both operate daily year-round. The low-rise building is comfortable and rooms have views of either the pool or the tropical gardens. All rooms were refurbished in November 2000. Family quarters sleep up to five in two separate rooms, and some have kitchenettes. The big range of activities make this a great value place for families. The center of Surfers Paradise and the patrolled beach are a few blocks across the highway. Some rooms are near the highway, so ask for a quiet spot.

122 Ferny Ave., Surfers Paradise, QLD 4217. ⓒ **1800/074 111** in Australia, 1800/221 4542 in the U.S. and Canada, 0181/283 4500 in the U.K., 0800/44 4422 in New Zealand, or 07/5579 4444. Fax 07/5579 4492. www.mercuresurfers.com.au 405 units. A$170 (U.S.$110.50) double; A$230–$190 (U.S.$149.50–$123.50) family room. Additional person A$22 (U.S.$14). Children under 16 stay free in parents' room if they use existing bedding. Free crib. Ask about special packages. AE, DC, MC, V. **Amenities:** 2 restaurants, bar; 4 outdoor pools; 2 tennis courts; exercise room; Jacuzzi; sauna; childcare center and kids' club; concierge; tour desk; babysitting. *In room:* A/C, TV with free and pay-per-view movies, kitchenette (family studios only), coffeemaker, hair dryer, iron.

GOOD-VALUE VACATION APARTMENTS

Apartments make good sense for families and for any traveler who is prepared to self-cater to save money. Because the Gold Coast has a dramatic over-supply of apartments that stand empty outside school vacations, you can get a spacious modern unit with ocean views for the cost of a low-priced mid-range hotel. The complexes listed below are particularly good values. Apartment block developers got in quick to snag the best beachfront spots when the Gold Coast boomed in the 1970s, so it's apartment complexes, not hotels, that have the best ocean views.

Bahia Beachfront Apartments ⓡ *Value*   You get champagne views at a beer price at this 14-story apartment complex 800 meters (½ mile) north of the center of Surfers Paradise. Units are big and airy, and simply but neatly furnished with linoleum tiles, a big modern kitchen, and combined bathroom/laundry. Front-facing apartments have a mirrored rear wall to reflect the ocean. Like many apartments on the Gold Coast, these are not air-conditioned, but the sea breeze is a good substitute on all but the hottest days. Corner apartments have two balconies, and only units in the southwest corner of the building and on the first two floors miss out on the sea view. A patrolled beach is just across the road.

154 The Esplanade, Surfers Paradise, QLD 4217. ⓒ **07/5538 3322.** Fax 07/5592 0318. www.bahia.com.au. 30 units. High season A$127 (U.S.$82.55) double 1-bedroom apt, A$172 (U.S.$111.80) double 2-bedroom apt. Low season A$98 (U.S.$63.70) 1-bedroom apt, A$135 (U.S.$87.75) 2-bedroom apt. Additional person A$15 (U.S.$9.75) extra. Weekly rates and discounts on stays of 3 nights or more available. AE, DC, MC, V. **Amenities:** Large outdoor wading pool; outdoor spa; sauna; tour desk; car-rental desk; massage; dry cleaning. *In room:* TV, fax, kitchen, iron.

Trickett Gardens Holiday Inn *(Value)* This clean, well-maintained three-story apartment block 100 meters (a few hundred ft.) from the beach and 2 blocks from Cavill Mall is not a member of the Holiday Inn chain, but rather a family-run concern. It's hard to beat for location, price, and comfort. The one- and two-bedroom painted-brick apartments have modest but neat furnishings, and are spacious and airy. Each has a balcony overlooking the pool, Jacuzzi, and barbecue under the bougainvillea and palms.

24–30 Trickett St., Surfers Paradise, QLD 4217. (C) **1800/074 290** in Australia, or 07/5539 0988. Fax 07/5592 0791. www.trickettgardens.com.au. 33 units (all with shower only). High season (Dec 26 to mid-Jan) A$132 (U.S.$85.80) double 1-bedroom apt, A$160 (U.S.$104) double 2-bedroom apt. Low season A$100 (U.S.$65) double 1-bedroom apt, A$108 (U.S.$70.20) double 2-bedroom apt. Additional person A$20 (U.S.$13). A$6 (U.S.$4.20) for children under 3 with extra bedding. MC, V. Free underground security parking. **Amenities:** Outdoor pool (heated in winter); spa; tour desk; car-rental desk; in-room massage; babysitting; same-day dry cleaning; nonsmoking rooms. *In room:* A/C, TV, dataport, kitchen, fridge, hair dryer, iron, safe.

WHERE TO DINE

The Gold Coast is full to the rafters with good restaurants. Many stylish new restaurants and cafes, most reasonably priced, are springing up around **Surf Parade** and **Victoria Avenue** at Broadbeach, as well as in the nearby **Oasis shopping mall.** Another of the trendy spots to be seen dining is in the stylish **Marina Mirage** shopping center opposite the Sheraton on Sea World Drive at Main Beach, or at one of the hip **Tedder Avenue** cafes in Main Beach.

THE GOLD COAST AFTER DARK

There's a genuine Rolls-Royce parked in the corner at **Rolls** nightclub at the Sheraton Mirage, Sea World Drive, Main Beach ((C) **07/5591 1488**)—you can reserve it as your booth for the night. A mixed-age crowd of sophisticated locals rubs shoulders with hotel guests. There is a A$5 (U.S.$3.50) cover; the club opens Friday and Saturday night. At 10:30pm they push back the tables at **Saks,** Marina Mirage, Sea World Drive, Main Beach ((C) **07/5591 2755**) and this elegant cafe/wine bar turns into a dance floor for fashionable 20- and 30-somethings. Friday, Saturday, and Sunday are the coolest nights to turn up, and there's a live band Sundays; no cover.

It's not as big some Vegas casinos, but **Conrad Jupiters Casino,** Gold Coast Highway, Broadbeach ((C) **07/5592 1133**), has plenty to keep the gambler amused—88 gaming tables and 1,100-plus slot machines with roulette, blackjack, Caribbean stud poker, baccarat and minibaccarat, craps, Pai Gow, and Sic Bo, as well as the classic Aussie two-up. Downstairs the 1,100-seat Jupiter's Theatre stages floor shows and live song performances; and there are nine bars, including an English-style pub. Of the six restaurants, the good-value Food Fantasy buffet is outrageously popular, so be prepared to wait. The casino is open 24 hours. You must be 18 to enter, and smart, casual dress is required.

10 The Gold Coast Hinterland: Back to Nature

The cool, green Gold Coast hinterland—the "green behind the gold," as the tourism spin doctors are fond of putting it—is only a half-hour drive from the Coast, but it is a world away from the neon lights, theme parks, and crowds. Up here, at an altitude of 500 to 1,000 meters (about 1,500–3,500 ft.), the tree ferns drip moisture, the air is crisp, and there's no pressure to do anything too quickly.

Mt. Tamborine shelters several villages known for their craft shops, galleries, cafes, and lovely B&Bs. Easy walking trails wander from the streets through rain forest and eucalyptus woodland, and as you drive you will discover magnificent views.

The impressive 20,200-hectare (50,500-acre) **Lamington National Park** lies to the south of Mt. Tamborine. The park, at around 1,000 meters (3,328 ft.) above sea level, is a refreshing eucalyptus and rain-forest wilderness criss-crossed with walking trails. It's famous for its rich, colorful bird life, wallabies, possums, and other wildlife. The road to the park is full of twists and tight turns, and as you wind higher and higher, gnarled tangled vines and dense eucalyptus and ferns make a canopy across the road, so dark you need your car headlights on. The park is about 90 minutes from the coast—but once you're ensconced in your mountain retreat, the world will seem remote.

The hinterland is close enough to the Gold Coast and Brisbane to make a pleasant day trip, but you will almost certainly want to stay overnight, or longer, once you breathe that restorative mountain air.

MT. TAMBORINE
40km (24 miles) NW of Surfers Paradise; 70km (42 miles) S of Brisbane

Craft shops, teahouses, and idyllic mountain vistas are why visitors come to Mt. Tamborine. The mountaintop is more a plateau than a peak, and it's home to a string of villages, all a mile or 2 apart—Eagle Heights, North Tamborine, and Mt. Tamborine proper. Many of the shops and cafes are only open Thursday, Friday, and weekends.

ESSENTIALS
GETTING THERE   From the Gold Coast, head to Nerang and follow the signs that say Beaudesert. The Mt. Tamborine turnoff is off this road. Alternatively, head up the Pacific Highway to Oxenford and take the Mt. Tamborine turnoff, the first exit after Warner Bros. Movie World. Many tour operators run minibus and four-wheel-drive day trips from the Gold Coast, and some also run tours from Brisbane.

VISITOR INFORMATION   Head to the **Gold Coast Tourism Bureau** (see "Visitor Information" in the "Gold Coast" section above) to stock up on information and tourist maps before you head out. Brisbane Tourism outlets (see "Visitor Information" in chapter 5) also have information. Once you arrive, the **Tamborine Mountain Information Centre** is in Doughety Park, where Geissmann Drive becomes Main Western Road in North Tamborine (© **07/5545 3200**). It's open daily from 10:30am to 3:30pm.

EXPLORING THE MOUNTAIN
With a map at hand, you are well equipped to drive around Mt. Tamborine's roads to admire the wonderful views over the valleys and to poke around in the shops. New Age candles, homemade soaps, maple-pecan fudge, framed tropical watercolors, German cuckoo clocks, and Aussie antiques are some of the things you can buy in the mountain's crafty stores. The best place to shop is the quaint strip of galleries, cafes, and shops known as Gallery Walk on Long Road, between North Tamborine and Eagle Heights. Eagle Heights has few shops but great views back toward the coast. North Tamborine is mainly a commercial center where you still find the odd nice gallery or two. Mt. Tamborine itself is mainly residential.

Allow time to walk some of the trails that wind through forest throughout the villages. Most are reasonably short and easy. The Mt. Tamborine Information Centre has maps marking them.

WHERE TO STAY

Tamborine Mountain Bed & Breakfast Elizabeth Finnemore's restful timber home has stunning 180° views to the ocean from the breakfast balcony. Laze by the open fire in the timber-lined living room, or out on the lovely veranda where rainbow lorikeets, kookaburras, and crimson rosellas flit about over the bird feeders. The ferny gardens have four purpose-built rustic timber rooms, each individually decorated in Edwardian/cottage style and linked to the house by covered walkways. Elizabeth will lend hair dryers. The rooms are heated in winter. The Queensland automobile association, the RACQ, awards the place five stars. No smoking indoors.

19–23 Witherby Crescent, Eagle Heights, QLD 4721. © 07/5545 3595. Fax 07/5545 3322. www.tmbb. com.au. 4 units (one with bath, others shower only). A$80–$110 (U.S.$52–$71.50) double; A$135–$160 (U.S.$87.75–$104) double on Sat nights. Rates include full breakfast. AE, MC, V. Free parking. No children allowed. *In room:* A/C, TV/VCR, small fridge, coffeemaker, iron available.

LAMINGTON NATIONAL PARK

70km (42 miles) W of Gold Coast; 115km (69 miles) S of Brisbane

Subtropical rain forest, 2,000-year-old, moss-covered Antarctic beech trees, giant strangler figs, and misty mountain air characterize Lamington's high narrow ridges and plunging valleys. Its great stretches of dense rain forest make it one of the most important subtropical parks in southeast Queensland, and one of the loveliest. The park has 160 kilometers (96 miles) of walking trails that track through thick forest, past ferny waterfalls, and along mountain ridges with soaring views across green valleys. The trails vary in difficulty and length, from 1-kilometer (½-mile) strolls up to 23-kilometer (14-mile) treks. The park is a haven for bird lovers who come to see and photograph the rosellas, bowerbirds, rare lyrebirds, and other species that live here, but that's not the only wildlife you will see. Groups of small wallabies, called pademelons, graze outside your room. In summer you may see giant carpet pythons curled up in a tree or large goannas sunning themselves on rock ledges. Near streams you may be stopped by a hissing Lamington spiny crayfish, an aggressive little monster 6 inches long, patterned in royal blue and white. The park comes alive with owls, possums, and sugar-gliders at night.

Most visitors are fascinated by the park's Antarctic beech trees, which begin to appear above the 1,000-meter (3,330-ft.) line. Like something from a medieval fairy tale, these mossy monarchs of the forest stand 20 meters (66 ft.) tall and measure up to 8 meters (26 ft.) in girth. They are survivors of a time when Australia and Antarctica belonged to the supercontinent, Gondwana, when it was covered by wet, tropical rain forest. The species survived the last Ice Age, and the trees at Lamington are about 2,000 years old, suckered off root systems about 8,000 years old. The trees are a 2½ hour walk from O'Reilly's Rainforest Guesthouse (see below).

TIPS FOR EXPLORING LAMINGTON NATIONAL PARK

The easiest way to explore the park is to base yourself at **O'Reilly's Rainforest Guesthouse** in the Green Mountains section of the park, or at **Binnaburra Mountain Lodge** in the Binnaburra section (see "Where to Stay & Dine," below). Most of the trails lead from one or the other of these resorts, and a 23-kilometer (14-mile) **Border Trail** connects them; it follows the New South Wales–Queensland border for much of the way, and can be walked by most reasonably fit folk in a day. Guided walks and activities at both resorts are for house guests only; however, both properties welcome day visitors who just want to walk the trails for free. Both have inexpensive cafes for day-trippers.

It is a good idea to bring a torch (flashlight) and maybe binoculars for wildlife spotting. The temperature is often 4°C to 5°C (10°F–20°F) cooler than on the Gold Coast, so bring a sweater in summer and bundle up in winter when nights get close to freezing. September through October is orchid season, and the frogs come out in noisy abundance in February and March.

GETTING THERE   By Car   O'Reilly's is 37 kilometers (22¼ miles) from the town of Canungra. The road is very twisty and winding, so take it slowly, allow yourself an hour from Canungra to reach O'Reilly's, and plan to arrive before dark. Binnaburra is 35 kilometers (21 miles) from Nerang via Beechmont, or 26 kilometers (15½ miles) from Canungra, on a similarly winding mountain road. From the Gold Coast go west to Nerang, where you can turn off to Binnaburra via Beechmont, or go on to Canungra where you will see the O'Reilly's and Binnaburra turnoffs. From Brisbane, follow the Pacific Highway south and take the Beenleigh/Mt. Tamborine exit to Mt. Tamborine. From there follow the signs to Canungra. Allow a good 2½ hours to get to either resort from Brisbane, and 90 minutes from the Gold Coast. Binnaburra sells unleaded fuel; O'Reilly's has emergency supplies only.

By Coach   The **Mountain Coach Company** (© 07/5524 4249) does daily transfers to O'Reilly's from the Gold Coast, leaving the airport at 8am, picking up at hotels along the way, and arriving at O'Reilly's at 12:30pm. The fare is A$44 (U.S.$28.60) adults round-trip. The return trip leaves O'Reilly's at 2:30pm, arriving at the airport by 5:30pm. **Allstate Scenic Tours** (© 07/ 3003 0700) makes a coach run from outside the Roma Street Transit Centre in Brisbane every day except Saturday at 9:30am, arriving at O'Reilly's at 12:30pm. It costs A$44 (U.S.$28.60) adults round-trip.

The Binnaburra resort runs a shuttle from the Gold Coast that costs A$22 (U.S.$14.30) per adult, half price for kids ages 5 to 14, each way. It runs on demand and should be booked when making accommodation bookings.

VISITOR INFORMATION   The best sources of information on hiking are O'Reilly's Rainforest Guesthouse and Binnaburra Mountain Lodge (see "Where to Stay & Dine" below for both); ask them to send you copies of their walking maps. There is a national-parks information office at both properties. For detailed information on hiking and camping in the park, contact the ranger at Lamington National Park, Green Mountains section (which is at O'Reilly's), via Canungra, QLD 4211 (© 07/ **5544 0634**).

WHERE TO STAY & DINE

The rates at these two mountaintop retreats include all activities, morning and afternoon tea, and supper; those at Binnaburra include three meals a day. There is little to choose between them. The rooms are cozier at Binnaburra, and its lounge and dining room are more modern and attractive; the family-owned O'Reilly's is a little homier and more welcoming. Both properties offer ample walking trails of a similar type and distance; guided walks, including nighttime wildlife-spotting trips; hearty food; and a restful, enjoyable experience. Look into the special-interest workshops both properties run throughout the year, which can be anything from gourmet weekends to mountain-jogging programs.

Binnaburra Mountain Lodge *(★★ (Kids*   Binnaburra is every bit the postcard-perfect mountain lodge. The original cabins, built in 1935, are still in use today;

they've been outfitted with modern comforts, but not 20th-century "inconveniences," such as telephones, radios, or clocks. All the accommodations have pine-paneled walls, floral bedcovers, heaters, and electric blankets. The most attractive and spacious are the mud-brick and weatherboard Acacia cabins, which have private bathrooms and the best views over the Numinbah Valley. There are two kinds of less-expensive Casuarina cabins—the nicest are the small and very cozy huts with a pitched ceiling, a washbasin, and a nice aspect into the forest and over the valley. Less atmospheric are the bunkroom-style rooms that sleep four to six people—good for families and groups of friends. Guests in Casuarina cabins share bathroom facilities, which include a Jacuzzi. Meals are served in the lovely stone-and-timber dining room. Seating is communal, so you get to meet other travelers. Free tea and coffee is on the boil all day. There is also a craft shop, a natural history library, and conference rooms.

Of the 21 trails leading from the lodge, 9 are short walks of less than 6 kilometers (3½ miles). The 12 longer trails range from a 9-kilometer (5½-mile) walk through "dry" rain forest to the 23-kilometer (14-mile) Border Trail to O'Reilly's. On Tuesday the resort buses hikers to O'Reilly's so they can spend the day walking back to Binnaburra. The lodge also conducts abseiling (rappelling) for anyone from beginners to advanced adventurers. Evening diversions might consist of parlor games, a weekly bush dance, or slide presentations on local natural history. Kids can entertain themselves in the excellent playground.

Beechmont via Canungra, QLD 4211. ℂ 1800/074 260 in Australia, or 07/5533 3622. Fax 07/5533 3747. www.binnaburralodge.com.au. 41 cabins, 22 with bathroom (shower only). A$250–$378 (U.S.$162.50–$245.70) double. Single supplement A$22 (U.S.$14.30) per night for 1–2 nights, A$11 (U.S.$7.15) for 3 or more nights; A$55 (U.S.$35.75) children 5–16. No sole use at Christmas and Easter holiday times. Rates decrease with every night you stay. Rates include all meals and activities. Ask about 2-, 3-, 4-, 5- and 7-night packages. Min. 2-night stay weekends, 3-night stay public holidays. AE, DC, MC, V. **Amenities:** Restaurant, bar; free kids' club Sat and school vacations for 5–14-year-olds; babysitting; coin-operated laundry. *In room:* minibar, fridge, coffeemaker, no phone.

O'Reilly's Rainforest Guesthouse 🐾🐾 (Kids)

Highlights of your stay will be the chance to hand-feed brilliantly colored rain-forest birds every morning and the fact that the staff will unfailingly remember you by name for your entire stay. Nestled high on a cleared plateau, the buildings are closed in on three sides by dense tangled rain forest and open to picturesque mountain views to the west. The rain forest begins right at the parking lot, from which 19 trails fan out through the bush. For those who don't want to venture too far, the **Treetop Walk** is just a few meters (yards) from the resort. You can walk the 15-meter-high (50-ft.-high) suspension bridge through the forest canopy, and climb to the two tree-top observation decks 30 meters (100 ft.) above ground for unbelievable views. One of the nicest trails is the 7.6-kilometer (4½-mile) round-trip to **Elabana Falls,** which takes about half a day. The staff run half-day and full-day guided walks, and half-day four-wheel-drive bus trips. Every night there is a slide show on the area's wildlife or history. You may also enjoy spot-lighting walks to see possums, glow-worms, and, in season, luminous fungi. Sometimes in summer there are cliff-top campfire nights with steaks cooked over the fire.

The timber-resort complex is inviting rather than grand, but up-market new suites and the refurbishment of older rooms have added a touch of luxury in the past year. The comfortable guest lounge has an open fire and is scattered with old-fashioned sofas, chairs, and an upright piano. The six rooms in the Tooloona block, which dates from the 1930s, have communal bathrooms and basic furniture. The motel-style Elabana rooms have en suite bathrooms. The 37 Bithongabel rooms have the best views and also have en-suite bathrooms. Six family rooms in this block have bunks for kids, and two rooms have wheelchair access. The newest, and most expensive, rooms are the Canopy Suites, which are twice as large as any of the other rooms and have such luxuries as a king-size four-poster bed, fireplace, spa, library, audio system and bar. At meal times, the maitre d' assigns you to a table in the dining room, so you get to meet other guests. If you do not buy a meal package, buffet breakfast costs A$22 (U.S.$14.30), lunch costs A$26 (U.S.$16.90), and a three-course dinner is A$37 (U.S.$24.05). Before dinner, guests head to the hexagonal timber bar, perched up high for great sunset views and half-price cocktails (5–6:30pm). Among other facilities are a cafe and gift shop, a basketball court, and free tea, coffee, and cookies all day.

Via Canungra, Lamington National Park Rd., Lamington National Park, QLD 4275. ℭ 1800/688 722 in Australia, or 07/5544 0644. Fax 07/5544 0638. www.oreillys.com.au. 52 units. A$108–$137 (U.S.$70–$89) single; A$177–$274 (U.S.$115–$178) double. Canopy Suites A$191 (U.S.$124) per person. Additional person A$22 (U.S.$14.30); children 17 and under stay free in parents' room if they use existing bedding. Free crib. Rates include all activities. Rates decrease with every night you stay. Min. 2-night stay weekends, 3-night stay long weekends, 4-night stay Easter and Christmas. Ask about packages for stays of 2 nights or more. Meal plans A$69 (U.S.$44.85) adults, A$34 (U.S.$22.10) children 10–17, A$17 (U.S.$11.05) children 4–9 for 3 meals per day; 2-meal packages available. AE, DC, MC, V. **Amenities:** Restaurant, bar; outdoor pool; day/night tennis court; Jacuzzi; sauna; kids' club for over-5s on weekends and school vacations; game room; babysitting; coin-operated laundry.

The Red Centre

by Natalie Kruger

The Red Centre is the landscape many of us conjure up when we think of the Outback—vast horizons, red sand as far as the eye can see, mysterious monoliths, cloudless blue sky, harsh sunlight, and the rhythmic twang of the didgeridoo. It's home to sprawling cattle ranches; ancient low mountain ranges; "living fossil" palm trees that survived the Ice Age; cockatoos and kangaroos; red gorges; pretty water holes; and, Ayers Rock, which the Aborigines call Uluru. Aboriginal people have lived here for tens of thousands of years, long before the Pyramids were a twinkle in a Pharaoh's eye, but the Centre is still largely unexplored by non-Aboriginal Australians. A single highway cuts from Adelaide in the south to Darwin in the north, and a few paved roads and four-wheel-drive tracks make a lonely spider web across it; but there are many areas where non-Aborigines have never set foot.

Alice Springs is the only big town in Central Australia. So let's get one thing straight—Alice Springs and Uluru are *not* side by side. Countless tourists wander into the Alice Springs visitor center after lunch, and say they want to "go see the Rock this afternoon." Uluru is 462 kilometers (289 miles) away. You can see it in a day from Alice, but it takes a big effort.

The Red Centre is more than just a Rock, though. Give yourself a few days to experience all there is out here—visiting the impressive Olgas near Ayers Rock, walking the rim of Kings Canyon, riding a camel down a dry riverbed, poking around Aboriginal rock carvings, swimming in gorge water holes, or staying at an Outback homestead. Many friends and colleagues in the tourism industry share my opinion that a stay in Alice Springs gives you an better flavor for the Outback than Uluru. If you base yourself in Alice, it's easy to radiate out to less crowded but still beautiful attractions like Palm Valley, Ormiston Gorge, and Trephina Gorge Nature Park, each easily handled as a day trip. Too many visitors jet in, snap a photo of the Rock, and head home, only to miss the essence of the desert.

1 Exploring the Red Centre

VISITOR INFORMATION The **Central Australian Tourism Industry Association** (see "Visitor Information" under "Alice Springs," later in this chapter) can send you a brochure pack. It is your best one-stop source of information.

Most of the Red Centre lies within the Northern Territory. The **Northern Territory Tourist Commission** (NTTC), Tourism House, 43 Mitchell St., Darwin, NT 0800 (© **13 61 10** for trip planning inquiries in Australia, or 08/8999 3900 administration; **www.ntholidays.com**) maintains a site tailored for North Americans (**www.insidetheoutback.com**), and yet another (**www.ozoutback.com**)

The Red Centre

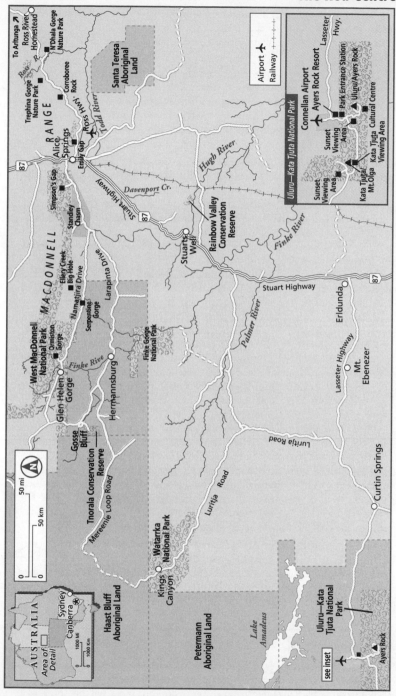

Legend:
Airport ✈
Railway ┼─┼─┼─┼

To Artunga ↗
Ross River Homestead
N'Dhala Gorge Nature Park
Santa Teresa Aboriginal Land

Trephina Gorge Nature Park
Corroboree Rock
RANGE
Alice Springs
Emily Gap
Simpson's Gap
Standley Chasm
Ross Hwy.
Todd River

Uluru–Kata Tjuta National Park
Connellan Airport ✈
Ayers Rock Resort
Lasseter Hwy.
Park Entrance Station
Uluru/Ayers Rock
Sunset Viewing Area
Kata Tjuta Cultural Centre Viewing Area
Sunset Viewing Area
Kata Tjuta/ Mt.Olga

Davenport Cr.
Stuart Highway
Hugh River
Rainbow Valley Conservation Reserve
Stuarts Well
Finke River

MACDONNELL
Ellery Creek Big Hole
Larapinta Drive
Namatjira Drive
Serpentine Gorge
West MacDonnell National Park
Ormiston Gorge
Glen Helen Gorge
Finke River
Hermannsburg
Finke Gorge National Park
Gosse Bluff
Tnorala Conservation Reserve

Stuart Highway
Palmer River
Erldunda
Lasseter Highway
Mt. Ebenezer
Luritja Road
87

50 mi
50 km
0
0

Mereenie Loop Road
Luritja Road
Watarrka National Park
Kings Canyon
Haast Bluff Aboriginal Land

Petermann Aboriginal Land
Lake Amadeus

Curtin Springs
Uluru–Kata Tjuta National Park
Ayers Rock
see inset ✈

AUSTRALIA
Sydney
Canberra
Area of Detail
1000 Mi
1000 Km
0
0

for young and student travelers. The commission publishes a helpful annual guide to Central Australia that details many hotels, tour operators, car-rental companies, and attractions, and operates a division that offers package deals on complete trips.

WHEN TO GO   April/May and September/October have warm sunny days (coolish in May, hot in Oct). Winter (that's June–Aug) means cold days, a sharp wind, and nights as cold as freezing point. Summer (Nov–Mar) is ferociously hot and best avoided. In summer, limit exertions to early morning and late afternoon, and choose air-conditioned accommodations. Rain is rare but can come at any time of year.

DRIVING TIPS   The **Automobile Association of the Northern Territory (AANT)**, 79–81 Smith St., Darwin, NT 0800 (© **08/8981 3837**), offers reciprocal emergency breakdown service to members of affiliated overseas automobile associations and dispenses maps and advice from its Darwin office. It has no office in the Red Centre. For **road conditions**, call © **1800/246 199** in Australia for a 24-hour recorded report.

Only a handful of highways and arterial roads are sealed (paved) roads in the Northern Territory. A conventional two-wheel-drive car will get you to 95% of all you want to see, but consider renting a four-wheel-drive for complete freedom. All the big car-rental chains rent them. Some attractions are on unpaved roads good enough for a two-wheel-drive car, but your car-rental company will not insure a two-wheel-drive for driving on them.

Outside settled areas, the Northern has no speed limit, but before you hit the gas pedal, consider the likely risk of hitting wild camels, kangaroos, and protected native wildlife. Locals stick to a comfortable 120 kilometers-per-hour (75 mph) or less. Avoid driving at night, early morning, and late afternoon when 'roos feed; beware cattle lying down on the warm bitumen at night. A white road sign bearing a black circle outline crossed by a diagonal black line indicates the point when speed restrictions no longer apply.

Road trains and fatigue caused by driving long distances are two other major threats. For details on safe driving, review the tips in the "By Car" section of "Getting Around Australia," in chapter 2.

If you plan to "go bush" in remote regions not covered by this guide, you may need a permit to cross Aboriginal land from the relevant Aboriginal lands council. This can be a drawn-out bureaucratic affair taking weeks, so plan ahead. The Northern Territory Tourist Commission (above) can put you in touch with the appropriate council. All good road maps mark Aboriginal lands clearly.

OTHER TRAVEL TIPS   **Always carry drinking water.** When hiking, carry 4 liters (about a gallon) per person per day in winter, and a liter (¼ gal.) per person per hour in summer. Wear a broad-brimmed hat, high-factor sunscreen lotion, and insect repellent.

Bring warm clothing for chilly evenings in winter.

Tips **Buzz Off!**

Uluru is notorious for plagues of flies in summer. Don't be embarrassed to cover your head with the fly nets sold in souvenir stores—you'll look like the Dreamtime Beekeeper from Outer Space, but there will be "no flies on you, mate," an Aussie way of saying you are doing the right thing.

TOUR OPERATORS   No end of coach, minicoach, and four-wheel-drive tour operators run tours taking in Alice Springs, Kings Canyon, and Ayers Rock. They depart either Alice Springs or Ayers Rock, offering accommodations ranging from spiffy resorts, comfortable motels, and basic cabins to shared bunkhouses, tents, or swags (sleeping bags) under the stars. Most pack the highlights into a 2- or 3-day trip, though leisurely trips of 6 days or more are available. Many offer one-way itineraries between Alice and the Rock (via Kings Canyon if you like), or vice versa, which allows you to avoid backtracking.

Among the reputable companies are **AAT Kings** (✆ **1800/334 009** in Australia, or 03/9274 7422 for the Melbourne central reservations office; www.aatkings.com.au), which specializes in mainstream coach tours but also has four-wheel-drive camping itineraries; **Alice Springs Holidays** (✆ **1800/801 401** in Australia, or 08/8953 1411; www.alicespringsholidays.com.au), which does upscale soft-adventure tours for small groups; **Sahara Outback Tours** (✆ **08/ 8953 0881;** www.saharatours.com.au), which conducts affordable camping safaris in small groups for all ages; and **Discovery Ecotours** (formerly Uluru Experience and Alice Experience) (✆ **1800/803 174** in Australia, or 08/8956 2563; www.ecotours.com.au), which specializes in ecotours for small groups. Coach operator **Greyhound Pioneer** (✆ **13 20 30** in Australia) provides inexpensive tours.

Tailormade Tours (✆ **08/8952 1731**; www.members.ozemail.com.au/ ~tmade/) and **VIP Travel Australia** (✆ **1800/806 412** in Australia, or 08/8956 2388; www.vipaustralia.com.au) customize luxury tours utilizing stretch limos, minicoaches, and four-wheel-drives, and offer upscale treats like private desert barbecues and champagne tailgate dinners overlooking the Rock or the Olgas.

You can book Sahara Outback Tours and Tailormade Tours via **Alice Springs Tour Professionals** (✆ **08/8953 0666;** www.alicetourprofessionals.com.au), a one-stop shop that represents a number of Alice Springs–based tour and sightseeing companies.

Aboriginal Desert Discovery Tours (✆ **08/8952 3408;** www.aboriginalart. com.au), owned by Alice Springs Aboriginal people, teams up its Aboriginal guides with Alice-based tour companies to offer tours with an Aboriginal slant.

2 Alice Springs

462km (289 miles) NE of Ayers Rock; 1,491km (932 miles) S of Darwin; 1,544km (965 miles) N of Adelaide; 2,954km (1,846 miles) NW of Sydney

"The Alice," as Australians fondly dub it, is the unofficial capital of Outback Australia. In the early 1870s, a handful of telegraph-station workers struggled nearly 1,000 miles north from Adelaide through uncompromising desert to settle by a small spring in what must have seemed like the end of the earth. Alice Springs, as the little place was called, was nothing but a few huts built around a repeater station on the ambitious telegraph line that was to link Adelaide with Darwin and the rest of the world.

Today Alice is a city of 27,000 people, with supermarkets, banks, and the odd nightclub. It's a friendly, rambling, unsophisticated kind of place. No matter what direction you come from, you will soar for hours over a vast, flat, unchanging landscape to get here. That's why folks are so surprised when they reach Alice Springs and see low but dramatic mountain ranges, rippling red in the sunshine. Many people excitedly mistake them for Ayers Rock, but that baby is almost 300 miles down the road. These hills, jutting their craggy faces up against the streets, are the **MacDonnell Ranges.**

Alice Springs

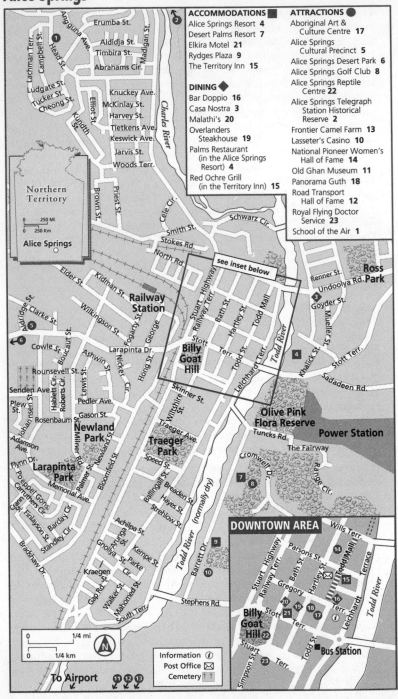

ACCOMMODATIONS ■
Alice Springs Resort **4**
Desert Palms Resort **7**
Elkira Motel **21**
Rydges Plaza **9**
The Territory Inn **15**

DINING ◆
Bar Doppio **16**
Casa Nostra **3**
Malathi's **20**
Overlanders
    Steakhouse **19**
Palms Restaurant
    (in the Alice Springs
    Resort) **4**
Red Ochre Grill
    (in the Territory Inn) **15**

ATTRACTIONS ●
Aboriginal Art &
    Culture Centre **17**
Alice Springs
    Cultural Precinct **5**
Alice Springs Desert Park **6**
Alice Springs Golf Club **8**
Alice Springs Reptile
    Centre **22**
Alice Springs Telegraph
    Station Historical
    Reserve **2**
Frontier Camel Farm **13**
Lasseter's Casino **10**
National Pioneer Women's
    Hall of Fame **14**
Old Ghan Museum **11**
Panorama Guth **18**
Road Transport
    Hall of Fame **12**
Royal Flying Doctor
    Service **23**
School of the Air **1**

Northern
Territory

0   250 Mi
0   250 Km

Alice Springs

see inset below

Ross
Park

Railway
Station

Billy
Goat
Hill

Olive Pink
Flora Reserve

Power Station

The Fairway

Newland
Park

Traeger
Park

Larapinta
Park

DOWNTOWN AREA

Billy
Goat
Hill

Bus Station

Information ⓘ
Post Office ✉
Cemetery ✝✝

To Airport

360

Many tourists visit Alice only to get to Ayers Rock, but Alice has plenty of charms all its own, albeit mostly of a small-town kind. The red folds of the MacDonnell Ranges hide lovely gorges with shady picnic grounds. A planned 250-kilometer (156-mile) hiking trail is partly ready for your boots now. There is an old gold-rush town to poke around in, quirky little museums, wildlife parks, a couple of cattle stations (ranches) that welcome visitors, a couple of nice day trips out of town, and one of the world's top-10 desert golf courses. You could easily fill 2 or 3 days in the area.

This is the heart of the Aboriginal Arrernte people's country, and Alice is a rich source of tours, shops, and galleries for anyone with an interest in Aboriginal culture, art, or simple souvenirs. There is a sad side to the town's Aboriginal riches. Not every Aboriginal succeeds in splicing his or her ancient civilization with the 21st century, and the result is dislocated communities living in the riverbed with only alcohol for company.

ESSENTIALS
GETTING THERE   By Plane   Qantas (© 13 13 13 in Australia) or its subsidiary **Airlink** (book through Qantas) fly direct from Sydney, Adelaide, Darwin, Cairns, Broome, and Ayers Rock. Flights from most other cities connect via Sydney or Adelaide. **Airnorth** (© 1800/627 474 in Australia, or 08/8945 2866) does a "Centre Run" from Darwin via Katherine and Tennant Creek every day except Sunday.

The **Alice Springs Airport Shuttle** (© 1800/621 188 in the Northern Territory, or 08/8953 0310) meets all major flights (but not always those from small towns like Tennant Creek) and transfers you to your Alice hotel door for A$10 (U.S.$5.50) one-way or A$17 (U.S.$9.35) round-trip, per person. A taxi from the airport to town, a distance of 15 kilometers (9 miles), is around A$25 (U.S.$13.75).

By Train   The *Ghan* train, named after Afghani camel-train drivers who carried supplies in the Red Centre last century, makes a 2-day trip from Sydney or Melbourne via Adelaide to Alice every week. The twice-weekly Adelaide–Alice stretch takes roughly 24 hours. It is treeless and empty, if fascinatingly so, so don't be concerned you'll miss it by overnighting on the train. The train has sleeper berths. For fares and schedules, call **Great Southern Railway** (© 13 21 47 within Australia, or 08/8213 4592; www.gsr.com.au) or see chapter 2 for its booking agencies abroad. There is no other train to Alice.

By Bus   Greyhound Pioneer (© 13 20 30 in Australia) and **McCafferty's** (© 13 14 99 in Australia) run from Adelaide and Darwin. It's about a 19½-hour trip from Adelaide, and the fare is around A$160 (U.S.$88). The 21-hour trip from Darwin costs about A$175 (U.S.$96.25). Greyhound does a daily 5¾-hour run from Ayers Rock; the fare is around A$71 (U.S.$39.05). It also does a daily trip from Kings Canyon for $54.

By Car   Alice Springs is on the Stuart Highway linking Adelaide and Darwin. Allow a very long 2 or a more comfortable 3 days to drive from Adelaide; the

---

Tips Safety in the Centre
Alice is a safe place, but steer clear of dark streets and the riverbed at night, as teenage kids like to accost people and make a nuisance of themselves.

same goes from Darwin. From Sydney, connect to the Stuart Highway via Broken Hill and Port Augusta north of Adelaide; from Cairns head south to Townsville, then west via the mining town of Mt. Isa to join the Stuart Highway at Tennant Creek. Both routes are long, dull, and best avoided. From Perth it is an even longer, duller drive across the Nullarbor Plain to connect with the Stuart Highway at Port Augusta.

VISITOR INFORMATION The **Central Australian Tourism Industry Association (CATIA) Visitor Information Centre,** 60 Gregory Terrace, Alice Springs, NT 0870 (© **08/8952 5800;** www.centralaustraliantourism.com), is the official one-stop shop for bookings and touring information for the entire Red Centre, including Alice Springs, Kings Canyon, and Uluru-Kata Tjuta National Park (Ayers Rock). It is also the visitor center for the Parks & Wildlife Commission of the Northern Territory, and dispenses National Park notes. It's open Monday through Friday from 8:30am to 5:30pm and from 9am to 4pm weekends and public holidays. It also has a desk at the airport.

SPECIAL EVENTS The town hosts a couple of bizarre events. The **Camel Cup** camel race takes place on second Saturday in July. On a Saturday in late September, folks from hundreds of miles around turn out for the **Henley-on-Todd Regatta.** They cheer on the proud owners of gaudily decorated, home-made bottomless "boats" as they race them on foot down the dry Todd River bed. Well, what else do you do on a river that flows only 3 days a year? See chapter 2 for more details on this event.

GETTING AROUND Virtually all tours pick you up at your hotel.

If your itinerary traverses unpaved roads, as it may do in outlying areas from Alice, you will need to rent a four-wheel-drive, as regular cars will not be insured on an unpaved road surface. However, a regular car will get you to most attractions. **Avis** (© 08/8953 5533), **Budget** (© 08/8952 8899), **Delta Europ-Car** (© 08/8955 5994), **Hertz** (© 08/8952 2644), local company **Outback Auto Rentals** (© 1800/652 133 in Australia, or 08/8953 5333), and **Thrifty** (© 08/8952 9999) all rent conventional and four-wheel-drive vehicles. You may get a better deal on car rental by going through booking agent **The Outback Travel Shop** (© **08/8955 5288;** www.outbacktravelshop.com.au) in Alice Springs, as it negotiates bulk rates with most Alice car rental companies.

Hertz, Thrifty Car Rental, and Outback Auto Rentals rent complete **camping kits** holding everything you need, including a tent, sleeping bags, and a gas stove. A kit will cost around A$11 (U.S.$6.05) per person per day. Book them in advance. Camping gear usually only fits into four-wheel-drive vehicles, not sedans.

Many national campervan rental outfits have Alice offices, including **Britz Campervan Rentals** (© **08/8952 8814**), **Hertz Campervans** (© **08/8953 5333**), and **Maui Rentals** (© **08/8952 8049**).

The best way to get around town without a car is aboard the **Alice Wanderer** bus (see "Organized Tours," below). Taxi fares are exorbitant, presumably because there's only one main outfit in town, **Alice Springs Taxis** (© **13 10 08**).

CITY LAYOUT **Todd Mall** is the heart of town. Most shops, businesses, and restaurants are here or within a few blocks' walk. Most hotels, the casino, the golf course, and many of the town's attractions are a mile or two out of town. The dry Todd River "flows" through the city a couple of blocks east of Todd Mall.

SEEING THE SIGHTS IN ALICE

Aboriginal Art & Culture Centre   Set up by the local Southern Arrernte Aboriginal people, this center houses a small but intriguing museum with exhibits on Aboriginal life. It displays a timeline of the Aboriginal view of history since "contact," as the arrival of Europeans is called. It's worth a visit if you're interested in indigenous cultures. It sells some artifacts and art. Allow anywhere from 15 minutes to 1 hour.

86 Todd St. ℂ 08/8952 3408. Admission A$2 (U.S.$1.10). Daily 8am–5pm.

Alice Springs Cultural Precinct   At least one or two of the attractions clustered here will probably pique your interest. All are within close walking distance of one another. The **Museum of Central Australia** mostly shows local fossils, natural history, and meteorites. Some impressive Aboriginal and contemporary Aussie art is shown at the **Araluen Centre,** the town's performing arts center; check out the "Honey Ant Dreaming" stained-glass window in its foyer. Aviation nuts may want to browse the old radios, several aircraft, and wreckage in the **Aviation Museum,** which preserves the Territory's aerial history. You can buy stylish craft works, and sometimes catch the artists at work, in the *Territory Craft* gallery. You may want to amble among the outdoor sculptures, including the 15-meter (49-ft.) *Yeperenye Dreamtime Caterpillar,* or among the gravestones in the cemetery, where "Afghani" (Pakistani) camel herders are buried facing Mecca. There is a picnic area, but save your picnic for the Alice Springs Telegraph Station Historical Reserve (below).

Larapinta Dr. at Memorial Ave., 2km (1¼ miles) south of town. ℂ **08/8951 1120.** Incorporating the Museum of Central Australia, Araluen Centre (ℂ 08/8951 1122 box office), Central Australian Aviation Museum, Territory Craft, and the Memorial Cemetery. Admission to precinct (includes admission to all attractions) A$7 (U.S.$3.85) adults, A$4 (U.S.$2.20) children 5–16, seniors, and students, A$18 (U.S.$9.90) family. Daily 10am–5pm. Closed Christmas and Good Friday. Take a cab or the Alice Wanderer bus (see "Organized Tours," below).

Alice Springs Desert Park ⚶   By means of an easy 1.6-kilometer (1-mile) trail through three reconstructed natural habitats, this impressive wildlife and flora park shows you 120 or so of the animal species that live in the desert around Alice, but that you won't spot too easily in the wild (including kangaroos you can walk amongst). Most are small mammals (like the big-eared bilby), reptiles (like the cute thorny devil lizards), and birds. Don't miss the excellent **Birds of Prey** ⚶⚶ show at 10am and 3:30pm. Allow 2 to 3 hours.

Larapinta Dr., 6km (3¾ miles) west of town. ℂ **08/8951 8788.** Admission A$18 (U.S.$9.90) adults, A$9 (U.S.$4.95) students and children 5–16, A$40 (U.S.$22) family. Daily 7:30am–6pm (last suggested entry 4pm; 'roo and emu exhibit closes 4:30pm). Closed Christmas. **Desert Park Transfers** (ℂ 08/8952 4667) provides round-trip transfers from anywhere in Alice for A$30 (U.S.$16.50) adults, A$25 (U.S.$13.75) students and seniors, A$20 (U.S.$11) kids 5–16, A$77 (U.S.$42.35) family. Includes park admission.

Alice Springs Reptile Centre *(Kids)*   Kids can walk around with pythons or bearded dragons (lizards) on their shoulders, all day if they want, at this Aussie reptile park. The easy-going proprietor lifts up the cages' glass fronts for better photos, and lets kids hand-feed bugs to the animals at feeding time. Some 30 species are on display, including the world's deadliest snake—Australia's inland taipan—and big goannas. Allow an hour.

9 Stuart Terrace (opposite the Royal Flying Doctor Service). ℂ **08/8952 8900.** Admission A$7 (U.S.$3.85) adults, A$4 (U.S.$2.20) children under 17, A$20 (U.S.$11) family. Daily 9am–5pm. Closed Christmas and New Year's Day.

Earning a Degree from Didgeridoo University

Fancy yourself as a Ray Charles of the desert? Then Didgeridoo University, at the Aboriginal Art & Culture Centre (see above) is the place for you.

Local Aboriginal Paul Ah Chee-Ngala set up his "campus" to satisfy an ever-growing demand from world travelers to master the didgeridoo's evocative rhythms. In truth, the university is an alcove in the culture center, and the degree takes just 1 hour. Classes begin every day at 1pm and cost A$11.50 (U.S.$6.35) adults, A$5.50 (U.S.$3) kids (or are free as part of the Centre's half-day tour described in "Organized Tours," below). Paul guarantees you will make kangaroo hopping sounds on the darn thing within the hour. The trick is to breathe in and out at the same time, a technique known as "circular breathing."

When buying a didgeridoo, keep in mind there is no such thing as a "good" or a "bad" one. The diameter, the wood used, and the unique surface of the instrument's insides are what makes each one unique. The pitch of the instrument can vary from a high wail on G to a deep and somber A; the shorter the instrument, the higher the pitch.

If you can't take a "degree" in Alice, learn to play the thing in your own living room via an audio lesson on the center's website, www.aboriginalart.com.au. The site sells didgeridoos, too.

Alice Springs Telegraph Station Historical Reserve 🔍 *Finds* Alice Springs began life as this charming telegraph repeater station in 1871, set by a pretty water hole amid red bouldery hills, sprawling gums full of parrots, and mercifully green lawns. An oasis in the harsh Alice landscape, it's a place tourists often overlook. Arm yourself with the free map, or join a free 45-minute tour, and wander around the old station master's residence; the telegraph office, with its Morse code machine tap-tapping away; the shoeing yard packed with blacksmith's equipment; and the stables, housing vintage buggies and saddlery. By the time you arrive, you may be able to "telegraph" e-mails to your friends from the on-site computer. May through October, "kitchen maids" in period dress serve scones (biscuits) and damper from the original wood-fired ovens. The park has pet camels, and sometimes orphaned kangaroo joeys. Allow a good hour, more to walk one of the several hiking trails leading from the extensive grounds. This is a lovely picnic spot. There is a gift shop and coffee and snacks for sale, too.

On the Stuart Hwy. 4km (2½ miles) north of town (beyond the School of the Air turnoff). ✆ 08/8952 3993. Free admission to picnic grounds and trails; station A$6.25 (U.S.$3.45) adults, A$4.75 (U.S.$2.60) seniors and students, A$3.25 (U.S.$1.80) children 5–15. Daily 8am–5pm (picnic grounds and trails open until 9pm). Station closed Christmas; picnic grounds open 365 days a year. Take a cab or the Alice Wanderer bus (see "Organized Tours," below) or the 4km (2½-mile) riverside pedestrian/bike track that starts near the corner of Wills Terrace and Undoolya Rd.

National Pioneer Women's Hall of Fame With a collection of photographs, domestic items, and other memorabilia, this engrossing museum tells the stories of more than 100 Aussie women who were pioneers in their fields, be they Olympic gold medalists, priests, or pilots.

The Old Courthouse, 27 Hartley St. ✆ 08/8952 9006. Admission A$2.20 (U.S.$1.20) adults, free for children under 15. Daily 10am–5pm. Closed mid-Dec to Feb 1.

Royal Flying Doctor Service   Alice is a major base for this airborne medical service that treats people living and traveling in the vast Outback. An interesting 20-minute tour runs every half-hour, featuring a video and a talk in the communications room; allow another 30 minutes or so to browse the small museum. Some of the taped conversations between doctors and patients are intriguing. There is a nice garden cafe and a gift shop.

8–10 Stuart Terrace (at the end of Hartley St.). © 08/8952 1129. Admission A$5.50 (U.S.$3) adults, A$2.20 (U.S.$1.20) children 6–15. Mon–Sat 9am–5pm (last tour departs 4pm); Sun and public holidays 1–5pm. Closed Christmas and New Year's Day.

School of the Air   Sitting in on school lessons may not be your idea of a vacation, but this school is different—it broadcasts by radio to a 1,300,000-square-kilometer (501,800-sq.-mile) "schoolroom" of 140 children on Outback stations. That's a classroom as big as Germany, Great Britain, Ireland, New Zealand, and Japan combined—or twice the size of Texas. The key attraction is to watch and listen in when classes are in session on weekdays, but outside class hours you may hear taped classes, and browse the kids' artwork, photos, video, touchscreens, and many other displays in the well put together visitor gallery. Free 30-minute tours run throughout the day.

80 Head St. (2.5km/1½ miles from town). © 08/8951 6834. Admission A$3.50 (U.S.$1.90) adults, A$2 (U.S.$1.10) seniors and children 5–16, A$12 (U.S.$6.60) family. Mon–Sat and public holidays 8:30am–4:30pm; Sun 1:30–4:30pm. Closed Christmas, Boxing Day (Dec 26), and New Year's Day. Bus: 3, or take the Alice Wanderer (see "Organized Tours," below).

ORGANIZED TOURS

AROUND TOWN & OUT IN THE DESERT   The **Alice Wanderer** bus (© **1800/66 9111** in Australia, or 08/8952 2111) does a running loop of town attractions every 70 minutes from 9am, with the last departure at 4pm. Hop on and off as you please, and enjoy the commentary from the driver. It departs daily from the southern end of Todd Mall. Tickets are sold on board and cost A$25 (U.S.$13.75) for adults, A$22.50 (U.S.$12.40) for seniors and students, and A$12.50 (U.S.$6.90) kids 4 to 14. Call for a free pickup from your hotel.

The bus calls at most of the attractions listed above, plus the **Road Transport Hall** of Fame; the **Old Ghan Museum,** housing the original *Ghan* train that plied the Adelaide–Alice Springs line from 1929 to 1980; and **Panorama Guth,** an art gallery housing a 360° painting by artist Henk Guth of central Australian landscapes.

Many Alice-based companies offer minicoach or four-wheel-drive day trips and extended tours not only of Alice, but also of outlying areas including the East or West Macs, Hermannsburg and Finke Gorge National Park. Among the well-regarded ones are: **Discovery Ecotours** (© **08/8956 2563;** www. ecotours.com.au); **Alice Springs Holidays** (© **1800/801 401** in Australia, or 08/8953 1411; www.alicespringsholidays.com.au); and **Alice Springs Tour Professionals** (© **1800/673 391** in Australia, or 08/8953 0666; www. alicetourprofessionals.com.au), a one-stop shopping for a number of reliable tour operators and adventure outfitters. See also "Exploring the Red Centre," at the beginning of this chapter, for companies running tours throughout the area.

Several Alice companies run tours by Harley Davidson motorcycle, or fun four-wheel-drive quad-bikes.

ABORIGINAL TOURS   Several companies offer tours on which you can experience some aspects of Aboriginal culture. I recommend those offered by the **Aboriginal Art & Culture Centre** (see "Seeing the Sights in Alice," above). All their tours have Aboriginal guides. Their **half-day tour** ⊙★ features an explanation of the Dreamtime creation era; a gentle bush tucker walk; a chance to throw a boomerang and spear; talks about tools and weapons over billy tea and damper; and a dance performance at which you can have a go yourself, and have your photo taken with the dancers. You may have seen these very dancers performing in the opening ceremony of the Sydney 2000 Olympic Games. Threaded through all this is an ongoing discussion of Aboriginal culture, beliefs, fascinating family relationships, and a view of history both ancient and modern through Aboriginal eyes. You have a chance to buy art during the morning. The experience wraps up with a 1-hour didgeridoo lesson at 1pm. The tour departs daily at 8am and costs A$82.50 (U.S.$45.40) adults and A$44 (U.S.$24.20) children under 12 (including hotel pickup).

CAMEL SAFARIS   You might not associate camels with Australia, but the camel's ability to get by without water was key to opening up the arid inland parts of the country to European settlement in the 1800s. With the advent of cars, they were released into the wilds, and today there are more than 200,000 of them roaming central Australia's deserts. Australia even exports them to the Middle East! **Frontier Camel Tours** (© **1800/806 499** in Australia, or 08/8953 0444) runs a fun 1-hour **Camel Ramble** ⊙★ down the dry Todd River bed that finishes with a browse through the interesting black-and-white photos, videos, and camel memorabilia in the Frontier Camel Farm's museum and shop. With hotel transfers it costs A$49 (U.S.$26.95) for adults and A$27 (U.S.$14.85) for kids 6 to 12. It departs daily at 2pm April through October, and at 3pm November through March. Kids under 6 can join the ride if the cameleer on duty agrees.

HOT-AIR BALLOON FLIGHTS   Dawn balloon flights above the sprawling desert are popular in Central Australia. You have to get up 90 minutes before dawn, though. Several companies offer flights. **Outback Ballooning** (© **1800/ 809 790** in Australia, or 08/8952 8723) is one of the most upscale. A 1-hour flight followed by champagne breakfast in the bush costs A$260 (U.S.$143), or A$208 (U.S.$114.40) for kids under 17. Kids under 6 are discouraged, because they cannot see over the basket. Allow all morning, by the time you get back to your hotel.

ACTIVE PURSUITS

BIKING   A gently undulating 17-kilometer (11-mile) **bike trail** weaves from John Flynn's Grave on Larapinta Drive, 7 kilometers (4 miles) west of town, through the bushland and desert foothills of the MacDonnell Ranges to Simpson's Gap (see "West MacDonnell National Park," below). **Centre Cycles** (© **08/8953 2966**) on Lindsay Avenue at Undoolya Road rents bikes for A$9.90 (U.S.$5.45) for 4 hours (plus a A$50/U.S.$27.50 refundable deposit). *Note:* Carry water, because the two taps en route are a long way apart. Bike in cooler months only.

BUSHWALKING   The 250-kilometer (156-mile) **Larapinta Trail** winds west from Alice through the sparse red ranges, picturesque semi-desert scenery, and rich bird life of the West MacDonnell National Park (see "Road Trips from Alice Springs," later in this chapter). It is still under construction, but many sections are ready for your boots now. Sections range from easy to hard. The shortest is 8 kilometers (5 miles), ranging up to several 23- to 29-kilometer (14- to 18-mile) stretches. Trail maps and information are dispensed by the **Parks & Wildlife Commission of the Northern Territory** office in Alice Springs

(© 08/8951 8211), or the **CATIA Visitor Centre** (see "Visitor Information," earlier in this chapter). Camp facilities are simple at best on popular routes, nonexistent on less traveled sections. Always carry drinking water. The trail may close in extremely hot summer periods.

Alice Wanderer Centre Sightseeing Tours (© **1800/66 9111** in Australia, or 08/8952 2111) runs transfers to road access points along the trail, where you can mostly pick up a choice of 1-, 2-, or 3-day hikes. Several outfitters run guided, supported hikes along trail sections.

GOLF   The **Alice Springs Golf Club** ⚐, 1 kilometer (just over half a mile) from town on Cromwell Drive (© **08/8952 5440**), boasts a Thomson-Wolveridge course rated among the world's top desert courses by touring pros. The course opens from sunup to sundown. For nine holes you will pay A$25 (U.S.$13.75), plus A$16.50 (U.S.$9.10) for clubs, and A$16.50 (U.S.$9.10) for a cart, which many locals don't bother with. It's best to book a tee time.

SHOPPING AT THE SOURCE FOR ABORIGINAL ART

Alice Springs is the best place in Australia to buy **Aboriginal art & crafts** ⚐. You will find no shortage of stuff to buy: linen and canvas paintings, didgeridoos, spears, clapping sticks, coolamons (a dish used by women to carry anything from water to babies), wooden animal carvings, baskets, and bead jewelry, as well as books, CDs, and all kinds of non-Aboriginal merchandise printed with Aboriginal designs. Prices can soar into the thousands of dollars for large canvases by world-renowned painters, but you will find plenty of small works for under A$250 (U.S.$137.50). Major artworks sell unmounted for ease of shipment, which most galleries arrange on your behalf. Store hours can vary with the seasons and the crowds, so it pays to check ahead.

See artists at work when you drop by **Jukurrpa Artists**, on Stott Terrace between Gap Road and Leichhardt Terrace (© **08/8953 1052**). This Aboriginal women's cooperative studio/gallery sells the "pattern and dot" paintings of the Western Desert style, plus craft items such as carvings and jewelry, and weapons and tools.

Aboriginal-owned **Warumpi Arts,** 105 Gregory Terrace (© **08/8952 9066**), sells wooden artifacts, seed necklaces, and canvas and linen paintings in the dramatic, earth-hued designs of the Papunya people, who live 250 kilometers (156 miles) west of Alice. Another Aboriginal-owned gallery, **Papunya Tula Artists,** 78 Todd St. (© **08/8952 4731**), sells paintings on canvas and linen from Papunya and other artists living in the desert as far as 700 kilometers (438 miles) west of Alice Springs.

Several stores on Todd Mall sell affordable Aboriginal art & souvenirs. The biggest, the **Original Dreamtime Gallery,** 63 Todd Mall (© **08/8952 8861**), stocks a huge selection, and packs, mails, and insures your purchases free of charge anywhere in the world. It also shows visiting exhibitions of Aboriginal art.

Arunta Art Gallery & Bookshop, 70 Todd St. (© **08/8952 1544**) stocks a great range of books on Aboriginal art, language, and archaeology, as well as Australian history, geology, wildlife, and biographies.

If you're interested in investing in serious artwork, speak to Roslyn Premont, proprietor of **Gallery Gondwana,** 43 Todd Mall (© **08/8953 1577**). She has written a book on desert art, and her gallery sells only top-notch works.

A big range of art, didgeridoos, artifacts, music, and books is sold by the **Aboriginal Art & Culture Centre** (see "Seeing the Sights in Alice," above) via its website at **www.aboriginalart.com.au.**

Today's Aboriginal bands mix ancient and hip new rhythms to create some wonderful sounds. For the country's biggest range of indigenous music, head to the **CAAMA (Central Australian Aboriginal Media Association)** ✿ store at 101 Todd St. (© **08/8952 9207**), inside the association's studios. It also stocks books on Aboriginal art and issues; videos in PAL and NTSC format (on everything from how to fix your broken-down Ford the bushman's way in the Outback, to Aboriginal people's memories of their first contact with "white man"); children's books with Aboriginal story lines; a line of Aboriginal-print fabrics, clothes, diaries, stationery, and greeting cards; Aboriginal artifacts and jewelry; and cute Yamba the Honey Ant dolls, modeled after a kids' character on the local Aboriginal television station, Imparja.

WHERE TO STAY

Alice's hotel stock is not grand. Many properties have dated rooms and only modest facilities, no match for the gleaming standard of **Ayers Rock Resort** (described later in this chapter). Despite the fact that is not the most expensive place in town, **Rydges Plaza Resort Alice Springs** (listed under "Moderate," below) is the ritziest place to stay. You may pay lower rates than those listed below in the summer off-season December through March, and sometimes even as late as June. Peak season typically runs July through October or November.

EXPENSIVE

Alice Springs Resort ✿   This friendly, well-run low-rise property is a 3-minute walk from town over the Todd River. Ask for one of the standard rooms smartly renovated in 2001 (the unrenovated ones are airy and perfectly comfortable, but those bright green carpets and dated peach floral curtains are hard on the eye!), or go for the big deluxe rooms built in 1999. All the standard rooms are being progressively renovated. In summer, it's nice to repair to the attractive pool under a couple of desert palms after a hot day's sightseeing. A fire glows in the Gumtree Lounge bar on nippy winter evenings.

34 Stott Terrace, Alice Springs, NT 0870. © **1800/805 055** in Australia, or 08/8951 4545. Fax 08/8953 0995. www.alicespringsresort.com.au. 144 units (108 shower only). A$200–$234 (U.S.$110–$128.70) double. Extra person A$25 (U.S.$13.75). Children under 12 stay free in parents' room with existing bedding. Ask about packages with Ayers Rock Resort and/or Kings Canyon Resort. AE, DC, MC, V. Free parking. Airport shuttle. **Amenities:** Restaurant (Palms, recommended in "Where to Dine," below), 2 bars; solar-heated outdoor swimming pool; bike rental; concierge; tour desk; secretarial services; limited room service; in-room massage; babysitting; laundry; same-day laundry/dry-cleaning service. *In room:* A/C, TV with pay movies, minibar, hair dryer, iron.

Bond Springs Outback Retreat ✿ *(Finds)*   This working 1,515-square-kilometer (585-sq.-mile) cattle station is a great place to get a taste of Outback life with a real Aussie family. A reader said it reminded her of the kind of place you'd see in *The Thornbirds*. Proprietor Janice Heaslip welcomes guests to her homestead, inviting them to join hearty country dinners with the family and accommodating them in simple but appealingly decorated rooms or self-contained cottages. A TV is located in the guest lounge. The Heaslips run a good range of day trips, overnight bush camps, and tours throughout the Red Centre, making this a good base for a Red Centre stay. Ask about 3- and 5-day packages, some combining tours and accommodations at Kings Canyon Resort, and Ayers Rock Resort also. No smoking indoors.

25km (16 miles) north of Alice Springs (P.O. Box 4, Alice Springs, NT 0870). © **08/8952 9888.** Fax 08/9853 0963. www.outbackretreat.com.au. 5 units (3 with bathroom, 2 sharing a private bathroom). A$220–$264 (U.S.$121–$145.20) double. Rates include full breakfast. Dinner A$49.50 (U.S.$27.20) per person extra. MC, V.

Closed Christmas–New Year. Transfers from Alice Springs A$40 (U.S.$22) from town, A$80 (U.S.$44) from airport, one-way, per vehicle. *Note:* All but the last 6km (3³/₄ miles) of the road to the station are paved; while car-rental companies do not allow driving on unpaved roads, they usually permit it on this stretch. Check with your company. **Amenities:** Outdoor swimming pool; outdoor tennis court; laundry. *In room:* A/C, fridge, coffeemaker (in cottages), hair dryer, no phone.   •

MODERATE

Rydges Plaza Resort Alice Springs ℛ *Value*   Located next to the golf club and a walk from Lasseter's Casino, this is one of Alice's fanciest resorts. Three stories of rooms wrap around the pool and ample sun deck, all spacious and refurbished in 2001. Every room has a balcony, some looking onto the pool, some back toward town, others over the red ranges. Barbecues take place every lunch and dinner around the pool September through March.

Barrett Dr. (1.5km/1 mile from town center), Alice Springs, NT 0870. ℂ **1800/226 466** in Australia, 0800/446 187 in New Zealand, or resort direct 1800/675 212 in Australia, or 08/8950 8000. Fax 08/8953 0475. www.rydges.com.au. 235 units. A$160–$215 (U.S.$88–$118.25) double; A$350–$500 (U.S.$192.50–$275) suite. Extra person A$25 (U.S.$13.75). Children under 13 free in parents' room with existing bedding. Ask about packages. Free crib. AE, DC, MC, V. Free parking. Airport shuttle. **Amenities:** Restaurant, bar; heated outdoor pool; 2 day/night tennis courts; exercise room with plunge pool; Jacuzzi; sauna; bike rental; tour desk; secretarial service; 24-hour room service; babysitting; laundry; same-day laundry/dry-cleaning service. *In room:* A/C, TV with pay movies, dataport, minibar, hair dryer, iron.

The Territory Inn   This pleasant hotel is smack bang in the center of town. Rooms in the newer wing are your standard quality motel-style variety, all clean, large, and decorated nicely enough. Those in the original wing are small and a little dark; they have a pretty heritage theme with floral bedcovers and lace curtains. The courtyard has a barbecue, and the front desk loans hair dryers. The tiny pool and Jacuzzi are tucked away in a utilitarian corner, so this is not the place for chilling out poolside; stay here to be within walking distance of shops and restaurants. Room service is from the Red Ochre Grill (see "Where to Dine," below).

Leichhardt Terrace (backing on to Todd Mall), Alice Springs, NT 0870. ℂ **1800/089 644** in Australia, or 08/8950 6666. Fax 08/8952 7829. www.aurora-resorts.com.au. 108 units (all with shower only, 1 suite with Jacuzzi). A$140–$150 (U.S.$77–$8.25) double; A$210 (U.S.$115.50) suite. Extra person A$20 (U.S.$11). Children under 14 stay free in parents' room using existing bedding. AE, DC, MC, V. Free parking. Hotel provides transfers from airport A$10 (U.S.$5.50) per person, round-trip. Airport shuttle. **Amenities:** Very small heated outdoor pool; Jacuzzi; tour desk; limited room service; babysitting; laundry; same-day laundry/dry-cleaning service. *In room:* A/C, TV with pay movies, minibar, iron.

INEXPENSIVE

Desert Palms Resort ℛ *Value*   Right next to Lasseter's Casino and the Alice Springs Golf Club (to which guests enjoy honorary social membership), these cabins set behind manicured palms and pink bougainvillea are one of the cheeriest places to stay in Alice. Don't be deterred by their poky prefab appearance; inside they are surprisingly large, well-kept, and inviting, with a pine-pitched ceiling, a minikitchen, a sliver of bathroom sporting fresh white tiles, and a pert little furnished front deck. A pretty pool with its own little island is out front, and out back is a free barbecue. The pleasant staff at the front desk loans hair dryers, processes your film, and sells basic grocery and liquor supplies.

74 Barrett Dr. (1km/just over ¹/₂ mile from town), Alice Springs, NT 0870. ℂ **1800/678 037** in Australia, or 08/8952 5977. Fax 08/8953 4176. www.saharatours.com.au/despalms.htm. 80 units (all with shower only). A$92 (U.S.$50.60) double. Extra person A$10 (U.S.$5.50). AE, DC, MC, V. Airport shuttle. Free coach station/train station/airport shuttle twice daily; free resort-to-town shuttle 4 times daily. **Amenities:** Small outdoor pool; half-size tennis court; tour desk; laundry; same-day laundry/dry-cleaning service. *In room:* A/C, TV, kitchenette.

Elkira Motel   The best rooms at a low price we can recommend in the heart of town are at this unpretentious but clean Best Western motel. None are flashy, but all were partly renovated in 1998. Deluxe rooms have a little more space than the standard rooms, and some of those have microwaves and a toaster. Ask for a room away from the road, because the traffic is noisy during the day. The A$85 (U.S.$46.75) budget rooms are too dated and tiny to consider. There is a modest pool with a barbecue area under big trees, and a reasonably priced restaurant.

65 Bath St. (opposite Kmart), Alice Springs, NT 0870. ℂ **1800/809 252** in Australia, or 08/8952 1222. Fax 08/8953 1370. www.elkira.com.au. 58 units (some with shower only). A$110–$120 (U.S.$60.50–$66) double. Extra person A$15 (U.S.$8.25); extra child under 3 A$5 (U.S.$2.75). AE, DC, MC, V. Free parking. Airport shuttle. **Amenities:** Restaurant; outdoor pool; tour desk; limited room service; laundry; same-day laundry/dry-cleaning service. *In room:* A/C, TV, dataport, fridge, hair dryer.

WHERE TO DINE
EXPENSIVE

A 1-hour sunset camelback ride down the dry Todd River, past eucalyptus while black cockatoos whirl overhead, is part of the **Take a Camel out to Dinner** nights offered by **Frontier Camel Tours** (ℂ **1800/806 499** in Australia, or 08/8953 0444; www.cameltours.com.au) in Alice Springs. The ride is followed by a tasty three-course meal of kangaroo sausages, smoked camel, wattleseed beer bread, and seasonal "bush tucker" samples like peppercress or native mistletoe, barramundi, or steak; and dessert, plus wine and beer. Dinner is served at the company's camel farm, where you can browse its camel museum and shop. The cost of A$98 (U.S.$53.90) for adults and A$75 (U.S.$41.25) for children 6 to 12 includes pickup from your hotel. The ride and dinner runs nightly, at 4pm April through October, and 5pm November through March. The company also does a breakfast version of this ride.

Several companies run outdoor "bush" dinners that you may find fun. Camp Oven Kitchen's has one of the best reputations. Sit down at white-clothed, lamp-lit slab tables in a fire-lit clearing just outside town to soup and damper, kangaroo kebabs, roast beef cooked in a camp oven over the fire, golden syrup dumplings with ice cream, and billy tea. The evening features a night sky talk and bush ballads. The meal, including transfers from your hotel but not drinks, costs A$82 (U.S.$45.10) for adults and A$66 (U.S.$36.30) for kids under 12. It departs 5:30pm May through August, 6pm September through April. Call **Alice Springs Holidays** (ℂ **08/8953 1411;** www.alicespringsholidays.com.au).

Overlanders Steakhouse ℛ STEAK/AUSSIE TUCKER   This landmark on the Alice dining scene is famous for its "Drover's Blowout" menu, which assaults the megahungry with soup and damper, then a platter of crocodile vol-au-vents, camel and kangaroo fillet, and emu medallions—these are just the *appetizers*— followed by Scotch fillet or barramundi, followed by dessert. There's a regular menu with a 700-gram (1-lb., 10-oz.) steak, plus lots of lighter fare like oysters or spinach crêpes. The barn-like interior is Outback all through, from the rustic bar to the saddlebags hanging from the roof beams. An "Overlanders' Table" seats solo diners together.

72 Hartley St. ℂ **08/8952 2159.** Reservations required in peak season. Main courses A$18.50–$25.50 (U.S.$10.20–$14); Drover's Blowout A$44 (U.S.$24.20). AE, DC, DISC, MC, V. Daily 6–10pm.

Palms Restaurant ℛℛ MODERN AUSTRALIAN   Ask the locals for the best chow in town, and this is where they'll send you. It serves sophisticated fare, like catch of the day done in a carrot and blood orange beurre blanc. Bush tucker creeps onto the menu, in dishes like the peppered kangaroo fillet with sweet potato mash, braised witlof and a native plum glaze. A lighter menu operates for lunch. The wine list is split between decent easy-drinkers at reasonable prices, and a "Premium" connoisseurs' list carrying some wonderful Australian labels, even Henschke's Hill of Grace, which some say is Australia's best red. Live piano music plays nightly. No smoking inside until 9pm.

At the Alice Springs Resort, 34 Stott Terrace. © **08/8951 4545.** Reservations recommended at dinner. Main courses A$24.50–$27.50 (U.S.$13.50–$15.15). AE, DC, MC, V. Daily 6am–9:30pm.

MODERATE
Malathi's Restaurant & Sean's Irish Bar ASIAN/WESTERN Located in
an unprepossessing building a couple of blocks from Todd Mall, Malathi's serves up an eclectic assortment of Asian dishes plus a few Aussie choices, such as grain-fed steak. The Asian food is outstanding. I can recommend the lamb korma, a kind of mild curry. You might want to try the Lakshmi King prawns cooked in Indian flavors, or the Thai coconut curry. Vegetarians have some good choices. They do take-out, too. The bar serves cheap Irish stews, live bands (sometimes), and Guinness (always!). The restaurant has a wine list, but permits BYO wine at A$5 (U.S.$2.75) corkage per bottle.

51 Bath St. (opposite Kmart). © **08/8952 1858.** Reservations recommended. Main courses A$14.60–$27.50 (U.S.$8.05–$15); many dishes under A$21 (U.S.$11.55). AE, DC, MC, V. Restaurant Mon–Sat 5:30–10pm or later. Bar daily 3:30–9:30pm.

Red Ochre Grill ✿ GOURMET BUSH TUCKER If you've never tried wallaby mignons on a bed of native pasta and polenta cake with a native berry and red wine cream sauce, or barramundi baked in paperbark with wild lime and coriander butter, here's your chance. The chef at this upscale chain fuses native Aussie ingredients with dishes from around the world. Although it might seem a touristy formula, the food is mouthwatering. Dine in the contemporary interior fronting Todd Mall, or outside in the attractive courtyard.

Under the Territory Inn on Todd Mall. © **08/8952 9614.** Reservations recommended at dinner. Main courses A$9–$21 (U.S.$4.95–$11.55) lunch; A$15–$22.50 (U.S.$8.25–$12.40) dinner; buffet breakfast A$12.50–$16 (U.S.$6.90–$8.80). AE, DC, MC, V. Daily 6:30am–10pm.

INEXPENSIVE
Bar Doppio ✿ EAST-MEETS-WEST CAFE FARE If you're in need of a
dose of cool—style, that is, as well as air-conditioning—this laid-back arcade cafe is the place to chill over good coffee and feast on cheap, wholesome food. Sacks of coffee beans are stacked all over, gypsy music plays, no tables and chairs match, and the staff doesn't care if you sit here all day. It's largely vegetarian, but fish and meat figure on the blackboard menu. Try lamb chermoula cutlets on Gabriella potatoes with rocket, red onion and tomato salad, chickpea curry, warm Turkish flatbread with dips, or spuds with hot toppings. Hot and cold breakfast choices stay on the menu until 11am. They do take-out. BYO.

2 and 3 Fan Arcade (off the southern end of Todd Mall). © **08/8952 6525.** Reservations accepted at dinner only. Main courses A$7–$16 (U.S.$3.85–$8.80); sandwiches average A$6 (U.S.$3.30). No credit cards. Mon–Fri 7:30am–5:30pm; Sat 7:30am–4:30pm; Sun 10am–4:30pm; dinner Fri–Sat only 6–9pm. Closed holidays and Christmas to New Year.

Casa Nostra ✿✿ Value ITALIAN The only difference between this cheery
homespun family eatery and every other Italian restaurant in the world is that this one has autographed photos of Tom Selleck pinned to the wall. Judging by his scrawled praise, Tom loved eating here (when on location in Alice filming

Quigley Down Under) as much as the locals do. You've seen the red-checked tablecloths and the basket-clad chianti bottles before, but the food is surprisingly good. A long list of pastas (like the masterful carbonara), pizzas, and chicken and veal dishes are the main offerings. All meals can come as take-out. BYO.

Corner of Undoolya Rd. and Sturt Terrace. (*C*) 08/8952 6749. Reservations strongly recommended. Main courses A$11–$17.50 (U.S.$6.05–$9.65). MC, V. Mon–Sat 5–10pm. Closed Christmas to end of Jan.

3 Road Trips from Alice Springs

The key attraction of a day trip into the MacDonnell Ranges is unspoiled natural scenery and few crowds. Many companies run coach or four-wheel-drive tours of a half day or a day, sometimes overnight, to the West and East Macs. Some appear in "Organized Tours," earlier in the "Alice Springs" section. Expect to pay about A$100 (U.S.$55) for a full-day trip.

THE WEST MACDONNELL RANGES *&*

WEST MACDONNELL NATIONAL PARK The approximately 300-kilometer (188-mile) round-trip drive west from Alice Springs into West MacDonnell National Park is a stark but picturesque trip to a series of red gorges, semi-desert country, and the occasional peaceful swimming hole.

From Alice, take Larapinta Drive west for 18 kilometers (11 miles) to the 8-kilometer (5-mile) turnoff to **Simpson's Gap,** a water hole lined with ghost gums. Black-footed rock wallabies hop out on the cliffs in the late afternoon (so you may want to time a visit here on your way back to Alice). There are a couple of short trails, including a 500-meter (⅓-mile) Ghost Gum circuit, and a 17-kilometer (11-mile) round-trip trail to Bond Gap. Swimming is not permitted. The place has an information center/ranger station and free barbecues.

Twenty-three kilometers (14 miles) further down Larapinta Road, 9 kilometers (5½ miles) down a turnoff, is **Standley Chasm** (*C* 08/8956 7440). This rock cleft is only a few meters wide but 80 meters (262 ft.) high, reached by a 10-minute creekside trail. Aim to be here at midday, when the walls glow orange in the overhead sun. A kiosk sells snacks and drinks. Admission is A$5.50 (U.S.$3) for adults and A$4.50 (U.S.$2.50) seniors and children 5 to 14. The Chasm is open from 8am to 6pm daily, with last entry at 5pm (closed Christmas).

Six kilometers (3¾ miles) past Standley Chasm, you can branch right onto Namatjira Drive, or carry on to Hermannsburg Historical Precinct (see below). Assuming you take Namatjira Drive, you'll head 42 kilometers (26 miles) on to **picturesque Ellery Creek Big Hole.** The spring-fed water is so nippy that the tourism authority warns swimmers to take a flotation device in case of cramping. A 3-kilometer (2-mile) walking trail explains the area's geological history.

Eleven kilometers (7 miles) farther along Namatjira Drive is **Serpentine Gorge,** where a trail leads up to a lookout for a lovely view of the ranges through the gorge walls. Another 12 kilometers (7½ miles) on are **ochre pits,** which Aboriginal people quarried for body paint and for decorating objects used in ceremonial performances. Twenty-six kilometers (16 miles) farther west, 8 kilometers (5 miles) from the main road, is **Ormiston Gorge and Pound** (*C* 08/8956 7799 for the ranger station/visitor center). This is a good spot to picnic, swim in the wide deep pool below red cliffs, and walk a choice of trails, such as the 30-minute Ghost Gum Lookout trail or the easy 7-kilometer (4-mile) scenic loop (allow 3–4 hr.). The water is warm enough to swim in the summer. You can camp here for A$6.60 (U.S.$3.65) per adult, and A$3.30 (U.S.$1.80) per kid

Road-Trip Tips for the East & West Macs

Facilities are scarce outside Alice, so bring food (a picnic perhaps, or meat to barbecue), drinking water, and a full gas tank. Leaded, unleaded, and diesel fuel is sold at Glen Helen Lodge, Hermannsburg, and Ross River Homestead. Wear walking shoes.

Many of the water holes dry up too much to be good for swimming—those at Ellery Creek, Ormiston Gorge and Glen Helen are the most permanent. Being spring-fed, they can be intensely cold, so take only short dips to avoid cramp and hypothermia, don't swim alone, and be careful of underwater snags. Don't wear sunscreen because it pollutes drinking water for native animals.

Two-wheel-drive rental cars will not be insured on unsealed (unpaved) roads—that means the last few miles into Trephina Gorge Nature Park, and the 11-kilometer (7-mile) road into N'Dhala Gorge Nature Park, both in the East Macs. If you are prepared to risk it, you will probably get into Trephina in a two-wheel-drive car, but you will need a four-wheel-drive for N'Dhala and Arltunga. The West MacDonnell road is paved to Glen Helen Gorge; a few points of interest may require driving for short lengths on unpaved road. Before setting off, drop into the CATIA Visitor Information Centre (see "Visitor Information," under Alice Springs, earlier in this chapter) for tips on road conditions, and for details on the free ranger talks, walks, and slide shows that take place in the West and East Macs April through October. Entry to all sights, parks and reserves, except for Standley Chasm, is free.

5 to 15. The campground has no powered sites but does have hot showers, toilets, and free barbecues.

A couple of miles on is **Glen Helen Gorge,** where the Finke River cuts through the ranges, with more gorge swimming, a walking trail, guided hikes, and helicopter flights. Modest **Glen Helen Resort (℗ 1800/896 110** in Australia, or 08/8956 7489; www.melanka.com.au) has 25 motel rooms (A\$143/U.S.\$78.65) double; bunkhouses for four (A\$19/U.S.\$10.45 per person) and campgrounds (A\$9/U.S.\$4.95 per person for a tent site, and A\$22/ U.S.\$12.10 double for a powered campsite); a restaurant serving three meals a day; a bar; and barbecues for which they sell meat packs.

HERMANNSBURG HISTORICAL PRECINCT   An alternative to visiting the West Mac gorges is to stay on Larapinta Drive all 128 kilometers (80 miles) from Alice Springs to the old **Lutheran Mission** at the **Hermannsburg Historical Precinct (℗ 08/8956 7402).** Some maps will show this route as an unpaved road, but it is now paved. Settled by German missionaries in the 1870s, this is a tiny cluster of pretty farmhouse-style mission buildings that have been restored. There are a museum, a gallery housing landscapes by famous Aussie artist Albert Namatjira, and tearooms serving a fabulous apple strudel from an old German recipe. The Mission is open daily from 9am to 4pm (from 10am November through March). Admission to the precinct with tea or coffee is A\$4.50 (U.S.\$2.50) for adults, A\$3 (U.S.\$1.65) for school-age kids, or A\$12 (U.S.\$7.50) for a family, plus A\$3.50 (U.S.\$1.95) per adult or A\$2.50

(U.S.$1.40) per child for a guided gallery tour, which departs every hour. The precinct is closed from December 24 to January 2 or 3, and on Good Friday.

FINKE GORGE NATIONAL PARK   Just west of Hermannsburg is the turnoff to the 46,000-hectare (113,620-acre) **Finke Gorge National Park,** 16 kilometers (10 miles) to the south on an unpaved road. The park is most famous for **Palm Valley,** where groves of rare Livistona mariae cabbage palms have survived since central Australia was a jungle millions of years ago. You will need a four-wheel-drive to explore this park. Four walking trails between 1.5 kilometers (1 mile) and 5 kilometers (3 miles) take you among the palms or up to a lookout over cliffs; one is a signposted trail exploring Aboriginal culture. There is a campsite about 4 kilometers (2½ miles) from the palms; it has showers, toilets, and free barbecues. Collect your firewood outside the park. Camping is A$6.60 (U.S.$3.65) for adults, A$3.30 (U.S.$1.80) for kids 5 to 15. For information, call into the CATIA Visitor Information Centre in Alice Springs before you leave, because there is no visitor center in the park. The ranger station (© **08/8956 7401**) is for emergencies only.

THE EAST MACDONNELL RANGES

Not as many tourists tread the path on the Ross Highway into the East Macs, but if you do, you'll be rewarded with lush walking trails, fewer crowds, and traces of Aboriginal history. I even spotted wild camels on my visit. At the end of the drive, 86 kilometers (54 miles) from Alice, is the dinky-di (that's Australian for "authentic"—as is "fair dinkum") **Ross River Homestead** (see "Where to Stay," below), where day-trippers are welcome. The homestead stages a boomerang-throwing and whip-cracking experience over billy tea and damper from 10am to noon daily for A$5.50 (U.S.$3) per person, so consider heading there first, then dropping in on the attractions below as you return.

The first points of interest are **Emily Gap,** 10 kilometers (6 miles) from Alice, and Jessie Gap, 7 kilometers (4 miles) on, a pretty picnic spot. You can cool off in the Emily Gap swimming hole if there is any water. Don't miss the "Caterpillar Dreaming" Aboriginal art on the wall, on your right as you walk through.

At **Corroboree Rock,** 37 kilometers (23 miles) farther on, you can make a short climb up this rocky outcrop that was important to local Aborigines. The highly polished rock "seat" at the hole high up in it means Aboriginal people must have used this rock for eons.

Twenty-two kilometers (13¾ miles) on is the turnoff to **Trephina Gorge Nature Park,** an 18-square-kilometer (7-sq.-mile) beauty spot with peaceful walking trails ranging from 45 minutes to 4½ hours. The last 5 kilometers (3 miles) of the 9-kilometer (5.5-mile) access road into the park are unpaved, but you can make it in a conventional car.

N'Dhala Gorge Nature Park, 10 kilometers (6 miles) past Trephina Gorge Nature Park, just before you reach Ross River Homestead, houses an "open-air art gallery" of rock carvings, or petroglyphs, left by the Eastern Arrernte Aboriginal people. An interesting 1.5-kilometer (1-mile) signposted trail explains the Dreamtime meanings of a few of the 6,000 rock carvings, hundreds or thousands of years old, that are thought to be in this eerily quiet gorge. A four-wheel-drive vehicle is a must to traverse the 11-kilometer (7-mile) access road.

The Ross Highway is paved all the way to Ross River Homestead.

WHERE TO STAY

Ross River Homestead   This fair dinkum, 100-year-old station offers both day visitors and overnight guests a condensed taste of Outback life. Overnight accommodations are rustic, roomy log cabins; there are also basic quad-share bunkhouses, with shared bathrooms, and shady campgrounds with a general store.

The whitewashed original homestead has been converted to an atmospheric restaurant with Edwardian furniture, open for breakfast, lunch, and dinner at moderate prices. Entry to the homestead, its rustic restaurant and bar, the barbecue, four bushwalking trails, and kangaroo enclosure is free (get feed for them from the stables); so are the pool and Jacuzzi if you patronize the bar or restaurant. Horse and camel rides are available at a moderate extra fee (half-hour, half-day, and full-day), as are 30-minute wagon rides. The homestead sometimes does 2-hour horse and camel rides to camp-oven cookouts under the stars. Call to check if any are scheduled. It's best to book all activities ahead.

Ross Hwy., 86km (54 miles) east of Alice Springs (P.O. Box 3271), Alice Springs, NT 0871. ℂ 1800/241 711 in Australia, or 08/8956 9711. Fax 08/8956 9823. www.rossriver.goau.net. 48 units, 30 with bathroom (shower only). Cabin A$79 (U.S.$43.45) double. Extra person A$16 (U.S.$8.80). Bunkhouse quad-share A$22.50 (U.S.$12.40) per person with linen. Unpowered campsite A$4.50 (U.S.$2.50) per adult; powered campsite A$9 (U.S.$4.95) per adult. Lower rates for kids in bunkhouses and campgrounds. AE, DC, MC, V. Coach transfers from Alice Springs A$110 (U.S.$60.50) per person, round-trip. **Amenities:** Restaurant, bar; small outdoor pool; Jacuzzi. *In room:* A/C, no phone.

4 Kings Canyon ⋆

Anyone who saw the Australian movie *The Adventures of Priscilla, Queen of the Desert* will remember the stony plateau the transvestites climb to gaze over the majestic plain below. You can stand on that very same spot (wearing sequined underpants is optional) at **Kings Canyon** ⋆ in **Watarrka National Park** (ℂ **08/8956 7460** for park headquarters). As the crow flies, it is 320 kilometers (200 miles) southwest of Alice Springs. The red sandstone walls of the canyon drop 100 meters (about 330 ft.) to rock pools and centuries-old gum trees. There is little to do here except walk the dramatic canyon rim for a sense of the peaceful emptiness of the Australian Outback.

GETTING THERE   No regular flights operate, but **Ayers Rock Scenic Flights** (ℂ **08/8956 2345**) does an aerial day trip from Ayers Rock Resort that incorporates a guided canyon walk at A$425 (U.S.$233.75) per adult, A$390 (U.S.$214.50) per child 3 to 12.

Murray Cosson's Australian Outback Flights (ℂ **08/8952 4625;** www.australianoutbackflights.com.au) and **Wright's Air** (ℂ **08/8995 5670**) both offer aerial day trips on a charter basis from Alice Springs. An 8-hour day with Murray Cosson including a flight over Gosse Bluff meteorite crater, the rim walk, and lunch is A$407 (U.S.$223.85) per person (based on a minimum two passengers).

Greyhound Pioneer (ℂ **13 20 30** in Australia) and coach tour company **AAT Kings** (ℂ **08/8952 1700** in Alice Springs or 08/8956 2171 in Ayers Rock) make daily coach transfers from Ayers Rock; Greyhound's fare is cheapest at A$54 (U.S.$29.70).

Numerous **coach** and **four-wheel-drive** tour outfits call at Kings Canyon from Alice Springs or Ayers Rock, with time allowed for the rim walk. See "Exploring the Red Centre," at the beginning of this chapter, for recommended companies.

With a four-wheel-drive, you can get to Kings Canyon from Alice Springs on the unpaved Mereenie Loop Road.

The regular route is the 480-kilometer (300-mile) trip from Alice Springs south via the Stuart Highway, then west onto the Lasseter Highway, then north and west on the Luritja Road. All three roads are paved. Uluru (Ayers Rock) is 306 kilometers (191 miles) to the south on a paved road; from Yulara, take the Lasseter Highway east for 125 kilometers (78 miles), then turn left onto Luritja Road for 168 kilometers (118 miles) to Kings Canyon Resort. The resort sells leaded and unleaded petrol and diesel.

Uluru Motorcycle Tours (© **08/8956 2019;** www.ozemail.com.au/ ~uluruharleys) will take you there on a 1-day charter tour by Harley Davidson from Ayers Rock Resort, with you as a passenger or in the driver's seat.

GETTING AROUND   **AAT Kings** provides a guided rim or creek-bed walk from Kings Canyon Resort, 7 kilometers (4 miles) away, for A$40 (U.S.$22) per adult, A$20 (U.S.$11) kids under 15, round-trip. It departs daily at 6:15am October through March, 7am April through September. You can book this through AAT Kings or the resort.

EXPLORING THE PARK

The way to explore the canyon is on the 6-kilometer (3¾-mile) **walk** up the side (short but steep!) and around the rim. Even if you're in good shape, it's a strenuous 3- to 4-hour hike. It leads through a maze of rounded sandstone formations called the Lost City, across a bridge to a fern-fringed pocket of water holes called the Garden of Eden, and back along the other side through more sandstone rocks. There are lookout points en route. If you visit after the odd rainfall, the walls teem with waterfalls. In winter, don't set off too early, because sunlight doesn't light up the canyon walls to good effect until midmorning.

If you're not up to making the rim walk, take the shady 2.6-kilometer (1.6-mile) round-trip trail along the mostly dry **Kings Creek bed** on the canyon floor. It takes about an hour. Wear sturdy boots, because the ground can be very rocky. This walk is good for very young kids and travelers in wheelchairs for the first 700 meters (half a mile).

Both walks are signposted. Avoid the rim walk in the middle of the day between September and May, when it's too hot.

You can also explore the park from an Aboriginal viewpoint with **Lilla Aboriginal Tours** (book through Kings Canyon Resort). Aboriginal guides take you on an easy 1-kilometer (just over half a mile) walk to sacred caves and rock-painting sites. You learn about the artworks, hear the Dreamtime events that created the land around you, discover plant medicines and food, and have a go at throwing a spear and a boomerang. The tour lasts 1½ to 2 hours and departs at 9am and 4pm daily (closed mid-Dec to mid-Jan) from the Lilla community, 14 kilometers (9 miles) from Kings Canyon Resort. The resort does transfers for A$20 (U.S.$11) per person, round-trip, or A$30 (U.S.$16.50) for two of you. The tour costs A$38.50 (U.S.$21.20) for adults, A$33 (U.S.$18.15) for seniors and students, and A$27.50 (U.S.$15.20) kids ages 5 to 16.

Professional Helicopter Services (© **08/8956 7873;** www.phs.com.au) makes 15-minute scenic flights over the canyon for A$90 (U.S.$49.50) per person.

WHERE TO STAY & DINE

Apart from campgrounds, the only place to stay in Watarrka National Park is at Kings Canyon Resort.

Kings Canyon Resort ℛ   This attractive, low-slung complex 7 kilometers (4 miles) from Kings Canyon blends into its surroundings. All but four of the larger deluxe rooms are new (1999) and have great desert views from glass-enclosed Jacuzzis. The remaining rooms are typical hotel rooms, comfortable enough, with restful range views from the balcony; they were refurbished in 2001. The double/twin, quad and family lodge rooms are an adequate low-budget choice, with a communal kitchen and bathroom facilities. The resort has a well-stocked minimart where you can buy meat to cook on the barbecues, where live entertainment plays some nights. A ranger gives a slide show several nights a week. Internet access is available to guests.

Luritja Rd., Watarrka National Park, NT 0872. (Ⓒ) **1800/817 622** in Australia, or 08/8956 7442. Fax 08/8956 7426. www.voyages.com.au. 164 units (128 with bathroom, of which 32 have Jacuzzis); 72 powered campsites and tent sites. High season (July–Nov) A$320–$378 (U.S.$176–$207.90) hotel room double; low season (Dec–June) A$256–$321 (U.S.$140.80–$176.55) hotel room double. Extra adult A$25 (U.S.$13.75). Children under 16 stay free in parents' room with existing bedding. High season A$97 (U.S.$53.35) lodge room double; A$163 (U.S.$89.65) quad-share; A$180 (U.S.$99) family (to sleep 5). Low season A$95 (U.S.$52.25) lodge room double; A$158 (U.S.$86.90) quad-share; A$173 (U.S.$95.15) family. No children in lodge rooms unless you book entire room. Tent sites A$26 (U.S.$14.30) double; powered sites A$29 (U.S.$15.95) double. Extra person A$11 (U.S.$6.05) adults, A$5 (U.S.$2.75) children 6–15 in powered campsite. Children under 16 dine free at breakfast and dinner buffets at Carmichael's with an adult. Ask about packages in conjunction with Ayers Rock Resort and Alice Springs Resort. AE, DC, MC, V. **Amenities:** Restaurant, cafe, 2 bars; 2 outdoor swimming pools; outdoor day/night tennis court; volleyball court; bike rental (from nearby gas station); tour desk; limited room service; guest laundry. *In room:* A/C, TV, fridge. Hotel only: TV with pay movies, minibar, hair dryer, iron.

5 Uluru-Kata Tjuta National Park (Ayers Rock/The Olgas) ⓡ

462km (289 miles) SW of Alice Springs; 1,934km (1,202 miles) S of Darwin; 1,571km (976 miles) N of Adelaide; 2,841km (1,765 miles) NW of Sydney

Ayers Rock is the Australia tourism industry's pinup icon, a glamorous red stone that has probably been splashed on more posters than Cindy Crawford has been on magazine covers. Just why people trek from all over the world to gawk at it is a bit of a mystery. For its size? Hardly, for nearby Mt. Conner is three times as big. For its shape? Probably not, when most folks agree the neighboring Olgas are more picturesque. You can put its popularity down only to the faint shiver up the spine and the indescribable sense of place it evokes in anyone who looks at it. Even taciturn Aussie bushmen reckon it's "got somethin' spiritual about it."

Ayers Rock is commonly known by its Aboriginal name, Uluru. In 1985 the **Uluru-Kata Tjuta National Park** ⓡ was returned to its Aboriginal owners, the Pitjantjatjara and Yankunytjatjara people, together known as the Anangu, who continue to manage the property jointly with the Australian government. People used to speculate that the Rock was a meteorite, but we now know it was formed by conglomerate sediments laid down 600 to 700 million years ago in an ancient inland sea and thrust up above ground 348 meters (1,141 ft.) by geological forces. With a circumference of 9.4 kilometers (6 miles), the Rock is no pebble, especially because two-thirds of it is thought to be underground. On photos it looks like a big smooth blob. In the flesh, it's more interesting—dappled with holes and overhangs, and its sides are draped with curtains of stone, creating little coves hiding water holes and Aboriginal rock art.

Don't think a visit to Uluru is just about snapping a few photos and going home. You can walk around the Rock, climb it (although the owners prefer you don't), fly over it, ride a camel to it, motorcycle around it on a Harley-Davidson, trek through the Olgas, eat in an outdoor restaurant, tour the night sky, and join Aboriginal people on guided walks. As we wrote, the Rock's resort management company (see "Where to Stay & Dine," below) was about to introduce four-wheel-drive eco day tours to outlying beauty spots in the desert currently not visited by many folks. Details were not available, but you may want to look into these excursions when planning your trip, as they promise to be interesting. Give yourself at least a full day in the Uluru area; you could easily fill two or three.

Isolation (and a lack of competition?) makes things like accommodations, meals and transfers expensive at Ayers Rock. An coach tour or four-wheel-drive camping safari is often the cheapest way to see the place. The "Exploring the Red Centre," at the beginning of this chapter, for recommended tour companies.

ESSENTIALS
GETTING THERE   By Plane   Qantas (𝒞 13 13 13 in Australia) or its subsidiary **Airlink** (book through Qantas) fly to Ayers Rock (Connellan) Airport direct from Sydney, Alice Springs, Perth, and Cairns. Flights from other ports go via Alice Springs. The airport is 6 kilometers (3¾ miles) from Ayers Rock Resort. A free shuttle ferries all resort guests, including campers, to their door.

By Bus   Greyhound Pioneer (𝒞 13 20 30 in Australia) makes a daily trip from Alice Springs (trip time: 5½ hr.), dropping you to your hotel door at Ayers Rock Resort. The fare is around A$71 (U.S.$39.05).

By Car   Take the Stuart Highway south from Alice Springs 199 kilometers (124 miles), and turn right onto the Lasseter Highway for 244 kilometers (153 miles) to Ayers Rock Resort. The Rock itself is 18 kilometers (11 miles) farther on. (Everyone mistakes the flat-topped mesa they see en route for Ayers Rock; it's Mt. Conner.)

If you want to rent a car in Alice Springs and drop it at Ayers Rock, brace yourself for a one-way penalty. Only Avis, Hertz, and Thrifty have Uluru depots: Thrifty charges a one-way fee of A$110 (U.S.$60.50) for bookings under 3 days; Hertz charges A$137 (U.S.$75.35) for bookings under 7 days; and Avis charges A$137 (U.S.$75.35) for bookings of 2 days or less.

VISITOR INFORMATION   For information before you leave home, contact the **Central Australian Tourism Industry Association (CATIA),** 60 Gregory Terrace, Alice Springs (𝒞 08/8952 5800; www.centralaustraliantourism.com), or drop in to its **Visitor Information Centre** if you visit Alice Springs. One of the best online sources is Ayers Rock Resort's site (**www.ayersrockresort. com.au**; click on "Activities" for things to see and do).

The **Ayers Rock Resort Visitor Centre,** next to the Desert Gardens Hotel (𝒞 08/8957 7377), has displays on the area's geology, wildlife, and Aboriginal

---

Tips The Rock in a Day?

It's a loooong day to visit Uluru in a day from Alice by road. Many organized coach tours pack a lot—perhaps a Rock base walk or climb, the Olgas, the Uluru-Kata Tjuta Cultural Centre, and a champagne sunset at the Rock—into a busy trip that leaves Alice around 5:30 or 6am and gets you back late at night. **Murray Cosson's Australian Outback Flights** (𝒞 08/ 8952 4625; www.australianoutbackflights.com.au) does an aerial day trip from Alice Springs that includes scenic flights over Kings Canyon, Gosse Bluff meteorite crater, and Lake Amadeus; a rental car at Ayers Rock; National Park entry fee; and lunch. It costs A$512 (U.S.$281.60) per person (based on a minimum two passengers).

Consider a day trip only between May and September. At other times, it's too hot to do much between early morning and late afternoon.

heritage, plus a souvenir store selling books and videos. It's open daily from 8:30am to 7:30pm. You can book tours at the **tour desk** in every hotel at Ayers Rock Resort, or visit the **Ayers Rock Resort Tour & Information Centre** (© **08/8957 7324**) at the shopping center in the resort complex. It dispenses information on and books tours as far afield as Kings Canyon and Alice Springs. It's open daily from 7:30am to 8:30pm.

One kilometer (just over half a mile) from the base of the Rock is the **Uluru-Kata Tjuta Cultural Centre** ⌖ (© **08/8956 3138**), owned and run by the Anangu, the Aboriginal owners of Uluru. It uses eye-catching wall displays, frescoes, interactive recordings, and videos to tell about Aboriginal Dreamtime myths and laws. It's worth spending some time here to understand a little about Aboriginal culture. A National Park desk has information on ranger-guided activities; animal, plant, and bird-watching checklists; and there is a cafe; a souvenir shop; and two Aboriginal arts and crafts galleries. It opens daily from early in the morning to after sundown; exact hours vary from month to month.

PARK ENTRANCE FEES Entry to the Uluru-Kata Tjuta National Park is A$16.25 (U.S.$8.95) per adult, free for children under 16, valid for 3 days. The cost of the pass is included in many organized tours.

ETIQUETTE The Anangu ask you not to photograph sacred sites or Aboriginal people without permission, and to approach sacred sites quietly and respectfully.

GETTING AROUND

Getting around the park is expensive. Ayers Rock Resort runs a **free shuttle** every 15 minutes or so around the resort complex from 10:30am to after midnight, but to get to the Rock or the Olgas, you will need to take transfers, join a tour, or have your own wheels.

BY SHUTTLE Uluru Express (© **08/8956 2152**) provides a minibus shuttle from Ayers Rock Resort to and from the Rock about every 50 minutes from before sunrise to sundown, and several times a day to the Olgas. Cheapest is a lap of Uluru and a sunset viewing for A$25 (U.S.$13.75); most expensive is a trip to the Olgas with time to walk the Valley of the Winds, followed by sunset back at the Rock, for A$50 (U.S.$27.50). All fares are round-trip.

BY CAR If there are two of you, the easiest and cheapest way to get around is likely to be renting a car. All roads in the area are paved, so a four-wheel-drive is unnecessary. Expect to pay around A$70 to A$95 (U.S.$38.50 to $52.25) per day for a medium-size car. Rates drop a little in low season. Most car-rental companies give you the first 100 kilometers (63 miles) free, then charge A27.5¢ (U.S.15¢) per kilometer after that. Take this into account, because the round-trip from the resort to the Olgas is just over 100 kilometers (63 miles), and that's without driving about 20 kilometers (13 miles) to the Rock and back. Only **Avis** (© **08/8956 2266**), **Hertz** (© **08/8956 2244**), and **Thrifty** (© **08/8956 2030;** book four-wheel-drives through its Darwin office at 08/8924 0000) have outlets at Ayers Rock. All rent regular cars and four-wheel-drives.

Booking agent **The Outback Travel Shop** ⌖ (© **08/8955 5288;** www.outbacktravelshop.com.au) in Alice Springs often has better deals on car-rental rates than you'll get by booking direct.

BY ORGANIZED TOUR Several tour companies run a big range of daily sunrise and sunset viewings, circumnavigations of the Rock by coach or on foot, guided walks at the Rock or the Olgas, camel rides, observatory evenings, visits

---

Tips Water, Water . . .

Water taps are scarce and kiosks non-existent in Uluru-Kata Tjuta National Park. Always carry your own drinking water when sightseeing.

---

to the Uluru-Kata Tjuta Cultural Centre, and innumerable permutations and combinations of all these. Some do "passes" containing the most popular activities. Virtually every company picks you up at your hotel. Among the most reputable are **Discovery Ecotours** (formerly Uluru Experience and Alice Experience), AAT Kings, Tailormade Tours and **VIP Travel Australia** (see "Exploring the Red Centre" at the start of this chapter for details).

ABORIGINAL TOURS Because **Anangu Tours** ⚘ (📞 **08/8956 2123;** www.anangutours.com.au) is owned and run by the Rock's Aboriginal owners, its tours give you firsthand insight into Aboriginal culture. Tours are in the Anangu language, translated to English by an interpreter. They are not cheap, but if you are going to spend money on just one tour, these guys are a good choice.

The company does a **Kuniya** walk, where you visit the Kata Tjuta Cultural Centre and the Mutitjulu water hole at the base of the Rock, learn about bush foods, and see rock paintings, before watching the sun set over Uluru. It departs daily at 2:30pm March through October, 3:30pm November through February, and it costs A$79 (U.S.$43.45) for adults and A$54 (U.S.$29.70) for children with transfers, or A$47 (U.S.$25.85) for adults and A$24 (U.S.$13.20) for kids without. Ask about family discounts, and slightly cheaper rates for doing more than one tour.

For an Aboriginal insight into the Rock without paying for a tour, join the free **Mala Walk** ⚘ (see "Walking, Driving, or Busing Around It," below); it discusses Aboriginal culture and is often led by an Aboriginal park ranger.

DISCOVERING AYERS ROCK

AT SUNRISE & SUNSET Sunset is the peak time to catch the Rock's beauty, when oranges, peaches, pinks, reds, and then indigo and deep violet creep across its face as if it were a giant opal. Some days it's fiery, other days the colors are muted. A sunset viewing carpark is located on the Rock's western side. Plenty of sunset and sunrise tours operate from the resort. A typical sunset tour is that offered by **AAT Kings** (📞 **08/8956 2171**), which departs 90 minutes before sunset, includes a free glass of wine with which to watch the "show," and returns 20 minutes after sundown; the cost is A$29 (U.S.$15.95) for adults, A$15 (U.S.$8.25) for children 4 to 14.

At sunrise the colors are less dramatic, but many folks enjoy the spectacle of the Rock unveiled by the dawn to birdsong. You'll need an early start—most tours leave about 75 minutes before sunup.

CLIMBING IT Aborigines refer to tourists as "minga"—little ants—because that's what we look like crawling up Uluru. Climbing this thing is no picnic—there's sometimes a ferociously strong wind that can blow you right off, the walls are almost vertical in places so you have to hold onto a chain, and it can be freezing cold or insanely hot. Quite a few people have died climbing the rock from heart attacks, heat stress, or simply falling off, so if you're not in good shape, have breathing difficulties, heart trouble, or high or low blood pressure, or are just plain scared of heights, don't do it. The Rock is closed to climbers during bad weather; when temperatures exceed 36°C (97°F), which they often do

Dinner in the Desert

Ayers Rock Resort's **Sounds of Silence** ⭐ dinner is hugely popular. In an outdoor clearing, you'll sip champagne and nibble canapés as the sun sets over the Rock to the strains of a lone didgeridoo, then sit at white-clothed, candlelit tables to a barbecue of kangaroo, barramundi, and emu, and Aussie wines. After dinner, the lanterns fade, the didgeridoo falls silent, and you are left with stillness. It is the first time some big-city folk have ever heard silence. Next, an astronomer points out the constellations of the Southern Hemisphere's Milky Way. Sounds of Silence is held nightly, weather permitting, and costs A$105 (U.S.$57.75) for adults and A$52.50 (U.S.$28.90) for children under 15 (kids under 10 are not encouraged), including transfers from the resort. It's mighty popular, so book 3 months ahead in peak season. Book through Ayers Rock Resort (see "Where to Stay & Dine," below).

between November and March; and when wind speed exceeds 25 knots, so climb in the stillness of early morning. Wherever you go at Uluru and the Olgas, *bring lots of drinking water with you from the resort.*

If that doesn't put you off, you'll be rewarded with views of the plain, the Olgas, and Mt. Conner. The surface is rutted with ravines about 2.5 meters (8 ft.) deep, which demand some scrambling. The climb takes at least 1 hour up for the fit, and 1 hour down. Less sure-footed mountaineers should allow 3 to 4 hours all told.

Note: The Anangu do not like people climbing Uluru, because the climb follows the trail their ancestral Dreamtime Mala men took when they first came to Uluru. They allow people to climb but strongly prefer that they don't.

WALKING, DRIVING, OR BUSING AROUND IT The easy 9.4-kilometer (6-mile) **Base Walk** circumnavigating Uluru takes about 2 hours, but allow time to linger around the water holes, caves, folds, and overhangs that make up its walls. A shorter walk is the easy 1-kilometer (just over half a mile) round-trip trail from the **Mutitjulu** parking lot to the pretty water hole near the Rock's base, where there is some rock art. The **Liru Track** is another easy trail; it runs 2 kilometers (1¼ miles) from the Cultural Centre to Uluru, where it links with the Base Walk.

Make time for the free daily 2-kilometer (1¼-mile) **Mala Walk** ⭐, where the ranger, who is often an Aborigine, explains the Dreamtime myths behind Uluru, talks about Aboriginal lifestyles and hunting techniques in days past, and explains the significance of the rock art and other sites you see along the way. The 90-minute trip leaves the Mala Walk sign at the base of the Uluru climb at 10am May through September, and at a cooler 8am October through April.

Before setting off on any walk, it's a good idea to arm yourself with the self-guided walking notes available for A$1.10 (U.S.60¢) from the Cultural Centre (see "Visitor Information," above).

A paved road runs around the Rock.

Most companies offer base tours. As an example, **Discovery Ecotours** (formerly Uluru Experience) (© **08/8956 2563**) conducts two guided base tours that give you an insight into natural history, rock art, and Dreamtime beliefs. Both arrive in time for sunrise: one is a 5-hour walk, the other is a 4-hour tour in a four-wheel-drive vehicle that incorporates short walks to the Rock base and a stop at the Uluru-Kata Tjuta Cultural Centre. Both include the park entry fee and breakfast, and cost A$98 (U.S.$53.90) for adults and A$65 (U.S.$35.75) for children 6 to 15. Kids under 6 are free but their meals are not included. The 5-hour walk is not suited to kids under 10.

FLYING OVER IT   Several companies do scenic flights by light aircraft or helicopter over Uluru and/or the Olgas, nearby Mt. Conner, the vast white salt pan of Lake Amadeus, and as far as Kings Canyon. Helicopters don't land on top of the Rock, however. As a guide to the flights available, **Professional Helicopter Services** (✆ **08/8956 2003**) does a 12- to 15-minute flight over Uluru for A$90 (U.S.$49.50) per adult. Kids under 13 usually pay half-price (that depends more. on their weight than their age). **Ayers Rock Scenic Flights** (✆ **08/8956 2345**) does a 110-minute Uluru/Olgas/Lake Amadeus/Kings Canyon "joyflight" for A$275 (U.S.$151.25) adults, A$235 (U.S.$129.95) kids 3 to 12.

MOTORCYCLING AROUND IT   Harley Davidson tours are available as sunrise or sunset rides, laps of the Rock, and various other Rock and/or Olgas tours with time for the Olgas walks. A blast out to the Rock at sunset with **Uluru Motorcycle Tours** (✆ **08/8956 2019**) will set you back A$135 (U.S.$74.25) with a glass of champagne. They drive the bike, you sit behind and hang on. Self-ride tours are available, too, at a hefty price.

VIEWING IT ON CAMELBACK   They say a soul travels at the same pace as a camel; it's certainly a peaceful way to see the Rock. **Frontier Camel Tours** (✆ **1800/806 499** in Australia, or 08/8956 2444) makes daily forays aboard "ships of the desert" to view Uluru at sunrise and sunset. Amble through red sand dunes with great views of the Rock, dismount to watch the sun rise or sink over it, and ride back to the depot for billy tea and yummy beer bread in the morning, or champagne in the evening. The 2-hour rides depart Ayers Rock Resort 1 hour before sunrise, or 1½ hours before sunset, and cost A$85 (U.S.$46.75) per person, including transfers from your hotel. Each day between 10:30am and midday you can visit the depot's camels and display free of charge and take a short camel ride for A$10 (U.S.$5.50) for adults, A$5 (U.S.$2.75) for kids 6 to 12, or A$25 (U.S.$13.75) for a family.

EXPLORING THE OLGAS

Although not everyone has heard of massive **Mt. Olga** ⍟ (or "the Olgas"), a sister monolith an easy 50 kilometers (31 miles) drive west of Uluru, many folks who have say she's lovelier and more mysterious, and I agree. Known to the Aborigines as Kata Tjuta or "many heads," the Olgas' 36 momentous red domes bulge out of the earth like turned clay on a potter's wheel. The tallest dome is actually 200 meters (656 ft.) higher than Ayers Rock. The Olgas are more important in Aboriginal Dreamtime legend than Uluru.

Two walking trails take you in among the domes: the 7.4-kilometer (4½-mile) **Valley of the Winds** ⍟ walk, which is fairly challenging and takes 3 to 5 hours,

---

Tips Travel Tip

Most tourists do Uluru in the mornings and the Olgas in the afternoon. Reverse the order (that is, do the Valley of the Winds walk in the morning and visit Uluru in the afternoon) and you'll find both places a little more silent and spiritual.

and the 2.6-kilometer (1½-mile) **Gorge walk,** which is easy and takes about an hour. The Valley of the Winds trail is the more rewarding in terms of scenery. Both have lookout points and shady stretches. The Valley of the Winds trail is closed when temperatures rise above 36°C (97°F).

WHERE TO STAY & DINE

Ayers Rock Resort not only is in the township of Yulara—it is the township. Located about 20 kilometers (13 miles) from the Rock, outside the national park boundary, it is the only place to stay. It is an impressive, contemporary complex, built to a high standard, very efficiently run and attractive. Because everyone either is a tourist or lives and works here, it has a village atmosphere— with a supermarket; a banking agency; a post office; a news agency; babysitting services; a medical center; a salon; several gift, clothing, and souvenir shops; a gas station; and a cinema.

You have a choice of six places to stay within the complex, from hotel rooms and apartments to bunkhouses and campsites—and probably luxury tents by the time you read this (see below). In keeping with this village feel, no matter where you stay, even in the campground, you are free to use all the pools, restaurants, and other facilities of every hostelry, except the rather glamorous Sails in the Desert pool, which is reserved for Sails guests.

Ayers Rock Resort, Alice Springs Resort, and Kings Canyon Resort are managed by **Voyages Hotels & Resorts.** You can book accommodations for all three properties through the central reservations office in Sydney (© **1300/139 889** in Australia, or 02/9339 1040; fax 02/9332 4555; www.voyages.com.au). Ask about packages for stays at one, two, or all three resorts.

High season is from July 1 to November 30. Book well ahead then.

A A$55-million (U.S.$30.25-million) resort refurbishment program has been taking place throughout 2001 and into 2002. Construction work was not expected to inconvenience guests greatly. Details on the new accommodation options that the program will produce appear in the listings, below.

A tour desk, same-day dry-cleaning and laundry service, and babysitting are available at every hostelry and campground.

As well as the dining options within the hotels below, the resort's small shopping center has the pleasant **Gecko's Café,** which offers wood-fired pizzas, pastas and sandwiches; a bakery; an ice-creamery; and a take-out joint. Sails in the Desert, Desert Gardens and the Outback Pioneer Hotel & Lodge can provide picnic hampers and breakfast backpacks. Kids under 15 dine free at any of the hotels' buffets in the company of an adult.

VERY EXPENSIVE

Some time in 2002, the resort plans to build a A$8-million (U.S.$4.4-million) luxury safari camp in the dunes a mile or two from the resort complex. It will have 15 "six star" air-conditioned tents, all with private bathrooms, and a balcony boasting views of the Rock. Details were sketchy at press time, but A$8 million on 15 tents works out to more than A$530,000 (U.S.$291,500) per tent, so they promise to be pretty special! Rates were not set as we wrote, but they will be pegged higher than the tariff at Sails in the Desert hotel, below.

Sails in the Desert 👉👉   This is the top-of-the-range hotel choice with elegant, contemporary rooms that were renovated in 1999 in the rich timber-and-stone tones of the desert and Aboriginal art. You do not see the Rock from your room, but most guests are too busy sipping cocktails by the big free-form pool to care. The pool area is shaded by eye-catching white "sails" and surrounded by sun lounges on inviting green lawns. The lobby art gallery regularly has Aboriginal artists-in-residence. The beautiful Kuniya restaurant serves elegant a la carte fine-dining fare with novel bush tucker ingredients; Winkuku is a smart a la carte and buffet venue; and the lively Rockpool serves alfresco Thai fare poolside.

Yulara Dr., Yulara, NT 0872. ℭ 08/8957 7888. Fax 08/8957 7474. 232 units (6 with Jacuzzis). High season A$464–$543 (U.S.$255.20–$286.65) double; A$819 (U.S.$450.45) suite. Low season A$427–$498 (U.S.$234.85–$273.90) double; A$760 (U.S.$418) suite. Extra person A$25 (U.S.$13.75). AE, DC, MC, V. Free airport shuttle. **Amenities:** 3 restaurants, bar; large outdoor swimming pool; 2 outdoor day/night tennis courts; limited room service. *In room:* A/C, TV with pay movies, dataport, minibar, hair dryer, iron.

EXPENSIVE

Desert Gardens Hotel 🐾   Apart from the new luxury tents (above), this is the only hotel with views of the Rock (rather distant ones), from some of the 60 deluxe rooms. The accommodations are not as lavish as those at Sails in the Desert, but they're just as comfortable, and done up with elegant furnishings. By early 2002, a further 58 new rooms should have been built, and the existing 100 standard rooms refurbished with new bathrooms, new bedding, and new carpets. The pleasant White Gums restaurant serves a la carte flame grill and buffet meals.

Yulara Drive, Yulara, NT 0872. ℭ 08/8957 7888. Fax 08/8957 7716. 160 units (100 with shower only). High season A$383–$449 (U.S.$210.65–$246.95) double. Low season A$355–$418 (U.S.$195.25–$229.90) double. Extra person A$25 (U.S.$13.75). AE, DC, MC, V. Free airport shuttle. **Amenities:** Restaurant, 2 bars; outdoor swimming pool; limited room service; laundry. *In room:* A/C, TV with pay movies, minibar, hair dryer, iron.

Emu Walk Apartments 🐾   These bright, contemporary apartments have full kitchens, laundries, separate bedrooms, and roomy living areas, and are serviced daily. There's no restaurant or pool; but Gecko's Café and the market are close, and you can cool off in the Desert Gardens Hotel pool next door.

Yulara Dr., Yulara, NT 0872. ℭ 08/8957 7888. Fax 08/8957 7742. 59 apts (all with shower only). High season A$359 (U.S.$197.45) 1-bedroom apt; A$445 (U.S.$244.75) 2-bedroom apt for 4. Low season A$330 (U.S.$181.50) 1-bedroom apt; A$410 (U.S.$225.50) 2-bedroom apt. Extra person A$25 (U.S.$13.75). AE, DC, MC, V. Free airport shuttle. **Amenities:** Limited room service. *In room:* A/C, TV with pay movies, kitchen, minibar, hair dryer, iron.

Outback Pioneer Hotel and Lodge   A happy, all-ages crowd congregates at this mid-range collection of hotel rooms, cabins, bunkrooms, and dorms. The decent-size motel-style hotel rooms got a smart refurbishing in 1999; some have a sink and microwave. By early 2002, 30 new rooms are likely to be built, offering clean, simple accommodation with private bathrooms, at a rate cheaper than the

---

Moments When You See the Southern Cross for the First Time . . .

Light pollution is extremely low out in the Red Centre, so the night sky is a dazzler. At the Ayers Rock Observatory, you can check out your zodiac constellation and take a 1-hour tour of the Southern Hemisphere heavens (they're different from the Northern Hemisphere stars).

To visit the observatory, you must join a tour with **Discovery Ecotours** (formerly Uluru Experience) (ℭ **1800/803 174** in Australia, or 08/8956 2563), which provides hotel pickup and a tour. Tours depart twice a night; times vary. It costs A$30 (U.S.$16.50) for adults, A$22 (U.S.$12.10) for children 6 to 15, and A$63 (U.S.$34.65) for a family.

hotel rooms but above the existing cabins. The existing cabins have double beds and bunks, and shared bathroom and kitchen facilities. Out by the pool, are plenty of lounge chairs, and there will be an Internet lounge by the time you arrive. The Bough House Restaurant does buffets, and there is a dirt-cheap poolside kiosk selling burger-style fare; but what seems like the entire resort gathers nightly at the great-value **Outback Pioneer Barbeque** 𝒢𝒢. This rustic barn with big tables, lots of beer, and live music is the place to join the throngs throwing a kangaroo steak or emu sausage on the communal cook-it-yourself barbie.

Yulara Dr., Yulara, NT 0872. ℭ 08/8957 7888. Fax 08/8957 7615. 125 units, all with private bathroom; 12 cabins, none with bathroom; 36 quad-share bunkrooms and 2 40-bed single-sex dorms, none with bathroom. High season A$348 (U.S.$191.40) double; $154 (U.S.$84.70) cabin. Low season A$318 (U.S.$174.90) double; A$145 (U.S.$79.75) cabin. Extra person A$25 (U.S.$13.75). Bunkroom bed A$40 (U.S.$22), dorm bed A$32 (U.S.$17.60), year-round. No children under 16 in bunkhouses unless you book entire room. AE, DC, MC, V. Free airport shuttle. **Amenities:** 2 restaurants, 2 bars; outdoor swimming pool. *In room:* A/C. Hotel and cabins only: TV (with pay movies in hotel), fridge. Hotel only: minibar, hair dryer, iron. Phones in hotel rooms only.

INEXPENSIVE

Moderately priced cabins and inexpensive bunkhouse and dorm beds are available at the Outback Pioneer Hotel and Lodge, above.

Note: Some time in 2002, Spinifex Lodge (below) was due to be converted into a moderately priced boutique hotel. According to the resort, it will have 100 small but high-quality "funky" rooms and a pool; rates were not set at press time. After the conversion takes place, you will find clean, affordable lodgings in the 30 new rooms built in late 2001 at the Outback Pioneer Hotel and Lodge (see above).

Ayers Rock Campground   Instead of red dust you get blissfully green lawns at this campground, which has barbecues, a playground, Internet access, and clean communal bathrooms and kitchen. If you don't want to camp but you want to travel cheap, consider the cabins. They're clean, modern, and a great value; each has a kitchenette, petite dining furniture, a double bed, and four bunks. By the time you arrive, new cabins with private bathrooms should be available. **Thrifty** (ℭ **08/8956 2030**) at Uluru rents a complete camping kit with sleeping bags, tents, cooking equipment, and so on, to its customers for A$35.50 (U.S.$19.55) per day for two people; book it ahead. **Hertz** (ℭ **08/ 8956 2244**) rents camping gear if you rent a large four-wheel-drive for a week or more.

Yulara Dr., Yulara, NT 0872. ℭ 08/8956 2055. Fax 08/8956 2260. 220 tent sites, 198 powered sites, 14 cabins (none with bathroom). A$132 (U.S.$72.60) cabin for up to 6 people. A$24.20 (U.S.$13.30) double tent site; A$28.60 (U.S.$15.75) double, A$35 (U.S.$19.25) family powered site. Additional person A$11 (U.S.$6.05) adults, A$5.50 (U.S.$3) children 5–15. AE, DC, MC, V. Free airport shuttle. **Amenities:** Outdoor swimming pool; laundry; kiosk. *In room* (Cabins): A/C, TV, fridge, no phone.

Spinifex Lodge 𝒢   As we wrote, this lodge consisted of clean, cool, smartly furnished twin/double rooms and bunkrooms. If you can handle shared bathrooms, they are your best budget-wise bet outside the camping area. There's no pool, but you can use the one at nearby Desert Gardens. There's no restaurant, but a few eateries and the market are next door. See the note above about the conversion of this lodge to a more expensive hotel in 2002.

Yulara Dr., Yulara, NT 0872. ℭ **08/8957 7888**. Fax 08/8957 7755. 34 units and 34 quad-share bunkhouses, none with bathroom. High season A$152 (U.S.$83.60) double or bunkhouse. Low season A$142 (U.S.$78.10) double or bunkhouse. Extra person A$25 (U.S.$13.75). AE, DC, MC, V. Free airport shuttle. **Amenities:** Laundry. *In room:* A/C, TV with Kiosk, pay movies, kitchenette.

8

The Top End

by Natalie Kruger

The "Top End" is the term Aussies use to refer to the vast sweep of barely inhabited country from Broome on the west coast of Western Australia to Arnhemland in the Northern Territory and eastern Queensland. It is the place Mick "Croc" Dundee called home, a genuine last frontier, a place of wild beauty and, sometimes, hardship.

The rugged northwest portion of Western Australia is known as the Kimberley, where beef-cattle farming, pearl farming, and tourism thrive in a rocky moonscape of red cliffs, waterfalls, mighty rivers, sparse gums, and wetland lagoons. Here you can visit a million-acre cattle station rich in ancient Aboriginal rock-art sites, tour the world's largest diamond mine, cruise the lush Ord River to see hundreds of native birds, ride a camel on the beach and shop for the world's biggest South Sea pearls.

The northern reaches of the Northern Territory are more populated than the Kimberley, but only just. Darwin, the capital, is a smallish city, rich, modern, and tropical. Katherine, to its south, is a small farming town famous for a beautiful river gorge. Here you can drop by on an Aboriginal community, explore vast cattle stations, canoe jungly rivers, and soak in natural thermal pools. To the east of Darwin and Katherine is Kakadu National Park, home to wetlands, crocodiles, and millions of birds—one-third of the country's bird species, in fact. Farther east still is Arnhemland, a stretch of rocky ridges and flooding rivers owned by Aboriginal people. Few white folks ever penetrate here.

Life is a bit different in the Top End than elsewhere in Australia, especially in the Northern Territory. It has a slightly lawless image, which I suspect Territorians enjoy cultivating among tenderfoot Aussies from the south. The isolation, the humidity in the summer Wet Season, monsoonal floods, human-eating crocodiles, and other dangers breed a tough guy and girl.

1 Exploring the Top End

Read "Exploring the Red Centre," at the start of chapter 7; it contains information on traveling the entire Northern Territory.

VISITOR INFORMATION The **Northern Territory Tourist Commission** (NTTC), Tourism House, 43 Mitchell St., Darwin, NT 0800 (© **13 61 10** for trip-planning enquiries in Australia, or 08/8999 3900 for administration) can supply you with information on Darwin, Litchfield National Park, Kakadu National Park, Katherine, and any other destinations in the Territory. As well as its main website, **www.ntholidays.com**, it maintains a second site tailored for North Americans, **www.insidetheoutback.com**, and yet another, **www.ozoutback. com**, for young and student travelers. It publishes a helpful annual guide to the

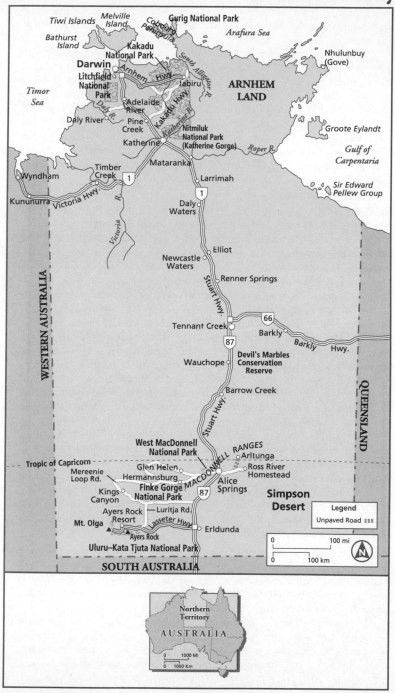

The Northern Territory

Tiwi Islands

Melville Island

Bathurst Island

Gurig National Park

Cobourg Peninsula

Arafura Sea

Kakadu National Park

South Alligator R.

Arnhem Hwy.

Darwin

ARNHEM LAND

Nhulunbuy (Gove)

Litchfield National Park

Jabiru

Timor Sea

Adelaide River

Daly R.

Kakadu Hwy.

Daly River

Pine Creek

Katherine R.

Groote Eylandt

Katherine

Nitmiluk National Park (Katherine Gorge)

Roper R.

Gulf of Carpentaria

Mataranka

Sir Edward Pellew Group

Wyndham

Timber Creek

1

Larrimah

Kununurra

Victoria Hwy.

Victoria R.

1

Daly Waters

WESTERN AUSTRALIA

Elliot

Newcastle Waters

Renner Springs

Stuart Hwy.

66

Tennant Creek

Barkly

Barkly Hwy.

QUEENSLAND

87

Wauchope

Devil's Marbles Conservation Reserve

Barrow Creek

Stuart Hwy.

West MacDonnell National Park

MACDONNELL RANGES

Arltunga

Tropic of Capricorn

Glen Helen

Ross River Homestead

Mereenie Loop Rd.

Hermannsburg

Alice Springs

Kings Canyon

Finke Gorge National Park

87

Simpson Desert

Luritja Rd.

Ayers Rock Resort

Lasseter Hwy.

Mt. Olga

Erldunda

Ayers Rock

Uluru–Kata Tjuta National Park

SOUTH AUSTRALIA

Legend

Unpaved Road ▦▦

0   100 mi

0   100 km

Northern Territory

AUSTRALIA

1000 Mi

1000 Km

Top End that details many hotels, tour operators, rental-car companies, and attractions, and a separate fishing guide. The Commission operates a division that offers package deals on complete trips.

The **Tourism Top End information centre** in Darwin and the **Katherine Region Tourist Association** (listed in the "Darwin" and "Katherine" sections of this chapter) can also supply useful information about the entire Top End and the Kimberley, not just their respective local regions. Your best source of information on the Kimberley region is the **Kimberley Tourism Association** (© 08/ 9193 6660; it shares the Broome Tourist Bureau's website at www. ebroome.com), or the **Broome Tourist Bureau** and the **Kununurra Tourist Bureau** (both listed in section 5 of this chapter). As the Kimberley lies within Western Australia, you can also contact the **Western Australian Tourism Commission's tourist information line** (© 1300/361 351 in Australia, or 08/9483 1111; www.westernaustralia.net).

WHEN TO GO   Most folks visit the Top End in the winter **Dry Season** ("the Dry"). Not a cloud will grace the sky, more than likely, and temperatures will be comfortable, even hot in the middle of the day. The Dry runs roughly from **late April to the end of October.** It is high season, so book every tour, hotel, or campsite in advance.

The **Wet Season** ("the Wet") runs November (sometimes as early as Oct) through March or April, sometimes a few weeks longer in the Kimberley. While it does not rain 24 hours a day, it comes down in buckets when it does, usually for an hour or two each day, mainly in the late afternoon or during the night. The land floods as far as the eye can see, the humidity is murderous, and the temperatures hit nearly 40°C (104°F). The floods cut off many attractions, sometimes suddenly, and some tour companies shut up shop for the season. Cyclones may hit the coast during the Wet, with the same savagery and frequency as hurricanes hit Florida. Many people find the "build-up" to the Wet in October and November, when clouds gather but do not break, to be the toughest time.

Having said all that, the Wet is my favorite time to travel. Waterfalls become massive torrents, fork lightning storms crackle across the afternoon sky, the land turns green, cloud cover keeps the worst of the sun off you, crowds vanish, and I find the place has an eerie, isolated exoticism to it. Keep your plans flexible to account for floods, take it slow in the heat, and carry loads of drinking water. Even if you normally camp, sleep in air-conditioned accommodations now. Book tours ahead, because most will operate on a reduced schedule. See the tips about traveling in the Wet, below.

GETTING AROUND   The **Automobile Association of the Northern Territory** (AANT), 79–81 Smith St., Darwin, NT 0800 (© 08/8981 3837), and the **Royal Automobile Club** of Western Australia (RACWA), 228 Adelaide Terrace, Perth, WA 6000 (© 08/9421 4444), are both good sources of maps and road advice (link to their websites via www.aaa.asn.au).

Always carry 4 liters (1 gal.) of **drinking water** per person a day when walking (increase to 1 liter/¼ gal. per person per hr. in summer). Wear a broad-brimmed hat, high-factor sunscreen lotion, and insect repellent containing DEET (Aerogard and RID brands both contain it) to protect against the dangerous Ross River Fever virus carried by mosquitoes in these parts.

Deadly **marine stingers** (see "Dangerous Wildlife & Other Hazards," in chapter 2) put a stop to ocean swimming in the Top End from roughly October to April or May.

Tips **Croc Alert!**

Saltwater crocodiles are a serious threat in the sea, estuaries, lakes, wetlands, waterfall pools, and rivers of the Top End—even hundreds of kilometers inland. They may be called "saltwater" crocs, but they live in fresh water, too. Never jump in the water or stand on the bank unless you want to be lunch.

TRAVELING IN THE WET   Some roads will be underwater throughout the Wet, while others can flood unexpectedly, leaving you cut off for hours, days, or even months. Flash floods pose dangers to unwary motorists. Don't cross a flooded road unless you know the water is shallow, the current very gentle, and the road underneath intact. Never wade into the water, because crocodiles may be present. If you're cut off, the only thing to do is wait, so it's smart to travel with food and drinking water in remote parts. Check road conditions every day by calling the **Northern Territory Department of Transport & Works' 24-hour recorded report on road conditions** (© 1800/246 199 in Australia) or in the Kimberley, by calling **Western Australia's Main Road department** (© 1800/013 314 in Australia); dropping into or calling the AANT (above) in Darwin during office hours; or tuning in to the local radio stations as you drive. Local tour companies, tourist bureaus, and police stations should also be able to help.

TOUR OPERATORS   Organized tours can bust the hassles posed by distance, isolation, and Wet floods in the Top End, and the guide will show and tell you things you almost certainly would not discover on your own. Plenty of companies run coach, minibus, and four-wheel-drive tours between Broome, Kununurra, Darwin, and even Alice Springs. A loop through Darwin, Litchfield National Park, Kakadu National Park, and Katherine is a popular triangle that shows you a lot in a short time.

Reputable companies include **AAT Kings** (© 1800/334 009 in Australia, or 03/9274 7422; www.aatkings.com.au); **Odyssey Safaris** (© 08/8948 0091; www.odysaf.com.au); **Sahara Outback Tours** (© 1800/806 240 in Australia, or 08/8953 0881; www.saharatours.com.au); and **Adventure Tours** (© 08/8936 1300; www.adventuretours.com.au).

VIP Travel Australia (© 1800/806 412 in Australia, or 08/8956 2388; www.vipaustralia.com.au) does luxury organized and tailor-made tours.

Katherine-based **Far Out Adventures** *☎* (© 08/8972 2552; www.farout.com.au) does four-wheel-drive camping adventures for groups of no more than six passengers into Kakadu, Darwin, Arnhemland, Litchfield National Park, Katherine, the Kimberley, and more remote regions across the Top End. Join an organized tour, or have proprietor/guide Mike Keighley tailor a private adventure to suit your interests and your budget. Touring with Mike is a bit like having Crocodile Dundee take you hiking, fishing, meeting, or even hunting with Aboriginal people, four-wheel-driving through the bush, canoeing, seeing Aboriginal rock art, taking optional extras like scenic flights, and swimming under (croc-free) waterfalls. He is one of a select group of operators with Australia's Advanced Eco Tour Accreditation and Savannah Guide status, and he has a tremendous knowledge of the Top End's geography, Aboriginal culture, and ecology. Fun and personal, his trips are accompanied by good wine (sometimes in wonderful locations like on a bird-filled lagoon at sunset) and "bush gourmet" meals. Highly recommended.

For details of tour operators running from Darwin to Broome, see "The Kimberley" section, later in this chapter.

2 Darwin

1,489km (923 miles) N of Alice Springs

Named after the founder of evolution himself, Australia's northernmost capital (pop. 97,750), full of proud white civic buildings adorned with pink bougainvillea, has a touch of Asian exoticism about it. It's a modern tropical capital—extremely modern, actually, because most of it was rebuilt after Cyclone Tracy wiped out the city on Christmas Eve 1974. Don't bother bringing along a jacket and tie here. Shorts and sandals will get you most places—even the swankiest official state invitations stipulate dress as "Territory Rig," meaning long pants and a short-sleeved open-necked shirt for men.

The city is most commonly used as a gateway to Kakadu National Park, Katherine Gorge, and the Kimberley. Australians look at you askance when you say you're visiting this place ("What the heck are you going to do in Darwin?"), but truth is, most Aussies have never been there. I really like Darwin's mix of frontier rawness, scenic beauty, and surprisingly sophisticated food. Give yourself at least a day to wander the pleasant streets and parklands, visit the wildlife attractions, and maybe explore the city's World War II history. The wetlands fishing in outlying regions is excellent, and the shopping for Aboriginal art and the Top End's illustrious South Sea pearls is good. An easy day trip away is **Litchfield National Park**, one of the Territory's best-kept secrets, boasting the kind of beautiful waterfalls to swim under that you only see on holiday brochures.

ESSENTIALS

GETTING THERE   Qantas (© 13 13 13 in Australia) serve Darwin daily from most state capitals; flights either are direct or connect in Alice Springs. Qantas also flies direct from Cairns. **Airlink** (book through Qantas) makes a direct Broome–Darwin flight. Airnorth (© **1800/627 474** in Australia, or 08/8945 2866) flies from Alice Springs via Tennant Creek and Katherine. There are also direct international flights to Darwin from Asia.

Darwin Airport Shuttle Services (© **1800/358 945** in the Northern Territory, or 08/8981 5066) meets every flight and delivers to any hotel between the airport and city (including The Summer House and the MGM Grand) for A$7.50 (U.S.$4.15) one-way or A$13 (U.S.$7.15) round-trip. Children 6 to 13 pay A$4.50 (U.S.$2.50), or A$8 (U.S.$4.40) round-trip. Bookings aren't essential. A cab to the city is around A$18.50 (U.S.$10.20). **Avis, Budget, Hertz,** and **Thrifty** have airport desks (see "Getting Around," below, for telephone numbers).

Greyhound Pioneer (© 13 20 30 in Australia) and **McCafferty's** (© 13 14 99 in Australia) both make a daily coach run from Alice Springs, and McCafferty's has a second daily service from Tennant Creek. The trip from Alice takes around 21 hours, and the fare is A$175 (U.S.$96.25). Greyhound also has daily service from Broome via Kununurra and Katherine; this trip takes around 26½ hours and costs A$230 (U.S.$126.50). Both companies run from Cairns via Townsville and Tennant Creek.

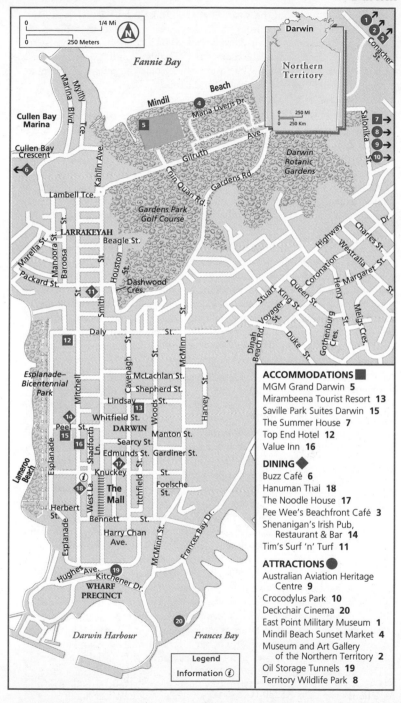

Darwin

ACCOMMODATIONS ■
MGM Grand Darwin **5**
Mirambeena Tourist Resort **13**
Saville Park Suites Darwin **15**
The Summer House **7**
Top End Hotel **12**
Value Inn **16**

DINING ◆
Buzz Café **6**
Hanuman Thai **18**
The Noodle House **17**
Pee Wee's Beachfront Café **3**
Shenanigan's Irish Pub,
    Restaurant & Bar **14**
Tim's Surf 'n' Turf **11**

ATTRACTIONS ●
Australian Aviation Heritage
    Centre **9**
Crocodylus Park **10**
Deckchair Cinema **20**
East Point Military Museum **1**
Mindil Beach Sunset Market **4**
Museum and Art Gallery
    of the Northern Territory **2**
Oil Storage Tunnels **19**
Territory Wildlife Park **8**

Legend
Information ⓘ

Darwin is at the end of the Stuart Highway. Allow at least 2 very long days, 3 to be comfortable, to drive from Alice. The nearest road route from the east is the long and extremely dull Barkly Highway, which connects with the Stuart Highway at Tennant Creek, 922 kilometers (572 miles) south. The nearest road from the west is the Victoria Highway, which joins the Stuart Highway at Katherine, 314 kilometers (195 miles) to the south.

There is no train service to Darwin.

VISITOR INFORMATION   The official visitor center is run by **Tourism Top End,** Knuckey Street at Mitchell Street, Darwin, NT 0800 (© **08/8981 4300;** info@drta.com.au). It is the place to go for maps, bookings, national park notes, and information on not just Darwin but Top End regions throughout the Northern Territory, including Arnhemland, Katherine, and Kakadu and Litchfield National Parks. It stocks information on the Kimberley, too, although a limited amount. It's open Monday through Friday from 8:30am to 5:45pm, Saturday from 9am to 2:45pm, and Sunday and public holidays from 10am to 1:45pm.

CITY LAYOUT   The city heart is the **Smith Street pedestrian mall.** One street over is the **Mitchell Street Tourist Precinct** with backpacker lodges, cheap eateries, and souvenir stores. Two streets past that is the harborfront **Esplanade.** In the **Old Wharf precinct,** a walk from town, are a couple of tourist attractions, a jetty popular with local fishermen, and a working dock. **Cullen Bay Marina** is a happening "millionaire's row" of restaurants, cafes, and expensive boats; it's about a 25-minute walk northwest of town. A couple of miles northwest of town is **Fannie Bay,** where you'll find the Botanic Gardens, sailing club, golf course, museum and art gallery, and casino.

GETTING AROUND   For car and four-wheel-drive rentals, call **Avis** (© 08/ 8981 9922), **Budget** (© 08/8981 9800), **Delta EuropCar** (© 08/8941 0300), **Hertz** (© 1800/89 1112 in the Northern Territory, or 08/8941 0944), or **Thrifty** (© 08/8924 0000).

Darwinbus (© **08/8924 7666**) is the local bus company. Its 1-day Tourcard allows unlimited travel on the network until midnight for A$5 (U.S.$2.75) per adult, A$2.50 (U.S.$1.40) kids 5 to 14. The city terminus is on Harry Chan Avenue (behind the Commonwealth Bank and Qantas buildings). Get timetables there, or from the Tourism Top End visitor center (see "Visitor Information" earlier in this chapter).

The **Tour Tub bus** (© **1800/63 2225** in Australia, or 08/8981 5233) does a loop of most city attractions and major hotels between 9am and 4pm daily. Hop on and off as often as you like all day for A$25 (U.S.$13.75) for adults, A$15 (U.S.$8.25) for children ages 4 to 12. It departs the Knuckey Street end of Smith Street Mall, opposite Woolworths. The **Territory Shuttle** (© **08/8928 1155**) is a minibus service that picks you up and drops you off anywhere in the Darwin area—hotels, attractions, shops, the wharf precincts, the 'burbs, and so on. It will come by as promptly as it can when you call, or you can pre-book it. It runs daily and usually 24 hours Wednesday through Saturday. The fares are low; a trip within the downtown area or out as far as the MGM Grand casino and Mindil Beach Sunset Markets will set you back just A$2 (U.S.$1.10) per person.

Darwin Day Tours (© **08/8924 1124**) has a range of sightseeing tours.

Darwin Radio Taxis (© **131 008**) is the main cab company. The flagfall is A$3.10 (U.S.$1.70), or A$3.70 (U.S.$2.05) on weekends and holidays. Taxi stands are at the Knuckey Street and Bennett Street ends of Smith Street Mall.

EXPLORING DARWIN

Darwin's parks, harbor, and tropical clime make it lovely for strolling in during the Dry. It's worth picking up the free map from the tourist office of a Historical Stroll of 17 points of interest around town. The **Esplanade** makes a pleasantly short and shady saunter and the 42-hectare (104-acre) **Darwin Botanic Gardens** (© **08/8981 1958**), on Gardens Road 1.5 kilometers (a mile) from town, has paths through palms, orchids, every species of baobab in the world, and mangroves. Entry is free daily. Take bus no. 4 or 6; the buses drop you at the Gardens Road entrance, but you might want to walk straight to the visitor center near the Geranium Street entrance to pick up self-guiding maps to the gardens' Aboriginal plant-use trails.

The pleasant 5-kilometer (3-mile) trail along **Fannie Bay** from the MGM Grand to the East Point Military Museum is also worth doing. Keep a lookout for some of the 2,000 wild wallabies on the east side of the road near the museum.

Darwin has two wildlife parks worth visiting. At the **Territory Wildlife Park** (© **08/8988 7200**), 61 kilometers (38 miles) south of Darwin at Berry Springs, you can take a free shuttle or walk 6 kilometers (3¾ miles) of bush trails to see native Northern Territory wildlife in wonderfully re-created natural habitats including monsoon rain-forest boardwalks, lagoons with bird-hides, a walk-through aviary, a walk-through aquarium housing sting rays and sawfish, and a nocturnal house with marsupials such as cute bilbies. Bats, birds (many of them wild), spiders, crocs, frill-neck lizards, kangaroos, and other creatures also make their home here (but not koalas, because they don't live in the Territory). A program of animal talks runs throughout the day. Go first thing to see the animals at their liveliest, and allow 4 hours to see everything, plus traveling time. The grounds are a nice picnic spot. Open daily from 8:30am to 6pm (last entry at 4pm), and closed Christmas. Admission is A$18 (U.S.$99.90) for adults, A$12.60 (U.S.$6.95) for seniors, A$9 (U.S.$4.95) for students and children 5 to 16, and A$40 (U.S.$22) for a family. Take the Stuart Highway for 50 kilometers (31 miles) and turn right onto the Cox Peninsula Road for another 11 kilometers (7 miles). If you don't have your own wheels, the cheapest way to get there is aboard the **Rainbow Down the Track and Back** (© **08/8948 4248**) bus service that runs direct to the park for A$25 (U.S.$13.75) per person, round-trip, free for kids under 7. It departs daily outside the McCafferty's/Greyhound Pioneer coach terminal at 67–69 Mitchell St. (behind the Darwin YHA hostel) at 8 and 10:45am, returning at 12:30 and 4pm. It's best to book.

In addition to housing an interesting crocodile museum, **Crocodylus Park** (© **08/8922 4500**), a 15-minute drive from town at 815 McMillan's Rd., Berrimah (opposite the police station), holds croc-feeding sessions and free guided tours at 10am, noon, and 2pm. It also has a few other species such as monkeys and turtles on display. It's open daily from 9am to 5pm (closed Christmas). Admission is A$19.50 (U.S.$10.75) for adults, A$16 (U.S.$8.80) for seniors and students, A$10 (U.S.$5.50) for children 4 to 16, and A$49 (U.S.$26.95) for a family. Take bus no. 5 (Mon–Fri only).

THE DARWIN SHOPPING SCENE

Darwin's best buys are Aboriginal art and crafts, pearls, opals, and diamonds.

For a good range of authentic Aboriginal artworks and artifacts at reasonable prices, check out **Raintree Aboriginal Fine Arts**, 20 Knuckey St. (© **08/8941 9933**). For a heavyweight investment in works by internationally sought-after artists, visit the Aboriginal-owned **Aboriginal Fine Arts Gallery,** on the second floor on the corner of Knuckey and Mitchell streets ((*C* **08/8981 1315**). Its website at **www.aaia.com.au** is a useful guide to art and artists.

The world's best South Sea pearls are farmed in the Top End seas. Buy, or just drool in the window, at **Paspaley Pearls,** off Smith Street Mall on Bennett Street ((*C* **08/8982 5555**). **The World of Opal,** 44 Smith St. Mall ((*C* **08/8981 8981**), has a re-creation of an opal mine in their showroom. If you fancy a pink diamond (the world's rarest) from the Argyle Diamond Mine in Kununurra (see later in this chapter), you can get them at **Creative Jewellers,** 27 Smith St. Mall ((*C* **08/8941 1233**), an Argyle-appointed supplier which buys direct from the mine. They also stock the champagne diamonds for which Argyle is renowned and other Argyle diamond colors, as well as South Sea pearls and opals. They try to fashion pieces for overseas visitors in a short time frame to match your traveling schedule.

The **Museum and Art Gallery of the Northern Territory,** Conacher Street, Fannie Bay ((*C* **08/8999 8201**), also holds an attraction for crocodile fans—the preserved body of **Sweetheart,** a 5.1-meter (17-ft.) human-eating saltwater croc captured in Kakadu National Park. The museum and gallery have good sections on Aboriginal, Southeast Asian, and Pacific art and culture. Gallery and museum are open from 9am to 5pm Monday through Friday, and 10am to 5pm weekends and public holidays (closed Christmas and Good Friday). The cafe has lovely bay views. Admission is free to the permanent exhibits. Take bus no. 4 or 6.

Darwin was an Allied supply base during World War II, when many American airmen were based here. The **East Point Military Museum,** East Point Road, East Point ((*C* **08/8981 9702**), housed in a World War II gun command post, plays a video of the 1942–43 Japanese bombing of Darwin and has small but fine displays of photos, memorabilia, artillery, armored vehicles, weaponry old and new, and gun emplacements right outside. Open daily from 9:30am to 5pm (closed Christmas and Good Friday). Admission is A$9 (U.S.$4.95) for adults, A$8 (U.S.$4.40) for seniors, A$4.50 (U.S.$2.50) for children under 16, and A$25 (U.S.$13.75) for a family.

Even if you are not a military or aircraft buff you may still enjoy the excellent **Australian Aviation Heritage Centre** ⊛, 557 Stuart Hwy., Winnellie ((*C* **08/ 8947 2145**). A B-52 bomber on loan from the United States is the prized exhibit, but the center also boasts a B-25 Mitchell bomber, Mirage and Sabre jet fighters, rare Japanese Zero fighter wreckage, and funny, sad and heart-warming (and heart-wrenching) displays on World War II and Vietnam. Hours are daily from 9am to 5pm (closed Christmas and Good Friday). Admission is A$11 (U.S.$6.05) for adults, A$7.50 (U.S.$4.15) for seniors and students, A$6 (U.S.$3.30) for children 6 to 12, and A$28 (U.S.$15.40) for a family. The Centre is 10 minutes from town; take the no. 5 or 8 bus.

Empty **World War II oil storage tunnels** ((*C* **1800/63 2225** in Australia, or 08/8981 5233) on Kitchener Drive in the Old Wharf precinct, house a collection of black-and-white photographs of the war in Darwin, each lit up in the dark. It's a simple but haunting attraction worth a visit. Admission is $4.50 per person. The tunnels are closed December 10 to 27 and all of February. They open from 9am to 5pm daily May through October; November through April, hours are Tuesday through Friday from 10am to 2pm, weekends and holidays from 10am to 4pm.

On the Esplanade stands a monument to the destroyer *U.S.S. Robert E. Peary,* which went down in Darwin Harbour, with a loss of 88 lives.

The Top End's wetlands and warm oceans are **fishing heaven** ☆. The big prey is barramundi. Loads of charter boats conduct jaunts of up to 10 days in the river and wetland systems around Darwin, Kakadu National Park, and into remote Arnhemland. The same company that runs Darwin's Tour Tub bus also runs the **Northern Territory Fishing Office** (✆ **1800/63 2225** outside Darwin in Australia, or 08/8981 5233), a booking agent for a number of fishing charter boats offering barramundi day trips and extended wetland safaris, reef fishing, light tackle sportfishing, fly fishing, and estuary fishing. They also rent skipper-yourself fishing boats and tackle. A day's barra fishing on wetlands near Darwin will cost you around A$220 (U.S.$121) per person; for an extended barra safari, budget about A$400 (U.S.$220) per person per day. If you simply want to cast a line in Darwin Harbour for trevally, queenfish and barra, they will take you out for A$75 (U.S.$41.25) per person for a half day, or A$135 (U.S.$74.25) per person for a full day.

WHERE TO STAY

April through October is the peak Dry Season; hotels usually drop their rates November through March, which is the Wet Season.

EXPENSIVE

MGM Grand Darwin ☆ *Value* Attached to Darwin's casino on Fannie Bay, this rather grand hotel is well priced for such an upscale place. The whole complex resembles a tropical palace with its white blocky architecture and 18 acres of gardens on Mindil Beach. It's worth paying the A$27.50 (U.S.$15.15) extra to guarantee an ocean-facing room in the Dry season so you can watch Darwin's great sunsets. The rooms are a cocktail of European-style/contemporary Spanish furniture, and the tropical elegance of timber louvers and potted palms. Tennis courts are next door, the Botanic Gardens are nearby, and a 9-hole public golf course is across the road. A long-ish beachside stroll brings you to the Museum and Art Gallery, and the Mindil Beach Sunset Markets take place right outside on Thursday nights. A free shuttle runs four times a day to the city, which is a A$7.50 (U.S.$4.15) cab ride away.

Gilruth Ave., The Gardens, Darwin, NT 0800. ✆ **1800/89 1118** in Australia, or 08/8943 8888. Fax 08/8943 8999. www.mgmgrand.com.au. 96 units. A$196 (U.S.$107.80) double; A$299–$700 (U.S.$164.45–$385) suite. Extra person A$44 (U.S.$24.20). Children under 14 stay free in parents' room with existing bedding. AE, DC, MC, V. Free valet and self-parking. Bus: 4, 6. **Amenities:** 3 restaurants (Asian, Modern Australian, cafe-style), 4 bars, nightclub; outdoor swimming pool; children's pool; exercise room; Jacuzzi; sauna; concierge; tour desk; business center; 24-hr. room service; massage; babysitting; laundry; same-day dry-cleaning/ laundry service. *In room:* A/C, TV with pay movies, minibar, hair dryer, iron.

Saville Park Suites Darwin ☆☆ This recently built (1998) eight-floor hotel and apartment complex, in town a block from Smith St. Mall and overlooking the Esplanade, is one of Darwin's most comfortable, elegant lodgings. Lime green, turquoise and sunny yellow lobby armchairs shout up-to-the-minute style, carried over in a more muted way in the contemporary-style rooms (mostly spacious studio, one-, two- or three-bedroom apartments, serviced daily, with a kitchen and internal laundry). Those on the higher floors have sea views. A pantry stocking service does your grocery shopping. "Premium" apartments have CD players and dataports, and you can request a Nintendo playstation. There are also hotel rooms, lacking a balcony but still a good size.

88 The Esplanade at Peel St., Darwin, NT 0800. ✆ **1800/681 686** in Australia or 08/8943 4333. Fax 08/8943 4388. www.savillesuites.com.au. 204 units. A$163 (U.S.$89.65) double; A$179.50 (U.S.$98.75) studio apt; A$190–$218 (U.S.$104.50–$119.90) 1-bedroom apt; A$300–$327.50 (U.S.$165–$180.15) 2-bedroom apt;

Tips Where Can I Swim?

It makes you sigh, but crocodiles render Darwin's lovely beaches a no-swim zone year-round. Locals sunbathe on Casuarina Beach, and swim within view of the sea in Lake Alexander on Alec Fong Lim Drive in East Point Reserve. It's that or hit the hotel pool!

A$355–$382.50 (U.S.$195.25–$210.40) 3-bedroom apt. Additional person A$27.50 (U.S.$15.15). Children under 15 stay free in parents' room with existing bedding. AE, DC, MC, V. Free parking. **Amenities:** Restaurant, bar; outdoor swimming pool; Jacuzzi; bike rental; concierge; tour desk; secretarial services; salon; limited room service; babysitting; same-day dry-cleaning/laundry service. _In room:_ A/C, TV with pay movies, kitchen (in apartments), minibar, hair dryer, iron.

MODERATE

Mirambeena Tourist Resort   You're just a stone's throw (a quarter of a mile's walk) from the city center at this modern hotel complex, where the tempting swimming pools, the Jacuzzis, and the treetop restaurant, all shaded by the leaves of a sprawling strangler fig, have a castaway island feel. All rooms were refurbished in 1998 to a high standard; each is a decent size and has some kind of garden or pool view. Town houses with kitchenettes are good for families, if you can handle sharing the compact bathroom with your kids.

64 Cavenagh St., Darwin, NT 0800. © **1800/891 100** in Australia, or 08/8946 0111. Fax 08/8981 5116. www.mirambeena.com.au. 225 units (all with shower only). High season (Apr–Sept) A$152–$195 (U.S.$83.60–$107.25) double; A$230 (U.S.$126.50) town house (sleeps 4). Low season (Oct–Mar) A$117–$148 (U.S.$64.35–$81.40) double; A$180 (U.S.$99) town house. Extra person A$25 (U.S.$13.75). Children under 3 stay free. AE, DC, MC, V. Free parking for limited cars, plus on-street parking. Bus: 4, 5, 6, 8, or 10. **Amenities:** Restaurant, poolside cafe, 2 bars; 2 outdoor swimming pools (in a single complex); children's pool; exercise room; 2 Jacuzzis; bike rental; game room; minigolf; tour desk; secretarial services; limited room service; babysitting; laundry; same-day dry cleaning/laundry service. _In room:_ A/C, TV with free movies, minibar (on request), fridge, hair dryer, iron, safe.

The Summer House _(★★ (Finds_   A groovy, stylish tropical hideaway is a rare thing in the rough-and-ready Territory, but that's what Jill Farrand has created in her home in this converted apartment block. The place is in a leafy suburb 3 kilometers (2 miles) from town, on the local bus route, or a $2 shuttle ride away. Two roomy suites sport white walls, trendy polished concrete floors, and wrought-iron furniture (one has giant Balinese armchairs and 3-meter-/10-ft.-high exotic flower arrangements), while a third has a retro look. All have louvered windows to encourage a breeze, hip mosaic bathrooms, and one or two bedrooms, a living area, and a kitchenette. VCRs are available. Jill delivers a nice continental breakfast. A Jacuzzi in the jungly garden is great for cooling off on hot nights. Gay and lesbian guests are welcome. No smoking indoors.

3 Quarry Crescent, Stuart Park (P.O. Box 104, Parap, NT 0820). © **08/8981 9992.** Fax 08/8981 0009. www.bed-and-breakfast.au.com/SummerHouseBandB.htm (note: not "com.au"). 3 units (all with shower only). A$140 (U.S.$77) double; A$220 (U.S.$121) 2-bedroom apt (sleeps 4). Rates include continental breakfast. Rates without breakfast A$120 (U.S.$66) double; A$180 (U.S.$99) apt. AE, MC, V. Free parking. Bus: 5, 6, 8, or 10. From the airport, take the Stuart Hwy. 5km (3 miles) to Stuart Park; turn left onto Woolner Rd., immediately right onto Iliffe St., right onto Armidale St., and immediately left onto Quarry Crescent. **Amenities:** Jacuzzi, laundry. _In room:_ A/C, TV, kitchenette, hair dryer, iron, no phone.

INEXPENSIVE

Top End Hotel   This two-story Best Western hotel has a quiet ambience, despite the trendy complex of bars, restaurant, sports-betting outlets, and a liquor store on one side. Most of the rooms face a rectangular saltwater swimming pool surrounded by an inviting lawn, sun lounges, and tall palms rather than the bar complex. The front desk sells breakfast and dinner meat packs for you to cook up on the barbie. Rooms were renovated in 2000, and each is a good size, with quality fittings, and a furnished patio or balcony. You're just across the road from the Esplanade (where fish come in to shore at high tide to be handfed by visitors), close to restaurants, and a 1-kilometer (half-mile) stroll from Smith Street Mall.

Mitchell St. at Daly St., Darwin, NT 0801. ℂ 1800/626 151 in Australia, or 08/8981 6511. Fax 08/8941 1253. www.bestwestern.com.au. 40 units (all with shower only). Dry Season A$121 (U.S.$66.55) double; A$132 (U.S.$72.60) triple. Wet Season A$115 (U.S.$63.25) double; A$125 (U.S.$68.75) triple. Extra person A$20 (U.S.$11) in Dry, A$10 (U.S.$5.50) in Wet. AE, DC, MC, V. Free parking. Bus: 4, 5, 6, 8, or 10. **Amenities:** Restaurant, 3 bars; outdoor swimming pool; tour desk; room service at breakfast; babysitting; laundry; same-day dry cleaning/laundry service. *In room:* A/C, TV w/ free movies, fridge.

Value Inn *(Value* The cheerful rooms at this neat little hotel in the Mitchell Street Tourist Precinct are extremely compact but tidy, and have colorful modern fittings. Each room is just big enough to hold both a queen-size and a single bed, and a small writing table. The views aren't much, but you'll probably spend your time in the cafes along the street. Smith Street Mall and the Esplanade walking path are 2 blocks away. There are a public pay phone, a coffee vending machine and an iron on each floor, and a teensy garden swimming pool off the car park.

50 Mitchell St., Darwin, NT 0800. ℂ 08/8981 4733. Fax 08/8981 4730. www.valueinn.com.au. 93 units (all with shower only). Dry Season A$77 (U.S.$42.35) double. Wet Season A$60 (U.S.$3.30) double. No charge for extra person. AE, MC, V. Limited free parking. **Amenities:** Outdoor swimming pool. *In room:* A/C, TV, fridge, no phone.

WHERE TO DINE

Cullen Bay Marina, a 25-minute walk from town or a short cab ride, is packed with cool restaurants and cafes. If it's Thursday, don't even think about eating anywhere other than the **Mindil Beach Sunset Market** ⭐⭐ (see the box, "Cheap Eats & More!"). The cool crowd hangs at **Roma Bar,** 30 Cavenagh St. (ℂ 08/8981 6729), for good coffee and cheap nosh; it's open from 7am to 5pm Monday through Friday, from 8am to 2pm weekends.

EXPENSIVE

Buzz Café ⭐⭐ MODERN AUSTRALIAN   Local movers and shakers come to this busy outdoor venue to move, shake, and enjoy the terrific views over the marina from the deck. There are some more terrific views from inside the men's bathroom (no, I don't mean views of the guys—girls, get a male to take you in there and see what I mean!). The food is flavorsome East-meets-West fare like jungle curry of chicken with snake beans and green peppercorns, or pan-fried barramundi on potato mash in a lemon butter sauce; the rib-eye fillet steak is a good choice. Lots of folks wash it down with a cocktail (try the mango daiquiris).

At the Cullen Bay Marina. ℂ 08/8941 1141. Reservations recommended in the Dry. Main courses A$16.50–$28.50 (U.S.$9.10–$15.70); "nothing over A$15 (U.S.$8.25)" lunch menu Mon–Fri. AE, DC, MC, V. Mon–Fri noon–2am, Sat–Sun 10:30am–2am (including brunch). Bus: 4 or 6.

Hanuman Thai ⭐⭐ CONTEMPORARY THAI/NONYA/ TANDOORI Sporting elegant black walls, this city restaurant works hard as a business-lunch venue by day and as a popular rendezvous for couples, families, and more business folk by night. You can rely on it to serve up sophisticated dishes cooked with skill, such as marinated chicken wrapped in pandan leaves with a mild chili and malt sugar sauce, and grilled local Gulf prawns with a sauce of crushed coriander and coconut milk sprinkled with kaffir lime leaf julienne. There is also a separate tandoori menu. Service is prompt and polite.

28 Mitchell St. ℭ **08/8941 3500**. Reservations recommended. Main courses A$16.50–$23.10 (U.S.$9.10–$12.70). AE, DC, MC, V. Mon–Fri noon–2:30pm; daily 6:30–10:30 or 11pm.

Pee Wee's Beachfront Café ✿ MODERN AUSTRALIAN   Surrounded on three sides by jungly forest, this modern steel-and-glass venue affords views of the turquoise Fannie Bay from just about every table, inside, out on the deck, or down on the lawn. The place mixes sophisticated meals with a laid-back ordering system where you check your selections off the menu and hand it in, then the waitstaff bring your meal to the table. Some of the dishes have a Creole twist—like Cajun-spiced porterhouse steak with mango curry crème fraîche. Many appetizers, like the mushroom risotto or the Thai squid salad, can be ordered in a main course portion. Try to arrive in time to watch the sun set.

Alec Fong Lim Dr., East Point Reserve (4km/2½ miles from town). ℭ **08/8981 6868**. Reservations recommended. Main courses A$17.50–$24 (U.S.$9.65–$13.20). AE, DC, MC, V. Daily 6pm to late; call for opening hours for lunch (Dry Season only). No bus; a cab fare from the city is about A$15 (U.S.$8.25).

MODERATE
Shenannigan's Irish Pub, Restaurant & Bar ✿ IRISH PUB FARE   Hearty Irish stews and braised beef and Guinness pies (plus the odd pint of Guinness itself) gets everyone in the mood for eating, talking, and dancing at this convivial bar/restaurant. A friendly mix of solo travelers, families, seniors, and backpackers eat and drink in atmospheric wooden booths, standing up at bar tables, or by the fire. As well as hearty meat dishes, there is lighter stuff like salmon salad or vegetarian brochettes, and nightly specials, such as chicken and chili pasta or poached barramundi in white wine sauce with fries and salad.

69 Mitchell St. at Peel St. ℭ **08/8981 2100**. Reservations recommended. Daily specials A$9.50–$14 (U.S.$5.25–$7.70). Main courses A$8.80–$19.80 (U.S.$4.85–$10.90). AE, DC, DISC, MC, V. Meals daily noon–2:30pm; 6–9pm (snack menu 3–5:30pm); bar open daily 11am–2am.

⟨ *Value* **Cheap Eats & More!**

If it's Thursday, join the entire city (well, 8,000 locals, anyhow) at the **Mindil Beach Sunset Market** ✿✿ to feast at the 60 terrific (and cheap!) Asian, Greek, Italian and Aussie food stalls, listen to live musicians, wander among almost 200 arts-and-crafts stalls, and mix and mingle with the masseurs, tarot-card readers, and street performers as the sun sets into the sea. The action runs from 5 to 10pm in the Dry (approximately May–Oct). A smaller market of about 50 stalls runs Sunday between about mid-May and late September from 4 to 9pm. The markets' season changes from year to year, so if you're visiting Darwin on the seasonal cusp in April or September, check whether they have started or ended by calling the organizers (ℭ **08/8981 3454**). The beach is about a A$7.50 (U.S.$4.15) cab ride from town, or take bus no. 4, or call the **Territory Shuttle** (ℭ **08/8928 1155**), which charges A$2 (U.S.$1.10) per person from downtown. The Tour Tub's last run of the day at 4pm (see "Getting Around," earlier in the chapter) goes by the markets.

⌒ *Moments* Lizards and Sunsets

A good spot to catch Darwin's Technicolor sunsets is the super-casual **Darwin Sailing Club,** Atkins Drive on Fannie Bay (© **08/8981 1700**). Ask the manager to sign you in. Dine on affordable meals outdoors while a family of goannas (monitor lizards) swirls around your feet looking for meaty scraps (told you it was casual). The bar is open from 10am until midnight, and until 2am Friday and Saturday. The cafes and restaurants of **Cullen Bay Marina** are a good place to be day or night, but especially for Dry Season sunsets. If it's Thursday, you are mad to be anywhere except the **Mindil Beach Sunset Markets** ⭐⭐ (described earlier).

INEXPENSIVE

The Noodle House CHINESE Twenty Aussie bucks will buy you a huge feed at this unpretentious eatery just around the corner from Smith Street Mall. Tummy-fillers like pineapple-and-chicken fried rice or shredded-beef fried rice are especially cheap. The long menu lists many meat dishes, such as Szechuan beef or chicken and roast duck, and there are the usual Chinese soup suspects. The decor isn't the stuff of romance, but the place has a friendly atmosphere. BYO.

33 Knuckey St. © 08/8941 1742. Main courses A$7.70–$22 (U.S.$4.25–$12.10); most approx. A$12 (U.S.$6.60). AE, MC, V. Mon–Sat 11am–2pm; daily 6–10pm.

Tim's Surf 'n' Turf ⭐ *Value* STEAK/SEAFOOD Locals fairly bash down the door to get into this unpretentious restaurant housed under a cheap motel on the city fringe. The modest surroundings are not the attraction, so what is? Hearty, no-nonsense food cooked well, and served in portions big enough to feed an army. No namby-pamby steaks here—Tim's steaks are monsters up to 700 grams (25½ oz.), over an inch thick, and grain-fed (a boon in Australia, where the beef is mostly grass-fed and hence a little chewy). Garlic prawns, crocodile schnitzel, lasagna, oysters, quiche, and roast of the day are typical menu items. There are meals for kids, too. A second Tim's on the Bay at Cullen Bay (© **08/8981 4666**) serves hearty buffets for A$25 (U.S.$13.75) adults; kids pay A$1 (U.S.55¢) for every year of their age up to 14.

In the Asti Motel, Smith St. at Packard Place. © 08/8981 9979. Main courses A$7–$21 (U.S.$3.85–$11.55) (many dishes around A$12/U.S.$6.60); seafood platter for 2 A$28.50 (U.S.$15.70). MC, V. Daily 7–9:30am, noon–2pm, and 5:30–9:30pm. Bus: 4 or 6.

DARWIN AFTER DARK

Lie back in a deckchair at the **Deckchair Cinema** (© **08/8981 0700**) to watch Aussie hits, foreign films, and cult classics under the stars. Movies are screened Wednesday through Sunday in the Dry (Apr or May–Oct or Nov) with late sessions Friday and Saturday nights. It is off Mavie Street behind Old Stokes Hill Power Station near the Wharf (about a 20-min. walk from the center of town). Tickets are A$12 (U.S.$6.60).

The gaming tables at the **MGM Grand Casino,** Gilruth Avenue, Mindil Beach (© **08/8943 8888**), are in play from noon until 3:30am, until 5:30am Saturday and Sunday. Slot machines are in play 24 hours. The dress regulation allows neat jeans, shorts and sneakers, but men's shirts must have a collar. **Sweetheart's,** also in the MGM Grand, is a popular nightclub attracting ages 18 to 45.

A SIDE TRIP TO LITCHFIELD NATIONAL PARK 🏍🏍
120km (74 miles) S of Darwin

An easy 90-minute drive south of Darwin is a miniature Garden of Eden full of forests, waterfalls, rocky sandstone escarpments, glorious swimming holes, and prehistoric cycads that look like they walked off the set of Jurassic Park. Litchfield National Park is much smaller (a mere 146,000 hectares/360,620 acres) and much less famous than its big sister, Kakadu, yet most folks would say it is prettier.

The park's main attractions are the spring-fed swimming holes, like the magical plunge pool at **Florence Falls** 🏍🏍🏍, 29 kilometers (18 miles) from the forest. It's quite a 15-minute hike down stairs to the water, so the easily accessible pool at **Wangi Falls** 🏍, 49 kilometers (30 miles) from the eastern entrance, actually gets more crowds (it's another beautiful spot, surrounded by cliffs and forests with a pretty viewpoint from the top). More idyllic swimming grottos are to be had 4 kilometers (2½ miles) from Florence Falls at **Buley Rockhole,** a series of cute birdbath-like rock holes and waterfalls. You can't swim at Tolmer Falls, but during the Wet when they're flowing, take the boardwalk about 400meters (1,312 ft.) to the lookout and see the falls cascade down red cliffs.

There are a number of manageably short walking trails through the park, too, such as the half-hour Shady Creek Circuit from Florence Falls up to the car park.

Parts of the park are also home to thousands of **"magnetic" termite mounds** 2 meters (6.5 ft.) high, so called because they run north-south to escape the fierce midday heat. There is a display hut about them and a viewing point 17 kilometers (10½ miles) from the park's eastern entrance.

Most of the park's swimming holes are regarded as crocodile-free; the same is *not* true of the Finniss and Reynolds rivers in the park, so no leaping into those!

To get there from Darwin, head south for 86 kilometers (53 miles) on the Stuart Highway and follow the park turnoff on the right through the town of Batchelor for 34 kilometers (21 miles). A number of minicoach and four-wheel-drive day trips run from Darwin. Katherine-based tour operator **Travel North** (© **1800/089 103** in Australia, or 08/8971 9999) runs a day tour to Litchfield that starts in Darwin and ends in Katherine, which is a convenient way to combine sightseeing and transport if you plan to visit both towns. Crowds of local Darwinites can shatter the peace on weekends, especially in the Dry season, but the park is still worth visiting on a Saturday or Sunday, crowds or no crowds.

The **Parks & Wildlife Commission** district office in Batchelor, on the corner of Nurdina Street and Pinaroo Crescent (© **08/8976 0282**), has maps and information; most locations of interest in the park have signboards. Entry to the park is free.

Roads to most swimming holes in the park are paved, although a few areas are accessible only by four-wheel-drive. In the Wet Season (approximately Nov–Apr), some roads in the park may be closed, usually the four-wheel-drive ones, and the Wangi water hole may be off-limits due to turbulence and strong currents. Check with the Parks & Wildlife Commission office before you leave Darwin during this time.

There are simple campsites at a number of locations throughout the park. The camping fee is A$6.60 (U.S.$3.65) for adults, A$3.30 (U.S.$1.80) for kids under 16. A kiosk at Wangi Falls sells basic supplies, but stock up on fuel and alcohol in Batchelor.

3 Kakadu National Park ⊛

257km (159 miles) E of Darwin

Kakadu National Park ⊛, a World Heritage area, is Australia's largest national park at whopping 1,755,200 hectares (4,335,344 acres).

Cruising the lily-clad wetlands to spot fearsome crocodiles, plunging into exquisite natural swimming holes, hiking through spear grass and cycads, fishing for prized barramundi, soaring in a light aircraft over torrential waterfalls during the Wet Season, photographing the thousands of birds flying over the eerie red sandstone escarpment that juts 200 meters (650 ft.) above the floodplain, and admiring some of Australia's most superb Aboriginal rock-art sites—these are the activities that draw people to Kakadu. Some 275 species of birds and 75 species of reptiles inhabit the park, making it one of the richest wildlife habitats in the country. To nature-loving Aussies, Kakadu is a true ecological jewel. So it is, but be aware that the hefty distances between points of interest in the park, and that sameness that infects so much Australian landscape, can detract from Kakadu's appeal for some folks. Wildlife here is not the breathtaking equivalent of an African game park, where herds roam the plains. It is best in the late Dry around September and October, when crocs and birds gather around shrinking water-holes. Wildlife viewing is not particularly good in the Wet Season, when birds disperse widely and you may not see a single croc.

The name "Kakadu" comes from "Gagudju," the group of languages spoken in the northern part of the park. It is thought that Aboriginal people have lived in this part of the world for 50,000 years. Today, Aborigines manage the park as its owners, in conjunction with the Australian government. This is one of the few places in Australia where some Aborigines stick to a fairly traditional lifestyle of hunting and living off the land. You won't see them, because they keep away from prying eyes, but their culture is on display at a cultural center and at rock-art sites. Kakadu and the vast wilds of Arnhemland to the east are the birth-place of the "x-ray" style of art for which Aboriginal artists are famous.

JUST THE FACTS
VISITOR INFORMATION   Both of the park entrances—the northern station on the Arnhem Highway used by visitors from Darwin and the southern station on the Kakadu Highway for visitors from Katherine—hand out free visitor guides with maps, and in the Dry they issue a timetable of free ranger-guided bushwalks, art-site talks, and slide shows taking place that week.

Park headquarters is at the **Bowali Visitor Centre** (✆ **08/8938 1120**) on the Kakadu Highway, 5 kilometers (3 miles) from Jabiru, 100 kilometers (62 miles) from the northern entry station, and 131 kilometers (81 miles) from the southern entry station. This architecturally attractive, environmentally friendly Outback-style center shows a running program of good 1-hour videos on the park's natural history and Aboriginal culture, stocks maps and free park notes, has a library and interesting displays, has information officers on hand to help you plan your visit (they provide tour times, costs and contact telephone numbers, but do not make bookings), and has a gift shop and a cafe. You may want to spend a good hour or so here, more to see a video. It is open daily from 8am to 5pm.

You can also book tours and get information at the **Jabiru Travel Centre,** Shop 6, Tasman Plaza, Jabiru, NT 0886 (✆ **08/8979 2548;** wendymchugh@ bigpond.com.au).

Before you arrive, you can find information on Kakadu, and book tours to it, at the Tourism Top End visitor information centre in Darwin. You can also contact the rangers at **Kakadu National Park** (© **08/8938 1120;** KakaduNationalPark@ea.gov.au). A Kakadu website was under construction as we wrote; the only other website for visitors to the park is the Northern Territory Tourist Commission's site at **www.ntholidays.com**, but it has only limited details.

WHEN TO GO   Kakadu has two distinct seasons: Wet and Dry. The Dry Season May through October is overwhelmingly the best time to go, thanks to temperatures around 30°C (86°F) and sunny days. Many tours, hotels, and even campsites are booked out a year in advance at this time, so don't travel without reservations.

In the Wet Season, November through April, floodwaters cover much of the park, some attractions are cut off all season or unexpectedly for days, and the heat and humidity are extreme. Some tour companies do not run during the Wet, and ranger talks, walks, and slide shows are not offered. The upside is that the crowds vanish, the brownish vegetation bursts into green, waterfalls swell from a trickle to a roar, and lightning storms are spectacular, especially in the very hot "build-up" to the season in October and November. The landscape can change dramatically from one day to the next as floodwaters rise and fall, so be prepared for surprises, both nice ones (like giant flocks of geese that are here today, gone tomorrow) and unwelcome ones (like blocked roads). Although it can pour down all day, it's more common for the rain to fall in late-afternoon storms and at night. Take it easy in the humidity and don't even think about camping in this heat—stay in air-conditioned accommodations.

GETTING THERE   Follow the Stuart Highway 34 kilometers (21 miles) south of Darwin, and turn left onto the Arnhem Highway all the way to the park's northern entrance station. The trip takes 2½ to 3 hours. If you're coming from the south, turn off the Stuart Highway at Pine Creek onto the Kakadu Highway, and follow the Kakadu Highway for 79 kilometers (49 miles) to the park's southern entrance station. **Greyhound Pioneer** (© **13 2030** in Australia) makes a daily run from Darwin stopping at Jabiru, Cooinda, and all park accommodations for A$40.70 (U.S.$22.40).

A big range of coach, minibus, and four-wheel-drive tours and camping safaris usually taking 1, 2 or 3 days depart from Darwin every day. These are a good idea, because many of Kakadu's geological, ecological, and Aboriginal attractions come to life only with a guide, and the best water holes, lookouts, and wildlife-viewing spots change dramatically from month to month, even from day to day.

FEES & REGULATIONS   The park entry fee of A$16.25 (U.S.$8.95) per adult is valid for 14 days. Children 15 and under enter free.

LOGISTICAL TIPS   Kakadu is a big place—about 200 kilometers (124 miles) long by 100 kilometers (62 miles) wide—so spend at least a night. Day trips are available from Darwin, but it's too far and too big to see much in a day.

Most major attractions are accessible in a conventional two-wheel-drive vehicle on sealed (paved) roads, but a four-wheel-drive vehicle allows you to get to more falls, water holes, and campsites. Car-rental companies will not permit you to take two-wheel-drive vehicles on unpaved roads. **Thrifty** (© **08/8979 2552**) rents cars at the Gagudju Crocodile Holiday Inn; otherwise, rent a car in Darwin. If you four-wheel-drive it in the Wet Season (Nov–Apr), always check

(Tips   Never Smile at a You-Know-What

The Aboriginal Gagudju people of the Top End have long worshipped a giant crocodile called Ginga, but the way white Australians go on about these reptilian relics of a primeval age, you'd think they worshipped 'em, too. There is scarcely a soul in the Northern Territory who will not earbash you with his or her own particular croc story, and each one you hear will be weirder and taller than the last.

Aussies may be good at pulling your leg with tall tales, but when they warn you not to swim in crocodile country, they're not kidding. After all, crocodiles are good at pulling your leg, too—literally. Here are some tips:

1. There are two kinds of crocs in Australia, the highly dangerous and enormously powerful saltwater or "estuarine" kind, and the "harmless" freshwater kind, which will attack only if threatened or accidentally stood on. Saltwater crocs can and do swim in the ocean, but live in fresh water.
2. Don't swim in *any* waterway, swimming hole, or waterfall unless you have been specifically told that it is safe. Take advice only from someone authoritative like a recognized tour operator or a park ranger. You can never be sure where these critters lurk from year to year, because every Wet Season crocs head upriver to breed and spread out over a wide flooded area. As the floodwaters subside in the Dry, they are trapped in whatever waterway they happen to be in at the time—so what was a safe swimming hole last Dry Season might not be so croc-free this year.
3. Never stand on or walk along a riverbank, and stand well back when fishing. A 20-foot croc can be 1 inch beneath the surface of that muddy water yet remain utterly invisible. He moves fast, so you won't see him until you're in his jaws.
4. Plant your campsite and clean fish at least 25 meters (82 ft.) back from the bank.

And if you come face to face with a crocodile? There is little you can do. Just don't get into this situation in the first place!

floodwater levels on all roads, paved and unpaved, at the **Bowali Visitor Centre** (✆ **08/8938 1120**). The Bowali Visitor Centre, many main attractions such as Nourlangie and Yellow Water Billabong, and the towns of Jabiru and Cooinda usually stay above the floodwaters year-round.

Facilities are limited. The only town of any size is **Jabiru** (pop. 1,455), a mining community where you can find banking facilities. The only other real settlements are the park's four accommodation houses.

SEEING THE HIGHLIGHTS
EN ROUTE TO KAKADU

En route to the park, stop in at the lovely **Fogg Dam Conservation Reserve** (✆ **08/8988 8009** is the ranger station), 25 kilometers (15½ miles) down the Arnhem Highway plus 7 kilometers (4 miles) off the highway. Here you'll get a close-up look at geese, finches, ibis, brolgas, and other wetland birds from look-outs looking over ponds of giant lilies, or leading through monsoon forests to viewing blinds. There are two lookouts on the road, and three walks, two at 2.2 kilometer (1½ miles) round-trip, and one at 3.6 kilometer (2¼ miles) round-trip. Entry is free every day of the year. (Crocs live here, so don't swim, and keep well away from the water's edge).

Four kilometers (2½ miles) down the Arnhem Highway at Beatrice Hill, you may want to stop at the **Window on the Wetlands Visitor Centre** (© **08/8988 8188**), a hilltop center with views across the Adelaide River floodplain and dis-plays and touch-screen information on the wetlands' ecology. It's free and open daily from 7:30am to 7:30pm.

Just past Beatrice Hill on the highway at the Adelaide River (you can't miss the statue of a grinning croc), you can join the **Original Jumping Crocodiles cruise** (© **08/8988 8144**) aboard the Adelaide River Queen to watch wild croc-odiles leap out of the water for hunks of meat dangled over the edge by the boat crew. While some eco-tourists disapprove of making the animals "perform" for food, crocs typically only move fast when they attack or eat, so you're unlikely to witness their immense power unless you take this cruise. Reader Mari Fagin of Okla-

---

A Bird-Watching Tip

Early morning and late after-noon are the best times for bird watching, when the birds flock to water holes to drink.

---

homa City, Oklahoma, says it was one of the highlights of her Australian vaca-tion. "After seeing little crocodile 'action' on our Yellow Waters Cruise, it was awesome and a bit sobering to see the speed and agility of these monsters in pur-suit of food," she writes. The 90-minute cruise departs 9, 11am, 1, and 3pm May through August, and 9, 11am, and 2:30pm September through April (closed Dec 24 and 25). It costs A$33 (U.S.$18.15) for adults, and A$18 (U.S.$9.90) for children 5 to 15.

TOP PARK ATTRACTIONS

WETLANDS CRUISES One of the biggest attractions in the park is **Yellow Water Billabong,** a lake 50 kilometers (31 miles) south of the Bowali Visitor Centre at Cooinda (pop. 20). It's rich with freshwater mangroves, paperbarks, pandanus palms, water lilies, and swathes of birds gathering here to drink—sea eagles, honking magpie geese, kites, china blue kingfishers, and jacanas, called "Jesus birds" because they seem to walk on water as they step across the lily pads. This is also one of the best places in the park to spot saltwater crocs. Cruises in canopied boats with a running commentary depart near Gagudju Lodge Cooinda six times a day from 6:45am in the Dry (May–Nov) and 7am in the Wet (Dec–Apr). A 90-minute cruise costs A$33 (U.S.$18.15) for adults and A$15 (U.S.$8.25) for children 2 to 14. A 2-hour cruise (available in the Dry only) costs A$38 (U.S.$20.90) for adults and A$16.50 (U.S.$9.10) for children. Book through **Gagudju Lodge Cooinda** (see "Where to Stay & Dine," below).

In the Wet, when the Billabong floods to join up with Jim Jim Creek and the South Alligator River, the bird life spreads far and wide over the park and the crocs head upriver to breed, so don't expect wildlife viewing to be spectacular.

Another good cruise is the **Guluyambi Aboriginal Culture Tour** (© **1800/ 089 113** in Australia, or 08/8979 2411 for booking agent Kakadu Tours) on the East Alligator River, which forms the border between Kakadu and isolated Arnhemland. Unlike the Yellow Water journey, which focuses on crocs, birds, and plants, this cruise tells you about Aboriginal myths, bush tucker, and hunting techniques. The cruise lasts 1 hour and 45 minutes and leaves at 9, 11am, 1, and 3pm daily May through October. The schedule shifts to a half-day cruise on the Magela Creek system late in the Wet (usually not until Feb 1, floodwaters permitting), with a climb of Ubirr Rock thrown in. Transportation to the boat in the Dry Season is not included, so you will need to get yourself to the departure point; in the Wet, the trip picks up from the Gagudju Crocodile Holiday Inn at 10am. The Dry cruise costs A$30 (U.S.$16.50) for adults and A$15 (U.S.$8.25) for children 4 to 14. The Wet cruise costs A$80 (U.S.$44) per person, A$65 (U.S.$35.75) for kids.

ABORIGINAL ART & CULTURE   There are as many as 5,000 art sites throughout the park, though for cultural reasons, the Aboriginal owners make only a few accessible to visitors. Although dating such old paintings is always controversial, it is thought some paintings may be 50,000 years old. The two best are **Nourlangie Rock** and **Ubirr Rock.** Nourlangie, 31 kilometers (19 miles) southeast of the Bowali Visitor Centre, features "x-ray" style paintings of animals and a vivid, energetic striped Dreamtime figure of **Namarrgon** ☆, the "Lightning Man," and modern depictions of a white man in cowboy boots, a rifle, and a sailing ship. You'll also find rock paintings at **Nanguluwur,** on the other side of Nourlangie Rock, and a variety of excellent art sites at Ubirr Rock, which is worth the 250-meter (820-ft.) steep climb for the additional art sites higher up the cliff, and for the views of the floodplain.

Ubirr Rock can be cut off in the Wet, but the views of afternoon lightning storms from the top at that time are breathtaking.

Unlike most sites in Kakadu, Ubirr is not open 24 hours—it opens at 8:30am April through November and at 2pm December through March, and closes every day at sunset. There is a 1.5-kilometer (1-mile) signposted trail past Nourlangie's paintings (short trails into the art sites shoot off it), an easy 1.7-kilometer (1-mile) trail from the carpark into Nanguluwur, and a 1-kilometer (0.6-mile) circuit track at Ubirr. Access to all of these sites is free.

Displays and videos of the bush tucker, Dreamtime creation myths, and lifestyles of the local Bininj Aboriginal people are on show at the **Warradjan Aboriginal Cultural Centre** ☆ (✆ **08/8979 0051**) at Cooinda. This circular building was built in the shape of a pig-nose turtle at the direction of the Aboriginal owners. There are also a quality gift shop selling items like didgeridoos, bark paintings by local Aboriginal artists, and baskets woven from pandanus fronds. The center is open from 9am to 5pm daily, and admission is free. It is connected to Gagudju Lodge Cooinda and the Yellow Water Billabong by a 1-kilometer (½-mile) trail.

SCENIC FLIGHTS   Scenic flights over the floodplains and the surprising rain-forest-filled ravines of the escarpment are worth doing if the strain is not too great on your wallet. They're much more interesting in the Wet than the Dry, when the floodplains spread and Jim Jim Falls and Twin Falls swell from their Dry Season trickle to a roaring flood. They are no match for, say, Niagara Falls, but they are impressive nonetheless. From the air is also the best way to appreciate the clever crocodile shape of the Gagudju Crocodile Holiday Inn. **North Australian Helicopters** (✆ **1800/898 977** in Australia, or 08/8972 1666) does flights from Jabiru from A$137.50 (U.S.$75.65), but to see Jim Jim and Twin Falls, you must take the flight costing A$412.50 (U.S.$226.90) per person. **Kakadu Air** (✆ **1800/089 113** in Australia, or 08/8979 2411) does fixed-wing flights from Jabiru and Cooinda for A$75 (U.S.$41.25) per person for 30 minutes, or A$125 (U.S.$68.75) per person for an hour.

SWIMMING, FISHING & BUSHWALKING IN THE PARK

In the eastern section of the park rises a massive red sandstone escarpment that sets the stage for two waterfalls, **Jim Jim Falls** and **Twin Falls.** In the Dry, the volume of water may not be all that impressive, but their settings are magical. Both are accessible by four-wheel-drive only, and neither is open in the Wet.

WHERE CAN I SWIM?

Folk swim at spots that are generally regarded as croc-free, such as Jim Jim, Twin Falls, and other water holes, such as Gubara (it's a long walk to it, but it can be lovely in the Wet), Maguk, and Koolpin Gorge. However, you do so at your own risk. Although rangers survey the swimming holes at the start of the season, and crocodiles are in any case territorial creatures that stick to one spot and rarely leave the water, there can never be an ironclad guarantee that a saltwater crocodile has not moved into a popular swimming hole. A good indication that the hole is croc-free is the presence of many other people already swimming in the water hole. Crocs tend to eat whatever's going pretty much immediately, so if there are people swimming happily, the pool is almost certainly croc-free! Macabre it may be, but it's a tool many people use to gauge a pool's safety. Ask at the Bowali Visitor Centre which pools are croc-free that year (it can change from year to year) before setting off into the park. If you are unsure about a water hole's safety, the only place rangers recommend you swim is your hotel pool. Water hole depths change dramatically with the season; some that are great swimming in the Wet might be too shrunken in the Dry, for example. Check with the Bowali Visitor Centre for the swimming spots that are best at the time you visit.

A 1-kilometer (½-mile) walk over rocks and through rain forest leads to a **deep green plunge pool** ⊛ at Jim Jim Falls, 103 kilometers (64 miles) from the Bowali Visitor Centre. The water is wrapped by an almost perfectly circular 150-meter (490-ft.) cliff. Allow 2 hours to drive the final 60 unpaved kilometers (37 miles) off the highway. Due to floodwaters, Jim Jim Falls may not open until as late as June. **Swimming** ⊛ at nearby Twin Falls is great, too. The falls descend into a natural pool edged by a sandy beach, surrounded by bush and high cliffs.

Kakadu Gorge and Waterfall Tours ⊛ (book through Gagudju Lodge Cooinda; ⊘ **08/8979 0145**) run an excellent small-group day trip to the falls for active people. You bushwalk into Jim Jim Falls for a swim and morning tea, four-wheel-drive through the bush, and then paddle in a tandem canoe past a "friendly" freshwater crocodile (the kind that does not typically attack humans) to Twin Falls for swimming and lunch. Tours depart daily from Jabiru and Cooinda May through November and cost A$130 (U.S.$71.50) for adults,

---

Moments A Swim in the Falls

Remember the idyllic pool that Paul Hogan and Linda Koslowski plunged into in *Crocodile Dundee?* That was **Gunlom Falls,** about 170 kilometers (105 miles) south of the Bowali Visitor Centre. A climb to the top of the falls rewards you with great views of southern Kakadu. It is generally regarded as croc-free, and therefore safe for swimming. Access is by four-wheel-drive only; it is cut off in the Wet.

(*Tips* **Bushwalking in Comfort**

Plan to walk in the early morning or late afternoon, especially during the Wet, because the heat dehydrates you quickly. To camp at an undesignated campsite on an overnight walk, you will need a permit from the rangers at the Bowali Visitor Centre, which can take a week to arrange.

A$110 (U.S.$60.50) for kids 4 to 14 (no kids under 4 allowed). Book in advance for July, the busiest month.

Kakadu's wetlands are brimful of barramundi, and there is nothing Territorians like more than to hop in a tin dinghy barely big enough to resist a croc attack and go looking for them. **Kakadu Fishing Tours** (book through **Gagudju Lodge Cooinda;** (© **08/8979 0145**) take you fishing in a 4.75-meter (15½-ft.) sportfishing boat. Tours depart from Jabiru, 5 kilometers (3 miles) east of the Bowali Visitor Centre, and cost A$120 (U.S.$66) per person for a half day (A$190/U.S.$104.50 if there is only one of you) and A$240 (U.S.$132) per person for a full day. They also do fly-fishing.

A wide-ranging collection of **bush and wetlands walking trails** lead throughout the park, including many short strolls and six half- to full-day treks. Typical trails include a 600-meter (less than ½-mile) amble through the Manngarre Monsoon Forest near Ubirr Rock, an easy 3.8-kilometer (2½-mile) circular walk at the Iligadjar Wetlands near the Bowali Visitor Centre, or a tough 12-kilometer (7½-mile) round-trip trek through rugged sandstone country at Nourlangie Rock.

One of the best wetlands walks is at **Mamukala wetlands,** 29 kilometers (18 miles) from Jabiru. Countless thousands of magpie geese feed here, especially in the late Dry Season around October. An observation platform gives you a good view of them, and a sign explains the dramatic seasonal changes the wetlands undergo. Choose from a 1-kilometer (0.6-mile) or 3-kilometer (1.8-mile) round-trip meander. The Bowali Visitor Centre sells hiking-trail maps. There are also some challenging unmarked trails along creeks and gorges, for which you will need good navigational skills.

CAMPING IN THE PARK

There are 16 national park campgrounds, all mostly near popular billabongs and wetlands, plus three commercial campgrounds attached to accommodation houses. Five of the national park campgrounds have hot showers and toilets; the rest are free "bush camps" with no showers and only basic toilets, or none. A ranger visits these campgrounds daily to collect a nightly fee of A$5.40 (U.S.$3) per person, free for kids under 16. Inquire at the park entry stations or at the Bowali Visitor Centre for a map marking campgrounds. To camp at undesignated campgrounds you will need a permit.

You need a four-wheel-drive to reach some national park campgrounds, and most are closed in the Wet.

WHERE TO STAY & DINE

High season is usually from April 1 to November 30.

Gagudju Crocodile Holiday Inn (ℛ   Some people think this hotel is gross kitsch; others declare it an architectural masterpiece. It was built to the specifications of its owners, the Gagudju Aboriginal people, in the form of their spirit ancestor, a giant crocodile called "Ginga." The building's entrance is the "jaws," the two floors of rooms are in the "belly," the circular car park clusters are "eggs," and so on. Love it or hate it, it is the most luxurious place to stay in Kakadu. Inside, it's a normal hotel with smallish but comfortable modern rooms (though I think the hair dryers could have been crocodile-shaped, too, don't you?). Guests can access the town's 9-hole golf course, tennis courts, and Olympic-size swimming pool a few blocks away. The lobby doubles as an art gallery selling the works of local Aborigines. The restaurant serves nice meals with a few native "bush tucker" ingredients thrown in. You are central to many Park attractions from here. A bush-walking trail leads to the Bowali Visitor Centre.

Flinders St. (5km/3 miles by road east of Bowali Visitor Centre), Jabiru, NT 0886. ℂ 1800/808 123 in Australia; or **Bass Hotels & Resorts**, 800/835 7742 in the U.S. and Canada, 0800/897 121 in the U.K., 1800/553 155 in Ireland, 0800/801 111 in New Zealand, or 08/8979 2800. Fax 08/8979 2707. www.basshotels.com. 110 units. A$330 (U.S.$181.50) double. Rates are often reduced in the Wet. Extra adult A$33 (U.S.$18.15). Children and teenagers under 20 stay free in parents' room with existing bedding. Free crib. AE, DC, MC, V. **Amenities:** Restaurant, 2 bars (1 serving pizza); small outdoor pool; tour desk; car-rental desk; secretarial services; 24-hr. room service; babysitting; laundry. *In room:* A/C, TV with free movies, minibar, hair dryer, iron.

Gagudju Lodge Cooinda   This modest but pleasant lodge set among tropical gardens is at the departure point for Yellow Water Billabong cruises. You will probably stay in the simply furnished tile-floor bungalows, which are big and comfortable. The front desk loans hair dryers and can arrange babysitting. There are also "budget rooms"—just bunk beds (four have double beds) in an air-conditioned corrugated iron demountable (portable cabin) with shared bathrooms. They rent on a "per bed" basis, so you may share with a stranger.

The lodge is something of a town center, so there is a general store, gift shop, currency exchange, post office, fuel, and other useful facilities. Cook up a 'roo steak in the nightly do-it-yourself barbecue in the satisfyingly rustic and ultra-casual Barra Bar & Bistro, or go for the bush tucker a la carte meals at lunch or dinner in **Mimi's** ℱ, which has a really nice "bush-sophisticated" ambience. The Barra Bistro does full buffet breakfast and an all-day snack menu, with live entertainment in the Dry Season. Scenic flights take off from the lodge's airstrip, and the Warradjan Aboriginal Cultural Centre is a 15-minute walk away.

Kakadu Hwy. (50km/31 miles south of Bowali Visitor Centre), Jim Jim, NT 0886. ℂ 1800/500 401 in Australia; or **Bass Hotels & Resorts**, 800/835 7742 in the U.S. and Canada, 0800/897 121 in the U.K., 1800/553 155 in Ireland, 0800/801 111 in New Zealand, or 08/8979 0145. Fax 08/8979 0148. www.sphc.com.au. 48 bungalows (all with shower only), 84 budget rooms (none with bathroom), 57 powered and 310 unpowered campsites. Bungalow A$198 (U.S.$108.90) double. Extra person A$27.50 (U.S.$15.15); children under 14 stay free. Budget room A$30.50 (U.S.$16.80) per bed. A$13 (U.S.$7.15) per adult, powered campsite; A$10 (U.S.$5.50) per adult, unpowered campsite. Children under 14 stay free in campsite. Rates in bungalows and budget rooms are often reduced in the Wet Season. AE, DC, MC, V. **Amenities:** Small outdoor pool; tour desk; laundry. *In room* (bungalows only): A/C, fridge.

4 Katherine

314km (196 miles) S of Darwin; 512km (320 miles) E of Kununurra; 1,177km (736 miles) N of Alice Springs

The key draw to the farming town of Katherine (pop. 9,450) is Katherine (Nit-miluk) Gorge. It's a small gorge by the standards of, say, the Grand Canyon, but its dramatic sheer orange walls dropping to a tranquil blue-green river make it a peaceful and pretty place, all the more so because it's an unexpected delight in the middle of the dry Arnhemland plateau that stretches to the horizon.

The gorge and its surrounding river ecosystem are located in the 292,008-hectare (721,269-acre) **Nitmiluk National Park.** In the Dry, the gorge is a haven not just for cruisers but also for canoeists, who must dodge the odd fresh-water crocodile (the kind that are regarded as "friendly") as they paddle up between its walls. In the Wet, the gorge can become a foaming torrent at times, and jet-boating is sometimes the only way to tackle it. Hikers will find nice trails any time of year throughout the park. Farther afield from Katherine are hot springs to soak in, natural water holes to swim in, uncrowded rivers to canoe, and Aboriginal communities where visitors can make dot paintings and find bush tucker.

ESSENTIALS

GETTING THERE   **Airnorth** (℗ **1800/627 474** in Australia, or 08/8945 2866) flies from Darwin, and from Alice Springs via Tennant Creek.

McCafferty's (℗ **13 14 99** in Australia) and **Greyhound Pioneer** (℗ **13 20 30** in Australia) stop in Katherine on their Darwin–Alice Springs and Alice Springs–Darwin routes, which both companies run once or twice a day. Greyhound also calls daily from Broome via Kununurra. It's about a 4½-hour trip from Darwin, costing A$48 (U.S.$30.35); from Alice it's about a 14-hour journey for which the fare is A$162 (U.S.$89.10); and the journey of around 22 hours from Broome costs A$204 (U.S.$112.20).

Katherine is on the Stuart Highway, which links Darwin and Alice Springs. From Alice Springs, allow a good 2 days to make the drive. The Victoria Highway links Katherine with Kununurra to the west. There is no direct route from the east; from, say, Cairns, you need to go via Townsville, Mt. Isa and Tennant Creek, a long and dull journey. There is no train to Katherine.

VISITOR INFORMATION   The **Katherine Region Tourist Association,** Stuart Highway at Lindsay Street, Katherine, NT 0850 (℗ **08/8972 2650;** visitor@krta.com.au), has information on things to see—not only all around Katherine, but as far afield as Kakadu National Park and the Kimberley. It's open Monday through Friday from 8:30am to 6pm and weekends from 10am to 3pm in the Dry season; in the Wet it's open Monday through Friday from 9am to 5pm. It was due to launch a website (**www.krol.com**) at press time.

The **Nitmiluk Visitor Centre** (℗ **08/8972 1886**) on the Gorge Road, 32 kilometers (20 miles) from town, dispenses information on the Nitmiluk National Park and sells tickets for gorge cruises, which depart right outside. The ranger station is here also. The Centre has maps; displays on the park's plant life, birds, geology, and Aboriginal history; a gift shop; and a cafe. It's open daily from 7am to 7pm, sometimes closing a little earlier in the Wet. Entry to the park is free.

GETTING AROUND   **Budget** (℗ **08/8971 1333**), **Hertz** (℗ **08/8971 1111**), and **Thrifty** (℗ **08/8972 3183**) have outlets in Katherine.

Travel North (℗ **1800/089 103** in Australia, or 08/8971 9999) makes transfers from Katherine hotels to the cruise, canoe, and helicopter departure points at the Nitmiluk Visitor Centre. Round-trip fares are A$18 (U.S.$9.90) per person, adult or child. In fact, most Katherine activities and attractions can be booked through Travel North. The company runs many local tours and activities such as horseback cattle musters, visits to an old homestead, half-day trips to Mataranka Thermal Pools (see below), and tour packages of up to 5 days taking in Katherine, Darwin, Litchfield and Kakadu National Parks, and outlying Aboriginal communities.

For personalized tours both off the beaten path and around town, contact **Far Out Adventures** ★ (℗ **08/8972 2552**), described below.

EXPLORING KATHERINE GORGE (NITMILUK NATIONAL PARK)

Cruising the gorge in an **open-sided boat** is the most popular way to appreciate its beauty. Katherine Gorge is actually a series of 13 gorges, but most cruises ply only the first two, because the second gorge is the most photogenic.

All cruises are operated by Travel North, above. Most folks take the 2-hour cruise, which departs four times a day and costs A$34 (U.S.$18.70) for adults and A$13.50 (U.S.$7.45) for children 5 to 15. There is also a 4-hour cruise at least once daily, although you will probably be satisfied with 2 hours, and an 8-hour cruise/hike safari to the fifth gorge (available from about May–Oct only). Wear sturdy shoes; because each gorge is cut off from the next by rapids, all the cruises involve some walking along the bank to transfer to a boat in the next gorge.

In the height of the Wet Season, the cruises may not operate on days when the floodwaters really start to swirl. Instead, Travel North runs a **jet boat** those days as far as the third gorge. This 45-minute adventure costs A$39 (U.S.$21.45) for adults and A$29 (U.S.$15.95) for kids 5 to 15. Departure times vary from day to day with the floodwater conditions.

Cruising is nice, but in a **canoe** ✿ you can discover sandy banks and waterfalls, and get up close to the gorge walls, the birds, and those crocs (don't worry, they're the freshwater kind that are not typically regarded as dangerous to humans). The gorges are separated by rocks, so be prepared to carry your canoe quite often. You may even want to camp out on the banks overnight. A half-day canoe rental from Travel North is A$28 (U.S.$15.40) for a single canoe and A$42 (U.S.$23.10) for a double. Canoeing the gorge is popular, so book canoes ahead, especially in the Dry season.

Guided paddles are a good idea as you will learn and see more. The most knowledgeable company is **Gecko Canoeing** ✿ (© **1800/634 319** in Australia, or 08/8972 2224), whose tours are accredited for their ecotourism content. Gecko's owner/guide, Martin Wohling, has attained Australia's elite "Savannah Guide" ecotour guide status. He mostly does 3- to 5-day canoeing/camping safaris on the Katherine River, but he will pick you up from your accommodation for a 1-day escorted canoe safari at a cost of A$140 (U.S.$77) per person. The company also runs canoeing and camping safaris (with any other activities you like thrown in such as mountain biking, rock climbing, wildlife photography, hiking, or fishing) of up to 12 days in little-explored wildernesses across the Top End, such as the Flora and Daly River systems near Katherine, the Kimberley, and ultra-remote Arnhemland, and sea-kayaking adventures around the equally remote Cobourg Peninsula northeast of Darwin.

Some 100 kilometers (62 miles) of **hiking trails** crisscross Nitmiluk National Park, ranging in duration from 1 hour to the lookout to 5 days to Edith Falls (see below). Trails—through rocky terrain and forests, past water holes and along the gorge—depart the Nitmiluk National Park ranger station, located in the Nitmiluk Visitor Centre, where you can pick up trail maps. Overnight walks require a deposit of between A$20 and $50 (U.S.$11 and $27.50) per person, and a A$3.30 (U.S.$1.80) per-person camping permit, payable at the Nitmiluk Visitor Centre.

One of the nicest spots in the Park is actually 42 kilometers (26 miles) north of Katherine, 20 kilometers (12½ miles) off the Stuart Highway. **Edith Falls** ✿ is a real Eden of natural (croc-free) swimming holes bordered by red cliffs, monsoonal forest, and pandanus palms. Among the couple of bushwalks leading from the Falls is a 2.6-kilometer (1½-mile) round-trip trail, which takes about 2 hours, and incorporates a dip at the upper pool en route.

More than the gorge itself, the aerial views of the ravine-ridden Arnhem Plateau, which stretches uninhabited to the horizon, are arresting. **North Australian Helicopters** (© **08/8972 1666**) does flights of 3, 5, and all 13 gorges for between A$55 (U.S.$30) and A$137.50 (U.S.$75.65) per person, adult or child. Take at least a five-gorge flight to get a sense of Australia's wild vastness. In the Wet it also makes flights from Katherine to see Jim Jim Falls in Kakadu National Park.

ABORIGINAL CULTURE TOURS, HOT SPRINGS & MORE

On a 1-day visit to the **Manyallaluk Aboriginal community** *&*, a 90-minute drive southeast from Katherine, you chat with Aboriginal people about how they balance traditional ways with modern living; take a short bushwalk to look for native medicines and bush tucker like green ants (they're refreshing!); try lighting a fire with two sticks, weaving baskets, throwing spears, painting on bark, and playing a didgeridoo; take a dip in a natural water hole; and buy locally made Aboriginal art and artifacts at better prices than you may find elsewhere. Lunch is a barbecue featuring stuff like high-grade kangaroo fillet, kangaroo tail, Scotch fillet steak, or barramundi cooked on hot coals. Some visitors rush into these tours and expect the community to be a kind of Aboriginal Disney World theme park with a new attraction every 10 minutes, but that's not how it is. It's an unstructured experience (this is the community's home), so it's up to you to take part. A 1-day tour from Katherine costs A$132 (U.S.$72.60) for adults and A$70 (U.S.$3.85) for children 5 to 15, or A$99 (U.S.$54.45) adults and A$65 (U.S.$35.75) for kids if you drive yourself. The last 35 kilometers (22 miles) of road is unsealed (unpaved), for which rental cars will be insured only if they are four-wheel-drive. The tour runs Monday through Friday around April through September; hours may be reduced, or the place may close, in the Wet. Call ahead before setting off no matter what the time of year, as sometimes the place closes for ceremonies or other cultural reasons. Call Manyallaluk: The Dreaming Place (© **08/8975 4727**), or book through Travel North, above.

About 110 kilometers (69 miles) south of Katherine, you can soak your aches away at the **Mataranka Thermal Pools.** This man-made pool is fed by 34°C (93°F) spring water, which bubbles up from the earth naturally at a rate of 16,495 liters (4,123¾ gallons) per minute! It's a little paradise, surrounded by palms, pandanus, and a colony of flying foxes. The pools are open 24 hours and admission is free. They are 7 kilometers (4 miles) along Homestead Road, which is off the Stuart Highway 1½ kilometers (1 mile) south of Mataranka township. They make a welcome stop on the *looong* drive from Alice Springs.

If you can't be bothered driving to Mataranka, you can soak in the pleasantly warm **Katherine Hot Springs,** under shady trees 3 kilometers (2 miles) from town on Riverbank Drive. Entry is free. At the **School of the Air,** Giles Street (© **08/8972 1833**), you can sit in on an 800,000-square-kilometer (262,400-sq.-mile) "classroom" as children from the Outback do their lessons by radio. Forty-five-minute tours begin on the hour from 9am up to and including 2pm (there's no tour at noon). Tours also run during school holidays and public holidays minus the on-air classes. The school is open Monday through Friday from 9am to 3pm from mid-March until mid-December. Admission is A$5 (U.S.$2.75) for adults and A$2 (U.S.$1.10) for school-age kids.

Mike Keighley of **Far Out Adventures** *&* (© **08/8972 2552**) runs numerous eco- and cultural tours around Katherine, which he tailors to your interests. One of his best is his **"Never Never"** ⟨⁂⟩ tour, an all-day chill-out on a beautiful patch of the 5,000-square-kilometer (1,930-sq.-mile) Elsey Station, 140 kilometers (88 miles) southeast of Katherine, made famous as the setting of the Aussie book and film *We of the Never Never.* Meet children of the Mangarrayi Aboriginal people, sample bush tucker, learn a little bush medicine, and swim in a vine-clad natural "spa-pool" in the Roper River. Mike has been accepted as an honorary family member of the Mangarrayi people and is a mine of information about Aboriginal culture and the bush. He can extend this trip into an overnight camp/canoe safari to Elsey Falls and the water lilies on Red Lily Lagoon.

When he's not out on tour, Mike runs atmospheric croc-spotting campfire cruises on the Katherine River Monday, Wednesday, and Friday through Sunday nights April through October. They cost A$50 (U.S.$27.50) per adult and A$25 (U.S.$13.75) for kids, including a great barbecue dinner, and guitar and didgeridoo music.

WHERE TO STAY & DINE

The Nitmiluk National Park ranger station in the Nitmiluk Visitor Centre has maps of available "bush campsites" throughout the park. These are very basic sites—no showers, no soaps or shampoos allowed because they pollute the river system, and simple pit toilets or none at all. Most are beside natural swimming holes. You must stop for a camping permit from the ranger station beforehand; the camping fee is A$3.30 (U.S.$1.80) per person per night.

Travel North (see above) runs the **Nitmiluk Gorge Caravan Park** next to the Nitmiluk Visitor Centre, where wallabies often hop into the shady grounds. Fees are A$8 (U.S.$4.40) per adult, A$5 (U.S.$2.75) per child for a tent site, and A$20 (U.S.$11) double for a powered site.

Knotts Crossing Resort   At this low-key resort, you have a choice of huge, well-furnished motel rooms, some with kitchenettes, minibars, and in-room dataports and fax machines; cabins with a kitchenette inside and their own private bathrooms just outside the door; or campgrounds, all located among the tropical landscaping. The "village" rooms are a good penny-wise choice, built in 1998 and smartly furnished with a double bed and bunks, a kitchenette, and joint veranda facing a small private pool with a barbecue. Locals meet at the casual bar beside the pool, and Katie's Bistro is one of the smartest places to eat in town.

Corner Giles and Cameron sts., Katherine, NT 0850. ⟨℗⟩ 1800/222 511 in Australia, or 08/8972 2511. Fax 08/8972 2628. www.knottscrossing.com.au. 123 units (some with shower only; cabins have adjacent private bathroom), 75 powered and unpowered campsites. A$75 (U.S.$41.25) double cabin; A$85 (U.S.$46.75) double "village" room; A$120–$145 (U.S.$66–$79.75) double motel room; A$135 (U.S.$74.25) family of 4, motel family room. Extra person A$10 (U.S.$5.50) adult and A$5 (U.S.$2.75) child under 13, cabin or village room; A$10 (U.S.$5.50) per extra adult, motel room. AE, DC, MC, V. Complimentary transfers from airport or bus stop. **Amenities:** Restaurant, bar, free BBQs; 2 outdoor pools (1 large and attractive, 1 small); Jacuzzi; tour desk; car-rental desk; limited room service; self-service laundry; same-day dry cleaning/ laundry service. *In room:* A/C, TV with pay movies, fridge, no phone in cabins.

5 The Kimberley: A Far-Flung Wilderness ⟨⁂⟩

Most Aussies would be hard pressed to name a single settlement, river, or mountain within the Kimberley, so rarely visited and sparsely inhabited is this vast wilderness. This is an old, old land of red, rocky plateaus stretching for thousands of square miles, jungly ravines, endless bush, crocodile-infested wetlands, spooky-looking boab trees with trunks shaped like bottles, lily-filled rock pools, lonely

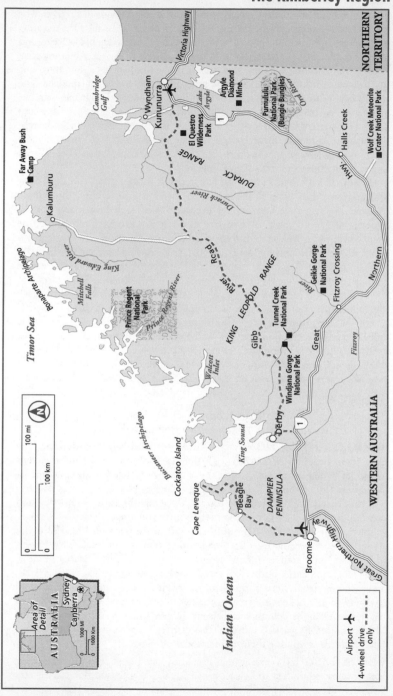

The Kimberley Region

NORTHERN TERRITORY

WESTERN AUSTRALIA

Victoria Highway

Wyndham

Kununurra

Lake Argyle

Argyle Diamond Mine

Purnululu National Park (Bungle Bungles)

Ord River

Wolf Creek Meteorite Crater National Park

Halls Creek

El Questro Wilderness Park

DURACK RANGE

Durack River

Kalumburu

Far Away Bush Camp

Cambridge Gulf

Bonaparte Archipelago

King Edward River

Mitchell Falls

Timor Sea

Prince Regent National Park

Prince Regent River

Rd Gibb River

KING LEOPOLD RANGE

Tunnel Creek National Park

Windjana Gorge National Park

Geikie Gorge National Park

Fitzroy Crossing

Northern

Great

Fitzroy

Walcott Inlet

Cockatoo Island

Buccaneer Archipelago

King Sound

Beagle Bay

Cape Leveque

DAMPIER PENINSULA

Derby

Broome

Great Northern Highway

Indian Ocean

100 mi

100 km

AUSTRALIA

Area of Detail

Sydney

Canberra

1000 Mi

1000 Km

Airport

4-wheel drive only

island-strewn coastline, droughts in winter, and massive floods in summer. The dry, spreading scenery might call to mind Africa or India. In the Dry, the area's biggest river, the Fitzroy, is bone dry, but in the Wet, its swollen banks are second only to the Amazon in the volume of water that surges to the sea. Aqua and scarlet are two colors that will hit you in the eye in the Kimberley—a luminous aqua for the sea, and the fiery scarlet of the fine soil hereabouts called "pindan." The area is famous for Wandjina-style Aboriginal rock art depicting people with circular hair-dos that look more than a little like beings from outer space. It is also known for another kind of rock art known as "Bradshaw figures," stick-like representations of human forms, which may be the oldest art on earth. A mere 25,000 people live in the Kimberley's 420,000 square kilometers (162,120 sq. miles). That's three times the size of England.

The unofficial capital of the East Kimberley is **Kununurra.** It's a small agricultural town that serves as the gateway to wildlife river cruises; the **Bungle Bungles** ⍟, a massive labyrinth of beehive-shaped rock formations; and **El Questro** ⍟⍟, a million-acre cattle station where you can hike, fish, and cruise palm-filled gorges by day and sleep in comfy permanent safari tents or glamorous homestead rooms by night (it's open from Apr to early Nov). The main town in the West Kimberley is the Outback port of **Broome** ⍟ whose waters give up the world's biggest and best South Sea pearls. Linking Kununurra and Derby, near Broome, is the Gibb River Road, an isolated four-wheel-drive track through cattle-station country that is becoming popular with adventure travelers.

Off the West Kimberley coast lies a jigsaw puzzle of 10,000 or more barely inhabited islands, the **Bonaparte** ⍟ and **Buccaneer Archipelagos** ⍟, the last named in honor of the pirate's pirate, William Dampier, who sailed here in 1688. In fact, much of the appeal of the this coastline lies in the knowledge that few Westerners have laid eyes on it since the first explorers of the 17th century.

ESSENTIALS

The Kimberley lies within Western Australia, so see "Exploring the State," at the start of chapter 9 for general tips on getting around in the state.

VISITOR INFORMATION The **Kimberley Tourism Association,** P.O. Box 554, Broome, WA 6725 (© **08/9193 6660;** www.ebroome.com/kimberley), supplies information on the entire region. The **Kununurra Tourist Bureau** and the **Broome Tourist Bureau** (which appear later in this chapter) also handle inquiries on things to see and do across the entire Kimberley, and you can drop into their information offices once you arrive.

Best of the Kimberley (© **1800/450 850** in Australia, or 08/9192 6070; www.kimberleytravel.net) is a Broome-based marketing co-operative for 18 reputable Kimberley tour operators, including four-wheel-drive safari operators, aerial tour companies, bushwalking and horse riding operators, cruise vessels, and accommodation houses. It sells off-the-shelf packages and a huge range of day trips, tours and activities, and specializes in personalized vacations. Visits to the remote Dampier Peninsula to fish and go mud-crabbing with an Aboriginal family, and self-fly packages around this vast region for private pilots (aircraft hire included) are among their more unusual offerings.

GETTING AROUND Enormous distances, high petrol costs (often A$1 per liter or more, equivalent to U.S.$2 per U.S. gal.), Wet Season floods, and very limited roads and other facilities can make traveling the Kimberley expensive and time-consuming. The place has lots of attractions that are so remote that they can be reached only by aerial tours or charter boats. Many more sights are accessible only on unpaved roads, for which your two-wheel-drive rental car is not insured and which it probably can't handle, so if you don't want to rely on tours, rent a four-wheel-drive (available in Broome and Kununurra). Allow for an average speed of 60 kilometers per hour (37.5 mph) on the area's rough unsealed roads, and never exceed 80 kilometers per hour (50 mph), because unexpected dips and smooth patches can take you by surprise. Most outfits will allow one-way rentals between Broome and Kununurra, or vice versa, at a ball-park surcharge of A$350 to $550 (U.S.$192.50–$302.50). Check Thrifty's one-way fee when planning your trip, as at press time, Thrifty was considering a circuit system whereby one-way fees would be lowered or eliminated. Review "Road Conditions & Safety," "What If Your Vehicle Breaks Down?," and "Tips for Four-Wheel Drivers," in the "Getting Around Australia" section of chapter 2, before setting off.

Kimberley Camping & Outback, 338 Frederick St., Broome (© **1800/645 909** in Australia, or 08/9193 5909) sells and rents every piece of camping equipment you need, from tents and "mozzie" (mosquito) nets to cooking utensils, plus outdoor clothing. A complete camping kit starts at A$29.50 (U.S.$16.25) per day for two people; weekly rates are available.

Taking a guided four-wheel-drive camping or accommodated safari is a neat way to sidestep the challenges of Kimberley travel. Safaris depart Broome, Kununurra, or Darwin, and last between 2 days and 2 weeks. A popular route is the cross-Kimberley journey between Broome and Kununurra, or vice versa. If you opt for this route, look for tours that traverse the Gibb River Road, rather than the scenically dull highway via Halls Creek and Fitzroy Crossing. The Gibb River Road is an adventurous unpaved "back road" between Kununurra and Broome that offers gorges, low red ranges, swimming holes (ask directions to croc-free ones and swim nowhere else), walking trails, barramundi fishing, and campsites or basic homestead accommodation on vast cattle stations (ranches). Most safaris run only in the Dry Season, April/May through October/November. Respected operators include **East Kimberley Tours** (© **1800/682 213** in Australia, or 08/9168 2213; www.eastkimberleytours.com); **Kimberley Wilderness Adventures** (© **1800/804 005** in Australia, or 08/9192 5741; www.kimberleywilderness.com.au); **Adventure Tours** (© **1300/654 604** in Australia, or 08/8936 1300; www.adventuretours.com.au); and **Australian Pinnacle Tours** (© **08/9417 5555;** www.pinnacletours.com.au).

Broome Aviation (© **1300/13 6629** in Australia, or 08/9192 1369; www.broomeaviation.com) and **King Leopold Air** (© **08/9193 7155;** www.kingleopoldair.com.au), both based in Broome, and **Alligator Airways** (© **08/9168 1333;** www.alligatorairways.com.au) and **Slingair Heliwork** (© **1800/095 500** in Australia, or 08/9169 1300; www.slingair.com.au), both based in Kununurra, run a range of flight-seeing tours all over the Kimberley, lasting from a couple of hours to several days. Some flights incorporate sightseeing on the ground, hiking in national parks, four-wheel-drive trips, overnights at fishing camps, or calls into vast cattle stations. Slingair offers a Kimberley Airpass.

KUNUNURRA

827km (517 miles) SW of Darwin; 1,032km (645 miles) E of Broome

Given the arid conditions in the Kimberley, it's quite a surprise to swoop over a field of sugarcane as you come in to land at Kununurra. This rather ramshackle little town (pop. 5,000) is an agricultural center created by the damming of the mighty Ord River to form **Lake Argyle.**

Kununurra itself (the name is Aboriginal for "Meeting of Big Waters") has little to spark your interest, but it is the gateway to several outstanding attractions. A cruise or canoe trip down the **Ord River** to see wild birds, dramatic cliffs, and crocs is a must. So is a flight over, or a hike into, the **Bungle Bungles (Purnululu National Park)** 𝒜, monumental orange domes of rock that look like giant beehives. The world's biggest diamond mine is not in South Africa but out in the rugged Kimberley wilds near Kununurra, and it can be visited by air every day. The town is also a gateway to **El Questro Wilderness Park** 𝒜𝒜, a million-acre cattle station (ranch) where you can hike magnificent gorges, fish, cruise rivers, ride horses, and see some of Australia's most breathtaking Aboriginal art. It is open from April to early November, closed over summer due to the Wet season.

ESSENTIALS
GETTING THERE   There is no train to Kununurra. **Greyhound Pioneer** (℡ **13 20 30** in Australia) serves the town daily from Broome and daily from Darwin via Katherine. From Broome the trip takes about 15 hours, and the one-way fare is A$156 (U.S.$85.50); from Darwin, the trip time is around 9 hours, and the fare is A$117 (U.S.$64.35).

Kununurra is 512 kilometers (320 miles) west of Katherine on the Victoria Highway. The Great Northern Highway from Broome connects with the Victoria Highway 45 kilometers (28 miles) west of Kununurra. The Gibb River Road is an alternative four-wheel-drive scenic route from Derby near Broome; it connects with the Great Northern Highway 53 kilometers (33 miles) west of town.

VISITOR INFORMATION   The **Kununurra Tourist Bureau** is at Coolibah Drive, Kununurra, WA 6743 (℡ **08/9168 1177;** kununurratb@bigpond.com). Its hours change with the crowds and the season and are not the same from year to year, but it usually opens from 8am to 5pm Monday through Friday, from 8am to 2pm Saturday, and from 8am to noon in the Dry. Its Wet season hours are usually from 9am to 4pm weekdays, closed weekends.

GETTING AROUND   Avis (℡ **08/9169 1258**), **Budget** (℡ **08/9168 2033**), **Hertz** (℡ **08/9169 1424**), and **Thrifty** (℡ **08/9169 1911**) all rent four-wheel-drive vehicles. Hertz rents camping gear also. At press time, no company in town rented campervans.

WHAT TO SEE & DO
ON THE ORD RIVER   Several cruise outfits will offer you the option of cruising the Ord River or Lake Argyle, a massive man-made blue inland sea ringed by stony red cliffs and bigger than 19 Sydney Harbours, but go for the Ord. The Ord River is one of the most picturesque waterways in Australia, lined by bulbous red cliffs in parts, and teeming with all kinds of wetland birds and freshwater crocodiles. Jeff Haley of **Triple J. Tours** 𝒜 (℡ **08/9168 2682**) runs excellent cruises along it. There are several itineraries, and they vary from Dry season to Wet, but the most popular starts with a 70-kilometer (44-mile) coach ride and commentary to Lake Argyle, a wander through a historic homestead, then the 55-kilometer (34-mile) cruise back to Kununurra. The boat travels fast and is a bit noisy, but Jeff pulls in at numerous tranquil spots. This costs A$95 (U.S.$52.25) for adults and A$55 (U.S.$30.25) for children 4 to 15, including pickup from your hotel. It takes most of the day.

Big Waters Kimberley Canoe Safaris (℡ **1800/641 998** in Australia, or 08/9169 1998; www.adventure.kimberley.net.au), offers a popular 3-day self-guided canoeing/camping safari down the Grade 1 (that means "gentle") Ord River in two-person Canadian canoes. It costs A$135 (U.S.$74.25) per person. The company also rents canoes for folks who want to explore on their own.

A day on the river to fish for barramundi with **Greg Harman's Ultimate Adventures** (© 08/9168 2310) costs around A$230 (U.S.$126.50) per person, more if there is only one of you. Greg also does trips of up to 10 days to remote fishing camps.

DIAMONDS IN THE ROUGH   Turning out an impressive 38 million carats a year—that's more than 8 tons of pure diamond—is the world biggest diamond mine, the **Argyle Diamond Mine**, 176 kilometers (110 miles) from Kununurra. It is the only mine in the world to produce the rare pink diamond in commercial quantities, as well as champagne, cognac, yellow, green, and white rocks. During a 3½- to 4-hour visit, you will see rough and polished gems in the viewing room, see gems get extracted from the huge open-cut mine (as long as safety conditions permit), and, if you like, buy diamonds. For security reasons, you must join an organized aerial tour with **Belray Diamond Tours** (© 08/ 9168 1014), which you can also book through **Slingair Heliwork** (© 1800/ 095 500 in Australia, or 08/9169 1300). I'd recommend you opt for a flight that covers the nearby Purnululu National Park (Bungle Bungles) and Lake Argyle as well, an option costing A$325 (U.S.$178.75). Belray Diamond Tours does a coach trip Thursdays only June through September, but it's a 2½-hour drive each way. Kids under 12 are not permitted on mine tours.

SPENDING THE DAY AT EL QUESTRO WILDERNESS PARK ⍣⍣   You do not have to stay at El Questro (see "Where to Stay," below) to enjoy the wonderful facilities. When aristocratic Englishman Will Burrell bought this million-acre cattle station (ranch) in 1991, he turned it into a kind of Outback holiday camp where anyone from the international celebrities to humble four-wheel-drive enthusiasts could revel in its rugged beauty. Although it's a working farm, guests don't get involved in the cow side of things. Instead, they go barramundi fishing and heli-fishing in croc-infested wetlands and rivers, soak under palm trees in the thermal waters of Zebedee Springs, hike gorges, some of which hide pockets of rain forest, take half-day four-wheel-drive fishing safaris, cruise tranquil Chamberlain Gorge, ride horses across stony plains, photograph red rocky ranges, join rangers on bird-watching or "bush-tucker" tours, or explore a rich lode of Aboriginal rock paintings. It's an unspoiled, primeval place.

El Questro is open from April 1 to early November (it closes in the Wet November through March). Visitors must purchase a 7-day Wilderness Park Permit to enter, which costs A$12.50 (U.S.$6.90), or A$5.50 (U.S.$3) if you go only as far as Emma Gorge. Children under 12 enter free. Buy permits from El Questro's office in Kununurra, on Banksia Street, where the staff will give you a map and point out all there is to see and do, or at the Station Township. The Township acts as a kind of headquarters—most tours and activities depart here, and it's where you can buy basic road and other supplies and fuel, and rent four-wheel-drives and camping gear. Consider renting a four-wheel-drive in Kununurra or at the Station Township. Guests at Emma Gorge pay A$60 (U.S.$33) per person round-trip (A$120/U.S.$66 if there's only one of you) to transfer to join tours and activities departing the Station Township (these transfers are free for Homestead guests), so while it is not crucial to have your own four-wheel-drive, it is certainly less costly. Having your own vehicle also means you can explore independently. The Station Township rents them for A$123 to $168

(U.S.$67.65–$92.40) per day, plus A28¢ (U.S.15¢) per kilometer after the first 100 kilometers (best to book them ahead as the fleet size is limited).

If you're short on time, the station's 12-hour ranger-guided day trips from Kununurra are a good idea. They include the highlights of a Chamberlain Gorge cruise to see Aboriginal Wandjina rock art and a soak in Zebedee Springs, plus a gorge walk, lunch at the Station Township restaurant, and four-wheel-drive transfers, for A$145 (U.S.$79.75) per person. Ask staff to identify which swimming spots are croc-free, and don't swim anywhere else!

You pay for most activities—between A$33 (U.S.$18.15) for a 1-hour horse ride to A$550 (U.S.$302.50) for a half-day's saltwater heli-fishing. Typical prices are A$40 (U.S.$22) for a gorge cruise, A$50 (U.S.$27.50) for a 4-hour four-wheel-drive trip to watch the sun set over the Cockburn Range while you sip champagne and eat melons, or A$175 (U.S.$96.25) for a half-day four-wheel-drive barramundi-fishing trip. The rangers are friendly and knowledgeable. The tour desk also arranges such off-station activities as day trips on the Ord River or around Kununurra, trips to the Argyle diamond mine and the Bungle Bungles, and extended tours throughout the Kimberley as far afield as Mitchell Falls.

WHERE TO STAY
At El Questro
El Questro Bungalows   These basic but comfortable cabin-style rooms located by the store at the heart of the Station Township are good for anyone without their own transportation, as tours depart from right outside. The nicest are the eight new-ish ones with balconies overlooking the Pentecost River. The Steakhouse restaurant and bar serves three meals a day of the steak and barramundi kind, and there is often live music around the campfire. A swimming hole is nearby. The front office loans hair dryers.

See contact details below. 12 bungalows (all with shower only). A$170 (U.S.$93.50) per bungalow (sleeps 4). The Bungalows are 110km (69 miles), about 90 min., from Kununurra. **Amenities:** Restaurant, bar; tour desk; 4-wheel-drive rental desk; laundry. In room: A/C, fridge.

El Questro Homestead 𝒜𝒜𝒜   Perched over the Chamberlain River on the edge of a gorge, this homestead is one of the world's most luxurious yet simple getaways. Visitors (make that wealthy visitors—no one else could afford those astronomical rates!) come for the sense of seclusion and the wilderness experience. You stay in airy rooms furnished in a blend of Aussie country style and Indonesian antiques, with a view of the gardens and the river from your veranda. The premier suite even has a bath on the veranda! Guests relax outside or in the inviting TV lounge. Everyone dines at one big communal table at breakfast and lunch. At dinner you dine at tables for two set up wherever you like—halfway down the gorge cliff face overhanging the river, out by the pool, and so on. The Station Township is 9 kilometers (5½ miles) away.

See contact details below. 6 units (shower only; 1 with veranda tub). A$725–$825 (U.S.$398.75–$453.75) *per person* per night (including all meals, open bar, laundry service, and all activities except helicopter flights). Min. 2-night stay. The homestead is 119km (74 miles) from Kununurra (about 1 hr. 45 min.). Round-trip 4-wheel-drive transfers from Kununurra A$150 (U.S.$82.50) per person (scheduled) or A$300 (U.S.$165) per person (private). Air transfers from Kununurra, Broome, Darwin, Alice Springs, and Ayers Rock available on request—baggage limit can be as little as 5kg (11lbs.) on flights from Kununurra or Darwin. Children under 16 not permitted. **Amenities:** Home-style kitchen "restaurant," free alcoholic beverages; small attractive outdoor swimming pool; tennis court; Jacuzzi; tour bookings; laundry. In room: A/C, hair dryer.

El Questro Wilderness Park 𝒜𝒜   In addition to the options listed in this section, **there's Black Cockatoo Riverside Camping.** Forty-five riverside camp locations near the station store are available for a nightly charge of A$12.50

(U.S.$6.90) per adult, free for children under 12. Campers share shower facilities and a laundry, and use the bungalows' restaurant. An extra 28 more secluded riverside campsites are within a 6 kilometers (3¾ miles) drive. No bookings are taken for campsites. The Wilderness Park Permit fee is included in the rate at all accommodation choices, except at the campground.

Gibb River Road, approx. 100km (62 miles) southwest of Kununurra (P.O. Box 909, Kununurra, WA 6743). **Accor,** ℂ **1300/65 65 65** in Australia, 1800/221-4542 in the U.S. and Canada, 020/8283 4500 in the U.K., 0800/44 4422 in New Zealand, or ℂ 08/9169 1777. Fax 08/9169 1383. www.elquestro.com.au. Consists of the 3 separate facilities described in this section. 4-wheel-drive transfers for guests from Kununurra, driven by a ranger who gives a commentary en route, cost A$144 (U.S.$79.20) per adult round-trip to Emma Gorge only, or A$180 (U.S.$99) to the Station Township. Children under 12 pay half price. To get there, take the Great Northern Highway 58km (36 miles) toward Wyndham, then the (unsealed) Gibb River Road 25km (15½ miles) to Emma Gorge Resort (which is 2km/1¼ miles along an access road), or a further 27km (17 miles) to the station store. All of the accommodations accept AE, DC, MC, and V. All have public pay phones only, not in-room phones (or TVs).

Emma Gorge Resort 🏕🏕   This neatly kept oasis of cute permanent tents mounted on lush lawns under pandanus palms at the foot of the soaring red Cockburn Range is a great way to "camp" in the wilderness without sacrificing comfort. Although they are "only" tents, accommodations are comfortable, with wooden floors, electric lights, fans, insect screens, nice firm beds with quilts, and torches (flashlights) for getting around at night. Those without bathrooms share clean and modern facilities. Reception stocks stuff like sunscreen and souvenirs, and lends hair dryers. The rustic restaurant serves up gourmet bush-tucker meals that would put many big-city restaurants to shame, and has a retractable roof for stargazing. Free to guests is access to a 1.6-kilometer (1-mile) trail along lush Emma Gorge to the natural swimming hole and trickling waterfall enclosed by 46-meter (150-ft.) cliffs. The Station Township is 27 kilometers (17 miles) away.

See contact details above. 45 tent cabins (27 with bathroom, shower only). A$133–$182 (U.S.$73.15–$100.10) double; A$198 (U.S.$108.90) Deluxe tent (sleeps 4). Emma Gorge is 85km (53 miles), an hour's drive, from Kununurra. **Amenities:** Restaurant, bar; small outdoor swimming pool; tour desk; laundry.

In Kununurra
Country Club Hotel   Just down the road from the tourist bureau, this low-rise hotel is your best bet among Kununurra's modest choice of accommodations. Set in tropical gardens, it has a lovely shaded pool with sun lounges and a bar, and a couple of simple dining and bar venues. The rooms are nothing flashy, but they're neat and clean, with plenty of space. The front desk loans hair dryers.

47 Coolibah Dr., Kununurra, WA 6743. ℂ **08/9168 1024.** Fax 08/9168 1189. www.countryclubhotel.com.au. 88 units (all with bathroom, 8 with tub). Dry Season (Apr–Oct) A$158.60 (U.S.$87.25) double; A$209.60 (U.S.$115.30) 2-bedroom apt. Wet Season (Nov–Mar) A$140 (U.S.$77) double; A$209.60 (U.S.$115.30) 2-bedroom apt. Extra person A$22.60 (U.S.$12.45). Children under 17 stay free in parents' room. AE, DC, MC, V. **Amenities:** 2 restaurants (1 casual grill, 1 Chinese), 3 bars; outdoor swimming pool; tour desk; laundry. *In room:* A/C, TV, fridge.

PURNULULU (BUNGLE BUNGLES) NATIONAL PARK 🏕
Rising out of the landscape 250km (156 miles) south

Rising out of the landscape 250 kilometers (156 miles) south of Kununurra are thousands of enormous sandstone domes 200 to 300 meters (656–984 ft.) high called the Bungle Bungles. Thought to be named after either "bundle bundle" grass or the bungle beetle, the Bungle Bungles get their distinctive orange-and-gray stripes from algae found in the permeable layers and mineral graining in non-permeable layers. The formations are 360 million years old.

The domes look spectacular from the air—that's the way most people see them, and it's the only way to see them in the Wet, because the park is closed to ground traffic from January 1 to March 31, sometimes later. As the waters subside, the soaring gorges and forested creeks at the base of the Bungle Bungles are accessible to hikers. Highlights are the beehive-shaped walls of Cathedral Gorge, the rock pool at Frog Hole Gorge, and palm-filled Echidna Chasm. Keep an eye peeled for rainbow bee-eaters, flocks of budgerigars, rare nail-tailed wallabies, and euros, a kind of kangaroo. It's a lonely, quiet, contemplative, and dramatic place.

VISITOR INFORMATION   For information call the state **Department of Conservation and Land Management (CALM)** (℡ **08/9168 4200**) in Kununurra; there is a **visitor centre/ranger station** (℡ **08/9168 7300**) in the park.

GETTING THERE & GETTING AROUND   Most folks take a scenic flight over the park in a light aircraft from Kununurra offered by **Slingair Heliwork** (℡ **1800/095 500** in Australia, or 08/9169 1300) or **Alligator Airways** (℡ **1800/632 533** in Australia, or 08/9168 1333). The flight takes about 2 hours, incorporates a flight over Lake Argyle and the impressive Argyle Diamond Mine, and costs A$185 (U.S.$101.75) per adult. Both companies also do combined air/hiking day trips, though they're pricey at between A$425 and $580 (U.S.$233.75 and $319) per person. Alligator Airways does a 2-day aerial/hiking/camping trip incorporating the Argyle diamond mine tour. **East Kimberley Tours** (see "Getting Around," earlier in the Kimberley section) runs an array of four-wheel-drive and fly/four-wheel-drive camping and hiking safaris into the park, including some 1-day "express" versions.

BROOME 🏊
2,389km (1,493 miles) N of Perth; 1,859km (1,161 miles) SW of Darwin

Part rough Outback town, part glam seaside resort, the pearling port of Broome 🏊 (pop. 11,000) is a hybrid of Australia and Asia you won't see anywhere else. Chinese and Japanese pearl divers used to work the pearling luggers in this isolated little town in the old days, and as the Chinese settled here, they affixed their distinctive architecture to typical Australian buildings. The result is a main street so cute it could be a movie set, with neat rows of Australian corrugated iron stores wrapped by verandas and trimmed with Chinese peaked roofs.

The people are a unique mixture, too, because Anglo-Saxon/Irish Aussies and Chinese, Filipino, and Malayan pearl workers often married Aboriginal women. The Japanese tended to return home rather than settle here, but not all of them made it. Cyclones, the "bends," sharks, and crocodiles all took their toll. The Japanese legacy in the town is a rather eerie divers' cemetery with Asian inscriptions on 900 rough-hewn headstones.

For such a small and remote place, Broome is surprisingly sophisticated. Walk the streets of Chinatown and you'll rub shoulders with Aussie tourists, itinerant workers, Asian food-store proprietors, tough-as-nails cattle hands, and well-heeled visitors from Europe and America downing good coffee at a couple of trendy cafes. Broome's South Sea pearls are still its bread and butter, but the old-timber pearling luggers have been replaced with gleaming high-tech vessels equipped with helipads and stainless-steel security doors.

To be honest, it's kinda hard to explain Broome's appeal. There is not much to do here, but it's a nice place to be. You can shop for pearls, and it's a good base for exploring the wider Kimberley. But most people simply come to laze by the jade-green Indian Ocean on Cable Beach, ride camels along the sand as the sun plops into the sea, fish the unplundered seas, mosey around the art galleries and jewelry stores, and soak up the gorgeous reds, blues, and greens of the Kimberley coast.

ESSENTIALS

GETTING THERE   Airlink (book through **Qantas** © 13 13 13 in Australia) flies direct from Perth, Darwin, and Alice Springs. The trip to Broome from Sydney and other state capitals is a depressingly lengthy affair via Perth, or via Alice Springs and/or Darwin.

Greyhound Pioneer (© **13 20 30** in Australia) has a daily service from Perth that takes around 32 hours. The fare is A$266 (U.S.$146.30). Greyhound's daily service from Darwin via Katherine and Kununurra takes around 24 hours; the one-way fare is A$230 (U.S.$126.50).

There is no train service to Broome.

Broome is 34 kilometers (21 miles) off the Great Northern Highway, which leads from Perth in the south, Kununurra to the east. Many companies (including those in Kimberley's "Essentials", above) run four-wheel-drive camping safaris to Broome on the Gibb River Road, an alternative unpaved Outback scenic route from Kununurra.

VISITOR INFORMATION   The **Broome Tourist Bureau** is on the Great Northern Highway (locals call it the Broome Highway) at Bagot Street, Broome, WA 6725 (© **08/9192 2222;** www.ebroome.com/tourism). It's open Monday through Friday from 8am to 5pm daily. On Saturday, Sunday, and public holidays, it opens from 9am to 4pm in the Dry, and from 9am to 1pm in the Wet.

Book hotels and tours well in advance of the peak June-through-August season.

GETTING AROUND   Avis (© 08/9193 5980), **Broome Broome Car Rentals** (© 1800/676 725 within Western Australia, or 08/9192 2210), **Budget** (© 08/9193 5355), **Delta Europcar** (© 08/9193 7788), **Hertz** (© 08/9192 1428), and **Thrifty** (© 08/9193 6787) all rent conventional cars and four-wheel-drives. Hertz rents car-top tents that affix to the larger four-wheel-drive's, and it rents full camping-gear kits; Thrifty also rents camping gear. Among the campervan-rental companies are **Delta Europcar** (see above; it is the agent for the national Apollo campervan chain), and **THL Rentals** (© 08/9192 2647), which rents both Britz and Maui campervans.

The **Town Bus** (© **08/9193 6585**) does an hourly loop of most attractions starting at 7:10am and finishing at 6:35pm daily, rising to half-hourly from June to mid-September. A single fare is A$2.70 (U.S.$1.50), and a day pass is A$8.50 (U.S.$4.70).

Broome Taxis (© **08/9192 1133**) operates the airport shuttle; book ahead if you want a transfer to your hotel door. For a cab call **Roebuck Taxis** (© **1800/ 880 330**).

Several coach or four-wheel-drive companies run a variety of day tours of the town, plus trips of a day or several days to natural attractions farther afield like Windjana and Geikie Gorges, Tunnel Creek, and the Dampier Peninsula (described in "Beyond Broome," below).

WHAT TO SEE & DO

Head to **Chinatown,** in the town center on Carnarvon Street and Dampier Terrace, when you arrive to get a feel for the town. It's not all that Chinese anymore, but most shops, cafes, and galleries are here.

Probably the most popular Dry Season pastime is lazing on the 22 glorious white sandy kilometers (14 miles) of **Cable Beach** ⚔. The beach is 6 kilometers (3¾ miles) out of town; the town bus runs there regularly. A beach hut near Cable Beach Club Resort Broome (see "Where to Stay & Dine," below) rents beach and water-sports equipment in the Dry. In the Wet season about November through April, the water is off-limits due to deadly marine stingers—it's incredibly frustrating! Crocodiles, on the other hand, do not like surf, so you should be safe swimming here. Make a point of being at the beach for at least one of the magnificently rosy sunsets in the Dry, when the sun sinks into the sea behind the romantic outlines of pearling luggers.

A novel way to experience the beach is on camelback. Several outfits operate; the most popular time is at sunset as the sun drops over the ocean. A 1-hour sunset ride with **Red Sun Camel Safaris** (℄ **1800/18 4488** within Western Australia, or 08/9193 7423) costs A$33 (U.S.$18.15) adults, A$22 (U.S.$12.10) kids 11 to 16, and A$11 (U.S.$6.05) for kids 6 to 10. Kids under 6 pay A$10 (U.S.$5.50), but they must ride with an adult.

Four-time state surf champ **Josh Parmateer** ⚔ (℄ **0418/958 264**) gives 2-hour surf lessons on the beach through July and August for A$80 (U.S.$44) per person, or A$40 (U.S.$22) per person for two. He supplies the boards and the wet suits; the lessons are great fun and worth it to hear Josh's ripper Aussie accent!

Don't miss the **Pearl Luggers** ⚔⚔, 31 Dampier Terrace (℄ **08/9192 2059**). A 75-minute session here includes a look over two restored Broome pearling luggers, a browse through a small, well-equipped pearling museum, and a riveting and hilarious talk about pearl diving as it used to be by former pearl divers, including Richard "Salty" Baillieu. Salty is so entertaining it's worth timing your visit for the days he's on duty. Admission is A$16.50 (U.S.$9.10) adults, A$15 (U.S.$8.25) seniors and students, A$9 (U.S.$4.95) for kids 8 to 17. The attraction opens from 9am to 5pm May through October, from 10am to 3:30pm November through April; tours run 9, 11am, and 2pm in the Dry, and 11am and 2pm in the Wet. Closed Christmas.

A **dinosaur footprint** 120 million years old is on show at very low tide on the cliff at Gantheaume Point, 6 kilometers (3¾ miles) from town. The town authorities have set a plaster cast of it higher up on the rocks, so you can see it anytime. Bring your camera to snap the point's breathtaking palette of glowing scarlet cliffs, white beach, and jade-turquoise water.

You should also take a peek at the haunting **Japanese pearl divers' cemetery** on Port Drive. Entry is free.

Moments **Stairway to the Moon**

You've heard of a stairway to heaven? Well, Broome has a stairway to the moon. On the happy coincidence of a full moon and a 10-meter (32¾-ft.) tide (which happens about 3 consecutive nights a month Mar–Oct), nature treats the town to a special show, as the light of the rising moon falls on the rippled sand and mudflats in Roebuck Bay, looking for all the world like a "staircase to the moon." The best place to see it is from the cliff-top restaurant at the **Mangrove Hotel** (see "Where to Stay & Dine," below), or from the food and craft markets held at Town Beach. Live music plays at the Mangrove most staircase nights, including a didgeridoo player to accompany the rising moon.

During a tour of the **Willie Creek Pearl Farm** (✆ **08/9192 6300**), 38 kilometers (24 miles) north of town, you will see the delicate process of an oyster getting "seeded" with a nucleus to form a pearl, learn about pearl farming, and learn what to look for when buying a pearl. You can also buy them in the showroom The tour costs A$25 (U.S.$13.75) adults, A$12 (U.S.$6.60) children 6 to 16. Book first. The road to the farm is four-wheel-drive-only, and tides can cut it off; coach tours operate.

If you have not seen any crocs in the wild during your travels, you can see them on a 1-hour tour at the **Malcolm Douglas Broome Crocodile Park,** next to Cable Beach Club Resort Broome, Cable Beach Road (✆ **08/9192 1489**). Admission is A$15 (U.S.$8.25) for adults, A$12 (U.S.$6.60) for seniors and students, A$8 (U.S.$4.40) for kids 5 to 15, and A$38 (U.S.$20.90) for a family. Tours run once or twice daily, but hours vary with the seasons, so call ahead.

Several art galleries sell vivid oil and watercolor Kimberley landscapes and a small range of Aboriginal art. A historic pearling master's house, **Matso's,** 60 Hamersley St. (✆ **08/9193 5811**), stocks the biggest range of European and Aboriginal paintings, sculpture, pottery, carvings, and books in its Monsoon Gallery. It has a lovely veranda cafe and boutique brewery turning out unusual recipes like alcoholic ginger beer. The gallery is open daily from 10am to 5pm; the cafe is open daily from 8am until late.

On Saturday from 8am to 1pm, browse the **markets** in the gardens of the colonial Courthouse at the corner of Frederick and Hamersley streets. It used to be the official station for the cable from Broome to Java. Don't bet the ranch on this tale being gospel, but locals like to tell you that when the British authorities packed up the building materials for the courthouse in Britain and addressed it to "The Kimberley," they meant them to end up in the Kimberley, South Africa. Instead, the stuff arrived in the Kimberley, Australia. The town kept the building and so can proudly lay claim to having Australia's only Zulu-proof courthouse.

A number of boats run sunset cruises on Roebuck Bay or off Cable Beach. **Fishing** ⟨⚓ for trevally, Spanish mackerel, barracuda, barramundi, queenfish, tuna, shark, sailfish, marlin, salmon (in the May–Aug run), and reef fish is excellent around Broome; fly- and sportfishing are also worth a try. Rent tackle and try your luck from the deep-water jetty near Town Beach 2 kilometers (1¼ miles) south of town, or join one of several charter boats running day trips. **FAD Game Fishing Charters** (✆ **08/9192 3998**) and **Lucky Strike Charters** (✆ **08/9193 7375**) are two of the respected ones. **Pearl Sea Coastal Cruises** (see "Boating the Kimberley Coast," below) runs extended live-aboard fishing trips up the coast. Cyclones, rain, high winds, and strong tides can restrict fishing December through March.

More than one-third of Australia's bird species live in the Kimberley. The blue, green, yellow, and violet Gouldian finch, Nankeen night heron, tawny frogmouth, and hundreds more species get "twitchers," as locals affectionately dub bird watchers, excited. **The Broome Bird Observatory** research station (✆ **08/9193 5600**), 25 kilometers (16 miles) out of town on Roebuck Bay, monitors the thousands of migratory wetlands birds that gather here from Siberia. It offers 2½-hour tours from Broome, and has basic accommodations and camping facilities for real enthusiasts.

Australia's "first family" of pearling, the Paspaleys, sell their wonderfully elegant jewelry at **Paspaley Pearls,** Carnarvon Street at Short Street (✆ **08/9192 2203**). **Linney's** is another reputable jeweler nearby.

Don't leave without taking in a recent-release movie at the adorable **Sun Pictures** outdoor cinema, Carnarvon Street near Short Street (© **08/9192 1077**). Built in 1916, these are the oldest "picture gardens" in the world, where the audience sits in (saggy) canvas deck chairs. Films are even screened through the rain in the Wet. Tickets are A$12 (U.S.$6.60). Open nightly except Christmas.

WHERE TO STAY & DINE

Cable Beach Club Resort Broome 🌟🌟🌟   For some Aussies, a visit to Broome is just an excuse to stay at this chic Chinatown-meets-Outback resort, which blends Australian frontier architecture and decor—corrugated iron walls inside as well as out, verandas, Aboriginal art—with Chinese elements like red and green latticework, pagoda roofs, silky red bathrobes, and Asian cotton bedcovers. The huge standard rooms are gorgeous and have a decent-size living area and balcony. Bungalows (which sleep five or six) were renovated in 2000; they have central bedrooms wrapped on three sides by a veranda, and kitchens. For glamour, it's tough to match the I'm-a-colonial-pearling-master suites, lavishly decked out with eye-popping antique Asiatica and valuable Australian art. These are truly to die for, so ask about suite packages, which offer remarkably good value. A dune blocks true sea views, because the authorities won't allow buildings visible from the sand. Unlike many resorts I can name, this one has a choice of dining venues worth eating in. It is a 5-minute drive or a 6-kilometer (3¾ miles) bus ride into town.

Cable Beach Rd., Broome, WA 6725. © **1800/099 199** in Australia, or 08/9192 0400. Fax 08/9192 2249. reservations@cablebeachclub.com. 263 units (some with shower only). High season (July–Sept) A$345–$445 (U.S.$189.75–$244.75) double; A$299–$575 (U.S.$164.45–$316.25) bungalow. Slight discounts in Apr–June; significantly lower rates Oct–Mar. Lower rates for a 3-night stay. Ask about packages. Extra person A$38 (U.S.$20.90). Children under 20 stay free with existing bedding. AE, DC, MC, V. Airport shuttle A$6 (U.S.$3.30) per person return. Town bus. **Amenities:** 5 restaurants (fine-dining, casual grill, colonial-style all-day dining venue, pasta bar, and Mongolian stir-fry; the grill and Mongolian venue close in the Wet), cafe, bar, bar service to pool; large outdoor swimming pool and an adults-only pool chilled in humid Wet season; 8 floodlit tennis courts (4 indoor); well-equipped health club offering a variety of massages, yoga, float tank, personal trainers (even cardio-boxing!); Jacuzzi; kids' club for kids 3–12; guest-activities program; concierge; tour desk; business center; limited room service; in-room massage; babysitting; laundry; same-day dry cleaning/laundry service; art gallery/pearl boutique. *In room:* A/C, TV w/ pay movies, fridge, hair dryer, iron.

Mangrove Hotel 🌟   The best views in Broome are across Roebuck Bay from this modest but appealing cliff-top hotel 5 minutes' walk from town. It's worth hightailing it back from sightseeing just to watch dusk fall over the bay from the lovely **Tides Garden** 🌟 restaurant, where tables and chairs are set out on the lawns under the palms and along the cliff edge. It's popular with locals for fresh, affordable food, and Charter's restaurant inside is one of Broome's best. There's no faulting the clean, well-kept, roomy Deluxe rooms with sea views. Sixteen new extra-large "Executive Suite" rooms were added recently (they have dataports); there are also three suites with kitchenettes, separate bedrooms, and Jacuzzis; and two two-bedroom apartments. The swimming pools and Jacuzzis are set in the lawns overlooking the bay. The town bus stops across the road.

120 Carnarvon St., Broome, WA 6725. © **1800/094 818** in Australia, or 08/9192 1303. Fax 08/9193 5169. www.mangrovehotel.com.au. 70 units, all with bathroom (65 with shower only, 3 with Jacuzzi). High season (Apr–Oct) A$143–$187 (U.S.$78.65–$102.85) double; A$220–$275 (U.S.$121–$151.25) suite; A$264 (U.S.$145.20) 2-bedroom apt. Low season (Nov–Mar) A$121–$165 (U.S.$66.55–$92.95) double; A$198–$253 (U.S.$108.90–$139.15) suite; A$242 (U.S.$133.10) 2-bedroom apt. Extra person A$33 (U.S.$18.15). Children under 3 stay free. Ask about packages in the Wet Season. AE, DC, MC, V. Courtesy car from airport. **Amenities:** 2 restaurants, 2 bars; 2 outdoor swimming pools; 2 Jacuzzis; tour desk; secretarial services; limited room service; laundry; same-day dry cleaning/laundry service. *In room:* A/C, TV with movies, fridge, hair dryer, iron.

BEYOND BROOME

North of Broome, the Kimberley gets really wild. It's a place with almost no human settlement, best suited to those who love exploring nature at its most raw and isolated. Swimming in the ocean and rivers is off-limits due to crocodiles, except in croc-free rock-pools.

Stretching 220 kilometers (138 miles) north of Broome, the **Dampier Peninsula** is home to several Aboriginal communities that sell artworks, and a wonderful pearl-shell church built by missionaries.

The 350-million-year-old walls of **Windjana Gorge**, 240 kilometers (150 miles) east of Broome reveal fossilized marine creatures laid down in the Devonian period. A trail leads you past the walls, which rise up to 100 meters (328 ft.) above the desert floor. The 30-meter- (98-ft.-) high walls of **Geikie Gorge** (pronounced *Geek*-ee), 418 kilometers (261 miles) east of Broome, are part of the same ancient coral-reef system as Windjana, which you explore by walk trails or a short cruise run by rangers. Either gorge can be explored on a long day trip from Broome.

The 10,000 or more islands of the **Buccaneer and Bonaparte Archipelagos** ⭑ are mostly uninhabited except for **Cockatoo Island Resort**, P.O. Box 444, Darwin, NT 0801 (© **08/8946 4455;** cockatooisland@bigpond.com.au), several hundred kilometers (a couple hundred miles) north of Broome, a glamorously simple hideaway that puts guests in salmon-pink former miners' huts perched high on a rock wall over the sea. Fishing, taking nature walks, and lazing by the clifftop pool are the main activities. The sight of the archipelago's red rocky islands and the clouds reflecting in the jade-green sea is wonderful from the air.

Much farther north are the tidal whirlpools, gorges, and rain-forested waterfalls of **Walcott Inlet;** the utter isolation of the gorges, rock plateaus, and river of the 600,000-hectare (1,482,000-acre) **Prince Regent Nature Reserve;** and the "Prince Regent Nature Reserve" four tiers of the picturesque **Mitchell Falls.**

There are no roads to most of these places (except for four-wheel-drive tracks to the Dampier Peninsula and Mitchell Falls), so you need to explore by scenic flight from Broome or Kununurra or by boat. July through September or later, plane and boat passengers often spot humpback whales along this coast.

BOATING THE KIMBERLEY COAST

Boating this vast and unspoiled Kimberley coastline is a true adventure. Here you can go fishing in rivers no one has even named yet, hike through spectacular gorges, laze on isolated beaches, see Aboriginal rock art, eat oysters fresh off the rocks, spot giant marine turtles, shower under waterfalls, swim in the odd croc-free rain-forest pool, and generally feel the wilderness is yours for a while. But extremely strong tidal currents of up to 11 meters (36 ft.), high cliffs, sharks, and saltwater crocodiles all pose dangers, so you should be reasonably fit and independent to travel by boat. This is a big region, so you will need to take an extended charter trip lasting anywhere from 5 to 14 days.

Half a dozen or so boat operators run fishing and adventure trips from Broome or Derby 221 kilometers (138 miles) north, or from Darwin. Some incorporate short inland expeditions on foot, or by light aircraft or four-wheel-drive. North Star Charters, below, even travels with its own helicopter for flight-seeing and heli-fishing. Some boats take scuba divers to Rowley Shoals, a marvelous outcrop of coral reef and giant clams 260 kilometers (163 miles) west off Broome. Find a vessel that suits you—some offer comfortable private cabins, while others are camp-on-the-beach jobs. **North Star Charters** (© **08/9192 1829;** www.NorthStarCharters.com.au) and **Pearl Sea Coastal Cruises** (© **08/ 9192 3829;** www.pearlseacruises.com), both operating from Broome, are the first kind; **Buccaneer Sea Safaris** (© **08/9191 1991;** www.westnet.com. au/buccaneer/) operating out of Derby is the second. Contact the Broome Tourist Bureau for an up-to-date list of the boats plying the coast, because some boats come and go from year to year.

The **Coral Princess** makes 10-day Broome–Darwin or reverse voyages April through September. It's a 35-meter (115-ft.) motorized catamaran carrying no more than 48 passengers in standard and deluxe staterooms or in budget cabins (all with bathrooms en suite). Facilities include a Jacuzzi, sun deck, cocktail bar, and dining room. The voyages depart about 10 times a year and give you the opportunity to go ashore at least once a day to swim (in croc-free pools only), fish, hike in spectacular scenery, croc-spot on river cruises, have a barbecue on an island beach, take optional scenic helicopter flights over the Mitchell Falls, or see Aboriginal art. Fares in 2001 ranged from A$4,865 to $5,710 (U.S.$2,675.75–$3,140.50) per person, twin-share. Contact **Coral Princess Cruises,** Breakwater Terminal, Sir Leslie Thiess Drive, Townsville, QLD 4810 (© **1800/079 545** in Australia, or 07/4721 1673; www.coralprincess.com.au); in the United States and Canada, contact S.H. Enterprises, 245-M, Mt. Hermon Road #B, Scotts Valley, CA 05066 (© **800/441-6880,** or 831/335-4954; Coralpss@aol.com).

9

Perth & Western Australia

by Natalie Kruger

Many international visitors—heck, many east-coast Australians—never make the trek to Western Australia. It's too far away, too expensive to fly to, too big when you get there, they say. That's all true, especially the bit about it being big (2.5 million sq. km, or 965,000 sq. miles), but don't dismiss a trip out of hand. Flights need not be expensive (not if you're an international traveler flying on air-pass coupons—see chapter 2), and some of Australia's best snorkeling and diving, cutest historic towns, most splendid natural scenery, and most fantastic wine regions are here. Every spring (that's Sept–Nov Down Under), a good deal of the state is carpeted in masses of wildflowers. The capital, **Perth** ⏧, has great food, a fabulous outdoor life of biking and beaches, plenty of smallish museums that are well worth a look, and a beautiful historic port called Fremantle.

The **Southwest** ⏧⏧ "hook" of the state, below Perth, is the prettiest part of Western Australia to visit, and also the easiest region to visit outside of Perth. Massive stands of karri and jarrah trees stretch to the sky, the surf is world-class, and the coastline is wave-smashed and rugged. The Southwest's Margaret River region turns out some of Australia's most acclaimed wines. En route to the Southwest is a special phenomenon—a visit by **wild dolphins** ⏧⏧ to the town of Bunbury. You can swim with them, if the creatures happen to be in the mood for socializing.

Head east 644 kilometers (400 miles) inland from Perth and you strike what, in the 1890s, was the richest square mile of gold-bearing earth the world has ever seen. The mining town of **Kalgoorlie** ⏧, still Australia's biggest gold producer (nearly 2,000 oz. a day), is a place of ornate 19th-century architecture. If Australia has an answer to the Wild West, then Kalgoorlie is it.

Head well north of Perth and you're in the Outback. Orange sand, scrubby trees, and spiky grass called spinifex are all you see for hundreds of miles. About 850 kilometers (531 miles) north of Perth, **wild dolphins** ⏧ make daily visits to the shores of Monkey Mia. Another 872 kilometers (545 miles) on is one of Australia's best-kept secrets, a 260-kilometer (163-mile) coral reef called **Ningaloo** ⏧⏧, stretching along the isolated Outback shore. It's a second Great Barrier Reef, undiscovered by world travelers or even Aussies themselves.

EXPLORING THE STATE

VISITOR INFORMATION   The **Western Australian Tourism Commission (WATC)** is the official source of information on touring the state. Its website (www.westernaustralia.net) provides a good overview, but it does not yet have a thorough rundown on what to see and do. You may find the **Australian Tourist Commission's** website (www.australia.com), or the web pages of local tourism boards (found under "Visitor Information" in each regional section of this chapter) more useful. Private company **Visit WA** (℡ **08/9581 5666;** www. visitwa.com.au) offers an online tour-planning service, and claims to try to reply within 48 hours to any e-mailed question about traveling in the state.

Also contact the WATC's **Perth Visitor Centre** in Perth, which dispenses information about the whole state, and makes bookings. See section 1 of this chapter for contact information. In Perth, drop by the **"W.A. Naturally"** store (℡ **08/9430 8600**) run by the state Department of Conservation and Land Management (CALM) for information on the state's national and marine parks (or go to CALM's website at www.calm.wa.gov.au).

WHEN TO GO Perth is blessed with long, dry summers and mild wet winters. You'll want warm gear in the Southwest winters, but temperatures rarely hit the freezing point. Much north of Perth, summer is hell, when temperatures soar well into the 40s°C (over 104°F–120°F). Avoid these parts from December to March; February is worst. Winter (June–Aug) in the mid-, northern, and inland reaches of the state is pleasantly cool—warm enough for ocean swimming—and sometimes even hot.

GETTING AROUND Before you plan a whirlwind driving tour of this state, consider the distances (it's three times as big as Texas) and the mostly arid, flat, and monotonous countryside. The Southwest forests make pretty driving; elsewhere, you should fly, unless you want to count sheep in all those vast brown paddocks you will be driving past.

If you do hit the road, remember that Western Australia is largely devoid of people, gas stations (keep the gas tank full), and emergency help. Road trains and wildlife pose a road threat more so here than in any other state. Avoid driving at night, dusk, and dawn—all prime animal feeding times. Read "Road Conditions & Safety," in "Getting Around Australia" in chapter 2, before setting off.

The **Royal Automobile Club of Western Australia (RACWA),** 228 Adelaide Terrace, Perth, WA 6000 (℡ **08/9421 4444;** www.aaa.asn.au), is a good source of maps and motoring advice. For a recorded road-condition report, call the state **Main Roads Department** (℡ **1800/013 314** in Australia).

Airlink (℡ **08/9225 8383,** or book through Qantas; www.qantas.com.au) is the state's major regional airline.

Greyhound Pioneer (℡ **13 20 30** in Australia) is the only interstate coach company serving Western Australia. It travels the highway from Adelaide over to Perth, then up the coast to Broome and across to Darwin; it also travels the remote inland Newman Highway calling at Outback mining towns.

The only train to Western Australia from outside the state is the *Indian Pacific* ⊕, from Sydney via Adelaide and Kalgoorlie to Perth (see "Getting Around Australia," in chapter 2). Inside the state, long-distance trains run only in the southern third. They are operated by **WAGR** (℡ **13 10 53** in Western Australia, 1800/099 150 in Australia but outside Western Australia, or 08/9326 2000; www.wagr.wa.gov.au) from Perth to Bunbury 2¼ hours south of Perth, Northam an hour or so eastward in the Avon Valley, and Kalgoorlie. WAGR also runs coach services to the Southwest and the southern coast.

All major car- and motorhome-rental companies have offices in Perth.

TOUR OPERATORS Between them, Western Australia's two biggest coach tour companies, **Australian Pinnacle Tours** (℡ **1800/999 304** in Australia, or

Western Australia

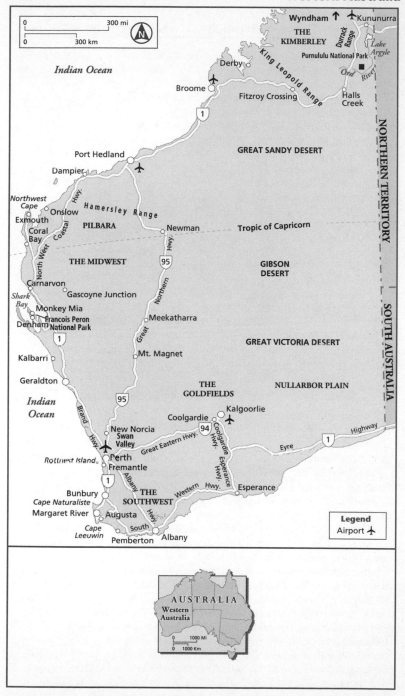

Indian Ocean

Wyndham
THE KIMBERLEY
Kununurra
Durack Range
Lake Argyle
Purnululu National Park
Ord River
Derby
King Leopold Range
Broome
Fitzroy Crossing
Halls Creek
1
GREAT SANDY DESERT
NORTHERN TERRITORY
Port Hedland
Dampier
Northwest Cape
Onslow
Hamersley Range
PILBARA
Newman
Tropic of Capricorn
North West Coastal Hwy.
Exmouth
Coral Bay
THE MIDWEST
95
GIBSON DESERT
Carnarvon
Gascoyne Junction
Shark Bay
Monkey Mia
Francois Peron National Park
Denham
1
Meekatharra
Great Northern Hwy.
GREAT VICTORIA DESERT
SOUTH AUSTRALIA
Kalbarri
Mt. Magnet
Geraldton
Indian Ocean
THE GOLDFIELDS
NULLARBOR PLAIN
95
Kalgoorlie
Coolgardie
New Norcia
Swan Valley
94
Great Eastern Hwy.
Coolgardie Hwy.
Eyre
Highway
1
Brand Hwy.
Rottnest Island
Perth
Fremantle
Esperance Hwy.
Western Hwy.
Esperance
1
Bunbury
Cape Naturaliste
Margaret River
Augusta
THE SOUTHWEST
Albany Hwy.
South Hwy.
Cape Leeuwin
Pemberton
Albany

Legend
Airport ✈

AUSTRALIA
Western Australia

0   1000 Mi
0   1000 Km

0   300 mi
0   300 km

N

Moments **Tiptoeing Through the Wildflowers** ✿✿

Every year from August to mid-November, the southern half of Western Australia is blessed with a carpet of 12,000 species of white, yellow, mauve, pink, red, and blue wildflowers.

This annual burgeoning is accompanied by wildflower shows and festivals in country towns throughout the state, and coach- and rail-tour companies go into overdrive ferrying petal enthusiasts from all around Australia and the globe on wildflower tours. The blossoms can be easily explored on day trips from Perth, or on longer jaunts of up to 5 days or so. September and October are the peak months.

If time is short, you can see ample blossoms right in Perth at the Kings Park & Botanic Garden, which conducts free guided walks through its 2,000 species during its 10-day Wildflower Festival every September.

Because Australian flora is adapted to desert conditions, it tends to sprout on dry, sunny days following a rain shower. The Western Australian Tourism Commission's Perth Visitor Centre (see "Visitor Information," in section 1 of this chapter) can keep you up to speed on whatever hot spot is blooming brightest that week, and they can book you on one of the many coach and rail wildflower tours. The Commission annually produces a helpful 32-page **Wildflower Holiday Guide** brochure that describes many detailed self-drive wildflower routes, accommodation houses and events en route, and wildflower tour operators. It is downloadable from the Commission's website (www.westernaustralia.net).

Interstate buses and trains and hotels fill up fast in wildflower season, so book ahead.

08/9221 5411; www.pinnacletours.com.au) and **Feature Tours** (© **1800/999 819** in Australia, or 08/9479 4131; www.ft.com.au) visit Perth and its surroundings, the Southwest, Monkey Mia, the Northwest Cape, and attractions about a day's drive away, such as Wave Rock (a large wave-shaped rock) and the Pinnacles (weird limestone formations in the desert). Australian Pinnacle Tours also does four-wheel-drive tours. **Overland 4WD Safaris** (© **08/9524 7122;** www.overland.com.au) runs four-wheel-drive safaris from Perth throughout the state with an off-the-beaten-track bent.

Aerial tours make sense in W.A. Look into the personalized or pre-set tours offered by **Complete Aviation Services** (© **1800/632 221** in Australia, or 08/9478 2749; www.casair.com.au) or **Kookaburra Air** (© **08/9354 1158;** www.kookaburra.iinet.net.au). Both do tours from Perth throughout Western Australia, including the Kimberley (described in chapter 8 in this book), and the Northern Territory's Top End and the Red Centre.

Landscope Expeditions ✿✿ is an excellent tour program run by the state Conservation and Land Management Department, or **CALM** (© **08/ 9380 2433** is the University of Western Australia, which handles bookings; fax 08/9380 1066 for a free schedule; or check it out at www.calm.wa.gov.au). It has you assisting CALM scientists on research projects, such as reintroducing endangered native species to the Shark Bay World Heritage region, observing solar eclipses from a boat in the remote Houtman Abrolhos Islands, or learning about 17th-century Dutch shipwrecks on the treacherous Zuytdorp Cliffs.

1 Perth ⟨★⟩

4,405km (2,753 miles) W of Sydney; 2,389km (1,493 miles) S of Broome

If you like Sydney, I bet you'll like Perth. It has the same silver skyscrapers glinting under a blue sky, the same youthful, energetic outdoorsy vibrancy, and, like Sydney, the sparkling ocean and glorious white beaches are just a bus ride from downtown. Perth likes to boast it gets more sunshine than any other city in Australia, some 300 days a year. Outside Sydney, I'd say Perth is the most interesting capital city to visit in Australia. Far from being one of those drab capitals that exists only to serve the state's economy, Perth has lots of fun stuff to do. Wander through the impressively restored historic warehouses, museums, and working docks of bustling **Fremantle;** stock up at the plentiful Aboriginal art and souvenir stores; visit some great art galleries and museums; eat at some of the country's best restaurants (no, they're not all in Sydney and Melbourne); go snorkeling and sea kayaking with wild sea lions; bushwalk through a 1,000-acre park in the middle of the city; and pedal your bike to a great snorkeling spot on **Rottnest Island** ⟨★★⟩, a miniature reef resort 19 kilometers (12 miles) offshore.

More than most other Aussie capitals, Perth gives you several good choices of side trips, too: Drop in on the Benedictine monks in the Spanish Renaissance monastery town of **New Norcia** ⟨★⟩, nip out to the Swan Valley vineyards 20 minutes from town, or spend a few days in **Margaret River** ⟨★★⟩ country, one of Australia's most revered wine regions. The long, dry summer is the best time to visit; winter is rainy.

ORIENTATION

ARRIVING   By Plane   Qantas (⟨©⟩ **13 13 13** in Australia) flies at least once a day, if not more often, from all mainland state capitals, either direct or with mostly only one stop. **Airlink** (⟨©⟩ **08/9225 8383,** or book through Qantas; www.qantas.com.au) flies direct from Alice Springs, and from Cairns via Ayers Rock. Airlink also flies from Broome and operates flights from many small towns within Western Australia.

Perth International Airport is 20 kilometers (12.5 miles) northeast of the city, and the Qantas domestic terminals are 8 kilometers (5 miles) closer. All have ATMs, showers, baby-change rooms, lockers, a post box (the news agencies sell stamps), and a limited range of tourist information. Internet kiosks and currency-exchange bureaus are in the international and Qantas domestic terminals. The international terminal has mobile (cell) telephones for rent.

Avis (⟨©⟩ 08/9277 1177 domestic terminal, 08/9477 1302 international terminal), **Budget** (⟨©⟩ 08/9277 9277), **Delta EuropCar** (⟨©⟩ 08/9277 9144), **Hertz** (⟨©⟩ 08/9479 4788), and **Thrifty** (⟨©⟩ 08/9464 7333) all have desks at both terminals.

Feature Tours runs the **airport-city shuttle** (⟨©⟩ **1800/999 819** in Australia, or 08/9479 4131), which meets all international and interstate flights. It does not specifically meet intrastate flights. There is no need to book. City transfers from the international terminal cost A$11 (U.S.$6.05) for adults, A$7 (U.S.$3.85) children under 15. Domestic terminal-city transfers are A$9 (U.S.$4.95) for adults and A$5.50 (U.S.$3) for kids. Transfers between the domestic and international terminals are A$5.50 (U.S.$3) for adults, and

A$3.30 (U.S.$1.80) for kids. Round-trip fares work out a little cheaper. Qantas runs a free bus between terminals for its transferring passengers. The **Fremantle Airport Shuttle** (© 08/9383 4115) operates 12 services a day from the airport to hotels, motorhome-rental offices, or anywhere else in Fremantle you want to go; you must book in advance. The fare is A$15 (U.S.$9.25), or A$12 (U.S.$6.60) per person for two or more people traveling together, and A$28 (U.S.$15.40) for a family.

Public buses no. 36, 37, 39, 302, and 556 run to the city from the domestic terminal only. No buses run from the international terminal. A taxi to the city is about A$25 (U.S.$13.75) from the international terminal and A$20 (U.S.$11) from the domestic terminal; that will include a A$1 (U.S.55¢) fee for picking up a taxi at the airport.

By Train   The epic 3-day journey to Perth from Sydney via Broken Hill, Adelaide, and Kalgoorlie aboard the *Indian Pacific* ✺, operated by Great Southern Railway, is an experience in itself. The train runs twice a week in each direction. The one-way fare ranges from A$1,499 (U.S.$824.45) in first class with meals and en suite bathroom, to A$1,199 (U.S.$659.45) in perfectly comfy second class (meals cost extra, and bathrooms are shared), down to A$459 (U.S.$252.45) for the sit-up-all-the-way coach class (not a good idea on this long trip). Connections are available from Melbourne on The Overland train. Fares may be higher, usually from September to mid-November, during the peak of Western Australia's wildflower season. See "Getting Around Australia," in chapter 2, for contact details in Australia and abroad. The **Prospector** train makes the 7¾ hour trip from Kalgoorlie daily; call **WAGR** (© **13 10 53** in Western Australia, 1800/099 150 in Australia from other states in the country, or 08/9326 2000).

All long-distance trains pull into the East Perth Terminal, Summers Street off Lord Street, East Perth. A taxi to the city center costs about A$10 (U.S.$5.50).

By Bus   Greyhound Pioneer (© **13 20 30** in Australia) runs coach services 5 days a week from Sydney via Adelaide (trip time: about 55 hr. from Sydney, about 34 hr. from Adelaide). It also has service daily from Darwin via Kununurra and Broome (trip time: about 55 hr.). Traveling from Alice Springs requires a connection in Adelaide. The Sydney–Perth fare is A$341 (U.S.$326.40) and Darwin–Perth is A$496 (U.S.$272.80).

By Car   There are only two road routes from interstate—the 2,389-kilometer (1,493-mile) route from Broome in the north, and the 2,708-kilometer (1,693-mile) odyssey from Adelaide, which includes hundreds of miles along some of the world's straightest road on the treeless Nullarbor Plain. Arm yourself with an up-to-date road map before setting off. It's not a bad idea to contact the South Australian or Western Australian state auto clubs (listed under "Getting Around Australia," in chapter 2) for advice on crossing the lonely Nullarbor. Both routes cross mostly featureless and semi-desert, sheep ranches or wheat fields most of the way, with very few towns en route. For that reason, I don't recommend either!

VISITOR INFORMATION   The Western Australian Tourism Commission's **Perth Visitor Centre,** Albert Facey House, 469 Wellington St. on the corner of Forrest Place (© **1300/361 351** in Australia, or 08/9483 1111; www.western australia.net), is the official visitor information source for Perth and the state. It's open Monday through Thursday from 8:30am to 6pm (5:30pm in winter May–July), Friday from 8:30am to 7pm (6pm in winter), Saturday from 8:30am

Perth

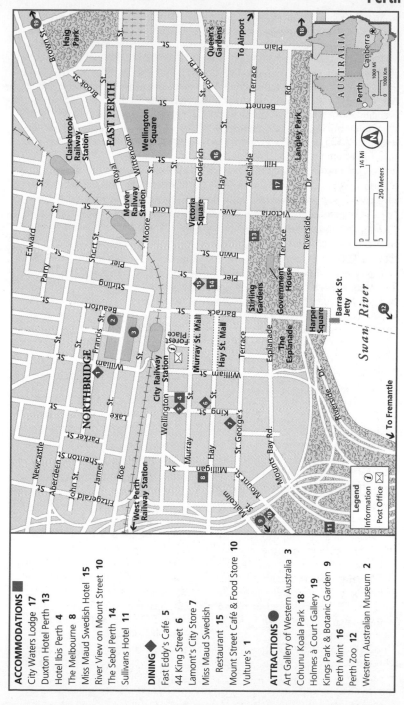

to 5pm (4:30pm in winter), and Sunday from 10am to 5pm (3pm in winter). Another source of information and maps (plus a free booking service) is **Perth Tourist Lounge,** Level 2, Carillon Arcade off 207 Murray Street Mall (© **08/ 9229 2238**), open Monday through Saturday from 9am to 5:30pm and Sunday from noon to 4pm.

A good source of ideas on nature-based activities and attractions in the state's national and marine parks is the **"W.A. Naturally"** center, 47 Henry St., Fremantle, WA 6160 (© **08/9430 8600**), run by the state Department of Conservation and Land Management (CALM)—check out their website at **www.calm.wa.gov.au.** The center is open every day except Tuesday from 10am to 5:30pm.

For an untouristy lowdown on the city's restaurants, cultural life, shops, bars, nightlife, festivals, concerts, and the like, buy the excellent local glossy quarterly magazine *Scoop* (A$8.90/U.S.$4.90; www.scoop.com.au) or pick up the free color newspaper, *Perth Weekly.* Both are available in bigger newsagents, and you can pick up *Perth Weekly* in cafes, tour desks, and other such places around town.

CITY LAYOUT   The city center is 19 kilometers (12 miles) upriver from the Indian Ocean, on the north bank of a broad reach of the Swan River. **Hay Street** and **Murray Street** are the two major thoroughfares, 1 block apart; both are bisected by pedestrian malls between William and Barrack streets. It helps to know that Adelaide Terrace and St. Georges Terrace are one and the same street. The name change occurs at Victoria Avenue.

MAPS   Of the many free pocket guides to Perth available at tour desks and in hotel lobbies, *Your Guide to Perth & Fremantle* has the **best street map,** because it shows one-way streets, public toilets and telephones, taxi stands, post offices, police stations, and street numbers, as well as most attractions and hotels. The **Royal Automobile Club of Western Australia** (see "Exploring the State," at the start of this chapter) is a good source of maps to the entire state, as is the **Perth Map Centre,** 2nd floor, Shafto Lane at 884 Hay St. (© **08/9322 5733**). You will find tourist maps at the Perth Visitor Centre and the Perth Tourist Lounge (see "Visitor Information," above).

NEIGHBORHOODS IN BRIEF

City Center   The central business district (called the CBD in Australia) is home to shops and department stores. A good introduction to Perth's charms is to take in the views from the pedestrian/bike path that skirts the river along Riverside Drive. Within walking distance on the western edge of town is Kings Park & Botanic Garden.

Northbridge   Just about all of Perth's nightclubs, and a good many of its cool restaurants, bars, and cafes, are in this 5-block precinct just north of the railway line, within easy walking distance of the

city center, or take the free Blue CAT buses. It's roughly bounded by James, Beaufort, Aberdeen, and Lake streets. What locals call the Cultural Centre—an umbrella term that means the Western Australian Museum, the Art Gallery of Western Australia, the State Library, and the Perth Institute of Contemporary Arts—is here, too.

Subiaco   This well-heeled suburb is on the other side of Kings Park from the city. Saturday morning just wouldn't be the same for Perth's see-and-be-seen crowd without a stroll through "Subi's" village-like concoction of cafes, markets, upscale boutiques, antique shops, and art galleries. Most of the action is near the intersection of Hay Street and Rokeby (pronounced Rockerby) Road. Take the train to Subiaco station.

Fremantle Not only is "Freo" Perth's working port, it's also Perth's second city heart, and a favorite weekend spot to relax, eat, shop, and sail. A 1980s restoration of long-neglected Victorian warehouses turned Freo into a marvelous living example of a 19th-century seaport—like San Francisco's Fisherman's Wharf

without the stale commercial taint. Fremantle is 19 kilometers (12 miles) downriver on the mouth of the Swan.

Scarborough Beach One of Perth's prize beaches, 12 kilometers (7½ miles) north of the city center. The district is a little tatty with that over-supply of cheap take-out food out-lets that seem to plague Aussie beaches, but if you like sun, sand, and surf, this is the place to be. You will find bars, restaurants, and surf-gear rental stores here. Allow 15 to 20 minutes to get there by car, 35 minutes on the bus.

GETTING AROUND

BY PUBLIC TRANSPORTATION **Transperth** runs Perth's buses, trains, and ferries. For route, closest bus stop, and timetable information, call © **13 62 13** in Western Australia, or drop into the Transperth InfoCentres at the Plaza Arcade off Hay Street Mall, the Perth Railway Station, the Wellington Street bus station, or the City Bus Port on Mounts Bay Road. You can transfer from bus to ferry to train on one ticket within its expiry time of 90 minutes or 2 hours. Travel costs A$1.80 (U.S.$1) in one zone (to Subiaco, for instance), and A$2.70 (U.S.$1.50) in two, which gets you most places, including Fremantle. Non-Australian seniors and students don't qualify for discounted fares; kids ages 5 to 14 do.

By Bus The Wellington Street Bus Station, centrally located next to Perth Railway Station at Forrest Place, and the City Bus Port on the western edge of the city on Mounts Bay Road, are the two main depots. The vast majority of buses travel along St. Georges Terrace. Drivers do not always stop unless you hail. Buy tickets from the driver. Buses run from about 5:30am until about 10:30 or 11:30pm, depending on the route.

The best way to get around town is on the silver, free **CAT** (Central Area Transit) buses that run a continual loop of the city and Northbridge. The Red CAT runs east-west every 5 minutes, Monday through Friday from 6:50am to 6:20pm, and once every 45 minutes from 10am to 6:15pm weekends. The Blue CAT runs north-south as far north as Northbridge and south to Barrack Street Jetty every 8 minutes from 6:50am. The last Blue CAT service is at 6:20pm Monday through Thursday, and on Friday it continues every 15 minutes from 6:20pm until 1:05am Saturday morning. Saturdays it runs from 8:30am to 1am (Sun morning) every 12 minutes, and Sundays every 12 minutes from 10am to 5pm. Look for the silver CAT bus stops. Transperth InfoCentres (see above) dis-pense free route maps.

The Perth Tram Co. tours (see "Whale-Watching Cruises, Tram Trips & Other Tours," later in this chapter) are a good way to get around, too.

By Train Trains are fast, clean, and safe. They start from about 5:30am and run every 15 minutes or even more often during the day, and every half hour at night until midnight. NightRider trains depart Perth at 1 and 2am Friday and

(Tips A Free Ride

A welcome freebie in Perth is the **Free Transit Zone** (FTZ). You can travel free on trains and buses within this zone at any hour, day or night. It is bounded by Kings Park Road, Fraser Avenue, Thomas Street, and Loftus Street in the west; Newcastle Street in the north; and the river in the south and east. Basically, this means you can travel to Kings Park, Northbridge, east to major sporting grounds, and anywhere in the city center free. Signs mark the FTZ boundaries; just ask the driver if you're unsure.

MultiRider passes give you 10 trips at a savings of 15%; they come in a range of prices good for various numbers of zones. A **DayRider** pass allows 1 day's unlimited travel after 9am on weekdays and all day on weekends and public holidays, and costs A$6.90 (U.S.$3.80). If you're a family, it may be worth getting a MaxiRider, valid for a 2-hour journey to any destination and back for a group of seven people with a maximum of two adults. MaxiRiders are aimed at Perth families and so are valid only weekends, public holidays, after 9am weekdays, and during Western Australian school holidays, after 6pm year-round Monday through Thursday, and after 3:30pm Friday. They cost A$6.90 (U.S.$3.80). Passes, collectively known as FastCards, are sold at Newspower newsagents and at Transperth InfoCentres. To use the passes, validate them in the machines located on board in the case of buses, and on the platform or wharf in the case of trains and ferries.

Saturday night (meaning Sat and Sun morning), and 3am December through March, stopping at all stations on all lines. All trains leave from Perth Railway Station opposite Forrest Place on Wellington Street. Buy your ticket before you board, at the vending machines on the platform.

By Ferry   You will probably use ferries only to visit Perth Zoo. They run every half hour or so, more often in peak hour, every day from 6:50am weekdays and 7:50am weekends and public holidays, until 7:15pm (or until 9:15pm on Fri and Sat nights in summer between Sept and Apr) from the Barrack Street Jetty to Mends Street in South Perth. Buy tickets before you board from the vending machine on the wharf. The trip takes 7 minutes.

By Taxi   Perth's two biggest taxi companies are **Swan Taxis** (© **13 1330**) and **Black & White Taxis** (© **13 1008**). Ranks are located at Perth Railway Station, and at both ends of Hay Street Mall.

By Car   Perth's signposting is notorious for telling you where you have been, not where you are going—for example, some interstate highways are announced with insignificant signs more suited to a side street.

CarePark, 152–158 St. Georges Terrace between William Street and King Street (© **08/9321 0667**) charges A$2.60 (U.S.$1.45) per hour and is open Monday through Friday from 6am to 8pm (until midnight Fri), and Saturday and Sunday from 8:30am to 6:30pm. The maximum charge between 5pm and midnight Friday, and all day Saturday or Sunday, is A$5 (U.S.$2.75).

The major car-rental companies are **Avis** (© 08/9325 7677), **Budget** (© 08/9322 1100), **Delta EuropCar** (© 08/9226 0026), **Hertz** (© 08/9321 7777), and **Thrifty** (© 08/9464 7444). All except Hertz also have outlets in Fremantle. **ATC Rent-A-Car** (© 08/9325 1833) is a locally owned outfit with offices in Monkey Mia and Broome; it also rents camping kits.

 FAST FACTS: **Perth**

American Express The bureau, located at 645 Hay Street Mall (© **08/9261 2711**), is open Monday through Friday from 9am to 5pm and Saturday from 9am to noon.

Business Hours Banks are open Monday through Thursday from 9:30am to 4pm and until 5pm Friday. Shopping hours are usually from 9am to 5:30pm Monday through Friday (until 9pm on Thurs in the suburbs and Fremantle, and until 9pm Fri in the city), and from 9am to 5pm on Saturday. On Sunday most major stores (but not all) open from noon to 4pm or later in the city, and from noon to 6pm in Fremantle.

Currency Exchange Go to the American Express office (see above) or **Interforex,** Shop 24, London Court off Hay Street Mall (© **08/9325 7418**), open daily from 9am to 6pm, and until 9pm Friday. Interforex has a Fremantle bureau at the corner of William Street and Adelaide Street (© **08/ 9431 7022**), open daily from 8am to 8pm.

Dentist **Forrest Chase Dental Centre** (© **08/9221 2777**) is on the Upper Walkway Level, Forrest Chase shopping complex, 425 Wellington St. opposite Perth Railway Station. Open daily from 8am to 8pm, it can be reached after hours at © **08/9383 1620.**

Doctor **Central City Medical Centre** is on the Perth Railway Station concourse, 420 Wellington St. (© **08/9221 4747**, or 08/9225-1100; this number diverts to an on-call doctor after hours). It is open daily from 7am to 7pm.

Embassies/Consulates The **United States Consulate-General** is at 16 St. Georges Terrace (© **08/9231 9400**). The **Canadian Consulate** is at 267 St. Georges Terrace (© **08/9322 7930**). The **British Consulate-General** is at 77 St. Georges Terrace (© **08/9221 5400**). The Irish **Consulate-General** is at 10 Lilika Rd., City Beach (© **08/9385 8247**).

Emergencies Dial © **000** for fire, ambulance, or police in an emergency. This is a free call, and no coins are needed from a public phone.

Hospitals **Royal Perth Hospital** in the city center has a public emergency/ casualty ward (© **08/9224 2244**). Enter from Victoria Square, which is accessed from Murray Street.

Luggage Storage/Lockers The **City Place Rest Centre** (© **08/8229 2989**) rents small lockers for A$3.30 (U.S.$1.80) per day, suitcase-size lockers for A$6.05 (U.S.$3.30), and offers showers with towel and soap supplied for A$4.40 (U.S.$2.40). It's on the Perth Railway Station concourse, 420 Wellington St. (next to the Central City Medical Centre), open Monday through Thursday from 7am to 10pm, Friday and Saturday from 7am to midnight, and Sunday from 7am to 9pm. The **Perth Tourist Lounge** (see "Visitor Information" earlier in the chapter) also stores luggage, and there are baggage lockers at the international and domestic terminals at the airport.

Pharmacies **Forrest Chase Pharmacy** (© **08/9221 1691**), on the upper level of the Forrest Chase shopping center, 425 Wellington St. (near the dentist's office listed in "Dentist," above) is open Monday through Thursday from 8am to 7pm (and until 9pm Fri), Saturday from 8:30am to 6pm, and Sunday from 10am to 6pm. **Shenton Pharmacy,** 214 Nicholson Rd., Subiaco (© **08/9381 1358** business and after hours), will deliver across Perth.

Police Dial © **000** in an emergency. **City Police Station,** 1 Hay St., East Perth (© **08/9222 1048**), the **City Watch** police bureau at Perth Railway Station, and **Fremantle Police Station,** 45 Henderson St. (© **08/9430 1222**), are open 24 hours. To be connected to the nearest station, dial © **13 14 44.**

Safety Perth is safe, but steer clear of the back streets of Northbridge at night, even if you are not alone, because groups of teenage boys have been known to pick fights.

Time Zone Western Australian time (WST) is GMT plus 8 hours and has no daylight saving. This means it is normally 2 hours behind Sydney, 3 October through March when New South Wales goes to daylight saving. Call © **1194** for the exact local time.

Weather Call © **1196** for a recorded local weather forecast.

WHERE TO STAY

Perth has loads of hotels in the city center. That means competition can be high, especially Friday through Sunday when the staple clientele of business travelers dries up, so ask about lower rates on weekends. Ask, and you may strike a good deal on weeknights, too, if business is slow across town. Many hotels throw a free breakfast or some other value-add into midweek overnight packages. Most hotels have rooms for travelers with disabilities.

IN THE CITY CENTER
Very Expensive
Duxton Hotel Perth 👫👫   The best uninterrupted views of the Swan River from a hotel room are found from the south side rooms at this chic 21st-century-meets-Art-Deco hotel, centrally located downtown. Only a few years old as a hotel, the place was created out of old tax office chambers. A sandstone portico fronts the bronze-paneled lobby with its Siena marble floor, and the rooms sport blond oak furniture with 1930s curves, elegant marquetry, and ample bathrooms. Superior rooms have extra-large bathrooms (some with Jacuzzis); executive-level rooms have TVs in the bathroom, CD players, and a fax and printer; and suites have separate living rooms. Make time to see and be seen lazing around that petite heated swimming pool colonnaded like a Roman bath.

1 St. Georges Terrace (at Victoria Ave. next to Perth Concert Hall), Perth, WA 6000. © **1800/681 118** in Australia, or 08/9261 8000. Fax 08/9261 8020. www.duxton.com. 306 units (several with shower only). A$360–$440 (U.S.$198–$242) double; A$470(U.S.$258.50) suite. Extra person A$27.50 (U.S.$15.15). Children under 16 stay free in parents' room with existing bedding. Ask about packages and special upgrade rates. AE, DC, DISC, MC, V. Valet parking A$15 (U.S.$7.50); no self-parking. Bus: Red CAT Stop 11 "Victoria Ave." Airport shuttle. **Amenities:** Restaurant; bar; health club and spa; concierge; business center; 24-hr. room service; in-room massage; babysitting; self-service laundry; same-day dry cleaning/laundry service; executive-level rooms. *In room:* A/C, TV with pay movies, dataport, minibar, hair dryer, iron.

Expensive
The Sebel Perth ⟨⚑⟩ Right in the middle of town, the Sebel has the biggest standard hotel rooms in Perth, and a friendly ambience that's a welcome contrast to the frosty hauteur of many five-star properties. Nice touches are everywhere—like a free gift with every stay (such as trendy locally made soap), free tea and coffee in the lobby every morning, and a weekly General Manager's cocktail party. All 86 standard rooms were thoroughly refurbished in 2000. All have big desks, walk-in closets, bathrobes, armchairs or sofas, and windows that open for fresh air. Suites have a separate sitting room. Every Monday, Wednesday, and Friday at 6:15am, you, three other guests, and a senior member of management can jump into the hotel's "Cottesloe Express" Rolls Royce and motor in style to fabulous **Cottesloe Beach** ⟨⚑⟩, 20 minutes away for a swim, a walk, or a jog. They get you back to the hotel by 7:40am or so. Overnight packages are often less than half the "rack" rates we quote below.

37 Pier St., Perth, WA 6000. ⟨✆⟩ Mirvac, **1800/999 004** in Australia, or 08/9325 7655. Fax 08/9325 7383. www.mirvac.com.au. 119 units. A$260 double (U.S.$143); A$300 (U.S.$165) suite. Extra person A$25 (U.S.$13.75). Children under 12 stay free in parents' room with existing bedding. Ask about weekend, overnight, honeymoon, and suite packages. AE, DC, MC, V. Free valet and self-parking. Train: Perth. Bus: Red CAT Stop 12 "Town Hall East"; Blue CAT Stop 4 "Town Hall" or 5 "Murray St. Mall East." Airport shuttle. **Amenities:** Restaurant, poolside bar-cum-cafe; heated outdoor swimming pool; access to a nearby health club; free bike rental; concierge; tour desk; secretarial services; 24-hr. room service; babysitting; guest laundry and laundry service, same-day dry cleaning service. *In room:* A/C, TV with pay movies, dataport, minibar, coffeemaker, hair dryer, iron.

Moderate
The Melbourne ⟨⚑⟩ ⟨Value⟩ This 1897 hotel in Perth's posh downtown West End, thoroughly restored to its ornate gold rush–era originality in 1997, is a great value, because its facilities and rooms match most five-star hotels. The public areas and restaurant have a New Orleans theme, aided by original trappings like decorative pressed metal ceilings and floral carpets. Rooms favor modern convenience but retain a hint of the South with wooden blinds, summery friezes, and brass-trimmed fans. Suites are a single room with a sitting area. Go for the outside rooms (those on the second floor open onto the wide veranda), as inside rooms lack views. The hotel rents infrared keyboards to access the Internet via the TV for A$7 (U.S.$3.85) per day. The atmospheric streetfront Mississippi's Bar is a happening place to be on Friday nights.

Corner of Hay and Milligan sts., Perth, WA 6000. ⟨✆⟩ **1800/68 5671** in Australia, or 08/9320 3333. Fax 08/9320 3344. www.melbournehotel.com.au. 36 units (all with shower only). A$165 (U.S.$90.75) double; A$185 (U.S.$101.75) suite. Extra person A$20 (U.S.$11). Children under 12 stay free in parents' room. Ask about overnight packages. AE, DC, MC, V. Valet parking A$8 (U.S.$4.40); no self-parking. Bus: Red CAT Stop 18 "QVI." Airport shuttle. **Amenities:** Restaurant, cafe, bar; access to a nearby health club; concierge; secretarial in-room services; limited room service; same-day dry cleaning/laundry service; babysitting. *In room:* A/C, TV, dataport, non-alcoholic minibar, hair dryer, iron.

Miss Maud Swedish Hotel ⟨⚑⟩ Staying at this adorable hotel right in the heart of town is like staying at Grandma's. Never mind that the bedspread clashes with the carpet, and the paint's peeling off the door (the rooms are gradually getting refurbished, anyhow). You're here for the homey ambience, the cozy rooms sporting wall-size murals of Scandinavian pine forests, and a staff that's more polite and on the ball than those in most five-star hotels. The front desk is staffed 24 hours. A private sun deck is tucked away as a little surprise up among the rooftops. The real Miss Maud, Maud Edmiston, wants guests to feel they are in a European family hotel like in her Swedish homeland, and she succeeds. A fabulous full buffet breakfast is included at Miss Maud Swedish Restaurant downstairs (see "Where to Dine," below).

97 Murray St. (at Pier St.), Perth, WA 6000. © 1800/998 022 in Australia, or 08/9325 3900. Fax 08/9221 3225. www.missmaud.com.au. 52 units (40 with shower only). A$112–$150 (U.S.$61.60–$82.50) double. Extra person A$15 (U.S.$8.25). Rates include full smorgasbord breakfast. AE, DC, MC, V. Discounted parking A$7 (U.S.$3.85) at the Kings Hotel carpark 1 block away on Hay St. between Pier and Irwin sts. Bus: Red CAT Stop 1 "Pier St."; Blue CAT Stop 5 "Murray St. Mall East." Airport shuttle. **Amenities:** Restaurant/bar, take-out pastry shop; tour desk; limited room service; self-serve laundry; laundry/dry cleaning service. *In room:* A/C, TV, minibar, hair dryer.

Sullivans Hotel   This family-owned hotel about 1.5 kilometers (1 mile) from town is popular with Europeans for its small-scale ambience. Despite being on the main road into the city, none of the rooms seems to be noisy. They're simply furnished with laminate fittings, not glamorous but clean and roomy. Larger deluxe rooms come with desks, safes, and balconies with views over parkland and the freeway to the river. There are also two-bedroom apartments with kitchenettes. Out back is a pleasant little swimming pool with a sun deck and bar-becue. Bikes are free, the restaurant is affordable, and the front desk has free 24-hour Internet access for guests. Some rooms have dataports. The Swan River is a stroll away, the city is a 10-minute walk, and Kings Park is a short, steep climb up the hill.

166 Mounts Bay Rd., Perth, WA 6000. © 1800/99 9294 in Australia, or 08/9321 8022. Fax 08/9481 6762. www.sullivans.com.au. Perth@sullivans.com.au. 68 units (66 with shower only). A$110–$130 (U.S.$60.50–$71.50) up to 4 people in room; A$150 (U.S.$82.50) 2-bedroom apt. Ask about packages. Weekly rates available. AE, DC, MC, V. Free parking. Bus: 71, 72, or 78 (the hotel is within the Free Transit Zone). Airport shuttle. **Amenities:** Restaurant/bar; tour desk; limited room service both for meals and drinks from the bar (no delivery charge); babysitting; self-service laundry; same-day laundry/dry cleaning service. *In room:* A/C, TV with free movies, hair dryer.

Inexpensive

Hotel Ibis Perth 🎯 *Value*   Ibis is one of those reputable chain brands of the "four-star facilities at a three-star price" variety. Shops, cinemas, and Hay Street Mall are just a block or two away from this hotel. Last year the neat, no-frills rooms here were thoroughly renovated with funky colors and high-quality beds. The rooms are only small, but a room this decent in this location for this price can't be beaten.

334 Murray St. (between William and King sts.), Perth, WA 6000. © 08/9322 2844; Accor, 1300/88 4400 in Australia, 1800/221-4542 in the U.S. and Canada, 020/8283 4500 in the U.K., or 0800/44 4422 in New Zealand. Fax 08/9321 6314. www.accorhotels.com.au. 192 units (all with shower only). A$85 (U.S.$52.25) double. Extra person A$27 (U.S.$43.60). Children under 13 stay free in parents' room with existing bedding. AE, DC, MC, V. Discounted self-parking A$9.90 (U.S.$5.45) at the nearby Queen Street Carpark. Bus: Red CAT Stop 15 "Murray St. Mall West"; Blue CAT Stop 17 "Hay Street Mall West." Airport shuttle. **Amenities:** Restaurant, bar; discounted rates at a nearby gym; tour desk; babysitting; self-service laundry; same-day laundry/dry cleaning service. *In room:* A/C, TV with pay movies, hair dryer, iron.

River View on Mount Street 🎯 *Value*   On a quiet leafy street a short walk from the city and Kings Park, these roomy studio apartments in a 1960s block were refurbished in 1999 with trendy new kitchens and bathrooms, fresh carpets and curtains, and smart-looking fittings. The result is great style at a great price. Some have distant views of the river a few blocks away. Maid service is weekly. The helpful on-site managers loan hair dryers and irons. You can breakfast at the excellent **Mount Street Café** downstairs (see "Where to Dine," below), which also sells prepared curries and deli items. By the time you get there, an elevator may be installed so you won't have to hike your baggage as far as the top (third) floor. No smoking.

42 Mount St., Perth, WA 6000. © **08/9321 8963.** Fax 08/9322 5956. www.riverview.au.com (not "riverview.com.au."). 50 units (all with shower only). A$85–$95 (U.S.$46.75–$58) apt (some sleep up to 3). Weekly rates available. AE, DC, MC, V. Limited free parking. Bus: Red CAT Stop 18 "QVI" (located over the freeway footbridge accessed from the corner of St. Georges Terrace and Milligan St.). Airport shuttle. **Amenities:** Cafe; tour desk; self-service laundry; laundry/same-day dry cleaning service. *In room:* A/C, TV, dataport.

ON THE BEACH

Hotel Rendezvous Observation City Perth ⚗ One of the few beachside places to stay in Perth is this 17-story complex right on the never-ending sands of Scarborough Beach. Its no-fuss ambience makes it popular with vacationing Aussies. All the rooms, which were renovated in 1998, have balconies with ocean views. Some rooms have dataports, and most suites have separate sleeping quarters. Among the entertainment venues is a British-style pub popular with locals, a live music lounge, and a dance club.

The Esplanade, Scarborough Beach, WA 6019. © **1800/067 680** in Australia, or 08/9245 1000. Fax 08/9245 1345. www.rendezvous.com.au. 333 units. A$215–$320 (U.S.$118.25–$176) double; A$550 and up (U.S.$302.50 and up) suite. Extra person A$45 (U.S.$24.75). Children under 18 stay free with existing bedding. Ask about overnight packages. AE, DC, MC, V. Valet parking A$20 (U.S.$11); self-parking A$7 (U.S.$3.85). A daily courtesy shuttle operates between the hotel, Perth city, Burswood Casino, Fremantle, and a local shopping mall. Bus: 400. **Amenities:** 3 restaurants, cafe, 3 bars; large heated free-form outdoor swimming pool, children's pool; 2 outdoor day/night tennis courts; health club; Jacuzzi; sauna; limited water-sports-equipment rentals; bike rental; childcare center; concierge; tour desk; small shopping arcade; salon; 24-hr. room service; in-room massage; babysitting; self-service laundry; same-day laundry/dry cleaning service; executive-level rooms. *In room:* A/C, TV with pay movies, minibar, hair dryer, iron.

IN FREMANTLE

There's a perpetual holiday atmosphere in this picturesque port city. Although you're 19 kilometers (12 miles) from Perth's city center, public transport connections are good, so you could happily explore all of Perth from here—and most of the top attractions are in Freo anyhow. There are good restaurants and a happening nightlife, too.

Danum House ⚗⚗ Friendly hostess Christine Sherwin has created a welcoming haven in her beautiful Federation (ca. 1909) home, a walk from town. One room, decked out in heritage reds and greens, opens onto a cottage garden. The other very large room has an ornate mantle, floral wallpaper, long drapes, and that most colonial of furnishings, a daybed, as well as a real bed for sleeping. Both sport antiques, ornate ceiling roses and cornices, fireplaces, high ceilings and fans, and have a private entrance. Even the bathrooms (one en suite, one with private access) share the colonial decor. Christine serves a hearty breakfast, and you can relax in the comfy lounge over books, CDs, free coffee, and complimentary port and chocolates. Hair dryers and irons are available. No smoking.

6 Fothergill St. (at Bellevue Terrace), Fremantle, WA 6160. © **08/9336 3735.** Fax 08/9335 3414. www.staywa.net.au/ads/danum (note: e-mail to danum@iinet.net.au). 2 units (both with shower only). A$90–$110 (U.S.$49.50–$60.50) double. Min. 2-night stay. Rates include full breakfast. MC, V. Ample on-street parking. Train: Fremantle. Fremantle airport shuttle (see "Arriving: By Plane," above). Children not permitted. *In room:* TV.

Esplanade Hotel Fremantle ⚗ Freo's best hotel is this low-rise 1897 colonial building wrapped by two verandas, centered around a buzzing four-story atrium lobby. A new 1996 wing blends in seamlessly. The nicely maintained rooms have views of the street, the pool, or the distant harbor across a park. Some have dataports. Of the several suite styles, only the Harbour Suite has a separate bedroom. The attractive larger pool in the courtyard is a good place to chill out without getting buffeted by the pesky local sea breeze, the "Fremantle Doctor." It's a minute's walk to Freo's cafes, shops, and attractions.

Marine Terrace at Essex St., Fremantle, WA 6160. ℂ 1800/998 201 in Australia, or 08/9432 4000. Fax 08/9430 4539. www.esplanadehotelfremantle.com.au. 259 units (some with shower only). A$239–$315 (U.S.$131.45–$173.25) double; A$369.50–$451 (U.S.$203.25–$248.05) suite. Rates for online reservations are considerably lower. Extra person A$33 (U.S.$18.15). Children under 13 stay free with existing bedding; cribs free. Ask about packages. AE, DC, MC, V. Valet parking A$15 (U.S.$8.25); no self-parking. Train: Fremantle. Fremantle Airport Shuttle (see "Arriving: By Plane," above). **Amenities:** Restaurant, cafe, bar; 2 heated outdoor swimming pools; exercise room; 3 Jacuzzis; sauna; bike rental; concierge; tour desk; business center; 24-hr. room service; in-room massage; babysitting; self-service laundry; same-day laundry/dry cleaning service. *In room:* A/C, TV with pay movies, minibar, hair dryer, iron.

WHERE TO DINE

An array of upscale choices, plus terrific, cheap ethnic spots makes Perth's restaurant scene as sophisticated as Sydney's and Melbourne's—which is to say, it's great. You'll find many of my recommendations in "restaurant city," Northbridge.

For an inexpensive pasta, a Turkish bread sandwich, or excellent coffee and cake, you can't beat Perth's homegrown **DOME** chain of cafes. You will spot their dark green logo at Trinity Arcade between Hay Street Mall and St. Georges Terrace (ℂ **08/9226 0210**); 149 James St., Northbridge (ℂ **08/9328 8094**); 13 S. Terrace, Fremantle (ℂ **08/9336 3040**); 19 Napoleon St., Cottesloe (ℂ **08/9383 1071**); 26 Rokeby Rd., Subiaco (ℂ **08/9381 5664**); and on Rottnest Island (ℂ **08/9292 5026**).

Western Australian law bans smoking in enclosed public spaces, including restaurants.

IN THE CITY CENTER
Expensive
Fraser's ⋆⋆⋆ *(Moments)* MODERN AUSTRALIAN/SEAFOOD   What a sensational view from this hilltop restaurant! The city skyscrapers and Swan River look so close you could almost reach out and touch them—and even better, the victuals match the vista. Executive chef Chris Taylor's sure hand with seafood, which composes about 70% of the long menu, has made the place a finalist in national "restaurant of the year" awards more than once. Seared Atlantic salmon with choy sum, abalone mushrooms, and lemon soy is typical. The duck is legendary. The spiced beef chunks with eggplant pahie (curry) and lentil dahl accompanied by chutney and yogurt salsa was possibly the best meal I've ever had. To maximize the view, ask for a seat on the terrace.

Fraser Ave. (near the Information Kiosk), Kings Park. ℂ 08/9481 7100. Reservations required. Main courses A$22–$45 (U.S.$12.10–$24.75); average A$26 (U.S.$14.30). AE, DC, MC, V. Daily 7am–late. Closed Good Friday. Bus: 33 stops outside the Information Kiosk. Red CAT Stop 25 "Havelock Street" is 1 block to the north of the gates.

Moderate
44 King Street ⋆⋆ MODERN AUSTRALIAN   Socialites and hip corporate types adorn this sophisticated hangout, whose interior is a mix of industrial design and European cafe with dark timber tables, exposed air ducts, and windows onto the street. The daily changing menu has weird and wonderful choices with exotic ingredients. Charred Malay coconut swordfish with pasenbor salad, or beetroot risotto with seared venison and quince are typical lunch or dinner choices. Not only does the menu helpfully list two wine suggestions for each dish, but it also does taster-size glasses from around A$3 (U.S.$1.65) to

A$8.50 (U.S.$4.70) from a 200-strong wine list. Lots of folks drop in just for coffee, roasted on-site, and the famous cakes. All meals are available as take-out.

44 King St. ℂ **08/9321 4476**. Reservations not accepted. Grazing menu A$3.50–$12.50 (U.S.$1.95–$6.90) breakfast, A$10–$26.50 (U.S.$5.50–$14.60) lunch and dinner. AE, DC, MC, V. Daily 7am–midnight. Bus: Red CAT Stop 28 "King Street"; Blue CAT Stop 1 "Cloisters."

Miss Maud Swedish Restaurant *Value* INTERNATIONAL   "Good food and plenty of it" is the motto at Miss Maud's (Edmiston) homey establishment, and the crowds packing the place prove it works. Most diners skip the long a la carte menu and go straight for the smorgasbord. At breakfast, that means 50 dishes including pancakes cooked before your eyes. At lunch and dinner you can tuck into soup, 10 salads, a big range of seafood (including oysters at dinner), cold meats, roasts, hot vegetables, pasta, cheeses, European-style breads, half a dozen tortes, fruit, and ice cream—65 dishes in all. Service is fast and polite.

97 Murray st. at Pier St. (below Miss Maud Swedish Hotel). ℂ **08/9325 3900**. Reservations recommended. Smorgasbord breakfast A$16.95 (U.S.$9.30) Mon–Sat, A$17.95 (U.S.$9.90) Sun and public holidays; lunch A$24.95 (U.S.$13.70) Mon–Sat, A$25.95 (U.S.$14.30) Sun and public holidays; dinner A$30.95 (U.S.$17) Sun–Fri, A$34.95 (U.S.$28.60) Sat and public holidays. Cheaper smorgasbord prices for children 4–13. A la carte main courses, sandwiches, and light meals A$5.75–$19.50 (U.S.$3.15–$10.70). Dine and leave by 7:15pm Mon–Sat for a A$5 (U.S.$2.75) discount. AE, DC, MC, V. Open all day for coffee and cake. Meals daily 6:45–10am, noon–2:30pm, 5:30–7pm, and 7:15–10pm (until about 11:30pm weekends). Bus: Red CAT Stop 1 "Pier St."; Blue CAT Stop 5 "Murray St. Mall East."

Mount Street Café and Food Store ★★ MODERN AUSTRALIAN   Chef Toby Uhlrich turns out yummy dine-in and take-out fare from this charming alfresco cafe on the edge of the central business district. Come for dinners like milk-fed veal with black-currant glaze on spinach fettuccine; lunches and breakfasts are equally fresh and delicious. Dine inside at a few tables, or out on the shaded stone terrace. Drop by anytime for cakes and good coffee, but be prepared to fight the regulars for a table. BYO.

Under the "River View on Mount Street" apts, 42 Mount St. ℂ **08/9485 1411**. Reservations recommended Thurs–Sun. Main courses A$9.50–$25 (U.S.$5.20–$13.75); many meals under A$15 (U.S.$8.25) at breakfast and lunch. MC, V. Daily 7:30am–5pm (until 11pm Fri). Bus: Red CAT Stop 18 "QVI" (located over the freeway footbridge accessed from corner of St. Georges Terrace and Milligan St.).

Inexpensive
Fast Eddy's Café FAST FOOD   A hefty menu of steaks, burgers, sandwiches, soups, pancakes, sundaes, milk shakes, and full fry-up brekkies are served all hours at this popular local chain. The fun interior is decked out with 1930s soap-powder posters and Coca-Cola advertisements. One side is table service;

Finds **Great Take-Out**

It's a take-out joint, not a restaurant, but some of the tastiest dishes in Perth are at **Lamont's City Store** ★★, 172 St. Georges Terrace at King Street (ℂ **08/9321 9907**). Grab some veal ravioli with goat's cheese, roast capsicum, and eggplant, or a gourmet sandwich, and find a shady tree to eat under. Many meals are under $15 (U.S.$8.25), sandwiches even less. They also sell their own label of wine. It is open Monday through Friday from 7am to 8pm. You can eat more of chef Kate Lamont's scrumptious food at her eponymous restaurants at 11 Brown St., East Perth (ℂ **08/9202 1566**), and in the Swan Valley (see "Side Trips from Perth," later in this chapter).

the same food minus the side-orders will cost you about half the already low prices, at the Victorian-era-meets-1950s counter service diner and take-out section on the other side.

454 Murray St. (at Milligan St.). ℂ 08/9321 2552. Main courses A$5–$15 (U.S.$2.75–$8.25). MC, V. Daily 24 hr. Red CAT Stop 27 "Milligan St."

IN NORTHBRIDGE

Vultures 𝒜 ECLECTIC/MODERN AUSTRALIAN This roomy, relaxed, and groovy "coffee lounge cum restaurant" has a knack of suiting all occasions and all folk, from couples doing a romantic dinner in the streetside courtyard to teenage nightclubbers hanging out after a big night. The place is scattered with funky bric-a-brac from Indian eagle totems to Balinese four-poster wedding beds—you can even sit inside them on cushions and eat at a low coffee table, instead of at the regular tables. The main courses are surprisingly sophisticated and skillfully cooked for such a casual joint—kangaroo fillet with caramelized baby onions and a lavender honey glaze is typical. There is also plenty of light stuff like roast-chicken nachos or pastas. Rainbow-colored cocktails are a specialty.

Francis St. at William St., Northbridge. ℂ 08/9227 9087. Reservations recommended for dinner Fri–Sat. Main courses A$14.50–$24.50 (U.S.$8–$13.45); dine-in or take-out sandwiches at lunch A$6.60–$8.30 (U.S.$3.65–$4.50). Kids' menu A$7 (U.S.$3.85). AE, DC, MC, V. Sun–Thurs noon–1am; Fri–Sat noon–2am or later. Bus: Blue CAT Stop 9 "TAFE."

ON THE BEACH

The Blue Duck 𝒜𝒜 INTERNATIONAL/PIZZAS For ocean views and a lively atmosphere, it's hard to beat this casual restaurant perched right over the sand. Although the interior lacks the balcony's panoramic position, it has an upbeat seaside ambience and is just as packed as the porch. The all-day menu has lots of light choices like chargrilled chicken salad, as well as steaks, grilled fish, gourmet burgers, and wood-fired pizzas with creative toppings. The store is licensed to sell alcohol, but you can also BYO (bottled wine). By the time you read this, the managers should also be running a "beach shack"–style cafe down the street at 149 Marine Parade, serving up "cheap and cheerful" food in a breezy ambience with a small veranda over the beach—good just for coffee, or an easy meal.

151 Marine Parade, North Cottesloe. ℂ 08/9385 2499. Reservations recommended. Main courses A$3.90–$13.50 (U.S.$2.15–$7.40) breakfast, A$11.50–$26.50 (U.S.$6.30–$14.60) all-day menu (many meals under A$20/U.S$11). Buffet breakfast Sat–Sun and public holidays A$13–$19 (U.S.$7.15–$10.45). Kids' menu A$7–$9 (U.S.$3.85–$4.95). AE, DC, MC, V. Daily 6am–late (from 6:30am in winter). Bus: 71, 72, 73, or 883.

Indiana Tea House 𝒜 MODERN AUSTRALIAN The colonial Asian trappings at this delightful turn-of-the-20th-century bathhouse-turned-restaurant on Cottesloe Beach (bamboo birdcages, plaster lions, and palms) make me want to head straight for the tropical timber bar and order a Singapore Sling. Actually, the tasteful stucco building with bay windows and wooden floors is new— it just looks old. The menu mostly sticks to straightforward basics like Thai green curry, Texan ribs, or seafood pasta. This place is just as popular with business folk cutting deals as it is with arty types browsing the papers over their cafe latte. It does breakfast on weekends. Go in the daytime to make the most of those ocean views, or at sunset.

99 Marine Parade (on Cottesloe Beach opposite Forrest St.), Cottesloe. ℂ 08/9385 5005. Reservations recommended. Main courses A$14.85–$38.50 (U.S.$8.15–$21.15); many meals under A$30 (U.S.$16.50). Seafood platter for 2 A$92.50 (U.S.$50.90). AE, DC, MC, V. Mon–Fri 10am–late, Sat–Sun 8am–late; open all day for coffee. Bus: 71, 72, 73, or 883.

> ## Tips Java Joints
>
> Don't leave Freo without a "short black" (that's an espresso) or a "flat white" (coffee with milk) at the port's "cappuccino strip" on South Terrace. On weekends this street bursts at the seams with locals flocking to alfresco Italian-style cafes serving good java and excellent foccacia, pasta, and pizza. **DOME, Old Papa's,** and **Gino's** are three to look for.

IN FREMANTLE

There's a Fremantle branch of **Fast Eddy's** (see above) at 13 Essex St. (© 08/9336 1671) and another **Miss Maud Swedish Restaurant** (see above) at 33 S. Terrace (© 08/9336 1599), though this branch serves only the breakfast buffet on weekends.

La Pizzeria WOOD-FIRED PIZZA/SEAFOOD   Freo has loads of restaurants, but this joint has an upbeat and easy ambience with its terrazzo tables, groovy concrete and timber floor, and a stainless-steel bar. Wood-fired pizzas come straight from the funky oven at the rear, bearing toppings like grilled eggplant, roast capsicum, and mushrooms. Traditional pastas and seafood main courses get served up, too. Licensed to serve alcohol but you can also BYO beer and wine.

95 Market St. (behind Gino's Café on South Terrace). © 08/9430 6126. Pizzas A$13–$18 (U.S.$7.15–$9.90); main courses A$16–$22 (U.S.$8.80–$12.10). AE, DC, MC, V. Mon–Thurs noon–10pm, Fri–Sun noon–10.30pm. Train: Fremantle.

WHAT TO SEE & DO IN PERTH

AQWA (Aquarium of Western Australia) *Kids*   You won't catch performing dolphins a la Sea World, but there's plenty to see here, including a moving walkway through an underwater tunnel of sharks, rays, turtles and fish; a touch pool that even has a (small!) shark; and lots of aquariums that showcase the marine life of the Western Australian coast, including pretty leafy sea dragons, coral reefs, jellyfish, cuttlefish, sea snakes, crocodiles, and deadly stonefish that look remarkably like stones. Keepers feed the sharks and the touch-pool creatures daily, and a program of talks and movies on marine creatures is scheduled throughout the day. For A$85 (U.S.$46.75), qualified divers can dive with sharks, and for A$75 (U.S.$41.25), anyone over 12 years of age can swim with fur seals (bring snorkel mask or goggles for this). Book both experiences weeks in advance. Allow half a day here.

Sorrento Quay at Hillarys Boat Harbour, 91 Southside Dr., Hillarys. © 08/9447 7500. Admission A$19 (U.S.$10.45) adults, A$15 (U.S.$8.25) seniors and students, A$9 (U.S.$4.95) children ages 3–14, free for children under 3, A$50 (U.S.$27.50) for a family of 2 adults, 2 children; A$31 (U.S.$17.05) for a family of 1 adult, 2 children. Daily 9am–5pm; until 9pm Wed (Nov–Apr). Closed Christmas. Train and bus: Take Joondalup train line to Warwick, transfer to bus 423. By car, take Mitchell Freeway 23km (14 miles) north, turn left into Hepburn Ave. and carry on to roundabout at entrance to Hillarys Boat Harbour; AQWA is at the western end of the harbour.

Art Gallery of Western Australia   Most outstanding among this state gallery's international and Australian works is the Aboriginal art collection, regarded as the finest in Australia. A free tour of a particular collection runs once or twice a day, Tuesday through Friday and Sunday; call for times.

47 James St. (enter near the walkway opposite Perth Railway Station), Northbridge. © 08/9492 6600 administration, or 08/9492 6622 recorded information line. Free admission. Entry fee may apply to special

exhibitions. Daily 10am–5pm; from 1pm Anzac Day. Closed Christmas, New Year's, and Good Friday. Train: Perth. Bus: Blue CAT Stop 7 "Museum."

Cohunu Koala Park   Not all states in Australia permit **koala cuddling,** but Western Australia does, and this large park set in bushland is a good place to try it. You can also feed 100 kangaroos, wallabies, and emus wandering in natural enclosures, see wombats and dingoes, walk through an aviary housing Aussie native birds and see wild water birds on the ponds. The Caversham Wildlife Park in the Swan Valley (see "Side Trips from Perth" later in the chapter) has a bigger and more intriguing range of native species, but it does not allow koala cuddling.

Off Mills Rd. E., Gosnells (or located in the suburb of Martin on some maps). © 08/9390 6090. Admission A$18 (U.S.$9.90) adults, A$16.20 (U.S.$8.90) seniors and students, A$9 (U.S.$4.95) children 5–14, A$48.60 (U.S.$26.75) family. Koala-cuddling photos A$15–$25 (U.S.$8.25–$13.75), or A$10 (U.S.$5.50) if you take the photo yourself. Daily 10am–5pm; koala photo sessions 10am–4pm. Closed Christmas. Train: Gosnells on Armadale line plus a cab of about A$13 (U.S.$7.15). By car: Take Riverside Dr. across Swan River onto Albany Hwy., follow for approx. 25km (16 miles) to Gosnells, turn left onto Tonkin Hwy. and right ½ mile later onto Mills Rd. E. (approx. 35-min. drive from city). A cab from the city is approx. A$37 (U.S.$20.35).

Holmes à Court Gallery   This glamorous riverside gallery exhibits rotating exhibitions from one of the country's most outstanding private art collections, that of Janet Holmes à Court, Australia's richest woman. Many of the works are Aboriginal or by well-known Australian artists such as Sidney Nolan. The shop sells some impressive craft pieces.

11 Brown St., East Perth. © 08/9218 4540. Free admission. Wed–Fri 11am–5pm, Sat–Sun 11am–6pm. Closed Christmas and Good Friday. Train: Claisebrook.

Kings Park & Botanic Garden   Smack bang against the city center and Swan River is this 400-hectare (988-acre) hilltop park of botanic gardens and uncultivated bushland. Here you can inspect weird and wonderful Western Australian flora, get to know the solitude of the Australian bush, and bike, hike, or drive an extensive network of roads and trails. Visiting the spring wildflower displays (which peak in Sept and Oct) is a highlight on many Perth residents' calendars. There are barbecue and picnic facilities, several extensive playgrounds, bikes for rent (behind the Visitor Information Centre), tearooms, and the incomparable Fraser's (see "Where to Dine," above).

Pick up self-guiding maps from the Visitor Information Centre, or join one of the daily free guided walks departing from the giant Karri Log outside it. Walks depart 10am and 2pm and take 1½ hours, or 2 or 3 hours on bushwalks. The **Perth Tram Co.** (© **08/9322 2006**) runs 1-hour tours of the park and neighboring University of Western Australia in replica 1899 wooden trams. Tours depart daily from outside the Information Kiosk on Fraser Avenue at 11am, 12:15, 1:15, and 2:15pm. Tickets cost A$12 (U.S.$6.60) for adults, A$10 (U.S.$5.50) for seniors, A$6 (U.S.$3.30) for children under 15, and A$30 (U.S.$16.50) for families. Buy tickets on board. You can stop en route and rejoin a later tram if you like.

Fraser Ave. off Kings Park Rd. © 08/9480 3659 information kiosk, or 08/9480 3600 administration. Free admission. Daily 24 hr. The Information Kiosk on Fraser Ave. inside the park is open daily from approx. 9:30am–4:30pm (closed Christmas). It is staffed by volunteers so these hours are not always exact. Bus: 33 stops outside the Information Kiosk and extends into the park on Sat afternoon, and much of the day Sun and public holidays. Red CAT Stop 25 "Havelock Street" is 1 block north of the gates.

Perth Mint ⚘   This lovely historic building—built in the 1890s to mint currency from the Kalgoorlie gold rush—produced the victors' **gold medals** in the

Moments **Picture Perfect**

For the only photo of Perth you'll need, snap the view over the city and river from the War Memorial in Kings Park—it's superb day or night.

Sydney 2000 Olympic Games. Bullion is still traded here today. The key event is a gold pour demonstration (on the hour from 10am weekdays, and from 10am to noon inclusive on weekends). You can also see samples of the 2000 Olympics medals, engrave a medallion with your own message, handle a 400-ounce gold bar, see gold coins being minted, and ogle the country's biggest collection of nuggets. A 30-minute free guided tour departs half an hour before every pour. A shop sells gold coins and nugget jewelry.

310 Hay St. at Hill St., East Perth. © 08/9421 7277. Admission A$6.50 (U.S.$3.60) adults, A$5.50 (U.S.$3) seniors and students, A$3.30 (U.S.$1.80) school-age children; free admission to the shop. Mon–Fri 9am–4pm; Sat–Sun and public holidays 9am–1pm. Closed Christmas, New Year's Day, ANZAC Day (Apr 25), and Good Friday. Red CAT Stop 10 "Perth Mint."

Perth Zoo *(Kids* This is a good place to see kangaroos, koalas, numbats, wombats, quokkas, emus, echidnas (the Aussie answer to the porcupine), dingoes, possums, snakes, frogs, and just about every other kind of Aussie wildlife, mostly housed in themed natural habitats, or in a walk-through aviary in the birds' case. There's plenty of exotic animals, too, including orangutans, Rothschild's giraffes, zebras, lions, rhinos, and Sumatran tigers. Feeding demonstrations and talks run throughout the day. Koala cuddling is not permitted; for that, head to Cohunu Koala Park (see above).

20 Labouchere Rd., South Perth. © 08/9474 3551 for recorded information, or 08/9367 7988 administration. Admission A$13.20 (U.S.$7.25) adults, A$6.60 (U.S.$3.65) children 4–15, A$35.75 (U.S.$19.60) family. Daily 9am–5pm. Ferry: Barrack St. Jetty to Mends St. Jetty, South Perth. Bus: 35.

Western Australian Museum *(Kids* Kids will like the dinosaur gallery, the drawers full of insects in the lobby, the blue-whale skeleton on the well-stocked aquatic zoology floor, the bizarre "megamouth" shark preserved in a tank set in the ground in the courtyard, and assorted other examples of Australia's weird natural creatures. The main attraction for grown-ups is one of the best collections of Aboriginal artifacts and rare photographs in the country. Allow 90 minutes to see most highlights.

Francis St. at Beaufort St. (or enter off James Street Mall), Northbridge. © 08/9427 2700. Free admission (donation requested); fee may apply to temporary exhibitions. Daily 9:30am–5pm; ANZAC Day (Apr 25) and Boxing Day (Dec 26) 1–5pm. Closed Christmas and Good Friday. Train: Perth. Bus: Blue CAT Stop 8 "Museum."

HITTING THE BEACHES

Perth shares Sydney's good luck in having beaches in the metropolitan area—19 of them, in fact, laid end to end along the 35-kilometer (22-mile) Sunset Coast from Cottesloe in the south to Quinns Rocks in the north. Mornings are best, because a strong afternoon wind, known as the "Fremantle Doctor," can be unpleasant, especially in summer. Always swim between the red and yellow flags, which denote a "safe swimming" zone.

On weekends and public holidays from the last Saturday in September to the last Sunday in April, Bus no. 582 stops hourly during the day at most beaches from Fremantle to Hillarys. It operates in both directions. You can take a surfboard under 2 meters (6½ ft.) on the bus.

These are the three most popular:

COTTESLOE   This pretty crescent, graced by the delightful Edwardian-style Indiana Tea House (see "Where to Dine," above), is Perth's most fashionable beach. It has safe swimming and a small surf break. A couple of good cafes are nearby. Train: Cottesloe, then a walk of several hundred meters. Bus: 71, 72, 73, or 883.

SCARBOROUGH   Scarborough's white sands stretch for miles from the base of the Hotel Rendezvous Observation City Perth. Swimming is generally safe, and surfers are always guaranteed a wave, although inexperienced swimmers should take a rain check when the surf is rough. The busy shopping precinct across the road means there's always somewhere to buy lunch and drinks. Bus: 400.

TRIGG   Surfers like Trigg best for its consistent swells. Bus: 400 to Scarborough, then a 10-minute walk north.

A DAY OUT IN FREMANTLE 🏴🏴

The heritage port precinct of **Fremantle,** 19 kilometers (12 miles) from downtown Perth on the mouth of the Swan River, is probably best known outside Australia as the site of the 1987 America's Cup challenge. Just before that event, the city embarked on a major restoration of its gracious but derelict warehouses and Victorian buildings. Today "Freo" is a bustling district of 150 National Trust buildings, alfresco cafes, museums, galleries, pubs, markets, and shops in a masterfully preserved historical atmosphere. It's still a working port so you will see fishing boats unloading and yachts gliding in and out of the harbor. The ambience is so authentic that locals make a beeline for the place every weekend, resulting in a wonderful hubbub of buzzing shoppers, market-stall holders, java drinkers, yachties, tourists, and fishermen. Allow a full day to take in even half the sights—and don't forget to knock back an ale or two on the verandas of one of the gorgeous old pubs.

ESSENTIALS

GETTING THERE   Parking is plentiful, but driving is frustrating in the maze of one-way traffic. Most attractions are within walking distance (or hop aboard the free CAT bus, below), so take the train to Fremantle station and explore on foot.

A nice way to get to Freo and see Perth's river suburbs at the same time is on the cruises run by several companies once or twice a day from Barrack Street Jetty. See "Whale-Watching Cruises, Tram Trips & Other Tours," later in this chapter, for cruise operators. A cruise with Boat Torque Cruises is A$15 one-way (U.S.$8.25).

GETTING AROUND   The easiest way to explore is on foot. Elaine Berry, of the Western Australian Maritime Museum (see below), leads a 90-minute **walking tour** for A$11 (U.S.$6.05) for adults, A$8 (U.S.$4.40) for seniors, and A$3.30 (U.S.$1.80) for school-age kids; you must book by calling the museum ℂ **08/9431 8455,** or Elaine at home (ℂ 08/9336 1906) on weekends. She schedules the tours for a day and time to suit you.

The silver Fremantle CAT bus makes a running loop of local attractions every 10 minutes Monday through Friday from 7am to 7pm, and every 8 minutes Thursday and Friday from 3pm to 10pm. On weekends and most public holidays it runs every eight minutes from 10am to 10pm. It is free and departs from the train station.

Fremantle Ghost Walks (© **08/9484 1133** is the booking agent, BOCS; 08/9336 1916 for inquiries) leads 1-hour spook saunters Monday (of the Fremantle Arts Centre, once an asylum for the insane) and Wednesday (of 10 haunted buildings) at 8pm; tickets are A$15 (U.S.$8.25) adults, A$12 (U.S.$6.60) seniors and students, and A$10 (U.S.$5.50) kids ages 6 to 15, plus a BOCS telephone booking fee of A$6.60 (U.S.$3.65) per booking.

VISITOR INFORMATION   The **Fremantle Tourist Bureau** is located in Town Hall, Kings Square at High Street, Fremantle, WA 6160 (© **08/9431 7878**). It's open Monday through Saturday from 9am to 5pm (until 4pm Saturdays in winter) and Sunday noon to 4:30pm. The best website is that of the Fremantle Council, www.fremantle.wa.gov.au.

SEEING THE SIGHTS IN FREMANTLE

You'll want to explore some of Freo's excellent museums and other attractions below, but take time to stroll the streets and admire the 19th-century offices and warehouses, many now painted in rich, historically accurate colors. As soon as you arrive, wander down to the docks—either Victoria Quay, where sailing craft come and go, or Fishing Boat Harbour off Mews Road, where the boats bring in their catches—to get a breath of salt air.

Freo's best **shopping** is arts and crafts, from hand-blown glass to Aboriginal art to alpaca-wool clothing. Worth a look are the assorted art, craft, and souvenir stores on High Street west of the mall; those in the **E Shed markets** on Victoria Quay (open Fri–Sun only, and public holidays that fall on a Mon, 9am–6pm); and Bannister Street **CraftWorks,** 81–12 Bannister St., an arts cooperative where you often spy the artists at work (open from 11am to 5:30pm; closed Mon). The **Fremantle Markets,** 74 S. Terrace at Henderson Street (© **08/9335 2515**), mostly sell cheap imported handicrafts, jewelry, homewares, and clothing, as well as inexpensive food. They're open Friday from 9am to 9pm, Saturday from 9am to 5pm, and Sunday and any public holidays that fall on a Monday from 10am to 5pm.

The most popular watering holes are the **Sail & Anchor,** 64 S. Terrace (© **08/9335 8433**), which brews its own Brass Monkey Stout; the **Norfolk,** 47 S. Terrace at Norfolk Street (© **08/9335 5405**); and the beautifully restored front bar and garden courtyard at **Phillimore's Café & Bar** at His Majesty's Hotel, on Phillimore Street at Mouat Street (© **08/9335 9596**). The happening "cappuccino strip" on South Terrace is good for people-watching.

Fremantle Arts Centre   Housed in a striking neo-Gothic 1860s building built by convicts, this center contains one of Western Australia's best contemporary arts-and-crafts galleries with a constantly changing array of works. A shop sells crafts from Western Australia, a bookstore stocks Australian art books and literature, and the courtyard cafe is the perfect place to hang out. Free concerts play on the lawn every Sunday between October and April from 2 to 4pm.

1 Finnerty St. © **08/9432 9555.** Free admission. Daily 10am–5pm. Closed Christmas and Good Friday, Boxing Day (Dec 26), and New Year's Day.

Fremantle History Museum ⚐   Housed in a convict-built former lunatic asylum next to the Fremantle Arts Centre, this small but densely packed museum uses lots of old photographs and personal possessions to paint a realistic picture of what life was like for Fremantle's first settlers, the Aboriginal people they displaced, and later generations up to the present day.

1 Finnerty St. at Ord St. (part of the Fremantle Arts Centre, see above). © 08/9430 7966. Free admission (donation requested). Sun–Fri 10:30am–4:30pm; Sat and public holidays 1–5pm. Closed for 1 week Christmas–Jan 2, and Good Friday.

Fremantle Prison 🏛️ Even jails sported attractive architecture back in the 1850s. This picturesque limestone jail, built to house 1,000 inmates by convicts who no doubt ended up inside it, was a maximum-security prison until 1991. To see cells now re-created in the style of past periods of the jail's history, bushranger (highwayman) Joe Moondyne's "escape-proof" cell, the gallows, the workshops, the chapel, the hospital, the jailers' houses, and cell walls featuring some wonderful artwork by the former inmates, take the 75-minute tour, or guide yourself with an audio headset. An additional 45-minute tour visits the women's prison every hour, after the main tour. You must book for the Wednesday- and Friday-night **candlelight tours** 🏛️ which take 90 minutes.

1 The Terrace. © 08/9430 7177. Free admission to courtyard. Tours A$12 (U.S.$6.60) adults, A$9.50 (U.S.$5.20) seniors and students, A$4.80 (U.S.$2.65) children 6–15, A$28.80 (U.S.$15.85) families; candlelight tours Wed and Fri. A$14.40 (U.S.$7.90) adults, A$12 (U.S.$6.60) seniors and students, A$7.20 (U.S.$3.95) children, A$36 (U.S.$19.80) families. Daily 10am–6pm. Main tours run every 30 min. from 10am; last tour 5pm. Women's prison tours run every hour from 11:30am; last tour 4:30pm. Candlelight tours Wed and Fri 7pm (winter) or 7:30pm (summer). Closed Christmas and Good Friday.

The Roundhouse This 12-sided jail is the oldest public building in the state (built around 1830). It won't take long to have a look. There are no displays or memorabilia, but it's worth a visit for history's sake, and for the sea views on the other side. The time cannon just to its west, a replica of a gun salvaged from an 1878 wreck, is fired and a **time ball** dropped at 1pm daily, just as it was in the 1800s, from a deck overlooking the ocean. You might be that day's honorary gunner chosen from the crowd!

Arthur Head (enter over the railway line from High St.). No phone. Admission by gold coin donation, A$1 or A$2 (U.S.55¢ or $1.10). Daily 10:30am–3:30pm. Closed Good Friday and Christmas.

Western Australian Maritime Museum 🏛️🏛️ If you are fascinated by deep-sea treasure, you will love this museum's tales of old wrecks and displays of pieces of eight, glassware, cannon and other items recovered off the treacherous Western Australian coast. The museum is renowned worldwide for its leading work in maritime archaeology. Displays date from the 1600s, when Dutch explorers became the first Europeans to encounter Australia. One of the best displays is the appalling tale of the *Batavia,* wrecked north of Perth in 1629, where most of the survivors were massacred by a handful of mutineers.

In mid-2002, the museum plans to move from its current premises in a two-story historic stone warehouse to modernistic new premises on Victoria Quay in Fremantle. The new premises will have both a historic and modern-day focus. It will look at Fremantle's history and present-day operations as a port, signaling and piloting, navigation ancient and modern, current sailing technology, naval defense, sea trade, and Aboriginal maritime heritage. It will house historic or rare boats, including *Australia II* (the Aussie yacht that won the America's Cup) and the *Ovens* submarine (located in Slip Street) which is open for tours. The existing museum in Cliff Street, to be renamed the Shipwrecks Museum, will continue to display its wonderful old wreck and treasure exhibits.

Until mid-2002: Cliff St. © 08/9431 8444. Free admission (donation requested). Daily 9:30am–5pm. Anzac Day (April 25) and Boxing Day (Dec 26) 1–5pm. Free guided tours daily 10, 11am, 2, and 3pm. Closed Christmas and

Good Friday. After mid-2002: Forrest Landing on western end of Victoria Quay. Museum admission prices and opening hours not set at press time. *Ovens* submarine tours: A$8.80 (U.S.$4.85) adults, A$5.50 (U.S.$3) seniors and students, A$3.30 (U.S.$1.80) children under 11, A$22 (U.S.$12.10) family. Fri–Sat 11am–5pm; Sun 10am–5pm; last tour 4pm.

WHALE-WATCHING CRUISES, TRAM TRIPS & OTHER TOURS

Boat Torque Cruises (© 08/9221 5844), **Golden Sun Cruises** (© 08/9325 1616), and **Oceanic Cruises** (© 08/9325 1191) run an assortment of morning, afternoon, sunset, luncheon, dinner, half-, and full-day cruises on the Swan River, some as far as Fremantle, and to historic homes and vineyards in the Swan Valley. Oceanic Cruises does a cruise to see wild sea lions at Carnac Island just off Fremantle. **Captain Cook Cruises** (© 08/9325 3341) also runs cruises on the Perth–Fremantle route, and does an Aboriginal cultural cruise that includes a guided bushland walk.

September through November, Perth's waters are alive with southern right and humpback **whales** returning from the north with their calves. To join a 2- or 3-hour jaunt to watch them, contact Boat Torque Cruises, Oceanic Cruises, or the **Rottnest Express ferry** (© 08/9335 6406), which does whale-watch trips between ferry runs. Departure days and times vary from year to year with every cruise operator, so check ahead. Prices range from A$22 (U.S.$12.10) on the Rottnest Express up to around A$35 (U.S.$19.25) for the other companies, and about half price for kids. Most depart Fremantle; Boat Torque also does them from Hillarys Boat Harbour (near the AQWA aquarium; see "What to See & Do in Perth," above). The company provides coach connections to Hillarys from Perth.

The Perth Tram Co. (© 08/9322 2006) makes a daily guided running loop of the city, the casino, and Kings Park in replica 1899 wooden trams; hop on and off as often as you wish. Tickets, which you buy on board, cost A$15 (U.S.$8.25) for adults, A$13 (U.S.$7.15) for seniors, A$7 (U.S.$3.85) for children under 15, and A$37 (U.S.$20.35) families. City–casino, city–Kings Park and casino–Kings Park single legs are also available. Join anywhere; the tram starts at 565 Hay St. at 9:40am and makes six 90-minute loops a day.

Feature Tours (© 1800/999 819 in Australia, or 08/9479 4131; www.ft.com.au) runs half-day and full-day coach tours to many attractions in and around Perth.

ACTIVE PURSUITS

BIKING   Perth's superb bike-track network stretches for miles along the Swan River, through Kings Park, around Fremantle, and all the way down the beaches. There is a great 9.5-kilometer (6-mile) track around Perth Water, the broad expanse of river in front of the central business district, that starts at the Swan River on Riverside Drive in the city and goes over the Causeway bridge, back along the other bank and over the bridge at the Narrows back to the city. The state Department of Transport's cycling division, Bikewest, publishes a range of useful bike-route maps to the city. They are available in bike shops, most newsagents, and the **Perth Map Centre,** 2nd floor, Shafto Lane at 884 Hay St. (© 08/9322 5733).

An hour's rental with **Koala Bike Hire,** located in the carpark behind Fraser's restaurant in Kings Park (© 08/9321 3061), is A$5 (U.S.$2.75), or A$16 (U.S.$8.80) for the day, which includes a helmet (required by law in Australia), lock, and maps of Kings Park.

GOLF   Most convenient to the city is Burswood Park Golf Course, part of the **Burswood International Resort Casino,** across the river from town on the

Great Eastern Highway, Burswood (© **08/9362 7576** for the pro shop). A 9-hole round is just A$13.20 (U.S.$7.25) weekdays and A$16.50 (U.S.$9.10) weekends. A cart for 9 holes is A$22 (U.S.$12.10), and club rental is A$16.50 (U.S.$9.10).

Even more scenic are the 27 championship fairways designed by Robert Trent Jones, Jr., at **Joondalup Resort,** Country Club Boulevard, Connolly, a 25-kilometer (15½-mile) drive north of Perth (© **08/9400 8811** is the pro shop); and **The Vines** in the Swan Valley (© **08/9297 3000** for the resort, or 08/9297 0777 for the pro shop), which has two 18-hole bushland courses. It was ranked No. 1 Resort Golf Course in Australia by *Golf Australia* magazine in 2001. Kangaroos often come onto both courses. Expect to pay between A$45 to $55 (U.S.$24.75–$30.25) for 9 holes at either resort, and A$90 (U.S.$49.50) at Joondalup on weekends.

SAILING   The tallest Tall Ship in Australia, the lovely three-masted barquentine *STS Leeuwin II* (© **08/9430 4105**), sails from B Shed at Victoria Quay, Fremantle, when it is not out on extended voyages around Australia. You may be one of up to 100 passengers, but you still get the chance to try your hand at sailing the way it used to be done. Leisurely day trips from 10am to 3pm are A$99 (U.S.$54.45) for adults and A$50 (U.S.$27.50) for children under 12. The ship sometimes does 3-hour sails at breakfast (with champagne), in the afternoon, or at dusk.

Experienced sailors can sail on Wednesday afternoons in summer from about 3 to 5pm with members of the **Royal Perth Yacht Club,** Australia II Drive, Crawley (© **08/9389 1555;** ask for the sailing administrator), if there is a place free aboard. It's not spinnaker sailing on Wednesdays, so the action is at an easy pace. All-white dress standards apply.

SCUBA DIVING & SNORKELING   Just 19 kilometers (12 miles) off Perth, Rottnest Island's corals, reef fish, wrecks, and limestone caverns, in 18- to 35-meter (59- to 128-ft.) visibility, are a gift from heaven to Perth divers and snorkelers. Contact **Rottnest Malibu Diving** (© **08/9292 5111**) on Rottnest Island (see "Side Trips From Perth," below) to rent gear or join a dive trip. **Diving Ventures,** at 384 S. Terrace, Fremantle (© **1800/655 330** in Australia, or 08/9430 5130; www.dventures.com.au), also conducts dive day trips from Perth to Rottnest Island, and also to the wreck of the HMAS Swan off Dunsborough in the state's Southwest, a 75-meter-long (250-ft.-long) destroyer which was scuttled for divers' pleasure a couple of years ago. A day trip costs A$150 (U.S.$82.50) or A$155 (U.S.$85.25) with two dives, including all gear. The company also does 2-day live-aboard trips to Rottnest, and "introductory" dives for any adventurer without dive qualifications who wants to try the sport, in the company of an instructor. It also rents scuba gear and conducts dive courses. It has a city outlet at 222 William St., Northbridge, in Perth.

SURFING   You will find good surfing at many city beaches, Scarborough and Trigg in particular. See the "Hitting the Beaches" section, earlier in this chapter. Rottnest Island (see "Side Trips from Perth," below) also has good breaks. **Murray Smith Surf Centre,** Shop 14, Luna Maxi Mart, Scarborough (© **08/ 9245 2988**), rents long boards for A$20 (U.S.$11) for half a day or A$30 (U.S.$16.50) for the day, plus a A$100 (U.S.$55) refundable deposit. They also rent body boards. **Surfing WA** (© **08/9448 0004**) runs hour-long surfing classes for A$35 (U.S.$19.25) per person, or A$50 (U.S.$27.50) for two people. Boards and wet suits are provided. Lessons run daily at a time and place to suit you, at any beach where there are waves. That usually turns out to be Trigg or Scarborough.

THE SHOPPING SCENE

Most shops are located downtown on the parallel **Hay Street** and **Murray Street malls,** located 1 block apart, and in the network of arcades running off them such as the Plaza, City, Carillon, and the Tudor-style **London Court** arcades. Off Murray Street Mall on Forrest Place is the **Forrest Chase shopping complex,** housing the Myer department store and boutiques on two levels. Add to your collection of international designer brands on posh **King Street.**

If you want to avoid the chains, spend half a day in fashionable **Subiaco** ✿ or "Subi," where Hay Street and Rokeby Road are lined with smart boutiques, home accessories shops, art galleries, cafes, antique shops, and markets. The Colonnade shopping center at 388 Hay St. showcases groovy young Aussie fashion designers in its Studio 388 section.

Fremantle's shopping is mostly limited to a good selection of crafts, markets, and Aboriginal souvenirs.

Shops are open until 9pm on Friday in the city, and until 9pm on Thursday in Subiaco and Fremantle.

ABORIGINAL ARTS & CRAFTS   Creative Native, 32 King St. (© 08/9322 3398), stocks Perth's widest range of Aboriginal arts and crafts. Upstairs is a gallery selling original works by some renowned Aboriginal artists. There's another branch at 65 High St., Fremantle (© 08/9335 6995).

Indigenart, The Mossenson Gallery, 115 Hay St., Subiaco (© 08/9388 2899), and 82 High St., Fremantle (© 08/9335 2911), stocks works on canvas, paper, and bark, as well as artifacts, textiles, pottery, didgeridoos, boomerangs, and sculpture, by world-famous and lesser-known Aboriginal artists from all over Australia. Dedicated collectors should find something they like here.

JEWELRY   Western Australia is renowned for farming the world's best **South Sea pearls** off Broome, for Argyle **diamonds** mined in the Kimberley, and for being one of the world's biggest **gold** producers.

Artisans of the Sea, corner of Marine Terrace and Collie Street, Fremantle (© 08/9336 3633) sells elegant South Sea pearl and gold jewelry.

Some of Perth's other leading jewelers, where you can buy opals, Argyle diamonds, and Broome pearls, are family-owned sister stores, **Costello's,** Shop 5–6, London Court (© 08/9325 8588), and **Swan Diamonds,** Shop 4, London

---

Finds Desert Designs

Aboriginal artist **Jimmy Pike** grew up in Western Australia's Sandy Desert and was one of the first to start transferring his Dreamtime art and designs to fabrics, in 1981. To buy colorful clothing and accessories bearing designs by Jimmy, visit the **Desert Designs** boutique at 114 High Street Mall, Fremantle (© 08/9430 4101), or order online at www.ddesigns.com.au. The cute children's gear has won the state fashion awards for the last 2 years in a row. For original paintings and limited-edition prints not only by Jimmy, but by other Aboriginal artists, visit the **Japingka Gallery,** 47 High St., Fremantle (© 08/9335 8265). It also stocks didgeridoos, artifacts, and stunning high-quality hand-tufted woolen floor rugs, mostly in Jimmy's designs.

Court (© **08/9325 8166**), and also **Linneys,** 37 Rokeby Rd., Subiaco (© **08/ 9382 4077**).

For opals to suit all budgets, head to the Perth outlet of national opal retailer, **Quilpie Opals,** Shop 6, Piccadilly Arcade off Hay Street Mall (© **08/9321 8687**).

PERTH AFTER DARK

Scoop and the *Perth Weekly* (see "Visitor Information," earlier in this chapter) are good sources of information on public festivals and concerts, performing arts, classical music, exhibitions, and the like. Your best guide to hip dance clubs, rock concerts, gig listings, art-house cinemas, theater and art galleries is the free *X-press newspaper,* available at pubs, cafes, and music venues in town. The *West Australian* and *Sunday Times* newspapers publish a limited amount of entertainment information, including cinema guides.

Two major booking agents handle bookings to most of the city's major performing arts, entertainment, and sporting events: the performing arts-oriented **BOCS** (© **1800/193 300** in Australia for bookings or events information, or 08/9484 1133; www.bocsticketing.com.au) and the sports- and family-entertainment-oriented **TicketMaster 7** (© **13 61 22** for sporting events, 13 61 66 for performing arts, or 13 61 00 for all other events; www. ticketmaster7.com.au). Book opera, ballet, the orchestra, and the Black Swan Theatre Company (see below) through BOCS.

THE PERFORMING ARTS   The **West Australian Opera Company** (© **08/ 9321 5869** administration, or 08/9265-0950 bookings) and **West Australian Ballet** (© **08/9481 0707** administration) usually perform at **His Majesty's Theatre,** 825 Hay St., a restored "grande dame" venue from the early 1900s. Perth's leading theatrical company, the **Black Swan Theatre Company** (© **08/9388 9388** administration), plays at various theatres around town. The **West Australian Symphony Orchestra** (© **08/9326 0000** administration and bookings) usually performs at the **Perth Concert Hall,** 5 St. Georges Terrace next to the Duxton Hotel. This hall has the best acoustics of any such venue in Australia, such acts as the London Philharmonic, comedian Billy Connolly, and legendary blues guitarist B. B. King have performed here.

Perth is an outdoors kinda place. In summer, look for outdoor concerts or jazz at **Perth Zoo** (© **08/9474 3551** for recorded information, or 08/9367 7988 administration), movies at Perth's several outdoor cinemas, and open-air concerts, plays, and movies in **Kings Park** (© **08/9480 3600**).

PUBS, BARS & NIGHTCLUBS   Northbridge houses most of city's lively pubs and dance clubs. Don't forget Freo has good pubs, too (we recommend three in "A Day Out in Fremantle," earlier in this chapter).

For a trendy take on the traditional corner pub, head to **The Brass Monkey,** 209 William St. at James Street, Northbridge (© **08/9227 9596**). Downstairs are several bars including a wine bar serving gourmet pizzas, and a beer garden; upstairs, stand-up comedy plays Wednesday night in the Monkey Bar for a A$10 (U.S.$5.50) cover.

In Subiaco, suits flock to the "Subi," also known as the **Subiaco Hotel,** 465 Hay St. at Rokeby Road, Subiaco (© **08/9381 1028**), a popular historic pub with a stylish cafe. It's big on Friday night.

Metropolis City Concert Club, 146 Roe St., Northbridge (© **08/9228 0500**), is a huge complex of dance floors and bars over several levels, where live Aussie and touring bands play. If your "dancing 'til 6am" days are over but you still know how to hit the dance floor, hit it at **Margeaux's,** a nightclub popular with 30-, 40- and 50-somethings, located in the Perth Parmelia Hilton, 14 Mill St. (© **08/9215 2000**). It opens Wednesday, Friday, and Saturday nights.

THE CASINO   A 2,300-seat theatre that hosts the likes of Tom Jones and opera singer Andrea Bocelli is located in the **Burswood International Resort Casino,** on the Great Eastern Highway just over the river from the city (© **08/9362 7646** for information, or call BOCS for bookings—see above). Live bands, disco, cabaret performers, or karaoke play nightly in the Cabaret Nightclub free, and there are nine restaurants and five bars within the resort/casino complex. On the gaming floor are 126 tables, 1,160 video gaming machines, a VIP players' room, and a Keno Lounge. Except for Christmas Day, Good Friday, and Anzac Day, the casino is open 24 hours. Dress standards are smart casual—jeans and T-shirts are fine, no shorts or sandals after 7pm. It's about a A$13 (U.S.$7.15) cab ride from the city, or take a train to Burswood station.

2 Side Trips from Perth

ROTTNEST ISLAND: GETTING FACE-TO-FACE WITH THE FISHES *⊀⊀*
19km (12 miles) W of Perth

The delightful wildlife reserve of Rottnest Island just off the Perth coast is like the city's own Great Barrier Reef in miniature. Its jewel-bright turquoise waters, warm currents, rocky coves, and many sheltered beaches harbor **coral reefs** and 360 kinds of fish that make for fabulous snorkeling. You may spot humpback whales September through December, and dolphins surfing the waves anytime. The island is also home to 10,000 **quokkas,** cute otter-like marsupials that reach up to your knees. A wonderful thing about Rottnest is that there are no cars. Everyone gets around by bike (or bus, if you tire of pedaling over the mostly moderate-grade hills). The island is 11 kilometers (7 miles) long and 4.5 kilometers (3 miles) across at its widest point.

ESSENTIALS
GETTING THERE   Boat Torque Cruises (© **08/9221 5844**) and **Oceanic Cruises** (© **08/9325 1191**) each operate services at least three times a day from Perth (trip time: about 1 hr., 45 min.), and between four and seven times a day from Fremantle (trip time: about 25 min.). The **Rottnest Express ferry** (© **08/9335 6406**) runs four or five times a day from Fremantle only. Round-trip fares from Perth average about A$60 (U.S.$33), or about A$38 (U.S.$20.90) from Fremantle. Boat Torque and Oceanic pick you up free from most Perth and Fremantle hotels. You pay about A$5 (U.S.$2.75) more if you return on a later day. Most boat operators offer day-trip and accommodation packages, as well as straight transfers.

Kookaburra Air (© **08/9354 1158;** www.kookaburra.iinet.net.au) and **Rottnest Air Taxi** (© **1800/500 006** in Australia, or 08/9292 5027; www.rottnest.de) provide aerial transfers. A round-trip transfer in a four-seater aircraft with Rottnest Air Taxi is A$180 (U.S.$99) for the plane.

VISITOR INFORMATION   Information is dispensed by the **Rottnest Island Visitor Centre** (© **08/9372 9752**), which is right at the end of the jetty on the island. The centre is run by the **Rottnest Island Authority** (© **08/9432 9300;** www.rottnest.wa.gov.au). The Perth Visitor Centre (see "Visitor Information" in the Perth section, earlier in this chapter), also has information.

GETTING AROUND   Ferries pull into the jetty in the main town, called "Settlement" at Thomson Bay. **Rottnest Bike Hire** (© **08/9292 5105**), next to the Rottnest Hotel near the jetty, rents 2,300 bikes in every size, speed, and type imaginable, as well as holders for everything from surfboards to babies. An 18-speed bike is A$20 (U.S.$11) for a 24-hour day (plus a A$25/U.S.$13.75 refundable deposit), including a helmet (compulsory in Oz) and lock. There is no need to book a bike.

The yellow **Bayseeker** bus does half-hourly circumnavigations calling at all the best bays. An all-day ticket costs A$5.50 (U.S.$3) for adults, A$3.30 (U.S.$1.80) for seniors and students, A$2.20 (U.S.$1.20) children 4 to 12, and A$13.20 (U.S.$7.25) for families. Buy tickets on board.

A free bus runs regularly between the airport and the five small communities around the island.

ISLAND ORIENTATION TOURS

Many first-time visitors take the **2-hour Island Bus Tour** because it is a good introduction to the bays and the island's cultural and natural history—and because it includes a stop to see the quokkas. It costs A$13.20 (U.S.$7.25) for adults, A$9.90 (U.S.$5.45) for seniors and students, A$6.60 (U.S.$3.65) for kids 4 to 12, and A$35.20 (U.S.$19.35) families of four. Departure times vary, but you can expect them to run twice a day, usually around 10:30am and 1:30pm. Buy tickets from the Visitor Centre.

SNORKELING, DIVING, SURFING & FISHING

Most people come to Rottnest to snorkel, swim, surf, dive, or fish. As soon as you arrive, rent a bike and your preferred aquatic gear, and pedal around the coast until you come to a beach that suits you. (Don't forget to carry drinking water and food, because the only shops are at Settlement.) The Basin, Little Parakeet Bay, Little Salmon Bay, and Parker Point are good snorkel spots. The Visitor Centre sells A$5.50 (U.S.$3) maps to suggested **snorkel trails** in many bays. Surfers should try Cathedral Rocks or Strickland Bay. Fishermen will catch squid, salmon, and tailor, as well as all kinds of reef fish. The island's dive shop, **Rottnest Malibu Diving** (© **08/9292 5111**), near the jetty, rents snorkel gear, dive gear, wet suits, surfboards, body boards, aqua-bikes, and fishing tackle to use off the beach. The company conducts two daily trips to some of the 100-plus dive sites around Rottnest. Some feature limestone caverns and some of the island's 14 shipwrecks. A shore or boat dive with all gear included is A$60 (U.S.$33). If you have never dived before but want to try, a 1- to 2-hour theory lesson followed by a boat dive is A$135 (U.S.$74.25).

A couple of operators run glass-bottom-boat tours and sea-kayak tours; no one offered fishing tours at press time.

FOR HISTORY BUFFS

Rottnest has quite a bit to offer history buffs, who may want to walk (45-min. trip), cycle, or take the train to the Oliver Hill 1930s gun emplacements, which has intact 9.2-inch guns and battery tunnels housing an engine room, a plotting room, and observation posts. You can explore the 1.5-kilometer (1-mile) heritage trail on your own (buy a map from the Visitor Centre for A$2.20/U.S.$1.20), or take a guided 1-hour tour on the hour between 11am and 2pm inclusive. The train fare, which includes the tour except for the last trip of the day, costs A$9.90 (U.S.$6.10) for adults, A$6.60 (U.S.$3.65) for seniors and students, A$4.95 (U.S.$2.70) for children 4 to 12, and A$26.40

(U.S.$14.50) for families. It departs from the station near the Visitor Centre hourly from 10:30am to 2:30pm inclusive.

Volunteer guides run free 1-hour historical walking tours of architectural points of interest around Thomson Bay, many of them built in the 19th century, like the Governor's residence, the chapel, the octagonal prison, the small museum (open daily from 11am to 4pm), and the former Boys' Reformatory. They depart from the Environment Office at 11:30am and 2:30pm daily. Another 1-hour heritage trail takes you to the memorial marking de Vlamingh, the Dutch explorer who named the island Rott Enest (Rat Nest) in 1696 when he mistook quokkas for varmints. Self-guiding maps to both these trails are sold at the Visitor Centre for a dollar or so.

WHERE TO STAY & DINE

Call the **Rottnest Island Authority's accommodation booking service (© 08/ 9432 9111)** to book one of the island's 250-plus holiday homes, apartments, cabins, historic cottages, or the campground. Don't expect anything new or upscale. Water and electricity restrictions mean no accommodation is air-conditioned. Book well in advance all through summer; accommodation during the peak Western Australian school vacation times is allotted on a ballot system, for which you must submit an application form.

Apart from the very nice restaurants at the hotels listed below, the casual tea-rooms, and a couple of lackluster take-out joints, your only other dining option is the excellent DOME cafe at the jetty.

Shoulder season is usually April through May, and again September through November or December. Winter is June through August.

Rottnest Hotel   This appealing 1864 building near the jetty, once the state governor's summer residence, is now the local pub where day-trippers gather in the sports bar or the large open-air beer garden to admire the ocean views over an ale or two. The building contains pleasant, modern motel-style rooms reno-vated 5 years ago, some with a small patio and sea views. Apart from the Lake-side units at Rottnest Lodge, below, these are the best hotel rooms on the island. New managers were to be appointed around press time, so rates and some serv-ices and amenities may change. No smoking indoors.

Rottnest Island, WA 6161. © 08/9292 5011. Fax 08/9292 5188. rottnesthotel@axismgt.com.au. 18 units (all with shower only). Peak (Christmas to Jan) A$178–$199 (U.S.$97.90–$109.45) double; summer (Feb to mid-April, Sept–Dec) A$157–$178 (U.S.$86.35–$97.90) double; shoulder (mid-April to May) A$135–$155 (U.S.$74.25–$85.25) double; winter (June–Aug) A$110–$135 (U.S.$60.50–$74.25) double. Extra person A$30 (U.S.$16.50). Rates include continental breakfast. Ask about mid-week packages in winter. AE, DC, MC, V. **Amenities:** Upscale restaurant, a cook-your-own BBQ, sports bar, beergarden, cocktail bar. *In room:* TV, fridge, no phone.

Rottnest Lodge Resort   The Lakeside Units at this former colonial barracks and prison are Rottnest's most luxurious accommodations, built new in 1989 with flagstone floors, cream painted brick walls, bright contemporary furnish-ings, and a living area. Some have salt-lake views, not always pretty when the water dries up. I'd avoid the remaining Deluxe, Standard, and Family rooms, which sleep from 2 to 10, in the historic quarters; they are mostly dark, viewless, and small. You are just a few minutes' stroll from the jetty and Visitor Centre here.

Rottnest Island, WA 6161. © 08/9292 5161. Fax 08/9292 5158. www.rottnestlodge.com.au. 80 units (all with shower only). High season (mid-Dec to late Jan) A$185–$250 (U.S.$101.75–$137.50) double. Shoulder (Feb–Apr, Sept to mid-Dec) A$175–$230 (U.S.$96.25–$126.50) double. Winter (May to early Sept)

A$140–$185 (U.S.$77–$101.75) double. Additional person A$40 (U.S.$22) extra. Ask about packages. AE, DC, MC, V. **Amenities:** Upscale restaurant, 2 bars; a small, pretty lagoon-style swimming pool. *In room:* TV, fridge; hair dryer and iron in Lakeside Units only.

IN PURSUIT OF THE GRAPE IN THE SWAN VALLEY ⃰
20km (13 miles) NE of Perth

Twenty minutes from the city center is the Swan Valley, home to two of Australia's biggest wine labels. In all there are 30 or so wineries along with a wildlife park, antique shops, a few arts-and-craft galleries, several good restaurants, and Australia's best golf resort. Some restaurants and wineries close Monday and Tuesday.

Lord Street from the Perth city center becomes Guildford Road and takes you to the small historic Art Deco town of Guildford at the start of the Swan Valley. The **Guildford and Swan Valley Tourist Information Centre** is at 111 James St., Guildford (© **08/9379 9420;** www.swanvalley-holiday.com.au). It's open daily from 9am to 5pm. Several companies (see "Whale-Watching Cruises, Tram Trips & Other Tours," above) run coach day tours or day cruises from Perth, and local companies run tours by London black cab or Rolls Royce. The winery at **Sandalford Caversham Estate** (© **08/9374 0000**) runs its own upscale cruise from Perth daily that includes a two-hour winery tour, three-course lunch matched to wines, wine tasting en route and at the winery, a souvenir wine glass, and a wine-education kit.

TOURING THE WINERIES & OTHER THINGS TO DO
Most Swan wineries are small family-run affairs, but an exception is **Houghton's,** Dale Road, Middle Swan (© **08/9274 5100**), Western Australia's oldest, biggest, and most venerable winery. The big-beamed timber cellar has old wine-making machinery on show, and there are beautiful picnic grounds (especially nice in Nov when mauve jacaranda trees blossom gloriously), a cafe, and an art gallery selling works by local artists. The other big-name winery is **Sandalford Caversham Estate,** 3210 W. Swan Rd., Caversham (© **08/9374 9374**). You may want to take its 90-minute winery tour, which takes you along walkways over the hi-tech production areas. The A$15 (U.S.$8.25) fee includes a tasting of premium wine and a wine-education kit. It runs three times daily. The winery also has a good gift shop, a pretty vine-covered casual dining area, and a pleasant restaurant. Both wineries' cellar doors are open daily for free tastings from 10am to 5pm.

The popular **Margaret River Chocolate Company** has an outlet at 5123 W. Swan Rd. (near the Reid Highway), West Swan (© **08/9250 1588**), open daily from 10am to 5pm. It does sales and tasting, and you can see it being made through the viewing window.

Perth Zoo is much bigger and brighter than this small, rather dilapidated little place, but the **Caversham Wildlife Park,** Arthur Street (but enter from Victoria Street and follow the signs), West Swan (© **08/9274 2202**) has a nonetheless intriguing collection of 200 species of mostly Western Australian wildlife you may not see elsewhere in Australia. You can stroke koalas (but not hold them, because the owner believes it stresses them), cuddle wombats and joeys sometimes, feed kangaroos, pet farm animals, and take a camel ride for A$4 (U.S.$2.20). It's open daily from 9am to 5pm, closed Christmas. Admission is A$9.50 (U.S.$5.20) for adults, A$7.50 (U.S.$4.10) for seniors and students, and A$4.50 (U.S.$2.40) for children 2 to 14.

Lovers of old stuff should browse the **junk-shop strip on James Street,** in Guildford (most shops are open daily), or visit **Woodbridge,** a beautifully restored and furnished 1883 manor house at Ford Street, in West Midland (© **08/9274 2432**). The house is open to the public daily (closed Wed) from 1 to 4pm; closed all July for restorative maintenance, and Christmas, Boxing Day (Dec 26) and Good Friday. Admission is A$3.85 (U.S.$2.10) for adults, A$1.65 (U.S.90¢) for seniors and school-age children, and A$8.80 (U.S.$4.85) for a family. Its river-view tearooms open for lunch.

Ladies, one of Perth's best boutiques, the **Swan Valley Boutique** (© **08/9377 2070**) is in the unlikely location of 4 Johnson St., Guildford; it serves coffee while you try on clothes by big-name Aussie fashion designers.

WHERE TO STAY

Hansons Swan Valley ☆☆ "At last!" some of you will cry as you step into the sleek entry hall—it's a B&B that's not down-on-the-farm hokey or drowning in chintz. Instead, these rooms have stark white walls and groovy furniture a la Philippe Starck. Most rooms have king-size beds; all have bathrobes and mini-bars stocked with cheeses, chocolates, and other goodies. Hair dryers and irons are available. Former advertising executives Jon and Selina Hanson purposely built this house to create a slick B&B of the kind they would like to stay in themselves, and it works. It is set on a 10-hectare (25-acre) farm. It also has great breakfasts and dinners. No smoking indoors.

60 Forest Rd., Henley Brook, WA 6055. © **08/9296 3366.** Fax 08/9296 3332. www.members.iinet. net.au/~hansons. 10 units (6 with Jacuzzis and shower, 4 with shower only). A$175–$250 (U.S.$96.25–$137.50) double. Rates include full breakfast. Ask about packages. AE, DC, MC, V. Take West Swan Rd. to Henley Brook and turn right at Little River Winery into Forrest St. Hansons is on the left at the end of the road. No children under 15. **Amenities:** Dining room; small outdoor swimming pool; limited room service; in-room massage (with 48 hr. notice); laundry/dry cleaning service. *In room:* A/C, TV/VCR, minibar.

Novotel Vines Resort ☆ This rural retreat was rated the best resort golf course in Australia by *Golf Australia* magazine in 2001, and it is the most upscale place to stay in the Swan Valley. Every room or apartment in the low-rise accommodation has a balcony looking onto one of two picturesque 18-hole courses where kangaroos often join the players. The rooms are of a high standard, if a bit stiff and citified for my taste. The suites are a room with a living area and spa baths.

Verdelho Dr., Belhus near Upper Swan, WA 6069. © Accor, **1300/65 6565** in Australia, 800/221 4542 in the U.S. and Canada, 020/8283 4500 in the U.K., 0800/44 4422 in New Zealand, or 08/9297 3000. Fax 08/9297 3333. www.vines.com.au. 103 units. A$204–$415 (U.S.$112.20–$228.25) double; A$265–$415 (U.S.$145.75–$228.25) suite; A$285 (U.S.$156.75) 2-bedroom apt; A$395 (U.S.$217.25) 3-bedroom apt. Extra person A$27.50 (U.S.$15.10). Children under 16 stay free in parents' room with existing bedding. Ask about packages. AE, DC, MC, V. Take West Swan Rd. to the Upper Swan and turn left on to Millhouse Rd. The resort entrance is about 1.5km (almost 1 mile) on the right. **Amenities:** 2 restaurants (1 open Fri and Sat night only); a large outdoor swimming pool; 4 all-weather tennis courts (2 floodlit); 2 squash courts; exercise room with supervised workouts; Jacuzzi; concierge; tour desk; hairdresser; limited room service; same-day laundry/ dry cleaning service. *In room:* A/C, TV with pay movies, dataport; minibar, hair dryer, iron.

WHERE TO DINE

The dining room at **Hansons** ☆ (see "Where to Stay," above) is only a small room at the rear of the house, but the flavors are big. It is open to the public daily from 8 to 10:30am and from 7pm until late. Main courses, such as peppered eye fillet, field mushrooms and roast roma tomatoes with a caper and blue brie butter, average A$23 (U.S.$16.25). Breakfast is a gourmet a la carte menu. Reservations are a good idea.

Lamont's Winery, Restaurant & Gallery ⓚⓚ MODERN AUSTRALIAN
This highly regarded restaurant is housed in a rustic timber building at Lamont
Winery. Full-flavored main courses such as chargrilled beef with roast tomatoes
and salsa verde, and hearty desserts such as chocolate tart with praline ice cream,
ensure that lots of regulars make the drive from Perth. Marron, a local crustacean,
is a specialty. An alfresco menu serves up casual fare like pizza or antipasto to eat
outside at the farm tables. A gallery on the grounds shows Western Australian art
and crafts.

85 Bisdee Rd., Millendon near Upper Swan. ⓒ **08/9296 4485.** Reservations recommended, especially for
dinner. Main courses A$24.75–$28.90 (U.S.$13.60–$15.90). Alfresco menu A$8.80–$15.40 (U.S.$4.85–
$8.45). AE, DC, MC, V. Wed–Sun 10am–5pm; open for dinner 1st Sat of the month 6:30pm–late. Closed
Christmas–New Year's Day. Take the Great Northern Hwy. to Baskerville near Upper Swan, take a right onto
Haddrill Rd. for 1.6km (1 mile), right onto Moore Rd. for 1km (just over ½ mile), and right onto Bisdee Rd.

NEW NORCIA: A TOUCH OF EUROPE IN AUSTRALIA ⓚ
132km (83 miles) N of Perth

It's the last thing you expect to see in the Australian bush—a Benedictine
monastery town with elegant European architecture, a fine museum, and a collection of Renaissance art—but New Norcia is no mirage. Boasting a population
of 55 (when everyone's at home, that is), this pretty town and the surrounding
8,000-hectare (19,760-acre) farm were established in 1846 by Spanish Benedictine missionaries. Visitors can tour beautifully frescoed chapels, marvel at one of
the finest religious art collections in Australia, stock up on famous New Norcia
nutcake straight from the monastery's 120-year-old wood-fired ovens, and
attend prayers with the 18 monks who live here.

New Norcia is an easy 2-hour drive from Perth. From downtown, take Lord
Street, which becomes Guildford Road, to Midland; here join the Great Northern Highway to New Norcia. Government rail organization **WAGR** (ⓒ **13 10
53** in Western Australia, 1800/099 150 from the interstate, or 08/9326 2000)
runs a coach service (there is no rail line) Sunday, Tuesday, and Thursday from
Perth for A$13.85 (U.S.$7.60) one-way. **Greyhound Pioneer** (ⓒ **13 20 30** in
Australia) coaches run from Perth Friday and Sunday for A$37 (U.S.$20.35).
Note that coach schedules will probably require you to stay at least overnight, if
not longer, in order to have time to see anything. Check ahead if you plan to
travel on a public holiday or during Western Australian school vacations,
because schedules sometimes change then. Day tours from Perth are available.

Conference groups can book the town solid, so reserve accommodations and
tours in advance, especially in wildflower season August through October.

You can get information at the **New Norcia Tourist Information Centre,**
New Norcia, WA 6509 (ⓒ **08/9654 8056;** www.newnorcia.wa.edu.au), in the
Museum and Art Gallery, just off the highway behind St. Joseph's, beside the
Trading Post and Roadhouse. Its hours are those of the museum and gallery (see
below).

EXPLORING THE TOWN & MONASTERY
The New Norcia Tourist Information Centre's intriguing 2-hour walking tours
are a must. Tickets cost A$12 (U.S.$6.60) for adults and A$5.50 (U.S.$3) for
children 12 to 17, free for younger children. Tours depart daily except Christmas
at 11am and 1:30pm, and they allow time for you to attend prayers with the
monks if you wish. The guide strolls you around some of the town's 27 National
Trust–classified buildings and gives an insight into the monks' lifestyle. You will
also see the delightful frescoes in the old monastery chapel and in St. Ildephonsus's

and St. Gertrude's colleges. Much of the monastery is closed to visitors, but the tour does show you the fruit gardens and a glimpse of the men-only courtyard. Heritage walking-trail maps sold for A$3.30 (U.S.$1.80) at the Tourist Information Centre include more buildings not visited on the tour, such as the octagonal apiary.

The **museum and art gallery** ✿ is full of relics from the monks' past—old mechanical and musical instruments, artifacts from the days when New Norcia was an Aboriginal mission, gifts to the monks from the Queen of Spain, and an astounding collection of paintings by Spanish and Italian artists. The oldest I saw was dated 1492. Give yourself at least an hour here, easily more. The museum and gallery are open daily from 9:30am to 5pm August through October, and from 10am to 4:30pm November through July (closed Christmas). Admission is A$4.50 (U.S.$2.50) for adults, A$3.50 (U.S.$1.95) for seniors and students, and A$1 (U.S.55¢) for children 6 to 12.

Apart from joining the monks for 15-minute prayers in the monastery five times a day (noon and 2:30pm are the most convenient for day visitors), you can join them for Mass in the Holy Trinity Abbey Church Monday through Saturday at 7:30am and on Sunday at 9am.

WHERE TO STAY & DINE
New Norcia Hotel   When they thought a Spanish royal visit to New Norcia was imminent in 1926, the monks built this grandiose white hotel fit for, well, a king. Sadly, the royals never materialized, and the building fell into disrepair. Only the grand central staircase, soaring pressed-metal ceilings, and imposing Iberian facade hint at the splendor that was. Three years ago, new carpets, curtains, and beds were put in, but be prepared for rather grim rooms. Only one has an en suite, air-conditioning, and a TV. Still, it's kinda nice to eat a meal at the rather dated bar or the charmingly faded Dining Room, and to sit on the football-size front veranda upstairs. The bar gets jumping on Friday and Saturday nights when local farmers come to town. This is the only place to stay in town. No smoking.

Great Northern Hwy., New Norcia, WA 6509. ℂ **08/9654 8034.** Fax 08/9654 8011. hotel_nn@hotmail.com. 17 units (1 only with bathroom). A$70 (U.S.$38.50) double without bathroom, A$90 (U.S.$49.50) double with bathroom. Extra person A$11 (U.S.$6.05). AE, MC, V. **Amenities:** Restaurant, meals served at the bar, bar. *In room:* Fridge, iron, no phone.

3 Margaret River & the Southwest: Wine Tasting in the Forests ✿✿

Margaret River: 290km (181 miles) S of Perth

Say "Margaret River" to Australians and they reply "great wine!" with their eyes all lit up. The area's 42 wineries nestle among statuesque forests of karri, the world's third-tallest tree. The wineries contribute only around 1% to Australia's wine output, yet they turn out some 10% of the country's top-notch "premium" wines. Not even most Aussies know about the Southwest's other drawing cards, though—like the spectacular surf breaks on the 130-kilometer (81-mile) coast from Cape Naturaliste in the north to Cape Leeuwin on the southwest tip of Australia; the coastal cliffs, perfect for abseiling (rappelling) and rock climbing; and the honeycomb of limestone caves filled with stalagmites and stalactites. Whales pass by June through December, wildflowers line the roads August through October, and wild birds, kangaroos, and cute shingle-backed lizards are everywhere. If you like hiking, pack your boots, because there are plenty of trails,

Taking a Dip with Flipper ★★

The wild dolphins that come to Monkey Mia's shore (see "The Midwest & the Northwest: Where the Outback Meets the Sea," later in this chapter) are justly famous. But just 2½ hours' drive south of Perth, en route to Margaret River, is a place where you can *swim* with these creatures. And the tourist hordes that invade Monkey Mia are largely absent!

At the **Dolphin Discovery Centre** in the seaside town of Bunbury, about three, sometimes as many as 16, bottle-nosed dolphins come into shore in Koombana Bay. You can swim with them free of charge in the "interaction zone" on the beach in front of the Centre, under the watchful eye of volunteer guides. The water is only waist-deep so you can stand if you like. You must not chase them, but you can pat them if they come near, and the dolphins are free to touch you. The Centre rents wet suits (A$10/U.S.$5.50) and snorkel gear (A$5/U.S.$2.75). Bookings are not necessary.

From November to April the Centre runs **2-hour boat tours** to swim with some of the bay's 100-plus dolphins in deeper water for A$80 (U.S.$44); you must be over 12. **Naturaliste Charters** (© **08/9755 2276**) runs excellent 90-minute **dolphin watch cruises** twice daily from the Centre; they cost A$25 (U.S.$13.75) adults, A$22 (U.S.$12.10) seniors and students, and A$18 (U.S.$9.90) kids ages 4 to 12. The Centre has showers, a cafe, and a good little eco-display on the dolphin life-cycle; admission to that is A$5 (U.S.$2.75) adults, A$3 (U.S.$1.65) seniors and students, and A$2 (U.S.$1.10) kids 4 to 17. The Centre is open from 8am to 5pm (Oct–May) and from 10am to 3pm (June–Sept). The Centre is located on Koombana Drive, Bunbury (© **08/9791 3088;** visit www.bunburytourism.org.au).

Monkey Mia's world fame as a dolphin spot means it draws big crowds, so rangers strictly control interaction with the dolphins. You are unlikely to get to touch or swim with dolphins there. So why go all the way to Monkey Mia? Because sightings are almost guaranteed every day. At Bunbury, dolphins don't show up about a third of the time (the best chance of seeing them is 8am–noon). *Note:* You can hand-feed wild dolphins at **Tangalooma Wild Dolphin Resort** near Brisbane (see chapter 5).

from a 15-minute stroll around Margaret River township, to a 6-day **Cape-to-Cape trek** ★ along the sea cliffs. The Southwest is truly one of Australia's last great wildernesses, and one of my favorite parts of the country.

Like wine regions the world over, the Southwest has more than its fair share of cozy B&Bs, arts-and-crafts galleries, and some super restaurants. Plan to stay at least 2 days.

ESSENTIALS

GETTING THERE   It's a 3½-hour drive to Margaret River from Perth; take the inland South Western Highway (the quickest route) or the tad more scenic

Old Coast Road to Bunbury, where you pick up the Bussell Highway to Margaret River.

Airline service to Margaret River ceased in 2001, but check with the tourism association (see "Visitor Information," below) to see if it has resumed when you visit. **Leeuwin Estate** winery (book through the Fremantle office; © **08/9430 4099;** www.leeuwinestate.com.au) does "Flying Visit" day and overnight trips from Perth. A day trip including return flights, three-course a la carte lunch at its excellent restaurant (wine costs extra), winery tour and tasting, and a district tour costs A$313 (U.S.$172.15) per person.

Southwest Coachlines (© **08/9324 2333,** or 1800/800 530) runs a daily service, and two on weekends and public and Western Australian school holidays, to Margaret River from Perth for A$24.70 (U.S.$13.60). There is no train, but government rail organization **WAGR** (© **13 10 53** in Western Australia, 1800/099 150 in Australia from interstate, or 08/9326 2000) runs a coach service from Perth, twice daily every day except Saturday. It takes over 5 hours, and on some services you transfer by local bus (which does not run Sun or public holidays) to a different coach in Bunbury. You could also connect to this coach service in Bunbury by taking WAGR's twice-daily *Australind* train from Perth to Bunbury—it shaves travel time down to a bit over 4½ hours. Fares are A$26.15 (U.S.$14.40) with either mode. WAGR schedules can differ on a public holiday or during Western Australian school vacations.

VISITOR INFORMATION   You will pass many wineries before you get to Margaret River township, but it's worth heading first to **the Augusta Margaret River Tourism Association** information center to pick up a winery guide. It's on the Bussell Highway at Tunbridge Street, Margaret River, WA 6285 (© **08/ 9757 2911;** www.margaretriverwa.com). It is open daily from 9am to 5pm.

GETTING AROUND   Nine kilometers (5½ miles) past Busselton, which marks the start of the Southwest, the Bussell Highway makes a sharp left and heads south among the wineries through Vasse, then 25 kilometers (15½ miles) on through the tiny village of Cowaramup, 11 kilometers (7 miles) farther through Margaret River proper, and 43 kilometers (27 miles) on to windswept Cape Leeuwin and the tiny fishing port of Augusta on Australia's south coast.

A car is close to essential. Only **Avis** (© **1800/679 880** within Australia for reservations in the Southwest, or 08/9757 3686) has an office in Margaret River.

Several companies run sightseeing, adventure, and winery tours from Margaret River or Perth.

TOURING THE WINERIES

Fans of premium wines (and who isn't?) will have a field day in the Southwest. Cabernet sauvignon and merlot are the star red varieties, while chardonnay, semillon, and sauvignon blanc are the pick of the bunch among whites. Most

---

Tips A Wine-Buying Tip

The place to buy wine if you want to take it out of Australia is the **Margaret River Regional Wine Centre,** 9 Bussell Hwy., Cowaramup (© **08/ 9755-5501**), because most wineries don't deliver internationally. It stocks just about every local wine, does daily tastings of select vintages, sells maps, visitor guides and winery guides, and has an expert staff to help you purchase wisely, and even tailor your day's foray. It is open Monday through Saturday from 10am to 7pm, and Sunday from noon to 6pm (closed Christmas, Good Friday, and sometimes New Year's Day). Order off its website at www.mrwines.com.

---

wineries offer free tastings from 10am to 4:30pm daily. Most wineries cluster north of Margaret River township, around Cowaramup.

The region's top winery is **Leeuwin Estate** 🔆, Stevens Road, Margaret River (© **08/9757 6253**). It has a towering reputation, especially for chardonnay; its Art Series label is among the country's best. Interesting winery tours are scheduled three times a day. A relative newcomer, **Voyager Estate,** Stevens Road, Margaret River (© **08/9757 6354**), has exquisite rose gardens and a South African Cape Dutch–style cellar. These wines are gaining a good reputation. Other good labels to look for are Arlewood Estate, Cape Mentelle, Cullen Wines, Devil's Lair, Evans & Tate, Lenton Brae, Pierro (at least one wine writer claims it makes Australia's best chardonnay) and Sandalford Wines. Vasse Felix winery makes two highly drinkable "quaffers"—Aussie slang for easy-drinking, inexpensive wines—called Theatre Red and Theatre White. They are served in the London West End theatres owned by the winery's proprietor, Janet Holmes à Court, Australia's wealthiest woman.

BEYOND THE WINERIES: CAVES, BUSH TUCKER & MORE

Five of the Southwest's 350 or so limestone caves are open to the public, all with elaborate stalactite formations. Before or after you visit one, call at the excellent **CaveWorks** eco-interpretive center at Lake Cave, Caves Road, 15 kilometers (9 miles) south of Margaret River's Wallcliffe Road (© **08/9757 7411**), open daily except Christmas from 9am to 5pm. Entry is free if you tour Lake, Jewel, Mammoth, or Moondyne caves, or else A$3 (U.S.$1.65) for adults, A$2 (U.S.$1.10) for children ages 4 to 15.

Lake Cave, right outside CaveWorks and 300 steps down an ancient sinkhole, contains a tranquil pond in which exquisite stalactites are reflected. Four kilometers (2½ miles) north along Caves Road is **Mammoth Cave,** where you can see the fossilized jaw of a baby zygotaurus trilobus, an extinct giant wombat. **Jewel Cave,** 8 kilometers (5 miles) north of Augusta on Caves Road, is the prettiest. Tours of Lake and Jewel and self-guided tours of Mammoth cost A$14 (U.S.$7.70) for adults, A$5.50 (U.S.$3) for children 4 to 15. A 7-day Grand Pass to all three plus CaveWorks saves you money. Mammoth is open from 9am to 5pm (last tour at 4pm); tours of Lake and Jewel run hourly from 9:30am to the last tour at 3:30pm. Sometimes extra tours are scheduled during school vacations. The caves are open every day except Christmas. Book tours through CaveWorks.

Just next to Jewel Cave is **Moondyne Cave,** an "adventure cave" where you get down and dirty crawling on your hands and knees, in the protective clothing supplied. This 2-hour experience costs A$27.50 (U.S.$15.10) for adults and

A$19 (U.S.$10.45) for kids (kids under 10 are not permitted, and an adult must accompany kids ages 10–16). Tours depart daily at 2pm; book through Cave-Works 24 hours ahead. A similar adventure tour taking about 2½ hours is offered at **Ngilgi Cave,** Caves Road, Yallingup (© **08/9755 2152**), for A$35 (U.S.$19.25) for anyone over 14. It departs daily at 9:30am; book 24 hours ahead. Ngilgi's main chamber has beautiful translucent stalactite "shawls," which anyone can explore on a semi-guided tour. This costs A$14 (U.S.$7.70) for adults and A$5 (U.S.$2.75) children 5 to 17, and runs half-hourly from 9:30am, with the last tour at 3:30pm (4pm during school vacations, 4:30pm during Christmas school vacations). The cave opens every day except Christmas.

Food-based attractions are opening up in the area all the time. You can pick your own kiwi, raspberries, and other fruit at **The Berry Farm,** 222 Bessell Rd. outside Margaret River (© **08/9757 5054**), or buy them ready-made as attractively packaged sparkling, dessert, and port wines; jams; and vinegars. At the **Margaret River Chocolate Factory,** Lot 21, Harman's Mill Rd., Metricup (© **08/9755 6555**) near the Cowaramup wineries, you can do free tastings, watch the candy making through a window, and of course, buy the stuff.

Allow time to browse the area's arts-and-crafts galleries, too. One of the most upscale is **Gunyulgup Galleries,** Gunyulgup Valley Drive near Yallingup (© **08/9755 2177**), which has elegant jewelry, glass, ceramics, and artworks.

Greg Miller of **Adventure Plus** (© **08/9361 5497,** or 0419/961 716 mobile phone) arranges all kinds of outdoor adventures from abseiling and rock climbing coastal cliffs, to caving, canoeing, hiking, mountain biking, and camping. He welcomes beginners. Prices vary with the activity; expect to pay around A$105 (U.S.$57.75) for a day's action. Plenty of **hiking trails** are suited to you, whether you want an easy stroll to a whale-watch lookout, an afternoon's ramble through the forest, or an overnight trek. The tourist information center in Margaret River (see "Visitor Information") sells trail maps, including maps to all the open sections of the Cape-to-Cape cliff-edge walk from Cape Naturaliste to Cape Leeuwin.

Try to make time for one of two tours offered by **"Bushtucker Woman"** **Helen Lee** ⋒ (© **08/9757 1084,** or 0419/91 1971). On one tour, she has you canoeing up the river, exploring a cave, and eating smoked emu, grub paté (I'm not kidding), and other Aboriginal delicacies on a river island. It runs from 10am to 2pm (no tour Tues and Thurs in winter), and costs A$35 (U.S.$19.25) for adults and A$17 (U.S.$9.35) for kids under 16. Her winery tour has an alternative bent incorporating short karri-forest walks, insights into organic wine making, tastings of 50 wines at five wineries, a visit to Leeuwin Estate's herb garden, and a picnic lunch of bush tucker and local cheeses, hams, and dips. She'll teach you things like how vaporized peppermint oil from the native

---

Moments Scenic Drives

Boranup Drive ⋒ is a magical detour off Caves Road through towering karris (though please keep in mind that your rental car is not insured on its unpaved surface). It departs Caves Road 6 kilometers (3¾ miles) south of Mammoth Cave and rejoins it after a 14-kilometer (8¾-miles) meander. **Caves Road** is a picturesque 106-kilometer (66-mile) north-south drive through forest and farms, from Busselton in the north to Augusta on Cape Leeuwin in the south.

trees condenses on the grapes to create the distinctive flavor of Margaret River whites. The 5-hour tour departs daily at noon and costs A$45 (U.S.$24.75), adult or child.

Surfing lessons 𝒢 from four-time Western Australian professional surfing champion **Josh Parmateer** (℗ **08/9757 3850** or 0418/958 264) are a must—take it from this surf virgin! Two-hour lessons in the gentle waist-deep surf at Prevelly Park Beach, 9 kilometers (5½ miles) west of Margaret River, run daily and cost A$80 (U.S.$44) per person, or A$40 (U.S.$22) per person for two. Lessons run September through June. If you are already a Master of the Surf Universe, try the legendary Smiths Beach or the Three Bears (Mama, Papa, and Baby) break at Yallingup, the double-barreled North Point at Gracetown, or the plentiful breaks at Prevelly Park. **Beach Life,** 117 Bussell Hwy., Margaret River (℗ **08/9757 2888**), rents boards for A$40 (U.S.$22) for 24 hours.

June through December **whales** play just offshore all along the coast. There is a whale lookout near the Cape Naturaliste lighthouse. Daily 3-hour whale-watching cruises with **Naturaliste Charters** 𝒢 (℗ **08/9755 2276**) depart June through September from Augusta (where you'll also see fur seals and often dolphins). September through December, cruise departures switch to Dunsborough, where whales rest their calves. The boat is fitted with an underwater camera connected to a TV and a hydrophone, so you can see and hear the creatures. Cruises cost A$45 (U.S.$24.75) for adults, A$42 (U.S.$23.10) for seniors and students, and A$35 (U.S.$19.25) for children 4 to 12. Children under 4 are free.

WHERE TO STAY

It's not the prettiest village in the Southwest, but **Margaret River** has the advantage of banks, a supermarket, and a few restaurants and shops. The blink-and-you'll-miss-it hamlet of **Cowaramup,** 11 kilometers (7 miles) north of Margaret River township, is closer to more wineries and has a general store, a cafe, and one or two interesting craft shops. **Vasse** is a tiny settlement at the northern edge of the Southwest, 36 kilometers (22½ miles) north of Margaret River. Some places may demand a minimum 2-night stay on weekends.

IN MARGARET RIVER

Basildene Manor 𝒢   This lovely National Trust–classified farmhouse was built by the local lighthouse keeper in 1912 out of local stone. Following a supremely tasteful refurbishment in 1997 by the friendly proprietors, Garry Nielsen and Julie Whittingham, it's now a gentrified B&B with attractive bedrooms. Some lead off an impressive jarrah gallery overlooking the cozy "Main Hall" with its open fire. Suites are large rooms with their own sitting areas, and eight of them added in 1999 have spa baths. A stylish, cooked breakfast is served in the pretty conservatory overlooking the 14-acre grounds, and your hosts point you along a walking trail to spy on a mob of kangaroos. No smoking indoors.

Lot 100 Wallcliffe Rd. (2km/1¼ miles west of town), Margaret River, WA 6285. ℗ **08/9757 3140.** Fax 08/9757 3383. www.basildene.com.au. 17 units (all with shower only, 8 with Jacuzzis also). A$193–$289 (U.S.$106.15–$158.95) double. Rates include full breakfast. AE, DC, MC, V. No children under 15. **Amenities:** Same-day laundry/dry cleaning service. *In room:* A/C, TV/VCR, non-alcoholic minibar, hair dryer, iron.

Heritage Trail Lodge 𝒢   Although they're on the highway and "in" Margaret River (within walking distance of restaurants), this cute row of salmon-pink cabin-style rooms, built in 1997, are huddled in a serene karri forest, out of sight of town. Inside, each spacious unit has king double or king twin beds and a fabulous double Jacuzzi (even the room for people with disabilities), from which you can see the forest. The rooms back onto 35-minute bushwalk trail. Welcoming proprietors Hugh and Maxine Beckingham serve up a delicious breakfast of cereals, yogurt, and local jams, cheeses, and breads in the sunny pine dining room. 'Roos even hop into the carpark sometimes. No smoking indoors.

31 Bussell Hwy. (400m north of town), Margaret River, WA 6285. ℰ 08/9757 9595. Fax 08/9757 9596. www.heritage-trail-lodge.com.au. 10 units (all with shower and Jacuzzi). A$210–$249 (U.S.$115.50–$136.95) double. Extra person A$35 (U.S.$19.25). Rates include continental breakfast. Ask about midweek packages. AE, DC, MC, V. Children under 16 not permitted. *In room:* A/C, TV, minibar, coffeemaker, hair dryer, iron.

IN COWARAMUP

The Noble Grape   English cottage gardens surround this B&B, recently built in a colonial style. Each well-maintained room is motel-like, but homey and welcoming with a modern bathroom, heating, ceiling fans, a comfy sitting area, and a small rear patio opening onto bird-filled trees. One caters to travelers with disabilities. Although you're on the highway here, I found the rooms quiet. Hair dryers are at reception. No smoking indoors.

Lot 18, Bussell Hwy., Cowaramup, WA 6284. ℰ and fax 08/9755 5538. www.babs.com.au/noblegrape. 6 units (all with shower only). A$99–$110 (U.S.$54.45–$60.50) double. Additional person A$22 (U.S.$12.10). Rates include continental breakfast. AE, DC, MC, V. **Amenities:** Self-service laundry. *In room:* TV, minibar, no phone.

IN VASSE

Newtown House   Set in lavender and rose gardens nice for lazing in after a hard day's wine tasting, this National Trust–listed 1851 homestead has four pretty rooms with "contemporary country" decor, furnished with wrought-iron table and chairs, pine furniture, and cute touches like potpourri "dream sacks" on your pillow. All have ceiling fans. The fixings for a gourmet continental breakfast are sent up to your room the night before. Don't miss the excellent restaurant (see "Where to Dine," below). No smoking indoors.

Bussell Hwy. (9km/5½ miles past Busselton), Vasse, WA 6280. ℰ and fax 08/9755 4485. 4 units (all with shower only). A$137.50 (U.S.$75.65) double. Rates include continental breakfast. AE, DC, MC, V. The property is on the right just after the Bussell Hwy. turns left (south). Children not permitted. **Amenities:** Restaurant. *In room:* TV, minibar, coffeemaker, no phone.

WHERE TO DINE

Good restaurants are attached to a number of wineries, including Vasse Felix, Driftwood Estate, and Brookland Valley Vineyard. Most outstanding is **Leeuwin Estate's restaurant** ☆☆, Stevens Road, Margaret River (ℰ 08/9757 6253); it has terrific food, it's cozy in winter, and in summer its wide deck overlooking lawns is just the place to be for lunch.

Stock up for a picnic at the supermarket in Margaret River. Cape Mentelle and Vasse Felix both have shady picnic areas beside a brook.

Newtown House ☆☆ MODERN FRENCH/AUSTRALIAN   The Southwest boasts some of the best restaurants in Australia, and this is one of 'em. Folks come from far and wide to savor chef Stephen Reagan's skill in preparing such dishes as rare local venison with roast pears, beetroot, and red wine glaze. Desserts are no letdown, either—caramel soufflé with lavender ice cream and hot caramel sauce is typical. Located in a historic homestead, the restaurant consists of two simple, intimate rooms with sisal matting and contemporary, boldly colored walls. Even better, it's BYO. Drop by for morning or afternoon tea, if you like.

Bussell Hwy. (9km/5½ miles past Busselton), Vasse. ℰ 08/9755 4485. Reservations recommended, especially at dinner. Main courses A$19.50–$24.50 (U.S.$10.75–$13.50) lunch; A$26.50–$31.50 (U.S.$14.60–$17.35) dinner. AE, DC, MC, V. Tues–Sat 10am–4pm and 6–10:30pm or later.

The Valley Café (★) MODERN AUSTRALIAN   Voted most popular Southwest cafe in 1998, 1999, and 2000, this pleasant place serves up stylish fare with views over the countryside. Lunch might be risotto with Augusta smoked chicken, sun-dried capsicum (bell pepper), and shaved Parmesan. Dinner might be cured Atlantic salmon with polenta, asparagus, and caramelized balsamic vinegar. Courses are "Medium" and "Large," so you can eat light if you wish, or just come for coffee and cake. BYO.

Carters Rd. (near Caves Rd.), Margaret River. (℃) **08/9757 3225.** Reservations recommended. Main courses A$18–$29.50 (U.S.$9.90–$16.25); average A$24 (U.S.$13.20). AE, MC, V. Wed–Sun 10am–4pm, Fri–Sat (and Sun on 3-day weekends) 6–10pm.

4 The Goldfields (★)

595km (372 miles) E of Perth

After Paddy Hannan struck gold in 1893, the wheat-belt town of Kalgoorlie found itself sitting on the "Golden Mile," the richest square mile of gold-bearing earth in the world, at the time. Today **Kalgoorlie** (★) (pop. 32,000) is still an Outback gold-rush boomtown, a mixture of yesteryear charm and 21st-century corporate gold fever. The town is perched literally on the edge of the Super Pit, the world's biggest open-cut gold mine, currently 4.5 kilometers (3 miles) long, 1.5 kilometers (1 mile) wide, and 290 meters (951 ft.) deep. It yields up to 850,000 ounces of the precious yellow stuff every year—over 2,000 ounces a day. An estimated 13 million ounces is still in the ground. Hardly surprisingly, Kalgoorlie Consolidated Gold Mines, which operates the pit, is Australia's biggest gold producer.

Walking down the wide streets fronted with wrought-iron lace verandas is like stumbling onto a Western movie set. Countless bars still do the roaring trade they notched up in the 1890s—only now they serve suited-up gold-mining executives from Adelaide and Perth.

Life on the Golden Mile is not so lively for everyone, however. Just down the road 39 kilometers (24 miles) is **Coolgardie** (pop. 1,100), another 1890s goldrush boomtown where the gold ran out in 1963. The town's semi-abandoned air is a sad foil to Kalgoorlie's brash energy; but much of the lovely architecture remains, so you can just wander the gracious streets and a few small museums for a pleasant nostalgia buzz.

ESSENTIALS

GETTING THERE   **Airlink** (℃ **08/9225 8383,** or book through Qantas at 13 13 13 in Australia) flies to Kalgoorlie from Perth daily. Airlink flies direct from Adelaide.

Greyhound Pioneer (℃ **13 20 30** in Australia) makes the 8-hour trip five times a week from Perth for A$102 (U.S.$56.10). Greyhound's service from

---

(*Fun Fact* **Gold in the Streets!**

In Kalgoorlie's young days, its streets were paved with a blackish spoil from the mining process called "tellurides." When someone realized tellurides contain up to 40% gold and 10% silver, those streets were ripped up in one big hurry. The city fathers had paved the streets with gold and didn't even know it!

Adelaide runs 5 days a week, takes around 24 hours, and costs A$226 (U.S.$124.30). **Goldrush Tours** (© **1800/62 0440** in Australia, or 08/9021 2954) runs a 6¾-hour express coach service from Perth every day except Monday for $78 (U.S.$42.90).

Kalgoorlie is a stop on the 3-day *Indian Pacific* ⚷ train service, which runs between Sydney and Perth through Adelaide twice a week in both directions. See section 11, "Getting Around Australia," in chapter 2, for contact details. The *Prospector* train makes 10 trips a week from Perth to Kalgoorlie for A$52.65 (U.S.$28.95). Call the government rail organization **WAGR** (© **13 10 53** in Western Australia, 1800/099 150 in Australia from interstate, or 08/9326 2000).

From Perth, take the Great Eastern Highway. If you want to make the extremely dull 2,182-kilometer (1,364-mile) journey on the Eyre Highway from Adelaide, which features the longest straight stretch of highway in the world on the empty Nullarbor Plain, contact the South Australian or Western Australian state auto clubs listed under "Getting Around Australia," in chapter 2, for advice. There are only a handful of small towns and gas stops en route.

VISITOR INFORMATION   The **Kalgoorlie-Boulder Tourist Centre,** 250 Hannan St., Kalgoorlie, WA 6430 (© **1800/00 1880** in Australia, or 08/9021 1966; www.kalgoorlieandwagoldfields.com.au), dispenses information on Kalgoorlie, Coolgardie, and outlying ghost towns and regions. Boulder is a suburb of Kalgoorlie. The center's walking-trail map to the town's architecture, which sells for a few dollars, is worth buying. The center is open Monday through Friday from 8:30am to 5pm, and Saturday, Sunday, and public holidays from 9am to 5pm. The **Coolgardie Tourist Bureau,** 62 Bayley St., Coolgardie, WA 6429 (© **08/9026 6090**), is open daily from 9am to 5pm.

GETTING AROUND   Avis (© **08/9021 1722**), **Budget** (© **08/9093 2300**), **Hertz** (© **08/9093 2211**), and **Thrifty** (© **08/9021 4722**) have offices in Kalgoorlie. The Tourist Centre also sells an exclusive A$16 (U.S.$8.80) round-trip taxi fare to Hannans North Historic Mining Reserve.

As well as offering coach, four-wheel-drive, and four-wheel-drive tag-along bush tours of Kalgoorlie, Coolgardie, and outlying ghost towns, local tour operators will take you gold prospecting in outlying regions. Tours range from half a day up to several days.

WHAT TO SEE & DO
As you might guess, gold is a common thread running through many of the town's attractions. One of the best is **Hannans North Historic Mining Reserve** ⚷, Broad Arrow Road, 6 kilometers (3¾ miles) north of the Tourist Centre on the Goldfields Highway (© **08/9091 4074**), where you can venture underground in an old mine, pan for gold, watch a fascinating gold pour, see a video in a re-created miner's tent, and pore over an extensive collection of mining memorabilia, old shaft heads, machinery, and huts in a re-created miners' village. It's fun, and the exhibits are well done. The admission fee is A$16.50 (U.S.$9.10) for adults, A$12 (U.S.$6.60) for seniors and students, A$8.50 (U.S.$4.70) for kids ages 5 to 15, and A$42 (U.S.$23.10) for a family. It is open daily 9am to 4:30pm (closed Christmas, Boxing Day—that's Dec 26—and New Year's Day). Allow 3 hours. Beside Hannan's North is the new **Mining Hall of Fame** mining museum. Not yet opened as we wrote, it promises to be an impressive place with five interactive galleries focusing on mining's modern high-tech face. It has a gallery each on how prospecting is done, how big business mining is conducted, geology, the economy,

and the Australian mining industry's influential individuals. Opening hours and admission prices were not set at press time.

The **Museum of the Goldfields,** 17 Hannan St. (© **08/9021 8533**), is worth a look for the first 400-ounce gold bar minted in town, nuggets and jewelry, and historical displays. It is open daily from 10am to 4:30pm, closed Christmas and Good Friday. Admission is free (donation requested). Allow an hour.

Don't leave town without ogling the awesome **Super Pit** open-cut mine—it makes giant dump trucks look like ants. The lookout is at Outram Street in Boulder, off the Goldfields Highway. It's open daily from about 4 or 5am to about 7pm. A blast takes place daily; check the time with the visitor center. Entry is free.

When they're not digging money out of the ground, hard-bitten locals gamble for it at the **Bush Two-Up School.** The game is a simple bet on a penny landing heads or tails—hardly exciting stuff, but it shows you a bit of local color. The school was due to move to new premises as we wrote; check with the tourist center. It opens daily around 5pm to dusk (closed Christmas and Good Friday). Admission is free. Kids under 18 are not permitted.

The **Royal Flying Doctor Service** (RFDS; © **08/9093 7500**) base at Kalgoorlie-Boulder Airport is open for visitors to browse memorabilia, see a video, and look over an aircraft if one is in. It is open Monday through Friday from 11am to 3pm. Admission is by donation.

Full-blood Aboriginal Geoffrey Stokes of **Yamatji Bitja Aboriginal Bush Tours** (© **08/9093 3745** or 0407/378 602) grew up the Aboriginal way in the bush. On his full-day four-wheel-drive tours, you'll forage for bush tucker, learn Aboriginal bushcraft, and do things like eat witchetty grubs, cook kangaroo over a fire, or track emus. Tours cost A$80 (U.S.$44), half price for kids 4 to 12. Geoff also does twilight campfire evenings, and overnight or longer tours in the bush.

Candidate for "Kalgoorlie's Most Unusual Attraction" award goes to **Langtrees 181,** 181 Hay St. (© **08/9026 2181**), a working brothel styled into a sex industry museum in the heart of Kalgoorlie's (in)famous red-light district. For the most part housed in corrugated iron sheds festooned with colored lights, this neck of town is a popular drive-by spot among the blue-rinse bus-tour set, who get a kick out of returning the cheery waves of the workers standing in their doorways. Ninety-minute tours, fun rather than sleazy, of some of the 12 themed rooms cost A$25 (U.S.$13.75). Tours depart 11am, 3, and 7pm daily.

Wandering Coolgardie's quiet streets, which are graced with historic facades, is a pleasant stroll back in time. More than 100 signboards erected around the place, many with photos, detail what each site was like in the town's heyday at the turn of the century.

The **Goldfields Exhibition,** 62 Bayley St. (© **08/9026 6090**), tells the town's story in a lovely 1898 building once used as the mining warden's courthouse (the Tourist Bureau is also here). Admission is A$3.30 (U.S.$1.80) for adults, A$2.75 (U.S.$1.50) for seniors, A$1.10 (U.S.60¢) for children under 16, or A$7.70 (U.S.$4.25) for a family. It's open daily except Christmas from 9am to 5pm. Coolgardie also has a couple of small museums, including a neat little pharmaceutical museum, a railway museum, and a National Trust–owned 1895 house open for tours, now restored with period interiors.

The **Coolgardie Camel Farm,** 4 kilometers (2½ miles) west of Coolgardie on the Great Eastern Highway (© **08/9026 6159**), leads rides through the bush on the mode of transport they used in the goldfields in the old days—camels.

WHERE TO STAY

Mercure Hotel Plaza Kalgoorlie   Mining execs like the practical comforts, upscale restaurant (which I can recommend), and walking distance to the lively main street at this four-story property. The rooms are neat and spacious, and some have modest city views. The cocktail lounge has a nice clubby buzz in the evenings.

45 Egan St., Kalgoorlie, WA 6430. © **1300/65 6565** in Australia, 800/221-4542 in the U.S. and Canada, 020/8283 4500 in the U.K., 0800/44 4422 in New Zealand, or 08/9021 4544. Fax 08/9091 2195. www.accorhotels.com.au. 100 units (all with shower only). A$181–$197 (U.S.$99.55–$108.35) double; A$290 (U.S.$159.50) suite. Extra person A$25 (U.S.$13.75). Ask about weekend packages. AE, DC, MC, V. **Amenities:** Restaurant, bar; modest outdoor pool; tour desk; secretarial services; limited room service; self-service laundry; same-day laundry/dry cleaning service. *In room:* A/C, TV with pay movies, minibar, coffeemaker, hair dryer, iron.

WHERE TO DINE

Akudjura ⊕ MODERN AUSTRALIAN   The Italianate outdoor terrace under sailcloth and the timber floors, curved silver bar, and blond-wood furniture make this Kalgoorlie's first groovy restaurant. Bright young waitstaff provide snappy service from a long and stylish menu featuring items like chicken Caesar salad, smoked salmon fettuccine, kangaroo steak, and seafood dishes (yep, even in the desert) like Tasmanian salmon in a citrus and coriander dressing. Lighter fare is available outside meal hours.

418 Hannan St. (next to Hannan's View Motel). © **08/9091 3311**. Reservations recommended. Main courses A$13.20–$31.90 (U.S.$7.25–$17.55); lunch averages A$12.50 (U.S.$6.90). AE, DC, MC, V. Daily 7am–approx. 10pm.

5 The Midwest & the Northwest: Where the Outback Meets the Sea ⊛

The Midwest and Northwest coasts of Western Australia are treeless, riverless semi-desert, occupied by vast sheep stations and only a handful of people. Temperatures soar into the 40s°C (over 115°F) in summer, and the Outback sand burns bright orange in the blazing sun. But it's not the land you come here for—it's what's in the sea that you're interested in. Since the 1960s, a pod of **bottle-nosed dolphins** has been coming into shallow water at **Monkey Mia** ⊕, the World Heritage–listed Shark Bay Marine Park, to greet delighted shore-bound humans. Their magical presence has generated worldwide publicity and drawn people from every corner of the globe.

Another 872 kilometers (545 miles) by road north on the Northwest Cape, adventure seekers from around the world come to **snorkel with awesome whale sharks** ⊕—measuring up to 18 meters (59 ft.) long—every fall (Mar to early June). The Cape's parched shore and green waters hide an even more dazzling secret though—a second barrier reef 260 kilometers (163 miles) long and 2 kilometers (1¼ miles) wide called **Ningaloo Marine Park** ⊕⊕. It protects 250 species of coral and 450 kinds of fish, dolphins, mantas, whales, turtles, and dugongs (manatees) in its 5,000 square kilometers (1,640 sq. miles). Some folks say Ningaloo is as good, if not better, than the Great Barrier Reef. Even the Great Barrier Reef can't beat Ningaloo Reef's proximity to shore—just a step or two off the beach delivers you into a magical underwater garden. What is so amazing about the reef is not that it is here, but that so few people know about it—a mere 8,000 tourists a year. To you, that means beaches pretty much to yourself, seas teeming with life because pesky humans haven't scared it away, unspoiled scenery, and a genuine sense of the frontier.

The Midwest and Northwest are lonely, remote, and really too hot to visit between November and March. The best time to visit is April through October, when it is still warm enough to swim, though snorkelers might want a wet suit June through August. Both regions are too far south to get the Top End's sticky Wet Season, and humidity is always low. Facilities, gas, and fresh water are scarce, and distances immense in this neck of the woods, so be prepared.

SHARK BAY (MONKEY MIA) 𝄢
853km (533 miles) N of Perth; 1,867km (1,167 miles) S of Broome

Monkey Mia's celebrity dolphins may not show on time—or at all—but they rarely pass up a visit. Apart from these delightful sea mammals, Shark Bay's waters absolutely heave with fish, dolphins, turtles, the world's biggest population of dugongs (10,000 at last count), manta rays, sea snakes, and, June through October, humpback whales. On the tip of the Peron Peninsula, which juts out like the middle prong of a "W" into the Shark Bay Marine Park, is **Francois Peron National Park.** The park is home to many endangered species, white beaches composed entirely of shells, and "living fossils"—rock-like structures on the shore (called stromatolites) that are actually Earth's first life. The bay's only town is the one-time pearling town of **Denham** (pop. 500), 129 kilometers (81 miles) from the main coastal highway, which has a hotel or two, a bakery, a news agency, and a few fishing-charter and tour operators. There is no settlement, only a pleasant but basic resort (see below), at Monkey Mia.

ESSENTIALS
GETTING THERE **Western Airlines** (© **1800/998 097** in Australia, or 08/9277 4022) flies two or three times a week from Perth to Shark Bay Airport (also called Monkey Mia Airport), 18 kilometers (11 miles) from Monkey Mia Dolphin Resort. The **Shark Bay Airport Bus** (© **08/9948 1358**) meets every flight and transfers you to Monkey Mia Dolphin Resort (see "Where to Stay & Dine," below) for A$7.70 (U.S.$4.25) per person one-way.

There is no train to Shark Bay. **Greyhound Pioneer** (© **13 20 30** in Australia) travels once or twice a day from Perth, daily from Broome, and three times a week from Exmouth via Coral Bay, to the Overlander Roadhouse at the Shark Bay turnoff on the North West Coastal Highway. These services connect (sometimes with a wait of hours) with a 2-hour coach trip to Monkey Mia Dolphin Resort, not always at convenient times. The trip from Perth costs A$131 (U.S.$72.05). From Exmouth, it's a 7-hour trip to the Overlander Roadhouse, and from Broome, 22½ hours through featureless landscape—not recommended.

Beware of wildlife on the lonely, uninteresting 9- to 10-hour drive from Perth, and keep the gas tank full. From Perth take the Brand Highway 424 kilometers (265 miles) north to Geraldton, then the North West Coastal Highway for 280 kilometers (175 miles) to the Overlander Roadhouse. Turn left onto the Denham–Hamelin Road and follow it for 152 kilometers (95 miles) to Monkey Mia, which is 27 kilometers (17 miles) past Denham. If you want to break the journey, the **Mercure Inn Geraldton,** Brand Highway, Geraldton, WA 6530 (© **08/9921 2455**), has smart, clean motel rooms. Rates are A$105 (U.S.$57.75) double; specials are available most nights.

Numerous coach, four-wheel-drive, and aerial tours run from Perth. **World Heritage Tours & Travel** (© **08/9581 5666;** book via sister tour-planning operation; visit WA at www.visitwa.com.au) offers a wide range.

VISITOR INFORMATION   Wide-ranging ecological information on Shark Bay Marine Park, Francois Peron National Park, and Hamelin Pool Marine Nature Reserve, as well as details on local tour details, is available at the **Dolphin Visitor Centre** (© **08/9948 1366**) within Monkey Mia Dolphin Resort (see "Where to Stay & Dine," below). Videos run throughout the day, and researchers (who are mostly from American universities) give free talks and slide shows most nights. The centre is run by the state Department of Conservation and Land Management (www.calm.wa.gov.au). The official visitor information outlet is the **Shark Bay Tourist Association's Centre** at 71 Knight Terrace, Denham, WA 6537 (© **08/9948 1253;** www.sharkbay.asn.au), open daily from 8am to 5pm (until 6pm in winter), though you will probably find the Dolphin Visitor Centre just as helpful.

Also check the website of the **Gascoyne Tourism Association** (© **08/9941 3000;** www.gta.asn.au), an umbrella body marketing the Midwest and Northwest. It has no streetfront visitor center.

GETTING AROUND   Shark Bay Car Hire (© **08/9948 1247**) delivers cars and four-wheel-drives to the airport and the resort from its Denham office. Several companies run tours to all the main attractions.

FAST FACTS   Admission to the Monkey Mia Reserve, in which Monkey Mia Dolphin Resort is located, is A$6 (U.S.$3.30) per adult, A$2 (U.S.$1.10) per child 7 to 16, and A$12 (U.S.$6.60) for a family. If you stay longer than 2 days and a night, you need a 4-week pass costing A$9 (U.S.$4.95) for adults, A$4 (U.S.$2.20) kids, and A$22 (U.S.$12.10) for a family.

ATMs and banks are non-existent. A banking agency is located within the post office in Denham.

MEETING THE DOLPHINS

At 7am guests at Monkey Mia Dolphin Resort are already gathering on the beach in quiet anticipation of the dolphins' arrival. By 8am three or more dolphins usually show, and they come and go until the early afternoon. Because of the crowds the dolphins attract (about 40 people a session in low season, coachloads in high season), a park ranger instructs everyone to line up knee-deep in the water as the playful swimsters cruise by your legs. You may not approach them or reach out to pat them, but they come up to touch people of their accord sometimes. Feeding times are different each day so the dolphins won't become dependent on the food. Once the crowd disperses, savvy swimmers dive into the

---

Tips Where Should I Go to See the Dolphins?

The main advantage to making the trek to **Monkey Mia** to see dolphins is that sightings are virtually guaranteed every day. But it's crowded, and rangers strictly monitor behavior with the dolphins—not the interactive frolic you might have imagined. At **Bunbury** ★★, a 2½-hour drive south of Perth, you can _swim_ with wild dolphins (see "Taking a Dip with Flipper," earlier in this chapter). Here the critters show up near shore only about two-thirds of the time. But the daily dolphin-watch cruise into deeper water has an almost 100% sighting success rate.

water just up the beach outside the no-swimmers-allowed Dolphin Interaction Area, because the dolphins may head there after the "show." Apart from the Monkey Mia Reserve entry fee, there is no charge to see the creatures.

A GREAT SEA-LIFE CRUISE, LIVING "FOSSILS" & MORE

Don't do what so many visitors do—see the dolphins, then shoot back to Perth. Stay for cruise to see Shark Bay's incredible marine life on the sailing catamaran *Shotover* ℱ (ⓒ 1800/24 1481 in Australia, or 08/9948 1481). During a 2½-hour dugong (manatee) cruise, we saw a hammerhead shark, a baby great white, two very large sea snakes that we hauled out of the water for a closer look, three turtles, oodles of dolphins beside the boat, and a baby dugong riding on its mum's back. Every passenger is given polarized sunglasses, which help you spot underwater animals. Sometimes you see dozens of dugongs (though they leave the area from mid-May to Aug). The cruise departs 1pm daily from Monkey Mia Dolphin Resort and costs A$49 (U.S.$26.95). The Shotover also does a fascinating 2-hour dolphin cruise at 10:30am—worth doing even if you already saw the dolphins on the shore. Children 7 to 16 pay half price on cruises, free for younger kids.

On your way in or out of Monkey Mia, stop by **the Hamelin Pool Historic Telegraph Station** (ⓒ 08/9942 5905), 41 kilometers (25½ miles) from the highway turnoff. A small museum houses old equipment, farming tools, and historical odds and sods from the 19th-century days when Monkey Mia was a repeater station on a telegraph line. The A$5.50 (U.S.$3) admission fee to the museum includes an explanation of the nearby **stromatolites,** rocky formations about a foot high that were created by the planet's first oxygen-breathing cells—in other words, Earth's first life. You might want to skip the museum, but wander down to **Shell Beach** and have a look at them. You may find them something of an anticlimax, but following the signposted boardwalk over their tidal zone in Hamelin Pool (a shallow part of Shark Bay) proves them a little more interesting. The "sand" on the beach consists of zillions of teensy white shells, which were quarried as bricks to build some of the local buildings. There is a cafe and gift store here, too.

You can explore the saltpans, dunes, coastal cliffs, short walking trails, and old homestead in the nearby 52,500-hectare (129,675-acre) Francois Peron National Park, either alone (you will need a four-wheel-drive) or on a half- or full-day tour—although not everyone will appreciate the park's harsh scenery. You should easily spot wallabies, birds, and emus, and you may see turtles, dolphins, rays, dugongs, and, in season, whales from the cliffs. Other activities in the region include half- and full-day game and deep-sea-fishing trips from Denham, scuba diving, excursions to the deserted beaches and 180-meter (600-ft.) cliffs of nearby Dirk Hartog Island, and a couple of pearl-farm tours.

WHERE TO STAY & DINE

Monkey Mia Dolphin Resort   Set right on the very beach the dolphins visit daily, this oasis of green lawns and palms doubles as a town settlement. Most comfortable are the spacious air-conditioned motel rooms; safari tent "canvas condos" with carpeted floors, bathrooms, electricity, a fridge, and a separate kitchen/dining area from the bedroom (but no air-conditioning); and air-conditioned demountable "park homes" with cooking facilities. The pleasant open-sided all-day restaurant overlooks the sea. Most tours in the area depart from the resort. A 1.5-kilometer (1-mile) nature trail leads from the resort.

Monkey Mia Rd., Shark Bay (P.O. Box 119, Denham, WA 6537). © **1800/653 611** in Australia, or 08/9948 1320. Fax 08/9948 1034. www.monkeymia.com.au. Tent sites: 58 powered sites; 10 on-site caravans; 6 "canvas condo" permanent tents to sleep 6; 13 park homes to sleep 6, none with bathroom; 72 motel rooms. A$35.20–$57.20 (U.S.$19.35–$31.45) for 2–4 people sharing caravan rented from resort; A$79.20 (U.S.$43.55) up to 4 people in canvas condo; A$90.20 (U.S.$49.60) up to 4 people in park home; A$157.30–$179.30 (U.S.$86.50–$98.60) double or triple, motel room. Extra person A$4.40–$11 (U.S.$2.40–$6.05). Linen A$11 (U.S.$6.05) per person in park homes, canvas condos, and caravans for duration of stay. Lower rates Feb 1–Mar 31 (excluding Easter) and May 1–June 30 except in on-site vans. Weekly rates available. AE, DC, MC, V. **Amenities:** Restaurant/bar, take-out cafe; small outdoor swimming pool; 2 outdoor tennis courts; Jacuzzi (fed by naturally warm underground water); volleyball court; snorkel gear; tour desk; well-stocked minimarket; self-service laundry. *In room:* Fridge. Phones and hair dryers in motel rooms only.

THE NORTHWEST CAPE
1,272km (795 miles) N of Perth; 1,567km (979 miles) S of Broome

Driving along the only road on the Northwest Cape is like driving on the moon. Hundreds of red anthills taller than you march away to the horizon, sheep and 'roos threaten to get under the wheels, and the sun beats down from a harsh blue sky. On the Cape's western shore is coral-filled **Coral Bay** (pop. 120), a tiny cluster of dive shops, backpacker lodges, a low-key resort, and charter boats nestled on sand so white, water so blue, and ochre dust so orange you think the townsfolk computer-enhanced it. Stretching north of town are deserted sandy beaches edged by coral. On the Cape's east coast is **Exmouth** (pop. 2,500), born in 1967 as a support town to the nearby Harold E. Holt Naval Communications Station, a joint Australian/United States center. Apart from whale-shark diving, the main reason you come here is to scuba dive and snorkel in Ningaloo Marine Park. You can also take four-wheel-drive trips over the arid Cape Range National Park, which covers much of the cape, and surrounding sheep stations. Ningaloo Marine Park stretches from Bundegi Beach on the Cape's east coast around its northern tip and down its western side.

Exmouth and Coral Bay are 150 kilometers (94 miles) apart. Coral Bay is several degrees cooler than Exmouth and has divine diving, swimming, and snorkeling right on the doorstep; a restaurant and take-out or two, and a bar or two; a small supermarket; and little else. It has no ATMs. Exmouth is hot, dusty, and charmless, but it has more facilities, including a supermarket, an ATM, an outdoor cinema, rental cars, a swimming beach 1 kilometer (just over half a mile) away, and one or two smarter accommodations and dining options. Most tours not having to do with the reef, such as four-wheel-drive safaris, leave from Exmouth. Both places have plenty of dive, snorkel, fishing and whale-watch companies. Wherever you stay, it's best to book ahead in whale-shark season (from Mar to early June). Carry drinking water everywhere you go.

ESSENTIALS
GETTING THERE **Northwest Regional Airlines** (© **1300/136 629** in Australia, or 08/9192 1369; www.northwestregional.com.au) flies from Broome. A shuttle bus meets every flight and takes you to your Exmouth hotel for A$16.50 (U.S.$9) one-way. It does not take bookings (have the cash on you; there's no ATM at the airport). **Coral Bay Adventures** (© **08/9942 5955**) makes transfers, on demand, from the airport to Coral Bay, approximately 120 kilometers (75 miles) away, for A$85 (U.S.$46.75) adults, A$40.50 (U.S.$22.30) children under 13, one-way.

Greyhound Pioneer (© **13 20 30**) operates three services a week from Perth (trip time: close to 17 hr.). The fare is A$180 (U.S.$99) to Coral Bay and A$200

(U.S.$110) to Exmouth. A cheaper but less convenient route is Greyhound's daily Perth–Broome service, which connects with a local bus service to Exmouth at the turnoff on the highway at Giralia in the wee hours of the morning. The Perth–Exmouth fare in that case is A$168 (U.S.$92.40).

There is no train.

The 14-hour drive from Perth (plus rest stops) is through lonely country on a two-lane highway. Check that your contract allows you to drive your rental car this far north. Wildlife will be thick on the ground, and gas stations thin. From Perth, take the Brand Highway north to Geraldton, 424 kilometers (265 miles), then the North West Coastal Highway for 623 kilometers (389 miles) to Minilya gas station; the Exmouth turnoff is 7 kilometers (4 miles) north of Minilya. Exmouth is a further 225 kilometers (141 miles) along the cape from the turnoff. Overnight at the Mercure Inn Geraldton, listed in "Getting There," under "Shark Bay (Monkey Mia)," above, or in Carnarvon, the only town between Geraldton and Exmouth. Everything else that looks like a town on your map is just a gas station. I don't recommend the even longer, lonelier drive from Broome.

VISITOR INFORMATION   The **Exmouth Tourist Bureau,** Murat Road, Exmouth, WA 6707 (© **1800/287 328** within Western Australia, or 08/9949 1176; www.exmouth-australia.com), is open daily from 8:30am to 5pm, or from 10am to 3pm on weekends November through March. The **Milyering Visitors Centre,** 52 kilometers (32½ miles) northwest of Exmouth, is the Cape Range National Park's information center, run by the Department of Conservation and Land Management (CALM), but you can pick up a hiking-trail map of the park from CALM's office in Nimitz Street in Exmouth. Local tour operator **Coral Bay Adventures** runs a tour information and booking center in the Coral Bay Supermarket, Coral Bay Arcade, Coral Bay, WA 6701 (© **08/9942 5955;** coralbay@bigpond.com.au).

Also check the website of the **Gascoyne Tourism Association** (© **08/9941 3000;** www.gta.asn.au), the umbrella tourist board for the Midwest and Northwest. It has no streetfront visitor center.

The entry fee to the Cape Range National Park, payable at the Milyering Visitor Centre, is A$9 (U.S.$4.95) per vehicle.

There is only one ATM cash machine on the Cape, in Exmouth.

GETTING AROUND   Tours and dive operators pick up from either Exmouth or Coral Bay accommodations, but not usually both. The roads to Exmouth and Coral Bay are paved, and so is the only road around the Cape's coast. **Avis** (© **08/9949 2492**), **Budget** (© **08/9949 1534**), **Hertz** (© **08/9949 2792**), and local operator **Allen's Car Hire** (© **08/9949 2403**) have offices in Exmouth; there is no car rental in Coral Bay.

Ningaloo Reef Bus (© **08/9949 1776**) runs from Exmouth hotels to various beaches around the cape, calling at the Milyering Visitors Centre en route. It runs every day except Thursday April through September, and Tuesday, Wednesday, Friday and Sunday October through March. The round-trip fare to the snorkel beauty spot of Turquoise Bay is A$22 (U.S.$12.10), including the Park entry fee.

DIVING WITH WHALE SHARKS 🐟🐟

"Diving" is not the correct term for this activity, because it's by snorkeling that you get close to these leviathans of the deep. Whale sharks are sharks, not whales, and they are the world's biggest fish, reaching an alarming 12 to 18 meters (39–59 ft.) in length. Terrified? Don't be. Their gigantic size belies a gentle nature (whew!) and swimming speed; despite having a mouth big enough to swallow a boatload of snorkelers in one go, they eat plankton (again, whew!). Several boat operators take people out to swim alongside the fish when they appear from mid-March to early June. A trip with one of the longest established whale-shark companies, **Exmouth Diving Centre** (© 1800/655 156 in Australia, or 08/9949 1201; www.exmouthdiving.com.au) or its Coral Bay sister company, **Ningaloo Reef Diving Centre** (© 08/9942 5824; www.users. bigpond.com/ningaloo), costs A$295 (U.S.$162.25) and takes a day. Most boats stop at reefs for more snorkeling, and some incorporate scuba dives.

DIVING, SNORKELING, FISHING & FOUR-WHEEL-DRIVE TOURS

Scuba dive the Cape's unspoiled waters, and you will see marvelous reef formations, grouper, manta rays, octopus, morays, potato cod (which you can hand-feed), and other marvels at a dozen or more sites. Divers often spot humpback and false killer whales and large sharks, while snorkelers may see dolphins, dugongs, and turtles. Loads of dive companies in Exmouth and Coral Bay rent gear and run daily dive trips and learn-to-dive courses, including the two listed in "Diving with Whale Sharks," above. A 2-dive day trip costs around A$120 (U.S.$66) with all gear supplied.

Three great snorkeling spots are: right off the shore at Coral Bay; Bundegi Beach, 14 kilometers (nearly 9 miles) north of Exmouth; and at beautiful **Turquoise Bay** , a 60-kilometer (37½-mile) drive from Exmouth. In deeper waters off Coral Bay, you can snorkel with harmless **manta rays** with a "wingspan" up to 7 meters (23 ft.). Companies in either town run manta and reef-snorkel trips, and rent snorkel gear. The Cape has loads of deserted swimming beaches; for safety's sake, never swim alone.

Reef fish, tuna, and Spanish mackerel are common catches in these waters, and black, blue, and striped marlin run outside the reef September through January. Up to a dozen boats operate reef and **game-fishing day trips** out of Exmouth and Coral Bay, and tackle and tin fishing dinghies are easily rented in either town.

Green and loggerhead **turtles** lay eggs at night November through February or March on the Cape's beaches. Take a flashlight and go looking for them, or join one of several turtle-watch tours from either town. August through October, boats run cruises from either town to spot **humpback whales.**

Because the Cape has few roads, and even fewer sights along the way, I recommend an off-road 240-kilometer (150-mile) four-wheel-drive escapade with **Neil McLeod's Ningaloo Safari Tours** (© 08/9949 1550). You will explore the arid limestone ridges of 50,581-hectare (124,935-acre) Cape Range National Park, snorkel Turquoise Bay, climb up a lighthouse, and cruise orange-walled Yardie Creek Gorge to spot rock wallabies—snacking on Neil's mum's fruitcake along the way. I have never seen so many 'roos in one place, including big reds. This full-day trip departs your Exmouth hotel at 7:30am and costs A$135 (U.S.$74.25) for adults and A$95 (U.S.$52.25) for children under 13.

WHERE TO STAY & DINE
IN EXMOUTH
Potshot Hotel Resort   The grounds are hot and dusty, but the building is a modern complex, right in town. The cocktail bar around the pool is the only shady place in town to enjoy a drink, which explains its popularity with locals.

The restaurant is scant on atmosphere but has a long menu, good food, and a nice wine list. The brick motel rooms are cool and spacious; the homestead rooms are smaller, older, and more basic; there are two-bedroom apartments; and across the road are recently built three-bedroom apartments.

Murat Rd., Exmouth, WA 6707. © **08/9949 1200.** Fax 08/9949 1486. potshot@nwc.net.au. 97 units (all with shower only). High season (Apr–Oct) A$89 (U.S.$48.95) double homestead room; A$126 (U.S.$69.30) 4 people in motel room. Low season A$85 (U.S.$46.75) double in homestead room; A$118 (U.S.$64.90) 4 people in motel room. Year-round A$137 (U.S.$75.35) 4 people in 2-bedroom apt; A$185 (U.S.$101.75) 4 people in 3-bedroom apt. Maid service in apts A$22–$33 (U.S.$12.10–$18.15) per day. AE, DC, MC, V. **Amenities:** 3 small swimming pools; self-service laundry. *In room:* A/C, TV, fridge. Hair dryers and irons available at front desk. Homestead rooms have no phones.

IN CORAL BAY

Ningaloo Reef Resort   This low-rise complex of motel rooms, studios, and apartments stands out as the best place to stay among Coral Bay's profusion of backpacker hostels. Located on a blissfully green lawn with a swimming pool overlooking the bay, the rooms are nothing fancy or new, but they're clean, with views toward the bay and the pool. The place has a nice communal air, thanks to the bar doubling as the local pub. Hair dryers and irons are available at front desk.

At the end of Robinson St., Coral Bay, WA 6701. © **08/9942 5934.** Fax 08/9942 5953. www.williams. com.au/resort.htm. 34 units, all with bathroom (shower only). A$132–$137.50 (U.S.$72.60–$75.65) double; A$165–$280 (U.S.$90.75–$154) apt. Extra person A$11 (U.S.$6.05) adults, A$4.50–$11 (U.S.$2.50–$6.05) child. Weekly rates available. MC, V. **Amenities:** Restaurant, bar; small outdoor pool; self-service laundry. *In room:* A/C, TV, no phone.

10

Adelaide & South Australia

by Marc Llewellyn

Adelaide has a major advantage over the other Australian state capitals in that it has Outback, vineyards, major wetlands, animal sanctuaries, a major river, and mountain ranges virtually on its doorstep. Meals and lodgings are also cheaper in Adelaide than in Sydney or Melbourne. If you plan to travel outside the city, then a trip to one of the wine-growing areas has to be on your itinerary, since Australian wines have been taking home many of the most important international wine prizes over the last few years. Of all the wine areas, the **Barossa Valley** ✿ is the nearest to Adelaide and the most interesting. Centered on Tanunda, the Barossa is known for its German architecture as well as its dozens of pretty hamlets, fine restaurants, and vineyards offering cellar-door tastings. If you want to see animals instead of, or in addition to, grapes, you're in luck. You're likely to come across the odd kangaroo or wallaby near the main settlements, especially at dusk, or you could visit one of the area's many wildlife reserves. Otherwise head out into the Outback where animals abound, or over to **Kangaroo Island,** without a doubt the best place in Australia to see concentrated numbers of native animals in the wild.

Another place well worth visiting is the craggy **Flinders Ranges,** some 460 kilometers (285 miles) north of Adelaide. Though the scenery along the way is mostly unattractive grazing properties devoid of trees, the Flinders Ranges offer an incredible landscape of multicolored rocks, rough-and-ready characters, and even camel treks in the semi-desert. On the other side of the mountains, the real Outback starts.

The **South Australian Outback** is serenely beautiful, with giant skies, wildflowers after the rains, red earth, and little water. Out here you'll find bizarre opal-mining towns, such as **Coober Pedy,** where summer temperatures can reach 50°C (122°F) and where most people live underground to escape the heat.

If you prefer your landscape with more moisture, head to the **Coorong,** a water-bird sanctuary rivaled only by Kakadu National Park in the Northern Territory (see chapter 8).

EXPLORING THE STATE

VISITOR INFORMATION The **South Australia Travel Centre,** 18 King William St. (✆ **1300/655 276** in Australia, or 08/8303 2033; fax 08/8303 2249; southaustralia.com), is the best place to collect information on Adelaide and South Australia. It's open weekdays from 8:30am to 5pm and weekends from 9am to 2pm. Also try www.adelaide.on.net, and www.adelaide.sa.gov.au, though you'll need to install Acrobat Reader to get any real information.

For general information about South Australia's national parks contact the **Department of Environment and Natural Resources Information Centre,**

Australis House, 77 Grenfell St., Adelaide 5000 (© **08/8204 1910**). It's open Monday through Friday from 9am to 5pm.

GETTING AROUND   South Australia, at four times the size of the United Kingdom, has a lot of empty space between places of interest. The best way to see it is by car, though a limited rail service connects Adelaide with some areas. The Stuart Highway bisects the state from south to north; it runs from Adelaide through the industrial center of Port Augusta (gateway to the Flinders Ranges), and onwards through Coober Pedy to Alice Springs in the Red Centre. The Eyre Highway travels westwards along the coastline and into Western Australia, while the Barrier Highway enters New South Wales just before the mining city of Broken Hill (see chapter 4). The Princes Highway takes you east to Melbourne. You should seek travel advice from the **Royal Automobile Association of South Australia** (RAA), 41 Hindmarsh Square, Adelaide, SA 5000 (© **13 11 11** in South Australia only, or 08/8202 4500; www.raa.net), if you are planning to drive into the Outback regions. The RAA provides route maps and emergency breakdown service.

Qantas (© **13 13 13** in Australia) flies to Adelaide from the other major state capitals.

Both **Greyhound Pioneer** (© **13 20 30** in Australia) and **McCafferty's** (© **13 14 99** in Australia) operate bus service within South Australia. Within the state the largest operator is **Stateliner** (© **08/8415 5555**).

1 Adelaide

Adelaide, "The City of Churches," has a reputation as a sleepy place, full of parkland and surrounded by vineyards. In many ways it's something of a throwback to the comfortable lifestyle of 1950s Australia—a lifestyle that the more progressive state capitals have left behind.

Numerous parks and gardens, wide tree-lined streets, the River Torrens running through its center, sidewalk cafes, colonial architecture, and, of course, the churches help make it a pleasant, open city, perfect for strolling or bicycling.

Though the immigrant population has added a cosmopolitan flair to the restaurant scene, Adelaide still has a feeling of old England about it. That's not surprising when you learn that Adelaide was the only capital settled entirely by English free settlers rather than convicts, and that it attracted plenty more after World War II, when Brits flocked here to work in the city's car parts and domestic appliance industries.

But it was earlier immigrants, from Germany, who gave Adelaide and the surrounding area a romantic twist. Arriving as refugees from their religious-torn country in the 1830s, German immigrants brought with them their wine-making skills, and established wineries. Today, more than one-third of all Australian wine—including some of the world's best—comes from areas mostly within an hour's drive from Adelaide. As a result, Adelaidians of all socio-economic groups are more versed in wine than even the French and regularly compare vintages, wine-growing regions, and wine-making trends.

Any time of the year is a good time to visit Adelaide, though May through August can be chilly and December and January hot.

ESSENTIALS
GETTING THERE   By Plane   Qantas (© **13 13 13** in Australia; www. qantas.com.au) flies to Adelaide from all other Australian state capitals. Adelaide International Airport is 5 kilometers (3 miles) west of the city center. Major

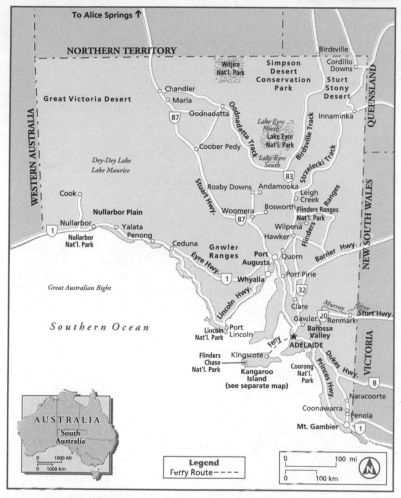

car-rental companies (Avis, Budget, Hertz, and Thrifty) have desks in both the international and domestic terminals.

The **Transit Bus** (© **08/8381 5311;** www.transitregency.com.au) links the airport with major city hotels and the rail and bus stations. On weekdays, buses leave the terminals at 30-minute intervals from 5:00am to 9:30pm, and on weekends and public holidays hourly (on the half-hour). Adult tickets are A$6.60 (U.S.$4.30) one-way and A$11 (U.S.$7.20) round-trip. Child tickets cost A$2.20 (U.S.$1.40) each way.

A taxi to the city will cost around A$17 (U.S.$11).

By Train The **Keswick Interstate Rail Passenger Terminal,** located 2 kilometers (1¼ miles) west of the city center, is Adelaide's main railway station. The terminal has a small snack bar and a cafe.

Call **Great Southern Railways** (© **08/8213 4530**) for information and bookings for all trains described below, or check out the timetables and fares on their website (www.gsr.com.au).

One of the great trains of Australia, The *Indian Pacific* transports passengers from Sydney to Adelaide (trip time: 28 hr.) and from Perth to Adelaide (trip time: 36 hr.) twice a week on Monday and Thursday. Tickets from Sydney to Adelaide are A$549 (U.S.$357) for adults and A$374 (U.S.$243) for children in first class; A$439 (U.S.$285.35) for adults and A$264 (U.S.$172) for children in an economy sleeper; and A$176 (U.S.$114) for adults and A$79 (U.S.$51) for children in coach. From Perth to Adelaide it costs A$1,099 (U.S.$714) for adults and A$748 (U.S.$484) for children in first class; A$879 (U.S.$571) for adults and A$528 (U.S.$343) for children in an economy sleeper; and A$283 (U.S.$184) for adults and A$128 (U.S.$83) for children in coach.

The other legendary Australian train is The *Ghan,* which runs from Sydney to Melbourne then on to Adelaide and up to Alice Springs weekly November through April and twice a week May through October. Trip time from Alice Springs to Adelaide is 20 hours; from Sydney to Adelaide is 24.5 hours; from Melbourne to Adelaide is 11.5 hours. Tickets from Melbourne to Adelaide are A$364 (U.S.$237) for adults and A$249 (U.S.$162) for children in first class; A$156 (U.S.$101) for adults and A$124 (U.S.$81) for children in an economy sleeper; and A$57 (U.S.$37) for adults and A$33 (U.S.$21.45) for children in an economy seat. From Alice Springs to Adelaide it costs A$780 (U.S.$507) for adults and A$531 (U.S.$345) for children in first class; A$624 (U.S.$156) for adults and A$375 (U.S.$244) for children in an economy sleeper; and A$197 (U.S.$128) for adults and A$89 (U.S.$58) for children for an economy seat. From Sydney to Adelaide it costs A$547 (U.S.$356) for adults and A$374 (U.S.$243) for children in first class; A$439 (U.S.$285) for adults and A$264 (U.S.$172) for children in an economy sleeper; and A$176 (U.S.$114) for adults and A$79 (U.S.$51) for children in an economy seat.

The return (round-trip) fare for the trains above works out to either twice the single (one-way) fare, or just a few dollars cheaper. Full-time students with a recognized student card from any institution travel for child prices on all trains.

The *Overlander* provides daily service between Adelaide and Melbourne (trip time: 12 hr.). From Melbourne to Adelaide ticket prices are A$156 (U.S.$101) for adults and A$124 (U.S.$81) for children in first class, and A$57 (U.S.$37) for adults and A$33 (U.S.$64) for children in an economy seat.

By Bus   Intercity coaches terminate at the central bus station, 101 Franklin St. (© **08/8415 5533**), near Morphett Street in the city center.

Adventurous types should consider traveling to Adelaide from Melbourne (or vice versa) on the **Wayward Bus,** operated by the Wayward Bus Touring Company, P.O. Box 7076, Adelaide, SA 5000 (© **1800/882 823** in Australia, or 08/8232 6646; www.waywardbus.com.au). These 21-seat buses make the trip in 3½ days via the Great Ocean Road; the fare is A$290 (U.S.$188) with backpacker's accommodations and around A$410 (U.S.$266) with motel accommodations. You spend around 3 hours a day on the bus, and the driver acts as your guide. A picnic or cafe lunch each day and entry to national parks are included in the fare. You can leave the trip and rejoin another later. Reservations are essential. Wayward Bus also runs a 4-day trip from Alice Springs to Adelaide, via Coober Pedy and the Flinders National Park (and vice versa) leaving twice weekly. This includes 2 nights camping and 2 nights in a bunkhouse. The trip costs A$395 (U.S.$257) from Adelaide to Coober Pedy, and A$770 (U.S.$500) from Adelaide to Alice Springs.

By Car   To drive from Sydney to Adelaide takes roughly 20 hours via the Hume and Sturt Highways; from Melbourne it takes around 10 hours via the

Adelaide

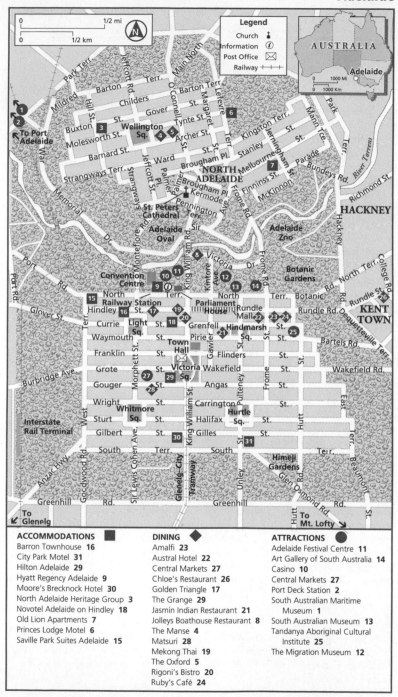

Legend
Church
Information
Post Office
Railway

AUSTRALIA
Adelaide

NORTH ADELAIDE
HACKNEY
KENT TOWN

ACCOMMODATIONS
Barron Townhouse **16**
City Park Motel **31**
Hilton Adelaide **29**
Hyatt Regency Adelaide **9**
Moore's Brecknock Hotel **30**
North Adelaide Heritage Group **3**
Novotel Adelaide on Hindley **18**
Old Lion Apartments **7**
Princes Lodge Motel **6**
Saville Park Suites Adelaide **15**

DINING
Amalfi **23**
Austral Hotel **22**
Central Markets **27**
Chloe's Restaurant **26**
Golden Triangle **17**
The Grange **29**
Jasmin Indian Restaurant **21**
Jolleys Boathouse Restaurant **8**
The Manse **4**
Matsuri **28**
Mekong Thai **19**
The Oxford **5**
Rigoni's Bistro **20**
Ruby's Café **24**

ATTRACTIONS
Adelaide Festival Centre **11**
Art Gallery of South Australia **14**
Casino **10**
Central Markets **27**
Port Deck Station **2**
South Australian Maritime Museum **1**
South Australian Museum **13**
Tandanya Aboriginal Cultural Institute **25**
The Migration Museum **12**

The Adelaide & Womadelaide Festivals

Adelaide is home to Australia's largest performing arts festival, the **Adelaide Festival,** which takes place over 3 weeks in March during even-numbered years. The festival includes literary and visual arts as well as dance, opera, classical music, jazz, cabaret, and comedy. The festival encompasses Writers' Week and a fringe comedy festival.

In February and March of odd-numbered years the 3-day **Womadelaide Festival** of world music takes place. Crowds of 60,000 or more turn up to watch Australian and international artists.

For more information on the Adelaide Festival check out the website at www.adelaidefestival.org.au, and for the Adelaide Fringe Festival visit www.adelaidefringe.com.au.

Great Ocean Road and Princess Highway; from Perth it takes 32 hours via the Great Eastern and Princess Highways; and from Alice Springs it takes 15 hours of remote driving on the Stuart Highway. For more information on driving distances consult www.auinfo.com/distancecalc_process.asp.

VISITOR INFORMATION   Head to the **South Australia Visitor and Travel Centre,** 18 King William St. (© **1300 655 276** in Australia, or 08/8303 2033; fax 08/8303 2249), for maps, travel advice, and hotel and tour bookings. It's open weekdays from 9:30am to 5pm and weekends from 9am to 2pm. There's also an information booth on Rundle Mall (© **08/8203 7611**) open daily from 10am to 5pm.

CITY LAYOUT   Adelaide is a simple city in which to find your way around because of its grid-like pattern, which was planned down to each wide street and airy square by Colonel William Light in 1836. The city's official center is **Victoria Square,** where you'll find the Town Hall. Bisecting the city from south to north is the city's main thoroughfare, **King William Street.** Streets running perpendicular to King William Street change their names on either side, so that Franklin Street, for example, changes into Flinders Street. Of these cross streets, the most interesting to the visitor are the restaurant strips of **Gouger Street** and **Rundle Street,** the latter running into the pedestrian-only shopping precinct of Rundle Mall. Another is **Hindley Street,** with its inexpensive restaurants and nightlife. On the banks of the River Torrens just north of the city center, you'll find **Adelaide Plaza,** the home of the Festival Centre, the Convention Centre, and the Adelaide Casino. Bordering the city center on the north and south are **North Terrace,** which is lined with galleries and museums and leads to the Botanic Gardens, and **South Terrace.**

Follow King William Street south and you'll be chasing the tram to the beachside suburb of **Glenelg;** follow it north, and it crosses the River Torrens and flows into sophisticated **North Adelaide,** an area crammed with Victorian and Edwardian architecture. The main avenues in North Adelaide, **O'Connell and Melbourne streets,** are lined with restaurants, cafes, and bistros that offer the tastes of a multicultural city.

To the northwest of the city center is **Port Adelaide,** a seaport and the historic maritime heart of South Australia—home to some of the finest colonial buildings in the state, as well as good pubs and restaurants.

GETTING AROUND   By Bus   Adelaide's public bus network is divided into three zones, and fares are calculated according to the number of zones traveled. The city center is classed as Zone 1. The fare in Zone 1 is A$1.60 (U.S.$1) from 9am to 3pm on weekdays and A$2.80 (U.S.$1.80) most other times. You can buy tickets on board the bus or at kiosks around the city. You can pick up free metro information and get timetable and destination information over the phone, or in person at the **Passenger Transport Board Information Centre** (© **08/8210 1000**), on the corner of Currie and King William streets. It's open Monday through Saturday from 8am to 6pm and Sunday from 10:30am to 5.30pm.

The **CityLoop bus** (number 99C) operates free bus service every 15 minutes (Mon–Thurs 8:30am–6pm; Fri to 9pm and Sat to 5pm) around the city center, along North Terrace, East Terrace, Grenfell Street, Pulteney Street, Wakefield Street, Grote Street, Morphett Street, Light Square, Hindley Street, and West Terrace. Another free bus, **the Bee Line** (number 99B), runs along North Terrace, down King William Street to Victoria Street. Routes are well signposted. All city free buses are wheelchair-accessible.

Bus numbers 181 and 182 run from the city to North Adelaide.

The **Adelaide Explorer bus** (© **08/8364 1933;** www.adelaideexplorer.com. au) stops at 10 sights around town, including Glenelg, and costs A$29 (U.S.$18.85) for adults, A$18 (U.S.$11.70) for children, and A$65 (U.S.$42.25) for families of four. The full loop takes a leisurely 3 hours, with commentary, and you can get on and off when you want. The first bus departs from 38 King William St., on the corner of Rundal Mall (next to Haigh's Chocolates) at 9am. The company will pick you up from your hotel between 8 and 8:30am if you call ahead, and will also pick you up and drop you off at the airport (with your luggage) as part as the daily fare. Ring or e-mail ahead. Buy tickets on the bus.

By Tram   The **Glenelg Tram** runs between Victoria Square and the beachside suburb of Glenelg. Tickets are valid for 2 hours and cost A$1.60 (U.S.$1) for adults and A80¢ (U.S.52¢) for children 5 to 14 from 9am to 3pm, and A$2.80 (U.S.$1.80) for adults and A$1 (U.S.65¢) for children at other times. The journey takes 29 minutes.

By Taxi & Car   The major cab companies are **Yellow Cabs** (© **13 22 27** in South Australia only), **Suburban** (© **08/8211 8888**), and **Amalgamated** (© **08/8223 3333**). **Access Cabs** (© **1300/360 940** in South Australia only) offers wheelchair taxis.

Major car-rental companies in the area are **Avis,** 136 North Terrace (© **08/ 8410 5727**); **Budget,** 274 North Terrace (© **08/8223 1400**); **Hertz,** 233 Morphett St. (© **08/8231 2856**); and **Thrifty,** 296 Hindley St. (© **08/8211 8788**).

The **Royal Automobile Association of South Australia (RAA),** 41 Hindmarsh Sq. (© **13 11 11** in South Australia, or 08/8202 4500; www.raa.net), has route maps and provides emergency breakdown services.

(Value A Money-Saving Transit Pass

If you plan to get around the city via public transportation, it's a good idea to purchase a **Daytrip ticket,** which covers unlimited travel on buses, trams, and city trains within the metropolitan area for 1 day. The pass costs A$5.60 (U.S.$3.65) for adults and A$2.80 (U.S.$1.80) for children 5 to 15 and are available at most train stations, newsstands, and the **Passenger Transport Board Information Centre** (© **08/8210 1000**).

FAST FACTS: Adelaide

American Express The **Amex** office, at 13 Grenfell St. (© **08/8202 1400**), is open during normal business hours.

Business Hours Generally, banks are open Monday through Thursday from 9:30am to 4pm and Friday from 9:30am to 5pm. Stores are generally open Monday through Thursday from 9am to 5:30pm, Friday from 9am to 9pm, Saturday from 9am to 5pm, and Sunday from 11am to 5pm.

Currency Exchange Banks and hotels, the casino, and the Myer department store in Rundle Mall all cash traveler's checks. The **Thomas Cook** office is at 45 Grenfell St. (© **08/8212 3354**).

Dentist Contact the **Australian Dental Association Emergency Information Service** (© **08/8272 8111**), open weeknights from 5pm to 9pm, and Saturday and Sunday from 9am to 9pm. It will put you in touch with a dentist. You can also contact the office of **Dr. Brook**, 231 North Terrace (© **08/8223 6988**), who is available during normal business hours.

Doctor Contact the **Royal Adelaide Hospital,** on North Terrace (© **08/8222 4000**). **The Travellers' Medical & Vaccination Centre,** 29 Gilbert Place (© **08/8212 7522**), offers vaccinations and other travel-related medicines.

Drugstores See "Pharmacies" below.

Emergencies Dial © **000** to call an ambulance, the fire department, or the police in a emergency.

Hospitals The **Royal Adelaide Hospital,** North Terrace (© **08/8222 4000**), is located in the city center.

Hot Lines Call the **Crisis Care Centre** at © **13 16 11;** the **Royal Automobile Association of South Australia (RAA)** at © **08/8202 4500;** and the **Disability Information and Resource Centre** at © **08/8223 7522.**

Internet Access The **Ngapartji Multimedia Centre,** 211 Rundle St., (© **08/8232 0839**), offers e-mail and Internet access Monday through Thursday from 8:30am to 9pm, Friday and Saturday from 9am to 10pm, and Sunday from noon to 7pm.

Lost Property If you've lost something on the street, contact the nearest police station. For items left on public transport contact the **Lost Property Office,** on the main concourse of the Adelaide Railway Station on North Terrace (© **08/8218 2552**); it's open Monday through Friday from 9am to 5pm.

Luggage Storage/Lockers There are luggage lockers at Adelaide Airport in the domestic terminal. At the **Central Bus Station** on Franklin Street (© **08/8415 5533**) luggage lockers cost A$2 (U.S.$1.30) for 24 hours.

Pharmacies Called "chemist shops" in Australia. **Burden Chemists,** Shop 11, Southern Cross Arcade, King William St. (© **08/8231 4701**), is open Monday through Thursday from 8am to 6pm, Friday from 8am to 8pm, and Saturday from 9am to 1pm.

Post Office The **General Post Office (GPO),** 141 King William St., Adelaide, SA 5000 (© **08/8216 2222**), is open Monday through Friday from 8am to 6pm and Saturday from 8:30am to noon. General delivery mail (poste restante) can be collected Monday through Friday from 7am to 5:30pm and from 9am to 1pm on Sunday.

Restrooms Public restrooms can be found at the Central Market Arcade, between Grote and Gouger streets, in both Hindmarsh and Victoria squares, and at James Place (off Rundle Mall).

Safety Adelaide is a very safe city, though it's wise to avoid walking along the River Torrens and through side streets near Hindley Street after dark.

WHERE TO STAY

The **South Australia Travel Centre** (see "Visitor Information," above) can supply information on B&Bs and homestays around the state. Satellite or cable TV is rare in South Australian hotels, though some provide pay-per-view movies.

IN THE CITY CENTER
Very Expensive

Hyatt Regency Adelaide 🏵🏵   The 20-story Hyatt Regency is in the heart of the city and is part of the complex that includes the Adelaide Festival Centre, the Casino, the Exhibition Hall, and the Convention Centre. The property overlooks the River Torrens and nearby parklands, and there are some wonderful views from the higher floors. What I like about the Hyatt is that it doesn't scrimp, which shows in the attention to detail in the rooms. Guests staying in the club-level Regency rooms get a good complimentary breakfast and free evening drinks and canapés. Waves, a cabaret/nightclub, offers a lively combination of video, disco, and live music; it's free for hotel guests, though it can be dull and the drinks are expensive. Afternoon tea is served in the stylish Atrium Lounge, which gets surprisingly full as the night wears on.

North Terrace, Adelaide, SA 5000. © **13 12 34** in Australia, 800/233-1234 in the U.S. and Canada, or 08/8231 1234. Fax 08/8231 1120. www.hyatt.com. 367 units. A$250–$300 (U.S.$162–$195) double (depending on season and availability); A$300–$340 (U.S.$195–$221) Regency Club City View (including breakfast); A$320–$360 (U.S.$221–$234) Club River Park View (including breakfast); A$390 (U.S.$253.50) Executive Suite; A$840 (U.S.$546) Deluxe Suite. Extra person A$50 (U.S.$32.50). Ask about packages and lower weekend rates. Children under 18 stay free in parents' room. AE, DC, MC, V. Parking A$15 (U.S.$9.75). **Amenities:** 3 restaurants (Modern Australian, buffet, Japanese), lounge, bar, nightclub; good outdoor swimming pool; excellent health club and spa; concierge; business center; 24-hr. room service; massage; babysitting; laundry service. *In room:* A/C, TV with pay movies, minibar, hair dryer, iron, high-speed Internet access.

Expensive

Barron Townhouse   Friendly staff and garish china flamingos welcome you to this uninspiring-looking concrete block. It's a 10- to 15-minute walk from the center of town, 5 minutes from the casino, and not far from the nightclub and red-light district. Rooms are spacious and comfortable enough, so it's certainly a choice worth considering despite the decor.

164 Hindley St., Adelaide, SA 5000. © **1800/888 241** in Australia, 800/624-3524 in the U.S. and Canada, 0800/892 407 in the U.K., 0800/803 524 in New Zealand, or 08/8211 8255. Fax 08/8231 1179. www.barron townhouse.com.au. 68 units. A$132 (U.S.$85.80) standard double; A$176 (U.S.$114.40) deluxe double; A$186 (U.S.$121) executive room; A$140 (U.S.$91) family. Extra person A$18 (U.S.$11.70). Children under 12 stay free in parents' room. Lower rates in off-season and weekends. Ask about package deals. AE, DC, MC, V. Free parking. **Amenities:** Restaurant; nonsmoking rooms. *In room:* A/C, TV, minibar, coffeemaker, iron.

City Park Motel   The rooms in this first-floor motel just outside the city center have modern furnishings and nice bathrooms with a shower. Some rooms have private balconies. Also on the premises is a separate bathroom with a tub. The best room is number 45. Downstairs there's a new cocktail bar, nightclub, and bistro.

> ## _Tips_ Plan Ahead
>
> If you plan to be in town during the biennial Adelaide Festival make sure
> you book your accommodations well in advance. Accommodations can
> also get pretty scarce during the Christmas and New Year's period, so it's
> wise to book well in advance then, too.

471 Pulteney St., Adelaide, SA 5000. ℂ 08/8223 1444. Fax 08/8223 1133. 18 units, 14 with bathroom
(shower only). A$55 (U.S.$35.75) double without bathroom; A$75 (U.S.$48.75) double with bathroom. Extra
person A$10 (U.S.$6.50). AE, DC, MC, V. Free parking. The tram to Glenelg stops just around the corner, and
3 streets up is a bus stop for the free City Loop bus. **Amenities:** Restaurant (bistro), bar, nightclub; room service. _In room:_ A/C, TV, minibar, coffeemaker, iron.

Hilton Adelaide 🏨🏨   The Hilton is a luxurious establishment situated on
Victoria Square and just around the corner from a whole host of restaurants on
Gouger Street. The lobby is polished marble with a cascading fountain and
piano music tinkling throughout. Guest rooms are pleasant with all you might
expect from a classy establishment. There are 11 rooms specially equipped for
travelers with disabilities. The Hilton has fabulous deals—A$210 (U.S.$136.50)
for standard and $235 (U.S.$142.75) for executive rooms—"subject to availability" (which means when it's not full). Five floors of mostly executive rooms
were totally refurbished in early 2001. I was surprised to find Charlie's Bar—full
of photos of famous Charlies—virtually empty even on a Saturday night. At a
pinch I'd probably choose the Hyatt (above) for the extensive views, but there's
not much difference between them.

233 Victoria Square, Adelaide, SA 5000. ℂ 08/8217 2000. Fax 08/8217 2001. www.hilton.com. 380 units.
A$325–$335 (U.S.$211–$217.75) double; A$440 (U.S.$286) executive floor; A$650 (U.S.$422.50) suite. Extra
person A$45 (U.S.$29.25). Children under 12 stay free in parents' room. AE, DC, MC, V. Parking A$16
(U.S.$10.40). The tram stops in front of the hotel; a bus stop is adjacent. **Amenities:** 2 restaurants, bar; heated
outdoor pool; health club; concierge; business center; salon; 24-hr. room service; massage; babysitting;
laundry/dry cleaning service. _In room:_ A/C, TV with pay movies, modem port and fax (in business rooms),
minibar, hair dryer, iron.

Moore's Brecknock Hotel   Adelaide's original Irish pub, built in 1851, still
attracts a lot of Irish who come here for the great selection of beer and reasonably priced home-style cooking—it reputedly serves Adelaide's best hamburgers.
It's also very popular with American guests who use the hotel accommodations
upstairs as a base from which to discover Kangaroo Island and other parts of the
state. The Brecknock is about 4 blocks from Victoria Square and is run by Kerry
Moore and his Canadian wife Tricia. There are live bands downstairs on Friday,
Saturday, and Sunday evenings, but the music finishes at 1am on Friday and
Saturday, and 10pm on Sunday, so you shouldn't have too much trouble sleeping. Rooms are large and pleasantly done out in old-world style. Each has a double and a single bed, and a sink, with the bathrooms down the hall.

Associated with the hotel, next door, is **Nomads Backpackers (08/8211
8985;** www.nomads-backpackers.com.au).

401 King William St., Adelaide, SA 5000. ℂ 08/8231 5467. Fax 08/8410 1968. 10 units, none with bathroom. A$60 (U.S.$39) double; A$80 (U.S.$52) triple. Rates include continental breakfast. AE, DC, MC, V. Free
parking. The tram to Glenelg stops in front of the hotel. **Amenities:** Restaurant, 3 bars; bike rental; tour desk;
car-rental desk; coin-op laundry; nonsmoking rooms. _In room:_ A/C, fax, fridge, coffeemaker, iron, safe.

Novotel Adelaide on Hindley   Only a short stroll from the center of town,
the Novotel is a pretty good value, especially if you happen to be staying on the

weekend when the rates go down. Otherwise, it's not as classy as either the Hyatt or the Hilton. What you get for your money is a good, recently renovated, bright room. Ask at the reception desk for a robe, as they aren't included in the standard rooms.

65 Hindley St., Adelaide SA 5000. ℭ **08/8231 5552.** Fax 08/8237 3800. www.accorhotel.com. 217 units. Midweek A$202 (U.S.$131) double; A$245 (U.S.$156) suite. Weekend A$150 (U.S.$97.50) double; A$193 (U.S.$125.45) suite. Ask about package deals. Children under 15 stay free in parents' room. AE, DC, MC, V. Parking A$17 (U.S.$11). **Amenities:** Casual brasserie, bar; heated outdoor pool; health club; concierge; business center; 24-hr. room service. *In room:* A/C, TV with pay movies, modem and fax, minibar, hair dryer; iron.

Saville Park Suites Adelaide ⋆

You can't miss this conglomerate of russet-red bricks just on the outskirts of the city center (about a 10-minute walk). Rooms are nice and spacious, if a bit formal, which is not surprising since the place is popular with business travelers. On the premises is the Zipp Restaurant and Wine Bar, where Tommy Chang serves up an innovative menu.

255 Hindley St., Adelaide SA 5000. ℭ **1800/882 601** in Australia, or 08/8217 2500. Fax 08/8217 2519. www.savillesuites.com.au. 141 units. A$142 (U.S.$92.30) studio; A$187 (U.S.$121.55) 2-bedroom suite. Up to 2 people in studio and 4 in other units. AE, DC, MC, V. Parking A$5 (U.S.$3.25). **Amenities:** Restaurant; free access to nearby City Gym; outdoor spa; concierge; tour desk; car-rental desk; room service (7–9am and 5–10:30pm); babysitting; laundry; same-day dry cleaning; nonsmoking rooms. *In room:* A/C, TV with pay movies, dataport, kitchen, minibar, fridge, hair dryer, iron.

IN NORTH ADELAIDE

This suburb across the river is an interesting place to stay because of its nice architecture and good restaurants. It's about a 10-minute bus ride from the city center.

Expensive

North Adelaide Heritage Group ⋆⋆⋆ Finds

It's worth coming all the way to Adelaide just for the experience of staying in one of these out-of-this-world apartments, cottages, and suites. Each of the 18 separate properties in North Adelaide and Eastwood are fabulous. I recommend particularly the former Friendly Meeting Chaple Hall, which was once the headquarters of the mouth-watering "Albert Lodge No. 6 of the Independent Order of Oddfellows, Manchester Unity Friendly Society and the Court Huntsman's Pride No. 2478 of the Ancient Order of Foresters Friendly Society." The structure is a small, simple gabled hall of blue-stone rubble trimmed with brick and resembles a small church. Built in 1878, it's stocked with period pieces and antiques and rounded off with a modern, fully stocked kitchen; a huge spa bath; a queen-size bed; and a CD player and TV.

Another standout place is the George Lowe Esquire unit. This huge 19th-century apartment is also stocked with antiques, has a huge four-poster bed, a separate bathroom, a lounge, and a full kitchen. Guests also have use of nice gardens. Owners Rodney and Regina Twiss have added all those little touches that make you feel like home, from magazines liberally piled up everywhere to bacon and eggs in the fridge. All properties are within easy walking distance of the main attractions in the area. The company has just bought the old North Adelaide Fire Station and has renovated it into three separate apartments.

Office: 109 Glen Osmond Rd., Eastwood, SA 5063. ℭ **08/8272 1355,** or 0418/289 494 (mobile phone). Fax 08/8272 1355. www.adelaideheritage.com. 19 units. A$145–$330 (U.S.$94.25–$214.50) double, depending on accommodation. Extra person A$60–$85 (U.S.$39–$55.25). Children under 12 A$30 (U.S.$19.50). AE, DC, MC, V. *In room:* A/C, TV, fridge, coffeemaker, hair dryer, iron.

Old Lion Apartments ⋆

These pleasant apartments are located inside a renovated brewery. The complex is about a 15-minute walk from the city center and is on a direct bus route. Rooms are spacious, with high ceilings, and come with a kitchenette, a living room, French doors separating bedrooms from living quarters, a shower and bath, and a good-size balcony. All apartments also have use of a washing machine and dryer. VCRs and videos are available for rent at the front desk. Continental breakfast costs A$8.50 (U.S.$5.50) extra.

9 Jerningham St., North Adelaide, SA 5006. ℂ 08/8223 0500. Fax 08/8223 0588. reservations@majestic apartments.com.au. 57 units. A$148 (U.S.$96.20) 1-bedroom apt; A$164.50 (U.S.$107) 2-bedroom apt; A$203 (U.S.$132) 3-bedroom apt. Extra adult A$16.50 (U.S.$10.75), extra child 3–12 A$5.50 (U.S.$3.60). AE, DC, MC, V. Parking A$5 (U.S.$3.25). Bus: 184, 224, 226, 228, or 229. **Amenities:** Concierge; room service. *In room:* A/C, TV (VCRs and videos by request), fridge, coffeemaker, iron, laundry.

Princes Lodge Motel   One of the best motels in Adelaide, the Princes Lodge looks more like a large private home than your typical simple brick roadside structure. Rooms are nicely decorated and generally come with a double and a single bed. There are three family rooms available, one of which has a double and three singles, while another has six beds in one room. The motel is within walking distance of the restaurant strip on O'Connell Street, and a A$6 (U.S.$3.90) taxi ride from the city center.

73 Lefevre Terrace, North Adelaide 5006. ℂ **08/8267 5566.** Fax 08/8239 0787. princeslodge@senet.com.au. 21 units. A$55 (U.S.$35.75) double with separate private bathroom; A$66 (U.S.$42.90) with attached bathroom. Rates include continental breakfast. AE, DC, MC, V. Bus: 222 from Victoria Square (with pickups along King William St.). **Amenities:** Golf course nearby; tour desk; car-rental desk; coin-op laundry. *In room:* A/C, TV, dataport, fridge, hair dryer.

IN GLENELG

I'd recommend anyone, without hesitation, to stay in Glenelg rather than in the city center. The journey to the city center by car or tram takes less than 30 minutes, and the airport is less than 10 minutes away. Add to this the sea, the lovely beach, the fun fair, the great shops, the good pub, and the nice accommodations, and you have a perfect place to ease up on your holiday.

Atlantic Tower Motor Inn   If you're looking for relatively inexpensive accommodations near the beach, this is your place. You can't miss this tubular building not far from the sea, with its slowly revolving restaurant on the 12th floor. Rooms are simple, but very bright, and have nice park views through large windows. Each room has a double and a single bed. The Deluxe rooms are a bit nicer and come with baths rather than just showers. Suites have two rooms and excellent views; the most expensive have a spa tub. The gently turning Rock Lobster Cafe upstairs is open for lunch on Thursday, Friday, and Sunday (no lunch on Sat) and dinner every evening.

760 Anzac Hwy., Glenelg, SA 5045. ℂ **08/8294 1011.** Fax 08/8376 0964. www.atlantic.com.au. 27 units (20 with shower only). A$86 (U.S.$56) double; A$106 (U.S.$69) deluxe double; A$145 (U.S.$94.25) suite. Extra person A$12 (U.S.$7.80). Children under 15 stay free in parents' room. AE, DC, MC, V. Free parking. Hotel is 1 block from tram stop 20. **Amenities:** Restaurant; tour desk; car rental; laundry service; same-day dry cleaning. *In room:* A/C, TV, fax, kitchenette (suites only), hair dryer, iron.

Stamford Grand Adelaide 🏨🏨   A classic Adelaide photo is certainly of the trams awaiting passengers in front of the imposing facade of the Stamford Grand. Located right on the beach, this classy hotel offers nice rooms with modern furnishings; many overlook the beach, the ocean, and the pier. The Pier and Pines is a very popular bar that's almost bursting with youngish crowds most nights; for a more mellow scene, there's Horizons piano bar, which offers quality live music particularly on weekends.

Moseley Square (P.O. Box 600), Glenelg, SA 5045. ℂ **1800/882 777** in Australia, or 08/8376 1222. Fax 08/ 8376 1111. 240 units. A$322 (U.S.$209) double; A$349–$546 (U.S.$227–$355) suite. Children under 12 stay free in parents' room. AE, DC, MC, V. Parking A$10 (U.S.$6.50). The tram from Adelaide stops in front of the

---

Finds Something Different—Dining Tours

If you like good food and wine, but can't decide on just one restaurant, try one of **Graeme Andrews' tours** (© 08/8336 8333, or 0412/842 242 (mobile); fax/message 08/8336 4075; www.food-fun-wine.com.au). He offers eight food and food-and-wine tours showcasing the Central Market, Chinatown, and Gouger Street restaurant precincts. Prices start from A$28 (U.S.$18). Private tours are also available on request.

---

hotel. **Amenities:** 2 restaurants (Modern Australian, Thai), 2 bars; good indoor swimming pool; health club and spa; concierge; business center; 24-hr. room service. *In room:* A/C, TV with pay movies, minibar, hair dryer, iron.

WHERE TO DINE

With more than 600 restaurants, pubs, and cafes, Adelaide boasts more dining spots per capita than anywhere else in Australia. Many of them are clustered in particular areas, such as Rundle Street in the city and Gouger Street and North Adelaide—where you'll find almost every style of cuisine you can imagine. For cheap noodles, laksas, sushi, and cakes head to Adelaide's popular Central Markets (© 08/8203 7494), behind the Adelaide Hilton Hotel between Gouger and Grote streets.

Because of South Australia's healthy wine industry, you'll find that many of the more expensive restaurants have extensive wine lists—though with spicier foods, it's probably wiser to stick with beer, or a fruity white in a pinch. Many Adelaide restaurants allow diners to bring their own wine (BYO), but most charge a steep corkage fee to open your bottle—A$6 (U.S.$3.90) or so is not uncommon.

IN THE CITY CENTRE
Very Expensive

The Grange 🍴🍴 MODERN AUSTRALIAN   The Grange is an open-plan restaurant specializing in contemporary food by Adelaide's most influential chef, Cheong Liew. Liew offers an innovative fusion of Western and Asian ingredients, rounded off with an extensive wine list. The menu begins with a choice of two starters, among them Liew's signature dish "The four dances of the sea"—an antipasto of fish, octopus in a garlic sauce, prawn sushi, raw cuttlefish, and black noodles. For the next course you could choose baby abalone, or lobster baked with bourbon and lime, or even Japanese quail filled with chestnuts and Chinese mushrooms. If there are two of you dining, then you might want to check the menu a day in advance, as some of the dishes for two require 24 hours' notice.

In the Hilton Adelaide, 233 Victoria Square. © 08/8217 2000. Reservations required. 3-course dinner A$81 (U.S.$52.65); 4 courses A$97 (U.S.$63). AE, DC, MC, V. Tues–Sat 7–10:30pm.

Moderate

Amalfi ITALIAN   Come here for good Italian cooking at reasonable prices served up in a lively atmosphere. The pizzas are the best in Adelaide—though a little expensive—and consistently good veal and pasta dishes are always on the menu. Be sure to check out the daily specials board, where you can pick out a very good fish dish or two.

29 Frome St. (just of Rundle St.). © 08/8223 1948. Reservations recommended. Main courses A$13.50–$16.50 (U.S.$8.80–$10.70). AE, DC, MC, V. Mon–Thurs 11:30am–3pm and 5:30–11pm (until midnight Fri); Sat 5:30pm–midnight.

Austral Hotel MODERN AUSTRALIAN   This large pub, with its dark timber and forest-colored wallpaper, is a pleasant place for a good-value pub meal. You can either eat at the bar, outside on the street, or in the dining room. The bistro serves burgers, fish and chips, pastas, laksas, and Thai curries. The restaurant is a bit more upscale and offers risotto, handmade crab ravioli, beef fillets, chicken dishes, venison, paella, and baby octopus.

205 Rundle St. (?) **08/8223 4660.** Reservations recommended. Main courses A$6.50–$13.50 (U.S.$4.20–$8.80) in bistro and A$14.90–$22 (U.S.$9.70–$14.30) in restaurant. AE, MC, V. Mon–Thurs noon–3pm and 5:30–9:30pm; Fri–Sun noon–10pm.

Golden Triangle THAI/LAOS/BURMESE   From Thai chicken laksa and Burmese beef curry to tom-yum soup and Indonesian Nasee Goreng, the Golden Triangle serves the lot. This grotto-like joint is dark, cramped, and badly furnished—with sea-green walls, a Buddha in the corner, and just 10 tables—but all this only serves to emphasize the wonderfully authentic food that will blow your socks off. Dinner specials—including a starter and main course (except seafood); a glass of wine, fruit juice, or coffee; and a ticket thrown in for the nearby movie complex—cost just A$22.50 (U.S.$14.60).

106a Hindley St. (?) **08/8211 8222.** Reservations recommended. Main courses A$9.50–$15 (U.S.$6.20–$9.75). AE, DC, MC, V. Daily noon–2:30pm and 5pm until last customer.

Jasmin Indian Restaurant NORTH INDIAN   Prices have crept up as this place has gotten more popular, but this family-run Adelaide institution a block south of Rundle Mall is still a good value—and it won the Restaurant Association's award for best Indian restaurant in 2000. Indian artifacts and signed cricket bats from visiting Indian teams decorate the walls. The atmosphere is comfortable yet busy, and the service is professional. The house special is the very hot beef vindaloo, but all the old favorites, such as tandoori chicken, butter chicken (a big seller here), lamb korma, and malabari beef with coconut cream, ginger and garlic, are here, too. Mop it all up with naan bread, and cool your palate with a side dish of raita. The suji halwa, a semolina pudding with nuts, is the best I've tasted. Smoking is not permitted.

31 Hindmarsh Square. (?) **08/8223 7837.** Reservations recommended. Main courses A$16.90–$18.90 (U.S.$11–$12.30). Lunch banquet A$27 (U.S.$17.55); dinner banquet A$33 (U.S.$21.45). AE, DC, MC, V. Tues–Fri noon–3pm; Tues–Sat 5:30–10pm.

Jolleys Boathouse Restaurant ✿ MODERN AUSTRALIAN   Jolleys is nicely situated on the banks of the River Torrens, with views of boats, ducks, and black swans. Business people and ladies-who-lunch rush for the three outside tables for a bit of alfresco dining, but if you miss out, the bright and airy interior, with its cream-colored tablecloths and director's chairs, isn't too much of a letdown. You might start with the intriguing goat's curd ravioli with red pesto and chives. Moving on, you could tuck into the roasted duck with hazelnut risotto (close your eyes to the peaceful quacking out on the river if you can). The banana and cardamom soufflé for dessert is wicked.

Jolleys Lane. (?) **08/8223 2891.** Reservations recommended. Main courses A$20–$24.50 (U.S.$13–$16). Lunch A$22 (U.S.$14.30) for 1 course, A$34.50 (U.S.$22.40) for 2 courses, and A$42.50 (U.S.$27.60) for 3 courses. AE, DC, MC, V. Daily noon–2:30pm; Mon–Sat 6:30–9.30pm.

Matsuri ✿ JAPANESE   I really like the atmosphere in this very good Japanese restaurant on the popular Gouger Street restaurant strip. The food is prepared by Takaomi Kitamura, world-famous ice sculptor and sushi master. The sushi and sashimi dishes are some of the best in Australia. Monday night is "sushi festival night," when sushi is half price. During happy hour Wednesday through Sunday, sushi is 30% off if you place your order before 7pm (you can pre-order over the phone and eat later). Other popular dishes include vegetarian and seafood tempura, yose nobe (a hot pot of vegetables, seafood, and chicken), and chawan mushi (a steamed custard dish). The service is friendly and considerate. Corkage fee is a steep A\$4.50 (U.S.\$2.90) a bottle.

167 Gouger St. ℂ 08/8231 3494. Reservations recommended. Main courses A\$8.60–\$23 (U.S.\$5.60–\$15). AE, DC, MC, V. Fri noon–2pm; Wed–Mon 5:30–10pm.

Mekong Thai THAI/MALAYSIAN/HALAL *Value*   Though this place is not much to look at—with simple tables and chairs, some outside in a portico— it has a fiery reputation for good food among in-the-know locals. The food is spicy and authentic, and the portions are filling. It's also a vegetarian's paradise, with at least 16 meat-free mains on the ethnically varied menu. It's Adelaide's only fully halal (suitable for Muslims) restaurant.

68 Hindley St. ℂ 08/8231 2914. Main courses A\$10.90–\$12.90 (U.S.\$7–\$8.40). AE, DC, MC, V. Daily 5:15pm–late.

Rigoni's Bistro ITALIAN   Located on a narrow lane west of King William Street, this traditional Italian trattoria is often packed at lunch, though less frantic in the evening. It's big and bright with high ceilings and russet quarry tiles. A long bar runs through the middle of the dining room; brass plates mark the stools of regular diners. The food is very traditional and quite good. The chalkboard menu often changes, but you are quite likely to find lasagna, veal in white wine, marinated fish, and various pasta dishes. There's also an extensive salad bar with a variety of antipasto and an outside dining area.

27 Leigh St. ℂ 08/8231 5160. Reservations recommended. Main courses A\$14.50–\$22 (U.S.\$9.50–\$14.30); antipasto bar (lunch only) A\$11.50–\$13.75 (U.S.\$7.50–\$8.90). AE, DC, MC, V. Mon–Fri noon–2:30pm and 6:30–10pm, Sat 6.30–10pm.

Ruby's Café ℱ MODERN AUSTRALIAN   Situated in suitably unpretentious surroundings for a former market cafe catering to the local workers, Ruby's is an Adelaide institution. It still has its laminated tables and the "no spitting, no coarse language" sign behind the bar, despite being far more upmarket than that. Basically, you get a very good restaurant meal in an old cafe atmosphere at very good prices. Served up are filling curries and fancier pasta dishes, hearty meals such as lamb shanks, and quite a few vegetarian options. For dessert I recommend the toffee pudding with toffee sauce. The menu changes every 6 weeks.

255b Rundle St. ℂ 08/8224 0365. Main courses A\$10.50–\$19.50. AE, MC, V. Sun 9am–5pm and 6:30–11.30pm; daily 6:30–11:30pm.

IN NORTH ADELAIDE

The Manse ℱℱ SEAFOOD   Swiss chef Bernhard Oehrli has a fine touch when it comes to seafood, and I recommend this place wholeheartedly. The surroundings are neat and gracious, with a log fire inside to keep you warm in winter and room to dine outside on the sidewalk on sunnier days. As for the food, the scallops here are almost fresh enough to waddle off the warmed cucumber base and head for sea, while the rare tuna in Japanese-style tempura is so delicate it literally melts in your mouth. If you want something other than seafood, then you can't go wrong with the duck or veal dishes. For dessert try the warm chocolate gâteau or the rhubarb gratin with ice cream.

142 Tynte St., North Adelaide. ℂ 08/8267 4636. Reservations recommended. A\$30 (U.S.\$19.50) for 2 courses. AE, DC, MC, V. Tues–Fri noon–3pm; Mon–Sat 6:30–10pm. Bus: 182, 224, 226, 228, or 229.

The Oxford ⭐ MODERN AUSTRALIAN   This restaurant has won nearly twice as many gold medals for cooking as Mark Spitz won for swimming (seven golds in 1972 Olympic Games, by the way). The Oxford is highly praised for its creative, contemporary food in a range of mixed-up styles. It's big and busy and housed in a renovated, character-filled 1870s building. Inside you'll find crisp white tablecloths, a single page menu, and a stainless steel kitchen whipping up steam. The signature dishes are the red-roasted spatchcock (a small chicken) with water chestnut, chicken-and-cashew-nut spring roll, black-bean mayonnaise, and coconut broth; and the wonderful Caesar salad. Other favorites include satay fried chicken; jellyfish with Moroccan-spiced salsa; and poached prawns with natural oysters, served with wasabi, nori rolls, and soy dressing. The wine list is extensive.

101 O'Connell St., North Adelaide. ℂ 08/8267 2652. Reservations recommended, especially for lunch and dinner Fri and dinner Sat. Main courses A$14.50–$20.50 (U.S.$9.40–$13.30). AE, DC, MC, V. Mon–Fri noon–3pm; Mon–Sat 6–10pm or later. Bus: 182, 22, 224, 226, 228, or 229.

SEEING THE SIGHTS

Adelaide is a very laid-back city. It's not jam-packed with tourist-oriented attractions like some of the larger state capitals, though the Migration Museum (see below) is easily one of the best museums in Australia. The best way to enjoy this pleasant city is to take things nice and easy. Take a walk beside the River Torrens, take the tram to the beachside suburb of Glenelg, and spend the evenings sipping wine and sampling some of the country's best alfresco dining.

THE TOP ATTRACTIONS

Art Gallery of South Australia ⭐   Adelaide's premier public art gallery has a good range of local and overseas works and a fine Asian ceramics collection. Of particular interest are Charles Hall's *Proclamation of South Australia 1836*, Nicholas Chevalier's painting of the departure of explorers Burke and Wills from Melbourne; several examples of works by Australian painters Sidney Nolan, Albert Tucker, and Arthur Boyd; and some excellent contemporary art. The bookshop has an extensive collection of art publications. Allow 1 to 2 hours.

North Terrace. ℂ 08/8207 7000. Free admission. Daily 10am–5pm. Guided tours Mon–Fri 11am and 2pm; Sat–Sun 11am and 3pm. Closed Christmas Day. Bus: City Loop.

The Migration Museum ⭐ *(Finds)*   This tiny museum, dedicated to immigration and multiculturalism, is one of the most important and fascinating in Australia. With touching, personal displays, it tells the story of the waves of immigrants who have helped shape this multicultural society, from the boatloads of convicts who came here in 1788 to the ethnic groups who have been trickling in over the past 2 centuries. Allow 1 hour.

82 Kintore Ave. ℂ 08/8207 7580. Admission by donation. Mon–Fri 10am–5pm, Sat–Sun and public holidays 1–5pm. Closed Good Friday and Christmas. Bus: Any to North Terrace.

South Australian Maritime Museum   Over 150 years of maritime history are commemorated in this Port Adelaide museum. Most of the exhibits can be found in the 1850s Bond Store, but the museum also incorporates an 1863 lighthouse and three vessels moored alongside Wharf No. 1, just a short walk away. The fully rigged replica of the 54-foot ketch *Active II* is very impressive. Allow 1½ hours. Port Adelaide is approximately 30 minutes from the city center by bus.

126 Lipson St., Port Adelaide. ℂ 08/8207 6255. Admission A$8.50 (U.S.$5.50) adults, A$3.50 (U.S.$2.30) children, A$22 (U.S.$14.30) families. Daily 10am–5pm. Closed Christmas. Bus: 151 or 153 from North Terrace in the city (opposite Parliament House) to Stop 40 (Port Adelaide). Train: Port Adelaide.

South Australian Museum 𝄞 The star attraction of this interesting museum is the new Australian Aboriginal Cultures Gallery which opened in March 2000. On display is an extensive collection of utensils, spears, tools, bush medicine, food samples, photographs, and the like. Also within the museum is a sorry-looking collection of stuffed native animals (sadly also including a few extinct marsupials, including the Tasmanian Tiger); a good collection of Papua New Guinea artifacts; and excellent mineral and butterfly collections.

If you're interested in learning even more about the exhibits, take one of the Behind-the-Scenes Tours. The tours are conducted after museum hours and cost A$12 (U.S.$7.80) for adults. Allow 2 hours.

On North Terrace between the State Library and the Art Gallery. 𝄞 08/8207 7500. Free admission. Daily 10am–5pm. Closed Good Friday and Christmas.

Tandanya Aboriginal Cultural Institute 𝄞𝄞 This place offers a great opportunity to experience Aboriginal life through Aboriginal eyes. Exhibits change regularly, but all give insight into Aboriginal art and cultural activities. At noon every day there's a didgeridoo performance. A shop sells Aboriginal art and books on Aboriginal culture, while a cafe on the premises serves up several bush tucker (native food) items. Allow 1 hour.

253 Grenfell St. 𝄞 08/8223 2467. Admission A$4 (U.S.$2.60) adults, A$3 (U.S.$1.95) children 13 and under, A$10 (U.S.$6.50) families. Daily 10am–5pm. Bus: City Loop.

THE FLORA & THE FAUNA

Adelaide Zoo *Kids* To be honest, if you've already experienced the wonderful Melbourne Zoo, or even Taronga Zoo in Sydney, it's probably not worth your while coming here. But if this is going to be your only chance to see a kangaroo in captivity, then plan a visit here. Of course, other Australian animals live at the zoo, too, and the nicely landscaped gardens and lack of crowds make it a pleasant place for an entertaining stroll. The zoo houses the only pygmy blue-tongue lizard in captivity in Australia, a species thought to be extinct since the 1940s, until a specimen was discovered inside the belly of a dead snake. Allow 1 hour.

Frome Rd. 𝄞 08/8267 3255. Admission A$12 (U.S.$7.80) adults, A$7 (U.S.$4.55) children. Daily 9:30am–5pm. Bus: 272 or 273 from Currie Street to bus stop 2 (5 min.).

Botanic Gardens You'll feel like you're at the true heart of the city when you stroll through the huddles of office workers having picnic lunches on the lawns here. Park highlights include a broad avenue of shady Moreton Bay figs, duck ponds, giant water lilies, an Italianate garden, a palm house, and the Bicentennial Conservatory—a large glass dome full of rain-forest species. You might want to have lunch in the Botanic Gardens Restaurant (𝄞 **08/8223 3526**) surrounded by bird song and lush vegetation, right in the center of the park; it's open daily from 10am to 5pm.

North Terrace. 𝄞 08/8223 9311. Free admission. Mon–Fri 8:30am–4pm, Sat–Sun 10am–5pm.

FOR TRAIN BUFFS

Port Dock Railway Museum This former Port Adelaide railway yard houses Australia's largest and finest collection of locomotive engines and rolling stock—with around 104 items on display including some 30 engines. Among the most impressive trains on show are the gigantic "Mountain" class engines, and so-called "Tea and Sugar" trains that once ran between railway camps in remote parts of the desert. Entrance includes a train ride. Allow 1½ hours.

Lipton St., North Adelaide. (✆ 08/8341 1690. Admission A$9 (U.S.$5.85) adults, A$3.50 (U.S.$2.30) children, and A$20 (U.S.$13) families. Daily 10am–5pm. Bus: 151 or 153 from North terrace, opposite Parliament House, to stop number 40 (approx. 30-min. journey).

ORGANIZED TOURS

Grayline Day Tours (✆ **1300 858 687** in Australia; www.grayline.com) operates a city sightseeing tour for A$39 (U.S.$25.35) for adults and A$19.50 (U.S.$12.70) for children. It operates from 9:30am to noon every day except Sunday. The bus can pick you up at your hotel. Grayline also does other tours taking in central Adelaide with either Hahndorf or Cleland Wildlife Park included, as well as tours to the Flinders ranges and Kangaroo Island.

The **Adelaide Explorer** (✆ **08/8364 1933;** www.adelaideexplorer.com.au) is a replica tram that circles the city, stopping off at a number of attractions along the way, including Glenelg. The full route takes 2¾ hours to complete; you can get on or off along the route and rejoin another tram later on. Buses depart from 38 King William St. daily on the hour in summer, and every hour and a half in winter. Tickets are A$35 (U.S.$22.75) for adults and A$20 (U.S.$13) for children 6 to 14, and A$80 (U.S.$52) for a family. Ask about family discounts.

ENJOYING THE GREAT OUTDOORS

BIKING   Adelaide's parks and riverbanks are very popular with cyclists. Rent your bicycle from **Linear Park Hire** (✆ **018/844 588** mobile phone). The going rate is A$15 to $20 (U.S.$9.75 to $13) for 24 hours, including helmet, lock, and baby-seat (if needed). **Recreation SA** (✆ **08/8226 7301**) publishes a brochure showing Adelaide's bike routes. Pick one up at the **South Australia Travel Centre** (see "Visitor Information" earlier in chapter). **The Map Shop,** 6 Peel St. (✆ **08/8231 2033**), is also a good source for maps.

HIKING & JOGGING   The banks of the River Torrens are a good place for a jog. The truly fit and/or adventurous, might want to tackle the **Heysen Trail,** a spectacular 1,600-kilometer (992-mile) walk through bush, farmland, and rugged hill country that starts 80 kilometers (50 miles) south of Adelaide and goes to the Flinders Ranges by way of the Adelaide Hills and the Barossa Valley. For more information on the trail, visit the **South Australia Travel Centre** (see "Visitor Information" earlier in chapter).

GOLF   The **City of Adelaide Golf Course** (✆ **08/8267 2171**) is quite close to town and has two short 18-hole courses and a full-size championship course. Greens fees are A$14 to $16.80 (U.S.$9.10 to $10.90) weekdays and A$16.20 to $19 (U.S.$10.50 to $12.35) weekends, depending on the course, Monday through Friday, plus A$3 (U.S.$1.95) extra on weekends. Club rental is available. Ask about cheaper after-4pm prices.

TAKING IN AN AUSSIE RULES GAME & OTHER SPECTATOR SPORTS

CRICKET   The **Adelaide Oval** (✆ **08/8300 3800**), on the corner of War Memorial Drive and King William Street, is the venue for international matches during the summer season.

FOOTBALL   Unlike in New South Wales, where Rugby League is the most popular winter sport, here in Adelaide you'll find plenty of Australian Rules fanatics. Games are usually played on a Saturday either at the **Adelaide Oval** (see above) or at **Football Park** (✆ **08/8268 2088**), on Turner Drive, West Lakes. The home teams are the Adelaide Crows and the Port Adelaide Power. Games are played February through October, with the finals held in September

---

(*Finds*) **Shopping for Opals**

South Australia is home to the world's largest sources of white opals (the more expensive black opals generally come from Lightning Ridge in northern New South Wales). There are plenty of places to buy around town, but **Opal Field Gems,** 33 King William St. (© **08/8212 5300**) is one of the best. As a rule, you're not going to find any bargains, so just buy what you like (and can afford—good opals cost many thousands of dollars).

---

and October. Tickets must be purchased well in advance from **BASS** (© **13 12 46** in South Australia, or 08/8400 2205).

THE SHOPPING SCENE

Rundle Mall (between King Williams and Pulteney streets) is Adelaide's main shopping street. This pedestrian-only thoroughfare is home to all the big names in fashion.

Adelaide's Central Markets (© **08/8203 7494**), behind the Adelaide Hilton Hotel between Gouger and Grote streets, make up the largest produce market in the Southern Hemisphere. They're a good place to shop for vegetables, fruit, meat, fish, and the like, although the colorful markets are worth popping into even if you're not looking for picnic fixings. The markets, held in a huge warehouse-like structure, are open Tuesday from 7am to 5:30pm, Thursday from 11am to 5:30pm, Friday from 7am to 9pm, and Saturday from 7am to 3pm. **Market Adventures** (© **08/8336 8333,** or mobile 0412/842 242; fax/ message 08/8336 4075) runs behind-the-scenes tours of the markets every Tuesday and Thursday at 10:30am and 1:30pm, Friday at 10am and 2pm, and Saturday at 8:30am. Tours cost A$28 (U.S.$18.20) for adults and A$15 (U.S.$9.75) for children 3 to 11. Phone for directions. The company also runs a Dawn Market Tour of the markets at 7:15am every Tuesday, Thursday, Friday, and Saturday for A$49 (U.S.$31.85) including breakfast.

The six-story **Myer Centre,** next door to the Myer department store, 22–38 Rundle Mall, has a Body Shop (on the ground floor), for beauty products; an Australian Geographic shop (on level 3), for top-quality Australiana; and Exotica (level 2), where you can find unusual futuristic gifts.

Just off Rundle Mall, at Shop 6 in the City Cross Arcade, is **L'Unique** (© **08/ 8231 0030**), a good craft shop selling South Australian pottery, jewelry, woodcraft, hand-blown glass, and original paintings.

Elsewhere, the renowned **Jam Factory Craft and Design Centre,** in the Lions Art Centre, 19 Morphett St. (© **08/8410 0727**), sells an excellent range of locally made ceramics, glass, furniture, and metal items. You can also watch the craftspeople at work here.

For the best boots in Australia, head to the **R.M. Williams** shop on Gawler Place (© **08/8232 3611**) for the best simple boots you're ever likely to find, as well as other Aussie fashion icons, including Akubra hats, moleskin pants, and Driza-bone coats.

ADELAIDE AFTER DARK

The *Adelaide Advertiser* lists all performances and exhibitions in its entertainment pages. The free tourist guide *Today in Adelaide,* available in most hotels, also has information. Tickets for theater and other entertainment events in Adelaide can be purchased from **BASS ticket outlets** at the following locations:

Festival Theatre, Adelaide Festival Centre, King William Road; Centre Pharmacy, 19 Central Market Arcade; Verandah Music, 182 Rundle St.; and on the 5th floor of the Myer department store, Rundle Mall. Call BASS at ℂ **13 12 46** in South Australia or 08/8400 2205.

THE PERFORMING ARTS

The major concert hall in town is the **Adelaide Festival Centre,** King William Road (ℂ **08/8216 8600** for general inquiries; 08/8400 2205 for box office). The Festival Centre encompasses three auditoriums: the 1,978-seat Festival Theatre, the 612-seat Playhouse, and the 350-seat Space Centre. This is the place in Adelaide to see opera, ballet, drama, orchestral concerts, the Adelaide Symphony Orchestra, plays, and experimental drama.

The complex also includes an outdoor amphitheater used for jazz, rock-'n'-roll, and country music concerts; an art gallery; a bistro; a piano bar; and the Silver Jubilee Organ, the world's largest transportable concert-hall organ (built in Austria to commemorate Queen Elizabeth II's Silver Jubilee).

The Adelaide Repertory Festival presents a season of five productions a year, ranging from drama to comedy, at the **Arts Theatre,** 53 Angus St. (ℂ **08/8221 5644**). Playwrights Alan Ayckbourne and Terrence Ratagan are among the many who have had plays performed here. The theatre, which is just a short walk away from many hotels and restaurants, is also the home of the Metropolitan Musical Theatre Company, which presents two musical comedy productions a year. Tickets cost around A$16 (U.S.$10.40) for adults and A$11 (U.S.$7.15) for children.

Her Majesty's Theatre, 58 Grote St. (ℂ **08/8216 8600**), is a 1,000-seat venue opposite Central Markets that presents drama, comedy, smaller musicals, dance, opera, and recitals. Tickets are generally A$30 to $55 (U.S.$19.50 to $35.75).

THE BAR & CLUB SCENE

Adelaide's nightlife ranges from twiddling your thumbs to nude lapdancers. For adult entertainment (clubs with the word "strip" in the name) head to **Hindley Street**—there are a few pubs there, too, but I wouldn't recommend them. For information on gay and lesbian options, pick up a copy of the *Adelaide Gay Times.*

As for all-age pubs, the locals will point you toward **The Austral,** 205 Rundle Street (ℂ **08/8223 4660**); **The Lion,** at the corner of Melbourne and Jerningham streets (ℂ **08/8367 0222**); and the **British Hotel,** 58 Finniss St. (ℂ **08/8267 2188**), in North Adelaide, where you can cook your own steak on the courtyard barbecue. Also popular with both visitors and locals alike is the **Earl of Aberdeen,** 316 Pulteney St., at Carrington Street (ℂ **08/8223 6433**), a colonial-style pub popular for after-work drinks. **The Port Dock,** 10 Todd St., Port Adelaide (ℂ **08/8240 0187**), was licensed as a pub in 1864 and has kept up with tradition ever since; it even brews four of its own beers and pumps them directly to its three bars with old English beer engines. Most pubs are open from 11am to midnight.

TRYING YOUR LUCK AT THE CASINO

Right next to the Adelaide Hyatt, and dwarfed by the old railway station it's situated in, is the **Adelaide Casino,** North Terrace (ℂ **1800/888 711** in Australia, or 08/8212 2811). The casino has two floors of gaming tables and slot machines, as well as four bars and several dining options, including a fast-food station and the excellent Pullman buffet restaurant. The casino is open Sunday through Thursday from 10am to 4am and Friday and Saturday from 10am to 6am.

2 Side Trips from Adelaide

THE BAROSSA: ON THE TRAIL OF THE GRAPE

More than a quarter of Australia's wines, and a disproportionate number of top labels, originate in the Barossa and Eden valleys—collectively known as the **Barossa.** Beginning just 45 kilometers (28 miles) northeast of Adelaide and easily accessible, the area has had an enormous influence on the city's culture. In fact, Adelaidians of all socio-economic levels partake in more wine talk than the French. The area was first settled by German settlers from Silesia, who came to escape religious persecution. They brought with them their particular brand of culture, their food, and their vines. They also built the Lutheran churches that dominate the Barossa's skyline. With the help of wealthy English aristocrats, the wine industry went from strength to strength. Today, there are more than 50 wineries in an area that still retains its German flavor.

The focal points of the areas are **Angaston,** the farthest away from Adelaide; **Nuriootpa,** the center of the rural services industry; and **Tanunda,** the nearest town to the city. Each has interesting architecture, craft and antique shops, and specialty food outlets. If you are adventurous, you might want to hire a bike in Adelaide and take it on the train to **Gawler,** and cycle through the Barossa. Other options are exploring the area by hot-air balloon, Harley-Davidson motorcycle, or limousine.

ESSENTIALS

WHEN TO GO   The best times to visit the Barossa are in the spring (September and October), when it's not too hot and there are plenty of flowering trees and shrubs, and in the fall (Apr and May), when the leaves turn red. The main wine harvest is late summer/early autumn (Feb and Mar). The least crowded time is winter (June, July, and Aug).

GETTING THERE   If you have a car (by far the most flexible way to visit the Barossa), I recommend taking the scenic route from Adelaide (the route doesn't have a specific name, but it's obvious on any map). It takes about half an hour longer than the Main North Road through Gawler, but the trip is well worthwhile. Follow the signs to Birdwood, Springton, Mount Pleasant, and Angaston.

So Much Wine, So Little Time

If you have the choice of exploring either the Barossa or the Hunter Valley in New South Wales (see chapter 4), I recommend the **Barossa,** which despite being a little more touristy, has more to offer in terms of history and architecture.

Another famous wine-producing region is the **Coonawarra,** 381 kilometers (236 miles) southeast of Adelaide and near the border with Victoria; it's particularly convenient if you're driving from Melbourne. The area is just 12 kilometers (7 miles) long and 2 kilometers (just over 1 mile) wide, but the scenic countryside is crammed with historical villages and 16 wineries. The **Clare Valley,** 135 kilometers (84 miles) north of Adelaide, is another pretty area; it produces some outstanding examples of cool-climate wine.

Drinking & Driving—Don't Do It!

Australia's drunk-driving laws are strict and rigidly enforced. If you'll be chasing the grape around the Barossa, choose a designated driver or take a guided tour.

Public buses run infrequently to the major centers from Adelaide. There are no buses between wineries.

ORGANIZED TOURS FROM ADELAIDE   Various companies run limited sightseeing tours. One of the best, **Grayline Day Tours** (© **1300 858 687;** www.grayline.com), offers a day trip visiting three wineries and other attractions every day. It costs A$75 (U.S.$48.75) for adults and A$37 (U.S.$24) for children, including a restaurant lunch. It also offers a daylong Grand Barossa Tour stopping off at two wineries, the Adelaide Hills and Hahndorf. This costs A$85 (U.S.$55.25) for adults and A$49.50 (U.S.$32) for children, and heads out Mondays through Wednesdays and Fridays in summer (Wed and Fri in winter). Both tours depart at 9am from the bus terminal at 101 Franklin Street, Adelaide.

VISITOR INFORMATION   The excellent **Barossa Wine and Visitor Centre,** 66–68 Murray St., Tanunda, SA 5352 (© **08/8563 0600;** www.barossaregion.org), is open Monday through Friday from 9am to 5pm, and Saturday and Sunday from 10am to 4pm. It's worth popping into the center's small audiovisual display for an introduction to the world of wine; entry is A$2.75 (U.S.$1.80) for adults, free for children. You'll need a least an hour to look around.

Wines are often cheaper at the **Tanunda Cellars 'bottleshop',** or retail outlet, located at 14 Murray Street, Tanunda (© **08/8563 3544;** tanundacellars@dove.com.au) than at the winery door. This historic 1858 stone bottleshop also houses one of Australia's finest collections of vintage wines, so pop in if you really appreciate wines.

TOURING THE WINERIES

With some 48 wineries offering free cellar-door tastings and/or daily tours charting the wine-making process, you won't be stuck for places to visit. All wineries are well-signposted. Below are just a few of my favorite places, but don't be shy about just stopping whenever you come across a winery that takes your fancy. A tip: Try a sparkling red. It may turn up noses elsewhere, and it takes some getting used to, but bearing in mind the world's wine industry now hangs on Australia's every wine offering, it may well be the great tipple of the future.

Orlando   This large winery was established in 1847 and is today the home of many award-winning brands. Its big seller is the well-known Jacobs Creek brand, now sold worldwide. Premium wines include the Lawson Shiraz and the Jacaranda Ridge Cabernet, and new vintages of either will set you back at least A$45 (U.S.$29.25) a bottle. There is an opal shop, a craft shop, and a picnic area with barbecues.

Barossa Hwy., Rowland Flat. © **08/8521 3140.** Mon–Fri 10am–5pm, Sat–Sun and public holidays 10am–4pm.

Penfolds   Australia's biggest wine producer churns out some 22.5 million liters (5.8 million U.S. gal.) from this one winery every year. Penfolds also owns other wineries all over the country. It all started when Dr. Christopher Rawson

The Barossa

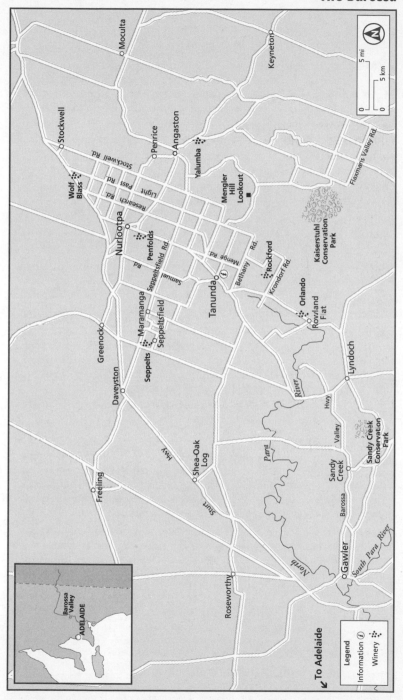

Legend

Information ⓘ

Winery ⋮⋮⋮

← **To Adelaide**

planted a few vines in 1844 to make wine for his patients. The winery now houses the largest oak barrel maturation cellars in the Southern Hemisphere. Nuriootpa. ✆ 08/8301 5400. Mon–Sun 10am–4:30pm.

Rockford   Most of the buildings here were constructed in 1984 out of recycled local materials, but you'd never know. The wine is pressed between mid-March and the end of April, in the traditional way with machinery from the turn of the 20th century. It's a fascinating sight. Demand for Rockford wines, especially the Basket Pressed Shiraz, far exceeds supply. Krondorf Rd., Tanunda. ✆ 08/8563 2720. Mon–Sat 11am–5pm.

Seppelts   This National Trust–listed property was founded in 1857 by Joseph Seppelt, an immigrant from Silesia. The wine tour around the gardens and bluestone buildings is considered one of the best in the world. Check out the family's giant Romanesque mausoleum on a nearby slope, skirted by planted roadside palms, built during the 1930s recession to keep winery workers employed. Seppeltsfield. ✆ 08/8562 8028. Adults A$5 (U.S.$3.25), children 5–16 A$2 (U.S.$1.30). Mon–Fri 10am–5pm, Sat–Sun 11am–5pm. Tours hourly Mon–Fri 11am–3pm, Sat–Sun 11:30am, 1:30, and 2:30pm.

Wolf Blass   This winery's Germanic-style black-label vintages have an excellent international reputation, while its cheaper yellow-label vintages are the toast of many a Sydney dinner party. The small Wolf Blass museum is worth a peek. Strut Hwy., Nuriootpa. ✆ 08/8568 7300. Mon–Fri 9am–5pm, Sat–Sun 10am–5pm.

Yalumba   This winery was built in 1849, making it the oldest family-owned wine-making business in Australia. It's also huge. Look out for the sad-looking Himalayan bear in the corner of the large tasting room; following a run-in with a hunting rifle, it's been Yalumba's advertising gimmick. The winery's Signature Red Cabernet-Shiraz is among the best you'll ever taste. Eden Valley Rd., Angaston. ✆ 08/8561 3200. www.yalumba.com.au. Mon–Fri 8:30am–5pm, Sat 10am–5pm, Sun noon–5pm.

WHERE TO STAY

There are plenty of standard motels and lots of interesting B&Bs throughout the Barossa, some with rooms for as little as A$60 (U.S.$39). Weekends often find rooms are often booked out and prices higher than weekdays. The **Barossa Wine and Visitor Centre** (see "Visitor Information," above) can provide information on additional accommodation choices and off-season deals.

Barossa Park Motel   Unlike your average motor inn, this one is set well back from the road within its own large grounds. The rooms are quite large, and some interconnect, which can be handy if you are traveling with a family. All rooms are comfortable and clean, and have a queen-size bed and at least another single. All have connecting bathrooms with a shower. Executive doubles are slightly plusher. Barossa Valley Hwy., Lyndoch (P.O. Box 370, Lyndoch, SA 5351). ✆ 08/8524 4268. Fax 08/8524 4725. 34 units. A$90 (U.S.$58.50) double; A$100 (U.S.$65) executive double; A$146 (U.S.$95) including dinner. Extra adult A$13 (U.S.$8.50), extra child under 12 A$8 (U.S.$5.20). Ask about packages. AE, DC, MC, V. **Amenities:** Restaurant; outdoor pool; spa; games room. *In room:* A/C, TV, minibar, coffeemaker, iron.

Barossa Valley (SA) Tourist Park   This very peaceful place is set way back from the road and abuts a nature lake and wildlife reserve. The cabins are simple affairs but come with just about everything you'll need for a pleasant enough stay. Cabins have a combination of doubles, singles, and bunk beds. If you don't have your own linen you'll be charged A$5 (U.S.$3.25) per single bed and A$10 (U.S.$6.50) per double.

Penrice Rd., Nuriootpa 5355. ℂ 08/8562 1404. Fax 08 85622 615. www.barossa.touristpark.com.au. 27 cabins, 19 with bathroom. A$30 (U.S.$19.50) double without bathroom; A$45–$60 (U.S.$29.25–$39) double with bathroom. Extra adult A$5 (U.S.$3.25), extra child 3–15 A$3 (U.S.$1.95). AE, DC, MC, V. **Amenities:** Pool (nearby); 2 tennis courts; laundry. *In room:* A/C, TV, kitchenette, coffeemaker, iron.

Collingrove Homestead 𝒶𝒶𝒶 *Finds*   In my opinion, Collingrove is not just the best country-house experience in the Barossa but, dare I say it, anywhere in Australia. It was originally the home of John Howard Angas, one of those involved in the initial settlement of South Australia. Built in 1856, additions were made as Angas's successful sheep business prospered. The hallway is festooned with spears, artillery shells, rifles, oil-painted portraits, and the mounted heads of various stags and tigers. English oak paneling and creaky floorboards add a certain nuance, and the cedar kitchen, library, glorious dining room, and various other places are all bursting with antiques and knickknacks. What the quaint, individually decorated guest rooms lack in modern amenities—no phones or TVs—they make up for in charm. The modern communal spa is set in the old stables, with its flagstone floors and old horse harnesses; there's also a flagstone-floored tennis court. Even if you don't stay here, visitors can indulge in Devonshire tea on the terrace daily for A$5 (U.S.$3.25) and can tour the property Monday through Friday from 1 to 4:30pm and Saturday and Sunday from 11am to 4:30pm. The tour costs A$4 (U.S.$2.60) for adults and A$1.50 (U.S.$1) for children. Sunday brunch is also popular. Dinner by prior arrangement for guests costs $95 per person.

Eden Valley Rd., Angaston, SA 5353. ℂ 08/8564 2061. Fax 08/8564 3600. www.collingwoodhomestead. com.au. 6 units, 4 with bathroom. A$170 (U.S.$110) double without bathroom; A$210–$250 (U.S.$136.50–$162.50) double with bathroom. Rates include full breakfast. AE, DC, MC, V. **Amenities:** Restaurant; tennis court; spa; in-room massage; babysitting; nonsmoking rooms. *In room:* TV with pay movies (room 5 only), minibar (room 5 only), hair dryer.

The Hermitage of Marananga 𝒶   This is far and away the best of the area's motels. The rooms are awkwardly shaped but have been recently renovated. Each has a small balcony. The main building is old-fashioned and bursting with character. It's also cool in the heat of summer. Outside there are fantastic views over the valley and to the ranges beyond. Good walks lead around the property, and at dusk you'll see plenty of kangaroos in the surrounding fields. The new apartment has a private balcony overlooking the vineyards, a separate bedroom, and a double sleeper sofa in the living room.

Corner of Seppltsfield and Stonewell rds., Marananga, SA 5351. ℂ 08/8562 2722. Fax 08/8562 3133. thehermitage@dove.net.au. 11 units, including 1 apt. A$190 (U.S.$123.50) double; A$230 (U.S.$149.50) spa room; $230 (U.S.$149.50) apt. Rates include breakfast. AE, DC, MC, V. **Amenities:** Restaurant; swimming pool; spa. *In room:* A/C, TV, minibar, coffeemaker.

Marble Lodge 𝒶𝒶   Wake up and smell the roses—there are plenty of them in the beautiful gardens surrounding this romantic historic property (as well as a tennis court, and several deer and kangaroos). Away from the main house is a lodge made of local marble that's divided into two suites. The larger suite has two rooms and an open fireplace. The second is basically a large bed/sitting room, with an open fireplace. Both suites have access to the shared spa bath and are tastefully furnished in antiques. There's always fresh fruit, homemade biscuits, and chocolates in the room, and it's a 5-minute walk to three local restaurants. A double room, with shared bathroom, is sometimes available in the homestead itself.

21 Dean St., Angaston, SA 5351. (℃) **08/8564 2478.** Fax 08/8564 2941. www.marblelodge.com.au. 2 units. A$170 (U.S.$110.50) suite. Rate includes breakfast, bottle of champagne, and minibar drinks. MC, V. **Amenities:** Tennis court; spa; e-mail facilities; laundry service; nonsmoking rooms. *In room:* A/C, TV with pay movies, fax, dataport, fridge, coffeemaker, hair dryer, iron.

WHERE TO DINE

The Barossa prides itself on its cuisine as well as its wine, so you'll find plenty of places of note to eat, many of them serving up traditional German foods in line with the area's heritage. Put the **1918 Bistro & Grill,** 94 Murray St., Tanunda (℃ **08/8563 0405**) on top of your list. Appetizers, ranging in price from A$8.90 (U.S.$5.80) to A$13 (U.S.$8.45), are enough to fill you up. I recommend the baked mushrooms. Another hot spot, for lunch or dinner, is **Vintner's Bar & Grill,** Nuriootpa Road, Angaston (℃ **08/8564 2488**); the wine list here is six pages long! Main courses cost A$15 (U.S.$9.75) to A$19 (U.S.$12.35). Both restaurants serve essentially Modern Australian cuisine. You'll find perhaps the valley's best German-style bakery in Lyndoch, the **Lyndoch Bakery,** on the Barossa Highway (℃ **08/8524 4422**). In Angaston you must stop off at the **Angas Park Hotel,** 28 Murray St. (℃ **08/8562 1050**), which serves up home-cooked meals.

THE ADELAIDE HILLS

Only a 25-minute drive from Adelaide and visible even from the main shopping street, you'll find the tree-lined slopes and pretty valleys, orchards, vineyards, winding roads, and historic townships of the **Adelaide Hills.** You might want to walk part of the Heysen Trail (see "Enjoying the Great Outdoors" in the Adelaide section earlier in this chapter), browse through the shops in Hahndorf, stop in Melba's Chocolate Factory in Woodside, or visit Cleland Wildlife Park or Warrawong Sanctuary. Otherwise, it's a nice outing just to hit the road and drive. Should you decide to stay overnight, the area offers lots of cozy B&Bs.

ESSENTIALS

GETTING THERE   The Adelaide Hills are just 25 minutes from Adelaide by car via Greenhill and Glen Osmond roads. **Adelaide Sightseeing** (℃ **08/8231 4144**) runs outings to the gorgeous little town of Hahndorf (see below) as well as to Cleland Wildlife Park. An afternoon excursion to Hahndorf costs A$30 (U.S.$13.65) for adults and A$20 (U.S.$13) for children; the tour to Cleland costs A$26 (U.S.$16.90) for adults and A$20 (U.S.$13) for children, including park entry.

VISITOR INFORMATION   Visitor information and bookings are available through the **Adelaide Hills Tourist Information Centre,** 41 Main St., Hahndorf (℃ **08/8388 1185**). It's open Monday through Friday from 9am to 4pm. Otherwise, detailed maps are available at the **South Australia Travel Centre** in Adelaide.

WOODSIDE: CHOCOLATE LOVERS UNITE!

Visitors come here for **Melba's Chocolate Factory,** Henry Street (℃ **08/8389 7868**), where chocoholics will find a huge range of handmade chocolates to tempt the tastebuds. Melba's is part of Heritage Park, a complex that includes a wood turner, a cheese maker, a ceramics studio, a leather maker, and a craft shop. It's open Monday through Friday from 10am to 4pm; and Saturday, Sunday, and public holidays from noon to 5pm.

MYLOR: GETTING BACK TO NATURE

Mylor is located 25 kilometers (15 miles) southeast of Adelaide, and 10 kilometers (6 miles) south of Mt. Lofty via the town of Crafters. Here you'll find the **Warrawong Sanctuary,** Stock Road, Mylor (P.O. Box 1135), Stirling, SA 5152; © **08/8370 9197;** fax 08/8370 8332; www.efl.com.au). Unlike in many other wildlife parks, the animals here are not kept in enclosed runs. Instead, park founder Dr. John Wamsley took a 35-acre tract of former farming land, replanted it with natural bush, fenced it off, and went around shooting the introduced rabbits, cats, dogs, and foxes that plague much of Australia. Then the good doctor took to reintroducing animals native to the site—such as kangaroos, various types of wallabies, bandicoots, beetongs, platypuses, possums, frogs, birds, and reptiles. They are all thriving, not only because he eliminated their unnatural predators, but also because he re-created waterways, rain forests, and black-water ponds. The animals roam free, and you're guided through on 1½-hour dawn or sunset walks that costs A$18 (U.S.$11.70) for adults and A$12 (U.S.$7.80) for children. There's a restaurant on the premises, and you can even stay overnight in large cabins with bathrooms, wall-to-wall carpeting, and air-conditioning. The cabins cost A$125 (U.S.$81.25) per person with both dawn and dusk tours, a two-course dinner, and breakfast.

Compared to **Cleland Wildlife Park** (see below), there is less variety of animals here (you won't find any koalas for example), but it's more educational and you get the feeling that you're in the wild rather than in a zoo.

HAHNDORF: GERMAN HERITAGE, CRAFTS & MORE ✿

This historic German-style village is one of South Australia's most popular tourist destinations. The town, located 29 kilometers (18 miles) southeast of Adelaide, was founded in 1839 by Lutherans fleeing religious persecution in their homeland of eastern Prussia. They brought with them their wine-making skills, foods, and architectural inheritance and put it all together here. Hahndorf still resembles a small German town in appearance and atmosphere, and is included on the World Heritage List as a Historical German Settlement. Walking around you'll notice St. Paul's Lutheran Church, erected in 1890. The Wool Factory, L'Unique Fine Arts & Craft, and Bamfurlong Fine Crafts are all worth checking out and are all within walking distance of Main Street.

Busway Travel (© **08/8410 6888;** fax 08/8410 3833) operates half-day tours daily to Hahndorf, including a German lunch, and a visit to Mt. Lofty summit (see below). Tours cost A$28 (U.S.$18.20) for adults and A$19 (U.S.$12.35) for children. Tours leave from the Busway Travel offices on Bank Street, off North Terrace, in Adelaide.

Where to Stay

The Hahndorf Resort ✿   This large resort has a variety of accommodations available, as well as approximately 80 caravan and tent sites. Here too are fully self-contained, air-conditioned cabins, and motel-style rooms with queen-size beds (some have an extra single) and a shower. The chalets look like they're straight out of Bavaria; each can accommodate from two to five people in either one or two bedrooms. All have a full kitchen and an attached bathroom with shower. Some of them overlook a small lake. The spa chalets are larger and, of course, come with a spa bath. A few emus, kangaroos, and horses run around in an animal sanctuary.

145A Main St., Hahndorf, SA 5245. © **08/8388 7921.** Fax 08/8388 7282. 60 units. A$60.50 (U.S.$39) cabin; A$86.90 (U.S.$56.50) motel room; $97.90–$165 (U.S.$63.70–$107.25) chalet. A$11 (U.S.$7.15) extra adult; A$5.50 (U.S.$3.60) extra child. AE, DC, MC, V. **Amenities:** Restaurant; outdoor swimming pool; 2 putting greens; half-size tennis court; small gym; bike rental; room service; laundry. *In room:* A/C, TV, kitchenette, mini-bar, coffeemaker, iron.

Where to Dine

Karl's German Coffee Shop $\mathcal{R}$ GERMAN   Pop into this Bavarian beer-cellar-style eatery at anytime of day for good homemade cakes and coffee. At lunch, the ploughman's lunch goes down well, as do the German sausages with sauerkraut. Dinner favorites include seafood, steaks, and chicken dishes.

17 Main St., Hahndorf. © 08/8388 7171. Main courses A$3.90–$10.50 (U.S.$2.55–$6.80) at lunch; A$8.90–$13.90 (U.S.$5.80–$9) at dinner. AE, DC, MC, V. Wed–Sun 11am–10pm and public holidays.

OAKBANK: A DAY AT THE RACES

This is the spot for the Adelaide hills' biggest event, the **Easter Oakbank Racing Carnival,** part of the Australia-wide "picnic races" that take place in small towns throughout the nation. The Oakbank horse races attract crowds in excess of 70,000 a day over the long Easter weekend. General admission is A$9 (U.S.$5.85), plus another A$5 (U.S.$3.25) for admission to the grandstand. The **Oakbank Racing Club** (© **08/8212 6279**), is just off the main road; you can't miss it.

Where to Stay

Adelaide Hills Country Cottages $\mathcal{R}\mathcal{R}$ These three self-contained cottages have won several tourism awards, including the 1998 Australian Tourist Commission award for hosted accommodation in Australia—which is quite a big deal. They are 1 kilometer (0.6 miles) apart and are surrounded by 150 acres of scenic countryside. The Apple Tree cottage, from around 1860, sleeps up to five, has a spa bath and antiques, and overlooks an orchard and a lake; the Gum Tree Cottage sleeps four and has wonderful country views; and the Lavender Fields Cottage also sleeps up to four and overlooks a lily-fringed duck pond. All of the cottages have open fireplaces and fully equipped kitchens. This is a great place to relax and a good base for exploring the area. You'll get a couple of free drinks and a fruit basket upon arrival.

P.O. Box 100, Oakbank, SA 5243. © 08/8388 4193. Fax 08/8388 4733. www.ahcc.com.au. 5 cottages. A$160–$230 (U.S.$104.75–$149.50). Extra person A$60. Rates include provisions for breakfast. A 1-night rate will include a surcharge of A$30 (U.S.$19.50). Ask about lower weekly rates. AE, DC, MC, V. Oakbank is 30 min. from Adelaide, 7 min. from Hahndorf, and less than an hr. from the Barossa Valley. **Amenities:** Spa; laundry. *In room:* A/C, TV/VCR, kitchen, stocked fridge (with breakfast items), coffeemaker, hair dryer, iron, mobile phones for rent.

MT. LOFTY: VIEWS & 'ROOS

Visitors make the pilgrimage to the top of the 2,300-foot (690m) **Mt. Lofty,** 16 kilometers (10 miles) southeast of Adelaide, for the panoramic views over Adelaide, the surrounding Adelaide plains, and the Mt. Lofty Ranges. There are several nice bushwalks from the top. You can find the **Summit Restaurant** (© **08/8339 2600**) up here, too; it's open for lunch daily and dinner Wednesday through Sunday. Main courses cost between A$13.90 and A$19.90 (U.S.$9 to $12.95) and include roasted field mushrooms on polenta, roast duck breast with black rice, and veal porterhouse. In the same building is the **Summit Cafe,** selling good sandwiches and cakes, and Devonshire tea for A$6 (U.S.$3.90). The restaurant runs a limo service to Adelaide and back for up to four people for A$80 (U.S.$52) round-trip.

Almost at the top of Mt. Lofty, off Summit Road, is the **Cleland Wildlife Park** (© **08/8339 2444**). Here you'll find all the usual Australian animals on offer—including the largest male red kangaroo I've ever seen. Though the park is not nearly as good as similar wildlife parks elsewhere in Australia, it does have a very good wetlands aviary. One of the drawbacks of Cleland is that it's got some unimaginative enclosures, most notably the one for the Tasmanian devils. The park is open daily from 9:30am to 4:30pm. Visitors can meet at the Tasmanian devil enclosure at 2pm and join the animal feed run by following a tractor around the park as it drops off food.

Admission to Cleland is A$9.50 (U.S.$6.20) for adults, A$5.50 (U.S.$3.60) for children 3 to 14, and A$23.50 (U.S.$15.30) for families. Koala holding is allowed during the photo sessions held daily from 2 to 4pm daily (but not on very hot summer days); on Sunday and public holidays there's an additional session from 10am to noon. The privilege will cost you A$10 (U.S.$6.50) per photo. A kiosk and restaurant are on the premises.

It's a bit of a hassle getting to either place by public transport. To get to the Mount Lofty Lookout take Bus 163 Monday through Friday, and number 165 on weekends from Currie Street in the city. Ask the driver to drop you off at "Crafters." The trip takes 30 minutes. From there you'll need to take a short taxi ride to the top, so prearrange pick up with **Tony's Taxi's** at © **08/8388 5988.**

To get to Cleland take Bus 822 from Currie Street and get off at bus stop 19b. There are only two services daily, at 10am and noon, Monday through Friday. Take the 10am bus and ask the bus driver for the exact return time. The trip to Cleland takes 40 minutes.

3 Kangaroo Island ★★★

110km (68 miles) South of Adelaide

There is nowhere better than Kangaroo Island to see Australian marsupials in the wild. Spend a few days on the island with the right guide and you can walk along a beach past a colony of sea lions; spot hundreds of New Zealand fur seals playing together; creep through the bush on the trail of wallabies; stroke semi-tame kangaroos; spot sea eagles, black swans, sacred ibis, pelicans, fairy penguins, the rare glossy cockatoo and other birds; come across goannas and the island's lone emu; pick out bunches of koalas hanging sleepily in the trees above your head; and, if you're lucky, see platypus, echidna, bandicoots, reclusive pygmy possums—the list goes on.

The secrets to Kangaroo Island's success are its perfect conditions; the most important of which is the fact that there are no introduced foxes or rabbits to take their toll on the native inhabitants or their environment. The island was also never colonized by the dingo—Australia's "native" dog—which was believed to have been introduced from Asia some 4,000 years ago. About one-third of the island is unspoiled national park, and there are plenty of wildlife corridors to give the animals a chance to move about the island, lessening the problems of inbreeding.

While the animals are what most people come to see, no one goes away without also being impressed by the scenery. Kangaroo Island has low mallee scrubland, dense eucalyptus forests, rugged coastal scenery, gorgeous beaches, caves, lagoons, and black-water swamps. The effect of 150 years of European colonization has taken its toll, though. In South Australia as a whole some 27 mammal, 5 bird, 1 reptile, and 30 plant species have become extinct since the state was discovered by the English seafarer Matthew Flinders in 1802.

The island's history is a harsh one. Aboriginal people inhabited the island as early as 10,000 years ago but abandoned it for unexplained reasons. In the 19th century it was settled by pirates, mutineers, cutthroats, deserters from English,

French, and American ships, and escaped convicts from the eastern colonies. Sealers also arrived and took a heavy toll on the local seal and sea lion population—in just 1 year, 1803–04, they managed to kill more than 20,000 of these animals. Between 1802 and 1836, Aboriginal women from both the mainland and Tasmania were kidnapped, brought to Kangaroo Island, and forced to work catching and skinning seals, kangaroos, and wallabies, and lugging salt from the salt mines.

In 1836, Kangaroo Island became the first place in South Australia to be officially settled. The state's capital was Kingscote, until it was abandoned a couple of years later in favor of Adelaide. In spite of its early settlement, Kangaroo Island had very few residents until after World War II, when returned soldiers set up farms here. Today, more than a million sheep are raised on the island. The island also acts as an official bee sanctuary to protect the genetic purity of the Ligurian bee, introduced in 1881 and believed to be the only place in the world where this strain of bee survives.

ISLAND ESSENTIALS

WHEN TO GO   The best time to visit Kangaroo Island is between November and March (though you'll have difficulty finding accommodations over the Christmas school holiday period). July and August tend to be rainy, and winter can be cold (though often milder than on the mainland around Adelaide). Many companies offer 1-day trips to Kangaroo Island from Adelaide, but I would strongly advise you to tailor your holiday to spend at least 2 days here, though 3 or even 5 would be even better. There really is a lot to see, and you won't regret spending the extra time.

GETTING THERE   As this book went to press, Ansett and its subsidiaries (including **Kendell,** the only airline to service Kangaroo Island), filed for bankruptcy. It is unclear whether another airline will take over this route; if you want to get here by plane, I recommend contacting Qantas (✆ **13 13 13** in Australia; www.qantas.com.au) to see what kind of regional service is available. The flight from Adelaide to Kangaroo Island usually takes about 25 minutes.

If you prefer to go there by sea, **Kangaroo Island SeaLink** (✆ **13 13 01** in Australia, or 08/8202 8688; www.sealink.com.au), operates two ocean-going, vehicle, and passenger ferries four times daily (sometimes 10 times in peak periods) from Cape Jervis on the tip of the mainland to Penneshaw on Kangaroo Island. The trip takes 40 minutes and costs A$64 (U.S.$41.60) round-trip for adults, A$32 (U.S.$20.80) for children 3 to 14, and A$138 (U.S.$90) for cars. Connecting bus service from Adelaide to Cape Jervis is provided at an extra A$32 (U.S.$20.80) for adults round-trip, and A$16 (U.S.$10.40) for children. Count on 3 hours for the whole trip from Adelaide if you take the connecting bus. SeaLink also run a range of island tours, including the 2-day/1-night "Ultimate Touring Adventure" which costs from $249 (U.S.$161.85) per person twin share.

VISITOR INFORMATION   Tourism Kangaroo Island, The Gateway Information Centre, Howard Drive, Penneshaw (P.O. Box 336, Penneshaw, Kangaroo Island, SA 5222; ✆ **08/8553 1185;** fax 08/8553 1255; www.tourkangarooisland.com.au), has plenty of maps and information and can book accommodations and island tours. For more information on the island's national parks contact the **National Parks and Wildlife Service (NPWS)** office, 39 Dauncey St. (P.O. Box 39), Kingscote, SA 5223 (✆ **08/8553 2381;** fax 08/8553 2531), open Monday through Friday from 9am to 5pm.

Tips   **An Island Bargain**

I'd advise buying an **NPWS Island Pass** if you'll be exploring the island on your own. It costs A$28 (U.S.$18.20) for adults, A$22 (U.S.$14.30) for children, and A$77 (U.S.$50) for families and includes guided tours of Seal Bay, Kelly Hill Caves, Cape Borda, and Cape Willoughby; also included is access to Flinders Chase National Park, where a A$13 (U.S.$8.45) charge per vehicle is usually levied. The pass doesn't cover penguin tours or camping fees.

In addition, hotel and motel staff generally carry a stack of tourist brochures and can point you in the right direction as far as where to go and what to see.

ISLAND LAYOUT   Kangaroo Island is Australia's third largest island, at 156 kilometers (97 miles) long and 57 kilometers (35 miles) wide at its widest point. The distance across the narrowest point is only 2 kilometers (1.25 miles). Approximately 3,900 people live on the island. More than half the population lives on the northeast coast of the island in one of the three main towns: Kingscote (pop. 1,800), Penneshaw (pop. 250), and American River (pop. 200). The island's major attractions, however, are located farther from the mainland; Flinders Chase National Park is in the far west, Lathami Conservation Park is on the north coast, and Seal Bay and Kelly's Caves are on the south coast.

GETTING AROUND   Apart from a bus service which connects Kingscote, Penneshaw, and American River, there is no public transport on the island. An **Airport Shuttle Service** (© 08/8553 2390) can transport you from Kingscote Airport to your Kingscote accommodation. The 15-minute trip costs A$11 (U.S.$7.15) for adults and A$6 (U.S.$3.90) for children. The shuttle meets all Kendell flights.

Major roads between Penneshaw, American River, Kingscote, and Parndana are paved, as is the road to Seal Bay. Most other roads are made of ironstone gravel, and can be very slippery if corners are approached too quickly. All roads are accessible by two-wheel-drive vehicles, but if you're bringing over a rental car from the mainland make sure your policy allows you to drive on Kangaroo Island's roads. Avoid driving at night—animals rarely fare best in a car collision.

Cars rental agencies on the island include **Budget** (© 08/8553 3133 or 08/8553 1034; fax 08/8553 2888), **Hertz & Kangaroo Island Rental Cars** (© 1800 088 296 in Australia, or 08/8553 2390; fax 08/8553 2878). You can pick up cars at the airport or ferry terminals.

ORGANIZED TOURS   If you want to keep expenses down, you can't go wrong with one of the tours organized by **Penneshaw Youth Hostel,** 43 North Terrace, Penneshaw, Kangaroo Island, SA 5222 (© 08/8553 1284; fax 08/8553 1295; advhost@kin.on.net). The most popular includes an afternoon pick up from the main bus station in Adelaide, coach and ferry to the island, a penguin tour that evening, and dorm accommodation (you can pay a little extra to upgrade to a double room, but book ahead). The next day involves 10 hours of touring, taking in most of the main attractions. That evening you return to Adelaide. The tour—entitled "the Sunset Tour"—costs A$176 (U.S.$114.40).

Another interesting tour arranged by these guys includes a dive (novices should contact the hostel to find about basic training). This costs A$265 (U.S.$172.25).

More expensive options include a tour by **Kangaroo Island Wilderness Tours** (② **08/8559 2220;** fax 08/8559 2288), which operates several small four-wheel-drive vehicles (maximum six people) and takes visitors around the islands on very informative 1-day trips costing A$205 (U.S.$133.25) per person, including transfers, an excellent lunch with wine, and park entry fees. Two-, three-, and four-day trips, with all meals and accommodations included, cost A$513 (U.S.$333.45), A$821(U.S.$533.65), and A$1,129 (U.S.$733.85) respectively.

Another excellent operator is **Adventure Charters of Kangaroo Island,** Playford Highway, Cygnet River, SA 5223 (② **08/8553 9119;** fax 08/8553 9122), with the knowledgeable and gregarious Craig Wickham at the helm. Day trips cost A$225 (U.S.$146.25) a day with a big lunch, or A$402 (U.S.$261.30) for a 1-day safari including Kendell flights from and to Adelaide.

Kangaroo Island Odysseys, P.O. Box 494, Penneshaw, SA 5222 (② **08/ 8553 1311;** fax 08/8553 1294) offers a similar day trip in small vehicles for A$215 (U.S.$139.75) per person, including lunch.

EXPLORING THE ISLAND

The island is much bigger than you might think, and you can spend a fair bit of time just getting from one place of interest to the next. Of the many, many places to see on the island, **Flinders Chase National Park** ⍟ is one of the most important. It took 30 years of lobbying until reluctant politicians finally agreed to preserve this unique western region of the island in 1919. Today, it makes up around 17% of the island and is home to true wilderness, some beautiful coastal scenery, two old lighthouses, and plenty of animals. Bird-watchers have recorded at least 243 species of birds here. Koalas are so common in parts that they're almost falling out of the trees. Platypus have been seen, but you'll probably need to make a special effort and sit next to a stream in the dark for a few hours for any chance of spotting one. In the works are plans to develop a series of walking trails, boardwalks, and platypus observation hides at the Rocky River Waterhole, which should greatly increase visitors chances of viewing the elusive critters. Kangaroos, wallabies, and brush-tailed possums, on the other hand, are so tame and numerous that the authorities were forced to erect a barrier around the Rocky River Campground to stop them from carrying away picnickers' sandwiches!

The most impressive coastal scenery can be found at **Cape du Couedic** at the southern tip of the park, where millions of years of crashing ocean have created curious structures—like the hollowed-out limestone promontory called Admiral's Arch and the aptly named Remarkable Rocks, where you'll see huge boulders balancing on top of a massive granite dome. At Admiral's Arch there is a colony of some 4,000 New Zealand fur seals that are easily spotted playing in the rock pools and resting on the rocks. During rough weather this place can be spectacular. Recently, the road from Rocky River Park Headquarters to Admiral's Arch and Remarkable Rocks was paved to within 4 kilometers (2.5 miles) of Rocky River. A new parking lot and loop trail also has been developed at Remarkable Rocks. There's also a new road, parking lot, and trail system around the Cape du Couedic heritage lighthouse district.

Don't Feed the Animals, Please

Don't feed *any* native animals. Kangaroos and wallabies might beg for food, but they are lactose-intolerant and can go blind, or catch disease, from being fed human food.

Culling Koalas—A National Dilemma

Koalas are cute. They're fluffy, they're sleepy, and they're awesomely cuddly. The problem is they eat an awful lot. In the early 1920s, 18 koalas were introduced to Kangaroo Island, where they had never existed before. Over the years, without predators and disease, and with an abundant supply of their favorite eucalyptus trees, they have prospered. By 1996, there were an estimated 4,000 koalas on the island, and their favorite trees were looking decidedly ragged. Some of the koalas were already suffering; some people even claimed the animals were starving to death.

The South Australian Government decided the only option was to shoot Australia's ambassador to the world. The public outcry was enormous; Japan even threatened to advise their citizens to boycott Down Under. But what could be done? Some scientists maintained that the koalas could not be relocated to the mainland because there were few places left to put them. Conservationists blamed Kangaroo Island's farmers for depleting the island of more than 50% of its vegetation. The koala is endangered, and the smaller northern variety is threatened with extinction in New South Wales; and the larger subspecies in Victoria, which includes the Kangaroo Island koalas, are also under threat. A compromise was reached; the koalas are to be trapped and neutered, a few thousand per year, until their numbers stabilize. A few conscientious farmers will plant more trees. Other farmers will, no doubt, continue to see the koalas as pests.

Elsewhere on the island, you shouldn't miss out on the unforgettable experience of walking through a colony of Australian sea lions at Seal Bay. The **Seal Bay Conservation Park** was declared in 1972, and these days some 100,000 people visit it each year. Boardwalks have been built through the dunes to the beach to reduce the impact of so many feet. The colony consists of about 500 animals, but at any one time you might see up to 100 basking with their pups here. The rangers who supervise the area lead guided trips throughout the day, every 15 to 30 minutes from 9am to 4:15pm. If you come here without a coach group, you must join a tour. Tours cost A$10 (U.S.$6.50) for an adult and A$7 (U.S.$4.55) for children.

Lathami Conservation Park, just to the east of Stokes Bay, is a wonderful place to see wallabies in the wild. Just dip in under the low canopy of casuarina pines and walk silently, keeping your eyes peeled, and you're almost certain to spot them. If you're fortunate you may even come across a very rare glossy cockatoo—it's big and black and feeds mainly on casuarina nuts.

Another interesting spot, especially for bird watchers, is **Murray Lagoon,** on the northern edge of Cape Gantheaume Conservation Park. It's the largest lagoon on the island and an important habitat for thousands of water birds. Contact the NPWS (see "Visitor Information," above) for information on a ranger-guided Wetland Wade.

If you want to see **fairy penguins**—tiny animals that stand just 33 centimeters (13 in.) tall—forget the touristy show at Phillip Island near Melbourne. On

Kangaroo Island you get to see them in a totally natural environment. Tours are conducted nightly by the NPWS (see "Visitor Information," above) and cost A$10 (U.S.$6.50) for adults and A$7 (U.S.$4.55) for children. Times of tours change seasonally, so call NPWS to confirm. Tours of a colony near Penneshaw gather at the Interpretive Centre adjacent to the penguins, and tours of the Kingscote colony meet at the reception desk of the Ozone Hotel.

For a fabulous day **boat fishing** for everything from King George Whiting, trevally, and snapper to mullet and mackerel contact **Kangaroo Island Fishing Charters** (© **08/8553 5247**). A day out costs $110 (U.S.$71.50), including lunch.

Finally, Kangaroo Island is renowned for its fresh food, and across the island you'll see signs beckoning to you to come and have a taste of cheese, honey, wine, or such like. One place worth stopping off at is **Clifford's Honey Farm** (© **08/8553 8295**), which is open daily from 9am to 5pm. The farm is the home of the protected Ligurian honeybee, found nowhere else on earth but on the island.

WHERE TO STAY

There are more than 40 places to choose from on the island, from cozy B&Bs to campgrounds. If you feel like sleeping out in one of 40 self-contained cottages or coastal lodgings, then contact **Kangaroo Island Remote and Coastal Farm Accommodation** (© **08/8553 1233;** fax 08/8553 1190; www.ki-ferry connections.com). Standards vary and prices range from A$65 to A$100 (U.S.$42.25 to $65) for each property. The staff can also arrange lodgings in local farms, homes, and B&Bs for A$60 to $110 (U.S.$39 to $71.50) for a double with breakfast.

The NPWS (see "Visitor Information," above) also offers basic but comfortable lodgings for rent, including relatively isolated **lighthouse cottages** 🏨🏨 at Cape Willoughby, Cape Borda, and Cape du Couedic, from A$21 to $36.50 (U.S.$13.65–$23.75) per adult per night—though the minimum charge per stay is between A$49 and $110 (U.S.$31.85 and $71.50) a cottage.

If you're on a super-tight budget, head to the **Penneshaw Youth Hostel,** 43 North Terrace, Penneshaw, Kangaroo Island, SA 5222 (© **08/8553 1284;** fax 08/8553 1295), with dorm beds for A$16 (U.S.$10.40) and doubles for A$38 (U.S.$24.70). It costs A$1 (U.S.65¢) less for YHA members.

Camping is allowed only at designated sites for a minimal fee, the main place being at Rocky River in Flinders Chase National Park.

IN & NEAR KINGSCOTE

Ozone Seafront Hotel   The best known of Kangaroo Island's lodging alternatives, the Ozone gets its name from the aroma from the sea—which virtually laps at its door. It's a nice, centrally located choice offering comfortable rooms with plenty of space; the majority of the more expensive ones have water views of Nepean Bay. Family rooms have a double bed and two single beds.

The Foreshore (P.O. Box 145), Kingscote, SA 5223. © **08/8553 2011.** Fax 08/8553 2249. www.ozonehotel. com. 37 units. A$104–$127 (U.S.$67.60–$82.55) double; A$116–$139 (U.S.$75.40–$90) triple. Extra person A$12. AE, DC, MC, V. **Amenities:** 2 restaurants, 3 bars; outdoor pool; golf course nearby; spa; sauna; baby sitting; laundry service. *In room:* A/C, TV, unstocked fridge, coffeemaker, hair dryer, iron.

Wisteria Lodge 🏨   All rooms at the modern and definitely unglamorous-looking Wisteria Lodge are standard motel-type, boosted by ocean views over Nepean Bay. Deluxe rooms offer a spa bath and queen-size beds. Reservations are essential for the restaurant.

7 Cygnet Rd., Kingscote, SA 5223. ℂ **08/8553 2707.** Fax 08/8553 2200. www.wisterialodge.com.au. Reservations can be made through Flag Inns (ℂ **800/624-3524** in the U.S. and Canada, 0800/892 407 in the U.K., 0800/803 524 in New Zealand, 13 24 00 in Australia). 20 units. A$130 (U.S.$84.50) double; A$148 (U.S.$96.20) triple; A$165 (U.S.$107.25) double spa room; A$185 (U.S.$120) triple spa room. Extra adult A$18–$20 (U.S.$11.70–$13); extra child 3–12 A$14–$17 (U.S.$9.10–$11). Breakfast A$11.50 (U.S.$7.50) extra. Ask about money-saving packages (with transport to the island, transfers, meals, and day tours). AE, DC, MC, V. **Amenities:** Restaurant; outdoor pool; half tennis court; spa; children's center; car-rental desk; limited business center; laundry/dry cleaning service; nonsmoking rooms. *In room:* A/C, TV, minibar, coffeemaker, hair dryer.

IN AMERICAN RIVER

Popular with fishermen and located 37 kilometers (23 miles) from Kingscote, American River lacks a beach but offers black swans on Pelican Lagoon instead. Wild wallabies abound, and egrets, magpies, and cockatoos offer early morning wake-up calls.

Casuarina Holiday Units   These simple, country-style units are not flash, but they offer a clean and cozy budget option. Each comes with a double bed, two singles, and an attached shower.

9 Ryberg Rd., American River, SA 5221. ℂ and fax **08/8553 7020.** 6 units. A$60 (U.S.$39) double; A$50 (U.S.$32.50) for more than 1 night. MC, V. **Amenities:** Children's playground; laundry; barbecue; fish-cleaning facilities. *In room:* TV.

Kangaroo Island Lodge ⚡   Though Kangaroo Island Lodge was originally built in 1801, renovations in late 1999 have so completely overhauled the place that you would be hard pressed to find anything rustic remaining. What you have though is a very nicely appointed property with pleasant, quiet motel-style rooms, a good swimming pool, spa and sauna, and a nice restaurant and bar (mains average $17.50/U.S.$11.40). The lodge looks over Pelican Lagoon (rightly famous for its pelicans), but it's a little too far away from it to make the water-view double rooms really worth the extra cost.

Scenic Road, American River, SA 5221. ℂ **08/8553 7053.** Fax 08/8553 7030. www.kangarooislandlodge. com.au. 38 units. A$157 (U.S.$102) water-view doubles; A$127 (U.S.$82.55) poolside double. A$17 (U.S.$11) extra person. AE, DC, MC, V. **Amenities:** Restaurant; outdoor pool; unlit tennis court; spa; sauna; tour desk; car-rental desk; room service (breakfast and dinner); coin-op laundry; nonsmoking rooms. *In room:* A/C, TV, kitchen, unstocked fridge, hair dryer, iron.

Wanderers Rest   This pleasant guest house is set on a hillside with panoramic views across the sea to the mainland. It has large, comfortably furnished rooms with balconies. All rooms come with king-size beds that convert to twins. You get a shower, but no tub. Breakfasts are hearty, packed lunches are available, and dinnertime can be a hoot, with guests sipping beers and wine around the dining room table and tucking into King George whiting caught that day. There are other meals available, such as steak, lamb chops, local oysters, and a vegetarian stir-fry.

Bayview Road (P.O. Box 34), American River, SA 5221. ℂ **08/8553 7140.** Fax 08/8553 7282. www. wanderersrest.com.au. 9 units. A$174 (U.S.$113) double; A$224 (U.S.$145.60) triple. Rates include full breakfast. Ask about value packages and ferry transport deals. AE, DC, MC, V. Children under 12 not accepted. **Amenities:** Restaurant; outdoor pool; spa; games room; tour desk; coin-op laundry. *In room:* TV, minibar.

IN PARNDANA

Developed by soldier-settlers after World War II, Parndana today is a rural service center situated a 25-minute drive from Seal Bay and Stokes Bay, and just around the corner from Parndana Wildlife Park, which has more than 50 aviaries with collections of native and other birds, some of them rare and protected.

The Open House ☆ The best thing about the Open House is mealtimes, when the guests get together and sit around a communal table and tuck into delicious home-cooked meals. The rooms—two with double beds, one with a queen size bed, one with two singles, and a family room sleeping up to four— are comfortable and homey and come with a private bathroom with shower. The very friendly owner, Sarah Wall, took over the house in June 1998, soon after she moved here, but she can already offer excellent advice on what to do around the island, and whips up a mean packed lunch for A$22 (U.S.$14.30).

70 Smith St., Parndana, SA 5221. © 08/8559 6113. Fax 08/8559 6088. 4 units. A$129 (U.S.$83.90) per person with dinner and breakfast included; A$99 (U.S.$64) per person with just breakfast included. A$99 (U.S.$64) per child under 14 with dinner and breakfast included; A$80.50 (U.S.$52.30) per child with just breakfast included. MC, V. **Amenities:** Restaurant; tour desk; laundry facilities.

OTHER PLACES
Hanson Bay Cabins ☆ *Finds* Located on the southwest coast of the island on the South Coast Road, Hanson Bay Cabins are a row of four comfortable log cabins perched above a fabulous beach. The cabins each have a large picture window facing the southern ocean, and come with a full kitchen, a bathroom, two bedrooms (including a double bed and three singles in all), and a wood stove. Bring your own food and supplies from Kingscote, American River, or Penneshaw. The ocean can get really wild and dramatic around here with strong offshore winds whipping up the sand and spray. The cottages are near to most of the major attractions so make a good base. Salmon are often caught off the beach.

Hanson Bay Company, P.O. Box 614, Kingscote, SA 5225. © 08/8853 2603. Fax 08/8853 2673. 6 units. A$110–$120 (U.S.$71.50–$78) cabin for 2. $17 (U.S.$11) each extra adult. A$11 (U.S.$7.15) extra child. There's a A$17 (U.S.$11) surcharge for staying only 1 night. AE, DC, MC, V. *In room:* Kitchen; fridge; coffeemaker; hair dryer; iron.

WHERE TO DINE
You'll find that most accommodations on Kangaroo Island provide meals for guests (at an additional cost, usually). In addition, most day tours around the island include lunch. You'll find a few cheap take-out booths scattered around the island at the most popular tourist spots. For lunch you could get sandwiches at the deli on Dauncey Street, behind the Ozone Hotel, in Kingscote.

IN PENNESHAW
Cape Willoughby Café ☆☆ LOCAL PRODUCE This fabulous restaurant is perched on a cliff-top on the far eastern tip of the island, right next to Cape Willoughby Lighthouse (an attraction in itself). One wall is all glass, and there's a veranda outside with terrific ocean views. King George Whiting is a specialty, as are the desserts (the sticky date pudding is mouthwatering). 45-minute tours of the lighthouse leave from the lighthouse office at 10, 11am, 12:30, and 2pm daily. They cost $6 (U.S.$3.90) for adults, A$4.50 (U.S.$2.90) for children, and A$16.50 (U.S.$10.70) a family.

Cape Willoughby. © 08/8553 1333. Main courses A$12–$17 (U.S.$7.80–$11). AE, DC, MC, V. Open 10am–4pm for coffee and cakes, and noon–3pm for lunch. Booking essential for lunch.

Dolphin Rock Café FAST FOOD Plastic tables and chairs and budget meals are what's offered here. Very popular with backpackers are the budget meals including individual pizzas, and french fries and gravy. Also on offer are fish-and-chips, hamburgers, and roasted chicken. Across the road, the fairy penguins come in at dusk.

43 North Terrace (next to the YHA). © 08/8553 1284. Main courses A$3–$9.50 (U.S.$1.95–$6.20). AE, MC, V. Winter Wed–Mon 7:30am–7:30pm; summer daily 7am–8:30pm.

4 Outback South Australia

South Australia is the driest state in Australia. This is well borne out once you leave behind the parklands of Adelaide and head into the interior. The Outback is as harsh as it is beautiful. Much of it is made up of stony desert, salt pans, and sand hills, roamed by kangaroos and wild goats. After spring rains, though, the area can burst alive with wildflowers.

It was always difficult to travel through these parts, and even today there are only four main routes that traverse it. One of them, the **Birdsville Track,** is famed in Outback history as the trail along which stockmen once drove their herds of cattle south from Queensland. Another, the **Strzelecki Track,** runs through remote sand dune country to Innaminka and on to Coopers Creek. Both of these tracks cut through the "dog fence"—a 5,600-kilometer- (3,500-mile-) long barrier designed to keep dingoes out of the pastoral lands to the south.

If you follow the **Stuart Highway,** or the **Oodnadatta Track,** you'll pass the mining towns of Coober Pedy, Andamooka, and Mintabie, where people from all over the world have been turned loose in the maddening search for opal. Out here, too, are national parks, such as the daunting Simpson Desert Conservation Park, with its seemingly endless blood-red sand dunes and spinifex plains; and Lake Eyre National Park, with its dried-up salt pan that, during the rare event of a flood, is a temporary home to thousands of water birds.

THE FLINDERS RANGES NATIONAL PARK 𝒻
460km (285 miles) N of Adelaide

The dramatic craggy peaks and ridges that make up the Flinders Ranges rise out of the South Australian desert country. The colors of the rock vary from deep red to orange, with sedimentary lines easily visible as they run down the sides of cliffs. Much of the greenery around here is stunted arid land vegetation. Ever since the introduction of a devastating rabbit virus in 1996, and with the continued culling of hundreds of thousands of wild goats, shoots and saplings that for decades were nibbled away before they grew up have started to turn what was once bare land back into bush. The most remarkable attraction is **Wilpena Pound,** a natural circle of cliff faces that form a gigantic depression on top of a mountainous ledge. The wind whipping over the cliff edges can produce some exhilarating white-knuckle turbulence if you fly over it in a light aircraft. Kangaroos and emus can sometimes be seen wandering around the park, but outside the park kangaroos are heavily culled.

ESSENTIALS
GETTING THERE By car, you can take Highway 1 out of Adelaide to Port Augusta (3½ hr.), then head east on Route 47 via Quorn and Hawker (another 45 min.). It's another hour to Wilpena Pound. Alternatively, take the scenic route (it doesn't have a specific name) through the Clare Valley (around 5 hr.):

Tips An Outback Travel Warning

If you intend to drive through the Outback, take care. Distances between points of interest can be huge, and water supplies, petrol, food, and accommodations are far apart. Always travel with a good map and plenty of expert advice. If you plan to travel off-road, a four-wheel-drive vehicle is a must.

From Adelaide head to Gawler and then through the Clare Valley; follow signs to Gladstone, Melrose, Wilmington, and Quorn.

Premier Stateliner (© **08/8415 5555;** www.premierstateliner.com.au) runs five buses every day from Adelaide to Port Augusta for A$34.80 (U.S.$22.60) one-way. The company also runs buses to Wilpena Pound via Hawker and Quorn, leaving Adelaide at 8:30am on Wednesday and 11am on Friday. Fares each way are A$44.40 (U.S.$28.90) to Quorn, A$58.20 (U.S.$38) to Hawker, and A$62.60 (U.S.$40.70) to Wilpena Pound. Buses return to Adelaide from Wilpena Pound at 11am on Thursday, 7:15pm on Friday (arriving in Adelaide at 5am), and 3:05pm on Sunday.

One of the best tour operators to the national park from Adelaide is **Wallaby Tracks Adventure Tours** (© **1800/639 933** or 08/8648 6655; fax 08/8648 6898; www.headbush.mtx.net). The company's 3-night mountain safari, including camping, costs A$299 (U.S.$194), while a 2-night Weekend Escape package departing Adelaide every Friday afternoon and returning Sunday night costs A$199 (U.S.$129.35). It also runs trips to the Flinders from Port Augusta and Quorn, as well as a 10-day Australian bush expedition from Adelaide to Alice Springs called **Heading Bush Adventures** *⚐*. On this tour you get to experience the Flinders Ranges, the Oodnatta Track, Coober Pedy, the Simpson Desert, Ayres Rock, the Olgas, Kings Canyon, and Aboriginal communities. This remarkable trip costs A$985 (U.S.$640), including meals and bush camping, and focuses on Aboriginal culture. These tours are run by Andu Lodge (see below).

Another good operator is **Banksia Adventures** (© **08/8236 9141;** www.banksia-adventure.com.au), which has 1-, 2-, or 4-day trips to the Flinders, either in hotels or camping. The 1-day trip, including a hotel, costs A$195 (U.S.$126.75), the 2-day trip A$525 (U.S.$341.25), and the 4-day trip A$835 (U.S.$542.75). Camping is about 25% cheaper. This company also offers camping trips to salty Lake Eyre when it floods (it flooded in 2000 and was due to flood again at the time of writing), as well as the Great Aussie Pub Crawl. On this trip you fly by light plane from Adelaide and visit remote Outback pubs. You stay overnight at good hotels including The Prairie Hotel in the Flinders and underground at Coober Pedy. The trip costs A$3,795 (U.S.$2,466) and is all inclusive (with as much beer as you can drink).

Covering a huge slice of the Outback from Adelaide is another great operator, **South Australian Scenic Tours** (© **08/8289 3970;** jpayne@camtech.net.au), which hits the rough dirt roads and heads off on 10-day trips up the Birdsville Track to remote townships and historic sites. You continue along the Strezelecki Track to Innamincka (where the explorers Burke and Wills came to a tragic end), cruise on Cooper Creek, and also take in the Sturt Stony Desert and the Flinders Ranges. Expect to see plenty of wildlife, including kangaroos, emus, and possibly even the very rare yellow-footed rock wallaby. The trip costs A$2,167 (U.S.$1,408).

Most operators will also make up personalized tours on request.

VISITOR INFORMATION   Before setting off, contact the **Flinders Ranges and Outback of South Australia Regional Tourism Association (FROSATA)** at P.O. Box 2083, Port Augusta (© **1800/633 060** in Australia), for advice on roads and conditions. I strongly recommend a visit to the **Wadlata Outback Centre** at 41 Flinders Terrace, Port Augusta (© **08/8642 4511**), an excellent, award-winning interactive museum and information center. The museum costs A$7 (U.S.$4.55) for adults and A$4.50 (U.S.$2.90) for children and is open

Monday through Friday from 9am to 5:30pm, and Saturday and Sunday from 10am to 4pm.

In Hawker, both the Mobil service station and the post office also act as information outlets.

GETTING AROUND If you decide to explore on your own using a rental car, I recommend renting one in Adelaide before setting out. **Kev's Kamel Kapers** (© **0419/839 288** mobile phone) offers remarkable 2-hour sunset camel safaris for A$25 (U.S$16.25); half-day excursions for A$50 (U.S.$32.50); and full-day safaris including a champagne lunch for A$80 (U.S.$52) for adults and A$60 (U.S.$39) for children under 16. Overnight camel treks are available, and on weekends and public holidays 15-minute rides cost just A$5 (U.S.$3.25). The tours only run from March to the end of October and leave from Hawker (call beforehand for exact pick-up spot). Kev is often unreachable, so check with the tourist association for his whereabouts.

WHERE TO STAY

Andu Lodge 🛴 This fabulous backpackers' lodge is one of the best in Australia. Situated in Quorn, in the central Flinders Ranges (42km [26 miles] from Port Augusta), this upscale former hotel is air-conditioned in summer, heated in winter, and has nice clean rooms (dorms sleep six). There's also a nice TV room, a laundry, a computer for e-mailing, and a kitchen area. The hostel offers transfers from Port Augusta for A$10 (U.S.$6.50) each way and runs a range of trips with an emphasis on Aboriginal culture and ecotourism. Guests can also rent mountain bikes. Quorn (pop. 1,300) was where the old Ghan railway used to start and finish from, and where part of the movie *Gallipoli* was filmed. The town has four friendly pubs, all serving meals from A$6.50 to $7.50 (U.S.$4.20 to $4.90). The lodge also offers 1-, 2-, and 3-day tours of the Ranges.

12 First St., Quorn, SA 5043. © **1800/639 933** in Australia, or 08/8648 6655. Fax 08/8648 6898. www.head bush.mtx.net. 64 units. A$50 (U.S.$32.50) double; A$82 (U.S.$53.30) family room (sleeps 4); A$22 (U.S.$14.30) dorm bed. AE, DC, MC, V. **Amenities:** Tour desk; coin-op laundry; nonsmoking rooms.

Prairie Hotel 🛴🛴 *Finds* If you are going to stay anywhere near the Flinders Ranges stay here. This tiny, tin-roofed, stone-walled pub offers a memorable experience and is well worth the dusty 89-kilometer (55-mile) drive north alongside the Ranges from Hawker on the A83. A new addition to the pub contains nice rooms, each with a queen-size bed and a shower. The older-style rooms are smaller and quaint. Three units have spa tubs. The bar out front is a great place to meet the locals and other travelers (who all shake their heads in wonder that this magnificent place is still so undiscovered). Meals here, prepared by "Flinders Feral Food," are top-notch—very nearly the best I've had in Australia. Among their specialties are kangaroo tail soup to start and a mixed grill of emu sausages, camel steak, and kangaroo as a main course. The owner's brother runs remarkable scenic flights over Wilpena Pound and out to the salt lakes. From here you could head to the township of William Creek for a side trip to see the giant salt lake, Lake Eyre, and then onwards west to Coober Pedy.

Corner of High St. and West Terrace, Parachilna, SA 5730. © **08/8648 4844.** Fax 08/8648 4606. www.prairie hotel.com.au. 12 units. A$125–$170 (U.S.$81.25–$110.50) double; A$225 (U.S.$146.25) double with spa bath. Extra person A$35–$45 (U.S.$22.75–$29.25). Rates include light breakfast. AE, DC, MC, V. **Amenities:** Restaurant, bar. *In room:* A/C, minibar, coffeemaker.

Wilpena Pound Resort The nearest place to the Wilpena Pound itself, this partly refurbished resort almost monopolizes the overnight tourist market around here. Standard rooms are adequate and offer respite from the summer heat. The self-contained units come with a stovetop, a microwave, a basin, and cooking utensils. The resort also operates a campground. Campsites cost A$22 (U.S.$14.30) per night for two people with power and A$18 (U.S.$11.70) per night for two people without power, and A$4 (U.S.$2.60) for each extra person. There are some good walks around the area. Also on offer are half-hour scenic flights over the Ranges for A$95 (U.S.$61.75) per person for two, or A$80 (U.S.$52) per person for 20 minutes. They also operate four-wheel-drive tours of the area.

Wilpena Pound, SA 5434. © **1800/805 802** in Australia, or 08/8648 0004. Fax 08/8648 0028. www.wilpena pound.com. 60 units. A$105–$150 (U.S.$68–$97.50) double; A$165 (U.S.$107) self-contained units. Extra adult A$22 (U.S.$6.50); extra child 2–14 A$6–$7 (U.S.$3.90–$4.55). AE, DC, MC, V. **Amenities:** Restaurant, bar; pool; game room; tour desk. *In room:* A/C, TV, kitchenette, coffeemaker.

WHERE TO DINE

The **Old Ghan Restaurant** on Leigh Creek Road, Hawker (© **08/8648 4176**), is open for lunch and dinner Wednesday through Sunday; the restaurant used to be a railway station on the Ghan railway line to Alice Springs before the line was shifted sideways due to flooding. The food here is unexciting, but the home-made pies have a following. If you find yourself in Port Augusta, the area's main town, head to the **Standpipe Motor Inn** (© **08/8642 4033**) for excellent Indian food. The rooms here are nice enough, and quiet, and cost A$80 (U.S.$52) for a double.

COOBER PEDY

854km (529 miles) NW of Adelaide; 689 km (427 miles) S of Alice Springs

Tourists come to this Outback opal-mining town for one thing: the people. More than 3,500 people, from 44 nations, work mainly underground here—the majority suffering from the so-called opal fever, which keeps you digging and digging on the trail of the elusive shimmering rocks. Though some residents are secretive and like to keep to themselves, many others are colorful characters all ready to stop for a chat and spin a few yarns.

Historically, Coober Pedy was a rough place, and it still has a certain Wild West air about it. The first opal was found here in 1915, but it wasn't until 1917 when the Trans Continental Railway was completed, that people began seriously digging for opal. Since then, they have mainly lived underground—not surprising when you encounter the heat, the dust, and the flies for yourself.

The town got its name from the Aboriginal words "kupa piti," commonly thought to mean "white man in a hole." Remnants of the holes left by early miners are everywhere, mostly in the form of bleached-white hills of waste called "mullock heaps." Unfortunately, it's rather discouraged for tourists to wander around the old tailing sites on account that the locals get fed up when tourists fall down the mine shafts.

As for the town itself, there isn't that much to look at, except a couple of underground churches, some casual restaurants, a handful of opal stores, and the necessary service-type businesses. In the center of town you'll find lots of outdoor buildings; the hotels and youth hostel have above-ground entrances but rooms before ground. These places are all within stumbling distance of each other on the main highway.

ESSENTIALS

GETTING THERE   **Kendell Airlines** (© **1800/338 894** in Australia, or 08/ 8231 9567) has daily flights to Coober Pedy from Adelaide. **Greyhound-Pioneer**

(*C* **13 20 30** in Australia) runs services from Adelaide to Coober Pedy for A$76 (U.S.$49.40) for adults and A$61 (U.S.$39.65) for children one-way. The trip takes about 12 hours. The bus from Alice Springs to Coober Pedy costs A$75 (U.S.$48.75) for adults and A$60 (U.S.$39) for children. Passengers bound for Ayres Rock transfer at Erldunda.

If you drive from Adelaide it will take you about 9 hours to reach Coober Pedy along the Stuart Highway. It will take you another 7 hours to drive the 700 kilometers (437 miles) to Alice Springs.

VISITOR INFORMATION The **Coober Pedy Tourist Information Centre,** Hutchinson St., Coober Pedy (*C* **08/8672 5298,** or 1800/637 076 in Australia) is open Monday through Friday from 8:30am to 5pm (closed public holidays).

SEEING THE TOWN
Desert Cave Hotel (*C* **08/8672 5688**) runs tours for both guests and other tourists exploring the opal fields and township; including visits to an underground mine, a home, and potteries, as well as a tour of the underground Serbian Church. You also get to witness an opal-cutting demonstration and "noodle" through the mullock heaps. The 4-hour tour costs A$39 (U.S.$25.35) for adults, A$19.50 (U.S.$12.70) for children, and A$95 (U.S.$61.75) for families.

If you want to see parts of Australia that most Australians never see, join an honest-to-goodness **Mail Run** *&* for a 12-hour journey out into the bush. Tours leave every Monday and Thursday from **Underground Books** (*C* **08/8672 5558**) in Coober Pedy (yep, it's a bookshop underground) and travel along 600 kilometers (372 miles) of dirt roads to Oodnatta and William Creek cattle station, stopping off at five different stations along the route. It can get pretty hot and dusty outside (think endless horizons of flat lands), but it's relatively comfortable inside the air-conditioned four-wheel-drive, and you'll have the chance to see such wildlife as eagles, emus, and the ever-present kangaroos. Bring your own lunch, or buy it along the way. Tours cost A$75 (U.S.$48.75) for adults and A$55 (U.S.$35.75) for children under 12, though kids might find the long trip difficult. This could easily be one of the most memorable experiences you have in Australia, for its up-close-and-personal look at life in the bush.

WHERE TO STAY
The Backpacker's Inn at Radeka's Downunder Motel *&* Whereas all other "underground" rooms in Coober Pedy are actually built into the side of a hill, the centrally located hostel here is actually underground—some 6.5 meters (21 ft.) directly below the topside building, that is. This makes for nice all-year-round temperatures. Odd-looking dorms have no doors and are scooped out of the rock. They contain just four beds, though there are two large dorms sleeping up to 20 people. The twin rooms are simply furnished but pleasant. The motel rooms are quite comfortable and come with attached bathrooms with a shower. Some have a kitchenette. Room 9 is huge with a double and two sets of bunk beds. All motel rooms are dug out of the side of a hill. Radeka's also runs a good opal tour.

1 Oliver St., Coober Pedy, SA 5723. *C* **08/8672 5223.** Fax 08/86725821. 150 units, 9 motel rooms. Dorm beds A$17 (U.S.$11); motel rooms A$88 (U.S.$57) double. A$12 (U.S.$7.80) extra person. AE, MC, V. Free parking. **Amenities:** Restaurant, bar; TV and video room; pool table; kitchen/dining room; tour desk.

The Desert Cave Hotel Though not the only underground hotel in the world (there's another wonderful one in White Cliffs in New South Wales), this

(Moments) A Fabulous Four-Wheel-Drive Adventure

With a hired vehicle from Adelaide, it's a day's drive north through the **Clare Valley wine region** to the **Prairie Hotel** (see above). Stop off along the way for a traditional Aussie lunch at **Bluey Blundstone's Café** 🍴 in Melrose (ⓒ **08/8666 2173**). The next day it's a 3- to 4-hour drive to **William Creek,** an unusual Outback town with a take-out restaurant and pub/hotel. Just 20 kilometers (12.4 miles) before you reach town is a turnoff to **Lake Eyre,** a giant salt lake which flooded in 2000, and again in 2001, and should hold water for a couple of years. **Wrightsair** offers 1-hour flights over Lake Eyre for A$110 (U.S.$71.50) per person. Call mobile ⓒ **0418 336 748.** Camping beside the lake is a magical experience. The next day it's a 166-kilometer (103-mile) drive to **Coober Pedy** (see above), and from there it's a 9-hour drive back to **Adelaide.**

is the only one with a pool and spa. Personally, I find the place to be a little soulless and in need of refurbishment. The bar's "pokie" machines are noisy, and you can hear your neighbors in the next room (heaven help you if the TV is turned up loud enough for you to hear). The hotel can arrange transfers from the airport (A$6.50).

Hutchison St., Coober Pedy (P.O. Box 223, Coober Pedy, SA 5723). ⓒ **1800 088 521** in Australia, or 08/8672 5688. Fax 08/8672 5198. www.desertcave.com.au. 50 units (19 underground). A$175 (U.S.$113.75) double; A$195 (U.S.$126.75) family room sleeping 5. Extra person A$20 (U.S.$13). Ask about packages. AE, DC, MC, V. Free parking. **Amenities:** Restaurant, bar; golf nearby; health club with spa; tour desk; car-rental desk (Thrifty only); room service (6–9:30pm); laundry/dry cleaning service. *In room:* TV with free movies, dataport, minibar, coffeemaker, hair dryer, iron.

WHERE TO DINE

The **Opal Inn** (ⓒ **08/8672 5054**) offers good-value counter meals of the typical pub-grub variety. Head to **Traces** (ⓒ **08/8672 5147**), the township's favorite Greek restaurant, for something a bit different.

5 The Coorong

Few places in the world attract as much wildfowl as the **Coorong,** one of Australia's most precious sanctuaries. The Coorong is made up of an area that includes the mouth of the Murray River, the huge Lake Alexandrina, the smaller Lake Albert, and a long, thin sand spit called the Younghusband Peninsula. A small, but by far the most scenic, part of this area is encompassed in the **Coorong National Park.** The area is under constant environmental threat due to pollutants coming south via the Murray River from the farmlands to the north. It still manages, however, to play host to large colonies of native and visiting birds, such as the Australian pelican, black swans, royal spoonbills, greenshanks, and the extremely rare hooded plover.

If it were possible to count all the birds here you'd probably run out of steam after some 45,000 ducks, 5,000 black swans, 2,000 Cape Barren geese, and 122,000 waders. This last figure is even more significant when you consider it corresponds to a total South Australian population of waders standing at 200,000, and an overall Australian population of some 403,000.

Add to these figures the thousands of pelicans—with around 3,000 birds nesting here annually it's the largest permanent breeding colony in Australia—and countless gulls, terns, and cormorants, and you'll soon realize why the Coorong and the adjoining Lower Murray Lakes form one of the most important waterbird habitats in Australia.

The national park, which stands out starkly against the degraded farmland surrounding it, is also home to several species of marsupials, including wombats.

The best time to visit the Coorong is in December and January, when the lakes are full of migratory birds from overseas. However, plenty of birds can be spotted year-round. *Note:* Binoculars and patience are highly recommended.

ESSENTIALS

GETTING THERE   The best way to visit the Coorong is by car, though a guided tour of the area is highly recommended once you arrive at either the main settlement of Goolwa on the western fringe of the waterways, or at Meninge, on the eastern boundary. From Adelaide follow the Princes Highway along the coast.

VISITOR INFORMATION   The **Goolwa Tourist Information Centre,** BF Lawrie Lane, Goolwa ((*C* **08/8555 1144;** www.alexandrina.sa.gov), has information on the area and can book accommodations. It's open from 9am to 5pm daily.

GETTING AROUND   The best operator in the area is **Coorong Nature Tours** (*C* **08/8574 0037,** or 0428 714 793 mobile phone; www.lm.net.au/~coorongnat/), based in Narrung. The tours are run by David Dadd, a delightful, unassuming Cockney, who fell in love with the Coorong when he arrived at the age of 11. He offers memorable 1-, 2-, and 3-day tours of the area, with pickup either in Meningie or Adelaide. Full-day tours cost A$132 (U.S.$86) per person from Meningie or A$185 (U.S.$120.25) per person from Adelaide. Reservations are essential.

WHERE TO STAY

There are plenty of hotels, B&Bs, campgrounds, and caravan parks in Goolwa and along the main road that runs parallel to the national park. One of the ones I prefer is the **Goolwa Camping and Tourist Park,** 40 Castle Rd., Goolwa, SA 5214 (*C* **08/8555 2144**). It has 70 caravans and a large area for tents. A two-berth van costs A$25 (U.S.$16.25) a night, and a six-berth A$35 (U.S.$22.75) for the first two people and A$5 (U.S.$3.25) for an extra adult or A$3 (U.S.$1.95) for an extra child. Bring your own bedding.

Grahams Castle Resort   This former conference center is classified as a three-star backpacker's accommodation. Rooms are very basic with two single beds, heating, and a shower shared between two rooms. It's very popular with budget groups, so it could get noisy.

Corner of Castle and Bradford sts., Goolwa, SA 5214. (*C* **08/8555 3300,** or 1800 243 303 in Australia. Fax 08/8555 3828. 22 units. A$15 (U.S.$9.75) per person. AE, DC, MC, V. **Amenities:** Restaurant, bar; outdoor pool; tennis court; tour desk; room service.

Poltalloch ✩✩   Located smack dab in the middle of nowhere on the eastern edge of the Coorong, Poltalloch is a working farm property—with plenty of cows, ducks, chickens, and dogs wandering about—that seems more like a village. The whole place is classified by the National Trust of South Australia, and history is evident everywhere, from the cottages once used by farm hands to the giant wooden shearing shed and other outbuildings crammed with relics from the past.

You can stay in a choice of five cottages scattered across the property. The Shearer's Hut is a stone cottage that sleeps up to nine people; the Overseers stone cottage sleeps up to eight people; the Boundary Rider's Cottage is built of timber, iron, and stone, and sleeps five; and the Station Hand's Cottage sleeps four. The Shearer's Quarters is mainly for large groups and sleeps 12. All of the units are modern and comfortable inside and have their own kitchen facilities and barbecues. I stayed in the Station Hand's Cottage, which was once the home of Aboriginal workers. I loved the mix of rural feeling and modern conveniences.

There's a private beach on the property if you want to swim in the lake, and guests have the use of a dingy, a canoe, and a Ping-Pong table. Fascinating historical tours of the property cost A$9 (U.S.$5.85) for adults, and A$4.50 (U.S.$2.90) for children with a minimum charge of A$27 (U.S.$17.55). Bookings are essential. Breakfast provisions are available for A$13 (U.S.$8.45) per person. Coorong Nature Tours will pick you up from here for no extra charge. There's plenty of bird life on and around the property.

Poltalloch. P.M.B.3, Narrung via Tailem Bend, SA 5260. ℂ **08/8574 0088.** Fax 08/8574 0065. www.poltalloch.com.au. 3 units. A$95–$165 (U.S.$61.75–$107.25) per cottage. Extra person A$25 (U.S.$16.25). MC, V. **Amenities:** Tennis court. *In room:* TV, coffeemaker.

11

Melbourne

by Marc Llewellyn

Melbourne (pronounced *Mel*-bun), the capital of Victoria and Australia's second-largest city, with a population well over 3 million, is a cultural melting pot. For a start, more people of Greek descent live here than in any other city except Athens. Chinese, Italian, Vietnamese, and Lebanese immigrants have all left their mark on Melbourne. In fact, almost one-third of Melburnians were born overseas or have parents who were born overseas. With such a diverse population, and with trams rattling through the streets and a host of stately European architecture surrounding you, you could easily forget you're in Australia at all.

Melbourne has a reputation of being at the head of the pack when it comes to shopping, restaurants, fashion, music, nightlife, and cafe culture. It frequently beats out other state capitals in bids for major international concerts, plays, exhibitions, and sporting events, such as the Formula One Grand Prix.

The city also revels in a healthy rivalry with its northern neighbor, Sydney, but it's interesting to note that almost every Melbournian adores their city—often described as the "most livable" in the world—whereas Sydneysiders are mostly half-hearted in their praise for their own abode.

Melbourne's roots go back to the 1850s, when gold was found in the surrounding hills. British settlers took up residence and have since prided themselves on coming freely to their city, rather than having been forced here in convict chains. The city grew wealthy and remained largely a conservative bastion until World War II, when another wave of immigration, this time mainly from southern Europe, made it a more relaxed place.

1 Orientation

ARRIVING

BY PLANE Melbourne's main international and domestic airport is **Tullamarine Airport,** located 22 kilometers (14 miles) northwest of the city center. If you're traveling from Sydney, the flight will take you around 1 hour 20 minutes. It's a 5-minute walk between the international and domestic terminals. If you are flying within Australia with either Impulse Airlines or Virgin Blue, you'll find they depart from the international terminal rather than the domestic terminal (you'll not be able to buy duty-free goods though if you're flying on these airlines). Travelers information desks are open on both levels of the international terminal building from 6am until the last flight. There are snack bars, a restaurant, currency-exchange facilities, and duty-free shops in the international terminal. There's also a post office, open daily from 9am to 5pm, but stamps are available from vending machines after hours, as well as mail boxes. ATM cash machines are available at both terminals. Showers are on the first floor of the international area. Baggage trolleys are free in the international baggage claim hall but cost A$2 (U.S.1.30) if hired in the car park, departure lounge, or the domestic terminal. Baggage lockers cost A$4 to $8 (U.S.$2.60–$5.60) per day, depending on size.

Thrifty (© **03/9330 1522,** or 1800 652 008 in Australia), **Budget** (© **13 27 27** in Australia), **Avis** (© **03/9338 1800,** or 1800 225 533 in Australia), and **Hertz** (© **03/9379 9955,** or 13 30 39 in Australia), all have rental desks at the airport.

Skybus (© **03/9662 9275**) picks up passengers in front of the baggage claim area every 30 minutes from 6:40am to 11:40pm, and hourly 11:40pm to 6:40am. The trip into the center takes around 35 minutes and costs A$10 (U.S.$6.50) one-way for adults and A$4.50 (U.S.$2.90) for children under 15. The service travels direct to Spencer Street Railway Station, where free shuttle buses transfer you to city hotels. When you want to return to the airport, book the Skybus service a few hours in advance and allow at least 40 minutes for traveling time. Buy tickets onboard, or from Skybus desks outside the baggage claim areas.

A taxi to the city center takes about 30 minutes and costs around A$35 (U.S.$22.75).

BY TRAIN   Interstate trains arrive at **Spencer Street Railway Station,** at Spencer and Little Collins Streets (5 blocks from Swanston Street in the city center). Taxis and buses connect with the city. The **Sydney–Melbourne XPT** travels between Australia's two largest cities daily; trip time is 10½ hours. The full fare (booked on the day of travel) is A$110 (U.S.$71.50) in economy, or A$77 (U.S.$50) (booked 2 days in advance), A$66(U.S.$43) (booked a week in advance), and A$55 (U.S.$35.75) (booked 2 weeks in advance). The first-class fare is A$154 (U.S.$100) (on day of travel), A$107.80 (U.S.$70) (2 days in advance), A$92.40 (U.S.$60) (a week in advance), and A$77 (U.S.$50) (2 weeks in advance). A first-class sleeper costs $231 (U.S.$150) (booked on day of travel), A$184.80 (U.S.$120) (2 days in advance), A$169.40 (U.S.$110) (a week in advance), and A$154 (U.S.$100) (2 weeks in advance). Students presenting an ISIC international student card travel at "a week in advance price" in all categories, even if booked on the day. Call **Countrylink** on © **13 22 32,** or access their website at www.countrylink.nsw.gov.com.au.

The *Overlander* provides daily service to and from Melbourne and Adelaide (trip time: 12 hr.). Fares are A$57 (U.S.$37) in economy and A$105 (U.S.$68) for a first-class sleeper. You can transport your car on the *Overlander* for A$110 (U.S.$71.50). Call Great Southern Railway on © **13 21 47,** or check their website at: www.gsr.com.au.

Daylink services also connect Melbourne with Adelaide. This trip is by train from Melbourne to Bendigo, and bus from Bendigo to Adelaide. Total trip time is 11 hours, and the fare is A$52 (U.S.$33.80) in economy and A$60.50 (U.S.$39) in first-class.

The ***Canberra Link*** connects Melbourne with the nation's capital, and consists of a train journey from Melbourne to Wadonga, and bus from there to Canberra. The journey takes around 11 hours and costs A$50 (U.S.$32.50) in economy, and A$65.80 (U.S.$42.80) in first-class.

For train information and reservations for the daylink services to Adelaide and Canberra call **V/Line** (© **13 61 96** in Australia, or 03/9619 5000), or visit their website on: www.vlinepassenger.com.au.

BY BUS   Several bus companies connect Melbourne with other state capitals and regional areas of Victoria. Among the biggest operators are **Greyhound**

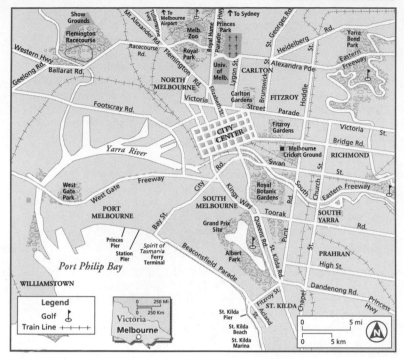

Pioneer (℡ **13 20 30** in Australia, or 03/9600 1687) and **McCafferty's** (℡ **13 14 99** in Australia, or 03/9670 2533). Greyhound Pioneer buses depart and arrive at Melbourne's Transit Centre, at 58 Franklin St. McCafferty's coaches depart and arrive from the Spencer Street Bus Terminal at 205 Spencer St., on the western side of the city, just north of the Spencer Street Railway Station. New arrivals can take a tram or taxi from the station to their hotel. **V/Line buses** (℡ **13 22 32** in Australia), which travel all over Victoria, also depart from the Spencer Street Bus Terminal.

BY CAR You can drive from Sydney to Melbourne along the Hume Highway, though a much nicer route is via the coastal Princes Highway, for which you will need a minimum of 2 days, with stops. For information on all aspects of road travel in Victoria, contact the **Royal Automotive Club of Victoria** (℡ **03/9790 3333**).

VISITOR INFORMATION

The first stop on any visitor's itinerary should be the **Victorian Visitors Information Center,** Melbourne Town Hall, Swanston Street, at the corner of Little Collins Street (℡ **13 28 42** in Australia—a recorded list of attractions and numbers, and consultants to help with accommodation; www.visitvictoria.com). You'll find everything you need here, and the staff can make reservations for accommodations and tours. The center is open Monday through Friday from 9am to 6pm and Saturday and Sunday from 9am to 5pm. The Melbourne Greeter Service operates from the Town Hall, too. This service connects visitors to enthusiastic local volunteers who offer free one-on-one orientation tours of the city. Book at least 3 days in advance on © **03/9658 9524** (fax 03/9654 1054), and make sure you state your interests.

You'll find some information services at **The National Trust Shop,** Shop 21, Block Arcade, 282 Collins St. (© **03/9654 7448**), and at **Information Victoria,** 356 Collins St. (© **1300/366 356**). Staffed information booths are also found in Bourke Street Mall, Flinders Street Station (on the corner of Flinders Street and Swanston Walk), and at the Queen Victoria Markets (on the corner of Therry and Queen streets).

Good websites on the city include CitySearch Melbourne (melbourne.city search.com.au); and www.melbourne.org.

CITY LAYOUT

Melbourne is situated on the Yarra River and stretches inland from Port Philip Bay, which lies to its south. Look at a map, and you'll see a distinct central oblong area surrounded by Flinders Street to the south, Latrobe Street to the north, Spring Street to the east, and Spencer Street to the west. Cutting north-to-south through its center are the two main shopping thoroughfares, Swanston Street and Elizabeth Street. A series of cross-streets, including Bourke Street Mall, a pedestrians-only shopping thoroughfare, runs between the major thoroughfares. If you continue south along Swanston Street, and over the river, it turns into St. Kilda Road, which runs to the coast. The central area is surrounded by Melbourne's various urban "villages," including South Yarra, Richmond, Carlton, and Fitzroy. The seaside suburb of St. Kilda has a rather scruffy beach. If you've visited Sydney, you'll find Melbourne's city center to be smaller and far less congested with people and cars.

NEIGHBORHOODS IN BRIEF

Melbourne is huge. At more than 6,110 square kilometers (3,788 sq. miles), it's one of the biggest cities in the world. Below are the areas of most interest to visitors:

City Center Made up of a grid of streets north of the Yarra River, the city center is bordered to the south by Flinders Street and to the north by Latrobe Street. The eastern and western borders are Spring Street and Spencer Street, respectively. There's some good shopping around here, charming cafes, and in recent years an active nightlife has sprung up with the opening of a swath of fun bars. The gateway to the city is the imposing Flinders Street Station, with its dome and clock tower.

Chinatown This colorful section of the city center is centered on Little Bourke Street between Swanston and Exhibition streets. The area marks Australia's oldest permanent Chinese settlement, dating from the 1850s, when a few boarding houses catered to Chinese prospectors lured by the state's gold rushes. Plenty of cheap restaurants crowd its narrow alleyways. Tram: Any to the city.

Carlton North of the city center, Carlton is a rambling inner-city suburb famous for the Italian restaurants strung along Lygon Street with outdoor seating—though the quality of the food served is variable. It's the home of the University of Melbourne, so there's a healthy student scene. From Bourke Street Mall count on a 15-minute walk to reach the restaurant strip. Tram: 1 or 22 from Swanston St.

Fitzroy A ruggedly bohemian place, 2 kilometers (1¼ miles) north of the city center, Fitzroy is raw and funky, filled with students and artists and popular for people-watching. Fitzroy revolves around Brunswick Street, with its cheap restaurant scene, busy cafes, late-night bookshops, art galleries, and pubs. Around the corner, on Johnston Street, are tapas bars, Flamenco restaurants, and Spanish clubs. Tram: 11 from Collins Street.

Richmond One of Melbourne's earliest settlements is a multicultural quarter based around historic streets and back lanes. Victoria Street is reminiscent of Ho Chi Minh City, with Vietnamese sights, sounds, aromas, and restaurants everywhere. Bridge Road is a bustling fashion precinct. Tram: 48 or 75 from Flinders Street to Bridge Road; 70 from Batmans Avenue at Princes Bridge to Swan Street; 109 from Bourke Street to Victoria Street.

Southgate This flashy entertainment district on the banks of the Yarra River opposite Flinders Street Station (linked by a pedestrian bridge) is home to the giant Crown casino —Australia's largest gaming venue—which offers themed restaurants, bars, cafes, nightclubs, cinemas, and designer shops. On the city side of the river is the new Melbourne Aquarium. All are a 10-minute stroll from Flinders Street Station. Tram: 8 from Swanston Street.

St. Kilda Hip and bohemian in a shabby sort of way, this seaside suburb (6km/4 miles south of the city center) has Melbourne's highest concentration of restaurants, ranging from glitzy to cheap, and some superb cake shops and delis. The Esplanade hugs an unremarkable beach (with brown waters) and is the scene of a lively Sunday crafts market. Ackland Street houses

many of St. Kilda's restaurants. Tram: 10 or 12 from Collins Street; 15 or 16 from Swanston Street; 96 from Bourke Street.

South Yarra/Prahan This posh part of town is crammed with chic boutiques, cinemas, nightclubs, and galleries. Chapel Street is famous for its well-heeled eateries and designer fashion houses, while Commercial Road is popular with the gay and lesbian community. Just of Chapel Street in Prahan is Greville Street, a bohemian enclave featuring retro boutiques and music outlets. Every Sunday the Greville Street Market offers arts, crafts, secondhand clothes, and jewelry from noon to 5pm. Tram: 8 or 72 from Swanston Street.

South Melbourne One of the city's oldest working-class districts, South Melbourne is known for its historic buildings, old-fashioned pubs and hotels, and markets. Tram: 12 from Collins Street; 1 from Swanston Street.

The River District The muddy-looking Yarra River runs southeast past the fabulous Botanic Gardens and nearby to other attractions such as The Victorian Arts Centre, the National Gallery of Australia, the Sydney Myer Music Bowl and the Melbourne Cricket Ground (MCG), all outlined later in this chapter.

Williamstown A lack of extensive development has left this outer waterfront suburb with a rich architectural heritage centered on Ferguson Street and Nelson Place—both reminiscent of old England. On the Strand overlooking the sea are a line of bistros and restaurants, and a World War II warship museum. Ferry: from Southgate, the World Trade Center, or St. Kilda Pier.

Value **Money-Saving Transit Pass**

The Getabout Travelcard, which can be used by two adults and up to four children, is good 1 day of travel on Saturdays and Sundays only. It costs A$9.50 (U.S.$6.20). Buy it at newsagents.

---

2 Getting Around
BY PUBLIC TRANSPORTATION

Trams, trains, and buses are operated by The Met. Generally, tourists and locals travel around the city and to the outlying suburbs by tram.

BY TRAM Melbourne has the oldest tram network in the world. Trams are still an essential part of the city, and a major cultural icon. There are some 700 mostly green-and-yellow trams running over 325 kilometers (200 miles) of track. Instead of phasing out this non-smoggy method of transport out, Melbourne is busily expanding the network.

Tram travel within the city and to all suburbs mentioned in this chapter costs A$1.50 (U.S.$1) for adults, A80¢ (U.S.52¢) for children for a single journey. Or you could buy a **2-Hour Metcard** good for unlimited transport on buses or trains for up to 2 hours. The 2-Hour Metcards cost A$2.40 (U.S.$1.60) for adults and A$1.35 (U.S.$90) for children. If you plan to pack an awful lot in then try the **Zone 1 Metcard Daily ticket,** which allows travel on all transport within the city center and surrounding suburbs mentioned in this chapter from 5:30am to midnight (when transportation stops). It costs A$4.60 (U.S.$3) for adults and A$2.40 (U.S.$1.60) for children. **Metcard Weekly tickets** cost A$20 (U.S.$13) for adults and A$9.95 (U.S.$6.50) for children.

Buy single-trip and 2-hour tram tickets at ticket machines on trams, special ticket offices (such as at the tram terminal on Elizabeth Street, near the corner of Flinders Street), at most newsagents, and at Metcard vending machines at many railway stations. A Metcard needs to be validated by the Metcard Validator machine on the tram, station platforms, or onboard buses before each journey; the only exception to this is the 2-hour Metcard ticket purchased from a vending machine on a tram, which is automatically validated for that journey only. Vending machines on trams only accept coins—but give change—whereas larger vending machines at train stations give change up to A$10 (U.S.$6.50).

You can pick up a free route map from the Victorian Visitors Information Center, in the Town Hall on Swanston Street, or at the **Met Information Centre,** 103 Elizabeth St., at the corner of Collins Street (© **13 16 38** in Australia; www.victrip.com.au). The latter is open Monday through Friday from 8:30am to 4:30pm, and Saturday from 9am to 1pm.

The **City Circle Tram** is the best way to get around the very center of Melbourne—and it's free. These burgundy-and-cream trams travel a circular route between all the major central attractions, and past shopping malls and arcades. The trams run, in both directions, every 10 minutes between 10am and 6pm, except Good Friday and Christmas Day. City Circle Tram stops are marked with a burgundy sign.

Trams can be hailed at numbered green-and-gold tram-stop signs. To get off the tram, press the red button located near handrails, or pull the cord running above your head.

BY EXPLORER BUS

City Explorer (© 03/9650 7000) operates double-decker London-style buses that pick up and drop off at 21 stops around the city, including the Melbourne Aquarium, Crown Casino, Queen Victoria Markets, Captain Cook's Cottage, Chinatown, the Melbourne Zoo, and the Botanic Gardens, among others. There's full commentary on board. You can hop on and off as often as you want during the day. A bus returns to each stop half-hourly. The first bus leaves Town Hall on Swanston Street at 9:30pm and the last leaves at 2:30pm. Tickets cost A$30 (U.S.$19.50) for adults, A$25 (U.S.$16.25) for students and YHA members, A$15 (U.S.$9.75) for children under 14, and A$75 (U.S.$18.75) for a family of five. Buy them from the driver or at the booth outside the Visitor Information Centre, near Melbourne Town Hall.

BY TAXI

Cabs are plentiful in the city, but it may be difficult to hail one in the city center late Friday and Saturday nights. Taxi companies include **Silver Top** (© 13 10 08, or 03/9345 3455), **Embassy** (© 13 17 55, or 03/9277 3444), and **Black Cabs Combined** (© 13 22 27). A large, illuminated rooftop light shows a cab is free. For wheelchair-accessible cabs call the **Central Booking Office** (© 1300/364 050) at least a day in advance.

BY CAR

Driving in Melbourne is not fun. Roads can be confusing, there are trams and aggressive drivers everywhere, and there is a strange rule about turning right from the left lane at major intersections (which leaves the left-hand lane free for oncoming trams and free for through traffic). Here, you must wait for the lights to turn amber before turning. Also, you must always stop behind a tram if it stops, as passengers usually step directly into the road. Add to this the general lack of parking spaces and expensive hotel valet-parking charges, and you'll know why it's better to get on a tram instead. For road rules pick up a copy of the Victorian Road Traffic handbook from bookshops, or from a Vic Roads office (© 13 11 71 in Australia for the nearest office).

Major car-rental companies include **Avis,** 400 Elizabeth St. (© 03/9663 6366); **Budget,** 398 Elizabeth St. (© 03/9203 4844); **Hertz,** 97 Franklin St. (© 03/9698 2555); **Delta,** 110 A'beckett St, (© 03/9600 9025); and **Thrifty,** 390 Elizabeth St. (© 03/9663 5200). Expect to pay from A$30 (U.S.$19.50) a day for a small car.

 FAST FACTS: Melbourne

American Express The main Amex office is at 233 Collins St. (© 03/9633 6333). It's open Monday through Friday from 9am to 5:30pm, and Saturday from 9am to noon.

Business Hours In general, stores are open Monday through Thursday 9am to 5:30pm, Friday from 9am to 9pm, Saturday from 9am to 5:30pm, and Sunday from 10am to 5pm. The larger department stores stay open on Thursday evening until 9pm. Banks are open Monday through Thursday from 9:30am to 4pm, and Friday from 9:30am to 5pm.

Camera Repair Vintech Camera Repairs, 5th Floor, 358 Lonsdale St. (✆ 03/9602 1820, or 0418/515 662 mobile phone), is well regarded.

Dentist Call the Dental Emergency Service (✆ 03/9341 0222) for emergency referral to a local dentist.

Doctor The "casualty" department at the Royal Melbourne Hospital, Grattan Street, Parkville (✆ 03/9342 7000) responds to emergencies. The Traveller's Medical & Vaccination Centre, 2nd Floor, 393 Little Bourke St. (✆ 03/9602 5788), offers full vaccination and travel medical services.

Consulates The following English-speaking countries have consulates in Melbourne: United States, Level 6, 553 St. Kilda Rd. (✆ 03/9526 5900); United Kingdom, Level 17, 90 Collins St. (✆ 03/9650 4155); and Canada, 1st Floor, 123 Camberwell Rd., Hawthorn (✆ 03/9811 9999).

Drugstores See "Pharmacies," below.

Emergencies In an emergency, call ✆ 000 for police, ambulance, or the fire department.

Internet Access Melbourne Central Internet, Level 2, Melbourne Central, at the corner of Elizabeth and Latrobe streets (✆ 03/9663 8410) is open Monday through Thursday from 10am to 6pm, Friday from 10am to 7pm, Saturday from 10am to 5:30pm, and Sunday from 11am to 5pm. Another option is Global Gossip, 440 Elizabeth St., City (✆ 03/9663 0511), open daily from 8am to 1am.

Lost Property Contact your nearest police station, or call in at the Melbourne Town Hall, Swanston Street, City (✆ 03/9658 9774).

Pharmacies The McGibbony & Beaumont Pharmacy is in the Grand Hyatt hotel complex, 123 Collins St. (✆ 03/9650 1823). It's open Monday through Thursday from 8am to 6:30pm, Friday from 8am to 7pm, Saturday from 9:30am to 2:30pm, and Sunday from 9:30am to noon.

Post Office The General Post Office (G.P.O.) is at the corner of Bourke Street Mall and Elizabeth Street (✆ 03/9203 3042). It's open Monday through Friday from 8:15am to 5:30pm, and Saturday from 10am to 3pm. Poste Restante hours are the same.

Safety St. Kilda might be coming up in the world, but it's still wise not to walk around there late at night. Parks and gardens can also be risky at night, as can the area around the King Street nightclubs.

Taxes Sales tax, where it exists, is included in the price, as is the 10% Goods and Services Tax (GST). There is no hotel tax as yet in Melbourne.

Telephones For Directory Assistance call ✆ 1223; for International Directory Assistance call ✆ 1225.

Weather Call ✆ 1196 for recorded weather information.

3 Where to Stay

Getting a room is generally easy enough on weekends, when business travelers are back at home with their families. You need to book well in advance, however, during the city's hallmark events (say, the weekend before the Melbourne Cup, and during the Grand Prix and the Ford Australia Open). Hostels in the St. Kilda area tend to fill up quickly in December and January.

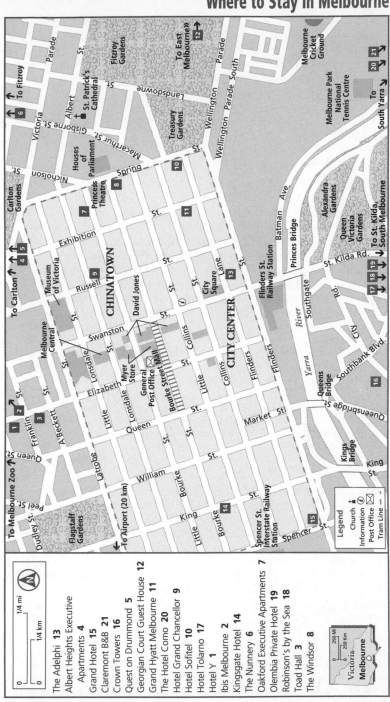

Where to Stay in Melbourne

The Adelphi **13**
Albert Heights Executive Apartments **4**
Grand Hotel **15**
Claremont B&B **21**
Crown Towers **16**
Quest on Drummond **5**
Georgian Court Guest House **12**
Grand Hyatt Melbourne **11**
The Hotel Como **20**
Hotel Grand Chancellor **9**
Hotel Sofitel **10**
Hotel Tolarno **17**
Hotel Y **1**
Ibis Melbourne **2**
Kingsgate Hotel **14**
The Nunnery **6**
Oakford Executive Apartments **7**
Olembia Private Hotel **19**
Robinson's by the Sea **18**
Toad Hall **3**
The Windsor **8**

Once considered dead after offices closed for the day, the city center has been rejuvenated in recent years, and you'll feel right in the heart of the action if you stay here. Otherwise, the various suburbs are all exciting satellites, with good street life, restaurants, and pubs—all just a quick tram ride from the city center. (Transportation from the airport to the suburbs is a little more expensive and complicated than to the city center, however.)

If you arrive without booked accommodation contact the travelers information desks (© 03/9297 1814), located on both floors of the international terminal and open daily from 6am to last flight. Both they, and the **Victorian Visitor Information Centre,** in the Melbourne Town Hall (© 03/9650 7721), provide last-minute bookings without a booking fee.

IN THE CITY CENTER
VERY EXPENSIVE

Crown Towers *๙๙*   One of Melbourne's finest hotels, Crown Towers is part of the Crown Casino complex, which opened in 1997 on the banks of the Yarra River. The hotel itself is grand and impressive. People often gasp audibly as they enter the huge glittering lobby paved in black marble. Superior guest rooms occupy floors 5 through to 15; those above the 10th floor have spectacular city views. Deluxe rooms, which run up to the 28th floor, are exactly the same except with better views. Rooms are very large, with thick carpets, a walk-in closet, in-room fax and safe, and an enormous bathroom with spa tub and its own TV. The hotel's only fault is that it's a 15-minute walk from the main shopping streets, though trams do stop right outside.

Crown Casino offers 24-hour gambling. The 900-seat Showroom offers live entertainment nightly. A 14-screen cinema complex open 24 hours and three cabaret theaters are also part of the complex.

8 Whiteman St., Southbank, Melbourne 3006. © **13 21 38** in Australia, or 03/9292 6868. Fax 03/9292 6600. www.crownltd.com.au. 500 units. A$560 (U.S.$364) double; A$900–$1,500 (U.S.$585–$975) suite. Extra person A$50 (U.S.$32.50). Children under 12 stay free in parents' room. AE, DC, MC, V. Parking A$20 (U.S.$13). **Amenities:** 3 restaurants (traditional Japanese, Cantonese, Italian); Olympic-size indoor pool; health club; concierge; tour desk; car-rental desk; business center; 24-hr. room service; massage; babysitting; laundry service; same-day dry cleaning; nonsmoking rooms; executive rooms. *In room:* A/C, TV with pay movies, dataport, minibar, coffeemaker, hair dryer, iron.

Grand Hyatt Melbourne *๙๙*   The Grand Hyatt is a glitzy, glamorous affair, situated in the best part of town, just a short walk from Swanston Street, Elizabeth Street, and Chinatown. Rooms are large and luxurious, and come with a nice-size marble bathroom and all those details you'd expect from a five-star establishment (though oddly there's no iron and ironing board). Prices vary with the view, which can be almost Hong Kong–like over the city from the top floors. Regency Club guests get free sushi and drinks in the evening, snacks all day, and a complimentary breakfast. Monsoon's is a late-night disco.

123 Collins St., Melbourne, VIC 3000. © **1800/339 494** in Australia, 800/233-1234 in the U.S. and Canada, or 03/9657 1234. Fax 03/9650 3491. www.melbourne.hyatt.com. 547 units. A$550 (U.S.$357) Hyatt Guest double; A$570 (U.S.$370) deluxe double; A$600 (U.S.$390) Regency Club double; A$840–$3,300 (U.S.$546–$2,145) suite. Extra person A$50 (U.S.$32.50). Children under 18 stay free in parents' room. Ask about lower weekend rates and packages. AE, DC, MC, V. Parking A$21 (U.S.$13.65). **Amenities:** 2 restaurants (Modern Australian, bistro); very large indoor pool; 2 tennis courts; health club; concierge; tour desk; car-rental desk; business center; 24-hr. room service; in-room massage; babysitting; laundry service; same-day dry cleaning; nonsmoking room; executive-level rooms. *In room:* A/C, TV with pay movies, dataport, minibar, coffeemaker, hair dryer.

Hotel Sofitel 𝄍𝄍 I guarantee you'll like this beautiful luxury hotel, located in the best area of Collins Street, just a short walk from the major shopping and business area. The hotel features a glass-topped atrium that allows natural light to flood in. Rooms are large and very pleasant, with high-quality furniture, two TVs, and a large bathroom with a tub/shower combination. More expensive rooms have two walls of tall windows and magnificent views over the city. The service is very impressive.

25 Collins St., Melbourne, VIC 3000. ℭ **1300/65 65 65** in Australia, 800/221-4542 in the U.S. and Canada, 0800/44 4422 in New Zealand, or 03/9653 0000. Fax 03/9650 4261. www.sofitelmelbourne.com.au. 363 units. A$383 (U.S.$250.25) double; A$445–$1,700 (U.S.$289–$1,105) suite. Extra person A$44 (U.S.$28.60). Children under 16 stay free in parents' room. Ask about lower weekend rates and other packages. AE, DC, MC, V. Parking A$26 (U.S.$16.90). **Amenities:** 2 restaurants (Modern French, brasserie), 1 bar; exercise room; spa; concierge; tour desk; car-rental desk; business center; shopping arcade; 24-hr. room service, babysitting; laundry service; same-day dry cleaning; nonsmoking rooms. *In room:* A/C, TV/VCR, dataport, minibar, coffeemaker, hair dryer, iron.

The Windsor 𝄍𝄍 The Windsor is Australia's only surviving authentic "grand" hotel. It opened in 1883 as, literally, The Grand and was restored to its original condition by Oberoi Hotels International. The charmingly upper-crust establishment oozes sophistication and has hosted such notable guests as Lauren Bacall, Katharine Hepburn, Muhammad Ali, and Omar Sharif. The lobby is luxuriously carpeted, and the staff very friendly and efficient. Standard rooms are comfortable, with high ceilings and tasteful furnishings. Each has a good-size bathroom. Deluxe rooms are twice as big, and many have good views of Parliament House and the Melbourne Cathedral. Suites are huge and furnished with antiques. Guests can choose from among 10 types of pillows, including an aromatherapy version filled with rose petals and herbs. The Windsor is a member of both Leading Hotels of the World and Small Luxury Hotels of the World.

The Grand Ballroom, with ornate ceilings, leather furniture, gorgeous carpets, and plenty of gold leaf, is the most impressive place to eat in all of Melbourne; it's open to non-guests for an unlimited buffet lunch at Fridays at noon.

103 Spring St., Melbourne, VIC 3000. ℭ **1800 033 100** in Australia, or 03/9633 6000. Fax 03/9633 6001. www.thewindsor.com.au. 180 units. A$380 (U.S.$247) standard double; $480 (U.S.$271.70) superior double; A$550 (U.S.$307.45) deluxe double; from A$650 (U.S.$393) suite. AE, DC, MC, V. Parking A$20 (U.S.$13). **Amenities:** Restaurant (Modern Australian), 2 bars; health club; concierge; 24-hr. room service; laundry service; babysitting; business center. *In room:* A/C, TV with pay movies, minibar, coffeemaker, hair dryer, iron.

EXPENSIVE

The Adelphi 𝄍 It may be worth staying in this designer boutique hotel, a minute's walk from the city center, just for the experience of taking a dip in its top-floor 25-meter lap-pool, which juts out from the end of the building and hangs over the city streets below. The pool has a glass bottom, so you can watch pedestrians below as you float upside down. The rooms are similarly modernist, with colorful leather seating and lots of burnished metal. While I highly recommend this place for its architectural intrigue, on my last stay the front desk staff was as spiky as the furniture.

187 Flinders Lane, Melbourne, VIC 3000. ℭ **03/9650 7555.** Fax 03/9650 2710. www.adelphi.com.au. 34 units (most with shower only). A$275 (U.S.$178.75) standard double; A$295 (U.S.$191.75) deluxe double; A$495 (U.S.$321.75) executive suite. Rates include breakfast. AE, DC, MC, V. Extra person A$45 (U.S.$29.25). Free on-street parking. **Amenities:** Restaurant (Modern Australian), bar; fantastic outdoor pool; exercise room; sauna; bike rental; concierge; tour desk; business center; babysitting; same-day dry cleaning; nonsmoking rooms; executive rooms. *In room:* A/C, TV, dataport, minibar, coffeemaker, hair dryer, iron.

Grand Hotel *ℛℛ*   This majestic former railway department headquarters is striking for its remarkable scale and imposing Italianate facade. Building started on the six-story site in 1887, and additions were still being made in 1958. It finally became a hotel in late 1997, and is now managed by Sofitel. Suites have plush red Pullman carpets, a full kitchen with a dishwasher, a CD player, a second TV in the bedroom, and great views over the railway tracks—though rooms are whisper quiet. All rooms are similar but vary in size, though some have balconies. Many of the suites are split level, with bedrooms on the second floor.

33 Spencer St., Melbourne, VIC 3000. ℂ 1300/361 455 in Australia, or 03/9611 4567. Fax 03/9611 4655. www.accorhotel.com. 118 units. A$228–$435 (U.S.$148–$282.75) studio suite; A$248–$475 (U.S.$161–$309) 1-bedroom suite; A$358–$590 (U.S.$232.70–$383.50) 2-bedroom suite; A$448–$800 (U.S.$291–$520) 3-bedroom suite. Extra person A$44 (U.S.$28.60). Children under 14 stay free in parents' room. Ask about weekend and seasonal packages. AE, DC, MC, V. Parking A$13 (U.S.$8.45). Tram: 48 or 75 from Flinders St. **Amenities:** Restaurant (Modern Australian); bar; golf course nearby; exercise room; spa; sauna; concierge; tour desk; car-rental desk; 24-hr. room service; in-room massage; babysitting; laundry service; same-day dry cleaning; nonsmoking rooms. *In room:* A/C, TV with pay movies, dataport, kitchen, minibar, unstocked refrigerator, coffeemaker, hair dryer, iron.

MODERATE

Hotel Grand Chancellor   The great advantage of this hotel is that it's right in the heart of the action, on the very edge of Chinatown. The staff is very friendly, the heated swimming pool on the roof is pleasant on a hot summer day, and the views from the roof and some of the higher rooms are noteworthy. Generally though, the rooms remind me of any good motel room anywhere.

131 Lonsdale St., Melbourne, VIC 3000. ℂ 1800/331 006 in Australia, or 03/9656 4000. Fax 03/9662 3479. www.hotelchancellor.com.au. 160 units. A$200–$250 (U.S.$130–$162.50) double. Extra person A$25 (U.S.$16.25). Ask about weekend packages and lower rates through Aussie auto clubs. Children under 15 stay free in parents' room. AE, DC, MC, V. Parking A$15 (U.S.$9.75). **Amenities:** Restaurant (Modern Australian); bar; large rooftop swimming pool; sauna; concierge; tour desk; business center; 24-hr. room service; coin-op laundry; same-day dry cleaning; nonsmoking rooms. *In room:* A/C, TV with pay movies, dataport, minibar, coffeemaker, hair dryer, iron.

Oakford Executive Apartments *ℛℛ*   These serviced apartments, located inside an 1884 National Trust–listed building, are some of the best I've seen, and are a good alternative for travelers who want to cook their own food. The spacious apartments come with full kitchens, including a dishwasher. Those in the south block are older in style but still have contemporary furnishings. Those in the north block are new and a bit more upscale; they're set farther back from the road, too. More than half the units have a tub, but specify when booking to make sure. Another option to consider is the well-placed **Oakford on Lygon** *ℛℛ*, on Lygon Street (ℂ **03/8341 4777;** about a 10 min. walk from the city center). The rooms here have no kitchen but offer great value and I highly recommend them.

24 Little Bourke St., Melbourne, VIC 3000. ℂ 1800/818 237 in Australia, or 03/9663 2888. Fax 03/9639 1537. www.oakford.com. 82 apts. A$140–$270 (U.S.$91–$175.50) studio; A$176–$271 (U.S.$114.40–$176.15) 1-bedroom apt; A$211–$325 (U.S.$137.15–$211.25) 2-bedroom apt; A$226–$325 (U.S.$146.90–$211.25) split-level 3-bedroom apt. Extra person A$22 (U.S.$14.30). Ask about weekend packages, corporate rates, and long-term stays. AE, DC, MC, V. Parking A$10–$20 (U.S.$6.50–$13). **Amenities:** Restaurant (Modern Australian); small outdoor pool; exercise room; spa; sauna; business center; room service (7am–10pm); dry cleaning; nonsmoking rooms. *In room:* A/C, TV with pay movies, dataport, kitchen, minibar, unstocked refrigerator, coffeemaker, hair dryer, iron.

Ibis Melbourne *ℛ* *Value*   The good-value Ibis is right next door to the bus station and a short walk from the central shopping areas. The four-star rooms are spacious, immaculate, and bright, and have an attached shower. Apartments come with kitchenettes and a tub. All guests have free use of the swimming pool, sauna, and spa just up the road at the Melbourne City Baths.

15–21 Therry St., Melbourne, VIC 3000. © **03/9639 2399,** or 1300/65 65 65 in Australia, 800/221-4542 in the U.S. and Canada, 0800/44 4422 in New Zealand. Fax 03/9639 1988. www.accorhotel.com. 250 units (some with shower only). A$109–$114 (U.S.$70.90–$74) double (depending on high/low season); A$139–$145 (U.S.$90–$94) 1-bedroom apt; A$186–$198 (U.S.$120–$128) 2-bedroom apt. Additional person A$27 (U.S.$17.50). Children under 12 free in parents' room. Ask about package deals. AE, DC, MC, V. Parking A$8 (U.S.$5). **Amenities:** Restaurant (International), bar; coin-op laundry; nonsmoking rooms. *In room:* A/C, TV with pay movies, unstocked refrigerator, coffeemaker, hair dryer, iron.

INEXPENSIVE

Hotel Y   All rooms at the Y are sparsely furnished and not overly large, and as such do not represent such great value. The most expensive doubles and triples have been refurbished recently and have a TV, a refrigerator, and air-conditioning. The one-bedroom apartment has a queen-size bed with an en-suite bathroom, and the lounge has a double pullout bed and a small kitchenette. A cafe on the premises serves breakfast, lunch, and light snacks. The Y welcomes both women and men. The hotel is situated right near the Queen Victoria Market and is a short tram ride down Elizabeth Street or a 10-minute walk from the city center.

YWCA Melbourne, 489 Elizabeth St., Melbourne, VIC 3000. © **1800/249 124** in Australia, or 03/9329 5188. Fax 03/9329 1469. melb@ywca.org.au. 60 units. A$93–$115 (U.S.$60–$74.75) double; A$104–A$126 (U.S.$67.60–$89) triple; A$170 (U.S.$110) apt (for 2 people). Additional person A$16.50 (U.S.$17.50). AE, DC, MC, V. No parking. **Amenities:** Cafe; kitchen; TV room; coin-op laundry. *In room:* A/C (more expensive rooms only), TV, refrigerator.

Kingsgate Hotel   Melbourne's only city-based two-and-a-half-star hotel is a 10-minute walk from the city center. It's an interesting place, which feels like a very basic B&B, though a total refurbishment in late 2000/early 2001—"to attract airline staff"—gave it a better look. From the outside, the hotel resembles a terrace building, but inside it's a maze of corridors and rooms. The staff is very friendly. The least-expensive "economy" rooms are for backpackers only. They're dark and have two single beds and a hand basin; there's barely enough room to swing a backpack. Pricier "executive" rooms, however, are light, spacious, and have a bouncy double bed (or two twins) and an en-suite bathroom. A cooked breakfast costs A$7 (U.S.$4.50) extra. The 15 or so deluxe quad rooms have a double bed and two singles.

131 King St., Melbourne, VIC 3000. © **03/9629 4171** or 1300 73 41 71. Fax 03/9629 7110. www. kingsgatehotel.com.au. 225 units (104 with bathroom). A$69–$99 (U.S.$22.90–$64) double; A$89–$119 (U.S.$57.90–$77) triple; A$139 (U.S.$90) deluxe quad. AE, DC, MC, V. Parking A$5.50 (U.S.$3.50) a day at Crown Casino, a 5-min. walk away. **Amenities:** Tour desk; executive-level rooms. *In room:* TV.

Toad Hall ⊕ *Value*   "It's one of the best in Australia" is what one well-traveled guest said of Toad Hall. I have to agree; this 1858 mansion is an excellent value. It's just down the road from Queen Victoria Market and a few minutes' walk to the main shopping areas. Dorms are segregated by sex, with four to six bunk beds in each. Doubles and twins are small, but like the dorms, are clean and quite comfortable, with springy beds. I really liked the large communal kitchen, dining room, and outdoor courtyard.

441 Elizabeth St., Melbourne, VIC 3000. © **03/9600 9010.** Fax 03/9600 9013. www.toadhall-hotel.com.au. toadhall.hotel@bigpond.com. 85 dorm beds in 16 rooms; 8 doubles, 4 with bathroom; 12 twin rooms, 2 with bathroom. A$60 (U.S.$39) double/twin without bathroom; A$90 (U.S.$58) double/twin with bathroom; A$25 (U.S.$16.25) dorm bed (A$1/U.S.$65¢ discount per dorm, and A$2/U.S.$1.30 per double/twin for YHA members). MC, V. Parking A$6 (U.S.$3.90). **Amenities:** 3 TV lounges; tour desk; coin-op laundry. *In room:* Coffeemaker.

IN CARLTON

Albert Heights Executive Apartments ☞ For good, moderately priced accommodations with cooking facilities, so you can cut down on meal costs, you can't go wrong with the Albert Heights, a favorite of American travelers. It's in a nice area of Melbourne, a few minutes walk from the city center. There are parks at each end of the street. Each self-contained unit in this brick building is large and attractive. If you want your own space, or are traveling with your family, you can use the sofa bed in the living room. Each unit comes with a full kitchen with a microwave (no conventional oven), dining area, and large bathroom.

83 Albert St., East Melbourne, VIC 3002. ⓒ **1800/800 117** in Australia, or 03/9419 0955. Fax 03/9419 9517. www.albertheights.com.au. 34 units. A$130 double (U.S.$84.50). Additional person A$20 (U.S.$13). Ask about special deals. AE, DC, MC, V. Free parking. Tram: 42 or 109; or a 10-min. walk to city. **Amenities:** Small outdoor pool; spa; 24-hr. room service; babysitting; dry cleaning; laundry service. *In room:* A/C, TV, kitchen, unstocked refrigerator, hair dryer.

Georgian Court Guest House The comfortable Georgian Court's appearance hasn't changed much since it was built in 1910—and it's still fits like a favorite shirt. The sitting and dining rooms both have high ceilings, and offer old-world atmosphere. The bedrooms, furnished with little more than plain pine furniture and a double bed, still have charm. Most rooms were renovated in 2000.

21 George St., East Melbourne, VIC 3002. ⓒ **03/9419 6353.** Fax 03/9416 0895. www.georgiancourt.aunz. com. 31 units, 21 with bathroom. A$93 (U.S.$60.45) double without bathroom; A$117 (U.S.$76) double with bathroom. A$10–$20 (U.S.$6.50–$13) surcharge during busy periods, such as the Melbourne Grand Prix and other major sporting events. Additional person A$24 (U.S.$15.60); children under 15 A$13 (U.S.$8.45) extra. Rates include buffet breakfast. AE, DC, MC, V. Free parking. Tram: 75 from Flinders St., or 48 from Spencer St. Georgian Court is behind the Hilton, a 15-min. walk from the city center. **Amenities:** Access to nearby health club; tour desk; car-rental desk; coin-op laundry; same-day dry cleaning; nonsmoking rooms. *In room:* A/C, TV, fax, unstocked refrigerator, coffeemaker, hair dryer, iron, safe.

Quest on Drummond Very nice and functional three-star self-catering apartments at a decent price are what you'll find at this good, semibudget option. All apartments are modern and clean, and come with a full kitchen. One-bedroom apartments also have a sofa bed. Breakfast packs are available on request, but no reception is on the premises (though the management is only a phone call and a 2-min. walk away). It's within walking distance of the city center.

371 Drummond St., Carlton, VIC 3053. ⓒ 03/9486 1777. Fax 03/9482 2649. www.questapartments.com.au. 10 units. A$115 (U.S.$74.75) studio apt; A$126 (U.S.$82) 1-bedroom apt. AE, DC, MC, V. Off-street parking. Tram: 1 or 22 from Swanston St. **Amenities:** Access to nearby health club; babysitting; coin-op laundry; nonsmoking rooms. *In room:* TV, kitchen, unstocked refrigerator; coffeemaker, iron.

IN FITZROY

The Nunnery ☞ *Value* This former convent is an exceptional budget accommodation. Set in a terrace on the city's edge, the Nunnery is perfectly situated near the restaurant and nightlife scenes on Lygon Street and Brunswick Street, in nearby Carlton. Rooms vary in size from three-bed dorms to 12-bed in former nun's cells. Twin rooms come with either two singles or a set of bunks. All have basic furnishings and share bathrooms. Some second-floor rooms have good views over the neighboring Royal Exhibition Buildings and the city skyline. There's a large guest kitchen, a small courtyard where you can eat breakfast, Internet access, and a large sitting room filled with couches, a fireplace, and a TV. A new boutique wing opened in November 2000 and has two doubles for A$85 (U.S.$55), five family rooms, and a single for A$65 (U.S.$42). These rooms are a nicer than those in main section but still have shared facilities.

116 Nicholson St., Fitzroy, Melbourne, VIC 3065. (C) **1800 032 635** in Australia, or 03/9419 8637. Fax 03/ 9417 7736. www.bakpak.com/nunnery.com.au. 30 units, none with bathroom. A$45 (U.S.$29) single; A$55–$65 (U.S.$35.75–$42) double; A$80 (U.S.$52) triple. A$19–$25 (U.S.$12–$16) dorm bed. MC, V. Off-street parking. Tram: 96 from the city to East Brunswick (stop 13). **Amenities:** Tour desk; kitchen; lounge. *In room:* Coffeemaker.

IN ST. KILDA

Hotel Tolarno ⓖ   The quirky Hotel Tolarno is right in the middle of St. Kilda's cafe and restaurant strip, and a long stone's throw away from the beach. The whole place was renovated and expanded in 1998 and has a new foyer and breakfast room and lounge. Rich red carpets bedeck the corridors throughout this 1950s-to-1960s retro-style building. Rooms vary, but all are modern and nice. Some of the most popular rooms are in the front of the building and have balconies overlooking the main street. The more expensive of those come with a separate kitchen and lounge. Suites vary from one and two bedroom, and don't have balconies, though some have Jacuzzis.

42 Fitzroy St., St. Kilda, Melbourne, VIC 3182. (C) **03/9537 0200.** Fax 03/9534 7800. www.hoteltolarno. com.au. 31 units. A$114 (U.S.$74) standard double, A$139 (U.S.$90) balcony double; A$180–$260 (U.S.$117–$169) suite (sleeps up to 4). Additional person A$20 (U.S.$13). AE, DC, MC, V. On-street parking. Tram: 16 from Swanston St.; 96 from Flinders St. (about a 15-min. ride). **Amenities:** Restaurant (Modern Australian), bar; concierge, nonsmoking rooms. *In room:* A/C, TV, dataport, kitchenette, refrigerator, coffeemaker, hair dryer, iron.

Olembia Private Hotel   This sprawling Edwardian house, built in 1922, is set back from a busy St. Kilda street behind a leafy courtyard. It's popular with tourists, business travelers, and young families; and everyone gets together for the frequent video nights, wine and cheese parties, and barbecues. The clean bedrooms are simply furnished, with little more than a double bed, or two singles, a desk, a hand basin, and a wardrobe. Guests share six bathrooms. There's a very comfortable sitting room, and a courtyard area with barbecues. The Olembia is near St. Kilda beach and the host of restaurants lining Acland Street.

96 Barkly St., St. Kilda, Melbourne, VIC 3182. (C) **03/9537 1412.** Fax 03/9537 1600. www.olembia.com.au. 23 units, none with bathroom. A$48 (U.S.$31) single; A$68 (U.S.$44) double. AE, MC, V. Free parking. Tram: 96 from Bourke Street to stop 138. **Amenities:** Bike rental; coin-op laundry; nonsmoking rooms.

Robinson's by the Sea ⓖⓖ *(Finds)*   If you want something special, Robinson's by the Sea fits the bill. Both the management and pet dog are incredibly friendly at this 1870s heritage B&B just across from the beach. They encourage an evening social scene, and downstairs you'll find a comfortable, antiques-filled living room, and a dining room. Four of the five bedrooms are located upstairs. Each unit is unique. The Eastern Room has a four-poster queen-size bed and Indian and Chinese furniture, whereas the Rose Room is decorated with patterned flowers and pastel colors. The units all share three communal bathrooms, one with a tub and shower, a second with a shower, and the third with a Jacuzzi tub and shower. There are wood floorboards and fireplaces throughout.

335 Beaconsfield Parade, St. Kilda, Melbourne, VIC 3182. (C) **03/9534 2683.** Fax 03/9534 2683. www. robinsonsbythesea.com.au. wendyr@alphalink.com.au. 5 units, none with bathroom. A$143–$185 (U.S.$93–$120) double. Rates include cooked breakfast. AE, DC, MC, V. Free parking. Tram: 112 to Cowderoy St., St. Kilda. **Amenities:** Laundry service; nonsmoking rooms. *In room:* TV, coffeemaker, hair dryer.

IN SOUTH YARRA

Claremont B&B   The high ceilings and the mosaic tiles in the lobby welcome visitors into the interior of this old-world hotel, which reopened in 1995 after a complete overhaul. It's an attractive place, though sparsely furnished. The two-star-rated rooms are comfortable enough, and each comes with either a double or a single bed. There is no elevator in this three-story building with 72 stairs, so it could be a bad choice for travelers with disabilities.

189 Toorak Rd., South Yarra, VIC 3141. ℂ 03/9826 8000, or 03/9286 8222. Fax 03/9827 8652. www. melbaccom.com.au. 80 units, none with bathroom. A$56 (U.S.$36) single; A$68 (U.S.$44) double. Additional person A$10 (U.S.$6.50) extra. Children stay free in parents' room. Rates include continental breakfast. AE, DC, MC, V. On street parking. **Amenities:** Coin-op laundry; nonsmoking rooms. *In room:* TV.

The Hotel Como 𝒦𝒦𝒦   Winner of many tourism awards, the Hotel Como deservedly basks in its reputation for excellent service and terrific accommodations. Accommodations include studio rooms (some with shower only), one-room suites (some with kitchen or kitchenette), one- or two-bedroom suites (all with kitchen, some with an office) and luxurious (and pricey) penthouse and executive suites. Some units have a private Japanese garden. The hotel is especially adept at accommodating business travelers: all rooms have video-conferencing capability, and three complimentary limousines carry guests to the city center each weekday morning. Weekend packages are a very good value.

630 Chapel St., South Yarra, Melbourne, VIC 3141. ℂ 1800/033 400 in Australia, 800/552-6844 in the U.S. and Canada, or 0800/389 7791 in the U.K., 0800/446 110 in New Zealand, or 03/9825 2222. Fax 03/9824 1263. www.hotelcomo.com.au. 107 units. A$570 (U.S.$370) studio; A$650 (U.S.$422.50) 1-bedroom suite; A$770 (U.S.$500) 2-bedroom suite; A$900 (U.S.$585) penthouse; A$1,270 (U.S.$825.50) Como/Executive Suite. Ask about weekend package deals. AE, DC, MC, V. Parking $15 (U.S.$9.75). **Amenities:** 2 restaurants (Modern Australian, brasserie), bar; good indoor pool; health club; concierge; tour desk; business center; 24-hr. room service; massage; babysitting; laundry service; currency exchange. *In room:* A/C, TV with pay movies, dataport, minibar, coffeemaker, hair dryer, iron.

4 Where to Dine

Melbourne's ethnically diverse population ensures a healthy selection of international cooking styles. Chinatown, in the city center, is a fabulous hunting ground for authentic Chinese, Malaysian, Thai, Indonesian, Japanese, and Vietnamese fare, often at bargain prices. Carlton has plenty of Italian cuisine, but generally the outdoor restaurants on Lygon Street are aimed at unsuspecting tourists, and are generally overpriced and disappointing, so avoid them; Richmond is crammed with Greek and Vietnamese restaurants; and Fitzroy has cheap Asian, Turkish, Mediterranean, and vegetarian food. To see and be seen, head to Chapel Street or Toorak Road in South Yarra, or to St. Kilda to take in the sea breeze and join the throng of Melbournians dining out along Fitzroy and Ackland streets. Most of the cheaper places in Melbourne are strictly BYO (bring-your-own wine or beer). Smoking is currently possible in cafes and restaurants, but moves are afoot to ban the practice, so think twice if you want to risk annoying fellow patrons.

IN THE CITY CENTER
EXPENSIVE
Flower Drum 𝒦𝒦𝒦 CANTONESE   Praise pours in from all quarters for this upscale choice situated just off Little Bourke Street, Chinatown's main drag. Take a slow elevator up to the restaurant, which has widely spaced tables (perfect for politicians and businesspeople to clinch their deals). Take note of the specials— the chefs are extremely creative and utilize the best ingredients they find in the markets each day. The signature dish here is the Peking duck, although the buttered garfish is my favorite. The king crab dumplings in soup is a great starter. You can also prearrange a banquet for two or more diners; you'll be served more unusual dishes (such as abalone). One- or 2-day advance notice is required.

Where to Dine in Melbourne

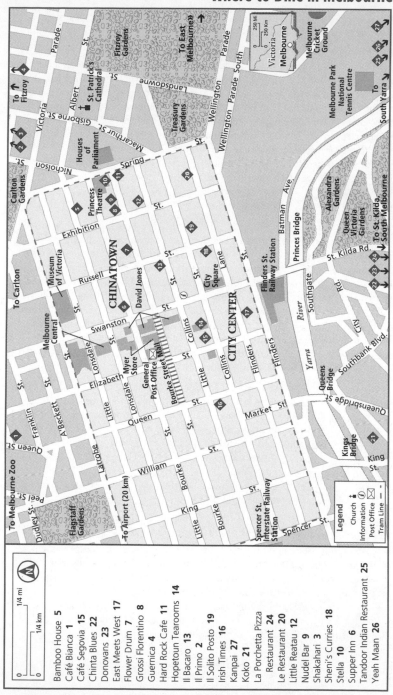

Legend
- Church
- Information
- Post Office
- Tram Line

Bamboo House **5**
Café Bianca **1**
Café Segovia **15**
Chinta Blues **22**
Donovans **23**
East Meets West **17**
Flower Drum **7**
Grossi Florentino **8**
Guernica **4**
Hard Rock Cafe **11**
Hopetoun Tearooms **14**
Il Bacaro **13**
Il Primo **2**
Il Solito Posto **19**
Irish Times **16**
Kanpai **27**
Koko **21**
La Porchetta Pizza Restaurant **24**
Le Restaurant **20**
Little Reatau **12**
Nudel Bar **9**
Shakahari **3**
Sheni's Curries **18**
Stella **10**
Supper Inn **6**
Tandoor Indian Restaurant **25**
Yeah Maan **26**

17 Market Lane. (℃ **03/9662 3655.** Reservations required. Main courses A$27–$45. AE, DC, MC, V. Mon–Sat noon–2:30pm and 6–11pm, Sun 6–10:30pm.

Koko 𝔤𝔤 JAPANESE   Though you'll find plenty of Japanese sushi and noodle bars around Chinatown, there's nothing quite like raw fish eaten with a bit of panache. A visit to Crown Casino can be a memorable experience in itself, but stop off here and you'll wish you could remember these tastes forever. The restaurant has a mixed contemporary/traditional decor, with a goldfish pond in the center of the main dining room and wonderful views over the city. There are separate teppanyaki grills and screened tatami rooms where you sit on the matted floor. If you can manage the boiled eel with rice then go for it. Otherwise the yaki udon, or the cooked "sushi" of roast chicken, duck, prawns, and rare beef is popular. A choice of 10 sakes helps digestion.

Level 3, Crown Towers, Southbank. (℃ **03/9292 6886.** Reservations required. Main courses A$25–$30 (U.S.$16.25–$19.50). AE, DC, MC, V. Daily for lunch from noon–2:30pm and dinner from 6:30–10.:30pm.

Le Restaurant 𝔤𝔤𝔤 MODERN AUSTRALIAN   You might not want to leave the hotel once you've experienced the Sofitel's magnificent dining options. If having the wonderful Café La on the premises wasn't enough, it is blessed with Le Restaurant, one of Melbourne's premier fine-dining choices. The service is exquisite, the cuisine inventive, and the views fixating. The dishes here are well crafted and combine wonderful flavors and colors. The menu changes regularly, but you might find the King Island crayfish in a crust of kaffir leaf and morel dust served up with scallop ravioli, shiitake mushroom, and tarragon essence. The enormous wine list is mostly populated with expensive vintages.

In the Hotel Sofitel, 35th floor, 25 Collins St., City. (℃ **03/9653 0000.** Reservations recommended. Main courses A$32–$40 (U.S.$20.80–$26). AE, DC, MC, V. Tues–Sat 7–10:30pm.

Stella 𝔤 MODERN AUSTRALIAN   This relaxed eating spot is made all the nicer by the cushion-scattered benches and moody lightning. The food is imaginative, and you could end up eating the likes of barramundi (a fish) on kipfler potatoes with a rocket pesto, cumin and coriander-scented pork fillet with spinach, potatoes, and green tomato chutney. The desserts, such as the baked chocolate pudding, are quite expensive at between A$15 to $18 (U.S.$9.75–$11.70), but are a taste sensation.

159 Spring St., City. (℃ **03/9639 1555.** Reservations required. Main courses A$23–$28 (U.S.$14.95–$18.20). AE, DC, MC, V. Mon–Fri noon–3pm; Mon–Sat 6–11pm.

MODERATE

Bamboo House 𝔤 NORTHERN REGIONAL CHINESE/CANTONESE   If Flower Drum (see below) is full (or breaks your budget), try this place, which is esteemed by both the Chinese community and local business big shots. The service here really is a pleasure, and the food (especially the delicious chicken with shallot sauce) is worth writing home about. The waiters are all eager to help you construct a feast from the myriad Cantonese and northern Chinese dishes. (Don't leave without a taste of the duck in plum sauce!) Other popular dishes include pan-fried dumplings, spring onion pancakes, and the signature dish, Sichuan smoked duck.

47 Little Burke St. (℃ **03/9662 1565.** Reservations recommended. Main courses A$17–$24 (U.S.$11–$15.60). AE, DC, MC, V. Mon–Fri noon–3pm; Mon–Sat 5:30–11pm; Sun 5:30–10pm.

Grossi Florentino ITALIAN   Under the management of the Grossi family, the restaurant formerly known solely as Florentinos has perked up to become probably the best Italian restaurant in Melbourne. It's split into three separate sections, with a casual bistro downstairs, next to the Cellar bar (where you can pick up a bowl of pasta for around A$10 (U.S.$6.50), while upstairs you can find the fine dining restaurant with its chandeliers and murals reflecting the Florentine way of life. On the menu here you could find veal shanks braised with tomato and red wine on a bed of saffron, as well as typical Italian risotto, seafood, and steak dishes.

80 Bourke St. ⓒ 03/9662 1811. Reservations recommended. Main courses $16–$35 (U.S.$10.40–$22.75). AE, DC, MC, V. Mon–Fri noon–3pm; Mon–Sat 6–11pm.

Il Bacaro 𝄐 ITALIAN   Walk into Il Bacaro and you'll feel you've been transported to Venice. Dominated by a horseshoe-shaped bar, it's jam-packed with small tables and weaving waiters carrying dishes like carpaccio of tuna or semolina gnocchetti with duck ragout. The pasta dishes and the risotto of the day always go down well, as do the salad side dishes. It's often crowded at lunch with local businesspeople digging deep into the excellent wine list.

168–170 Little Collins St. ⓒ 03/9654 6778. Reservations recommended. Main courses A$19.80–$26.80 (U.S.$12.87–$17.40). AE, DC, MC, V. Mon–Fri noon–4pm; Mon–Sat 6pm–midnight.

Il Solito Posto NORTHERN ITALIAN   This sunken restaurant is split into two parts. The casual bistro has a blackboard menu offering good pastas, soups, and salads. Then there's the sharper and more upmarket trattoria, with its a la carte menu offering the likes of steak, fish, and veal dishes. The coffee is good, too.

Basement of 113 Collins St. (enter via George Parade). ⓒ 03/9654 4466. Reservations recommended. Main courses A$8.50–$13 (U.S.$5.50–$8.45) in bistro, A$18.50–$27.50 (U.S.$12–$17.90) in trattoria. AE, DC, MC, V. Mon–Sat 7:30am–1am.

Irish Times IRISH/MODERN AUSTRALIAN   An Irish bar more authentic than most, the Irish Times is a character-filled eating and drinking escape from the rush of the city outside, which serves up generous portions and Guinness on tap. Popular dishes include the warm chicken salad, mussels in a creamy broth, Caesar salad, and Irish dishes such as "boxty"—patties of mashed potato, leak, and onion with an accompanying tomato relish. There's a live band on Thursday and Friday evenings from 9:30pm and on Saturday from 10:30pm.

427 Little Collins St. ⓒ 03/9642 1699. Reservations advisable. Main courses $8.50–$18 (U.S.$5.50–$11.70). AE, DC, MC, V. Open Sun–Tues 11am–midnight; Wed–Sat 11am–3am. Not BYO.

Nudel Bar NOODLES   A favorite with city slickers, the Nudel Bar serves up a variety of noodle dishes to the crowded tables and bar. Examples of what you might find here are cold spicy green tea noodles, *mee goring* (a noodle dish with peanuts and here, often chicken) and sticky rice pudding is a favorite for dessert.

76 Bourke St. ⓒ 03/9662 9100. Reservations advisable Fri and Sat evenings. Main courses $12.90–$17.80 (U.S.$8.40–$11.60). AE, DC, MC, V. Open Mon–Fri 11am–10:30pm; Sat 11am–11pm; Sun 4–10:30pm.

INEXPENSIVE

Café Bianca 𝄐 *Finds* PIZZA   Inside the main market building, past the meat and fish sellers, and farther on past a range of cake and deli stalls is the best little pizza take-out in Australia. It's tiny, and there's nowhere to sit, but who has time to hang around with so much to see anyway? All the pizzas, including such gourmet concoctions as chicken tandoori pizza, fresh asparagus pizza, and potato and herb pizza, are homemade. Don't be fooled by the pretenders to the pizza crown that can be found nearby.

Store 97–98, Queen Victoria Market. No phone. Main courses A$2.60–$3.80 (U.S.$1.70–$2.50). No credit cards. Market hours.

Café Segovia *★★ (Finds* CAFE   Café Segovia is one of the most atmospheric cafes in Australia, with a smoky, sensual interior reminiscent of Spain. Seating is also available outside in the arcade itself, but you'll have to come early at lunchtime to nab a chair. Typical cafe food is on offer, such as focaccias, cakes, and light meals.

33 Block Arcade. ℭ **03/9650 2373.** Main courses A$8–$13 (U.S.$5.20–$8.50). AE, DC, MC, V. Mon–Fri 7:30am–11pm, Saturday 8am–6pm, Sunday 9am–5pm.

East Meets West ASIAN/FAST FOOD   This little place is great for a quick Indian curry, a plate of noodles, some spring rolls, or fish-and-chips. It's simple and cheap, with a few small tables. The curries are delicious and come in medium and large portions.

271 Flinders Lane. ℭ **03/9650 8877.** Main courses A$5.50–$7 (U.S.$3.60–$4.55). AE, DC, MC, V. Mon–Fri 10am–6:30pm, Sat 10:30am–2:30pm.

Hard Rock Cafe AMERICAN   You know the drill here. The ubiquitous Hard Rock serves up large portions of typical theme-restaurant fare—nachos, T-bone steaks, chicken, salads, and burgers—in a rock-'n'-roll atmosphere. Bottomless soft drinks are served, but there are no free refills for coffee. The music can get overpoweringly loud here.

1 Bourke St. (next to The Windsor Hotel). ℭ **03/9633 6193.** Reservations recommended. Main courses A$9.75–$19.95 (U.S.$6.85–$13.95). AE, DC, MC, V. Daily noon–midnight.

Hopetoun Tearooms *★* CAFE   The first cup of coffee served in this Melbourne institution left the pot in 1891. It's all very civilized here, with green-and-white Regency wallpaper and marble tables. The cakes are very good; the sandwiches go for A$4.50 to $6.50 (U.S.$2.90–$4.25) and the focaccias for A$7 to $8.50 (U.S.$4.50–$5.50). Scones, croissants, and grilled food are also available.

Shops 1 and 2, Block Arcade. ℭ **03/9650 2777.** Main courses A$4.50–$8.50 (U.S.$2.90–$5.55) (min. charge A$5/U.S.$3.25 per person noon–2pm). Mon–Thurs 8:30am–5pm, Fri 8:30am–6pm, Sat 10am–3:30pm. Closed Sunday. AE, DC, MC, V.

Little Reatau TEX-MEX   Typical Tex-Mex cooking is served up inside the blood-red walls of this dimly lit restaurant. The house specialty is the chicken fajitas (chicken marinated in tequila and lime with tortillas, salad, salsa, and sour cream). There's an interesting cocktail selection available for A$6 to $8.50 (U.S.$3.90–$5.50).

68 Little Collins St. ℭ **03/9654 5917.** Reservations recommended. Main courses A$10.50–$16 (U.S.$6.80–$10.40). AE, DC, MC, V. Daily 5:30pm–7am (limited menu 11pm–5am); Tues–Fri noon–2:30pm.

Sheni's Curries SRI LANKAN   This tiny, very busy place (it seats 30) offers a small range of excellent-value, authentic Sri Lankan curries. You can either dine here or take your lunch special to go. Choose between three vegetable dishes and a choice of meat and seafood dishes. All meals come with rice, three types of chutney, and a papadam. You can also buy extra items such as samosas and roti.

Shop 16, 161 Collins St. (on the corner of Flinders Lane and Russell St., opposite the entrance to the Grand Hyatt). ℭ **03/9654 3535.** Lunch specials A$4.50–$7 (U.S.$2.90–$4.55). No credit cards. Mon–Fri 11am–4pm.

Supper Inn CANTONESE   Head here if you get the Chinese-food munchies late at night. It's a friendly place with a mixed crowd of locals and tourists chowing down on such dishes as steaming bowls of congee (a rice-based porridge), barbecued suckling pig, mud crab, or stuffed scallops. Everything's authentic, not like some of the Westernized slop you often get served.

15 Celestial Ave. © 03/9663 4759. Reservations recommended. Main courses A$9–$12 (U.S.$5.85–$7.80). AE, DC, MC, V. Daily 5:30pm–2:30am.

CARLTON

Il Primo ⚵ SOUTHERN EUROPEAN   This restaurant is tucked away in a pair of historic houses in the Italian sector of Carlton. There are three dining areas in all, all cozy, with antique bricks, wood-beamed ceilings, and tiled floors. It feels like you're dining in a wine cellar, and indeed, there's a great wine list, including a range of unlabeled local wines at rock-bottom prices. The menu changes regularly, but you'll see the likes of veal parmigiana, warm kangaroo salad, fish, garlic prawns, risotto, and a dozen or pastas. Live jazz brings in the customers every night from 10 or 11pm to closing time.

242 Lygon St., Carlton. © 03/9663 6100. Reservations recommended. Main courses A$16.80–$27.50 (U.S.$11–$18). AE, DC, MC, V. Sun–Tues 6:30am–1am, Wed–Sat 6:30am–3am. Tram: 1, 15, 21, or 22 traveling north on Swanston St. (Stop 12).

Trotters ⚵ CAFE   If you want a great breakfast and you're staying in Carlton, then Trotters is easily the best place you'll come across. All the classics include bacon and eggs, homemade cakes and croissants, as well as good coffee. Seating is both indoors and out.

400 Lygon St, Carlton. © 03/9347 5657. Main courses A$4.50–$8 (U.S.$2.90–$5.20). AE, DC, MC, V. Open Mon–Fri 7:30am–10pm, Sat 8am–10pm, Sun 9:30am–10pm. Tram: Any tram going north along Swanston St. toward Melbourne University.

A VEGETARIAN DELIGHT IN CARLTON

Shakahariu VEGETARIAN   Good vegetarian food isn't just a meal without meat; it's a creation in its own right. At Shakahari you are assured of a creative meal that's not at all bland. The large restaurant is quite low-key, but the service can be a bit inconsistent. The Sate Samsara (skewered, lightly fried vegetables and tofu pieces with a peanut dip) is a winner, as is the couscous, served in a vast earthenware pot. Also served up are curries, croquets, tempura avocado, and veggie burgers (on a plate with salad, not in a bun).

201–203 Faraday St., Carlton. © 03/9347 3848. Main courses A$12.50 (U.S.$8.10). AE, DC, MC, V. Mon–Sat noon–3:30pm; Sun–Thurs 6–9:30pm; Fri–Sat 6–10:30pm. Tram: Any tram going north along Swanston St. toward Melbourne University.

FITZROY

Guernica ⚵⚵ MODERN AUSTRALIAN   Dimly lit and featuring a giant print of Picasso's famous 1936 painting, this restaurant serves up some exciting dishes, many jazzed up with a healthy tingle of spice or pepper. Choices range from chili-salted calamari, chargrilled ocean trout, and chargrilled beet fillet— though the gourmet additions on your plate make them all even more appetizing than they sound. The desserts are some of the best in town and include the marvelous palm-sugar caramelized rice pudding with toasted coconut ice cream. Check out the blackboard selections of good Australian wines by the glass. The restaurant is nonsmoking in the evenings until 10pm.

257 Brunswick St., Fitzroy. © 03/9416 0969. Reservations recommended. Main courses A$20–$25.50 (U.S.$13–$16.60). AE, DC, MC, V. Sun–Fri noon–3pm; daily 6–10:30pm. Tram: 11 from Collins St., or 86 from Bourke St.

SEASIDE DINING IN ST. KILDA

Chinta Blues MALAYSIAN   Head to this very popular eatery if you're looking for simple, satisfying food with a healthy touch of spice. The big sellers are the laksa, the mei goreng, the chicken curry, the sambal spinach, and a chicken dish called ayam blues. Lots of noodles, too. It's very busy, especially at lunch.

6 Acland St., St. Kilda. ℂ 03/9534 9233. Reservations recommended. Main courses A$10–$19. AE, MC, V. Mon–Wed noon–2:30pm and 6–10pm; Thurs–Sat noon–2:30pm and 6–10:45pm; Sun noon–9:45pm. Tram: 16 from Swanston St. or 96 from Bourke St.

Donovans 𝒢𝒢 MODERN MEDITERRANEAN   Donovans is so near the sea that you expect the fish to jump through the door and onto the plate—and indeed, you do get extremely fresh seafood. The restaurant is all higgledy-piggledy and charming, with lots of cushions, a log fire, and the sound of jazz and breakers on the beach. The menu includes a mind-boggling 53 dishes, so you are sure to find something to suit your fancy. Favorites include the swordfish fillet with warm onion relish, or the home-style fish stew, big enough for two, with generous amounts of prawns, clams, mussels, and fish. If you're not a big fish-eater, then choose from several pasta and meat dishes.

40 Jacka Blvd., St. Kilda. ℂ 03/9534 8221. Reservations recommended. Main courses A$23–$32 (U.S.$14.90–$20.80). Daily noon–10:30pm. AE, DC, MC, V. Tram: 12 from Collins St., 16 from Swanston St., 94 or 96 from Bourke St.

La Porchetta Pizza Restaurant PIZZA   This very busy, quite large, and very noisy pizza joint is a very good value. There are some 22 different pizzas to choose from, with the largest ranging in price from A$6 to $7.80 (U.S.$4.20–$4.50) being just large enough to fill two. A range of pasta dishes cost from A$6 to $9 (U.S.$4.20–$6.30). Chicken, seafood, veal, and steaks are also on the menu. The heart-pounding pace here means it's not for the faint-hearted.

80 Acland St., St. Kilda. ℂ 03/9534 1888. Main courses A$5–$13.50 (U.S.$3.20–$8.80). No credit cards. Sun–Thurs 11am–midnight, Fri–Sat 11am–2am. Tram: 16 from Swanston St. or 96 from Bourke St.

MORE ETHNIC EATS IN SOUTH YARRA

Kanpai JAPANESE   You have to book early in the day to get a seat at this very popular restaurant on the Chapel Street restaurant strip. The sushi and sashimi dishes are very fresh, and the miso soup is well worth plundering with your chopsticks. There's a good vegetarian selection, too.

569 Chapel St., South Yarra. ℂ 03/9827 4379. Reservations recommended. Main courses A$12–$34 (U.S.$7.80–$22). (average price A$12.50/U.S.$8.10). AE, DC, MC, V. Daily noon–11pm. Tram: 6, 8, or 72 from Swanston St.

Tandoor Indian Restaurant 𝒢 INDIAN   This basic Indian restaurant was far less crowded than many of the others on the Chapel Street strip when I last visited—all I can say is that the "in" crowd didn't know what they were missing. The curries here are rich and spicy, with the vegetarian paneer-butter masala and the cheese kofta being some of the best I've tasted in Australia. Some dishes, such as the crab masala curry, are truly inspirational. The main courses are quite large, so you'll probably not need a first course, but I highly recommend side dishes of naan bread (one per person) and a cucumber raita to cool the palate.

517 Chapel St., South Yarra. ℂ 03/9827 8247. Reservations recommended Fri and Sat night. Main courses A$9–$17 (U.S.$5.85–$11). AE, DC, MC, V. Tues–Fri noon–2:30pm; daily 6–11pm. Tram: 6, 8, or 72 from Swanston St.

Yeah Maan 𝒢 CARIBBEAN   Is this the coolest restaurant in Australia or what? Calypso music wafts amid the homemade triangle-backed chairs, diners wait in the lounge for a table to become free, palm trees sway—and the food! Wow! The whole place is rockin', mon, with the 75 seats almost continually occupied. The authentic Trinidadian goat curry is a must, as is the Barbados burrito. The Jamaican KFC (chicken marinated for 2 days in approximately 30 spices and then smoked), and the Jumbo-Jumbie cassava shoestring fries (cassava is similar to a potato), are very, very popular. An upstairs dining room was due to open in late 2001. The staff is ultra-friendly.

340 Punt Rd. (at Fawkner St.), South Yarra. (℃ **03/9820 2707.** Reservations not accepted. Main courses A$13–$18.50. MC, V. Tues–Sat 6–11:30pm. Tram: 6, 8, or 72 from Swanston St.

5 Seeing the Sights

Melbourne may not have as many major attractions as Sydney, but visitors come here to experience the contrasts of old-world architecture and the exciting feel of a truly multicultural city.

If you'd like to see the city aboard a leisurely cruise, call **Melbourne River Cruises** (℃ **03/9614 1215** Mon–Fri, or 03/9650 2055 on weekends). This company offers a 2½-hour round-trip cruise on the Yarra River costing A$16.50 (U.S.$10.70) for adults, A$8.80 (U.S.$5.70) for children ages 3 to 12, A$13.20 (U.S.$8.60) concession, and A$41.80 (U.S.$27) for a family.

THE TOP ATTRACTIONS

Gold Treasury Museum   Designed by the architect J.J. Clarke (when he was only 19) and built in 1857, The Old Treasury Building is an imposing neoclassical sandstone building which once housed precious metal from the Ballarat and Bendigo gold rushes. The gold was stored in eight thick-walled vaults underground and protected by iron bars. The "Built on Gold" Exhibition within the vaults themselves is a high-tech multimedia show featuring videos and displays showing how the gold was dug up, sold, transported, and housed. In the basement are the restored living quarters of a caretaker who lived there from 1916 to 1928. The ground floor is taken up by the "Melbourne: A City Built On Gold" display which shows how Melbourne was built using the profits from the gold rushes. A temporary exhibition gallery on the premises can feature anything from prints to gold-thread embroidery. Allow 1 hour.

Old Treasury Building. Spring St. (top of Collins St.) (℃ **03/9651 2233.** A$7 (U.S.$4.55) adults, A$3.50 (U.S.$2.30) children, A$18 (U.S.$11.70) family. Mon–Fri 9am–5pm; weekends and public holidays10am–4pm.

IMAX Theatre *(Kids)*   This eight-story movie screen rivals the world's largest screen at Sydney's Darling Harbour. The movies shown here are shot with special giant-format cameras. Recent subjects have been outer space, the African Serengeti, and the deep oceans.

Melbourne Museum Complex, Rathdowne St., Carlton. (℃ **03/9663 5454.** Admission from A$13.95 (U.S.$9) adults, A$9.95 (U.S.$6.50) children. Daily 10am–10pm. Tram: 1 or 22 from Swanston St.

Tips A Few Sightseeing Suggestions

Much of Melbourne's appeal comes from soaking up the atmosphere on a walk around the city. But if you have time to see only one major attraction, by all means make it the **Melbourne Zoo.** Other can't-miss sights include the **Rialto Towers Observation Deck,** the **National Gallery of Victoria,** and the **Botanic Gardens.** If you have time, head to **Phillip Island** to see the fairy penguins.

Melbourne Aquarium   Opened in early 2000, the Melbourne Aquarium is a much smaller version of the one in Sydney. Stretched over three levels, it features a large Barrier Reef–type exhibit, some interesting jellyfish displays, and an enormous walk-through tank filled with larger fish, sharks, and rays. Altogether though it was pretty disappointing and didn't live up to the hype. Allow 30 minutes.

A Money-Saving Tip

If you're a student, a senior over 60, or a YHA member, you can often receive hefty discounts on entrance fees to attractions in Australia. Just carry some relevant identification, and always remember to ask!

Corner of King & Flinders sts, opposite Crown Casino. ℂ **03/9620 0999.** Admission A$19 (U.S.$12.40) adults, A$9 (U.S.$5.90) children under 16, A$49 (U.S.$12) family of 5. Open 9am–6pm.

Melbourne Zoo 𝒦𝒦 *Kids*   This place is a must-see. Built in 1862, it's the oldest zoo in the world, and still among the best. There are some 3,000 animals here, including the ever-popular kangaroos, wallabies, echidnas, koalas, wombats, and platypus. Rather than being locked up in tiny cages, most animals are set in almost natural surroundings or well-tended gardens. Don't miss the wonderful butterfly house, with its thousands of colorful Australian butterflies flying around; the enormous freeflight aviary; the lowland gorilla exhibit; and the tree-top monkey displays. Allow at least 1 hour if you just want to see the Australian natives and around 2½ hours for the whole zoo.

Elliot Ave., Parkville. ℂ **03/9285 9300** or 03/9347 9530. Admission A$16.40 (U.S.$10.70) adults, A$8.10 (U.S.$5.30) children under 14, A$44.30 (U.S.$28.80) family. Daily 9am–5pm. Free guided tours Mon–Fri 10am–3pm, Sat–Sun 11am–4pm (go to the Friends of the Zoo Office to arrange tours). Tram: 55 or 56 going north on William St. to stop 25; 18, 19, or 20 from Elizabeth St. to Stop 16 (then it's a short walk to your left following signposts). Train: Royal Park Station. Bus: City Explorer.

National Gallery of Victoria 𝒦   This is the best place in Victoria to view Aboriginal art, as well as colonial Australian, Asian, and European works. Look for works by artists such as Sidney Nolan, Russell Drysdale, and Tom Roberts; there are also a few works by Rembrandt, Picasso, Manet, and Turner. A free Aboriginal arts tour starts at 2pm every Thursday. There is a cafe and a restaurant on the premises. The Australian collection is due to move to a new building in Federation Square, on the corner of Flinders and Swanston in May 2001, and the whole gallery will be packed up and moved to its original home at 180 St. Kilda Road in November 2002. Allow 1 hour.

285–321 Russell St. ℂ **03/9208 0203.** Free general admission; call about special exhibits. Daily 10am–5pm. Closed Good Friday and Christmas. Tram: any southbound tram on Swanston St.

Old Melbourne Gaol 𝒦𝒦 *Finds*   I love this cramped former prison with its tiny cells and spooky collection of death masks and artifacts relating to 19th-century prison life. Some 135 hangings took place here, including that of the notorious bandit (and Australian hero) Ned Kelly, in 1880. The scaffold where he was hung is still in place, and his gun, as well as a suit of armor used by a member of his gang, is on display. The jail closed in 1929. The display profiles of former prisoners give a fabulous perspective of what it was like to be locked up here. Chilling night tours run every Sunday and Wednesday (call ahead and check the schedule); they cost A$18 (U.S.$11.70) for adults and A$10 (U.S.$6.50) for children (though the tour is not recommended for children under 12). Allow 1 hour or more.

Melbourne Attractions

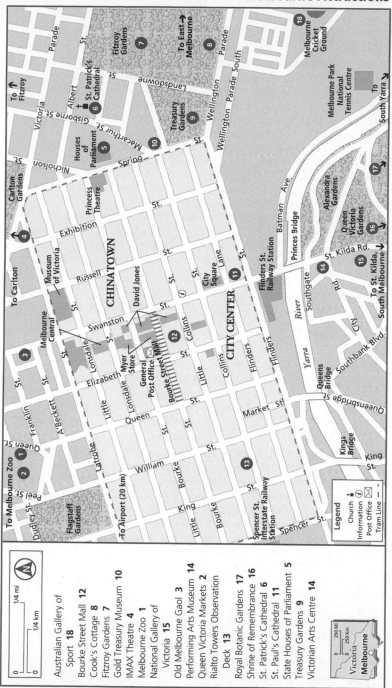

Australian Gallery of
  Sport **18**
Bourke Street Mall **12**
Cook's Cottage **8**
Fitzroy Gardens **7**
Gold Treasury Museum **10**
IMAX Theatre **4**
Melbourne Zoo **1**
National Gallery of
  Victoria **15**
Old Melbourne Gaol **3**
Performing Arts Museum **14**
Queen Victoria Markets **2**
Rialto Towers Observation
  Deck **13**
Royal Botanic Gardens **17**
Shrine of Remembrance **16**
St. Patrick's Cathedral **6**
St. Paul's Cathedral **11**
State Houses of Parliament **5**
Treasury Gardens **9**
Victorian Arts Centre **14**

Legend
Church ✝
Information ⓘ
Post Office ⊠
Tram Line - - -

Russell St. ☎ **03/9663 7228.** www.vicnet.net.au/~omgaol. Admission A$9.90 (U.S.$6.40) adults, A$6.60 (U.S.$4.30) children, A$27.50 (U.S.$17.85) families. Daily 9:30am–4:30pm. Tram: City Circle tram to corner of Russell and Latrobe sts.

Queen Victoria Markets ✿ The Queen Vic is a Melbourne institution covering several blocks. There are hundreds of indoor and outdoor stalls, where you can find virtually anything from live rabbits to bargain-basement clothes. The markets can get cramped, and there's a lot of junk to sort through, but you'll get a real taste of Melbourne and its ethnic mix here. Look out for the interesting delicatessen section, and cheap eateries. Allow at least an hour.

Two organized 2-hour tours of the market take in its food and heritage. The Foodies Dream Tour departs every Tuesday, Thursday, Friday, and Saturday at 10am and costs A$22 (U.S.$14.30) and A$15 for children under 15, including sampling. The Heritage Market Tour departs on the same days but at 10:30am and includes morning tea. It costs A$16.50 (U.S.$10.70) for adults, and "would most likely bore children to death," according to the guide. Call ☎ 03/9320 5822 for reservations.

Between Peel, Victoria, Elizabeth, and Therry sts. on the northern edge of the city center. ☎ **03/9269 5822.** Tues–Thurs 6am–2pm, Fri 6am–6pm, Sat 6am–3pm, Sun 9am–4pm. Tram: any tram traveling north along William St. or Elizabeth St.

Rialto Towers Observation Desk From this observation deck, near the top of the tallest building in the Southern Hemisphere, you get magnificent 360° views of the whole of Melbourne and beyond. See if you can spot the Melbourne Cricket Ground (MCG) and the new Crown Casino. A 20-minute film costing A$2 (U.S.$1.30) shows you what you're looking at, but you might as well just take a map up with you and figure it out for yourself. Of interest are the displays telling about life in Melbourne, past and present. There's a licensed cafe here, too. Allow 1 hour.

Rialto Building, 55th Floor, Collins St. (between William and King sts.). ☎ **03/9629 8222.** Admission A$9.90 (U.S.$6.40) adults, A$5.50 (U.S.$3.60) children, A$27.50 (U.S.$17.90) families. Sun–Thurs 10am–10pm, Fri–Sat 10am–11pm. Tram: Any tram on Collins St.

Rippon Lea House Museum & Historic Garden This grand Victorian house, 8 kilometers (5 miles) from the city center, is worth a visit to get a feel for old-money Melbourne. Boasting dozens of rooms, Rippon Lea House was built by socialite Sir Frederick Thomas Sargood between 1868 and 1903; a pool and ballroom were added in the 1930s. Though the Romanesque architecture is interesting (note the stained glass and polychrome brickwork), the real attraction is the surrounding 13 acres (5.3 hectares) of gorgeous landscaped gardens, which include a conservatory, a lake, a lookout tower, an orchard, and extensive flower beds and ornate shrubbery. If you're here on a weekend, a public holiday, or during school vacations, you might like to drop into the tearoom, which is open from 11am to 4pm. Allow 2 hours.

192 Hotham St., Elsternwick. ☎ **03/9523 6095.** Admission A$9 (U.S.$5.85) adults, A$5 (U.S.$3.25) children 5–16, A$20 (U.S.$13) families of up to 6. Daily 10am–5pm (house closes at 4:45pm). Daily guided tours of house every ½ hour 10:30am–4pm and tour of estate at 2pm. Closed Good Friday and Christmas Day. Tram: 67 to Stop 40, then walk up Hotham St. Bus: 216/219 from Bourke and Queen sts. in the city to Stop 4. Train: Sandringham Line from Flinders Street Station to Rippon Lea Station.

St. Pauls Cathedral Built in 1880-92 from the designs of William Butterfield, a famous English Gothic revival architect, the Anglican St. Pauls Cathedral is noteworthy for its highly-decorative interior and English organ built by T.S Lewis. Gold mosaics cover the walls, Victorian tiles the floors, there are intricate wood carvings, wonderful stained-glass windows, and the cathedral sports the second highest spire (at 98m/321½ ft.) in the Anglican Communion. The tallest spire, by the way, is on top of Salisbury Cathedral in England (123m/403½ ft.). A boy's choir sings at 5:10pm Monday through Friday during school times, and twice on Sunday at 10:30am and 6pm. Outside is a statue of Matthew Flinders, the first sailor to navigate the Australian mainland between 1801 and 1803 in the *Tom Thumb*. Allow 15 minutes.

Flinders and Swanston sts. 𝄐 **03/9650 3791.** Daily 7:30am–6pm.

St. Patrick's Cathedral   Though lacking the intricacy of design of St. Pauls, the Roman Catholic St. Patrick's is another interesting Gothic Revival construction with exceptional stained-glass windows. Built between 1858 and 1940 (consecrated in 1897), St. Patrick's was closely associated with immigrants from Ireland escaping the mid-19th-century potato famine. In the courtyard out front is a statue of the Irish patriot Daniel O'Connell. Allow 15 minutes.

Cathedral Place. 𝄐 **03/9662 2233.** Mon–Fri 6:30am–6pm; weekends 7:15am–7:30pm.

State Houses of Parliament   Now the home of the Victorian Parliament, this imposing monument to Victorian (as in Queen Victoria) architecture at the top of a run of sandstone steps was built in 1856. Between the time of Australian Federation, in 1900, to 1927, it was used as the National Parliament. When the State Government is in session—generally on Tuesday afternoon and all day Wednesday and Thursday between March and July, and again between August and November—you can view the proceedings from the public gallery. However, you should ring ahead and check as sitting times do vary. During non-sitting times both the extremely opulent Upper House and the less ornate Lower House chambers are open to the public. Allow 30 minutes.

Spring St. 𝄐 **03/9651 8568.** Mon–Fri 9am–5pm. Free guided tours 10, 11am, noon, 2, 3, and 3:45pm on weekdays when parliament is not in session. Bookings advisable.

PARKS & GARDENS

The **Royal Botanic Gardens** 𝄐𝄐, 2 kilometers (1¼ miles) south of the city on Birdwood Avenue, off St. Kilda Road (𝄐 **03/9252 2300**), are the best of their type in Australia and well worth a few hours wander. More than 40 hectares (100 acres) of gardens are lush and blooming with more than 12,000 plant species from all over the world. Don't miss a visit to the oldest part of the garden, the Tennyson Lawn, with its 120-year-old English elm trees. Other special corners include a fern gully, camellia gardens, an herb garden, rain forests packed with fruit bats, and ponds full of ducks and black swans. You can either discover the gardens by wandering at your own pace (most plant species are labeled, so you'll know what you're seeing), or you can take one of the free guided walks that leave the national Herbarium Building, F Gate, Sunday through Friday at 11am and noon. Bring snacks and your picnic blanket to Shakespeare in the Park, a popular summer event in the gardens. Performances occur in January and February, and tickets cost around A$30 (U.S.$19.50). Call 𝄐 **03/9252 2300** for details. The gardens are open November through March from 7:30am to 8:30pm, in April from 7:30am to 6pm, May through August from 7:30am to 5:30pm, September through October from 7:30am to 6pm. Admission is free. To get there, catch the tram on Route 8, traveling south on St. Kilda Road, and get off at Stop 21. Allow 2 to 4 hours.

Nearby, in King's Domain, take a look at **Victoria's first Government House,** Latrobe's Cottage (𝄐 **03/9654 5528**). It was built in England and transported to

Australia brick by brick in 1836. Admission is A$2 (U.S.$1.30) per person. The cottage is open from 11am to 4pm every Monday, Wednesday, Saturday, and Sunday. On the other side of Birdwood Avenue is the **Shrine of Remembrance,** a memorial to the servicemen lost in Australia's wars. It's designed so that at 11am on Remembrance Day (Nov 11), a beam of sunlight hits the Stone of Remembrance in the Inner Shrine. Note the eternal flame in the forecourt. King's Domain is Stop 12 on the Route 15 tram traveling south along St. Kilda Road.

In Fitzroy Gardens, off Wellington Parade, is **Cook's Cottage** (© **03/9419 4677**), which was moved to Melbourne from Great Ayton, in Yorkshire, England, in 1934 to mark Victoria's centenary. It's claimed (with some debate) that Captain Cook lived here between his long voyages. Inside, it's spartan and cramped, not unlike a ship's cabin. Admission is A$3 (U.S.$1.95) for adults, A$1.50 (U.S.$1) for children 5 to 15, and A$7.50 (U.S.$4.90) for families of up to six. It's open daily from 9am to 5pm. Also east of the central business district are the Treasury Gardens. Look for the memorial to John F. Kennedy near the lake. Treasury Gardens and Fitzroy Gardens can be reached by Tram 75 traveling east along Flinders Street. Get off at Stop 14 for Treasury Gardens and Stop 14A for Fitzroy Gardens.

6 Enjoying the Great Outdoors or Catching an Aussie Rules Football Match

OUTDOOR ACTIVITIES

BALLOONING   **Melbourne by Balloon,** Balloon Sunrise Office, 41 Dover St., Richmond (© **03/9427 7596;** fax 03/9427 7597), offers flights over the city plus a champagne breakfast once you've hit the ground again. Dawn flights cost A$225 (U.S.$146.25) for adults, and A$155 (U.S.$100.75) for children under 12 (but if they're under 1.2 meters (4 ft.) tall they won't be able to see over the basket). Advance reservations are essential.

BIKING   Extensive bicycle paths wind through the city and suburbs. For details on the 20 most popular routes, pick up a copy of **Melbourne Bike Tours,** published by Bicycle Victoria (© **03/9328 3000;** fax 03/9328 2288; www.bv.com.au), available at most bookshops. Bicycle Victoria also runs several major cycling tours throughout the state every year.

Bike Now, 320 Toorak Rd., South Yarra (© **03/9826 6870**), rents bicycles for A$15 (U.S.$9.75) for 2 hours, A$20 (U.S.$13) for 4 hours, A$30 (U.S.$19.50) for a full day, and A$70 (U.S.$45.50) for a week. The shop is open weekdays from 9am to 7pm, Saturday from 9am to 5pm, and Sunday from 11am to 5pm. Take tram 8 to Toorak Road.

You can also rent a bike from **Hire a Bike** at St. Kilda Pier (© **03/9531 7403**); non-Australians must show their passports.

GOLF   One of the best public golf courses in Australia is **Yarra Bend,** Yarra Bend Road, Fairfield (© **03/9481 3729**). Greens fees are about A$15 (U.S.$9.75), and club rental is an extra A$10 (U.S.$6.50) for a half set and A$25 (U.S.$16.25) for a full set.

The exclusive **Royal Melbourne Golf Club,** in the suburb of Black Rock, 24 kilometers (15 miles) from the city center, is rated as one of the world's 10 best golf courses. It's open to members only, but if you belong to a top-notch golf club at home, you might be able to wheedle your way in.

For more information on golf in Victoria, contact the **Victorian Golf Association,** 15 Bardolph St., Burwood (© **03/9889 6731**).

IN-LINE SKATING The promenade in St. Kilda is the most popular place to strap on a pair of skates. You can rent all you need at **Rock'n'n'Roll'n,** 11a Fitzroy St., St. Kilda (✆ **03/9525 3434**). The first hour costs A$8 (U.S.$5.20). Successive hours are less expensive.

TENNIS The venue for the Australian Open, the **Melbourne Park National Tennis Centre,** on Batman Avenue (✆ **03/9286 1244**), is a great place to play tennis. When tournaments are not scheduled, its 22 outdoor courts and four indoor courts are open to the public. You can rent courts Monday through Friday from 7am to 11pm, and Saturday and Sunday from 9am to 6pm. Charges range from A$14 to $30 (U.S.$9.10–$19.50) per hour, depending on the court and time of day (outdoor courts are cheapest). Show courts 1, 2, and 3 are also for rent at the same prices. Racquets are also available for A$3 (U.S.$1.95).

SPECTATOR SPORTS

CAR RACING The annual **Australian Formula One Grand Prix** takes place in early March. Call TicketMaster (✆ **13 61 22** in Australia), or the Grand Prix Hotline (✆ **13 16 41** in Australia, or 03/9258 7100) for information on tickets, accommodations, and airfares. Also check out the Grand Prix's website at www.grandprix.com.au.

CRICKET From October through March, cricket's the name of the game in Melbourne. The **Melbourne Cricket Ground** (MCG), Brunton Avenue, Yarra Park, Jolimont (✆ **03/9657 8879**), once the main stadium for the 1956 Melbourne Olympic Games, is perhaps Australia's most hallowed cricket field. The stadium can accommodate 97,500 people. For the uninitiated, "one-day" games are the ones to look out for; "Test" games take several days to complete. Buy tickets at the gate or in advance from TicketMaster (✆ **13 61 22** in Australia; www.ticketmaster.com.au).

Tours of the MCG and its museum leave every half hour daily from 10am to 3pm. The Australian Gallery of Sport and the Olympic Museum are also at the MCG. The Olympic Museum traces the development of the modern Olympics with individual display sections for each city.

FOOTBALL Melbourne's number-one sport is **Australian Rules Football—** or simply, "the footy"—a skillful, but often violent, ball game the likes of which you've never seen (unless you have ESPN). Melbourne sports 10 of the 16 Australian Football League (AFL) teams, with the others coming from Adelaide, Perth, Sydney, and Brisbane. The season starts on the third weekend in March and ends with the Grand Final on the last Saturday in September. The most accessible grounds are at The Melbourne Cricket Ground (MCG)—take tram 75 along Wellington Parade, and the Optus Oval at Carlton (tram 19 from Elizabeth Street). Tickets cost around A$12 (U.S.$7.80) per person, or A$30 (U.S.$19.50) for a family of four. For game information, call **AFL Headquarters** at ✆ **03/9643 1999.** Buy tickets at **TicketMaster** (✆ **13 61 22** in Australia; www.ticketmaster.com.au).

HORSE RACING The **Melbourne Cup,** run on the first Tuesday in November, has been fought for by the best of Australia's thoroughbreds (and a few from overseas) since 1861. Melbourne society puts on a show when they all dress up for the occasion, and it seems that the entire nation stops in its tracks to at least tune in on TV.

The city has four race tracks: **Flemington** (which holds the Melbourne Cup), on Epson Road in Flemington (✆ **03/9371 7171**); **Moonee Valley,** on McPherson Street in Mooney Ponds (✆ **03/9373 2222**); **Caulfield,** on Station

Street in Caulfield (© **03/9257 7200**); and **Sandown,** on Racecourse Drive in Springvale (© **03/9518 1300**). If you're staying in the city center, Flemington and Moonee Valley tracks are the easiest to get to. Take tram 57 from Flinders Street to reach the Flemington racetrack, and catch tram 59 from Elizabeth Street to travel to Moonee Valley.

TENNIS   The **Australian Open,** one of the world's four Grand Slam events, is played during the last 2 weeks of January every year at the Melbourne Park National Tennis Center, on Batman Avenue (© **03/9286 1234**). Tickets for the Australian Open go on sale in mid-October and are available through **Ticketek** (© **03/9299 9079**) and also on the Open's website, www.ausopen.org. Guided tours of the center are offered from April through October, Wednesday through Friday, when events aren't scheduled. Tours cost A$5 (U.S.$3.25) for adults and A$2.50 (U.S.$1.60) for children. To get there, take a train from the Flinders Street Station to Richmond Station and catch the special Tennis Center tram from there.

7 Shopping

Ask almost any Melbournite to help you plan your time in the city, and they'll advise you to shop 'til you drop. All of Australia regards Melbourne as a shopping capital—it's got everything, from famous fashion houses to major department stores and unusual souvenir shops. If you're coming from Sydney, I say save your money until you get to Melbourne, and then indulge!

Start at the magnificent city arcades, such as the **Block Arcade** (running between Collins and Little Collins streets), which has more than 30 shops, including the historic Hopetoun Tearooms (see "Where to Dine" above), and the Royal Arcade (stretching from Little Collins Street to the Bourke Street Mall). Then hit the courts and lanes around **Swanston Street** and the huge **Melbourne Central shopping complex** between Latrobe and Lonsdale streets.

Next, take your wallet as you fan out across the city, taking in **Chapel Street** in South Yarra, for its Australian fashions; and **The Jam Factory,** 500 Chapel St., South Yarra (© **03/9826 0537**), which is a series of buildings with a range of shops and food outlets, including a branch of the U.S.-based Borders, as well as 16 cinema screens. Get there on tram no. 8 or no. 72 from Swanston Street.

There's also **Toorak Road** in Toorak, for Gucci and other high-priced, high-fashion names; Bridge Road in Richmond for budget fashions; Lygon Street in Carlton for Italian fashion, footwear, and accessories; and Brunswick Street in Fitzroy for a more alternative scene.

Serious shoppers might like to contact **Shopping Spree Tours** (© **03/9596 6600**), a company that takes you to all those exclusive and alternative shopping venues, manufacturers, and importers you wouldn't be likely to find by yourself. Tours depart Monday through Saturday at 8:30am and cost A$60 (U.S.$39) per person including lunch and a visit to the Rialto Observation Deck.

MELBOURNE SHOPPING FROM A TO Z
ABORIGINAL CRAFTS
The Aboriginal Gallery of the Dreaming   This place stocks an extensive range of acrylic dot paintings and represents more than 120 artists. Boomerangs, didgeridoos, pottery, jewelry, bark paintings, prints, books, and music are also available. 73–77 Bourke St., City. © **03/9650 3277**.

Aboriginal Handcrafts Didgeridoos, bark paintings, boomerangs, and so forth are sold here, with the profits going to Aboriginal colleges. Mezzanine floor, 130 Little Collins St. © 03/9650 4717.

CRAFTS

An interesting arts-and-crafts market is held on The Esplanade in St. Kilda on Sunday from 9am to 4pm. Take tram no. 16 from Swanston Street or no. 96 from Bourke Street.

The Australian Geographic Shop Head here for high-quality Australiana, including crafts, books, and various gadgets. Shop 130, Melbourne Central, 300 Londsdale St. © 03/9639 2478.

DEPARTMENT STORES

Daimaru With 6 floors of interesting merchandise, including Asian foodstuffs and top-label fashions, Daimaru is giving the more established department stores a run for shoppers' money. In the Central Melbourne complex. © 03/9660 6666.

David Jones Like Myer, its direct competition, David Jones (or DJ's as it's affectionately known) also spans 2 blocks and offers similar goods. 310 Bourke St. Mall, City. © 03/9643 2222.

Myer The grand dame of Melbourne's department stores has 12 floors of household goods, perfume, jewelry, and fashions stretching over 2 blocks. (It claims to be the fifth largest store in the world.) There's a good food section on the ground floor offering, among other things, good sushi. 314 Bourke St. Mall, City. © 03/9661 1111.

FASHION

High-fashion boutiques also line the eastern stretch of Collins Street between the Grand Hyatt and the Hotel Sofitel, and Chapel Street in South Yarra. In addition, many thousands of retail shops and factory outlets are dotted around the city, many of them concentrated on Bridge Road near Punt Road and Swan Street near Church Street in Richmond. You'll be able to find designer clothes, many just last season's fashions, at a fraction of the original price.

Country Road County Road is one of Australia's best-known names for men's and women's fashion. The cool, classic looks don't come cheap, but the quality is worth it. County Road also sells designer cooking equipment and house wares. 252 Toorak Rd., and other sites, including Chapel St., South Yarra. © 1800/801 911 in Australia, or 03/9824 0133.

Mortisha's Looking for something to wear to your next Goth party? Then don't miss this satin-lined, coffin-like store selling everything from vampy velvet dresses to original bridal wear. You can also find some very unusual jewelry and accessories to complete your Addams Family look. Shop 8–10, Royal Arcade, City. © 03/9654 1586.

Overseas Designer Warehouse This place sells end-of-run and last season's high fashions. The stuff is still pretty expensive, but you can find a few bargains if you really search. 18 Ellis St., South Yarra (off Chapel St., between Toorak and Commercial rds.). © 03/9824 0399.

Paddington Coat Factory Exquisite high-fashion clothes made by young Australian designers—Andrea Yasmin, Susie Mooratoff, and Lara Agnew—go for A$39 to $500 (U.S.$25.30–$325) at this Melbourne sister store of the one in Paddington, Sydney. 461–463 Chapel St., South Yarra. © 03/9827 4004.

Death by Chocolate

If you love chocolate, sign up now for the Chocolate Indulgence Walk and the Chocolates & Other Desserts Walk by calling ℭ **03/9815 1228** or 0412/158 017. The former takes you on a tasting tour of Cadbury's, Myer, New Zealand Natural Ice Creamery, Chocolate Box, and Darrell Lea, and finishes off over chocolate cake at a cafe. This 2-hour tour leaves every Saturday at 12:30pm and costs A$22 (U.S.$14.30) for adults (children under 6 go free). The latter tour includes sampling plenty of ice creams and chocolates around town as you tour kitchens and talk to chefs. The tour finishes with afternoon tea at the Grand Hyatt. This tour leaves every Saturday at 2:30pm and also costs A$22 (U.S.$14.30). A third tour has been recently added, the Coffee and Café Walk, during which you try coffee and pastries at some of Melbourne's grooviest cafes. This tour also costs A$22 (U.S.$14.30). Bookings are essential.

R.M. Williams   Head here for genuine Australian gear: great boots, Driza-bone coats, and Akubra hats. In the Melbourne Central complex. ℭ **03/9663 7126.**

Saba   Australian designer Joseph Saba has several very vogue, very expensive boutiques for men and women in Melbourne, including one for each sex on Chapel Street (nos. 538 and 548) in South Yarra. This store caters to both men and women. 236 Collins St., City. ℭ **03/9654 3524.**

Sam Bear   Sam Bear is another good bet for Outback-style fashions: Driza-bone coats, Akubra bush hats, R.M. Williams boots and clothing, and Blundstone boots (my favorite). They also sell a solid range of camping equipment. 225 Russell St., City. ℭ **03/9663 2191.**

Surf, Dive 'N Ski Australia   As well as surfboards, boogie boards, and sunglasses, this store stocks a wide range of hip and happening beach wear, all at reasonable prices. All the big names in Australian surf wear can be found here, including Ripcurl, Quicksilver, and Billabong. The Jam Factory, Chapel St., South Yarra. ℭ **03/9826 4071.**

Vegan Wares   Instead of leather, Vegan Wares uses microfibre to create tough, stylish shoes, handbags, and belts. It's not just for vegetarians; carnivores enjoy browsing here, too. 78 Smith St., Collingwood. ℭ **03/9417 0230.**

FOODSTUFFS
Haigh's Chocolates   Indulge in some 50 types of Australia's best chocolate, from milk to dark to fruit flavored. I recommend the Sparkling Shiraz truffle if you need a serious treat. Two locations: 26 Collins St. ℭ **03/9650 2114;** and Shop 26, the Block Arcade, 282 Collins St. ℭ **03/9654 7673.**

Suga–Melbourne Candy Kitchen   If you have a sweet tooth, you're likely to spend a fortune at this traditional little candy shop that makes its goodies right before your very eyes. Rock candy is a specialty, and you can even get your name (or the name of someone back home) spelled out in its center. Shop 20, Royal Arcade, City. ℭ **03/9663 5654.**

JEWELRY

Altman & Cherny   Even if you're not in the market to buy, it's worth coming here to check out "Olympic Australia," the largest precious-gem opal in the world. It was found in Coober Pedy in South Australia in 1956 and is valued at A$2.5 million (U.S.$1.6 million). The store offers tax-free shopping for tourists armed with a passport and international airline ticket. 120 Exhibition St., at the corner of Little Collins St. ℂ 03/9650 9685.

Dinosaur Designs   Dinosaur Designs is taking the jewelry design world by storm with its range of very artistic jewelry made out of resin. The shop has modern house wares as well. None of it's cheap, but the odd item won't break the bank. 562 Chapel St., South Yarra. ℂ 03/9827 2600.

Portobello Lane of South Yarra   Proprietor Robyn Meate specializes in locally produced and imported sterling silver jewelry with lots of beads and glass. Some of the designs are quite intricate. Pieces cost from A$40 to $200 (U.S.$26–$130). 405 Chapel St., South Yarra. ℂ 03/9827 5708.

8 Melbourne After Dark

Melbourne can be an exciting place once the sun has set. The pubs here are far better than those in Sydney. Friday and Saturday nights will see most pubs (of both the trendy and the down-to-earth variety) packed to the rafters, and at lunchtimes those that serve food are popular, too. To find out what's hot and happening, check the entertainment guide included in *The Age*, Melbourne's daily broadsheet, each Friday.

THE PERFORMING ARTS

Melbourne is the most dynamic performing arts city in Australia. Its theaters offer the whole gamut from offbeat independent productions to large-scale musicals the like you'd find on Broadway. The city is also the home of the most prestigious festivals, with the annual **Melbourne Fringe Festival** (held over the first 3 weeks in Oct) and the annual **Melbourne International Comedy Festival** (from the end of Mar to roughly the end of Apr) attracting the best of Australian and international talent.

The Melbourne International Comedy Festival sees venues all over the city putting on performances, while the Fringe Festival sees the streets, pubs, theaters, and restaurants playing host to everyone from jugglers and fire-eaters to musicians and independent productions covering all art forms. Try to get tickets if you're in town during either festival, but keep in mind that hotels fill up fast at these times. For more information about these festivals consult their relevant websites (www.melbournefringe.org.au; www.comedyfestival.com.au).

Another good time to plan your visit is during the annual **Melbourne International Film Festival** (from mid-July to the end of the first week in Aug), when new releases, shorts, and avant-garde movies are shown at varying venues around the city. For details or to check schedules call up the festival's website (www.melbournefilmfestival.com.au).

For information on upcoming theater productions and reviews check out www.stageleft.com.au, or the official government entertainment information site (www.melbourne.vic.gov.au/news/events/events/). The latter site shows what's on in the theater world for 2 months in advance, as well as what's happening in dance, film, comedy, music, exhibitions, sports, and tours.

The best place to buy tickets for everything from theater to major sporting events, as well as obtain details on schedules, is **TicketMaster** (✆ **13 28 849** or 1800/062 849 in Australia, or 03/9299 9079; www.ticketmaster.com.au).

THE HEART OF MELBOURNE'S CULTURAL LIFE

Victorian Arts Centre ✿✿   The towering spire atop the Theaters Building of the Victorian Arts Center, on the banks of the Yarra River, crowns the city's leading performing-arts complex. Beneath it, the State Theatre, the Playhouse, and the Fairfax present performances that are the focal point of Melbourne's cultural life.

The *State Theater,* seating 2,079 on three levels, can accommodate elaborate stagings of opera, ballet, musicals, and more. The **Playhouse** is a smaller venue that often hosts the Melbourne Theatre Company. The **Fairfax** is more intimate still, and is often used for experimental theater or cabaret.

Adjacent to the Theaters Building is the **Melbourne Concert Hall,** home of the Melbourne Symphony Orchestra and the State Orchestra of Victoria, and often host to visiting orchestras. Many international stars have graced this stage, which is known for its excellent acoustics.

Guided 1-hour tours of the Concert Hall and the theaters are offered Monday through Saturday at noon and 2:30pm and Saturday at 10:30pm and noon. They cost A$10 (U.S.$6.50) for adults, A$7.50 (U.S.$4.90) for children, and A$23 (U.S.$14.95) for families. Backstage tours on Sunday at 12:15pm cost A$13.50 (U.S.$8.80). Children under 11 are not allowed. Call ✆ **03/9281 8000** between 9:30am and 5pm for information.

100 St. Kilda Rd. ✆ **03/9281 8000,** or 13 61 66 for ticket purchase. www.artscentre.net.au. Tickets for State Theatre A$40–$110 (U.S.$26–$71.50); Playhouse and Fairfax A$30–$59 (U.S.$19.50–$38.35); Concert Hall A$40–$80 (U.S.$26–$52).

ADDITIONAL VENUES & THEATERS

Check *The Age* to see what productions are scheduled during your visit. Odds are that the leading shows will be produced in one of the following venues:

The Comedy Club   The Comedy Club is another Melbourne institution. Come here to see local and international comedy acts, musicals, and special shows. Dinner and show Friday through Saturday A$40 to $45 (U.S.$26–$29.25) depending on performer; show only Thursday through Saturday approximately A$20 (U.S.$13). Level 1, 380 Lygon St., Carlton. ✆ **03/9348 1622.**

Comedy Theatre   The Comedy Theatre, with its ornate Spanish Rococo interior, manages to feel intimate even though it seats more than 1,000 people. Plays and musicals usually fill the bill, but dance companies and comedians also appear. 240 Exhibition St., City. ✆ **03/9209 9000.**

Value Half-Price Tickets

Buy your tickets for entertainment events, including opera, dance, and drama, on the day of the performance from the Half-Tix Kiosk in Bourke Street Mall (✆ **03/9650 9420**). The booth is open Monday from 10am to 2pm, Tuesday through Thursday from 11am to 6pm, Friday from 11am to 6:30pm, and Saturday from 10am to 2pm. Tickets must be paid for in cash. The available shows are displayed each day on the booth door, and you can't get show information over the phone.

The Forum Theatre   The Forum hosts well-known bands and international comedians. Tables and chairs are set up in cabaret-style booths, from which you can order drinks and meals from the bar. 154 Flinders St., City. ✆ 03/9299 9700.

Her Majesty's Theatre   A fire destroyed the original theater here, but the current structure still retains the original facade and the Art-Deco interior added during a 1936 renovation. Musicals, such as the Australian premier of *Chicago*, frequent the boards. 219 Exhibition St., City. ✆ 03/9663 3211.

The Princess Theatre   This huge facility hosts extravaganza productions. The theater opened its doors in 1886, and it still retains a dramatic marble staircase and ornate plaster ceilings. 163 Spring St., City. ✆ 03/9299 9800.

The Regent Theatre   Built in 1929, the regent fell into disrepair, and its stage was dark for 25 years. Now, after a recent A$35-million (U.S.$22.75-million) renovation, it's been restored to its former glory. It recently staged lavish production of *Showboat*. Tickets are available in the United States through ATS Tours at ✆ 800/423-2880. The theater offers a range of dining packages. 191 Collins St., City. ✆ 03/9299 9800.

Sydney Myer Music Bowl   This enormous outdoor entertainment center is run under the auspices of the Victorian Arts Center Trust and hosts opera, jazz, and ballet in the warmer months (and ice skating in the winter!). It underwent extensive renovations in 2000. King's Domain, Alexandra Ave., City. ✆ 03/9281 8360.

THE CLUB & MUSIC SCENE

Melbourne's nightclub scene is centered along King Street, though in-places come and go month by month. It's best just to follow the crowds. Otherwise, the following options are more enduring in their appeal.

Bobby McGee's Entertainment Lounge   If you want a fun night out, head for the restaurant section of Bobby McGee's, then hit the dance floor at the disco. The restaurant has good American-style food served by waiters in fancy dress, while the disco area is open from 5pm to the wee hours (the music, a mix of the popular dance hits of the moment, starts pounding at 9pm). The disco is popular with the 22-to-35 crowd after work, while the younger set flocks in after 10pm. You'll see lots of business suits on Thursday and Friday nights; dress is casual but smart on other nights. In the Rydges Melbourne Hotel, 186 Exhibition St. ✆ 03/9639 0630. Cover A$5 (U.S.$3.25) Mon and Thurs–Sat after 8pm; free for hotel guests.

Chasers   One for the 20-somethings, Chasers goes wild to techno and retro in a spacious main dance room. 386 Chapel St., South Yarra. ✆ 03/9827 6615.

Metro   An institution on the Melbourne clubbing scene, Metro is large and stylish and popular for its dance, pop, and alternative sounds. It re-opened in November 2000 with a revamp. Expect queues. 20 Bourke St., City. ✆ 03/9663 4288.

Monsoon's Entertainment Studio   Dress up a bit to blend in with the crowd at the upscale Monsoons. Hotel guests and well-heeled locals dance to Top 40 tunes, or check out visiting jazz or cabaret performers on Friday and Saturday nights (Thurs night is funk night). One Sunday and Wednesday every month the nightclub is open for special theme nights. In the Grand Hyatt Melbourne, 123 Collins St. ✆ 03/9657 1234. Cover A$15 (U.S.$9.75); free for hotel guests.

Revolver   Mostly techno music, though bands play on weekends with dancing later. 229 Chapel St., Prahan. ✆ 03/9521 5985.

WHERE TO SHARE A PINT

Something fun to do if you want a few drinks and to meet a few people is to take one of the **City Pub Walks** (✆ **03/9384 0655** or 0412/085 661). The 2½- to 3-hour walks stop off a variety of interesting pubs and bars where you can sample the local brews (at your own expense). Tours leave from "under the clocks" at Flinders Railway Station at 6:30pm Tuesday and Thursday.

Bridie O'Reillys   Bridie O'Reillys is one of Melbourne's best Irish pubs, complete with traditional dark wood decor and good beer. The two-level pub has 19 different beers on tap (seven of them Irish). There is live Irish music every night from around 9pm. The place gets quite crowded on weekends. 62 Little Collins St. (just off Exhibition St.). ✆ **03/9650 0840.**

The Charles Dickens Tavern   Come here for a touch of Olde England in the heart of the city. The homey pub has two bars and a restaurant serving good pub grub (traditional roasts and pies as well as some lighter dishes). 290 Collins St., City (between Elizabeth and Swanston sts.). ✆ **03/9654 1821.**

The Cricketers Club Bar   Locals come to this popular English-style pub in this five-star hotel to lift a glass surrounded by the relics of Australia's summer passion. Glass cases are packed full of cricket bats, pads, and stumps, whereas the plush green carpets and solid mahogany woodwork give the place a touch of class. In the Windsor Hotel, 103 Spring St. ✆ **03/9653 0653.**

The Esplanade Hotel   Long-established as a pub-rock and serious drinking venue, this fun place offers bands most nights—free in the front bar, and with a small cover charge out back. 11 Upper Esplanande, St. Kilda. ✆ **03/9534 0211.**

The Mitre Tavern *(Finds)*   This place is almost as good as a traditional English pub—if they'd only put some good carpets on the floor. Still, it's atmospheric and centrally located. The outdoor courtyard is perfect for lunch on a sunny day. 5 Bank Place (between Queen and William sts. and Collins and Little Collins sts.). ✆ **03/9670 5644.**

The Night Cat   A stylish place offering jazz or lounge music most nights, the Night Cat stays open late but gets pretty crowded, so go early to get a table. 141 Johnston St, Fitzroy. ✆ **03/9417 0090.**

The Prince St. Kilda   This pub is a legend among the locals. Though recently refurbished, it retains its original rough-at-the-edges appearance. Bands play most nights, some of them big names. 29 Fitzroy St., St. Kilda. ✆ **03/9536 1111.**

The Punters Club   There are plenty of pubs on Brunswick Street to chose from, but if you're into music and young crowds you'll probably end up at this grungy bar along with everyone else. Its nicotine-stained ceilings, dingy interior, and bar stools are nothing special, but the vibe is good, and it has a back section which often features live up-and-coming bands for a cover charge of around $A10 (U.S.$6.50). 376 Brunswick St, Fitzroy. ✆ **03/9417 3006.**

Anyone for Cocktails?

For a touch of sophistication and spectacular views, drop into the cocktail bar on the 35th floor of the **Hotel Sofitel**, at 25 Collins St. (✆ **03/9653 0000**). Otherwise, the **Windsor Hotel**, at 103 Spring St. (✆ **03/9653 0653**) offers drinks and cocktails in an atmosphere of Old World charm.

The Young and Jacksons Hotel You probably won't think much of the rough-and-tumble downstairs here, so head upstairs see the naked *Chloe*. The famous painting was brought to Melbourne for the Great Exhibition in 1880. The pub, which was built in 1853 and started selling beer in 1861, has a few years on the *Chloe*, who was painted in Paris in 1875. She has a special place in the hearts of customers and has spawned hundreds of copies that have found their way to far-flung places. At the corner of Flinders and Swanston sts. ℂ 03/9650 3884.

THE CASINO

Crown Casino Australia's largest casino is a plush affair open 24 hours. You'll find all the usual roulette and blackjack tables and so on, as well as an array of poker machines. There are some 25 restaurants and 40 bars on the premises. Clarendon St., Southbank. ℂ 03/9292 6868.

9 Side Trips from Melbourne

DANDENONG RANGES

40km (25 miles) E of Melbourne

Melburnites traditionally do a "day in the Dandenongs" from time to time, topping off their getaway with Devonshire tea with scones and jam at one of the many cafes en route. Up in the cool, high country you'll find native bush, famous gardens, the Dandenong Ranges National Park, historic attractions such as the Puffing Billy vintage steam train, and plenty of restaurants and cozy B&Bs. The Dandenong Ranges National Park is one of the state's oldest, set aside in 1882 to protect its Mountain Ash forests and lush tree-fern gullies.

Auswalk, P.O. Box 516, Jindabyne, NSW 2627 (ℂ 02/6457 2220; fax 02/6457 2206; monica@auswalk.com.au) offers a 4-day/3-night, self-guided tour of the Dandenongs for two or more people, including accommodations, most meals, a ride on the Puffing Billy steam train (see below), national park entrance fees, vehicle transfers, and an itinerary and maps. The tour costs around A$590 (U.S.$383) per person but could be a little cheaper depending on the season.

Parkwood Personalised Tours (ℂ 03/5334 2428; www.oztour.com; info@oztour.com) runs personalized day and multiday tours of the Yarra Valley as well as other places in Victoria, and the Great Ocean Road, staying at quaint B&B guesthouses or boutique hotels, from $60 (U.S.$39) per hour.

GETTING THERE To get to the area, take the Burwood Highway from Melbourne, then the Mt. Dandenong Tourist Road, which starts at Upper Ferntree Gully and then winds its way through the villages of Sassafras, Olinda, Mount Dandenong, and Kalorama to Montrose. If you take a turnoff to Sherbrook, or extend your journey into a loop taking in Seville, Woori Yallock, Emerald, and Belgrave you'll see a fair slice of the local scenery.

VISITOR INFORMATION The **Dandenong Ranges & Knox Visitor Information Centre,** 1211 Burwood Hwy., Upper Ferntree Gully, VIC 3156 (ℂ 1800/645 505 in Australia, or 03/9758 7522; fax 03/9758 7533) is open daily from 9am to 5pm.

NATURE WALKS

Most people come here to get out of the city for a pleasant bushwalk (hike), so in that way it's the equivalent of Sydney's Blue Mountains. Some of the better walks include the easy 2.5-kilometer (1½-mile) stroll from the **Sherbrook Picnic Ground** through the forest, and the **Thousand Steps** and the **Kokoda Track Memorial Walk,** a challenging rain-forest track from the Fern Tree Gully

Mapping Out Your Side Trips

For a map of the area surrounding Melbourne, please consult the "Victoria" map in chapter 12.

Picnic Ground up One Tree Hill. Along the way are plaques commemorating Australian troops who fought and died in Papua New Guinea in World War II.

FOR GARDENING BUFFS

Bonsai Farm   If you don't like to crane your neck when it comes to looking at trees, then visit this large display of petite bonsais. Some of them are many decades old and cost a pretty penny.

Mt. Dandenong Tourist Rd., Mt. Dandenong. © 03/9751 1150. Free admission. Wed–Sun 11am–5pm. Transportation: See William Ricketts Sanctuary below.

National Rhododendron Gardens   From September through November, thousands of rhododendrons and azaleas burst into bloom in these magnificent gardens. There are 42 lovely hectares (103 acres) in all, with a 3-kilometer (2-mile) walking path leading past flowering exotics and native trees as well as great vistas over the Yarra Valley. A tearoom is open every day during spring and on weekends at other times. Visitors flock here in summer for the glorious walks, and again in autumn when the leaves are turning.

The Georgian Rd., Olinda. © 03/9751 1980. Admission Sept 1–Nov 30 A$6.70 adults, A$2.20 (U.S.$1.40) children 10–16, A$13.50 (U.S.$8.80) family of 5; Dec 1–Aug 31 A$5.60 (U.S.$3.60) adults, A$2.20 (U.S.$1.40) children, A$13.50 (U.S.$8.80) family. Open daily 10am–4:30pm. Closed Christmas Day. Train to Croydon and then Bus no. 688 to the gardens, or train to Belgrave and Bus number 694.

Tesselaar's Bulbs and Flowers   There are literally tens of thousands of flowers on display here, all putting on a flamboyantly colorful show in the spring (Sept and Oct). Expect to see a dazzling variety of tulips, daffodils, rhododendrons, azaleas, fuchsias, and ranunculi. Bulbs are on sale at discount prices at other times.

357 Monbulk Rd., Silvan. © 03/9737 9305. Admission during tulip festival, A$9.50 (U.S.$6.20) adults, children under 16 admitted free if accompanied by an adult; free for everyone rest of the year. During tulip festival (approx. Sept 12–Oct 11) daily 10am–5pm; rest of year Mon–Fri 8am–4:30pm, Sat–Sun 1–5pm. Take the train to Lilydale and then Bus no. 679.

William Ricketts Sanctuary   This wonderful garden, set in a forest of mountain ash, features clay figures representing the Aboriginal Dreamtime. The sculptures were all created over the lifetime of sculptor William Ricketts, who died in 1993 at the age of 94. The garden encompasses fern gullies and waterfalls spread out over 13 hectares (33 acres), though the sculptures occupy just .8 hectares (2 acres).

Mt. Dandenong Tourist Rd., Mt. Dandenong. © 03/9751 1300. Admission A$5.60 (U.S.$3.70) adults, A$2.20 (U.S.$1.40) children 10–16, A$13.50 (U.S.$8.80) families of 5. Daily 10am–4:30pm. Closed Christmas. Train to Croydon then Bus no. 688 to the sanctuary.

FOR TRAIN BUFFS

Puffing Billy Railway *Kids*   For just about a century, the Puffing Billy steam railway has been chugging over a 13-kilometer (8-mile) track from Belgrave to Emerald Lake. Passengers take trips on open carriages and are treated to lovely views as the train passes through forests and fern gullies and over a National Trust–classified wooden trestle bridge. Trips take around an hour each way. Trains leave at 10:30, 11:15am, noon, and at 2:30pm on weekdays; and at

10:30, 11:45am, 1:30, and 3:15pm on Saturday and Sunday. A further stretch of track to Gembrook was opened in 1998. Daily trips to Gembrook take an extra 45 minutes and cost A$25 (U.S.$16.25) for adults, A$14 ($9.10) for children, and A$72 (U.S.$46.80) for families. Night trains also run on occasional Saturday nights.

Belgrave Station, Belgrave. ℭ 03/9754 6800 for 24-hr. recorded information. Admission A$18 (U.S.$11.70) adults, A$10 (U.S.$6.50) children 4–16, A$51 (U.S.$33) families of 5. Operates daily except Christmas. Train from Flinders Street Station in Melbourne to Belgrave; the Puffing Billy station is a short walk away.

WHERE TO DINE

Churinga Café CAFE   This is a nice place for a quick lunch or morning or afternoon tea. It has nice gardens and is just across from the William Ricketts Sanctuary. You can get everything here from curries to traditional British fare. Devonshire tea costs A$6 (U.S.$3.90).

1381 Mt. Dandenong Tourist Rd., Mt. Dandenong. ℭ 03/9751 1242. Main courses A$12.95–$13.95 (U.S.$8.40–$9). AE, DC, MC, V. Sat–Wed 10:30am–4:30pm.

Wild Oak Café MODERN AUSTRALIAN   For good home cooking you can't beat this cozy cafe. The food could include the likes of chargrilled steak, smoked Atlantic salmon rissotto, Linguini with prawns, and Cajun chicken. The restaurant has a few vegetarian selections and a roaring log fire in winter.

232 Ridge Rd., Mt. Dandenong. ℭ 03/9751 2033. Main courses A$16–$19 (U.S.$10.40–$12.35). DC, MC, V. Daily 10am–10pm.

YARRA VALLEY
61km (38 miles) E of Melbourne

The Yarra Valley is a well-known wine-growing region just east of Melbourne. It's dotted with villages, historic houses, gardens, craft shops, antique centers, and restaurants, as well as dozens of wineries. There are some good bushwalks around here and the Healesville Sanctuary is one of the best places in Australia to see native animals.

ESSENTIALS
GETTING THERE   McKenzie's Bus Lines (ℭ 03/9853 6264) operates a bus service from Lilydale Railway Station to Healesville (catch a train from Melbourne's Spencer Street Station to Lilyvale; the trip takes about an hour). Buses connect with trains roughly 12 times a day; call for exact connection times.

If you're driving, pick up a detailed map of the area from the Royal Automotive Club of Victoria (ℭ 03/9790 3333) in Melbourne. Maps here are free if you're a member of an auto club in your home country, but remember to bring along your membership card. Alternatively, you can pick up a map at the tourist office. Take the Maroondah Highway from Melbourne to Lilydale and on to Healesville. The trip takes around an hour and 15 minutes.

VISITOR INFORMATION   Pick up details on what to see and where to stay at the **Yarra Valley Visitor Information Centre,** Old Court House, Harker Street, Healesville (ℭ 03/5962 2600; fax 03/5962 2040). It's open daily from 9am to 5pm.

EXPLORING THE VALLEY
There are three principal roads in the valley: the Melba Highway, Maroondah Highway, and Myers Creek Road, which together form a triangle. Within the triangle are three smaller roads, the Healesville Yarra Glen Road, Old Healesville Road, and Chum Creek Road, which all access wineries. Most people start their

tour of the Yarra Valley from Lilydale and take in several cellar-door tastings at vineyards along the route.

Balloon Aloft (© **1800/028 568** in Australia) offers dawn balloon rides over the wineries for A$195 (U.S.$126.75) for adults and A$130 (U.S.$84.50) for children over 8. The flight includes a champagne breakfast. Peregrin Adventures (© **03/9662 2800;** www.peregrin.net.au; travelcentre@peregrin.net.au) also has balloon flights over the valley, with free pickup from Adelaide for A$195 (U.S.$126.75) on weekends and A$175 (U.S.$113.75) on weekdays. Peregrin can also arrange accommodations.

Healesville Sanctuary ⓖ *(Finds)* Forget about seeing animals in cages—this preserve is a great place to spot native animals in almost natural surroundings. You can see wedge-tailed eagles, dingoes, koalas, wombats, reptiles, and more, all while strolling through the peppermint-scented gum forest, which rings with the chiming of bell birds. The sanctuary was started in 1921 by Sir Colin McKenzie, who set it up as a center to preserve endangered species and educate the public. There's a gift shop, a cafe serving light meals, and picnic grounds.

Badger Creek Rd., Healesville. © **03/5957 2800.** Fax 03/5957 2870. www.zoo.org.au. Admission A$16.40 (U.S.$10.60) adults, A$12.20 (U.S.$7.90) concession, A$8.10 (U.S.$5.20) children, A$44.30 (U.S.$28.70) family, up to 4 kids. Daily 9am–5pm. Train from Flinders Street Station to Lilydale, then Bus no. 685 to the sanctuary.

WHERE TO STAY & DINE

Melba Lodge ⓖ These stylish, modern accommodations opened in Yarra Glen, in the heart of the Yarra Valley wine region, in early 1999. Of the six luxurious bedrooms, four have queen-size beds, and two have king-size beds and a spa; all have private bathrooms. There's a comfortable lounge with an open fire, and a billiard room. The lodge is only a few minutes' walk from historic Yarra Glen, which has antique shops and a craft market. There are plenty of restaurants and wineries around, too. It's a short drive to the Healesville Sanctuary.

939 Melba Highway, Yarra Glen, VIC 3775. © **03/9730 1511.** Fax 03/9730 1566. www.melbalodge. citysearch.com.au. 6 units. A$150 (U.S.$97.50) Queen room; A$180 (U.S.$117) King room. Rates include cooked breakfast. AE, MC, V. Transportation: See the Healesville Sanctuary above. **Amenities:** Spa; nonsmoking rooms. *In room:* A/C, TV, hair dryer.

Sanctuary House Motel Healesville This place is very handy for visiting the sanctuary and even better if you want to relax and sample some good Yarra Valley wine. Just 400 meters (440 yd.) from the Healesville Sanctuary, Sanctuary House is set in some 4 hectares (10 acres) of beautiful bushland. The rooms are motel-style and come with all the essentials.

Badger Creek Rd. (P.O. Box 162 Healesville, VIC 3777). © **03/5962 5148.** Fax 03/5962 5392. 12 units. A$70–$75 (U.S.$45.50–$48.75) double. Extra adult A$20 (U.S.$13); extra child A$10 (U.S.$6.50). AE, DC, MC, V. Transportation: See the Healesville Sanctuary above. **Amenities:** Restaurant (home-cooked meals); small pool; spa; sauna; games room; laundry service; nonsmoking rooms. *In room:* A/C, TV.

PHILLIP ISLAND: PENGUINS ON PARADE ⓖ
139km (86 miles) S of Melbourne

Philip Island's **penguin parade,** which happens every evening at dusk, is one of Australia's most popular animal attractions. There are other (less crowded) places in Australia where watching homecoming penguins feels less staged—Kangaroo Island in South Australia comes to mind—but at least the little ones and their nesting holes are protected from the throngs by guides and boardwalks. Nevertheless, the commercialism of the Penguin Parade puts a lot of people off— busloads of tourists squashed into a sort of amphitheater is hardly being one with nature. Phillip Island also offers nice beaches, good bushwalking, and a seagull rookery. If you have the time, you could spend at least 2 days here.

ESSENTIALS

GETTING THERE   Most visitors come to Phillip Island on a day trip from Melbourne and arrive in time for the Penguin Parade and dinner. Several tour companies run day trips. Among them are **Gray Line** (© 03/9663 4455), which operates penguin trips daily departing Melbourne at 1:30pm and returning at around 11:30pm. Tours cost A$79.50 (U.S.$51.60) for adults and A$39.75 (U.S.$25.80) for children. Gray line also offers full-day trips including the Dandenong Ranges and a ride on the Puffing Billy Steam Train.

   Down Under Day Tours (© 03/9650 2600), offers a similar half-day tour for A$79.50 (U.S.$51.70) for adults and A$39.50 (U.S.$25.70) for children; tours depart Melbourne at 1:30pm and return at 11:30pm. It also offers a day-long trip that combines a Melbourne sightseeing tour with the penguin tour for A$106 (U.S.$68.90) for adults, and A$53 (U.S.$34.45) for children, and a half-day combined Dandenong Ranges/Phillip Island tour costing A$96 (U.S.$62.40) for adults and A$48 (U.S.$31.20) for children.

   An excellent budget option is a half-day trip with **Melbourne Sightseeing** (© 03/9663 3388). Tours depart Melbourne daily at 1:30pm and include visits to a cattle farm where you can hand-feed kangaroos, the Koala Conservation Centre, a seal colony, as well as the Penguin Parade. The coach returns to Melbourne at 10:30pm. The trip costs A$75 (U.S.$48.75) for adults (A$49/U.S.$31.85 with a YHA card) and A$38 (U.S.$24.70) for children. For the same price, an express bus leaves Melbourne at 5:30pm (returning at 11pm) and travels directly to the Penguin Parade.

   Auswalk, P.O. Box 516, Jindabyne, NSW 2627 (© 02/6457 2220; fax: 02/6457 2206; monica@auswalk.com.au), offers a 4-night self-guided tour of Phillip Island for two or more people for A$760 (U.S.$494) per person. The price includes accommodations, most meals, park and entrance fees to the main places of interest, some vehicle transfers, an itinerary, and maps.

   If you're driving on your own, it's an easy 2-hour trip from Melbourne along the South Gippsland Highway and then the Bass Highway. A bridge connects the highway to the mainland.

   V/Line trains (© 13 22 32 in Australia, or 03/9619 5000) run in summer from Flinders Street Station to Phillip Island via Dandenong. The trip takes 2 hours and 15 minutes and costs A$13.40 (U.S.$8.70).

VISITOR INFORMATION   The **Phillip Island Information Center,** Phillip Island Tourist Road, Newhaven (© 1300/366 422 in Australia, or 03/5956 7447), is an attraction in itself, with interactive computer displays, relevant information, dioramas giving visitors a glimpse into the penguin's world, and a theaterette. It's open daily from 9am to 5pm (to 6pm in the summer).

EXPLORING THE AREA

Visitors approach the island from the east, passing through the town of **Newhaven.** Just a little past Newhaven is the Phillip Island Information Center.

   The main town on the island, **Cowes** (pop. 2,400), is on the far north coast. It's worth taking a stroll along its Esplanade. The Penguin Parade is on the far southwest coast.

   The tip of the west coast of the Summerland Peninsula ends in a interesting rock formation called **The Nobbies.** This strange-looking outcropping can be reached at low tide by a basalt causeway. You'll get some spectacular views of the coastline and two offshore islands from here. On the farthest of these islands is a population of up to **12,000 Australian fur seals,** the largest colony in Australia (bring your binoculars). This area is also home to thousands of nesting silver gulls.

On the north coast you can explore **Rhyll Inlet,** an inter-tidal mangrove wetland, where you can see wading birds such as spoonbills, oystercatchers, herons, egrets, cormorants, and the rare bar-tailed godwit and the whimbrel.

Bird-watchers will also love **Swan Lake,** another important breeding habitat for wetland birds.

Elsewhere, walking trails lead through heath and pink granite to **Cape Woolamai,** the island's highest point, where there are fabulous coastal views. September through April the cape is home to thousands of short-tailed shearwaters, or muttonbirds as they are sometimes called.

If you really want to see a bit of the island (instead of just seeing the parade and dashing off), consider taking one of the 15 different tours offered by **Mike Cleeland** and his **Island Nature Tours,** RMB 6080, Cowes, Phillip Island, VIC 3922 (© **03/5956 7883**).

Koala Conservation Centre ⭐   Koalas were introduced to Phillip Island in the 1880s and at first they thrived in the predator-free environment. However, overpopulation, the introduction of foxes and dogs, and the clearing of land for farmland, townships, and roads, have all taken their toll. Though today you can still see a few koalas in the wild, the best place to find them is at this sanctuary, which was set up for research and breeding purposes. Visitors can get quite close to them, especially on the elevated boardwalk, which lets you peek into their treetop homes. For the best viewing come around 4pm, when the ordinarily sleepy koalas are on the move.

At Fiveways, Phillip Island Tourist Road, Cowes © **03/5956 8300.** A$5.60 (U.S.$3.60) adults, A$2.60 (U.S.$1.70) children under 16, A$13.80 (U.S.$9) family, up to 4 kids. Daily 10am–5pm.

Phillip Island Penguin Reserve ⭐ *Kids*   The Penguin Parade takes place every night of the year at dusk, when hundreds of little penguins appear at the water's edge, gather together in the shallows, and waddle up the beach toward their burrows in the dunes. They're the smallest of the world's 17 species of penguins, standing just 33 centimeters (13 in.) high, and they're the only penguins that breed on the Australian mainland. Fences and viewing stands were erected in the 1960s to protect the nesting areas. Flash photography is banned because it scares the little guys. Wear a sweater or jacket, since it gets chilly after the sun goes down. A kiosk selling food opens an hour before the penguins turn up.

If you get to Phillip Island on your own and don't have your own car, the **Penguin Parade Bus** (© **03/5952 1042,** or 0417/360 370) will pick you up from your accommodation in time to see the action. The round-trip price is A$19 (U.S.$12.40) for adults and A$11 (U.S.$7.10) for children and includes a pre-booked ticket for the Penguin Parade.

Summerland Beach, Phillip Island Tourist Road, Cowes © **03/5956 8300.** www.penguins.org.au. Admission A$13 (U.S.$8.45) adults, A$6.50 (U.S.$4.20) children 4–13, A$32 (U.S.$21) families, up to 4 children. Visitor center opens 10am; penguins arrive at sunset. Reservations for the Penguin Parade are essential in summer when tickets can be difficult to get, and on weekends and public holidays year-round.

WHERE TO STAY
Penguin Hill Country House B&B   This private home with views over sheep paddocks to Bass Strait is within walking distance of the Penguin Parade. Each room has good views and is stocked with antiques (as is much of the house) and

queen-size beds. Two have an attached bathroom with shower, and the third has a private bathroom across the hall. There's a TV and a phone in the cozy lounge. The hosts can pick you up from Cowes.

At Backbeach and Ventnor rds. (RMB 1093, Cowes, Phillip Island, VIC 3922). © and fax **03/5956 8777.** 3 units. A$120 (U.S.$78) double. Rates include cooked breakfast. MC, V. Not suitable for children. **Amenities:** TV lounge. *In room:* Hair dryer.

Rothsaye on Lovers Walk 𝕽𝕽 The penguins are just down the road and the beach is right on the doorstep—who could ask for anything more? The two suites here are adjuncts to the owner's home, and the one-bedroom cottage is set slightly apart. All rooms come with antiques and king-size beds. You also get a fruit basket, free fishing gear, beach chairs and umbrellas, magazines, and fresh flowers. Lovers Walk, a romantic floodlit path, leads from the doorstep to the center of Cowes. The owners also have a new beachside property nearby called Abaleigh on Lovers Walk. The two gorgeous apartments here come with a kitchen, barbecue, and good water views. They cost A$215 (U.S.$139) a night.

2 Roy Ct., Cowes 3922. © and fax **03/5952 2057.** www.rothsaye.com. 2 suites, 1 cottage. A$130–$150 (U.S.$84.50–$97.50) suite; A$145–$170 (U.S.$94–$110.50) cottage. MC, V. Children not allowed. **Amenities:** Golf course nearby; tour desk; nonsmoking rooms. *In room:* A/C (portable), TV/VCR, kitchen, laundry, coffeemaker, hair dryer, iron.

AROUND PORT PHILLIP BAY

West of Melbourne, the Princes Freeway (or M1) heads toward Geelong via a bypass at Werribee. To the east of Melbourne, the Nepean Highway travels along the coast to the Mornington Peninsula as far as Portsea. If you have time to stay the night, you can combine the two options, heading first down to the Mornington Peninsula (see below) and then taking the car and passenger ferry from Sorrento to Queenscliff (see below).

WERRIBEE

This small country town is 32 kilometers (20 miles) southwest of Melbourne, a 30-minute drive along the Princes Freeway. Trains run from Melbourne to Werribee station; a taxi from the station to the zoo will cost around A$5 (U.S.$3.25).

The Mansion at Werribee Park Known as "the palace in the paddock," this 60-room Italianate mansion was built in 1877. It was quite the extravagant project in its day. In addition to touring the house, you may like to stroll around the grounds and have a picnic; it's surrounded by 132 hectares (325 acres) of bushland fronting the Werribee River. You can also pre-arrange to take one of the popular carriage rides that make their way through the property. Allow 1 to 2 hours.

K Rd., Werribee. © **13 19 63** in Australia, or 03/9741 2444. Free admission park and picnic grounds; admission to mansion A$11 (U.S.$7) adults, A$6.50 (U.S.$4.20) concession, A$5.50 (U.S.$3.60) children 5–15, A$28.60 (U.S.$18.60) families. Nov–Mar daily 10am–5pm; Apr–Oct daily 10am–4pm. Closed Christmas.

Victoria's Open Range Zoo at Werribee From inside your zebra-striped safari bus you can almost touch the mainly African animals that wander almost freely over the plains—no depressing cages here. This high-caliber open-air zoo is closely associated with the Melbourne Zoo. There is also a walk-through section featuring African cats, including cheetahs, and monkeys. The safari-bus tour takes 50 minutes.

K Rd., Werribee. © **03/9731 9600.** www.zoo.org.au. Admission A$16.40 (U.S.$10.60) adults, A$12.20 (U.S.$7.90) concession, A$8.10 (U.S.$5.20) children, A$44.30 (U.S.$28.80) families. Daily 9am–5pm (the entrance gate closes at 3:30pm). Safari tours hourly 10am–4pm.

GEELONG

Victoria's second largest city, Geelong, lies 72 kilometers (45 miles) southwest of Melbourne. It's an industrial center, not really of note to visitors except as the home of the National Wool Museum. Geelong is a 45-minute drive from Melbourne. There's a regular train service, and the museum is a couple of blocks from the station.

You can pick up brochures and book accommodations through the **Geelong Great Ocean Road Visitor Information Center,** Stead Park, Princes Highway, Geelong (© **03/5275 5797,** or 1800/620 888 in Australia). The office is open daily from 9am to 5pm.

National Wool Museum   For Australians in colonial time, the sheep was the lifeblood of the nation, providing food and warm wool, profits to the landlords, and jobs to shearers, stockmen, and farmhands. This fascinating museum tells the story, from how sheepdogs work to how the sheep are sheared. You'll also see an interesting collection of gadgets used to create products from wool. There is also a reconstructed shearers' hut and a 1920s mill workers' cottage, as well as a specialty wool store, a gift shop, and a bistro. Allow up to 2 hours.

26 Moorabool St., Geelong. © **1800/620 888** in Australia, or 03/5227 0701. A$8 (U.S.$5.20) adults, A$6.50 (U.S.$4.20) concession, A$4 (U.S.$2.60) children under 16, A$22 (U.S.$14.30) families. Daily 9:30am–5pm. Closed Christmas and Good Friday.

THE MORNINGTON PENINSULA

The Mornington Peninsula, a scenic 40 kilometers (25 miles) stretch of windswept coastline and hinterland 80 kilometers (50 miles) south of Melbourne, is one of Melbourne's favorite day-trip and weekend-getaway destinations. The coast is lined with good beaches and thick bush consisting almost entirely of tea trees (early colonists used it as a tea substitute). The Cape Shanck Coastal Park stretches along the peninsula's Bass Strait foreshore from Portsea to Cape Shanck. It's home to gray kangaroos, southern brown bandicoots, echidnas, native rats, mice, reptiles, bats, and many forest and ocean birds. The park has many interconnecting walking tracks providing access to some remote beaches.

Along the route south you could stop off at the **Morning Peninsula Regional Gallery,** 4 Vancouver St., Mornington (© **03/5975 4395**), to check out the work of famous Australian artists (open Tues–Sun 10am–5pm), or visit Arthurs Seat State Park to take a short hike or ride a chair lift to a 300-meter (1,000-ft.) summit offering glorious views over the surrounding bush. At Sorrento, take time out to spot pelicans on the jetty, or visit the town's many galleries.

Also on the Mornington Peninsula is Australia's oldest and most famous maze, **Ashcombe Maze & Water Gardens,** Red Hill Road, Shoreham (© **03/ 5989 8387**), which also has extensive water and woodland gardens. There is even a rose maze made out of 1,300 rose bushes, which is spectacular when in full bloom over the spring and summer months. There's also pleasant cafe with indoor and outdoor dining. The park is open daily from 10am to 5pm; admission is A$7 (U.S.$4.60) for adults, and A$4 (U.S.$2.60) for children.

GETTING THERE   From Melbourne, take the Mornington Peninsula Freeway to Rosebud, and then the Point Nepean Road. If you want to cross Port Phillip Bay from Sorrento to Queenscliff, take the **Queenscliff Sea Road Ferry** (© **03/5258 3255;** fax 03/5258 1877), which operates daily every 2 hours from 8am to 6pm (there's an 8pm ferry on Fri and Sat from mid-Sept to mid-Dec and daily from mid-Dec until Easter Thurs). Ferries from Queenscliff operate from 7am to 5pm (plus a 7pm ferry on days listed above). The fare is A$32 to $34

(U.S.$20.80–$22.10) for cars depending on season, plus A$3 (U.S.$1.90) for adults, A$2 (U.S.$1.30) for children 5 to 15, and A$1 (U.S.65¢) for children 4 and under. Passenger-only fares are A$7 (U.S.$4.50) for adults, A$5 (U.S.$3.25) for children 5 to 15, and A$1 (U.S.65¢) for children under 4. The crossing takes 35 to 40 minutes.

VISITOR INFORMATION The **Peninsula Visitor Information Center,** Point Nepean Road, Dromana (℃ **1800/804 009** in Australia, or 03/5987 3078), has plenty of maps and information on the area and can also help book accommodations. It's open daily from 9am to 5pm. You can get more information on this and all the other Victorian National Parks on ℃ **13 19 63,** or via the Internet on www.parks.vic.gov.au.

Where to Stay & Dine

The Portsea Hotel The rooms in this typical Australian motel right on the seafront are done up in country-style furnishings. The standard twin rooms are basic; all share bathrooms. En-suite doubles have a double bed and an attached bathroom with shower. The outdoor beer garden is pleasant on a sunny day.

3746 Point Nepean Rd., Portsea, Vic 3944. ℃ **03/5984 2213.** Fax 03/5984 4066. www.portseahotel.com.au. 25 units, 6 with bathroom. A$115.50 (U.S.$75) double without bathroom; A$143 (U.S.$93) double with bathroom; A$176 (U.S.$114) bay-view suite. Rates are around 20% cheaper in winter. AE, DC, MC. V. **Amenities:** Restaurant (bistro), 3 bars; golf course nearby; tour desk; laundry service. *In room:* A/C, TV (in 6 rooms with bathroom only), unstocked refrigerator (in rooms with bathroom), coffeemaker.

12

Victoria

by Marc Llewellyn

Australia's southernmost mainland state is astoundingly diverse. Within its boundaries are 35 national parks, encompassing every possible terrain, from rain forest and snowcapped mountain ranges to sun-baked Outback desert and a coast where waves crash dramatically onto rugged sandstone outcroppings.

Melbourne (see chapter 11) may be this rugged state's heart, but the mighty Murray River, which separates Victoria from New South Wales, is its lifeblood, providing irrigation for vast tracks of semi-desert land.

Most visitors to Victoria start out exploring Melbourne's cosmopolitan streets, then visit a few local wineries, before heading for the gold fields around the historic city of Ballarat. Lots of them only experience a fraction of Victoria as a blur whizzing by the window of their rental car, but this wonderful and not overly touristed region is worth a closer look.

Visitors with more time might make their way inland to the mountains (perhaps for skiing or bushwalking at Mt. Hotham or Falls Creek), or seek out the wilderness of the Snowy River National Park. Others head to the Outback, to the Grampians National Park, and onward to Mildura through open deserts and past pink lakes and red sand dunes.

Lots of options await, and because much of it is out in the country, you'll find prices for accommodations very affordable. Whatever itinerary you choose, you're sure to find adventure and dramatic scenery.

See "Side Trips from Melbourne," in chapter 11, for information on Phillip Island, the Mornington Peninsula, the Dandenong Ranges, and the Yarra Valley.

EXPLORING THE STATE

VISITOR INFORMATION   Pick up brochures and maps at the Victorian Visitors Information Centre (see chapter 11, "Melbourne"), or call the **Victorian Tourism Information Service** (© **13 28 42**) from anywhere in Australia to talk to a consultant about your plans. The service, open daily from 8am to 6pm, will also send out brochures. If you need information along the way, look for blue road signs with a yellow information symbol.

GETTING THERE   V/Line (© 13 61 96 in Victoria, 13 22 32 in New South Wales, or 03/9619 5000) runs a limited network of trains to various places in Victoria, continuing trips to most major centers with connecting buses. Several bus companies connect Melbourne with regional areas of Victoria; the biggest operators are **Greyhound Pioneer** (© **13 20 30** in Australia, or 03/9600 1687) and **McCafferty's** (© **13 14 99** in Australia, or 03/9670 2533).

Victoria

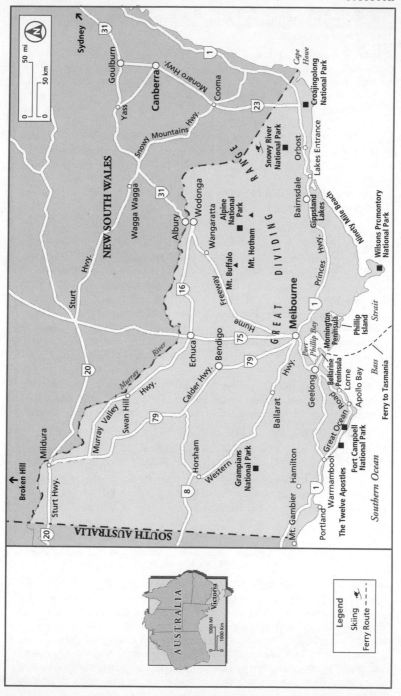

1 Ballarat: Gold-Rush City ✵✵

113km (70 miles) W of Melbourne

Ballarat, Victoria's largest inland city (pop. 90,000), is all about gold. In 1851, two prospectors found gold nuggets scattered on the ground at a place known as, ironically, Poverty Point. Within a year, 20,000 people had drifted into the area, and Australia's El Dorado gold rush had begun.

In 1858, the second-largest chunk of gold ever discovered in Australia (the Welcome Nugget) was found, but by the early 1860s, most of the easily obtainable yellow metal was gone. Larger operators continued digging until 1918, and by then Ballarat had developed enough industry to survive without mining.

Today, you can still see the gold rush's effects in the impressive buildings, built from the miners' fortunes, lining Ballarat's streets. If you're interested in seeing another former mining town, head 1½ hours north to Bendigo, a small city filled with elaborate public buildings constructed with the gains from the gold rush.

ESSENTIALS

GETTING THERE   From Melbourne, Ballarat is a 1½-hour drive via the Great Western Highway. **V/Line** (© **13 61 96** in Victoria, 13 22 32 in New South Wales, or 03/9619 5000) runs trains between the cities every day, and the trip takes less than 2 hours. The one-way fare is approximately A$17 (U.S.$11) for adults and A$9 (U.S.$5.85) for children. Ask about family-saver fares. A public bus connects the Ballarat train station with the town center.

Several sightseeing companies offer day trips from Melbourne. **Melbourne Sightseeing** (© **03/9663 3388**) offers one of the most affordable choices, a full-day tour that costs A$98 (U.S.$63.70) for adults and A$49 (U.S.$31.80) for children.

VISITOR INFORMATION   The Ballarat Visitor Information Centre at 39 Sturt St. (at the corner of Albert Street), Ballarat, VIC 3350 (© **1800/648 450** in Australia, or 03/5320 5741; www.ballarat.com), is open daily from 9am to 5pm.

SEEING THE SIGHTS

Ballarat contains many reminders of the gold-rush era, but it all really comes to life in the colonial-era re-creation on Sovereign Hill.

Ballarat Fine Art Gallery   After you've learned the story of the Eureka uprising (see below), you may find it moving to come here and see the original Eureka flag. This provincial gallery also houses a large collection of Australian art, including works by Sydney Nolan, Fred Williams, and Russell Drysdale. Look out for Tom Roberts' *Charcoal Burners* and Phillip Fox's *Love Story.*

40 Lydiard St. N., Ballarat. © **03/5331 5622.** Admission A$4 (U.S.$2.60) adults, A$2 (U.S.$1.30) students, A$1 (U.S.65¢) children 6–16. Daily 10:30am–5pm. Closed Good Friday and Christmas.

Blood on the Southern Cross ✵   This 80-minute show re-creates the Eureka Uprising, one of the most important events in Australia's history, in a breathtaking light-and-sound show that covers Sovereign Hill's 25 hectares (62 acres). Bring something warm to wear, because it can get chilly.

After gold was discovered, the government devised a system of gold licenses, charging miners a monthly fee, even if they came up empty-handed. The miners had to buy a new license every month, and corrupt gold-field police (many of whom were former convicts) instituted a vicious campaign to extract the money.

When license checks intensified in 1854, even though most of the surface gold was gone, resentment flared, and prospectors began demanding political reforms, such as the right to vote, parliamentary elections, and secret ballots.

The situation exploded when the Eureka Hotel's owner murdered a miner but was set free by the government. The hotel was burned down in revenge, and more than 20,000 prospectors joined together, burned their licenses in a huge bonfire, and built a stockade over which they raised a flag.

Troops arrived at the "Eureka Stockade" the following month, but by then only 150 miners remained behind its walls. The stockade was attacked at dawn, and in the 15-minute skirmish, 24 miners were killed and 30 wounded. The civil uprising forced the government to act: The licenses were replaced with "miners rights" and cheaper fees, and the vote was introduced to Victoria.

At Sovereign Hill, Bradshaw St. © 03/5333 5777. www.sovereignhill.com.au. Reservations required. Admission A$29 (U.S.$18.85) adults, A$15 (U.S.$9.80) children 5–15, A$79.50 (U.S.$51.70) family. Other packages include daytime entry to Sovereign Hill: A$48.50 (U.S.$31.50) adults, A$25 (U.S.$16.25) children, A$136 (U.S.$88.40) families. Call ahead for information about other packages. 2 shows nightly Mon–Sat (times vary seasonally). Closed early Aug.

Eureka Stockade Centre   You can't miss this building with its huge sail, signifying the flag of the Southern Cross, which was raised above the original miners' stockade. Relive the action of the battle through multimedia displays. The Contemplation Room, where you are asked to think about Australian history while listening to a trickling water soundscape, is a bit too hokey for me.

Eureka St. © 03/5333 1854. Admission A$8.80 (U.S.$5.70) adults, A$4.60 (U.S.$3) children, A$24.20 (U.S.$15.75) families of 6. Open every day 9am–5pm. Closed Christmas and Mon except public holidays.

The Gold Museum   This interesting museum houses a large collection of gold nuggets found at Ballarat, as well as alluvial deposits, gold ornaments, and coins. There are also gallery displays relating to the history of gold mining in the area. One hour should be enough to take in the museum.

Bradshaw St. (opposite Sovereign Hill), Ballarat. © 03/5337 1107. Admission included with Sovereign Hill ticket; otherwise A$6.30 (U.S.$4) adults, A$3.10 (U.S.$1.95) children. Open daily 10am–5:30pm.

Sovereign Hill Goldmining Township 🅡🅡 _Kids_   Australia's best outdoor museum transports you back to the 1850s and the heady days of the gold rush. More than 40 stone-and-wood reproduction buildings, including shops and businesses on the re-created Main Street, sit on this 25-hectare (62-acre) former gold-mining site. There are also tent camps around the diggings on the lowest part of the site, which would have been the outskirts of town. There are lots to see and do here, so expect to spend at least 4 hours.

The Township bustles with actors in period costumes going about their daily business. In addition to seeing how miners and their families lived, visitors can pan for real gold, watch lessons in Victorian classrooms, ride in horse-drawn carriages, and watch potters, blacksmiths, and tanners make their wares.

On top of Sovereign Hill are the mine shafts and their pithead equipment. The fascinating tour of a typical underground gold mine takes around 45 minutes.

The Voyage to Discovery museum has various artifacts from the gold rush, dioramas of mining scenes, and interactive computer displays.

A restaurant and several cafes, coffee shops, and souvenir stores can be found around the site.

Bradshaw St. © 03/5331 1944. Admission (including mine tour and admission to Gold Museum) A$25 (U.S.$16.25) adults, A$12 (U.S.$7.80) children 5–15, A$65 (U.S.$42.25) families (2 adults and up to 4 children), free for children under 5. Daily 10am–5pm. Closed Christmas. Bus: From Ballarat catch the Buninyong bus.

WHERE TO STAY

The Ansonia 🅡   This boutique hotel in a restored Victorian building sports a glass atrium that runs the length of the property and is filled with plants and wicker chairs. Studio rooms are simply but comfortably furnished, and have nice polished floorboards. The executive doubles are larger and a little plusher. The two family rooms can sleep four people in two bedrooms. There is a comfortable library and sitting room with an open fire and tea and coffeemaking facilities, and plenty of flowers and art are scattered everywhere. Smoking is not allowed on the property.

32 Lydiard St. S., Ballarat 3350. © **03/5332 4678.** Fax 03/5332 4698. www.ballarat.com/ansonia. 20 units. A$130 (U.S.$84.50) double; A$145 (U.S.$94.25) executive double; A$170 (U.S.$97.50) suite; A$210 (U.S.$136.50) family room; A$210 (U.S.$136.50) apt. AE, DC, MC, V. Free parking. **Amenities:** Restaurant (home cooking); babysitting; laundry service; same-day dry cleaning; nonsmoking rooms. *In room:* A/C, TV, dataport, hair dryer, iron.

Ballarat Heritage Homestay ⚮ *(Finds* If you'd enjoy staying in a historic cottage, you might want to try Ballarat Heritage Homestay. Some of these Victorian and Edwardian cottages date back to the gold-rush days. All of them are very different, but all have a historic feel. Three cottages have claw-foot tubs, and one has a Jacuzzi. Generally there's a queen and a double, and sometimes two singles in each cottage. All the cottages have three bedrooms, open fires, and gas heating. The B&B room has a queen-size bed and sole use of a lounge.

185 Victoria St. (P.O. Box 1360, Ballarat Mail Centre, VIC 3354). © **1800/813 369** in Australia, or 03/5332 8296. Fax 03/5331 3358. 5 cottages, 1 B&B unit. A$175 (U.S.$113.75) for 2 people for 1-night weekend stay (available for some cottages only); A$275–$350 (U.S.$178.75–$227.50) for 2-night weekend stay; A$145–$160 (U.S.$94.25–$104) 1-night weekday stay. Rates include breakfast. Extra adult A$30 (U.S.$19.50); extra child under 18 A$15 (U.S.$9.65). AE, DC, MC, V. **Amenities:** TV lounge. *In room:* Kitchen, hair dryer, iron.

The Sovereign Hill Lodge The colonial-style wooden buildings adjacent to the Sovereign Hill Goldmining Township were built to resemble an 1850s Government Camp that was used to control (and tax) the mine fields. The Residence building has rooms with queen-size beds and a set of single bunks, and the Offices building has heritage rooms with four-poster beds and plenty of Baltic pine furnishings, some with Jacuzzis. There are eight double rooms in the Superintendent's house, while the Barracks houses dorm rooms that sleep up to eight people (A$16/U.S.$10.40 for YHA members; A$18/U.S.$11.70 for non-members). There's a bar, 24-hour reception, and a game room on the grounds. Guests get a 10% discount off entry to Sovereign Hill.

Magpie St., Ballarat 3350. © **03/5333 3409.** Fax 03/5333 5861. istiff@sovereignhill.austasia.net. 37 units. A$115 (U.S.$74.75) double or family room; A$126–$142 (U.S.$82–$92.30) heritage room. Extra person A$12.50 (U.S.$8.10). Ask about packages. AE, DC, MC, V. Free parking. **Amenities:** Restaurant (Modern Australian), bar; spa (in heritage room); babysitting, laundry service, nonsmoking rooms. *In room:* A/C, TV, iron.

WHERE TO DINE

Lake Pavilion Restaurant Café INTERNATIONAL I like this restaurant across from the Botanical Gardens and on the shores of Lake Wendouree. The Lake Pavilion was constructed in 1890 and still has that old-world atmosphere, with polished floorboards and high ceilings. You can eat either indoors or outside, but either way you have some good views across the gardens and the lake. The menu includes pizzas, focaccia sandwiches, various pasta dishes, salads, steaks, and seafood. It's licensed but you can also bring your own wine. A kiosk adjacent to the restaurant sells cheap snacks.

Wendouree Parade (across from the Botanical Gardens). © **03/5334 1811.** Main courses around A$11 (U.S.$7.15). AE, MC, V. Daily 9am–6pm. Bus: 15 Mon–Sat.

Robin Hood Family Bistro BISTRO   The Robin Hood is located in a big old pub—not exactly a place where you'd expect to find a bistro catering to healthy eating. The bistro, though, is a past winner of the Real Meal Award, handed out by the Australian Hoteliers Association and aimed at promoting healthier pub food. Everything here is made with low-fat/low-cholesterol ingredients. On the menu you'll find steak-and-kidney pie, beef curry, and several types of steak. Not healthy so far, perhaps, but there's an extensive salad bar, and all main courses come with a healthy dollop of vegetables.

33 Peel St. N. ⓒ 03/5331 3348. Reservations recommended Fri–Sat. Main courses A$8–$20 (U.S.$5.20–$13). AE, DC, MC, V. Daily 11:30am–2pm and 5:30–8pm.

2 The Great Ocean Road: One of the World's Most Scenic Drives ⍟⍟

Geelong: 75km (46½ miles) SW of Melbourne; Torquay: 94km (58 miles) SW of Melbourne; Port Campbell National Park: 285km (177 miles) SW of Melbourne; Peterborough: 200km (160 miles) SW of Melbourne

The Great Ocean Road—which hugs the coast from Torquay, and onwards through Anglesea, Lorne, Apollo Bay, and Port Campbell, until it ends at Peterborough—is one of Australia's most spectacular drives (many say it's the best). The scenery along the 106-kilometer (64½-mile) route includes huge cliffs, ocean vistas, beaches, rain forests, and some incredible rock formations. The settlements along the highway are small, but they offer a number of accommodation choices.

The best way to travel along the Great Ocean Road is to drive yourself at a leisurely pace, stopping off wherever your fancy takes you. The main attractions are in the coastal Port Campbell National Park, so don't be surprised if you're not overly impressed until you get there. If you are traveling on to Adelaide, you could stop off for 1 night along the Great Ocean Road, and spend another night in the Coorong in South Australia (see chapter 10).

ESSENTIALS

ORGANIZED TOURS   Melbourne Sightseeing (ⓒ **03/9663 3388**) offers a bus trip featuring the highlights of the Great Ocean Road. The buses leave from Melbourne daily at 8:15am and return at 8:30pm—which is a journey I wouldn't like to attempt in a day. Tours cost A$97 (U.S.$63) for adults—A$54 (U.S.$35) if you have a YHA card—and A$49 (U.S.$31.80) for children. The trip can be stretched out over 2 days with overnight accommodation; the price for the overnight trip ranges between A$136 and $170 (U.S.$88.40 and $110.50) depending on where you choose to stay. **Grayline Sightseeing Tours** (ⓒ **03/9663 4455**) also has daily trips that cost A$102 (U.S.$66.30) for adults and A$51 (U.S.$33) for children.

Another option worth considering is a 2-day excursion with **Let's Go Bush Tours** (ⓒ **03/9662 3969**), which departs Melbourne every Wednesday and Saturday. The trip is less rushed than others, and you get to stay in the company's own house situated on the highest point of the Great Ocean Road. The trip costs A$99 (U.S.$64.30), including dinner, breakfast, and accommodation.

Wild-Life Tours (ⓒ **1300 650 288** or 03/9747 1882; www.wildlifetours. com.au) offers a 3-day Great Ocean Road tour from Melbourne, including a visit to The Grampians, for A$135 (U.S.$87.75). The company also offers a 2-day trip from Melbourne to Adelaide along the Great Ocean Road for A$129 (U.S.$83.80) one-way. Prices do not include accommodation or food. Inquire about discounts.

V/Line (© **13 61 96** in Victoria, 13 22 32 in New South Wales, or 03/9619 5000) runs a special combined train/coach Coast Link service as far as Warrnambool, via Geelong, Lorne, Apollo Bay, and Port Campbell. The train leaves Melbourne every day at 8:50am, 12:40, and 6:08pm—but check before just turning up—and then you transfer onto a bus at Geelong. The bus tours the Great Ocean Road, stopping off at various lookout points (and for lunch) and then carries on to Warrnambool. The round trip costs A$52.80 (U.S.$34.30) for adults and A$26.40 (U.S.$17) for children on Tuesday, Wednesday and Thursday, and A$75.40 (U.S.$49) for adults and A$37.70 (U.S.$24.50) for children on other days. Ask about family-saver fares.

VISITOR INFORMATION Most places along the route have their own information centers. If you're coming from Melbourne, stop at the Geelong & Great Ocean Road Visitors Centre, Stead Park, Princess Highway, Geelong, VIC 3220 (© and fax **03/5275 5797**; www.greatoceanrd.org.au). You can book accommodations here, which you should do in advance, especially in summer. There's also a visitor center at the National Wool Museum, 26 Moorabool St., Geelong (© **1800/620 888** in Australia, or 03/5222 2900).

Along the route, the **Park Information Centre,** at Port Campbell National Park, Norris Street, Port Campbell (© **03/5598 6382**), is also a good place to pick up brochures. It also has some interesting displays and an audio-visual show of the area. It's open from 10am to 4:30pm daily.

If you're approaching from the north, visit the **Camperdown Visitor Information Centre,** "Court House," Manifold Street, Princes Highway, Camperdown (© **03/5593 3390**). It's open Monday through Friday from 9:30am to 5pm, Saturday from 9:30am to 4pm, and Sunday from 11am to 4pm.

EXPLORING THE COASTAL ROAD

Along the route you might want to stop off at Torquay, a township dedicated to surfing. The main surf beach here is much nicer than the one farther down the coast in Lorne. While in Torquay, check out **Surfworld,** Surfcoast Plaza Beach Road, West Torquay (© **03/5261 4606**), which has interactive exhibits dealing with surfboard design and surfing history, and video of the world's best surfers. Admission is A$6.50 (U.S.$4.20) for adults, A$4.50 (U.S.$2.90) for children, and A$17.50 (U.S.$11.40) for families. Bells Beach, just down the road, is world-famous in surfing circles for its perfect waves.

Lorne has some nice boutiques and is a good place to stop off for lunch or stay the night. The stretch from Lorne to Apollo Bay is one of the most spectacular sections of the route, as the road narrows and twists and turns along a cliff edge with the ocean on the other side. Apollo Bay is a pleasant town that was once a whaling station. It has good sandy beaches and is more low-key than Lorne.

Next, you come to the Angahook-Lorne State Park, which protects most of the coastal section of the Otway Ranges from Aireys Inlet, just south of Anglesea, to Kennett River. It has plenty of well-marked rain-forest walks and picnic areas at Shelly Beach, Elliot River, and Blanket Bay. There's plenty of wildlife around here.

About 13 kilometers (8 miles) past Apollo Bay, just off the main road, you can take an elevated stroll through the rain forest on the Maits Rest Rainforest Boardwalk. A little farther along the main road, an unpaved road leads north past Hopetoun Falls and Beauchamp Falls to the settlement of Beech Forest. Seven kilometers (4¼ miles) farther along the main road another unpaved road heads off south for 15 kilometers (9 miles) to a windswept headland and the Cape Otway Lighthouse. Built by convicts in 1848, the 100-meter-tall (328-ft.-tall) lighthouse is open to tourists daily. Admission is A$6.50 (U.S.$4.20) for adults and A$3.50 (U.S.$2.30) for children. It's open daily from 9am to 5pm. Ask about guided tours.

Back on the main road again, your route heads inland through an area known as Horden Vale, before running to the sea again at Glenaire—there's good surfing and camping at Johanna, 6 kilometers (3¾ miles) north of here. Then the Great Ocean Road heads north again to Lavers Hill, a former timber town. Five kilometers (3 miles) southwest of Lavers Hill is the small Melba Gully State Park, where you can spot glowworms at night and walk along routes of rainforest ferns. Keep an eye out for one of the last giant gum trees that escaped the loggers—it's some 27 meters (88½ ft.) in circumference and is estimated to be more than 300 years old.

The next place of note is Moonlight Head, which marks the start of the "Shipwreck Coast"—a 120-kilometer (74-mile) stretch of coastline running to Port Fairy that claimed more than 80 ships in only 40 years at the end of the 19th century and the beginning of the 20th.

Just past Princetown starts the biggest attraction of the entire trip, **Port Campbell National Park** ⩗⩗. With its sheer cliffs and coastal rock sculptures, it's one of the most immediately recognizable images of natural Australia. You can't miss the **Twelve Apostles,** a series of rock pillars that stand in the foam just offshore. Other attractions are the **Blowhole,** which throws up huge sprays of water; the **Grotto,** a baroque rock formation intricately carved by the waves; **London Bridge,** which looked quite like the real thing until the center crashed into the sea in 1990 (leaving a bunch of tourists stranded on the wrong end); and the **Loch Ard Gorge. Port Fairy,** a lovely fishing town once known as Belfast by Irish immigrants who settled here to escape the potato famine, is also on the Shipwreck Coast.

Not far past the town of Peterborough the Great Ocean Road heads inland to Warrnambool to eventually join the Princes Highway heading toward Adelaide.

WHERE TO STAY ALONG THE WAY

The **Great Ocean Road Accommodation Centre,** 136 Mountjoy Parade, Lorne, VIC 3232 (© **03/5289 1800**), rents out cottages and units along the route.

IN LORNE

Lorne is a good option for a night's rest. Though the beach and water are nothing special, there are plenty of restaurants.

Cumberland Lorne Conference & Leisure Resort ⩗ *Value* This sporty resort, built in 1988 but already crumbling around the edges, stands out like a sore thumb from its location between the sea and the foothills of the Otway Ranges. Still, I highly recommend it, as it's good value for money and quite luxurious. Every apartment has a queen-size bed and a foldout sofa bed, a large kitchen, a laundry, a Jacuzzi, a balcony, and free in-house movies. All units have large bathrooms with a shower/tub combination. More than half of the rooms have panoramic ocean views; the rest look out onto gardens. Two-bedroom apartments have two extra single beds, and split-level penthouses have two Jacuzzis and two balconies.

150–178 Mountjoy Parade, Lorne, VIC 3232. © **1800/037 010** in Australia, or 03/5289 2400. Fax 03/5289 2256. www.cumberland.com.au. 99 units. Summer A$270–$295 (U.S.$175.50–$191.75) 1-bedroom apt; A$315–$340 (U.S.$204.75–$221) 2-bedroom apt; A$370–$395 (U.S.$240.50–$256.75) penthouse. Off-season A$210–$235 (U.S.$136.50–$168) 1-bedroom apt; A$265–$285 (U.S.$172.25–$185.25) 2-bedroom apt; A$325–$345 (U.S.$211.25–$224.25) penthouse. Ask about packages. AE, DC, MC, V. **Amenities:** Restaurant (bistro); small indoor pool; 2 tennis courts (lit for nightplay); exercise room; spa; sauna; water-sports rental; children's center; concierge; tour desk; business center; 24-hour room service; in-room massage; babysitting; same-day dry cleaning; nonsmoking rooms. *In room:* TV with pay movies, iron, kitchenette, unstocked refrigerator, coffeemaker, hair dryer.

Great Ocean Road Cottages *Kids*   This complex has it all, although with so many people around (and quite a few children), it can be a little noisy in summer. There's a set of self-contained cottages, set away from each other in a quiet patch of bushland, about a 5-minute walk from the town center. Each cottage is a two-story wooden hut with a double bed, two twin beds, and a pullout mattress. There's also a bathroom and a full kitchen. Just down the road is Waverley House, a historic mansion that has been divided into seven apartments. All of them are nice, but they vary enormously in size and furnishing.

Also on the property is **Great Ocean Road Backpackers,** which offers dorm-style accommodation for A$18 (U.S.$11.70) for YHA members and A$21 (U.S.$13.60) for non-members. They also have a few family rooms (discounts apply to all backpacker beds for YHA members).

10 Erskine Ave. (P.O. Box 60), Lorne, VIC 3232. © **03/5289 1070.** Fax 03/5289 2508. greatoceanrdcots@ iprimus.com.au. 10 cottages, 7 apts, dorms sleeping 33. A$195 (U.S.$126.75) cottages summer, A$115 (U.S.$74.75) off-season; A$110–$160 (U.S.$71.50–$104) standard apts, depending on season; A$180–$200 (U.S.$117–$130) spa apts, depending on season; A$255–$295 (U.S.$146.25–$191.75) suite. AE, DC, MC, V. **Amenities:** Bike rental. *In room:* A/C (cottages only), kitchenette (cottages only).

IN APOLLO BAY

Bayside Gardens   Right opposite the beach, with good ocean views from the front rooms, Bayside Gardens is a pleasant place to stay—and you can save money on meals by cooking in your own kitchen. The units all have a separate bedroom with a double bed, a lounge area, a full kitchen, and an attached bathroom with shower. Rooms at the front can be noisy if you're not used to living beside an ocean. There are wood fires in some of the units, and all rooms are centrally heated. Fry your fish on the barbecues scattered around in the 1½-acre grounds. It's a 10-minute walk to town.

219 Great Ocean Rd., Apollo Bay, VIC 3233. © and fax **03/5237 6248.** baysidegardens@iprimus.com.au. 10 units. A$70–$110 (U.S.$45.50–$71.50) 1-bedroom apts. Higher rates apply Christmas, Jan, Easter, and public holidays. MC, V. Min. 1-week stay in Jan. MC, V. **Amenities:** Coin-op laundry; nonsmoking rooms. *In room:* TV, kitchen, unstocked refrigerator.

IN PORT CAMPBELL

Macka's Farm *Finds* *Kids*   This working farm is located inland from the Twelve Apostles (continue on from the Twelve Apostles for 2 kilometers/1¼ miles and turn off at the sign for Macka's farm—it's another 4 kilometers/2½ miles inland from there). The units all have kitchens, so you can cook up your own feast. Otherwise, you can order meals by prior arrangement outside peak season, or visit one of the nearby restaurants. Rooms sleep between six and eight people in a mixture of singles and doubles. There's no TV—but who needs it when there are lots of pigs, cows, ducks, and chickens running around? Overall, it's a great farm experience.

RSD 2305 Princetown Rd., Princetown, VIC 3269. © **03/5598 8261.** Fax 03/5598 8201. macka's@netcam. com.au. 3 units. A$85–$100 (U.S.$55.25–$65) double, depending on season. Extra person A$15 (U.S.$9.75). MC, V. *In room:* Iron, kitchen, unstocked refrigerator, coffeemaker, hair dryer.

WHERE TO DINE IN LORNE

Arab Restaurant *R* INTERNATIONAL   This popular bistro serves some of the best food along this part of the coast. The house specialty is chicken Kiev, but you can also tuck into dishes such as the fish of the day or chicken schnitzel. The apple crumble is delicious.

Mount Joy Parade. ⓒ **03/5289 1435.** Reservations recommended. Main courses A$10.50–$18.50 (U.S.$6.80–$12). AE, DC, MC, V. Mon–Fri 9am–9pm, Sat 8am–11pm, Sun 7:30am–10pm. Closed Christmas.

Marks ⚔ INTERNATIONAL   Lorne's best restaurant is a classy joint with simple wooden chairs and tables set in an elegant fashion in a cool, yellow-walled interior. Dishes includes fried calamari salad, spicy octopus, risotto, and the intriguing oven-baked vine-wrapped goat cheese and macadamia nut parcel on eggplant paté with red capsicum purée. The bar is open for coffee and drinks all day.

Mount Joy Parade. ⓒ **03/5289 2787.** Main courses A$9–$17.50 (U.S.$5.85–$11.40). AE, DC, MC, V. Daily noon–2:30pm (only Sat–Sun in winter) and 6–8:30pm.

Ozone Milk Bar ⟨Value⟩ AUSTRALIAN MILK BAR   An Ozzie icon, milk bars are a kind of downmarket cafes that sell everything from milk shakes and pies to newspapers. This one sells good pies and quiche, a limp-looking and bland-tasting veggie burger I wouldn't recommend, chicken-fillet burgers, cookies, ice cream, and small homemade cakes. The milk shakes are particularly good. You can sit inside or around three small tables outside. There's a Thai place next door, but it's very unwelcoming.

Mount Joy Parade. ⓒ **03/5289 1780.** Menu items A$1.80–$4 (U.S.$1.20–$2.60). No credit cards. Daily 7am–6pm (to 11pm Christmas to the end of Jan).

3 The Murray River ⚔

Mildura: 544km (337 miles) NW of Melbourne; Albury-Wadonga: 305km (189 miles) N of Melbourne; Echuca: 210km (130 miles) N of Melbourne

The Murray is Australia's version of the Mississippi River. Though it's a rushing torrent of white water at its source in the Snowy Mountains, it becomes slow moving and muddy brown by the time it becomes the meandering border between Victoria and New South Wales. The Darling River, which starts off in Queensland, feeds the Murray; together they make Australia's longest river.

The Murray was once used by Aborigines as a source of food and transportation, and later the water was plied by paddle steamers, laden with wool and crops from the land it helped irrigate. In 1842, the Murray was "discovered" by explorers Hamilton Hume and William Howell on the first overland trek from Sydney to Port Phillip, near Melbourne. As Hume later wrote, on their trek the explorers "suddenly arrived at the bank of a very fine river—at least 200 feet wide, apparently deep, the bank being 8 or 9 feet above the level, which is overflowed at the time of flood . . . In the solid wood of a healthy tree I carved my name." You can still see the carved initials on a tree standing by the river bank in Albury, on the border between the two states.

ESSENTIALS

GETTING THERE   Most visitors cross the river during an overland drive between cities. There are two routes to get to the Murray from Melbourne: Either take the Calder Highway to Mildura, which is a 6-hour drive, or take the 2½-hour route down the Midland Highway to Echuca. Traveling from Melbourne to Mildura is only practical if you're continuing on to Broken Hill, which is 297 kilometers (184 miles) north of Mildura. Those in a hurry to get to and from Sydney can travel via the river-straddling twin towns of Albury-Wadonga on the Hume Highway (about a 12-hr. trip with short stops).

V/Line (✆ **13 61 96** in Victoria, 13 22 32 in New South Wales, or 03/9619 5000) runs regular train services to Mildura, Echuca, and Albury-Wadonga.

VISITOR INFORMATION   The **Echuca and Moama and District Visitor Information Centre,** 2 Heygarth St., Echuca, VIC 3564 (✆ **1800/804 446** or 03/5480 7555; fax 03/5482 6413; www.echucamoama.com), has plenty of maps and detailed information about local accommodations and river cruises. It's open daily from 9am to 5pm. The **Mildura Visitor Information & Booking Centre,** 180–190 Deakin Ave., Mildura, VIC 3502 (✆ **1800/039 043** or 03/5021 4424; fax 03/5021 1836; tourism@mildura.vic.gov.au), offers similar services. It's open Monday through Friday from 9am to 5:30pm and weekends from 9am to 5pm. If you're passing through Albury, you might want to contact the **Gateway Visitors Information Centre,** Gateway Village, Lincoln Causeway, Wadonga, VIC 3690 (✆ **1800/800 743** or 02/6041 3875; fax 02/6021 0322), open daily from 9am to 5pm.

RIVER CRUISES & OTHER FUN STUFF

IN MILDURA   Mildura is one of Australia's most important fruit-growing areas. There was a time, however, when this was just semi-arid, red dust country. The area bloomed due to a little ingenuity and, of course, the Murray. The original irrigation system consisted of two imported English water pumps and the manual labor of hundreds of newly arrived immigrants, who were put to work clearing the scrub and digging channels through the new fields. Today, the hungry land soaks up the water.

Several paddle steamers leave from Mildura wharf. One of the nicest boats is the **PS *Melbourne*** (✆ **03/5023 2200;** fax 03/5021 3017), which was built in 1912 and is still powered by steam. It offers 2-hour trips leaving at 10:50am and 1:50pm. The fare is A$18.50 (U.S.$12) for adults and A$7.50 (U.S.$4.90) for children (free for children under 5).

The PS *Melbourne*'s sister ship, the ***Rothbury,*** was built in 1881, but its steam-driven engine has been replaced by a conventional engine. It churns out a winery cruise every Thursday from 10:30am to 3:30pm, stopping off at a winery for tastings and a barbecue lunch. The trip costs A$42 (U.S.$27.30) for adults and A$20 (U.S.$13) for children. The Rothbury has evening dinner cruises every Thursday from 7 to 10pm for A$40 (U.S.$26) for adults and A$18 (U.S.$11.70) for children. You can also take the paddleboat to the Golden River Zoo (see below) during school holiday periods leaving Mildura Wharf at 9:50am on Wednesday morning (returning at 3pm). The trip costs A$32 (U.S.$20.80) for adults and A$16 (U.S.$10.40) for children 5 to 14, including zoo.

On dry land, the **Golden River Zoo,** Flora Avenue, Mildura (✆ **03/5023 5540;** www.goledriverzoo.com.au) is a pleasant place to see native animals. The zoo fronts onto the river 4 kilometers (2½ miles) from the city center down 11th Street. The animals here virtually follow you around (on the lookout for food) as you walk through their large enclosures. Admission is A$15 (U.S.$9.80) for adults and A$8 (U.S.$5.20) for children, including a free barbecue lunch at noon and a free tractor-train ride down to the river at 1:30pm and an animal show. The zoo is open daily, except Christmas Day, from 10am to 5pm.

IN ECHUCA   In Echuca, another paddle steamer option is the ***Emmylou*** (✆ **03/5480 2237;** fax 03/5480 2927; www.emmylou.com.au). A 2-day/ 2-night cruise leaves the Port of Echuca Wednesday at 6pm and returns at noon on Friday (but check sailings beforehand). The cruise includes a visit to the Barmah, an area famous for its wetlands and the largest red gum trees in the world, or depending on river levels will include a stop at Perricoota Station. The trip costs A$415 to $435 (U.S.$269.75–$282.75) per person, depending on cabin. Children 4 to 14 receive a 25% discount. An overnight trip also leaves on Saturday at 6pm and returns at 10am on Sunday. It costs A$195 to $210 (U.S.$126.75–$136.50) per person including breakfast; dinner is extra. The *Emmylou* also offers various day trips costing A$15 (U.S.$9.75) for adults and A$7.50 (U.S.$4.90) for kids for 1 hour, and A$18 (U.S.$11.70) for adults and A$9 (U.S.$5.90) for kids for 1½ hours.

The **Port of Echuca** (© 03/5482 4248; www.portofechuca.org.au) is definitely worth a look. The three-level red gum wharf was built in 1865 and is still used by paddle steamers. The Port owns the PS *Adelaide*, the oldest operating wooden-hulled paddle steamer in the world (1866), the PS *Pevensey* (1911), and the PS *Alexander Arbuthnot* (1923). One-hour cruises on the latter two are offered daily at 10:15, 11:30am, 1, 2:15, and 3:30pm for A$15 (U.S.$9.90) for adults and A$6.50 (U.S.$4.20) for children. You can also take a look around the wharf on a guided tour, priced at A$10 (U.S.$6.50) for adults and A$6.50 (U.S.$4.20) for children. Ask about combined and family prices. Outside the Port, in the Echuca Port Precinct, there are various things to do, including horse and carriage rides and old penny arcade machines in Sharpes Magic Movies, located in an old riverboat warehouse.

TRIPS INTO THE OUTBACK   If you want to get out into the Outback, then trips from Mildura with **Mallee Outback Experiences,** P.O. Box 82, Nichols Point, VIC 3501 (©/fax **03/5021 1621,** or mobile 0418/521 0030) are well worth the effort. The company offers two trips. The first goes to **Mungo National Park** *✿*, which is famous for its red sand dunes and shifting sands, and which I highly recommend you go and see. The second is to **Hattah National Park,** which has some gorgeous river plains, Murray River lakes, pine forests, and more mallee scrub. The Mungo trip leaves every Wednesday and Saturday, and the Hattah National Park trip every Friday. All trips cost A$55 (U.S.$35.75) for adults, A$33 (U.S.$21.45) for children, and A$132 (U.S.$85.80) for a family of five.

You can get to these two national parks on your own, but it's best to have a four-wheel-drive vehicle—even better if you go with an experienced guide. Mungo National Park is a unique, arid region located 110 kilometers (68 miles) northeast of Mildura, off the Sturt Highway. People come here to see the Walls of China, a strange moonscape of intricately weathered red sand. The walls edge onto Lake Mungo, which was once a huge freshwater lake during the last Ice Age, but is now dry. A 60-kilometer (37-mile) driving tour starting at the visitor center at the park's entrance takes you across the lake bed to the Walls of China. There are several short walks in the park leading off from the campsites at the park entrance. Call the **National Parks & Wildlife Service NSW** (© **1300 361 967** in Australia) for more information on Mungo. Just outside the park, the **Mungo Lodge** (© **03/5029 7297;** www.mungoldg@ruralnet.net.au) offers affordable motel accommodation and a casual restaurant.

WHERE TO STAY
IN MILDURA

Mildura Grand Hotel *✿✿✿*   This huge 19th-century hotel is right in the center of Mildura, overlooking the Murray River. Double rooms are comfortable, and many have been recently refurbished. Suites are bigger, and some have balconies and garden views. State suites are plush and come with a king-size bed.

The Presidential suite (the most expensive) is Art-Deco inspired, with a large marble bathroom and spa.

Seventh St., Mildura, VIC 3500. © 1800/034 228 in Australia, or 03/5023 0511. Fax 03/5022 1801. www. milduragrand.com.au. 102 units. A$110–$143 (U.S.$71.50–$92.95) Grand Room double; A$176–$462 (U.S.$114.40–$300) suite. Rates include breakfast. Additional person A$22 (U.S.$14.30). Ask about packages. AE, DC, MC, V. **Amenities:** 3 restaurants (Italian, pizza cafe, bistro, 4 bars; large outdoor pool; golf course nearby; access to nearby health club, spa, sauna; 24-hour concierge; shopping arcade; 24-hour room service; in-room massage; laundry service; dry cleaning; nonsmoking rooms; executive rooms. *In room:* A/C, TV with pay movies, minibar, coffeemaker, hair dryer, iron.

IN ECHUCA
Echuca Gardens B&B and YHA   There are evening gatherings around the piano at this popular two-story log cabin B&B, as well as a pretty neat hot tub in the front yard surrounded by murals and landscaped water gardens. Rooms are decorated in native flower themes, and all of them have balconies. Two rooms have showers in the bathroom, and another has a shower on the second floor. It's a short stroll from the B&B to either the river or a state forest. The YHA has a basic twin room inside and three tent-like cabins outside, one with a double bed and the other with two singles. There are also three basic dorm rooms with beds going for A$18 (U.S.$11.70) for YHA members and A$21.50 (U.S.$14) non-members.

103 Mitchell St., Echuca, VIC 3564. © 03/5480 6522, or 0419 881 054 mobile. Fax 03/5482 6951. www. echucagardens.com.au. 6 units (3 in B&B and 3 in hostel). B&B room A$140 (U.S.$91) weekends, A$120 (U.S.$78) weekdays. Rates include breakfast. MC, V. **Amenities:** Spa; sauna; nonsmoking rooms. *In room:* A/C, hair dryer.

IN ALBURY
Hume Country Golf Club Motor Inn   This is a good place to stop if you're making the long trip north to Sydney. Just on the New South Wales side of the border, this motor inn has typical motel rooms and two very large family rooms, one sleeping five the other seven. Suites are also large and come with a Jacuzzi tub. All rooms overlook the 27-hole golf course, where a round of golf costs A$20 (U.S.$13).

736 Logan Rd., Albury, NSW 2640. © 02/6025 8233. Fax 02/6040 4999. humegolfmotel@primus.com.au. 25 units. A$82 (U.S.$53.30) double; A$90 (U.S.$58.50) family room; A$115 (U.S.$74.75) suite. Extra person A$10 (U.S.$6.50). AE, DC, MC, V. **Amenities:** Golf course on the premises; babysitting; coin-op laundry; non-smoking rooms. *In room:* A/C, TV, iron, unstocked refrigerator, coffeemaker, hair dryer, iron.

4 The Southeast Coast

The Princes Highway wanders down the coast from Sydney just past Eden, then darts across into Victoria, passing through the logging town of Orbost, and then dipping down toward Lakes Entrance. The highway continues to the southwest, swooping in an arch to Melbourne.

This region's most interesting sights are Wilsons Promontory National Park, and—to a lesser extent—the Snowy River National Park.

WILSONS PROMONTORY NATIONAL PARK 𝒜
200km (124 miles) SE of Melbourne

"The Prom," as it's called, is Victoria's best-loved national park. Dipping down into Bass Strait, the park—which was named after a prominent London businessman—marks the southernmost point on Australia's mainland. It's thought to once have been joined to Tasmania by a land bridge. The best time to visit the park is from late September to early December, when all the bush flowers are in bloom.

Visitors come here for the spectacular granite mountains, the thick forests and vast plains, and some of the country's best beaches. Wildlife abounds in the park, including plenty of koalas, kangaroos, wallabies, possums, echidnas, wombats, and emus. You can hand-feed crimson rosellas at the capital of the Prom, Tidal River, but you'll find little more here than the national park's **Tourist Information Center** (© **1800/350 552** in Australia, or 03/5680 9555) and camping and caravan grounds. There are plenty of trails leading away into the mountains: Following the longer trails can turn into a 2- or 3-day excursion, though shorter day hikes are possible. One of the best trails is the 1-hour Mt. Oberon walk, which starts from the Mt. Oberon parking lot and offers superb views. Visitors also rave about the Squeaky Beach Nature Walk, a 1½-hour walk from Tidal River to the next bay and back.

There are some 30 beaches in the park, some of which are easily accessible. Norman's Beach in Tidal River is the most popular, and it's the only one recommended for swimming. No snorkeling or lifeguards are at these beaches, but they're gorgeous.

ENTRY FEES   Park entry costs A$9 (U.S.$5.90) for cars, which you pay at the park entrance gate, 30 kilometers (18 miles) north of Tidal River. The gate is open 24 hours, but if you arrive late and the collection station is closed, pay the following morning at Tidal River.

GETTING THERE   From Melbourne, take the South Gippsland Highway (B440), turning south at Meeniyan and again at Fish Creek or Foster. The route is well-signposted. Tidal River is 30 kilometers inside the park boundary.

There's no public transportation to the park. You can, however, take the V/Line bus from Melbourne to Foster (fare: A$21.30/U.S.$13.85), which is 60 kilometers (37 miles) north of the park. In Foster, you can stay at the **Foster Backpackers Hostel,** 17 Pioneer St., Foster, VIC 3960 (© **03/5682 2614**). It's basically a private home with a few spare rooms; the two doubles cost A$44 (U.S.$28.60), and dorm beds go for A$19 (U.S.$12.35). There are also 2 fully self-contained apartments for $55 (U.S.$35.75). The owner offers daily transport to Tidal River for A$22 (U.S.$14.30) each way; the trip takes around 45 minutes.

WHERE TO STAY

The national park's Tourist Information Center operates 17 self-contained cabins costing A$118.50 to $129.50 (U.S.$77–$84.20) a night for two, depending on season. They can accommodate up to six people; each extra adult costs A$17.20 (U.S.$11.20) and child A$11 (U.S.$7.15). In addition, five "Lorikeet" units cost A$58.30 to $93 (U.S.$37.90–$60.45) a night for two and A$93.50 to A$134 (U.S.$60.80–$87) for three or four (higher prices in summer). For bookings call © **03/5680 9500** or fax 03/568 09516.

Waratah Park Country House   If you don't feel like roughing it, this is the only place within the park that will do. Rooms, with king-size beds and double spas, offer stunning views over Wilsons Promontory and a dozen or so islands. The food here is excellent, too. The hotel is also next to the new Cape Liptrap Coastal Park, home to some 120 species of birds.

It's a friendly place, and the hosts will sit down with you and go through the things you want to do while in the area. A V/Line coach operates from

Melbourne to Fish Creek (about 10 min. away), and the owner will pick you up from the bus station.

Thomson Rd., Waratah Bay, VIC 3959. © 03/5683 2575. Fax 03/5683 2275. www.wpe.com.au. 6 units. A$78 (U.S.$50.70) including breakfast; A$115 (U.S.$75) Sun–Thurs (including 4-course dinner and breakfast); A$280 (U.S.$182) for weekend package including 2 nights' lodgings, 2 breakfasts, and 2 4-course dinners. All rates are per person. AE, MC, V. **Amenities:** Restaurant (International); babysitting (for dinner time only); laundry (in room); nonsmoking rooms. *In room:* TV, unstocked refrigerator, coffeemaker, hair dryer.

5 The High Country

Victoria's High Country is made up of the hills and mountains of the Great Dividing Range, which runs from Queensland, through New South Wales, to just before Ballarat, where it drops away and reappears in the dramatic mountains of the Grampians, in the western part of Victoria. The range separates inland Australia from the greener coastal belt. The highest mountain in the Victorian segment of the range is Mt. Bogong, which at just 1,988 meters (6,621 ft.) is minuscule by world mountain standards.

The main attractions of the High Country are its natural features, which include moorland and typical mountainous alpine scenery. It's also popular for its outdoor activities, including hiking, canoeing, white-water rafting, and rock climbing. The High Country is also the home of the Victorian ski fields, based around Mt. Buller, Mt. Stirling, Falls Creek, Mt. Buffalo, and Mt. Hotham. If you plan to go walking here make sure you have plenty of water and sunscreen, as well as a tent and a good-quality sleeping bag. As in any alpine region temperatures can plummet dramatically. In summer, days can be very hot, and nights very cold.

SNOWY RIVER NATIONAL PARK

390km (242 miles) NE of Melbourne

The Snowy River National Park, with its lovely river scenery and magnificent gorges, protects Victoria's largest forest wilderness areas. The Snowy River was once a torrent worthy of Banjo Patterson's famous poem, but since Snowy Mountain Hydro-Electric came along and erected a series of dams, it's become a mere trickle of its former self.

GETTING THERE & GETTING AROUND   There are two main access roads to the park, the Gelantipy Road from Buchan and the Bonang Freeway from the logging township of Orbost. MacKillop's Road (also known as Deddick River Road) runs across the park's northern border from Bonang to a little south of Wulgulmerang. Around MacKillop's Bridge, along MacKillop's Road, is some spectacular scenery, and the park's best campgrounds, set beside some nice swimming holes and sandy river beaches. The Barry Way leads through the main township of Buchan, where you'll find some of Australia's best caves.

VISITOR INFORMATION   The main place to get information on Snowy River National Park and Alpine National Park is the Buchan Caves Information Centre, in the Buchan Caves complex. It's open daily from 9am to 4pm (closed Christmas). Otherwise, call Parks Victoria (© 13 19 63 in Victoria, or 03/5155 9264).

EXPLORING THE BUCHAN CAVES

The **Buchan Caves** (© 03/5155 9264) are set in a scenic valley that is particularly beautiful in autumn, when all the European trees are losing their leaves. Tourists can visit the Royal and Fairy caves (which are quite similar), with their fabulous stalactites and stalagmites. There are several tours daily: April to September at 11am, 1, and 3pm; October to March at 10, 11:15am, 1, 2:15, and 3:30pm. Entry to one cave costs A$10 (U.S.$6.50) for adults, A$5 (U.S.$3.25) for children ages 5 to 16, and A$25 (U.S.$16.25) for families of five.

To reach the caves from the Princes Highway, turn off at Nowa Nowa (it's well-signposted), or if you're coming south from Jindabyne in New South Wales (see chapter 4) follow the Barry Way, which runs alongside the Snowy River.

Want to feel like the Man from Snowy River? **Snowy Mountain Rider Tours,** Karoonda Park, Gelantipy (© **03/5155 0220;** fax 03/5155 0308), offers half-day rides in the Snowy River National Park for A$60 (U.S.$39), and full-day tours for A$120 (U.S.$78) including lunch. Four-day trips including camping and all meals costs A$520 (U.S.$338). The company also arranges rafting on Snowy River for A$120 (U.S.$78) a day including lunch.

ALPINE NATIONAL PARK ☞☞
333km (200 miles) NE of Melbourne, 670km (402 miles) SW of Sydney

Victoria's largest national park at 646,000 hectares (2,494 sq. miles), the Alpine National Park connects the High Country areas of New South Wales and the Australian Capital Territory (ACT). The park's scenery is spectacular, encompassing most of the state's highest mountains, wild rivers, impressive escarpments, forests, and high plains. The flora is diverse; in all, some 1,100 plant species have been recorded within the park's boundaries, including 12 not found anywhere else. Walking here is particularly good in spring and summer, when the Bogong High Plains are covered in a carpet of wildflowers. Other impressive walking trails include the 5.7-kilometer (3½-mile) route through Bryce Gorge to The Bluff, a 200-meter (356-ft.) high rocky escarpment with panoramic views. Of the numerous other walking tracks in the park, the most well known is the Alpine Walking Track, which bisects the park for 400 kilometers (240 miles) from Walhalla to the township of Tom Groggin, on the New South Wales border. There are plenty of access roads into the park, though some close in winter.

If you are a keen walker, you could strap on your boots and see the area by foot. **Ecotrek** (© **08/8383 7198;** ecotrek@ozemail.com.au) offers an 8-day Bogong Alpine Traverse trek, including 4 nights camping and 3 nights in ski lodges. You carry your own pack, but the pain is worth it for the incredible panoramic views of peaks, plains, and forested valleys. The trek costs A$1,150 (U.S.$747.50), including round-trip transport to Melbourne. The company also offers a 5-day trek that involves camping and day walks through extremely rugged country. It costs A$630 (U.S.$409.50), including round-trip transport to Melbourne.

Horse treks are another option for seeing the area. One of the best operators is **Stoney's Bluff & Beyond Rides** (© **03/5775 2212;** www.stoneys.com.au).

GETTING THERE   The Alpine National Park can be accessed by several routes from Melbourne, including the Great Alpine Road (B500), the Kiewa Valley Highway (C531), and the Lincoln Road from Heyfield. Get to The Bluff from Mansfield along the Maroodah Highway.

HITTING THE SLOPES: THE HIGH COUNTRY SKI RESORTS
Most of the **Victoria's ski areas** ☞ are in, or on the edge of, the Alpine National Park (see above). The ski season in the Victorian High Country lasts June through October, with July and August being the most popular months.

MT. HOTHAM
373km (231 miles) NE of Melbourne

Mt. Hotham (1,750m/5,740 ft.) is an intimate ski resort significantly smaller than those at Falls Creek (see below). There are eight lifts, offering runs from beginners to advanced. It also offers some good off-piste (off-trail) cross-country skiing, including a route across the Bogong High Plains to Falls Creek. Some of the lifts are quite far apart, although there's a free "zoo cart" and bus transport system in winter along the main road. Resort entry costs A$20 (U.S.$13) per car for a day, payable at the resort entry gates, or at the Mount Hotham Resort Management office (see "Visitor Information" below). Ski tickets are available from Mount Hotham Skiing Company (© **03/5759 4444**). Full-day lift tickets cost between A$59 and $72 (U.S.$38.35 and $46.80) for adults and A$33 and $39 (U.S.$21.45 and $25.35) for children, depending on time of season. Combined lift and ski-lesson tickets are also available.

GETTING THERE   From Melbourne, take the Hume Highway via Harrietville, or the Princes Highway via Omeo. The trip takes around 5½ hours (the trip is slightly quicker on the Hume Highway). Fly to Mt. Hotham Airport from Melbourne and Sydney with Qantas (© **13 13 13**).

   Trekset Mount Hotham Snow Service (© **03/9370 9055**), runs buses to Mt. Hotham daily during the ski season departing Melbourne's Spencer Street Coach Terminal at 9am. The trip takes 6 hours and costs A$70 (U.S.$45.50) one-way or A$105 (U.S.$68.25) round-trip. You need to book in advance.

VISITOR INFORMATION   **Mount Hotham Resort Management,** Great Alpine Road, Mt. Hotham (© **03/5759 3550**), is as close as you'll come to an information office. It has plenty of brochures. It's open daily from 8am to 5pm in during the ski season, and Monday through Friday from 9am to 5pm at other times.

WHERE TO STAY   The **Mt. Hotham Accommodation Service** (© **1800/ 032 061**; www.mt-hotham-accommodation.com.au), can book rooms and advise you on special deals during both off-peak and peak periods, including flights. Another option is **Falls Creek Reservations Centre** (© **1800 453 525** in Australia). During the ski season, most places will want you to book for an entire week. Prices are significantly lower in the non-ski season. The general Mt. Hotham web page is **www.mthotham.com.au**.

FALLS CREEK 𝄞
375km (225 miles) NE of Melbourne

One of Victoria's best ski resorts, and my favorite, Falls Creek is situated on the edge of the Bogong High Plains overlooking the Kiewa Valley. This compact alpine village is the only one in Australia where you can ski from your lodge to the lifts and back again from the ski slopes. The nightlife is also very good in the ski season, with plenty of party options as well as a range of walk-in lodge restaurants.

   The ski fields are split into two parts, the Village Bowl and Sun Valley, with 17 lifts in all covering more than 90 trails. There are plenty of intermediate and advanced runs, as well as a sprinkling for beginners. You'll also find some of Australia's best cross-country skiing here; Australia's major cross-country skiing event, the Kangaroo Hoppet, is held here on the last Saturday in August every year. Entry to the resort costs A$6 (U.S.$3.90). Full-day lift tickets cost from A$59 to $75 (U.S.$38.35–$48.75) for adults and A$33 to $39 (U.S.$21.45–$25.35) for children depending on the time you ski (July 31–Aug 31 is the most expensive time, and June and after mid-Sept is the cheapest). Combined lift and ski lesson tickets are also available. Call the **Falls Creek Ski Lifts** (© **03/5758 3280**) for details. The ski lifts can also organize accommodation options.

Falls Creek is also a pleasant place to visit in summer, when you can go bush-walking, horseback riding, and trout fishing. **Angling Expeditions** (© and fax **03/5754 1466**) is the best option for fly-fishing for trout in the alpine area during spring, summer, and fall. Trips last from 3 hours to all day and are suitable for everyone from beginners to experts. Overnight trips are also available. Horse-back riding operators include **Falls Creek Trail Rides** (© **03/5758 3655**) and **Bogong Horseback Adventures** (© **03/5754 4849**).

GETTING THERE   **Pyles Coaches** (© **03/5754 4024**) runs buses to the ski resort from Melbourne every day during the ski season (from the end of June to the end of Sept), departing Melbourne at 9am and Falls Creek at 5pm. The round-trip fare is A$100 (U.S.$65) for adults and A$75 (U.S.$48.75) for children and includes the resort entrance fee. The company also runs shuttle buses to and from Albury just over the border in New South Wales (accessible by train from Sydney), and between Mt. Beauty and Falls Creek. Bookings are essential.

If you're driving from Melbourne take the Hume Highway to Wangaratta, and then through Myrtleford and Mt. Beauty to Falls Creek. The trip takes around 4½ hours. From Sydney take the Hume Highway to Albury-Wodonga and follow the signs to Mt. Beauty and the snowfields. If you arrive in the ski season, a resort worker will direct you to a car park, and bring you back to the resort entrance, from where you can take a caterpillar-tracked "troop-carrier" to your hotel, or attempt the (probably) short but slippery, walk yourself.

VISITOR INFORMATION   The **Falls Creek Information Centre,** 1 Bogong High Plains Rd., Falls Creek (© **03/5758 3490**), is open daily from 8am to 5pm. Buy your lift tickets in the booth next door, between mid-June and October.

Where to Stay & Dine

Falls Creek is a year-round resort, with a good range of accommodations available at all times, though it tends to fill up fast during the ski season. As you might expect room rates are significantly higher during the ski season. The **Falls Creek Reservation Centre** (© **1800/45 35 25** in Australia or 03/5758 3100; fax 03/5758 3337; www.fallscreek.net; accom@fallscreek.albury.net.au) can tell you what deals are on offer and can book rooms for you. The cheapest winter option is the very basic **Frying Pan Inn,** P.O. Box 55, Falls Creek, VIC 3699 (© **03/5758 3390;** fax 03/5758 3416), right in the village next to the ski lifts. Bunks in four- or six-bed rooms cost A$58 (U.S.$37.70) per night Sunday through Thursday, and A$68 (U.S.$44.20) Friday through Saturday, in the ski season. Packages are available.

If you fancy a self-contained apartment or free-standing chalet then try the **Frueauf Village** complex (© **03/9593 6125;** www.fvfalls.com.au). These 28 spanking new properties were built in 2001 (some to be completed in 2002). In peak season they work out at about A$100 (U.S.$65) per person per night for two or more.

Feathertop Alpine Lodge ✿ *Finds*   I really like this pleasant old-fashioned ski lodge nestled among the gum trees. Hosts Pip and Mark Whittaker have made it into one of the friendliest getaways in the mountains, and its relatively small size makes it easy to get to know a few of the other guests. Rooms are functional yet cozy, and sleep two to four people. All have showers attached. The lounge room is large and comfortable with good views, a well-stocked bar, and a library.

Parallel St. (P.O. Box 259), Falls Creek, VIC 3699. ℂ 03/5758 3232. Fax 03/5758 3514. www.ski.com.au/
feathertop. 10 units. Winter A$95–$185 (U.S.$61.75–$120.25); summer A$70 (U.S.$45.50). Rates are per person and include dinner and breakfast. MC, V. **Amenities:** Restaurant (country cooking); small indoor pool;
4 tennis courts (summer only); exercise room; sauna; children's program (winter only); tour desk; business
center; in-room massage (winter only); babysitting; coin-op laundry; nonsmoking rooms.

Summit Ridge Alpine Lodge   Summit Ridge is a large four-and-a-half star
property made from local rock and timber. It caters to discerning guests. All
rooms are quite nice, if a little stark. The mezzanine suites are split-level with the
bedroom upstairs; they have king-size beds and an attached bathroom with tub.
There's a large lounge and dining room on the ground floor and a small library
on the second. If the mist holds out there are some fine valley views. The hosts
pay a lot of attention to detail, and the homemade bread is worth an early rise.
The restaurant excels in fine dining. The owner can take you out on early-
morning ski runs.

Schuss St., Falls Creek, VIC 3699. ℂ 03/5758 3800. Fax 03/5758 3833. sunridge@fallscreek.albury.net.au.
Winter A$135–$230 (U.S.$87.75–$149.50) queen room per person. Summer A$110 (U.S.$71.50) per person.
AE, DC, MC, V. Rates include breakfast and dinner. Children 5–14 25% off adult rate. Children under 5 not
allowed. **Amenities:** Restaurant (Modern Australian), bar; exercise room; sauna; spa; in-room massage;
babysitting; coin-op laundry. *In room:* TV, minibar, coffeemaker, hair dryer.

MT. BUFFALO NATIONAL PARK ⭐⭐
350km (210 miles) NE of Melbourne

Based around Mt. Buffalo, this is the oldest national park in the Victorian High
Country, declared in 1898. The scenery around here is spectacular, with huge
granite outcrops and plenty of waterfalls. As you ascend the mountain you pass
through dramatic vegetation changes, from tall snow gum forests to subalpine
grasslands. In summer, carpets of silver snow daisies, royal bluebells, and yellow
Billy Button flowers bloom on the plateau. Animals and birds here include wallabies and wombats, cockatoos, lyrebirds, and mobs of crimson rosellas, which
congregate around the campsite at Lake Catani (popular for swimming and
canoeing). Other popular sports around and about include advanced hang gliding and some very serious rock climbing. There are also more than 90 kilometers (54 miles) of walking trails.

Mt. Buffalo is also home to Victoria's smallest ski resort, with just five lifts, and
a vertical drop of 157 meters (515 ft.). There are also 11 kilometers (6½ miles)
of marked cross-country ski trails.

ENTRY FEES & LIFT TICKETS   Entry to Mt. Buffalo ski resort is A$20
(U.S.$13) per car. Full-day lift tickets cost around A$39 (U.S.$25.35) for
adults, A$25 (U.S.$16.25) for children under 15, and A$15 (U.S.$9.75) for
children under 8. Combination lift and ski lesson packages are available. Buy lift
tickets at the park offices (ℂ 13 19 63 in Victoria, or 03/5756 2328) between
9am and 3pm.

GETTING THERE   From Melbourne take the Hume Freeway (M31) to
Wangaratta, then follow the Great Alpine Road to Porepunkah. From there follow the Mount Buffalo Tourist Road.

VISITOR INFORMATION   The nearest visitor information center is in the
town of Bright. Find the **Bright Visitor Information Centre** at 1A Delaney
Ave., Bright (ℂ 03/5755 2275).

WHERE TO STAY
Mt. Buffalo Chalet ⭐⭐ *Finds*   This rambling mountain guesthouse was built
in 1910 and retains a wonderful old-world feel. Guesthouse rooms, which have

a mixture of double, twin, and bunk beds, are reminiscent of the 1930s. Rooms with views across the valley have better furnishings. There's a large lounge room and a game room, both with open fireplaces. Meals are available for non-guests for A$35 (U.S.$22.75) for three courses. The chalet was up for sale as this book went to press, so new owners may change facilities and rates.

Mt. Buffalo National Park, VIC 3740. ℂ **1800/037 038** in Australia or 03/5755 1500. Fax 03/5755 1892. www.mtbuffalochalet.com.au. 97 units, 72 with bathroom (some with shower only). A$129 (U.S.$83.85) guest house without bathroom; A$156 (U.S.$101.40) room with bathroom; A$184 (U.S.$119.60) view room with bathroom; A$198 (U.S.$128.70) suite. Rates are per person and include breakfast and dinner, guided walks, evening activities, and park entry. Higher rates Christmas to mid-Jan and Easter weekend. AE, DC, MC, V. **Amenities:** Restaurant (Modern Australian), bar; 2 grass tennis courts; exercise room; spa; sauna; canoe rental; bike rental; kids' club on weekends and school holidays; activities desk; massage; babysitting; coin-op laundry; nonsmoking rooms. *In room:* Unstocked refrigerator, coffeemaker.

6 The Northwest: Grampians National Park

260km (161 miles) NW of Melbourne

One of Victoria's most popular attractions, the rugged **Grampians National Park** rises some 1,000 meters (3,280 ft.) from the plains, appearing from the distance like some kind of monumental island. The park, which is an ecological meeting place of Victoria's western volcanic plains and the forested Great Dividing Range, contains one-third of all the wildflowers native to Victoria and most of the surviving Aboriginal rock art in southeastern Australia. Almost 200 species of birds, 35 different species of mammals, 28 species of reptiles, 11 species of amphibians, and 6 species of freshwater fish have been discovered here. Kangaroos, koalas, emus, gliders, and echidnas can be easily spotted.

There are some awesome sites in the Grampians, including Reeds Lookout and The Balconies, which are both accessible by road, and the Wonderland Range, which offers walking tracks leading past striking rock formations and massive cliffs to waterfalls and more spectacular lookouts.

The main town in the Grampians is Halls Gap, which is situated in a valley between the southern tip of the Mt. Difficult Range and the northern tip of the Mt. William Range. It's a good place to stock up on supplies. The Wonderland Range, with its stunning scenery, is close to Halls Gap, too. There are plenty of short strolls and longer bushwalks available.

A must-do stop on the park is the **Brambuk Aboriginal Living Cultural Centre** ⍟ (ℂ **03/5356 4452**), adjacent to the park visitor center (see below). It offers an excellent introduction to the area's Aboriginal history and accessible rock-art sites. A 15-minute movie highlighting the local Aboriginal history costs A$4 (U.S.$2.60) for adults and A$2.50 (U.S.$1.60) for children. Otherwise, entrance to the center is free. The center is open daily from 10am to 5pm.

ESSENTIALS

GETTING THERE   By car, the park is accessed from the Western Highway at Ararat, Stawell (pronounced Storl), or Horsham. Alternatively, you can access the southern entrance from the Glenelg Highway at Dunkeld. The western areas of the park are reached from the Henty Highway (A200).

V/Line (ℂ **13 61 96** in Victoria, 13 22 32 in New South Wales, or 03/9619 5000) has a daily train and bus service to Halls Gap from Melbourne (the train goes to Stawell, and a connecting bus takes you to your destination). The trip takes around 4 hours.

GETTING AROUND   Paved roads include the **Grampians Tourist Road,** which cuts through the park from Dunkeld to Halls Gap; the **Mt. Victory Road**

from Halls Gap to Wartook, and the **Roses Gap Road,** which runs from Wartook across to Dadswells Bridge on the Western Highway. Many other roads in the park are unpaved, but most are passable with a two-wheel-drive car.

Grampians National Park Tours (℗ **03/5356 6221**) offers all-day, four-wheel-drive tours of the park, stopping off at Aboriginal rock-art sites, waterfalls, and lookouts. There's not much walking involved, but you certainly get the chance to spot native animals and ferret around among the native flora. The tour includes lunch and morning and afternoon tea, and costs A$75 (U.S.$48.75).

Auswalk, P.O. Box 516, Jindabyne, NSW 2627 (℗ **02/6457 2220;** fax 02/ 6457 2206; monica@auswalk.com.au), organizes self-guided tours through the park. A 6-night tour for two or more people costs A$1,090 (U.S.$708) per person including accommodation, most meals, national-park fees, some vehicle transfers, a half-day four-wheel-drive tour, an itinerary, and maps.

VISITOR INFORMATION   The **Grampians National Park Visitor Centre** (℗ **03/5356 4379**), 2.5 kilometers (1½ miles) south of Halls Gap, is open daily from 9am to 5pm. It has plenty of maps and brochures, and the rangers can advise you on walking trails and camping spots.

WHERE TO STAY

You can hire a caravan or a cabin for the night at **Halls Gap Caravan Park** (℗ **03/5356 4251**). Caravans cost A$39.50 to $45.10 (U.S.$25.70–$29.25) and cabins A$49.50 to $61.60 (U.S.$32.20–$40), depending on season. They also offer self-contained units from A$61.60 to A$99 (U.S.$40–$64.35), and log cabins from A$126.50 to $137.50 (U.S.$82.25–$90). Another option is the **Halls Gap Lakeside Caravan Park** (℗ **03/5356 4281**), which is 5 kilometers (3 miles) from town on the shores of Lake Bellfield. Cabins cost A$45 to $95 (U.S.$29.25–$61.75) depending on rooms and season.

The Mountain Grand Guesthouse and Business Retreat   A couple of years ago this old-fashioned guesthouse was pretty run-down, but recent refurbishment by the new owners has brought it up to a comfortable three and a half–star standard. These days it's promoting itself as a business retreat, and as such tourists who turn up get all the benefits of those added little corporate extras, such as exceptional service. The guesthouse offers a special weekend-getaway package costing A$218 (U.S.$141.70) for two, with a Devonshire tea, a three-course dinner, a buffet breakfast, a gourmet picnic lunch, and champagne and chocolates thrown in.

The rooms are quite small, but furnished with country-style furniture and double beds. All have an attached bathroom. Larger family rooms, some of which have a whirlpool, were renovated in 1999. There are several lounge rooms and "conversion nooks," all with TVs and dataports.

Grampians Tourist Rd. ℗ **03/5356 4232.** Fax 03/5356 4254. mtgrand@netconnect.co.au. 10 units. A$109 (U.S.$70.85) double (min. 2-nights on weekend). Rates include breakfast. AE, DC, MC, V. **Amenities:** 2 restaurants (International, cafe-style), 2 bars; free laundry. *In room:* A/C, unstocked refrigerator, coffeemaker, iron.

13

Canberra

by Marc Llewellyn

If you mention you're heading to Canberra (pronounced *Can*-bra, with very open vowels), most Australians will raise an eyebrow and say "Why bother?" Even many Canberrans will admit that it's a great place to live but they wouldn't want to visit.

So what is it about Canberra that draws so much lackluster comment? Simply put, Australians aren't used to having things so nice and ordered. In many ways, Canberra is like Washington, D.C., or any new town that was a planned community from the start. Some see its virtues as of the bland variety: The roads are wide and in good order, the buildings are modern, and the suburbs are pleasant and leafy. Canberra is also the seat of government and the home of thousands of civil servants— enough to make almost any free-thinking, individualist Aussie shudder.

But to me, Canberra's differences from other Australian cities are the very things that make it special. The streets aren't clogged with traffic, and there are plenty of opportunities for safe biking—try that in almost any other city center, and you'll be dusting the sides of cars and pushed onto the sidewalks in no time. There are plenty of open spaces, parklands, and fascinating monuments, and there is an awful lot to see and do—from museum and gallery hopping to ballooning with a champagne glass in your hand or boating on Lake Burley Griffin. You can certainly pack a lot in a few days' visit.

Canberra was born after the Commonwealth of Australia was officially created in 1901. Melbourne and Sydney, even then jockeying for preeminence, each put in their bid to become the new federal capital. In the end, Australian leaders decided to follow the example of their U.S. counterparts by creating a federal district; in 1908 they chose an undeveloped area between the two cities.

Designing the new capital fell to Chicago landscape architect Walter Burley Griffin, a contemporary of Frank Lloyd Wright. The city he mapped out was christened Canberra (a local Aboriginal word meaning "meeting place"), and by 1927, the first meeting of parliament took place. The business of government was underway.

1 Orientation

ARRIVING

BY PLANE   **Qantas** (© **13 13 13** in Australia, or 02/ 9691 3636) runs frequent daily services to Canberra. A new operator, **Impulse Airlines** (© **13 13 81** in Australia; www.impulse.com.au) offers cut-price seats to Canberra from both Sydney and Brisbane. It's well worth checking their website and booking online.

The Canberra Airport is about 10 minutes from the city center. Car-rental desks can be found here, as well as a currency exchange, a bar, and a bistro.

Stamps are sold at the newsagent (newsstand), and a mailbox is provided for cards and letters. The airport lacks lockers, showers, and a post office.

Canberra City Sites and Tours (𝄢 **0418/628 633,** mobile only) meets most planes, but make sure you phone them before you arrive. They charge A$6 (U.S.$3.90) per person for a trip to city-center hotels.

BY TRAIN   A nice way to see some of the countryside while you're in Australia is to take the train. **Countrylink** (𝄢 **13 22 32** in Australia; www.countrylink. nsw.gov.au) runs three Canberra Xplorer trains daily between Sydney and Canberra. The 4-hour trip costs around A$70 (U.S.$45.50) in first class and A$50 (U.S.$32.50) in economy; children are charged half price, and a return trip costs double. Many people make use of Countrylink transport/hotel packages (call **Countrylink Holidays** at 𝄢 **13 28 29**), which can save you quite a bit of money. There's a range of hotels to choose from in Canberra costing between A$90 and $190 (U.S.$58.50–$123.50) a night for a couple, and if you book in advance (they recommend 2 weeks), you can save up to 40% on the train fare (through a Rail Escape package), too. Find the Countrylink office at Wynyard CityRail Station.

From Melbourne, the **Canberra Link,** run by **V/Line** (𝄢 **136 196** in Australia), involves a 5-hour bus trip and a 3½-hour train trip. It costs A$55 (U.S.$35.75) for adults and A$34 (U.S.$22.10) for children and students.

Canberra Railway Station (𝄢 **02/6239 7039**) is on Wentworth Avenue, Kingston, about 5 kilometers (3 miles) southeast of the city center.

BY BUS   **Greyhound Pioneer** (𝄢 **13 20 30** in Australia; www.greyhound. com.au) runs six services a day from Sydney to Canberra. Tickets cost A$35 (U.S.$22.75) for adults, A$32 (U.S.$20.80) for students with an ISAC card, and A$28 (U.S.$18.20) for children 3 to 14; the trip takes 4 to 4½ hours.

From Melbourne, tickets to Canberra cost A$56 (U.S.$36.40) for adults, A$50 (U.S.$32.50) for students, and A$45 (U.S.$29.25) for children. (Advanced purchase fares can save you up to 35%.)

Murrays Australia (𝄢 **13 22 51** in Australia) runs three services a day from Sydney to Canberra for A$35 (U.S.$22.75) for adults and A$18.70 (U.S.$12.20) for children. Ask for YHA member discounts. Several sightseeing companies in Sydney, including **AAT King's, Murrays,** and **Australia Pacific Tours,** offer day trips to Canberra as well.

Intercity buses arrive at **Jolimont Tourist Centre,** at the corner of Northbourne Avenue and Alinga Street, in Canberra City.

BY CAR   The ACT (Australian Capital Territory) is surrounded by the state of New South Wales. Sydney is 306 kilometers (190 miles) northeast, and Melbourne is 651 kilometers (404 miles) southwest of Canberra. If you drive from Sydney via the Hume and Federal Highways, the trip will take 3½ to 4 hours. From Melbourne, take the Hume Highway to Yass, then switch to the Barton Highway; the trip will take about 8 hours.

VISITOR INFORMATION

The **Canberra Visitors' Centre,** 330 Northbourne Ave., Dickson (𝄢 **02/6205 0044**), dispenses information and books accommodations. The office is open Monday through Friday from 9am to 5:30pm, and Saturday and Sunday from 9am to 4pm. The official government website (www.canberratourism.com.au) is worth checking out.

SPECIAL EVENTS   A host of free events—from concerts to competitions— are part of the annual **Canberra National Multicultural Festival** held in the

Canberra

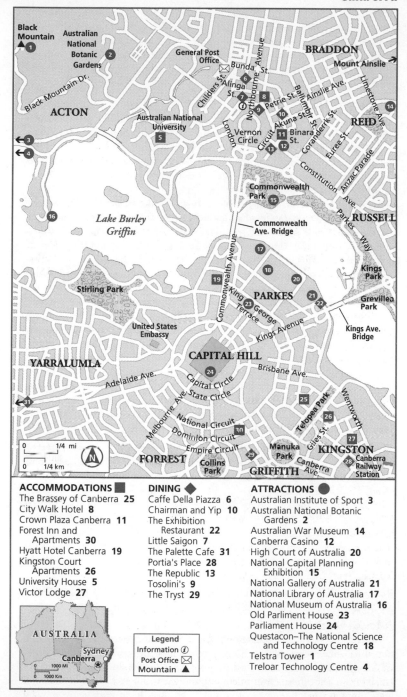

Black Mountain ▲①
Australian National Botanic Gardens ②
General Post Office ✉
ACTON
Black Mountain Dr.
Australian National University ⑤
Childers St.
Bunda St. ⑥
Alinga St. ⑦
Northbourne Avenue
⑧ **Petrie St.**
⑨ ⑩ **Akuna St.**
Ballumbir St.
Ainslie Ave.
BRADDON
Mount Ainslie
Limestone Ave.
⑭
REID
Vernon Circle
London Circuit
⑪ **Binara St.**
⑬ ⑫
Coranderrk St.
Euree St.
Constitution Ave.
Anzac Parade
Commonwealth Park ⑮
Commonwealth Ave. Bridge
Parkes Way
RUSSELL
③
④
⑯
Lake Burley Griffin
Commonwealth Avenue
⑰
King George Terrace
⑱
⑲
Stirling Park
PARKES
⑳
㉑
㉒
Kings Park
Grevillea Park
Kings Ave. Bridge
United States Embassy
㉓
Kings Avenue
YARRALUMLA
CAPITAL HILL
㉔
Capital Circle
State Circle
Brisbane Ave.
Adelaide Ave.
㉛
Melbourne Ave.
National Circuit
Dominion Circuit
Empire Circuit
㉕
㉖
㉗
Tetopea Park
Giles St.
Wentworth
KINGSTON
Canberra Railway Station
㉘
FORREST
Collins Park
㉚
㉙
Manuka Park
Canberra Ave.
GRIFFITH

0 — 1/4 mi
0 — 1/4 km

ACCOMMODATIONS ■
The Brassey of Canberra **25**
City Walk Hotel **8**
Crown Plaza Canberra **11**
Forest Inn and Apartments **30**
Hyatt Hotel Canberra **19**
Kingston Court Apartments **26**
University House **5**
Victor Lodge **27**

DINING ◆
Caffe Della Piazza **6**
Chairman and Yip **10**
The Exhibition Restaurant **22**
Little Saigon **7**
The Palette Cafe **31**
Portia's Place **28**
The Republic **13**
Tosolini's **9**
The Tryst **29**

ATTRACTIONS ●
Australian Institute of Sport **3**
Australian National Botanic Gardens **2**
Australian War Museum **14**
Canberra Casino **12**
High Court of Australia **20**
National Capital Planning Exhibition **15**
National Gallery of Australia **21**
National Library of Australia **17**
National Museum of Australia **16**
Old Parliment House **23**
Parliament House **24**
Questacon–The National Science and Technology Centre **18**
Telstra Tower **1**
Treloar Technology Centre **4**

AUSTRALIA
Sydney
Canberra
0 — 1000 Mi
0 — 1000 Km

Legend
Information ⓘ
Post Office ✉
Mountain ▲

first 3 weeks of March. The fun includes Canberra Day (a local public holiday—always the third Mon in Mar), a hot-air balloon fiesta, fireworks displays, food and wine promotions, plenty of music, and a large range of activities organized by Australia's ethnic mix. Visitors could find it a little more difficult to book accommodations during this time, but you should always be able to find something.

CITY LAYOUT

The first thing that strikes a visitor to Canberra is its park-like feel (amazing, since there was barely a tree on the original site). Half a dozen avenues radiate from **Capital Hill,** where the Parliament House stands. Each of these broad, tree-shaded streets leads to a traffic circle, from which yet more streets emanate. Around each hub, the streets form a pattern of concentric circles—not the easiest layout for visitors trying to find their way.

Another of Canberra's most notable features is **Lake Burley Griffin,** a man-made lake created by damming the Molonglo River. The centerpiece of the lake is the **Captain Cook Memorial Jet,** a spire of water that reaches 147 meters (482 ft.) into the air. Wedged between Commonwealth Avenue and Kings Avenue is the suburb of **Parkes,** also known as the National Triangle. Here you'll find many of the city's most impressive attractions, such as the National Gallery of Australia, the High Court of Australia, and the National Science and Technology Center (all sites here can be accessed via www.nationaltriangle.com.au/tri).

Canberra's main shopping district is on the other side of the lake, centered around Northbourne Avenue, one of the city's main thoroughfares. Officially labeled Canberra City, this area is more commonly known as **"Civic."** Northeast of Civic is **Mount Ainslie,** with the Australian War Memorial at its foot; from its summit there are spectacular views of the city and beyond. Another good lookout point is from the top of the **Telstra Tower** on Black Mountain, reached by Black Mountain Drive. All the embassies and consulates are concentrated in the suburb of **Yarralumla,** east of Capital Hill, while most of the other suburbs are filled with pleasant homes and small retail areas.

2 Getting Around

BY CAR   Advantage Car Rentals, 74 Northbourne Ave. (corner of Barry Drive) (© **02/6257 6888,** or 1800 504 460 in Australia), has cars from A$35 (U.S.$22.75) per day, including 200 kilometers (124 miles) per day. **Budget** (© **02/6257 1305**), **Hertz** (© **02/6249 6211**), and **Thrifty (02/6248 9081)** have desks at the airport.

If you decide to rent your own wheels, you might follow one or more of the six tourist drives marked with signs; pick up details from the Canberra Visitors' Centre.

BY TAXI   Canberra's only taxi company is **Canberra Cabs** (© **13 22 27**).

BY BUS   Canberra's bus system is coordinated by **ACTION** (© **02/6207 7611;** www.action.gov.au). The central bus terminal is on Alinga Street, in Civic, 200 Scollay St., Tuggeranong, ACT. The bus system divides Canberra into three zones; travel within the city center is in Zone One, which will cost A$2.30 (U.S.$1.50) for adults one-way and A$1.20 (U.S.80¢) for children 5 to 15. If you travel through more than one zone, it will cost A$4.40 (U.S.$2.90) for adults and A$2.30 (U.S.$1.50) for children. Ask the driver when you board the bus just to make sure how much you should pay.

Weekly tickets cost A$19.80 (U.S.$13) for Zone One and A$38 (U.S.$24.70) for all three zones; children ride half price. Ten-Ride tickets cost A$18.40 (U.S.$11.90) for one zone or A$36.80 (U.S.$24) for all zones. Purchase all tickets on the bus or from most newsagents and ACTION interchanges.

For timetable information, call ACTION from 7am to 9pm Monday through Saturday, and from 8am to 6pm Sunday. Pick up bus route maps at bus interchanges, newsagents, and the Canberra Visitors' Center.

Canberra City Sightseeing Tours (✆ **0500 505 012**) has double-decker buses, which pull in at 11 attractions around the city. Visitors can get off and on when they like. An all-day ticket costs A$25 (U.S.$16.25) for adults and A$12.50 (U.S.$8.15) for children.

BY BICYCLE   Canberra is unique in Australia for its extensive system of cycle tracks—some 120 kilometers (74 miles) of them—which makes sightseeing on two wheels a very pleasurable experience. See "Outdoor Pursuits," later in this chapter, for details on bike rental.

 FAST FACTS: Canberra

American Express   The office at **Centerpoint,** Shop 1, 185 City Walk (at the corner of Petrie Plaza), Civic (✆ **02/6247 2333**), is open Monday through Friday from 9am to 5pm, and Saturday from 9am to noon.

Business Hours   Banks are generally open Monday through Thursday from 9:30am to 4pm and Friday from 9:30am to 5pm. Stores and offices are open Monday through Friday from 9am to 5:30pm. Many shops stay open on weekends and until 9pm Fridays.

Car Rentals   See "Getting Around," above.

Climate   The best time to visit Canberra is in spring (Sept–Nov) or autumn (Mar–May). Summers are hot and winters can get pretty cold.

Currency Exchange   Cash traveler's checks at banks, at **American Express** (above), or at **Thomas Cook,** at the Petrie Plaza entrance of the Canberra Centre (✆ **02/6257 2222**), open Monday through Friday from 9am to 5pm and Saturday from 9:30am to 12:30pm.

Dentist   Canberra lacks a dental emergency referral service. A reputable dentist in the center of town is **Lachland B. Lewis,** Level 3, 40 Allara St., Civic (✆ **02/6257 2777,** and for emergency calls only on 02/6295 9495 on weekends).

Doctor   The **Capital Medical Centre,** 2 Mort St., Civic (✆ **02/6257 3766**), is open Monday through Friday from 8:30am to 4:30pm. A standard consultation costs A$30 (U.S.$19.50). The **Travellers' Medical & Vaccination Centre,** Level 5, 8–10 Hobart Place, Civic (✆ **02/6257 7154**), offers vaccinations and travel medicines. Standard consultations cost from A$39.50 (U.S.$26).

Drugstores   See "Pharmacies," below.

E-mail   The **National Library,** Parkes Place, Parkes (✆ **02/6262 1111**), has e-mail facilities available during opening hours: Monday through Thursday 9am to 5pm.

Embassies/Consulates   The **British High Commission** is located at Old Parliament House Annex, Parkes (✆ **02/6270 6666**). The **Canadian High**

Commission is at Commonwealth Avenue, Yarralumla (✆ **02/6270 4000**); the **U.S. Embassy** is found at Moonah Place, Yarralumla (✆ **02/6214 5600**); and the **New Zealand High Commission** is at Commonwealth Avenue, Yarralumla (✆ **02/6270 4211**).

Emergencies Call ✆ **000** for an ambulance, the police, or the fire department.

Eyeglasses For repairs, glasses, and contact lenses try **OPSM Express**, shop 5, Lower Ground Floor, The Canberra Centre, Civic (✆ **02/6249 7344**). It's open 9am to 5:30pm weekdays (to 9pm on Fri) and 9am to 4pm on Saturday.

Hospitals For medical attention, go to the **Canberra Hospital**, Yamba Drive, Garran (✆ **6244 2222**), or call the **Accident & Emergency Department** on ✆ **02/6244 2324** (24 hr.).

Hot Lines In Canberra you have access to the **Rape Crisis Centre** (✆ 02/6247 2525); **Drug/Alcohol Crisis Line** (✆ 02/6205 4545, 24 hr.); **Lifeline Crisis Councelling** (✆ 13 11 14); **Salvation Army Councelling Service** (✆ 02/9331 6000); **Poison Information Centre** (✆ 02/6285 2852); and **National Roads & Motorists Association (NRMA)** (✆ 13 21 32).

Pharmacies The **Canberra Centre Pharmacy**, Civic (✆ **02/6249 8074**) is open during general shopping hours.

Photographic Needs **Fletchers Fotographics**, Shop 2, 38 Akuna St., Civic (✆ **02/6247 8460**), is the best place to buy camera gear and films. They also repair cameras and sell secondhand equipment.

Police See "Emergencies," above.

Post Office The **Canberra GPO**, 53–73 Alinga St., Civic (✆ **02/6209 1680**), is open Monday through Friday from 8:30am to 5:30pm. The Poste Restante address is c/o Canberra GPO, ACT 2601.

Restrooms Found near the city bus exchange, City Hall, London Circuit.

3 Where to Stay

Canberra has a good scattering of places to stay, and generally accommodations are much cheaper than in most other state capitals. Many people travel to Canberra during the week, so many hotels offer cheaper weekend rates to put heads on beds. You should always ask about special deals. The rates given below are rack rates, or what the hotels hope they'll get on a good day—you can often get a room for less.

VERY EXPENSIVE

Hyatt Hotel Canberra ✰✰   Visiting heads of state and pop stars make this their residence of choice when staying in Canberra, and it's not hard to see why. It has a great location, being only a 2-minute drive from the city center, in the shadow of Parliament House and between Lake Burley Griffin and the Parliamentary Triangle. Originally the Hotel Canberra, it was opened in 1924 and was based on the low-slung "prairie" design of the now-destroyed Imperial Hotel in Tokyo. For many years the Hyatt was an important part of Canberra's social and political life, with key decisions affecting all Australians being consistently made over drinks in the bar. All staff members wear 1920s costumes to add to the atmosphere.

Some 39 rooms are in the original two-story section. The rooms have more historic appeal, but they are darker than their more modern counterparts, which were added in the 1980s. Standard rooms have a king-size bed and large marble bathrooms. They all come with all the little luxuries you'd expect from a hotel of this class.

Commonwealth Ave., Yarralumla, ACT 2600. © **13 12 34** in Australia or 02/6270 1234; 800/233-1234 in the U.S. and Canada; 0181/335 1220 in London or 0845/758 1666 elsewhere in the U.K.; 0800/44 1234 in New Zealand, or 02/6270 1234. Fax 02/6281 5998. 249 units. A$380 (U.S.$247) standard double; A$605 (U.S.$435.50) executive suite; A$1,200 (U.S.$780) Diplomatic Suite. Extra person A$28 (U.S.$18.20). Children under 18 stay free in parents' room. Ask about weekend packages and special rates. AE, DC, MC, V. Free parking. **Amenities:** Cafe, 2 restaurants (Modern Australian, buffet); indoor pool; tennis court; extensive health club and spa; bike rental; concierge; business center; 24-hr. room service; laundry. *In room:* A/C, TV with pay movies, minibar, hair dryer, iron, safe.

EXPENSIVE

Crowne Plaza Canberra ✦✦   This centrally located hotel, formerly the Parkroyal Canberra (it changed owners in mid-2001), is right next door to the National Convention Centre and Canberra Casino. Its car-orientated approach makes it a little inconvenient for pedestrians, but the gardens at the back are good for early morning strolls. Rooms face onto oval internal balconies that look down to the restaurants below. Standard rooms are user-friendly and comfortable; most come with one queen-size bed or two doubles. Parkview doubles look over the gardens. Weekend rates drop dramatically here. For example the standard rooms drop from $300 to $190, with breakfast thrown in too.

1 Binara St., Canberra ACT 2601. © **1800/020 055** in Australia or 02/6247 8999. Fax 02/6257 4903. www.crowneplaza.com. 295 units. A$300 (U.S.$195) standard double; A$315 (U.S.$204.75) parkview double; A$425–$500 (U.S.$276–$325) suite. Extra person A$35 (U.S$22.75). Lower weekend rates. Children under 15 stay free in parents' room. AE, DC, MC, V. Free parking. **Amenities:** Restaurant (Modern Australian, buffet), bar; medium-size pool; health club; concierge; business center; 24-hr. room service; laundry service. *In room:* A/C, TV, minibar, hairdryer, iron, safe.

MODERATE

The Brassey of Canberra ✦   Rooms in this 1927 heritage-listed building, formerly a boardinghouse for visiting government officials, are large, quiet, and somewhat plush. The garden bar and piano lounge are popular. Other good points include its proximity to Parliament House and other major attractions, and the hearty breakfasts. The hotel underwent extensive renovations in early 2000, which included the remodeling of many of the doubles into larger heritage rooms.

Belmore Gardens, Barton, ACT 2600. © **02/6273 3766.** Fax 02/6273 2791. www.brassey.net.au. 81 units. A$162 (U.S.$105.30) double, or A$192 (U.S.$124.80) for a family room; A$182 (U.S.$118.30) heritage double, or A$225 (U.S.$146.25) for a heritage family room. Rates include full breakfast. Check for specials. AE, DC, MC, V. Free parking. Bus: 36 (get off outside the National Press Club). **Amenities:** Restaurant (Modern Australian). *In room:* A/C (in heritage rooms only), TV, minibar, hair dryer, iron.

Forest Inn and Apartments   The Forest Inn is far from fancy, but it's close to the Manuka shops and restaurants and Parliament House. The outside of this 1960s property looks tacky, but the interior has been recently refurbished. The motel-style rooms are small and colorless, but clean; the apartments are nicer and have full-size kitchens, so for the same price I'd go for one of these. Two-bedroom apartments are perfect for families, and even the one-bedroom apartments have a single bed in the living room.

30 National Circuit, Forrest, ACT 2603. ℂ 1800/676 372 in Australia, or 02/6295 3433. Fax 02/6295 2119. www.forestinn.com.au. 102 units. A$110 (U.S.$71.50) motel room; A$150 (U.S.$97.50) 1-bedroom apt; A$175 (U.S.$113.75) 2-bedroom apt. AE, DC, MC, V. Free parking. Bus: 39 (get off at the Rydges Hotel). *In room:* A/C, TV, minibar, hair dryer, iron.

Kingston Court Apartments ⊛ Situated about 1 kilometer (½ mile) from the Parliamentary Triangle and 6 kilometers (3½ miles) from Civic, this apartment complex is a good option if you're looking for the comforts of home. The apartments are modern and very spacious and come with a full kitchen, a washing machine and dryer, a balcony, and a courtyard. The rooms underwent a full renovation in 2000.

4 Tench St., Kingston, ACT 2604. ℂ 1800 655 754 in Australia, or 02/6295 2244. Fax 02/6295 5300. www. kingstonterrace.com.au. 36 units. A$155 (U.S.$100.75) apt for 2. Extra adult A$17 (U.S.$11), extra child A$6 (U.S.$3.90). AE, DC, MC, V. Free parking. Bus: 38. **Amenities:** Small pool; half-size tennis court; in-room laundry. *In room:* A/C, TV/VCR, kitchen, minibar, fridge, iron.

University House ⊛ University House, situated less than 2 kilometers (1¼ miles) from the city center, offers a pleasant alternative to run-of-the-mill hotels in a similar price bracket. Large twin rooms come with two single beds; suites have a sitting room and a queen-size bed; the one-bedroom apartments have a bedroom with a queen-size bed, a sitting room, and a kitchenette; and the two-bedroom apartments are huge, with two large bedrooms, a dining room, a lounge room, and a full kitchen. All units have bathrooms with a shower and a tub.

The hotel at the Australian National University, Balmain Crescent, Acton (G.P.O. Box 1535, Canberra, ACT 2601). ℂ 1800/814 864 in Australia, or 02/6249 5211. Fax 02/6249 5252. www.anu.edu.au. 104 units. A$118 (U.S.$76.70) twin; A$124 (U.S.$80.60) suite; A$128 (U.S.$83.20) 1-bedroom apt; A$185 (U.S.$120.25) 2-bedroom apt. Ask about packages, especially during low season. AE, DC, MC, V. Free security parking. Bus: 34. **Amenities:** Restaurant (Modern Australian), cafe; 2 tennis courts; bike rentals; babysitting. *In room:* TV.

INEXPENSIVE

City Walk Hotel You can hardly get closer to the city center than at this former YWCA-turned-budget-travel hotel. Being right near the Jolimont Tourist Centre bus interchange, it picks up a lot of business from backpackers and budget travelers arriving by bus from other parts of the country. The rooms are pretty basic, but clean. There are five double rooms with shared bathrooms, and three of these also have two extra single beds. One room (room 204) has air-conditioning. Family rooms sleep up to 10 people, all in one room. The hotel has a bunch of communal facilities for the weary traveler, including a kitchen, telephone, tea- and coffeemakers, and a lounge area with TV and VCR.

2 Mort St., Civic, ACT 2601. ℂ 02/6257 0124. Fax 02/6257 0116. www.citywalkhotel.citysearch.com.au. 55 units, 18 with bathroom (shower only). A$60 (U.S.$39) double without bathroom; A$70 (U.S.$45.50) double with bathroom; A$95–$125 (U.S.$61.75–$81.25) family room. Extra adult A$12 (U.S.$7.80); extra child stays free. A$22–$24 (U.S.$14.30–$15.60) dorm bed. MC, V. **Amenities:** Internet cafe; laundry. *In room:* TV, no phone.

Victor Lodge (*Value* Backpackers, parliamentary staff, and budget travelers frequent this friendly place, which is situated right next to Kingston shops and about a 15-minute drive from the city center. Rooms vary from dorms with three, four, or five beds, to modern, simple doubles. There are communal showers and toilets and a courtyard. The staff picks up guests from the train and bus stations daily and drops off guests in town every morning. It's a nice place overall, but you'll have to decide whether or not you want to put up with the short trek into the city.

The owners also own the reasonable Best Western motel next door, which has standby rates of A$89 (U.S.$57.85) for a double. Apparently, long-suffering parents often dump their teenage kids at the lodge and live it up at the motel.

29 Dawes St., Kingston, ACT 2604. © **02/6295 7777.** Fax 02/6295 2466. www.victorlodge.com.au. 29 units, none with bathroom. A$59 (U.S.$38.35) double; A$23 (U.S.$15) dorm bed. Rates include continental breakfast. MC, V. Free parking. Bus: 38, 39, or 50. **Amenities:** Bike rental; tour desk; nonsmoking rooms. *In room:* A/C, TV, iron.

4 Where to Dine

EXPENSIVE

The Exhibition Restaurant ★★ MODERN AUSTRALIAN   The Exhibition Restaurant (formerly the Mirrabook) sits on a lake edged with rushes and sculptures and full of goldfish. Add smoke machines (they call it a fog sculpture) on the far bank to send mysterious white eddies across the lake's surface toward your lakeside table, and you have a charming fantasy world in which to dine. The menu is small, with only a choice of four first courses, mains, and desserts. Mains could include roasted pheasant, pan-fried lamb loin stuffed with an almond mousse, a vegetarian option, and a veal fillet. The lemon meringue pie with a rhubarb base is a favorite.

Sculpture Garden of the National Gallery of Australia, Parkes. © **02/6273 2836.** Reservations recommended. Main courses at lunch A$20 (U.S.$13); fixed-price dinner A$38 (U.S.$24.70) 2 courses, A$48 (U.S.$31.20) 3 courses. AE, DC, MC, V. Daily noon–2:30pm; Thurs–Sat 6:30–10pm.

The Republic ★★ MODERN AUSTRALIAN   With stylish looks and a cutting-edge menu, The Republic is a top-class brasserie, serving up big, bold flavors in small nouvelle-cuisine-size servings. The pumpkin and sage risotto with toasted almond pesto is a firm favorite, as is the Atlantic salmon wrapped in prosciutto on herbed lentil spinach salad with yogurt dressing. Come here too for the chargrilled beef fillet with wild mushroom sauce and roasted garlic and the kangaroo on gingered pumpkin mash and harissa butter. To finish off, you shouldn't miss the homemade ice creams. A two-course "twilight" special meal, from 6pm (guests must depart by 8pm) is a great value at A$20 (U.S.$13) with a glass of wine. Expect Asian-influenced food, such as stir-fried noodles, and Malaysian chicken curry.

20 Allara St., Civic. © **02/6247 1717.** www.republic-restaurant.com.au. Reservations recommended. Main courses A$19–$26 (U.S.$12.35–$16.90). AE, DC, MC, V. Tues–Fri noon–3pm; Mon–Sat 6–10pm.

MODERATE

Chairman and Yip ★★ ASIAN AUSTRALIAN   This is, without doubt, Canberra's best restaurant. Upbeat and popular with political bigwigs, it really is the place to see and be seen. The fish specials are good and spicy, with combinations of chili, coriander, lemongrass, and galangal perking up your taste buds. I always go for the prawns with homemade chili jam, served on vermicelli noodles with mango salsa. Abalone and lobster also find their way onto the menu. The pannacotta is the signature dessert.

108 Bunda St., Civic. © **02/6248 7109.** Reservations required. Main courses A$16–$22 (U.S.$10.40–$14.30). AE, DC, MC, V. Sun–Fri noon–3pm; daily 6–11pm.

The Palette Café ★ CAFE/MODERN AUSTRALIAN   This is a great choice for lunch, especially since it's in the same building as Canberra's largest private art gallery. You can either eat inside, surrounded by artwork, or claim a table outside in the sunny courtyard. Standout dishes include grilled asparagus spears with Japanese scallops and almond hollandaise, and the chili-salted baby octopus. The Caesar salads are particularly good, as are the field mushrooms with a sauce of soy, Japanese rice wine, honey, and coriander. The etchings, paintings, and sculptures on display are of high quality and are well-priced.

Beaver Gallery, 81 Denison St., Deakin. © 02/6282 8416. Main courses A$12–$18 (U.S.$7.80–$11.70). AE, MC, V. Daily 10am–5pm.

Tosolini's ☆ CAFE/MODERN AUSTRALIAN   Since it's situated right next to the busy central bus terminal and close to the major shopping areas, Tosolini's really pulls in the passing crowd. You can sit out on the sidewalk terrace and watch the world go by. The eggs Benedict served here at breakfast could be the best A$7.50 (U.S.$4.90) you've ever spent. Lunchtime fare is almost as good. Both the battered flathead and the pan-fried broad bill (both are local fish) are tasty, but Tosolini's really made its name with its pastas and focaccias.

Corner of London Circuit at East Row, Civic. © 02/6247 4317. Main courses A$14.50–$18 (U.S.$9.40–$11.70). AE, DC, MC, V. Daily 7:30am–5pm (Tues–Sat until 10:30pm).

The Tryst ☆☆ *Finds* MODERN AUSTRALIAN   The personal touches and service really shine through at The Tryst, and the food is consistently delicious. The restaurant is tastefully decorated in an upscale cafe style, with the kitchen staff on show as they rustle up some of the capital's best tucker. It's also relaxed, feeling more communal than intimate on busy nights. My favorite dish is the Atlantic salmon served with beurre blanc sauce and potatoes, but other popular dishes include the eye fillet steak, and the pumpkin risotto. If you have room left for dessert, don't miss out on the sticky date pudding served with hot butter-scotch sauce, pralines, and ice cream—it's as good as it sounds. Otherwise, the long list of daily specials that complement the extensive menu could keep you busy for weeks.

Bougainville St., Manuka. © 02/6239 4422. Reservations recommended. Main courses A$15–$23 (U.S.$9.75–$15). AE, DC, MC, V. Daily noon–2:30pm; Mon–Sat 6–10pm.

INEXPENSIVE

Caffe Della Piazza ☆ ITALIAN/CAFE   Good eating isn't hard to find in Canberra, but this place is up there with the best. It won several awards for its Italian-inspired cooking, including the catering industries award for the best restaurant in the state (there's nothing like being judged by your peers). The restaurant offers both indoor and outdoor dining in pleasant surrounds, and is a good place to pop in for a light meal and a coffee, or something more substantial. Pastas here cost around A$11 (U.S.$7.15), and the best seller is chicken breast strips in a machi-ato sauce. You need to book early for Friday or Saturday evenings.

19 Garema Place, Civic. © 02/6248 9711. Reservations recommended. Main courses A$6.50–$17.50 (U.S.$4.20–$11.40). AE, DC, MC, V. Daily 10:30am–midnight.

Little Saigon *Value* VIETNAMESE   This spacious restaurant has minimalist decor and floor-to-ceiling windows offering views of the busy city center. Tables are set up on either side of an indoor pond, and there's a bar in the back of the restaurant. The menu is vast, with lots of noodle dishes as well as spicy seafood, duck, chicken, pork, beef, and lamb selections. The top seller is the lemongrass and chili chicken.

Alinga St. and Northbourne Ave., Civic. © 02/6230 5003. Main courses A$12–$15 (U.S.$7.80–$9.75). AE, DC, MC, V. Daily 10am–3pm and 5–10:30pm.

Portia's Place CANTONESE/MALAYSIAN/PEKING   A small restaurant serving up excellent traditional cookery, Portia's Place often fills up early and does a roaring lunchtime trade. The best things on the menu are the lamb ribs in shang tung sauce, the King Island fillet steak in pepper sauce, the flaming pork (brought to your table wrapped in foil and bursting with flames), and the Queensland trout stir-fried with snow peas.

11 Kennedy St., Kingston. © 02/6239 7970. Main courses A$9.80–$18.80 (U.S.$6.40–$12.20). AE, DC, MC, V. Daily noon–2:30pm; Sun–Wed 5–10pm, Thurs–Sat 5–10:30pm.

5 Seeing the Sights

Australian Institute of Sport   This institution provides first-class training and facilities for Australia's elite athletes. Tours, led by one of the institute's athletes, include visits to the gymnasium, basketball courts, and Olympic swimming pool to see training in progress. There is also a fascinating interactive sports display where visitors can test their sporting skills.

Leverrier Crescent, Bruce. © 02/6214 1444. Admission A$12 (U.S.$7.80) adults, A$6 (U.S.$3.90) children, A$33 (U.S.$21.45) families. Tours leave the AIS shop Mon–Fri at 11:30am and 2:30pm, and Sat–Sun at 10, 10:20, 11:30am, 1, and 2:30pm. Bus: 80 from city center.

Australian War Memorial ☆☆   This monument to Australian troops who gave their lives for their country is truly moving and well worth a visit. Artifacts and displays tell the story of Australia's conflicts abroad. You won't soon forget the exhibition on Gallipoli, the bloody World War I battle in which so many Anzac (Australian and New Zealand Army Corps) servicemen were slaughtered. The Hall of Memory is the focus of the memorial, where the body of the Unknown Soldier lies entombed (his remains were brought back from a World War I battlefield in 1993). The Memorial also holds one of the largest collections of Australian art in the world, including works by Tom Roberts, Arthur Streeton and Grace Cossington-Smith. Recently added exhibits include a film showing the surrender of Singapore, projected onto the actual table on which the surrender was signed, and a simulated ride aboard an original Lancaster bomber.

At the head of Anzac Parade on Limestone Ave. © 02/6243 4211. Free admission. Daily 10am–5pm (when the Last Post is played). Closed Christmas. Guided tours at 10, 10:30, 11am, 1:30, and 2pm. Bus: 233, 302, 303, 362, 436, or 901.

Canberra Deep Space Communication Complex ☆   This information center, which stands beside huge tracking dishes, is a must for anyone interested in space. There are plenty of models, audio-visual recordings, and displays, including a genuine space suit, space food, and archive film footage of the Apollo moon landings. The complex is still active and is tracking and recording results from the Mars Pathfinder, Voyager 1 and 2, and the Cassini, Soho, Galileo, and Ulysses space exploration projects, as well as providing a vital link with NASA spacecraft. This is a great stop-off on the way back from the Tidbinbilla Nature Reserve just up the road (see below).

Tidbinbilla, 39km (23¼ miles) southwest of Civic. © 02/6201 7880. www.cdscc.nasa.gov. Free admission. Summer daily 9am–8pm; rest of year daily 9am–5pm. No public bus service, but several tour companies offer programs that include the complex.

High Court of Australia   The High Court, an impressive concrete-and-glass building that overlooks Lake Burley Griffin and stands next to the National Gallery of Australia, was opened by Elizabeth II in 1980. It is home to the highest court in Australia's judicial system and contains three courtrooms, a video display, and a huge seven-story-high public hall. When the court is in session, visitors can observe the proceedings from the public gallery. Call or e-mail for session details.

Overlooking Lake Burley Griffin, Parkes Place. © 02/6270 6811. Jpelle@hcourt.gov.au. Free admission. Mon–Fri 9:45am–4:30pm. Closed public holidays. Bus: 34.

Finds **Up, Up & Away**

Balloon Aloft (© **02/6285 1540**) offers fabulous 45-minute sunrise flights over Canberra Monday through Friday for A$155 (U.S.$100.75) for adults and A$100 (U.S.$65) for children 6 to 12, including a champagne breakfast on touchdown. On weekends an hour-long trip costs A$220 (U.S.$143) for adults and A$140 (U.S.$91) for children, including breakfast at the Hyatt Hotel. It costs A$25 (U.S.$16.25) less each day if you don't want breakfast.

Dawn Drifters (© **02/6285 4450**; fax 02/6281 5315; www.dawn drifters.com.au) will also send you soaring over the city. One-hour champagne flights with breakfast cost A$155 (U.S.$100.75) for adults Monday through Friday and A$195 (U.S.$1126.75) on weekends and public holidays. Children go for 40% of the adult price. Breakfast is A$15 (U.S.$9.75) extra.

National Capital Exhibition   If you want to find out more about Canberra's beginnings—and get a memorable view of Lake Burley Griffin, the Captain Cook Memorial Water Jet, and the Carillon in the bargain—then head here. The displays are well done, and there's a film that provides an overview of the city's design.

On the lake shore at Regatta Point in Commonwealth Park. © **02/6257 1068**. Free admission. Daily 9am–6pm (5pm in winter).

National Gallery of Australia   Linked to the High Court by a pedestrian bridge, the National Gallery showcases both Australian and international art. The permanent collection and traveling exhibitions are displayed in 11 separate galleries. You'll find paintings by big names such as Claude Monet and Jackson Pollock, and Australian painters Arthur Boyd, Sidney Nolan, Arthur Streeton, Charles Condor, Tom Roberts, and Albert Tucker. The exhibition of Tiwi islander burial poles in the foyer is also interesting (the Tiwi Islands include Melville and Bathurst islands off Darwin), and there's a large collection of Aboriginal bark paintings from central Australia. A sculpture garden surrounding the gallery has 24 sculptures and is always open to the public.

Parkes Place. © **02/6240 6502**. www.nga.gov.au. Free admission (except for major touring exhibitions). Daily 10am–5pm. Guided tours daily at 11am and 2pm; Thurs and Sun at 11am there's a free tour focusing on Aboriginal art. Bus: 36 and 39 from Old Parliament House, or 34 from Parkes Place in front of the High Court.

National Museum of Australia   This, the first official all-encompassing museum dedicated to the nation of Australia, opened in 2001. Using state-of-the-art technology and hands-on exhibits, the museum is based on three main themes: Australian society and its history since 1788; the interaction of people with the Australian environment; and Aboriginal and Torres Strait Islander cultures and histories. In reality it doesn't so much rely on actual historic objects to tell the stories of Australia but on images and sound. Allow a couple of hours if it grabs you, and 30 minutes to rush around baffled if it doesn't.

Acton Peninsula (about 5km [3 miles] from the city centre). © **1800/026 132**, or 02/6208 5000. www. nma.gov.au. Free admission. Daily 9am–5pm.

Old Parliament House The seat of government from 1927 to 1988, the Old Parliament House is now home to regular exhibitions from the National Museum and the Australian Archives. The National Portrait Gallery is also here, and outside on the lawn is the Aboriginal Tent Embassy, which was set up in 1972 in a bid to persuade the authorities to recognize the land ownership claims of Aboriginal and Torres Strait Islander people. The red, black, and yellow Aboriginal flag first came to prominence here. Interestingly, the Australian Heritage Commission now recognizes the campsite as a place of special cultural significance.

On King George Terrace, midway between the new Parliament House (see below) and the lake. ℂ 02/6273 4723. Admission A$2 (U.S.$1.30) adults, A$1 (U.S.65¢) children, A$5 (U.S.$3.25) family. Daily 9am–5pm. Bus: 39.

Parliament House Conceived by American architect Walter Burley Griffin in 1912, but only built in 1988, Canberra's unmistakable centerpoint was designed to blend organically into its setting at the top of Capital Hill; only a national flag supported by a giant four-footed flag pole rises above the peak of the hill. In good weather, picnickers crowd the grass that covers the roof, where the view is spectacular. Inside are more than 3,000 works of Australian arts and crafts, and extensive areas of the building are open to the general public. Be sure to look out for a mosaic by Michael Tjakamarra Nelson entitled *Meeting Place,* which represents a gathering of various Aboriginal tribes, and can be found just inside the main entrance. There's also a 20-meter- (65½-ft.) long tapestry by Arthur Boyd in the Great Hall on the first floor and one of the four known versions of the Magna Carta in the Great Hall directly beneath the flag pole. Free 50-minute guided tours are offered throughout the day.

Parliament is usually in session Monday through Thursday between mid-February and late June, and mid-August to mid-December. Both the lower house—the House of Representatives (where the prime minister sits)—and the upper house—the Senate—have public viewing galleries. The best time to see the action is during Question Time, which starts at 2pm in the lower house. If you turn up early enough, you might be lucky and get a seat; otherwise make reservations for gallery tickets via the **sergeant-at-arms** (ℂ **02/6277 4889**), at least a day in advance. Free tours of the building go for 45 minutes and start at 9am (then follow every 30 min.).

Capital Hill. ℂ 02/6277 5399. Free admission. Daily 9am–5pm. Closed Christmas. Bus: 39.

Questacon—The National Science and Technology Centre *(Kids* Questacon offers some 170 hands-on exhibits that can keep you and your inner child occupied for hours. Exhibits are clustered into six galleries, each representing a different aspect of science. The artificial earthquake is a big attraction. The center is great for kids, but give it a miss if you've already visited the Powerhouse Museum in Sydney (see chapter 3).

King Edward Terrace, Parkes. ℂ 02/6270 2800. Admission A$10 (U.S.$6.50) adults, A$5 (U.S.$3.25) children, A$6.50 (U.S.$4.20) students, A$28 (U.S.$18.20) families. Daily 10am–5pm. Closed Christmas. Bus: 34.

Telstra Tower The tower, which rises 195 meters (644 ft.) above the summit of Black Mountain, has both open-air and enclosed viewing galleries that provide magnificent 360° views over Canberra and the surrounding countryside. Those who dine in the pricey, revolving **Tower Restaurant** (ℂ **02/6248 7096**) are thoughtfully entitled to a refund of their admission charge.

Black Mountain Dr. ℂ 02/6248 1911. Admission A$3.30 (U.S.$2.15) adults, A$1.10 (U.S.70¢) children. Daily 9am–10pm. No bus service.

Tidbinbilla Nature Reserve *Moments* This is a great place to see native animals such as kangaroos, wallabies, koalas, platypuses, and birds in their natural environment. Unlike other wildlife parks around the country, this one has plenty of space, so sometimes you'll have to look hard to spot the animals. (On a recent quick visit, I saw a few birds and not much else, but on previous visits I've been almost stomped on by kangaroos.) A guide is available from the visitor center. If you want to be sure to spot some animals, contact **Round About Tours** (© **02/6259 5999**), which runs day tours of the reserve for A$55 (U.S.$35.75), which includes a picnic lunch and afternoon tea. It also offers 2-hour kangaroo-spotting night tours for A$20 (U.S.$13).

Tidbinbilla. © **02/6237 5120**. Admission A$8.50 (U.S.$5.50) per vehicle day. Daily 9am–6pm (8pm in summer). Visitor center Mon–Fri 9am–4:30pm; Sat–Sun 9am–5:30pm. No public bus service, but several tour companies offer programs that include the reserve.

BOTANIC GARDENS & A NEARBY NATIONAL PARK

The **Australian National Botanic Gardens** *&*, Clunies Ross Street, Black Mountain, Acton (© **02/6250 9540**), are home to the best collection of Australian native plants anywhere. The gardens are situated on 51 hectares (125 acres) on the lower slopes of Black Mountain and feature a Eucalyptus Lawn containing more than 600 species of eucalyptus, a rain-forest area, a Tasmanian alpine garden, and self-guided walking tracks. Free guided tours depart from the visitor center at 11am on weekdays and 11am and 2pm on weekends. The gardens are open daily from 9am to 5pm (to 8pm in summer). The visitor center is open daily from 9:30am to 4:30pm. There's no bus service to the gardens.

The **Namadgi National Park** *&* covers almost half of the Australian Capital Territory. Parts of the park, which has high rolling plateaus, good trout-fishing streams, and dense forest, are just 30 kilometers (19 miles) from Canberra. Marked hiking tracks can be found throughout the park. Spring is the best time of year to visit for the prolific display of bush flowers. In the past, sections of the park were cleared for sheep grazing, but these days the pastures are popular with hundreds of gray kangaroos (they're easiest to spot in the early morning and late afternoon). At Yankee Hat, off the Nass/Boboyan Road, is an Aboriginal rock-art site. The **Namadgi Visitors Center** (© **02/6207 2900**), on the Nass/Boboyan Road, 3 kilometers (1¾ miles) south of the township of Tharwa, has maps and information on walking trails.

6 Outdoor Pursuits

BIKING With 120 kilometers (74 miles) of bike paths, Canberra is made for exploring on two wheels. Rent a bike from **Mr. Spoke's Bike Hire** on Barrine Drive near the ferry terminal in Acton (© **02/6257 1188**). Bikes for adults cost A$10 (U.S.$6.50) for the first hour and A$9 (U.S.$5.85) for each hour afterwards; rates are A$9 (U.S.$5.85) for kids, going down to A$8 (U.S.$5.20) for each subsequent hour.

BOATING **Burley Griffin Boat Hire,** on Barrine Drive near the ferry terminal in Acton (© **02/6249 6861**), rents paddle boats for A$20 (U.S.$13) per hour and canoes for A$14 (U.S.$9.10) per hour. **Row 'n' Ride,** near the Mac-Dermott Place Boat Ramp, Belconnen (© **02/6254 7838**), is open on weekends and school and public holidays and offers canoes from A$9 (U.S.$5.85) per hour, kayaks for A$10 (U.S.$6.50) per hour, and mountain bikes for A$9 (U.S.$5.85) per hour.

GLIDING   The **Canberra Gliding Club** (© **02/6257 1494** or 02/6452 3994) offers joy flights and trial instructional flights on weekends and public holidays from the Bunyan Airfield. Flights cost A$60 (U.S.$39).

SWIMMING   The indoor heated pool at the **Australian Institute of Sport** (© **02/6214 1281**), on Leverrier Crescent in Bruce, a short drive northwest of Civic, is open to the public at certain times during the day (call ahead to check schedules). Adults pay A$3.50 (U.S.$2.30) to swim, and children pay A$2 (U.S.$1.30). It's compulsory to wear swimming caps, which can be bought there for A$2.50 (U.S.$1.60). It costs A$6 (U.S.$3.90) to use the pool, spa, and sauna.

TENNIS   The **National Tennis and Squash Centre,** Federal Highway, Lyneham (© **02/6247 0929**), has squash courts available for A$11.50 to $15.50 (U.S.$7.50–$10) per hour, depending on when you want to play. Tennis courts can be booked for A$9.50 to $14.50 (U.S.$6.20–$9.40). The Australian Institute of Sport (see above) also rents courts.

7 Canberra After Dark

The **"Good Time"** section in Thursday's *Canberra Times* has listings on what's on offer around town.

Of the pubs in town, the best in the city center are the British-style **Wig & Pen,** on the corner of Limestone and Alinga Street (© **02/6248 0171**); the very popular **Moosehead's Pub,** at 105 London Circuit in the south of the city (© **02/6257 6496**); the **Phoenix,** at 21 East Row (© **02/6247 1606**), which has live music upstairs for a small cover charge; and **P.J. O'Reileys** (© **02/6230 4752**) on the corner of West Row and Alinga Street, an authentic-style Irish pub.

If you're looking to roll some dice, the **Casino Canberra,** in Glebe Park, 21 Binara St., Civic (© **1800/806 833** in Australia, or 02/6257 7074), is a small, older-style casino offering all the usual casino games from noon to 6am. Dress regulations prohibit leisure wear, running shoes, and denim, but overall it's a casual place to lose some money.

14

Tasmania

by Marc Llewellyn

The name "Tasmania" suggests an unspoiled place, with vast stretches of wilderness roamed by strange creatures like the Tasmanian devil. Many mainland residents still half-jokingly refer to their "country cousins" on this island as rednecks. In truth, most Tasmanians are hospitable and friendly people, lacking the harsh edge that big cities can foster. Most also care passionately for the magnificent environment they've inherited, decrying the belief that anything that moves deserves a bullet and anything that stands still needs chopping down.

Visitors to Tasmania are surprised by its size, though compared to the rest of Australia the distances are certainly more manageable. Dense rain forests, stony mountain peaks, alpine meadows, pine plantations, vast eucalyptus stands, and fertile stretches of farmland are all easily accessible, but you should still be prepared for several hours of concentrated driving to get you between the main attractions. Among Tasmania's chief attractions is its natural environment. More than 20% of the island has been declared a World Heritage Area, and nearly a third of the island is protected within its 14 national parks.

Tasmania's other main draw is its history. Remains of the Aboriginal people that lived here for tens of thousands of years are evident in isolated rock paintings, engraving, stories, and the aura of spirituality that still holds tight in places where modern civilization has not yet reached.

Europeans discovered Tasmania (or Van Diemen's Land, as it was once known) in 1642, when the great seafarer Abel Tasman set anchor off its southwest coast, although it wasn't identified as an island until 1798. Tasmania soon made its mark as a dumping ground for convicts, who were more often than not transported for petty crimes committed in their homeland. The brutal system of control, still evident in the ruins at Port Arthur and elsewhere, spilled over into persecution of the native population. Tragically, the last full-blooded Tasmanian Aborigine died in 1876, just 15 years after the last convict transportation. Most had already died of disease and maltreatment at the hands of the settlers.

1 Exploring Tasmania

VISITOR INFORMATION The **Tasmanian Travel and Information Centre** (© **1800/806 846** in Australia, or 03/6230 8233; www.tourism.tas.gov.au), operates visitor centers located in more than 30 towns throughout the state. It can arrange travel passes, ferry and bus tickets, car rental, cruises, and accommodations.

Pick up a copy of *Travelways,* Tourism Tasmania's tourist tabloid, for details on transportation, accommodations, restaurants, and attractions around Tasmania.

Tasmania

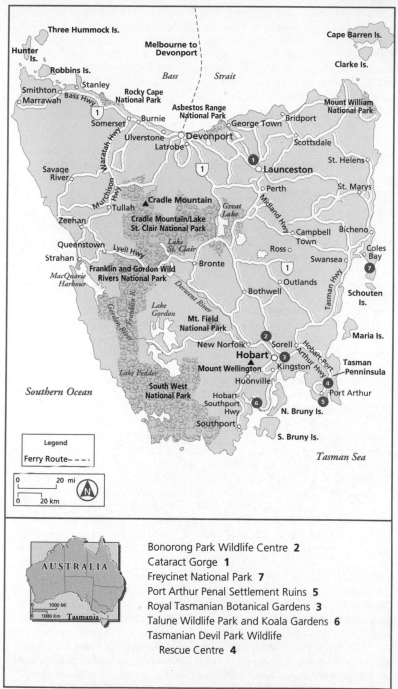

Legend

Ferry Route – – – –

0 ____ 20 mi
0 ____ 20 km

AUSTRALIA

0 ____ 1000 Mi
0 ____ 1000 Km   Tasmania

Bonorong Park Wildlife Centre **2**
Cataract Gorge **1**
Freycinet National Park **7**
Port Arthur Penal Settlement Ruins **5**
Royal Tasmanian Botanical Gardens **3**
Talune Wildlife Park and Koala Gardens **6**
Tasmanian Devil Park Wildlife
    Rescue Centre **4**

WHEN TO GO The best time to visit Tasmania is between mid-September and May, when the weather is at its best. By April nights are getting cold, the days are getting shorter and the deciduous trees are starting to turn golden. Winters (June–Aug), especially in the high country, can be quite harsh—though that's the best time to curl up in front of a blazing fire. The east coast is generally milder than the west coast, which is buffeted by the "Roaring 40s"—the winds that blow across the ocean and the 40° meridian, from as far away as Argentina.

The busy season for tourism here runs December through February, as well as during public holiday and school holiday periods. Unlike the rest of Australia, Tasmanian schools have three terms. Term dates are from the second week in February to the last week in May; the third week in June to the first week in September; and the fourth week in September to the first week in December.

GETTING THERE The quickest way to get to Tasmania is by air. **Qantas** (© **13 13 13** in Australia) flies from the mainland to Hobart and Launceston.

A more adventurous way to reach Tasmania is to take a boat across Bass Strait from the mainland. The quickest of these options is on the **DevilCat,** Australia's largest high-speed catamaran, which runs between Melbourne's Station Pier and George Town on Tasmania's north coast from roughly December 21 to April 16 (trip time: 6 hr.). Ferries depart Melbourne at 8:30am Monday, Thursday, and Saturday, arriving in George Town at 2:30pm. Return ferries depart George Town Tuesday, Friday, and Sunday at 2pm, arriving in Melbourne at 8pm.

One-way tickets cost between A$145 (U.S.$94.25) and A$175 (U.S.$113.75) for adults and A$92 to A$100 (U.S.$105–$65) for children under 16. Prices change regularly, and "specials" can be found on the website. Check the website or contact **TT-Line** (© **03/9206 6211;** www.tt-line.com.au). **Tasmanian Redline Coaches** (© **03/6336 1446,** or 1300/360 000 from within Tasmania, and 1800/030 033 from other states; www.redlinecoaches.com.au) link George Town with Launceston, 35 minutes away.

The car and passenger ferry *Spirit of Tasmania* plies the Tasman Sea between Melbourne's Station Pier and Devonport on the island's northwest coast. The ferry holds 1,300 passengers; it offers a dining room, a buffet bistro, a cafeteria, a pool, a sauna, and a disco. The ferry departs Melbourne every Monday at 7:30pm, Wednesday and Friday at 6pm (and Sun at 9am depending on demand). The trip takes 12 to 13 hours. Return trips leave Devonport every Saturday at 4pm, Tuesday and Thursday at 6pm (and Mon at 2am depending on demand).

Accommodation options vary from suites and double rooms, to two- and four-person bunk rooms, and large hostel-style units. A four-person suite costs A$270 to $368 (U.S.$175.50–$239.20) one-way for adults and A$98 to $118 (U.S.$63.70–$76.70) for children, depending on the season. A double costs A$227 to $289 (U.S.$147.55–$187.85) for all persons; a two-person or four-person bunk room from A$181 to $237 (U.S.$117.65–$154) for adults and A$90 to $118 (U.S.$58.50–$76.70) for children; and a hostel room (sleeping between 8 and 28 people) from A$124 to $158 (U.S.$80.60–$102.70) per person. Return fares cost double. To transport a car one-way costs an extra A$55 (U.S.$35.75) in peak season, and A$40 (U.S.$26) off-peak. Prices are highest during the school holiday periods of early December to the end of January, and during the 2 weeks over Easter. Make reservations through TT-Line (see above). You can also book tickets by calling **Inta-Aussie** at © **800/531-9222** in the United States or Canada.

Tasmanian Redline Coaches (℗ **03/6336 1446**) connect with each ferry. Standard single fares are A$34.80 (U.S.$22.60) for adults and A$17.40 (U.S.$11.30) for children 15 and under to Hobart, and A$14.40 (U.S.$9.40) for adults and A$7.20 (U.S.$4.70) for children to Launceston.

McCafferty's (℗ **13 14 99** in Australia) can organize coach travel from the eastern mainland states, with transfers to Tasmania by ferry.

GETTING AROUND   The regional airline **Tasair** (℗ **1800/062 900** in Australia; www.tasair.com.au) flies to most major settlements in Tasmania. **Par Avion** (℗ **03/6248 5390;** www.paravion.com.au) concentrates on the southwest World Heritage areas of the state and also operates tours.

Statewide coach services are provided by **Tasmanian Redline Coaches** (℗ **03/6336 1446**), and **Tassielink** (℗ **03/6272 6611,** or 1300/300 520 in Australia; www.tigerline.com.au). Associated with Tassielink are **Tigerline Coaches** (contactable by same phone and website), which offer a series of coach tours to major places of interest. **Hobart Coaches** (℗ **1800/030 620** in Australia, or 03/6234 4077) runs trips around the Hobart area.

The cheapest way to get around by coach is to buy a travel pass to get you around the island. The Tassie Link Explorer Pass, which can be used on all Tassielink routes, comes in four categories: A 7-day pass good for travel within 15 days is A$150 (U.S.$97.50); a 14-day pass good for travel within 20 days is A$210 (U.S.$136.50); a 21-day pass valid for travel in 30 days is A$250 (U.S.$162.50).

Driving a car from Devonport on the north coast to Hobart on the south coast takes less than 4 hours. From Hobart to Strahan on the west coast also takes around 4 hours, while the journey from Launceston to Hobart takes about 2 hours. The **Royal Automobile Club of Tasmania (RACT),** at Murray and Patrick streets in Hobart (℗ **13 27 22** in Tasmania), can supply you with touring maps.

TOUR OPERATORS   Dozens of operators run organized hiking, horse trekking, sailing, caving, fishing, bushwalking, diving, cycling, rafting, climbing, kayaking, or canoeing trips in Tasmania. For a full listing, see the "Outdoor Adventure" section of *Travelways,* the Tasmanian tourist board's publication (see "Visitor Information" above).

One of the best operators is **Tasmania Adventure Tours** (℗ **1300/654 604** in Australia; www.adventuretours.com.au). They offer a 3-day East Coast Explorer tour from Devonport, taking in Launceston, Freycinet National Park, and Port Arthur, before finishing in Hobart. The tour costs A$320 (U.S.$208). Their 3-day Wild and Green West Coast Tour departs Hobart and goes to Mount Field National Park, Strahan, Tullah, and Cradle Mountain National Park before ending in Devonport. This tour costs A$340 (U.S.$221). For a

---

Tips **Drive Carefully**

Driving in Tasmania can be dangerous; there are more accidents involving tourists on Tasmania's roads than anywhere else in Australia. Many roads are narrow and bends can be tight, especially in the mountainous inland regions—where you may also come across black ice early in the morning or at anytime in winter. Marsupials are also common around dusk, and swerving to avoid them has caused countless crashes.

National Park Entry Fees

A Tassie Holiday Pass costs A$33 (U.S.$21.45) and allows entry for a car and passengers to all Tasmania's national parks for a period of 2 months. Pedestrians, cyclists, motorcyclists and coach passengers pay $13.20 (U.S.$8.58) for 2 months. Occasional users can buy a 24-hour pass costing $9.90 (U.S.$6.45) per car, while walkers, cyclists, motorcyclists and coach passengers pay $3.30 (U.S.$2.15) per day. Passes are available at all major national parks and Tasmanian Visitor Information Centres. For more information contact the **Parks and Wildlife Service** at ✆ **03/6233 8203**. Look up the Tasmanian Parks and Wildlife Service's official website (www.parks. tas.gov.au) for great information on all Tasmania's national parks.

---

longer tour, their 6-day Taste of Tasmania Tour starts off in Devonport, takes in all the attractions in their other two tours, and ends up in Hobart. This tour costs A$630 (U.S.$409.50). Ring for departure days.

Peregrin Adventures (✆ **03/9662 2800**; www.peregrin.net.au) runs rafting tours of the Franklin River, which carves its way through some of the most beautiful, rugged, and inaccessible wilderness in the world. Two other good operators are **Rafting Tasmania** (✆ **03/6239 1080**; www.tasmaniaadventures. com.au), and the **Roaring 40's Ocean Kayaking Company** (✆ **1800/653 712** in Australia); both companies offer paddling expeditions lasting from 1 to 11 days. **Tasmanian Expeditions,** based in Launceston (✆ **1800/030 230** in Australia, or 03/6334 3477; www.tas-ex.com), runs a whole range of cycling, trekking, and rafting trips around the country, some starting or finishing in Hobart.

SUGGESTED ITINERARIES Planning my first trip to Tasmania, I'd pack my walking boots, raincoat, and shorts, and head off first to either **Launceston** or **Hobart,** the island's two main cities. I'd take in **Freycinet National Park** for its wonderful scenery and abundant wildlife, stop in at **Port Arthur** for its beautiful setting and disturbing convict past, and head to the central highlands for a stomp around **Cradle Mountain.** If I had more time, I'd drive to **Strahan** on the far west coast to discover the southwest wilderness, take some time off to go trout fishing in the central lakes, and head off to the quaint coastal towns of the north.

2 Hobart

198km (123 miles) S of Launceston

Tasmania's capital (pop. 126,000), second in age only to Sydney, is an appealing place well worth visiting for a couple of days. Hobart's main features are its wonderful harbor and the colonial cottages that line the narrow lanes of **Battery Point.** As with Sydney, Hobart's harbor is the city's focal point, attracting yachts from all over the world. Down by the waterfront, picturesque **Salamanca Place** bursts with galleries, pubs, cafes, and an excellent market on Saturdays. Europeans settled in Hobart in 1804, a year after Tasmania's first colony was set up at Risdon (10km/6 miles up the Derwent River).

ESSENTIALS

GETTING THERE **Qantas** (✆ **13 13 13** in Australia) carries passengers from the mainland. The trip from the airport to the city center takes about 20 minutes and costs about A$25 (U.S.$16.25) by taxi and A$7.50 (U.S.$4.90) by

Hobart

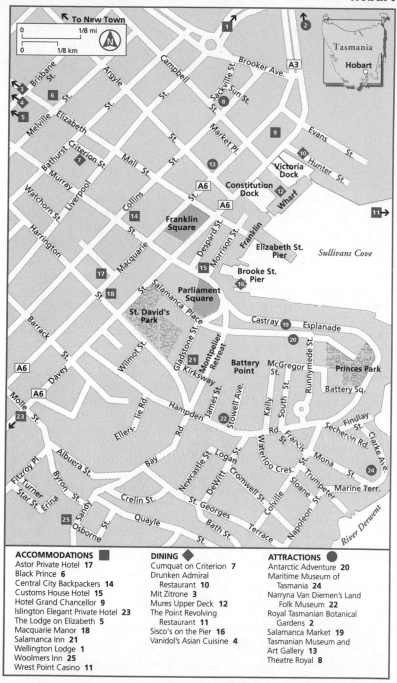

Tasmania
Hobart

To New Town

Sullivans Cove

River Derwent

ACCOMMODATIONS
Astor Private Hotel **17**
Black Prince **6**
Central City Backpackers **14**
Customs House Hotel **15**
Hotel Grand Chancellor **9**
Islington Elegant Private Hotel **23**
The Lodge on Elizabeth **5**
Macquarie Manor **18**
Salamanca Inn **21**
Wellington Lodge **1**
Woolmers Inn **25**
Wrest Point Casino **11**

DINING
Cumquat on Criterion **7**
Drunken Admiral
  Restaurant **10**
Mit Zitrone **3**
Mures Upper Deck **12**
The Point Revolving
  Restaurant **11**
Sisco's on the Pier **16**
Vanidol's Asian Cuisine **4**

ATTRACTIONS
Antarctic Adventure **20**
Maritime Museum of
  Tasmania **24**
Narryna Van Diemen's Land
  Folk Museum **22**
Royal Tasmanian Botanical
  Gardens **2**
Salamanca Market **19**
Tasmanian Museum and
  Art Gallery **13**
Theatre Royal **8**

Tasmanian Redline Coaches, 199 Collins St., Hobart (© **03/6336 1446**). Coaches drop you off at the Collins Street bus terminal or at any central city hotel.

Car and camper rental offices at the airport include **Hertz** (© **03/6237 1155**), **Advance** (© **1800/030 118** in Australia, www.advancecars.com.au), **Avis** (© **03/6248 5424**), **Budget** (© **03/6248 5333,** or 1300/362 848 in Australia), and **Thrifty** (© **1800/030 730** in Australia, or 03/6234 1341). Cars cost around A$55 (U.S.$35.75) for 1 day, A$50 (U.S.$32.50) per day for 2 days, A$45 (U.S.$29.25) per day for 4 days, and A$40 (U.S.$26) per day for a week or more. You might find even better bargains in town with lower-priced rental companies such as **Lo-Cost Auto Rent** (© **03/6231 0550** or 1800 03 0023) and **Range Rent-a-Bug** (© **03/6231 0300**).

VISITOR INFORMATION Information is available from the **Tasmanian Travel and Information Centre,** at Davey and Elizabeth streets (© **03/6230 8233**). It's open Monday through Friday from 8:30am to 5:15pm, Saturday and public holidays from 9am to 4pm, and Sunday from 9am to 1pm (9am–4pm Dec–Apr). You can pick up information on the State's National Parks at the **Lands Information Bureau,** 134 Macquarie St. (© **03/6233 8011**).

CITY LAYOUT Hobart straddles the Derwent River on the south coast of the Tasmania. Historic **Salamanca Place** and nearby **Battery Point** abut Sullivan's Cove, home to hundreds of yachts. The row of sandstone warehouses that dominate Salamanca Place date back to the city's importance as a whaling base in the 1830s. Tucked away behind Princes Wharf, Battery Point is the city's historic district, which in colonial times was the home of sailors, fishermen, whalers, coopers, merchants, shipwrights, and master mariners. The open ocean is about 50 kilometers (31 miles) farther down the river, though the Derwent empties out into Storm Bay, just 20 kilometers (12 miles) downstream. The central business district is on the west side of the water, with the main thoroughfares— **Campbell, Argyle, Elizabeth, Murray, and Harrington streets**—sloping down to the busy harbor. The Tasman Bridge and regular passenger ferries reach across the Derwent River. Set back from the city, but overlooking it, is the 1,270-meter- (4,191-ft.-) tall **Mount Wellington.**

GETTING AROUND Central Hobart is very small, and most of the attractions are in easy walking distance. **Metro Tasmania** (© **03/6233 4232** or 13 22 01; www.metrobus.com.au) operates a system of public metro buses throughout the city and suburban areas. Single tickets cost from A$1.30 to $3.30 (U.S.85¢– $2.15) depending on how far you're going. Day Tripper tickets can be used between 9am and 4:30pm and after 6pm during the week and all day on weekends; they cost A$3.40 (U.S.$2.20). Purchase tickets from bus drivers. If you plan on busing about, stop off at the Metro Shop situated in the General Post Office building on the corner of Elizabeth and Macquarie streets and pick up a timetable, brochures, and sightseeing information.

(Tips Staying Connected

It's relatively hard to find public access to the Internet in Hobart, but you can try **Drifters Internet Café,** Shop 9/33 Salamanca Place, Hobart (in Salamanca Galleria) (© **03/6224 3244**). The cafe charges A$5 (U.S$3.25) per half hour.

The **Roche-O'May ferry company** (© 03/6223 1914; www.ontas.com.au/cartela) operates morning and afternoon tea cruises, and lunch and dinner cruises on the *Cartela,* a wooden-hulled, former steam-powered ferry built in Hobart in 1912. Coffee cruises cost A$12 (U.S.$7.80) and lunch and dinner cruises A$24 (U.S.$15.60). Ring ahead for departure times. The company also runs a ferry service on the *Wanderer,* with coffee and tea and full commentary. It stops at the Wrest Point Casino, the Royal Tasmanian Botanical Gardens, Sullivan's Cove, and the old suburb of Belle Reeve. These ferries leave Brooke Street Pier on Franklin Wharf at 10:30am, noon, 1:30, and 3pm. The 1½-hour cruise costs A$10 (U.S.$6.50) for adults, A$5 (U.S.$3.25) for children, and A$25 (U.S.$16.25) for a family.

Driving here isn't the best idea. Parking is difficult in the city center, and the one-way streets can drive you crazy.

SPECIAL EVENTS   The **Sydney-to-Hobart Yacht Race,** starting in Sydney on December 26, fills the Constitution Dock Marina and general harbor area close to overflowing with spectators and party-goers when the ships eventually turn up in Tasmania. The race takes anywhere from 2 to 4 days, and the sailors and fans stay on to celebrate New Year's Eve in Hobart. Food and wine lovers indulge themselves after the race during the 2-month-long **Hobart Summer Festival,** which starts around December 28.

EXPLORING THE CITY & ENVIRONS

Simply strolling around the harbor and popping into the shops at Salamanca Place can keep you nicely occupied.

Also take a look around Battery Point, an area chock-full of colonial stone cottages. The area gets its name from a battery of guns set up on the promontory in 1818 to defend the town against potential invaders (particularly the French). Today, there are plenty of tearooms, antique shops, cozy restaurants, and atmospheric pubs interspersed between grand dwellings. One of the houses worth looking into is **Narryna Van Diemen's Land Folk Museum,** 103 Hampden Rd. (© 03/6234 2791), which depicts the life of upper-class pioneers. It's open Tuesday through Friday from 10:30am to 5pm and Saturday and Sunday from 2 to 5pm (closed July). Admission is A$5 (U.S.$3.25) for adults and A$2 (U.S.$1.30) for children. Also in this area is the **Maritime Museum of Tasmania,** 16 Argyle St. (© 03/6234 1427), one of the best museums of its type in Australia. It's open daily from 10am to 5pm, and admission is A$6.60 (U.S.$4.30) for adults, A$4 (U.S.$2.60) for children 4 to 16, and A$17.50 (U.S.$11.40) for a family.

The National Trust (© 03/6223 7570) offers a 3-hour **Battery Point Heritage Walk** leaving at 9:30am every Saturday from the wishing well in Franklin Square. It costs A$11 (U.S.$7.15) for adults and A$3 (U.S.$1.95) for children 6 to 16 and includes morning tea.

For magnificent views over Hobart and across a fair-size chunk of Tasmania, drive to **The Pinnacle** on top of Mount Wellington, about 40 minutes from the city center. Take a warm coat though; the wind in this alpine area can bite. An extensive network of walking trails offers good hiking around the mountain. Pick up a copy of *Mt. Wellington Day Walk Map and Notes* from the Department of Environment Tasmap Centre, on the ground floor of the Lands Building, 134 Macquarie St. (© 03/6233 3382).

THE TOP ATTRACTIONS

Antarctic Adventure 🌟 *Kids*   Hobart is the last port of call for expeditions to Antarctica. You can experience the cold continent yourself at this highly recommended attraction. It doesn't look like much at first, but I promise you'll be sucked in. You can experience an Antarctic blizzard, climb all over heavy machinery, experience a downhill ski simulator (I'm not sure how that fits in), and get computer access to Antarctic weather conditions and communications. The photos and other displays are also interesting. The irresistible stuffed huskies in the souvenir shop will take a hefty bite out of your wallet. Allow 1 to 2 hours.

Salamanca Square. ℂ **03/6220 8220.** Admission A$16 (U.S.$10.40) adults; A$13 (U.S.$8.45) students; A$8 (U.S.$5.20) children 4–13, A$40 (U.S.$26) families. Daily 10am–5pm. Closed Christmas.

Bonorong Park Wildlife Centre *(Kids)* I don't think I've ever seen so many wallabies in one place as I saw here—they were hopping all over the place. There are lots of other native animals around, too, including snakes, koalas, Tasmanian devils, and wombats. The Bush Tucker shed serves lunch, billy teas (basically tea brewed up in a metal pot with a gum leaf thrown in), and damper (Australian-style campfire bread). Koala cuddling isn't allowed in Tasmania, but if you're around at feeding times it's possible to stroke one—they're not as shy as you might think. Feeding times are 12:30 and 3pm daily. The park is on the side of a steep hill, so travelers in wheelchairs are likely to fare badly. Allow 1 hour.

Briggs Rd., Brighton. ℂ **03/6268 1184.** Admission A$8 (U.S.$5.20) adults, A$4 (U.S.$2.60) children under 15. Daily 9am–5pm. Closed Christmas Day. Bus to Glenorchy from the central bus terminal in Hobart (about 10 min.), then take Bus 125 or 126 to the park. Drive north on route 1 to Brighton; it's about 25 min. north of Hobart and well-signposted.

Cadbury Chocolate Factory Eat chocolates till they make you sick on this Willy Wonka–type trip. Book well ahead, because chocolate tours are very popular. Keep in mind you'll need to climb lots of stairs inside the factory. You can visit the factory on a ferry tour (details below), or go through Tasmanian Tours & Travel Tigerline (ℂ **1300/653 633** or 03/6272 6611), which runs half-day coach tours out of Hobart Monday through Friday from 9:30am. These cost A$29 (U.S.$18.90) for adults and A$18 (U.S.$11.70) for children.

Claremont, 12km (7 miles) north of Hobart. ℂ **1800/627 367** in Australia, or 03/6249 0333. Tours A$11 (U.S.$7.15) adults, A$5.50 (U.S.$3.60) children, A$27.50 (U.S.$18) families. Mon–Fri 8 (summer only), 9, 9:30, 10:30am, and 1pm.

Cascade Brewery Tours Cascade Premium is one of the best beers in the country, in my opinion. To see how this heady amber nectar is produced, head to Australia's oldest brewery and tag along on a fascinating 2-hour tour, which includes a stroll through the grand old Woodstock Gardens behind the factory.

Cascade Rd. ℂ **03/6221 8300.** Tours A$11 (U.S.$7.15) adults, A$4.50 (U.S.$2.90) children 5–12. Mon–Fri 9:30am and 1pm. Closed public holidays. Reservations required. Bus: 44, 46, or 49; get off at stop 18.

Fudge Factory and Historic Garden Tours *(Finds)* This is an interesting stopover if you're visiting either the Cascade Brewery or Mount Wellington. Not only do you get a trip around a very successful fudge-making factory, but also a guided tour around the remains of the women's prison next door. The tales told around here will make the hairs on your neck stand on end—like the fact that 17 out of every 20 children born within the walls of the institution died soon after birth, and that women who died were simply tossed into an unmarked mass grave. All the proceeds of the tour goes into preserving the prison. Allow 1½ hours.

Island Produce Confectionery, 16 Degraves St., South Hobart. ℂ **03/6223 3233.** Tours A$6 (U.S.$3.90) adults, A$3 (U.S.$1.95) children, A$15 (U.S.$9.75) families. Mon–Fri 8am–4pm. Tours begin at 10:30am (and 1:30pm during summer) Mon–Fri; reservations essential. (You can look around the gardens for free anytime if you make a purchase in the shop.) Bus: 44, 46, or 49 to South Hobart and Cascade Rd.; get off at stop 16.

Royal Tasmanian Botanical Gardens   Established in 1818, these gardens are known for English-style plant and tree layouts, a Japanese garden dominated by a miniature Mt. Fuji, and colorful seasonal blooming plants housed in the conservatory. A restaurant provides lunch and teas. Also here is a Botanical Discovery Centre (admission A$2/U.S.$1.30) and a Sub-Antarctic plant house. Allow 1 to 2 hours.

On the Queens Domain near Government House. ℂ 03/6234 6299. Admission: gardens free; conservatory A$2 (U.S.$1.30) donation. Daily 8am–6:30pm (until 5pm in winter). Bus: 17.

Tasmanian Museum and Art Gallery 𝒜   Come here to find out more about Tasmania's Aboriginal heritage, its history since settlement, and the island's wildlife. Traveling art exhibitions are mounted from time to time, but always on display are the paintings of the colonial era. The art gallery has a particularly impressive collection of paintings by Tom Roberts and by several convict artists. The pride of the entire collection, though, is *The Conciliation by Benjamin Duttereau*, the second-most painting of historical significance in Australia, after Tom Roberts' *Shearing of the Rams*, which you can see in the National Gallery of Victoria in Melbourne. Allow 1 to 2 hours.

40 Macquarie St. ℂ 03/6223 1422. Free admission. Daily 10am–5pm.

ORGANIZED TOURS

You'll get a good introduction to the city on the daily **Hobart Historic Walk** (ℂ **03/6225 4806**), a 2-hour leisurely stroll through historic Sullivan's Cove and Battery Point. Tours start at 10am daily from September through May and on request from June through August and cost A$17 (U.S.$11) for adults. Children under 12 are free. The tour requires a minimum of six people for a walk to go ahead; group discounts are provided.

Several companies run boat tours of the harbor. **Captain Fells Ferries** (ℂ **03/6223 5893**) offers a wide range of morning tea, lunch, afternoon, and dinner cruises. The company also runs Cadbury Factory Tours, which include coach transfers, a tour of the factory, a harbor cruise, and a two-course lunch for A$32 (U.S.$20.80) for adults and A$18 (U.S.$11.70) for children; these tours leave at 9:45am Monday through Thursday. Cruises depart from Franklin Wharf behind the wooden cruise-sales booths beside Elizabeth Street Wharf at the bottom of Elizabeth Street.

The Cruise Company (ℂ **03/6234 9294**) operates river trips along the Derwent to the Cadbury Chocolate Factory. Cruises depart at 10am Monday through Friday, returning at 2:30pm, and cost A$33 (U.S.$21.45) for adults, A$16 (U.S.$10.40) for children 5 to 15, and A$93 (U.S.$60.45) for a family, including entry and a guided tour of the factory; free for children under 5. The boat leaves from Brooke Street Pier. Also of interest is the company's 2-hour Ironpot Cruise (to the lighthouse of that name at the mouth of the Derwent). The scenic tour of the river leaves Brooke Street Pier at 2pm every Saturday and costs A$20 (U.S.$13) for adults; free for children under 15.

THE SHOPPING SCENE

If you are in Hobart on a Saturday don't miss the **Salamanca Market** 𝒜𝒜, in Salamanca Place—it's one of the best markets in Australia. Some 200 stalls offer everything from fruit and vegetables to crafts made from pottery, glass, and native woods. The market is open from 8:30am to 3pm.

Salamanca Place, 65 Salmanaca Place, itself has plenty of craft and souvenir shops that are worth exploring, though you pay for the privilege of buying them

---

⟨Tips **Booking Accommodations Online**

Just like elsewhere in Australia, you can save a lot of money in Tasmania by booking rooms online. **Asia Travel** (http://asiatravel.com/australia.html) offers substantial savings on some of the properties mentioned below if you book online. At the time of writing these included the Hotel Grand Chancellor in Hobart, the Colonial Motor Inn in Launceston, Freycinet Lodge, and Cradle Mountain Lodge.

---

in such a fashionable area. You could try **The Salamanca Collection** (② 03/ 6224 1341) for quality decorative arts, while the **Handmark Gallery,** 77 Salamanca Place (② 03/6223 7895), has a fine selection of wooden jewelry boxes and Art-Deco-style jewelry and pottery. The best bookshop in town is a beauty and sells a large range of new and secondhand books, many relating to Tasmania. Find the **Hobart Bookshop** at 22 Salamanca Square (② 03/6223 1803). For great chocolate and the best licorice, head to **Darrell Lea,** shop 36 in the Cat & Fiddle Arcade between Collins and Liverpool streets. There are plenty of other interesting shops here, too.

Store hours are Monday through Thursday from 9am to 6pm, Friday from 9am to 9pm, and Saturday from 9am to noon.

WHERE TO STAY

Hobart has some of the best hotels, guesthouses, and B&Bs in Australia. For something different, you can stay with a Tasmanian family either in town or at a farm in the country or arrange accommodations in one of the many boutique bed-and-breakfasts found throughout Tasmania. Contact **Heritage Tasmania Pty Ltd.,** P.O. Box 780, Sandy Bay, TAS 7005 (② 03/6233 5511; fax 03/6233 5510). Nightly bed-and-breakfast rates range from about A$60 (U.S.$39) to around A$160 (U.S.$104) for a double. There are 20 **YHA youth hostels** in Tasmania, including ones in Devonport (② 03/6424 5696), Bicheno (② 03/ 6375 1293), Coles Bay (② 03/6257 0115), Mt. Field National Park (② 03/ 6288 1369), Stanley (② 6458 1266), and Strahan (② 03/6471 7255). Most have dorms as well as inexpensive double rooms. The State office is located at 28 Critereon Street, Hobart (② 03/6234 9617).

VERY EXPENSIVE

Hotel Grand Chancellor ✿   If you prefer standard hotel accommodations to a stately old homestead, then you should book a room at this imposing property overlooking the yachts and fishing boats parked in Victoria Dock. Standard rooms are large and comfortable, with large polished granite bathrooms. More than 50% of the rooms have water views. Eight rooms are equipped for travelers with disabilities. The lobby is an impressive marble-and-granite construction complete with a large curved window to catch the action on the docks.

1 Davey St., Hobart, TAS 7000. ② 03/6235 4535. Fax 03/6223 8175. 234 units. A$260 (U.S.$169) double; A$365 (U.S.$237.25) executive suite. Extra person A$30 (U.S.$19.50). Children under 15 stay free in parents' room. AE, DC, MC, V. Free parking. **Amenities:** 1st-class restaurant specializing in innovative Tasmanian cuisine, relaxed lounge with good views; heated indoor pool; good health club; concierge; business center; salon; 24-hr. room service; massage; babysitting; laundry service. *In room:* A/C, TV with pay movies, dataport, minibar, hair dryer, iron.

Wrest Point Casino ✿✿   A A$23-million (U.S.$14.95-million) face-lift in 1998 completely transformed this Hobart icon, built in 1973, giving birth to

Australia's A$2-billion-a-year (U.S.$1.3-billion-a-year) casino industry. Situated beside the Derwent River, 3 kilometers (almost 2 miles) from the city center, the hotel complex looks out across the harbor and the city and up to Mount Wellington. All rooms feature fine Tasmanian oak furniture and plush carpets, and the more expensive rooms have exceptional views. While it may not be as convenient to the city center as the Hotel Grand Chancellor (though it's certainly walkable) the views in particular make it a class above. Adjacent to the casino is the 61-room Wrest Point Motor Inn, which has nice rooms costing between A$120 and $131 (U.S.$78 to $85). Taxis from Wrest Point to the city cost around A$7 (U.S.$4.55), and the bus operates to and from the city every 15 minutes.

410 Sandy Bay Rd., Sandy Bay, TAS 7005. © **03/6225 0112.** Fax 03/6225 3744. www.wrestpoint.com.au. 197 units. A$242–$264 (U.S.$157.30–$171.60) double; A$330 (U.S.$214.50) spa suite. Extra adult A$33 (U.S.$21.45). AE, DC, MC, V. Free parking. **Amenities:** 3 restaurants (Modern Australian, bistro, Asian), cocktail bar, lounge and bar, nightclub, sports bar; harbor boardwalk with indoor and outdoor entertainment; large indoor pool; 9-hole putting course; 2 tennis courts; good health club; children's playground; concierge; business center; 24-hr. room service; massage; babysitting; laundry service; boutique casino. *In room:* A/C, TV with pay movies, dataport, minibar, hair dryer, iron, safe.

EXPENSIVE

The Elms of Hobart   This lovely old National Trust–classified mansion is too far out of the city to walk to, and I think both the Islington and Macquarie Manor are nicer. However, it's just 500 meters (⅓ mile) from a wide range of restaurants situated along the popular North Hobart food strip. Each room has heritage appeal and is nicely furnished with antiques. There is a "grog" room where guests can help themselves to beers and wines on an honor system and a quaint front living room. Two outstanding features are the Tasmanian Oak staircase and paneling. Bedrooms at the front face onto the road and can be noisy. Smoking is not permitted.

52 Elizabeth St., North Hobart, TAS 7000. © **03/6231 3277.** Fax 03/6231 3276. 6 units. A$120–$178 (U.S.$78–$115.70) double. Rates include full breakfast. AE, DC, MC, V. Free off-street parking. The hotel is 2km (1¼ miles) from the city center. Bus: Any up Elizabeth St. from the city. Children over 10 accepted. **Amenities:** Restaurant, lounge. *In room:* TV.

Islington Elegant Private Hotel   This quiet 1845 private home is very popular with American travelers. Rooms are large and simple, each with a queen-size bed and TV. The Grand rooms are slightly roomier. Antiques, cedar woodwork, and elegant furnishings contribute to an air of gentility. French doors open onto a nice garden and a pool. The breakfast room is small and sunny, and the chessboard, piano, and open fire add charm to the front parlor. The last time I visited, the guests had found the place so relaxing they'd all retired for their afternoon snooze. Smoking is not permitted.

321 Davey St., Hobart TAS 7004. © **03/6223 3900.** Fax 03/6224 3167. www.historichouses.com.au. 8 units. A$170 (U.S.$110) standard double; A$180 (U.S.$117) Grand double. Rates include continental breakfast. AE, DC, MC, V. Free parking. The Islington is 1.5km (1 mile) from the city on the way to Mt. Wellington. Take the A6 Highway from the airport to Davey St.; it's important to stay in the right lane and go straight ahead when the road turns left. Bus: 44, 46, 48, or 49 from the city. Children not accepted. Free secure parking. **Amenities:** Outdoor pool. *In room:* TV, coffeemaker.

The Lodge on Elizabeth ⚑   The Lodge on Elizabeth is located in the second-oldest building in Tasmania, with some parts of it dating back to 1810. Originally a gentleman's residence, it later became the first private boy's school in Tasmania. It's well-situated just a 12-minute walk from Salamanca Place and is surrounded by restaurants. All rooms are decorated with antiques, and many are quite romantic, with four-poster beds. Standard rooms have just a shower, whereas the deluxe rooms come with more antiques and a large granite bathroom with a tub. Complimentary drinks are served in the communal living room in the evenings, and a good continental breakfast buffet goes for A$11.50 (U.S.$7.50).

249 Elizabeth St., Hobart, TAS 7000. ℂ **03/6231 3830.** Fax 03/6234 2566. www.thelodge.com.au. 13 units. A$129 (U.S.$74.75) standard double; A$139 (U.S.$90.30) deluxe double (with Jacuzzi). AE, DC, MC, V. **Amenities:** Laundry facilities. *In room:* TV, fridge, coffeemaker.

Macquarie Manor 𝕽𝕽 As soon as you walk into this classically colonial-style manor you'll know you want to stay. Macquarie Manor was built in 1875 as a doctor's surgery and residence. Extra rooms were added in 1950. Thick carpets and double-glazed windows keep the place very quiet, even though the Manor is on the main road. Rooms, which vary enormously, are comfortable and elegantly furnished. One room is suitable for people with disabilities. The staff is very friendly and will be happy to escort you around the premises in search of your favorite room. Check out the delightful dining room, and the drawing room complete with old couches and a grand piano. Parking is just to the left down the side of the main building. Smoking is not permitted.

172 Macquarie St., TAS 7000. ℂ **1800/243 044** in Australia, or 03/6224 4999. Fax 03/6224 4333. www.mac manor.com.au. 18 units (most with shower only). A$160 (U.S.$104) Heritage room; A$190 (U.S.$123.50) Heritage suite; A$210 (U.S.$136.50) Macquarie suite. Extra adult A$33 (U.S.$21.45). Extra child A$16.50 (U.S.$10.70). Rates include full breakfast. AE, DC, MC, V. Free parking. 2 blocks from central bus terminal. **Amenities:** Tour desk. *In room:* TV, minibar, coffeemaker, hair dryer.

Salamanca Inn Conveniently located on the edge of the central business district and toward the waterfront near Battery Point, Salamanca Inn features modern and pleasant apartments. The whole place was refurbished in 2000 and features queen-size beds, leather couches, Tasmanian oak furniture, galley-style kitchens, and spacious living areas. The more expensive suites are a bit plusher.

10 Gladstone St., Hobart, TAS 7000. ℂ **1800/030 944** in Australia, or 03/6223 3300. Fax 03/6223 7167. www.salamancainn.com.au. 68 units. A$198 (U.S.$128.70) 1-bedroom apt; A$220 (U.S.$143) 2-bedroom suite; A$260 (U.S.$169) 2-bedroom deluxe suite. Extra adult A$25 (U.S.$16.25), extra child 3–14 A$15 (U.S.$9.75). Ask about weekend and long-stay packages. AE, DC, MC, V. Free parking. Bus: Sandy Bay Road. **Amenities:** Restaurant, bar; indoor pool; spa; business center; room service; babysitting; laundry/dry cleaning service. *In room:* TV, free in-house movies, dataport, kitchenette, minibar, fridge, coffeemaker, hair dryer, iron.

MODERATE

Black Prince If you're looking for someplace centrally located, clean, and unfussy, then try the Black Prince, an American-influenced pub with a 1950s bent. All rooms come with a shower and a bathtub. Room 8 is the landlord's favorite here, because "it's nearer to the stairs so you don't have to walk too far" (presumably beneficial when you've had a few beers). Downstairs, the American-style bar called Joe's Garage is popular, especially on weekends. The American-influenced restaurant serves up budget-priced steaks and chicken dishes. Lunch is offered Monday through Friday, and dinner Monday through Saturday.

145 Elizabeth St., Hobart, TAS 7000. ℂ **03/6234 3501.** Fax 03/6234 3502. 10 units. A$70 (U.S.$45.50) double, including breakfast. AE, DC, MC, V. **Amenities:** Restaurant, bar. *In room:* TV, coffeemaker.

Wellington Lodge This charming Victorian-style town house (ca. 1885) is just a 10-minute walk (through Hobart's Rose Garden) from the main shopping area and Salamanca Place. It was refurbished in 1997 and is stocked with period antiques. Two rooms share a shower; the other two have their own separate private bathrooms. Complimentary port is served every evening in the guest lounge. Smoking is not permitted.

7 Scott St., Hobart, TAS 7000. ℂ **03/6231 0614.** Fax 03/6234 1551. www.wwt.com.au. 4 units, 2 with bathroom (shower only). A$100–$120 (U.S.$65–$78) double. Extra person A$30 (U.S.$19.50). Rates include full breakfast. MC, V. Free off-street parking. The airport bus will drop you off here, as will any bus to the Aquatic Center. Free parking. Children under 11 not accepted. *In room:* TV, coffeemaker, hair dryer.

Woolmers Inn   Situated 2 kilometers (1¼ miles) south of the city, Woolmers Inn offers cozy one- or two-bedroom units with fully equipped kitchens. One unit is suitable for travelers with disabilities. Sandy Bay is Hobart's main suburb; it's halfway between the casino and the city (within walking distance of Salamanca Place) and features a "golden mile" of boutique shopping. The inn was upgraded throughout 1999.

123–127 Sandy Bay Rd., Hobart, TAS 7000. ℂ **1800/030 780** in Australia, or 03/6223 7355. Fax 03/6223 1981. 36 units. A$121 (U.S.$78.65) 1-bedroom apt; A$148.50 (U.S.$96.50) 2-bedroom apt. Rates 10% higher from mid-Dec to end of Jan, and cheaper in winter. AE, DC, MC, V. Free parking. Bus: Catch the Sandy Bay (no number) bus from Elizabeth Street Mall on Elizabeth St. **Amenities:** Tour desk; coin-op laundry. *In room:* TV/VCR, kitchen, coffeemaker, iron.

INEXPENSIVE

Adelphi Court YHA Hostel   The Adelphi is a typical clean and friendly Australian youth hostel. All dorm rooms sleep four people. There is a communal kitchen, a dining room serving breakfasts, and a barbecue area. It's situated 3 kilometers (less than 2 miles) from the city center.

17 Stoke St., New Town (YHA Tasmania, G.P.O. Box 174, Hobart, TAS 7001). ℂ **03/6228 4829.** Fax 03/6278 2047. www.yha.com.au. 25 units, 2 with bathroom. A$53 (U.S.$34.45) per person twin/double without bathroom; A$63 (U.S.$40.95) double with bathroom; A$20 (U.S.$13) dorm bed. Non-YHA members pay A$3.50 (U.S.$2.30) per person extra. MC, V. Free parking. Bus: 15 or 16 from Argyle St. to stop no. 8A, or any bus from Stop E at Elizabeth Street Mall to bus stop no 13. **Amenities:** Common game and TV room; tour-booking desk; barbecue area; common kitchen.

Central City Backpackers   This place is typical of backpacker-type accommodations—cheap and cheerful, a little frayed around the edges, but right in the heart of things. The central shopping district is right outside the door, and it's only a short walk to the harbor.

138 Collins St., Hobart, TAS 7000. ℂ **1800/811 507** in Australia, or 03/6224 2404. Fax 03/6224 2316. www. centralbackpackers.com.au. 80 units. A$22 (U.S.$14.30) twin per person; A$44 (U.S.$28.60) double; A$18 (U.S.$11.70) dorm bed. Cash or traveler's checks only. 2-min. walk from central bus terminal. **Amenities:** Bar (open in summer); common room with e-mail and Internet access; pool table; kitchen; dining room; laundry facilities.

Customs House Hotel   You won't find a better value than the rooms above this historic sandstone pub overlooking the waterfront. Built in 1846, the property offers simple, colonial-style rooms, without luxuries such as a TV and telephone. Four have water views overlooking the old sailing ship the *May Queen*, which used to carry wood up the Derwent River. Other rooms look across Parliament House. Guests make the best of a shared TV room. Downstairs, a friendly public bar overlooks the water, and at the back of the building is a popular seafood restaurant known for its scallops.

1 Murray St., Hobart, TAS 7000. ℂ **03/6234 6645.** Fax 03/6223 8750. www.customshousehotel.com.au. 13 units, 2 with bathroom. A$75 (U.S.$48.75) double without bathroom; A$80 (U.S.$52) double with bathroom. Rates include continental breakfast. AE, DC, MC, V. **Amenities:** Communal kitchenette with fridge.

WHERE TO DINE

Tasmania is known for its fresh seafood, including oysters, crab, crayfish, salmon, and trout. Once cheap, in recent years prices have crept up to match or even surpass those on the mainland. Generally though, the food is of a good quality—as long as you avoid some of the cheaper fish-and-chip take-out joints on the waterfront (Flippers on Constitution Dock is an exception).

EXPENSIVE

Mures Upper Deck 𝒢 SEAFOOD This large and bustling waterfront restaurant offers great views of bobbing yachts as well as very fine seafood caught on the owner's very own fishing boats. I recommend starting with a bowl of potato soup, or the signature Mures Oysters topped with smoked salmon, sour cream, and salmon caviar. The most popular main courses are the blue-eye fillet Martinique—a Creole-inspired sweet fish curry with coconut cream and banana sauce—or the giant seafood platter for two. The best summer dessert on the menu is the restaurant's famous summer pudding, which almost bursts with berries. In winter, come here if only for the Granny Leatherwood Pudding—made of apples and Australian leatherwood honey and served with cinnamon ice cream. The complex also includes Lower Deck, a very popular self-service family restaurant where you can dine very well for under A$15 (U.S.$9.75).

Between Victoria and Constitution Docks, Hobart. ℂ **03/6231 2121.** Reservations recommended. Main courses A$19.50–$25 (U.S.$12.70–$16.25). AE, DC, MC, V. Daily noon–10pm.

The Point Revolving Restaurant TASMANIAN/AUSTRALIAN This revolving restaurant on the 17th floor of the Wrest Point Hotel Casino is known for its spectacular harbor and mountain views. Criticism of its consistency has led to a complete review of its cuisine over the last couple of years, but fortunately its specialties—prawns flambé in a curry sauce and the Caesar salad—have remained through regular menu upgrades. The crèpes Suzette dessert is also wonderful. The service is friendly and relaxed. This place is packed on weekends.

In the Wrest Point Hotel Casino, 410 Sandy Bay Rd. ℂ **03/6225 0112.** Reservations recommended. Main courses from A$11.50 (U.S.$7.50) at lunch, from $17 (U.S.$11) at dinner. Fixed-price 3-course lunch menu A$25.50 (U.S.$16.60); fixed-price 3-course dinner menu A$43 (U.S.$27.95) Fri–Sat or A$34 (U.S.$22) Sun–Thurs. AE, DC, MC, V. Daily noon–2pm and 6:30–9:30pm.

MODERATE

Drunken Admiral Restaurant 𝒢 SEAFOOD The Drunken Admiral, opposite the Hotel Grand Chancellor on the waterfront, is an extremely popular spot with tourists, and can get quite raucous on very busy evenings. The main attraction is its famous seafood chowder, swimming with anything that was on sale at the docks that morning. The large Yachties seafood grill is a full plate of squid, scallops, fish, mussels, and prawns, but there are plenty of simpler fish dishes on the menu, too. Otherwise splash out on Sperm Whale Sally's Shellfish Platter, or perhaps Captain Nimrod's Depth Charge Platter. The salad bar is spread in a sailing dingy and can be raided as often as you want, but it's rather uninteresting, so you'll probably be content with just one dip.

17–19 Hunter St. ℂ **03/6234 1903.** Reservations required. Main courses A$13.50–$22.90 (U.S.$8.80–$15). AE, DC, MC, V. Daily 6–10:30pm.

Mit Zitrone 𝒢𝒢 MODERN AUSTRALIAN Chef and owner Chris Jackman has earned quite a reputation in Tasmania. His twice-cooked eggs with chili-palm sugar are a huge seller, while the hot smoked blue-eye cod with ginger and wok-fried greens, and the chicken and mushroom sausages with wide noodles, spinach, and anchovy sauce are sensational. The informal restaurant, which is basically an old shop, has bright yellow citrus walls and wooden floors and furniture. You can also drop in for coffee and cake.

333 Elizabeth St., North Hobart. ⓒ **03/6234 8113**. Reservations recommended. Main courses A$15.50–$17 (U.S.$10–$11). AE, DC, MC, V. Mon–Sat 10am–2pm; Tues–Sat 6–10pm.

Sisco's on the Pier SPANISH/MEDITERRANEAN/INTERNATIONAL Sisco's has undergone a transformation from a typical Spanish eatery with roving guitar players to a more upmarket international affair in recent years. Today it's known for its paella, Morton Bay bugs (a kind of small crayfish) with chocolate, garlic prawns with squid-ink spaghetti, and chargrilled octopus. The restaurant is light and bright with a large outdoor balcony.

Upper Level, Murray Street Pier. ⓒ **03/6223 2059**. Reservations recommended. Main courses A$17–$18 (U.S.$11–$11.70). AE, DC, MC V. Mon–Fri noon–3pm; Mon–Sat 6pm–12am.

Vanidol's Asian Cuisine ASIAN Another restaurant very popular with both locals and tourists, Vanidol's serves up a variety of Thai, Indonesian, and Indian dishes. The beef salad with basil, chili, and mint is very good, as are the barbecue prawns served with a sweet tamarind sauce. The fish cooked in a light red curry sauce is another specialty. Smoking is not permitted between 6 and 9pm.

353 Elizabeth St., North Hobart. ⓒ **03/6234 9307**. Reservations recommended. Main courses A$13–$18. AE, MC, V. Tues–Sun 6 to around 11pm.

INEXPENSIVE

Cumquat on Criterion 🍴 *Value* MIXED ASIAN/AUSTRALIAN This cafe is an excellent breakfast venue, offering everything from egg on toast to traditional porridge with brown sugar. On the menu for lunch and dinner you could find Thai beef curry, laksa, a daily risotto, and chermoula-marinated fish. The desserts can be great. Vegetarians and vegans, and those on a gluten-free diet, are very well catered for, as are your average carnivores.

10 Criterion St. ⓒ **03/6234 5858**. Reservations recommended. Main courses A$7.50–$15 (U.S.$4.90–$9.75). No credit cards. Mon–Fri 8am–6pm.

HOBART AFTER DARK

Built in 1837, the 747-seat **Theatre Royal,** 29 Campbell St. (ⓒ **03/6233 2299**), is the oldest remaining live theater in the country. It's known for its excellent acoustics and its classical Victorian decor. Ticket prices vary depending on the performance, but A$25 (U.S.$16.25) is average.

If theater's not your thing, then you may be interested in the **Hobart Historic Pub Tour** (ⓒ **03/6225 4806**), which traces the city's early development through hotel drinking holes—an important part of life in Hobart early last century. The 2-hour tour takes in four pubs; visitors enjoy a drink in each as guides give a lively account of the building's unique place in Hobart's drinking history. Tours depart Sunday through Thursday at 5pm, and cost A$35 (U.S.$242.75), including a drink at each pub.

Opened in 1829 as a tavern and a brothel frequented by whalers, **Knopwood's Retreat,** 39 Salamanca Place (ⓒ **03/6223 5808**) is still a raucous place to be on Friday and Saturday evenings, when crowds cram the historic interior and spill out onto the streets. Light lunches are popular throughout the week, and occasionally you'll find jazz or blues on the menu.

My favorite drinking hole in Hobart is **Irish Murphy's,** 21 Salamanca Place (ⓒ **03/6223 1119**), an atmospheric pub with stone walls and lots of dark wood. Local bands play Friday and Saturday evenings.

If you want to tempt Lady Luck, head to the **Wrest Point Casino,** in the Wrest Point Hotel, 410 Sandy Bay Rd. (ⓒ **03/6225 0112**), Australia's first legal gambling club. Smart, casual attire required (collared shirts for men).

Moments Tasmania by Raft

A good way to experience Tasmania's natural beauty is to take a raft trip with **Rafting Tasmania,** P.O. Box 403, Sandy Bay, Tasmania 7006 (© **03/6239 1080;** fax 03/6239 1090; raftingtas@ozE-mail.com.au).

This company supplies all equipment, including high-quality rubber rafts for four or more people, trained guides, and camping equipment. The Franklin River is the company's specialty, and they have trips lasting 4, 7, and 10 days departing from Hobart. Each trip leaves on specific dates between mid-November and the first week or so of April, so you'll have to make plans in advance, or try potluck when you arrive. The Franklin River offers a real wilderness experience, with gorges, waterfalls, rain forests, pebble beaches, limestone cliffs, and rapids along the way. Trips cost A$950 (U.S.$617) for 4 days, A$1,250 (U.S.$812) for 7 days, and A$1,650 (U.S.$1,075) for 10 days.

An alternative is to take the company's 1-day rafting trip down the Picton River, not too far from Hobart. This trip costs A$115 (U.S.$80.50) and leaves Hobart Sundays year-round, and Tuesdays and Fridays between November and March.

A SIDE TRIP TO MOUNT FIELD NATIONAL PARK
80km (50 miles) NW of Hobart

Mount Field National Park ⚘ is one of the prettiest in Tasmania. It was proclaimed a national park in 1916 to protect a plateau dominated by dolerite-capped mountains and dramatic glaciated valleys. Mount Field West is the highest point at 1,417 meters (4,647 ft.), and in the central and western regions of the park in particular, there are examples of lakes and tarns formed in the ice age of 30,000 years ago. The most mountainous regions support alpine moorlands of cushion plants, pineapple and sword grass, waratahs, and giant pandani. You can get a good look at these changing environments on a 16-kilometer (10-mile) drive from the park entrance to Lake Dobson along an unpaved and often highly rutted road, which is not suitable for conventional vehicles in winter or after heavy rain.

Bennett's and rufous wallabies are common in the park, as are wombats, barred bandicoots, Tasmanian devils, and quolls. Platypuses inhabit the lakes. Birds common to the park include black cockatoos, olive whistlers, green rosellas, honeyeaters, currawongs, wedge-tailed eagles, and lyrebirds, which were introduced from Victoria in the 1930s. Also here are rare native hens, yellow wattlebirds, and dusky robins.

There are many walking trails in the park, including one to Tasmania's most photographed waterfalls, the spectacular 45-meter (147-ft.) **Russell Falls,** near the park's entrance. The walk to the falls along a paved, wheelchair-accessible track takes 15 minutes and passes ferns and forests, with some of Tasmania's tallest trees, mighty swamp gums up to 85 meters (278 ft.) high.

GETTING THERE   Tassielink (© **03/6272 6611,** or 1300 300 520 in Australia; www.tigerline.com.au) offers a daily service from December through March for A$35 (U.S.$22.75) one-way. By car, take the Lyall Highway from Hobart to the Gordon River and follow the signs after the township of Westerway.

WHERE TO STAY

National Park Hotel   Located 300 meters (984 ft.) inside the park, this typical one-story Aussie hotel has basic rooms, some with a sink. There's a TV in the lounge bar. The hotel can book horseback-riding expeditions within the park.

2366 Gordon River Road, National Park, TAS 7140. ℂ **03/6288 1103**. 7 units, none with bathroom. A$60 (U.S.$39) double. Rates include full breakfast. MC, V. **Amenities:** Bar, lounge; golf course nearby.

Russell Falls Holiday Cottages   These cottages are right at the entrance to the park in a rural setting with rolling fields. Each is spacious and comfortable, with an attached toilet and shower, as well as a lounge and dining room.

Lake Dobson Rd., National Park, TAS 7140. ℂ **03/6288 1198**. 4 units. A$66 (U.S.$42.90) for 2 people. Extra adult A$13 (U.S.$8.45), extra child under 16 A$8 (U.S.$5.20). MC, V. *In room:* Gas heat, TV, kitchen, fridge.

---

3 Port Arthur: Discovering Tasmania's Convict Heritage ⁂

102km (63 miles) SE of Hobart

Port Arthur, on the Tasman Peninsula, is one of Australia's prettiest harbors and houses the extensive remains of Tasmania's largest penal colony—essentially Australia's version of Devil's Island. It's the state's number-one tourist destination, and you really should plan to spend at least a whole day in this incredibly picturesque, yet haunting, place.

From 1830 to 1877, Port Arthur was one of the harshest institutions of its type anywhere in the world. It was built to house the settlement's most notorious prisoners, often prisoners who had escaped into the bush from lesser institutions. Nearly 13,000 convicts found their way here, and nearly 2,000 died while incarcerated. Port Arthur was, and still is, connected to the rest of Tasmania by a narrow strip of land called Eaglehawk Neck. Guards and rows of dogs kept watch over this narrow path, while the authorities circulated rumors that the waters around the peninsula were shark-infested. Only a few convicts ever managed to escape, and most of those either perished in the bush or were tracked down and hanged. Look out for the blowhole and other coastal formations, including Tasman's Arch, Devil's Kitchen, and the Tessellated Pavement, as you pass through Eaglehawk Neck.

ESSENTIALS

GETTING THERE   Port Arthur is a 1½-hour drive from Hobart via the Lyell and Arthur highways. **Tasmanian Tours & Travel Tigerline** (ℂ **1300/653 633** or 03/6272 6611; www.tigerline.com.au) runs trips from Hobart to the former penal settlement on Tuesdays, Wednesdays (in summer only), Thursdays, Fridays and Sundays. Tours cost A$57 (U.S.$37) for adults and A$35 (U.S.$22.75) for children 4 to 16; free for children under 4. Another option also takes in Bushmills Pioneer Settlement, a pioneer saw mill with old buildings, which features a narrow-gauge steam railway. It's near Port Arthur. This tour costs A$65 (U.S.$42.25) for adults and A$40 (U.S.$26) for children 4 to 16. Tours depart from 199 Collins St. at 9am and return around 5:30pm. Both trips include a guided tour of the Port Arthur site.

    Experience Tasmania (ℂ **03/6234 3336;** fax 03/6234 3166) also runs coach trips from Hobart to Port Arthur every Monday, Wednesday, Friday, and Sunday, leaving the Cruise Company ferry offices on Franklin Wharf at 9:15am and returning around 5pm. Tours cost A$50 (U.S.$32.50), A$60 (U.S.$39) or A$65 (U.S.$42.25) for adults; and A$32 (U.S.$20.80), A$37 (U.S.$24) or A$40 (U.S.$26) for children 5 to 16, depending on the tour. Children under 5 go free. All trips include a guided tour of the prison complex.

Finds **Something Spooky**

The excellent **Ghost Tours of Port Arthur** leave nightly by lantern at 6:30, 8:30, and 9:30pm (only 8:30pm during winter months) and cost A$13 (U.S.$8.45) for adults and A$8 (U.S.$5.20) for children. You can also purchase a Family ticket, costing A$34 (U.S.$22), which includes 2 adults and up to 6 children. Reservations are essential; call © **1800/659 101** in Australia.

EXPLORING THE SITE

The **Port Arthur Historic Site** 👁👁 (© **03/6251 2310;** fax 03/6251 2311), is large and scattered, with some 30 19th-century buildings (most of the main ones were damaged during bushfires in 1877, shortly after the property ceased to be a penal institution). You can tour the remains of the church, guard tower, model prison, and several other buildings. It's best to tour the area with a guide, who can graphically describe what the buildings were originally used for. Don't miss the fascinating museum in the old lunatic asylum, which has a scale model of the prison complex, as well as leg irons and chains.

The site is open daily from 9am to 5pm; admission is A$18 (U.S.$11.70) for adults, A$9 (U.S.$5.85) for children 4 to 7. The admission price includes a walking tour and a boat cruise around the harbor leaving eight times daily in summer. There is also a separate cruise to the **Isle of the Dead** off the coast of Port Arthur twice a day; some 1,769 convicts and 180 free settlers were buried here, mostly in mass graves with no headstones. The cruise costs an extra A$5 (U.S.$3.25) per person.

A new visitor center opened here in January 1999. The main feature is a fabulous **Interpretive Gallery,** which takes visitors through the process of sentencing in England to transportation to Van Dieman's Land. The gallery contains a courtroom, a section of a transport ship's hull, a blacksmith's shop, a lunatic asylum, and much more. Allow between 3 and 4 hours to explore the site and the gallery.

EN ROUTE TO PORT ARTHUR

On the way to Port Arthur you might want to stop off at the historic village of Richmond and at the Tasmanian Devil Park Wildlife Rescue Centre.

Richmond is just 26 kilometers (16 miles) northeast of Hobart and is the site of the country's oldest bridge (1823), the best preserved convict jail in Australia (1825), and several old churches, including St John's Church (1836)—the oldest Catholic church in the country. Richmond also has plenty of tearooms, craft shops, galleries, and antique stores.

Eighty kilometers (50 miles) from Hobart is the **Tasmanian Devil Park Wildlife Rescue Centre,** Port Arthur Highway, Taranna (© **03/6250 3230;** fax 03/6230 3406), which houses orphaned or injured native animals, including Tasmanian devils, quolls, kangaroos, eagles, and owls. The park is open daily from 9am to 5pm. Admission is A$12 (U.S.$7.80) for adults, A$6 (U.S.$3.90) for children, and A$30 (U.S.$19.50) for a family. Tasmanian devils are fed daily at 10, 11am, and 5pm. The adjoining World Tiger Snake Centre, a unique medical research project, contains some 1,500 highly venomous snakes.

WHERE TO STAY & DINE

Port Arthur Motor Inn   If you decide to stop over rather than drive all the way back to Hobart (remember marsupials get killed all the time on the roads at night—and they can do a lot of damage to a rental car), then this is a good choice. The rooms are attractive and overlook the historic site. Port Arthur ghost tour packages are available from here.

Port Arthur Historic Site, Arthur Hwy., Port Arthur, TAS 7182. © **1800/030 747** in Australia, or 03/6250 2101. Fax 03/6250 2417. portarthur@fc-hotels.com.au. 35 units. A$110 (U.S.$71.50) double. Extra person A$15 (U.S.$9.75). Children 11 and under stay free in parents' room. AE, DC, MC, V. Free parking. Bus: Hobart Coaches run from Hobart on weekdays. **Amenities:** Restaurant; kids's playground; coin-op laundry. *In room:* TV, coffeemaker, iron.

4 Freycinet National Park ★★

206km (129miles) NE of Hobart; 214km (134 miles) SW of Launceston

If you only have time to visit one place in Tasmania, make sure it's **Freycinet National Park.** The Freycinet Peninsula hangs down off the eastern coast of Tasmania. It's a place of craggy pink granite peaks, spectacular white beaches, wetlands, heathlands, coastal dunes, and dry eucalyptus forests. This is the place to come to spot sea eagles, wallabies, seals, pods of dolphins, and humpback and southern right whales during their migration to and from the warmer waters of northern New South Wales from May through August. The township of **Coles Bay** is the main staging post, and there are many **bush walks** in the area. The **Moulting Lagoon Game Reserve**—an important breeding ground for black swans and wild ducks—is signposted along the highway into Coles Bay from Bicheno. Some 10,000 black swans inhabit the lake, so it's very rare not to see them. Six kilometers (5.38 miles) outside town and inside the national park is the **Cape Tourville Lighthouse,** from where there are extensive views north and south along the coast and across several of the small islands in the Tasman Ocean.

The spectacular **Wineglass Bay** ★★, named as one of the world's top 10 beaches by *Outside* magazine, is a lovely spot for a walk.

ESSENTIALS

GETTING THERE   **Tasmanian Redline Coaches** (© **03/6336 1446**) runs between Hobart (199 Collins St.) and Bicheno, leaving Hobart at 10am on Monday and Wednesday, 12:30pm on Tuesday and Thursday, 2pm on Friday, and 10:30am on Sunday. The trip takes about 4½ hours. From Launceston (112 George St.) buses leave at 2pm Monday through Thursday, at 3:45pm on Friday, and 11am on Sunday, and take less than 3 hours. From Bicheno catch a local bus run by **Bicheno Coach Services** (© **03/6257 0293,** or mobile 0419 570 293). Buses leave at 9am and 3pm every day (except Sat, when there's no 3pm service). Buses also meet every coach from Hobart or Launceston, but you need to book in advance. **Tassielink** (© **03/6272 6611,** or 1300 300 520 in Australia; www.tigerline.com.au) runs buses from Launceston to Bicheno on Monday, Wednesday, Friday, and Sunday leaving at 8:30am. **Tasmanian Tours & Travel Tigerline** (© **1300/653 633** or 03/6272 6611; www.tigerline.com.au) offers a day trip to Freycinet with an optional walking trip to Wineglass Bay (see below) from both Hobart and Launceston, in summer only, on Friday and Sunday. It costs A$48 (U.S.$31) for adults and A$32 (U.S.$20.80) for children.

From Hobart it's about a 3-hour drive to the park.

VISITOR INFORMATION   The **Visitor Information Centre** (© **03/6375 1333;** fax 03/6375 1533) on the Tasman Highway at Bicheno can arrange tour bookings. Otherwise, the **Tasmanian Travel and Information Centre** in Hobart (© **03/6230 8383**) can supply you with maps and details. Daily entry to the park costs A$9 (U.S.$5.85) per vehicle.

EXPLORING THE PARK

If you only have time to do one walk, then head out from Freycinet Lodge on the 30-minute uphill hike past spectacularly beautiful pink granite outcrops to **Wineglass Bay Lookout** for breathtaking views. You can then head down to Wineglass Bay itself and back up again. The walk takes around 2½ hours. A longer walk takes you along the length of **Hazards Beach,** where you'll find plenty of shell middens—seashell refuge heaps—left behind by the Aborigines who once lived here. This walk takes 6 hours.

Tasmanian Expeditions (ⓒ **1800/030 230** in Australia, or 03/6334 3477; fax: 03/6334 3463; www.tas-ex.com) offers a 3-day trip from Launceston and back that includes 2 nights in cabins at Coles Bay. The trip includes guided walks to Wineglass Bay and Mt. Amor. The company also offers 6- and 12-night walking, rafting, and cycling trips.

Not to be missed is a trip aboard Freycinet Sea Charter's vessel *Kahala* (ⓒ **03/6257 0355;** fax 03/6375 1461), which offers whale-watching between June and September, bay and game fishing, dolphin watching, diving, scenic and marine wildlife cruises, and sunset cruises. Half-day cruises cost A$60 (U.S.$39) per person with a minimum of four adults onboard. Full day cruises cost A$100 (U.S.$65) per person.

WHERE TO STAY & DINE

Camping is available in the park itself for A$10 (U.S.$6.50) a tent, though water is scarce. For inquiries, call the **Parks and Wildlife Service** (ⓒ **03/6257 0107**).

Freycinet Lodge 𝒢𝒢   I can't praise the eco-friendly lodge enough. Comfortable one- and two-room cabins are spread unobtrusively through the bush and connected by raised walking tracks. Each has a balcony, and the more expensive ones have a huge spa tub (the deluxe cabins are newly furnished, and some have water views). Twenty cabins have their own kitchen. The main part of the lodge houses a lounge room and a truly excellent restaurant that sweeps out onto a veranda overlooking the limpid green waters of Great Oyster Bay. The lodge is right next to the white sands of Hazards Beach, and from here it's an easy stroll to the start of the Wineglass Bay walk.

Freycinet National Park, Coles Bay 7215. ⓒ **03/6257 0101.** Fax 03/6257 0278. www.frecinetlodge.com.au. 60 units. A$190 (U.S.$123.50) standard cabin; A$222 (U.S.$144) spa cabin; $255 (U.S.$165.75) deluxe spa cabin. AE, DC, MC, V. **Amenities:** 2 restaurants; bar; golf course nearby; tennis court; bike rental; activities desk; e-mail kiosk; coin-op laundry; nonsmoking rooms. *In room:* Fridge, hair dryer.

HOBART TO LAUNCESTON: THE "HERITAGE HIGHWAY"

By the 1820s several garrison towns had been built between Launceston and Hobart, and by the middle of the 19th century convict labor had produced what was considered to be the finest highway of its time in Australia. Today, many of the towns along the route harbor magnificent examples of Georgian and Victorian architecture. It takes about 2 hours to drive between Launceston and Hobart on the "Heritage Highway'" (officially known as the A1, or the Midland Highway) but you really need 2 days to fully explore.

ROSS 𝒢
121km (75 miles) N of Hobart; 78km (48 miles) S of Launceston

One of Tasmania's best preserved historic villages, picturesque Ross was established as a garrison town in 1812 on a strategically important crossing point on the Macquarie River. **Ross Bridge,** the third oldest in Australia, was built in

1836 to replace an earlier one made of logs. The bridge is decorated with Celtic symbols, animals, and faces of notable people of the time. It is lit up at night, and there are good views of it from a dirt track that runs along the river's north bank.

The town's **main crossroads** is edged by four historic buildings, humorously known as "temptation" (represented by the Man-o'-Ross Hotel), "salvation" (the Catholic church), "recreation" (the town hall) and "damnation" (the old jail). The **Ross Female Factory,** built in the early 1840s, consists of ruins, a few interpretive signs, and a model of the original site and buildings inside the original Overseer's Cottage. Entry is free. Women convicts were imprisoned here from 1847 to 1854.

At the **Tasmanian Wool Centre** and tourist information center on Church Street (② **03/6381 5466**), there is an exhibition detailing the growth of the region and the wool industry since settlement. It's open daily from 9am to 5pm (until 6pm Jan–Mar), and entry costs A$4 (U.S.$2.60) for adults, A$2 (U.S.$1.30) for children, and A$10 (U.S.$6.50) for a family.

WHERE TO STAY & DINE

Colonial Cottages of Ross 𝒢   To feel the part, why not stay in one of these delightful historic cottages. Apple Dumpling Cottage (ca. 1880) is a two-bedroom wooden cottage, sleeping four, with impressive sandstone fireplaces set on the edge of the village in a rural setting. The spacious Church Mouse Cottage (ca. 1840), set in an old Sunday School, sleeps just two. Captain Samuel's Cottage (ca. 1830), accommodates six people in three bedrooms, with two double and two single beds. Finally, Hudson Cottage (ca. 1850) sleeps four. All cottages have modern bathroom and kitchen facilities.

12 Church St., Ross, Tasmania 7209. ② 03/6381 5354. Fax 03/6381 5408. tim@tasmania.com. 4 units. A$110–$130 (U.S.$77.50–$84.50) for 2 (depending on cottage and season). A$20–$30 (U.S.$13–$19.50) extra person. MC, V. In room: TV.

The Ross Village Bakery and Inn   This old coaching inn, built in 1832, offers four homely rooms done out old English style. One room has a double bed, another a double and two singles, and a third a double which opens up onto a fourth with two singles (suitable as a family room). A separate lounge room has a TV and free tea, coffee, sherry, and cakes. The bakery on the premises is an excellent place for lunch, serving up things like filled baked potatoes and some of the best pies in Australia, baked in a wood-fired oven dating from 1860.

15 Church St., Ross, Tasmania 7209. ② 03/6381 5246. Fax 03/6381 5360. 4 units. rossbakery@vision.net.au. A$110 (U.S.$71.50). AE, MC, V. In room: Hair dryer.

5 Launceston 𝒢

198km (123 miles) N of Hobart

Tasmania's second largest city is Australia's third oldest after Sydney and Hobart. Situated at the head of the Tamar River, 50 kilometers (31 miles) inland from the state's north coast, and surrounded by delightful undulating farmland, **Launceston** is a pleasant city crammed with elegant Victorian and Georgian architecture and plenty of remnants from convict days. Unfortunately, short-sighted local and state governments are gradually overseeing the chipping away of its great architectural heritage in favor of the usual parking garages and ugly concrete monoliths. However, Launceston (pop. 104,000) is still one of Australia's most beautiful cities and has plenty of delightful parks and churches. It's also well placed as the gateway to the wineries of the Tamar Valley, the highlands and alpine lakes of the north, and the stunning beaches to the east.

ESSENTIALS

GETTING THERE   Qantas (© 13 13 13 in Australia) flies to Launceston from Melbourne and Sydney.

Tasmanian Redline Coaches depart Hobart for Launceston several times daily (trip time: around 2 hr., 40 min.). The one-way fare is A$19 (U.S.$12.35). Launceston is 1½ hours from Devonport if you plan to take the **Spirit of Tasmania ferry** from Melbourne across Bass Strait to Devonport. The bus ride from Devonport to Launceston costs around A$13 (U.S.$8.45).

The drive from Hobart to Launceston takes just over 2 hours on Highway 1.

VISITOR INFORMATION   The **Gateway Tasmania Travel Centre** on the corner of St. John and Paterson streets (© 03/6336 3133; fax 03/6336 3118; gateway.tas@microtech.com.au) is open Monday through Friday from 9am to 5pm, Saturday from 9am to 3pm, and Sunday and holidays from 9am to noon.

CITY LAYOUT   The main pedestrian shopping mall, Brisbane Street, along with St. John and Charles streets on either side, forms the heart of the central area. The Victorian-Italianate Town Hall is 2 blocks north on Civic Square, and opposite the red brick Post Office building dating from 1889. The Tamar River slips quietly past the city's northern edge and is crossed at two points by Charles Bridge and Tamar Street. City Park, to the northeast of the central business district, is a nice place for a stroll.

EXPLORING THE CITY & ENVIRONS

Launceston is easily explored by foot. A must for any visitor is a stroll with **Launceston Historic Walks** ❅ (© 03/6331 3679; harris.m@bigpond.com), which leave from the Gateway Tasmania Travel Centre Monday through Friday at 9:45am (weekend walks can also be arranged). The hour-long walk gives a fascinating insight into Launceston's history and costs A$10 (U.S.$6.50). **City Sights** (© 03/6336 3122), on the corner of St. John and Paterson streets, runs city tours daily by replica tram. Tours cost A$23 (U.S.$14.95) for adults and A$16 (U.S.$10.40) for children under 16. Otherwise, **Tasmanian Tours & Travel Tigerline** (© 1300/653 633 or 03/6272 6611) operates a half-day coach tour of the city on Mondays, Wednesdays, and Fridays from 9:30am.

A must see is **Cataract Gorge** ❅, the result of violent earthquakes that rattled Tasmania some 40 million years ago. It's a wonderfully scenic area just 10 minutes from Launceston. The South Esk River flows through the gorge and collects in a small lake traversed by a striking yellow suspension bridge and the longest single span chair lift in the world. The chair lift (© 03/6331 5915) is open daily from 9am to 4:30pm (except June 23–Aug 11, when it operates on Sat and Sun only), and costs A$5 (U.S.$3.25) for adults and A$3 (U.S.$1.95) for children under 16. Outdoor concerts are sometimes held on the lake bank. The hike to the Duck Reach Power Station takes about 45 minutes. Take good footwear and a raincoat. Other walks in the area are shorter and easier. The **Gorge Restaurant** (© 03/6331 3330) and the kiosk next door serve meals with glorious views from the outdoor tables.

Tamar River Cruises (© 03/6334 9900) offers lunch, afternoon, and evening buffet dinner cruises up the Tamar River from Home Point Wharf in Launceston.

Mountain biking is popular in this area. Contact **Tasmanian Expeditions** (© 1800/030 230 in Australia, or 03/6334 3477) for information on its 4- to 7-day trips along the east coast in summer. You can rent bicycles from the youth hostel at 36 Thistle St. (© 03/6344 9779) for A$11 (U.S.$7.15) per day for a touring bike or A$18 (U.S.$11.70) per day for a mountain bike. (Also hire bushwalking equipment, including boots, tents, sleeping bags, and stoves.)

The **Trevallyn State Recreation Area,** on the outskirts of Launceston off Reatta Road, is a man-made lake surrounded by a beautiful wildlife reserve with several walking tracks. There are barbecue facilities, picnic areas and a beach.

OTHER ATTRACTIONS

Aquarius Roman Baths   Adorned with gold, Italian marble, and works of art, this remarkable Romanesque structure is worth visiting just for the architectural experience. Indulge in warm, hot, and cold water baths; visit the steam room; or get a massage or a beauty makeover.

127 George St. ℂ 03/6331 2255. Admission to baths and hot rooms A$20 (U.S.$13) for 1, A$30 (U.S.$19.50) for 2. Treatments extra. Mon–Fri 8:30am–10pm, Sat–Sun 9am–6pm.

The Old Umbrella Shop   Built in the 1860s, this unique shop is the last genuine period store in Tasmania and has been operated by the same family since the turn of the 20th century. Umbrellas spanning the last 100 years are on display, while modern "brollies" and souvenirs are for sale. Allow 15 minutes.

60 George St. ℂ 03/6331 9248. Free admission. Mon–Fri 9am–5pm, Sat 9am–noon.

The Penny Royal World & Gunpowder Mill   This amusement park, with its sailboat, barges and trams, and historic gunpowder mills, is large enough to occupy an entire day. Admission also includes a tram ride and a trip up Cataract Gorge and the Tamar River on the paddle steamer MV *Lady Stelfox.*

Off Bridge Rd. ℂ 03/6331 6699. Admission A$19.50 (U.S.$12.70) adults, A$9.50 (U.S.$6.20) children. Family of 2 adults and up to 6 children A$49.50 (U.S.$32.20). Daily 9am–4:30pm. Closed Christmas.

The Queen Victoria Museum & Art Gallery   Opened in honor of Queen Victoria's Golden Jubilee in 1891, this museum houses a large collection of stuffed wildlife, including the extinct Tasmanian tiger, or thylacine. There are also temporary exhibits and historical items on display. Allow an hour.

Corner of Wellington and Paterson sts. ℂ 03/6323 3777. Free admission. Mon–Sat 10am–5pm, Sun 2–5pm.

Waverley Woollen Mills   Established in 1874 on a site 5 kilometers (3 miles) northeast of town, this business still uses a waterwheel to turn the looms that help make woollen blankets and rugs. Tours show how the process works. Everything from woolen hats to ties is sold on the premises. Allow an hour.

Waverley Rd. ℂ 03/6339 1106. Tours A$4 (U.S.$2.60) adults, A$2 (U.S.$1.30) children, A$12 (U.S.$7.80) families. Tours daily 9am–4pm (there's usually a 20-min. wait).

York Town Square Market   If you're in Launceston on a Sunday, try to visit the York Town Square Market. This marketplace specializes in craft items, many turned from local wood. It's a pleasant place to spend a sunny Sunday afternoon.

The rear of the Launceston International Hotel. No phone. Sunday 9am–5pm.

WHERE TO STAY
EXPENSIVE

Alice's Place & Ivy Cottage ✹✹✹   I highly recommend these two delightful cottages. Alice's Place, which sleeps two, was made entirely from bits and pieces of razed historic buildings. Ivy Cottage, on the other hand, is a restored Georgian house (ca. 1831). Both places are furnished with antiques and fascinating period bric-a-brac. Kitchens are fully equipped, and both units have large spa baths. Guests come and go as they please and stay here on their own (check in at the reception at 129 Balfour St.). Both cottages share the same garden. Also available for rent are five other cottages in a colonial Australian theme (some sleeping four), called **Alice's Hideaways;** and four cute cottages collectively known as **The Shambles.** A recent addition is **Aphrodites Delux Spa,** a very large and regal setup with a formal dining room.

129 Balfour St., TAS 7250. © **03/6334 2231.** Fax 03/6334 2696. 11 units. Alice's Place A$192 (U.S.$124.80), cottage for 1 or 2 people; Ivy Cottage A$192 (U.S.$124.80), cottage for 1 or 2 people. Shambles cottages A$157 (U.S.$102); Aphrodites $220 (U.S.$143) (2-night minimum stay). A$55 (U.S.$35.75) extra person. Rates include breakfast ingredients left in your fridge. AE, DC, MC, V. Free parking. *In room:* A/C, TV, kitchen, laundry facilities.

Launceston International ★★   This former Novotel hotel was about to undergo major refurbishment as this edition was being researched, so expect good things. In its previous guise it had some of the most comfortable and homey rooms of any major hotel in Australia, and that's not about to change, apparently. Standard rooms have two double beds or a king-size bed. The tavern, just off the lobby, is a popular watering hole. Smoking is not permitted.

29 Cameron St., Launceston, TAS 7250. © **03/6334 3434.** Fax 03/6331 7347. res.launceston@dogherty hotels.com.au. 162 units. A$205 (U.S.$133.25) double; A$230 (U.S.$149) spa room; A$290–$500 (U.S.$188.50–$325) suites. Children stay free in parents' room. Ask about packages. AE, DC, MC, V. Free parking. **Amenities:** Restaurant (deli/grill), bar; concierge; business center; salon; 24-hr. room service; babysitting; laundry service and self-service laundry. *In room:* A/C, TV, minibar, coffeemaker, iron.

York Mansions ★★★   If you feel that where you stay is as important to your visit as what you see, then you must stay here. Within the walls of the National Trust–classified York Mansions, built in 1840, are five very spacious apartments, each with a distinctly individual character. The Duke of York apartment is fashioned after a gentleman's drawing room, complete with rich leather sofa, antiques, and an extensive collection of historic books. The two-bedroom, light and airy Duchess of York unit has hand-painted silk panels and a spa tub. Each apartment is self-contained and has its own separate kitchen, dining room, living room, bedrooms, bathroom, and laundry. A CD player and large-screen TV add modern touches. The ingredients for a hearty breakfast can be found in the refrigerator. There's also a delightful cottage garden.

9–11 York St., Launceston, TAS 7250. © **03/6334 2933.** Fax 03/6334 2870. www.yorkmansions.com.au. 5 units. A$186–$216 (U.S.$121–$140) depending on apt. A$55 (U.S.$35.75) extra person. Rates include breakfast provisions supplied to your kitchen. AE, DC, MC, V. Free parking. **Amenities:** Laundry service. *In room:* TV/VCR, dataport, kitchen, minibar, coffeemaker, hair dryer, iron.

MODERATE
Innkeepers Colonial Motor Inn   Those who desire tried-and-true motel lodging will feel right at home at the Colonial, a place that combines old-world ambience with modern facilities. The rooms are quite large and have attractive furnishings. The Old Grammar School that stands next door has been incorporated into the complex, with the Quill and Cane Restaurant operating in what once was a schoolroom, and Three Steps On George, Launceston's liveliest nightspot, making use of the former boys' gym. Rooms are fairly standard and attract a large corporate clientele.

31 Elizabeth St., Launceston, TAS 7250. © **03/6331 6588.** Fax 03/6334 2765. 63 units. A$120 (U.S.$78) double; A$195 (U.S.$126.75) suite. Extra person A$15 (U.S.$9.75). Lower weekend rates. Children under 3 stay free in parents' room. AE, DC, MC, V. Free parking. **Amenities:** Restaurant, lounge; tour desk; laundry facilities. *In room:* A/C, TV, minibar, coffeemaker, hair dryer; iron.

Waratah on York ★★   The Waratah on York is a carefully renovated Victorian mansion, originally built in 1862 for Alexander Webster, an ironmonger by trade and mayor of Launceston in the 1860s and '70s. The current owners have spent considerable time and energy restoring the property to its former glory. Some of the original features—pressed brass ceiling roses and a staircase with a cast-iron balustrade—remain, while others have been faithfully re-created. Of the nine rooms, six come with a spa tub, one with a private balcony, and another with a private sunroom. All have high ceilings and ornate (but non-functional) fireplaces. The executive rooms have four-poster beds and sweeping views down upon the Tamar River.

12 York St., Launceston, TAS 7250. © **03/6331 2081.** Fax 03/6331 9200. waratahonyork@bigpond.com. 9 units. A$148 (U.S.$96.20) standard double; A$168 (U.S.$109) spa room; A$198 (U.S.$130) executive spa suite. Rates include continental breakfast. AE, DC, MC, V. Free off-street parking. **Amenities:** Bar, lounge with fireplace; laundry. *In room:* TV, coffeemaker, hair dryer.

INEXPENSIVE

Hillview House   The rooms at this restored farmhouse are nothing fancy, but are quite comfortable. They come with a double bed and a shower. The family room has an extra single bed; it's the nicest room and has the best views. The hotel overlooks the city, and the large veranda and colonial dining room both have extensive views over the city and the Tamar River.

193 George St., Launceston, TAS 7250. © **03/6331 7388.** Fax 03/6331 7388. 9 units. A$90 (U.S.$58.50) double; A$105 (U.S.$68.25) family room for 3. Rates include full breakfast. MC, V. **Amenities:** Laundry facilities. *In room:* TV.

Hotel Tasmania   Situated right in the heart of town, this budget hotel offers simple rooms with modern furnishings and attached showers. All the rooms were renovated in 1998, which helped win the hotel the Australian Hoteliers Association's award for the best budget pub-style accommodation in Tasmania. Downstairs there's a saloon-style bar with a cowboy theme.

191 Charles St., Launceston, TAS 7250. © **03/6331 7355.** Fax 03/6331 5589. www.saloon.com.au. 18 units. A$64 (U.S.$41.60) double. Rates include continental breakfast. Extra person A$19 (U.S.$12.35). AE, MC, V. Free on-street parking. **Amenities:** Restaurant, bar. *In room:* TV, fridge, coffeemaker.

Lloyd's Hotel   This older-style property offers comfortable lodging at a modest budget. It's centrally located, and the owners are friendly, interesting, and have traveled extensively, mainly through the United States. It was getting a bit grubby, so the refurbishment in 2001 was welcome.

23 George St., Launceston, TAS 7250. © **03/6331 4966.** Fax 03/6331 5589. 18 units (some with shower only). A$54 (U.S.$35) double. Rates include full breakfast. Extra person A$20 (U.S.$13). AE, MC, V. Free parking. **Amenities:** Coin-op laundry; nonsmoking rooms. *In room:* TV, fridge, coffeemaker.

WHERE TO DINE

You'll find most places to eat in Launceston don't have a fixed closing time; rather they close up shop when the last customer has been served and has eaten.

EXPENSIVE

Fee & Me Restaurant ✿✿ MODERN AUSTRALIAN   What is perhaps Launceston's best restaurant is found in a grand old mansion. The menu is structured so that diners choose a selection from five categories, each one moving from light to rich. An extensive wine list has been designed to complement selections for each course. A five-course meal could go something like this: Tasmanian smoked salmon with salad, capers, and a soft poached egg; followed by chili oysters with a coconut sauce and vermicelli noodles; then ricotta and goat cheese gnocchi with creamed tomato and red capsicum; followed by Asian-style duck on bok choy with a citrus sauce; topped off with a coffee and chicory soufflé. The dishes change frequently, so you never know what you might find.

Corner of Charles and Frederick sts. ℂ **03/6331 3195.** Reservations recommended. A$42 (U.S.$27.30) for 3 courses, A$48 (U.S.$31.20) for 4 courses, A$50 (U.S.$32.50) for 5 courses. AE, DC, MC, V. Mon–Sat 7–10:30pm.

MODERATE

O'Keefe's Hotel ASIAN/TASMANIAN   This pub-based eatery earns high praise for its variety of well-prepared dishes. You can choose between such delicacies as Thai curry and laksa, seafood dishes such as scallops, prawns, and sushi, and plenty of pastas and grills. There's also a range of good salads.

124 George St. ℂ **03/6331 4015.** Reservations recommended. Main courses A$10.50–$14.50 (U.S.$6.80–$9.40). AE, MC, V. Daily 11:30am–2pm and 5:30–11pm.

Shrimps 🛠 SEAFOOD   Shrimps offers the best selection of seafood in Launceston. Built in 1824 by convict labor, it has a classic Georgian exterior. Tables are small and well spaced, and the best meals are off the blackboard menu, which generally includes at least eight fish dishes. Usually available are wonderful Tasmanian mussels, whitebait, Thai-style fishcakes, and freshly split oysters. Everything is very fresh and seasonal.

72 George St. (at the corner of Paterson St.). ℂ **03/6334 0584.** Reservations recommended. Main courses A$14–A$19 (U.S.$9.10–$12.35). AE, DC, MC, V. Mon–Sat noon–2pm and 6:30–10pm.

Star Bar Cafe 🛠 MEDITERRANEAN   Many consider this Tasmania's best bistro. It offers a range of dishes, such as mee goreng, beetroot, and quail risotto; grilled octopus, steaks, and chicken livers; as well as popular pizzas and breads cooked in the large wood-fired oven. In winter, guests congregate around a large open fire.

113 Charles St. ℂ **03/6331 9659.** Reservations recommended. Main courses A$10.50–$17.50 (U.S.$6.80–$11.40). AE, MC, V. Mon–Wed 11am–11pm, Thurs–Sat 11am–midnight, Sunday noon–10pm.

INEXPENSIVE

Konditorei Cafe Manfred PATISSERIE   This German patisserie has recently moved to larger premises to keep up with demand for its sensational cakes and breads. It's also added an a la carte restaurant serving up the likes of pastas and steaks. Light meals include croissants, salads, and cakes. You can eat in or outside.

106 George St. ℂ **03/6334 2490.** Reservations not accepted. Light meals A$4–$5 (U.S.$2.60–$3.25); main courses A$9–$18 (U.S.$5.85–$11.70). AE, DC, MC, V. Mon–Thurs 9am–5:30pm, Fri 9am–late, Sat 10am–10:30pm.

A CAFE

Croplines Coffee Bar 🛠 *Finds*   If you crave good coffee, bypass every other place in Launceston and head here. It's a bit hard to find, and you may have to ask for directions, but basically it's behind the old Brisbane Arcade. The owners are dedicated to coffee, grinding their beans on the premises daily. If coffee's not your cup of tea, then try the hot chocolate—it's the best I've tasted.

Brisbane Court, off Brisbane St. ℂ **03/6331 4023.** Coffees and teas A$1.60–$2.40 (U.S.$1–$1.60). Cakes under A$2 (U.S.$1.30). AE, MC, V. Daily 8am–5:30pm.

6 Cradle Mountain & Lake St. Clair National Park 🗷🗷

85km (53 miles) S of Devonport; 175km (107 miles) NW of Hobart

The national park and World Heritage area that encompasses both Cradle Mountain and Lake St. Clair is one of the most spectacular regions in Australia and, after Hobart and Port Arthur, the most visited place in Tasmania. The 1,545-meter (5,199-ft.) mountain dominates the north part of the island, and the long, deep lake is to its south. Between them lie more steep slopes, button grass plains, majestic alpine forests, dozens of lakes filled with trout, and several rivers. **Mount Ossa,** in the center of the park, is Tasmania's highest point at 1,617 meters (5,336 ft.). The **Overland Track** (see below), links Cradle Mountain with Lake St. Clair and is the best known of Australia's walking trails. Another option in the area is a visit to the **Walls of Jerusalem National Park,** a high alpine area with spectacular granite walls, small lakes, and old-growth forest.

ESSENTIALS

GETTING THERE   Tassielink (© **03/6272 6611,** or 1300 300 520 in Australia; www.tigerline.com.au) runs buses to Cradle Mountain from Hobart, Launceston, Devonport, and Strahan. Round-trip Tassielink coach transfers from Launceston cost A$69 (U.S.$44.80) and leave daily in the summer at 8:30am. A special Overland Track service (also provided by Tassielink) drops off passengers at the beginning of the walk and picks them up at the end and costs A$69 (U.S.$44.80) round-trip, departing from Hobart. All coaches have commentary on board.

Maxwells Cradle Mountain–Lake St. Clair Charter Bus and Taxi Service (© and fax **03/6492 1431**) runs buses from Devonport and Launceston to Cradle Mountain from A$35 (U.S.$22.75), depending on how many people are onboard. The buses also travel to other areas nearby, such as the Walls of Jerusalem, as well as Lake St. Clair. Buses also run from the Cradle Mountain campground to the start of the Overland Track.

Motorists enter the park via the Lyall Highway from Hobart, via Deloraine or Poatina from Launceston, and via Sheffield or Wilmot from Devonport. Both Cradle Mountain and Lake St. Clair are well signposted.

VISITOR INFORMATION   The park headquarters, **Cradle Mountain Visitor Centre** (© **03/6492 1133;** fax 03/64 921120; www.parks.tas.gov.au), on the northern edge of the national park just outside Cradle Mountain Lodge, offers the best information on local walks and treks. It's open from 8am to 5pm (6pm in summer) daily.

EXPLORING THE PARK

Cradle Mountain Lodge (see "Where to Stay & Dine," below) runs a daily program of guided walks, abseiling (rappelling), rock-climbing, and trout-fishing excursions for lodge guests. There are also plenty of trails in the area that can be attempted by people equipped with directions from the staff at the park headquarters (see "Visitor Information," above). Be warned, though, that the weather changes quickly in the high country; so go prepared with wet-weather gear and always tell someone where you are headed. Of the shorter walks, the stroll to Pencil Pines and the 5-kilometer (3-mile) walk to Dove Lake are the most pleasant. Between June and October it's sometimes possible to cross-country ski in the park.

WHERE TO STAY & DINE

Cradle Mountain Lodge ★★   If you like luxury with your rain forests, then this award-winning lodge is the place for you. Cradle Mountain Lodge is simply marvelous. Just minutes from your bed are the giant buttresses of 1,500-year-old trees, moss forests, craggy mountain ridges, limpid pools and lakes, and hoards of scampering marsupials. The cabins are comfortable, the food excellent, the staff friendly, and the big open fireplaces well worth cuddling up in front of for a couple of days. Each modern wood cabin has a pot-bellied stove

Finds Hiking the Overland Track

The most well-known hiking trail in Australia is the **Overland Track** 🌟🌟, an 85-kilometer (53-mile) route between Cradle Mountain and Lake St. Clair. The trek takes between 5 to 10 days and goes through high alpine plateaus, buttongrass plains, heathland, and dense rain forests and passes glacial lakes, ice-carved crags, and waterfalls. The trek gives you a good look at the wild beauty of Tasmania's pristine wilderness, and although the first day is quite tough walking, you soon get into the rhythm. After climbing to Pelion Gap, the track gradually descends southwards toward the towering myrtle forests on the shores of Lake St Clair. There are many rewarding side trips, including the 1-day ascent of Mt. Ossa (1,617m/5,305 ft.), Tasmania's highest peak.

Several companies offer guided walks of the Overland Track from October through April, although simple public huts, on a first-come, first-served basis, and camping areas are available for those who wish to do it solo. Every summer up to 200 people a day start the trek. Most trekking companies employ at least two guides who carry tents and cooking gear, while you carry your sleeping bag, lunch, and personal belongings. Wet-weather gear is essential as heavy downpours can be frequent, and make sure your boots are well worn in to avoid blisters.

Tasmanian Expeditions (© 1800/030 230 in Australia, or 03/6334 3477; fax 03/6334 3463) offers great 3-day walking tours around Cradle Mountain, staying at Waldheim Cabins. The tours depart from Launceston and cost A$430 (U.S.$279), all-inclusive. Trips leave every Sunday and Wednesday between November and April, with extra trips from Christmas to the end of January. The company also offers a full 8-day trek on the Overland Track for A$995 (U.S.$646.75), all-inclusive, from Launceston (wet-weather gear costs A$55/U.S.$35.75 extra to rent). These trips depart every Saturday between November and April, with extra trips from late December to the end of January. Another trip, a 6-day Cradle Mountain and Walls of Jerusalem National Park trip, includes 3 nights of wilderness camping and 3 nights in a cabin. It costs A$840 (U.S.$546) and leaves every Sunday between October and April. Many people have reported this trek to be the highlight of their trip to Australia.

Craclair Tours (© and fax **03/6424 7833;** www.southcom.com. au/~craclair), also offers a quality 8-day Overland Track tour, including 5 nights of camping, between October and mid-April (leaving every Sun and Wed) for A$1,085 (U.S.$705).

For an organized trek in this area I recommend **Cradle Mountain Huts,** P.O. Box 1879, Launceston, TAS 7250 (© **03/6331 2006;** fax 03/ 6331 5525; cradle@tassie.net.au). Six-day walks cost A$1,450 (U.S.$942) for adults and A$1,350 (U.S.$877) for children 12 to 16; rates are all-inclusive and include transfers to and from Launceston. Children under 12 are not permitted. The huts are fully equipped, heated, and quite comfortable, with showers, a main living area, and a full kitchen. You get a good three-course meal every night. The treks leave every day between Christmas Day and early February, and around five times a week between November and April.

as well as an electric heater for chilly evenings, a shower, and a small kitchen. There are no telephones or TV in the rooms—but who needs them! Spa cabins come with carpets, a spa tub, and a balcony offering a variety of scenic views. Some have a separate bedroom. Two cabins have limited facilities for travelers with disabilities. Guests have the use of the casual and comfortable main lodge where almost every room has a blazing log fire.

G.P.O. Box 478, Sydney, NSW 2001. © 13 24 69 in Australia, 800/225-9849 in the U.S., 0171/805-3875 in the U.K., or 03/6492 1303. Fax 02/9299 2477. www.poresorts.com.au. 96 units. A$186 (U.S.$120.90) Pencil Pine cabin; A$240 (U.S.$156) spa cabin. Extra person A$26 (U.S.$22). Children under 3 stay free in parents' room. Ask about special winter packages. AE, DC, MC, V. Free parking. **Amenities:** Cafe, 2 bars; laundry facilities. *In room:* Kitchenette.

Waldheim Cabins   If you want a real wilderness experience then head for these cabins run by the Parks and Wildlife Service and located just 5 kilometers (3 miles) from Cradle Mountain Lodge. Nestled between button grass plains and temperate rain forest, they are simple and affordable and offer good access to plenty of walking tracks. Each cabin is equipped with heating, single bunk beds, basic cooking utensils, crockery, cutlery, and a gas stove. They are serviced by two composting toilets and showers. Generated power is provided for lighting between 6 and 11pm only. Stores and fuel can be bought at Cradle Mountain Lodge. Bring your own bed linen and toiletries.

Cradle Mountain Visitor Centre, P.O. Box 20, Sheffield, TAS 7306. © 03/6492 1110. Fax 03/6492 1120. 8 cabins (none with bathroom). A$60.50 (U.S.$39) 4-berth cabin for 2; A$71.50 (U.S.$46.50) 6-berth cabin for up to 3; A$82.50 (U.S.$53.60) 8-berth cabin for up to 3. Additional adult A$20.90 (U.S.$13.60); additional child A$9.90 (U.S.$6.40). MC, V. Collect cabin keys from the National Park Visitor Centre, just inside the boundary of the national park, between 8am–5:30pm daily.

LAKE ST. CLAIR ®

Australia's deepest natural freshwater lake is a narrow, 15-kilometer (9-mile) long waterway, fully enclosed within the Cradle Mountain–Lake St. Clair National Park. On the lake's southern edge is **Cynthia Bay,** site of an informative ranger station where you must register if you're attempting the Overland Track from this end, as well as a restaurant, cabin accommodation, and a backpackers' hostel (the latter are operated by **Lakeside St. Clair** at © **03/6289 1137**). National park

---

Moments A Lakeside Fishing Lodge

Tasmania's extensive hydroelectric schemes have created many new lakes, all seeded with some of the biggest wild brown and rainbow trout in the world. At **London Lakes Lodge** ®®®, it's all about low-key, high-action trout fishing; guides—one to every two people—take guests out on area lakes, rivers, and streams, offering personal tips and lessons. The lodge caters to just 10 guests in 5 simple twin-bedded rooms, each with an en suite bathroom; the chef here produces marvelous food. Such personalized attention doesn't come cheap; prices start at A$693 (U.S.$451) with guide, A$495 (U.S.$322) without guide, including meals, tackle, rods, clothing, and transportation. Prebooking is mandatory; contact Post Office, Bronte Park, TAS 7140 (© **03/6289 1159;** fax 03/6289 1122; www. londonlakes.com.au). *Note:* The lodge is so exclusive that the owners won't even post a road sign to tell you where it is; it's off the first dirt track after the Bronte Park turnoff on the road from Strahan to Hobart. The lodge is closed May through July.

---

rangers run several tours between Boxing Day and the end of February, including spotlighting tours and guided walks around the local area. Call ahead for details at ✆ 03/6289 1172.

7 The West Coast

296km (184 miles) NW of Hobart; 245km (152 miles) SW of Devonport

Tasmania's west coast is wild and mountainous with a scattering of mining and logging towns and plenty of wilderness. The pristine Franklin and Gordon rivers tumble through World Heritage Areas once bitterly contested by loggers, politicians, and environmentalists, whereas the bare, poisoned hills that make up the eerily beautiful "moonscape" of Queenstown show the results of intensive mining and industrial activity. Strahan ⊛ (pronounced Strawn), the only town of any size in the area, is the starting point for cruises up the Gordon River and ventures into the rain forest.

ESSENTIALS

GETTING THERE   Tassielink (✆ 03/6272 6611, or 1300 300 520 in Australia; www.tigerline.com.au) runs coaches between Strahan and Launceston, Devonport, and Cradle Mountain every Tuesday, Thursday, and Saturday (and also Sun to and from Hobart). The trip from Launceston takes over 8 hours. The drive from Hobart to Strahan takes about 4½ hours without stops. From Devonport, allow 3½ hours. Although the roads are good, they twist and turn quite dramatically and are particularly hazardous at night when marsupial animals come out to feed. The cheapest way to travel between these places is via bus with a **Tassie Wilderness Pass.**

VISITOR INFORMATION   **Strahan Visitors Centre,** on The Esplanade (✆ 03/6471 7622; fax 03/6471 7533), is open daily from 10am to 6pm in winter and to 8pm in spring and summer. It has good information on local activities. A good website of the area is www.westcoasttourism.com.au.

CRUISING THE RIVERS & OTHER ADVENTURES

Gordon River Cruises (✆ 03/6471 7187) offers a half-day trip daily at 9am, an afternoon cruise sailing at 2pm in the first 3 weeks of January, and a full-day trip from October 1 to the end of May. Cruises take passengers across Macquarie Harbour and up the Gordon River past historic **Sarah Island,** where convicts—working in horrendous conditions—were once used to log valuable Huon pine. A stop is made at **Heritage Landing,** where you can get a taste of the rain forest on a half-hour walk. The full-day cruise in the high season (Oct–May) includes lunch and a guided tour through the convict ruins on Sarah Island. Cruises depart from the Main Wharf on The Esplanade, in the town center.

   World Heritage Cruises (✆ 03/6471 7174; www.worldheritagecruises.com.au) offers daily all-year cruises leaving Strahan Wharf at 9am and returning at 3:30pm. The company's MV *Wanderer III* stops at Sarah Island, Heritage Landing, and the salmon and trout farm at Liberty Point. Meals and drinks are available on board. The cruises cost A$55 (U.S.$35.75) for adults; A$25 (U.S.$16.25) for children 5 to 14 (free for children under 5), and A$150 (U.S.$97.50) for a family of five. It also offers a half-day cruise between October 1 and April 31 starting at 9am and returning at 2pm (it doesn't stop at Sarah Island). This costs A$50 (U.S.$32.50) for adults, A$22 (U.S.$14.30) for children, and A$130 (U.S.$84.50) for a family.

Moments Dune Buggy Rides

What's more fun than scooting across the sand in a dune buggy? **Four-Wheelers** (© 03/6471 7622, or mobile 0419/508 175) offers exhilarating, 40-minute rides across the **Henty Sand Dunes** *Ⓡ*, about 10 minutes north of Strahan. Trips cost just A$35 (U.S.$22.75) for one adult and A$60 (U.S.$39) for two. Longer trips are also offered outside the hot summer months.

West Coast Yacht Charters (© 03/6471 7422) runs fishing trips from 9am to noon for A$40 (U.S.$26) negotiable, with fishing gear, bait, and morning tea included; crayfish dinner & fishing cruises from 6 to 8:30pm for A$50 (U.S.$32.50); and 2-day, 2-night sailing cruises for A$320 (U.S.$208) all-inclusive.

Although cruises are the main attraction in the area, you can also enjoy jet-boat rides, sightseeing in a seaplane that lands on the Gordon River, helicopter flights, and four-wheel-drive tours.

WHERE TO STAY & DINE

Franklin Manor *Ⓡ* Built in 1886 as the home of the harbormaster, this superior B&B offers standard rooms with queen-size beds, deluxe rooms with king-size ones, and a very plush executive deluxe room. Also on the premises are four delightful cottages, which allow you to really get away from it all. The main lounge is comfortable and warmed by a log fire, while the simple Huon-pine bar in the foyer and the wine cellar operate on the honor system. The specialties at the manor's restaurant include salmon, duck, seafood, beef, and venison.

The Esplanade, Strahan, TAS 7468. © 03/6471 7311. Fax 03/6471 7267. www.franklinmanor.com.au. 18 units, including 4 cottages. A$176 (U.S.$114.40) standard double; A$210 (U.S.$136.50) deluxe double or cottage; A$245 (U.S.$159.25) executive deluxe. Rates include breakfast. AE, DC, MC, V. Ask about winter deals. **Amenities:** Bar; laundry service. *In room:* TV, coffeemaker, iron.

Gordon Gateway Chalets These modern self-contained units are on a hill with good views of the harbor and Strahan township. Each has cooking facilities, so you can save on meal costs. The two-bedroom suites have a bathtub, and the studios have just a shower. Breakfast is provided on request. Guests have the use of a self-service laundry, a barbecue area, and a children's playground. One unit has facilities for travelers with disabilities.

Grining St., Strahan, TAS 7468. © 03/6471 7165. Fax 03/6471 7588. ggc@tassie.net.au. 19 units. A$100–$160 (U.S.$65–$104) studio; A$185–$195 (U.S.$120–$126.75) suite. Discounts in winter. MC, V. **Amenities:** Tour desk; massage; babysitting; coin-op laundry; nonsmoking rooms. *In room:* TV, kitchenette, fridge, coffeemaker, hair dryer, safe.

Ormiston House *ⓇⓇ* Ormiston House is a gem. Built in 1899 for the family that gave it its name, the present owners have made it into a sort of shrine to their predecessors. Each of the four rooms is styled to represent one of the original family members. Each room is intricately furnished and wallpapered in busy designs and comes with a good-size private bathroom. There's a nice morning room and a restaurant serving good food. The owners are very friendly and have plenty of time for their guests. Smoking is not permitted.

The Esplanade, Strahan, TAS 7468. © 03/6471 7077. Fax 03/6471 7007. www.ormistonhouse.com.au. 6 units. A$185–$245 (U.S.$120–$159.25) double. Extra person A$62 (U.S.$40.30). Rates include breakfast. AE, DC, MC, V. **Amenities:** Bar; lounge; laundry service. *In room:* TV, coffeemaker, iron.

STANLEY

140km (90 miles) W of Devonport; 430km (270 miles) NW of Hobart

Among the least well-known areas of Tasmania, the coastline east of Devonport can throw up some surprises. Not least of them is "The Nut," a kind of miniature Ayers Rock rising out from the sea and towering above the township of Stanley. The Nut is the remains of a volcanic plug that forced its way through a crack in the earth's crust some 12 million years ago. You can walk to the top or, if you're feeling brave, take a chair lift up for A$7 (U.S.$4.55) for adults, A$4.50 (U.S.$2.90) for children. A warning, though, don't attempt riding the chair lift back down again if you're afraid of heights—the descent is incredibly steep and there's no getting off! There's a small buggy up top that will take you on a tour of The Nut for A$6 (U.S.$3.90); free for children under 10.

WHERE TO STAY

The Old Cable Station 𝒜   Darryl Stafford, an ex-logger, and his wife Heather have turned the former exchange building for the telephone line coming over from the mainline into a very cozy B&B. The rooms are nice and comfortable; there are TVs in two rooms, but you'll probably spend all your time in the lounge room chatting around the fire anyway. Darryl is as Aussie as you can get and will keep you entranced for hours with his stories. Seal cruises are offered daily, weather permitting, for A$30 (U.S.$19.50). Home-cooked dinners are served daily in the restaurant.

Highfield Lane, Stanley, TAS 7331. ⓒ **03/6458 1312.** Fax. 03/6458 2009. 4 units. A$95 (U.S.$61.75) double; $130 (U.S.$84.50) spa suite. Rates include continental breakfast. AE, MC, V. **Amenities:** Restaurant, lounge; laundry service. *In room:* TV.

WHERE TO DINE

Hursey Seafoods SEAFOOD   There are plenty of people around who rate this little place as having the best seafood in Australia. Downstairs it's a casual cafe, where you choose what you want from fish tanks, while upstairs it's a more formal restaurant. An unusual specialty is muttonbird (shearwater), an oily seabird that you either like seeing flying around or like seeing on your plate. You can't have it both ways.

2 Alexander Terrace, Stanley. ⓒ **03/6458 1103.** Main course, cafe A$10 (U.S.$6.50), restaurant A$15 (U.S.$9.75). MC, V. Take-out/cafe 9am–6pm; restaurant 6–10pm.

Appendix:
Australia in Depth

by Marc Llewellyn

The land "Down Under" is a modern nation coming to terms with its identity. The umbilical cord with mother England has been cut, and the nation is still trying to find its position within Asia.

One thing it realized early on, though, was the importance of tourism to its economy. Millions flock here every year. You'll find Australians to be helpful and friendly, and services, tours, and food and drink to rival any in the world. Factor in the landscape, the native Australian culture, the sunshine, the animals, and some of the world's best cities—what more could you ask for?

1 Australia's Natural World

THE LAND OF THE NEVER-NEVER

People who have never visited Australia wonder why such a huge country has a population of just 19 million people. The truth is, Australia can barely support that many. About 90% of those 19 million people live on only 2.6% of the continent. Climatic and physical land conditions ensure that the only relatively decent rainfall occurs along a thin strip of land around Australia's coast. The vast majority of Australia is harsh Outback, characterized by salt bush plains, arid brown crags, shifting sand deserts, and salt lake country. People survive where they can in this great arid land because of one thing—the Great Artesian Basin. This saucer-shaped geological formation comprises about one-fifth of Australia's land mass, stretching over much of inland New South Wales, Queensland, South Australia, and the Northern Territory. Beneath it are massive underground water supplies stored during Jurassic and Cretaceous times (some 66–208 million years ago), when the area was much like the Amazon basin is today. Pressure brings water to the surface and allows sheep, cattle, and humans a respite from the dryness.

The Queensland coast is blessed with one of the greatest natural attractions in the world. The **Great Barrier Reef** stretches some 2,000 kilometers (1,240 miles) from off Gladstone in Queensland, to the Gulf of Papua, near New Guinea. It's relatively new, not more than 8,000 years old, though many fear that rising seawater, caused by global warming, will cause its demise. As it is, the non-native Crown of Thorns starfish and a bleaching process believed to be the result of excessive nutrients flowing into the sea from Australia's farming land, is already causing significant damage. The reef is covered in chapter 6.

AUSTRALIA'S FAUNA

NATIVE ANIMALS Australia's isolation from the rest of the world over millions of years has led to the evolution of forms of life found nowhere else. Probably the strangest of them all is the **platypus.** This monotreme, or egg-laying marsupial, has webbed feet, a duck-like bill, and a tail like a beaver's. It lays eggs, and the young suckle from their mother. When a specimen was first brought back to Europe, skeptical scientists insisted it was a fake—a concoction of several different animals sewn together. You will probably never see this shy, nocturnal creature in the wild, though there are a few at Sydney's Taronga Zoo.

Another strange one is the **koala.** This fluffy marsupial eats virtually indigestible gum leaves and sleeps about 20 hours a day. There's just one species, though those found in Victoria are substantially larger than their brethren in more northern climes. Australia is also famous for **kangaroos.** There are 45 different kinds of kangaroos and wallabies, ranging in scale from small rat-size kangaroos to the man-size red kangaroos.

The animal you're most likely to come across in your trip is the **possum,** named by Captain James Cook after the North American "opossum," which he thought they resembled (in fact they are from an entirely different family of the animal kingdom). The brush-tailed possum is commonly found in suburban gardens, including those in Sydney. Then there's the **wombat.** There are four species of this bulky burrower in Australia, but the most frequently found is the common wombat. You might come across the smaller hairy-nosed wombat in South Australia and Western Australia.

The **dingo,** thought by many to be a native of Australia, was in fact introduced—probably by Aborigines. They vary in color from yellow to a russet red, and are heavily persecuted by farmers. Commonly seen **birds** include the fairy penguin along the coast, black swans, parrots and cockatoos, and honeyeaters. **Tasmanian devils** can be found in (you guessed it) the island/state of Tasmania.

DANGEROUS NATIVES   Snakes are common throughout Australia, but you will very rarely see one. The most dangerous land snake is the taipan, which hides in the grasslands in northern Australia—one bite contains enough venom to kill up to 200 sheep. If by the remotest chance you are bitten, you must immediately demobilize the limb, wrapping it quite tightly (but not tight enough to restrict the blood flow) with a cloth or bandage, and head to the nearest hospital where antivenin should be available.

There are two types of **crocodile** in Australia: the harmless freshwater croc which grows to 3 meters (9.8 ft.); and the dangerous estuarine (or saltwater) crocodile, which reaches 5 to 7 meters (16.4–23 ft.). Freshwater crocs eat fish; estuarine crocs aren't so picky. *Never* swim in, or stand on the bank of, any river, swamp, or pool in northern Australia unless you know *for certain* it's croc-free.

Spiders are common all over Australia, with the funnel web spider and the red-back spider being the most aggressive. Funnel webs live in holes in the ground (they spin their webs around a hole's entrance) and stand on their back legs when they're about to attack. Red-backs have a habit of resting under toilet seats and in boots (car trunks), generally outside the main cities. Caution is a good policy.

If you go bushwalking, check your body carefully. **Ticks** are common, especially in eastern Australia, and can cause severe itching and fever. If you find one on you, dab it with methylated spirits or another noxious chemical. Wait a while and pull it out gently with tweezers, taking care not to leave the head behind.

Fish to avoid are stingrays, porcupine fish, stonefish, lionfish, and puffer fish. Never touch an **octopus** if it has blue rings on it, or a cone shell, and be wary of the very painful and sometimes deadly tentacles of the box **jellyfish** found along the northern Queensland coast in summer. If you happen to brush past one of these creatures, pour vinegar over the affected site immediately—local councils leave bottles of vinegar on the beach specifically for this purpose. Vinegar deactivates the stinging cells that haven't already affected you, but doesn't affect the ones that already have.

In Sydney, you might come across "stingers" or "blue bottles" as they are also called. These long-tentacled blue jellyfish can inflict a very nasty stinging burn that can last for hours. Sometimes you'll see warning signs on patrolled beaches. The best remedy if you are severely stung is to wash the affected water with fresh water and have a very hot bath or shower.

2 The People of Oz

It's generally considered that more races of people live in Australia at the present time than anywhere else in the world, including North America. Heavy immigration has led to people from some 165 nations making the country their home. In general, relations between the different ethnic groups have been peaceful. Today Australia is an example of a multicultural society, despite an increasingly vocal minority that believes that Australia has come too far in welcoming people from races other than their own.

THE ABORIGINES When Captain James Cook landed at Botany Bay in 1770 determined to claim the land for the British Empire, at least 300,000 Aborigines were already on the continent. Whether you believe a version of history that suggests the Aboriginal people were descendants of migrants from Indonesia to the north, or the Aboriginal belief that they have occupied Australia since the beginning of time, there is scientific evidence that people were using fire for cooking in present-day New South Wales at least 120,000 years ago.

At the time of the white "invasion" of their lands, there were at least 600 different, largely nomadic tribal communities, each linked to their ancestral land by **"sacred sites"** (certain features of the land, such as hills or rock formations). They were hunter-gatherers, spending about 20 hours a week harvesting the resources of the land, rivers, and the ocean. The rest of the time was taken up by a complex social and belief system, as well as by life's practicalities, such as making utensils, weapons, and musical instruments such as didgeridoos and clapsticks.

The basis of Aboriginal spirituality rests in the **Dreamtime** stories, in which everything—land, stars, mountains, the moon, the sun, the oceans, water holes, animals and humans—was created by spirits. Much Aboriginal art is related to their land and the sacred sites that are home to the Dreamtime spirits. Some Aboriginal groups believe these spirits came in giant human form, others believed they were animals, still more that they were huge snakes. According to Aboriginal custom, individuals can draw on the power of the Dreamtime spirits by re-enacting various stories and practicing certain ceremonies.

Aboriginal groups had encountered people from other lands before the British arrived. Dutch records from 1451 show that the Macassans, from islands now belonging to Indonesia, had a long relationship trading Dutch glass, smoking pipes, and alcohol for edible sea slugs from Australia's northern coastal waters, which they sold to the Chinese in the Canton markets. Dutch, Portuguese, French, and Chinese vessels also encountered Australia—in fact, the Dutch fashion for pointy beards caught on through northern Australia long before the 1770 invasion.

When the British came, bringing their **diseases** with them, coastal communities were virtually wiped out by smallpox. Even as late as the 1950s, large numbers of Aborigines in remote regions of South Australia and the Northern Territory succumbed to deadly influenza and measles outbreaks.

Though relationships between the settlers and local Aborigines were initially peaceful, conflicts over land and food soon led to skirmishes in which Aborigines were massacred and settlers and convicts attacked—Governor Phillip was speared in the back by an Aborigine in 1790.

Within a few years, some 10,000 Aborigines and 1,000 Europeans were killed in Queensland alone, while in Tasmania, a campaign to rid the island entirely of local Aborigines was ultimately successful, with the last full-blooded Tasmanian Aborigine dying in 1876. By start of the 20th century, the Aboriginal people were considered a dying race. Most left alive lived in government-owned reserves or Church-controlled missions.

Massacres of Aborigines continued to go largely or wholly unpunished into the 1920s, by which time it became official government policy to remove light-skinned Aboriginal children from their families and to forcibly sterilize young women. Many children of the "stolen generation" were brought up in white foster homes or church refuges and never reunited with their biological families—many with living parents were told that their parents were dead.

Today, there are some 283,000 Aborigines living in Australia, and a great divide still exists between them and the rest of the population. Aboriginal life expectancy can be 20 years lower than that of other Australians, with overall death rates between two and four times higher. A far higher percentage of Aboriginal people than other Australians fill the prisons, and despite a Royal Commission into Aboriginal Deaths in Custody, Aborigines continue to die while incarcerated.

A landmark in Aboriginal affairs occurred in 1992 when the High Court determined that Australia was not an empty land (*terra nullius*) as it been seen officially since the British invasion. The **"Mabo" decision** resulted in the **1993 Native Title Act,** which allowed Aboriginal groups, and the ethnically distinct people living in the Torres Strait islands off northern Queensland, to claim government-owned land if they could prove continual association with it since 1788. The later **"Wik" decision** determined that Aborigines could make claims on Government land leased to agriculturists. The federal government, led by the right-leaning Prime Minister John Howard, curtailed these rights following pressure from farming and mining interests.

Issues currently facing the Aboriginal population include harsh mandatory sentencing laws, enacted in Western Australia and the Northern Territory state governments in 1996 and 1997 respectively, which came to international attention in 2000. The Aboriginal community believes such laws specifically target them. When a 15-year-old Aboriginal boy allegedly committed suicide less than a week before he was due to be released from a Northern Territory prison in early 2000, and a 21-year-old Aboriginal youth was imprisoned for a year for stealing A$23-worth of fruit cordial and biscuits, Aboriginal people protested, activists of all colors demonstrated, and even the United Nations weighed in with criticism.

Added to this was the simmering issue of the federal government's decision not to apologize to the Aboriginal people for the "stolen generation." In March 2000, a government-sponsored report stated there was never a "stolen generation," and according to respected researchers on both sides of the fence, went on to markedly underestimate the amount of people personally affected.

Prior to the Sydney 2000 Olympic Games, a popular movement involving people of all colors and classes called for reconciliation and an apology to the Aboriginal people. In Sydney, an estimated 250,000 people marched across the Sydney Harbour Bridge. The Liberal (read "conservative") Government refused to bow to public pressure. Despite threats of boycotts and rallies during the Olympics, the Games passed without major disturbance, and a worldwide audience watched as Aboriginal runner Cathy Freeman lit the Olympic cauldron.

THE REST OF AUSTRALIA   "White" Australia was always used to distinguish the Anglo-Saxon population from that of the Aboriginal population.

These days, though, a walk through any of the major cities would show that things have changed dramatically. About 100,000 people emigrate to Australia each year. Of these, approximately 12% were born in the U.K. or Ireland, 11% in New Zealand, and more than 21% in China, Hong Kong, Vietnam, or the Philippines. Waves of immigration have brought in millions of people since the end of World War II. At the last census in 1996, more than a quarter of a million Australian residents were born in Italy, for example, some 186,000 in the former Yugoslavia, 144,000 in Greece, 118,000 in Germany, and 103,000 in China. So what's the typical Australian like? Well, he's hardly Crocodile Dundee.

3 Australian History 101

IN THE BEGINNING In the beginning there was the **Dreamtime**—at least according to the Aborigines of Australia. Between then and now, perhaps, the supercontinent referred to as **Pangaea** split into two huge continents called **Laurasia** and **Gondwanaland.** Over millions of years, continental drift carried the land masses apart. Laurasia gradually broke up and formed North America, Europe, and most of Asia. Meanwhile, Gondwanaland divided into South America, Africa, India, Australia and New Guinea, and Antarctica. **Giant marsupials** evolved to roam the continent of Australia: Among them were a plant-eating animal that looked like a wombat the size of a rhinoceros; a giant squashed-face kangaroo standing 3 meters (10 ft.) high; and a flightless bird the same size as an emu, but four times heavier. The last of these giant marsupials are believed to have died out some 40,000 years ago.

EARLY EXPLORERS The existence of Australia had been in the minds of Europeans since the Greek astronomer Ptolemy drew a map of the world in about A.D. 150 showing a large land mass in the south, which he believed had to be there to balance out the land in the northern hemisphere. He called it *Terra Australia Incognita*—the unknown south land.

Evidence suggests Portuguese ships reached Australia at least as early as 1536 and even charted part of its coastline. In 1606 William Jansz was sent by the Dutch East India Company to

Dateline

- **120,000 B.C.** Evidence suggests Aborigines living in Australia.
- **60,000 B.C.** Aborigines living in Arnham Land in the far north fashion stone tools.
- **24,500 B.C.** The world's oldest known ritual cremation takes place at Lake Mungo.
- **1606** Dutch explorer Willem Jansz lands on far north coast of Van Diemen's Land (Tasmania).
- **1622** First English ship to reach Australia wrecks on the west coast.
- **1642** Abel Tasman charts the Tasmanian coast.
- **1770** Capt. James Cook lands at Botany Bay.
- **1787** Capt. Arthur Phillip's First Fleet leaves England with convicts aboard.
- **1788** Captain Phillip raises British flag at Port Jackson (Sydney Harbour).
- **1788–1868** Convicts are transported from England to the colony of Australia.
- **1793** The first free settlers arrive.
- **1830** Governor Arthur lines up 5,000 settlers across Van Diemen's Land to walk the length of the island to capture and rid it of all Aborigines.
- **1850** Gold discovered in Bathurst, New South Wales.
- **1852** Gold rush begins in Ballarat, Victoria.
- **1853** The last convict arrives in Van Diemen's Land and to celebrate, the colony is renamed Tasmania after Abel Tasman.
- **1860** The white population of Australia reaches more than one million.
- **1875** Silver found at Broken Hill, New South Wales.

continues

open up a new route to the Spice Islands, and to find New Guinea, which was supposed to be rich in gold. He landed on the north coast of Queensland and fought with local Aborigines. Between 1616 and 1640, many more Dutch ships made contact with Australia as they hugged the west coast of what they called "New Holland," after sailing with the *westerlies* (west winds) from the Cape of Good Hope.

In 1642, the Dutch East India Company, through the Governor General of the Indies, Anthony Van Diemen, sent Abel Tasman to search out and map the great south land. During two voyages, he charted the northern Australian coastline and discovered Tasmania, which he named Van Diemen's Land.

THE ARRIVAL OF THE BRITISH

In 1697, English pirate William Dampier published a book about his adventures. In it, he mentions Shark Beach on the northwest coast of Australia as the place his pirate ship made its repairs after robbing ships on the Pacific Ocean. Sent to further explore by England's King William III, Dampier returned and found little to recommend.

Captain James Cook turned up in 1770 and charted the whole east coast in his ship HMS *Endeavor.* He claimed it for Britain and named it New South Wales, probably as a favor to Thomas Pennant, a Welsh patriot and botanist who was a friend of the *Endeavour's* own botanist, Joseph Banks. On April 29, Cook landed at Botany Bay, which he named after the discovery of scores of plants hitherto unknown to science. Turning northwards, Cook passed an entrance to a possible harbor where he noted there appeared to be safe anchorage. He named it Port Jackson after the Secretary to the Admiralty, George Jackson, but didn't explore much. Back in Britain, King George III was convinced Australia could

- **1889** Australian troops fight in the Boer War in South Africa.
- **1895** Banjo Patterson's *The Man from Snowy River* published.
- **1901** The six states join together to become the Commonwealth of Australia.
- **1902** Women gain the right to vote.
- **1911** Australian (non-Aboriginal) population reaches 4,455,005.
- **1915** Australian and New Zealand troops massacred at Gallipoli.
- **1927** The federal capital is moved from Melbourne to Canberra.
- **1931** The first airmail letters are delivered to England by Charles Kingsford Smith and Charles Ulm.
- **1931** The Arnham Land Aboriginal Reserve is proclaimed.
- **1932** Sydney Harbour Bridge opens.
- **1942** Darwin bombed; Japanese minisubmarines found in Sydney Harbour.
- **1953** British nuclear tests at Emu in South Australia lead to a radioactive cloud that kills and injures many Aborigines.
- **1956** Olympic Games held in Melbourne.
- **1957** British atomic tests conducted at Maralinga, South Australia. Aborigines again affected by radiation.
- **1962** Commonwealth government gives Aborigines the right to vote.
- **1967** Aborigines granted Australian citizenship and are counted in census.
- **1968** Australia's population passes 12 million following heavy immigration.
- **1971** The black, red, and yellow Aboriginal flag flown for the first time.
- **1973** Sydney Opera House completed.
- **1976** The Aboriginal Land Rights (Northern Territory) Act gives some land back to native people.
- **1983** Ayers Rock given back to local Aborigines, who rename it Uluru.
- **1983** Australia wins the Americas Cup, ending 112 years of American domination of the event.
- **1986** Queen Elizabeth II severs the Australian Constitution from Great Britain's.

continues

make a good colony. It would also reduce Britain's overflowing prison population, as England could no longer transport convicts to the United States of America following the War of Independence.

The First Fleet left England in May 1787, made up of 11 store and transport ships (none of them was bigger than the passenger ferries that ply modern-day Sydney Harbour from Circular Quay to Manly) led by Arthur Phillip. Aboard were 1,480 people, including 759 convicts. Phillip's flagship, *The Supply*, reached Botany Bay in January 1788, but Phillip decided the soil was poor and the surroundings too swampy. On January 26, now celebrated as Australia Day, he settled for Port Jackson (Sydney Harbour) instead.

SETTLING DOWN The convicts were immediately put to work clearing land, planting crops, and constructing buildings. The early food harvests were failures, and by early 1790, the fledgling colony was facing starvation.

Phillip decided to give some convicts pardons for good behavior and service, and even grant small land parcels to those who were really indus-

- **1988** Aborigines demonstrate as Australia celebrates its Bicentennial with a re-enactment of the First Fleet's entry into Sydney Harbour.
- **1991** Australia's population reaches 17 million.
- **1993** Sydney chosen as the site of 2000 Olympics.
- **1994** High Court *Mabo* decision overturns the principle of *terra nullius*, which suggested Australia was unoccupied at time of white settlement.
- **1995** Australians protest as France explodes nuclear weapons in the South Pacific.
- **1996** High Court hands down *Wik* decision, which allows Aborigines the right to claim some Commonwealth land.
- **1998** The right-wing One Nation Party, led by former fish-and-chip shop owner Pauline Hanson, holds the balance of power in Queensland elections on an anti-immigration and anti-Aboriginal platform.
- **2000** A 10% Goods and Services tax becomes part of everyday life in Australia. Business and consumer confidence evaporates; the country is jolted into an economic downturn.
- **2000** Sydney Olympics held; Aboriginal track and field star Cathy Freeman lights Olympic torch.

trious. In 1795, coal was discovered; in 1810 Governor Macquarie began extensive city building projects; and in 1813 the explorers Blaxland, Wentworth, and Lawson forged a passage over the Blue Mountains to the fertile plains beyond.

When gold was discovered in Victoria in 1852, and in Western Australia 12 years later, hundreds of thousands of immigrants from Europe, America, and China flooded into the country in search of their fortunes. By 1860, more than a million non-Aboriginal people were living in Australia.

The last 10,000 convicts were transported to Western Australia between 1850 and 1868, bringing the total shipped out to Australia to 168,000.

FEDERATION & THE GREAT WARS On January 1, 1901, the six states that made up Australia proclaimed themselves to be part of one nation, and the Commonwealth of Australia was formed. In the same ceremony, the first Governor General was sworn in as the representative of the Queen, who remained head of state. In 1914, Australia joined the mother country in war. In April the following year, the Australian and New Zealand Army Corps (ANZAC) formed a beachhead on the peninsula of Gallipoli in Turkey. The Turkish troops had been warned, and 8 months of fighting ended with 8,587 Australian dead and more than 19,000 wounded.

Australians fought in World War II in North Africa, Greece, and the Middle East. In March 1942, Japanese aircraft bombed Broome in Western Australia and Darwin in the Northern Territory. In May 1942, Japanese midget submarines entered Sydney Harbour and torpedoed a ferry before being destroyed. Later that year, Australian volunteers fought retreat through the jungles of Papua New Guinea on the Kokoda Trail against superior Japanese forces. Australian troops fought alongside Americans in subsequent wars in Korea and Vietnam and sent military support to the Persian Gulf conflicts.

RECENT TIMES Following World War II, mass immigration to Australia, primarily from Europe, boosted the population. In 1974 the left-of-center Whitlam government put an end to the White Australia policy that had largely restricted black and Asian immigration since 1901. In 1986 the official umbilical cord to Britain was cut when the Australian Constitution was separated from that of its motherland. Australia had begun the march to complete independence.

In 1992 the High Court handed down the "Mabo" decision that ruled that Aborigines had a right to claim government-owned land if they could prove a continued connection with it. The following year, huge crowds filled Sydney's Circular Quay to hear that the city had won the 2000 Olympic Games.

The Olympic city built new venues (some of which were temporary, others now used as arenas for professional and amateur sports). A new expressway and train link were built to connect the spruced-up airport to the city center, and Sydney welcomed thousands of international visitors to the 2-week extravaganza starting in September 2000. The Games put medal-winning Australian athletes Cathy Freeman and swimmer Ian Thorpe in the spotlight, and spurred a new wave of interest and tourism in the Land Down Under.

4 Aussie Eats & Drinks

THE EATS

It took a long time for the average Australian to realize there was more to food than English-style sausage and mashed potatoes, "meat and three veg," and a Sunday roast. It wasn't long ago that spaghetti was something foreigners ate, and zucchini and eggplant were considered exotic. Then came mass immigration, and all sorts of foods that people had only read about in *National Geographic*.

The first big wave of Italian immigrants in the 1950s caused a national scandal. The great Aussie dream was to have a ¼-acre block of land with a Hills Hoist (a circular revolving clothesline) in the backyard. When Italians started hanging their freshly made pasta out to dry on this Aussie icon, it caused a national uproar, and some clamored for the new arrivals to be shipped back. As Australia matured, Southern European cuisine became increasingly popular, until olive oil was sizzling in frying pans the way only lard had previously done.

In the 1980s, waves of Asian immigrants hit Australia's shores. Suddenly, everyone was cooking with woks. These days, this fusion of flavors and styles has melded into what's now commonly referred to as "Modern Australian"—a distinctive cuisine blending the spices of the east with the flavors of the west.

THE DRINKS

THE AMBER NECTAR The great Aussie drink is a "*tinnie*" (a can) of beer. Barbecues would not be the same without a case of tinnies, or "*stubbies*" (small bottles). In the hotter parts of the country, you may be offered a polystyrene cup in which to place your beer to keep it cool.

Australian beers vary considerably in quality, but, of course, there's no accounting for tastes. Among the most popular are Victoria Bitter (known as

'VB'), XXXX (pronounced "four ex"), Fosters, and various brews produced by the Tooheys company. All are popular in cans, bottles, or on tap (draft). My favorite beer is Cascade, a German-style beer that you will usually find only in a bottle. It's light in color, strong in taste, and made from Tasmanian water straight off a mountain. If you want to get plastered, try Coopers—it's rather cloudy in looks, very strong, and usually ends up causing a terrific hangover. Most Australian beers range from 4.8% to 5.2% alcohol.

In New South Wales, beer is served by the glass in a "schooner" and a smaller "midi"—though in a few places it's also sold in British measurements, by pints and half pints. In Victoria you should ask for a "pot," or the less copious "glass." In South Australia a "schooner" is the size of a NSW "midi," and in Western Australia a "midi" is the same size as a New South Wales midi, but a glass about half its size is called a "pony." Confused? My advice is to gesture with your hands like a local to show whether you want a small glass or a larger one.

THE VINO   Australian wine making has come a long way since the first grape vines were brought to Australia on the First Fleet in 1788. These days, more than 550 major companies and small winemakers produce wine commercially in Australia. Vintages from Down Under consistently beat competitors from other wine-producing nations in major international shows. The demand for Australian wine overseas has increased so dramatically in the past few years that domestic prices have risen, and new vineyards are being planted at a frantic pace.

Australian wines are generally named after the grape varieties from which they are made. Of the white wines, both the fruity chardonnay and riesling varieties; the "herbaceous," or "grassy" sauvignon blanc; and the dry semillon are big favorites. Of the reds, the dry cabernet sauvignon, the fruity merlot, the burgundy-type pinot noir, and the big and bold shiraz come out tops.

5 Recommended Books & Films
BOOKS

The earliest Australian literature consists mostly of poems and chanties that go on about how difficult it was to travel all the way over to the new land. Of the 19th-century writers, the one that stands above anyone else is the poet "Banjo" Patterson, whose epic poem *The Man from Snowy River* hit the best-seller list in 1895 (and was later made into a film).

The big names of the 20th century include Miles Franklin, who wrote *My Brilliant Career* (1901), the story of a young woman faced with the dilemma of choosing between marriage and a career. Outback adventures were at the heart of three classic Australian books printed later in the century. Colleen McCullough's *Thorn Birds* is a romantic epic about a Catholic priest who falls in love with a girl; *We of the Never Never* by Mrs. Aeneas Gunn, tells the story of a young woman who leaves the comfort of her Melbourne home to go and live on a cattle station in the Northern Territory; and *Walkabout* by James V. Marshall shows the relationship between an Aboriginal and two children who get lost in the bush. It was later made into one of Australia's most influential movies.

If you can find it, *The Long Farewell* by Don Charlwood tells amazing first-hand diary accounts of long journeys from Europe to Australia in the last century. A good historical account of the early days of settlement is Geoffrey Blainey's *The Tyranny of Distance,* first published in 1966. Robert Hughes's *The Fatal Shore: The Epic of Australia's Founding,* is a best-selling non-fiction study of the country's early days.

> **Fun Fact Witchetty Grubs, Lilly-Pillies & Other Good Eats**
>
> Soon after the First Fleet of European convicts and settlers landed in Sydney Cove on January 26, 1788, they starved. They thought the Australian bush was empty of nourishment, despite the well-fed and healthy Aboriginals all around them. Only in the past 10 years have Europeans awakened to the dazzling variety and tastes of "bush tucker," as native Aussie food is tagged. These days bush tucker is all the rage, and most every fashionable restaurant has worked wattleseed, lemon myrtle, or some other native taste sensation into its menu. Below is a list of those foods you are likely to encounter in trendy restaurants around the country:
>
> | BUSH TUCKER | EXPLANATION |
> | --- | --- |
> | Bunya nut | Crunchy nut of the bunya pine, about the size of macadamias. |
> | Bush tomato | Dry, small darkish fruit more like raisins in look and taste. |
> | Cranberry (native) | Small berry that tastes a bit like an apple. |
> | Kangaroo | Kangaroo is a red meat with a strong gamey flavor. Tender when correctly prepared, tough when it is not. Excellent smoked. |
> | Illawarra plums | Dark berry with a rich, strong, tangy taste. |
> | Kakadu plum | Wonderfully sharp tangy green fruit that boasts the highest recorded Vitamin C level of any food. |

Modern novelists include David Ireland, Elizabeth Jolley, Helen Garner, Sue Woolfe, and Peter Carey, whose *True History of the Kelly Gang*, a fictionalized autobiography of the famous outlaw Ned Kelly, garnered critical acclaim in 2001.

FILMS

Australia's movie industry has never been a slouch when it comes to producing beautifully made, intelligent dramas, as well as a quirky, off-beat comedies. All the films below are available on video. If you plan to buy any of them in Australia, note that Australia uses the PAL system, while the United States used the NTSC system; which means you'll have to get your videos converted.

For a sampling of Australian comedy: *The Adventures of Priscilla, Queen of the Desert* (1994). starring Terrence Stamp, follows three transsexuals who set out from Sydney in a bus called Priscilla to work their way across Australia. The anthropomorphic *Babe* (1994) features a young pig who wants to be a sheepherding dog. The darkly funny documentary *Cane Toads, An Unnatural History* (1987) illustrates the love/hate (mostly hate) relationship Australians have with this non-indigenous creature that has wreaked environmental havoc. And in *Reckless Kelly* (1993), Yahoo Serious is a wacky version of the notorious Australian bush-ranging bandit Ned Kelly. (Yahoo's 1988 hit *Young Einstein* was a strange tale of a Tasmanian apple farmer who plans to split the beer atom.)

Lemon aspen	Citrusy, light yellow fruit with a sharp tangy flavor.
Lemon myrtle	Gum leaves with a fresh lemony tang; often used to flavor white meat.
Lilly-pilly	Delicious juicy, sweet pink berry; also called a riberry.
Macadamia nut	Sweet white nut. Macadamias come from Australia, not Hawaii as most of us think.
Quandong	A tart, tangy native peach.
Rosella	Spiky red petals of a flower with a rich berry flavor; traditionally used by Europeans to make rosella jam.
Wattle-seed	Roasted ground acacia seeds that taste a little like bitter coffee; commonly used by Europeans in pasta or desserts.
Wild lime	Smaller and more sour than a regular lime; good in salads.

One ingredient you will *not* see on restaurant menus is **witchetty grubs;** most people are too squeamish to eat these fat, slimy white critters. They live in the soil or in old dead tree trunks and are a common protein source for Aboriginals. You only eat them alive, not cooked. If you are offered one in the Outback, either freak out (as most locals would do) or enjoy its pleasantly nutty taste as a reward for your bravery!

On the dramatic front, *Breaker Morant* (1980) stars Aussie icons Edward Woodward, Jack Thompson, and Bryan Brown in a true story of three mates who find themselves in the Boer War. Mel Gibson and Mark Lee are two young runners who join the army amidst the jingoism surrounding World War I in *Gallipoli* (1981). Kirk Douglas and Jack Thompson ride the ranges in a remake of *The Man from Snowy River* (1982), Banjo Patterson's famous poem about the chase of an escaped colt. Mel Gibson comes of age—and gains international stardom—as an ex-cop in a futuristic world in the Mad Max trilogy: *Mad Max* (1979), *The Road Warrior* (1981), and the best, *Beyond Thunderdome* (1985). *My Brilliant Career* (1979) is an award-winning film based on Miles Franklin's novel. In *Picnic at Hanging Rock* (1975), Rachel Roberts is one of three girls and a teacher who disappear while on a school trip into the bush. Pre-*Gladiator* Russell Crowe is a skinhead who, with his gang, takes to beating up Melbourne's Asian youth in *Romper Stomper* (1992). Jenny Agutter and David Gulpilil are the stars of *Walkabout* (1976), a visually evocative movie about a young girl and her brother who get lost in the desert and are befriended by a traditional Aborigine. It was re-released in 1998.

Index

A boriginal Art and
Culture Centre (Alice
Springs), 16, 363, 365–366
Aborigines (Aboriginal
culture), 8, 12, 639–640
  Adelaide, 495
  Alice Springs, 365–367
  arts and crafts
    Alice Springs, 367–368
    Darwin, 393–394
    Melbourne, 552
    Perth, 453
    Sydney, 160–161
  best places to learn about,
16–17
  Dreamtime Cultural Centre
(Rockhampton), 322
  Grampians National Park,
587
  Kakadu National Park, 405
  Kings Canyon, 376
  Mootwingee National Park,
220–221
  Mt. Coot-tha Aboriginal Art
Trail, 245
  Nitmiluk National Park,
411
  Tjapukai Aboriginal Cultural Park (Cairns), 16,
266–267
  tours, 16–17, 287–288,
365–366, 376, 380, 404,
470
  Umbarra Aboriginal
Cultural Centre (Wallaga
Lake), 16, 213–214
  Warradjan Aboriginal
Cultural Centre, 18
Abseiling (rappelling), 9,
42–43, 177, 178, 245
Accommodations
  bed and breakfasts, 22–23,
73
  best, 19–23
  farmstays, 74, 254
  tips on, 72–74
Active vacations, 40–49
  health, safety and outdoor
etiquette, 46–47

Adelaide, 479–498
  accommodations, 21,
487–491
  layout of, 484
  nightlife, 497–498
  organized tours, 496
  outdoor activities, 496
  restaurants, 491–494
  shopping, 497
  side trips from, 499–507
  sights and attractions, 17,
494–496
  transportation, 485
  traveling to, 480–482, 484
  visitor information, 484
Adelaide Festival of Arts, 38,
484
Adelaide Hills, 504
Adelaide Zoo, 495
Aerial tours (scenic flights),
2, 59. *See also* Hot-air
ballooning
  Ayers Rock, 382
  Kakadu National Park,
405–406
  the Kimberley, 417
  Kings Canyon, 376, 378
  Nitmiluk National Park,
411
  Red Centre, 3
  Whitsunday Islands, 314
Airfares, 55–56, 58
Airlie Beach, 3, 307, 308,
310, 315, 316–317
Airlines, 1–2, 54–58, 72
Air passes, 58–59
Albury, 577, 578, 580
Alice Springs, 39, 356,
359–375
  accommodations, 368–370
  layout of, 362
  organized tours, 365–366
  outdoor activities,
366–367
  restaurants, 370–372
  road trips from, 372–375
  shopping, 367–368
  sights and attractions, 16,
363–365
  special events, 362
  transportation, 362

  traveling to, 361–362
  visitor information, 362
Alice Springs Cultural
Precinct, 363
Alice Springs Desert Park,
363
Alice Springs Reptile Centre,
3, 363
Alice Springs Telegraph
Station Historical Reserve,
18, 364
Alpine National Park, 583
American Express, 74
  Brisbane, 233
  Melbourne, 529
  Sydney, 96
American River, 509, 513,
514
Amigo's Castle (Lightning
Ridge), 223–224
A.M.P. Centrepoint Tower
(Sydney), 142
Anangu Tours (Ayers Rock),
16, 380
Angahook-Lorne State Park,
574
Angaston, 23, 499
Anna Bay, 195
Antarctic Adventure
(Hobart), 611–612
Anzac Memorial (Sydney),
151
Apartment rentals, 2, 20–21,
52, 72–73
Apollo Bay, 574, 576
Aquarius Roman Baths
(Launceston), 627
AQWA (Aquarium of Western
Australia) (Perth), 445
Araluen Centre (Alice
Springs), 363
Archibald Fountain (Sydney),
151
Argyle Diamond Mine, 417
Artesian Bore Baths (Light-
ning Ridge), 224
Art galleries, Broken Hill,
219
Art Gallery of New South
Wales (Sydney), 148, 151

Art Gallery of South
Australia (Adelaide), 494
Art Gallery of Western
Australia (Perth), 445–446
Arthur Frommer's Budget
Travel Online, 71
Ashcombe Maze and Water
Gardens (Shoreham), 566
ATMs (automated-teller
machines), 34–35
Australia Day, 37
Australian Aviation Heritage
Centre (Darwin), 18, 394
Australian Ballet, 166
Australian Butterfly Sanctu-
ary (Kuranda), 10–11, 272
Australian Capital Territory
(ACT), 29
Australian Chamber Orchestra
(Sydney), 167
Australian Formula One
Grand Prix (Melbourne),
38
Australian Institute of Sport
(Canberra), 599
Australian Museum
(Sydney), 148
Australian National Botanic
Gardens (Acton), 602
Australian National Mar-
itime Museum (Sydney),
18, 141, 154
Australian Reptile Park
(Sydney), 144–145
Australian Surf Life Saving
Championships (Kurrawa
Beach), 38
Australian Tourist Commis-
sion (ATC), 30
Australian War Memorial
(Canberra), 19, 599
Australian Woolshed
(Brisbane), 240
Australia Zoo (Beerwah), 337
Auto racing, 38, 39–40, 551
Aviary, The (Kuranda), 272
Aviation Museum (Alice
Springs), 363
Ayers Rock (Uluru), 8, 12, 16,
27, 43, 56, 57, 356,
380–382. See also Uluru-
Kata Tjuta National Park
Ayers Rock Observatory, 384
Ayers Rock Resort, 3–4, 368,
378, 379, 381, 383

B allarat, 570–573
Ballarat Fine Art Gallery, 570
Ballooning. See Hot-air
ballooning
Balmain, 88

Balmain Market (Sydney),
165
Balmoral Beach (Sydney),
147
Barossa, the (Barossa and
Eden valleys), 9, 479, 499,
500–504
Barrington Tops National
Park, 22
Barron Falls, 270, 272
Barron River, 273, 274
Batemans Bay, 212–213
Beaches, 47. See also
specific beaches
best, 13
Beaver Cay, 258
Bedarra Island, 3, 19,
299–300
Bed and breakfasts and
guest houses, 22–23, 73
Beer, 644–645
Bellingen, 201
Belongil Beach, 204
Ben Boyd National Park, 214
Bicentennial Park (Sydney),
151
Big Banana Theme Park
(Coffs Harbour), 200
Big Pineapple (near
Nambour), 337
Biking and mountain biking,
43, 156, 178, 245, 273,
288, 366, 451, 496, 550,
602, 626–627
Bilgola Beach (Sydney), 157
Billabong Koala and Wildlife
Park (Port Macquarie),
198–199
Billabong Sanctuary (near
Townsville), 303
Bird-watching, 43–44, 410,
416
Alice Springs Desert Park,
363
best places for, 10, 11
Broome Bird Observatory,
423
Currumbin Wildlife Sanctu-
ary, 347
Healesville Sanctuary, 562
Kakadu National Park, 404
Kangaroo Island, 511–512
Kuranda, 272
Lamington National Park,
352
Mutton Bird Island, 200
Rainforest Habitat, 287
Birdworld (Kuranda), 272
Blackall Ranges, 337
Blackheath, 183–185
Blood on the Southern Cross
(Ballarat), 570–571

Blowhole, Kiama, 208
Blue bottles (jellyfish;
Portuguese-Man-o'-Wars),
27, 48, 146, 284, 445, 545,
638–639
Blue Mountains, 9, 15,
42–43, 152, 174–186
Boating. See Boat tours and
cruises; Canoeing; Kayak-
ing; Sailing
Boat tours and cruises, 2.
See also Whale-watching;
and other specific
destinations
to Australia, 57
Brisbane, 243–244
Clyde River, 212
Daintree River, 286–287
Dunk Island, 297
Gordon River and
Tasmania's west coast,
634–635
Great Barrier Reef,
258–259
from Cairns, 265
from Mission Beach,
295
from Townsville, 301
Green Island, 268–269
Kakadu National Park, 404
the Kimberley coast,
425–426
Kuranda, 272
Melbourne, 545
Murray River, 578
Narooma, 213
Nitmiluk National Park,
410
Shark Bay, 474
Sydney, 2, 154–155
Tamar River, 626
Bondi Beach (Sydney),
87–88, 113–114, 133–134,
146, 157
Bonorong Park Wildlife
Centre (Hobart), 612
Bonsai Farm (Mt. Dande-
nong), 559
Books, recommended, 645
Boranup Drive, 465
Botanic Gardens (Adelaide),
495
Bouderee National Park, 209
Bournda National Park, 214
Brisbane, 225–253
accommodations, 20, 23,
235–237
arriving in, 225–226, 228
layout of, 228–229
neighborhoods, 229
nightlife and entertain-
ment, 246–249

Brisbane *(cont.)*
   organized tours, 243–245
   outdoor activities, 245
   restaurants, 24, 237–240
   shopping, 246
   sights and attractions,
      240–243
   transportation, 229,
      232–233
   visitor information, 228
   what's new in, 3
Brisbane Botanic Gardens
   Mt. Coot-tha, 240
Brisbane City Gardens, 243
Brisbane Forest Park, 245
Brisbane Powerhouse-Centre
   for the Live Arts, 247
Broken Heads Nature
   Reserve, 204
Broken Hill, 12, 17, 218–223
Broken Hill City Art Gallery,
   219–220
Bronte Beach (Sydney), 147
Broome, 17, 20, 414,
   420–424, 428, 430–431
Broome Bird Observatory,
   423
Brunswick Street Markets
   (Brisbane), 246
Buccaneer and Bonaparte
   Archipelagos, 414, 425
Buchan Caves, 582–583
Buffalo, Mt., 586–587
Buley Rockhole, 400
Bunbury, 11, 462, 463, 473
Bundaberg, 258, 327–328
Bundeena Beach, 153
Bungee jumping, Cairns, 273
Bungle Bungles, 414,
   416–420
Burning Palms Beach, 153
Bushwalking (hiking), 42,
   177–178, 245, 296, 315,
   366–367, 410, 496, 559,
   583, 632. *See also specific
   destinations*
   basic tips, 47
   best places for, 15
Business hours, 74
Bus passes, 62
Bus travel, 61–63
Butterfly Sanctuary,
   Australian (Kuranda, near
   Cairns), 10–11, 272
Byron Bay, 203–207

C able Beach, 422
Cable Beach (Broome), 13
Cadbury Chocolate Factory
   (Hobart), 612

Cairns, 14, 254, 256,
   258–282
   accommodations, 19, 20,
      23, 274–277
   day trips to Great Barrier
      Reef, 265–266
   layout of, 264
   nightlife, 282
   restaurants, 24, 280–281
   sights and activities,
      266–268
   sights and attractions, 16
   transportation, 264
   traveling to, 262, 264
   visitor information, 264
Calendar of events, 37–40
Caloundra, 333
Camel trekking and safaris,
   43, 366, 370, 382, 422,
   471
Campervans (motorhomes),
   65–66
Canberra, 4, 589–603
   accommodations, 20,
      594–596
   arriving in, 589–590
   Floriade, 38–39
   layout of, 592
   nightlife, 603
   outdoor activities,
      602–603
   restaurants, 25, 597–598
   sights and attractions,
      599–602
   special events, 590, 592
   transportation, 592–593
   visitor information, 590
Canberra Deep Space Com-
   munication Complex, 599
Canoeing, 9–10, 28, 44–46,
   158, 274, 389, 406, 409,
   410, 416–417, 602
Canyoning, in the Blue
   Mountains, 177, 178
Cape Byron Lighthouse, 204
Cape du Couedic (Kangaroo
   Island), 510
Cape-to-Cape, 15, 462, 465
Cape Tourville Lighthouse,
   623
Cape Tribulation National
   Park, 287
Cape Woolamai, 563–564
Capricorn Coast, 320–329
Caravan parks, Hunter Val-
   ley, 190
Car racing, 38, 39–40, 551
Car rentals, 63–65
Cars and driving, 63–70. *See
   also* Four-wheel-driving
   auto clubs, 67–68
   breakdowns and getting
      lost, 69

driving rules, 66–67
drunk-driving laws, 188
emergency assistance, 69
floods and, 69
kangaroos and other
   wildlife, 68
Outback driving tips, 218
petrol (gasoline), 66, 69
road conditions and safety,
   68
road maps, 67
road signs, 67
road trains and, 69
on unpaved roads, 69
Cascade Brewery Tours
   (Hobart), 612
Casinos, 282, 350, 399, 455,
   498, 558, 619
Castle Hill (near Townsville),
   303
Cataract Gorge, 626
Cathedrals, the (Fraser
   Island), 331
Caversham Wildlife Park, 458
Caves (caving; spelunking),
   44, 176, 185, 321, 322,
   376, 461, 464–465, 582
Caves Beach, 210
Caves Road, 465
CaveWorks (Lake Cave), 464
Centennial Park (Sydney),
   151, 156
Central Tilba, 17, 213
Cessnock, 186–194
Champagne Pools, 331
Charters Towers, 300
Children, families with,
   52–53
Chinatown (Broome), 421
Chinese Garden (Sydney),
   141–142
City Hall (Brisbane), 241
Clare Valley, 499
Clarke's Beach, 204
Cleland Wildlife Park,
   505–506
Cliff Walk, 183–184
Climate, 35–36
Clovelly Beach (Sydney), 147
Club Crocodile Long Island,
   313
Clyde River, 212
Cobblers Beach (Sydney),
   148
Coffs Harbour, 199–203
Coffs Harbour Zoo, 200
Cohunu Koala Park (Perth),
   446
Colloroy Beach (Sydney), 157
Consulates, 75
Conway State Forest, 315

Coober Pedy, 12–13, 18, 479, 518–520
Coogee (Sydney), 147
Cook's Cottage (Melbourne), 550
Coolgardie, 468–471
Cooloola National Park (Great Sandy National Park), 336
Coonawarra, 499
Coorong, 479, 520–522
Coorong National Park, 520
Coral, 48
Coral Bay, 475, 476, 478
Coral reefs, 268. *See also* Great Barrier Reef
types of, 255
Coral Sea, 14
Corroboree Rock, 374
Cottesloe Beach, 13, 448
Cowaramup, 463–467
Cowes, 563
Cradle Mountain, 16, 22, 630–634
Credit cards, 35
Cricket, 158, 496, 551
Crocodiles, 11, 15, 48–49, 142, 265, 268, 286, 287, 296, 303, 310, 314, 337, 347, 386, 389, 396, 401, 403, 406, 420, 422, 425, 445, 638
Crocodylus Park (Darwin), 393
Hartley's Creek Crocodile Farm (Cairns), 267
Malcolm Douglas Broome Crocodile Park (Broome), 423
tours and cruises, 315, 404, 416
Crocodylus Park (Berrimah), 393
Cumberland Islands, 253
Currency and currency exchange, 33–34
Currumbin Wildlife Sanctuary, 11, 347
Customs House (Sydney), 148
Customs regulations, 32–33
Cycling. *See* Biking

D aintree National Park, 284, 286–287
Daintree Rain Forest, 269–273, 282, 291–292
Daintree River, 286–287
Dampier Peninsula, 425
Dance clubs, Sydney, 168–169

Dandenong Ranges National Park, 559–561
Darwin, 23, 390–400
Darwin Botanic Gardens, 393
David Fleay Wildlife Park, 347
Daydream Island, 312
Delprat's Mine, 220
Denham, 472
Department stores
Melbourne, 553
Sydney, 162
Didgeridoo University, 364
Dingoes, 144, 145, 200, 267, 268, 332, 347, 446, 447, 515, 562
Disabilities, travelers with, 51
Dolphins, 11, 196, 210, 213, 250, 252, 346, 427, 462, 471, 473–474, 623, 624
Dorrigo National Park, 201
Drayton Family Wines (Pokolbin), 188
Dreamtime Cultural Centre (Rockhampton), 322
Dreamworld (Coomera), 345
Drinking water, 69, 358, 381, 388
Driving rules, 66–67
Dromedary, Mount, 214
Drunk-driving laws, 188
Dunk Island, 253, 294, 295, 297–299
Duty-free shops, Sydney, 162

E ast Coast Blues and Roots Festival (Byron Bay), 204
East Macdonnell Ranges, 374
East Point Military Museum (Darwin), 394
Echuca, 578–580
Eden, 214
Eden Killer Whale Museum (Merimbula), 214
Edith Falls, 410–411
Electricity, 75
Eli Creek, 331
Elizabeth Bay House (Sydney), 148–149
Ellalong, 191
Ellery Creek Big Hole, 372
Ellis Beach, 278
El Questro Wilderness Park, 4, 414, 416, 417–418
Elsey Station, 12
Embassies and consulates, 75

Emergencies, 75
Emily Gap, 374
Entry requirements, 31–32
Escorted tours, 53–54
Eumundi Markets, 338
Eureka Stockade Centre (Ballarat), 571
Exmouth, 475–478

F alls Creek, 584–586
Falls Reserve, 183
Fannie Bay trail, 393
Farmer's markets, Brisbane, 246
Farmstays, 74, 254
Fashions (clothing)
Melbourne, 553–554
Sydney, 162–164
Featherdale Wildlife Park (Sydney), 145, 153
Film Festival, Melbourne International, 555
Film Festival, Sydney, 38
Films, Australian, 646–647
Finke Gorge National Park, 374
Fishing, 9, 44, 212, 213, 273, 314, 395, 407, 423, 425, 456, 477, 512, 585, 635. *See also specific destinations*
Fish to avoid, 48
Fitzroy Island, 269, 280
Flinders Chase National Park (Kangaroo Island), 510
Flinders Ranges, 22, 24–25, 479
Flinders Ranges National Park, 515–518
Florence Falls, 400
Floriade (Canberra), 38
Fogg Dam Conservation Reserve, 403–404
Food, 644
Football, 496–497, 551
Sydney, 159
Fort Denison, 138, 151
Four Mile Beach (Port Douglas), 13, 288
Four-wheel-driving (rentals, tours, and safaris), 9, 12, 16, 22, 45, 46, 64–67, 330–331, 336. *See also specific destinations*
tips for, 69–70
Fox Studios Australia (Sydney), 143
Francois Peron National Park, 472
Fraser Island, 22, 253, 329–332

Fremantle, 431, 441, 445, 448–451
Fremantle Arts Centre, 449
Fremantle History Museum, 449–450
Fremantle Markets, 449
Fremantle Prison, 450
Freycinet National Park, 15–16, 22, 623–625
Frommers.com, 71
Fudge Factory and Historic Garden Tours (Hobart), 612

Gasoline (petrol), 66, 69
Gawler, 499
Gay and lesbian travelers
information and resources, 51–52
Sydney, 38, 98, 169–170
Geelong, 565–566
Geikie Gorge, 425
George's Gold Mine (near Coffs Harbour), 200
Ghan train, 60–61
Gladstone, 256, 258, 324–325
Glass House Mountains, 333, 338
Glenbrook National Park, 176
Glengarry opal fields, 223
Glen Helen Gorge, 373
Gliding, 602
Gold Coast, 21, 22, 27, 44, 253, 341–355
accommodations, 348–350
hinterland, 350–355
nightlife, 350
restaurants, 350
theme parks, 345–347
transportation, 344
traveling to, 341–342
visitor information, 342
Golden River Zoo (Mildura), 578
Goldfields, 468–471
Goldfields Exhibition (Kalgoorlie), 470
Gold Museum (Ballarat), 571
Gold Treasury Museum (Melbourne), 545
Golf, 37–38, 44–45, 156–157, 213, 214, 221, 288, 315, 367, 451–452, 496, 550
Goolang River, 202
Gordon River, 634, 635
Government House (Sydney), 150
Grampians National Park, 587–588

Grawin opal fields, 223
Great Barrier Reef, 8, 253, 255–261
day trips to, 258–259
from Cairns, 265–266
from Mission Beach, 295
from Port Douglas, 285
from Townsville, 301
from Whitsunday Islands, 310–314
gateways to, 256, 258
health and safety warnings, 258
multiday cruises along, 259
scuba diving, 256, 259–261
when to visit, 255
Great Goat Race (Lightning Ridge), 223
Great Keppel Island, 3, 320, 321, 323–324
Great Ocean Road, 9, 29, 482, 573–577
Great Sandy National Park (Cooloola National Park), 336
Great South Pacific Express, 60
Green Island, 258, 268, 279
Gunlom Falls, 406

Hahndorf, 18, 505–506
Hamilton Island, 312, 318
Hannans North Historic Mining Reserve (Kalgoorlie), 469
Hartley's Creek Crocodile Farm (Cairns), 267
Hayman Island, 317–318
Hazards Beach, 624
Healesville Sanctuary, 562
Health concerns, 49
Health insurance, 49
Henley-on-Todd Regatta (Alice Springs), 39
Heritage Landing, 634
Hermannsburg Historical Precinct, 373–374
Heron Island, 3, 14, 258, 320, 325–327
Hervey Bay, 10
High Country (Victoria), 582–587
High Court of Australia (Canberra), 599
High season, 36
History of Australia, 641–644

Hobart, 21, 608–621, 624
Hole in the Wall Beach, 209–210
Holidays, 36–37
Holmes à Court Gallery (Perth), 446
Homebush Bay, 88
Hook Island, 312, 319
Horseback riding, 45, 184, 196, 201, 217, 288, 583, 585
Horse racing, 39, 159, 506, 551–552
Horse trekking, 9
Hostels, 52
Hot-air ballooning, 190, 366, 550, 561, 600
Hotham, Mt., 584
Houghton's (Middle Swan), 458
Hunter Estate Winery (Pokolbin), 188
Hunter Valley, 186–195
Hunter Valley Wine Society, 188
Huskisson, 209, 210
Hyams Beach (Jervis Bay), 13, 209
Hyde Park (Sydney), 151
Hyde Park Barracks Museum (Sydney), 143
Hydro Majestic Hotel (Medlow Bath), 183

Imax Dome Theatre (Townsville), 301
IMAX Theatre (Melbourne), 545
IMAX Theatre, Panasonic (Sydney), 142
Imperial Cave, 185
Indian Head, 331
Indian Pacific train, 5, 60, 61, 218, 428, 432, 469, 482
Information sources, 30
In-line skating, 157, 245, 550
Insurance, 50–51, 65
Isle of the Dead, 622

Jabiru, 402, 403, 405–408
Jellyfish (blue bottles), 27, 48, 146, 284, 445, 545, 638–639
Jenolan Caves, 177, 185–186
Jervis Bay, 10, 209–211
Jet lag, 56
Jewel Cave, 464

Jim Jim Falls, 406
Jindabyne, 215
Jock's Place (White Cliffs), 221–222
Johnnie Walker Classic, 37–38
Johnstone River, 273
Julian Rocks, 204

Kakadu National Park, 11, 15, 401–408
Kalgoorlie, 16–17, 427, 468–471
Kangaroo Island, 11, 479, 507–514
Kangaroos, 10, 68, 144, 145, 153, 176, 191, 198, 200, 209–211, 240, 241, 268, 269, 287, 303, 321, 337, 345, 347, 363, 446, 447, 458, 507, 508, 510, 515, 519, 546, 563, 566, 581, 587, 601, 602, 622, 638
Katherine, 16, 408–412
Katherine Gorge (Nitmiluk National Park), 408–412
Katherine Hot Springs, 411
Katoomba, 22, 174, 177, 178–182
Kayaking, 10, 44–46, 269, 296, 297, 315–316, 335–336, 410, 602, 608
Kiama, 208–209
Kimberley, the, 8, 20, 22, 412–426
Kings Canyon, 12, 375–377
Kingscote, 509, 512–514
Kings Creek bed, 376
Kings Park and Botanic Garden (Perth), 446
Kiwi Down Under Farm (near Coffs Harbour), 200–201
Koala Conservation Centre (Phillip Island), 564
Koala Park (Sydney), 145
Koalas, 11, 27, 29, 144, 195, 200, 240, 267, 268, 272, 303, 305, 306, 322, 336, 337, 345, 458, 507, 546, 562, 563, 581, 587, 601, 612, 638
   Billabong Koala and Wildlife Park (Port Macquarie), 198–199
   Kangaroo Island, 510, 511
   Koala Park (Sydney), 145
   Lone Pine Koala Sanctuary (Brisbane), 10, 241
   Perth, 446
   Phillip Island, 564

Kondalilla Falls, 338
Kosciuszko National Park, 215
Kununurra, 414, 415–419
Kuranda, 266, 269–274
Kuranda Scenic Railway, 271
Ku-ring-gai Chase National Park, 152
Ku-ring-gai Wildflower Garden (Sydney), 152
Kurrawa Beach, 38

La Boite Theatre (Brisbane), 247
Lady Elliot Island, 14, 328–329
Lady Jane Bay (Sydney), 148
Lake Cave, 464
Lake St. Clair National Park, 16, 630, 633
Lamington National Park, 15, 351, 352–355
Langtrees (Kalgoorlie), 470
Larapinta Trail, 15
Lathami Conservation Park (Kangaroo Island), 511
Launceston, 18, 21, 624, 625–630
Lee, "Bushtucker Woman" Helen, 465
Leeuwin Estate Winery, 463, 464
Leura, 183
Licuala Fan Palm track, 296
Lightning Ridge, 12, 223–224
Lindemans (Pokolbin), 189
Liquor laws, 75
Litchfield National Park, 390, 400
Little Marley Beach, 153
Living Desert Nature Park (near Broken Hill), 221
Lizard Island, 14, 279–280
Lofty, Mt., 506
Lone Pine Koala Sanctuary (Brisbane), 10, 241
Long Reef Beach (Sydney), 157
Lorne, 574–577
Lower Hunter, 186
Low Isles, 258
Low season, 36
Lucas Cave, 185

MacDonnell Ranges, 12, 359, 361, 366, 372–375
McGuigan Brothers Winery (Pokolbin), 189

McKenzie, Lake, 331
McWilliams Mount Pleasant (Pokolbin), 189
Magnetic Island, 304–306
Mail, 75
Main Beach (Byron Bay), 204
Main Beach (Gold Coast), 342, 344, 346, 348, 350
Main Beach (Noosa Heads), 335
Malcolm Douglas Broome Crocodile Park (Broome), 423
Maleny, 338
Mammoth Cave, 464
Mamukala wetlands, 407
Mangarrayi people, 16, 412
Manly (Sydney), 88, 114–116, 134–135, 147, 157
Manly to Spit Bridge Scenic Walkway (Sydney), 151
Mansion at Werribee Park, 565
Manyallaluk Aboriginal community (Katherine), 16, 411
Mapleton Falls, 338
Mardi Gras, Sydney Gay & Lesbian, 38
Margaret River, 23, 431, 461–468
   surfing, 10
Marineland Melanesia (Green Island), 268
Maritime Museum, Australian National (Sydney), 18, 141, 154
Maritime Museum, Western Australian (to be renamed Shipwrecks Museum after mid-2002) (Fremantle), 4, 18
Maritime Museum of Tasmania (Hobart), 611
Mataranka Thermal Pools, 411
MAXVISION Cinema (Katoomba), 179
Medlow Bath, 183
Melba's Chocolate Factory (Woodside), 504
Melbourne, 523–567
   accommodations, 20, 23, 530–538
   arriving in, 523–525
   Carlton, 526
      accommodations, 535–536
      restaurants, 542–543
   Chinatown, 526

Melbourne *(cont.)*
City Center, 526
accommodations, 532
restaurants, 538–542
Fitzroy, 526–527
accommodations, 536
restaurant, 543
layout of, 526
neighborhoods, 526–527
nightlife, 555–559
outdoor activities, 550–551
restaurants, 25, 538–544
St. Kilda, 527
accommodations,
536–537
restaurants, 543–544
shopping, 552–555
side trips from, 559–567
sights and attractions,
545–550
Southgate, 527
South Yarra/Prahan, 527
accommodations,
537–538, 544
special events, 38, 39
spectator sports, 551–552
transportation, 527–529
visitor information,
525–526
Melbourne Aquarium, 545
Melbourne Concert Hall, 556
Melbourne Cup, 39
Melbourne International
Film Festival, 555
Melbourne Zoo, 545, 546
Merimbula, 214–215
Merimbula Jazz Festival, 215
Michaelmas Cay, 258
Migration Museum
(Adelaide), 19, 494
Mildura, 578, 579–580
Mimosa Rocks National
Park, 214
Mining Hall of Fame
(Kalgoorlie), 4, 469–470
Mission Beach, 13, 17, 253,
254, 258, 260, 294–300
Mitchell Falls, 425
Money, 33–35
Monkey Mia (Shark Bay), 11,
471, 472–475
Mon Repos Turtle Rookery
(Bundaberg), 11, 326
Montague Island, 10, 213
Montville, 338
Mooloolaba, 333–336, 340
Moondyne Cave, 464–465
Mootwingee National Park,
220–221
Moreton Bay, 249
Moreton Island, 250, 252

Mornington Peninsula,
566–567
Mosman, accommodations,
116
Mossman Gorge, 286
Motorcycle tours, 156, 180,
376, 382
Moulting Lagoon Game
Reserve, 623
Mt. Buffalo National Park,
586–587
Mt. Coot-tha Aboriginal Art
Trail, 245
Mt. Hotham, 584
Mt. Tomah Botanic Gardens
(Katoomba), 179–180
Mount Field National Park,
620–621
Mount View Estate, 189
Mrs. Macquarie's Chair
(Sydney), 150
Mumbulla Mountain, 214
Murramarang National Park,
10, 211
Murray Lagoon (Kangaroo
Island), 511
Murray River, 577–580
Murwillumbah, 207–208
Museum and Art Gallery of
the Northern Territory
(Darwin), 394
Museum of Central Australia
(Alice Springs), 363
Museum of Contemporary
Art (MCA) (Sydney), 143
Museum of Sydney, 149
Museum of the Goldfields
(Kalgoorlie), 470
Museum of Tropical Queens-
land (Townsville), 300,
301–302
Museums. *See also specific
museums*
best, 18–19
Mutton Bird Island, 200
Mylor, 505

N amadgi National Park,
602
Nambour, 334, 337, 338
Nanguluwur, 405
Narooma, 213–214
Narrabeen Beach (Sydney),
157
Narryna Van Diemen's Land
Folk Museum (Hobart),
611
National Capital Exhibition
(Canberra), 599–600
National Gallery of Australia
(Canberra), 600

National Gallery of Victoria
(Melbourne), 546
National Museum of Aus-
tralia (Canberra), 4, 600
National Pass Walk, 183
National Pioneer Women's
Hall of Fame (Alice
Springs), 364
National Rhododendron
Gardens (Olinda), 560
National Wool Museum
(Geelong), 566
Native Guide Safari Tours,
16, 288
N'Dhala Gorge Nature Park,
374
Nelson Bay, 195
Newhaven, 563
New Norcia, 431, 460–461
New Norcia Museum and Art
Gallery, 18–19
New South Wales, 26–27,
173–224
Outback, 217–224
transportation, 173–174
visitor information, 173
what's new in, 2
Newstead House (Brisbane),
241
New Year's Eve, 37
Ngilgi Cave, 465
Nimbin, 205
Ningaloo, 15, 427
Ningaloo Marine Park,
471–472
Nitmiluk National Park,
408–412
Nobbies, The, 563
Noosa Heads, 333–335,
339–341
Noosa National Park, 336
North Stradbroke Island, 249
North Sydney Olympic Pool,
158
Northwest Cape, 11, 12, 471,
475–476
Nourlangie Rock, 405
Nuriootpa, 499
Nymboida River, 202

O akbank, 506
Oceanworld Manly (Sydney),
145, 153
Old Melbourne Gaol, 546
Old Parliament House
(Canberra), 600–601
Old Post Office (Medlow
Bath), 183
Old Sydney Town, 143
Old Umbrella Shop
(Launceston), 627

Olga, Mt. (the Olgas), 382–385
Olgas, the (Kata Tjuta), 8
Olsen's Capricorn Caverns (Rockhampton), 321–322
Olympic Park, Sydney, 143
Opals, 166, 223, 224, 393, 394, 453, 454, 497, 518, 519, 554
Opera Australia (Sydney), 167
Opera Queensland (Brisbane), 247
Ord River, 416
Orlando winery, 500
Ormiston Gorge and Pound, 372
Orpheus Island, 306–307
Otford, 153
Outback, the. *See also* Aborigines (Aboriginal culture)
    best places to experience, 12–13
    biking tours, 43
    New South Wales, 217–224
    South Australia, 479, 515–520
    Victoria, 579
Overland Track, 632
Overland train, 61

P acific Highway, 198–208
Package tours, 53–54
Paddington, 229, 237, 246
Paddington Bazaar (Sydney), 165
Paddy's Markets (Sydney), 165
Palm Beach (Sydney), 13, 147, 157
Palm Cove, 277–278, 282
Palm Valley, 374
Panasonic IMAX Theatre (Sydney), 142
Parasailing, 157, 288, 295, 346
Parliament House (Canberra), 601
Parndana, 513–514
Pearl Luggers (Broome), 422
Pebbly Beach, 10, 211
Penfolds winery, 500, 502
Penguins, 10, 29, 213, 511, 562, 564
Penneshaw, 509, 510, 512
Penny Royal World and Gunpowder Mill (Launceston), 627
Perth, 427, 431–455
    accommodations, 21, 23, 438–442
    arriving in, 431–432

beaches, 447–448
    layout of, 434
    neighborhoods, 434–435
    nightlife, 454–455
    restaurants, 24, 442–445
    shopping, 453–454
    side trips from, 455–461
    sights and attractions, 445–447
    transportation, 435–437
    visitor information, 432, 434
    what's new in, 4
Perth Mint, 446–447
Perth Zoo, 447
Peterson's Champagne House (Pokolbin), 189
Peterson's Vineyard (Mount View), 189
Petrol (gasoline), 66, 69
Phillip Island, 562–567
Phillip Island Penguin Reserve, 564
Pinnacle, the (Hobart), 611
Pittwater (Sydney), 147
Planetariums
    Sir Thomas Brisbane Planetarium and Cosmic Skydome (Brisbane), 243
    Sydney Observatory, 150
Platypus, 11, 144, 145, 269, 347, 505, 507, 510, 546, 601, 620, 637–638
Pokolbin, 186, 188, 189, 191–195
Police, 76
Port Arthur, 621–623
Port Campbell, 574, 576
Port Campbell National Park, 575
Port Dock Railway Museum (Adelaide), 495–496
Port Douglas, 14, 16, 17, 254, 256, 258, 260, 282–293
    accommodations, 289–293
    accommodations in or near, 20–21, 23
    day trips to Great Barrier Reef, 285
    market, 289
    restaurants, 293
    safety tips, 284
    transportation, 284–285
    traveling to, 284
    visitor information, 284
Port Fairy, 575
Port Jackson. *See* Sydney Harbour
Port Macquarie, 198–199
Port Phillip Bay, 565–566
Port Stephens, 195–197

Possums, 209, 210, 268, 269, 347, 351, 352, 447, 505, 507, 510, 581, 638
Powerhouse Museum (Sydney), 142, 153
Prince Regent Nature Reserve, 425
Princes Highway, 208–215
Puffing Billy Railway (Belgrave), 560
Purnululu National Park (Bungle Bungles), 416–420
Pylon Lookout (Sydney), 139

Q ueensland, 27, 253–355
    accommodations, 3
    exploring the coast, 254–255
    what's new in, 3
Queensland Art Gallery (Brisbane), 242
Queensland Ballet (Brisbane), 247
Queensland Cultural Centre (Brisbane), 242
Queenslander train, 61
Queensland Museum (Brisbane), 242
Queensland Orchestra (Brisbane), 248
Queensland Performing Arts Complex (QPAC) (Brisbane), 242, 247
Queensland Theatre Company (Brisbane), 247
Queen Victoria Building (QVB) (Sydney), 159
Queen Victoria Markets (Melbourne), 546, 548
Queen Victoria Museum and Art Gallery (Launceston), 627
Questacon-The National Science and Technology Centre (Canberra), 601

R ail passes, 61
Rail travel. *See* Train travel
Rainbow Beach, 333
Rainforestation Nature Park (Kuranda), 272–273
Rainforest Habitat, 287
Rain forests, 201, 204–205, 272–273, 297. *See also* Daintree Rain Forest; Wet Tropics Rain Forest
Raleigh International Raceway (near Coffs Harbour), 202
Ravenswood, 300

Red Centre, 27–28, 356–385.
    See also Alice Springs
    driving tips, 358
    tour operators, 359
    visitor information, 356,
        358
    what's new in, 3–4
    when to go, 358
Red Peak, 270
Reef HQ (Townsville), 302
Regions of Australia, 26–30
Restaurants, best, 24–25
Rhyll Inlet, 563
Rialto Towers Observation
    Desk (Melbourne), 548
Richmond, 622
Rippon Lea House Museum
    and Historic Garden
    (Melbourne), 548
River cruises. *See* Boat tours
    and cruises
Riverside Markets
    (Brisbane), 246
Road maps, 67
Road trains, 69
Rock climbing, Brisbane, 245
Rockford winery, 502
Rockhampton, 321–323
Rockhampton Botanic
    Gardens, 322
Rocks Market, The (Sydney),
    165
Ross, 624–625
Ross Bridge, 624–625
Ross River Homestead, 374
Rothbury Estate (Pokolbin),
    189
Rottnest Island, 14–15, 431,
    455–458
Roundhouse (Fremantle),
    450
Royal Botanic Gardens
    (Melbourne), 549
Royal Botanic Gardens
    (Sydney), 150
Royal Flying Doctor Service
    (Alice Springs), 365
Royal Flying Doctor Visitors
    Centre (Cairns), 267–268
Royal National Park,
    152–153
Royal Tasmanian Botanical
    Gardens (Hobart), 613
Runnymeade, 192
Russell Falls, 620

S afety, 46–49, 76
    Jervis Bay warning, 211
Sailing (yachting), 8, 45, 158,
    311–313, 452
St. Clair, Lake, 16, 633–634

St. Helena Island, 251
St. John's Anglican Cathedral
    (Brisbane), 243
St. Kilda, 23
St. Patrick's Cathedral
    (Melbourne), 549
St. Pauls Cathedral
    (Melbourne), 548–549
Sandalford Caversham
    Estate, 458
Sarah Island, 634
Scarborough Beach, 448
Scenic flights. *See* Aerial
    tours
Scenic Railway (Blue
    Mountains), 179
School of the Air (Alice
    Springs), 365
School of the Air (Broken
    Hill), 220
School of the Air
    (Katherine), 411
Sciencentre (Brisbane), 242
Scuba diving, 8, 40–42, 157,
    200, 204, 256, 259–261,
    269, 285, 328, 452, 456,
    477
    best places for, 14–15
Sea kayaking. *See* Kayaking
Seal Bay Conservation Park,
    511
Seasons, 35–36
Sea World (Main Beach),
    345, 346
Seniors, 52
Seppelts winery, 502
Serpentine Gorge, 372
75-Mile Beach, 331
Shark Bay (Monkey Mia),
    472–475
Shark Bay Marine Park, 471
Sharks, 146
    whale, 11, 471, 476–477
Shelly Beach (Sydney), 147
Shipwrecks Museum (named
    Western Australian
    Maritime Museum before
    mid-2002) (Fremantle),
    4, 18
Shrine of Remembrance
    (Melbourne), 549–550
Silverton, 220
Simpson's Gap, 372
Sir Thomas Brisbane Plane-
    tarium and Cosmic Sky-
    dome (Brisbane), 243
Skiing, 10, 215–216,
    583–586
Skyrail Rainforest Cableway,
    270–271
Skywalk (Dorrigo National
    Park), 201

Skyway (Katoomba), 179
Small Winemakers Centre
    (Pokolbin), 188
Smoking, 49–50
Snakes, 48
Snorkeling, 8, 11, 200, 256,
    268, 285, 311–312, 452,
    456, 471, 477
    best places for, 14–15
Snowy Mountains, 9,
    215–217
Snowy River National Park,
    582–583
South Australia, 29, 479–522
    Outback, 515–520
    transportation, 480
    visitor information,
        479–480
South Australian Maritime
    Museum (Adelaide), 494
South Australian Museum
    (Adelaide), 495
South Bank Craft and
    Lantern Markets
    (Brisbane), 246
South Bank Parklands
    (Brisbane), 243
Southeast Coast, 580–582
South Head (Sydney), 152
South Mission Beach, 297
South Molle Island, 312,
    319–320
South Stradbroke Island,
    250, 251–252
Sovereign Hill Goldmining
    Township, 571
Spiders, deadly, 47–48
Spirit of the Tropics train, 61
Stadium Australia (Sydney),
    144
Standley Chasm, 372
Stanley, 636
Star City (Sydney), 172
State Houses of Parliament
    (Melbourne), 549
State Library of NSW
    (Sydney), 149–150
St James Church (Sydney),
    149
St Mary's Cathedral
    (Sydney), 149
Strand, The (Townsville), 302
Students, 53
Sublime Point Lookout, 183
Summer Cloud Bay, 210
Sun, protection from the, 50
Sun-Herald City to Surf
    (Sydney), 38
Sunshine Coast, 253,
    333–341
Surfers Paradise, 13, 342,
    344, 348–350

Surfing, 10, 45, 157–159, 204, 335, 422, 452–453, 456, 466
Surfworld (West Torquay), 574
Survivor 2-The Australian Outbank, 274
Swan Lake, 563
Swan Valley, 24, 458–460
Swimming, 158, 406, 603
Sydney, 80–172
  accommodations, 19, 22, 99–117
  arriving in, 81, 83–84
  babysitters, 96
  bars, 170–171
  beaches, 146–148
  Bondi and southern beaches, 87–88
    accommodations, 113–114
    restaurants, 133–134
  business hours, 96
  cafes, 132
  casino, 172
  Central (City Centre), 87
    accommodations, 106–108
  Circular Quay, 85
    accommodations, 102–105
    restaurants, 120–122
  currency exchange, 97
  Darling Harbour, 86
    accommodations, 108–109
    restaurants, 128
    sights and attractions, 141–142
  Darlinghurst, 87
    accommodations, 111–112
    restaurants, 129–131
  dentists and doctors, 97
  emergencies, 97
  gay and lesbian travelers, 98, 169–170
  Glebe, 87
    accommodations, 112–113
    restaurants, 131
  harbor cruises, 154–155
  Harbour. *See* Sydney Harbour
  hospitals, 97
  Kings Cross and suburbs beyond, 86–87
    accommodations, 109–111
    restaurants, 129–131
  layout of, 84–85

  lost property, 98
  luggage storage, 98
  Manly, 88, 114–116, 134–135, 147, 157
  movies, 171–172
  neighborhoods, 85–88
  newspapers, 98
  Newtown, 87
    accommodations, 112
    restaurants, 133
  nightlife and entertainment, 2, 166–172
  North Shore, 88
  North Sydney, 88
    restaurant, 135
  organized tours, 155–156
  outdoor activities, 156–158
  Paddington, restaurants, 131–132
  Paddington/Oxford Street, 87
  parks and gardens, 150–153
  performing arts, 166–168
  pharmacies, 98
  picnic fare, 121
  post offices, 98
  restaurants, 24, 117–135
    BYO (bring your own), 117
  The Rocks, 85
    accommodations, 102–105
    restaurants, 122–126
    walking tour, 153
  safety, 99
  shopping, 159–166
    discount shopping, 160
  sights and activities, 135–154
    for kids, 153
    Privileges Card, 138
  sights and attractions, 8
  special events, 37–40
  Surry Hills restaurants, 128–129
  taxes, 99
  telephones, 99
  Town Hall, 85–86
    restaurants near, 126–128
  transportation, 89–96
    buses, 92–93
    car travel and rentals, 96
    CityRail trains, 93–94
    ferries and jetcats, 93, 138–139
    Metro Light Rail, 94

    metro monorail, 94
    money-saving passes, 89, 92
    taxis, 94
    timetable information, 89
    water taxis, 94, 96
  visitor information, 84
  walking tours, 155–156
  Watsons Bay, 88
  what's new in, 2
Sydney Aquarium, 142, 153
Sydney Festival, 37, 167
Sydney Film Festival, 38
Sydney Harbour (Port Jackson), 2, 138–140
Sydney Harbour Bridge, 37, 80, 85, 86, 139
  climbing, 140
Sydney Harbour National Park, 138, 151
Sydney International Airport, 81, 83
  accommodations, 116–117
Sydney International Aquatic Centre, 144, 158
Sydney Jewish Museum, 150
Sydney Observatory, 150
Sydney Olympic Park, 143–144
Sydney Opera House, 140–141, 166
Sydney Symphony Orchestra, 167
Sydney-to-Hobart Yacht Race, 159, 611

Tamarama (Sydney), 147, 157
Tamar River, 626, 627, 629
Tamborine, Mt., 350–352
Tamburlaine (Pokolbin), 189
Tamworth Country Music Festival, 37
Tandanya Aboriginal Cultural Institute (Adelaide), 17, 495
Tangalooma, 11
Tanunda, 499
Taronga Zoo (Sydney), 145–146, 153
Tasmania, 9, 29–30, 604–635
Tasmanian Devil Park Wildlife Rescue Centre, 622
Tasmanian devils, 200, 241, 507, 612, 620, 622, 638
Tasmanian Museum and Art Gallery (Hobart), 613
Taxes, 76–77

Telephone, 77–78
Telstra Tower (Canberra), 601
Tennis, 37, 158, 551, 552, 603
Territory Wildlife Park (Darwin), 393
Tesselaar's Bulbs and Flowers (Silvan), 560
Thala Beach, 292–293
Theater, 167–168, 247, 454, 498, 555–557, 619
Thredbo Village, 215, 216
Three Brothers, 183
Three Sisters (Katoomba), 179
Ticks, 48
Tidbinbilla Nature Reserve (Canberra), 601–602
Time zone, 78
Tinklers (Pokolbin), 189
Tipping, 78–79
Tjapukai Aboriginal Cultural Park (Cairns), 16, 266–267
Top End, 4, 28, 386–426
Torquay, 574
Tourist information, 30
Tours. See also Aerial tours; Boat tours and cruises; and specific destinations
escorted, 53–54
package, 53–54
Townsville, 23, 253, 256, 258, 260, 294, 300–304
Train travel, 2, 59–61
Brisbane and Queensland, 3
Kuranda Scenic Railway, 271
Port Dock Railway Museum (Adelaide), 495–496
Puffing Billy Railway, 560
Traveler's checks, 35
Traveling
around Australia, 57–70
to Australia
airlines, 54–55
cruises, 57
Travel-planning and booking websites, 70–72
Trephina Gorge Nature Park, 374
Trinity Beach, 277
Tropical Fruit World (near Murwillumbah), 207
Tully River, 9, 17, 45, 273–274, 294, 295–296
Turquoise Bay, 477
Turtles, 11, 255, 302, 306, 321, 323, 325, 326, 445, 471, 477

Tweed Valley, 207
Twelve Apostles, 575
Twin Falls, 406
Tyrell's (Pokolbin), 189

Ubirr Rock, 405
Ulladulla, 23, 210–212
Uluru-Kata Tjuta National Park (Ayers Rock/The Olgas), 12, 377–385. See also Ayers Rock
Umbarra Aboriginal Cultural Centre (Wallaga Lake), 16, 213–214
Underwater World (Mooloolaba), 336–337
Upolu Cay, 258
Upper Hunter, 186, 193

Valley of the Waters, 183
Vasse, 24, 466, 467
Vaucluse House (Sydney), 150
Victoria, 29, 568–588
Victorian Alps, 10
Victorian Arts Centre (Melbourne), 555–556
Victoria's first Government House (Melbourne), 549
Victoria's Open Range Zoo at Werribee, 565
Vincentia, 210
Visitor information, 30

Waddy Point, 331
Walcott Inlet, 425
Wallaga Lake, 16
Wangi Falls, 400
Warner Bros. Movie World (Oxenford), 346
Warning, Mount, 207–208
Warradjan Aboriginal Cultural Centre, 18, 405
Warrawong Sanctuary, 505
Watarrka National Park, 375–377
Wategos Beach, 204
Water, drinking, 69, 79, 358, 381, 388
Waverley Woollen Mills (Launceston), 627
Weather, 35–36
Websites, 30, 70–72
Wentworth Falls, 183
Werribee, 565
West Coast (Tasmania), 634–636

Western Australia, 28–29, 427–478
visitor information, 427–428
what's new in, 4
Western Australian Maritime Museum (to be renamed Shipwrecks Museum after mid-2002) (Fremantle), 4, 18, 450–451
Western Australian Museum (Perth), 447
West MacDonnell National Park, 372
West Macdonnell Ranges, 372–374
Wet 'n' Wild Water World (Oxenford), 346–347
Wet Tropics Rain Forest, 8, 11, 261, 269, 287. See also Cape Tribulation National Park; Daintree National Park; Daintree Rain Forest
Whales and whale-watching, 4, 10, 196, 202, 213, 214, 315, 451, 466, 477
Whale sharks, 11, 471, 476–477
White Cliffs, 21, 221
Whitehaven Beach, 13, 314
White-water rafting, 9, 17, 45, 202, 273–274, 295–296, 620
Whitsunday Coast and Islands, 8, 14, 15, 253, 258, 260, 307–320
accommodations, 20, 21, 316–317
choosing a base in, 310
exploring the islands and the Reef, 310–316
resorts, 317–320
restaurants, 317
seasons, 311
transportation, 308, 310
traveling to, 307–308
visitor information, 308
Wildflowers, 8–9, 152, 430, 446, 583, 587
Wildlife and wildlife viewing, 637–639. See also Bird-watching; and specific wildlife, wildlife parks and reserves
best places for, 10–11
car travel and, 68
tips on, 46–49
Wild World-The Tropical Zoo (Cairns), 268
William Ricketts Sanctuary (Mt. Dandenong), 560

Willie Creek Pearl Farm
    (Broome), 423
Wilpena Pound, 515
Wilsons Promontory
    National Park, 580–582
Windjana Gorge, 425
Windsurfing, Sydney, 158
Wineglass Bay, 623
Wineglass Bay Lookout, 624
Wines and vineyards, 9, 166,
    186, 188–190, 458–459,
    461, 463–466, 499, 500,
    502, 645
Wolf Blass winery, 502

Womadelaide Festival, 484
Wombats, 144, 145, 198,
    200, 241, 303, 347, 446,
    447, 458, 521, 546, 562,
    581, 586, 612, 620, 638
Wonderland Sydney, 144
Woodbridge (West Midland),
    459
Woodside, 504
Woongarra Marine Park
    (Bundaberg), 327–328
World War II oil storage
    tunnels (Darwin), 394

Yachting. See Sailing
Yacht Race, Sydney-to-
    Hobart, 159, 611
Yalumba winery, 502
Yamatji Bitja Aboriginal
    Bush Tours, 16–17, 470
Yarra Valley, 561–562
Year of the Outback (2002),
    1, 39
Yellow Water Billabong, 404
Yongala wreck, 14
York Town Square Market
    (Launceston), 627

FROMMER'S® COMPLETE TRAVEL GUIDES

Alaska
Amsterdam
Argentina & Chile
Arizona
Atlanta
Australia
Austria
Bahamas
Barcelona, Madrid & Seville
Beijing
Belgium, Holland & Luxembourg
Bermuda
Boston
British Columbia & the Canadian
   Rockies
Budapest & the Best of Hungary
California
Canada
Cancún, Cozumel & the Yucatán
Cape Cod, Nantucket &
   Martha's Vineyard
Caribbean
Caribbean Cruises & Ports of Call
Caribbean Ports of Call
Carolinas & Georgia
Chicago
China
Colorado
Costa Rica
Denmark
Denver, Boulder & Colorado Springs
England
Europe
European Cruises & Ports of Call
Florida
France

Germany
Great Britain
Greece
Greek Islands
Hawaii
Hong Kong
Honolulu, Waikiki & Oahu
Ireland
Israel
Italy
Jamaica
Japan
Las Vegas
London
Los Angeles
Maryland & Delaware
Maui
Mexico
Montana & Wyoming
Montréal & Québec City
Munich & the Bavarian Alps
Nashville & Memphis
Nepal
New England
New Mexico
New Orleans
New York City
New Zealand
Nova Scotia, New Brunswick &
   Prince Edward Island
Oregon
Paris
Philadelphia & the Amish Country
Portugal
Prague & the Best of the Czech
   Republic

Provence & the Riviera
Puerto Rico
Rome
San Antonio & Austin
San Diego
San Francisco
Santa Fe, Taos & Albuquerque
Scandinavia
Scotland
Seattle & Portland
Shanghai
Singapore & Malaysia
South Africa
South America
Southeast Asia
South Florida
South Pacific
Spain
Sweden
Switzerland
Texas
Thailand
Tokyo
Toronto
Tuscany & Umbria
USA
Utah
Vancouver & Victoria
Vermont, New Hampshire
   & Maine
Vienna & the Danube Valley
Virgin Islands
Virginia
Walt Disney World & Orlando
Washington, D.C.
Washington State

FROMMER'S® DOLLAR-A-DAY GUIDES

Australia from $50 a Day
California from $70 a Day
Caribbean from $70 a Day
England from $75 a Day
Europe from $70 a Day

Florida from $70 a Day
Hawaii from $80 a Day
Ireland from $60 a Day
Italy from $70 a Day
London from $85 a Day

New York from $90 a Day
Paris from $80 a Day
San Francisco from $70 a Day
Washington, D.C., from $80
   a Day

FROMMER'S® PORTABLE GUIDES

Acapulco, Ixtapa & Zihuatanejo
Alaska Cruises & Ports of Call
Amsterdam
Aruba
Australia's Great Barrier Reef
Bahamas
Baja & Los Cabos
Berlin
Big Island of Hawaii
Boston
California Wine Country
Cancún
Charleston & Savannah
Chicago
Disneyland

Dublin
Florence
Frankfurt
Hong Kong
Houston
Las Vegas
London
Los Angeles
Maine Coast
Maui
Miami
New Orleans
New York City
Paris

Phoenix & Scottsdale
Portland
Puerto Rico
Puerto Vallarta, Manzanillo &
   Guadalajara
San Diego
San Francisco
Seattle
Sydney
Tampa & St. Petersburg
Vancouver
Venice
Virgin Islands
Washington, D.C.

FROMMER'S® NATIONAL PARK GUIDES

Family Vacations in the National
   Parks
Grand Canyon

National Parks of the American
   West
Rocky Mountain
Yellowstone & Grand Teton

Yosemite & Sequoia/
   Kings Canyon
Zion & Bryce Canyon

Frommer's® Memorable Walks

Chicago	New York	San Francisco
London	Paris	

Frommer's® Great Outdoor Guides

Arizona & New Mexico	Northern California	Vermont & New Hampshire
New England	Southern New England	

Suzy Gershman's Born to Shop Guides

Born to Shop: France	Born to Shop: Italy	Born to Shop: New York
Born to Shop: Hong Kong, Shanghai & Beijing	Born to Shop: London	Born to Shop: Paris

Frommer's® Irreverent Guides

Amsterdam	Los Angeles	San Francisco
Boston	Manhattan	Seattle & Portland
Chicago	New Orleans	Vancouver
Las Vegas	Paris	Walt Disney World
London	Rome	Washington, D.C.

Frommer's® Best-Loved Driving Tours

Britain	Germany	New England
California	Ireland	Scotland
Florida	Italy	Spain
France		

Hanging Out™ Guides

Hanging Out in England	Hanging Out in France	Hanging Out in Italy
Hanging Out in Europe	Hanging Out in Ireland	Hanging Out in Spain

The Unofficial Guides®

Bed & Breakfasts and Country Inns in:	Florida with Kids	New Orleans
California	Golf Vacations in the Eastern U.S.	New York City
New England	The Great Smokey & Blue Ridge Mountains	Paris
Northwest		San Francisco
Rockies	Inside Disney	Skiing in the West
Southeast	Hawaii	Southeast with Kids
Beyond Disney	Las Vegas	Walt Disney World
Branson, Missouri	London	Walt Disney World for Grown-ups
California with Kids	Mid-Atlantic with Kids	Walt Disney World for Kids
Chicago	Mini Las Vegas	Washington, D.C.
Cruises	Mini-Mickey	World's Best Diving Vacations
Disneyland	New England & New York with Kids	

Special-Interest Titles

Frommer's Adventure Guide to Australia & New Zealand
Frommer's Adventure Guide to Central America
Frommer's Adventure Guide to India & Pakistan
Frommer's Adventure Guide to South America
Frommer's Adventure Guide to Southeast Asia
Frommer's Adventure Guide to Southern Africa
Frommer's Britain's Best Bed & Breakfasts and Country Inns
Frommer's France's Best Bed & Breakfasts and Country Inns
Frommer's Italy's Best Bed & Breakfasts and Country Inns
Frommer's Caribbean Hideaways

Frommer's Exploring America by RV
Frommer's Gay & Lesbian Europe
Frommer's The Moon
Frommer's New York City with Kids
Frommer's Road Atlas Britain
Frommer's Road Atlas Europe
Frommer's Washington, D.C., with Kids
Frommer's What the Airlines Never Tell You
Israel Past & Present
The New York Times' Guide to Unforgettable Weekends
Places Rated Almanac
Retirement Places Rated

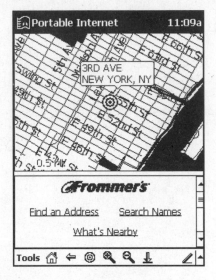